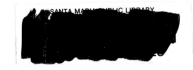

HANDGUNS 2002

14th Annual Edition

Edited by
Ken Ramage

Manuscripts, contributions and inquiries, including first class return postage, should be sent to the HANDGUNS Editorial Offices, Krause Publications, 700 E. State Street, Iola, WI 54990-0001. All materials received will receive reasonable care, but we will not be responsible for their safe return. Material accepted is subject to our requirements for editing and revisions. Author payment covers all rights and title to the accepted material, including photos, drawings and other illustrations. Payment is at our current rates.

CAUTION: Technical data presented here, particularly technical data on the handloading and on firearms adjustment and alteration, inevitably reflects individual experience with particular equipment and components under specific circumstances the reader cannot duplicate exactly. Such data presentations therefore should be used for guidance only and with caution. Krause Publications, Inc., accepts no responsibility for results obtained using this data.

Published by

700 E. State Street • Iola, WI 54990-0001
Telephone: 715/445-2214
Web: www.krause.com

Please call or write for our free catalog of publications.
Our toll-free number to place an order or obtain a free catalog is 800-258-0929
or please use our regular business telephone, 715-445-2214.

Library of Congress Catalog Number: 88-72115
ISBN: 0-87349-299-4

— HANDGUNS STAFF —

Ken Ramage, Editor
HANDGUNS
Firearms & DBI Books

Ross Bielema,
Associate Editor

Editorial Comments and Suggestions

We're always looking for feedback on our books. Please let us know what you like about this edition. If you have suggestions for articles you'd like to see in future editions, please contact.

Ken Ramage/Handguns
700 East State St.
Iola, WI 54990
email: ramagek@krause.com

About Our Covers...

On the Front...

The **Taurus PT 92 AFS**. This particular stainless steel model *(above)* is equipped with fixed 3-dot sights and chambered for the proven 9x19mm Parabellum cartridge. Like the other members of the PT 92 family, this autoloader carries a 5-inch barrel and incorporates an ambidextrous three-position safety. Magazine capacity is 10, plus one in the chamber. This design has been in the Taurus line for many years and, as reported in the company's literature, is based upon the *"...most extensively tested, duty-proven and widely used double-action autoloader design in history..."*

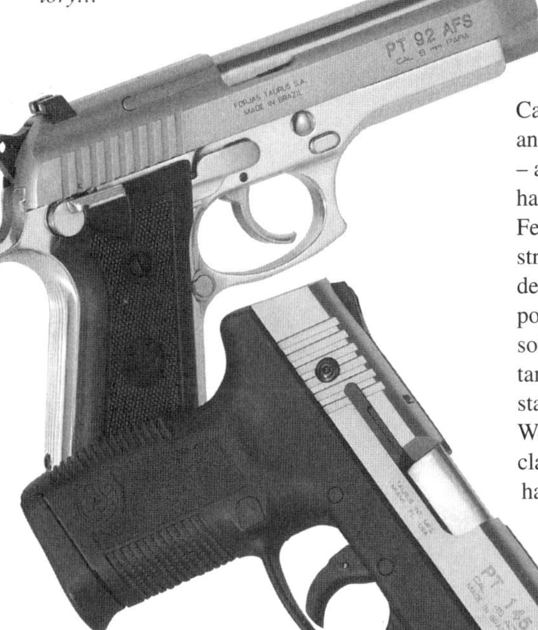

The **Model PT-145 Millennium**. The expanding line of lightweight polymer-framed Millennium pistols reflects their growing popularity. The double-action-only PT-145 *(below)* is chambered for the 45 ACP cartridge, carrying ten in the magazine plus one in the chamber. Other features include a 3-inch barrel, fixed 3-dot sights *(night sights available)*, choice of stainless steel or matte-finished blued slide and an integral key lock safety system.

On the Back...

The **Taurus Model 454SS6 Raging Bull** stainless steel five-shot revolver *(above)* chambered for the proven and powerful 454 Casull cartridge, is an excellent choice – and value – for handgun hunters. Features include a strong double-lockup cylinder design. The heavy-contour, vent-ribbed and ported barrel *(6-inch barrel shown)* and soft rubber "Cushion Insert" grips help tame recoil. Adjustable iron sights are standard. Taurus offers a special Weaver system scope base, designed to clamp onto the barrel's ventilated rib, to handily mount a scope *(as shown)*.

The **Model 85 Ultra Lite TI** is a recent addition to the Taurus line and, like the Model 85 family, is a five-shot revolver chambered for the 38 Special cartridge. Notable features include major components of titanium *(frame, cylinder, barrel, etc.)*, extended *(shrouded)* ejector rod and improved cylinder yoke latch. Sights are fixed: ramp front and square-notch rear. This particular model, stocked with soft rubber boot grips, features a 'bobbed' hammer and so operates double-action only.

For more information on these and other Taurus products, see your dealer or contact the company:

Taurus International Firearms
16175 NW 49th Avenue,
Miami, FL 33014
305-624-1115
www.taurususa.com

Handguns 2002

Handguns for Sport and Personal Protection 

CONTENTS

Page 33

Page 45

Page 93

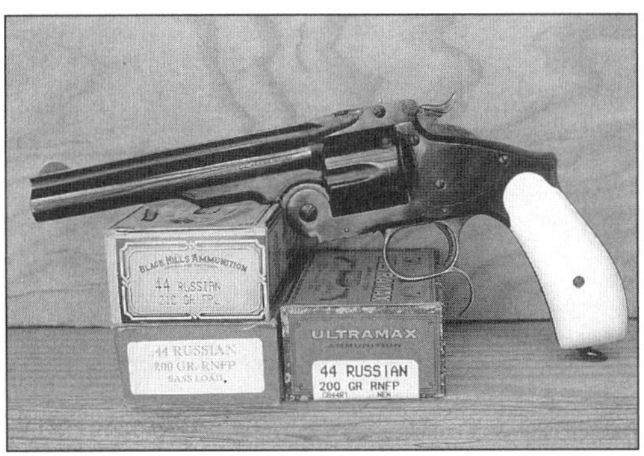

Page 101

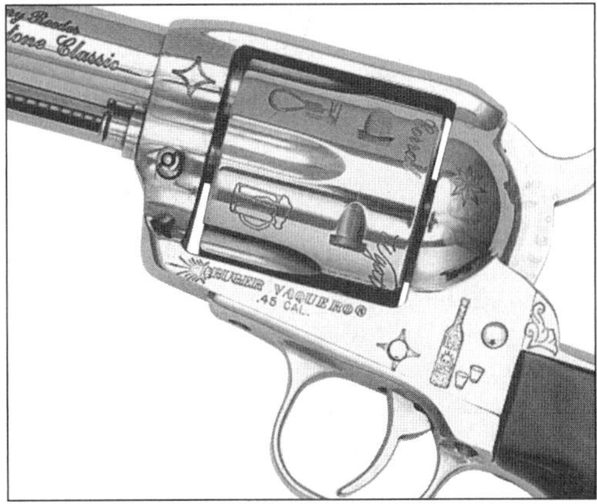

Page 137

Page 173

Page 201

New Autoloading Handguns

by John Malloy

THE PAST YEAR was one of great uncertainty for both makers and users of autoloading handguns.

There were many aspects. Lawsuits against firearms manufacturers (primarily those making semi-auto pistols), misuse of authority by public officials, media assaults against firearms ownership, and proposed anti-gun legislation at state and federal levels—all of these things played a part.

As the year 2000 went on, the November 7, 2000 elections were seen as a climax that would give an indication as to what the future might hold.

But even the elections added to the uncertainty, and it was over a month later before George W. Bush was finally acknowledged the President-elect. The election of Bush, who is basically pro-gun, should provide needed relief from the anti-gun policies of the Clinton-Gore administration. In the meantime, however, some state legislators and bureaucrats decided they were firearms experts, even when they had no understanding of handgun or ammunition terminology. States such as California, Maryland and Massachusetts initiated differing standards as to what pistols could be sold within their borders. The arbitrary and sometimes conflicting rules baffled many manufacturers. If other states come up with even different criteria, how can any handgun meet them all?

Some manufacturers have held off spending research time or money on new developments due to this uncertainty. Some have suspended certain models from production.

Yet, there is still much going on in the world of autoloading handguns. There are many new offerings. Most of these are variations on the 1911 theme, and the 45 ACP cartridge remains the most popular chambering for new offerings. Polymer frames have not lost their charm, and some interesting polymer/aluminum combinations have been introduced. Small 45s are very popular, but some new full-size variants have been introduced also. However, everything is not 1911 45s. There are also brand-new designs and brand-new cartridges

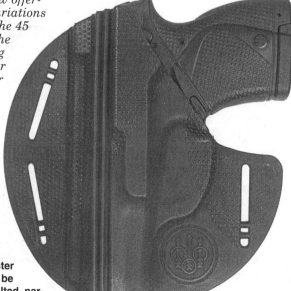

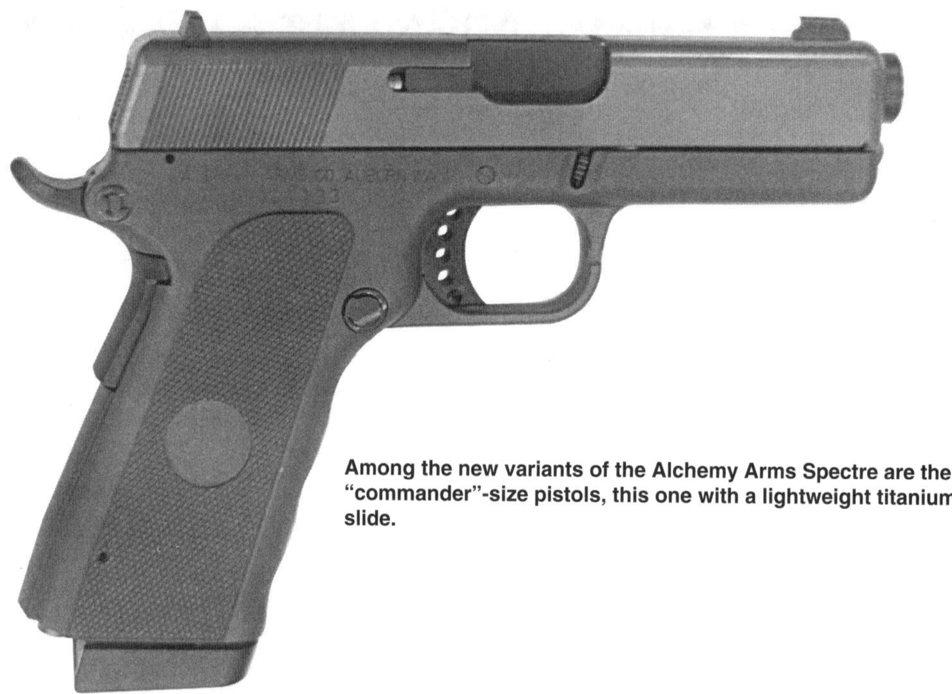

Among the new variants of the Alchemy Arms Spectre are the "commander"-size pistols, this one with a lightweight titanium slide.

Beretta offers a nifty new holster for their 9000S pistols—it can be used left or right, straight or tilted, narrow belt or wide.

being introduced. The 22-caliber pistol remains popular—both new pistols and conversion units are being introduced in the 22 Long Rifle (22 LR) chambering. New U. S. companies have been set up to market foreign products.

Due to litigation possibilities and state requirements, many manufacturers are offering or designing locking devices that can incapacitate their pistols.

The aftermarket industry is active and creative. Many new accessories for autoloading handguns are being offered.

The industry has become more involved with things electronic. Most companies involved with semiautomatic pistols now have websites or e-mail addresses to provide information about their products. To show that your writer is up with the times, these electronic contacts will be provided here.

Now, let's take a look at what the companies are doing:

ALCHEMY ARMS

Alchemy Arms' Spectre pistol was introduced only a year ago, but already variations are being introduced. The original 4.5-inch full-size model has been joined by a 4-inch version. The carbon- and stainless-steel slides in both lengths are now joined by those made of titanium. Titanium reduces the weight of a Spectre to 22 ounces.

Express sights (large bead, shallow notch) are standard now. Alchemy also plans to introduce new wide sights of their own design.

Attentive observers will note that the new full-size Spectres have a more rounded slide contour. Also, the takedown has been simplified and the trigger guard has been reshaped slightly. A notch in the front of the trigger guard serves as what the company calls a "digital safety." When not ready to shoot, the user can place his finger on the notch instead of on the trigger.

www.alchemyltd.com

ARMSCOR

This Philippine manufacturer makes a line of 1911-type pistols. The line consists of full-size (5"), "commander" (4") and compact (3.5") in blue, stainless and dual-tone finishes. Calibers are 45, 40 and 9mm. New for 2001 was a full-size 45-caliber "meltdown" variation, with all the edges rounded off.

www.armscor.com.ph

ARMS MORAVIA

The recently introduced CZ-G 2000 pistol now has a new U. S. importer. Anderson and Richardson Arms Co., of Fort Worth, TX, will handle the Czech-made pistol. The distinctively shaped pistol has a polymer frame and is available in 9mm and 40. It is a conventional Double Action (DA) with the decocker recessed into the slide.

arms@arms-moravia.cz

BERETTA

Beretta is celebrating its 475th anniversary in 2001, and rightfully considers itself the oldest firearms company in existence. Records in the company's archives show that in 1526, Bartolomeo Beretta sold 185 arquebus barrels to the Arsenal of Venice. (He received 296 ducats as payment.) From that point, the Beretta line has expanded.

The biggest news is the new Model 92 Millennium pistol. Based on the Model 92 design, it is single action, has a steel frame, frame-mounted safety (it can be carried cocked-and-locked), carbon-fiber grips and adjustable rear sight. The slide is the reinforced "Brigadier" type. It is finished in nickel alloy, with special engraving. Production will be limited to 2000 pistols, 1000 of which will be sold in the United States.

The 92/96 series pistols are now available in a Black Inox (black on stainless) variant. Finish is matte black with gray wraparound rubber grips.

Beretta's Cathy Williams demonstrates the new 9000S pistol, this version a double-action-only (DAO).

On the smaller end, the 3022 Alley Cat variation of its little Tomcat 32 is offered. It has Big Dot tritium express sights, and comes with a special inside-the-pants holster.

The Model 87 22-caliber target pistol has its adjustable sights mounted in a full-length top bar that will accept optical or electronic sights. A nice feature is that the pistol will stand upright when placed on a flat surface.

The 9000S, Beretta's first polymer-frame pistol, is now in full production. The 9000S, the first Beretta with a tilting-barrel locking system, now makes the company the only one to offer all three common locked-breech systems. (The 92/96 series has the dropping block, and the Cougar has the rotating

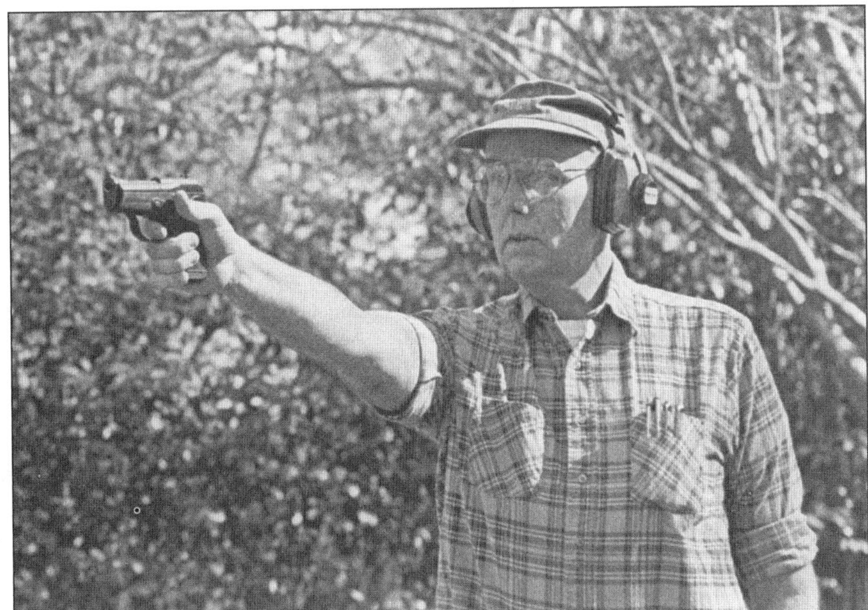

Malloy tries out a 40-caliber conventional DA Beretta 9000S in single-action mode. A separate DAO variant is also offered.

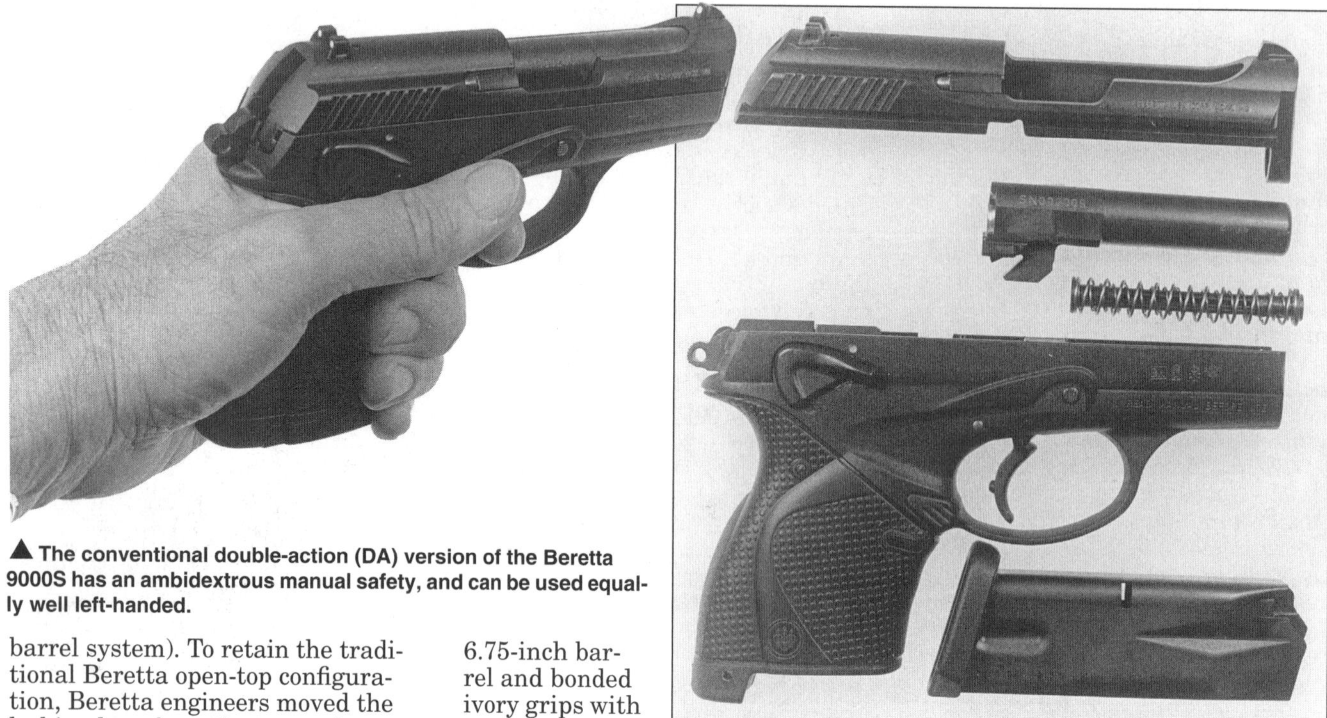

▲ The conventional double-action (DA) version of the Beretta 9000S has an ambidextrous manual safety, and can be used equally well left-handed.

The 9000S is Beretta's first tilting barrel locking system. It is cam-operated, and the lugs are at the bottom to maintain the traditional Beretta open-top appearance.

barrel system). To retain the traditional Beretta open-top configuration, Beretta engineers moved the locking lugs from the top to the lower side of the 9000S barrel. A clever holster is available for the 9000S—it can be used either right or left side, straight up or tilted forward, small belt or large belt.

A 22-caliber conversion kit is now offered for the 92/96 series 9mm and 40 S&W pistols.

www.berettausa.com

BROWNING

Browning is celebrating its 25th year of 22-caliber pistol production in Utah. Accordingly, this year the company is producing a 25th Anniversary Buck Mark pistol with a 6.75-inch barrel and bonded ivory grips with a scrimshaw pattern. 1000 will be made.

Other new items in the pistol line include Buck Mark "Color Camper" pistols. These will be made with red, blue or green frames. A limited run of 1200 pistols will be made in colors.

It is not really a pistol, but the Buck Mark line has also been expanded to include a semiautomatic carbine. By adding a longer barrel, wood forearm and shoulder stock, they have transformed the basic Buck Mark mechanism into a cute little carbine.

www.browning.com

BUL

Bul Transmark, of Israel, introduced a new 10-shot small 45 at the January 2001 SHOT Show. It uses a polymer frame and was so new Bul had not named it yet. It will not be sold in the U. S. under the Bul name. The company is also marketing parts for 1911-type pistols. Their "Warp Speed" kit of hammer, sear and disconnector is a high-quality, low-price set of parts that can be installed without fitting.

A "Slideless" pistol attracted considerable attention at the Bul display. The custom 9mm pistol had so much metal removed from the slide it almost seemed a cutaway model. It is claimed to have a very fast action, and the specimen shown was actually used in competition.

www.bultransmark.com

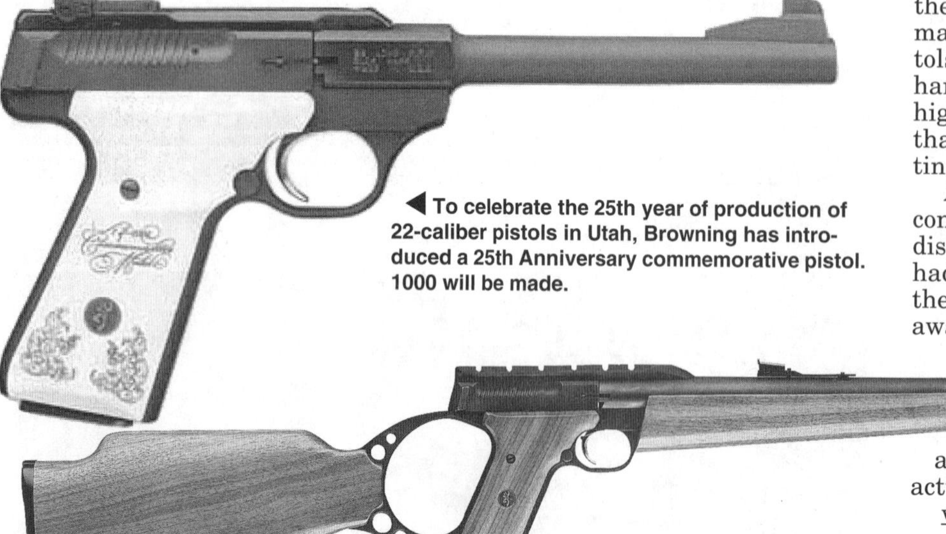

◀ To celebrate the 25th year of production of 22-caliber pistols in Utah, Browning has introduced a 25th Anniversary commemorative pistol. 1000 will be made.

▲ Browning's Buck Mark pistol is the basis for the new Buck Mark carbine. Not really a pistol, but sort of cute.

CASULL

Casull Arms, noted for big revolvers and powerful cartridges,

◀ The new Dan Wesson 1911-type Pointman pistols have given the company a position in the autoloader field as well as in revolvers.

▶ The new Firestorm 22 is a Bersa-style pistol handling the popular 22 Long Rifle (22LR) cartridge. Operation is conventional DA and capacity is 10+1.

has entered the world of semiautomatic pistols. The new Casull autoloader is a 1911-style pistol for, of course, a powerful new cartridge. The new bottleneck round is called the 38 Casull. It reportedly pushes a 124-grain bullet out at about 1800 feet per second (fps), while a 147-grain projectile leaves at about 1650 fps.

www.casullarms.com

CENTURY INTERNATIONAL

Century International's big news is their new line of 45-caliber 1911-style pistols. The guns are available in full-size and "commander" lengths in two styles. The standard model has a beavertail grip safety and extended controls. The Blue Thunder variant adds combat sights, full-length guide rod, a notched front strap, distinctively reshaped trigger guard and (in the full-size versions) an optional ported barrel.

Century also offers the Korean Daewoo "Tri-fire" pistols, in the full-size version, in 9mm and 40 S&W. The Arcus 9mm pistol is made in Bulgaria, and is available in full-size and compact versions. It is based on the venerable Browning High-Power mechanism, but includes a DA trigger and extended safety lever.

www.centuryarms.com

COLT

Colt continues to make its line of 1911-style pistols in 45 ACP only. One special edition model was displayed at the January 2001 SHOT Show, considered by some a reissue. It is a genuine Colt 1911A1 as it was made at the beginning of World War II. It is Parkerized, has the original mechanical construction (no late-model changes), and has the old wide hammer, and—glory be—a lanyard ring. The markings are the same as those of the original Colts of the early WWII period. However, if you look closely, you'll see the serial number has a "WK" prefix. They are the initials of Lt. Gen.

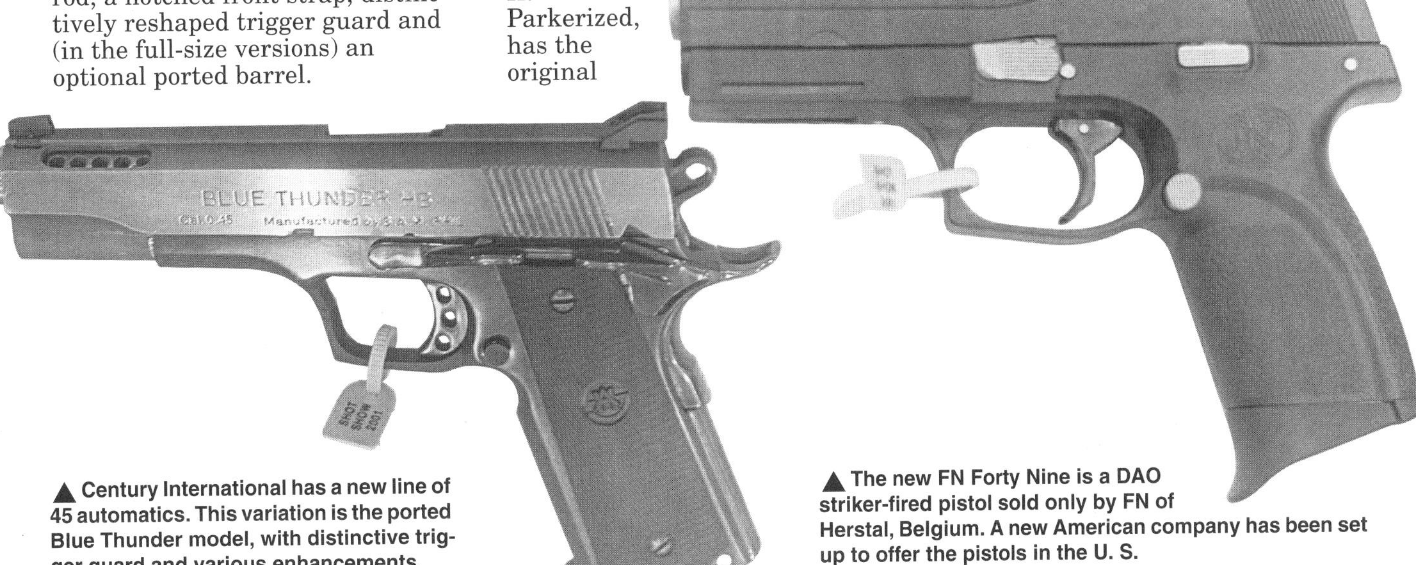

▲ Century International has a new line of 45 automatics. This variation is the ported Blue Thunder model, with distinctive trigger guard and various enhancements.

▲ The new FN Forty Nine is a DAO striker-fired pistol sold only by FN of Herstal, Belgium. A new American company has been set up to offer the pistols in the U. S.

A 380 Comp Gun? Well, why not? Hi-Point's new offering gives a new shooter a low-recoil way to get started. Two magazines are provided—an 8-shot finger-rest version, and a 10-shot extended one.

William Keyes, Colt's new head man, who supported the project.

It is a little off the subject of autoloading handguns, but many were glad to see a Python 357 revolver back in Colt's display. Plans were to reintroduce the Python during the second quarter of 2001, in a 6-inch stainless-steel version.

www.colt.com

CZ-USA

The CZ 75 and its variants continue to dominate the line for CZ. New at the 2001 SHOT Show were the CZ 75 Compact, now in 40 S&W as well as 9mm, and the CZ 75D (decocker) variants. The new decocker model eases the hammer down in two steps; this could be of real interest to those who have never really felt comfortable with the hammer of a loaded pistol slamming forward, no matter what assurances the safety devices provided.

Also available is a CZ 75 Compact "carry" pistol. This is a smooth-edged "meltdown" that many shooters seem to like nowadays. A new CZ 75M IPSC pistol has been introduced. In 40 S&W caliber, it is designed to meet Modified Class rules. It uses the full frame of the 45-caliber CZ 97, and has extended magazine release, compensator, blast deflector and other niceties.

The polymer-frame CZ 100, previously scheduled for United States introduction, will not be imported.

CZ offers a FirePoint sight with a red dot that stays permanently on. The expected life is over five years.

If you have looked at CZ pistols and have wondered why some models have the letter B suffix in the designation, be aware that it indicates that a new firing pin safety is installed. If you see a pin-filled hole in the rear portion of the slide, that also indicates the new safety.

www.cz-usa.com

DAN WESSON

Dan Wesson, a name associated with modern revolvers since 1968, introduced a line of 1911-type pistols in the year 2000. By January 2001, the variety of "Pointman" pistols had grown to eleven different models.

www.danwessonfirearms.com

FIRESTORM

FireStorm is a new name in the shooting world, introduced just last year, which offers new twists in established designs. Its first offering was a line of 1911-styled 45-caliber pistols. A new introduction in early 2001 was a new FireStorm pistol chambered for the 22LR cartridge. Based on the Bersa design, the new pistol has 10+1 capacity and measures about 4.7x6.6 inches. Matte and duo-tone finishes are offered. The FireStorm pistols are available through SGS Importers.

www.firestorm-sgs.com

FN

FN Herstal, of Belgium, sells some handguns in the rest of the world that Browning sells in the United States. The new FN Forty-Nine pistol (note that the first letters of the company name and the pistol model are the same), however, is sold only by FN. It is a departure from the traditional pistols based on the Browning 1935 "High Power." The FN is DAO, striker-fired – and with a polymer frame, yet.

The pistol feels good in the hand, with a slantier grip angle than that of the 1935-type pistols. The slide and barrel are of stainless steel, and a semigloss black finish is available. The polymer frame's forward edge is slotted for whatever accessories the shooter might desire.

The new pistol is offered in 9mm for now. Size is 5.7x7.7 inches, with a 4.25" barrel. Empty weight is about 26 ounces. Magazine capacity is 16 rounds for the rest of the world, 10 for the common folk in America. The Forty-Nine is offered through a new company, FN Manufacturing, Inc. of Columbia, SC.

billf@fnmfg.com

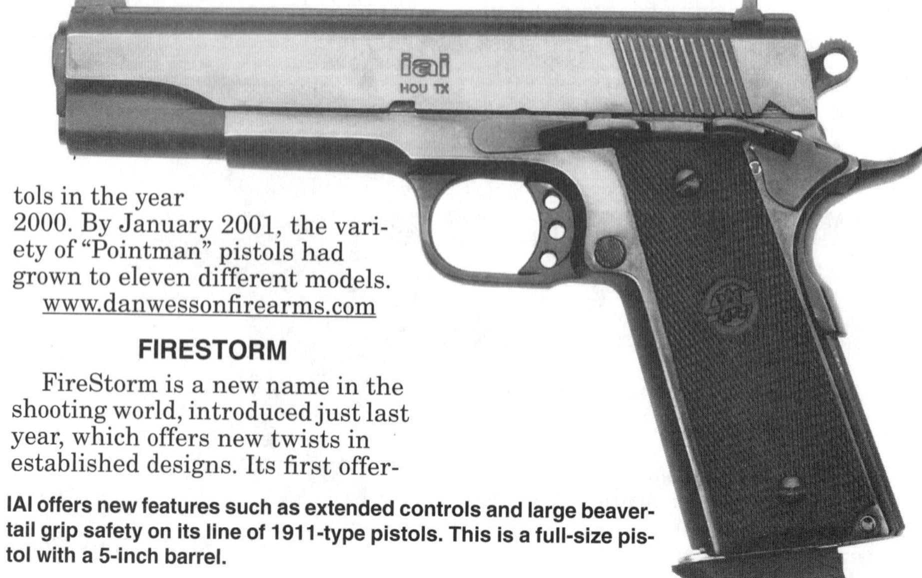

IAI offers new features such as extended controls and large beavertail grip safety on its line of 1911-type pistols. This is a full-size pistol with a 5-inch barrel.

GLOCK

Having filled most of the niches in its autoloading handgun plans, Glock has taken a temporary break from introducing new models this year. However, the company is working on a new internal lock, a prototype of which was present at the 2001 SHOT Show in New Orleans. This prototype device locked with a key through the butt, in the space behind the magazine. When locked, a protrusion at the rear of the grip can be seen or felt.

www.glock.com

Kahr Arms has expanded its polymer-frame offerings with the new P40, a lightweight pistol chambered for the 40 S&W cartridge.

HK

Heckler & Koch have introduced a new 40-caliber pistol in their USP Expert series. At present, this pistol is cataloged for law enforcement only. It has a magazine-well extension to funnel the magazine into place rapidly. The magazine is a special 16-round polymer one, which can be used by American law enforcement and the rest of the world. The extension can be removed, and a standard magazine can be used. So, it is possible that a 10-round "civilian" version might be forthcoming if the interest warrants it.

www.hecklerkoch-usa.com

Auto-Ordnance, now operated by Kahr, offers three 1911-style pistols, including this variant with wraparound grips.

HERITAGE

The nice little Heritage Stealth polymer-frame pistol has taken a sabbatical for now. Cowboy Action shooting has become popular enough that Heritage has expanded its single-action "Rough Rider" revolver line, and temporarily suspended production of the semiautos. A number of shooters have expressed the hope that the Stealth pistols—which have received good reviews for exceptional accuracy—will soon become available again.

www.heritagemfg.com

HIGH STANDARD

High Standard is offering a "Safety/Fast" shooting kit for its new line of 1911-type pistols. From the full-cock position, the hammer can be pushed forward, a bit like a Daewoo. However, the similarity ends there. The Safety/Fast system automatically engages the thumb safety when the hammer is pushed forward. Now, everything is locked—the hammer cannot be recocked, the trigger cannot be pulled, the slide cannot be moved. At this time a transfer-bar system prevents the hammer from contacting the firing pin. To get the pistol back into action, simply push the thumb safety down. The hammer is automatically recocked, and the pistol is ready to shoot. Pretty nifty.

www.highstandard.com

HI-POINT

Hi-Point Firearms has introduced a new 380 Comp Gun. The new pistol has a 4-inch barrel, adjustable sights and compensator on the muzzle. It comes with two magazines—an 8-round version with a finger rest, and a 10-round extended model. Why a 380? Hi-Point claims it is extremely accurate with very low recoil; perhaps a good way for a new shooter to get started at low cost. Unlike most previous models, the new pistol has a magazine disconnect safety and last-round hold-open. It is also available with a laser mounted to the compensator.

www.high-pointFirearms.com

IAI

IAI offers new features on its line of 1911-type pistols such as extended slide stop, safety and magazine release, beavertail grip safety, ambidextrous safety and beveled magazine well. The Houston-based company is now also the sole distributor for the South African RAP 401 (9mm) and RAP 440 (40 S&W) pistols, which are marketed as the IAI M-3000 and IAI M-4000 models, respectively.

www.israelarms.com

HS AMERICA

The HS 2000 pistol, introduced just last year, is now in production in 9mm. 40-caliber versions were scheduled for mid-2001. Recall that the Croatian-designed pistol has a polymer frame, a "Glock-type" trigger, and locks by a cam-operated tilting-barrel system. New features such as an accessory rail, front slide serrations, a shorter trigger pull and an outlined stippled grip are now standard. They will be phased in on current production.

Also added is a "read this" instruction notice of which American shooters have grown so fond. When bored with shooting, we can just stop and read our guns.

www.hsarms.com

Kel-Tec's Renee Goldman holds two of the many options of the company's popular lightweight P-32 pistol.

◀ To help preserve our firearms rights, Kimber offered a special Heritage Fund pistol. The company donated to the Hunting and Shooting Sports Heritage Foundation for each pistol sold.

▶ Kimber believes their new Ultra Ten II is the smallest, lightest 10-shot 45 around. The new pistol is the first to utilize Kimber's new grip-operated safety system.

KAHR

Kahr introduced its first polymer-frame 9mm pistol last year, and is filling out its polymer lineup. The new 40 S&W-caliber Kahr P40 was introduced at the January 2001 SHOT Show. The P40 weighs in at less than 19 ounces and measures about 4.5x6 inches, with a 3.5-inch barrel. The single-column 6-round magazine keeps the width down to less than an inch. Two magazines come with each pistol.

Recall that Kahr bought Auto-Ordnance two years ago, and with it the right to the 1911-type A-O Thompson pistols. Three versions are now in production: a Parkerized military version, a standard blued version, and a deluxe variant with wrap-around grips and 3-dot sights.

www.kahr.com

KEL-TEC

Kel-Tec has had such good response to the little 6.5-ounce P-32 pistol that they are trying to fill all possible niches of their customers' wants. The P-32 slide may now be had in a hard chrome finish as well as the standard black. The polymer frame is now available in a choice of five colors, in addition to the basic black. Options are silver grey, light blue, dark blue, tan and olive. Mix and match the slides and frames, and it would be possible to have an extensive collection of just P-32s.

www.kel-tec.com

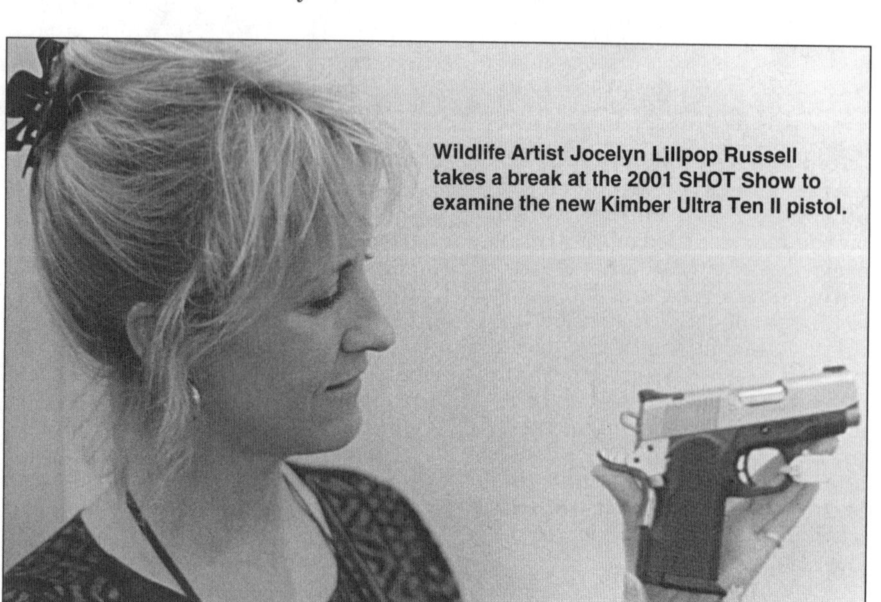

Wildlife Artist Jocelyn Lillpop Russell takes a break at the 2001 SHOT Show to examine the new Kimber Ultra Ten II pistol.

KIMBER

Kimber, reportedly the largest maker of 1911-style pistols, has added a new safety system. The firing pin block is now deactivated by movement of the grip safety, rather than the trigger. This allows the trigger to do the original job of releasing the hammer, without any additional parts going along for the ride that might change the pull. There is no difference in external appearance. The change was scheduled to be phased in during 2001, and the modified pistols will have a "II" designation after the model number.

Kimber designed a special Heritage Fund Edition 45 to help preserve our firearms rights. For each pistol purchased, the company donated $200 to the Hunting and Shooting Sports Heritage Foundation. Each owner also received an individual Heritage Fund membership.

Who offers the smallest, lightest 10-shot 45? Kimber believes their brand-new Ultra Ten II fits that description. At 24 ounces, with its aluminum-insert polymer frame, the new pistol holds a 10-round magazine for 10+1 capacity. Did you notice the "II" in the name? It is the first Kimber produced with the new safety system.

www.kimberamerica.com

KORTH

At its first SHOT Show display in recent years was the elegant German Korth pistol. A new company, Korth USA, has been formed to market the Korth in the United States. The clever design and beautiful machine work on the Korth variant displayed allows the use of four calibers to be used in a single pistol, with only changes of barrels. Even though they are of different dimensions and shapes, 9x19mm, 9x21mm, 357 SIG and 40 S&W cartridges can be handled in the Korth with the same magazine, slide, extractor, ejector and springs. A lot of thought went into this pistol.

www.korthusa.com

LES BAER

Les Baer Custom is offering a new variation of their 45-caliber Monolith pistol, which was introduced in 2000. Recall that the Monolith frame extends all the way forward to the front of the slide. The new variant is a 4.25-inch barrel pistol called the Comanche. It is available in standard weight and heavyweight styles, and is guaranteed to shoot 3-inch groups at 50 yards. Tritium night sights are included.

www.lesbaer.com

A new company, Korth USA, has been formed to market the elegant German Korth pistol in the United States.

LLAMA

Some years ago, the trend to smaller carry pistols, especially in 45 ACP, became evident. Llama got in on that trend and concentrated on their compact and subcompact "Minimax" 45s. But there are always those who like the original 1911 size and style. To appeal to them, Llama has reintroduced the government-size 45-caliber MAX-1 pistol, which has a matte black finish.

www.bersa-llama.com

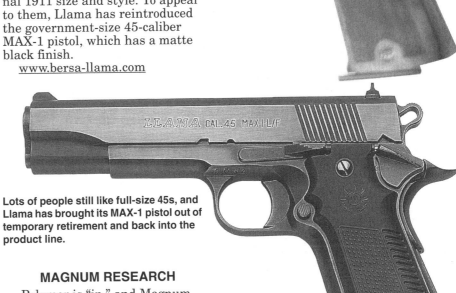

Lots of people still like full-size 45s, and Llama has brought its MAX-1 pistol out of temporary retirement and back into the product line.

MAGNUM RESEARCH

Polymer is "in," and Magnum Research has added a polymer-frame pistol to their Baby Eagle lineup.

Their big boomer, the Desert Eagle, now offers components to switch from one caliber to another almost instantly. Owners of Mark XIX Desert Eagles in 44 Magnum, 440 Cor-Bon, or 50 Action Express (50 AE) can now have the other calibers with just a barrel and magazine change. The 357 Magnum Desert Eagle can also convert to the other calibers, but that swap requires a bolt assembly change also. All chamberings are available with 6- or 10-inch barrels.

Titanium Gold finishes are now available on most of the pistol line, one of eight different finishes the company can provide.

www.magnumresearch.com

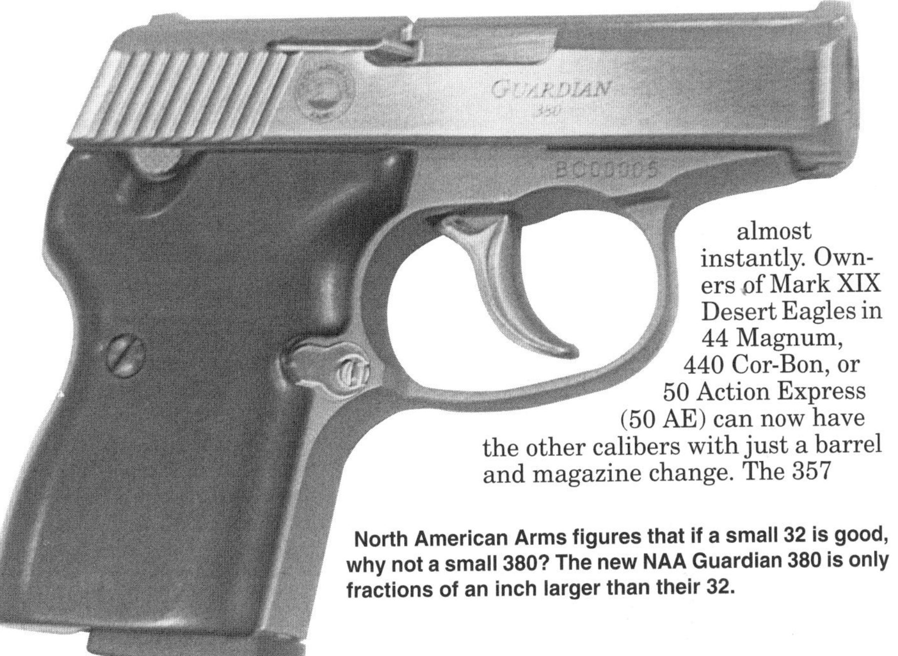

North American Arms figures that if a small 32 is good, why not a small 380? The new NAA Guardian 380 is only fractions of an inch larger than their 32.

NAA

North American Arms, long a maker of mini-revolvers, was a recent entry into the semi-auto pistol field just a few years ago. Its single offering—the 25-sized 32 Guardian pistol—was well received, so now the company has added another. If a small 32 is good, company officers apparently reasoned, would not a small 380 be better? Their new offering, displayed for the first time at the January 2001 SHOT Show, is the NAA

Introduced during the 1950s, the Whitney Wolverine was considered far ahead of its time. Now, Olympic Arms plans to reintroduce the racy-looking little pistol.

Tom Spithaler of Olympic Arms displays a 22-caliber Whitney Wolverine pistol. The company plans to bring back the neat little pistol, long out of production.

Guardian 380. The new 380 measures 3.5x4.75 inches, with a 2.5-inch barrel. Weight is less than 19 ounces. For comparison, the 32 is 3.3x4.35 inches, so the difference is about .4-inch longer grip and about .2-inch longer slide. Capacity of both pistols is 6+1.

A new version of the 32, the Guttersnipe, was unveiled at the same time. The catchy name comes from a hollow gutter along the tip of the slide. At the end of the gutter is a white dot. At the rear of the slide, on the sides of the gutter, are two white dots. Thus, the little pistol offers a 3-dot sight system without using any sights. Nothing protrudes and there is nothing to snag.

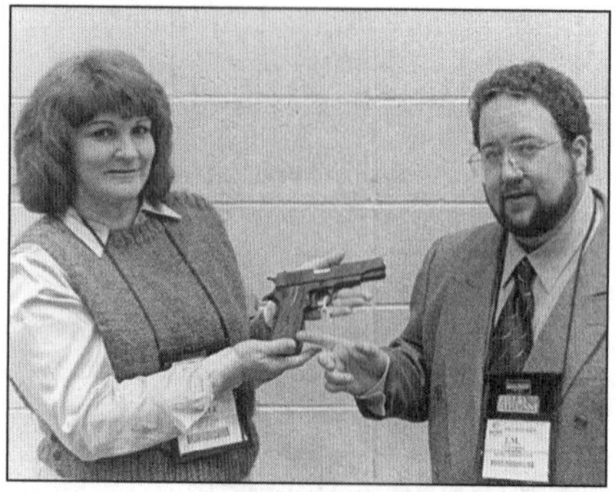

Pacific Armament's Joel Steinberg (*right*) points out features of the company's new line of 1911-type pistols to Gayle Grissett. Long a maker of parts, Pacific Armament now offers a variety of complete pistols.

Also available is an attachable laser that fastens to the front of the pistol and acts as a "deprinter," concealing the shape of the pistol when it is carried in a pocket.

www.naaminis.com

NOWLIN

The 40 Super cartridge, introduced last year, has great potential, and Nowlin has brought out a pistol for that recent cartridge. The new Maximum Hunter model was so new, only one sample was available to observe at the SHOT Show. With its 6-inch barrel, velocities are reported to be in the 1800 fps range.

Nowlin also demonstrated other new variations. The company's Compact Carry guns are 6+1 short-grip 1911 variants with 4.25-inch barrels.

A World Cup PPC pistol is available in 9mm, 38 Super, 9x23, 10mm, 40 S&W and 45 ACP. A nice feature is a set of sights that allows preset adjustments for the different PPC ranges.

www.nowlinguns.com

OLYMPIC ARMS

Remember the Whitney Wolverine, the racy-looking 22 pistol made back in the 1950s? Many said it was 50 years ahead of its time. Now that the half-century has passed, Olympic Arms believes it should be offered again.. Olympic had actually made most of the parts to begin manufacture, when disaster struck. The factory burned down, and the Wolverine project was dealt a big setback. As of early 2001, a new building was being constructed, and the Whitney Wolverine is indeed scheduled to reappear. Minor modifications to the safety will be made, but essentially the pistol will be an exact continuation of the original.

www.olyarms.com

PACIFIC ARMAMENT

A new line of 45-caliber 1911-type pistols has been introduced by Pacific Armament Corp. The company has been making FAL rifle receivers and 1911 parts, and is now offering it own series of complete pistols. Full-size (5") and commander-size (4.25") variants were available in early 2001, with shorter officer-size pistols and versions with 38 Super chambering in the works.

gunparts@att.net

PARA-ORDNANCE

Para-Ordnance, which began with—and gained recognition for—its double-column high-capacity 1911 frames, has introduced its first single-stack pistols. Designed to be slimmer for concealed carry, the first of the new series to be presented are compact, short-barrel DAO versions. The L6.45S is a 3.5-inch-barrel version, and the LL6.45S is a 3-incher. They have spurless "snag-free" hammers.

New variants of the LDA (Light Double Action) line, which was introduced two years ago, will be offered with manual safeties.

www.paraord.com

PROFESSIONAL ORDNANCE

Professional Ordnance, makers of the large but relatively light 223-caliber pistols, now offer a quick-detachable compensator for their new pistols. The company uses carbon-fiber upper and lower receivers to make a pistol fully 20 inches long that only weighs 46 ounces. The new compensator reduces muzzle rise, and so makes the pistol easier to shoot. A ball-

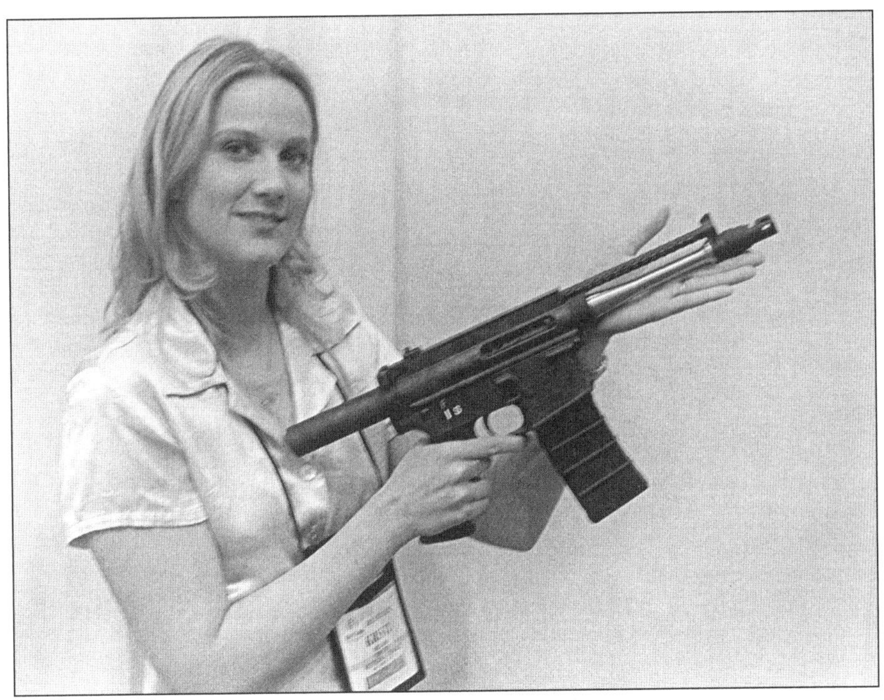

Kristi McGaha of Professional Ordnance demonstrates the new quick-detachable muzzle brake on the company's big 223-caliber pistol. Using carbon-fiber receivers, the 20-inch pistol weighs only 46 ounces.

type lock lets it go on or off the muzzle in seconds.

www.professional-ordnance.com

RUGER

Sturm, Ruger & Co.'s P-series polymer-frame guns have become mainstays in the firm's pistol line. One new variant was introduced at the 2001 SHOT Show. It is a P-95 DA with a conventional manual safety. The safety is ambidextrous and can be operated from either side.

www.ruger-firearms.com

S.A.M.

Shooters Arms Manufacturing, located in the Philippines, is offering a new long-frame 1911 variant. The front of the polymer double-stack frame extends to the front of the slide. The Falcon, as the new series is called, is available in full-size (5" barrel) or compact (4.25" barrel) variants. S.A.M. makes several variations of semiautomatic pistols, all based on the Colt 1911, and all chambered for the 45 ACP cartridge.

www.shootersarms.com.ph

Shooters Arms Manufacturing, located in the Philippines, offers 1911-type pistols. S.A.M.'s Richard Yuson holds the new Falcon, with frame extended to the front of the slide.

SIGARMS

In 2000, two German investors acquired Sigarms. The purchase included the Exeter, NH operation in the United States. As might be expected, some changes are taking place.

The elegant 9mm single-action P210, scheduled last year to fade into history, is now back in the line, and in a version with a new "American-style" pushbutton magazine release to replace the catch at the base of the grip. This new P210 has wood grips and adjustable sights. Three other variations are also offered with the original butt magazine release and different options of sights and barrel lengths.

In recent years, full-size service pistols seem not to have received much attention. However, the reliable full-size SIG P220, in 45 ACP, has been quietly available since 1975 while other models got the fanfare. Now, a new stainless-steel version has been introduced. The new P220ST is, like its blued predecessor, a 5.6x7.8-inch conventional DA pistol, with a 4.5-inch barrel.

The P226 is now also available as a 9mm Sport pistol for competition in which the lower recoil of the 9mm offers a recovery-time advantage. The new P226 has a heavy 5.6-inch barrel with a

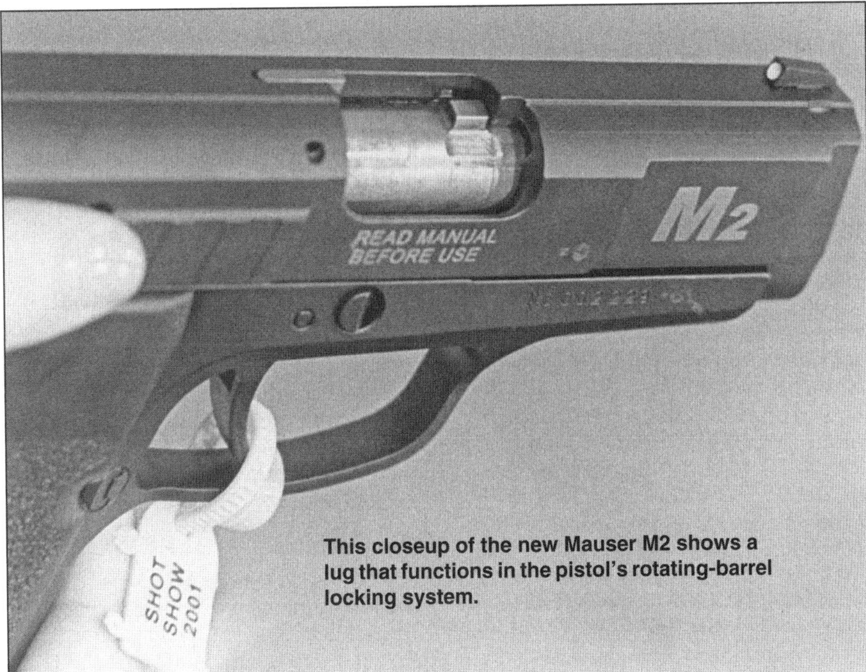

This closeup of the new Mauser M2 shows a lug that functions in the pistol's rotating-barrel locking system.

▶The 45-caliber SIG P220 has been quietly available for over a quarter-century without much fanfare. Now the full-size pistol is available in a new stainless-steel version. Here, Malloy fires an early P220, one of the first imported.

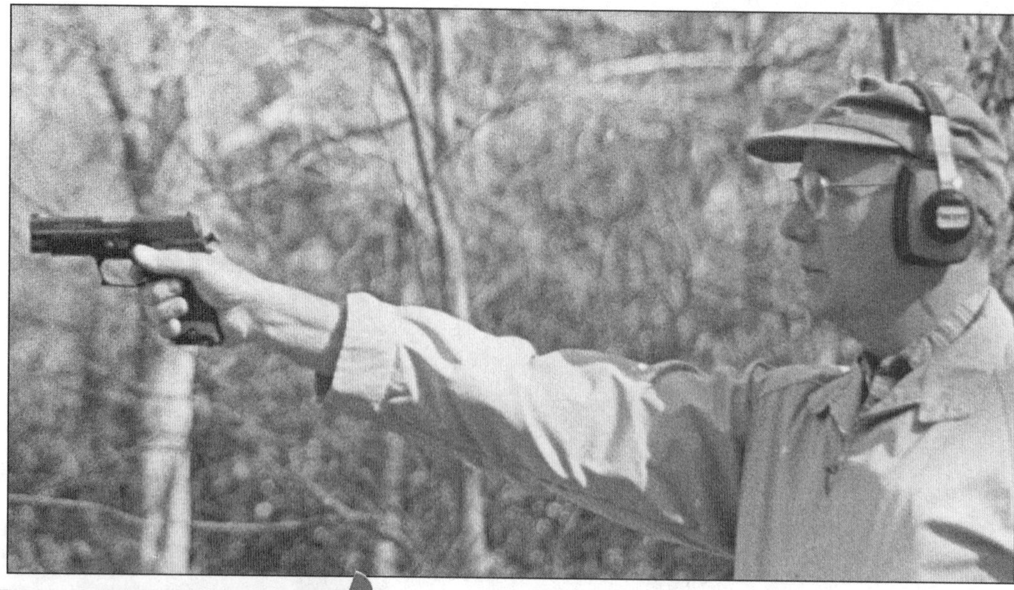

◀ The nice SIG P210 is back in the catalog, in a new version that includes a push-button magazine release.

◀ For competition in which fast recovery time is important, SIG offers the P226 Sport, a 9mm with 51-ounce weight.

◀ SIG's standby 45-caliber pistol, the venerable P220, is now available in a stainless-steel version.

weighted frame extension. The weight is upped to over 51 ounces. Capacity is the legal limit of 10+1.

SIG also offers the new rotating-barrel Mauser M2 pistol, a compact 5x6.8-inch size with a 3.5-inch barrel. At about 32 ounces, the M2 comes as a 45, 40S&W or 357 SIG. Capacity is 8+1 in 45, 10+1 in the other calibers.

www.sigarms.com

SMITH & WESSON

Smith & Wesson created considerable discussion in mid-2000 when the company reached an agreement with the Clinton administration. Ostensibly about safety, it actually concerned what they could make, how those products would be marketed and how the company would spend its money. The firearms community apparently did not favor such government control of a private industry. In October 2000, S&W's parent company, the Tomkins group, announced that Ed Schultz had stepped down as president and CEO. He was replaced by George Colclough, a 25-year S&W employee.

By early 2001, the company had dropped a number of items from the line, but had added some new ones, too. Several new semiautomatic pistols were added. The SW9P (9mm) and SW40P (40S&W) are ported pistols in the Sigma series. The new ported guns feature 3-dot sights and an accessory or equipment rail on the forward frame. The sides of the slides are polished bright.

For those who want something less bright, S&W has also gone the other way with its unported SW9G and SW40G pistols. Specifications are basically the same, but these are not bright. The polymer frame is NATO green, and a coating of Melonite black hides the stainless slide.

The 22-caliber models 22A and 22S pistols are now offered with "Hi-Viz" sights. They use light-gathering rods at the front sights that appear to the shooter as a bright orange or bright green dot.

www.smith-wesson.com

SOMMER & OCKENFUSS

The German company is known for its interesting rifle designs. At the January 2001 SHOT Show, SO introduced a new pistol, the P21.

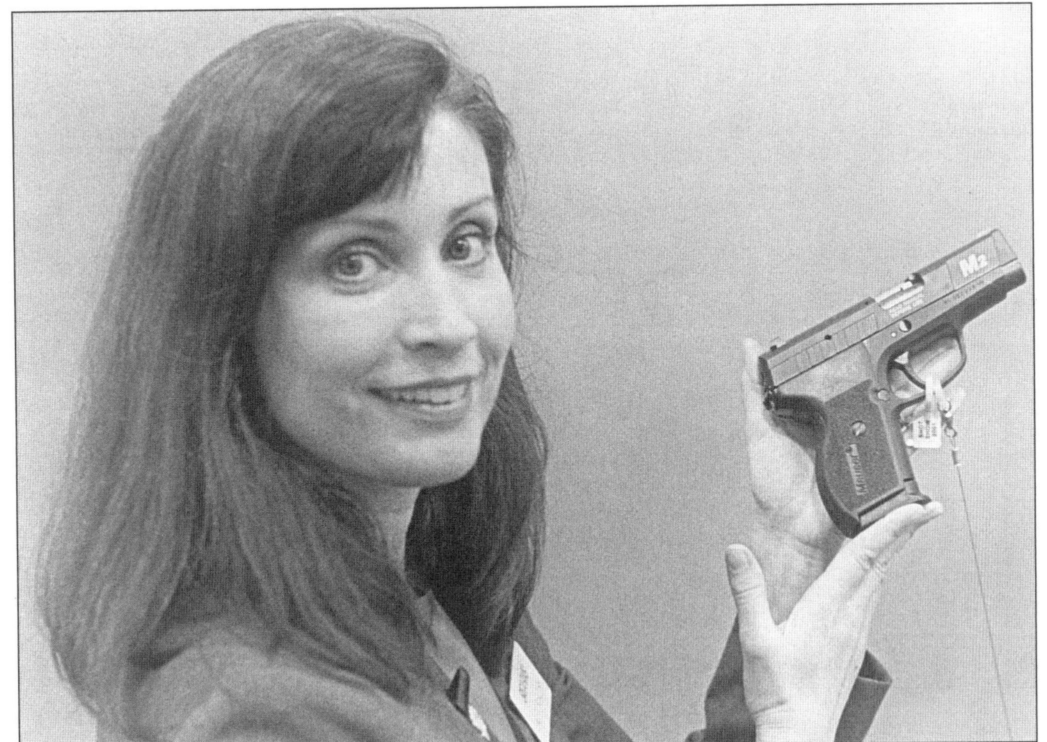

Sigarm's Laura Burgess displays a Mauser M2 pistol, which is marketed by Sigarms, along with the company's extensive line of SIG pistols.

The pistol is interesting for both design and ammunition.

At first observation, the pistol reminds one of the HK P7, as it has a long pivoted bar in the front strap of the grip frame. On the HK pistol, this was a cocking lever; on the SO P21, the lever is called a grip safety. When the SO pistol is grasped, it operates as a conventional double-action (DA) arm, that is, DA for the first shot, SA for succeeding shots. The difference with the P21 is that when the grip safety is released, the hammer is automatically uncocked and drops to the safety position.

As a compact pistol of about 4.7x6.5 inches, the P21 has its 3.1-inch barrel offered in more-or-less standard 9mm and 40 chamberings. However, SO also offers it with a new cartridge, the 224 HV. The new round is essentially an elongated 9mm case necked down to 22 caliber. The overall length is about that of the standard 9mm cartridge. A 40-grain jacketed bullet reportedly goes out at about 2000 feet per second. For comparison, that is faster than the 40-grain 22 Winchester Magnum Rimfire (22 WMR) fired from a rifle. Pretty zippy.

www.sommer-ockenfuss.de

SPRINGFIELD

Springfield has introduced an Internal Locking System (ILS) for their line of 1911-type pistols. The locking device uses a special key to make the pistol inoperable; a reverse turn of the key can put it back into service. The interesting thing about this system is that it is completely contained within the

Some models of the S&W 22-caliber pistol line are now offered with "Hi-Viz" sights.

There is now a ported S&W Sigma. The new SW40P and SW9P have barrel porting, three-dot sights and an accessory rail.

▶Here is the prototype of the new Sommer & Ockenfuss P21 pistol. The grip safety at the front of the grip allows the gun to fire as a conventional DA pistol. When the grip safety is released, the hammer lowers automatically.

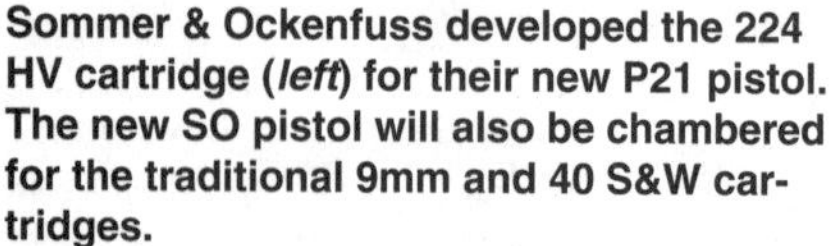

Sommer & Ockenfuss developed the 224 HV cartridge (*left*) for their new P21 pistol. The new SO pistol will also be chambered for the traditional 9mm and 40 S&W cartridges.

mainspring housing. Springfield began phasing these in on their products in February 2001 and planned to offer a retrofit kit soon afterwards. The installation requires no modification to the pistol.

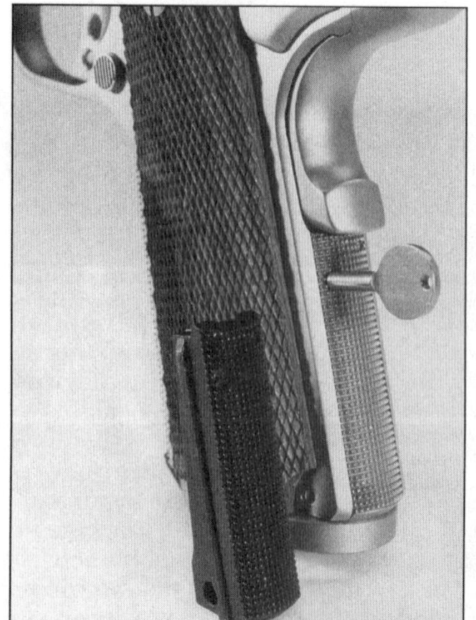

The new Integral Locking System (ILS) from Springfield Armory is a patented locking device that can disable a 1911-type pistol. It is contained entirely within the mainspring housing.

A new pistol, the TRP Operator, was introduced by Springfield at the January 2001 SHOT Show. The initials stand for Tactical Response Pistol, and the gun is based around the FBI-contract-pistol specifications. The "Operator" portion of the name refers to a special frame with a forged light/accessory rail at the front. The pistol carries most of Springfield's current enhancements, and it has the adjustable rear sight mounted in a forward position on the slide to prevent damage or snagging.

www.springfieldarmory.com

STEYR

The smaller "S" series Steyr pistol, introduced last year, is now in production. The first shipment of 9mms reached the United States in January 2001, with the 40 S&W variant coming soon after.

Steyr's importer, GSI of Trussville, AL, has offered an upgrade of a more consistent trigger assembly for the first group of "M"- series pistols sold. They have the serial numbers of the ones eligible for the upgrade.

The triangular sight system remains standard, but Steyr is con-

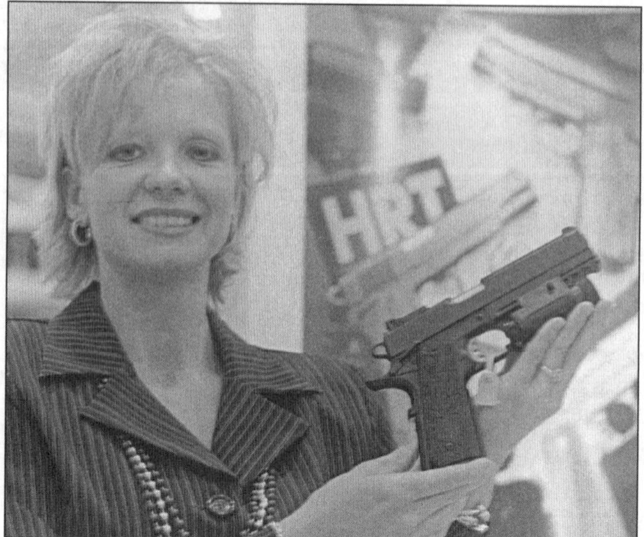

Springfield's Donna Rahn displays the armsmaker's new TRP Operator, a 45 with a special frame for accessory attachment. This specimen has a light installed.

The compact Steyr S-series pistols are now in full production.

sidering more sight options for the future.

www.GSIfirearms.com

STI

The V.I.P., a new 45 ACP pistol, was STI's offering for 2001. Based on the 1911, of course, the V.I.P. has an interesting aluminum frame with a double-stack polymer grip. The slide is stainless steel, sized to fit the 3.9-inch barrel. The combination of materials, says STI, makes a potent, lightweight, corrosion-resistant personal-defense firearm. Available in 45 ACP, the capacity is 10+1 and the weight is 25 ounces.

www.stiguns.com

TALON

A new company from Ennis, MT, Talon Industries has introduced pistols in the recent category of inexpensive subcompact polymer-frame carry pistols. Two models, the T-100 (380) and the T-200 (9mm) are offered. Each has a 10-round magazine, with a weight of 17 ounces. Overall size is 4.4x6 inches, and the barrel length is 3.3 inches. Locking is by a tilting-barrel system. Trigger mechanism is DAO.

talonind@3rivers.net

TAURUS

Handy little pistols and more ammunition options have given the 32 ACP a new lease on life in recent years. Now Taurus will have a 32 Automatic in their line. The new Taurus 32 is included in the polymer-frame Millennium series, and is designated PT 132. The little gun was too new to make it into the company's 2001 catalog, so keep an eye peeled for it.

The compact Millenium 45, the PT 145, was introduced last year, but ran into production delays. Quantity delivery of the compact 23-ounce 45 was rescheduled for summer 2001. For those who like a variety of sight options, it may be worth the wait, as night sights will be available when it arrives

www.taurususa.com

VALTRO

Whatever happened to the Valtro 45, the nice Italian-made 1911 design that was introduced several years ago? It had a slow manufacturing start, but is now in production. As of early 2001, the guns were coming out of Italy at the rate of about 100 a month. The pistols are offered in the United States by Valtro USA, of San Rafael, CA.

WALTHER USA

Some changes have been taking place at Walther USA since last year. The Hungarian-made PPK/E, announced last year to replace the PPK/S, will not be imported after all. Instead, the PPK/S, which was destined to fade into history, was slightly redesigned and was scheduled to be available by late summer 2001. The remaining stocks of the original-design PPK/S will be sold until they are gone.

Walther realizes that just about everyone can use a 22 pistol. A new offering, a 22-caliber version of the company's P99 pistol, was introduced in January 2001, with availability planned for April 2001. The new P22 is about 25 % smaller than the P99, but retains the same general appearance, although there are mechanical differences. The takedown, ambidextrous magazine release and interchangeable grip backstraps are similar, but the new 22 is hammer-operated, rather than striker-fired. Two versions were announced, a plinker with a 3.4-inch barrel and a more serious

The subcompact Talon pistol is a new entry in the field of inexpensive polymer-frame carry pistols. It is available in 9mm and 380.

Talon's Sharon Edwards points out the features of the Talon 9mm pistol to Sean Gilthorpe at the 2001 SHOT Show.

version with a weighted 5-inch barrel. The barrels are interchangeable, and the first 1000 will be offered in a kit with both barrels.
www.walther-usa.com

WILSON

Wilson Combat has introduced their KZ-45, a polymer-frame compact carry pistol. A prototype was shown at the January 2001 SHOT Show, and availability was planned for sometime in 2002. A 9+1 45, the new compact Wilson, based on the 1911 design, sports a 4.1-inch barrel. Although the magazine is of the staggered double-column type, the width is as thin as a standard 1911. The KZ-45 will come with an accuracy guarantee of 1.5 inches at 25 yards.
www.wilsoncombat.com

POSTSCRIPT

Innovative accessories for semi-automatic handguns have been recently introduced. Here are just a few of them:

Pearce Grips offers new items for the ever-popular 1911 pistols. A shooter who likes his present grip panels but would like front-strap finger grooves can get just the rubber front grooves. The Pearce product is a clever way to adapt the finger grooves without modification of the gun. Pearce also offers rubber grip panels, with moulded big-diamond checkering. These can be used by themselves or combined with the finger grooves for a good-feeling grip. www.pearcegrip.com

With the trend to legal-limit magazine capacity in smaller-size pistols, it sometimes becomes harder to load the magazines. There are good magazine loaders available, but generally different ones are required for different magazines. Magloader has introduced a clever new loading aid that will work with all magazines in calibers 32 through 45. The simple loader fits on the shooter's thumb, is easy to carry around, and works great. www.magloader.com

How about a magazine for magazines? The Redi-Clip is a nylon dispenser that holds five loaded magazines and allows them to be withdrawn one at a time. It can clip to a belt or can be otherwise mounted. www.Redi-Clip.com

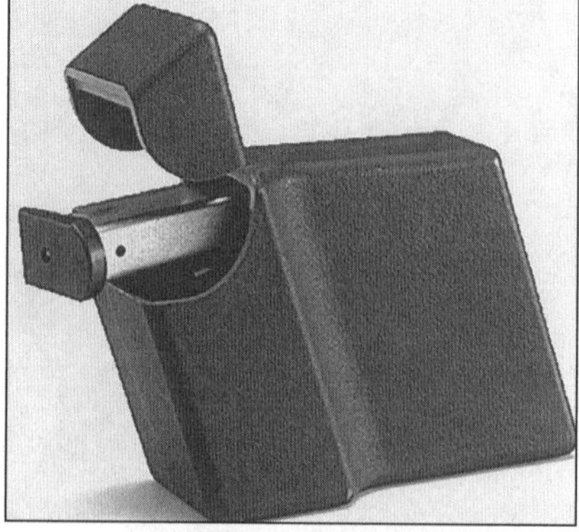

Among a plethora of new accessories is the Redi-Clip, sort of a magazine for pistol magazines.

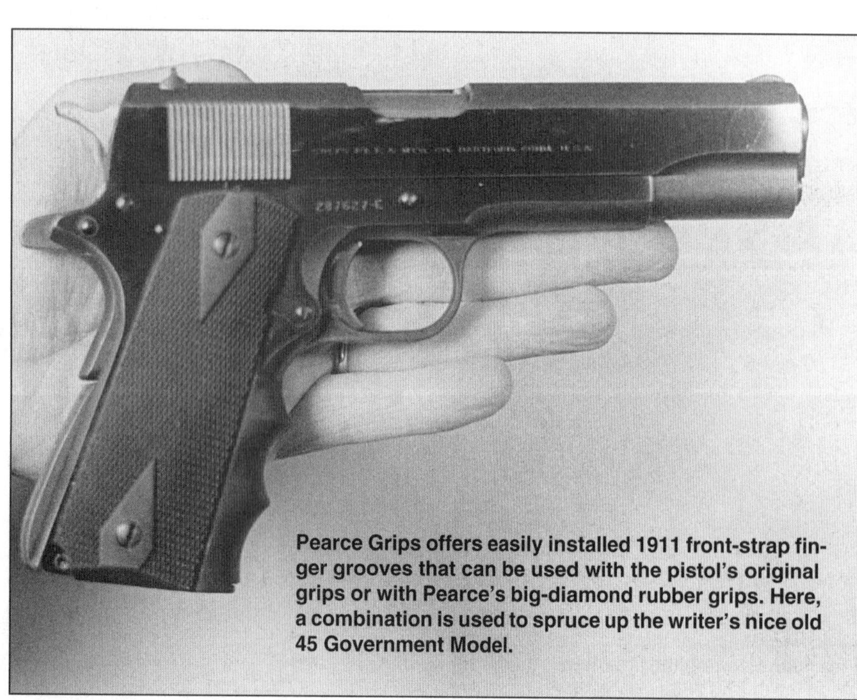

Pearce Grips offers easily installed 1911 front-strap finger grooves that can be used with the pistol's original grips or with Pearce's big-diamond rubber grips. Here, a combination is used to spruce up the writer's nice old 45 Government Model.

The Safety Fast shooting kit is available from Numrich Gun Parts for Colt 1911 and Browning High Power pistols. The modified pistol can be safely carried with hammer down on a chambered round. By depressing the manual safety, the hammer is automatically cocked and the pistol is ready to shoot. The kit comes with complete instructions and can be installed without modification to the gun.
info@gunpartscorp.com

"Pre-ban" high capacity pistol magazines are treasured items for those with high-capacity pistols. Yet, the magazines can lead a hard life, especially when used in certain types of pistol competition. It is a tragic loss if one is damaged beyond use. Now, the LaPrade Company offers legal replacement magazine bodies for damaged high-capacity Glock magazines. A shooter can put the internal parts of the unusable magazine into the new body and be back in action.

These are just a few of the accessories available for those who enjoy shooting autoloading pistols. A shooter can find an array of metallic sights, optical sights, electronic sights, lasers, grips, holsters, safety devices, specialized parts and magazines, not to mention such staples as ammunition and targets. We should never lose sight of the fact that autoloading handguns and their accessories provide both a creative and an economic boost to our nation. •

Update: Handgun Ammunition, Ballistics & Components

by Holt Bodinson

WHETHER YOUR INTEREST runs to autoloaders, cowboy guns, hunting or handloading, you'll find some interesting new handgun cartridges and components here from the world's leading makers.

Aguila

This year brings the introduction of Aguila's "smart bullet," the "IQ." The IQ is a dual-purpose, non-lead alloy bullet that breaks into 3 or 4 projectiles when fired directly at a gelatin block, while at the same time, offering cohesion and excellent penetration against hard surfaces such as glass and plastic. The IQ bullet is currently loaded in the 9mm, 45 ACP, and 40 S&W and will soon be released as a 170-grain, 2400 fps loading in the 454 Casull.

www.aguilaammo.com

Accurate Arms

No new powders this year—instead, AA has issued the 2nd Edition of its thoroughly unique *"Loading Guide."* In it is data for the XMP-5744 reduced load powder and XMR-4064. Both powders were developed after *Guide* Number 1 was published. A whole new section devoted to Cowboy Action Shooting loads has been added — plus loading data for the 300 Whisper, 7.62x25 Tokarev, 357 Sig, 400 CorBon, 44 Russian, 45 S&W Schofield and 460 Rowland. Lots of new bullets have been added, including the Remington 30-caliber Sabot! This is a *"must have"* reloading manual.

www.accuratepowder.com

Alliant's Green Dot is still Green Dot but it burns 50 percent cleaner.

Alliant Powder

Making a major push to improve the clean-burning characteristics of some to its classic powders, Alliant has reduced powder fouling by 50 percent in its Green Dot and Unique canister grades.

ww.alliantpowder.com

Barnes Bullets

Most computer-based ballistic programs seem to be developed by technocrats or computer nerds — not the Barnes program. Here is the easiest to use, most logical ballistics program available, and Barnes has just revised it. It's available as a download from Barnes' web site after one pays a reasonable fee for a user ID number. *Highly recommended.* Look for the 3rd edition of Barnes reloading manual to make its appearance mid-year — new data will include the XLC and VLC lines.

www.barnesbullets.com

Bismuth

Bismuth has transferred its non-toxic shotgun shell technology to the realm of frangible, non-toxic handgun ammunition. Their new 9mm, 40 S&W and 45 ACP projectiles are created by casting, swaging and then copper-plating a pure Bismuth core, thereby approximating the weight and recoil of lead ammunition. Upon impact, the Bismuth bullets disintegrate into Bismuth dust. Labeled *"Bismuth Reduced Hazard Ammunition,"* the new loads are recommended for high-risk environments — including nuclear, biological, chemical, precious cargo and personal defense situations—where ricochet and over-penetration is to be avoided. www-bismuth-notox.com

Black Hills Ammunition

New this year are a 9mm 124-grain JHP+P load at 1250 fps; a 165-grain Gold Dot or FMJ loading for the 40 S&W at maximum velocities; a 45 ACP +P load featuring the 230-grain Hornady XTP bullet at 950 fps; and for the cowboys and cowgirls, a 32 H&R Magnum (!) load featuring a 90-grain lead bullet at 750 fps. Anyway, Black Hills offers superior ammo at great prices.

www.black-hills.com

CCI-Speer

The aluminum-cased Blaser line is being expanded with 38 Special, 44 Special and 45 Colt "cowboy" loads. On the Speer side of the shop, the high-performance Gold Dot handgun line has been extended to include the 44 Special, 454 Casull and 50 Action Express, while the 25 and 32 auto cartridges with FMJs now grace the Lawman line. Speer has developed several new bullets this year — a 170-grain Gold Dot SP .357 and a 130-grain FNSP for the 7-30 Waters cartridge.

www.cci-ammunition.com

Cfventures

Here's a small mail order operation with a unique product — a *"soft"* gas check that can reduce

▼CCI is reviving the 22 WRF load with a 45-grain Gold Dot at 1300 fps.

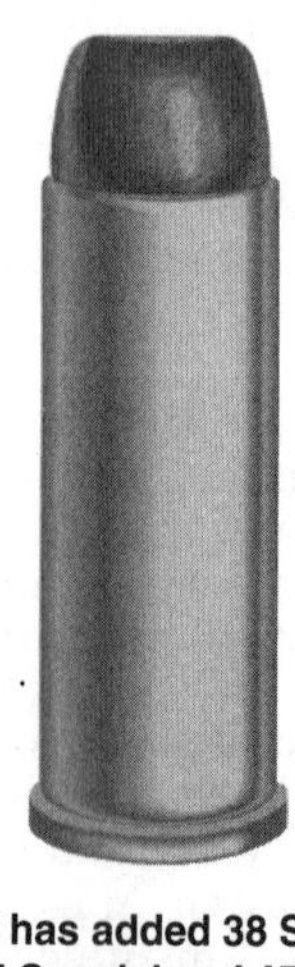

▲CCI has added 38 Special, 44 Special and 45 Colt cowboy action loads to its Blaser line.

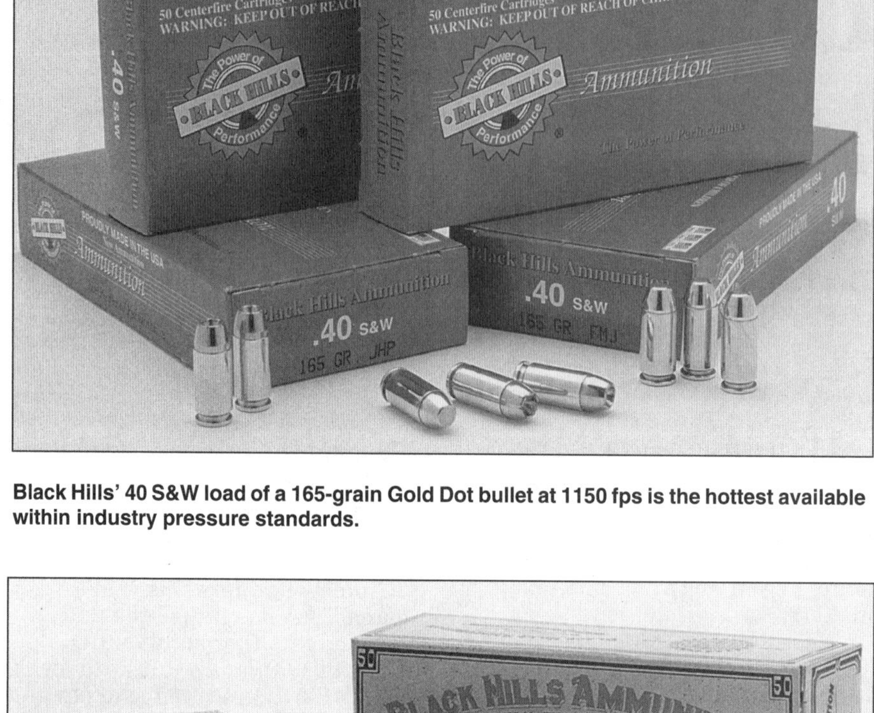

Black Hills' 40 S&W load of a 165-grain Gold Dot bullet at 1150 fps is the hottest available within industry pressure standards.

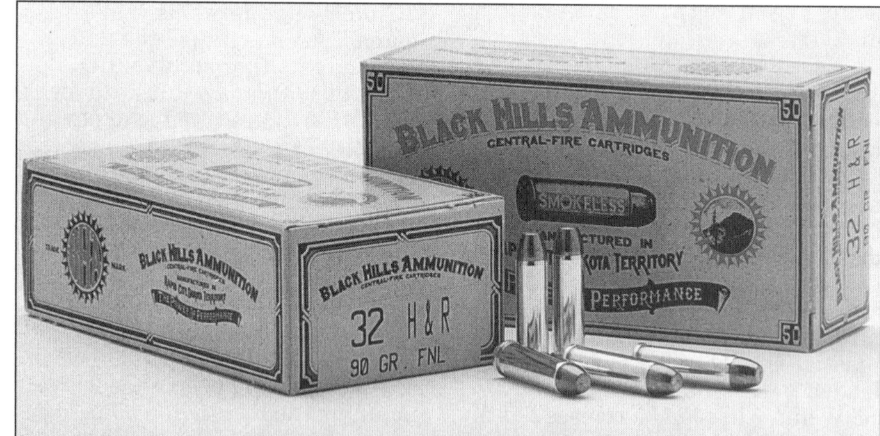

With the return of the 32 H&R to the Ruger Vaquero line, Black Hills offers the perfect cowboy action load – a 90-grain lead bullet at 750 fps.

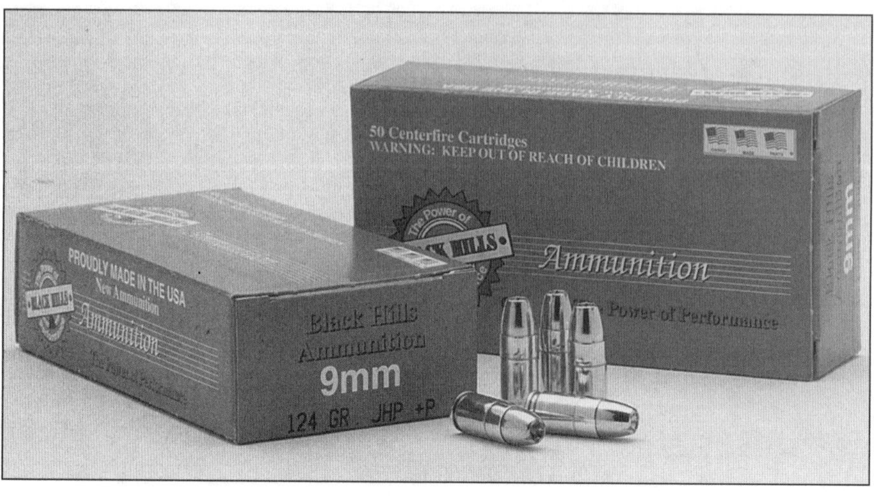

Black Hills' new 9mm+P load features a 124-grain Speer Gold Dot at a sizzling 1250 fps.

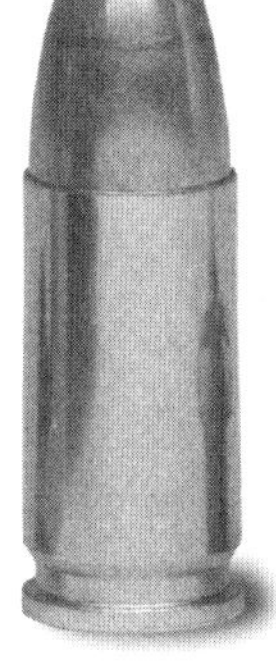
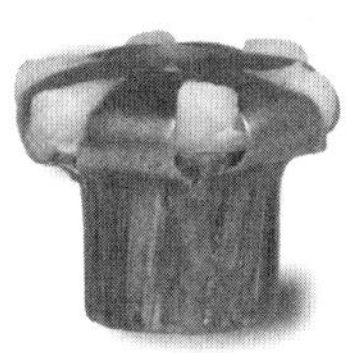

◀ Federal's expanding FMJ features a collapsing nose over an internal rubber core and is designed for police departments that prohibit HP ammo.

leading significantly. Actually it's a thin waxy sheet that is pressed cookie-cutter-style into the mouth of the case just before seating the bullet. Worth trying. Reach them at 509 Harvey Drive, Bloomington, IN 47403-1715.

Clean Shot Technologies

Clean Shot, the black powder substitute, is now offered in easy-to-handle 30- and 50-grain pellets for muzzleloading, or loading those cowboy action cartridges. Here's the smoke without the mess.
www.cleanshot.com

Federal

Federal was purchased by Blount recently and will continue to produce fine ammunition under the Federal label. The 9mm and 40 S&W have been given a revolutionary bullet that is actually an expanding FMJ featuring a collapsing internal rubber tip just under the nose.
www.federalcartridge.com

Garrett Cartridges

If you own a 44 Magnum revolver, Garrett delivers all the power you'll ever need for big-game hunting. Garrett loads super-hard cast bullets with broad meplats and of a weight-forward Hammerhead design that leaves adequate room in the case for powder. Garrett's 44 Magnum handgun loads are very impressive—a 310-grain bullet at 1325 fps and a 330-grain bullet at 1385 fps.
www.garrettcartridges.com

Hodgdon

No new powders this year but lots of new loading data in their "*Basic Reloaders Manual*" including 'Longshot' pistol loads.
www.hodgdon.com

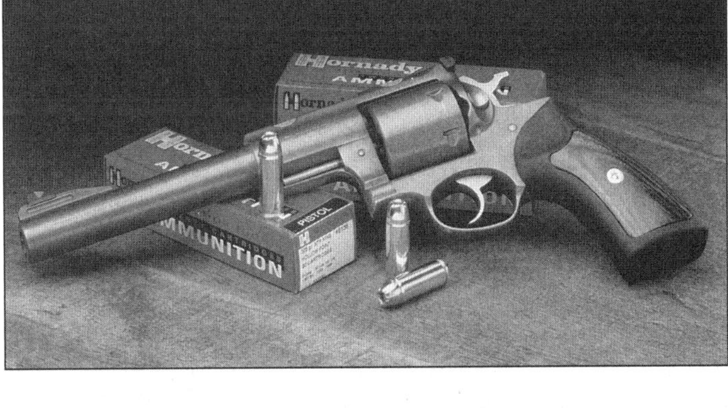

Hornady is introducing the new Ruger 480 cartridge, featuring a 325-grain XTP bullet at 1,350 fps.

Hornady

As a joint project with Ruger, Hornady released the 480 Ruger cartridge featuring a 325-grain XTP magnum bullet at 1,350 fps.
www.hornady.com

ITD Enterprises

ITD is working with Murom, Russia's largest primer maker, to market a line of non-hygroscopic, lead- and heavy metal-free primers that have at least a 25-year shelf life and which, according to HP White tests, exhibit uniform sensitivity and reliability. Stay tuned.
itdprime@aol.com

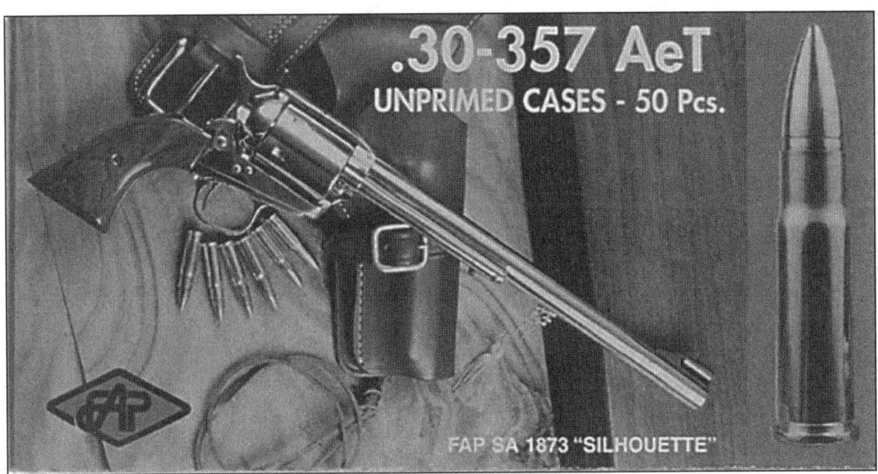

With a 123-grain bullet at 1992 fps, the 30-357 Aet should really perform in Pietta's new silhouette six-shooter.

Lapua

In addition to its new 6.5-284 brass, Lapua is introducing some very unique handgun cartridges this year. There's a rimmed, bottlenecked, 30-357 AeT cartridge sporting a 123-grain bullet at 1992 fps to be chambered in a single-action silhouette revolver made by Fratelli Pietta of Italy. In conjunction with Tanfoglio, Lapua has designed a heavy-walled 9mm case called the 9mm FAR. The purpose of the reinforced case is to permit the manufacture of a high velocity,

▲For handgun hunters, Nosler has designed a 90-grain 6mm Ballistic Tip that expands at more moderate velocities.

in-line barrel, blowback action pistol that will offer improved accuracy and performance. Finally, there's a rimless, heavy duty, 38 Super Comp version of the 38 Super Auto cartridge that should minimize reloading problems in progressive presses. Speaking about reloading, Lapua and Vihtavuori have released a 38-minute video entitled *"Reloading with the Masters"* featuring the champs — Leatham, Enos and Hobdell, who do some show-and-tell about reloading for competition.
www.lapua.com

▲Remington continues to expand its UMC Leadless line with the addition of the 40 S&W.

Nosler

This is a "Ballistic Tip" year for Nosler with the introduction of some great new calibers and grain weights. In the expanded Ballistic Tip line, there's a 90-grain 243 handgun-hunting bullet.
www.nosler.com

Old Western Scrounger

Dangerous Dave now carries the full Kynoch line, so if you need anything from 700 Nitro to 318 Wesley Richards, the *OWS* has it. Several new calibers have been added to the "obsolete" ammunition line — the 11mm French Ordnance Revolver and, for you Chicago Palm Pistol owners, the 32 Extra Short Rimfire. The new catalog's a scream, and filled with rare goodies.
www.ows-ammunition.com

Remington

With the interest in lead-free ammunition accelerating, Remington has added a UMC Leadless line that includes the 9mm, 380 Auto, 38 Special, 40 S&W and 45 Auto – and developed leadless frangible loads for the 38 Special and 357 Sig.
www.remington.com

Simunition

Simunition makes and distributes highly refined lines of non-lethal practice ammunition that can be fired in a trainee's personal service weapon. Some of the products are designed for face-to-face combat practice with padded clothing while others are for close-quarter combat target ranges.
www.simunition.com

SSK

SSK's radically *"blown-out"* '06 based single-shot pistol rounds now include the 257, 6.5 and 270 calibers.
www.sskindustries.com

Winchester

The economical USA Brand line also has been upgraded with the addition of jacketed hollow points for the 38 Special, 9mm, 357 SIG, 40 S&W and 45 Auto. And, to satisfy the demand for leadless loads, the WinClean pistol ammunition line has been expanded to include the 9mm Luger with either a 124- or 147-grain bullet and the 357 SIG loaded with a 125-grain WinClean projectile.
www.winchester.com

Wolf

As an importer of ammunition from Russia's Tula Cartridge Works, Wolf continues to expand the line of non-corrosive, steel-cased ammunition. A number of new loads and calibers are being added this year, including the 40 S&W, 223 Rem. HP, and match-grade brass-cased 22 rimfire.
www.wolfammo.com

It's been a busy year. ●

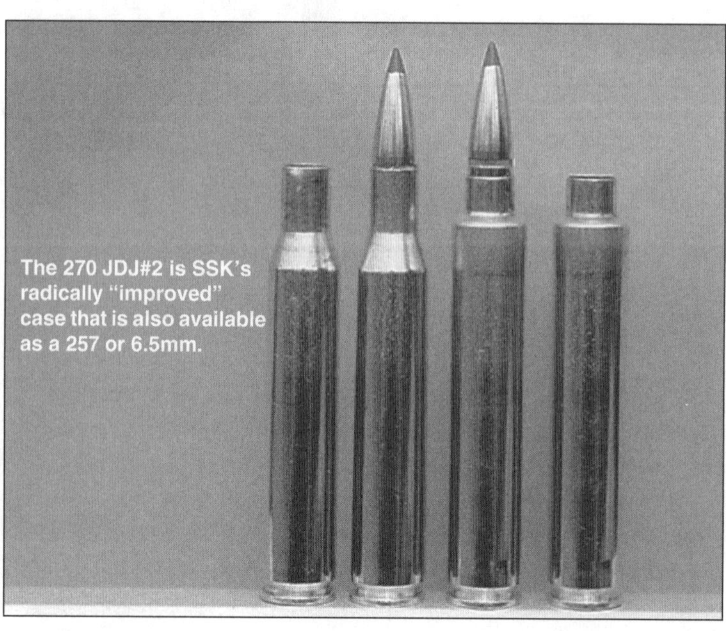

The 270 JDJ#2 is SSK's radically "improved" case that is also available as a 257 or 6.5mm.

Centerfire Handgun Cartridges — Ballistics & Prices

Notes: Blanks are available in 32 S&W, 38 S&W and 38 Special. "V" after barrel length indicates test barrel was vented to produce ballistics similar to a revolver with a normal barrel-to-cylinder gap. Ammo prices are per 50 rounds except when marked with an ** which signifies a 20 round box; *** signifies a 25-round box. Not all loads are available from all ammo manufacturers. Listed loads are those made by Remington, Winchester, Federal, and others. DISC. is a discontinued load. Prices are rounded to nearest whole dollar and will vary with brand and retail outlet. † = new bullet weight this year; "c" indicates a change in data.

Cartridge	Bullet Wgt. Grs.	VELOCITY (fps)			ENERGY (ft. lbs.)			Mid-Range Traj. (in.)		Bbl. Lgth. (in).	Est. Price/ box
		Muzzle	50 yds.	100 yds.	Muzzle	50 yds.	100 yds.	50 yds.	100 yds.		
221 Rem. Fireball	50	2650	2380	2130	780	630	505	0.2	0.8	10.5"	$15
25 Automatic	35	900	813	742	63	51	43	NA	NA	2"	$18
25 Automatic	45	815	730	655	65	55	40	1.8	7.7	2"	$21
25 Automatic	50	760	705	660	65	55	50	2.0	8.7	2"	$17
7.5mm Swiss	107	1010	NA	NA	240	NA	NA	NA	NA	NA	NEW
7.62mmTokarev	87	1390	NA	NA	365	NA	NA	0.6	NA	4.5"	NA
7.62 Nagant	97	1080	NA	NA	350	NA	NA	NA	NA	NA	NEW
7.63 Mauser	88	1440	NA	NA	405	NA	NA	NA	NA	NA	NEW
30 Luger	93†	1220	1110	1040	305	255	225	0.9	3.5	4.5"	$34
30 Carbine	110	1790	1600	1430	785	625	500	0.4	1.7	10"	$28
30-357 AeT	123	1992	NA	NA	1084	NA	NA	NA	NA	10"	NA
32 S&W	88	680	645	610	90	80	75	2.5	10.5	3"	$17
32 S&W Long	98	705	670	635	115	100	90	2.3	10.5	4"	$17
32 Short Colt	80	745	665	590	100	80	60	2.2	9.9	4"	$19
32 H&R Magnum	85	1100	1020	930	230	195	165	1.0	4.3	4.5"	$21
32 H&R Magnum	95	1030	940	900	225	190	170	1.1	4.7	4.5"	$19
32 Automatic	60	970	895	835	125	105	95	1.3	5.4	4"	$22
32 Automatic	60	1000	917	849	133	112	96			4"	NA
32 Automatic	65	950	890	830	130	115	100	1.3	5.6	NA	NA
32 Automatic	71	905	855	810	130	115	95	1.4	5.8	4"	$19
8mm Lebel Pistol	111	850	NA	NA	180	NA	NA	NA	NA	NA	NEW
8mm Steyr	112	1080	NA	NA	290	NA	NA	NA	NA	NA	NEW
8mm Gasser	126	850	NA	NA	200	NA	NA	NA	NA	NA	NEW
380 Automatic	60	1130	960	NA	170	120	NA	1.0	NA	NA	NA
380 Automatic	85/88	990	920	870	190	165	145	1.2	5.1	4"	$20
380 Automatic	90	1000	890	800	200	160	130	1.2	5.5	3.75"	$10
380 Automatic	95/100	955	865	785	190	160	130	1.4	5.9	4"	$20
38 Super Auto +P	115	1300	1145	1040	430	335	275	0.7	3.3	5"	$26
38 Super Auto +P	125/130	1215	1100	1015	425	350	300	0.8	3.6	5"	$26
38 Super Auto +P	147	1100	1050	1000	395	355	325	0.9	4.0	5"	NA
9x18mm Makarov	95	1000	NA	NA	NA	NA	NA	NA	NA	NA	NEW
9x18mm Ultra	100	1050	NA	NA	240	NA	NA	NA	NA	NA	NEW
9x23mm Largo	124	1190	1055	966	390	306	257	0.7	3.7	4"	NA
9x23mm Win.	125	1450	1249	1103	583	433	338	0.6	2.8	NA	NA
9mm Steyr	115	1180	NA	NA	350	NA	NA	NA	NA	NA	NEW
9mm Luger	88	1500	1190	1010	440	275	200	0.6	3.1	4"	$24
9mm Luger	90	1360	1112	978	370	247	191	NA	NA	4"	$26
9mm Luger	95	1300	1140	1010	350	275	215	0.8	3.4	4"	NA
9mm Luger	100	1180	1080	NA	305	255	NA	0.9	NA	4"	NA
9mm Luger	115	1155	1045	970	340	280	240	0.9	3.9	4"	$21
9mm Luger	123/125	1110	1030	970	340	290	260	1.0	4.0	4"	$23
9mm Luger	140	935	890	850	270	245	225	1.3	5.5	4"	$23
9mm Luger	147	990	940	900	320	290	265	1.1	4.9	4"	$26
9mm Luger +P	90	1475	NA	NA	437	NA	NA	NA	NA	NA	NA
9mm Luger +P	115	1250	1113	1019	399	316	265	0.8	3.5	4"	$27
9mm Federal	115	1280	1130	1040	420	330	280	0.7	3.3	4"V	$24
9mm Luger Vector	115	1155	1047	971	341	280	241	NA	NA	4"	NA
9mm Luger +P	124	1180	1089	1021	384	327	287	0.8	3.8	4"	NA
38 S&W	146	685	650	620	150	135	125	2.4	10.0	4"	$19
38 Short Colt	125	730	685	645	150	130	115	2.2	9.4	6"	$19
39 Special	100	950	900	NA	200	180	NA	1.3	NA	4"V	NA
38 Special	110	945	895	850	220	195	175	1.3	5.4	4"V	$23

Notes: Blanks are available in 32 S&W, 38 S&W and 38 Special. "V" after barrel length indicates test barrel was vented to produce ballistics similar to a revolver with a normal barrel-to-cylinder gap. Ammo prices are per 50 rounds except when marked with an ** which signifies a 20 round box; *** signifies a 25-round box. Not all loads are available from all ammo manufacturers. Listed loads are those made by Remington, Winchester, Federal, and others. DISC. is a discontinued load. Prices are rounded to nearest whole dollar and will vary with brand and retail outlet. † = new bullet weight this year; "c" indicates a change in data.

Group	Cartridge	Bullet Wgt. Grs.	VELOCITY (fps)			ENERGY (ft. lbs.)			Mid-Range Traj. (in.)		Bbl. Lgth. (in).	Est. Price/ box
			Muzzle	50 yds.	100 yds.	Muzzle	50 yds.	100 yds.	50 yds.	100 yds.		
38 cont.	38 Special	110	945	895	850	220	195	175	1.3	5.4	4"V	$23
	38 Special	130	775	745	710	175	160	120	1.9	7.9	4"V	$22
	38 Special Cowboy	140	800	767	735	199	183	168			7.5" V	NA
	38 (Multi-Ball)	140	830	730	505	215	130	80	2.0	10.6	4"V	$10**
	38 Special	148	710	635	565	165	130	105	2.4	10.6	4"V	$17
	38 Special	158	755	725	690	200	185	170	2.0	8.3	4"V	$18
	38 Special +P	95	1175	1045	960	290	230	195	0.9	3.9	4"V	$23
	38 Special +P	110	995	925	870	240	210	185	1.2	5.1	4"V	$23
	38 Special +P	125	975	929	885	264	238	218	1	5.2	4"	NA
	38 Special +P	125	945	900	860	250	225	205	1.3	5.4	4"V	#23
	38 Special +P	129	945	910	870	255	235	215	1.3	5.3	4"V	$11
	38 Special +P	130	925	887	852	247	227	210	1.3	5.50	4"V	NA
	38 Special +P	147/150(c)	884	NA	NA	264	NA	NA	NA	NA	4"V	$27
	38 Special +P	158	890	855	825	280	255	240	1.4	6.0	4"V	$20
357	357 SIG	115	1520	NA	NA	593	NA	NA	NA	NA	NA	NA
	357 SIG	124	1450	NA	NA	578	NA	NA	NA	NA	NA	NA
	357 SIG	125	1350	1190	1080	510	395	325	0.7	3.1	4"	NA
	357 SIG	150	1130	1030	970	420	355	310	0.9	4.0	NA	NA
	356 TSW	115	1520	NA	NA	593	NA	NA	NA	NA	NA	NA
	356 TSW	124	1450	NA	NA	578	NA	NA	NA	NA	NA	NA
	356 TSW	135	1280	1120	1010	490	375	310	0.8	3.50	NA	NA
	356 TSW	147	1220	1120	1040	485	410	355	0.8	3.5	5"	NA
	357 Mag., Super Clean	105	1650									NA
	357 Magnum	110	1295	1095	975	410	290	230	0.8	3.5	4"V	$25
	357 (Med.Vel.)	125	1220	1075	985	415	315	270	0.8	3.7	4"V	$25
	357 Magnum	125	1450	1240	1090	585	425	330	0.6	2.8	4"V	$25
	357 (Multi-Ball)	140	1155	830	665	420	215	135	1.2	6.4	4"V	$11**
	357 Magnum	140	1360	1195	1075	575	445	360	0.7	3.0	4"V	$25
	357 Magnum	145	1290	1155	1060	535	430	360	0.8	3.5	4"V	$26
	357 Magnum	150/158	1235	1105	1015	535	430	360	0.8	3.5	4"V	$25
	357 Mag. Cowboy	158	800	761	725	225	203	185				NA
	357 Magnum	165	1290	1189	1108	610	518	450	0.7	3.1	8-3/8"	NA
	357 Magnum	180	1145	1055	985	525	445	390	0.9	3.9	4"V	$25
	357 Magnum	180	1180	1088	1020	557	473	416	0.8	3.6	8"V	NA
	357 Mag. CorBon F.A.	180	1650	1512	1386	1088	913	767	1.66	0.0		NA
	357 Mag. CorBon	200	1200	1123	1061	640	560	500	3.19	0.0		NA
	357 Rem. Maximum	158	1825	1590	1380	1170	885	670	0.4	1.7	10.5"	$14**
40, 10mm	40 S&W	135	1140	1070	NA	390	345	NA	0.9	NA	4"	NA
	40 S&W	155	1140	1026	958	447	362	309	0.9	4.1	4"	$14***
	40 S&W	165	1150	NA	NA	485	NA	NA	NA	NA	4"	$18***
	40 S&W	180	985	936	893	388	350	319	1.4	5.0	4"	$14***
	40 S&W	180	1015	960	914	412	368	334	1.3	4.5	4"	NA
	400 Cor-Bon	135	1450	NA	NA	630	NA	NA	NA	NA	5"	NA
	10mm Automatic	155	1125	1046	986	436	377	335	0.9	3.9	5"	$26
	10mm Automatic	170	1340	1165	1145	680	510	415	0.7	3.2	5"	$31
	10mm Automatic	175	1290	1140	1035	650	505	420	0.7	3.3	5.5"	$11**
	10mm Auto. (FBI)	180	950	905	865	361	327	299	1.5	5.4	4"	$16**
	10mm Automatic	180	1030	970	920	425	375	340	1.1	4.7	5"	$16**
	10mm Auto H.V.	180†	1240	1124	1037	618	504	430	0.8	3.4	5"	$27
	10mm Automatic	200	1160	1070	1010	495	510	430	0.9	3.8	5"	$14**
	10.4mm Italian	177	950	NA	NA	360	NA	NA	NA	NA	NA	NEW

Notes: Blanks are available in 32 S&W, 38 S&W and 38 Special. "V" after barrel length indicates test barrel was vented to produce ballistics similar to a revolver with a normal barrel-to-cylinder gap. Ammo prices are per 50 rounds except when marked with an ** which signifies a 20 round box; *** signifies a 25-round box. Not all loads are available from all ammo manufacturers. Listed loads are those made by Remington, Winchester, Federal, and others. DtSC. is a discontinued load. Prices are rounded to nearest whole dollar and will vary with brand and retail outlet. † = new bullet weight this year; "c" indicates a change in data.

Cartridge	Bullet Wgt. Grs.	VELOCITY (fps)			ENERGY (ft. lbs.)			Mid-Range Traj. (in.)		Bbl. Lgth. (in).	Est. Price/ box
		Muzzle	50 yds.	100 yds.	Muzzle	50 yds.	100 yds.	50 yds.	100 yds.		
41 Action Exp.	180	1000	947	903	400	359	326	0.5	4.2	5"	$13**
41 Rem. Magnum	170	1420	1165	1015	760	515	390	0.7	3.2	4"V	$33
41 Rem. Magnum	175	1250	1120	1030	605	490	410	0.8	3.4	4"V	$14**
41 (Med. Vel.)	210	965	900	840	435	375	330	1.3	5.4	4"V	$30
41 Rem. Magnum	210	1300	1160	1060	790	630	535	0.7	3.2	4"V	$33
44 S&W Russian	247	780	NA	NA	335	NA	NA	NA	NA	NA	NA
44 S&W Special	180	980	NA	NA	383	NA	NA	NA	NA	6.5"	NA
44 S&W Special	180	1000	935	882	400	350	311	NA	NA	7.5"V	NA
44 S&W Special	200†	875	825	780	340	302	270	1.2	6.0	6"	$13**
44 S&W Special	200	1035	940	865	475	390	335	1.1	4.9	6.5"	$13**
44 S&W Special	240/246	755	725	695	310	285	265	2.0	8.3	6.5"	$26
44-40 Win. Cowboy	225	750	723	695	281	261	242				NA
44 Rem. Magnum	180	1610	1365	1175	1035	745	550	0.5	2.3	4"V	$18**
44 Rem. Magnum	200	1400	1192	1053	870	630	492	0.6	NA	6.5"	$20
44 Rem. Magnum	210	1495	1310	1165	1040	805	635	0.6	2.5	6.5"	$18**
44 (Med. Vel.)	240	1000	945	900	535	475	435	1.1	4.8	6.5"	$17
44 R.M. (Jacketed)	240	1180	1080	1010	740	625	545	0.9	3.7	4"V	$18**
44 R.M. (Lead)	240	1350	1185	1070	970	750	610	0.7	3.1	4"V	$29
44 Rem. Magnum	250	1180	1100	1040	775	670	600	0.8	3.6	6.5"V	$21
44 Rem. Magnum	250	1230	1132	1057	840	711	620	0.8	2.9	6.5"V	NA
44 Rem. Magnum	275	1235	1142	1070	931	797	699	0.8	3.3	6.5"	NA
44 Rem. Magnum	300	1200	1100	1026	959	806	702	NA	NA	7.5"	$17
44 Rem. Magnum	330	1385	1297	1220	1406	1234	1090	1.83	0.00	NA	NA
440 CorBon	260	1700	1544	1403	1669	1377	1136	1.58	NA	10"	NA
450 Short Colt/450 Revolver	226	830	NA	NA	350	NA	NA	NA	NA	NA	NEW
45 S&W Schofield	180	730	NA	NA	213	NA	NA	NA	NA	NA	NA
45 S&W Schofield	230	730	NA	NA	272	NA	NA	na			
45 Automatic	165	1030	930	NA	385	315	NA	1.2	NA	5"	NA
45 Automatic	185	1000	940	890	410	360	325	1.1	4.9	5"	$28
45 Auto. (Match)	185	770	705	650	245	204	175	2.0	8.7	5"	$28
45 Auto. (Match)	200	940	890	840	392	352	312	2.0	8.6	5"	$20
45 Automatic	200	975	917	860	421	372	328	1.4	5.0	5"	$18
45 Automatic	230	830	800	675	355	325	300	1.6	6.8	5"	$27
45 Automatic	230	880	846	816	396	366	340	1.5	6.1	5"	NA
45 Automatic +P	165	1250	NA	NA	573	NA	NA	NA	NA	NA	NA
45 Automatic +P	185	1140	1040	970	535	445	385	0.9	4.0	5"	$31
45 Automatic +P	200	1055	982	925	494	428	380	NA	NA	5"	NA
45 Super	185	1300	1190	1108	694	582	504	NA	NA	5"	NA
45 Win. Magnum	230	1400	1230	1105	1000	775	635	0.6	2.8	5"	$14**
45 Win. Magnum	260	1250	1137	1053	902	746	640	0.8	3.3	5"	$16**
45 Win. Mag. CorBon	320	1150	1080	1025	940	830	747	3.47			NA
455 Webley MKII	262	850	NA	NA	420	NA	NA	NA	NA	NA	NA
45 Colt	200	1000	938	889	444	391	351	1.3	4.8	5.5"	$21
45 Colt	225	960	890	830	460	395	345	1.3	5.5	5.5"	$22
45 Colt + P CorBon	265	1350	1225	1126	1073	884	746	2.65	0.0		NA
45 Colt + P CorBon	300	1300	1197	1114	1126	956	827	2.78	0.0		NA
45 Colt	250/255	860	820	780	410	375	340	1.6	6.6	5.5"	$27
454 Casull	250	1300	1151	1047	938	735	608	0.7	3.2	7.5"V	NA
454 Casull	260	1800	1577	1381	1871	1436	1101	0.4	1.8	7.5"V	NA
454 Casull	300	1625	1451	1308	1759	1413	1141	0.5	2.0	7.5"V	NA
454 Casull CorBon	360	1500	1387	1286	1800	1640	1323	2.01	0.0		NA
475 Linebaugh	400	1350	1217	1119	1618	1315	1112	NA	NA	NA	NA
480 Ruger	325	1350	1191	1076	1315	1023	835	2.6	0.0	7.5"	NA
50 Action Exp.	325	1400	1209	1075	1414	1055	835	0.2	2.3	6"	$24**

Freedom's Downsized 41 Magnum

Stainless steel winners: Freedom Arms' new Model 97 in 41 Magnum with a 2X Leupold pistol scope.

by Dick Williams

THERE WAS A time when even the briefest evaluation of a business or company included phrases like "quality products" and "customer satisfaction." But if you watch CNBC, the TV channel that covers business news all day long, discussions of companies focus on investor rather than consumer interest items, like earnings per share and stock prices. In many cases, a casual viewer might have no idea what products the subject company manufactures. We have become a "bottom line" audience; as long as a company makes money, it doesn't matter what products it makes. This is understandable, since a company that doesn't make a profit won't be making any products for very long. This philosophy, however, doesn't bode well for those of us with an interest in products of limited demand because, to satisfy our desires, it requires the manufacturer to examine a "niche" market, and it's difficult for large manufacturers to reliably predict serious profits in such a market. The end result is that manufacturers prefer to focus on high-volume products with more predictable revenues. For fans of the 41 Magnum, this philosophy has been a severe blow in terms of available handgun models in their preferred chambering. Would all 41 Mag shooters please stand and repeat a few words from an old advertising slogan: "*Thank you, Freedom Arms.*"

Actually, 41 "magnumists" owe the Wyoming revolver maker a double debt of gratitude. At the 1998 SHOT Show, Freedom introduced their Model 83 in 41 Magnum. This large-frame revolver, originally designed for the 454 Casull, easily handles the 41 Magnum–including some turbo-charged handloads that exceed similar factory ammunition by a few hundred feet per second. Some might say the Model 83 is a bit oversized for the 41 Magnum, given its origin as a launch platform for the mighty 454. Happily, Freedom is providing a delightful solu-

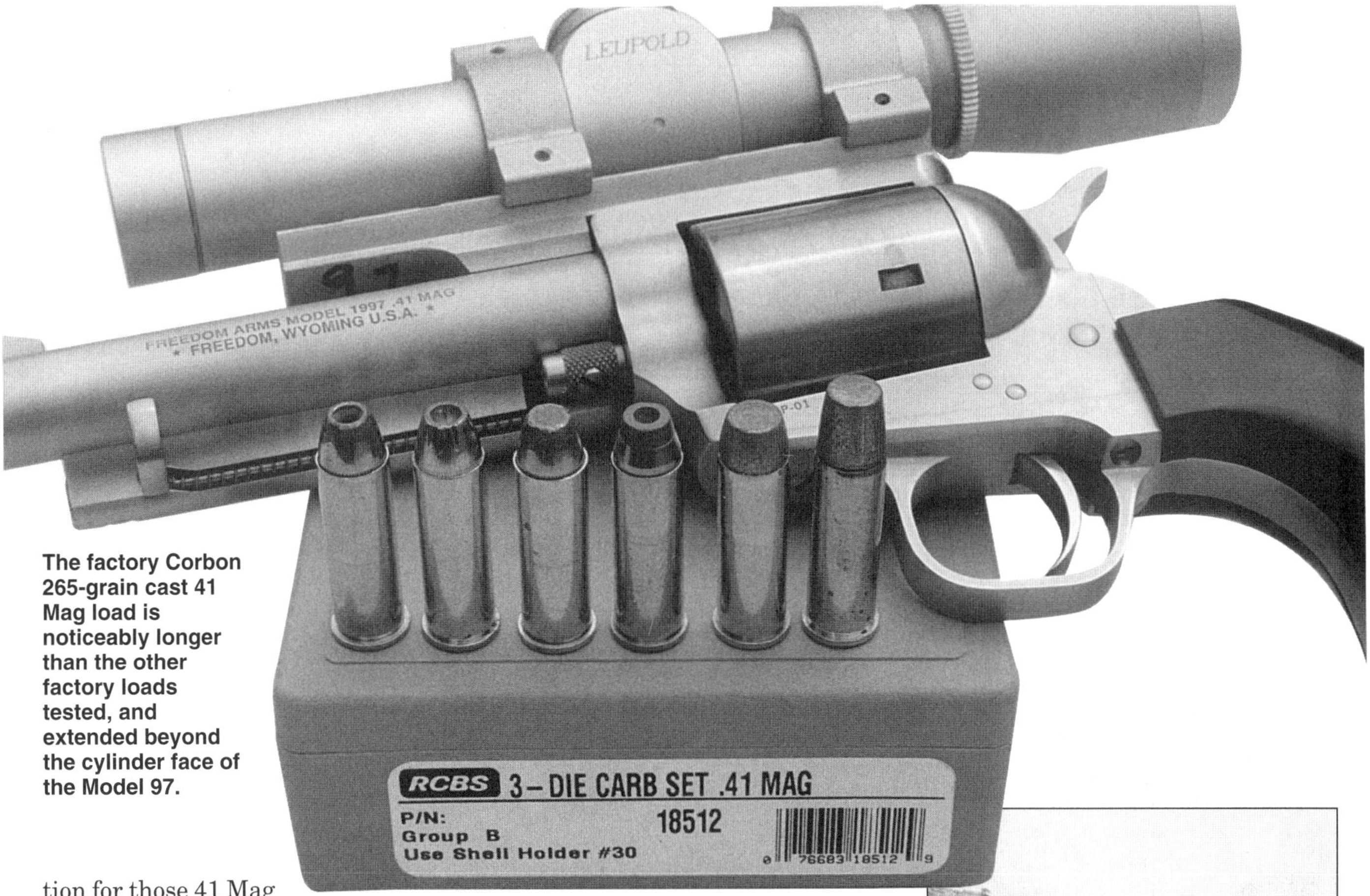

The factory Corbon 265-grain cast 41 Mag load is noticeably longer than the other factory loads tested, and extended beyond the cylinder face of the Model 97.

tion for those 41 Mag fans who share this view...their downsized Model 97 revolver is now being produced in 41 Magnum. This is the third chambering Freedom has chosen for their beautiful little revolver, following the five-shot 45 Colt/ACP introduced in 1998 and the original 357 Magnum six-shot offering in 1997. And, while the downsized Model 97 isn't designed to handle 454-level performance and pressures, it is a marvelously efficient handgun for handling factory-level 41 Magnum performance.

For openers, the Model 97 is built with all the precision and accuracy-enhancing features for which Freedom Arms has become famous. Considering the incredibly tight manufacturing tolerances, line-boring the chambers–and the hand-fitting and finishing throughout the gun–it is difficult to call this a "production" gun. Unlike the larger Model 83s, the smaller gun is not offered in a field grade; it is available only in the Premier grade. And, like the other Premier grades, grips are

Table 1: Ammunition Tests

Cartridge & Brand	Average Velocity/FPS (5 shots)	Group Size/ Inches @ 50 yards
Winchester 175 gr. Silvertip	1355 fps	>.75
Remington 170 gr. JHP	1595 fps	1.25 (4>.5)
Remington 210 gr. JSP	1343 fps	<1.25
Federal 210 gr. JHP	1381 fps	>1.25
Federal 250 gr. Cast	1195 fps	>1.25

Note: Corbon's 265-grain cast bullet load is too long for the Model 97 cylinder.

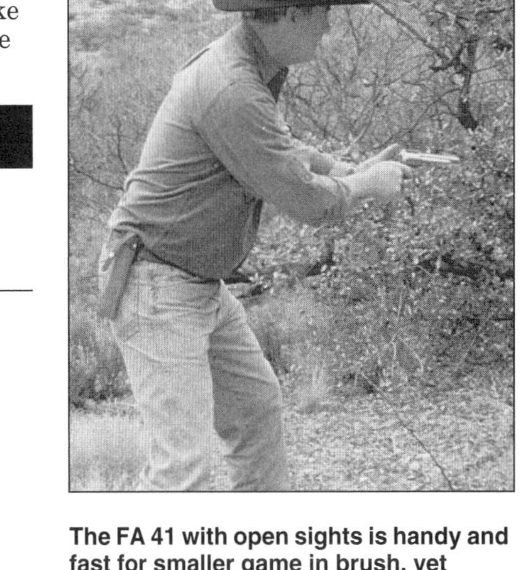

The FA 41 with open sights is handy and fast for smaller game in brush, yet adequately powerful for the Fall big-game hunt.

Difference in frame size between the downsized Model 97 and full-size Model 83 isn't overwhelming until you catch an end view of the two cylinders.

either laminated or black micarta. It comes with Freedom's adjustable rear sight and removable ramp front sight blades. Front sight blades are the same size as, and interchangeable with, the front sight blades on the larger Model 83s, but the rear sights are slightly smaller in keeping with the shorter, smaller topstrap of the Model 97.

Effective in 2000, there are three choices in barrel length: 4.25, 5.5 or 7.5 inches. The gun tested in this article is the original factory prototype with a "*NPXX*" serial number indicating a new product, non-production gun. It was equipped with a 5.5-inch barrel that so far has been my favorite length for this compact little belt gun–I have not yet tried the new, shorter barrel. Should you wish to install a scope, the rear sight can be removed from it's channel in the topstrap and replaced with SSK's excellent T'SOB base featuring Weaver-type slots. The base is slightly smaller than the SSK model used on the larger Freedom revolvers, but the mounting system is exactly the same and just as sturdy.

One might think Freedom had a choice of making the new 41 Mag with either a 5-shot or 6-shot cylinder *ala* the original 6-shot 357 Magnum or second generation 5-shot 45 Colt/ACP. But the 41 is an honest magnum with factory ammo operating pressures around the 40K psi level, and handloaders probably pushing the same parameters. The Model 97 cylinders measure a mere 1.575 inches outer diameter, but the 5-shot version in 41 Mag provides approximately .167 inch between chambers and .088-inch thick outer walls. For comparison purposes, the same dimensions on a Model 97 chambered for 357 Mag are 1.575-inches outer diameter, .133 inch between chambers, and .115-inch outer walls. Also the 5-shooter allows the location of bolt notches between chambers, rather than cutting into the thinnest part of the cylinder's outer wall directly over each chamber. The result is that strength and safety margins are maximized, always a good idea when dealing with magnums, particularly the larger caliber variety.

I commented briefly above on my preference for the 5.5-inch barrel on the Model 97 because of its suitability as a belt gun and its outstanding handling characteristics as an open-sighted revolver. However, accuracy testing was done with a 2X Leupold EER pistol scope mounted in a T'SOB base to minimize any visual deficiencies on my part in shooting the best possible 50-yard groups. A higher power scope would doubtless produce smaller groups, but the little Leupold is an excellent and realistic choice for optics on the short barrel version of this gun, and I would have no qualms in taking this setup hunting. (*I can't comment on mounting a scope on the shorter 4.25-inch barrel.*) In fact, game has already been harvested with this prototype gun and 2X Leupold scope both by Bob Baker, the president of Freedom Arms, and JoAnn Conn, a lady handgun hunter from Idaho. JoAnn has fired most of the different Freedom Arms revolvers except for the 475 Linebaugh, and has stated her preference for the 41 Magnum in the new Model 97. While she has hunted with both scoped and iron-sighted revolvers, her preference is for a low-power scope. If most of your handgun hunting/shooting is done with scopes, you might opt for the 7.5-inch barrel. The gun still has great balance but allows the use of a larger, higher-power scope without overwhelming the small-frame revolver or extending the objective lens in front of the muzzle. In all probability, you will gain some feet per second from the longer barrel but, as you can see in **Table 1**, the 5.5-inch barrel is no slouch in the velocity department. **Table 2** shows a comparison of 41 Magnum velocities between the 5.5-inch barrel Model 97 and a 7.5-inch barrel Freedom Arms Model 83 tested a couple of years ago.

Recognizing that felt recoil is quite subjective, a couple of comments in this area are worthwhile. First, bullet weight in factory ammo ranges from 170 grains to 265 grains, with 210 grains considered "standard" and quite suitable for most hunting. The heavyweight 41 Magnum Federal load of 250-grain cast bullet at just under 1200 fps felt much gentler to me than the heavyweight 300-grain Buffalo Bore 45 Colt loads fired in an earlier Freedom Arms Model 97. Interestingly, I could not test Corbon's 41 Magnum 265-grain cast bullet load because the round was too long for the Model 97 cylinder. Too bad, because the Corbon load produces higher velocity than the Federal ammo and performed beautifully in the large-frame Freedom 41 Magnum on some Arkansas razorbacks. If you do manage to crank up one of the super heavyweight bullets (like SSK's 295-grain cast slug) to the 1200 fps level in the smaller Freedom revolver, I suspect recoil will feel just like the same weight bullets at the same velocity in the 45 Colt-chambered Model 97. However, for all the standard weight loads, the 41 Mag's recoil was quite manageable, and not at all uncomfortable for me, while the heavyweight 45 Colt slugs were noticeably unpleasant.

Please don't think my failure to mention the 357 Magnum means I'm badmouthing this cartridge. I'm very fond of it and have used it successfully on the smaller varieties of "big" game. But the 41 Mag is an infinitely better choice for any kind of big-game hunting, and the versatile performance of available factory ammo makes it unnecessary for you to develop a custom load for a particular application. If you choose to use the heaviest loads, and their recoil adversely affects your performance, Magnaport has a number of porting systems that can bring the felt recoil down to an acceptable level.

As a trail gun the Model 97 has no equal, in my opinion. Fitted with either of the two short barrels, equipped with the adjustable iron sights, and carried on the hip in Freedom's own holster, it is a backcountry stroller's dream come true. Introduction of this little gun in 41 Magnum makes selection easy for the devoted 41-bore fans. Since I am not one of the 41 Mag faithful, it's difficult for me to argue selection of this chambering as

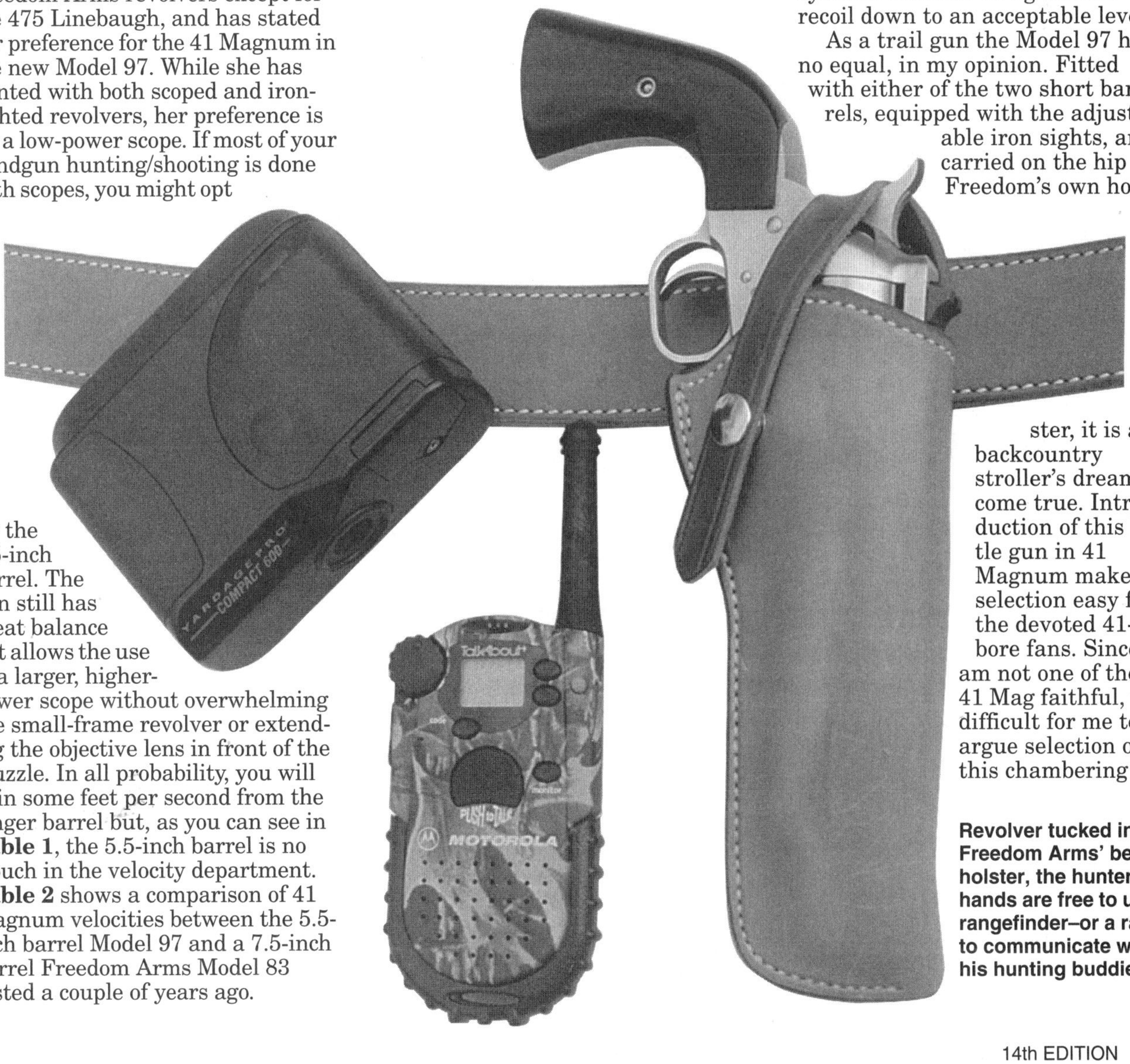

Revolver tucked into Freedom Arms' belt holster, the hunter's hands are free to use a rangefinder–or a radio to communicate with his hunting buddies.

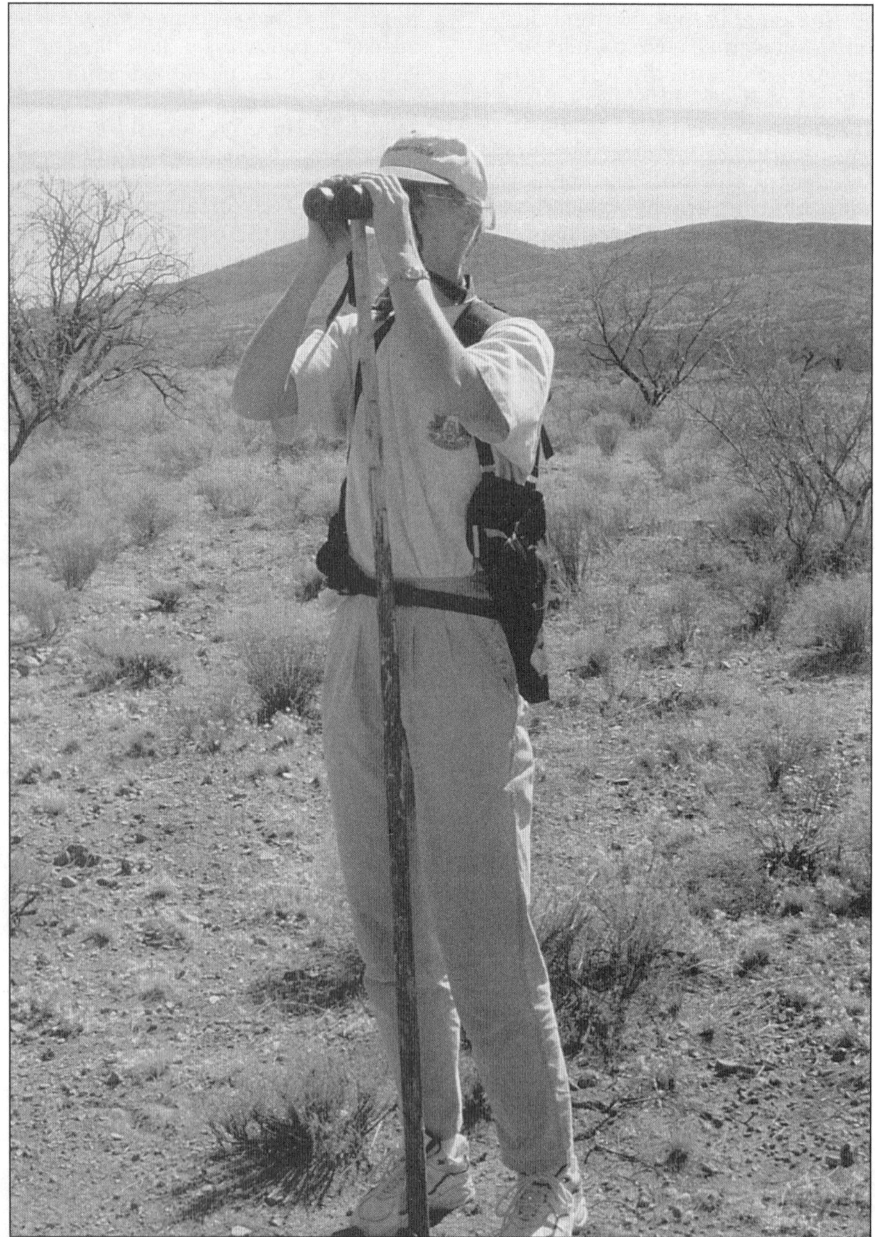

Whether in a compact belt rig with open sights or in a shoulder holster with some kind of optical sight, the small FA 41 Mag is a joy to carry afield, leaving the hunter's hands free for glassing.

Table 2: 41 Mag Velocity Comparisons - Model 97 and Model 83.

Cartridge & Brand	Model 97 w/ 5-in. bbl.	Model 83 w/ 7.5-in. bbl.
Winchester 175 gr. Silvertip	1355 fps	1380 fps
Remington 170 gr. JHP	1595 fps	1668 fps
Remington 210 gr. JSP	1343 fps	1376 fps
Federal 210 gr. JHP	1381 fps	1406 fps
Federal 250 Cast	1195 fps	1218 fps

"best of class" in trail guns. In the Southwest, where most of my hunting is rabbits and javelina with the occasional stretch to small deer, I like the pleasant shooting versatility and instant availability of ammo for the 357. It is cheap to reload and encourages practice. If one recognizes its limitations and hunts within them, it is a very satisfying handgun cartridge, especially in the Model 97.

On the other hand, I am a pretty serious 45 fan, and the availability of an extra cylinder that allows use of either 45 Colt or 45 ACP ammo is irresistible to me. Slow-moving, big-diameter bullets from the ACP are marvelously effective on small game and, with velocities up to 1000 fps available in factory ammo using well-constructed 230-grain slugs, the stubby little round becomes suitable for medium-size big game. Finally, stoked with Buffalo Bore 45 Colt ammo, featuring 300-grain bullets at 1200 fps from the 5.5 inch barrel, the Model 97 on your hip allows you to walk comfortably–if carefully–through bear country.

But depending on individual situations and needs, choosing the Model 97 chambered in 41 Magnum may be the best selection a shooter can make, at least to date. Equipped with just the one load of Federal 210-grain JHPs, a trail stroll can turn into a serious big-game handgun hunt with no changeover in cylinders or ammo. At slightly under 1400 fps from the Freedom belt gun, the Federal factory load's trajectory and power extend your hunting range to 100 yards or so, depending on the skill of the handgunner. And while small game destruction would be more than one desires, my experiences with Federal JHPs indicate their bullets don't expand violently on small, thin-skinned game. A head or shoulder shot on a rabbit still leaves the major edible parts for dinner. The trajectory of Federal's heavier cast bullet might shorten your hunting range a bit, but the hard cast bullets will do less damage on small game and provide better penetration on bigger game.

Yep, regardless of personal preferences, it's hard to make a case that either of the existing chamberings available in Freedom's Model 97 is quite as good as the newly-offered 41 Magnum. But the choice is up to you, and no matter how you struggle with the selection process, ain't it wonderful to have options? ●

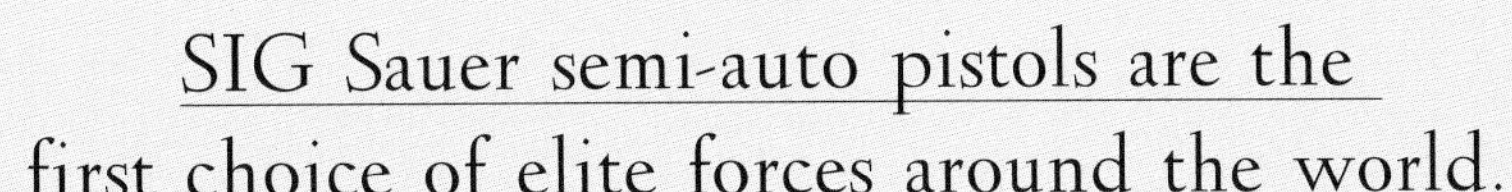

P226

P220 P229 P245

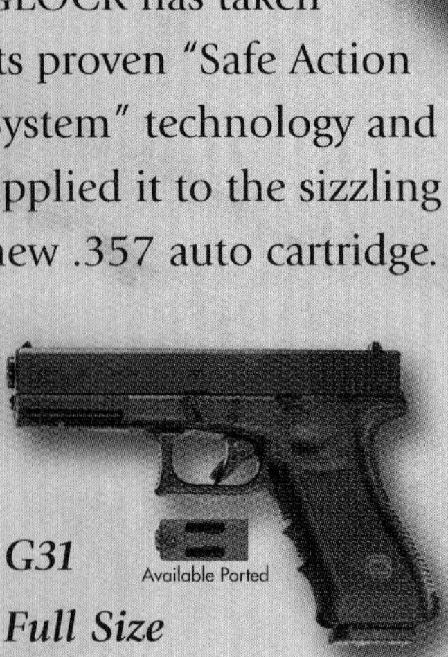

Innovative Walther P99 includes 3-mode trigger plus a gaggle of other desirable features.

James Bond Upgrade: The Walther P99

by Jerry Burke

IAN FLEMMING'S SPY-THRILLER books, first put to film in the 1960's, brought the Walther Model PPK ("Pocket Pistol *Kriminal*", designed for plainclothes detectives) into general public awareness. However, knowledgeable arms fanciers were already well aware of this landmark 1920's design, a smaller version of the slightly earlier Walther PP. Even in the recent 007™ film *Tomorrow Never Dies*©, James Bond did not abandon his trademark PPK. The Cold War's best-known fictional secret agent did, however, supplement his personal weaponry by appropriating the futuristic Walther Model P99 from the ill-gotten stores of a global evil. As he examined the new pistol, Bond mentioned he'd been after Her Majesty's Secret Service to provide him with one. But even before Walther's latest design appeared in advance 007 cinematic publicity, savvy handgunners were busy seeking out the innovative, rakish-looking P99 in numbers exceeding production capacity.

Walther was targeting the worldwide law enforcement and professional bodyguard markets when they set out to develop a state-of-the-art pistol for the new millennium. The result of this intensive effort is the Model P99, Walther's first leap into the "plastic" or polymer-frame pistol venue. Starting with the basics, the P99 is a double-action centerfire locked-breach, recoil-operated, linkless Browning-type, semi-automatic striker-actuated (hammerless) pistol, with 3 trigger modes. As is increasingly common, there is no traditional manual safety on the P99, although other safety features abound. Available in both 9mm Parabellum and 40 S&W calibers, design capacity in the former caliber is "16+1" (that's *sixteen*-rounds in a fully-loaded magazine plus an additional cartridge in the chamber); and, "12+1" in the latter. U.S. civilians are limited to "10+1"-round capacity in each caliber. Both high and limited-capacity magazines are capped with a polymer base, although of different size. Empty P99 weight-with-magazine is 24.7 oz. according to my scale, which makes the new Walther pistol just over an ounce heavier than the original, limited power/low capacity landmark Walther PP pocket pistol. Based on other handguns on the market and whose industry "yardstick" you use, the P99 can be considered either a full-size belt pistol or

SPECIFICATIONS:

Manufacturer: Carl Walther Waffenfabrik, Ulm/Donau, Germany.
Model Designation: P99.
Action Type: Double-action/single-action semi-automatic pistol.
Chambering: 9mm Parabellum and 40 Smith & Wesson.
Finish: Tenifer®-process finish, matte blue or matte silver slide. Polymer frame in black or military-style green.
Barrel Length: Four (4) inches.
Capacity: "16+1" design in 9mm Parabellum; "12+1" in 40 S&W. "10+1" U.S. civilian capacity in both calibers.
Sights: Four (4) front sights supplied with pistol, different heights; rear sight "*click*" windage adjustable.
Weight, Empty: 24.7 oz.
Length: 7.09 inches.
Width: 1.14 inches.
Height: 5.31 inches.
Standard Features: Trigger safety, internal striker/"drop" safety, three-mode action, cocking indicator, loaded-chamber indicator, slide-mounted decocker, replaceable backstraps (3 sizes), varying-height front sights (4), left/right magazine releases.
Standard Accessories: Spare magazine, front sight/backstrap replacement tools (2), cleaning rod, plastic foam-lined compartmentalized storage/carrying case, owner's manual, factory test target.
Available Factory Accessories: Trijicon® night sights, accessory-rail laser sights, accessory-rail flashlight, threaded barrel with cap for suppressors (*both operable and training/dummy models*) and flash hiders; plus, a variety of Walther-branded holsters.
Manufacturer's Suggested Retail Price: $799.

◀ Walther P99 with special "SD" (silenced) threaded barrel and Swiss-made suppressor installed. Both activated and training/dummy suppressors are factory available.

a compact carry gun. But whatever category you put it in, the Walther P99 is an intriguing handgun, packed with innovation and value-added features.

Two slide finishes are available, each boldly carrying the Walther name and "P99" model designation on the left side. While both versions are constructed of a carbon-based steel with tough Tenifer™ coating, one has a black matte appearance and the other a matte silver. Both finishes provide excellent protection against weather and wear. All other metal parts are "QPQ"-coated, providing excellent foul weather and perspiration protection. The slide is boldly futuristic, with relieved segments on both sides near the muzzle. Effective, angular finger grooves are located near the rear of the somewhat wide slide. There's also an ample ejection port, heavily relieved to ensure empty cartridge cases fly well clear of the action during the firing sequence. The top of the slide is finely grooved to reduce glare. Seriously innovative is the slide-mounted, press-bar decocker, located near the left rear of the slide above the finger grooves. Flush with the slide, this arrangement is quite effective; there's nothing to swing into position and no concern over whether or not the decocker automatically rebounds. Just press the ample bar and the striker decocks, putting the P99 trigger and action in true double-action mode. More about that later. In addition to the slide-mounted decocker, there are other notable slide assembly safety features housed within the slide assembly. When cocked, the red-tipped base of the striker extends slightly through a recess at the rear of the slide, making it easy to determine the condition of the striker by sight and by feel. In addition, the base of the extractor provides a "loaded chamber" indicator, again perceivable by sight and feel. When the extractor grips the base of a chambered cartridge, the rear of the extractor pivots into the slide, exposing a red patch on the extractor cutout in the slide. Again, this arrangement provides recognition both visually and by touch. Walther has also included a striker or "drop" safety on the P99 to guard against accidental discharge, and the trigger safety must be rotated out of engagement by normal action of the trigger finger before the firing sequence can begin.

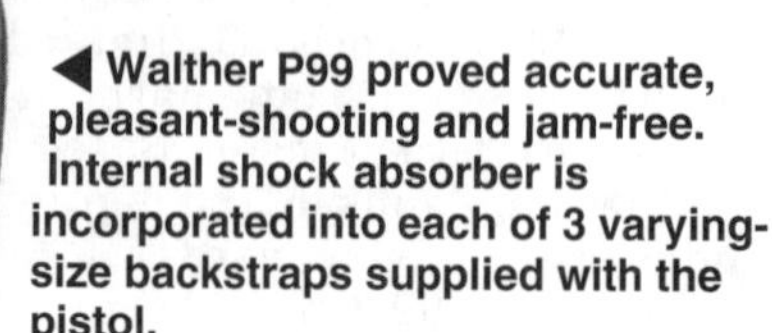

◀ Walther P99 proved accurate, pleasant-shooting and jam-free. Internal shock absorber is incorporated into each of 3 varying-size backstraps supplied with the pistol.

Another special slide-mounted feature is the sight system. Standard P99 sights are constructed of new-age polymer, forming a 3-dot picture with blade out front and a squared-off "U"-shaped notch at the rear. A mid-height front sight is installed at the factory; plus, an additional three (3) front sights of varying height are also included with each P99. A diminutive Allen wrench, also supplied with the pistol, makes sight swap-outs a veritable snap. The Allen wrench is used to release a set-screw inside the slide, and a multi-purpose plastic punch… yet again, supplied with the P99… is used to free the front sight from the slide. Alternate height front sights can then be installed, as needed. If you can't get vertically in the 10-ring with one of the supplied four (4) front sights, your marksmanship needs plenty of work. The P99's windage-adjustable rear sight is an absolute joy to work with, a feature easily appreciated if you've ever struggled with drift-adjustable sights—or click-adjustable models which don't hold their zero. On the Walther P99, a horizontally positioned, squared-off slotted screwhead on the right side of the rear sight is held in place by a vertical spring-loaded pin, also slotted to accept the square sides of the screwhead. A screwdriver can be used to rotate the square screwhead one side at a time. However, I found rear sight adjustment even easier, without the use of tools. With only a fingernail, the vertical pin holding the adjustment screwhead is easily depressed. With this accomplished, the P99's rear sight simply slides out of the sight groove. With the rear sight removed from the slide, the windage adjustment screwhead can again be turned using nothing more than a fingernail. The adjusted rear sight simply snaps back into place in reverse order. Metallic factory Trijicon™ night sights are also available from Walther in similar 3-dot configuration, and rear sight adjustment is identical to that described above for the standard polymer version.

Walther P99 is delivered with 3 interchangeable backstraps of varying size. Switch-out is easily accomplished by removal of a single pin at base of the backstrap.

Optional night sights have been added to this P99, but four different height front sights are supplied as original equipment; plus, the tools needed for sight and backstrap changes.

Moving on to the lightweight fiberglass-reinforced polymer frame, black is standard. The military-green P99M variation is also on the civilian market due to heavy demand for this extraordinary pistol. The frame is injection molded onto steel slide rails and other critical components requiring greater strength than even today's advanced plastics can provide. The famous Walther banner flies proudly on both sides of the grip, and the left side of the frame above the triggerguard declares the German sister cities of "Ulm/Do" as the site of manufacture, with "Do" being shorthand for "Donau." On the right side of the frame above the grip is a *"read the manual"* warning in both English and German. "Made In Germany", commercial German nitro (smokeless powder) proofmarks and Walther's stag antler Ulm/Do proof also appear on the right side of the frame. A world-renowned Italian designer noted for his winning ways with Olympic-grade target pistols created the grip on the P99, and it is superb. Efficient finger grooves grace the front of the grip, which flares at the bottom. A horizontal ribbed pattern coupled with vertical notching on the finger grooves help anchor the pistol in the shooter's hand, even when wet. Indentations on both sides of the grip provide an area for both right and left-hand shooters to secure their fingertips. Except for the finger grooves, the remaining three sides of the grip surface are covered with a two-size dot pattern, providing additional gripping properties without irritating the hand during extended shooting sessions. Directly behind the triggerguard, the gripframe is scooped on both sides to accommodate the trigger finger and thumb of the shooting hand, providing additional ambidextrous properties on the P99.

Dimensions of the P99 triggerguard are especially helpful for shooters with hands the size of a dinner plate, or when wearing gloves. Interior of the triggerguard is oval shaped with a "peak" midway along the bottom, just below the trigger tip. When starting well forward in the triggerguard, this "peak" helps guide the trigger finger onto the trigger and into firing position. The face of the triggerguard is horizontally grooved to help steady the pistol with the shooter's offhand, for those using that technique. Above and forward of the triggerguard, the frame has deep recessed "rails," designed to accommodate a variety of techno-special accessories like mini-flashlights and laser sights. Grooved dual polymer magazine release levers, blended into the bottom rear of the triggerguard, are easily activated by thumb or forefinger of either hand. The slide stop/release is located on the left of the frame above the grip and is supported by a well-designed shelf to help keep the pistol snag-free. Wrapping under the frame forward of the trigger is a grooved, one-piece "U"-shaped takedown catch, easily manipulated when field stripping is in order. Even the trigger and trigger safety are constructed of lightweight polymer, but the most intriguing part of the P99's frame is the backstrap; that is, *backstraps*... plural!

Installed on each Walther Model P99 is a mid-size, flexible backstrap with designed-in shock absorber which mates perfectly with the frame and continues the double-size dot pattern motif. Held in place near the base of the grip by a roll pin and at the top by a tab that fits into the frame, the backstrap blends precisely with the P99's frame. The medium-size backstrap alone will accommodate most hands, but Walther was dedicated to creating perfection... the ultimate solution to grip customization on a production pistol. To accomplish this lofty goal, two additional backstraps are supplied with each P99, with the primary difference being the thickness where the web of the hand makes contact with the pistol. Through these interchangeable backstraps, the forefinger's reach to the trigger is noticeably affected. Shooters with small hands will find the least meaty backstrap to their liking; conversely, a big hand or long fingers will appreciate the largest of the three backstrap inserts. Walther thoughtfully includes a plastic punch with the P99, suitable for easy removal and replacement of the backstrap roll pin without risking damage to the frame or backstrap inserts. To accommodate many law enforcement organizations outside the U.S., the rear base of two of the backstraps is deeply slotted where the retaining roll pin helps hold the backstrap in place. If you've ever had the urge to experience the use of a pistol lanyard, here's your chance!

◀ **Standard P99 equipment includes spare magazine, owners manual, factory test target and cleaning rod, all in a foam-lined plastic carrying/storage case.**

As if all this wouldn't qualify the Walther P99 as innovative, the 3-mode trigger puts Walther's latest product in a class all its own. A true professional's handgun, this is the first pistol to offer this combination of operational options, with each mode being practical as well as convenient. These trigger modes are perhaps best described by following the pistol through an action sequence. Of course, all three trigger conditions must first be mastered with the pistol empty, including the chamber. Pulling the slide fully to the rear with an empty magazine in the magazine well will activate the slide stop, holding the slide at the rear. This slide movement also cocks the striker. After replacing the empty magazine with a loaded one and tripping the slide stop, the slide will travel to its full forward position, or into "*battery*". In the process, the top cartridge is stripped from the magazine and loaded into the barrel chamber. The now-cocked striker will protrude slightly from the rear of the slide. This action also moves the trigger to the rear, placing it in traditional "*single-action*" mode. A relatively light pull of the trigger (approximately 4 lbs.) will now sequentially and repeatedly discharge the weapon until the last cartridge from the magazine is fired. If the P99 is not to be fired immediately, the shooter can simply press the slide-mounted decocker, causing

▼ **Special features on Walther P99 include slide-mounted decocker and red-tipped striker indicator. Trijicon® night sights seen here are optional.**

▼ **Four varying-height polymer front sights come standard with the P99. Walther even supplies the change-up tool. Optional Trijicon® front night sight seen here.**

Field stripping P99 is nearly effortless, as described in text. Seen here, 9mm American civilian 10-round magazine.

▶9mm P99 was designed for sixteen (16)-round magazine (*left*), 12-rounder in 40 S&W. American civilians are limited to 10-round magazine (*right*) in both calibers. For total loaded 9mm capacity, add one round in the barrel chamber, as displayed here.

two highly desirable things to happen. First, the striker will decock. Additionally, the trigger will return to a true *"double-action"* mode, requiring a relatively long and significantly strong pull (a distance of more than 1/2 inch, with a pull of nearly 12 lbs.) to cock and release the striker, firing the weapon.

That covers both the single and double-action modes on the P99, with trigger action similar in practice to any so-called traditional double-action/single-action pistol or revolver. But as indicated, there is a third professionally-oriented trigger condition, which I've dubbed, *"extended single-action"*. Walther based this trigger option on medical research involving human muscle reflex movement under stress. Trigger finger stress reflex reaction was pegged at approximately 5/16-inch; after that, the brain takes over intentional movement of the trigger finger. While trigger travel distance and the amount of pressure required makes true double-action least likely to produce an unintentional weapon discharge, it is also most likely to produce the least accuracy. For pinpoint special applications like anti-terrorist, SWAT Team and professional bodyguard duties, first-shot accuracy is paramount. Essentially, the *"extended single-action"* trigger condition is tied to the equally unique *"recock maneuver;"* again, my term. From the decocked condition with trigger fully forward, the *"recock maneuver"* cocks the pistol's striker, without ejecting a chambered cartridge. Pointing the handgun in a safe direction with trigger finger outside the triggerguard, the offhand is used to move the slide rearward approximately 3/8-inch. This cocks the striker, while the trigger remains in the full-forward position... ***but with a critical difference***! The trigger now only *appears* to be in the long, stout double-action mode; an effortless touch will move the trigger approximately 5/16th of an inch rearward and audibly *click* the trigger into the single-action position. From there, approximately 3/16-inch of single-action trigger pull will launch the P99's striker, firing a chambered round. This combination *"recock maneuver / extended single-action trigger"* option allows carrying the Walther P99 in true double-action mode, with the option of altering the pistol to every-shot-single-action... with antistress *"extended single-action"* trigger positioning... when time allows and the situation requires. But again, the shooter *MUST* be thoroughly aware that while the trigger *APPEARS* to be in double-action mode, such is *not* the case. The distance the trigger needs to travel to discharge the pistol is the same, but the required pressure is greatly diminished. Still, even after placing the trigger in this unique mode, use of the decocker will again return the P99 to true double-action.

Having thoroughly familiarized myself with an unloaded P99, I was ready for the range. Duly impressed with this Walther's potential, I rounded-up an array of test ammunition including cartridges manufactured by Black Hills, CCI, CORBON, Federal, Remington and Winchester. Contained therein were a variety of bullet configurations and velocity ratings, just to see if the P99 was finicky. The greatest product variety was by Black Hills Ammunition, including two 115-grain JHP rounds, one EXP (EXtra Power) and the other a true "+P;" a 124-grain JHP and an FMJ version in the same weight; and Black Hills Subsonic rounds with both JHP and FMJ 147-grain bullets. I included CCI's 124-grain TMJ Blazer cartridge, as well as their superb 9mm shotshell which contain approximately 230 #11 lead shot pellets in a plastic capsule. Three of CORBON's excellent "+P"

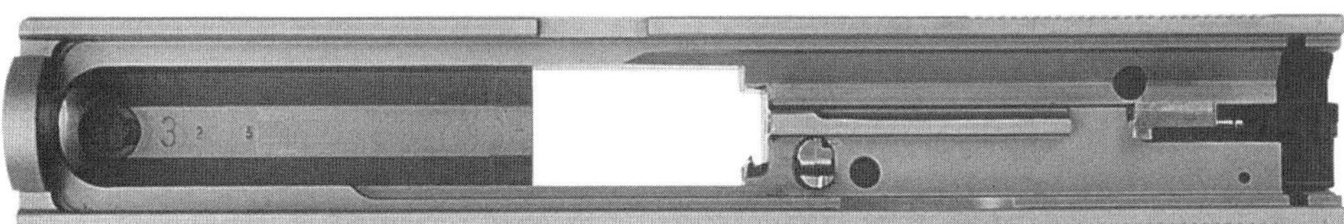

▲ Inside of P99's slide shows top quality manufacture with attention to detail, a Walther hallmark for more than 100 years.

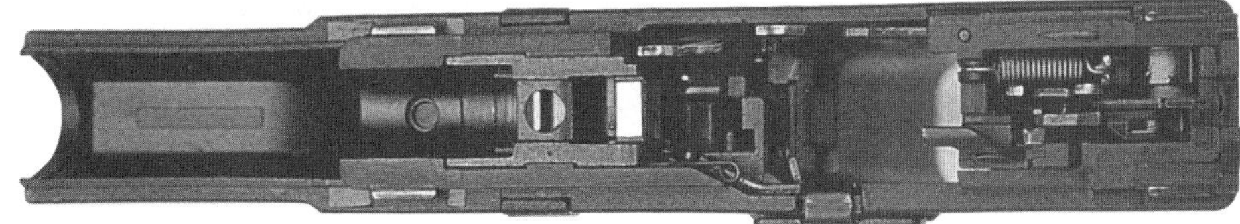

▲ P99's polymer frame is molded over steel slide rails. Frame-mounted components are easily cleaned with gun solvent and soft bristle brush.

products were selected for testing, in 90-, 115-, and 125-grain bullet weights. Federal's Classic Hi-Shok 115-grain JHP is indeed a classic, and I also selected Remington's exceptional Golden Saber 147-grain JHP for the test. I used 3 Winchester products, including one of the finest personal defense loads on the market, the Supreme SXT with 147-grain JHP projectile. Two additional products are new loadings from Winchester's USA-brand… a 124-grain FMJ and a 147-grain flat-nose fully jacketed bullet. *Americanizing* the 25-meter Walther factory test target, I selected 25 yards from a seriously stable but informal rest for academic testing. In separate sessions, I fired the P99 offhand from both 7 and 10 yards, more likely personal defense distances. I tried the CCI shotshells through the P99 at a poisonous snake-taming 8 feet. In total, I fired 1,000+ rounds through the futuristic 9mm Walther P99. Each time I chambered the pistol, I immediately pressed the slide-mounted decocker-bar to engrain the practice into my handling routine. As presented above, this puts the pistol in a true double-action mode, the condition I recommend at all times until the need or desire to fire the pistol is imminent. This also gave me an opportunity to try my hand at the *"recock"* action mode, wherein retracing the slide approximately 3/8-inch cocks the striker and places the trigger in *"extended single-action"*. Having both the standard issue polymer and factory night sights, I tried both. The standard sights worked just fine with the factory-installed, mid-height front sight from 7, 10 and 25 yards, although a modest amount of holdover was required at the farthest distance. The night sights ride a bit higher on the slide, and only one height front night sight is supplied, but the rear night sight retains the same excellent adjustable features as its polymer counterpart. For all practical purposes, the point of impact was not affected by the switch from standard polymer to metallic night sights.

On the sample pistol, trigger let-off was crisp and clean. In double-action, the trigger pull was less than 12 lbs. In single-action, 4 lbs. of pressure was necessary to send the cocked striker toward the chamber. In extended single-action mode, rearward trigger travel for that first +/- 5/16th-inch is accomplished with minimal resistance. The P99 efficiently and effectively digested all

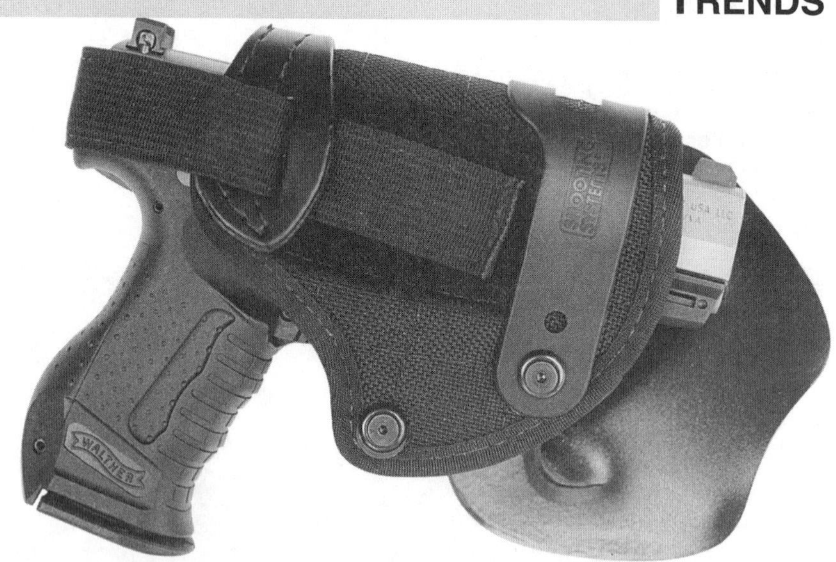

▲ Shooting System's new cross-draw paddle holster works well with the P99, especially when seated.

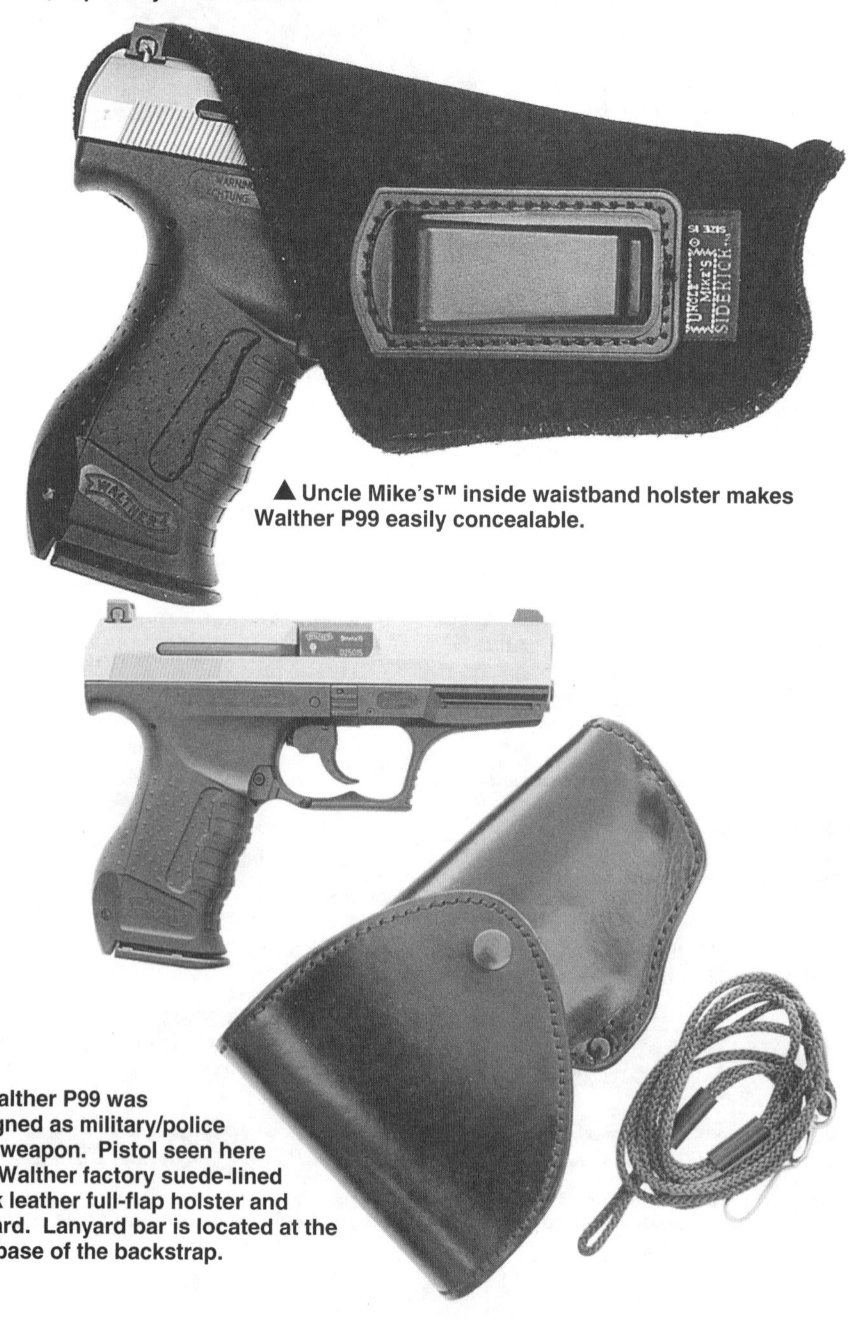

▲ Uncle Mike's™ inside waistband holster makes Walther P99 easily concealable.

▶Walther P99 was designed as military/police duty weapon. Pistol seen here with Walther factory suede-lined black leather full-flap holster and lanyard. Lanyard bar is located at the rear base of the backstrap.

At 10 yards, experienced handgunners can expect excellent off-hand results. Test P99 produced this 1-inch, "timed fire" target with CORBON's 9mm "+P" 125-gr. JHP cartridges.

From a solid rest, Walther P99 delivered 2 1/4-inch average groups from 25 yards with Winchester's new USA-brand 147-grain TCMC cartridge.

◀ The only factor limiting 7-yard combat accuracy with the P99 is the skill of the shooter.

brands and types of ammunition tested, from mild to "+P"; from full metal jackets to wide-mouth hollow-points. Every brand and type of ammunition tested performed expertly in the P99 at both 7 and 10-yard combat distances. Performance variations at these two distances were really insignificant from a practical application standpoint. At 25 yards, on-target performance predictably widened, but the P99 certainly proved itself worthy of carrying the famous Walther banner, as seen in the accompanying chart. Black Hill's 124-grain JHP produced the best groups in this particular test pistol. Whether for uniformed service, professional bodyguard work, legal civilian concealed carry or as a house gun, the Walther P99 will prove a most efficient tool and trustworthy companion.

Each of the polymer-frame pistols I've tested has suffered to some degree from a measure of muzzle flip, when compared to a comparable aluminum alloy or steel-frame gun. This effect seems the nature of the beast. The polymers used are as much as 85% lighter, yet stronger than steel. The recoil-absorbing elasticity of the space-age blend also creates a certain amount of whipping action. During the test phase, both the 16- and 10-round factory magazines were used. The P99 was fired one and two-handed; both with and without using the front of the triggerguard to help steady the pistol. It was also fired from the standard upright position and at various degrees of "*list*", left and right. I fired the pistol upside-down and even "*limp wristed*" the P99. After firing more than 1,000 rounds, not one malfunction was encountered.

The barrel and feeding ramp of the test P99 were swabbed with solvent and dried with a clean patch between each 5-shot group. But at the end of the test period, it was time for a serious clean up. Field stripping the pistol is simple and easy. First, make certain the pistol is unloaded, which means removing the magazine and making absolutely sure the chamber is empty. Next, depress the slide-mounted decocker to relieve spring tension on the striker. The "U"-shaped disassembly device is frame-mounted, wrapping under and on both sides of the frame in front of the trigger. Grasping the pistol in the shooting hand, with trigger finger outside the trigger-

▲ More than 1,000 rounds of 9mm ammunition were put through test Walther P99. Included, *from left-to-right:* Black Hills 147-gr. Subsonic JHP, 124-gr. Black Hills JHP, Black Hills 115-gr. JHP "+P", 115-gr. Black Hills JHP EXP, 124-gr. Black Hills FMJ, CCI shotshells with 230 #11 shot pellets, CCI 124-gr. Blazer FMJ, Federal 115-gr. JHP, Remington Golden Saber 147-gr. JHP, Winchester Supreme SXT 147-gr. JHP, Winchester USA-brand 147-gr. TCMC, Winchester USA-brand 124-gr. FMJ.

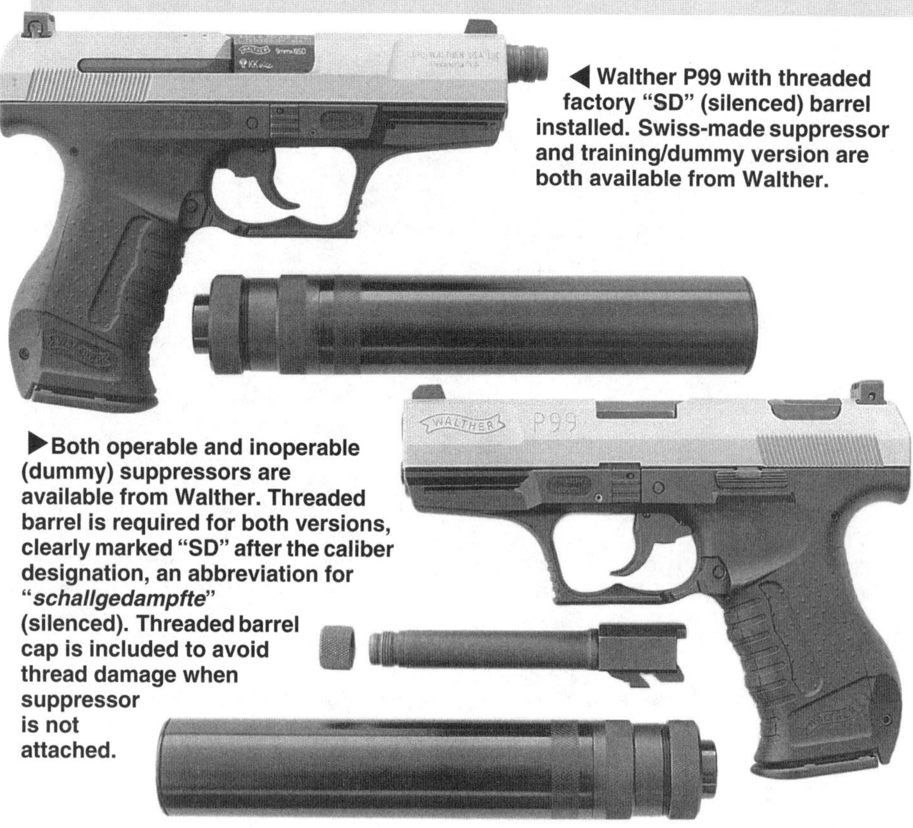

◀ Walther P99 with threaded factory "SD" (silenced) barrel installed. Swiss-made suppressor and training/dummy version are both available from Walther.

▶ Both operable and inoperable (dummy) suppressors are available from Walther. Threaded barrel is required for both versions, clearly marked "SD" after the caliber designation, an abbreviation for "*schallgedampfte*" (silenced). Threaded barrel cap is included to avoid thread damage when suppressor is not attached.

Walther P99 Test Firing Results

Ammunition.	Bullet Weight (grs.)	Bullet Type	MV.(fps)*	Group Size (ins.)**
Black Hills				
Subsonic	147	JHP	920	2.64
Standard	124	JHP	1085	2.57
+P	115	JHP	1250	3.32
EXP	115	JHP	1175	2.84
Subsonic	147	FMJ	935	2.93
"Blue" box	124	FMJ	1092	2.82
CCI				
Blazer	124	TMJ	1068	3.15
Shotshells	230 pellets	#11 lead shot.	1450***	52 hits in 8" circle****
CORBON				
+P	90	JHP	1472	3.46
+P	115	JHP	1312	2.73
+P	125	JHP	1240	3.12
Federal				
Classic, Hi-Shok	115	JHP	1090	2.72
Remington				
Golden Saber	147	JHP	946	2.78
Winchester				
Supreme	147	SXT (JHP)	961	3.03
USA Brand	147	FMJ-FN	930	2.85
USA Brand	124	FMJ	1072	3.37

LEGEND:

JHP = Jacketed Hollowpoint, **FMJ** = Full Metal Jacket, **TMJ** = Total Metal Jacket,SXT, **(JHP)** = Extreme Expansion Technology (Jacketed Hollowpoint),**FMJ-FN** = Full Metal Jacket-Flat Nose

*Shooting Chrony® chronograph used to determine velocity; equipment placed 8 feet from pistol muzzle.

**Average of 10, 5-shot groups fired at 25-yards from solid rest. Group size measured from center-to-center of two widest shots.

***Factory data.

****8 feet from target.

guard, use the thumb and forefinger of the off-hand to pull the disassembly device down slightly. This allows the slide to move effortlessly forward and off the frame without spring tension. From there, the recoil spring assembly and barrel are easily extracted from the slide. That's as far as I cared to disassemble the P99. Not because you can't remove the striker unit, but because I didn't find it necessary, even after firing hundreds of rounds. Using Birchwood Casey's aerosol Gun Scrubber® and Super Strength Bore Scrubber®, I had no problem reaching every area of the pistol that needed attention. Reassembly after a light application of Sheath® Rust Preventive, also by Birchwood Casey, and the P99 was again ready for carry or storage.

In addition to everything covered above, Walther delivers still more with each P99. There's a one-piece polymer cleaning rod, and the entire P99 package is sold in a compact, foam-lined plastic storage/carrying case. For Walther factory-authorized accessories, including night and laser sights, detachable light source, Walther-branded holsters, yet more backstrap options, threaded barrels, suppressors (both operable and training/dummy versions); and, yes... a lanyard, I heartily recommend Earl's Repair Service [(978) 851-2656; 437 Chandler Street/ rear, Tewksbury, MA 01876]. Earl's has been a Walther-exclusive emporium for more than 16 years. If you hurry, you might even be able to acquire one of the two limited edition P99 variations, a James Bond package and a "Year 2000" Commemorative. You'll find the service at Earl's impeccable; the products genuine Walther.

Regarding suppressors, formerly known as "silencers," the persistent misconception is that if a device to limit the sound associated with firing a bullet from a weapon is attached to the business end of the barrel, there is no sound associated with the discharge of the weapon. This mistaken belief is no doubt due to movie and television depictions of a "silenced" weapon being fired. While the sound associated with the firing of a cartridge is markedly reduced... using the proper ammunition... the sound of the hammer fall, plus firing pin or striker being placed in motion to make contact with a chambered

◀ **Walther P99 with special factory threaded barrel and suppressor installed. Accompanying cartridge box is marked "schallgedampfte" (silenced); barrel is also marked with the abbreviation "SD", after the caliber designation.**

▲ **Top quality, German-made Walther CP99 (*below*) is CO2 pistol, designed for inexpensive military/police training. Air pistol is identical to the 9mm/40 S&W-chambered versions in size, weight and handling qualities. Replaceable backstraps in three sizes are also included for realism.**

cartridge primer, remains unaltered. More noticeably, the sound of a semi-automatic pistol cycling is also unaffected by an attached barrel-mounted suppressor. An exception to the norm is an arrangement found on the 9mm S&W Military Mark 22 Model O, more commonly known as the "Hush Puppy," which includes a device for locking the slide in-place, effectively turning the semi-auto into a single-shot pistol.

The Walther factory offers a suppressor for the P99 in two forms. For authorized organizations and appropriately-licensed individuals, there is the functioning Swiss-made Brugger & Thomet Impuls II suppressor. Weight of the Impuls II is 10.56 oz.; length is 7.84 inches. For the collector, a "*shell*" or inoperable version is available, which is the same product in outside appearance, but obviously lacks the internal components and other features needed to make the device function as a suppressor. Walther also offers a threaded barrel, appropriately marked "SD" (silenced) after the caliber designation, which is needed to affix either version of the suppressor to the P99. As you would expect from any product worthy of the Walther banner, great care and thought have gone into both the design and manufacture of the P99 suppressor and threaded barrel. For openers, the suppressor is threaded in the opposite directly of the rifling in the barrel. As a result, each time the pistol is fired with the suppressor attached, the tendency is for the suppressor to tighten, not loosen, during the firing cycle. In addition, the threaded barrel does not allow for overtightening and eliminates possible stripping of the threads in the suppressor. The special "SD" barrel quickly and easily interchanges with the standard barrel, and with practice, the suppressor can be added in just a few seconds.

Walther has announced the addition of the "Quick Action" P99QA to the P99 line-up. For those preferring a single trigger/action pistol mode for precise, every-shot-the-same control in critical tactical situations, the P99QA offers a constant short stroke trigger pull for immediate action and accurate results. Also available is a top-quality, spitting image CO2 pistol designed for cost-effective law enforcement/military training and informal civilian practice sessions. The air gun includes many of the physical characteristics of the real P99, including weight, replaceable backstraps, trigger pull and more. Additionally, with demand for the P99 climbing, Smith & Wesson and Walther have entered into an agreement combining their design and manufacturing expertise to produce the Smith & Wesson Model SW99, with Walther-produced frame and slide/slide components and pistol assembly supplied by Smith & Wesson. There are enough subtle feature differences between these two pistols to offer handgunners similar but different products to consider while making a purchase decision.

Having for all practical purposes invented the double-action pistol mechanism in the late 1920s, Walther therein secured its financial success as well as a lofty place in firearms history. While Walther's P99 is not the first of the new wave polymer-frame pistols, it incorporates several unique characteristics and is loaded with value added features, especially appealing to the seasoned professional handgunner. Designed as a law enforcement/military tool, the P99... in either 9mm Parabellum or 40 S&W caliber... is just as useful for legal civilian concealed carry or as a house gun, adjustable to virtually every shooter's grip and shooting style. With the slide-mounted decocker, which allows the P99 to be placed in a true double-action mode, this is the first of the striker-equipped pistols with which I personally feel comfortable carrying chambered. And as for James Bond of Her Majesty's Secret Service... it's comforting to know he still insists on the very best of everything, including the newest Walther pistol! •

The Charter Arms Bulldog–

Absolutely the Biggest Bang for Your Hard-Earned Bucks

by Robert M. Hausman

THE NEW ENGLAND-MADE product line of Charter Arms, familiar to many long-time shooters, is again available under the new corporate moniker of "Charter 2000." Although this firm has had financial troubles over the past several years, the newly revitalized (and refinanced) company is moving full speed ahead with a slew of new products.

In keeping with tradition, the entire line is designed and engineered to yield high value for the dollar spent. In other words, great effort has been made to produce useful and practical no-frills firearms that the working man will not only want to own, but can afford to buy.

Probably the most famous product in the Charter Arms line was the "Bulldog 44," a compact, double-action five-shot 44 Special revolver chambered for the slow-moving but hard-hitting 44

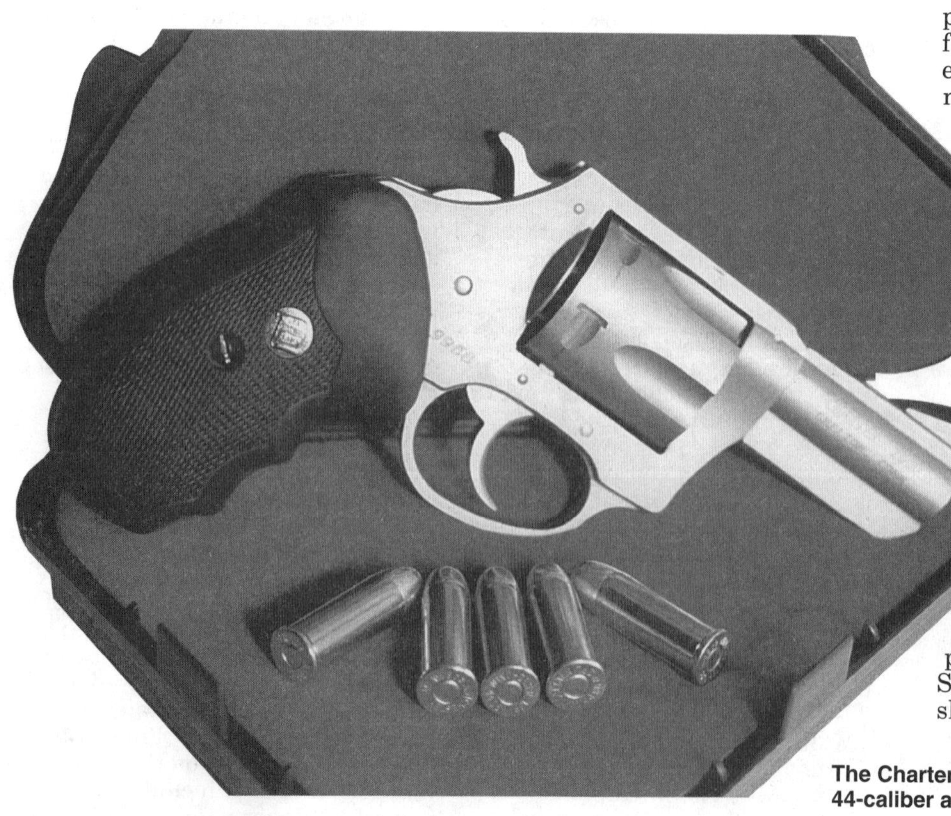

The Charter Bulldog offers five shots of hard-hitting 44-caliber ammunition.

Special cartridge. The Bulldog is a highly effective self-defense arm and one of Charter's top-selling products. Thankfully, it has been brought back and I recently received a test and evaluation sample.

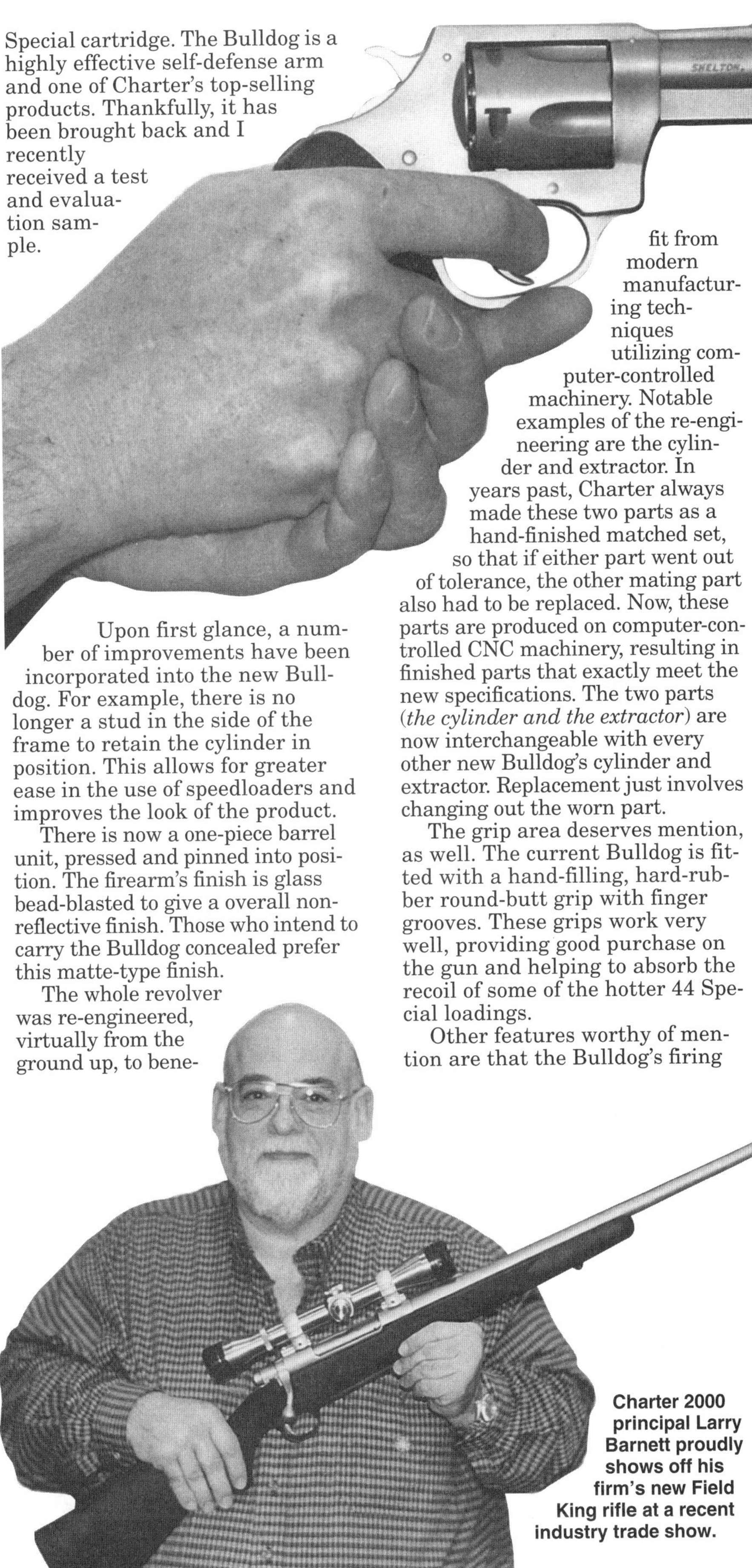

Though the Charter Bulldog 44 can be fired with one hand with most loads, the author recommends a two-hand hold whenever possible to deliver the greatest accuracy.

Upon first glance, a number of improvements have been incorporated into the new Bulldog. For example, there is no longer a stud in the side of the frame to retain the cylinder in position. This allows for greater ease in the use of speedloaders and improves the look of the product.

There is now a one-piece barrel unit, pressed and pinned into position. The firearm's finish is glass bead-blasted to give a overall nonreflective finish. Those who intend to carry the Bulldog concealed prefer this matte-type finish.

The whole revolver was re-engineered, virtually from the ground up, to benefit from modern manufacturing techniques utilizing computer-controlled machinery. Notable examples of the re-engineering are the cylinder and extractor. In years past, Charter always made these two parts as a hand-finished matched set, so that if either part went out of tolerance, the other mating part also had to be replaced. Now, these parts are produced on computer-controlled CNC machinery, resulting in finished parts that exactly meet the new specifications. The two parts (*the cylinder and the extractor*) are now interchangeable with every other new Bulldog's cylinder and extractor. Replacement just involves changing out the worn part.

The grip area deserves mention, as well. The current Bulldog is fitted with a hand-filling, hard-rubber round-butt grip with finger grooves. These grips work very well, providing good purchase on the gun and helping to absorb the recoil of some of the hotter 44 Special loadings.

Other features worthy of mention are that the Bulldog's firing pin is now made of unbreakable beryllium copper. Since it is spring-loaded, rather than fixed in position, the firing pin can handle repeated dry firing without sustaining damage. The 410 stainless frame, of solid one-piece construction, is considered stronger than the frame of revolvers constructed with a side-plate. The revolver locks in three places – at the cylinder hand, the cylinder stop and at the ejector rod collar.

The Bulldog's weight is 21 ounces (*stainless steel*), length: 7-1/4 inches; height: 5-3/4 inches. Options include a blue steel finish (actually 4130 steel with a black oxide coating), rather than stainless. A bobbed pocket hammer option is available in the stainless model only. The Bulldog is backed by an unlimited lifetime warranty to the original owner.

Other products in the line include the rebirth of the Charter Undercover 38 Special double-action revolver. Considered by many to be the finest American-made utility-grade service revolver, it's chambered for the venerable–but still very popular–38 Special round.

The Undercover is available in several variations, including both stainless and blue finishes. Shooters also have a choice of rubber or wood grips, and the option of a standard spurred hammer or a concealed hammer model. The Undercover is built to the same standards as the Bulldog, with a newly designed one-piece barrel and frame. Holding five rounds, the Undercover has a 2-inch barrel, beryllium copper firing pin and 8-groove rifling. Weight is 19-1/2 ounces, length 6-1/4 inches and height 4-1/4 inches. Unlike some other lower-priced snubbies, the ejector rod on the Undercover is fully shrouded to prevent it catching on clothing or being bent.

Yet another new Charter handgun product newly being introduced as this publication goes to press, is a 357 Magnum snub-nose revolver with a ported barrel. Called the "Magnum Pug," it is a five-shot, 2.2-inch barrel revolver

Charter 2000 principal Larry Barnett proudly shows off his firm's new Field King rifle at a recent industry trade show.

manufactured only in 410 stainless steel. Fitted with a traditional spurred hammer, it carries compact rubber grips, weighs only 20 ounces and is sold with a lifetime warranty to the original purchaser.

New Rifle Line

In a piece of news sure to get the attention of big-game hunters on a budget, Charter has gone into rifle production.

Charter's new Field King bolt-action rifles are built around a 400 series stainless Mauser-style long action and 22-inch stainless E.R. Shaw-made barrel as standard equipment. Available in 30-06, 270, 25-06 and 243, the rifle is fitted with a checkered, fiberglass-reinforced synthetic stock with cheekpiece. The trigger is fully adjustable for sear engagement and over-travel. Magazine capacity is 4 rounds.

The rifle's receiver is drilled and tapped for scope use (*no iron sights are provided*) and the rifle comes with a recoil pad and sling studs. Weight is 8 pounds. The U.S. Olympic rifle team supplier, Time Manufacturing, machines the rifle's receiver.

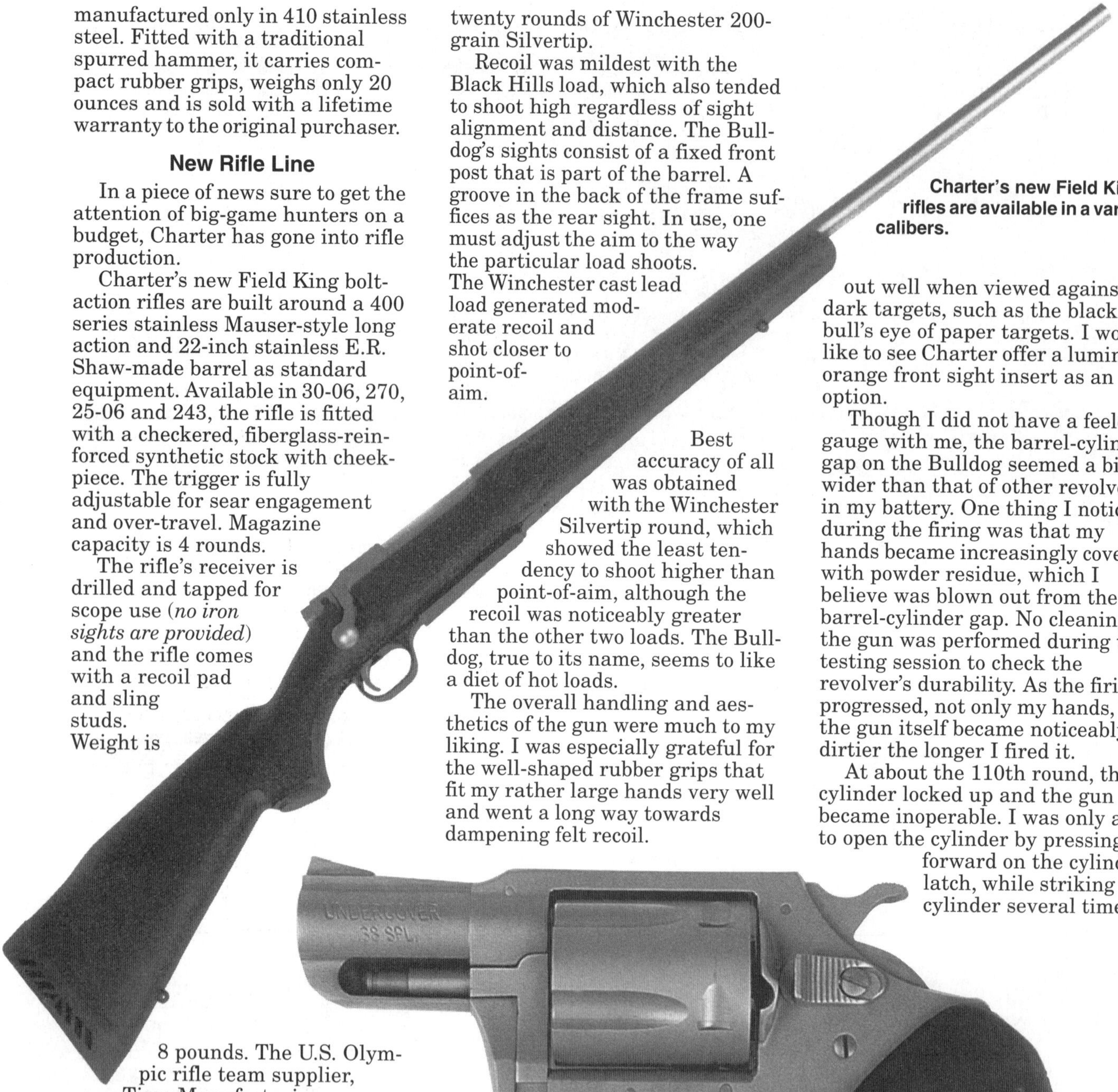

Charter also has a carbine version of the rifle available in 308 only. Produced in stainless or black finishes, barrel length is 20 inches with a factory-installed compensator.

Bulldog Test Fire

As mentioned, Charter sent out a sample Bulldog 44 for use in preparing this article. During an afternoon test fire session at an outdoor range, approximately 100 rounds (50 each) of Winchester 240-grain cast lead factory loads and Black Hills 210-grain lead loads were fired, plus an additional twenty rounds of Winchester 200-grain Silvertip.

Recoil was mildest with the Black Hills load, which also tended to shoot high regardless of sight alignment and distance. The Bulldog's sights consist of a fixed front post that is part of the barrel. A groove in the back of the frame suffices as the rear sight. In use, one must adjust the aim to the way the particular load shoots. The Winchester cast lead load generated moderate recoil and shot closer to point-of-aim.

Best accuracy of all was obtained with the Winchester Silvertip round, which showed the least tendency to shoot higher than point-of-aim, although the recoil was noticeably greater than the other two loads. The Bulldog, true to its name, seems to like a diet of hot loads.

The overall handling and aesthetics of the gun were much to my liking. I was especially grateful for the well-shaped rubber grips that fit my rather large hands very well and went a long way towards dampening felt recoil.

The matte silver-gray front sight (*on my stainless-finish sample*) tended to blur against light-colored targets. The silver sight does stand out well when viewed against dark targets, such as the black bull's eye of paper targets. I would like to see Charter offer a luminous orange front sight insert as an option.

Though I did not have a feeler gauge with me, the barrel-cylinder gap on the Bulldog seemed a bit wider than that of other revolvers in my battery. One thing I noticed during the firing was that my hands became increasingly covered with powder residue, which I believe was blown out from the barrel-cylinder gap. No cleaning of the gun was performed during the testing session to check the revolver's durability. As the firing progressed, not only my hands, but the gun itself became noticeably dirtier the longer I fired it.

At about the 110th round, the cylinder locked up and the gun became inoperable. I was only able to open the cylinder by pressing forward on the cylinder latch, while striking the cylinder several times

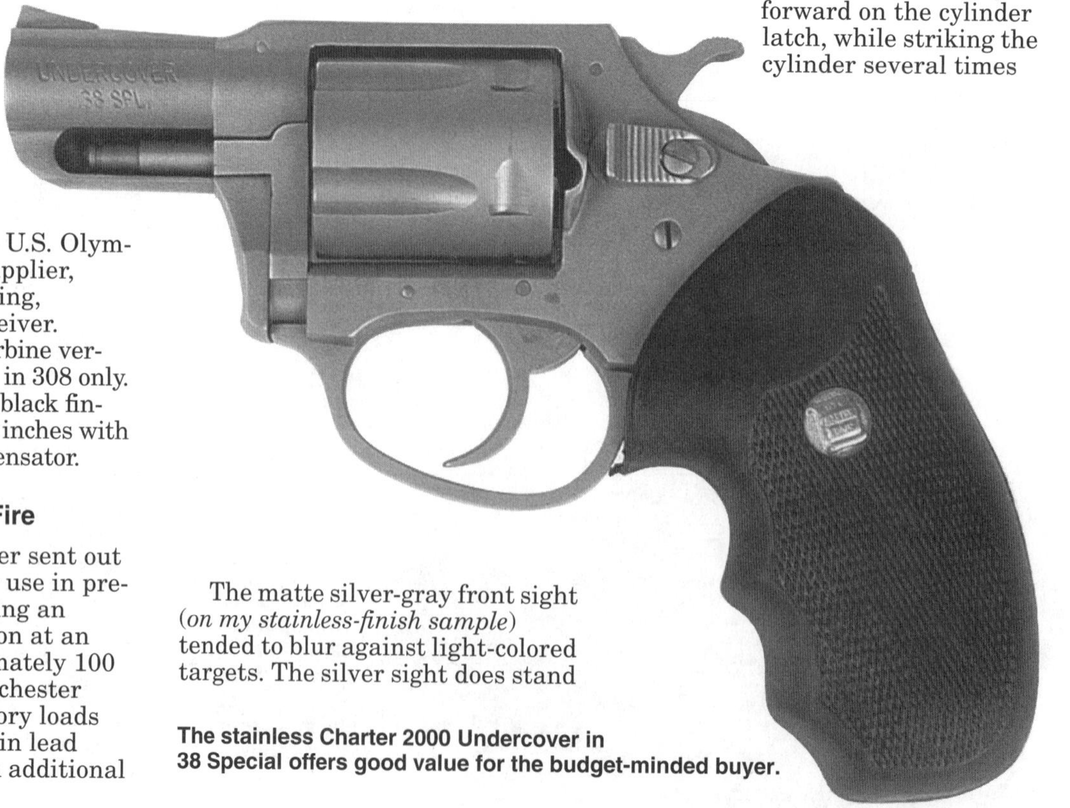

Charter's new Field King rifles are available in a variety of calibers.

The stainless Charter 2000 Undercover in 38 Special offers good value for the budget-minded buyer.

Traditional craftsmanship still goes into each Charter 2000 revolver.

with the end of a plastic-handled screwdriver.

By this time, both the interior and exterior of the gun had become covered with powder residue. I attribute the cylinder lockup problem to the accumulation of fouling. I applied some lubricant and wiped the gun off with a paper towel. The remaining approximately ten rounds were fired without incident.

The Bulldog was taken back to the office and given a thorough cleaning. The next afternoon, I went back to the range and fired an additional fifty rounds of cast lead and Silvertip hollowpoints with no stoppages.

I found the Bulldog to be a worthy choice for personal protection, either as a primary gun or as a backup. While I did not measure the trigger-pull weight, I found the feel of the trigger, in both single- and double-action modes, to be very controllable.

Most purchasers of utility-grade revolvers, such as the Bulldog 44, probably won't put as many rounds through it as I did in one test session. They also certainly won't need to fire over one hundred rounds, risking a fouling-induced stoppage, when calling upon the gun in a self-protection situation.

As an aside, at the same time I was working with the Bulldog 44, I also brought to the range a pair of domestically-produced, newly-designed double-action-only semi-auto pistols (*which shall remain nameless*) designed to be sold at about the same price as the Charter product. The first, a 9mm, had its trigger bar come out of alignment after firing only 35 rounds of standard full metal jacket ammunition. The second pistol, in 380 ACP, could not fire more than four rounds of ball ammo before a failure-to-feed stoppage. With 380 ACP Remington hollow points, it jammed every second round and, with Federal hollowpoints, it jammed almost every shot. Needless to say, both of these pistols were returned to the respective manufacturers.

When compared to these two sleek, but poorly functioning semi-autos, the Charter wheelgun's dirt-induced stoppage pales by comparison. The much more powerful 44 Special chambering of the Bulldog, combined with it's reliable revolving cylinder mechanism, make it a best bet for the self-defense-minded handgun shopper on a budget.

The sight of the gaping black hole of the Bulldog's muzzle and the large 44-caliber slugs visible in the piece's cylinder, may be enough to deter aggressors–without firing a shot.

Company Name Origin

The original Connecticut company, Charter Arms, was named in honor of the "Charter Oak," a large tree that once stood in Hartford, Connecticut, the state's capital. The tree became famous since Connecticut's original state charter was once hidden there so that the English governor could not destroy it.

Sir Edmund Andros came to Hartford in 1687 to seize the Connecticut charter by force, if necessary, and to make the colony part of a proposed "Royal Dominion of New England." An agreement was made by the colonists to turn over the charter to the king's representative at an evening council meeting.

During the meeting, the door to the council room flew open and a gust of wind blew out the candles illuminating the room. When the light was restored, the charter was gone. Patriot Joseph Wadsworth is believed to have been the one who hid the charter in the heart of a nearby oak tree. The document remained hidden until 1689, after James II fell from power, then it was retrieved and used as the supreme law until 1818. Charter 2000 is fulfilling its namesake by keeping the tradition of freedom alive with its production of no-nonsense working guns that fit into most everyone's budget. •

Model 657 L-O-N-G!

S&W's 41 Magnum ... A Long-Barrel Winner!

by Dave Workman

THE 41 REMINGTON Magnum is back prominently this year in the Smith & Wesson lineup and, for hunting handgunners or silhouette shooters who like a flat-shooting, hard-hitting, not-so-hard recoiling powerhouse, that is good news indeed.

Happy to admit that I would have crawled on my belly to both HANDGUNS 2002 editor Ken Ramage, and S&W's Ken Jorgensen, to get the chance to check this baby out. Fortunately, it didn't require that sort of groveling, just a visit with the two at the SHOT Show in New Orleans.

What followed turned into what might arguably be one of the most enjoyable, yet slightly frustrating, handgun tests this writer has ever done.

This all began when Jorgensen tipped me off in late 2000 that the company was planning to introduce a long-barreled 41 Magnum Model 657 wheelgun into its product line. A longtime fan of this cartridge (*I've killed two species of deer with this round after having been one of the earliest advocates for big game handgun hunting in my home state of Washington back in the early 1980s*), I have fired thousands of rounds through my two 41 Magnums, one a blued Model 57 Smith with 6-inch barrel and the other a Ruger Blackhawk with a 6.5-inch tube

41 Remington Magnum Roots

The cartridge, initially developed at the urging of the late Elmer Keith (who killed the first recorded big game with early Smith wheelguns in this chambering, on a much-publicized trek to Alaska), is a true .410 caliber (unlike the far more popular 44 Magnum, which actually measures .429-inch). In its current factory loadings, it clocks out of the muzzle in the 1,250-1,300 fps range with a 175-grain Silvertip from Winchester, a 250-grainer Federal and a 210-grain Remington load.

Like all other S&W handguns, this big boy comes in a lockable, padded case with Master keyed trigger lock.

With a 1.29-inch case length, and maximum cartridge length of 1.59-inch, in its heyday, the 41 Magnum could be fed with factory ammunition from several different companies. There were, in the beginning, two load levels: one for hunting and the other for law enforcement. Yep, Keith and others originally pitched this cartridge as a police round and, for a time, S&W actually made a 41 Magnum Model 58 with fixed sights, but it never really took off. Street cops just couldn't handle the recoil and there was a genuine concern about over-penetration in an urban environment, even with a mellowed "law enforcement" load that might easily have been called the "41

Mag Lite." I have seen the occasional Model 51 at gun shows, but they never impressed me because it is against live game and metal chickens that this cartridge really struts its stuff.

Alas — and here's the rub — factory fodder for the 41 Mag. just isn't all that available these days, and one might call this cartridge the *"Rodney Dangerfield magnum"* because it just don't get no respect.

Indeed, I cruised a couple of gun shops during the course of writing this piece, and there were not any 41 Magnum cartridge boxes on the shelf. I asked one guy about this, and the reply was a not-terribly-convincing, *"Oh, we just haven't gotten our order in."*

I called Remington, Federal and Winchester to ship me some test ammo, and none of it arrived in time for my evaluation. Fortunately, I had small supply of Winchesters, enough to do the test. But that's not the worst of it.

True story: I called my pal Allan Jones at Speer's plant in Lewiston, Idaho. A few years ago, Speer had cranked out a moderate 41 Magnum Blazer round that I had found to be a real sweet shooter, topped by a 200-grain Speer JHP that shot to point of aim out of both my wheelguns. Here's a rendition of that conversation:

Me: *"Allan, I need a couple of boxes of Blazer 41 Magnum."*

Allan: *"Well, we stopped doing that load a couple of years ago. We found out you were the only guy buying it."*

Ouch! But not so fast. I dug into my ammo cache and guess what I found? A nearly half-full box of those aluminum-jacketed cartridges that became part of this gun test, just for giggles. Winchester, Federal and Remington still brew loads for the 41 Magnum, but I had to rely on handloads for much of my shooting.

Of course, I had an ample supply of said handloads, using the Speer 200-grain JHP, the Hornady 210-grain XTP/JHP, some older Hornady 210-grain JHPs and Nosler's 210-grain JHP. My gun-writer colleagues may laugh me off the map for this, but I use the exact same powder charge: 17.5 grains of 2400 behind all of these projectiles. Why? Well, because it just works for me, okay? I've put a couple of deer in the freezer; the first with two lung shots (*the first being the Speer, the second being an XTP*) about an inch apart, through the brush downhill at about 25 yards, at a moving mule deer. The second was taken with a Nosler that nicked a shoulder blade and, in so doing, mushroomed perfectly and literally slammed the spike blacktail to the ground at about 30 yards.

So, for the handloader, there are many component bullets available, from everybody on the map. They are just not utilized much for factory ammunition, it would seem.

I've also shot both guns long-range at some impromptu pistol matches at a local gun range, smacking water-filled milk jugs at 125 yards with both the Smith and Ruger, so there's no doubt in my mind that the 41 Magnum is a cartridge that delivers the goods.

Well, so much for the cartridge and my history with it. Now, what about this S&W wheelgun?

One Awesome Six-Shooter

For openers, the new version of S&W's Model 657 is just plain awesome. They've put a 7.5-inch full underlug barrel on this stainless steel N-frame cannon, and left the cylinder unfluted. The tops of the

Specifications: Smith & Wesson Model 657

Manufacturer:
Smith & Wesson
2100 Roosevelt Avenue
P.O. Box 2208
Springfield, MA 01102-2208
(413) 781-8300

Model: 657

Barrel Length: 7.5 inches

Caliber: 41 Magnum

Capacity: Six rounds

Sights: Black front ramp, rear square-notch click-adjustable

Weight (empty): 52 ounces

OAL: 11 7/8 inches

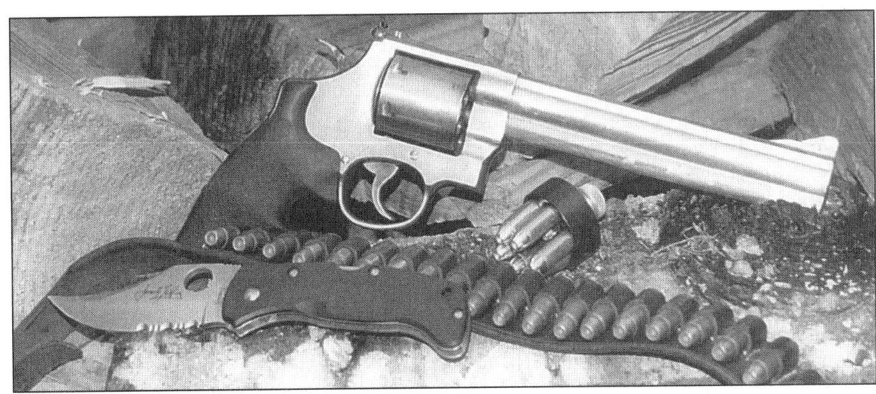

Now here's a hunting package: S&W Model 657 with HKS speedloader carrying six Winchester 175-grain Silvertips and gunbelt loaded with handloads carrying Hornady XTPs, and Spyderco's new Chinook folder by James A. Keating.

Performance Review: Smith & Wesson Model 657

Cartridge	Bullet type and Wt.	Vel.@ 10 yards	Group
Factory:			
Winchester	175 gr. Silvertip	1257	2.0
CCI/Blazer	200 gr. Speer JHP	1052	2.5
Handloads:			
Winchester brass	200 gr. Speer JHP	1135	2.75
Winchester brass	210 gr. Hornady JHP	1228	3.5
Winchester brass	210 gr. Nosler JHP	1157	2.0
Winchester brass	210 gr. Hornady XTP	1169	2.75

frame and barrel have a bead-blasted finish with the traditional S&W full-length serrations running from the frame to the front ramp. Both front and rear sights are matte black, while overall finish is a very appealing brushed satin. I would personally opt for a ramp front sight with a red insert.

'Smith designers must have been thinking of me when they installed a wide, smooth target trigger and wide, sharply checkered target hammer.

Unlike my personal Model 57, and a couple of Model 19 Smiths, this new gun is fitted with a frame-mounted, rebounding firing pin. Smith & Wesson began phasing in this firing pin a few years ago, and now it is standard issue. On my older models, the firing pin was still part of the hammer.

The crane-to-frame lockup was solid, and it just had the feel of sound engineering and finishing to it. In addition, that cylinder was impressive. Years ago, S&W stopped counter-boring its cylinders, but it's made little personal difference to me because every one of these revolvers I have ever fired, with or without counter-boring, shot just fine.

I carefully examined each of the six chambers and found them to be polished like mirrors. The full-length ejection rod/cylinder pin pressed spent cartridges out positively, and the cylinder revolved around it like a well-lubricated ball bearing.

Now for the feature on this gun that I just don't care for at all: the rounded grip frame. It's a pet peeve of mine that has nothing at all to do with the accuracy or reliability of this - or any other - S&W revolver, but I will never understand the reasoning behind Smith's decision a few years ago to round the grip frames on all their wheelguns.

The 41 Magnum is one healthy popgun, and despite the factory mounting of a superb one-piece Hogue finger-groove black rubber Monogrip with that marvelous raised-bump surface, I just think my hand likes a squared backstrap. However, I have had a set of Hogue panels on one of my 45 autos for a long time, and swear by them. If I have to settle for a round grip frame, this rubber grip makes it tolerable, though I would personally opt for a grip without the finger grooves.

To Hogue's credit, they mold a palm swell into each side of the grip, and that helps make for a comfortable hold. There is an S&W emblem molded into the top of the grip on both sides.

Newer S&W revolvers have firing pin in frame, where older models mounted pin on hammer. Author Workman doesn't care either way, so long as they go "*BANG!*" when trigger is pressed.

My test gun (*Ser. # CER4684*) came out of the box with one of the smoothest double-action trigger pulls I've ever felt, and in this realm, "*feel*" carries a lot of weight. It was better than that on my prized Model 57, and almost identical to the feel of my 6-inch Model 19.

Single-action trigger pull was dead-on crisp, with no discernible creep. The trigger broke at just under 5.5 pounds, which is too heavy for some folks, but okay by me on this type of handgun because it requires the shooter to put just that additional effort into concentration, what I call the 'brain-to-finger' coordination.

Of particular interest to that one handgun shooter out there who is interested in political correctness (*there's got to be at least one!*), each S&W handgun now comes from the factory in a lockable padded gun box, with a trigger lock from Master Lock. I found this appealing, particularly for handgunners who live in states where laws are now requiring them to lock up their pistols when not in use. S&W's system, with two locking "devices," is about as good as it gets to satisfy the hand wringers and, from a safety standpoint, it makes sense.

Now, the Good Part

Okay, we have extolled most of the virtues of the Model 657, save for one. It shoots!

My range sessions became so enjoyable I lost track of time - shooting groups, and finally plinking at tin cans just for something different to do.

Initial range testing over a Chrony chronograph showed that factory loads and my handloads clocked out of the bore in the 1,150-1,200 fps-range as expected. I got the tightest factory group with 175-

Author relied heavily on handloads for testing because factory 41 Magnum ammo is limited. Here's a sample mix of Workman's test fodder (*l-r*) CCI/Blazer 200 gr. JHP (*no longer produced*), Winchester 175-grain Silvertip JHP, Speer 200 gr., Nosler 210 gr. JHP, older Hornady 210 gr. JHP and Hornady 210 gr. XTP, all ahead of 17.5 grains of 2400.

grain Winchester Silvertips, and I just could not tell a heck of a lot of difference between the groups my handloads shot with the Speer, Nosler and Hornady projectiles.

Thanks to the healthy weight of that big full-lug N-Frame, recoil was not simply manageable, but surprisingly comfortable.

Out of the box, the big 'Smith shot low at 25 yards with everything I put through the tube, in some cases several inches low at 25 yards. Fiddling around with the rear click-adjustable sight fixed that in a jiffy, and then I settled down for shooting groups that ranged from a two-incher to one with an extreme spread of about 3.5 inches, which I attributed to the pains of getting used to a new gun. Once I settled down to shooting off a sandbag rest, I managed to put several two-holers through the Birchwood-Casey Shoot*N*C targets.

I'll admit that the nastiest recoil I got came out of one lot of handloads, some that I had brewed up using old-style Hornady 210-grain JHPs that have been replaced by the superb XTP. (*Years ago, I stocked up on enough .410 bullets to keep me shooting well into retirement, and those older Hornady pills are proof positive that even gun writers can be impulse shoppers!*)

I will also note that the velocities from that one handful of cartridges clocked about 100 fps faster than all the others, and that one just flat beats the heck out of me. As I noted earlier, I use the same powder charge in my handloads, and the 210-grain Noslers and XTPs clocked within 30-35 fps of the Speer 200-grainer over the Chrony, so I'll just have to sort that one out another time.

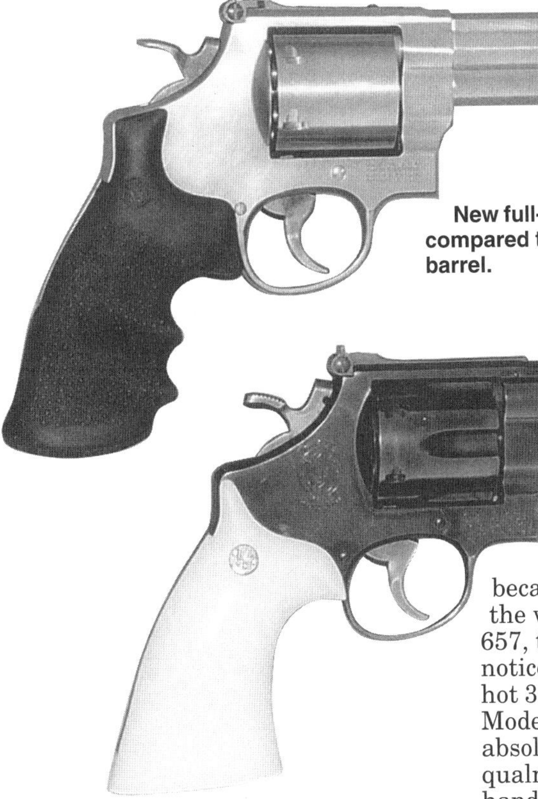

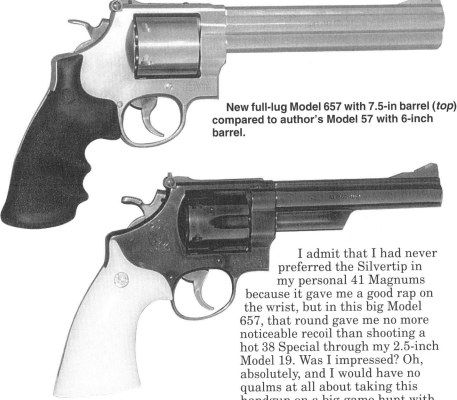

New full-lug Model 657 with 7.5-in barrel (*top*) compared to author's Model 57 with 6-inch barrel.

One target out of many. Three holes at lower left are from author's left-over Blazer ammo, while the tight little holes above are his handloads pushing 210-grain Noslers.

Second five-shot group was produced with Silvertips, which really impressed author.

I admit that I had never preferred the Silvertip in my personal 41 Magnums because it gave me a good rap on the wrist, but in this big Model 657, that round gave me no more noticeable recoil than shooting a hot 38 Special through my 2.5-inch Model 19. Was I impressed? Oh, absolutely, and I would have no qualms at all about taking this handgun on a big-game hunt with nothing but the Winchester factory load, leaving my handloads at home.

Now, for something healthier than deer, say a caribou or even an elk, that hefty 250-grain pill from Federal in its Premium cartridge would be my first choice if I was determined to anchor the quarry with a 41 Magnum.

Now, for serious work, a handgun hunter will give definite consideration to putting a scope on this gun, and there's plenty of room to accommodate one. It may make the gun awful heavy but, with the right shoulder holster, carrying it will be comfortable. I would recommend any handgun glass from Bushnell/Bausch & Lomb, Weaver, Simmons and Leupold.

Is this gun worth the suggested retail price? Of course, that is a subjective question seeking a subjective response. In my opinion, any straight-shooting 41 Magnum is worth buying, and if you find the price to your liking, pull out your wallet.

For die-hard devotees of the 41 Magnum, this revolver will be worth every penny. It shoots superbly, is well balanced and has an eye-catching profile. And it has the right size hole in the barrel. In this writer's book, it doesn't get much better than that. •

THE ENDURING GRACE OF THE K-FRAME

By Massad Ayoob

Certain guns adapt so well to their purpose that they are timeless. The Smith & Wesson K-frame is one of them.

IN 1899, SMITH & Wesson introduced their 38-caliber Military & Police Hand Ejector. It had a round butt, a tapered barrel and no front lug for the ejector rod. It was chambered, says S&W historian Roy Jinks, for the 32-20 and the newly developed 38 S&W Special. (*1*) Notes Jinks, "*Many engineering changes were made to this model during the course of its early production. The collector has classified these engineering changes, produced from 1899-1940, into eight model variations.*" (*2*)

Two of the biggest changes would occur subsequent to that. Late in WWII, after a sailor was killed when a Smith 38 went off when dropped, a new hammer block design was developed. In the immediate post-war years, a new "short-action" design replaced the long, smooth double-action mechanism that had previously been its hallmark. Though the length of trigger stroke and hammer fall were reduced, the smoothness remained. Since its inception, double-action trigger pulls were judged by the standard of the K-frame Smith & Wesson, and the short action did not change that.

In 1957, S&W added numeric designations to its products. The Military & Police 38 Special became the Model 10. Future engineering changes would be memorialized by altering the model number with a dash and a suffix. (*3*) The highest M&P number this writer has seen is "10-8," indicating at least eight changes since '57 in the Model 10 alone, and not counting adjustable sights or different calibers, which had different primary model numbers.

By 1985, gun authority Larry Wallack reported that S&W had produced more than six million K-frame revolvers. Colt, by contrast, produced only half as many 45 automatics in the period 1911-85. (*4*)

A star had been born. With several models still in the catalog in at least three calibers as of 2001, the K-frame would span the 19th, 20th and 21st century. With millions still in service, it remains an absolute classic.

One thing that makes a classic is... the manufacturers got it right from the beginning. As noted, there were many variations. S&W has catalogued barrel lengths from 2 inches to 8 3/8 inches, and chambered the K-frame for a wide variety of cartridges: 22 Long Rifle, 22 Magnum, 22 Jet, 32/20, 32 S&W Long, 32 Magnum, 38 S&W (British designation .380), 38 Special, 9mm Parabellum and 357 Magnum. The frames would be made of chrome-molybdenum ordnance gunsteel, stainless and aluminum (although not yet of Titanium and Scandium, at this writing). Finishes would be fine blue, ordinary blue and nickel; stainless, of course– and sometimes the finest gold filigree. They were Parkerized during WWII in the Victory Model series, and Lew Horton Distributors recently commissioned a special run of visually striking Model 10s with case-hardened frames.

For most of the 20th century, the K-frame revolver was the mainstay of the Smith & Wesson catalog. Only today does it seem to be in eclipse. At a recent lunch with S&W's public relations manager Ken Jorgensen, I heard Ken say, "Our best-selling revolvers are split between the little guns and the semi-big ones. The list goes J-frame, L-frame, J-frame..."

At the beginning, S&W kept the #1 maker, Colt, on their toes with this gun. By the end of WWII, Smith & Wesson was neck and neck with Colt in police revolver sales, and about to surpass them. A quarter century later, the S&W was utterly dominant. The guns American police carried were overwhelmingly K-frames, first in 38 Special and then, when legendary Border Patrol gun expert Bill Jordan convinced S&W president Carl Hellstrom to produce it in 1954, as the 357 Combat Magnum.

A history of the nation's leading handgun experts is a history of K-frame users. Elmer Keith thought it was the right size for a 22, though he normally carried one or another S&W 44 on a larger frame for serious business. Paul B. Weston, a high-ranking NYPD officer, crack shot and police science professor, had his choice between Colt and Smith 38s for both range and street.

In competition, he went back and forth between the two. On duty, the gun he chose to protect his life was a customized M&P.

"Skeeter" Skelton carried one or another 4- or 5-inch Combat Magnum for much of his distinguished career. Jim Cirillo of the NYPD Stakeout Squad became the most famous police gunfighter of modern times, and every armed criminal he shot down with a handgun fell to his K-frame Model 10 38 Special. Jim Wilson, the Texas sheriff who sort of inherited Skelton's mantle after Skeeter's untimely death, had always found it hard to choose between the K-frame Combat Magnum and the Colt 45 auto, so he always spent a lot of time with both. He would later nominate the Combat Magnum as the most important revolver of the 20th century. Long before then, legendary FBI agent Melvin Purvis brought a pair of Military & Police 38s to Chicago's Biograph Theater on the night he and his team brought down John Dillinger.

The bad guys who knew their hardware were smart enough to use K-frames, too. No Allied general of WWII was known to carry a Luger or a Walther, but when Hermann Goering was captured, he was said to be carrying a commercial-production 4-inch Smith & Wesson Military & Police 38 Special.

The K-frame has a longer history than the 1911 45 auto, obviously, and was produced in greater numbers for a longer continuous period than the Colt "Peacemaker." Indeed, one expert called the K-frame "the Peacemaker of the 20th century." I don't recall anyone arguing the point.

+P 38 Special ammo is not a problem in modern K-frames. These Model 10s with tapered barrel (*left*) or heavy barrel (*right*) are filled with "FBI loads" and will eat them up all day, says author.

X-ring group potential is built into these guns. This is a K-38 with S&W factory 6-inch barrel; only BoMar sight rib and Hogue Monogrips have been added. Ammo was Federal Match 38 Special wadcutter.

Secrets of Success

The K-frame's sweet double-action trigger stroke was one of its claims to fame. Ironically, the Colt double actions until 1969 were easier, smoother and crisper in single-action fire and, since most target shooting was done in single action mode, the Colt ruled that game. Many police chiefs and instructors thought that whatever worked best for the pistol team must be best for issue to the rank and file, and the Colt was thus the preferred brand for most of the first half of the 20th century.

It was not until after WWII that combat-style training became an imperative in the police establishment, and that meant double action. The Smith's stroke was not only shorter than the Colt's, but smoother–and absolutely consistent from first pressure to last. It was said by the experts that the Colt lent itself to a two-stage pull, trigger-cocking if you will, in which the practitioner brought the trigger most of the way back until the cylinder locked into place. The shooter then applied the rest of the press as if squeezing off a single-action shot. Predictably, this strategy did not lend itself to real-world defensive shooting. In NRA bullseye matches of the time, as now, "rapid fire" meant five shots in ten seconds. In the real world, rapid fire meant you were trying to fire five shots in close

J-frame Model 36 target version (*right*) may be as mechanically accurate as K-frame Model 10 (*left*), but ergonomics of the "K" make practical accuracy easier to extract.

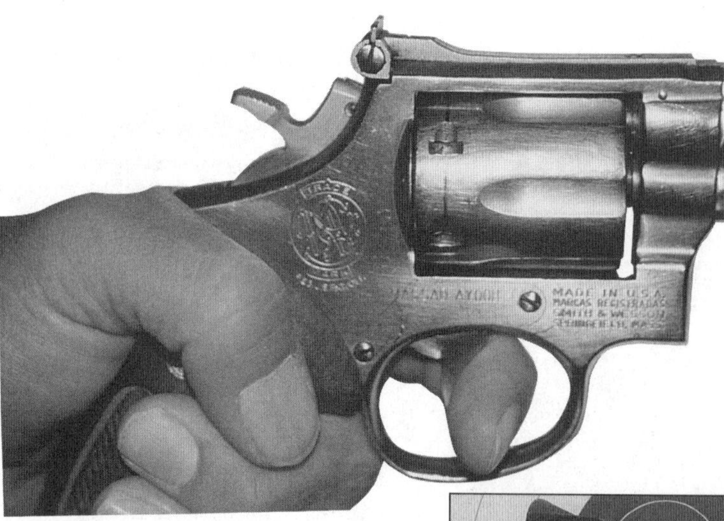

A key element of K-frame's success is trigger reach dimension. With web of hand high and centered on backstrap, distal joint of index finger is centered on trigger: ideal "grasping factors" for maximum control.

to *one* second before the criminal aiming his stolen gun at you could pull his trigger at all.

In this, the S&W excelled. Where Colt masters used the two-stage pull, S&W masters appreciated the single-stage double-action roll of the gun from Springfield, Massachusetts. This turned out to be what worked best in high-speed, high-stress shooting, and this is the main reason the S&W surpassed the Colt revolver in the police marketplace. Bill Ruger designed a similar one-stage pull into his double-action police revolver introduced circa 1970. It was for that reason (and its rugged reliability with Magnum loads) that Ruger was running a very close second to Smith, and Colt was a distant third in the service revolver market in the mid-80s, when the service revolver sales race became a moot point. US police were beginning their *en masse* switch to the semiautomatic duty pistol.

The Subtleties of Fit and Handling

There was much more to the K-frame's rise to prominence than just its exquisite double action trigger pull. Long before "ergonomics" and "human engineering" entered the language, the designers of the 1899 Hand Ejector had put together a gun that was absolutely perfect in shape for rapid fire in the average adult male hand. Company co-founder Daniel Baird Wesson and particularly his son Joseph are generally credited with these key elements of the K-frame's design, during the period 1896-99.

A few years ago I attended the briefing in which S&W introduced the Sigma pistol. They went to great lengths to explain the ergonomics study they had commissioned at a six-figure cost to determine average hand sizes and build a pistol to those dimensions. I sat in the audience going, *"Damn!"* It turned out that I *owned* one of those "average size adult male hands." Two of them, in fact.

K-frame's smooth double-action pull allows 50' groups like these from a well-worn M/15.

Thus, it was no surprise that the Sigma fit me perfectly. This explained something else. *So did the K-frame revolver!*

For maximum control of the handgun, experts agree, you want to hold it with the barrel directly in line with the long bones of your forearm. To control its double-action trigger, you want to be able to take this grasp, and feel the distal joint of your index finger make contact on the trigger. This gives the finger optimum leverage, since it is the ideal alignment of skeleto-muscular support structure for a smooth, straight-back pull against firm resistance. This means a fast and accurate shot. This is what "the revolver fitting the hand" is all about.

This is also why petite females with proportional hands, and males with short fingers, usually do their best with a gun that has a shorter "trigger reach" dimension than the K-frame revolver. It is also why people with big hands and long fingers do their best with such guns when they are fitted with custom grips that back the web of their hand away from the rear of the grip-frame, thus lengthening the trigger reach dimension.

There is one more design feature that many have felt in their favorite revolver without finding occasion to put it into words. The shape of the frame on the "K" is such that with the web of your hand at its highest point on the recurve of the backstrap, the axis of the barrel sits lower *vis-à-vis* the wrist and forearm than any other conventional service-size revolver. The lower the axis of the bore, the less the muzzle can rise in recoil.

I discovered something surprising early on in my shooting career. A fan of the N-frame revolver, whose much greater mass better absorbed recoil, I learned that while those "44-frame" sixguns kicked back into my hand less, the 38-frame "K-size" Smiths stayed on target better with the same hot 357 Magnum ammo. The reason was simple: the bore axis of the Model 19 K-frame Combat Magnum was lower, and gave the shooter more

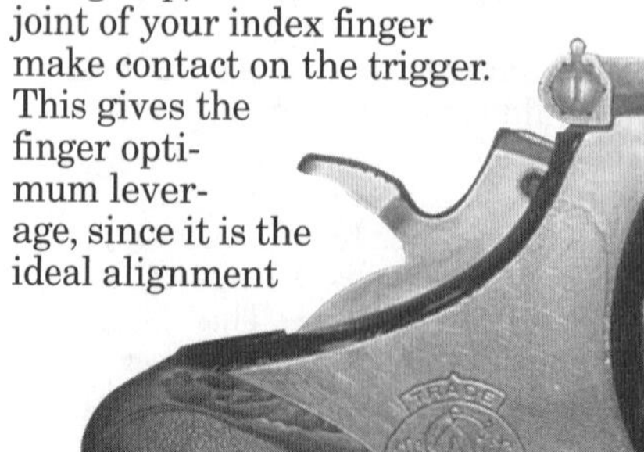

Adjustable sights have been available on K-frames from the beginning – 102 years. These adorn a Model 15 38 Special Combat Masterpiece, for decades, standard issue to L.A. cops, both city and county.

"Cop trade" M/15 was bought for $130 in 1998. Rough finish, perfect interior, glass-smooth action, and 1-inch groups at 25 yards. Only Hogue grips have been added.

leverage than did the Model 27 N-frame 357 Magnum.

Thus it was that the smaller, lighter K-frame could actually keep its most powerful rounds on target at a faster pace than the theoretically superior big, heavy N-frame with the same ammo. The K just hurt your hand more to do it.

Jerry Miculek used N-frame Smith & Wessons to set his speed records. However, you have to remember that Jerry came to fame shooting bowling pins at Second Chance, a game that requires powerful loads. I was there when Jerry started. *He began with a K-frame, the 8 3/8-inch barrel K-38 to be specific, and only switched to the bigger Smith in the same barrel length because his monster handloads were beating the 38-frame guns to death.*

Which leads us to the cardinal weakness of the K-frame concept, at least when chambered for the 357 Magnum cartridge.

No revolver has more after-market grip options than the "K." ***Left, from top:*** **Craig Spegel boot grips (M/13), Uncle Mike's (M/13) & home-modified Pachmayrs (M/15).** ***Right, from top,*** **Hogue Monogrip and Pachmayr Presentation, both on M/10s.**

Durability Factor

The K-frame was designed around a low-pressure black powder cartridge. It came to its greatest fame and glory as a 38 Special, a round that delivers maybe 17,000 psi pressure in a standard load and some 23,000 psi with a hot +P. Even with modern metallurgy, chambering it for the 357 Magnum was asking a lot. Industry pressure standards for the 357 run toward the mid-30,000 psi range and have been known to exceed 42,000 psi with certain 125-grain Magnum rounds.

Bill Jordan himself said the Model 19 Combat Magnum was intended to be shot mostly with 38 Specials, with the Magnum loads reserved only for serious business. Jordan, we will remember, is the man who conceptualized the K-frame in the 357 chambering and sold Smith & Wesson on the idea. However, by the 1970s, liability issues were forcing police to train intensively with the ammo they carried. Firearms instructors began to notice that the ordnance steel Model 19s were taking a beating, going "out of time" and occasionally splitting their forcing cones. This occurred mainly with the 125-grain full Magnum round. The K-frame handled +P 38 Special just fine.

Then came the stainless version of the Combat Mag, the Model 66. There hadn't been enough research done on the metallurgy. Stainless heats up faster than chrome-moly, and when steel heats, it expands. M66s began locking up at an epidemic rate. The factory went through three or four desperate fixes before they finally got the guns to work. By then, cops were looking for heavier-duty 357s, and were switching almost wholesale to S&W's L-frames, basically 41-frame guns, and Rugers. It was the K-frame's darkest hour.

Even today, most seasoned instructors will advise the person who carries a K-frame Magnum to shoot it in qualifications with Mag loads, to carry Mag loads, but to do most of their practice with 38 Special rounds.

A Personal View

At age eleven, my dad gave me a Ruger Standard 22 auto, and I learned with it to be comfortable shooting pistols. A year later it was swapped for a lighter High Standard Sentinel 22 and, with that, I

▶There's little to improve on a K-frame. Andy Cannon honed the action and polished the trigger surface on this M/66, removing trigger stop the factory put on target-grade models *(note empty slot in frame behind trigger)*, and shaved cylinder latch to prevent thumb-cutting from Magnum recoil.

learned to shoot and *hit*. But the year after, he gave me a Smith & Wesson K-22, and that was the instrument that taught me to shoot a handgun and hit *well*. By then I already had a 45 auto and would soon have my first 44 Magnum. But it was the K-22 that taught me that accurate handguns have to be lived up to.

Time went on. The police department that swore me in at age 23 issued the S&W Model 10, but we could carry something bigger. I started with a five-screw Smith 1955 Target revolver in 45 ACP, its barrel cut to 4 inches, and was soon carrying a Colt 45 auto. Before long I was into PPC, competing with a Power Custom revolver built on a Model 15 traded in by the Kansas City PD. This was my second "meaningful relationship" with a K-frame. I was about to have a third: in 1978, a new chief of police made us all carry the Model 66, the stainless Combat Magnum that had by then been adopted by the agency, and for the next two years that gun was my constant companion.

I didn't much like having a 357 forced down my throat when I preferred a 45 Auto. Our issue guns were the early, crappy ones from before S&W got "stainless" and "357 Magnum" to blend right, so I'd bought my own and had it slicked up and straightened out by Andy Cannon.

In 1980, I had this gun fitted with the Magna-Trigger device, which meant that it could only fire in the hand of an authorized person wearing a special ring. Wonder of wonders, it worked! This gun became my bedside home companion, since I had an active, smart three-year-old wandering about. For the first few years that I went into firearms training full time, I taught with it. It was a concept I wanted to demonstrate, and that made for one less gun to carry on road trips. I once shot the Bianchi Cup with it.

I don't usually nickname my guns, but this one became "Fluffy, the Pet Revolver." I called it that because it would only speak for its owner.

◀ Many consider 3-inch heavy barrel the optimum concealed carry format for K-frames, like this M/13, with recoil control vents added by Delta Vectors.

There were other K-frame 357s that I carried for a while, now that S&W had them working well. Model 13s in 3 inch and 4 inch, and a Model 65 in the latter length. All were nice...but all, including Fluffy, wound up having to be re-timed again and again from the hard pounding of constant shooting with 125-grain Magnum loads. None of mine split their forcing cones, thought I saw it happen with some others.

For a while, I was enamored of the 2-inch Model 12. It was a right brain, left brain thing. With the FBI load (158-grain all-lead hollow point +P) it was adequately powerful. This six-shot Airweight was deadly accurate and,

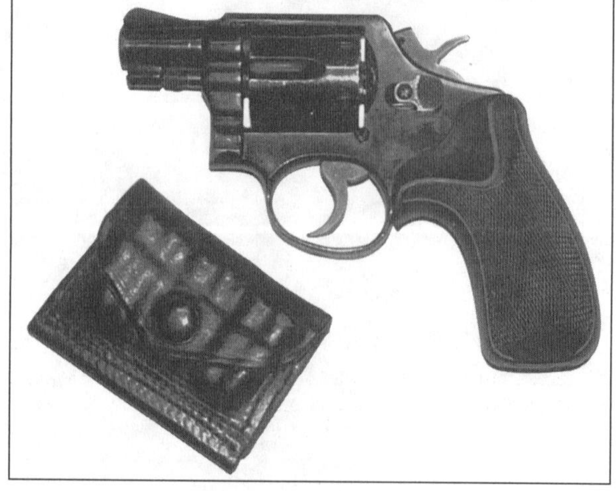

Ayoob always had a weak spot for this Model 12 Airweight M&P, with Pachmayr Compac grips that made fast shooting with +P easy. Ammo pouch is FBI-style DeSantis 2x2x2.

with Pachmayr Compac grips, a joy to shoot. Of course, it was exquisitely comfortable to carry on the hip. But there was a nagging feeling that I should carry something more potent as a main gun, and eventually, I stopped wearing it.

Twenty or so years ago, I showed up at Chapman Academy for the advanced class, pausing only to crush my trigger finger in a freak accident en route. It was no problem working my Colt 45 Auto southpaw, but I couldn't figure out how to load the magazines one-handed, something I *could* do with a revolver's speedloaders. Ray Chapman lent me his 6-inch Model 10 with Pachmayr grips, and that's what I shot the course with. It left me with fond memories, and one day I caught Ray in a weak moment when he wanted a compact 357 and traded him my 3-inch Model 65 for it. Ray, in turn, had bought the Model 10 as a trade-in from the Rhode Island State Police when they swapped their long-barrel 38s for Ruger 357s of the same length. I won a pistol match or two with it later, and I have it still, a memory of good times with good people.

The K-frame I'm most likely to use today is another police trade-in. I bought this Model 15 for $130 from Jack First's gun shop in Rapid City, South Dakota while out there for a trial deposition in 1998. It had been *"carried much and shot seldom,"* in Jeff Cooper's words; the finish was all but gone, yet the bore was clean and bright and it locked up as if it had just come out of the Performance Center. I took it home and promptly shot a one-inch group with it at 25 yards.

A few times a year, I teach a class with this gun and use it for the shooting demonstrations. I've shot it next to a mint late-production Model 15 with the heavier barrel, and couldn't tell the difference. This well-worn 38 Special makes the point that you don't have to blow the mortgage money to get a handgun that will shoot well enough to save your life. Which leads us to the next point...

Best Buy Trade-Ins

The K-frame is no longer the best-selling Smith & Wesson. But handguns are durable goods, millions of K-frames are out there, and while they're not the police standard anymore, the 38 and 357 K-models continue to protect literally millions of American homes. The wave of police departments switching to autos

+P "FBI loads," almost universally considered the best 38 Special defense rounds, aren't famous for accuracy, but these groups at 50' are ample. *Left*, M/13 357; *right*, M/15 38.

◀ In the 1980s, cops switched from K-frames to L-frames like this 686 to better handle these hot 125-grain 357 Magnum loads. Then came the semiautomatics...

flooded the market with traded-in service revolvers, and that pool remains deep. Go into a gun shop today and look at the used handguns with a copy of this publication in your hand, turned open to the catalog section. You'll see that the K-frame 38s and 357s are selling for proportionally less of their new value than almost any other defensive handguns of comparable quality and condition. (The single best buy seems to be the Model 10 38 Special with 4-inch barrel.)

If you'd rather buy new, no problem. The stainless Combat Magnum (M/66) and adjustable sight 38 Combat Masterpiece (M/67) remain in the catalog. The fixed sight 38s in blue (M/10) and stainless (M/64) are still with us, as is the 357 Magnum version of that Military & Police style. So, thankfully, is the exquisite K-22, the gun that defined the small-caliber target/sport revolver for more generations than any other. There are those who for political reasons are not comfortable buying Smith & Wessons at this time, and for them, Taurus and other makers offer identically shaped revolvers in 22, 38 and 357.

With a full century under its belt and a year of another century bracketing either side of that, this optimally-sized and highly functional revolver won't have the book closed on it any time soon. The enduring grace of the Smith & Wesson K-frame seems truly timeless. ●

(*1*) Jinks, Roy G., "History of Smith & Wesson," 1977, North Hollywood, CA: Beinfeld Press, P. 160.

(*2*) *Ibid.*, P. 160.

(*3*) Supica, Jim, and Nahas, Richard, "Standard Catalog of Smith & Wesson," 1996, Iola, WI: Krause Publications. Pp. 108-109.

(*4*) Wallack, L.R., "Thirty Million Handguns," *1985 Gun Digest*, Northbrook, IL: DBI Books, Pp. 108, 110.

"Drop-in" Glock

The most adaptable pistol?

by Paul Scarlata; Butch Simpson photos

WHEN IT FIRST hit the US market in the mid-1980s, it was greeted with derision by most shooters. The *"real steel & walnut"* crowd confidentially predicted that a *"plastic pistol"* would receive short shrift from knowledgeable shooters and, within a decade, would be a mere curiosity.

Well, that wasn't the first time the traditionalists made a bad call–and it probably won't be the last! There is little argument today that polymer-frame Glock pistols are some of the most popular - and influential - handguns on the market. Since their introduction, they have captured an enviable share of military, law enforcement and civilian handgun sales–worldwide. They say that "imitation is the sincerest form of flattery," and it must be true because there are few major players in today's highly competitive handgun industry that have not introduced a pistol with a polymer frame.

If one examines its qualifications, it is not difficult to fathom the Glock's burgeoning popularity:

Reliability - Glocks are widely recognized for their out-of-the-box reliability with all styles of bullets and both light and heavy loads. In addition, Glocks are famous for their ability to function when grunged-up with dirt and under the worst conditions Mother Nature (or man) can dish out.

Recoil Control - the Glock's polymer frame flexes and absorbs recoil force. This allows fast, accurate follow-up shots, something that is only accomplished with steel- or alloy-framed pistols by means of added weight, barrel porting or recoil-reducing devices.

Ergonomics - Glock's polymer frame does not require grip panels. This provides, despite the use of high-capacity magazines, a narrow grip frame suitable for persons with small hands.

Simplicity of Operation - Glock's patented "Safe-Action" trigger does away with the necessity of external manual safeties, leaving only three external controls: trigger, slide stop and magazine release. This means there are no levers or buttons to manipulate or grip safeties to depress. To my way of thinking simplicity of operation is of primary importance in a handgun used for police or defensive purposes.

High Capacity - Glock pistols were designed from the word *"go"* as high-capacity firearms. And while pre-ban high-capacity magazines can be expensive, it's been my experience that Glock *hi-caps* are more readily available - and usually at a lower price - than those for other handguns.

Economical - as they require fewer modifications than any other type of pistol, Glocks are the most affordable handgun for competitive shooting. And the vast majority of these modifications are generally of the drop-in variety, which allows a Glock shooter to modify one pistol, as necessary, for different disciplines. In contemporary parlance, this makes the Glock a "cross-training" pistol!

In recent years, a sizeable after-market industry has grown up to provide

The only "permanent" changes made to the G21 were the installation of a set of Heinie SlantPro "Straight-Eight" night sights and a Custom Glock Racing extended magazine release button. Set up like this, my G21 is used in GSSF *Amateur* and IDPA *Stock Service Pistol* matches.

As can be seen by this nicely perforated D-1 target, my G21 has proven very suitable for GSSF matches.

Glock shooters with a wide variety of parts, devices and services. Persons desiring to personalize their Glock to make it more suitable for home defense, CCW, police service or the various types of competitive shooting can choose from a wide selection of accessories that will allow them to go from *"Mild to Wild."*

In this regard, I want to examine a selection of some of those items I feel will make your Glock even more suitable for home/personal defense/police service than it already is. In addition, these parts will allow you to modify your Glock so you can compete in three of the more popular Action Pistol disciplines here in the USA.

For the purposes of this article, our test platform was one of the Austrian firm's biggest sellers on the U.S. market — the 45-caliber Glock 21. This particular 2nd Generation pistol was a police trade-in that came with factory fixed sights, an extended slide stop lever, the standard 5.5-pound trigger and two pre-ban, full metal-lined high-capacity magazines.

As a home/personal defense/police handgun, the Glock has few peers. The fact that it is carried by approximately 60% of American law enforcement agencies says more about its suitability then I could possibly relate on these pages! Since I purchased my G21 it has become one of my regular CCW handguns and while some might feel it is a bit too large for everyday concealed carry, I must disagree with them. While it's true that it is not a "small" pistol, it is a *LIGHT* pistol and, even when loaded with fourteen rounds of Cor-Bon 200-grain +P HP ammo, my G21 is lighter than a Commander-sized 1911 pistol that has only half the magazine capacity. With the proper holster–in this case a Don Hume H710 belt slide–it can be carried under light outer clothing, such as a Concealed Carry Clothiers vest.

As I believe one can be put in a 'disadvantageous' position, liability-wise, by using a modified handgun for defensive purposes, I only made two *"permanent"* changes to the G21 after purchase. The factory sighting equipment was replaced with a set of Heinie Slant-Pro "Straight Eight" sights. These night sights use a dual Tritium dot insert system and are easy to see, provide a sharp sight picture and fast target acquisition. I find them eminently suitable to both defensive and competitive shooting. As I don't have overly large hands, I also installed an extended magazine release produced by Matt Kartozian at Custom Glock Racing. Aside from these, when used for home defense or CCW, my G21 is as stock as a Glock can be!

But I am also an enthusiastic Action Pistol shooter and it wasn't very long before I got the urge to use my new Glock in competition. It was then that I became acquainted with the large selection of aftermarket drop-in parts that are available for the *Plastic Pistol* and how quickly - and inexpensively - I could modify my G21 so as to be competitive in a number of these fun disciplines.

Glock Sport Shooting Foundation (GSSF)

In 1992, Glock, Inc. began hosting a series of Action Pistol matches to show their appreciation for their customers' support and brand loyalty. There are twenty-six GSSF matches held around the country each year, each one attracting hundreds of Glock enthusiasts. Now it must mentioned–right up front–that GSSF matches are centered around "Stock Glock" pistols. This, very simply, means that except for specific modifications - if you can't get your pistol that way from Glock, it isn't Stock!

Of GSSF's four classes - *Amateur, Competition, Sub-Compact and Unlimited/Master* - all but the last require stock pistols. The rules do permit any sights consisting of a blade front and a U- or square-notch rear, refinished Glock pistols are OK; Pearce magazine extensions are legal and you may put rubber sleeves or skateboard tape on the grips. But for the techno-junkies among us, *Unlimited/Master* class permits just about any modification your bank account can handle–and you tend to see quite a few IPSC Race Glocks in *U/M* class!

As it is, my G21 is "legal" for use in *Amateur and Competition* classes, although I am thinking of a putting some non-slip tape on the grips for future matches. As *U/M* allows one much more leeway, when I shoot it I equip the G21 with Lightning Strike's Titanium striker, safety plunger and competition trigger (*a drop-in unit replacing the factory trigger and trigger bar; designed so that forward movement of the trigger ceases once the trigger resets, reducing overall trigger travel by almost*

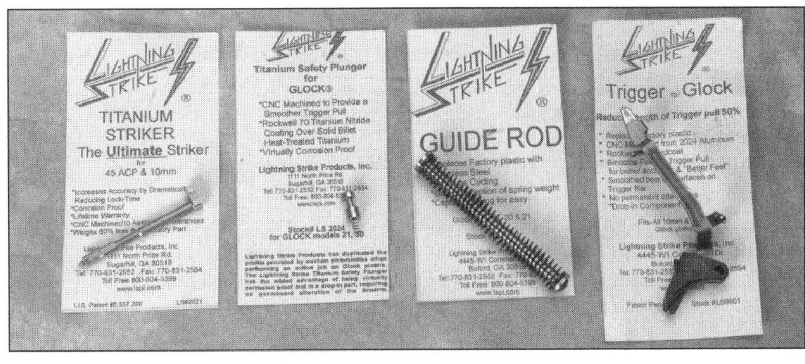

If I shoot IDPA *Custom Defensive Pistol* and USPSA's *Production* matches I drop in a Lightning Strike titanium striker and safety plunger, stainless steel guide rod with captive spring and Competition Trigger unit.

50%. In addition the safety lever on the face of the trigger is wider and more comfortable).

To help tame recoil and muzzle flip somewhat, the same firm's stainless guide rod is teamed up with a Taylor Freelance brass Seattle Slug grip weight. Trigger pull is further improved by installing a 3.5-pound connector. As GSSF does not have a Power Factor, using Winchester SuperClean NT ammunition loaded with "light" 170-grain bullets enhances recoil control.

As was pointed out above, all of these modifications to the G21 are drop-in items and can be done quickly with a minimum of tools–I *have done it between stages at GSSF matches*–and require no alterations whatsoever to the pistol's grip, frame or slide.

International Defensive Pistol Association (IDPA)

IDPA's website states that they provide a "*...forum for practical shooters in which truly practical equipment, techniques and courses of fire are mandated. Prior to Defensive Pistol there was no place at all to compete with common service pistols ... nor was there a shooting sport where your concealed carry holster could also be your match holster without handicapping yourself. Other shooting sports have become equipment "races," Defensive Pistol will not. If you're interested in using truly practical pistols, drawn from practical holsters to solve challenging and exciting defensive shooting problems, them Defensive Pistol is the sport for you.*"

Because of their popularity with police and civilian shooters, Glocks are one of the more common types of handguns seen at IDPA matches. All pistols used in IDPA must be able to fit inside a box measuring 8 3/4" x 6" x 1 5/8", and the G21 easily makes those limitations.

IDPA has five classes: *Stock Service Pistol, Enhanced Service Pistol, Custom Pistol, Stock Service Revolver and Back-Up Gun.* Now while the G21 in its stock configuration can be used in *Stock Service Pistol Class*, competitors in *Enhanced Service Pistol* and *Custom Defensive Pistol* classes are allowed to make certain modifications to their pistols: change sights to another notch and post type, change grips, internal accuracy work to include replacement of the barrel with one of factory configuration, internal reliability work, custom checkering, extended thumb and grip safeties, full-length guide rod manufactured of material no heavier than common steel, change trigger action parts to enhance trigger pull and magazine well extensions.

For *Custom Defensive Pistol* I would add the following to the G21: a 3.5-pound trigger connector–paired with the aforementioned Lightning Strike titanium striker, safety plunger and competition

For defensive purposes I favor Cor-Bon 200-grain +P JHP. With its "light" 170-grain bullet, Winchester's SuperClean NT is my preferred load for GSSF, IDPA *Stock Service Pistol* and USPSA Production matches. To ensure that I make the Power Factor - when I compete in IDPA's *Custom Defensive Pistol* and USPSA's *Limited* or *Limited 10* matches, I load my G21 with Black Hills 230-grain FMJ ammunition.

Safariland's 007 Competition Holster provides fast, snag-free presentations. Note how the 771 magazine pouches hold the spare mags away from the body for a fast reload.

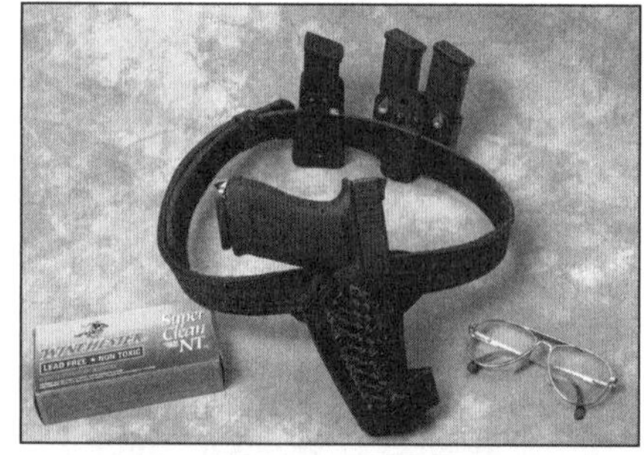

For USPSA *Production* I use another Safariland 007 Competition Holster with a 177 double- and 074 single-mag pouch - all worn behind the hip. I often use this same rig when shooting *Limited 10* matches.

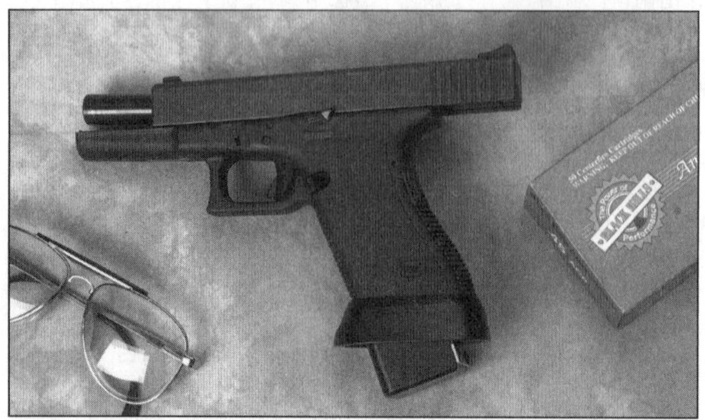

When USPSA's *Limited Class* is the game of the day a Lightning Strike flared magazine well joins the titanium striker and plunger, guide rod and Competition Trigger unit. So as to have a few extra rounds for those hard-to-reach targets, magazine extensions from Grams Engineering, Taylor Freelance and Lightning Strike give me an additional 5, 4 and 3 rounds.

With just the addition of a few drop-in parts, the G21 has shown itself to be eminently practical for USPSA's *Production Limited* and *Limited 10* matches.

trigger–would improve the trigger pull in addition to reducing lock time for improved accuracy. Lastly, the extended magazine release from Custom Glock Racing remains in place while the Lightning Strike guide rod provides a slight amount of additional weight up front to improve balance.

According to the guidelines in the IDPA rulebook, thus modified, my G21 would fit 'inside the box' and meet the requirements for use in the *Enhanced Service Pistol* class. *Custom Defense Pistol* has a strict Power Factor of 165,000 (determined by multiplying the bullet weight by velocity), so I use traditional hardball ammo in the G21 and have found Black Hills 230-grain FMJ fills the bill to perfection. As IDPA rules mandate the use of practical, concealable holsters, I wear the same Don Hume H710 holster and mag pouch I use for CCW.

United States Practical Shooting Association (USPSA)

USPSA is the U.S. branch of the International Practical Shooting Confederation (IPSC), the oldest and largest Action Pistol organization in the world. Unlike IDPA's purist theory, USPSA/IPSC has evolved into a more specialized sport and, while some feel it has strayed from its "practical" roots, tens of thousands of other shooters around the world find it the most fun of all the Action Pistol disciplines. Personally, I enjoy the multiple-target, high round-count stages and find the physical gyrations, movement, multiple reloads and contorted shooting positions challenging. I once heard this sport described as the only shooting discipline where you can *"Run & Gun & Have Fun"* all at the same time. My G21 has proven more than suitable for use in

For GSSF *U/M* class and USPSA's *Limited Ten* the flared magazine well is replaced with a Taylor Freelance "Seattle Slug." This brass grip weight helps hold down recoil and provides superior balance. As both disciplines have limits on magazine capacity, I use "Clintonista" ten-round magazines.

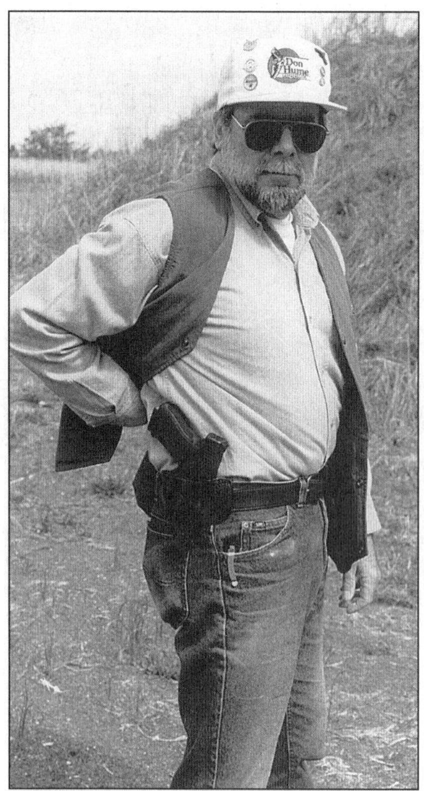

While some may feel the G21 is too large for concealed carry, with a Don Hume H710 holster it carries very comfortably...

...but is still readily accessible if needed.

...and can be concealed easily under this light-weight vest from Concealed Carry Clothiers.

USPSA's *Limited, Limited 10* and *Production Divisions*.

Production Division is aimed (*excuse the pun*) at those persons who want to try their hand at USPSA matches with basically "stock" factory pistols - and without the fancy holsters and ancillary equipment usually connected with this sport. For this reason, shooters only need to make a Minor Power Factor of 125, which can be accomplished with any pistol using a 9x19mm cartridge or larger (*Power Factors are determined by multiplying the bullet weight by velocity and then dividing by 1000*). The major caveat here is that the pistol must use a DA/SA, DAO or Safe Action trigger–no single-action pistols allowed. Modifications are limited to trigger work, sights and grips and the pistol cannot weigh more than 2 ounces above the listed factory weight. *Production Class* shooters cannot load more than ten rounds in their magazines, while holsters and spare magazines must be worn behind the hipbone.

When *Production Division* is the day's game, my G21 is equipped with the Lightning Strike striker, safety plunger, trigger unit and guide rod in addition to the 3.5-pound connector. As *Production* rules require the pistol and spare magazine be worn on or behind the hip, I have found the straight-up position of Safariland's tried and true 007 Competition Holster allows it to serve nicely, especially when worn on one of their super-comfortable 0282 contoured belts with 177 double- and 074 single-mag pouches. In an attempt to trim the edge held by those small-caliber shooters–each of my magazines are again filled with ten rounds of Winchester's light-recoiling Super-Clean NT ammunition.

As the name signifies, *Limited Division* limits the modifications one may make to their handgun. And while many shooters compete successfully with stock pistols, others hope to gain an edge by making whatever modifications are permissible. Unlike *Production*, *Limited* rules require a minimum caliber of .40/10mm to be able to claim a Major Power Factor of 165 with its scoring advantages, making our 45-caliber G21 a natural.

For *Limited* matches, in addition to the parts installed for *Production*, I add a Lightning Strike flared magazine well. This item not only facilitates rapid reloads but provides additional weight, length and width to the bottom of the grip for a more positive draw, better gun retention and recoil control. When used with magazine extensions from Lightning Strike, Taylor Freelance and Grams Engineering I now have - as the situation may demand - an additional three, four or five rounds for that occasional hard-to-hit (!) target while still keeping the overall length of the mags within *Limited* class' 140mm length rule.

Limited 10 combines aspects of both *Production* and *Limited* divisions. While the type of pistol, allowable modifications and Power Factor are the same as *Limited*, shooters may not load more than ten rounds in their magazines. While originally seen as a venue for single-stack 1911s, *Limited 10* can be shot with many types of pistols and my G21 fills the bill quite nicely by simply by replacing the mag well with the Seattle Slug and restricting myself to ten-round magazines.

And so there are not any questions about my making the power factor, I once again shoot that most respected of all 45 ACP loads – the Black Hills 230-grain FMJ. While I often use my *Production* holster set up for *Limited 10*, when I shoot

I use the G21, the Don Hume holster, mag pouch and Concealed Carry Clothiers vest when I compete in IDPA matches.

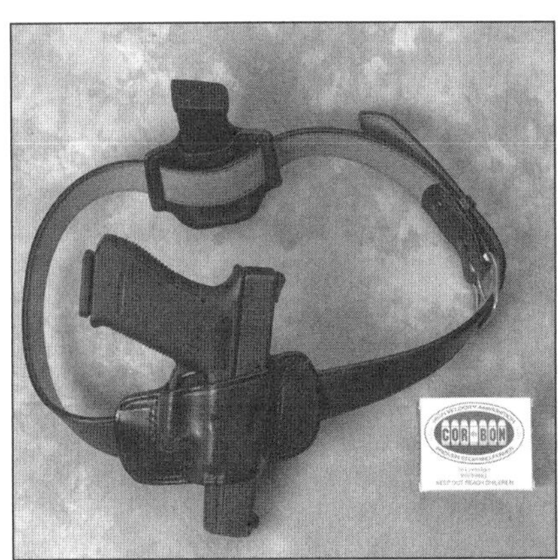

For both concealed carry and IDPA matches I team my G21 up with a Don Hume H710 holster, gun belt and mag pouch.

Limited I pair the G21 up with another Safariland 007 Competition holster–but this time spare magazines are carried in a pair of the same company's 771 magazine pouches, worn across the front of the body, and another 074 single-mag pouch on the side.

In conclusion, I have found Glock pistols to be some of the most practical, reliable and user-friendly of the many types of handguns I have carried and competed with over the past three decades. For personal/home defense or police/security work, their almost-legendary reliability and simplicity of operation makes them a natural choice for both the new shooter and the 'Old Hand.'

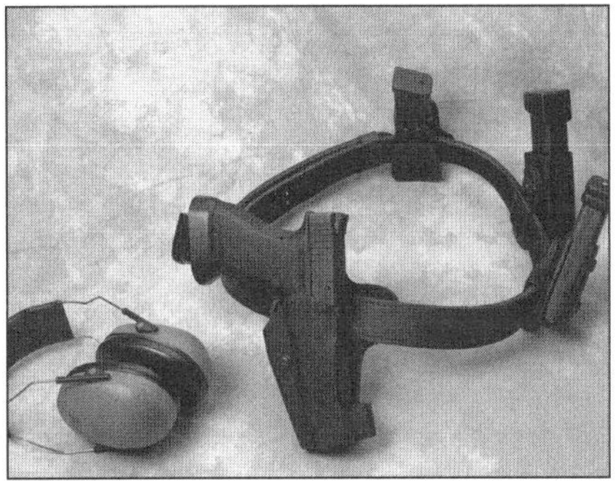

My USPSA *Limited* rig consists of a Safariland 007 Competition holster on a comfortable 0282 contoured belt with a pair of 771 magazine pouches worn across the front of the body and a 074 single-mag pouch on the side.

For all of you *wannabee*-Action Pistol competitors out there, the easiest way to get involved in this — the most fun of the shooting sports — is to buy yourself a Glock and, depending on just how mild - or wild - you want to be in your chosen discipline, modify your pistol accordingly. That way, the next time there is an Action Pistol match in your neck of the woods, you won't have to limit yourself to being a mere spectator. And when you are done, in a matter of a few minutes you can "un-modify" your Glock back to a practical personal/home defense or service handgun. Now, if that isn't the best of both worlds, I don't know what is!

I have tested all of the accessories mentioned in this article, using many of them in competition. While there are similar products available from other manufacturers and suppliers, I can only vouch for the quality and practicality of those with which I have personal experience. •

For further information:

Concealed Carry Clothiers - PO Box 237, Saunderstown, RI 02874-0237. Tel. 888-959-4500.

Custom Glock Racing - PO Box 3359, Danville, CA 94526. Tel. 602-241-8655.

Don Hume Leathergoods - PO Box 351, Miami, OK 74355. Tel. 800-331-2686.

Glock, Inc. - PO Box 369, Symrna, GA 30081. Tel. 770-432-1202.

Grams Engineering - 2435 Norse Ave., Costa Mesa, AZ 92627. Tel. 949-548-3745.

Heinie Specialty Products - 301 Oak St., Quincy, IL 62301. Tel. 217-228-9500.

Lightning Strike Products - 355 Brogdon Road #105, Suwanee, GA 30024. Tel. 800-804-5399.

Safariland, Ltd. - PO Box 51478, Ontario, CA 91761. Tel. 909-923-7300.

Two Colts and an Owl

by Larry S. Sterett

IN THIS WRITER'S opinion, one of the finest looking - and shooting - rimfire pistols ever manufactured was the Colt Woodsman Match Target, Second Issue. Some shooters may have a preference for the First Issue with the tapered barrel and one-piece walnut stock with extended sides. Regardless, the Woodsman has sired a number of more economical models with similar features, and at least one bastard with very little in common except for the caliber and magazine. This test-fire report takes a look at two of the rimfire Colts and an Owl that except for the markings could pass for a Colt.

The Colt Woodsman, introduced in 1915 as a target model with a 6-1/2 inch barrel, was discontinued in 1932. The first issue Match Target Woodsman was introduced in 1938 and only survived until World War II, after which it was replaced by the Second Issue with the heavy barrel. (The Match Target Woodsman, Second Issue, weighed 40 ounces, empty, and featured a 6-inch barrel, an overall length of 9-7/8 inches, and a height of 4-13/16 inches. Its sight radius was 8-13/16 inches.)

The first pistol test-fired in this report was one of the Huntsman models, which has features similar to the first issue Woodsman Target Model: no hold-open device and the stock style of the second issue. (*The safety can be used to lock the slide back, but it must be operated manually.*) Measuring 8-1/2 inches overall, with a barrel length of 4-5/8 inches, the Huntsman tipped the scales at 32 ozs. It's height stood at 4-3/4 inches. The sight radius measured 7-1/4 inches. (The sights consisted of a 0.100-inch wide front blade with serrated face, and a fixed rear with 0.103-inch square notch.)

The second Colt was the Colt 22, which bears little resemblance to the Woodsman, other than caliber and magazine capacity. Featuring a polymer frame, this pistol weighed in at 34 ozs., with an overall length of 8-11/16 inches and a barrel length of 4-1/2 inches. Its height measured 4-3/4 inches, and it had a sight radius of 7-1/2 inches. (*Unlike the Woodsman and its followers, the Colt 22 features interchangeable barrels, somewhat similar to that on some of the last original High Standards. A target barrel unit was available with a 6-inch barrel having an extended barrel rib with target sights, and a corresponding slide without a rear sight. The barrel/slide unit weighed 25 ozs. and provided a sight radius of 8-15/16 inches.*) The sights on the Colt 22 included a 0.120-inch blade integral with the 0.373-inch wide synthetic barrel rib, and a fixed rear having a 0.115-inch wide square notch.

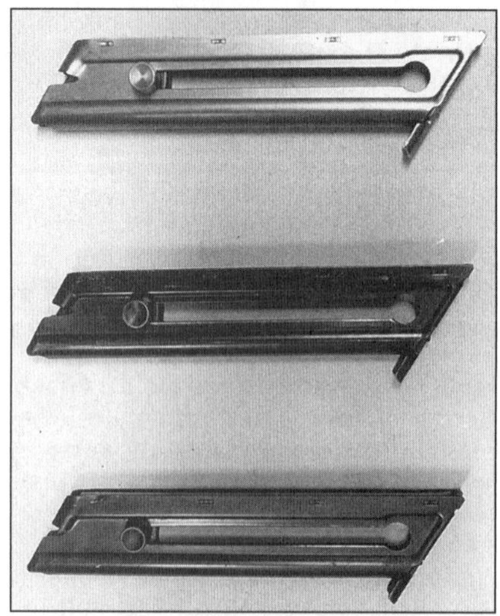

Which magazine is not a Colt? (The one in the middle.) *Left to right:* Colt Huntsman, I.J. Trailsman and Colt 22.

The Colt 22 has a cross-bolt safety just to the rear of the grip. When *'on,'* to the left it blocks the trigger and locks the slide in the forward position. When *'off,'* to the right, a red band around the cross-bolt is visible. (*When the pistol is cocked a red dot on the striker is visible.*)

The Iver Johnson Trailsman (*the Owl*) weighed 32 ozs. with a barrel length of 6 inches and an overall length of 9-7/8 inches. Its height measured 4-5/8 inches. It resembles the Colt Huntsman, except for having a slide hold-open device, and a push-button magazine release of the M1911 type. The sights consisted of a 0.100- inch blade front sight, identical to that on the Colt Huntsman, and a fixed rear with 0.063-inch square notch. (*Sight radius on the Trailsman measured 8-5/8 inches.*)

Both Colts and the Owl were blow-back operated, and chambered for 22 Long Rifle rimfire cartridges. Magazine capacity on all three pistols was ten rounds and the magazines were identical in construction; two were blued and one was stainless. The Colt Huntsman featured a manually-operated 'snap-back' magazine release on the butt of the grip, while the Trailsman had a push-button M1911 style magazine release on the frame just to the rear of the trigger. The Colt 22 also featured a magazine release button, but on the right side of the receiver, above the trigger where is easily reached with the trigger finger. (*The lever-type safeties on the Colt Huntsman*

***Top to bottom:* The Colt Huntsman 22 rimfire pistol with a barrel length of 4-5/8 inches. The stocks are not original, having been replaced some time in the past.**

Second is the Colt 22 with a barrel length of 4-1/2 inches. It features a polymer frame, interchangeable barrels, and a cross-bolt safety to the rear of the grip.

Third is the Iver Johnson Trailsman with a barrel length of 6 inches. Although almost identical to the Colt Huntsman there are noticeable differences, other than the barrel being pinned and its length. The Trailsman has a slightly different shape at the rear of the frame, plus the trigger face is serrated (*the Huntsman's trigger face is smooth*), it has a push-button magazine release and a hold-open slide stop. (*Both the Huntsman and Trailsman are shown with the safety 'on,' locking the slide forward.)*

and I.J. Trailsman are thumb-operated. They lock the slide in the forward position and block the trigger. They can be easily operated with the thumb of the right hand, while the Colt 22 requires the use of the second hand if the crossbolt safety is to be operated easily.)

All three pistols are called hammerless, but the Colt Huntsman and the I.J. Trailsman have enclosed hammers and firing pins. The Colt 22 is striker-fired. The Colt Huntsman barrel is threaded and screwed into the frame, while the I.J. Trailsman barrel slips into the receiver and is cross-pinned in place. The Colt 22 barrel has a stud on the bottom which fits into a recess on the receiver, and is secured by a setscrew.

The three pistols were checked for functioning and accuracy from the bench at 25 yards, using six brands of long rifle ammunition and loads. Five-shot groups were fired using a six-o'clock sight picture. No attempt was made to center the groups, but only to check sizes.

A total of eleven different loads were used by six different manufacturers. Seven of the loads would be considered match or target loads, including Federal's Silhouette and Gold Medal, Winchester's Super Silhouette and T-22, PMC's Scoremaster, CCI's Mini-Group and Remington's Club Extra. The three plinking or hunting loads were Remington's Hi-Speed with the 'golden bullet,' Federal's Hi-Power, and the Aguila Standard. The final load was the Aguila Subsonic.

It was anticipated the target loads would produce the smallest groups; this was only partially correct. The smallest group produced with the Colt Huntsman measured 1-3/8 inches, center-to-center, using the CCI Mini-Group load. (*The Winchester T-22 cartridges did well in this pistol also.*) However, the smallest group produced by the Colt 22 measured 1-3/32 inches, center-to-center, and was obtained Federal's Hi-Power. (*In addition, this pistol turned in some good groups using Winchester's Super Silhouettte, CCI's Mini-Group, Aguila's Subsonic, and Federal's Gold Medal Target.*) The I. J. Trailsman produced its smallest group, 1-9/16 inches, center-to-center, using the Federal Gold Medal load, but did well with the Federal Hi-Power, and the Aguila Standard loads.

The majority (36.4 percent) of the groups shot by the Colt Huntsman were in the two to three-inch range, while for the Colt 22 the majority (45.4 percent) were in the one to two-inch range. For the I.J. Trailsman the majority (63.4 percent) of its five-shot groups were in the two to three-inch range. The Huntsman was the only one of the three pistols to produce any groups measuring over four inches, one with a target load and one with a high velocity load. None of the pistols produced any groups measuring under an inch at 25 yards, but these were not target pistols, nor new, although the Colt 22 was definitely the newest of the three.

The pistols were intended as plinking or small-game hunting pistols, with recoil springs designed for use with standard and high-speed ammunition. For this reason no cartridges of the Viper, Stinger, etc. types were used. Even so, none of the three pistols performed flawlessly. Failures to feed from the magazine, '*stovepipes*' and failures to eject were most common with the target velocity cartridges. After the Trailsman misfired several times, it was found to have a dimple on the breech of the barrel caused by some earlier owner having dry-fired the pistol extensively without an empty case in the chamber. This, coupled with the difference in the case alloy of the different brands - and the sensitivity of the primers - produced more misfires than failures to feed or eject with this particular pistol.

Overall, the two Colts and the owl produced some good five-shot groups. With the correct ammunition all three could produce groups measuring just over an inch at 25 yards. The Huntsman groups were high and to the left of the bull, while the Trailsman groups were close to the point-of-aim, with a number of 10s being achieved. The Colt 22 shot slightly to the left of the point-of-aim, but on target vertically. (*The rear sights on all three pistols can be drifted laterally for windage, and those on the Trailsman and Colt 22 are secured with set screws.*) With a bit of fine tuning the three could become real 'fun guns,' especially when using SHOOT-N-C targets. ●

AMT AUTOMAG 440 CORBON Pistol

The AMT 440 Cor-Bon Magnum, as manufactured by Galena Industries, features a long slide and a barrel length of nearly seven inches. It weighs 50 ounces, empty.

by Larry Sterett

A CENTURY AGO the "world's most powerful autoloading pistol" was the Gabbett-Fairfax Mars, a real barn burner the British Navy found to be a bit too much for them to handle. It was an autoloader that fed from the rear of the magazine, used a rotary-locking breechbolt, and was chambered for a line of cartridges unique to its design.

The Mars remained "the pistol" in name, at least until the 44 AutoMag arrived nearly seven decades later. (*The "world's most powerful handgun" title may have moved in 1956 when Smith & Wesson introduced their Model 29 revolver chambered for the 44 Remington Magnum cartridge.*) However, the Auto Mag stayed in the limelight only briefly, as did the Mars. (The Auto Mag did make it into the movies, an accomplishment the Mars did not achieve.) Then the 475 Wildey was introduced (at least a couple of times). Again lots of high-powered press, but no longevity. Next came the 50 Action Express, available in AMT, Desert Magnum and L.A.R. autoloading pistols–plus two or more single-shot pistols and a revolver or two.

What may be the ultimate autoloading handgun/cartridge combination of the century is the latest AutoMag pistol chambered for the 440 Cor-Bon Magnum cartridge. (*This is not the original AutoMag with the fixed barrel and rotary-locking breech-bolt, but the later M1911-type with the long slide, no link, cam-down barrel minus recoil lugs forward of the chamber.*) The cartridge is the 50 Action Express case necked down to accommodate .429-inch diameters in weights up to at least 305 grains. (*Ammunition is custom loaded by Cor-Bon in Sturgis, South Dakota, and is available through dealers handling the Cor-Bon line.*)

The new 440 AutoMag pistol tested measured 10-7/8 inches long, with a barrel length of 6-13/16 inches, and tipped the scales at 50 ounces. (*The grip was fitted with walnut stocks having excellent cut checkering and a smooth center panel featuring the AMT logo. With a grip circumference of 5-13/16 inches, the pistol was comfortable to grasp, and actually felt relatively lightweight to this shooter.*)

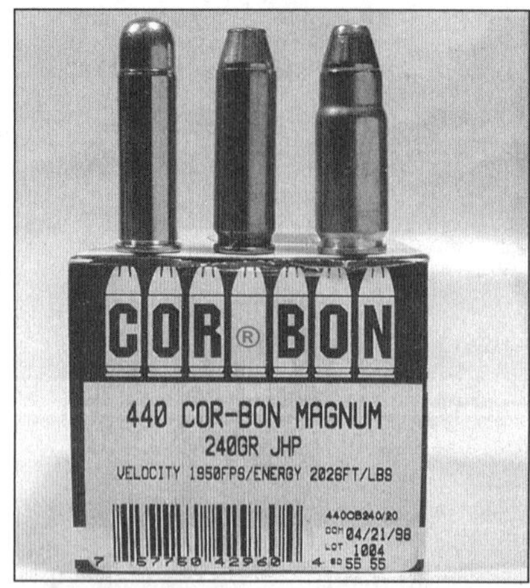

Left to right: A 44 Remington Magnum loaded by Cor-Bon with a 305-grain bullet, which is also loaded in the 440 Cor-Bon cartridge; an original 44 Auto Mag cartridge with 180-grain bullet; the 440 Cor-Bon loaded with a 240-grain jacketed hollow point bullet on a box of similar cartridges.

Height of the test pistol measured 5-5/16 inches from the top of the rear sight to the bottom of the magazine floorplate. Maximum thickness of the pistol measured 1-7/16 inches. The full-length slide is reduced slightly in width from 1.050-inch to 1.010-inch, beginning at approximately the end of the frame. (*This may reduce muzzle weight slightly, in addition to providing the pistol with a racy appearance.*) Topping the slide is a 0.440-inch wide, solid rib with a smooth, non-reflective finish. Gracing the muzzle end of the rib was a 0.135-inch wide blade front sight featuring a serrated face and a concave white dot. Inset into the rear of the rib was an Ellison-type rear sight, screw-adjustable for windage and elevation, with a 0.130-inch wide square notch and a white dot on each side. (*The combination of the front and rear dots provided a classic three-dot sight picture when properly aligned.*) Sight radius measured nine inches.

The 440 AutoMag features a hammer block safety on the left side of the slide. When the safety lever is parallel with the barrel, a bright red-colored dot is visible below the safety, indicating the '*fire*' mode. If there's a live round in the chamber, the hammer is cocked and the trigger pulled, the pistol will fire in this mode, as the hammer is free to strike the firing pin. If the safety lever is moved downward with the thumb, the red-colored dot is covered and a block of steel is placed between the hammer face and the firing pin. (*This method of safety movement, which is common to slide-mounted safeties, is directly*

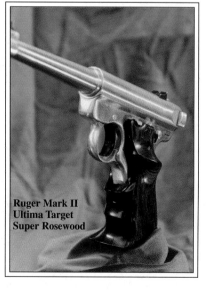

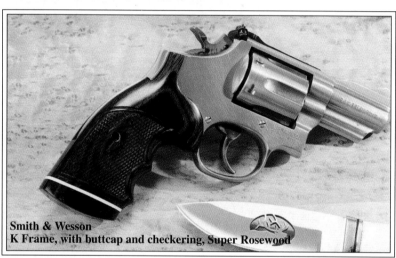

the opposite of M1911-type frame-mounted safeties, where upward is 'safe,' and downward is 'fire.')

The AutoMag frame features an extended tang to reduce 'bite' on the web of the shooting hand; the spur hammer doesn't extend below the tang when in the cocking or full recoil position. (*The slide stock and magazine release button are M1911 types, with the slide stop having a bit more thumb pad extension to increase leverage. Both, along with the hammer spur, are serrated to reduce thumb slippage.*)

The box magazine is stainless steel as is the entire pistol. The magazine floorplate, which at first glance appears removable is not. It is welded in place, probably to reduce the possibility of it suddenly moving elsewhere during recoil of the pistol. Capacity is five rounds, and the left side of the magazine is perforated to permit viewing the contents. High density orange-colored plastic is used for the magazine follower, and a plunger-style hold-open device is incorporated into the left side of the follower.

The trigger on the test gun measured 0.370-inch wide with the smooth face. (*The trigger guard is rather small, leaving little room for a gloved finger.*) Let-off measured a crisp 3-1/2 pounds, which is excellent for an out-of-the-box pistol.

The AutoMag features the regular M1911 type of takedown, with a barrel bushing and recoil spring plunger. An exception is the use of a full-length guide rod for the recoil spring. (*Both the barrel and the guide rod must removed from the slide toward the rear, due to their configurations.*) The barrel, which features eight-groove, right-hand rifling, does not have any M1911-type recoil lugs forward of the chamber area. (*The barrel extension butts solidly against the face of the slide breech when the slide is forward.*) The outside diameter of the barrel, forward of the chamber area, measured 0.635-inch; this was then reduced to 0.620-inch and increased again to 0.635-inch at the muzzle where it entered the barrel bushing. Result? Less barrel wobble in the bushing and increased accuracy.

Fit and finish on the test pistol was excellent. The frame and slide both had non-glare matte finishes, the frame silvered and the slide charcoal gray. The sights were finished black; the safety lever, slide stop, and magazine release matte silver.

The AMT 440 Cor-Bon field-strips basically the same way as a regular M1911. Fundamentally it has the same number of parts, except for being minus the link and having a full-length guide rod for the recoil spring. It does not feature locking lugs forward of the barrel chamber or breech.

Functioning and accuracy testing was done from the bench at 25 and 50 yards, although the cartridge and pistol have 100 yards-plus capability. Only three-shot groups were fired (*If game can't be secured with three shots or less with this cartridge, it's probably not the fault of the cartridge.*). Cor-Bon is the only commercial loader of the 440 Cor-Bon cartridge at present, and three different loads are available. These consist of a 240-grain jacketed hollow point at 1800 ft/second, a 260-grain Bonded-Core jacketed hollow point at 1700 ft/second, and a 305-grain round nose jacketed Penetrator round at 1600 ft/second. Listed muzzle energies for these loads range from 1670 foot-pounds to 1734 foot-pounds, respectively. The best the Mars could do, according to published velocities, was push a 140-grain 8.5mm bullet at 1750 ft/second for 952 ft-pounds of muzzle energy. (One load for the 45 Long Mars cartridge achieved 763 ft-pounds of muzzle energy by pushing a 250-grain bullet at 1250 ft/second.) The 440 Cor-Bon has almost double the muzzle energy of the "world's most powerful pistol" of a century ago. The lightest 440 Cor-Bon bullet weight currently loaded has nearly twice the weight of the 8.5mm Mars bullet and, when using the 305 grain, almost half again as much as the heaviest 45 Long Mars bullet. Double your pleasure.

Using a six o'clock hold on a seven-inch black bull, firing was from the bench with the wrists resting on a sandbag with the left hand under the pistol butt and cupped around the shooting hand. Starting with the 240-grain hollow points, the first cases from the two rounds *stovepiped* on ejection and the third didn't eject. Although the pistol had been field-stripped and the barrel cleaned prior to going to the range, the pistol was again disassembled and inspected. The barrel was clean, and the fired cases had flattened primers with a bit of firing pin drag, but had not cratered or 'flowed' onto the radius of the primer pocket. A pass with Hoppes through the barrel and a wipe-clean, a bit of Teflon lubricant on the frame rails and the AMT was again assembled ready for shooting. The cartridges were each inspected and wiped to make sure no sizing residue was present. The magazine was again loaded with the 240-grain hollow point rounds, and the slide stop pushed to chamber the first round. This apparently solved the problem: there were no more *stovepipes* and ejection was positive–except for one later case from the 260-grain soft point rounds failing to eject.

The smallest group at 25 yards measured 1-1/2 inches, center-to-center, and was shot using the 305-grain Penetrator load. With the 240-grain jacketed hollow point and 260-grain jacketed soft point loads, the smallest groups measured 2-5/16 and 2-5/8 inches, respectively. All the three-shot groups were with the seven-inch bulls, using the six o'clock hold, and only one group exceeded three inches in diameter, measured center-to-center.

Recoil with the Penetrator is noticeable, but not severe, raising the pistol from a horizontal position approximately eight to twelve inches. Ejection of the fired cases ranged from three to seven paces directly to the rear of the firing point, depending on the load.

The new AMT AutoMag chambered for the 440 Cor-Bon pistol is not a plinking pistol, but a great combination for use on deer-size game. The test gun was accurate, the Cor-Bon ammunition has plenty of knock-down power for such game and the recoil is not punishing; the recoil actually seemed milder than some 44 Magnum loads this shooter has fired in a number of revolvers. •

Rexio Single Shot 45/.410 Pistol

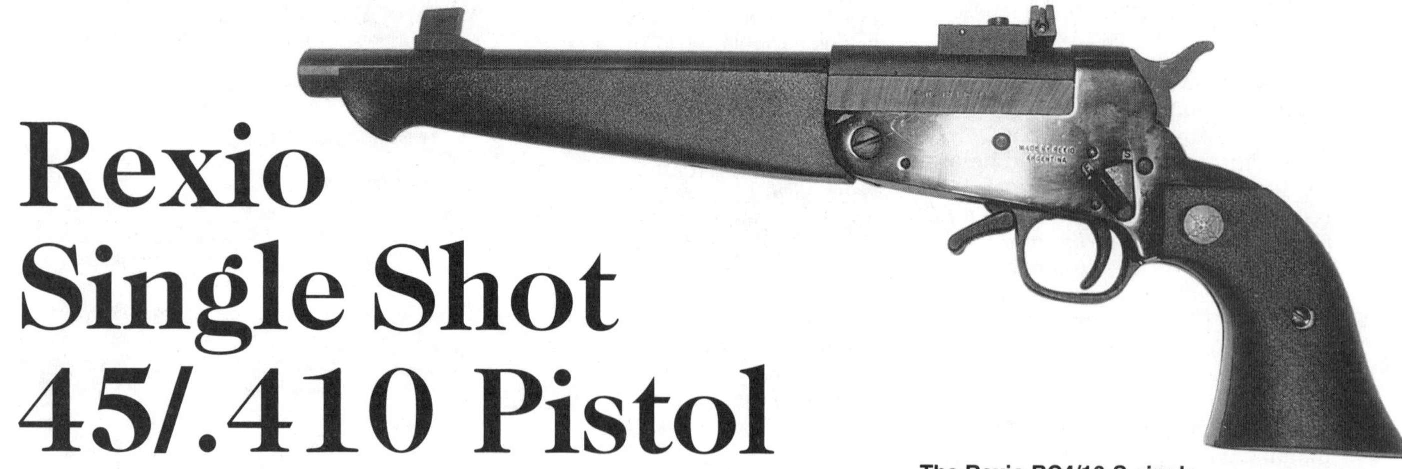

The Rexio RC4/10-S single shot 45/.410 pistol with the choke tube installed. Overall length of the pistol as shown is 14-1/4 inches.

by Larry Sterett

SINGLE-SHOT PISTOLS CHAMBERED for the .410 cartridge were relatively common in the U.K. at one time and, to a somewhat lesser degree in the U.S., with the H & R Handy Gun and the Crescent-Davis models probably being the most common. The Gun Control Act of 1934 brought their production to a halt, just as it did the Marble Arms Game Getter over/under models. Rifled barrel pistols chambered for the 45 Colt cartridge, but with an extended chamber capable of holding a .410-bore shotshell, are still available. (*The Thompson / Center Contender so chambered is the best known of such pistols.*)

Recently a new single shot 45/.410 pistol has become available to U. S. sportsmen. Manufactured in Argentina by Rexio, and imported into the U. S. by VAM Distributing Company of Wooster, Ohio, the pistol is the Model RC4/10-S, but is not so marked. (*The left side of the barrel breech is stamped Cal. 45 LC / 410, with the manufacturer, importer and serial number on the left and right sides of the frame, respectively.*)

Tipping the scales at 44 ounces, empty, the 10-S resembles a flat-sided Colt Single Action Army revolver, with one-piece frame featuring SAA-style grip, hammer spur, trigger and trigger guard. (*The frame is a non-ferrous alloy with a hard anodized glossy black finish.*). It's a single-action design with the hammer having only two positions, cocked and uncocked with the nose resting against the frame. (*A transfer bar prevents the face of the hammer from contacting the in-frame firing pin, until the pistol is actually fired.*) The hammer is powered by a spiral-wound spring.

Loading of the 10-S is similar to that of the T/C Contender, most single- and double-barrel shotguns and some early break-action revolver designs, such as the Smith & Wesson, Webley and Iver Johnson. The barrel is grasped with the fingers over the top, while pushing upward on the barrel release with the thumb. This permits the barrel to be pivoted downward, camming the extractor rearward at the same time, exposing the chamber for loading.

The steel barrel measured 9-3/16 inches long on the test pistol, with 6-1/16 inches of left-hand twist rifling. The muzzle end of the barrel is threaded and two screw-on tubes are provided, one for use with 45 Colt cartridges and one with .410 shotshells. With the .410 choke tube (1-17/32 inches long) installed, the barrel length measured 10-5/32 inches. (This tube, stamped *410*, features four straight lands and grooves. The lands are to retard and straighten the wad twist imparted by the barrel rifling. Bore diameter at the lands measured 0.395-inch, with the diameter at the grooves measuring 0.435-inch.) When shooting the 45 Colt cartridge in the 10-S, the 410 choke tube must be removed and the shorter tube, stamped *45 LC*, installed. This latter tube measured 1-5/32 inches long, providing a barrel length of 9-25/32 inches, and an overall length of 14-1/4 inches. (*Bore diameter of the 45 LC tube measured 0.452-inch.*)

The sights on the 10-S consisted of a 0.140-inch wide blade front with barrel band, and a 0.120-inch wide square notch rear. The rear sight is screw-adjustable for windage and elevation, and features a vertical white line on each side of the notch. (*The rear sight base is integral with the breech section of the barrel assembly.*) The sight radius measured 7-21/32 inches on the test gun.

The trigger on the 10-S is an investment casting, as is the hammer, safety, barrel release lever, barrel breech, front sight and rear sight. On the test gun the trigger measured 0.310-inch wide, with a smooth, slightly convex face, and a creeping let-off of seven pounds.

The 10-S features a thumb-activated lever safety on the left side of the frame. Forward is the '*fire*' mode, marked with the letter *F*, and to the rear is the '*safe*' mode, marked with the letter *S*. In the '*safe*' mode the trigger and hammer are both blocked; the trigger cannot be pulled and the hammer cannot be cocked.

The 10-S features a forearm and stocks of black, grain-surfaced black rubber. The forearm measured 6-13/16 inches on the test gun and featured a *schnable* tip, while the stocks have the characteristic Colt SAA shape with a bit of extra flare at the heel. The stocks also featured a brass-colored medallion with what appeared to be an 'X' imposed on a target, the trademark of the Rexio company. The stocks were comfortable, but the small SAA-style trigger guard doesn't leave much room for a gloved finger.

Checking of the Rexio for functioning and accuracy was done at 10 yards using .410 shotshells and 25 yards using 45 Colt cartridges. Fir-

The 10-S with the stocks removed revealing the spiral hammer spring, and the hammer cocked. The 45 Colt muzzle cap and the spanner wrench are to the left of the stocks.

ing with the 45 Colt cartridges was done from the bench, and only three-shot groups were fired, since it's doubtful much game will wait for additional shots from a single shot.

The .410 choke tube was installed on the barrel prior to patterning. First to be checked out was Winchester's AA Target load (MAX, 1/2, 8-1/2) containing an average of 241 pellets by actual count. (The 2-1/2-inch shell is the shortest .410 shell produced in the U.S., although some 2-inch .410 shells are loaded in the U.K. and elsewhere.) Using 12 square-inch targets as aiming points, the 10-S produced patterns averaged 84.6 percent within a 15-inch diameter (*176.7 square-inches*) circle.

The patterns were centered just over 1/2-inch above and 3-3/4 inches to the left of the point of aim, with the 12 inch aiming point containing an average of 22 pellets. (*This would be a good load for use on snakes, rodents, and even small game such as rabbits if the shooter was fast enough.*)

Remington's Express 3-inch .410 (MAX, 3/4,7-1/2) load containing 246 pellets of size 7-1/2 shot was checked next. (Due to the decreasing number of pellets, size 7-1/2 is about as large as is practical with the .410 in order to have sufficient pellets per shell. This shooter has used shells with size 6 in regular 3-inch chambered .410 shotguns, but not often.) Recoil with this load is a bit more, but not excessive. At ten yards the patterns averaged 69.9 percent of the pellets within a 15-inch circle, with an average of 14 size 7-1/2 pellets within the 12 in. aiming target. (*This would probably make a better rabbit load. Plus there are fewer pellets to bite into.*) The patterns were centered just under 2-1/2 inches above, and just over 3-1/2 inches to the left of, the point-of-aim.

Using .410 slug loads in the test gun was considered, but not for long. Why using a 1/5-ounce slug, when regular 45 Colt cartridges would produce better results, or at least should.

Replacing the .410 choke tube on the barrel with the 45 Colt muzzle cap, the 10-S was first tried with Winchester Super-X 45 cartridges loaded with 255-grain flat-nose lead bullets. At 25 yards, with the forearm resting in the padded 'V' of the pistol rest, the first three shots could have been covered by a small dinner plate. The creeping trigger pull didn't exactly help, but the 10-S is definitely not a target pistol. Continued firing finally produced a group measuring 6-3/4 inches in diameter, center-to-center; nothing to write home about, but better. Recoil was relatively mild, raising the pistol approximately four to six inches off the rest.

Switching to some handloads containing 250- and 240-grain Keith-style semi-wadcutter bullets did not produce much better results. Foam padding under the forearm did not alter the group sizes, and the smallest group obtained measured 6-13/16 inches, center-to-center, using the solid SWC bullets.

Recoil with the handloads, which were loaded to a few grains under maximum, was more pronounced, raising the 10-S approximately a foot off the rest. No jacketed loads were tried and it is possible brands other than Winchester might produced different results. Case extraction was easy, although none of the cases fell out of the chamber when the barrel was inverted. (*This could have caused by the chamber, both 45 Colt and .410 being rough, due either to a faulty reamer or dragging chips.*) Cartridges are lifted 0.150-inch by the extractor for manual removal, which is a bit difficult wearing gloves.

No attempt was made to center the groups, but only to obtain some sizes. The top of the front sight blade is more than 1/2-inch above the barrel, and using a six-o'clock sight picture the groups would normally center low. Not so with the 10-S. With the rear sight set in its lowest position, the groups were centered approximately a foot above the aiming point. Lowering the front sight by grinding or filing would raise the groups even more, as would raising the rear sight.

The front sight is on a collar, or band, which simply slips over the muzzle end of the barrel to be retained by the .410 choke tube or the 45 Colt muzzle cap. A stud on the underside of the sight collar centers the sight by mating with an indent on the underside of the barrel. To prevent the sight from wobbling, the choke tube/cap must be kept tight.

The 10-S has potential. Machining marks were still visible on the sides of the barrel breech and 'water table' of the frame, with mould parting lines visible on the hammer, trigger, barrel breech and barrel release lever. The heel of the extractor had an abrupt radius where it struck the face of the standing breech, but a larger radius or a gentle bevel would make closing the barrel assembly easier and reduce wear on the standing breech. Even the trigger could stand a bit of stoning, but this is best left undone by an amateur.

The 10-S is not a target pistol, although other 45 Colt loads might have produced smaller groups. It performed well with the light .410 loads, and might make a handy rabbit gun for a shooter wanting a bit of challenge, and it definitely is good for rodent and vermin control in a rural area. •

REXIO 10S Specifications

Model:	P1 RC4/10-S
Caliber:	45 Colt/.410
Barrel Length:	9-3/16 inches
Overall Length:	14-1/4 inches
Weight:	44 ounces
Trigger Let-Off:	7 pounds
Sight Radius:	8 inches
Height:	5-1/8 inches
Forearm:	6-13/16 inches

The 45 Auto Rim

Lots Of Punch In A Small Package!

By Chuck Taylor

THE END OF World War One marked a doldrum period in the U.S. firearms industry. The 1914-1918 "War To End All Wars" had indelibly marked millions of Americans, and pacifism and disarmament were thus the orders of the day. Military budgets were slashed to the bone, causing massive demobilization of existing personnel. Research and development programs dealing with new weapons were cancelled and even existing weapon systems were scrapped or reduced in number. Yes, it was a grim time for those who knew the folly of such utopian attitudes, for they also knew what would eventually result, but 1939 was at the time a long way off.

Above: **A great 45 Auto Rim lineup, *L to R*: For plinking or self-defense, the Factory Remington 230-grain RNL; for small to medium game, the Hornady 185 or 200-grain XTP JHP and 8.5-grains of Unique; and, finally for large or dangerous game, the Sierra 240-grain JHP with 14.0-grains of 2400 and the Keith 255-grain #452424 SWC cast from pure linotype and 14.5-grains of 2400.**

The U.S. firearms manufacturing community wasn't exempt from the mood of the time, either. Sales slumped, due in part to the vast quantities of military arms appearing on the surplus market. As a result, though one of the giants, Smith & Wesson, too, faced a difficult economic period. And in order to survive, they needed to get production moving again, and quickly.

A quick look at what they had "in house" showed a number of possibilities, the most attractive of which was the introduction of a new gun. Many returning WWI veterans had used Smith's highly successful M1917 45 ACP revolver and liked it immensely. Used with stamped-steel "half moon clips" to allow proper headspacing

▼First revolver to utilize the 45 AR when it first appeared in 1920 was the commercial version of Smith & Wesson's M1917 of World War One fame.

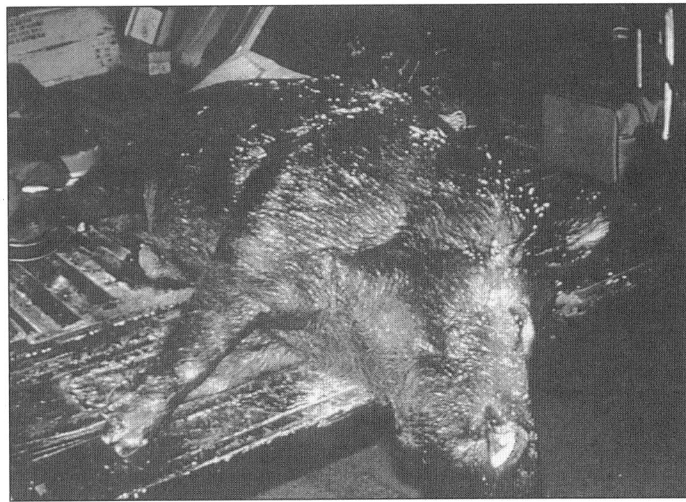

426-lb. record book Russian boar charged author but was stopped by 255-grain Keith SWC from his 6 1/2-inch S&W M25-2, allowing a quick *coup de grace* follow-up shot.

and extraction of the rimless 45 ACP service cartridge, it had performed admirably in the military environment and gained a substantial following among those who preferred revolvers to self-loaders.

Thus, in 1921, a commercial version of the M1917 was introduced, featuring an attractive, highly polished blued finish and checkered full-sized walnut stocks. This was a particularly good move for Smith, since the previous year, Peters Cartridge Corporation *(later absorbed by Remington)* had introduced a rimmed version of the 45 ACP specifically for use in the M1917 that eliminated the need for the half-moon clip.

Loaded with a lead 230-grain roundnose bullet to minimize wear on the shallow rifling of the M1917, the new cartridge, called the 45 Auto Rim, was loaded to identical specifications to 230-grain 45 ACP "hardball" and enjoyed immediate success. Accurate, potent and easy to handload, it stimulated sales of the commercial S&W M1917 sufficiently to allow its continued production until 1939, when Smith began concentrating on military contracts and ceased producing all commercial models.

After World War Two ended, the M1917 revolver was produced until 1949, when Smith's engineers and marketing executives decided to modernize it with a longer barrel, adjustable sights and better stocks. The new gun, dubbed the "Model 1950 45 Target" proved unpopular with most shooters who, by June, 1952, had purchased only 1162 of them. Something had to be done, so S&W added a 6 1/2-inch heavy barrel and on March 3, 1955, re-introduced it as the ".45 Hand Ejector Model Of 1955." So-modified, the new gun (later designated the M25) was successful and continued in production until the late 1980s, giving the ubiquitous 45 Auto Rim yet another lease on life.

In 1989, S&W resurrected the M25's basic design in stainless steel, adding a 5-inch underlugged barrel and rubber "combat" stocks, calling the result the M625, "Model Of 1989." Curiously, though the gun was immensely popular, only small numbers of them were produced, making it a much sought-after gun by not only shooters, but hunters and collectors alike.

Because both the M25 and M625 are essentially heavy-barreled versions of the heavy-framed M1917 and because its case wall is thicker than the 45 ACP, the 45 AR can withstand higher pressures and thus be loaded to power levels considerably above that of the factory

Performance Chart For Sample Loads For 45 Auto Rim

Bullet	Mfr	Wt	Powder	Chg	Vel: 5" bbl	6.5"bbl	Avg Ext sprd
HP	Speer	185	Unique	7.0	906	952	36
JHP	Horn	185	Unique	8.5	1093 * #	1145*#	27
JHP	Speer	185	Unique	8.5	1049 *	1101	29
JHP	Horn	200	Unique	8.5	1027 *+	046	31
JHP	Speer	200	Unique	7.0	869	910	38
JHP	Speer	200	Unique	8.0	1008 *#	1023 *#	32
JHP	Speer	225	Unique	6.2	841	864	84
RNL	R-P	230	Factory	N/A	761	802	16
FMJ	Speer	230	Unique	6.2	777	801	12
JHP	Sierra	240	2400	14.0	966 *+	1027+	29
SWC	Keith	255	Unique	7.0	844	886	31
SWC	Keith	255	2400	14.5	1083 *+ #	1137*+ #	11

NOTES
JHP: *Jacketed Hollow Point* **RNL:** *Round Nose Lead*
FMJ: *Full Metal Jacket* **SWC:** *Semi-Wad Cutter*
Test Guns: *Smith & Wesson M625-2 w/5-inch bbl & Smith & Wesson M25-2 w/6 1/2-inch bbl.* **CASES:** Remington **PRIMERS:** Remington #2 1/2
Chronograph: *Oehler Model 35P Skyscreen w/printer*
Temperature: *61 degrees Fahrenheit*
Altitude: *4665 ft.*
Humidity: *48%*
Barometric Pressure: *29.87*
** = denotes 1-inch or better Ransom Rest accuracy at 25 meters.*
+ = denotes pronounced recoil. Should be considered "+P" and, although safe, are therefore not recommended for use in Colt and S&W M1917 revolvers.
 # = denotes author's preferred loads.
BULLET TYPES: ***Speer*** *— Gold Dot JHP* **Hornady** *— XTP JHP* **Keith** *— Cast from pure linotype using original Lyman #452424 mold.*

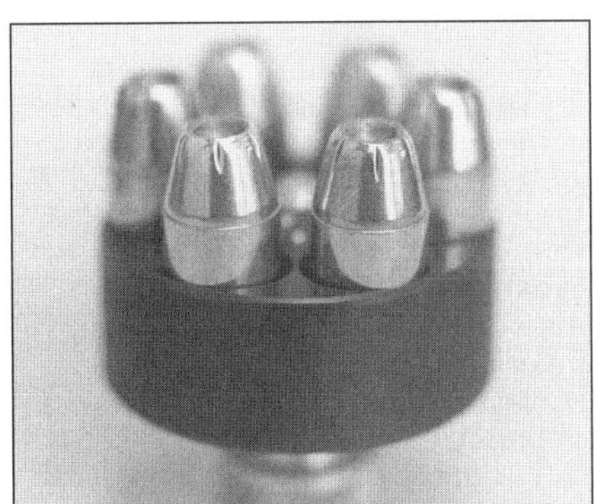

Close up view of Hornady 200-grain *XTP* JHPs in speed-loader. These provide spectacular expansion and performance on both small and medium-sized game.

For dealing with dangerous game like this black bear, the 255-grain Keith #452454 SWC cast of solid linotype and propelled by 14.5-grains of 2400 is a good load. Capable of 1-inch accuracy at 25 meters, it produces 1083 fps from a 5-inch barreled M625 and a whopping 1137 fps from a 6 1/2-inch M25-2.

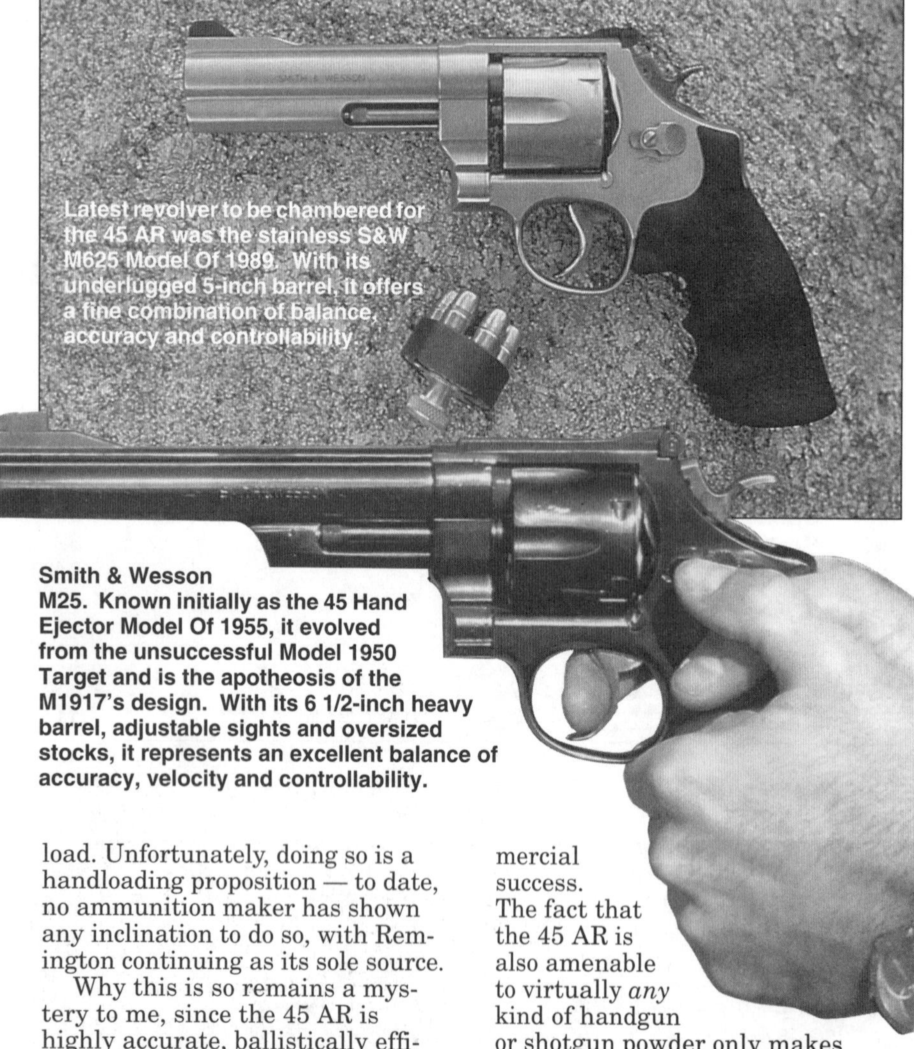

Latest revolver to be chambered for the 45 AR was the stainless S&W M625 Model Of 1989. With its underlugged 5-inch barrel, it offers a fine combination of balance, accuracy and controllability.

Smith & Wesson M25. Known initially as the 45 Hand Ejector Model Of 1955, it evolved from the unsuccessful Model 1950 Target and is the apotheosis of the M1917's design. With its 6 1/2-inch heavy barrel, adjustable sights and oversized stocks, it represents an excellent balance of accuracy, velocity and controllability.

load. Unfortunately, doing so is a handloading proposition — to date, no ammunition maker has shown any inclination to do so, with Remington continuing as its sole source.

Why this is so remains a mystery to me, since the 45 AR is highly accurate, ballistically efficient and easy to work with. Moreover, a huge array of 45 caliber lead and jacketed bullet designs are readily available, giving such a project immense potential for commercial success. The fact that the 45 AR is also amenable to virtually *any* kind of handgun or shotgun powder only makes the situation more inexplicable.

Of the many available powders, I've found Unique and 2400 the most versatile. A rather extensive data-gathering project lasting several years has brought me to the following loads. Each has a specific function and represents simple criteria – the best combination of accuracy, velocity, penetration, bullet expansion and weapon controllability. Actually, the only load that produces noteworthy recoil in either a M25 or M625 is the big Keith #454424 hard-cast SWC and 14.5-grains of 2400.

This load in particular is intended for use on large or dangerous game and generates an impressive 1083 fps from a 5-inch M625 or a whopping 1137 fps from a 6 1/2-inch M25-2 and shoots into 1 inch at 25 meters. Interestingly, it actually duplicates the performance of Elmer Keith's preferred high-intensity load for the much larger 45 Colt from a 7 1/2-inch Ruger Blackhawk (20 grains of 2400). On elk, moose, caribou, bear, wild boar or for "boondocking" in country where encounters with potentially dangerous critters are possible, it's tough to beat, providing excellent penetration, a full-caliber permanent wound channel and fine stopping power.

On two occasions, I've taken Russian boar in the 400-lb. class with this load and found that it slams through a boar's heavy hide, massive muscle and substantial bone mass, often putting him down even more quickly than many *rifle* cartridges. In one instance, the animal had been inadvertently cornered and was beginning a charge when hit. The pure-linotype Keith #452424 SWC struck him in the right shoulder as he spun towards me, shattered it, continued through the chest cavity and exited behind the right shoulder. Though enraged and beginning his rush, the boar was unable to remain on his feet and somersaulted diagonally forward, striking the ground in a cloud of dust, allowing me to administer a *coup de grace* shot to finish him.

Another nice load for big critters is the Sierra 240-grain JHP and 14.0-grains of 2400. It produces 966 fps from a 5-inch M625 or 1027 fps from a 6 1/2-inch M25-2 and is also capable of 1-inch accuracy at 25 meters. However, as with the aforementioned Keith load, recoil is substantial, though not by any means unmanageable.

For smaller game such as jackrabbits, coyotes, javelina and exotic or white tail deer, Hornady's 185-grain XTP JHP and 8.5-grains of *Unique* (1093 fps – 5-inch bbl; 1145 fps – 6 1/2-inch bbl) is excellent out to a full 100 meters or so, and pro-

Author with Javelina taken in the mountains near Prescott, Arizona with Hornady 185-grain *XTP* JHP/Unique load. Animal dropped in his tracks and had a 4-inch diameter exit wound.

For small game, such as jackrabbits or these prairie dogs, Hornady 185-grain *XTP* JHP/Unique load is spectacular.

Excellent Whitetail buck taken by Taylor on Tex-Mex border with a single broadside thoracic hit with Hornady 185-grain *XTP* JHP and 8.5-grains of Unique from 6 1/2-inch S&W M25-2 (1145 fps). Though shot from sixty meters, buck collapsed in his tracks and had succumbed by the time author reached him. Expanded bullet measured almost .90 caliber and was recovered from beneath hide on opposite side from impact.

duces spectacular bullet expansion, fine accuracy and only moderate recoil. In the last ten years, I've personally taken no less than a dozen Sika, Fallow, Axis and white-tail bucks with this load from a 6 1/2-inch S&W M25-2 at ranges of from fifteen to a full 80 meters.

All were one-shot kills, with only one animal moving more than ten meters from the spot where it was originally hit. This particular white tail buck managed to take two bounds (covering about 25-meters), then collapsed into a thicket of prickly-pear cactus, making for an interesting, though leisurely, recovery problem!

For larger mule deer, mountain lion and even elk, the Hornady 200-grain XTP JHP, also loaded over 8.5-grains of *Unique* (1049 fps – 5-inch bbl; 1046 fps – 6 1/2-inch bbl) is *highly* effective. A close friend of mine just took a trophy 200-lb. male mountain lion from 35 meters with this load, requiring only a single thoracic hit. After being hit, he took only two bounds, then collapsed and succumbed. Post-mortem bullet examination showed bullet expansion to nearly .75 caliber. Now, *that's* potent medicine, gents!

If you're a target shooter or plinker, Speer's 185-grain *Gold Dot* JHP and 7.0-grains of Unique (906 fps – 5-inch bbl; 952 fps – 6 1/2-inch bbl) demonstrates superb accuracy with almost no recoil. If you want just a *little* more punch, try the Gold Dot 230-grain JHP and 6.2-grains of Unique (777 fps – 5-inch bbl; 801 fps – 6 1/2-inch bbl). It, too, is very accurate, but hits just a bit harder downrange.

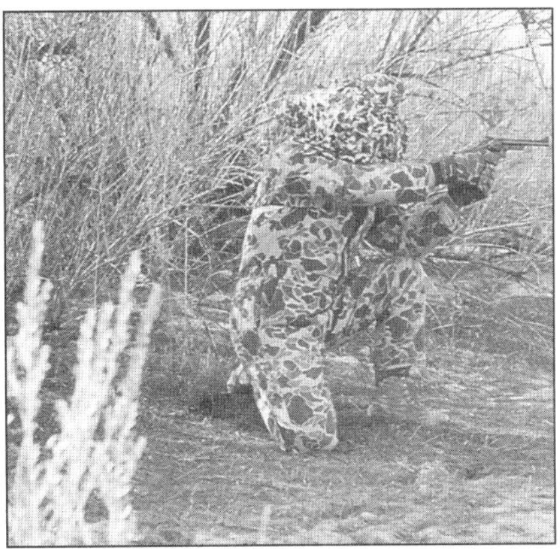

Full camo against silhouette-breaking background can help close the range for handgun hunters.

As you can see, careful handloading allows the 45 Auto Rim to reach exceptionally high levels of overall performance, making it a *most* satisfactory cartridge for nearly any kind of use. It can be used successfully against virtually any kind of game, for serious target shooting or for just bustin' beer cans on a Saturday morning while camping. Even with heavy loads, its recoil, though admittedly substantial, is nowhere near that generated by a 44 or 41 Magnum – a full-house 158-grain 357 load, perhaps, but no more. Yet, its accuracy with any load is nothing short of superb, making it a good choice indeed, suitable for nearly any shooting need.

So, if you prefer a cartridge that provides both versatility and performance without excessive recoil, give the 45 Auto Rim a try. Once you do, like me, you just might find yourself using it more often than anything else, and why not? Especially these days, cartridges with this kind of capability are hard to find. ●

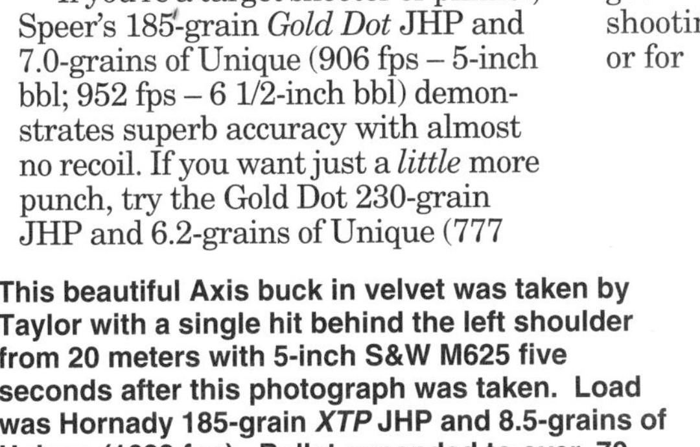

This beautiful Axis buck in velvet was taken by Taylor with a single hit behind the left shoulder from 20 meters with 5-inch S&W M625 five seconds after this photograph was taken. Load was Hornady 185-grain *XTP* JHP and 8.5-grains of Unique (1093 fps). Bullet expanded to over .70 caliber and was found on ground on exit side of animal.

Engraved and Custom Handguns

by Tom Turpin

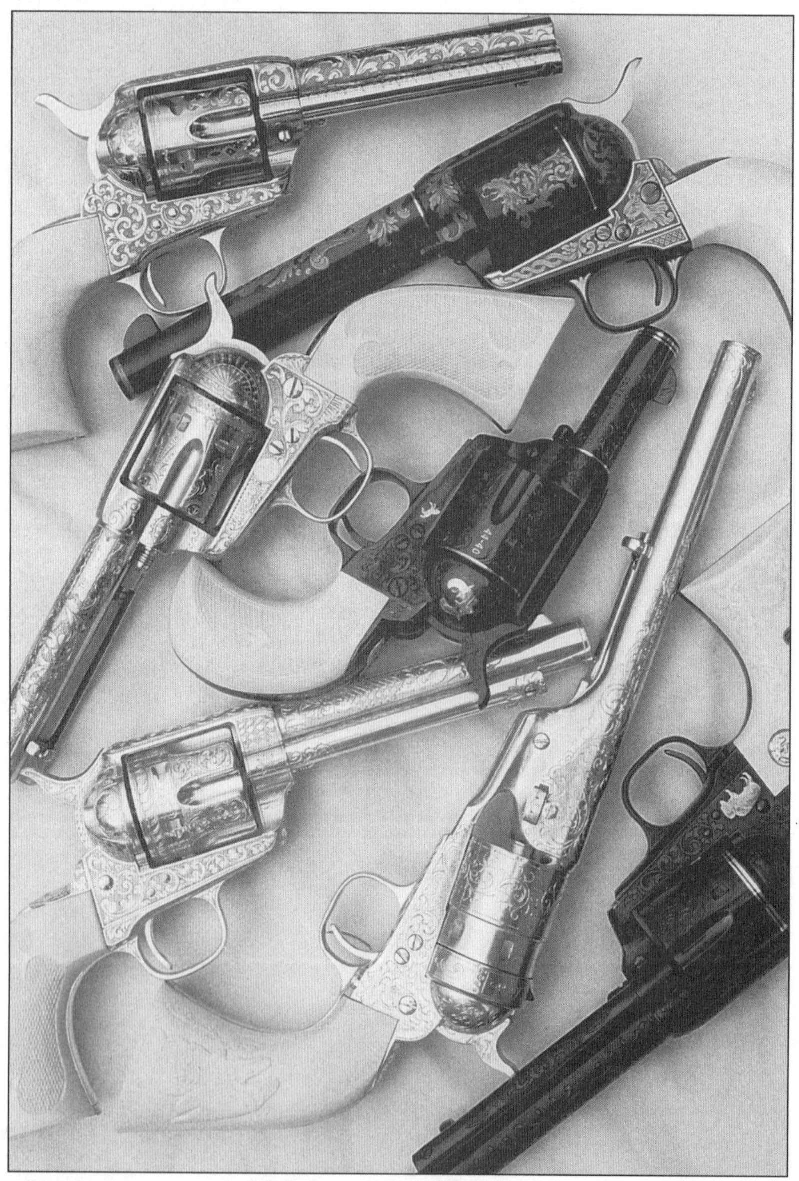

Colt Single Action revolvers from the Montana shop of Barry Lee Hands. Although Barry is very adept at engraving any type of firearm, he has done quite a number of Colt Single-Actions over the years. Still a very young man, he will surely adorn many more with his artistry before hanging up his engraving tools. *Photo by Barry Lee Hands.*

◀ ▼One of the old timers in the engraving craft is Buckeye native Floyd Warren. Turning 84 in July 2001, "Fiddling" Floyd still spends some time at the engraving bench even today. This Singer Contract Colt 45 was engraved by Warren for his wife in the mid-1960s. *Photo courtesy of Leslie Oliver.*

◀This FN Browning HiPower has been lavishly engraved and gold inlaid by Ron Collings. Mr. Collings is not well know nationally as he specializes mostly in production type engraving. His work is superb. *Photo courtesy R.J. Collings.*

▶Ron Collings turned out this extraordinary Colt 45. Heavily gold inlaid, the work is reminiscent of that turned out by Colt Master Engraver Gustave Young during the second half of the 1800s. *Photo courtesy of R.J. Collings.*

▼There is an old saying that "the Devil is in the details." That is very true in most endeavors, and it is certainly true in engraving. Sometimes, one comes across a piece that, viewed as a whole, looks impressive. However, when examined closely, they sometimes fall apart as the details - unseen from a distance - are not so well executed. This work, by German Master Engraver Claus Willig, will stand scrutiny from anyone. The gripcap treatment and the details on the barrel are both from a Ruger black powder revolver. Nothing is lost in examining the details of this engraving job. *Photo Courtesy of Claus Willig.*

▶A Colt Gold Cup Commander, Cal. 45 ACP, a rare gun. The magnificent engraving and gold work as well as the buffalo horn grips are the work of John Barraclough. John, when not farming avocados or working at the engraving bench, teaches the art of engraving at several community colleges around the country. *Photo by Walter Rickell Photography.*

Ralph Ingle turns out many engraved handguns from his Centerville, GA shop. This S&W revolver is an example of his work. In addition to the luxurious engraving, this S&W has also been fitted with elephant ivory grips which perfectly compliment the engraving. *Photo courtesy of Ralph Ingle.*

▼ ▶Some of the details of engravings by Ron Nott on a Colt Single Action revolver. Note that the scroll work is cleanly cut with no ragged edges and the gold line inlays are straight and not wavy. *Photos courtesy of Ron Nott.*

▲A Colt Single Action Army from the Pennsylvania shop of Ron Nott. Ron does exceptional work on all types of firearms and also on custom knives. Much of his work is devoted to the old Peacemaker though. *Photo courtesy of Ron Nott.*

▲ **A wonderful Colt Government Model 45 auto that has been lavishly engraved by Ray Viramontez. Ray spent a career in the US Air Force, engraving part-time. Since retiring from active duty a few years back, he has been at the bench full time. This is a good example of his artistry.** *Photo courtesy of Ray Viramontez.*

▲ **There are ornate engravings and then there are *really* ornate engravings. This piece, if it was of the correct era, would likely belong in the collection of French royalty or the Russian Czars. Since it is a modern Colt double-action revolver though, neither is the case. This really ornate revolver is the work of German engraver Wolfgang Tschinkowitz. Not only is this revolver ornate, it is also "X" rated. The other side of this revolver contains scenes that would make Playboy blush.** *Photo courtesy of Wolfgang Tschinkowitz.*

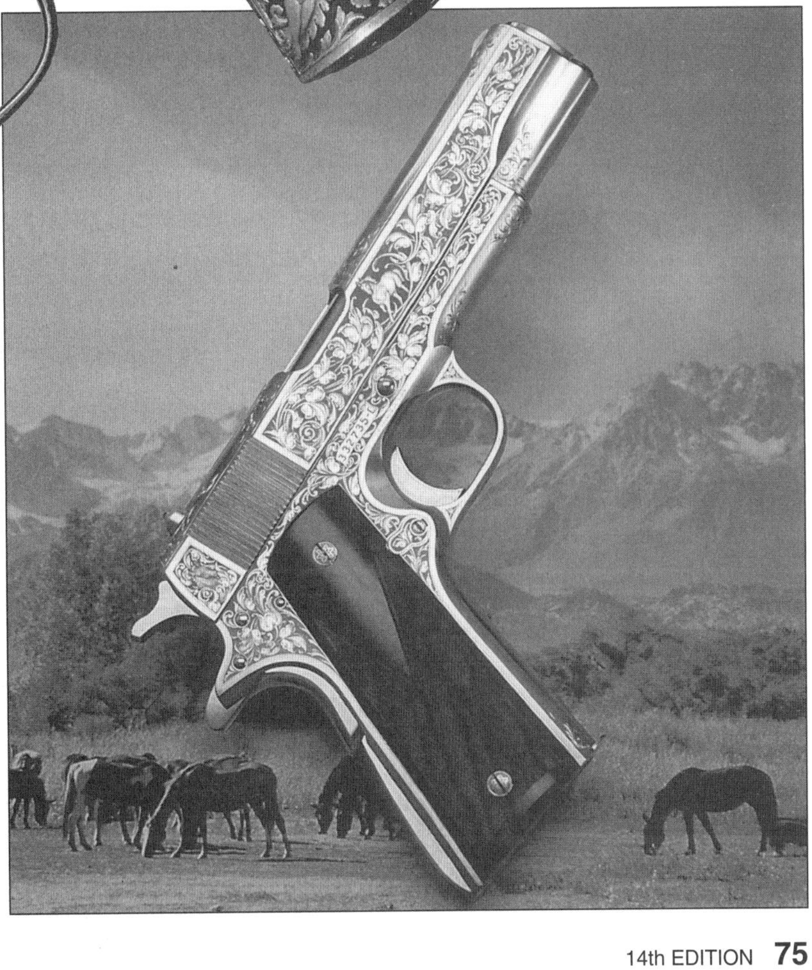

▶**This superb Colt Government Model .45 auto is from the Vermont shop of Winston Churchill. While there is much debate and subjectivity in discussing the quality of work turned out by various artisans, there is no one that I have ever talked to that didn't rate Winston among the top two or three engravers in all the world. Many rate him at the very top. There is no question that his work is impeccable.** *Photo courtesy of Winston Churchill.*

▲ **Ben Shostle has owned and operated a commercial gunshop in Indiana for many years. As an adjunct to his shop, he began doing custom gun work, including accepting commissions for engraving. Completely self-taught, his work is highly stylized. This Walther PPK is a good example of his work. Unfortunately, Ben has failing eyesight and has likely engraved his last firearm. We are much worse off as a result.** *Photo courtesy of Ben Shostle.*

▲ **A Thompson Center handgun as engraved and gold inlaid in the shop of Ray Viramontez. Ray has been laboring at the engraving bench for many years now. As a career US Air Force man, his bench moved with him for many years. It is now permanently located in Albany, Georgia - at least as permanently as can be predicted. Last I spoke with him, he had no intentions of moving again.** *Photo courtesy of Ray Viramontez.*

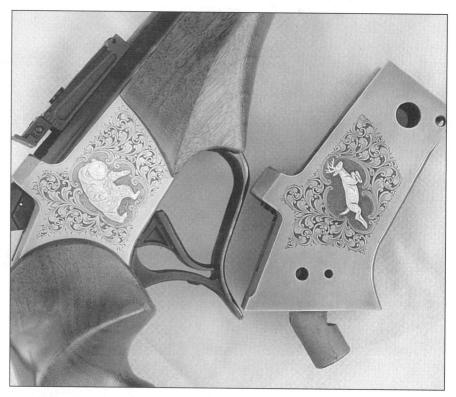

▼ **This S&W 357 Magnum is typical of the engraving artistry of Ray Viramontez. His Germanic training is evident in his styling, but not overpoweringly so. Ray has been plying his craft for many years now and like good wine, he just keeps getting better and better.** *Photo by Ray Viramontez.*

▶ **A fine engraver who will likely not be doing any future work due to failing eyesight is Hoosier resident Ben Shostle. Actually a Kentuckian by birth, Ben turned out many fine engraving jobs over the years. A former President of the Firearms Engravers Guild of America, Ben is a real craftsman and gentleman. These Lugers exemplify his work.** *Photo courtesy of Ben Shostle.*

▶ **Joe Rundell is one of the finest artisans in the business today. Not only does he execute glorious engraving, he also does carving and scrimshaw work - all exquisitely accomplished. This Colt Single Action is but an example of his work. Joe performed his artistry on a part-time basis for many years but now works at his craft full time. His shop is located in Clio, Michigan.** *Photo by Weyer of Toledo.*

▲ **New York engraver Martin Rabeno is primarily known for his superb period style work on Winchester lever action rifles. His work on this Colt Government Model 45 ACP is a bit of a departure from the norm. Even so, *aficionados* familiar with Marty's work, would recognize his engraving rather quickly, even on a 45 ACP. His artistry is always clean, sharply cut, and wonderfully executed.**
Photo courtesy of Martin Rabeno.

▼ **Some examples of the artistry of Montanan Barry Lee Hands. Barry engraved and photographed these Colt handguns. At one time and perhaps continuing, Barry did considerable work for the Colt factory.** *Photo by Barry Lee Hands.*

▲ **This S&W magnum revolver was beautified in the Arizona shop of Mel Wood. Known primarily as a custom knife engraver, this S&W exemplifies that he does embellish other than fine custom knives.**
Photo courtesy of Mel Wood.

The New Breed

The Development of Low-Priced Polymer Subcompact Carry Pistols

by John Malloy

The small, light Kel-Tec, offered in 9mm or 40 S&W, is easily controllable for repeat shots with a two-hand hold.

SHOOTERS SELDOM GET to see a whole new class of firearms appear and develop before their very eyes. In the last few years of the 1990s, however, that is exactly what happened.

Inexpensive subcompact polymer frame personal-protection pistols were introduced. They were initially chambered for the 9mm Luger (Parabellum) cartridge, which previously had found its place as a chambering for high-capacity full-size semiautomatic pistols.

The new subcompacts came from small manufacturers at a time when an interest in "carry" guns was beginning to grow. The new pistols were priced at a level that could be afforded by almost anyone concerned about personal safety—they were listed at roughly half the price of the traditional carry pistols from the major manufacturers. Before long, the new small centerfires had grown past just being offered in 9mm.

The three pistols that started this group were, in a way, the result of outside forces. Two major factors led to the offering of this new breed of firearms.

Certainly, the effect of the so-called Crime Bill of September 1994, with its ten-round limit on magazine capacity, was one. A full-size, large-capacity 9mm pistol loses some of its advantage without a large-capacity magazine. The stage was set for the introduction of new pistols that could offer a "legal limit" of ten rounds in a smaller, more compact package.

Another factor was the encouraging passage of right-to-carry legislation in a growing number of states. An increasing number of ordinary people who were able to be legally armed created a demand for more suitable pistols. Ordinary people, perhaps not in law enforcement, and perhaps not dyed-in-the-wool firearms enthusiasts, wanted pistols that had adequate power, didn't cost too much, were not very big, were not very heavy, and were easy to use.

Effective cartridges offered in the new breed of light subcompact pistols, from left: 9mm Luger, 40 Smith & Wesson, 45 ACP and 32 ACP.

▶Kel-Tec P-11, left view. The small, light 9mm carries a "legal limit" of 10+1 cartridges. Trigger mechanism is double-action only, with second-snap capability.

▲ Kel-Tec P-11, right view. The Kel-Tec, introduced in 1995, was the first of a new breed of light polymer-frame subcompact pistols chambered for desirable cartridges.

Three mechanically-different pistols, introduced a year apart, met these specifications.

The first of the new breed was the Kel-Tec P-11, a 9mm pistol introduced early in 1995. The Kel-Tec had a ten-shot magazine and could hold an additional cartridge in the chamber, for a capacity of 10+1. The option of eleven shots led to the P-11 model designation. The eleven shots could be put into a pistol with an unloaded weight of only 14 ounces.

The size of the pistol was about 4-1/8 inches high by 5-3/4 inches long. This size allows it to almost hide under a 4 x 6 note card. 4 x 6 has become a rule of thumb that has grown to indicate that a pistol is in the "subcompact" category. Because it is just a rule of thumb, a pistol is not excluded if a little sticks out here or there. (Generally, 5 x 7 indicates a "compact," and larger ones are "full size").

9mm pistols had been made in the general subcompact size before, but they had carried fewer shots and weighed substantially more. Also, to achieve small size, the earliest subcompact nines were of straight-blowback design, and the felt recoil was decidedly uncomfortable.

Kel-Tec CNC Inc., a small company in the unlikely location of Cocoa, Florida, solved all these problems. A polymer frame reduced weight and allowed a 10-shot double-column magazine in a frame only an inch wide. A scaled-down tilting-barrel locking system for its 3-inch barrel and a steel slide were combined to tame the recoil. The firing mechanism was double-action-only (DAO), of the type that allows additional falls of the hammer in case of a misfire. This feature is sometimes called "second-snap" capability.

Actually a tiny bit smaller and slightly lighter than a 38 Chiefs Special revolver, it held over twice as many shots. The new Kel-Tec pistol quickly developed a following.

Disassembly of the Kel-Tec P-11 shows the cam-actuated tilting-barrel locking system and the double-wound recoil spring.

◀ **Stealth, right view. In addition to the Glock-type trigger, the Heritage Stealth pistol also has an ambidextrous thumb-operated manual safety, easily reached from either side.**

▶ **Heritage Stealth, left view. The 1996 introduction of the Heritage Stealth 9mm pistol provided the second entry into the new breed of polymer subcompact carry pistols. This is the all-black version, known as the Stealth Shadow.**

Disassembly of the Stealth shows the piston attached to the front of the slide that retards its rearward motion. The piston rides in a gas cylinder beneath the barrel. When a shot is fired, powder gas tapped from the barrel pushes the piston forward as recoil attempts to move the slide back.

Another entry into the polymer subcompact niche came almost exactly a year later. In January of 1996, another Sunshine State company, Heritage Manufacturing, Inc., of Opa Locka, Florida, introduced the Stealth 9mm pistol.

At about 4-1/8 x 6-1/8, the Stealth was slightly larger than the Kel-Tec, but its design allowed a longer 3.9-inch barrel. At 20 ounces, it was light, although heavier than the Kel-Tec.

Except for its spot in the new polymer subcompact class, the Stealth has little similarity with the Kel-Tec. The Heritage Stealth is striker-fired. The trigger mechanism is partially cocked by the movement of the slide, and brought to full cock by the trigger. This general mechanism was introduced by the Austrian Roth-Steyr of 1907 and recently popularized by another Austrian pistol, the Glock, as "safe action." The system is generally called a "Glock-type" trigger mechanism. The Stealth's trigger pull is about 4 pounds. For those uncomfortable without a thumb-operated manual safety, an ambidextrous trigger-block safety is provided.

The barrel is fixed, and recoil is controlled by a gas-delay system. A gas piston attached to the front of the slide rides in a cylinder under the barrel. A port in front of the chamber vents gas into this cylinder when a shot is fired. This gas pushes forward on the piston, retarding the rearward movement of the slide until the pressure has dropped. The system comfortably reduces felt recoil, and the fixed barrel contributes to making the pistol a very accurate one for its size.

While the new small 9mm pistols were expanding into their niche, the full-size pistols were undergoing a period of change.

The federal 10-round limit on magazine capacity made the full-size 9mm autoloaders less useful.

◀ **The left view of the user-friendly Republic Arms Patriot shows its only external control, the magazine release behind the trigger guard.**

▲ **The 45-caliber Republic Arms Patriot, right view. The 1997 entry into the new breed was its largest caliber chambering. This is the all-black variant.**

The Republic Arms 45 uses a cam-operated tilting-barrel locking system. The single-wind recoil spring is held captive on its guide.

However, most full-size pistols that could handle the 9mm cartridge could be adapted to handle the 40 S&W round. The 40-caliber round, introduced a few years before, in 1990, had caught the interest of police officers and ordinary citizens alike. For the common folk, 10 rounds of 40 in a full-size pistol looked better than 10 rounds of 9mm, and a number of new 40-caliber pistols were introduced.

If a full-size 9 could become a 40, why not a subcompact 9? Both Kel-Tec and Heritage began work toward that end.

By mid-1997, Kel-Tec had successfully introduced a 40 S&W version. The larger-caliber Kel-Tec, given the model designation P-40, was only 5/32-inch longer than the original pistol. Weight went up two ounces, bringing the new 40 up from 14 to 16 ounces. At an even one pound, the new Kel-Tec was a very light 40. The fatter 40 S&W cartridges reduced the magazine capacity to 9, giving a total capacity of 9+1. Later, a magazine extension was offered to bring the P-40 to 10+1 capacity.

Heritage was right behind with their 40. By the first month of 1998, the new pistol, the Stealth C-4000, was being shipped. Because the Stealth was a slightly larger design to begin with, Heritage's 40-caliber was the same size and weight as their original 9mm version. The 40 magazine retained the full 10-shot capacity, making the Stealth 40 a full 10+1 pistol.

The arrival of the Kel-Tec in 1995 and the Stealth in 1996 gave

◀ Kel-Tec surprised the shooting world with the introduction of its little P-32, a 6-1/2 ounce locked-breech 32 ACP. Right view.

▶The left view of the Kel-Tec P-32 shows its only external control, the magazine release behind the trigger guard. Departing from the original Kel-Tec design, the P-32 has an internal slide lock.

the shooting world the first two entries into this new category.

Then, in early 1997, two years after the Kel-Tec's introduction and a year after the Stealth's debut, a new company from the other side of the country entered the polymer subcompact field. Republic Arms, of Chino, California, decided that if a 9 or a 40 is good, a 45 might be better.

The Republic Arms Patriot was offered as a 20-ounce locked-breech polymer frame pistol, chambered for the 45 ACP cartridge. The polymer frame was mated with a stainless-steel slide. Action was short-recoil, using a tilting-barrel locking system. Size is 4.75 x 6 inches, with a 3.25-inch barrel. The 45-caliber Patriot is only one inch wide.

The Republic pistol has a slightly longer grip than the other two, but we'll keep it in the subcompact class. Republic makes a departure from the "legal-limit" capacity of the Kel-Tec and Heritage pistols. The grip holds a single-column magazine that holds six rounds of 45 ACP, giving the pistol a capacity of 6+1. Seven rounds of 45 is a pretty good payload for a 20-ounce pistol.

The single-column magazine keeps the pistol slim, but because it is a modification of the 1911 Colt magazine, surplus 1911 magazines can sometimes be used as spares. They stick out a bit and Republic will obviously not guarantee functioning, as they will with their own magazines, but their use offers an option for people who have access to 1911 magazines. The longer grip is well-shaped and provides good recoil control for such a light pistol.

Mechanically, the Republic Patriot is striker-fired, with a DAO trigger that operates much as does a revolver trigger. Letoff occurs well before the trigger finger contacts the frame, and seems not to disturb sight alignment. Like the Kel-Tec, the Republic trigger allows second-snap capability.

After the introduction of this new breed of pistols by Kel-Tec, Heritage and Republic, some additional variations were added to each. As discussed, the first two manufacturers added 40-caliber versions to their original 9mm offerings. Kel-Tec also

Unusual for a 32, the Kel-Tec P-32 is a locked-breech pistol, using a tilting-barrel system. The locked-breech mechanism uses a very light slide, allowing the 6-1/2 ounce weight of the pistol.

▶The Republic's well-shaped polymer grip allows the recoil of the 45 ACP cartridge to be controlled for repeat shots with a two-hand grip.

introduced hard-chrome and Parkerized slides, with polymer frames colored to match. Heritage continued to offer black frames, but now with a choice of stainless steel, all-black or two-tone slides. Republic offered an all-black pistol, with a black Melonite finish on the stainless slide, as well as the original black-frame/stainless-slide version. It would seem that all the spaces in this new niche of polymer subcompact carry pistols had been pretty well filled.

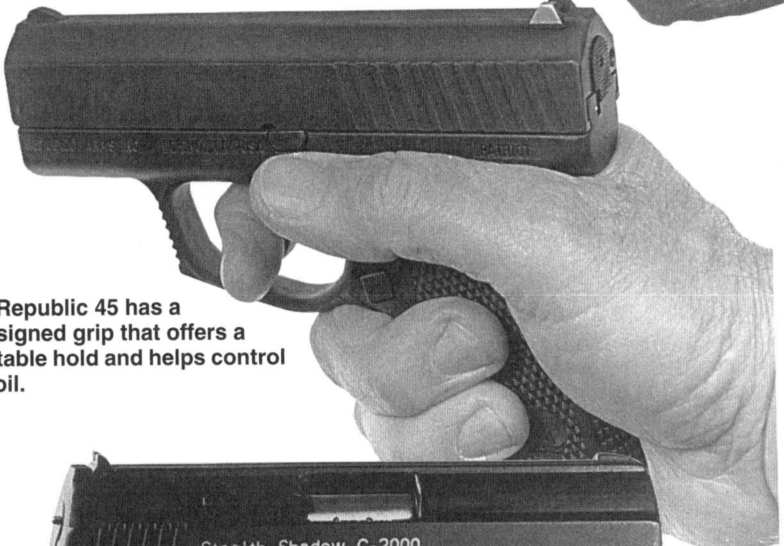

▶The Republic 45 has a well-designed grip that offers a comfortable hold and helps control felt recoil.

▲The only external controls of the Stealth design are the magazine release and the safety. The ambidextrous safety can be readily operated from either side.

Then, in February 1999, Kel-Tec surprised the shooting world by offering an entirely new pistol. They had modified their pistol's design and had scaled it down to 32 ACP caliber. Because of the recent popularity of 25-sized 32 pistols, the 32 ACP had again become a cartridge to be considered for personal defense.

The new Kel-Tec pistol was only 3/4-inch wide and weighed just a hair over 6-1/2 ounces. Unusual for a 32, the new Kel-Tec P-32 was a locked-breech design, using a tilting-barrel locking system. This locked breech system allows a very light slide. Coupled with the small polymer frame, it made for a very light little pistol. Some internal changes distinguish it from the original P-11 and P-40. The 32 does not have second-snap capability. To enhance slimness, the P-32 has an internal, rather than external, slide-lock. The single-column magazine gives the little pistol 7+1 capacity. The P-32 measures about 3-1/2 x 5, and has a 2-5/8 inch barrel.

Shall we include it in our consideration? Well, perhaps it does not exactly fit in with the other, more powerful, examples of this new breed, but it is certainly hard to ignore.

So these three pistols (all right, perhaps four pistols) have established a new niche in the firearms world.

Designed for personal protection and concealed carry by ordinary citizens, they made no pretense of being intended for military or police contracts. However, their small size, combined with satisfactory power, accuracy and reliability, have led some police officers to select them as personal firearms for off-duty carry.

True, these three small companies were not the first to offer polymer frames, or even small size. However, they put polymer frames, subcompact size and desirable calibers together and sold reliable pistols at prices affordable for ordinary people. They have carved out a new niche.

This new breed of personal pistols has had an influence on the entire firearms industry. In the past few years, other manufacturers have added polymer frames, smaller sizes, slimmer pistols and reduced-price offerings to their lines.

We are fortunate that the pioneers of this new breed were offered, and fortunate indeed to have been able to watch the development of this useful new category. ●

Built For The Street!

by Dave Workman

New S&W Model 66 variation has features that make it a great choice for personal defense

FOR SEVERAL YEARS before switching almost exclusively to a custom-built 45 Auto (see HANDGUNS 2001), one of my primary personal defense guns was a handsomely blued Smith & Wesson Model 19 Combat Magnum with a round butt and that wicked-looking 2.5-inch barrel.

Fired under low light conditions, that revolver would not only put its six 357 Magnum 125-grain JHPs into a target, but the muzzle flash would barbecue anything within ten feet! It rode with me on some interesting adventures in a Bianchi pancake holster or a Safariland upside-down shoulder rig, accompanied by a couple of HKS speedloaders. For a street sixgun, this one was, and still is, a winner.

A bit later on, S&W cooked up a stainless steel version of that famous K-frame and called it the Model 66, again with the 2.5-inch tube and familiar ramp front sight. It was just as good, but not better. Same caliber. Same smooth action. Same six rounds. Same barrel length.

This year, however, those clever gents at S&W have done something to spruce up the Model 66 that makes it perhaps the best of the genré, for a couple of reasons. It's got a 3-inch barrel (*not exactly a new option*) and it wears a Hi-Viz fiber optic front sight that lights up your sight picture remarkably well (*this is new!*). Folks who have been waiting for a straight-from-the-box street wheelgun that can easily do double duty in the woods for hunters, fishermen, hikers and backpackers–this may be your lucky day.

Smith & Wesson's Ken Jorgensen said this new Model 66-5 really caught his attention, same as mine. After my shooting session was completed, we traded notes in a long-distance conversation and it was obvious that he considered the fiber optic sight something special.

Sum Of Its Components

To really appreciate why this six-shooter stands apart from the crowd, one needs to take a close look at it, for the Model 66-5 is the sum of its components.

Like its predecessors, this one is built from stainless steel, from the butt to the muzzle. It wears a rear click-adjustable sight featuring a "V"-notch rear blade, while that front sight by Hi-Viz has its fiber optic component held firmly in its own steel frame. When even the slightest light hits that sight, it glows a brilliant green.

A couple of years ago, I did a story on various night sights for the HANDGUNS 2000 annual, and part of my research included snooping out the fiber optic alternatives to tritium. Hi-Viz dominates that market, and this new model definitely measures up to anything I could have recommended then, and even now. It is held into the ramp by a single pin. That 3-inch barrel has a cylinder pin shroud on the bottom, and full-length serrations from the frame to the front sight ramp.

Barrel-to-frame fit is excellent, and there is no visible difference in the tone of the brushed satin finish, as sometimes happens with components that are finished separately, then assembled. Finish on the barrel and frame top is bead blasted.

The crane swings the cylinder up smoothly and locks up tight in the traditional S&W fashion. This gun's cylinder is fluted, and the chambers look to have been carefully polished. It has a smooth combat trigger and semi-wide hammer spur with cut checkering. Both hammer and trigger have a case-hardened finish. The frame-mounted firing pin rebounds back into the frame after each shot, as the hammer also rebounds.

Mating of the side plate to the right side of the frame is second to

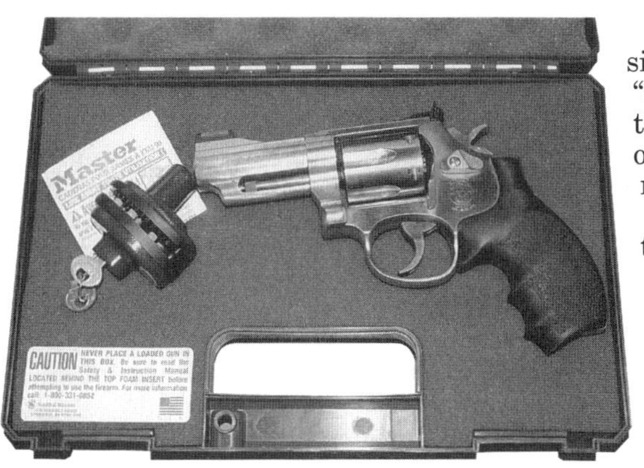

Smith & Wesson delivers its Model 66-5 in a lockable hard box with ample padding and a Master keyed trigger lock. In all, a great package.

none. Fit is as good as, or better, than other S&W revolvers I've used, and that's saying a lot. Over the years, I've seen only one 'Smith wheelgun where there was just a slight flaw in the sideplate, and it didn't have any adverse effect on this gun's ability to function. That's why I've kept it for over 20 years.

Pick up the Model 66-5 and you will be wrapping your palm around a jet-black finger-groove Hogue Monogrip that mates perfectly with the round butt frame, and is handsomely offset against the brushed stainless finish.

This Hogue grip has the S&W logo molded into the top on both sides, and Hogue's trademark "stippled" bumpy surface allows the shooter to keep a firm hold on this gun, even under the recoil of a full-house 357 load.

As to the particular grip on this pistol, I wasn't too keen on it, because it felt a little small to me, and that may be due to the finger groove profile. I don't care for finger-groove grips because they're a "one size fits all" answer to a problem that isn't that easily solved because there are lots of hands out there, of many different sizes. Mine is one of them. If I were to own this wheelgun, switching the grip– probably to another Hogue or Pachmayr–would be my first priority.

As for the action, it is typically Smith & Wesson smooth. The double-action stroke is a little stiff, but not beyond what I would expect from a brand new gun. Single action letoff is sharp and crisp, with no creep that I could discern and, during my test, I had lots of opportunity to feel that trigger break.

On the subject of triggers: like all S&W pistols, this one comes with a Master trigger lock of the keyed variety. Of all these locks, the keyed models are my favorite. Of course, they are not a panacea to firearms accidents, but if this addition to the package satisfies some anti-gunner –hey, I'm all for it! Besides, these trigger locks do provide a measure of gun safety for people who cannot afford a gun safe. Add to that the plastic gun boxes now supplied by S&W are padlock-lockable and you ve got more security than 90 percent of the shooting public.

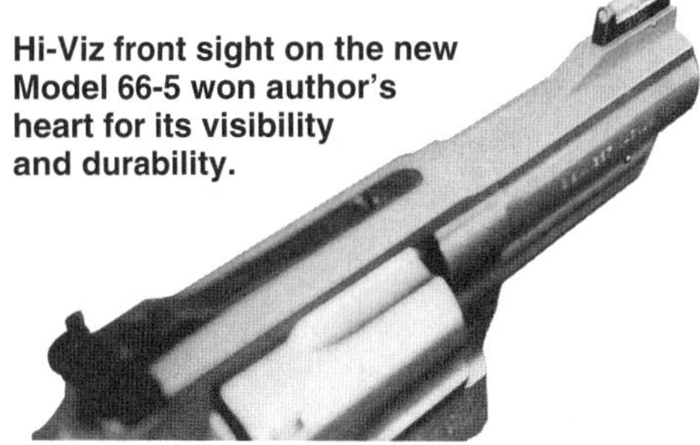
Hi-Viz front sight on the new Model 66-5 won author's heart for its visibility and durability.

Packing The 66-5

What makes a handgun good for personal protection, off-duty law enforcement, and trail carry is what I call its "pack-ability." Translation: How easy is it to carry this piece, in a good leather or nylon holster? How well does it ride on the hip? Is it cumbersome? Is it awkward? Can it be drawn fast and smoothly?

The textbook example of a scenario that just does not fit the gun would be putting a Desert Eagle in an ankle holster. (*Now watch Hollywood come up with this in the next action flick.*)

The quick answer is that the Model 66-5 is a hands-down winner. Thanks to that additional half-inch on the front end, this revolver seems better balanced in the hand than my personal Model 19.

How would I carry it? Go with a strong-side belt holster of the thumb-break variety, and leather would be my first choice simply because I like it as a holster material. However, for the purpose of this evaluation, I tried it in a nylon Uncle Mike's rig, and it worked out quite well.

Whether your choice is a high-ride or a pancake model, the belt holster is my best recommendation. There's enough of the gun's weight, and bearing surface, below the vertical center of gravity to keep this gun well-balanced, rather than making it too heavy either below the belt line, or in the grip area where it might tend to lean away from the body - thus *printing* on jacket, vest or open shirt worn to conceal the gun.

As a practical gun for carry, that's not even a serious subject for debate. The Model 66-5 is an out-

New S&W wheelgun (*top*) with 3-inch barrel compared to author's Model 19 with 2.5-inch tube and Pachmayr grips. Workman liked that longer barrel.

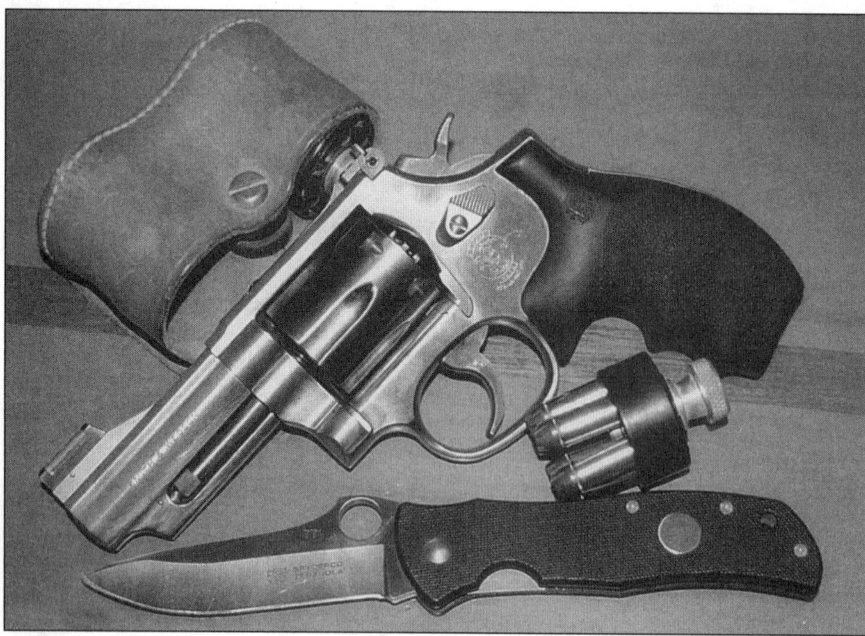

Winning combination in any close encounter of the worst kind: S&W's Model 66-5, HKS speedloaders carrying 357 Magnum cartridges in a well-used Bianchi carrier, and Spyderco's Terzuola knife.

standing choice for anyone who prefers a wheelgun to a semi-auto and, in many cases, it is far more practical for novices because there are fewer moving parts, it is simpler to operate, and it shoots pretty good, too. (More about that in a minute.)

It is superbly versatile due to the variety of ammunition out there, from lead wadcutters to frangibles in both 38 Special and 357 Magnum.

For veteran *pistoleros*, the Model 66-5 is going to be hard to resist, like eating only one potato chip. Anybody who has ever done serious work with a handgun is going to find it very difficult to not like this gun. It is well-built, it feels good in the hand thanks to its heft and, when the trigger is squeezed, it goes BANG! every time. Pick it up, and you just have to shoot it. Moreover, that is exactly what I did!

Home On The Range

It must be noted for the sake of accuracy that a lot of short-barreled handguns chambered in 357 Magnum are made to be carried a lot and fired very seldom. Happy to note that the Model 66-5 isn't one of them. This is one sturdy K-frame, and my guess is that it will take a heap of shooting.

I expected to get a little jolt from the selection of Plus-P ammo in 38 Special, and a good rap from the assorted 357 Magnums. I was happily surprised, as recoil was

Specifications: Smith & Wesson Model 66-5

Manufacturer:
Smith & Wesson
2100 Roosevelt Avenue
P.O. Box 2208
Springfield, MA 01102-2208
(413) 781-8300

Model: 66-5

Barrel Length: 3.2 inches

Caliber: 38 Special/357 Magnum

Capacity: Six rounds

Sights: Hi-Viz green dot fiber optic front, click-adjustable V-notch rear

Weight (empty): 37 ounces

OAL: 8 inches

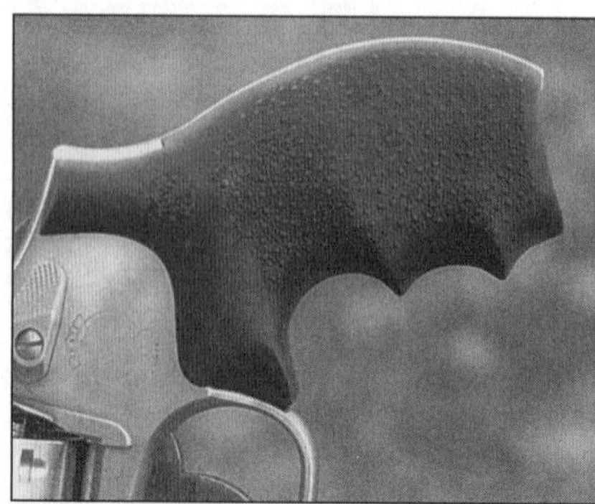

Hogue Bantam rubber one-piece grip was not author's favorite, due to finger groove profile. However, it's stippled surface and compact profile made it good for concealed carry.

not out of the realm of manageability. For sure, when packing full-house magnum loads in this wheelgun, you are definitely going to know it when the gun goes off. However, it will not go flying out of your hand.

I began the test with an assortment of 38 Special rounds, ranging from the relatively anemic 158-grain roundnose lead Blazer from CCI, to the sizzling 110-grainer from Cor-Bon. At a range of 15 yards, I shot groups with a spread that ranged from just over 2.5 inches to a spread of nearly 4.5 inches, the latter which I blame solely on myself for wobbling on the bag as the pistol went off.

Otherwise, my groups at 15 yards on a Birchwood-Casey Shoot'N*C targets averaged about 3 inches, and that could easily be brought down with ample practice and a determination of just which round works best through a particular specimen of this model series.

I immediately fell in love with that front sight. It delivered a sharp front sight image that glowed unmistakably green under less-than-ideal Pacific Northwest cloud cover. (*Everything you've read about a drought and dry winter up in the Pac-N'west earlier this year must be taken with a grain of salt. We did have some beautiful days. For some reason I cannot explain, my range trips seemed to coincide with clouds and, on one occasion, a downpour that made me miserable, but didn t do a thing to that stainless steel sixgun other than just make it wet.*)

So much for your weather report. I worked through a laundry list of 38 Specials that came from the "usual suspects" including Cor-Bon, Speer/Lawman, CCI/Blazer, Triton, Hornady, PMC, Remington and Winchester. As the brass began piling up around my feet, the revolver became more familiar to my hand and, despite the aforementioned grip problem, I got to the point of overlooking that one drawback, and just making that six-shooter hum.

Of all the loads, my test gun seemed to like the Hornady 140-grainer and Cor-Bon 158-grain lead hollowpoint best. I shot groups of slightly over two inches at 15 yards with both those rounds, so it appears that three-inch tube likes heavier bullets. I switched over to the 357 Magnums, and things began to get interesting.

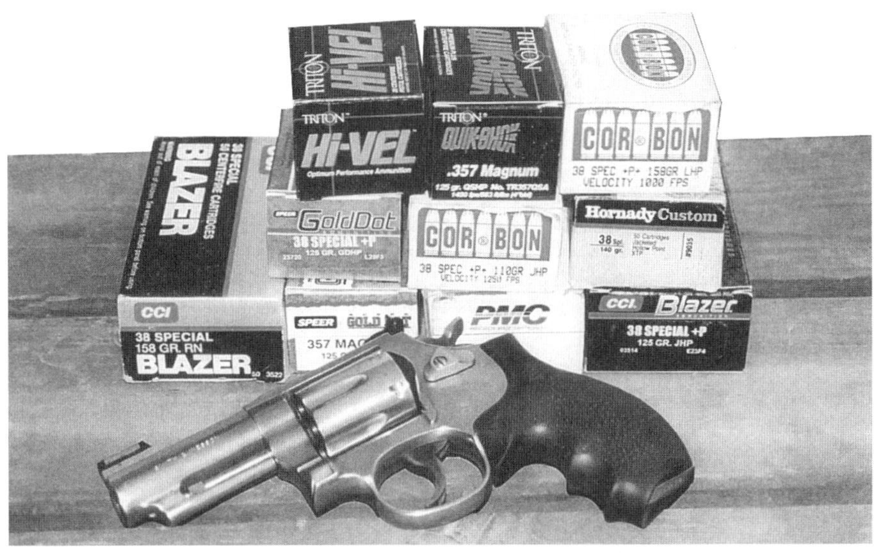

An assortment of ammunition went downrange during the test, and this is just a sampling. The Model 66-5 is versatile because of all the 38 Special and 357 Magnum loads on the market.

Performance Review: Smith & Wesson Model 66-5

Ammo Brand	Bullet & Cartridge	Velocity	Group @ 10yards
Speer Gold Dot	125 JHP / 38 Special +P	957.2	2.5
CCI/Blazer	158 RNL / 38 Special	732.3	3.0
Cor-Bon	110 JHP/ 38 Special	1238	2.5
Cor-Bon	158 LHP / 38 Special	1058	2.5
Triton Hi-Vel	110 JHP / 38 Special	1066	3.4
CCI / Blazer	125 JHP / 38 Special	971.3	4.0
Hornady	140 XTP / 38 Special	763.3	2.0
Speer Gold Dot	125 JHP / 357 Magnum	1141	3.0
Triton Hi-Vel	125JHP/357 Magnum	1218	3.5
Triton Quik-Shot	125JHP/357 Magnum	1273	3.5

Author found gun to shoot low out of the box. Here's his first results with a mix of Speer, Hornady, Triton ammunition.

There's a 2.5-inch group fired offhand from 10 yards, with a half-and-half load of Cor-Bon 158-grain LHP and Hornady 140-grain XTP rounds in 38 Special.

Even out of a 3-inch tube, velocity was impressive, ranging upwards from about 1,140 fps to well over 1,250 fps and one thing I noticed from the outset is that, out of the box, the Model 66-5 shot low. In some cases, horribly low. To wring out the gun before I got down to the real business of testing, I function-fired it and found the bullet impact at 15 yards to be three inches below point of aim. I was not terribly impressed, but simply adjusting the sights solves this dilemma. Windage was pretty much dead-on, and any flyers I just blamed on myself because, for the most part, the revolver put its shots in a ragged vertical string when I was doing my part. When I wasn't, the revolver–predictably–was all over the paper.

Firing from both one- and two-hand holds without a rest, at seven and ten yards, the Model 66-5 delivered round after round into the black, leaving me convinced that in a sudden emergency, any handgunner armed with this piece would be pretty well equipped.

Of the magnum loads, the one this gun seemed to prefer slightly over the others was Speer's Gold Dot 125-grainer. I punched a three-inch group with it at 15 yards initially, and during subsequent shooting, put together a handful of multiple-round one-holers that were pretty convincing. Like the commercials say, "your mileage may vary," but so far as this writer is concerned, it looks like the Gold Dots would probably be my first choice, followed rather closely by the Triton Hi-Vel and Hornady XTP, though in all honesty, any of the 357 factory fodder I chambered in this gun delivered impressive accuracy that would translate to gunfight survival, and small game or varmint mortality.

Of course, individual specimens of this model may perform better with a different round, so each shooter will simply have to experiment. I anticipate you will find the right solution, and enjoy plenty of range time in the process.

Bottom line on this wheelgun is that it is a great little investment, and for the suggested retail price, you are getting a very good package. •

According to defensive firearms theory, the "snubnose 38" should have long since been relegated to the gun museums. Instead, it remains among the most popular real-world carry guns.

The first defining "snubby" of the 20th century was this 1927 vintage Colt Detective Special...

... the second was the S&W Chiefs Special (1950 first model shown)...

WHY SNUBBIES WON'T DIE

by Massad Ayoob

COPS CALL IT simply "the two-inch," after the length of its barrel. Fiction writers have called them "snub-nose 38s," and so therefore does much of the populace. Another term was "belly gun," explained variously as *"you carry it next to your belly"* or *"it's so inaccurate, you have to shove it in the other guy's belly to hit him with it."* Most who own one just call it "the snubby."

This gun's time in America touches three centuries. It was with us for most of the cowboy years as a solid-frame "bulldog" or a top-break; the best of the latter probably being the S&W Safety Hammerless of the late 1870s. The defining small-frame 38 Special was introduced by Colt in 1927, and it was simply a two-inch barrel version of their Police Positive revolver in the same chambering. They called it the Detective Special, and it so typified the breed that for many *"detective special"* became a generic, trademark-violating term for the entire breed, like "frigidaire" and "kleenex" and "scotch tape."

... and the one that shaped what may be the new paradigm was this S&W AirLite Ti, introduced in 1998.

Roughly 75 years later, the experts tell us these guns are obsolete. 380 autos are just as potent, some say, since the 38's ballistics become less "Special" out of a two-inch barrel. 9mm Parabellum and even 40 S&W autos, we are told, can now be had in size envelopes roughly as small and light as the snubby, and much more efficient in terms of both firepower and per-shot stopping power.

"Obsolete, inefficient, doomed to disappear..." That's what they said about large automobiles. Big vehicles and small revolvers have sur-

vived the prediction of their doom for the same two reasons: they are convenient, and they tend to keep their owners alive when they collide with potential death.

The Scope of the Snubby

Twenty years ago, the four-inch barrel service revolver was the standard American law enforcement weapon, and many thought the semiautomatic duty pistol was a radical, *avant garde* trend that wouldn't last. The snub-nose 38 was the second most common weapon in the law-enforcement armory. (A nine-officer department might have a 12-gauge pump gun in each of the three patrol cars used by the rotating shifts, but it was a good bet that at least eight out of those nine officers owned a 38 snub for off-duty and/or backup carry.)

Today, 90% or more of police officers carry auto pistols to work…but the 38 snub is still the second most common weapon in police work. The reason is the same as before. "*The future of the revolver in law enforcement is as a backup handgun and a convenient off duty gun, almost always in a short-barrel, lightweight format,*" says Bert DuVernay, Director of the Smith & Wesson Academy.

There are some thirty states, at this writing, that have adopted a "shall issue" policy for permits to carry concealed handguns. Many of them require licensees to qualify with the gun they're going to carry, or something similar. This has allowed firearms instructors in those states to keep tabs on what the newly-enfranchised citizens have chosen for street hardware. Though we live in the time of the finest compact semi-autos ever available, one of the most popular carry guns is the two-inch barrel 38 Special revolver. In some jurisdictions, it's the single most common gun listed on the licenses.

"Aha," scoff some gun buffs. "That just shows you that ordinary people don't know as much about guns as we do." Not exactly, sports fans. Some of the top gun experts I know carry 38 snubs at least part of the time as their primary armament. Virtually all of them have snubs for backup.

"Hogwash," cry the hi-tech handgun buffs. "I've learned from the likes of John Farnam, Manny Kapelsohn, Chuck Taylor, and Jim Wilson. They carry manly, modern automatics." That's right to a point, but you haven't checked their ankles or jacket pockets lately, have you? I hang with these guys, have roomed with three of the four of them at matches or seminars and, to a man, they back up their Glocks, 1911s and whatnot with 38 snubs. John and Manny favor the lightweight Smiths with shrouded hammers, and while you might find Wilson without his Colt 45 on quiet days, you'll never find him without at least his Model 640 Centennial 38 in his front pants pocket. Taylor is partial to a de-horned S&W Model 12 Airweight for such purposes. Some other credentialed experts – Roy Huntington, Paul Scarlata, and Leroy Thompson to name three – have been known to carry that same six-shot Model 12 as a primary defense gun. A generation earlier, Jeff Cooper mentioned in his classic book "*Cooper on Handguns*" that he armed his lovely wife Janelle with a 2-inch S&W five-shot 38 Special, and used one himself when he had to carry under a snug-fitting business suit.

Let's look at a couple of other professionals. Walt Rauch has a hard-bitten background with the Secret Service and the Philadelphia Warrant Squad, and has been in more than his share of armed encounters. You'll generally find him carrying either a 1911 or a Glock in 10mm or 45 ACP. On the quietest days, or in the most politically-sensitive environments, you might find him without those guns…but not without one of his "hammerless" Smith 38s, which the rest of the time serves him as backup.

I remember a day at poolside relaxing after the Bianchi Cup with Evan Marshall and

Light, lighter, lightest. S&W Centennial 38 Specials, *from top:* all-steel Model 640 (20 oz.), aluminum-frame Airweight Model 442 (15 oz.) and AirLite Titanium (10.8 oz.).

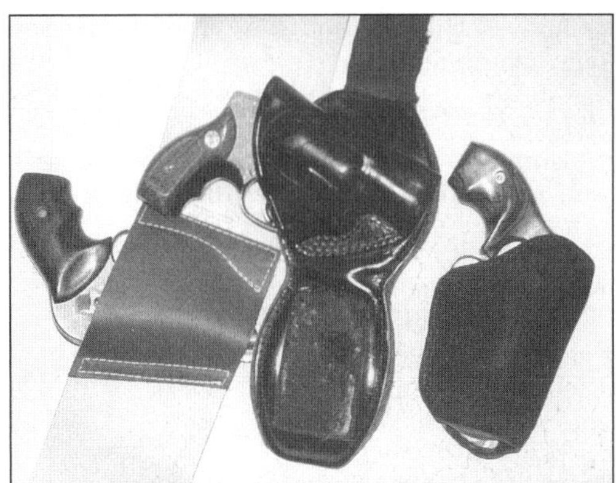

Ayoob explains in the article why rounded grip-frames of revolvers give faster draws from belly bands (S&W M/38 shown in Guardian brand), ankle holsters (M/640 shown in Alessi) and pocket holsters (M/342 shown in new Safariland).

The Crimson Trace LaserGrip fits the J-frame to the hand well, and gives another useful aiming option. *Top*, brushed nickel Model 442 AirWeight; *below*, AirLite Ti, both by S&W.

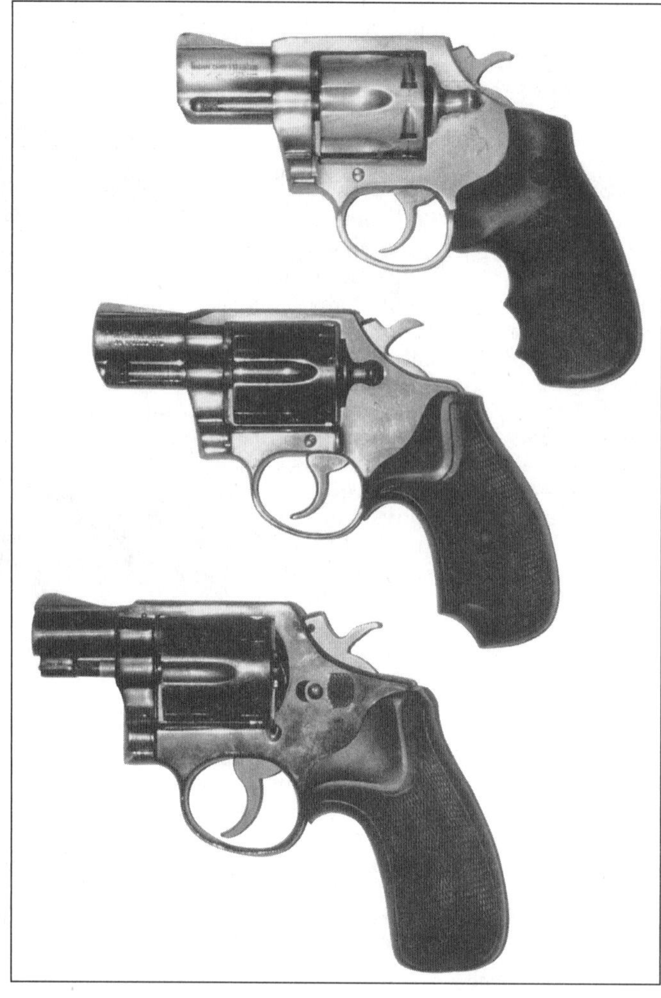

When concealment needs allow, hand-filling grips give maximum control of your hot-loaded snub. *From top*, Colt 357 Magnum carry with latest Hogues, and Pachmayr Compacs on Colt Detective Special (*center*) and S&W Model 12 Airweight. All these 2-inch guns are six-shooters.

some other industry professionals. One of them, knowing Evan's long history and multiple gunfights as a Detroit cop, asked him what the one best carry gun was. Evan replied, "*S&W Bodyguard Airweight 38.*" The man was shocked, because he knew Evan was a fan of 41 and 357 Magnums, and asked why. "*Because you can always have it with you,*" answered Evan. "*I've got mine on now.*" He had been sunbathing next to the hotel pool, and was wearing only swim trunks.

These professionals learned the hard way what the new shooters intuited in checking out their options at the gun shop. The 38 revolver can be loaded to adequate power with modern ammunition, is utterly reliable, is easy to load, unload and draw–and can be comfortably carried in light clothing in hot weather without anyone noticing.

The "Always" Factor

Sheriff Jim Wilson calls his 38 snub his "always gun" because he *always* has it on. When his 45 Government Model or his Combat Magnum is locked away at home, his little 38 will always be within reach. It's a reality he learned in a lifetime of doing dangerous work under the hot Texas sun.

My wife Dorothy has been licensed to carry for more than 30 years. She has her share of handgun trophies and is a shark with a 1911 45. She also can't fit that gun into a female executive wardrobe. I've given her enough high-tech autos to outfit a small police department. Her response has ranged from "*that's nice, dear*" to actually carrying one for a few days. Then, invariably, she goes back to her two-inch Colt 38. In a shoulder holster under her blazer or pants-suit jacket, or in a coat pocket in cooler weather, it's *there*.

I'm happy. Your mom and mine were right when they said, "A bird in the hand beats two in the bush." My wife is one mom who will add, "A 38 where you can reach it beats a 45 somewhere else." She speaks for a helluva lot of people who carry guns.

What A Snubby Can Do

An adult lifetime of studying gunfights tells me Evan Marshall is right: a 158-grain lead 38 Special +P hollowpoint–even out of a two-inch barrel revolver–hits with about the same fight-stopping authority as the legendary "GI hardball" round of the "Army 45." The reason this load works best out of short-barrel guns is that, being all-lead, it has no tough copper jacket to peel back, and

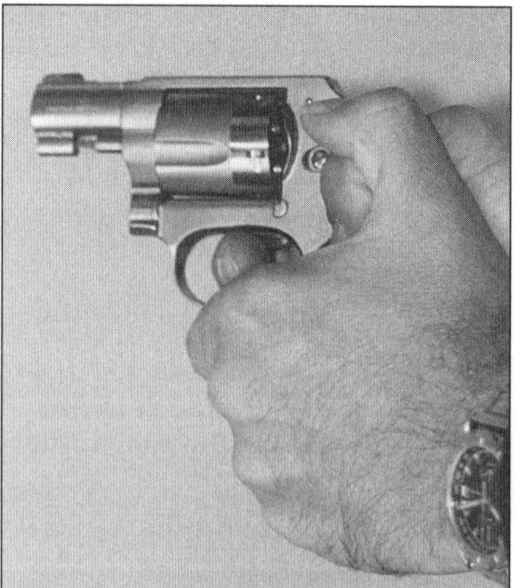

Author's preferred grasp of "belly gun" is shown on this 940. Both hands are in crush grip, firing hand thumb curled down for maximum strength, support thumb locked over it to bond hands together.

will usually open up at least somewhat even if heavy clothing is in the way, and even with velocity reduced by a short barrel.

A shroud-hammer 38 will fire its entire payload through a coat pocket, a handy place to have your gun (*with your hand on it, finger clear of the trigger guard of course)* when you're walking through a city parking lot after midnight. Any auto pistol will jam on the first shot if fired that way.

If you've carried both small revolvers and small autos in pockets, ankle holsters and belly-bands as I have for decades, you know why the revolver rules in those environments. An ankle holster holds the gun just a few inches off the ground where every step kicks dust up on it. Only a few "mil-spec" compact autos like the baby Glocks, Kahrs, and Kel-Tec P-11s can function when they're gritted up like that, but any good revolver will go six for six or five for five even if it's ***coated*** with dust. Pockets get filled with lint, etc. I've run across cases from Florida to Los Angeles where the good guy pulled a 380 from an ankle holster and had it jam after a shot or two. I've *never* seen that with a quality 38 snub.

Is the gun in your trouser pocket? If the pants fit you at all well, the gun will be held tight against your body. With the flat-sided auto, your fingers have to claw to get hold of it. The rounded grip shape of the small-frame revolver, on the other hand, guides your hand right into grasp-and-draw position. The same is true with belly-band holsters, and groin holsters like the popular Thunderwear. The same is true of some ankle holsters, too.

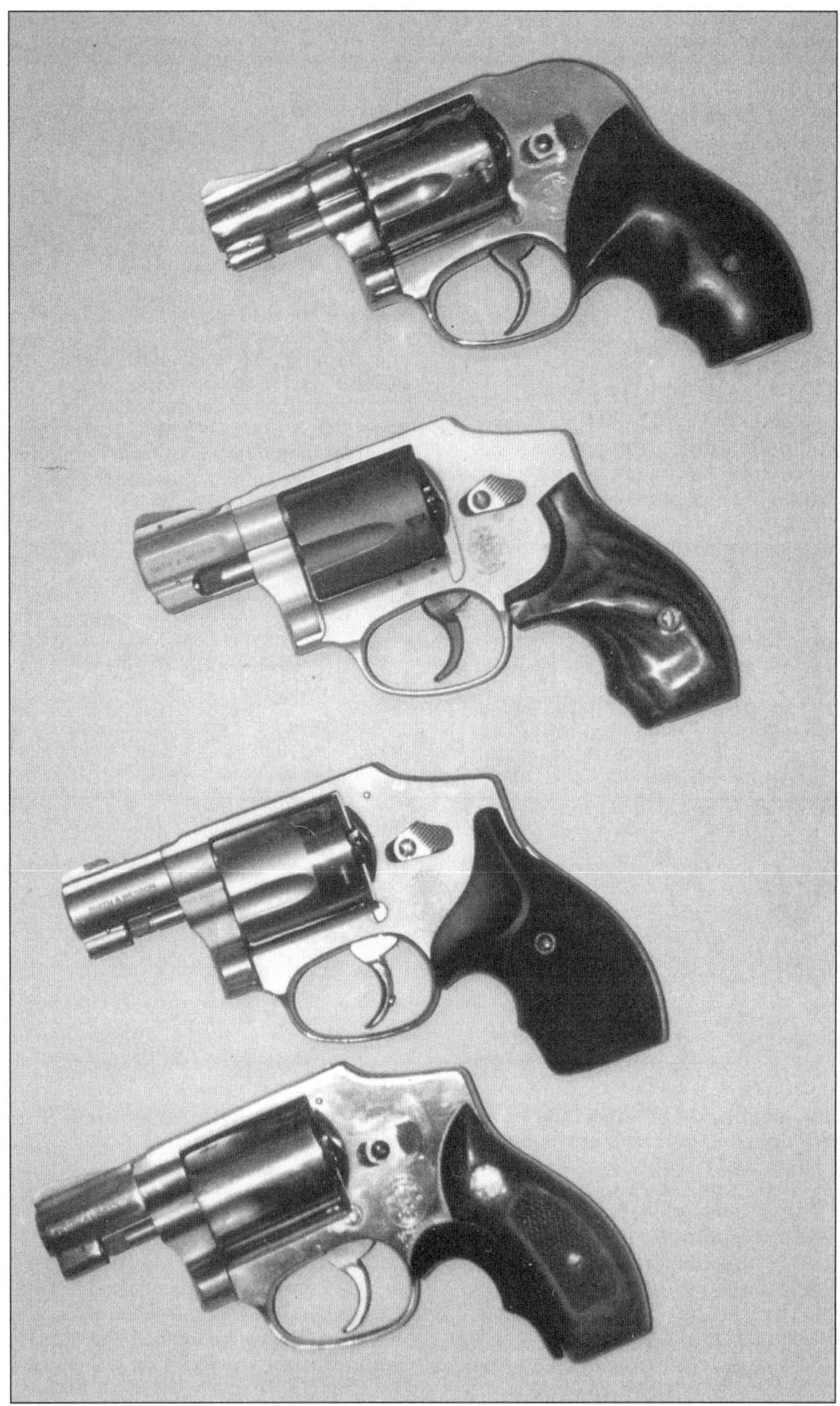

Compromise grips: maximum concealment with adequate control, all on J-frame S&Ws. *From top*, "secret service" from Eagle Grips on M/38; S&W's own laminated style on M/340; Uncle Mike's Boot grips on M/940 9mm; and (absolute minimum) standard Chiefs Special grips with Tyler grip adapter on M/640.

Retention Factor

A major anti-gun argument is, "If you carry a gun, the bad guy will get it away from you and shoot you with it." When the poison is disarming, the antidote is handgun retention, a concept long ago refined and proven by a master martial artist and police trainer named Jim Lindell in Kansas City, Missouri. Jim taught me his system in the mid-1970s, certified me to teach it in 1980, and certified me to train other instructors in it in 1990. That's a whole lot of full-power struggles for guns in the training environment, folks, and you learn some things there.

One thing I learned was that the toughest gun to take away from its legitimate owner is the snub-nose 38. A tiny automatic? The attacker doesn't have much to grab, but the good guy doesn't have much to hang onto, so it's a wash. But if there's any grip to the short-barrel revolver at all, most of the leverage is with the legitimate holder as the assailant struggles to get a purchase on that stubby barrel. His hand will probably roll over the muzzle. If you pull the trigger, you're probably dealing with a one-armed man, and your chances of winning the fight for your gun just got better still.

When carried as a backup gun, the 38 snub is also a "safety net" against a criminal disarm. In Buffalo, a criminal had dislocated a security guard's arm and knocked his service revolver to the sidewalk. As the felon reached for the gun, the guard drew his backup Charter Arms Undercover two-inch 38 and killed the attacker with a single shot. In Michigan, a suspect was overpowering a cop and pulling his 41 Magnum out of his holster when the officer drew his S&W Bodyguard Airweight from a hip pocket with his free hand, and fired the shot that saved his life and ended that of the would-be copkiller.

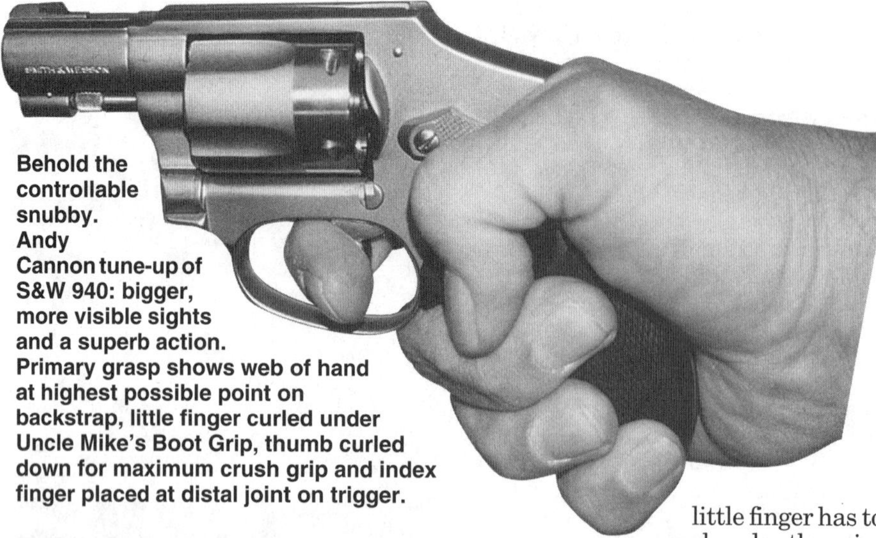

Behold the controllable snubby. Andy Cannon tune-up of S&W 940: bigger, more visible sights and a superb action. Primary grasp shows web of hand at highest possible point on backstrap, little finger curled under Uncle Mike's Boot Grip, thumb curled down for maximum crush grip and index finger placed at distal joint on trigger.

Getting the Most from the Belly Gun

"Belly guns" aren't exactly famous for accuracy. This is because they have a short sight radius and fairly small grips. The answer is simple: learn to aim the little thing, and have grips that give you a decent hold.

158-grain lead semi-wadcutter hollow-point +P is author's choice for ammo in 38 Special snub. Recoil is sharp, but impact on target equals GI 45 ball.

These guns will usually be used at close range. I practice a lot with the 'StressPoint Index', a sight picture in which the front sight is sitting above the rear sight instead of down in the notch. It gives you hits in a heart-size group from seven yards and closer and, up by itself, that little front sight becomes easy to see in dim light and stress situations. If you still can't get a sight picture, slap on a pair of LaserGrips. Crimson Trace makes this neat little product for small-frame, round-butt S&W, Taurus and Ruger revolvers. Your gun hand in normal grasp activates the button that sends the red dot to the target.

There are lots of after-market grips that improve your hold on these little guns. The big thing you want is something that will give you firm enough a grasp to keep the revolver from shifting in your hand when the hard recoil hits. For a gun that's going to be carried in a belt or shoulder holster, or kept in a lockbox, by all means get Pachmayr Compac grips: they give "big gun" feel and control, splendid leverage for weapon retention, and recoil absorption that has to be felt to be believed, particularly in their Decelerator variation. Hogue now offers some similar after-market grips.

For deep concealment, the above grips will get in the way. If hiding the gun thoroughly is the mission, you can't beat the small, finger-grooved grips developed by Craig Spegel. The little finger has to curl under the grip-frame, but that still leaves you with a surprisingly strong hold, and concealment is maximized. This design is used in the excellent Uncle Mike's Boot Grips that S&W furnishes now from the factory, and Eagle Grips has a similar design in wood that they call "secret service," in small letters.

Use a hard, crush grip to stabilize the firing platform. Curl your gun hand thumb down for maximum strength of grasp. If at all possible, put your support hand to work in the same max-force grip. Curl the support thumb over the firing thumb, to bond the hands together and keep them from separating when the recoil hits. The more the gun jolts in recoil, the more important it will be to get your upper body weight forward into the gun as you take your defensive stance.

There are numerous recoil- and muzzle jump-reducing options available, but most of them involve jets of burning gunpowder gases being directed upwards. If you have to fire with the snubby close to your body, these will be going right up into your face and eyes. You don't need me to tell you how quickly that can pass the point of diminishing returns.

A quality 38 snub is accurate. My wife's pet Detective Special once gave me six hits for six shots on a Colt silhouette target at 100 yards. This was not a fluke. In the third-level class at my school, Lethal Force Institute, we show students how to hit man-size targets at 100 yards with their carry guns. One attendee, Vince Dragone, shot the entire course with his daily carry gun, an Airweight Bodyguard S&W snub-nose. I don't think he missed the silhouette once.

The trick is to know where it shoots. Be sure the sights are true.

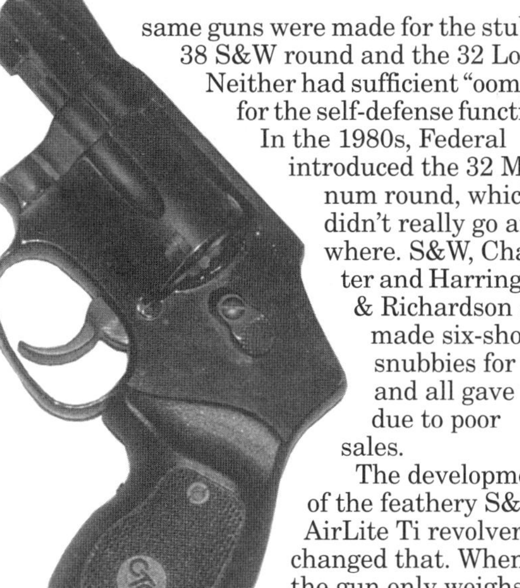

AirLite Ti, (*left*, at 10.8 ounces in Spegel Boot Grips) vs. Airweight (*right*, at 15 ounces with Crimson Trace LaserGrips). For balance of "*shootability* and *portability*," author favors the Airweight.

Then stabilize the gun and *smoooothly* roll that double-action trigger straight back.

Loading the 38 Special Snubby

As noted, that 158-grain lead semi-wadcutter hollow-point round at +P velocity seems to have the best record on the real-world streets, when you put all the accounts together. However, it's recoil is vicious in a small-frame gun, so much so that in the 11-ounce S&W Titanium, it is expressly forbidden. The reason is, the violent recoil jerks lead bullets loose from the mouths of their cases, bringing them forward enough to block the cylinder's rotation. Jacketed bullets, being more tightly crimped, don't have that problem.

In a Titanium gun, I like the fast Triton Quik-Shok 110 grain. It's a +P+ load, though, and still has lots of rearward momentum. If kick is a problem, the best low-recoil round I've seen is the Federal Nyclad Chief Special load, a 125-grain lead hollow point at sedate velocity with a soft Nylon coating. This bullet always seems to open, though the bullet is not as dynamic in tissue as the 158-grain lead +P.

There are, of course, other cartridges. Before there were 38 Special snubs, what were essentially the same guns were made for the stubby 38 S&W round and the 32 Long. Neither had sufficient "oomph" for the self-defense function. In the 1980s, Federal introduced the 32 Magnum round, which didn't really go anywhere. S&W, Charter and Harrington & Richardson all made six-shot snubbies for it–and all gave up due to poor sales.

The development of the feathery S&W AirLite Ti revolvers changed that. When the gun only weighs ten or eleven ounces, recoil of 38 Special rounds becomes stout, and +P is absolutely vicious. Gun expert Charlie Petty made the point that six rounds of 32 Mag that you can hit with beat heck out of five rounds of 38 +P that makes you flinch so badly that you'll miss. Soon, S&W was back happily making AirLite 32 Magnums that actually *sold*, and they were joined by Taurus, with their Ultra-Lite configuration. You can't argue with the logic.

The power has also gone upward, a trend that began when I convinced Bill Ruger to make his rugged little five-shot 38 snub for the 357 Magnum cartridge. S&W followed with five-shot J-frames, and soon Taurus introduced their similar Model 605. Colt's short-lived Magnum Carry was the Detective Special rendered as a six-shot 357, and it was an excellent gun whose loss is much lamented. The others are still with us, and more: S&W has recently introduced an 11-ounce 357 Magnum that is unequaled for power per ounce, but whose recoil makes it something close to a torture device in training.

Find a balance. For this writer, having shot extensively with the all-steel S&W Model 640 (20 ounces), the Airweight Model 442 (15 ounces), and the AirLite Ti (10.8 ounces), I split the difference between *shootability* and *portability*–and usually carry the Airweight as my backup 38. But each individual has to decide.

These guns are timeless. The Detective Special defined the concept in 1927. S&W redefined it as a smaller package, a five-shot 38 Special on a 32 frame, with their Chiefs Special introduced in 1950. The same firm may have given us the snubby of the 21st century with their AirLite of 1998.

The reason there are so many choices is because so many good people, cops and law-abiding armed citizens alike, are still buying these small, handy revolvers in droves.

Obsolete? On their way out? Not hardly. •

With 10+1 9mm rounds when fully loaded, this little Glock 26 is roughly the size and weight of a steel snubby, easier to shoot fast and straight, with as many rounds as a Detective Special and a Chiefs Special combined. Yet, author maintains, there are situations where the revolver has the advantage.

Both the 32 and 380 ACP versions of the Guardian are furnished with this zippered carrying case, with waistband clip, produced by De Santis Holster & Leather Goods. The available finger rest grip (*shown*) was found handy by the author, who has rather large hands. Non-finger rest (*flat-bottom*) grips are available as well.

NORTH AMERICAN ARMS has built its name and reputation by producing quality 22 rimfire mini-revolvers known for being "convenient, reliable and effective." The revolver line is popular among civilian and law enforcement gun buyers as a second and, in some cases, a third backup–as easy to deploy as to conceal.

The firm expanded its offerings in the mini-handgun market several years ago with the 1998 debut of the Guardian, a 6+1 capacity, high-grade autoloading pocket pistol designed to capitalize on the growing popularity of 32 ACP pocket pistols. Now the gun maker has gone one step further with the introduction of a new Guardian chambered for the more potent 380 ACP cartridge, resulting in perhaps the ideal combination of small size and greater stopping power.

The advent of the federal 1994 Crime Law,.which mandated a maximum 10-round cartridge capacity for handguns, has resulted in significant changes in the types of handguns available on the market. The trend in the handgun-manufacturing sector (since the passage of the Crime Law) has been to develop products that pack the most punch in the smallest possible package, since the selling point of high cartridge capacity has been removed.

There is demand for small, ultra-concealable pocket pistols that more than makes up for their chambered cartridges' ballistic shortcomings. This new 380 Guardian may offer the ideal combination of ultra-small size and ballistic performance to bridge the gap between small-caliber handguns unsuitable for self-defense and those chambered for more powerful cartridges–but in a larger, heavier format.

While small inexpensive pistols–chambered for such cartridges as the 22 LR, 25 ACP, 32 ACP and the 380 ACP–have been available for years, most are not considered suitable for serious self-defense use due to concerns regarding their durability and sensitivity to feeding all ammunition types (such pistols usually feed only ball ammunition reliably, not the more effective hollow-point rounds). There are some exceptions: the Walther PPK and PPK/S in 380 ACP, the Beretta Jetfire in 25 ACP, the Beretta Tomcat, Kel-Tec and the Seecamp pistols in 32 ACP.

The Guardian has a somewhat similar appearance to the Seecamp pistol, so a comparison of the two is in order. Both pistol designs have a fixed barrel and employ double recoil springs in a grooved, recessed chamber beneath the barrel, but the Guardian design has added a guide rod set in the center of the springs. Though a popular seller, the Seecamp pistol design is hampered (*in my opinion*) by its limited availability. The Seecamp also employs a European-style butt-mounted magazine catch/release requiring the magazine be manually pulled from the grip frame after the latch is released (*requiring the use of both hands*). This slows the reloading process considerably compared to the 1911-style frame-mounted button release employed on the North American Arms Guardian series. The Guardian's magazine release is designed to allow the magazine to drop free of the gun while the user's other hand readies a fresh magazine for insertion.

The Seecamp also was designed to function reliably with but a single brand of high-performance ammunition (the Winchester Silvertip). Due to most ball cartridges' greater length, they usually cannot be loaded into the Seecamp's magazine. In contrast, the Guardian pistols are designed to reliably handle all commercially-available 32 and 380 ammo.

The *NEW* North American Arms 380 ACP Guardian

From one of the most innovative and market-savvy handgun makers comes an upgraded, more potent pocket pistol

by Bob Hausman

Guardian Specs

The Guardian series is constructed largely of surgical-grade, 17-4 pH stainless steel, have fixed barrels (2.185 inches in the 32 ACP version and 2.5 inches in the 380 model). The magazine release is at the mid-point of the frame where it meets the bottom left corner of the triggerguard. This position permits fast magazine changes, and prevents accidentally releasing the magazine while deploying the pistol.

The Guardian pistol weighs (*unloaded*) 13.5 ounces in the 32 ACP model and 19 ounces in the 380 ACP version. Dimensions of the 32 ACP version are 4 1/4 inches overall length, width 7/8-inch, height 3 1/2 inches; with fixed low-profile sights and 6-round magazine capacity. Dimensions for the new 380 ACP model are 4 7/8 inches overall length, a width of 7/8-inch, height 3 1/2 inches; plus fixed low-profile sights and 6-round magazine.

While the new 380 ACP model is slightly longer, the most noticeable difference between it and the 32 ACP version is the weight; the 380 ACP Guardian is some 4.5 ounces heavier, unloaded. Depending on its application, the weight difference may be a deciding factor in choosing between the two chamberings for some Guardian pistol buyers. Though there is a weight increase, the balancing factor is that the 380 ACP cartridge offers better terminal ballistics than does the 32 ACP cartridge.

The new Guardian offers 6+1 rounds of upgraded (from the 32 ACP version) 380 ACP stopping power.

The choice is entirely up to the buyer, or one can do what the author did – acquire a pair of Guardian pistols, one in each chambering. That way, if one wants to travel light, you can pack the 32. When you are wearing heavier clothing, the 380 ACP may be the appropriate choice.

Both Guardian pistols were designed to represent the most effective balance of ballistic capability and package size. The trigger on both models operates in the double-action mode only. The pistols are furnished with a zippered nylon carrying case made by De Santis Holster & Leather Goods. Perfect for carrying in a briefcase or auto glove compartment, the case features an exterior metal clip, allowing attachment to trouser waistband or belt. The case interior includes a form-fitting nylon holster as well as a carrier for an extra magazine.

"*We have found there's great demand for products like the Guardian line,*" says Sandy Chisholm, North American Arms' president. "*Most of the other entries are greatly compromised by either availability or reliability, or both,*" he continues. "*We choose to invest a substantial amount of time and engineering resources to 'do it right' the first time. And to assure our customers and ourselves these are the finest pistols of their type available. I feel confident we've set a new standard for small, concealable pocket pistols and I invite the most critical comparisons between the Guardians and any other products on the market.*"

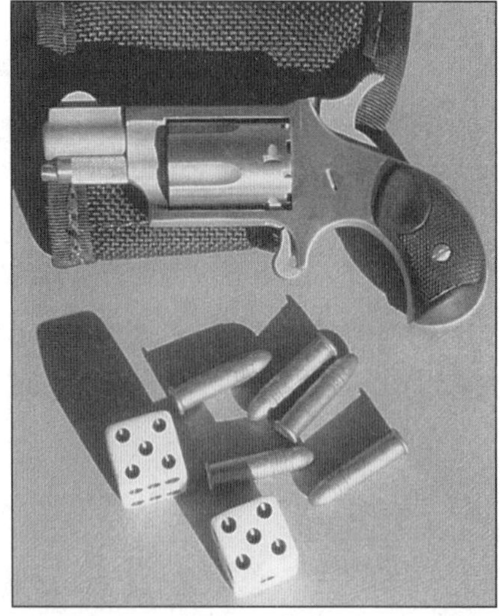

North American Arms' flagship product is its line of mini-revolvers reminiscent of the derringer pocket pistols carried by gamblers in the Old West.

Firing Test

During live-fire testing, the Guardian proved highly reliable, with a variety of various brands of 380 ACP ammunition tested. Accuracy was more than adequate for delivering hits, at 15 feet, within the center mass of life-sized silhouette targets. One novice woman shooter with small hands experienced some initial difficulty in pulling back the Guardian's trigger far enough to discharge the piece. This problem, though, was overcome by additional practice.

The sample pistol in 380 ACP did occasionally fail to completely eject the empty cartridge casing from the last round in the magazine. The 32 ACP Guardian also occasionally does the same thing. This is not a serious problem as the failure to eject completely occurs only on the last fired round and is easily cleared with a swipe of the hand. Otherwise, neither gun failed to fire when called upon to do so.

The Guardian pistols have no external manual safety lever and no grip safety. They are fired like a double-action revolver–by firmly and deliberately pulling the trigger. The average 10-pound trigger pull on production guns acts as a safety feature by ensuring the user will not cycle the trigger inadvertently. An external safety lever on such small pistols as the Guardian would be difficult to manipulate handily.

Disassembly

The Guardian series have one of the most straightforward and easy disassembly procedures of any similar product, in the author's experience. For normal cleaning, the Guardian is disassembled into four main components- frame, slide, mag-

Although possessing only rudimentary sights, the Guardian can be used as a plinker.

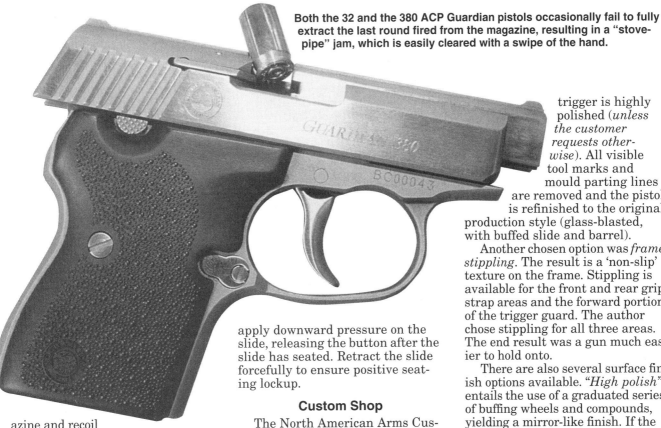

Both the 32 and the 380 ACP Guardian pistols occasionally fail to fully extract the last round fired from the magazine, resulting in a "stove-pipe" jam, which is easily cleared with a swipe of the hand.

azine and recoil spring assembly.

To field-strip for cleaning, first ensure the gun is not loaded. Next, remove the magazine; then depress and hold the spring-loaded slide release button, located above the right-side grip assembly beneath the serrations at the rear of the slide. Retract the slide one-half inch to clear the extractor from the chamber, and lift the slide up one inch at the rear to clear the barrel. Move the slide forward along the length of the barrel and remove it from the frame assembly (*at which point the recoil spring assembly will fall clear from the frame*).

To reassemble, insert the smaller-diameter inner recoil spring into the larger outer recoil spring and then insert the guide rod into the small end of the outer recoil spring. Insert the complete spring assembly into the grooved, recessed chamber beneath the barrel, spring guide rod forward. Position the slide atop the frame, with the forward bridge of the slide positioned in the channel beneath the barrel, capturing the recoil slide assembly behind it.

Move the slide a half-inch toward the rear and pull the trigger slightly, clearing the top of the hammer from beneath the firing pin retainer. Depress the slide release button and simultaneously apply downward pressure on the slide, releasing the button after the slide has seated. Retract the slide forcefully to ensure positive seating lockup.

Custom Shop

The North American Arms Custom Shop opened in the spring of 1999 to offer shooters a range of enhancements for their Guardian pistols. "*The Custom Shop gives our craftsmen a real opportunity to demonstrate their artistic engineering and machining skills*," notes Sandy Chisholm, the gunmaker's president. "*The Guardian in either caliber is the perfect platform for those interested in creating an heirloom or for adding performance options*."

This author recently decided to review the work of the facility by sending in his personally owned 32 ACP Guardian for performance enhancement modifications. The major work performed involved what the company calls the "*carry*" and "*stippling*" packages, as well as the application of a black coating to all exposed metal surfaces.

The "carry package" I chose was mainly a "*de-horning*" job, involved a comprehensive softening of all the crisp lines & sharp edges characteristic of a basic production gun. The most noticeable change was a generous 'breaking' and 'blending' of all 90-degree edges, particularly at the muzzle.

In addition, the profile of the trigger and the interior edges of the trigger guard are arched as gently as geometry allows, and the trigger is highly polished (*unless the customer requests otherwise*). All visible tool marks and mould parting lines are removed and the pistol is refinished to the original production style (glass-blasted, with buffed slide and barrel).

Another chosen option was *frame stippling*. The result is a 'non-slip' texture on the frame. Stippling is available for the front and rear grip strap areas and the forward portion of the trigger guard. The author chose stippling for all three areas. The end result was a gun much easier to hold onto.

There are also several surface finish options available. "*High polish*" entails the use of a graduated series of buffing wheels and compounds, yielding a mirror-like finish. If the "*full matte*" finish is chosen, all exterior surfaces are blasted with a combination glass bead and 120-grit aluminum oxide media to minimize reflectivity. Appointments include the hammer, trigger, magazine and slide releases, the extractor, mainspring plug and grip screws. The "full matte" finish, in combination with a black titanium nitride coating (*described below*), has become very popular with law enforcement officers.

I also specified a black coating for this pistol. Composed of vapor-deposited titanium nitride, it is as deep and lustrous as the finest bluing when applied to a highly polished surface. Conversely, when applied to a glass bead-blasted matte-finished gun, the black coating is wholly non-reflective for maximum covert carry. Additionally, with a hardness rating of 90 on the Rockwell scale, the coating delivers excellent wear and corrosion resistance, while providing lubricity between moving parts. Available in black or gold tones, chrome and bronze-colored coatings are available on special request. Selected areas–or the entire Guardian pistol–may be so coated.

Other Custom Shop options include the cutting of five serrations in the forward section of the

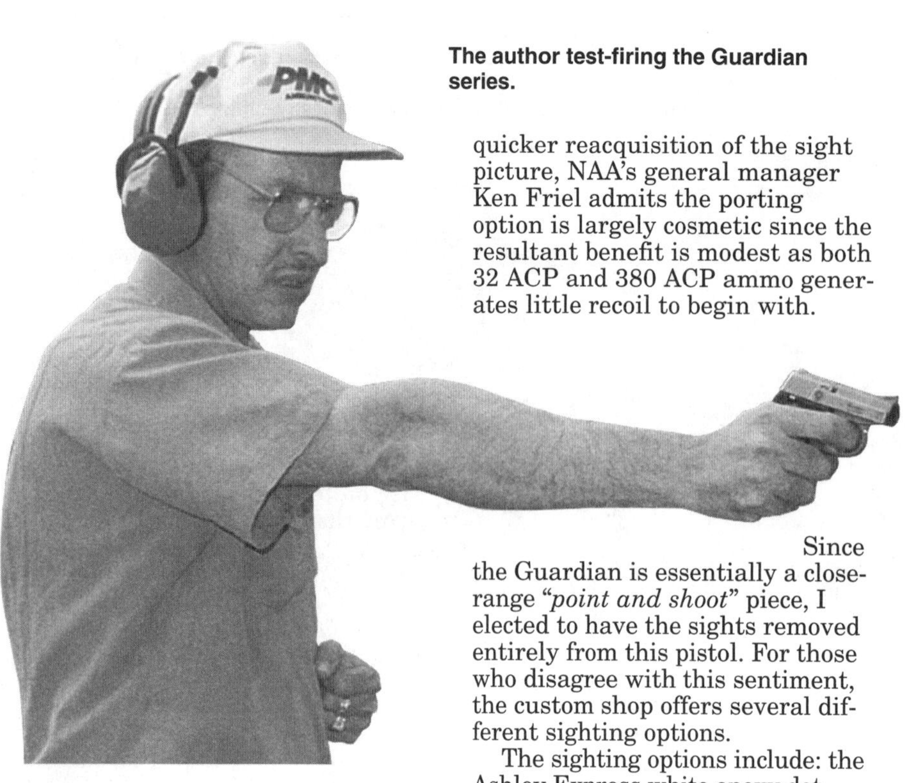

The author test-firing the Guardian series.

slide. Smith & Wesson Model 945-style 30-degree 'fish-scale pattern' serrations can also be ordered. Barrel porting, involving the drilling of four 1/16-inch diameter holes surrounded by a recessed apron, is yet another option. While intended to moderate muzzle flip and allow quicker reacquisition of the sight picture, NAA's general manager Ken Friel admits the porting option is largely cosmetic since the resultant benefit is modest as both 32 ACP and 380 ACP ammo generates little recoil to begin with.

Since the Guardian is essentially a close-range *"point and shoot"* piece, I elected to have the sights removed entirely from this pistol. For those who disagree with this sentiment, the custom shop offers several different sighting options.

The sighting options include: the Ashley Express white epoxy dot sights made of CNC-machined, heat-treated steel–with or without a tritium insert. Ashley Express Sights are available with a "standard" .110-inch diameter dot, or a "big"-sized dot of .160-inch diameter.

Another choice is the North Pass HiVis natural light-gathering sight. The light pipes used are injection molded of optical-quality plastic and engineered for interchangeability. The spring-loaded sight base is of steel, with a black oxide finish and a beryllium copper spring. Both orange and green light tubes are available in several different diameters to accommodate changing shooting conditions. Other available sights include Novak white dot models–with and without tritium inserts–as well as black and tritium sight options from the firm, Innovative Weaponry.

Company Background

The background history of this innovative gunmaker is worthy of note. North American Arms was originally founded under the name, "Rocky Mountain Arms," around 1974-75 in Salt Lake City, Utah by famed firearms designer/entrepreneur Dick Casull. Most readers will probably recognize his name from the bone-crushing handgun round he developed known as the "454 Casull" cartridge. Around 1976-77 the company's name was changed to North American Arms and it became part of the Tally Corp. of Newbury Park, California. North American Arms' plant was relocated from Salt Lake City to Provo, Utah in 1978 and in 1984 moved again to Spanish Fork, Utah.

In the 1986-87 period, Teleflex Corp. (*a large aerospace company*) bought North American Arms' parent, the Tally Corp. In 1992, Teleflex decided to sell the gunmaking company and Sandy Chisholm, a Teleflex employee, was given the task of finding a buyer. Chisholm became intrigued with the company and the firearms industry and wound up buying it himself. North American Arms moved back to Provo, Utah in 1994 and has been operated successfully by Chisholm ever since.

North American Arms' present ultra-modern plant comprises 30,000-square feet and has about 35 employees. Current production includes 30,000 to 35,000 of the various 22-rimfire mini-revolvers and about 15,000 Guardian pistols annually. All products are hand-finished and individually test-fired before leaving the plant.

Mini-Revolvers

North American Arms' other major product line is their selection of mini-revolvers. Constructed of stainless steel, the single-action, five-shot wheelguns range from a tiny 22 Short model, up through 22 Long Rifle and 22 Magnum versions with 1 1/8-, 1 5/8- and 2-inch barrels.

Introduced several years ago, the 32 ACP Guardian was North American Arms' first entry into the auto pistol market.

A size comparison between the author's customized 32 ACP Guardian (*left*) and the popular Kel-Tec 32, reveals the Guardian is smaller in overall dimensions.

There is even a 22 Magnum model furnished with an interchangeable 22 LR conversion cylinder. Some handgun *aficionados* across the country hold mini-pistol target matches, employing the 4-inch NAA Mini-Master Target models with fixed or adjustable sights. The "Companion" is a 22-caliber cap and ball version of the mini-revolver with the same single-action, five-shot, stainless steel construction.

While small in size, the mini-revolvers are equipped with a safety feature designed to prevent accidental discharge. The revolver's safety cylinder feature allows the guns to be carried fully loaded, with a round in each chamber. There are notches in the cylinder, between each chamber, and the hammer is lowered into one of these notches after the gun is loaded. When the hammer is pulled back to the firing position, the cylinder rotates to the next chamber.

Design Upgrades

North American Arms has instituted a number of improvements to the 32 ACP Guardian since the gun was first introduced in January 1998, and incorporated them into the new 380 ACP Guardian, as well. These include a slight increase in the finger contact surface of the trigger and smoothing of its edges, as well as increasing the size of the slide release button. A switch in vendors for the grips (to Hogue, Inc.) and magazines (to MEC-GAR) are two other changes. Changes have also been made to the drawbar return spring.

The most significant change is a re-engineered main (*hammer*) spring from the noted spring maker, Wolff, which reduces the weight of the trigger pull by two pounds. The trigger pull on production guns now averages about 10 pounds, which plant manager Friel feels is about the lightest it should be while still ensuring reliable ignition of a variety of ammo.

North American Arms will provide most of these components to owners of older Guardian pistols–free. Contact the factory (telephone: 801-374-9990; via the Internet: www.naaminis.com) for more information. Guns returned to the factory for warranty or Custom Shop work will automatically have these updates incorporated.

Aside from the customization and upgrade features, a wide range of accessories has been brought out for both versions of the Guardian, as well. These include Hogue hand-filling contoured grips in goncalo alves, pau ferro… as well as wine wood and simulated mother-of-pearl. There are also high-grade inside-the-pant, pocket- and ankle-holsters from a plethora of makers.

The array of customization options, component upgrades and accessories is extensive for the two models of the Guardian. While having built its name and reputation on finely-made mini-revolvers, North American Arms is betting the Guardian line will become its 'flagship' in the years ahead. As such, the arms maker has invested heavily in the customer service area, with the establishment of its Custom Shop, to ensure Guardian pistols will meet customers' aesthetic and practical self-defense needs. •

For more information, contact: North American Arms, Inc., 2150 South 950 East, Provo, Utah 84606 Tel: (800) 821-5783 web site: naaminis.com.

NAVY ARMS NEWMODEL RUSSIAN

by John Taffin

THIS IS ONE of those stories that ought to be true, although it isn't. Many times (*beginning in grade school, I think!*) I have read of the Grand Duke Alexis coming to America and shooting buffalo from horseback with Buffalo Bill Cody. Supposedly the Duke came over in 1869, had a great time hunting buffalo with both Bill Cody and George Custer, met General Sheridan, was totally enthralled with the Smith & Wesson 44 American, and placed a large order with Smith & Wesson for an improved version. The story is great–but untrue.

The Grand Duke did come over to hunt–but it was in 1872, not 1869; he did hunt with the men mentioned, and during the hunt he carried a Smith & Wesson already chambered in the new 44 Russian. Actually Smith and Wesson provided one of their new 44 Americans to his Imperial Majesty, the Czar of all the Russians, in 1869. Modifications were proposed (a great improvement in the Smith and Wesson 44 American) and a large order placed with Smith and Wesson for his Imperial Majesty's army.

In 1869 Smith & Wesson produced the first successful big-bore single-action revolver: the No.3 First Model American, a 44-caliber, six-shot, top-break, auto-ejecting six-gun. Cartridge cases were made of brass instead of copper and were centerfire instead of rimfire. The 44 Smith & Wesson American cartridge was loaded with 25 grains of blackpowder under a 218-grain bullet, delivering a muzzle velocity of 650 fps.

The coming together of Smith and Wesson and the Russians is certainly one of the great events in six-gun and cartridge history as the Russians made major improvements to the American revolver, as well as to its ammunition. The First Model Russian was identical to the Smith and Wesson American except for the chambering. With the Second Model Russian, the square stock and grip-frame of the American was rounded and reduced in diameter to make it more comfortable for use, a lanyard ring was added to the butt and a 'hump' was added to the backstrap to keep the gun from shifting in the hand when fired. With the Third Model, or New Model Russian, the 8-inch barrel was shortened to a more convenient 6 1/2 inches.

These old six-guns were magnificent. However, the Russians made the most significant contribution to the ammunition, a contribution from which we still benefit. The 44 Smith & Wesson American cartridge, while of centerfire design, was much like the 22 ammunition we still use today. That is, the bullet was of the heel-type (the base of the bullet smaller than the body, and inside the cartridge case). Both the bullet and the cartridge case thus had the same outside diameter. The Russians changed this. The bullet was made of uniform bearing surface diameter; lubrication placed in grooves in the bullet's body (that, in a loaded round, were *inside* the cartridge case) and the case mouth was crimped into a groove near the nose of the bullet. The powder charge was reduced to 23 grains (blackpowder, of course), bullet weight was increased from 218 grains to 246 grains (*today's 44 Magnum has been standardized at 240-250 grains*): the result was the magnificent 44 Russian, which soon gained a well-deserved reputation for accuracy.

Before the Grand Duke Alexis came over to hunt with Buffalo Bill, Smith and Wesson single actions chambered for the 44 Russian were already being produced.

Perhaps even more important, the New Model Russian revolver would soon evolve into the New Model Number Three; the 44 Russian cartridge would soon lead to the 44 Special, which then appears in the First Model Hand Ejector and the New Century Triple-Lock. Over the next fifty years, the Second, Third and Fourth Model Hand Ejectors and the 44 Special cartridge would evolve to become Smith & Wesson's greatest revolver and ammunition combination of all time, the 44 Magnum.

Production of Smith & Wesson single-action revolvers lasted from 1870 to 1912 with four basic models: The Americans (1870-1874), the Russians (1871-1878), the Schofields (1875-1877) and the New Model Number Threes (1878-1912). The Americans were made only in 44 S&W American, the Schofields only in 45 S&W, and the Russians only in 44 Russian–except for a few chambered in 44 Rimfire. For the most part the New Model Number Threes were 44 Russians, with a relative few being made in 16 other calibers from 32 S&W up to 455 Mark II.

Navy Arms has led the way in introducing replicas of single-action six-guns and lever-guns, giving us the first Smith & Wesson replica of the Schofield Model single action. Now they bring us the New Model Russian, chambered for the original 44 Russian cartridge.

The Navy Arms New Model Russian–or Model 3 Russian–is a faithful copy of the original, finished overall in a deep blue-black set off with a case-colored hammer, trigger guard and locking latch. Stocks are smooth European walnut, which I immediately replaced by shipping this newest of the replicas off to Raj Singh at Eagle Grips for the fitting of a pair of their UltraIvory grips. In fact, I sent not only the Russian Model, but Smith and Wesson's new Schofield Model as well. This synthetic material is about as close as one can get to real ivory, with a milky white color and realistic ivory grain. Combining the UltraIvory grips with the dark blue finish of the two single-action Smith and Wessons makes for a most striking appearance.

For authenticity it would be difficult to beat the Navy Arms New Model Russian 44, Smith and Wesson Model 3 Schofield 45 S&W and Black Hills Leather.

The 44 Russian evolved into the 44 Special which then spawned the 44 Magnum. Loading dies for the 44 Russian are available from RCBS.

Original 44 Russian brass was of the folded head, or balloon-style, originally used with blackpowder and has not been seen since before WW II. As they do with many of the old frontier cartridges, Starline now offers solid-head 44 Russian brass and Black Hills has modern 44 Russian ammunition with a 210-grain bullet clocking right at 750 fps. Ultramax also has a 44 Russian load, while Ten-X offers 44 Russian rounds as well as their 4-in-1 ammunition that can be used in 44 Russian, 44 Colt, 44 Special and 44 Magnum. The latter is offered both in smokeless and BPC (blackpowder cartridge) versions. Whether you are a reloader, or purchase your ammunition ready-made, there is no problem feeding the New Model Russian. Dies for reloading the 44 Russian are available from RCBS.

Quite often in the past, different reasons have been advanced as to why the Russians added the spur on the bottom of the trigger guard. It is strange looking, sometimes awkward

Performance Report

Navy Arms New Model Russian Revolver: 44 Russian; 6 1/2-inch barrel

Factory Load	MV/fps	Group/In.*
Black Hills		
210 Cowboy	745	1.5
Ultramax		
200 Cowboy	665	1.4
Ten-X		
4-in-1 200 BPC	640	2.3
Ten-X		
4-in-1 200	740	1.8

***Five shots at 50 feet.**

and, although Navy Arms maintained authenticity by including it in their replica model, I thought I would remove it as many original owners did. Now that I have used the New Model Russian, the spur–and the sights–tells me the Russians were not gunfighters, but marksmen. The sights are hard to see, requiring concentration–but they are precise. I also found if I placed my middle finger on the spur when firing the New Model Russian, the result was an incredibly steady hold. With this type of hold it is difficult to reach the hammer for a second shot–but perhaps it was rarely needed.

The New Model Russian from Navy Arms, with a suggested retail price of $745, is an easy-shooting, accurate historical six-gun. With the double-action style grip frame and the spur added to the bottom of the trigger guard it is (for me at least) the easiest single-action revolver to shoot offhand. In fact, I was surprised to find my *stand-on-your-back-legs-and-shoot-one-handed groups* rivaled my sandbag-rest groups. Perhaps the old-timers really knew something! •

There is no problem finding ammunition for the Navy Arms New Model Russian as Black Hills, Ten-X and Ultramax all offer factory loads.

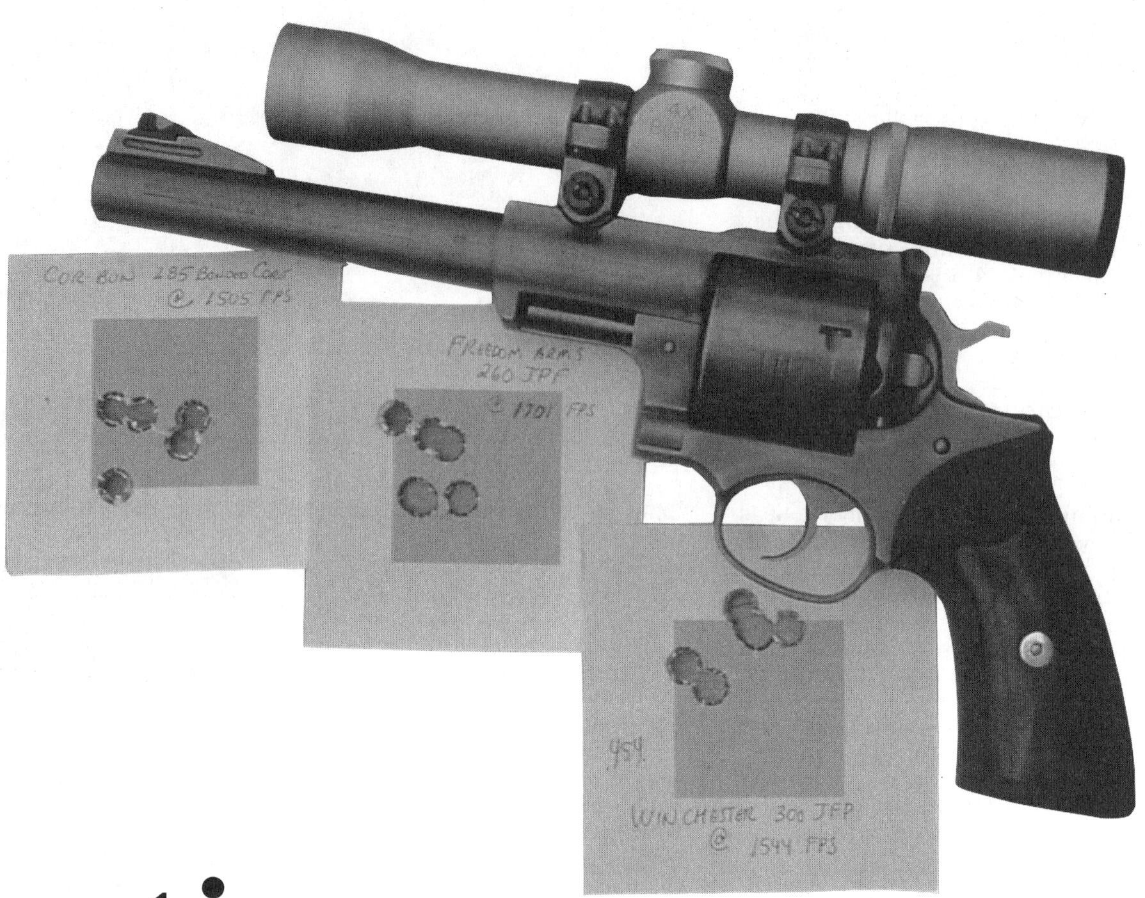

Above: **Ruger Redhawk 454 handles Cor-Bon's 454 loads with ease and accuracy.**

Hunting Sixguns & Ammo

by John Taffin

THE 1950s WERE the near-perfect time to be a teenager. It was the age of the custom car, the "Hot Rod"; movies still had easily-identifiable good guys and bad guys; TV, in its infancy, had not even arrived in many parts of the country; Ike was in the White House; Elvis sang music we could understand and identify with; instant communication meant talking to your neighbor–and firearms and kids were looked upon as a natural combination. By 1955 I knew six-guns would be a very important part of my life even though handgun hunting had not yet "arrived," and the only Magnum six-gun available was a 357 Magnum.

However, that was about to change. For 30 years a cowpoke out here in Idaho had been proclaiming that not only was a six-gun capable of taking big game cleanly, but he had accomplished it with his custom 44 Special six-gun loads.

For three decades Elmer Keith loaded 250-grain hard cast bullets over a heavy charge of #2400 powder, achieving 1100-1200 fps from a long-barreled six-gun. I have duplicated his old loads, using the balloon-head brass he had prior to 1950, his hard cast 44 Special "Keith" bullets and modern primers. That load clocks out at more than 1200 fps from a 7 1/2 inch single-action six-gun. All Keith wanted was to see his 44 Special offered as a factory load in a new six-gun. It happened at Christmas time in 1955. Smith & Wesson teamed up with Remington and the result was the Smith & Wesson 44 Magnum and Remington's first 44 Magnum loading. Keith had asked for a 250-grain bullet at 1200 fps; he received a 240-grain bullet traveling at well over 1400 fps–he was ecstatic. Those first 6 1/2 inch bright-blued S&W 44 Magnums (that began to arrive at gun shops in 1956) can only be described as magnificent; however, the ammunition needed to be "fixed" as the bullet was too soft for the velocity. Keith went to work using his 250-grain hard cast bullet

Ruger's Blackhawk was the first 45 Colt to permit use of heavier-than-standard 45 loads.

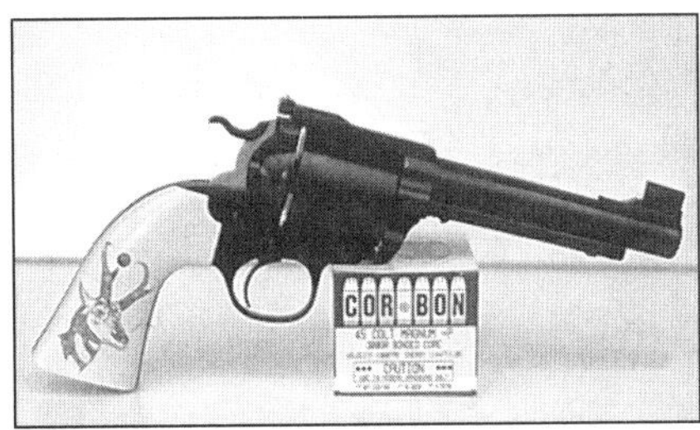

Ruger's 45 Bisley Blackhawk, customized by Jim Stroh, handles Cor-Bon's +P 45 loads with ease.

Buffalo Bore's Heavy 45 Colt loads and the Bisley Blackhawk make a fine hunting combination.

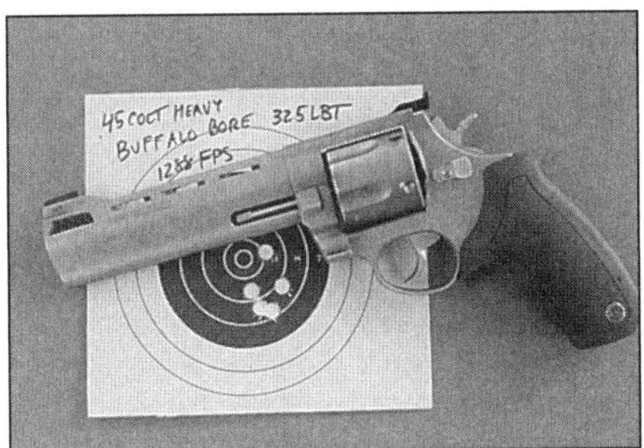

The Taurus Raging Bull 454 Casull also does quite well with Heavy 45 Colt loads from Buffalo Bore.

Cor-Bon's +P 45 Colt loads and Ruger's 45 Bisley Blackhawk will handle most big game any of us will ever encounter.

A great choice for turkeys (where legal) is Freedom Arms Model 83 357 Magnum and Black Hills 125-grain JHPs.

and favorite #2400 powder and the result was the Keith load: Lyman's original #429421 Keith bullet over 22.0 grains of #2400 for a full 1400 fps and, as Keith said, *less pressure, no barrel leading and greater accuracy.* It was–and is–a great handgun-hunting load.

The 44 Magnum has been *King of the Six-gun Cartridges* for nearly half a century. It is not as easy to control as its predecessor, the 357 Magnum, or it's offspring, the 41 Magnum–and it has been overshadowed in power by several new cartridges. However, it remains *THE* hunting handgun and hunting cartridge by which all others are judged. We will be taking a serious look at the current crop of hunting sixguns and factory loads available for them, looking chronologically from the 45 Colt through the 357, 44 and 41 Magnums–and then through the newer batch of big bores, right up to this year's brand new 480 Ruger. By no means an exhaustive encyclopedia–rather, a look at some of the best offered. Every six-gun and cartridge load mentioned has also been personally experienced.

45 COLT: This most versatile of all six-gun cartridges arrived in black powder form in 1873 in the now-legendary Colt Single Action Army with a 255-grain conical bullet at around 900 fps. This load proved to be too much to handle for most of the soldiers in the U.S. Cavalry so it was reduced to around 800 fps. For nearly a century this was the standard loading for the 45 Colt mainly because the original six-gun, the Colt Single Action Army, has paper-thin cylinder walls when chambered in the big 45. This all changed when Ruger introduced their 45 Colt revolver built on the 44 Magnum frame. For the first time we had a factory-chambered 45 Colt that could handle heavier loads safely. Reloaders soon found the Ruger 45 easily capable of handling 250-grain bullets at 1300 fps and 300-grain bullets at a full 1200 fps. The day of big-game hunting with the 45 Colt had arrived.

Ruger still offers the Blackhawk in 45 Colt with either 7 1/2- or easier-packing 4 5/8-inch barrel

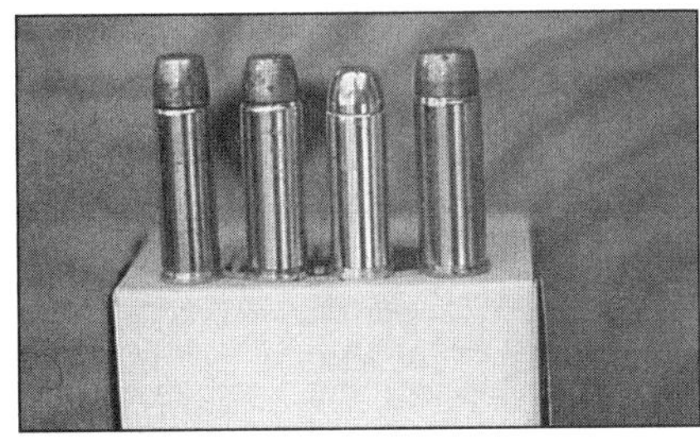

The Big Bores: 454 Casull, 475 Linebaugh, 480 Ruger and 500 Linebaugh.

lengths - and with either the original blued finish or weather-beating stainless steel. In any caliber for a packin' six-gun I prefer the shorter barrels but, where hunting is the main activity, I feel much better with a 7 1/2-inch barreled six-gun simply because it is easier to shoot accurately. My favorite Ruger–when it comes to the 45 Colt chamber in any hunting handgun–is the Bisley Model. Offered only in blue and with a 7 1/2-inch barrel, the grip frame of the Bisley Model combines the best features of the original Colt Bisley Single Action, Freedom Arms and Ruger Super Blackhawk grip frames. Felt recoil is highly subjective, as is the best grip frame design for handling it. More often than not, the Bisley Model grip frame handles recoil the best for the most shooters.

Ruger has recently gone double-action with the 45 Colt in their bull-strong Redhawk. Offered in stainless steel only with a choice of 5 1/2 and 7 1/2-inch barreled standard models, or a 7 1/2-inch scope-ready model complete with Ruger scope rings, the Redhawk will handle heavy factory 45 Colt loads with ease.

Freedom Arms revolvers are, without question, the finest factory-produced six-guns ever offered anytime, anywhere. Two frame sizes are offered in their stainless steel

The first six-guns designed with hunting in mind: Smith & Wesson's 8 3/8- and 6 1/2-inch 44 Magnum with grips by Roy Fishpaw, and the 357 Magnum stocked by BearHug.

S&W's modernized version of the 1950s 44 Magnum is this M629 PowerPort, with Hogue grips.

five-shot six-guns: the original Model 83 chambered in 454 Casull (available with an auxiliary 45 Colt cylinder), or the easy-packing smaller-framed Model 97 in 45 Colt. Standard barrel lengths for the former are 4 3/4, 6, 7 1/2 and 10 inches; while the smaller 45 is offered in 5 1/2 and 7 1/2-inch versions. All adjustable-sighted Freedom Arms single actions are made scope-ready by removing the rear sight.

I know of only two companies offering 45 Colt loads suitable for hunting big game where deep penetration is required: Buffalo Bore and Cor-Bon. All of Buffalo Bore's 45 Colt loads are advertised as "Heavy 45 Colt" and are for use only in modern heavy-duty 45 Colt sixguns. There are three standard offerings: for maximum penetration - a hard cast 325-grain LBT-LFN (*Lead Bullet Technology-Long Flat Nose*) at 1325 fps; penetration plus expansion - a 300-grain Speer PSP (*Plated Soft Point*) at 1300 fps. For smaller critters where expansion is more important than deep penetration, Buffalo Bore offers a 260-grain jacketed hollowpoint at 1450 fps. The fourth offering from Buffalo Bore, designed with the mid-framed Freedom Arms Model 97 45 Colt in mind, is a 300-grain Speer PSP at 1200 fps. This is also a good choice for those that hunt deer-sized critters with Ruger's Blackhawk; although potent, recoil is fairly mild.

The first two 45 Colt loads from Buffalo Bore are recommended for big game up to 1000 pounds on the hoof. Buffalo Bore's advertised velocities, unlike some that are taken in closed pressure barrels, are clocked from actual sixguns that would be used in the field. If anything, muzzle velocities are slightly on the conservative side. Witness the fact that in a 7 1/2 inch Ruger Redhawk 45 Colt, Buffalo Bore's 325-grain LBT clocked out at 1392 fps while the 300-grain Speer load does 1367 fps. If Buffalo Bore claims it, *it is*!

Cor-Bon's Peter Pi and Buffalo Bore's Tim Sundles are experienced handgun hunters–and know what works. Cor-Bon has long offered true handgun hunting ammunition for both sixguns and single shots. Currently Cor-Bon offers three 45 Colt Magnum +*P* loadings for handgun hunters. Both Buffalo Bore and Cor-Bon distinguish their serious 45 Colt hunting loads from the "normal" 45 Colt factory loads by using the terms *"Heavy .45 Colt" and ".45 Colt Magnum +P"*... and I cannot emphasize enough that these loads are for currently manufactured large-framed 45 Colt sixguns. They can also be used in any sixguns chambered in 454 Casull if the chambers are kept clean of any deposit build-up from the shorter 45 Colt brass which can make chambering the 454 brass difficult–and even raise pressures when the 454 rounds are fired.

Cor-Bon's 45 Colt hunting loads include a 265-grain Bonded Core HP at 1350 feet per second, a 300-grain Bonded Core jacketed softpoint at 1300 fps and a 335-grain Hard Cast rated at 1050 fps. In the same 45 Redhawk mentioned above, Cor-Bon's 265 is right on the money at 1350 fps while the 300-grain Bonded Core clocks just slightly under, at 1275 fps. Cor-Bon's Bonded Core process fuses the interior lead core to the outside jacket to keep both together for maximum penetration and expansion. Their *Hard Cast* and *Penetrators* are designed to perform as solids, giving maximum possible penetration on large and/or dangerous game.

357 MAGNUM: In 1935 Smith & Wesson collaborated with Winchester to bring out the first Magnum six-gun/ammunition combination. The first two revolvers, a 6 1/2 and an 8 3/4 inch, were built on the large-frame 44 Hand Ejector with specially heat-treated cylinder and frame and chambered for the lengthened 38 that had been christened the 357 Magnum. Those first loads were built around a 158-grain bullet–that proved too soft and leaded horribly–and a heavy charge of #2400 powder in a Winchester case, ignited by a large rifle primer. Col. Doug Wesson used those two revolvers to hunt big game such as elk, moose, and antelope. He also went to Alaska in search of brown bear but, in retrospect, he said he was glad he did not find one!

At 1500 fps from a long-barreled six-gun, the 357 Magnum was well beyond any factory chambered six-gun cartridge being offered. However, by this time several six-gunners of note who had discovered the 250-grain 44 Special at 1200 fps, looked at the new Magnum, tried it out, gave a collective yawn, and went back to their 44s. The true position of the 357 Magnum lies somewhere between Col. Doug Wesson's accomplishment and the requirements of the 44 Special *aficionados*.

I am somewhat conservative when using the 357 Magnum, and although I have taken deer-sized animals with it, it was up close and with hard cast bullets designed for maximum penetration. I do use the 357 Magnum a lot for turkey hunting, where legal, and my choice is Black Hills 125-grain jacketed hollowpoints, a scoped six-gun and placing the shots where the head meets the body.

For small deer these are excellent choices: Ruger's Bisley Model in 357 and 41 Magnum, Freedom Arms M83s in the same chamberings.

Even though Smith & Wesson no longer offers their large-frame 357 Magnum, eventually known as the Model 27, there are a number of excellent 357 Magnum six-guns offered to handgun hunters. The 357 Magnum lives on in Smith & Wesson's L-frame Model 686, a stainless steel, heavy underlug-barreled six-gun offered to hunters with either a 6- or 8 3/8-inch barrel length. The Model 686 has a well-deserved reputation for both durability and accuracy. It is also scope-ready when the rear sight assembly is removed.

Single action-style, Ruger offers the extremely strong Bisley Model with a 7 1/2-inch barrel, as well as the standard 6 1/2-inch Blackhawk in either blue or stainless. As with the 45 Colt, Freedom Arms has two frame sizes in 357 Magnum: the large-framed Model 83 with a five-shot cylinder, and the mid-framed Model 97 with a six-shot cylinder.

Virtually every ammunition manufacturer offers 357 Magnum loads. The 357 Magnum is a great defensive cartridge when used with 125-, 140- and 158-grain jacketed hollowpoints. For hunting, I would reserve these loads only for the smallest of critters that are no tougher than man. For any other hunting with the 357 Magnum I know of only three loads offered for deep penetration: Cor-Bon's 180-grain Bonded Core at 1265 fps and their 200-grain Hard Cast at 1200 fps. The third load is from Federal, a 180-grain hard cast known as a Cast Core rated at 1250 fps.

44 MAGNUM: That the 44 Magnum is King of the Sixguns is easily seen by the number of revolvers offered and great variety of factory ammunition to be had. Virtually every handgun manufacturer offers revolvers chambered in 44 Magnum and likewise for the ammunition manufacturers. Smith & Wesson no longer offers the original 44 Magnum (the Model 29). However, a stainless-steel version–the 629–lives on in both 6 inch and 8 3/8 inch versions for hunters… as well as the easy packin' 4 inch model. In addition to the standard 629, Smith & Wesson also has two heavy underlug-barreled 629s, the 6 1/2-inch *Power-Port* with factory-ported barrel and an excellent black post front sight; and the Classic DX porting but offered in either a 6 1/2 inch or 8 3/8 inch version. The latter is one of the most accurate 44 Magnums I have fired.

Ruger goes all-out when it comes to offering hunting handguns chambered in 44 Magnum. Single-action style we have the legendary Super Blackhawk which, in the 7 1/2-inch barreled blued version has been–and remains–the greatest bargain offered to handgun hunters. This is one case in which the shooter actually gets more than he pays for! First offered in 1959 as an improved version of the standard Blackhawk Model, it would be 25 years before any other barrel length or finish was offered. Today, shooters have a choice of blue or stainless steel versions and barrel lengths of 4 5/8, 5 1/2, 7 1/2 and 10 1/2 inches. I find the latter

Twenty-four whitetail deer, all one-shot kills, have fallen to this combination: Freedom Arms M83 44 Magnum; 7 1/2-inch barrel, Leupold 2X scope and Black Hills 240-grain JHP load.

Among the easiest big bores to shoot–due to their weight and grip design–are Raging Bulls from Taurus in 454 and 44 Magnum chamberings.

especially accurate and easy-shooting; however, when it comes to Ruger single actions in 44 Magnum I much prefer the Bisley Model, although it is offered only in a 7 1/2-inch blued version.

Ruger does not stop with single actions only. In the days of "Dirty Harry" and the great demand for Smith & Wesson's Model 29, handgunners often had to pay nearly double the retail price for the coveted double-action 44 Magnum. Smith & Wesson worked around the clock and still could not meet the demand for 44 Magnums. Ruger stopped all this nonsense by introducing their Redhawk, chambered in 44 Magnum. While Smith & Wesson used an existing frame, the 44 Hand Ejector, as the platform for the 44 Magnum in 1955, Ruger was able to deliver, in 1979, a larger, stronger magnum six-gun. The Redhawk has been so popular that, when it was "improved" by the introduction of the Super Redhawk in 1987, demand for the original double-action Ruger 44 Magnum kept it in the line. Both these big-bore six-guns remain in production today. Redhawk fanciers have a choice of blue or stainless-steel versions in 5 1/2- and 7 1/2-inch barrel lengths, the latter also offered scope-ready with integral *scallops* on the barrel rib to accept Ruger rings; those that prefer the larger Super Redhawk have only two choices, a 7 1/2- or 9 1/2-inch barreled, scope-ready, stainless-steel massive brute of a six-gun.

Freedom Arms also offers their Model 83 in 44 Magnum in stainless steel only and in all four standard barrel lengths. My most-used hunting handgun for whitetail deer is a scoped Freedom Arms 7 1/2 inch 44 Magnum combined with Black Hills Ammunition's 44 Magnum offering: a 240-grain jacketed XTP bullet from Hornady loaded to 1350 fps. For me, this is the ideal combination for Southern whitetails.

Finally, we have the double-action 44 Magnum six-guns from Wesson Firearms and Taurus. Dan Wesson also helped alleviate the demand for 44 Magnums with the introduction of their big-bore six-gun in the early 1980s. This large-framed revolver, with its interchangeable barrel system, soon won favor among hunters and silhouetters alike. Wesson Firearms is now under new management with new machinery and new dedication to produce excellent sixguns. With a Pistol Pak consisting of four barrels and shrouds in lengths of 4, 6, 8 and 10 inches, the 44 Magnum fancier is set up for any situation with a Wesson 44 Magnum.

Taurus went big-bore with the Model 44 in 1994. Offered in blue or stainless and barrel lengths of 4, 6 1/2 or 8 3/8 inches, this Brazilian-made 44 Magnum six-gun quickly gained a reputation for accuracy. My long-barreled test model consistently stays under three inches at 100 yards, from a sandbag rest. Three years after introducing their first 44 Magnum, Taurus had their second big-bore hunting revolver with the introduction of the Raging Bull. This five-shot revolver features a 6 1/2- or 8 3/8-inch heavily underlugged barrel, integral porting and, at four pound-plus weight with factory rubber finger-groove grips, is one of the *easiest-shooting* of the 44 Magnums offered.

As with the 357 Magnum, virtually every ammunition manufacturer offers quality 44 Magnum ammunition loaded with 240-grain jacketed hollowpoints that are certainly adequate for hunting small deer. I have already reported my choice of Black Hills Ammunition's 44 Magnum 240-grain JHP for this duty. Herein we are more concerned with heavy-duty ammunition designed for use with larger animals. Both Speer and Winchester take the standard 44 Magnum loading up a step with the former's 270-grain Gold Dot Hollow Point

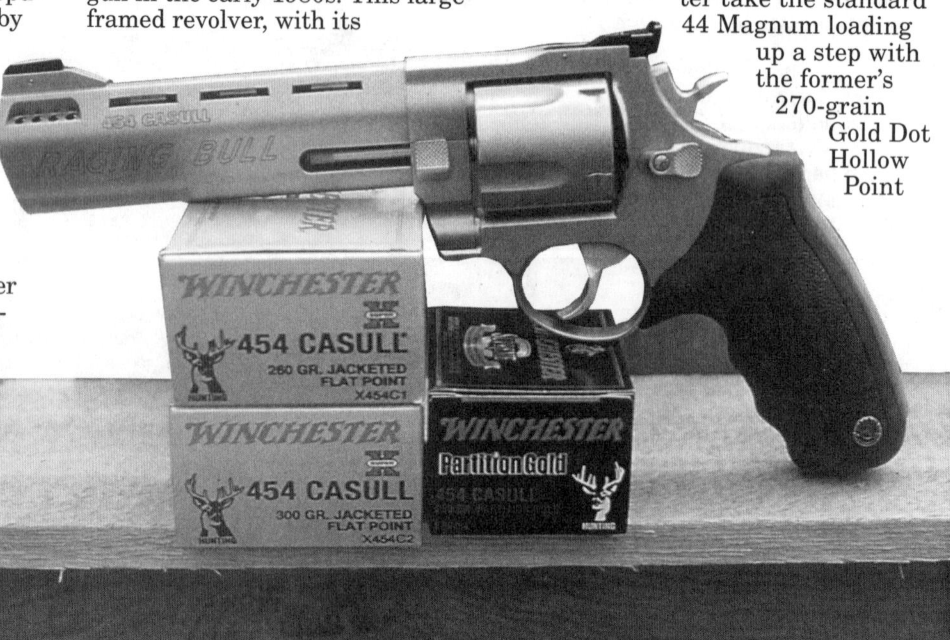

Taurus stainless steel Raging Bull 454 Casull and Winchester's 454 loads are favored by many handgun hunters for a combination of accuracy and power.

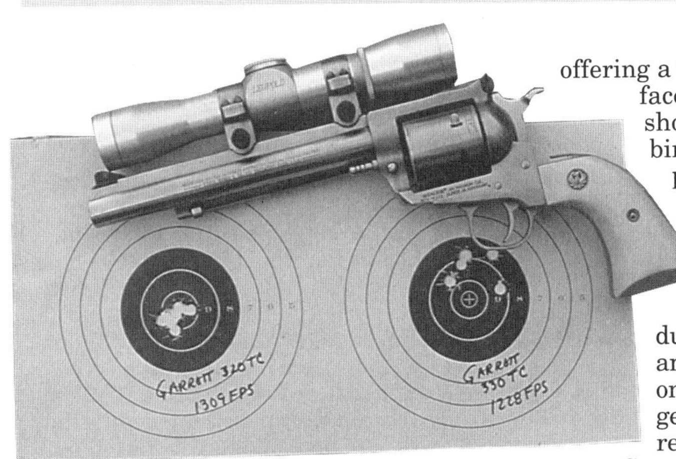

Good news for handgun hunters! Ruger is thinking of returning their scope-ready, heavy-barreled 44 Magnum Hunter Model to production.

which clocks at 1216 fps out of my 5 1/2-inch six-gun and the latter's 250-grain Partition Gold at 1327 fps from the same Ruger 44 Magnum. Both Black Hills and Federal contribute to 44 Magnum hunting loads with a 320-grain Hard Cast and a 300-grain Cast Core, respectively, both at 1250 fps; Hornady joins the heavy-bullet brigade in 44 Magnum with their 300-grain XTP-MAG at 1150 fps.

Buffalo Bore's offerings in 44 Magnum consist of three Heavy 44 Magnum loadings. First there is the above-mentioned 270-grain Speer Gold Dot loaded to 1450 fps; then a 300-grain Speer PSP (*Plated Soft Point*) at 1300 fps and finally, for maximum penetration, a 305-grain hard cast LBT-LFN (*Long Flat Nose*) rated at 1325 fps. As with the heavy bullet 45 Colt loads from Buffalo Bore, these 44s are recommended for big game up to 1000 pounds.

Cor-Bon has six 44 Magnum loads for specific purposes. First, we have the 240-grain jacketed hollowpoint at a full 1500 fps for small deer; then the tougher 260-grain Bonded-Core hollowpoint (1450 fps) that will work for most hunting situations, followed by the 280-grain Bonded-Core softpoint (1400 fps) for larger deer, including elk and moose.

The heavyweight heavy-duty loads from Cor-Bon for the 44 Magnum include a 300-grain jacketed softpoint at 1300 fps that is designed for expansion on soft-skinned game; the 305-grain Flat-Point Penetrator (1300 fps), a copper-jacketed solid for maximum penetration and, finally, the 320-grain Hard-Cast Flat Point (1270) offering a wide frontal surface for maximum shocking power combined with deep penetration.

Randy Garrett was one of the first, perhaps *the* first, to provide heavy-duty 44 Magnum ammunition for use on large and/or dangerous critters. Currently Garrett Cartridges offers two Super Hard Cast Hammerhead loadings: a 310-grain bullet at 1325 fps for use in all currently manufactured 44 Magnums, and a 330-grain +P Long Hammerhead at 1385 fps for use in Ruger's long-cylindered Redhawk and Super Redhawk. These loads are too long to fit in the cylinders of other 44 Magnum sixguns. Both loads are designed for maximum penetration and will shoot through most animals, broadside, and will penetrate deeply into the vitals from a frontal shot. Garrett's 44 Magnum bullets are of the LBT style rather than the Keith style and are cast from specially designed molds that give a *meplat*, or frontal surface, of .320-inch diameter for maximum shocking power.

41 MAGNUM: The 41 Magnum deserves a lot better treatment than it receives. First introduced by Smith & Wesson in the Model 57 in 1964, it was immediately chambered in Ruger's Blackhawk, made the transition to stainless steel with Smith & Wesson's Model 657 and was then chambered in Ruger's Redhawk and Bisley Models. Ruger's Blackhawk remains; however, the Bisley Model, the Redhawk and the Model 57 are all gone (*but worth searching out on the used market*), and the Model 657 remains only in a 6-inch version. Fortunately Freedom Arms saw fit to chamber both their models in 41 Magnum. Diehard 41 Magnum fans can at least have their cartridge in the finest factory sixguns ever offered. The most accurate six-gun I have fired in recent times is the Freedom Arms 10-inch 41 Magnum.

Both of the sixguns offered by Freedom Arms are five-shooters with the large-framed Model 83 capable of handling much heavier loads than any manufacturer is offering. The standard 210-grain jacketed hollowpoint 41 Magnum load offered by several manufacturers is certainly capable of handling small deer. However, Federal is the only company that presently offers a 41 Magnum loading with a heavyweight hard cast bullet. Their load features a 250-grain bullet at 1250 fps and, compared to the standard 210-grain jacketed hollowpoint, is a better choice for hunting when penetration is desired.

454 CASULL: Now we come to the really big-bore–I mean ***REALLY BIG-BORE***– sixguns! In the 1950s Dick Casull began experimenting with the 45 Colt, eventually building his own guns with five-shot cylinders to handle the pressures involved. When the time came to produce his 45 "Magnum," the case was lengthened and cartridge named the 454 Casull was chambered in the Model 83 Freedom Arms revolver. As did

A winning pair of 44s for handgun hunters: the Raging Bull from Taurus and the M644 from Wesson Firearms.

Jim Wilson of SHOOTING TIMES connected the next day--three for three!

the 357 Magnum in 1935 and the 44 Magnum in 1956, the 454 Casull revolutionized sixgunning in 1983. The first Magnum gave us a 158-grain bullet at over 1400 fps, the 44 Magnum did the same with the 240-grain bullet–and the 454 gave us a 260-grain bullet at 1800 fps!

To safely handle the pressures and power involved, Freedom Arms built a five-shot revolver with the emphasis on high-quality materials and tight tolerances. By doing this they were able to produce a five-shot 454 revolver only slightly larger than a Super Blackhawk. Available in standard barrel lengths of 4 3/4, 6, 7 1/2 and 10 inches, the Freedom Arms 454 from has become the truly serious hunter's hunting six-gun. For 15 years, except for a few sixguns from US Arms, the Freedom Arms was the only game in town when it came to the 454 Casull chambering. Now, within the past few years, both Taurus and Ruger have introduced double-action revolvers chambered for the biggest 45.

Taurus' five-shot Raging Bull is as described in the 44 Magnum report. To me it is one of the best looking sixguns Taurus has ever produced and, even in 454 chambering, is fairly easy to handle due to the weight (53 ounces), heavy barrel, porting and rubber grips. Ruger's Super Redhawk 454 six-gun is a true six-gun, which differs from their 44 Super Redhawk by incorporating specially heat-treated metals and a new finish. This Ruger has what they are calling a *target gray* finish on the stainless steel. With its hefty weight of 53 ounces and "Cushioned Grips," the 454 Super Redhawk is relatively easy to shoot in either the 7 1/2- or 9 1/2-inch barrel lengths, especially when a scope is mounted with the supplied rings.

Buffalo Bore offers two hard-cast and one jacketed bullet load for the 454 Casull. The jacketed version consists of Freedom Arms' 300-grain jacketed flat nose at 1625 fps; the two hard cast bullet loads are a 325-grain LBT-LFN at 1525 fps and a 360-grain LBT-WFN at 1425 fps. These loads will handle anything that walks!

Cor-Bon offers six loads for the 454, three designed for expansion plus penetration and three for the ultimate in penetration. Cor-Bon says of their first two Bonded Core designs, a 265-grain BC Hollow Point at 1800 fps and a 285-grain. BC Soft Point at 1700 fps: *"Upon impact they will expand, creating a devastating mushroom—plowing through tough hide and bone."* These two are followed by a 300-grain jacketed softpoint at 1650 fps.

For deepest penetration with the 454, Cor-Bon's 320-grain Flat –Point Penetrator, 335-grain Hard Cast Flat Point and 360-grain Flat Point Penetrator deliver 1600 fps, 1600 fps and 1500 fps, respectively. I clocked all Cor-Bon's 454 loads through a Freedom Arms 7 1/2-inch 454 in cold weather. Muzzle velocities averaged around 50 fps less than advertised–not out of line considering differences in sixguns, weather conditions and chronographs.

Finally, Winchester also manufactures the 454 Casull, though they have cut back on their offerings, only the 250-grain JHP at 1300 fps and the 300-grain JFP at 1625 fps now being offered. The latter is good for anything that is hunted while the former is in the 44 Magnum JHP class.

500 LINEBAUGH: This *biggest of the big*–and John Linebaugh's first wildcat–is still not offered in a factory-chambered revolver but is well represented by custom five-shot revolvers from John Linebaugh himself, as well as six-gunsmiths such as Hamilton Bowen, David Clements, Jack Huntington, Gary Reeder and Jim Stroh. We mention the 500 Linebaugh in this survey of factory sixguns and factory hunting loads simply because "factory" loads are available from Buffalo Bore. Three hard cast LBT designs: a 435-grain LFN at an easy-shootin' 950 fps; the same bullet at a full-bore 1300 fps; and a 440-grain WFN for maximum shocking power and penetration at 1250 fps; all joined by a 400-grain jacketed hollowpoint at 1400 feet per second. The foregoing loads are for critters up to 800 pounds, the other two are dependent upon shape. The LFN will do for animals up to 2000 pounds while the WFN (*with less penetrating ability*) is rated for critters up to 1200 pounds. So it is easy to see the effectiveness of handgun hunting loads is determined by caliber, weight, muzzle velocity and bullet shape.

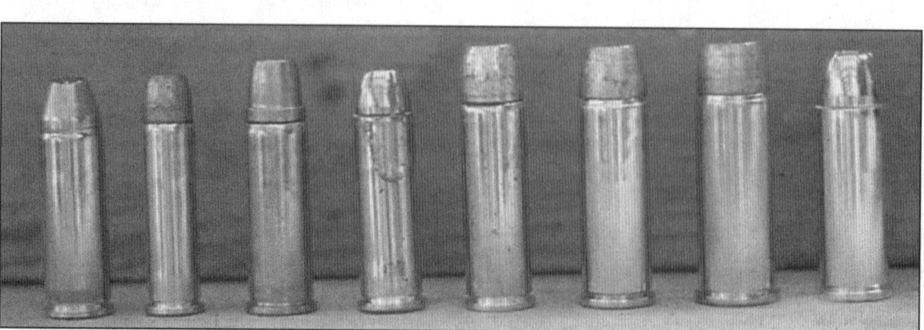

The lineup of handgun hunting cartridges: 45 Colt, 357 Magnum, 44 Magnum, 41 Magnum, 454 Casull, 475 Linebaugh, 500 Linebaugh and 480 Ruger.

Ruger 44 Magnum, 45 Colt Redhawk and 454 Super Redhawk--all for hunting the largest of big game.

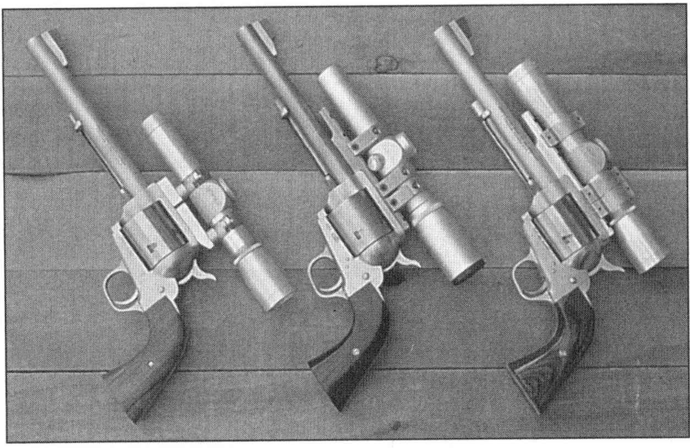

Freedom Arms Big Three for serious handgun hunters: 44 Magnum, 454 Casull and 475 Linebaugh.

475 LINEBAUGH: While Linebaugh's 500 is based on the 348 Winchester case cut to 1.4 inches, he turned to easily obtainable 45-70 brass for his 475 Linebaugh. This easy wildcat is made by trimming Winchester 45-70 brass to 1.4 inches, loading .475-inch bullets–and shooting. By using Winchester brass, it is not necessary to inside neck-ream the formed 475 Linebaugh brass. When Freedom Arms looked at chambering their Model 83 in 475 Linebaugh, the *hitch* was the rims of the wildcat brass were too large in diameter for the Freedom Arms cylinder. When Buffalo Bore offered 475 Linebaugh ammunition as a factory chambering, they trimmed the rims to fit in the Freedom Arms-sized cylinders. So we now have the excellent Model 83 offered in 475 Linebaugh in all standard barrel lengths, as well as six variations of 475 ammunition from Buffalo Bore.

The first game animal to fall to the new Ruger 480--wild hog taken by HANDLOADER's Brian Pearce.

As with the 500 Linebaugh, Buffalo Bore starts with an easy-shootin' loading of a 420-grain LBT-LFN at 950 fps. We call both the 475 and 500 Linebaugh at this muzzle velocity *"easy-shootin,"* but realize they are in the 44 Magnum recoil category and are serious hunting loads capable of shooting broadside through most commonly hunted critters. Next comes the two heavy-duty cast-bullet loads both at 1350 fps, both weighing 420 grains: one an LBT-LFN for maximum penetration and the other an LBT-WFN (*Wide Flat Nose*) for maximum shocking power. Due to the difference in penetrating ability, Buffalo Bore recommends the LFN for animals up to 2000 pounds and the WFN up to 1200 pounds. For those who prefer jacketed bullets there is a 400-grain jacketed softpoint at 1400 fps that falls into the same animal weight class as the first 950 fps/475 load and finally, two "custom" loadings of a 350-grain JHP at 1500 fps and a 440 LBT-WFN at 1325 fps.

THE 480 RUGER: Finally–brand new for this year we have the 480 Ruger, the first cartridge to bear the "Ruger" name. Chambered in the 454-styled Super Redhawk, the 480 is the 475 cut back to 1.275-inches and loaded by Hornady with a 325-grain XTP-MAG hollowpoint bullet to 1350 fps. We used this load on Texas wild hogs ranging from 125 to 190 pounds. Penetration was complete with a broadside shot on the 125-pound boar, but not on the 170- or 190-pound specimens. From this small sampling I would class this most interesting cartridge as a deer-sized cartridge with the same capabilities as a 44 Magnum loaded with a 300-grain JHP. I hope Hornady brings it out with a flat point bullet–or even a heavier bullet at a lower muzzle velocity–and that Ruger also chambers their Bisley Model in this newest cartridge.

It isn't too many years ago when handgun hunting was looked upon as stunt–even unsportsmanlike–by other shooters. No more. Handgun hunting is not only here to stay, it is as legitimate as any other type of hunting. We have the finest sixguns and ammunition ever available. It is up to us to match six-gun, ammunition and an honest appraisal of our skill to the quarry to ensure handgun hunting remains a respected part of hunting. •

Addresses Of Handgun Hunting Ammunition Manufacturers:

Black Hills Ammunition, PO Box 3090, Rapid City SD 57709; 1-605-348-5150

Buffalo Bore, PO Box 78, Carmen ID 83642; 1-208-756-8085

Cor-Bon, 1311 Industry Rd., Sturgis SD 57785; 1-800-626-7266

Federal Cartridge, 900 Ehlen Dr., Anoka MN 55303; 1-612-323-2300

Garrett Cartridges, PO Box 178, Chehalis WA 98532; 1-206-736-0702

Hornady, PO Box 1848, Grand Island NE 68802; 1-800-338-3220

Speer, PO Box 856, Lewiston ID 83501; 1-800-627-3640

Winchester, 427 N. Shamrock, Alton IL 62024; 1-618-258-3566

INTERESTING PRODUCT NEWS FOR THE ACTIVE SHOOTING SPORTSMAN

The companies represented on the following pages will be happy to provide additional information – feel free to contact them.

SWEETSHOOTER™ PREVENTS METAL CORROSION

Sweetshooter's micro-thin film penetrates the pores of barrels and other metal surfaces of firearms, blackpowder arms and knives to prevent corrosion and fouling. Once Sweetshooter™ fills the pores of these metal surfaces, there is no place for copper, lead, carbon and other deposits to collect, except on the film surface. Simply wipe them away! Users have found that Sweetshooter™ smoothes actions, reduces jamming, extends barrel life and improves accuracy. There is no need for immediate cleanup. Soaking of gun parts in solvent is eliminated, too.

While Sweetshooter™ is great for firearms and muzzleloaders, it will also prevent corrosion on knives, fishing tackle and tools, too.

NO MORE FOULING...GUARANTEED!

For information, call 1-800-932-4445 or visit their website at www.tecrolan.com

TECROLAN INC.

P.O. Box 14916, Fort Worth, TX 76117 • Phone: 940-325-6688 • Fax: 940-325-3636

FRIENDLY CLAY TARGET THROWERS

Trius Traps offer shooters superior quality, easy cocking, manual clay target traps. Singles, doubles plus piggy back doubles. Traps are factory-assembled and tested. Attach mount and main spring and you're ready to shoot. All adjustments made without tools. Birdshooter — quality at a budget price. Trius Model 92R — the original "Foot trap." Trapmaster — sit down comfort with pivoting action. The innovative 1-Step (shown) — almost effortless to use. Set arm without tension, place targets on arm and step on pedal to put tension on main spring and release target. High angle target retainer on all traps. Trius, satisfying shooters since 1955.

TRIUS TRAPS, INC.

Attn: Dept. SM'2001, P.O. Box 25, Cleves, OH 45002
Phone: 513-941-5682 • Web: www.triustraps.com

RAZOR SHARP

Finland has a harsh and challenging environment. Long ago, Finns developed a multi-purpose survival knife "the puukko." These basic tools are very sharp, light-weight and durable. Used for many daily tasks, these knives are still being used today.

Kellam Knives began to bring these knives into the worldwide marketplace. The "puukko" is an excellent tool that will endure for many decades. This year, one of their makers from the KP Smithy won Best Knifemaker in Finland. His family has been making knives since 1610 and comes from an award-winning tradition.

Kellam Knives offers the largest selection of quality knives made by the most respected knifemakers in Finland.

902 S. Dixie Hwy., Lantana, FL 33462
Phone: 561-588-3185 or 800-390-6918
Fax: 561-588-3186
Web: www.kellamknives.com
Email: info@kellamknives.com

SHOOTER'S MARKETPLACE

CONCEALABLE HOLSTER

The Concealable™ Holster, Belt and Magazine Carrier provide excellent comfort, style, and workability. The unique two-piece holster construction is contoured on the body side to the natural curve of the hip providing:

- A narrower profile
- Minimizing shifting
- Combat grip
- Comfortable fit
- Deep hand-molding

The 1-1/2" contour belt is fully lined and tapers to 1". The magazine carrier's stitched belt channel fits belts up to 1-1/2".

Available in black or Havana brown premium saddle leather. The holster sells for $85.00 + S&H. The Belt is $107.00 + S&H and the Magazine Carrier is $39.95 + S&H. Color catalog is $8.00.

Galco International "For those who demand the best...and know the difference."

GALCO INTERNATIONAL

2019 W. Quail Ave., Phoenix, AZ 85027

Phone: 623-434-7070 • Fax: 800-737-1725

1-800-US-Galco (874-2526) • www.usgalco.com

CATALOG #23

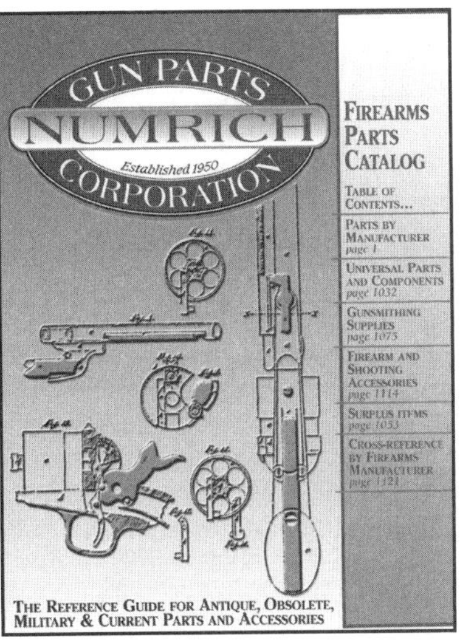

Catalog #23 is Numrich Gun Part Corporation's most recent edition. This 1152-page catalog features more than 450 schematics for use in identifying commercial, military, antique, and foreign guns. Edition #23 contains 180,000 individual items from our inventory of over 650 million parts and accessories, and is a necessity for any true gunsmith or hobbyist. It has been the industry's reference book for firearm parts and identification for over 50 years.

Order Item #RH-23 $12.95

U.S. Orders: Bulk Mail (Shipping charges included)

Foreign Orders: Air Mail-30 day delivery

or Surface-90 day delivery. (Shipping charges additional).

NUMRICH GUN PARTS CORPORATION

226 Williams Lane, West Hurley, NY 12491

Orders: (845) 679-2417 • Customer Service: (845) 679-4867

Toll-Free Fax: (877) Gun Parts

e-GunParts.com • E-mail: info@gunpartscorp.com

CLENZOIL FIELD & RANGE®

This is what museums, collectors, and competitive shooters are switching to in serious numbers.

Clenzoil Field & Range® is a remarkable one-step bore cleaner, lubricant, and long-term protectant that contains absolutely no teflon or silicone, so it never gets gummy or sticky.

A regional favorite for many years, Clenzoil is finally available nationwide. Clenzoil is signing up dealers daily, but your local shop may not carry it yet. If that's the case, you may order 24 hours a day by calling 1-800-OIL-IT-UP. Dealers may join the growing Clenzoil dealer network by calling 440-899-0482.

Clenzoil is a proud supplier to ArmaLite, Inc.

25670 First Street, Westlake, OH 44145

Phone: 440-899-0482 • Fax: 440-899-0483

GLASER SAFETY SLUG

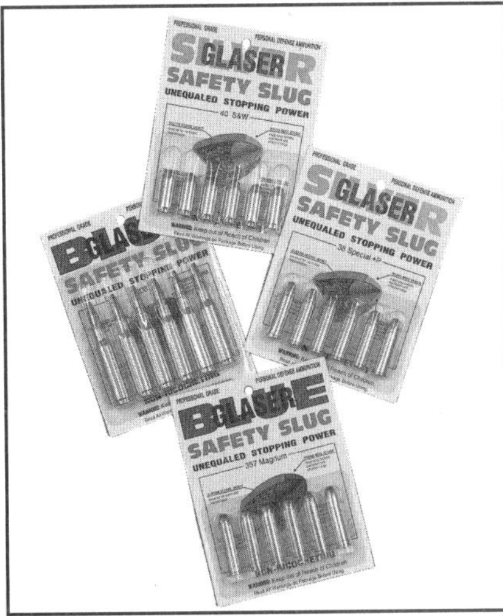

For over 25 years Glaser has provided a state-of-the-art personal defense ammunition used by the law enforcement and civilian communities. Available in two bullet styles, the Glaser Blue is offered in a full range of handgun calibers from 25 ACP to 45 Colt (including the 9mm Makarov and 357 Sig) and four rifle cailbers: 223, 308, 30-06 and 7.62x39. The Glaser Silver is available in all handgun calibers from 380 ACP to 45 Colt.

A complete brochure is available on the internet.

GLASER SAFETY SLUG, INC.

1311 Industry Road, Sturgis, SD 57785

Phone: 605-347-4544 • www.safetyslug.com

RIFLE AND PISTOL MAGAZINES

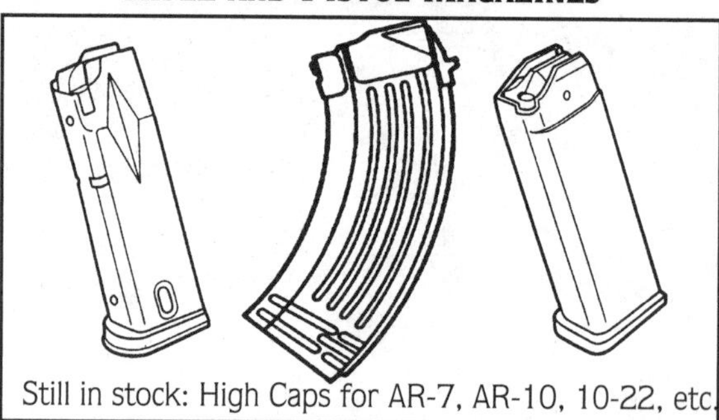
Still in stock: High Caps for AR-7, AR-10, 10-22, etc.

Forrest, Inc. offers shooters one of the largest selections of standard and extended high-capacity magazines in the United States. Whether you're looking for a few spare magazines for that obsolete 22 rifle or pistol, or wish to replace a reduced-capacity ten-shot magazine with the higher-capacity pre-ban original, all are available from this California firm. They offer competitive pricing especially for dealers wanting to buy in quantity. Gun show dealers are our specialty. G.I., O.E.M., factory or aftermarket.

Forrest Inc. also stocks parts and accessories for the Colt 1911 45 Auto pistol, the SKS and MAK-90 rifles as well as many U.S. military rifles. One of their specialty parts is firing pins for obsolete weapons.

Call or write Forrest, Inc. for more information and a free brochure. Be sure and mention *Shooter's Marketplace*.

FORREST, INC.
P.O. Box 326, Dept: #100, Lakeside, CA 92040
Phone: 619-561-5800 • Fax: 888-GUNCLIP
Web: www.gunmags.com

NEW MANUAL AVAILABLE

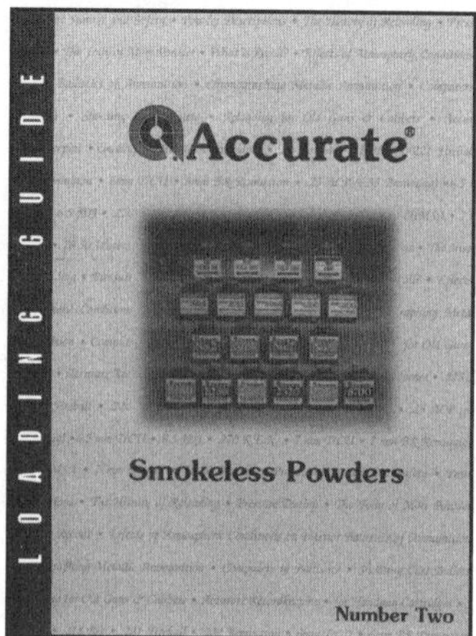

Accurate Powder's newest manual, Number Two, contains new data on powders XMR 4064 and XMP 5744, as well as a special section on Cowboy Action Shooting. In addition, the 400-page manual has loads for new cartridges, such as the .260 Rem., .300 Rem. Ultra Mag., .338 Rem. Ultra Mag., .357 Sig., .300 Whisper, .400 Corbon and more. It also includes many new bullets for the most popular cartridges as well as data for sabots in selected calibers. The price for the book is $16.95, plus $2.00 for shipping and handling in the continental U.S. To order a copy, call or write to:

ACCURATE ARMS
5891 Hwy. 230 W., McEwen, TN 37101
Phone: 1-800-416-3006 • Web: www.accuratepowder.com

6x18x40 VARMINT/TARGET SCOPE

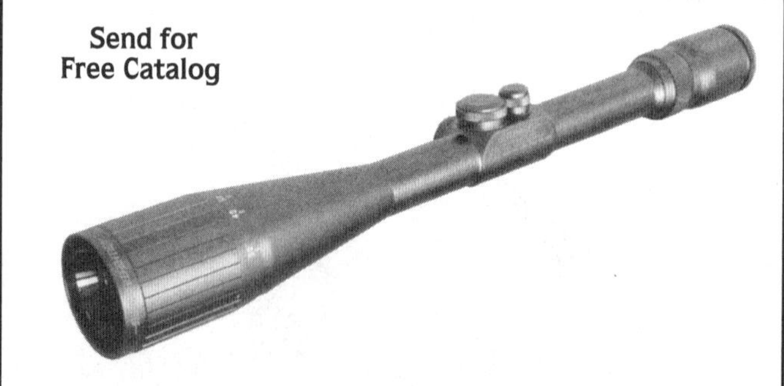

The Shepherd 6x18x40 Varmint/Target Scope makes long-range varmint and target shooting child's play. Just pick the ranging circle that best fits your target (be it prairie dogs, coyotes or paper varmints) and Shepherd's exclusive, patented Dual Reticle Down Range System does the rest. You won't believe how far you can accurately shoot, even with rimfire rifles.

Shepherd's superior lens coating mean superior light transmission and tack-sharp resolution.

This new shockproof, waterproof scope features 1/4 minute-of-angle clicks on the ranging circles and friction adjustments on the crosshairs that allow fine-tuning to 0.001 MOA. A 40mm adjustable objective provides a 5.5-foot field of view at 100 yards (16x setting). 16.5 FOV @ 6X.

SHEPHERD ENTERPRISES, INC.
Box 189, Waterloo, NE 68069
Phone: 402-779-2424 • Fax: 402-779-4010
E-mail: shepherd@shepherdscopes.com • Web: www.shepherdscopes.com

NYLON COATED GUN CLEANING RODS

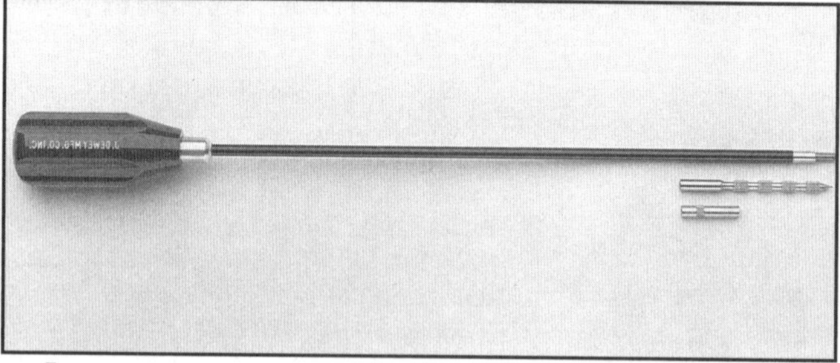

J. Dewey cleaning rods have been used by the U.S. Olympic shooting team and the benchrest community for over 20 years. These one-piece, spring-tempered, steel-base rods will not gall delicate rifling or damage the muzzle area of front-cleaned firearms. The nylon coating elmininates the problem of abrasives adhering to the rod during the cleaning operation. Each rod comes with a hard non-breakable plastic handle supported by ball-bearings, top and bottom, for ease of cleaning.

The brass cleaning jags are designed to pierce the center of the cleaning patch or wrap around the knurled end to keep the patch centered in the bore.

Coated rods are available from 17-caliber to shotgun bore size in several lengths to meet the needs of any shooter. Write for more information.

J. DEWEY MFG. CO., INC.
P.O. Box 2014, Southbury, CT 06488
Phone: 203-264-3064 • Fax: 203-262-6907
Web: www.deweyrods.com

SHOOTER'S MARKETPLACE

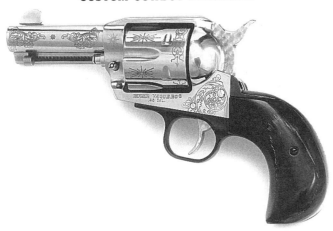

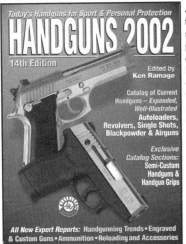

SHOOTER'S MARKETPLACE

ADVANCED MULTI-FUNCTION RIFLE

DSA offers a complete line of new U.S.-manufactured SA58 rifles. The SA58 rifle is a 21st-century version of the battle proven FAL. DSA is the only U.S. manufacturer of FAL-type rifles with upper and lower receivers machined from solid billets.

Firearm durability, reliability and shooter safety are vital components of the DSA design and manufacturing process. H.P. White Laboratory, Inc. excess pressure tested a SA58 rifle to 101,000 CUP with the receiver remaining undamaged! The SA58 is an incredibly strong and accurate multi-function rifle that can be accessorized to fit the personal needs of each shooter. Available in .308, .243, .260 and 7mm-08 calibers.

DSA carries a huge selection of FAL/SA58 parts and accessories, including two new, DSA exclusive items. The FAL Rail Interface Handguard has a 1913 Picatinny rail on all four sides for attaching accessories where the shooter wants them. The X Series FAL Buttstock gives the shooter a better rifle grip for precision shooting.

For more information, call for a catalog or check out the DSA Web site.

DSA, INC.

P.O. Box 370, Barrington, IL 60011

Phone: 847-277-7258 • Fax: 847-277-7259

Web: www.dsarms.com

ALASKAN HUNTER

Gary Reeder Custom Guns, builder of full custom guns, including custom cowboy guns, hunting handguns, African hunting rifles, custom Encores and Encore barrels, has a free brochure available or you can check out the large Web site at www.reedercustomguns.com. One of our most popular series is our Alaskan Hunter. This beefy 5-shot 454 Casull is for the serious handgun hunter and joins our 475 Linebaugh and 500 Linebaugh as our most popular hunting handguns. For more information contact:

GARY REEDER CUSTOM GUNS

2710 N Steve's Blvd., Suite 22, Flagstaff, AZ 86004

Phone: 520-526-3313

HIGH QUALITY OPTICS

One of the best indicators of quality is a scope's resolution number. The smaller the number, the better. Our scope has a resolution number of 2.8 seconds of angle. This number is about 20% smaller (better) than other well-known scopes costing much more. It means that two .22 caliber bullets can be a hair's breadth apart and edges of each still be clearly seen. With a Shepherd at 800 yards, you will be able to tell a four inch antler from a four inch ear and a burrowing owl from a prairie dog. Bird watchers will be able to distinguish a Tufted Titmouse from a Ticked-Off Field Mouse. Send for free catalog.

SHEPHERD ENTERPRISES, INC.

Box 189, Waterloo, NE 68069

Phone: 402-779-2424 • Fax: 402-779-4010

E-mail: shepherd@shepherdscopes.com • Web: www.shepherdscopes.com

COMBINATION RIFLE AND OPTICS REST

The Magna-Pod weighs less than two pounds, yet firmly supports more than most expensive tripods. It will hold 50 pounds at its low 9-inch height and over 10 pounds extended to 17 inches. It sets up in seconds where there is neither time nor space for a tripod and keeps your expensive equipment safe from knock-overs by kids, pets, pedestrians, or even high winds. It makes a great mono-pod for camcorders, etc., and its carrying box is less than 13" x 13" x 3 1/4" high for easy storage and access.

Attached to its triangle base it becomes an extremely stable table pod or rifle bench rest. The rifle yoke pictured in photo is included.

It's 5 pods in 1: Magna-Pod, Mono-Pod, Table-Pod, Shoulder-Pod and Rifle Rest. Send for free catalog.

SHEPHERD ENTERPRISES, INC.

Box 189, Waterloo, NE 68069

Phone: 402-779-2424 • Fax: 402-779-4010

E-mail: shepherd@shepherdscopes.com • Web: www.shepherdscopes.com

SHOOTER'S MARKETPLACE

FOLDING BIPODS

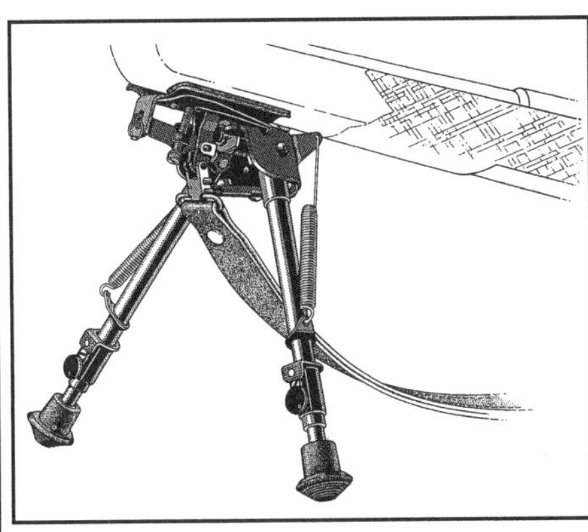

Harris Bipods clamp securely to most stud-equipped bolt-action rifles and are quick-detachable. With adapters, they will fit some other guns. On all models except the Model LM, folding legs have completely adjustable spring-return extensions. The sling swivel attaches to the clamp. This time-proven design is manufactured with heat-treated steel and hard alloys and has a black anodized finish.

Series S Bipods rotate 35° for instant leveling on uneven ground. Hinged base has tension adjustment and buffer springs to eliminate tremor or looseness in crotch area of bipod. They are otherwise similar to non-rotating Series 1A2.

Thirteen models are available from Harris Engineering; literature is free.

HARRIS ENGINEERING INC.

Dept: GD54, Barlow, KY 42024
Phone: 270-334-3633 • Fax: 270-334-3000
Web: www.cyberteklabs.com/harris/main/htm

PRECISION RIFLE REST

Bald Eagle Precision Machine Co. offers a rifle rest perfect for the serious benchrester or dedicated varminter.

"The Slingshot" or Next Generation has 60° front legs. The rest is constructed of aircraft-quality aluminum or fine-grain cast iron and weighs 12 to 20 lbs. The finish is 3 coats of Imron clear. Primary height adjustments are made with a rack and pinion gear. Secondary adjustment uses a mariner wheel with thrust bearings for smooth operation. A hidden fourth leg allows for lateral movement on the bench.

Bald Eagle offers approximately 150 rest combinations to choose from, including windage adjustable, right or left hand, cast aluminum or cast iron.

Prices: $165.00 to $335.00.

BALD EAGLE PRECISION MACHINE CO.

101-K Allison Street, Lock Haven, PA 17745
Phone: 570-748-6772 • Fax: 570-748-4443
Web: www.baldeaglemachine.com

WORLD CLASS EXHIBITION SHOOTING

Tom Knapp's exhibition shooting videos are now available.

Each video reveals explicit slow motion and unusual camera angles of Tom's unbelievable multi-gun routines.

Video #1: Tom's World Record in the semi-auto class, of shooting *9 hand-thrown* clay targets using no assistance. RT approx. 9 min. **Price $9.95 + $4.55 SH=$14.50 USD**

Video #2: Three segments (including video #1). Also, rare footage of Tom's aerial .22 rifle routines (including shooting aspirins from mid-air!) and a video library of Tom's live show shotgun routines. RT approx. 30 min. **Price $19.95 + $4.55 SH=$24.50 USD**

Video #3: Tom Knapp & Bill Dance. As seen on TNN's "*Bill Dance Outdoors*" program. Although Bill knew that Tom was going to demonstrate some of his .22 rifle shooting, he didn't know about the "trick" that Tom had in store for him! RT approx. 35 min. **Price$19.95 + $4.55 SH=$24.50 USD**

Mail your check or money order to the address below or you can make a secure credit card order for Tom's Videos & Shooting Accessories from Tom's Web site.

THE SHOOTIST INC.

14618 County Road 35, Elk River, MN 55330
Phone (763) 441-5634, Fax (763) 241-0056
E-mail: tjknapp@qwest.net • Web: www.tomknapp.net

DETACHABLE RINGS & BASES

A.R.M.S.® #22 Throw Lever Rings

All steel 30mm ring, secured with A.R.M.S.® dovetail system to an extruded aluminum platform. Built in no-mar patented buffer pads. Available in Low, Medium, and High height. Low height measures .925". Medium height measures 1.150". High height measures 1.450". Height is measured from the center of the optic to the bottom of the base.

Sugg. Retail $99.00
U.S. Patent No. 5,276,988 & 4,845,871
Item #37 to convert 30mm to 1",
Suggested Retail $29.00

Call for dealer or distributor in your area.

A.R.M.S., INC.

230 W. Center St., West Bridgewater, MA 02379
Phone: (508) 584-7816 • Fax: (508) 588-8045
E-mail: sswan37176@aol.com • Web: www.armsmounts.com

SHOOTER'S MARKETPLACE

AO Pro Express Sights

Uses proven Express Sight Principle with Big Dot Tritium or Standard Dot Tritium Front Sight with a vertical Tritium Bar within the Express Rear Sight. Ideal "flash sight alignment" stressed in defensive handgun courses. The tritium Express Rear enhances low-light sight alignment and acquisition. This improves a handgun for fastest sight picture in both normal and low light. Professional trainers rate it as the fastest acquisition sight under actual stress situations. Improves front sight acquisition for IDPA and IPSC shooting competition. Fits most handguns with factory dovetails; other models require dovetail front cuts. Also available in Adjustable Express Rear for Bomar, LPA, and Kimber.

Price: Pro Express Big Dot Tritium (or Standard Dot Tritium): $120.00

Price: Adjustable Pro Express Big Dot Tritium (or Standard Dot Tritium): $150.00

AO SIGHT SYSTEMS INC.

(Formerly: Ashley Outdoors)
2401 Ludelle, Fort Worth, TX 76105
Phone: 817-536-0136 • Fax: 800-536-3517

Custom Leather

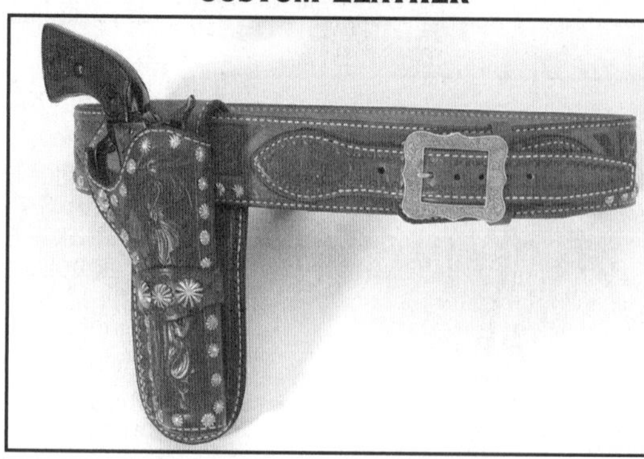

Rod Kibler Saddlery applies 25 years of saddle-making experience to the construction of fine holsters and belts. Kibler has found working on gun leather was a natural extension of saddle work.

Kibler, himself an active cowboy-action shooter, listens to other shooters and incorporates their ideas into his leatherwork for shooters.

Each of his rigs is extensively field-tested to ensure it will perform for the buyer. Several top national competitors have used Rod Kibler rigs for years.

Kibler adheres to old-time methods and quality standards. This commitment assures gun leather that meets the customer's standards, as well as Kibler's.

Only select, oak-tanned skirting leather is used.

The pictured rig is fully hand carved and lined with top-grain leather. The hardware includes solid sterling siver conchos and buckle.

ROD KIBLER SADDLERY

2307 Athens Road, Royston, GA 30662-3231 • Phone: 706-246-0487

e-GunParts.com

Numrich Gun Parts Corporation has expanded its website to include full e-commerce purchasing. Our new virtual storefront allows shopping for all your firearms parts and accessories by manufacturer and model. 180,000 items are available to purchase from our secure site, 24 hours a day, from anywhere in the world. You can now browse and buy within four clicks. The updated e-commerce site will also offer specials, new products, and inventory closeouts.

NUMRICH GUN PARTS CORPORATION

226 Williams Lane, West Hurley, NY 12491
Orders: 845-679-2417 • Customer Svc: 845-679-4867
Toll Free Fax: 877-Gun Parts • E-mail: info@gunpartscorp.com

The Gun Digest® Book of Modern Gun Values

11th Edition

Edited by Ken Ramage

Identify, evaluate and price any of the commonly encountered firearms made from 1900 to present. This specialized, heavily illustrated, expanded edition helps you easily identify and value older firearms found in gun shops, auctions, advertisements-or that old family gun you've just inherited. More than 7,500 post-1900 models are gathered by type then listed alphabetically. All prices are fully updated to mid-year. Includes more photos, and new sections covering mechanical inspection and (full-color) condition evaluation. New reference section lists books and associations for collectors.

Softcover • 8-1/2 x 11 • 640 pages
3,000+ b&w photos
Item# MGV11 • $24.95

To place a credit card order or for a FREE all-product catalog call

800-258-0929 **Offer DLB1**

M-F 7am - 8pm • Sat 8am - 2pm, CST

Krause Publications, Offer DLB1
P.O. Box 5009, Iola WI 54945-5009 • ***www.krausebooks.com***

Shipping & Handling: $4.00 first book, $2.00 each additional. Non-US addresses $20.95 first book, $5.95 each additional.
Sales Tax: CA, IA, IL, PA, TN, VA, WI residents please add appropriate sales tax.

SHOOTER'S MARKETPLACE

QUALITY GUNSTOCK BLANKS

Cali'co Hardwoods has been cutting superior-quality shotgun and rifle blanks for more than 31 years. Cali'co supplies blanks to many of the major manufacturers—Browning, Weatherby, Ruger, Holland & Holland, to name a few—as well as custom gunsmiths the world over.

Profiled rifle blanks are available, ready for inletting and sanding. Cali'co sells superior California hardwoods in Claro walnut, French walnut, Bastogne, maple and myrtle.

Cali'co offers good, serviceable blanks and some of the finest exhibition blanks available. Satisfaction guaranteed.

Color catalog, retail and dealer price list (FFL required) free upon request.

CALI'CO HARDWOODS, INC.
3580 Westwind Blvd., Santa Rosa, CA 95403
Phone: 707-546-4045 • Fax: 707-546-4027

CUSTOM RESTORATION/CASE COLORING

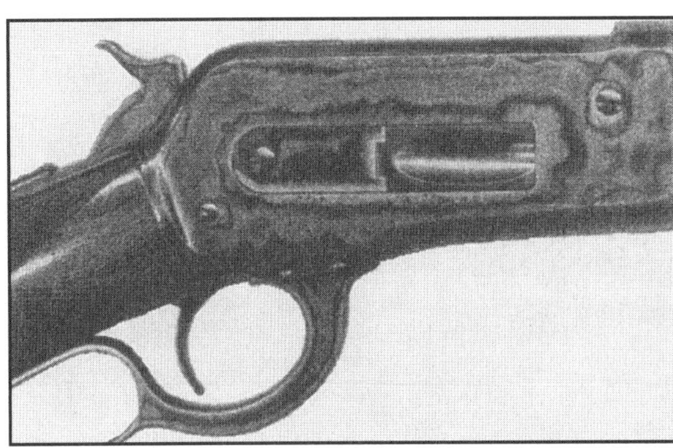

Doug Turnbull Restoration continues to offer bone charcoal case hardening work, matching the original case colors produced by Winchester, Colt, Marlin, Parker, L.C. Smith, Fox and other manufacturers. Also available is charcoal blue, known as Carbona or machine blue, a prewar finish used by most makers. "Specializing in the accurate recreation of historical metal finishes on period firearms, from polishing to final finishing. Including Bone Charcoal Color Case Hardening, Charcoal Bluing, Rust Blue, and Nitre Blue".

DOUG TURNBULL RESTORATION
P.O. Box 471, 6680 Rt 5&20, Dept SM2000
Bloomfield, New York 14469 • Phone/Fax: 716-657-6338
E-mail: turnbullrest@mindspring.com
Web: www.turnbullrestoration.com

FOR THE SERIOUS RELOADER...

Rooster Laboratories® makes two professional quality cannelure lubricants in 1" x 4" hollow or solid sticks, and in 2" x 6" solid. With a 220° F melting point, these lubes won't melt out and kill the powder, nor will they sweat oil. Using a lubrisizer heater, they flow consistently through the dieports, bond securely to the bullet, and harden quickly to a firm, tough finish.

- **ZAMBINI®** is a hard, tough lubricant, primarily for pistols.
- **HVR®** is for high velocity rifles, and is also excellent for pistols.

Contact Rooster Labs for prices, samples, and information on **Rooster Bright®** revolutionary ammonia-free case polish, plus a broad array of specialty bullet and case lubricants.

ROOSTER LABORATORIES®
P.O. Box 414605, Kansas City, MO 64141
Phone: 816-474-1622 • Fax: 816-474-1307
E-mail: roosterlabs@aol.com

WOLF® Performance Ammunition

•100% Guaranteed • Newly Manufactured • Reliable and Affordable

WOLF, Russia's highest quality ammunition, has expanded its product line to include six additional calibers .223 Rem HP, 7.62x39 SP, 7.62x54R, .22 Rifle (Match Target and Match Gold) and 40 S&W. WOLF's product line of reliable ammunition also includes: 7.62x39, 9mm Luger, .380 Auto, .45 Auto, .223 Rem (55 &62 GR.) and 5.45x39. All products are newly manufactured and non-corrosive. All **WOLF** Performance Ammunition comes with a full performance guarantee.

SSI
Sporting Supplies International, Inc

**2201 E. Winston, Suite K,
Anaheim, CA 92806
tel: 714.635.4246 • fax: 714.635.9276
www.wolfammo.com •
email:info@wolfammo.com**

"Your exclusive representative for WOLF Performance Ammunition and The Tula Cartridge Works and also suppliers of Novosibrirsk LVE Plant, Russia and SK Jagd-und, Germany."

SHOOTER'S MARKETPLACE

New Youth Shotgun

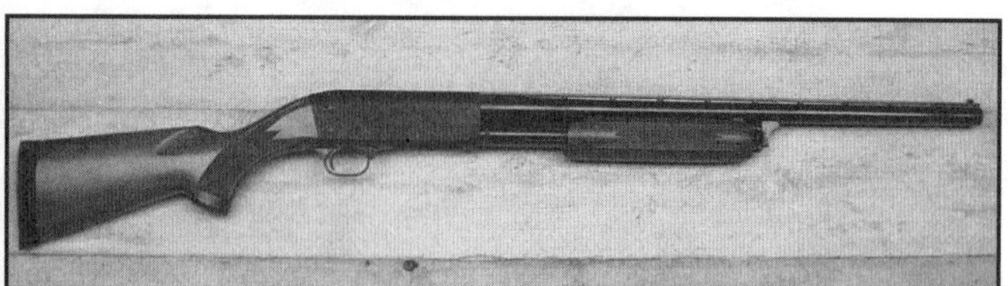

The Ithaca Model 37 Ultra Featherlight Youth model is based on the classic Model 37 pump-action shotgun, with bottom ejection and adaptability to either right- or left-handed shooters via a simple safety change. This new model uses a receiver machined from aircraft-grade aluminum to keep the gun's unloaded weight below five pounds, a definite benefit to younger shooters. The Youth model features a 22-inch barrel with interchangeable choke tubes and a vent rib. The American black walnut stock has a 12 3/4-inch length of pull over the ventilated recoil pad. For information, please contact:

ITHACA GUN® CO., LLC

901 Route 34B, King Ferry, NY 13081
Phone: 315-364-7171 • Fax: 315-364-5134
Web: www.ithacagun.com

New Deer Gun in 16-Gauge

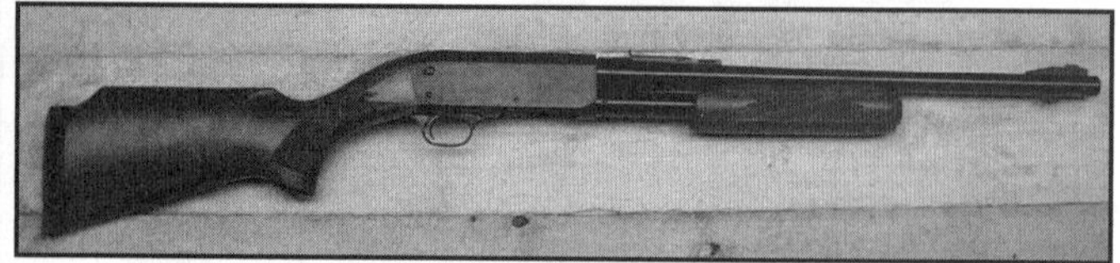

Ithaca Gun is introducing a new 16-gauge fixed-barrel Deerslayer II pump-action shotgun based on the proven Model 37 design.

Like the 12-gauge Deerslayer II, the new 16-gauge version is designed with scope use in mind, featuring a factory drilled and tapped receiver, a Monte Carlo stock and incorporates a free-floated, rifled barrel mated to the all-steel receiver to deliver rifle-like accuracy. The new Ithaca, and Lightfield's 16-gauge impact-discarding sabot ammunition, makes a hard-hitting, flat-shooting combination delivering energy comparable to that of a 12 gauge - from a lighter, easier-to-carry gun.

ITHACA GUN® CO., LLC

901 Route 34B, King Ferry, NY 13081
Phone: 315-364-7171 • Fax: 315-364-5134
Web: www.ithacagun.com

Versatile Scope

Waterproof; Multi-Coated; Speed Focus

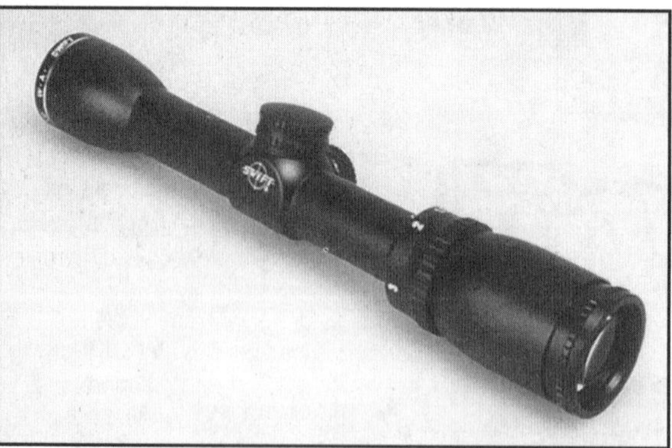

The 1.5-4.5x, 32mm Model 648M Swift *PREMIER*.
Considered by many to be the most versatile scope in our *Premier* line, works well on a shotgun or used as a black powder scope. It is often used in wooded areas for turkeys. It is effective on deer where rifles are permitted. Eye relief from 3.05 to 3.27. Crosshair and circle reticle make this rifle scope easy to focus on target, and ideal for turkey hunting. With black matte finish.

For more information, contact:

SWIFT INSTRUMENTS, INC.

952 Dorchester Avenue, Dept: GD, Boston, MA 02125
Phone: 617-436-2960 • Fax: 617-436-3232
E-mail: info@swiftoptics.com • Web: www.swift-optics.com

Model 676S Swift Premier

4-12X, 40 – WA – Waterproof – Multi-coated – Speed Focus

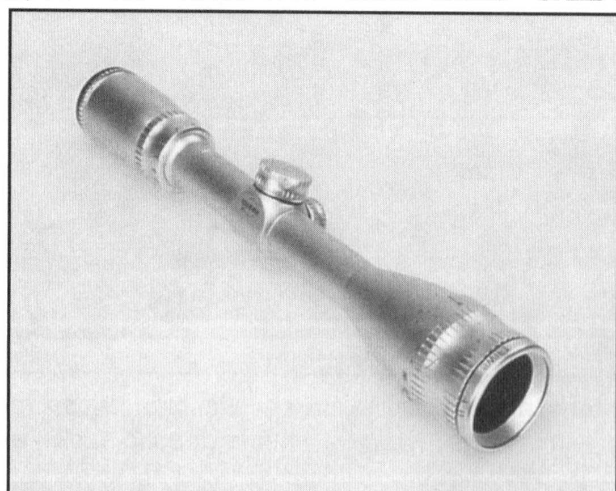

With a parallax adjustment from 10 yards to infinity this scope is highly adaptable and excellent for use as a varminting scope or on gas powered air rifles. Elevation and windage adjustments are full saddle on the hard anodized 1-inch tube. *Speed Focus* adjustment brings you on target easily. The objectives are multi-coated and the self-centering reticle in Quadraplex. Available in regular (676), matte (676M), and silver finish (676S). Gift boxed.

For more information, contact:

SWIFT INSTRUMENTS, INC.

952 Dorchester Avenue, Dept: GD, Boston, MA 02125
Phone: 617-436-2960 • Fax: 617-436-3232
E-mail: info@swiftoptics.com • Web: www.swift-optics.com

A New Trend in Gun Collecting: Guns That Can't Shoot!

INTERNATIONAL MILITARY ANTIQUES, INC. of New Jersey, the company that supplied the machine guns used in "*Saving Private Ryan*" and many other World War II block buster movies, has introduced a new trend in gun collecting. Historically significant NON-FIRING machine guns constructed from original G.I. military parts to BATF specifications, making them legally unrestricted by federal law and unconvertible to firing condition. Previously unavailable, these original weapons can complete any 20th century military collection without the extremely high cost, extensive paperwork and security measures that comes with operational machine gun ownership.

Spanning from the WWI water-cooled Maxim and Vickers guns through the myriad of weapons developed by many countries during two World Wars, including the legendary Nazi era MG34 and MG42 series light machine guns, I.M.A. has developed a range of some of the most famous and infamous weapons that forged the modern world we know today.

In addition, I.M.A. offers a vast range of other military-related materials, both original and high quality reproduction. Military holsters, complete with replicated markings together with belts, pouches, swords, helmets, and accoutrements from over 300 years of history cater to the requirements of the collector and reenactor alike.

With its parent company Fire-Power International, Ltd. of England supplying the lion's share of the ex-military equipment, I.M.A.'s offerings are often unique to the U.S. market.

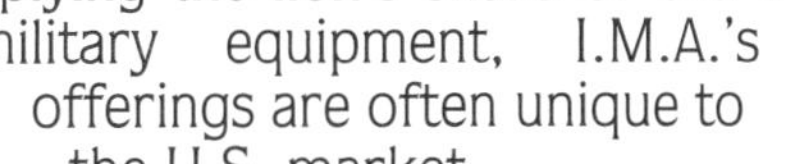

A mail order company operating from a 25,000 sq. ft. facility in New Jersey, the depth and scope of its inventory provides something for everyone. The often humorous but always highly accurate detailed cartoon illustrations by the renowned military artist SCOTT NOVZEN make I.M.A.'s advertisements and catalogs, or a visit to their website an added treat. Take a light hearted look at military history.

For further information contact:

INTERNATIONAL MILITARY ANTIQUES, INC.

Box 256, Millington, New Jersey 07946, U.S.A.

Phone: 908-903-1200 • Fax: 908-903-0106 • www.ima-usa.com

COWBOY ACTION

The closest you'll get to the Old West short of a time machine.

Join SASS® and preserve the spirit of the Old West. Members receive a numbered shooter's badge, alias registration, an annual subscription to *The Cowboy Chronicle*, and much more.

SINGLE ACTION SHOOTING SOCIETY™

Phone Toll Free: 1-877-411-SASS

Web: www.sassnet.com

JP ENTERPRISES, INC.

Manufacturer of professional grade semi-auto rifles for competitive shooters and law enforcement. In addition, they offer modifications on bolt rifles, Remington shotguns and Glock pistols using proprietary components and techniques to enhance performance. They also offer their complete line of high performance parts for rifles, pistols and shotguns for sale direct or through several major distributors such as Brownell's. In particular, their recoil eliminators for rifles and the JP precision trigger system for AR-type rifles are known for their outstanding performance and have become the choice for many professional level shooters. Last year, they introduced a new coil reduction system for Remington series shotguns that has received excellent feed back from the action shooting community. Their extensive web site can be seen at www.jpar15.com.

JP ENTERPRISES, INC.

P.O. Box 378, Hugo, MN 55378

Phone: 651-426-9196 • Fax: 651-426-2472

DO-ALL TRAPS

Do-All Traps has a variety of traps and targets for the weekend shooter or commercial range.

The heart of the Do-All Trap is a patented, pivoting adjustable throwing arm. Three simple adjusting bolts allow the arm to be positioned to throw any clay target from a 90-degree vertical springing teal to a ground-bouncing rabbit or standard pair of doubles, and everything in-between.

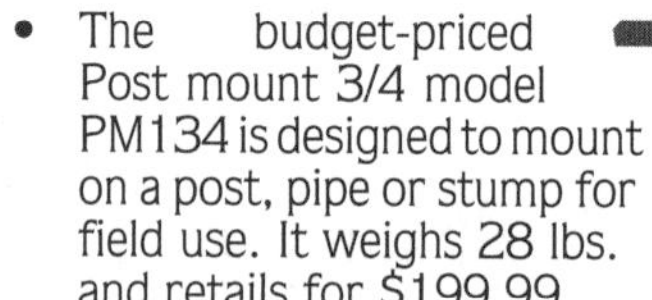

A sliding, adjustable-tension spring clip on the throwing arm adapts to standard, rabbit, 90mm (midi), 60mm (mini) or battue clays, and allows them to be thrown as singles, stacked doubles or nesting pairs. By varying spring tension, target selection and position of the targets on the throwing arms, the Do-All Trap can create any target presentation desired.

The frame of each Do-All Trap is 3-inch, heavy-duty steel tubing with robotic welds and a durable power-coat paint finish. Each model assembles in seconds and includes an adjusting wrench, protective ring-guard and 15-minute instructional video.

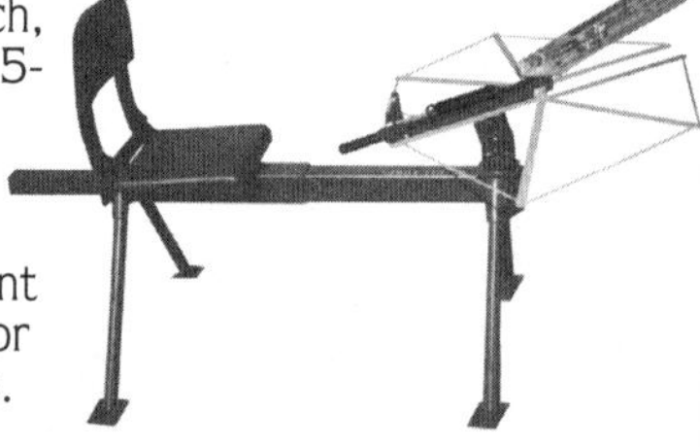

- The budget-priced Post mount 3/4 model PM134 is designed to mount on a post, pipe or stump for field use. It weighs 28 lbs. and retails for $199.99.
- The Single Trap model ST200 includes a fold-down chair, includes legs and also fits a trailer hitch. It weighs 47 lbs. and retails for $139.99.
- The Double Trap 3/4 Trap model DT534 has the same features as the Single Trap, but includes an extra throwing arm for report pairs. It can throw four targets at once. It weighs 94 lbs. and retails for $399.99.

Weekend rifle and airgun shooters will enjoy the fun of swinging targets with The Plinker and Plinker Jr.

The Plinker™ Target Systems

- The Plinker, designed to withstand .22 rimfire rounds, has four pendulum targets that swing up when shot. To reset, simply shoot the fifth "reset" target at the top. The 10-lb. steel unit retails for $34.99.
- The Plinker Jr. is similar to The Plinker, but made to withstand airgun pellets. It weighs 1 lb. and retails for $13.99.

8113 Moores Ln., Suite 1900-154, Brentood, TN 37027

Phone: 1-800-252-9247 or 615-269-4889

Fax: 800-633-3172 or 615-269-4434

E-mail: sales@do-alltraps.com • Web: www.do-alltraps.com

SHOOTER'S MARKETPLACE

PERFORMANCE AMMUNITION

For serious enthusiasts who demand quality and accuracy, Black Hills Ammunition offers high quality ammo at a reasonable price with good service. Black Hills Ammunition has been producing high quality rounds for over 20 years. They sell dealer-direct and pay all freight to the continental U.S. Minimum order in only one case. Satisfaction is guaranteed. Black Hills Ammunition specializes in match-quality 223 (both new and remanufactured), .308 Match, cowboy ammo and more. Performance is so good that the U.S. Army, Navy, Air Firce and Marines all use Black Hills.

Ask for it at your dealer, or contact them directly for purchase information.

BLACK HILLS AMMUNITION

P.O. Box 3090, Rapid City, SD 57709

Phone: 1-605-348-5150 • Fax: 1-605-348-9827

ADJUSTABLE APERTURE FOR GLASSES

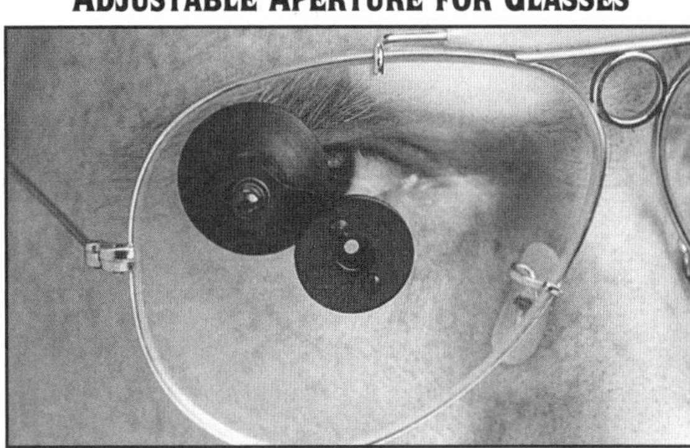

The Merit Optical Attachment is an instantly adjustable iris aperture that allows shooters to see their iron sights and target clearly. The adjustable aperture dramatically increases the eye's depth of focus, eliminating a fuzzy sight picture.

The Optical Attachment works with all types of glasses including bifocals and trifocals. It attaches securely with a small rubber suction cup. The aperture instantly adjusts from .022- to .156-inch in diameter to accommodate different light conditions. It is compact and lightweight.

Merit Corporation makes a full line of adjustable apertures for mounting in peep sights as well. Contact Merit Corporation for information and a free catalog.

MERIT CORPORATION

P.O. Box 9044, Schnectady, NY 12309

Phone: 518-346-1420

Web: www.meritcorporation.com

OBSOLETE AND HARD-TO-FIND AMMO

The Old Western Scrounger has been in the firearms business for 40 years, providing obsolete and hard-to-find ammunition and components, including European and double-rifle calibers. The company now carries the Kynoch line of ammo, ranging from the 318 Westley Richards to the 700 Nitro Express. Old Western Scrounger's own line of ammo covers almost any obsolete rifle or pistol caliber, including a 1 million-round run of the 5mm Remington Mag. (coming soon). The firm also is the exclusive carrier of RWS brass and other reloading components. In addition, Scrounger carries Fiocchi, Norma, Eley and RWS ammunition, as well as some old favorites. Free catalogs and free shipping are provided on orders over $25.00. Call the company if you need help determining which ammo is needed for a particular gun.

OLD WESTERN SCROUNGER, INC.

1540 Lucas Road, Yreka, CA 96097

Phone: 800-UPS-AMMO • Web: www.ows-ammunition.com

QUALITY CUSTOM KNIVES

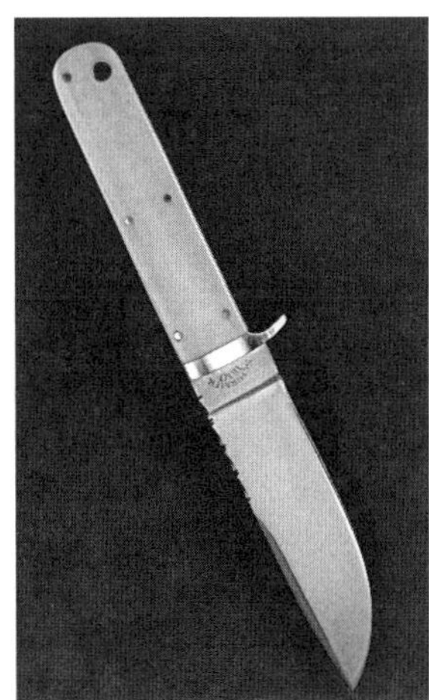

Mike Schirmer's lifelong interest in knives stems from his passion for hunting and since he lives in the heart of Montana's best big-game country, he has had plenty of opportunity to test his blades. Mike has also worked as an elk guide and a "buffalo skinner." (Call him to book a buffalo hunt.) All of Mike's knives, no matter how beautiful, are made to use. D2 is his favorite type of steel, but he will use other steels (including damascus) on special order. All types of handle material are available, as is engraving.

While the majority of his business is hunting knives, Mike also makes camp, fighting, and Old West Period knives. When you purchase a Mike Schirmer knife, you are getting a one-of-a-kind piece of working art that is destined to be a family heirloom. Mike usually has a few knives on hand for immediate delivery, or if you prefer, he will make a custom knife to your design.

For more information, contact Mike at:

RUBY MOUNTAIN KNIVES

P.O. Box 534,

Twin Bridges, MT 59754

Phone: 406-684-5868 • Email:

schirmer@3rivers.net

SHOOTER'S MARKETPLACE

CNC Machined Trigger Guard

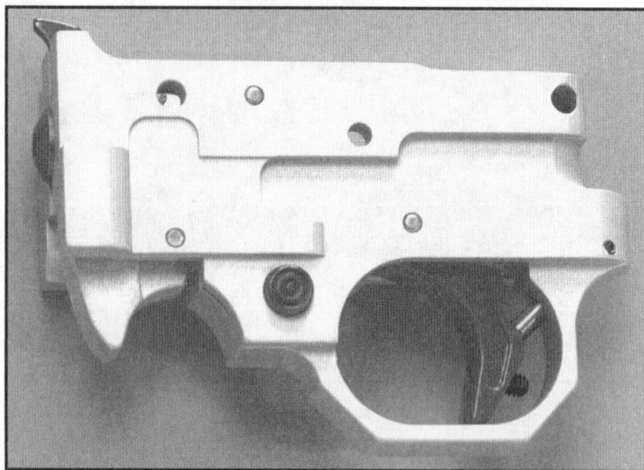

This is a complete CNC machined trigger guard equipped with precision EDM parts. It features an internal pretravel adjustment that is set at the factory in order to greatly reduce pretravel. This new match trigger guard is CNC machined from a solid billet of high strength aircraft aluminum. The hammer is a precision ground 440C stainless steel. The sear and disconnector are EDM manufactured parts. The trigger is black anodized and equipped with an overtravel adjustment screw. The trigger is reset internally. An automatic bolt release and an extended magazine release are also included.

VOLQUARTSEN CUSTOM LTD.

24276 240th Street, P.O. Box 397, Carroll, IA 51401
Phone: 712-792-4238 • Fax: 712-792-2542
E-mail: info@volquartsen.com • Web: www.volquartsen.com

CNC Machined Steel Competition Bolt

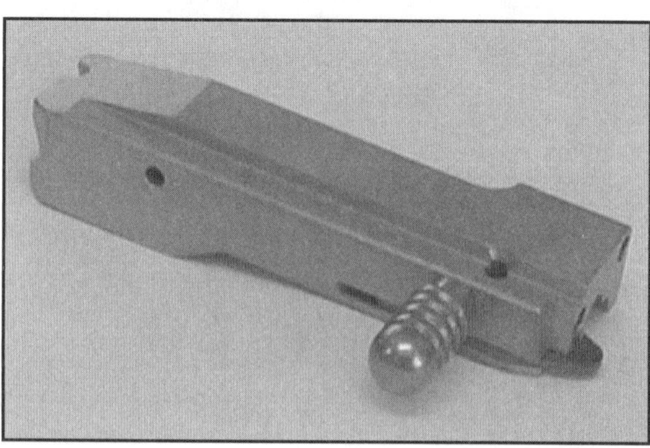

This bolt features hardened (60Rc) and tuned extractor for positive, consistent extraction. It also includes Volquartsen's own unique round titanium firing pin for faster lock time and to assure positive ignition. The new bolt also features interchangeable bolt handles. It is available with their streamline, compact stainless steel handle or a target knob (red or black) for easy cocking control. The bolt comes with Volquartsen's recoil rod and spring for ease of installation in either their stainless steel receiver or for the factory Ruger 10/22® receiver.

VOLQUARTSEN CUSTOM LTD.

24276 240th Street, P.O. Box 397, Carroll, IA 51401
Phone: 712-792-4238 • Fax: 712-792-2542
E-mail: info@volquartsen.com • Web: www.volquartsen.com

BREAK-FREE®
An Armor Holdings Company

Break-Free® is a leading manufacturer of synthetic-based cleaners, lubricants and preservative compounds for military weapon maintenance, law enforcement, civilian firearms, high performance sports equipment and industrial machinery. Break-Free's flagship product Break-Free CLP® was specifically developed to provide reliable weapon lubrication in battlefield conditions and to remove firing residues, carbon deposits and other firing contaminants. Moreover, Break-Free CLP® repels water and dirt and prevents corrosion, and keeps weapons combat ready in any condition – rain, snow, ice, mud, or sand.

Break-Free® has been an approved qualified source and quality supplier to militaries around the globe for over 20 years. To learn more about the Break-Free family of products, visit www.break-free.com or buy online at holsters.com.

BREAK-FREE®, INC.

13386 International Parkway
Jacksonville, FL 32218
Phone: 800-428-0588

M36 PlusOne™ Extension

Pearce Grip Inc., originators of the popular grip extension line for the Glock® sub-compact auto pistols, introduces the M36 PlusOne™ extension. This unit converts the Glock® model 36 (45 Auto) factory six-round magazine to a seven-round capacity and provides the extra finger groove for shooting comfort and control. The PlusOne™ replaces the factory magazine floor plate and is held securely to the magazine body with an external locking device that doubles as a contour blending feature completing the rear of the grip. This new extension is made from a high-impact polymer and incorporates the same texture and checkering pattern found on the pistol frame for a factory appearance. For more information or for a dealer near you contact:

PEARCE GRIP, INC.

P.O. Box 40367, Fort Worth, TX 76140
Phone: 800-390-9420 • Fax: 817-568-9707

SHOOTER'S MARKETPLACE

1911 MAGAZINE GUIDE

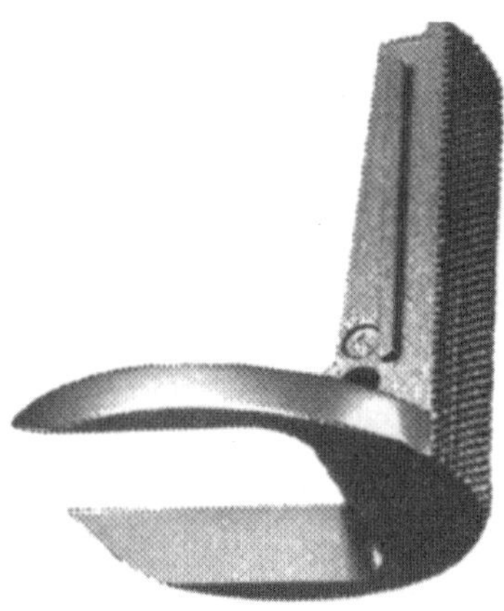

The S&A Mag Guide is the only one-piece magazine guide in the marketplace for 1911 pistols. It's the most popular and practical addition to the 1911 firearm. No frame modification, installs in minutes. Increases magazine opening 100%. 20LPI checkering for maximum grip, adds 1/4" length for extra leverage and recoil control. Will fit most 1911 clones, Colt, Springfield, Kimber, Auto-Ordnance, Norinco and Para Ordnance. Available in stainless steel or blued. Government and officer's models now available in hard anodized aluminum, neutral or black. $74.95 each.

SMITH & ALEXANDER, INC.

P.O. Box 496208, Garland, TX 75049

Phone: 1-800-722-1911 • Fax: 1-972-840-6176

E-mail: sa1911@gte.net • Website: wwwsmithandalexander.com

FINE GUN STOCKS

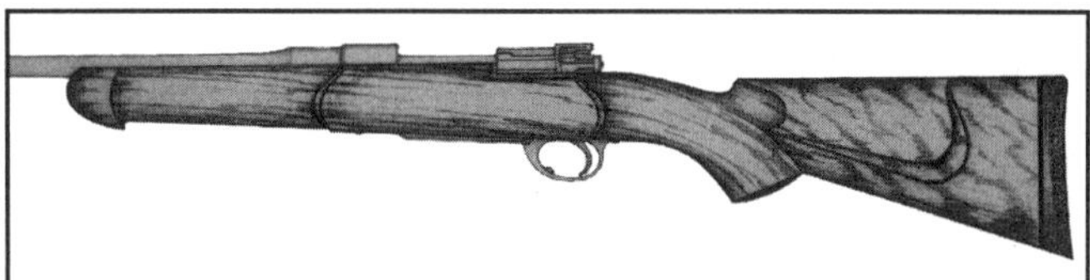

Manufacturing custom and production gunstocks for hundreds of models of rifles and shotguns—made from the finest stock woods and available in all stages of completion.

Visit www.gunstocks.com to view their bargain list of fine custom gunstocks. Each displayed in full color.

GREAT AMERICAN GUNSTOCK COMPANY

3420 Industrial Drive

Yuba City, CA 95993

Phone: 530-671-4570

Fax: 530-671-3906

Gunstock Hotline: 800-784-GUNS (4867)

Web: www.gunstocks.com

E-mail: gunstox@oro.net

BALLARD RIFLE IS BACK!

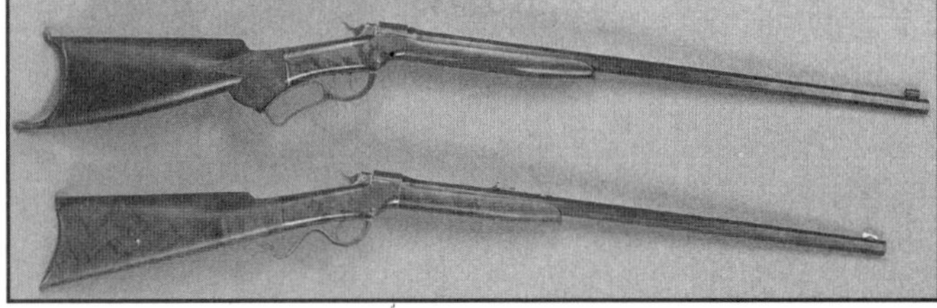

The Ballard rifle is back in production after more than 100 years. At the Cody, Wyoming factory, we have made a firm commitment to honoring the Ballard tradition of superior quality, fit and finish. Our craftsmen focus on that goal every day as they make Ballard rifles from the patent, in all original configuations.

Whether your interest is hunting, target shooting or Schuetzen shooting, there is a Ballard rifle to perfectly fit your needs. Please send for our color catalog of rifles, sights, parts, and bullet molds.

BALLARD RIFLES, LLC

113 W. Yellowstone Ave., Cody, WY 82414

Phone: 307-587-4914 • Fax: 307-527-6097

E-mail: ballard@wyoming.com

PERSONAL PROTECTION

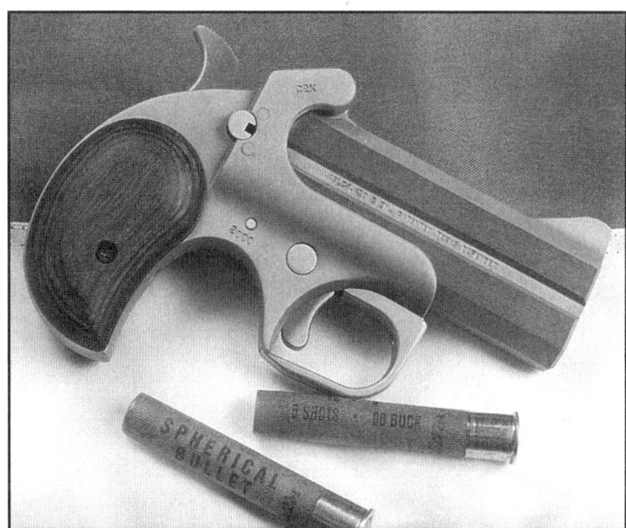

The Century 2000 Defender is designed for self-defense.

This Derringer-style pistol has a 3 1/2" double barrel, rebounding hammer, retracting firing pins, crossbolt safety, cammed locking lever, spring-loaded extractor and interchangeable barrels. 3" chambers for .45 Colt or .410 00 buckshot.

For further information, contact:

BOND ARMS, INC.

P.O. Box 1296, Granbury, TX 76048

Phone: 817-573-4445 • Fax: 817-573-5636

E-mail: bondarms@shooters.com • Web: www.bondarms.com

COMPLETE COMPACT CATALOG

HANDGUNS 2002

GUNDEX

GUNDEX

GUNDEX

GUNDEX

Ed Brown Classic

Ed Brown Classic Class A

BRILEY 1911-STYLE AUTO PISTOLS

Caliber: 9mm Para., 38 Super, 40 S&W, 10-shot magazine; 45 ACP, 8-shot magazine. **Barrel:** 3.6" or 5". **Weight:** NA. **Length:** NA. **Grips:** rosewood or rubber. **Sights:** Bo-Mar adjustable rear, Briley dovetail blade front. **Features:** Modular or Caspian alloy, carbon steel or stainless steel frame; match barrel and trigger group; lowered and flared ejection port; front and rear serrations on slide; beavertail grip safety; hot blue, hard chrome or stainless steel finish. Introduced 2000. Made in U.S. From Briley Manufacturing Inc.

Price: Fantom (3.6" bbl., fixed low-mount rear sight, armor coated lower receiver) . . . . from **$1,795.00**

Price: Fantom with two-port compensator . . . . from **$2,145.00**

Price: Advantage (5" bbl., adj. low-mount rear sight, checkered mainspring housing) . . . . from **$1,495.00**

Price: Versatility Plus (5" bbl., adj. low-mount rear sight, modular or Caspian frame) . . . . from **$1,695.00**

Price: Signature Series (5" bbl., adj. low-mount rear sight, 40 S&W only) . . . . from **$1,995.00**

Price: Plate Master (5" bbl. with compensator, lightened slide, Briley scope mount) . . . . from **$1,795.00**

Price: El Presidente (5" bbl. with Briley quad compensator, Briley scope mount) . . . . from **$2,195.00**

ED BROWN CLASSIC CUSTOM AND CLASS A LIMITED 1911-STYLE AUTO PISTOLS

Caliber: 45 ACP; 7-shot magazine; 40 S&W, 400 Cor-Bon, 38 Super, 9x23, 9mm Para. **Barrel:** 4.25", 5", 6". **Weight:** NA. **Length:** NA. **Grips:** Hogue exotic checkered wood. **Sights:** Bo-Mar or Novak rear, blade front. **Features:** Blued or stainless steel frame; ambidextrous safety; beavertail grip safety; checkered forestrap and mainspring housing; match-grade barrel; slotted hammer; long lightweight or Videki short steel trigger. Many options offered. Made in U.S. by Ed Brown Products.

Price: Classic Custom (45 ACP, 5" barrel) . . . . from **$2,750.00**

Price: Class A Limited (all calibers; several bbl. lengths in competition and carry forms) . . . . from **$2,250.00**

EUROPEAN AMERICAN ARMORY WITNESS AUTO PISTOLS

Caliber: 9mm Para., 9x21, 38 Super, 40 S&W, 45 ACP, 10mm; 10-shot magazine. **Barrel:** 3.55", 3.66", 4.25", 4.5", 4.75", 5.25". **Weight:** 26 to 38 oz. **Length:** 7.25" to 10.5" overall. **Grips:** Black rubber, smooth walnut, checkered walnut, ivory polymer. **Sights:** three-dot, windage-adjustable or fully adjustable rear, blade front. **Features:** Single and double action; polymer or forged steel frame; forged steel slide; field strips without tools; ergonomic grip angle; front and rear serrations on slide; matte blue and stainless steel finish. Frame can be converted to other calibers. Imported from Italy by European American Armory.

Price: Witness Full Size (4.5" bbl., three-dot sights, 8.1" overall) . . . . from **$399.00**

Price: Witness Compact (3.66" bbl., three-dot sights, 7.25" overall) . . . . from **$399.00**

Kimber Custom Compact CDP

Price: Carry-Comp (4.25" bbl. with compensator, three-dot sights, 8.1" overall) . . . . from **$439.00**

Price: Gold Team (5.25" bbl. with compensator, adjustable sights, 10.5" overall) . . . . from **$2,195.00**

Price: Silver Team (5.25" bbl. with compensator, adjustable sights, 9.75" overall) . . . . from **$999.00**

Price: Limited Class (4.75" barrel, adj. sights and trigger, drilled for scope mount) . . . . from **$999.00**

Price: P-Series (4.55" bbl., polymer frame in four colors, many porting and sight options) . . . . from **$379.00**

KIMBER CUSTOM 1911-STYLE AUTO PISTOLS

Caliber: 9mm Para., 38 Super, 9-shot magazines; 40 S&W, 8-shot magazine; 45 ACP, 7-shot magazine. **Barrel:** 5". **Weight:** 38 oz. **Length:** 8.7" overall. **Grips:** Black synthetic, smooth or double-diamond checkered rosewood, or double-diamond checkered walnut. **Sights:** McCormick low profile or Kimber adjustable rear, blade front. **Features:** Machined steel slide, frame and barrel; front and rear beveled slide serrations; cut and button-rifled, match-grade barrel; adjustable aluminum trigger; full-length guide rod; Commander-style hammer; high-ride beavertail safety; beveled magazine well. Other models available. Made in U.S. by Kimber Mfg. Inc.

Price: Custom (black matte finish) **$730.00**

Price: Custom Royal (polished blue finish, checkered rosewood grips) **$886.00**

Price: Custom Stainless (satin-finished stainless steel frame and slide) **$832.00**

Price: Custom Target (matte black or stainless finish, Kimber adj. sight) **$837.00**

SEMI-CUSTOM HANDGUNS — AUTOLOADERS

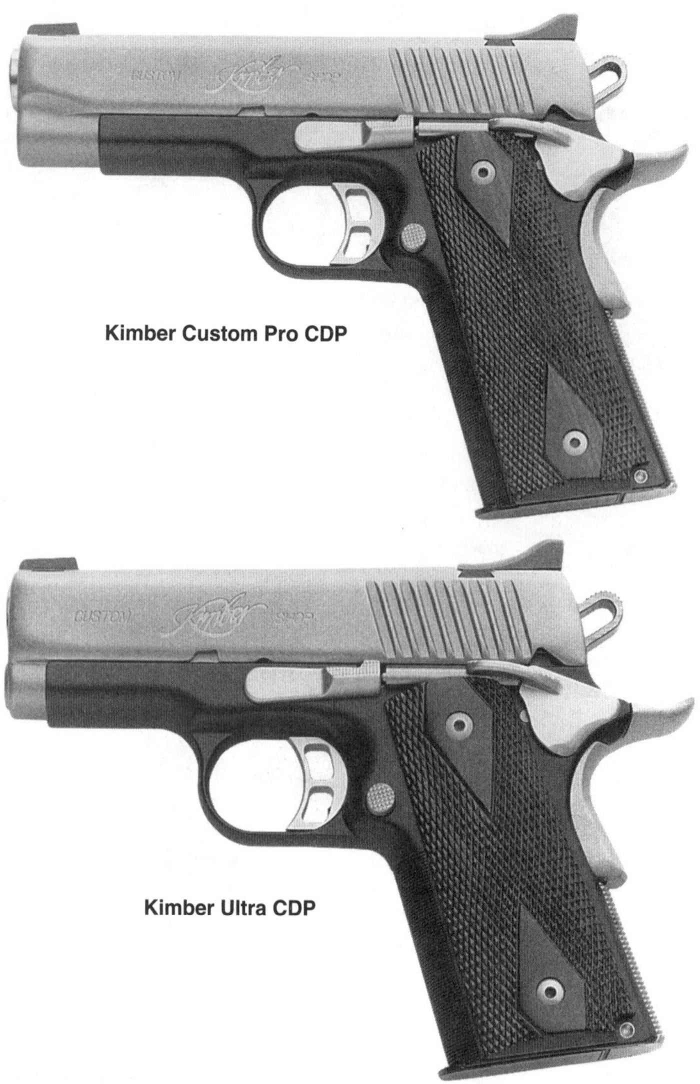

Kimber Custom Pro CDP

Kimber Ultra CDP

North American Arms Guardian with gold accents

Price: Custom Compact CDP (4" bbl., alum. frame, tritium three-dot sights, 28 oz.) **$1,142.00**
Price: Custom Pro CDP (4" bbl., alum. frame, tritium sights, full-length grip, 28 oz.) **$1,142.00**
Price: Ultra CDP (3" bbl., aluminum frame, tritium sights, 25 oz.). **$1,142.00**
Price: Gold Match (polished blue finish, hand-fitted barrel, ambid. safety) **$1,169.00**
Price: Stainless Gold Match (stainless steel frame and slide, hand-fitted bbl., amb. safety) **$1,315.00**
Price: Gold Combat (hand-fitted, stainless barrel; KimPro black finish, tritium sights) **$1,682.00**
Price: Gold Combat Stainless (stainless frame and slide, satin silver finish, tritium sights) **$1,623.00**
Price: Super Match (satin stainless frame, KimPro black finished, stainless slide) **$1,927.00**

LES BAER CUSTOM 1911-STYLE AUTO PISTOLS

Caliber: 9mm Para., 38 Super, 40 S&W, 45 ACP, 400 Cor-Bon; 7- or 8-shot magazine. **Barrel:** 4-1/4", 5", 6". **Weight:** 28 to 40 oz. **Length:** NA. **Grips:** Checkered cocobolo. **Sights:** Low-mount combat fixed, combat fixed with tritium inserts or low-mount adjustable rear, dovetail front. **Features:** Forged steel or aluminum frame; slide serrated front and rear; lowered and flared ejection port; beveled magazine well; speed trigger with 4-pound pull; beavertail grip safety; ambidextrous safety. Other models available. Made in U.S. by Les Baer Custom.

Price: Baer 1911 Premier II 5" Model (5" bbl., optional stainless steel frame and slide) . . . . from **$1,428.00**
Price: Premier II 6" Model (6" barrel) . . . . from **$1,595.00**
Price: Premier II LW1 (forged aluminum frame, steel slide and barrel) . . . . from **$1,740.00**
Price: Custom Carry (4" or 5" barrel, steel frame) . . . . from **$1,640.00**
Price: Custom Carry (4" barrel, aluminum frame) . . . . from **$1,923.00**
Price: Swift Response Pistol (fixed tritium sights, Bear Coat finish) . . . . from **$2,495.00**
Price: Monolith (5" barrel and slide with extra-long dust cover) . . . . from **$1,599.00**
Price: Stinger (4-1/4" barrel, steel or aluminum frame) . . . from **$1,491.00**
Price: Thunder Ranch Special (tritium fixed combat sight, Thunder Ranch logo) . . . . from **$1,620.00**
Price: National Match Hardball (low-mount adj. sight; meets DCM rules). . . . . from **$1,335.00**
Price: Bullseye Wadcutter Pistol (Bo-Mar rib w/ adj. sight, guar. 2-1/2" groups) . . . . from **$1,495.00**
Price: Ultimate Master Combat (5" or 6" bbl., adj. sights, checkered front strap). . . . . from **$2,376.00**
Price: Ultimate Master Combat Compensated (four-port compensator, adj. sights) . . . . from **$2,476.00**

NORTH AMERICAN ARMS GUARDIAN AUTO PISTOL

Caliber: 32 ACP, 6-shot magazine. **Barrel:** 2.18". **Weight:** 13.57 oz. **Length:** 4.36" overall. **Grips:** Checkered or smooth; cocobolo, kingwood, winewood, goncalo alves, pau ferro, white or black simulated mother of pearl. **Sights:** White dot, fiber optics or tritium (nine models). **Features:** Double action only; stainless steel frame and slide; barrel porting; frame stippling; forward striped or scalloped slide serrations; meltdown (rounded edges) treatment; slide/frame finishes available in combinations that include black titanium, stainless steel, gold titanium and highly polished or matte choices. From North American Arms Custom Shop.

Price: NAA-32 Guardian. **$359.00**
Price: Gold or black titanium finish . . . . add **$120.00**
Price: High-polish finish . . . . add **$150.00**
Price: Ported barrel . . . . add **$90.00**

SEMI-CUSTOM HANDGUNS — AUTOLOADERS

North American Arms Guardian with high polish finish

North American Arms Guardian with matte finish

Rock River Arms Elite Commando

Rock River Arms Standard Match

Rock River Arms National Match Hardball

ROCK RIVER ARMS 1911-STYLE AUTO PISTOLS

Caliber: 9mm Para., 38 Super, 40 S&W, 45 ACP. **Barrel:** 4" or 5". **Weight:** NA. **Length:** NA. **Grips:** Double-diamond, checkered cocobolo or black synthetic. **Sights:** Bo-Mar low-mount adjustable, Novak fixed with tritium inserts, Heine fixed or Rock River scope mount; dovetail front blade. **Features:** Chrome-moly, machined steel frame and slide; slide serrated front and rear; aluminum speed trigger with 3.5-4 lb. pull; national match KART barrel; lowered and flared ejection port; tuned and polished extractor; beavertail grip safety; beveled mag. well. Other frames offered. Made in U.S. by Rock River Arms Inc.

Price: Elite Commando (4" barrel, Novak tritium sights) . . from **$1,175.00**
Price: Standard Match (5" barrel, Heine fixed sights). . . . . from **$1,025.00**
Price: National Match Hardball (5" barrel, Bo-Mar adj. sights) . . . . from **$1,275.00**
Price: Bullseye Wadcutter (5" barrel, Rock River slide scope mount) . . . . from **$1,380.00**
Price: Basic Limited Match (5" barrel, Bo-Mar adj. sights) . . . . from **$1,395.00**
Price: Limited Match (5" barrel, guaranteed 1-1/2" groups at 50 yards). . . . . from **$1,795.00**
Price: Hi-Cap Basic Limited (5" barrel, four frame choices) . . . . from **$1,895.00**
Price: Ultimate Match Achiever (5" bbl. with compensator, mount and Aimpoint) . . . . from **$2,255.00**
Price: Match Master Steel (5" bbl. with compensator, mount and Aimpoint) . . . . from **$2,355.00**

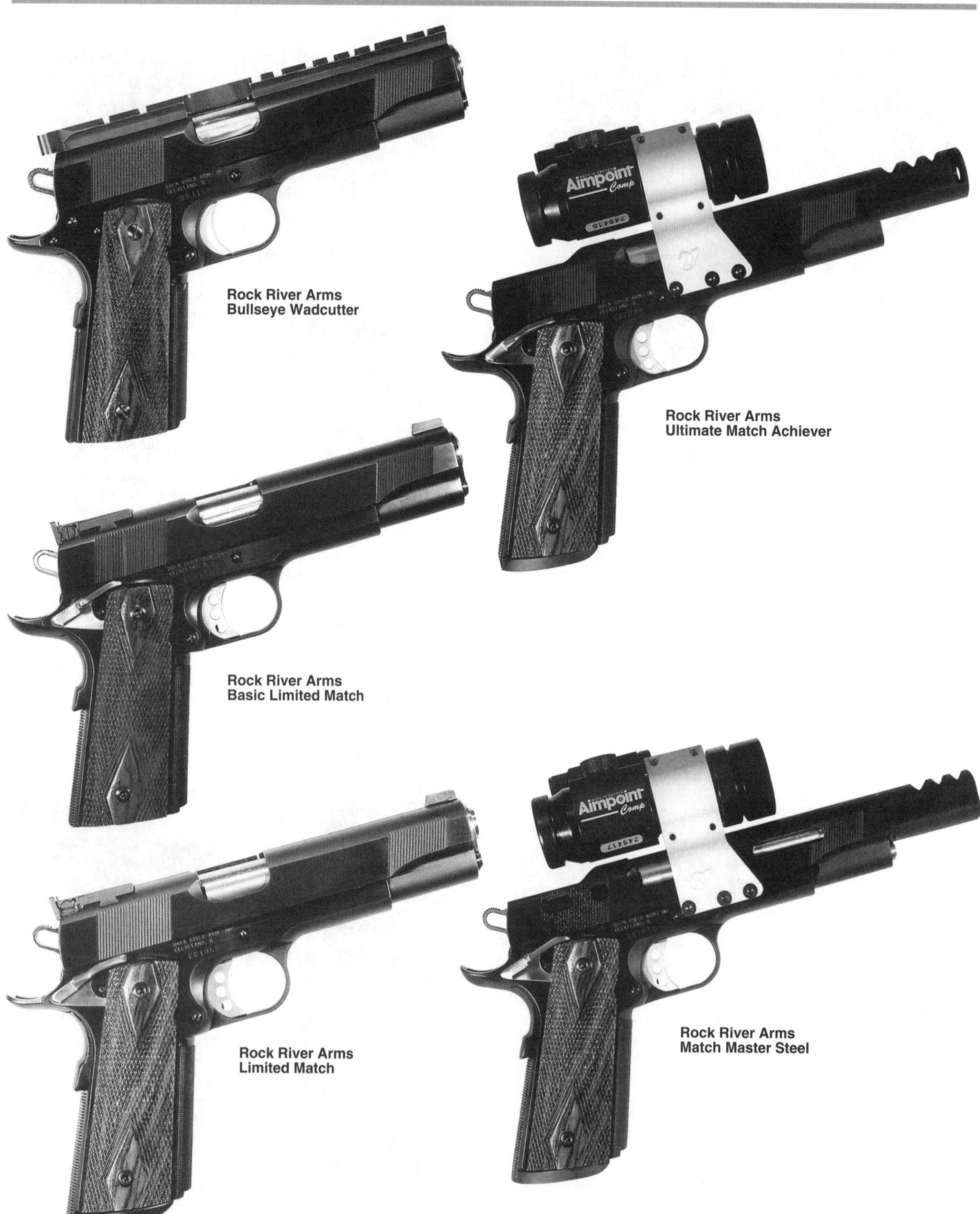

Rock River Arms
Bullseye Wadcutter

Rock River Arms
Ultimate Match Achiever

Rock River Arms
Basic Limited Match

Rock River Arms
Match Master Steel

Rock River Arms
Limited Match

Springfield Pro

Vektor SP1 Target

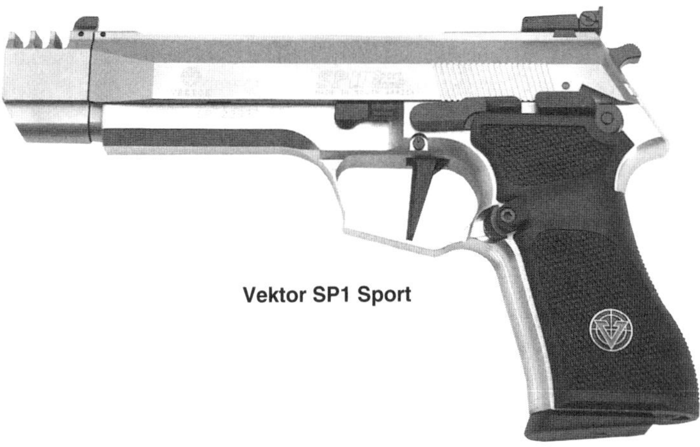
Vektor SP1 Sport

SPRINGFIELD ARMORY 1911-STYLE AUTO PISTOLS

Caliber: 9mm Para., 8- or 9-shot magazine; 45 ACP, 6-, 7-, 8- or 10-shot magazine; 45 Super, 7-shot magazine. **Barrel:** 3.5", 3.9", 5", 6". **Weight:** 25 to 41 oz. **Length:** 7" to 9.5" overall. **Grips:** Checkered cocobolo or synthetic. **Sights:** Novak low-profile, Novak tritium or adjustable target rear; blade front. **Features:** Parkerized, blued, stainless steel or bi-tone frame and slide; lightweight Delta hammer; match trigger; front and rear slide serrations; hammer-forged, air-gauged barrel; beavertail grip safety; extended thumb safety; beveled magazine well. Made in U.S. From Springfield Inc.

Price: Mil-Spec 1911-A1 (5" barrel, fixed three-dot sights, parkerized finish) **$610.00**

Price: Full-Size 1911-A1 (5" bbl., Novak fixed or adj. sights, steel or alum. frame) . . . . from **$648.00**

Price: Champion 1911-A1 (3.9" bbl., Novak fixed sights, steel or alum. frame) . . . . from **$669.00**

Price: Compact 1911-A1 (3.9" bbl., Novak fixed sights, alum. frame) . . . . from **$678.00**

Price: Ultra-Compact 1911-A1 (3.5" bbl., Novak fixed sights, steel or alum. frame) . . . . from **$669.00**

Price: Trophy Match 1911-A1 (5" or 6" bbl., adj. sights, blued or stainless) . . . . from **$1,089.00**

Price: Long Slide 1911-A1 (6" bbl., adj. sights, stainless, 45 ACP or 45 Super) . . . . from **$849.00**

Price: Full Size High Capacity (5" bbl., Novak fixed sights, two 10-shot magazines) . . . . from **$733.00**

Price: Ultra Compact High Capacity (3.5" bbl., Novak fixed sights, 10-shot mag.) . . . . from **$759.00**

Price: Tactical Response Pistol (3.9" or 5", Novak fixed sights, Teflon or stain.) . . . . from **$1,289.00**

Price: Professional Model (5" bbl., Novak three-dot tritium sights, Black-T finish) . . . . from **$2,395.00**

STI 2011 AUTO PISTOLS

Caliber: 9mm Para., 9x23, 38 Super, 40 S&W, 40 Super, 10mm, 45 ACP. **Barrel:** 3.4", 5", 5.5", 6". **Weight:** 28 to 44 oz. **Length:** 7" to 9-5/8" overall. **Grips:** Checkered, double-diamond rosewood or glass-filled nylon polymer (six colors). **Sights:** STI, Novak or Heine adjustable rear, blade front. **Features:** Updated version of 1911-style auto pistol; serrated slide, front and rear; STI skeletonized trigger; ambidextrous or single-sided thumb safety; blue or hard-chrome finish; etched logo and model name. From STI International.

Price: Competitor (38 Super, 5.5" barrel, C-More Rail Scope and mount) . . . . from **$2,499.00**

Price: Trojan (9mm, 45 ACP, 40 Super, 40 S&W; 5" or 6" barrel) . . . . from **$970.00**

Price: Edge 5.0" (40 S&W or 45 ACP; 5" barrel) . . . . from **$1,776.00**

Price: Eagle 5.0" (9mm, 9x23, 38 Super, 40 S&W, 10mm, 40 Super, 45 ACP; 5" bbl.) . . . . from **$1,699.00**

Price: Eagle 6.0" (9mm, 38 Super, 40 S&W, 10mm, 40 Super, 45 ACP; 6" bbl.) . . . . from **$1,795.40**

Price: BLS9/BLS40 (9mm, 40 S&W; 3.4" barrel, full-length grip) . . . . from **$843.70**

STI COMPACT AUTO PISTOLS

Caliber: 9mm Para., 40 S&W. **Barrel:** 3.4". **Weight:** 28 oz. **Length:** 7" overall. **Grips:** Checkered double-diamond rosewood. **Sights:** Heine Low Mount fixed rear, slide integral front. **Features:** Similar to STI 2011 models except has compact frame, 7-shot magazine in 9mm (6-shot in 40 cal.), single-sided thumb safety, linkless barrel lockup system, matte blue finish. From STI International.

Price: (9mm Para. or 40 S&W) . . . . from **$746.50**

VEKTOR SP1/SP2 AUTO PISTOLS

Caliber: 9mm Para., 40 S&W; 10-shot magazine. **Barrel:** 4", 4-5/8", 5", 5-7/8". **Weight:** 31.5 to 42 oz. **Length:** 7-1/2" to 11" overall. **Grips:** Black synthetic. **Sights:** Fixed, three-dot adjustable or scope mount; blade front. **Features:** Cold forged, polygon-rifled barrel; Aluminum alloy frame with machined steel slide; blued, anodized or nickel finish. Imported from South Africa by Vektor USA.

Price: SP1 Service Pistol (9mm Para., 4-5/8" barrel, fixed sights) . . . . from **$619.95**

Price: SP2 Service Pistol (40 S&W, 4-5/8" barrel, fixed sights) . . . . from **$649.95**

Price: SP1 Sport Pistol (9mm, 5" bbl. with compensator, combat sight, trigger stop) . . . . from **$849.95**

Price: SP1 Target Pistol (9mm, 5-7/8" bbl. with compensator, three-dot sights, adj. trigger) **$1,199.95**

Price: SP1 Ultra Sport (9mm, 5-7/8" bbl. with comp., integral Weaver rail, polymer mount) **$1,949.95**

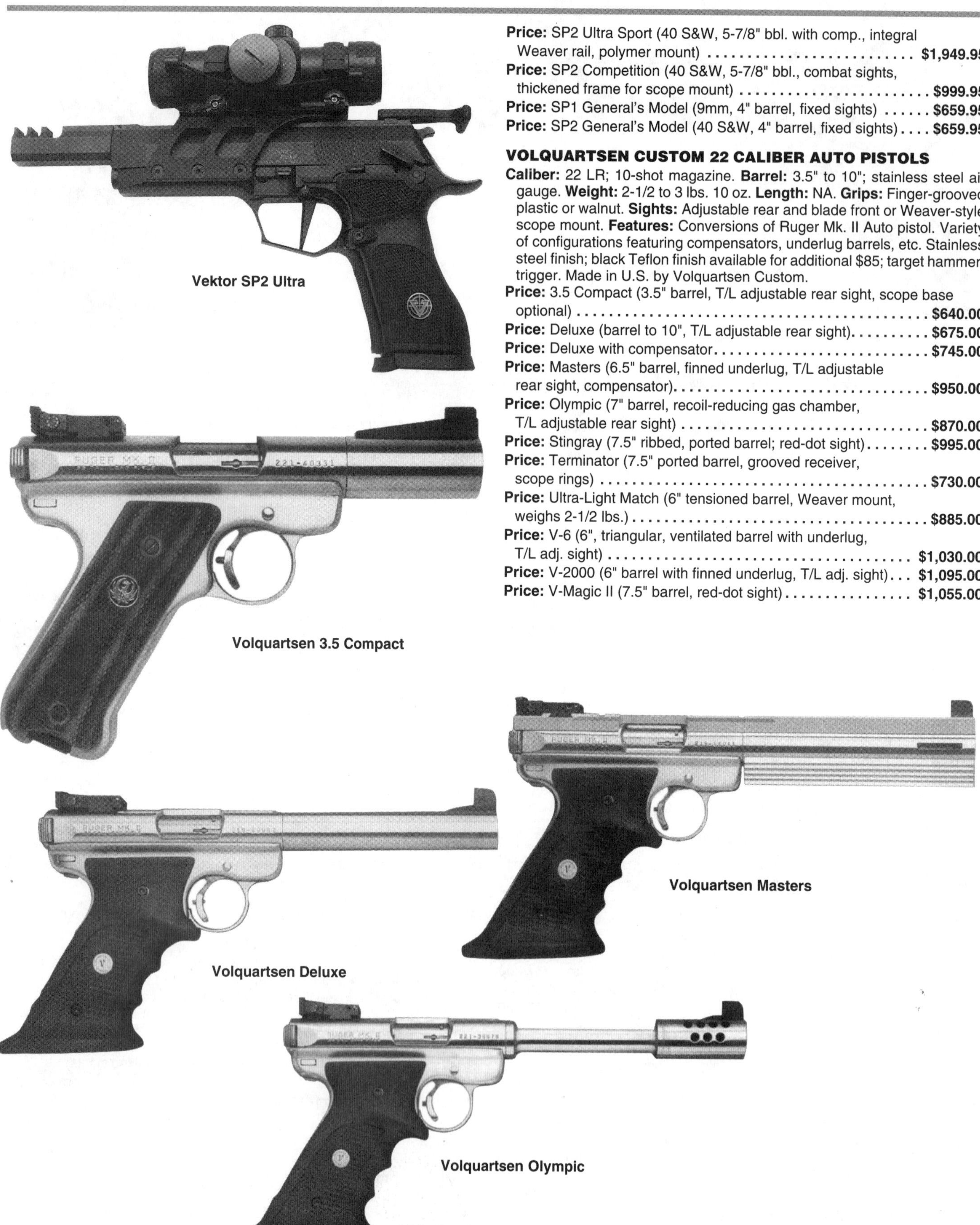

Vektor SP2 Ultra

Volquartsen 3.5 Compact

Volquartsen Masters

Volquartsen Deluxe

Volquartsen Olympic

Price: SP2 Ultra Sport (40 S&W, 5-7/8" bbl. with comp., integral Weaver rail, polymer mount) **$1,949.95**
Price: SP2 Competition (40 S&W, 5-7/8" bbl., combat sights, thickened frame for scope mount) **$999.95**
Price: SP1 General's Model (9mm, 4" barrel, fixed sights) **$659.95**
Price: SP2 General's Model (40 S&W, 4" barrel, fixed sights) **$659.95**

VOLQUARTSEN CUSTOM 22 CALIBER AUTO PISTOLS

Caliber: 22 LR; 10-shot magazine. **Barrel:** 3.5" to 10"; stainless steel air gauge. **Weight:** 2-1/2 to 3 lbs. 10 oz. **Length:** NA. **Grips:** Finger-grooved plastic or walnut. **Sights:** Adjustable rear and blade front or Weaver-style scope mount. **Features:** Conversions of Ruger Mk. II Auto pistol. Variety of configurations featuring compensators, underlug barrels, etc. Stainless steel finish; black Teflon finish available for additional $85; target hammer, trigger. Made in U.S. by Volquartsen Custom.

Price: 3.5 Compact (3.5" barrel, T/L adjustable rear sight, scope base optional) **$640.00**
Price: Deluxe (barrel to 10", T/L adjustable rear sight). **$675.00**
Price: Deluxe with compensator. **$745.00**
Price: Masters (6.5" barrel, finned underlug, T/L adjustable rear sight, compensator). **$950.00**
Price: Olympic (7" barrel, recoil-reducing gas chamber, T/L adjustable rear sight) **$870.00**
Price: Stingray (7.5" ribbed, ported barrel; red-dot sight). **$995.00**
Price: Terminator (7.5" ported barrel, grooved receiver, scope rings) **$730.00**
Price: Ultra-Light Match (6" tensioned barrel, Weaver mount, weighs 2-1/2 lbs.) **$885.00**
Price: V-6 (6", triangular, ventilated barrel with underlug, T/L adj. sight) **$1,030.00**
Price: V-2000 (6" barrel with finned underlug, T/L adj. sight) . . . **$1,095.00**
Price: V-Magic II (7.5" barrel, red-dot sight). **$1,055.00**

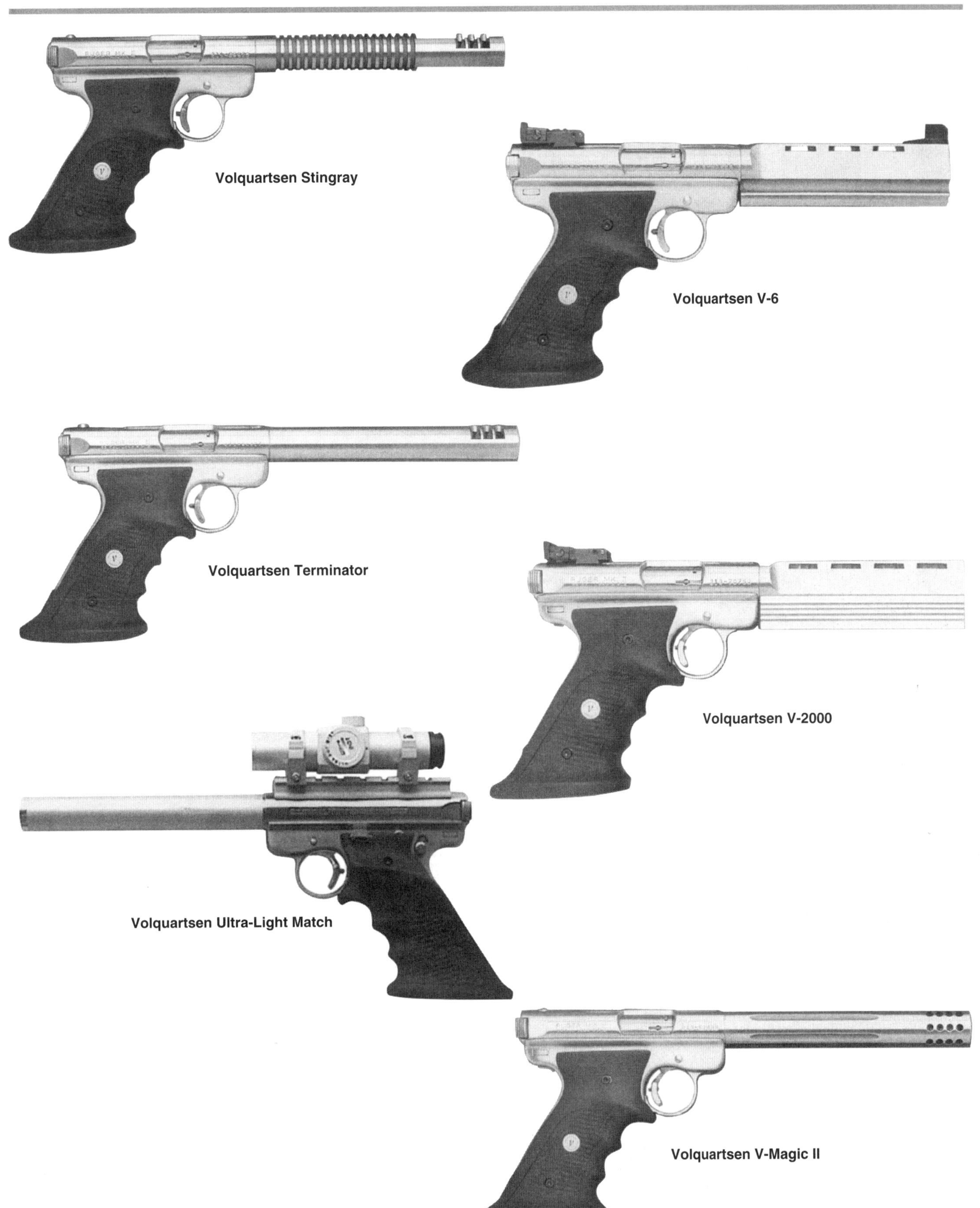

Volquartsen Stingray

Volquartsen V-6

Volquartsen Terminator

Volquartsen V-2000

Volquartsen Ultra-Light Match

Volquartsen V-Magic II

SEMI-CUSTOM HANDGUNS — REVOLVERS

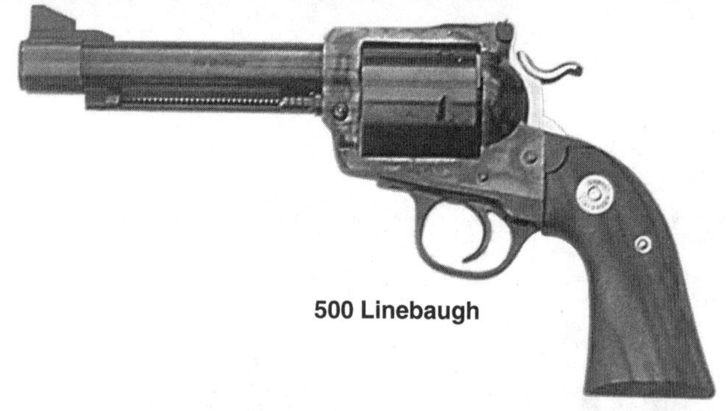
500 Linebaugh

44 Linebaugh Long

500 Linebaugh Long

475 Linebaugh

500 Linebaugh

500 Linebaugh

HANDGUNS

LINEBAUGH CUSTOM SIXGUNS REVOLVERS

Caliber: 45 Colt, 44 Linebaugh Long, 458 Linebaugh, 475 Linebaugh, 500 Linebaugh, 500 Linebaugh Long, 445 Super Mag. **Barrel:** 4-3/4", 5-1/2", 6", 7-1/2"; other lengths available. **Weight:** NA. **Length:** NA. **Grips:** Dustin Linebaugh Custom made to customer's specs. **Sights:** Bowen steel rear or factory Ruger; blade front. **Features:** Conversions using customer's Ruger Blackhawk Bisley and Vaquero Bisley frames. Made in U.S. by Linebaugh Custom Sixguns.

Price: Small 45 Colt conversion (rechambered cyl., new barrel) . . . . from **$1,000.00**

Price: Large 45 Colt conversion (oversized cyl., new barrel, 5- or 6-shot) . . . . from **$1,500.00**

Price: 475 Linebaugh, 500 Linebaugh conversions . . . . . . from **$1,500.00**

Price: Linebaugh and 445 Super Mag calibers on 357 Maximum frame . . . . from **$2,700.00**

GARY REEDER CUSTOM GUNS REVOLVERS

Caliber: 357 Magnum, 45 Colt, 44-40, 41 Magnum, 44 Magnum, 454 Casull, 475 Linebaugh, 500 Linebaugh. **Barrel:** 2-1/2" to 12". **Weight:** Varies by model. **Length:** Varies by model. **Grips:** Black Cape buffalo horn, laminated walnut, simulated pearl, others. **Sights:** Notch fixed or adjustable rear, blade or ramp front. **Features:** Custom conversions of Ruger Vaquero, Blackhawk Bisley and Super Blackhawk frames. Jeweled hammer and trigger, tuned action, model name engraved on barrel, additional engraving on frame and cylinder, integral muzzle brake, finish available in high-polish or satin stainless steel or black Chromex finish. Also available on customer's gun at reduced cost. Other models available. Made in U.S. by Gary Reeder Custom Guns.

Price: Gamblers Classic (2-1/2" bbl., engraved cards and dice, no ejector rod housing) . . . . from **$995.00**

Price: Tombstone Classic (3-1/2" bbl. with gold bands, notch sight, birdshead grips) . . . . from **$995.00**

Price: Doc Holliday Classic (3-1/2" bbl., engraved cards and dice, white pearl grips) . . . . from **$750.00**

Price: Ultimate Vaquero (engraved barrel, frame and cylinder, made to customer specs) . . . . from **$750.00**

Price: Black Widow (4-5/8" bbl., black Chromex finish, black widow spider engraving). . . . . from **$995.00**

Price: Cowboy Classic (stainless finish, cattle brand engraved, limited to 100 guns) . . . . from **$995.00**

Price: African Hunter (6" bbl., with or without muzzle brake, 475 or 500 Linebaugh) . . . . from **$1,395.00**

Price: Alaskan Survivalist (3" bbl., Redhawk frame, engraved bear, 45 Colt or 44 Magnum) . . . . from **$995.00**

Price: Ultimate Back-Up (3-1/2" bbl., fixed sights, choice of animal engraving, 475 Linebaugh, 500 Linebaugh) . . . . from **$1,295.00**

SEMI-CUSTOM HANDGUNS — REVOLVERS

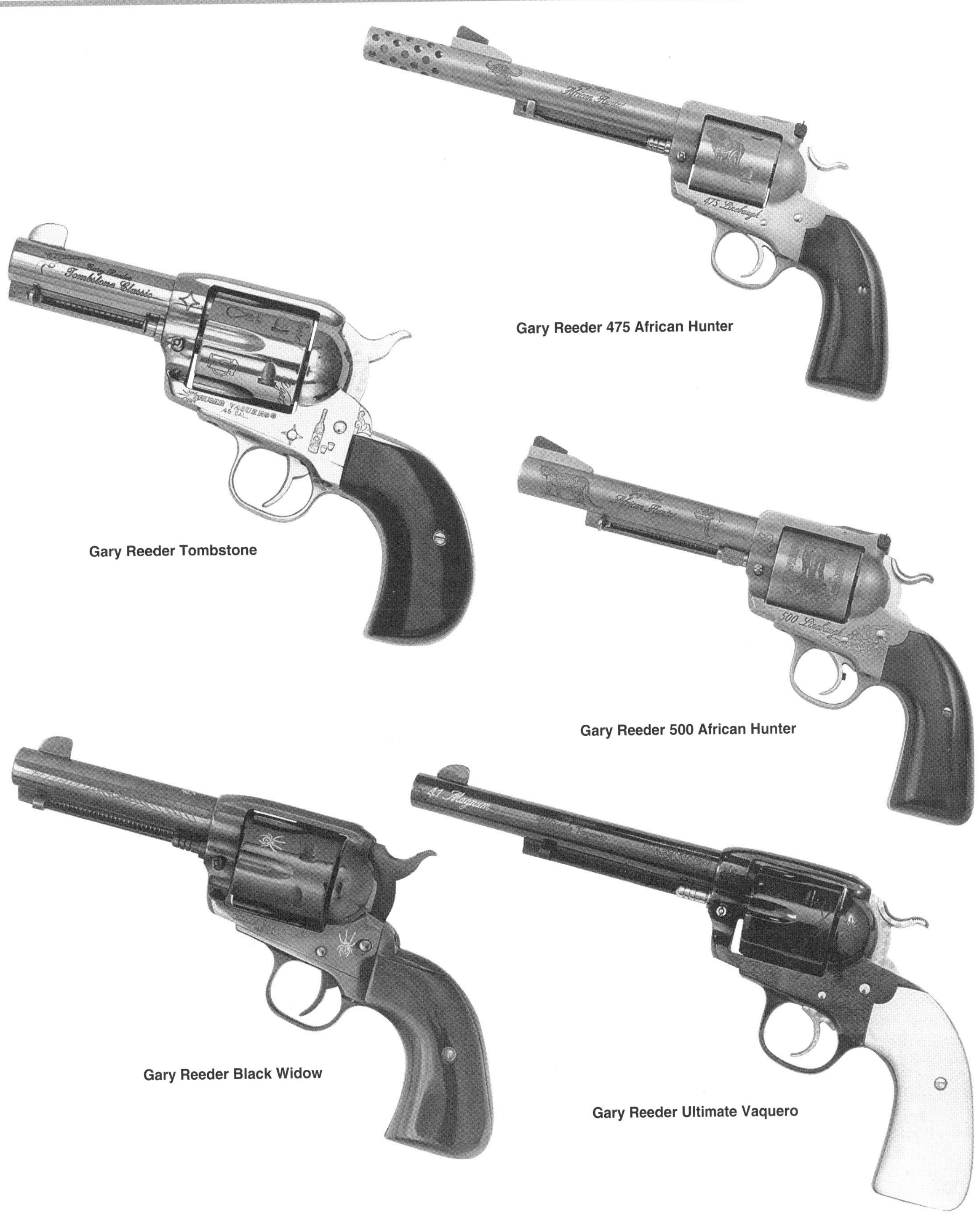

Gary Reeder 475 African Hunter

Gary Reeder Tombstone

Gary Reeder 500 African Hunter

Gary Reeder Black Widow

Gary Reeder Ultimate Vaquero

United State Fire-Arms Single Action Army

United States Fire-Arms SAA Bisley

United States Fire-Arms SAA Flat Top Target

United States Fire-Arms Omni-Snubnose

United States Fire-Arms Omni-Potent Six Shooter

HANDGUNS

UNITED STATES FIRE-ARMS SINGLE-ACTION REVOLVERS

Caliber: 32 WCF, 38 Special, 38 WCF, 41 Colt, 44 WCF, 44 Special, 45 Colt, **Barrel:** 2", 3", 4-3/4", 5-1/2", 7-1/2", 16". **Weight:** NA. **Length:** NA. **Grips:** Hard rubber, rosewood, stag, pearl, ivory, ivory Micarta, smooth walnut, burled walnut and checkered walnut. **Sights:** Notch rear, blade front. **Features:** Hand-fitted replicas of Colt single-action revolvers. Full Dome Blue, Dome Blue, Armory Blue (gray-blue), Old Armory Bone Case (color casehardened) and nickel plate finishes. Carved and scrimshaw grips, engraving and gold inlays offered. Made in U.S. From United States Fire-Arms Mfg. Co.

Price: Single Action Army (32 WCF, 38 Spec., 38 WCF, 41 Colt, 45 Colt, 44 Spec., 44 WCF) **$919.00**

Price: SAA Flat Top Target (extended blade front, drift-adj. rear sights. . . . . from **$995.00**

Price: SAA Bisley (Bisley grip and hammer) . . . . from **$995.00**

Price: Omni-Snubnose (2" or 3" barrel, lanyard loop, 45 Colt only) . . . . from **$1,120.00**

Price: Omni-Potent Six Shooter (lanyard loop on grip). . . . from **$1,125.00**

Price: New Buntline Special (16" bbl., skeleton shoulder stock, case, scabbard) . . . . from **$2,199.00**

Price: China Camp Cowboy Action Gun (4-3/4", 5-1/2" or 7-1/2" bbl., Silver Steel finish). . . . . from **$989.00**

Price: Henry Nettleton Cavalry Revolver (5-1/2" or 7-1/2" bbl., 45 Colt only) . . . . from **$1,125.00**

Price: U.S. 1851 Navy Conversion (7-1/2" bbl., color casehardened frame, 38 Spec. only). . . . . from **$1,499.00**

Price: U.S. Pre-War (SAA, Old Armory Bone Case or Armory Blue finish) . . . . from **$1,175.00**

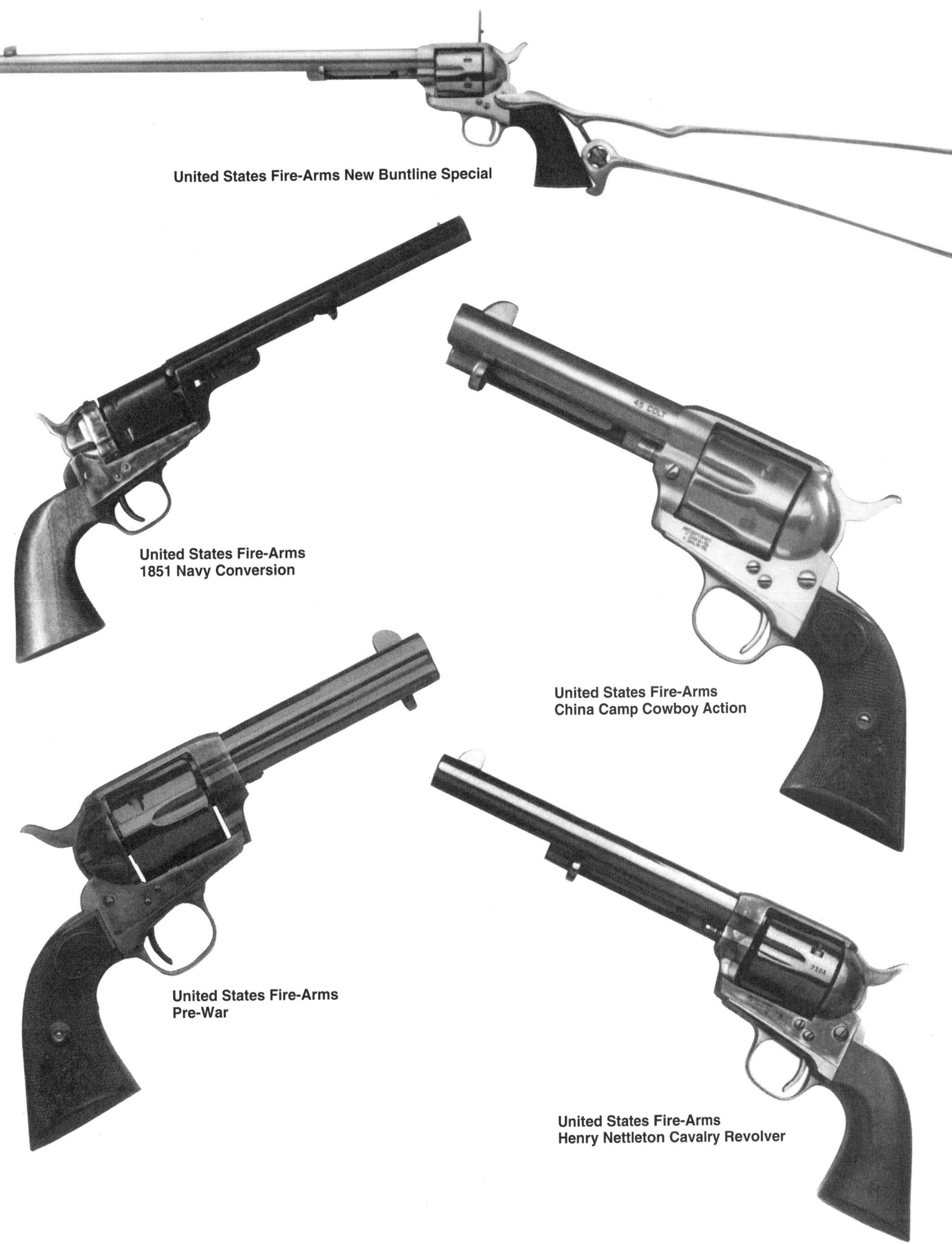

United States Fire-Arms New Buntline Special

United States Fire-Arms
1851 Navy Conversion

United States Fire-Arms
China Camp Cowboy Action

United States Fire-Arms
Pre-War

United States Fire-Arms
Henry Nettleton Cavalry Revolver

SEMI-CUSTOM HANDGUNS — SINGLE SHOT

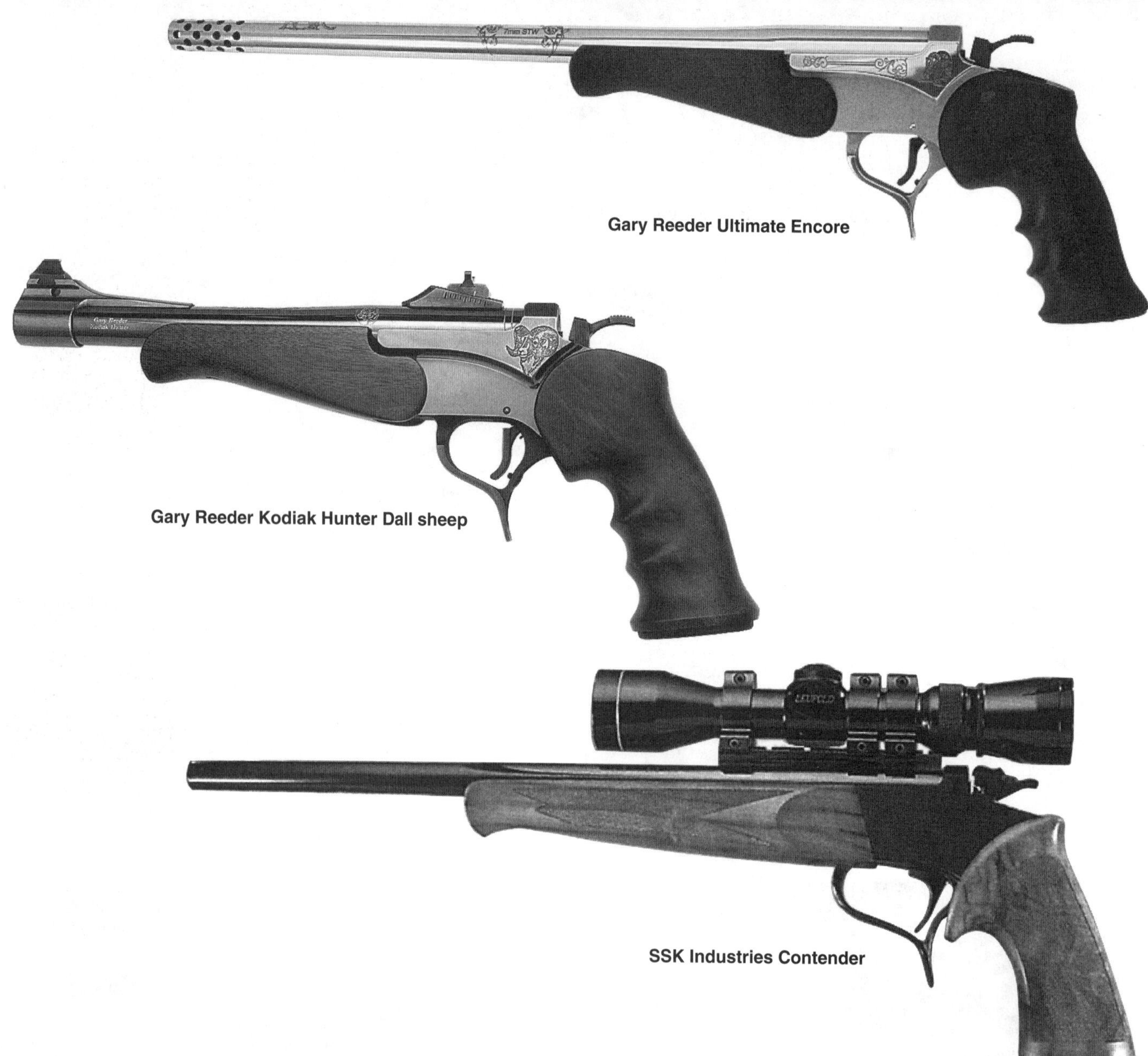

Gary Reeder Ultimate Encore

Gary Reeder Kodiak Hunter Dall sheep

SSK Industries Contender

GARY REEDER CUSTOM GUNS CONTENDER AND ENCORE PISTOLS

Caliber: 22 Cheetah, 218 Bee, 22 K-Hornet, 22 Hornet, 218 Mashburn Bee, 22-250 Improved, 6mm/284, 7mm STW, 7mm GNR, 30 GNR, 338 GNR, 300 Win. Magnum, 338 Win. Magnum, 350 Rem. Magnum, 358 STA, 375 H&H, 378 GNR, 416 Remington, 416 GNR, 450 GNR, 475 Linebaugh, 500 Linebaugh, 50 Alaskan, 50 AE, 454 Casull; others available. **Barrel:** 8" to 15" (others available). **Weight:** NA. **Length:** Varies with barrel length. **Grips:** Walnut fingergroove. **Sights:** Express-style adjustable rear and barrel band front (Kodiak Hunter); none furnished most models. **Features:** Offers complete guns and barrels in the T/C Contender and Encore. Integral muzzle brake, engraved animals and model name, tuned action, high-polish or satin stainless steel or black Chromex finish. Made in U.S. by Gary Reeder Custom Guns.

Price: Kodiak Hunter (50 AE or 454 Casull, Kodiak bear and Dall sheep engravings) . . . . from **$995.00**

Price: Ultimate Encore (15" bbl. with muzzle brake, grizzly bear engraving) . . . . from **$995.00**

SSK INDUSTRIES CONTENDER AND ENCORE PISTOLS

Caliber: More than 200, including most standard pistol and rifle calibers, as well as 226 JDJ, 6mm JDJ, 257 JDJ, 6.5mm JDJ, 7mm JDJ, 6.5mm Mini-Dreadnaught, 30-06 JDJ, 280 JDJ, 375 JDJ, 6mm Whisper, 300 Whisper and 338 Whisper. **Barrel:** 10" to 26"; blued or stainless; variety of configurations. **Weight:** Varies with barrel length and features. **Length:** Varies with barrel length. **Grips:** Pachmayr, wood models available. **Features:** Offers frames, barrels and complete guns in the T/C Contender and Encore. Fluted, diamond, octagon and round barrels; flatside Contender frames; chrome-plating; muzzle brakes; trigger jobs; variety of stocks and forends; sights and optics. Made in U.S. by SSK Industries.

Price: Blued Contender frame . . . . from **$263.00**

Price: Stainless Contender frame . . . . from **$290.00**

Price: Blued Encore frame . . . . from **$290.00**

Price: Stainless Encore frame . . . . from **$318.00**

Price: Contender barrels . . . . from **$315.00**

Price: Encore barrels . . . . from **$340.00**

Includes models suitable for several forms of competition and other sporting purposes.

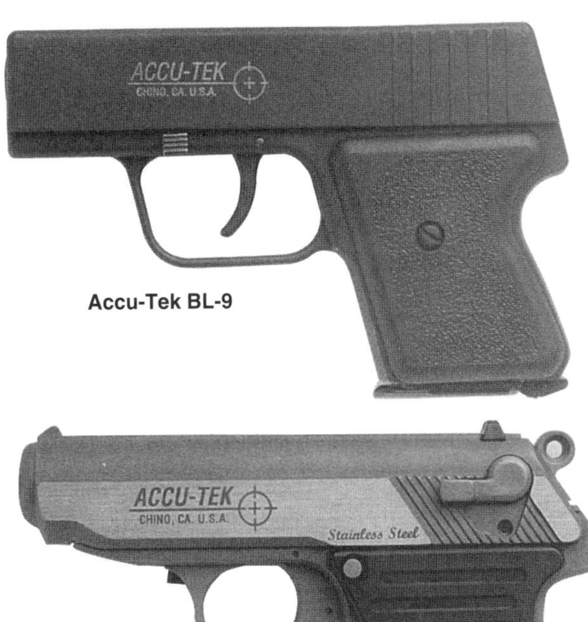

Accu-Tek BL-9

Accu-Tek HC-380

Accu-Tek AT-380

Accu-Tek XL-9

ACCU-TEK BL-9 AUTO PISTOL

Caliber: 9mm Para., 5-shot magazine. **Barrel:** 3". **Weight:** 22 oz. **Length:** 5.6" overall. **Stocks:** Black pebble composition. **Sights:** Fixed. **Features:** Double action only; black finish. Introduced 1997. Price includes cleaning kit and gun lock, two magazines. Made in U.S. by Accu-Tek.

Price: **$232.00**

Accu-Tek Model AT-32SS Auto Pistol

Same as the AT-380SS except chambered for 32 ACP. Introduced 1991. Price includes cleaning kit and gun lock.

Price: Satin stainless **$221.00**

ACCU-TEK MODEL AT-380 AUTO PISTOL

Caliber: 380 ACP, 5-shot magazine. **Barrel:** 2.75". **Weight:** 20 oz. **Length:** 5.6" overall. **Stocks:** Grooved black composition. **Sights:** Blade front, rear adjustable for windage. **Features:** Stainless steel frame and slide. External hammer; manual thumb safety; firing pin block, trigger disconnect. Introduced 1991. Price includes cleaning kit and gun lock. Made in U.S. by Accu-Tek.

Price: Satin stainless **$221.00**

ACCU-TEK MODEL HC-380 AUTO PISTOL

Caliber: 380 ACP, 10-shot magazine. **Barrel:** 2.75". **Weight:** 26 oz. **Length:** 6" overall. **Stocks:** Checkered black composition. **Sights:** Blade front, rear adjustable for windage. **Features:** External hammer; manual thumb safety with firing pin and trigger disconnect; bottom magazine release. Stainless steel construction. Introduced 1993. Price includes cleaning kit and gun lock. Made in U.S. by Accu-Tek.

Price: Satin stainless **$231.00**

ACCU-TEK XL-9 AUTO PISTOL

Caliber: 9mm Para., 5-shot magazine. **Barrel:** 3". **Weight:** 24 oz. **Length:** 5.6" overall. **Stocks:** Black pebble composition. **Sights:** Three-dot system; rear adjustable for windage. **Features:** Stainless steel construction; double-action-only mechanism. Introduced 1999. Price includes cleaning kit and gun lock, two magazines. Made in U.S. by Accu-Tek.

Price: **$248.00**

AMERICAN ARMS MATEBA AUTO/REVOLVER

Caliber: 357 Mag., 6-shot. **Barrel:** 4", 6", 8". **Weight:** 2.75 lbs. **Length:** 8.77" overall. **Stocks:** Smooth walnut. **Sights:** Blade on ramp front, adjustable rear. **Features:** Double or single action. Cylinder and slide recoil together upon firing. All-steel construction with polished blue finish. Introduced 1995. Imported from Italy by American Arms, Inc.

Price: **$1,295.00**

Price: 6" **$1,349.00**

AMT AUTOMAG II AUTO PISTOL

Caliber: 22 WMR, 9-shot magazine (7-shot with 3-3/8" barrel). **Barrel:** 3-3/8", 4-1/2", 6". **Weight:** About 32 oz. **Length:** 9-3/8" overall. **Stocks:** Grooved carbon fiber. **Sights:** Blade front, adjustable rear. **Features:** Made of stainless steel. Gas-assisted action. Exposed hammer. Slide flats have brushed finish, rest is sandblast. Squared trigger guard. Introduced 1986. From Galena Industries, Inc.

Price: **$429.00**

AMT AUTOMAG III PISTOL

Caliber: 30 Carbine, 8-shot magazine. **Barrel:** 6-3/8". **Weight:** 43 oz. **Length:** 10-1/2" overall. **Stocks:** Carbon fiber. **Sights:** Blade front, adjustable rear. **Features:** Stainless steel construction. Hammer-drop safety. Slide flats have brushed finish, rest is sandblasted. Introduced 1989. From Galena Industries, Inc.

Price: **$529.00**

AMT AUTOMAG IV PISTOL

Caliber: 45 Winchester Magnum, 6-shot magazine. **Barrel:** 6.5". **Weight:** 46 oz. **Length:** 10.5" overall. **Stocks:** Carbon fiber. **Sights:** Blade front, adjustable rear. **Features:** Made of stainless st3578eel with brushed finish. Introduced 1990. Made in U.S. by Galena Industries, Inc.

Price: **$599.00**

AMT Backup

Auto-Ordnance Deluxe

Auto-Ordnance 1911A1 Standard

Auto-Ordnance Pit Bull

AMT 45 ACP HARDBALLER II

Caliber: 45 ACP. **Barrel:** 5". **Weight:** 39 oz. **Length:** 8-1/2" overall. **Stocks:** Wrap-around rubber. **Sights:** Adjustable. **Features:** Extended combat safety, serrated matte slide rib, loaded chamber indicator, long grip safety, beveled magazine well, adjustable target trigger. All stainless steel. From Galena Industries, Inc.

Price: **$425.00**
Price: Government model (as above except no rib, fixed sights) . **$399.00**
Price: 400 Accelerator (400 Cor-Bon, 7" barrel) **$549.00**
Price: Commando (40 S&W, Government Model frame) **$435.00**

AMT 45 ACP HARDBALLER LONG SLIDE

Caliber: 45 ACP. **Barrel:** 7". **Length:** 10-1/2" overall. **Stocks:** Wrap-around rubber. **Sights:** Fully adjustable rear sight. **Features:** Slide and barrel are 2" longer than the standard 45, giving less recoil, added velocity, longer sight radius. Has extended combat safety, serrated matte rib, loaded chamber indicator, wide adjustable trigger. From Galena Industries, Inc.

Price: **$529.00**

AMT BACKUP PISTOL

Caliber: 357 SIG (5-shot); 38 Super, 9mm Para. (6-shot); 40 S&W, 400 Cor-Bon; 45 ACP (5-shot). **Barrel:** 3". **Weight:** 23 oz. **Length:** 5-3/4" overall. **Stocks:** Checkered black synthetic. **Sights:** None. **Features:** Stainless steel construction; double-action-only trigger; dust cover over the trigger transfer bar; extended magazine; titanium nitride finish. Introduced 1992. Made in U.S. by Galena Industries.

Price: 9mm, 40 S&W, 45 ACP **$319.00**
Price: 38 Super, 357 SIG, 400 Cor-Bon **$369.00**

AMT 380 DAO Small Frame Backup

Similar to the DAO Backup except has smaller frame, 2-1/2" barrel, weighs 18 oz., and is 5" overall. Has 5-shot magazine, matte/stainless finish. Made in U.S. by Galena Industries.

Price: **$319.00**

AUTO-ORDNANCE 1911A1 AUTOMATIC PISTOL

Caliber: 45 ACP, 7-shot magazine. **Barrel:** 5". **Weight:** 39 oz. **Length:** 8-1/2" overall. **Stocks:** Checkered plastic with medallion. **Sights:** Blade front, rear adjustable for windage. **Features:** Same specs as 1911A1 military guns—parts interchangeable. Frame and slide blued; each radius has non-glare finish. Made in U.S. by Auto-Ordnance Corp.

Price: 45 ACP, blue **$447.00**
Price: 45 ACP, Parkerized **$462.00**
Price: 45 ACP Deluxe (three-dot sights, textured rubber wraparound grips) **$455.00**

Auto-Ordnance 1911A1 Custom High Polish Pistol

Similar to the standard 1911A1 except has a Videki speed trigger, extended thumb safety, flat mainspring housing, Acurod recoil spring guide system, rosewood grips, custom combat hammer, beavertail grip safety. High-polish blue finish. Introduced 1998. Made in U.S. by Auto-Ordnance Corp.

Price: **$585.00**

Auto-Ordnance ZG-51 Pit Bull Auto

Same as the 1911A1 except has 3-1/2" barrel, weighs 36 oz. and has an over-all length of 7-1/4". Available in 45 ACP only; 7-shot magazine. Introduced 1989.

Price: **$470.00**

AUTAUGA 32 AUTO PISTOL

Caliber: 32 ACP, 6-shot magazine. **Barrel:** 2". **Weight:** 11.3 oz. **Length:** 4.3" overall. **Stocks:** Black polymer. **Sights:** Fixed. **Features:** Double-action-only mechanism. Stainless steel construction. Uses Winchester Silver Tip ammunition.

Price: . . . . **NA**

Baer Custom Carry

Baer Premium II

BAER 1911 CUSTOM CARRY AUTO PISTOL

Caliber: 45 ACP, 7- or 10-shot magazine. **Barrel:** 5". **Weight:** 37 oz. **Length:** 8.5" overall. **Stocks:** Checkered walnut. **Sights:** Baer improved ramp-style dovetailed front, Novak low-mount rear. **Features:** Baer forged NM frame, slide and barrel with stainless bushing; fitted slide to frame; double serrated slide (full-size only); Baer speed trigger with 4-lb. pull; Baer deluxe hammer and sear, tactical-style extended ambidextrous safety, beveled magazine well; polished feed ramp and throated barrel; tuned extractor; Baer extended ejector, checkered slide stop; lowered and flared ejection port, full-length recoil guide rod; recoil buff. Partial listing shown. Made in U.S. by Les Baer Custom, Inc.

Price: Standard size, blued $1,640.00
Price: Standard size, stainless $1,690.00
Price: Comanche size, blued $1,640.00
Price: Comanche size, stainless $1,690.00
Price: Comanche size, aluminum frame, blued slide $1,923.00
Price: Comanche size, aluminum frame, stainless slide $1,995.00

BAER 1911 PREMIER II AUTO PISTOL

Caliber: 9x23, 38 Super, 400 Cor-Bon, 45 ACP, 7- or 10-shot magazine. **Barrel:** 5". **Weight:** 37 oz. **Length:** 8.5" overall. **Stocks:** Checkered rosewood, double diamond pattern. **Sights:** Baer dovetailed front, low-mount Bo-Mar rear with hidden leaf. **Features:** Baer NM forged steel frame and barrel with stainless bushing; slide fitted to frame; double serrated slide; lowered, flared ejection port; tuned, polished extractor; Baer extended ejector, checkered slide stop, aluminum speed trigger with 4-lb. pull, deluxe Commander hammer and sear, beavertail grip safety with pad, beveled magazine well, extended ambidextrous safety; flat mainspring housing; polished feed ramp and throated barrel; 30 lpi checkered front strap. Made in U.S. by Les Baer Custom, Inc.

Price: Blued $1,428.00
Price: Stainless $1,558.00
Price: 6" model, blued, from $1,595.00

BAER 1911 S.R.P. PISTOL

Caliber: 45 ACP. **Barrel:** 5". **Weight:** 37 oz. **Length:** 8.5" overall. **Stocks:** Checkered walnut. **Sights:** Trijicon night sights. **Features:** Similar to the F.B.I. contract gun except uses Baer forged steel frame. Has Baer match barrel with supported chamber, Wolff springs, complete tactical action job. All parts Mag-na-fluxed; deburred for tactical carry. Has Baer Ultra Coat finish. Tuned for reliability. Contact Baer for complete details. Introduced 1996. Made in U.S. by Les Baer Custom, Inc.

Price: Government or Comanche length $2,240.00

Beretta 96

BERETTA MODEL 92FS PISTOL

Caliber: 9mm Para., 10-shot magazine. **Barrel:** 4.9". **Weight:** 34 oz. **Length:** 8.5" overall. **Stocks:** Checkered black plastic. **Sights:** Blade front, rear adjustable for windage. Tritium night sights available. **Features:** Double action. Extractor acts as chamber loaded indicator, squared trigger guard, grooved front- and backstraps, inertia firing pin. Matte or blued finish. Introduced 1977. Made in U.S. and imported from Italy by Beretta U.S.A.

Price: With plastic grips $669.00

Beretta Model 92FS/96 Brigadier Pistols

Similar to the Model 92FS/96 except with a heavier slide to reduce felt recoil and allow mounting removable front sight. Wrap-around rubber grips. Three-dot sights dovetailed to the slide, adjustable for windage. Weighs 35.3 oz. Introduced 1999.

Price: 9mm or 40 S&W, 10-shot $716.00
Price: Inox models (stainless steel) $771.00

Beretta Model 92FS 470th Anniversary Limited Edition

Similar to the Model 92FS stainless except has mirror polish finish, smooth walnut grips with inlaid gold-plated medallions. Special and unique gold-filled engraving includes the signature of Beretta's president. The anniversary logo is engraved on the top of the slide and the back of the magazine. Each pistol identified by a "1 of 470" gold-filled number. Special chrome-plated magazine included. Deluxe lockable walnut case with teak inlays and engraving. Only 470 pistols will be sold. Introduced 1999.

Price: $2,082.00

Beretta Model 92FS Compact and Compact Type M Pistol

Similar to the Model 92FS except more compact and lighter: overall length 7.8"; 4.3" barrel; weighs 30.9 oz. Has Bruniton finish, chrome-lined bore, combat trigger guard, ambidextrous safety/decock lever. Single column 8-shot magazine (Type M), or double column 10-shot (Compact), 9mm only. Introduced 1998. Imported from Italy by Beretta U.S.A.

Price: Compact (10-shot) $669.00
Price: Compact Type M (8-shot) $669.00
Price: Compact Inox (stainless) $734.00
Price: Compact Type M Inox (stainless) $721.00

Beretta Model 96 Pistol

Same as the Model 92FS except chambered for 40 S&W. Ambidextrous safety mechanism with passive firing pin catch, slide safety/decocking lever, trigger bar disconnect. Has 10-shot magazine. Available with three-dot sights. Introduced 1992.

Price: Model 96, plastic grips $669.00
Price: Stainless, rubber grips $734.00

HANDGUNS — AUTOLOADERS, SERVICE & SPORT

Beretta 950 Jetfire

BERETTA MODEL 80 CHEETAH SERIES DA PISTOLS

Caliber: 380 ACP, 10-shot magazine (M84); 8-shot (M85); 22 LR, 7-shot (M87). **Barrel:** 3.82". **Weight:** About 23 oz. (M84/85); 20.8 oz. (M87). **Length:** 6.8" overall. **Stocks:** Glossy black plastic (wood optional at extra cost). **Sights:** Fixed front, drift-adjustable rear. **Features:** Double action, quick takedown, convenient magazine release. Introduced 1977. Imported from Italy by Beretta U.S.A.

Price: Model 84 Cheetah, plastic grips **$576.00**
Price: Model 84 Cheetah, wood grips, nickel finish **$652.00**
Price: Model 85 Cheetah, plastic grips, 8-shot **$545.00**
Price: Model 85 Cheetah, wood grips, nickel, 8-shot **$609.00**
Price: Model 87 Cheetah, wood, 22 LR, 7-shot **$576.00**
Price: Model 87 Target, plastic grips **$669.00**

Beretta Model 86 Cheetah

Similar to the 380-caliber Model 85 except has tip-up barrel for first-round loading. Barrel length is 4.4", overall length of 7.33". Has 8-shot magazine, walnut grips. Introduced 1989.

Price: **$578.00**

BERETTA MODEL 950 JETFIRE AUTO PISTOL

Caliber: 25 ACP, 8-shot. **Barrel:** 2.4". **Weight:** 9.9 oz. **Length:** 4.7" overall. **Stocks:** Checkered black plastic or walnut. **Sights:** Fixed. **Features:** Single action, thumb safety; tip-up barrel for direct loading/unloading, cleaning. From Beretta U.S.A.

Price: Jetfire plastic, matte finish **$226.00**
Price: Jetfire plastic, stainless **$267.00**

Beretta Model 21 Bobcat Pistol

Similar to the Model 950 BS. Chambered for 22 LR or 25 ACP. Both double action. Has 2.4" barrel, 4.9" overall length; 7-round magazine on 22 cal.; 8 rounds in 25 ACP, 9.9 oz., available in nickel, matte, engraved or blue finish. Plastic grips. Introduced in 1985.

Price: Bobcat, 22 or 25, blue **$285.00**
Price: Bobcat, 22, stainless **$307.00**
Price: Bobcat, 22 or 25, matte **$252.00**

BERETTA MODEL 3032 TOMCAT PISTOL

Caliber: 32 ACP, 7-shot magazine. **Barrel:** 2.45". **Weight:** 14.5 oz. **Length:** 5" overall. **Stocks:** Checkered black plastic. **Sights:** Blade front, drift-adjustable rear. **Features:** Double action with exposed hammer; tip-up barrel for direct loading/unloading; thumb safety; polished or matte blue finish. Imported from Italy by Beretta U.S.A. Introduced 1996.

Price: Blue **$370.00**
Price: Matte **$340.00**
Price: Stainless **$418.00**
Price: Titanium **$572.00**

BERETTA MODEL 8000/8040/8045 COUGAR PISTOL

Caliber: 9mm Para., 10-shot, 40 S&W, 10-shot magazine; 45 ACP, 8-shot. **Barrel:** 3.6". **Weight:** 33.5 oz. **Length:** 7" overall. **Stocks:** Checkered plastic. **Sights:** Blade front, rear drift adjustable for windage. **Features:** Slide-mounted safety; rotating barrel; exposed hammer. Matte black Bruniton finish. Announced 1994. Imported from Italy by Beretta U.S.A.

Price: **$709.00**

Beretta M8000/8040 Cougar

Bersa Thunder 380

Price: D model, 9mm, 40 S&W **$739.00**
Price: D model, 45 ACP **$739.00**

BERETTA MODEL 9000S COMPACT PISTOL

Caliber: 9mm Para., 40 S&W; 10-shot magazine. **Barrel:** 3.4". **Weight:** 26.8 oz. **Length:** 6.6". **Grips:** Soft polymer. **Sights:** Windage-adjustable white-dot rear, white-dot blade front. **Features:** Glass-reinforced polymer frame; patented tilt-barrel, open-slide locking system; chrome-lined barrel; external serrated hammer; automatic firing pin and manual safeties. Introduced 2000. Imported from Italy by Beretta USA.

Price: 9000S Type F (single and double action, external hammer) **$551.00**
Price: 9000S Type D (double-action only, no external hammer or safety) **$551.00**

Beretta Model 8000/8040/8045 Mini Cougar

Similar to the Model 8000/8040 Cougar except has shorter grip frame and weighs 27.6 oz. Introduced 1998. Imported from Italy by Beretta U.S.A.

Price: 9mm or 40 S&W **$709.00**
Price: 9mm or 40 S&W, DAO **$739.00**
Price: 45 ACP, 6-shot **$739.00**
Price: 45 ACP DAO **$739.00**

BERSA THUNDER 380 AUTO PISTOLS

Caliber: 380 ACP, 7-shot (Thunder 380 Lite), 9-shot magazine (Thunder 380 DLX). **Barrel:** 3.5". **Weight:** 23 oz. **Length:** 6.6" overall. **Stocks:** Black polymer. **Sights:** Blade front, notch rear adjustable for windage; three-dot system. **Features:** Double action; firing pin and magazine safeties. Available in blue or nickel. Introduced 1995. Distributed by Eagle Imports, Inc.

Price: Thunder 380, 7-shot, deep blue finish **$248.95**
Price: Thunder 380 Deluxe, 9-shot, satin nickel **$291.95**

Browning Micro Buck Mark Standard

Calico M-110

Browning Buck Mark Challenge

BLUE THUNDER/COMMODORE 1911-STYLE AUTO PISTOLS

Caliber: 45 ACP, 7-shot magazine. **Barrel:** 4-1/4", 5". **Weight:** NA. **Length:** NA. **Grips:** Checkered hardwood. **Sights:** Blade front, drift-adjustable rear. **Features:** Extended slide release and safety, spring guide rod, skeletonized hammer and trigger, magazine bumper, beavertail grip safety. Imported from the Philippines by Century International Arms Inc.

Price: . . . . . $464.80 to $484.80

BROWNING HI-POWER 9mm AUTOMATIC PISTOL

Caliber: 9mm Para.,10-shot magazine. **Barrel:** 4-21/32". **Weight:** 32 oz. **Length:** 7-3/4" overall. **Stocks:** Walnut, hand checkered, or black Polyamide. **Sights:** 1/8" blade front; rear screw-adjustable for windage and elevation. Also available with fixed rear (drift-adjustable for windage). **Features:** External hammer with half-cock and thumb safeties. A blow on the hammer cannot discharge a cartridge; cannot be fired with magazine removed. Fixed rear sight model available. Includes gun lock. Imported from Belgium by Browning.

Price: Fixed sight model, walnut grips $680.00
Price: Fully adjustable rear sight, walnut grips $730.00
Price: Mark III, standard matte black finish, fixed sight, moulded grips, ambidextrous safety $662.00

Browning Hi-Power Practical Pistol

Similar to the standard Hi-Power except has silver-chromed frame with blued slide, wrap-around Pachmayr rubber grips, round-style serrated hammer and removable front sight, fixed rear (drift-adjustable for windage). Available in 9mm Para. Includes gun lock. Introduced 1991.

Price: $717.00

BROWNING BUCK MARK STANDARD 22 PISTOL

Caliber: 22 LR, 10-shot magazine. **Barrel:** 5-1/2". **Weight:** 32 oz. **Length:** 9-1/2" overall. **Stocks:** Black moulded composite with checkering. **Sights:** Ramp front, Browning Pro Target rear adjustable for windage and elevation. **Features:** All steel, matte blue finish or nickel, gold-colored trigger. Buck Mark Plus has laminated wood grips. Includes gun lock. Made in U.S. Introduced 1985. From Browning.

Price: Buck Mark Standard, blue $286.00
Price: Buck Mark Nickel, nickel finish with contoured rubber grips $338.00
Price: Buck Mark Plus, matte blue with laminated wood grips . . . $350.00
Price: Buck Mark Plus Nickel, nickel finish, laminated wood grips $383.00

Browning Buck Mark Camper

Similar to the Buck Mark except 5-1/2" bull barrel. Weight is 34 oz. Matte blue finish, molded composite grips. Introduced 1999. From Browning.

Price: $258.00
Price: Camper Nickel, nickel finish, molded composite grips $287.00

Browning Buck Mark Challenge

Similar to the Buck Mark except has a lightweight barrel and smaller grip diameter. Barrel length is 5-1/2", weight is 25 oz. Introduced 1999. From Browning.

Price: $320.00

Browning Buck Mark Micro

Same as the Buck Mark Standard and Buck Mark Plus except has 4" barrel. Available in blue or nickel. Has 16-click Pro Target rear sight. Introduced 1992.

Price: Micro Standard, matte blue finish $286.00
Price: Micro Nickel, nickel finish $338.00
Price: Buck Mark Micro Plus, matte blue, lam. wood grips $350.00
Price: Buck Mark Micro Plus Nickel $383.00

Browning Buck Mark Bullseye

Same as the Buck Mark Standard except has 7-1/4" fluted barrel, matte blue finish. Weighs 36 oz.

Price: Bullseye Standard, molded composite grips $420.00
Price: Bullseye Target, contoured rosewood grips $541.00

Browning Buck Mark 5.5

Same as the Buck Mark Standard except has a 5-1/2" bull barrel with integral scope mount, matte blue finish.

Price: 5.5 Field, Pro-Target adj. rear sight, contoured walnut grips $459.00
Price: 5.5 Target, hooded adj. target sights, contoured walnut grips $459.00

Buck Mark Commemorative

Same as the Buck Mark Standard except has a 6-3/4" Challenger-style barrel, matte blue finish and scrimshaw-style, bonded ivory grips. Includes pistol rug. Limited to 1,000 guns.

Price: Commemorative $437.00

CALICO M-110 AUTO PISTOL

Caliber: 22 LR. **Barrel:** 6". **Weight:** 3.7 lbs. (loaded). **Length:** 17.9" overall. **Stocks:** Moulded composition. **Sights:** Adjustable post front, notch rear. **Features:** Aluminum alloy frame; compensator; pistol grip compartment; ambidextrous safety. Uses same helical-feed magazine as M-100 Carbine. Introduced 1986. Made in U.S. From Calico.

Price: $570.00

CARBON-15 (Type 97) PISTOL

Caliber: 223, 10-shot magazine. **Barrel:** 7.25". **Weight:** 46 oz. **Length:** 20" overall. **Stock:** Checkered composite. **Sights:** Ghost ring. **Features:** Semi-automatic, gas-operated, rotating bolt action. Carbon fiber upper and lower receiver; chromemoly bolt carrier; fluted stainless match barrel; mil. spec. optics mounting base; uses AR-15-type magazines. Introduced 1992. From Professional Ordnance, Inc.

Price: $1,600.00
Price: Type 20 pistol (light-profile barrel, no compensator, weighs 40 oz.) $1,500.00

Carbon-15

Colt 1991 Model O Compact

Charles Daly M-1911-A1P

Colt XS Model O Commander

Colt XS Lightweight Commander

CHARLES DALY M-1911-A1P AUTOLOADING PISTOL

Caliber: 45 ACP, 7- or 10-shot magazine. **Barrel:** 5". **Weight:** 38 oz. **Length:** 8-3/4" overall. **Stocks:** Checkered. **Sights:** Blade front, rear drift adjustable for windage; three-dot system. **Features:** Skeletonized combat hammer and trigger; beavertail grip safety; extended slide release; oversize thumb safety; Parkerized finish. Introduced 1996. Imported from the Philippines by K.B.I., Inc.

Price: **$469.95**

COLT MODEL 1991 MODEL O AUTO PISTOL

Caliber: 45 ACP, 7-shot magazine. **Barrel:** 5". **Weight:** 38 oz. **Length:** 8.5" overall. **Stocks:** Checkered black composition. **Sights:** Ramped blade front, fixed square notch rear, high profile. **Features:** Matte finish. Continuation of serial number range used on original G.I. 1911 A1 guns. Comes with one magazine and moulded carrying case. Introduced 1991.

Price: **$645.00**

Price: Stainless.......... **$800.00**

Colt Model 1991 Model O Commander Auto Pistol

Similar to the Model 1991 A1 except has 4-1/4" barrel. Overall length is 7-3/4". Comes with one 7-shot magazine, molded case.

Price: Blue **$645.00**

Price: Stainless steel **$800.00**

COLT XSE SERIES MODEL O AUTO PISTOLS

Caliber: 45 ACP, 8-shot magazine. **Barrel:** 4.25", 5". **Weight:** NA. **Length:** NA. **Grips:** Checkered, double diamond rosewood. **Sights:** Drift-adjustable three-dot combat. **Features:** Brushed stainless finish; adjustable, two-cut aluminum trigger; extended ambidextrous thumb safety; upswept beavertail with palm swell; elongated slot hammer; beveled magazine well. Introduced 1999. From Colt's Manufacturing Co., Inc.

Price: XSE Government (5" barrel) **$950.00**

Price: XSE Commander (4.25" barrel) **$950.00**

COLT XSE LIGHTWEIGHT COMMANDER AUTO PISTOL

Caliber: 45 ACP, 8-shot. **Barrel:** 4-1/4". **Weight:** 26 oz. **Length:** 7-3/4" overall. **Stocks:** Double diamond checkered rosewood. **Sights:** Fixed, glare-proofed blade front, square notch rear; three-dot system. **Features:** Brushed stainless slide, nickeled aluminum frame; McCormick elongated-slot enhanced hammer, McCormick two-cut adjustable aluminum hammer. Made in U.S. by Colt's Mfg. Co., Inc.

Price: 45, stainless **$950.00**

COLT DEFENDER

Caliber: 40 S&W, 45 ACP, 7-shot magazine. **Barrel:** 3". **Weight:** 22-1/2 oz. **Length:** 6-3/4" overall. **Stocks:** Pebble-finish rubber wraparound with finger grooves. **Sights:** White dot front, snag-free Colt competition rear. **Features:** Stainless finish; aluminum frame; combat-style hammer; Hi Ride grip safety, extended manual safety, disconnect safety. Introduced 1998. Made in U.S. by Colt's Mfg. Co.

Price: **$773.00**

Colt Lightweight Commander

Coonan 357 Magnum

Colt Defender

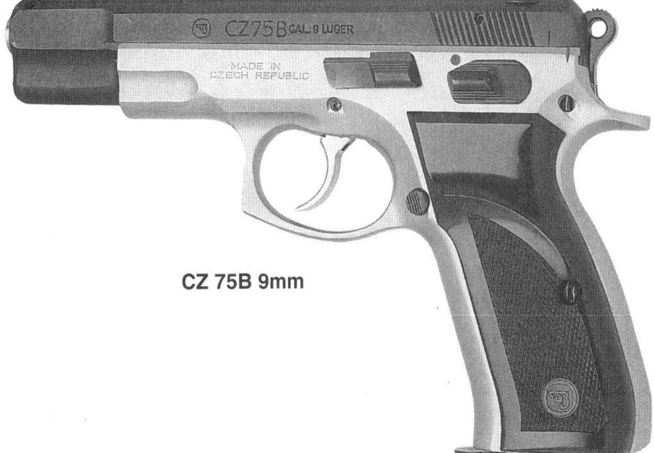

CZ 75B 9mm

COONAN 357 MAGNUM, 41 MAGNUM PISTOLS

Caliber: 357 Mag., 41 Magnum, 7-shot magazine. **Barrel:** 5". **Weight:** 42 oz. **Length:** 8.3" overall. **Stocks:** Smooth walnut. **Sights:** Interchangeable ramp front, rear adjustable for windage. **Features:** Stainless steel construction. Unique barrel hood improves accuracy and reliability. Link-less barrel. Many parts interchange with Colt autos. Has grip, hammer, half-cock safeties, extended slide latch. Made in U.S. by Coonan Arms, Inc.

Price: 5" barrel, from **$735.00**
Price: 6" barrel, from **$768.00**
Price: With 6" compensated barrel **$1,014.00**
Price: Classic model (Teflon black two-tone finish, 8-shot magazine, fully adjustable rear sight, integral compensated barrel) **$1,400.00**
Price: 41 Magnum Model, from **$825.00**

Coonan Compact Cadet 357 Magnum Pistol

Similar to the 357 Magnum full-size gun except has 3.9" barrel, shorter frame, 6-shot magazine. Weight is 39 oz., overall length 7.8". Linkless bull barrel, full-length recoil spring guide rod, extended slide latch. Introduced 1993. Made in U.S. by Coonan Arms, Inc.

Price: **$855.00**

CZ 75B AUTO PISTOL

Caliber: 9mm Para., 40 S&W, 10-shot magazine. **Barrel:** 4.7". **Weight:** 34.3 oz. **Length:** 8.1" overall. **Stocks:** High impact checkered plastic. **Sights:** Square post front, rear adjustable for windage; three-dot system. **Features:** Single action/double action design; firing pin block safety; choice of black polymer, matte or high-polish blue finishes. All-steel frame. Imported from the Czech Republic by CZ-USA.

Price: Black polymer **$472.00**
Price: Glossy blue **$486.00**

CZ 75B Decocker

Price: Dual tone or satin nickel **$486.00**
Price: 22 LR conversion unit **$279.00**

CZ 75B Decocker

Similar to the CZ 75B except has a decocking lever in place of the safety lever. All other specifications are the same. Introduced 1999. Imported from the Czech Republic by CZ-USA.

Price: 9mm, black polymer **$467.00**
New! **Price:** 40 S&W **$481.00**

CZ 75D Compact

CZ 85

CZ 83B

CZ 97B

CZ 75B Compact Auto Pistol

Similar to the CZ 75 except has 10-shot magazine, 3.9" barrel and weighs 32 oz. Has removable front sight, non-glare ribbed slide top. Trigger guard is squared and serrated; combat hammer. Introduced 1993. Imported from the Czech Republic by CZ-USA.

Price: 9mm, black polymer **$499.00**
Price: Dual tone or satin nickel **$513.00**
Price: D Compact, black polymer **$526.00**

NEW!

CZ 75M IPSC Auto Pistol

Similar to the CZ 75B except has a longer frame and slide, slightly larger grip to accommodate new heavy-duty magazine. Ambidextrous thumb safety, safety notch on hammer; two-port in-frame compensator; slide racker; frame-mounted Firepoint red dot sight. Introduced 2001. Imported from the Czech Republic by CZ USA.

Price: 40 S&W, 10-shot mag. **$1,498.00**
Price: CZ 75 Standard IPSC (40 S&W, adj. sights) **$1,038.00**

CZ 85B Auto Pistol

Same gun as the CZ 75 except has ambidextrous slide release and safety-levers; non-glare, ribbed slide top; squared, serrated trigger guard; trigger stop to prevent overtravel. Introduced 1986. Imported from the Czech Republic by CZ-USA.

Price: Black polymer **$483.00**
Price: Combat, black polymer **$540.00**
Price: Combat, dual tone **$487.00**
Price: Combat, glossy blue **$499.00**

CZ 85 Combat

Similar to the CZ 85B (9mm only) except has an adjustable rear sight, adjustable trigger for overtravel, free-fall magazine, extended magazine catch. Does not have the firing pin block safety. Introduced 1999. Imported from the Czech Republic by CZ-USA.

Price: 9mm, black polymer **$540.00**
Price: 9mm, glossy blue **$561.00**
Price: 9mm, dual tone or satin nickel **$561.00**

CZ 83B DOUBLE-ACTION PISTOL

Caliber: 9mm Makarov, 32 ACP, 380 ACP, 10-shot magazine. **Barrel:** 3.8". **Weight:** 26.2 oz. **Length:** 6.8" overall. **Stocks:** High impact checkered plastic. **Sights:** Removable square post front, rear adjustable for windage; three-dot system. **Features:** Single action/double action; ambidextrous magazine release and safety. Blue finish; non-glare ribbed slide top. Imported from the Czech Republic by CZ-USA.

Price: Blue **$378.00**
Price: Nickel **$378.00**

CZ 97B AUTO PISTOL

Caliber: 45 ACP, 10-shot magazine. **Barrel:** 4.85". **Weight:** 40 oz. **Length:** 8.34" overall. **Stocks:** Checkered walnut. **Sights:** Fixed. **Features:** Single action/double action; full-length slide rails; screw-in barrel bushing; linkless barrel; all-steel construction; chamber loaded indicator; dual transfer bars. Introduced 1999. Imported from the Czech Republic by CZ-USA.

Price: Black polymer **$607.00**
Price: Glossy blue **$621.00**

CZ 75/85 Kadet

Davis P-380

Davis P-32

CZ 100

Desert Eagle Mark XIX

CZ 75/85 KADET AUTO PISTOL

Caliber: 22 LR, 10-shot magazine. **Barrel:** 4.88". **Weight:** 36 oz. **Length:** NA. **Stocks:** High impact checkered plastic. **Sights:** Blade front, fully adjustable rear. **Features:** Single action/double action mechanism; all-steel construction. Duplicates weight, balance and function of the CZ 75 pistol. Introduced 1999. Imported from the Czech Republic by CZ-USA.

Price: Black polymer **$486.00**

CZ 100 AUTO PISTOL

Caliber: 9mm Para., 40 S&W, 10-shot magazine. **Barrel:** 3.7". **Weight:** 24 oz. **Length:** 6.9" overall. **Stocks:** Grooved polymer. **Sights:** Blade front with dot, white outline rear drift adjustable for windage. **Features:** Double action only with firing pin block; polymer frame, steel slide; has laser sight mount. Introduced 1996. Imported from the Czech Republic by CZ-USA.

Price: 9mm Para **$405.00**

Price: 40 S&W **$405.00**

DAVIS P-380 AUTO PISTOL

Caliber: 380 ACP, 5-shot magazine. **Barrel:** 2.8". **Weight:** 22 oz. **Length:** 5.4" overall. **Stocks:** Black composition. **Sights:** Fixed. **Features:** Choice of chrome or black Teflon finish. Introduced 1991. Made in U.S. by Davis Industries.

Price: **$98.00**

DAVIS P-32 AUTO PISTOL

Caliber: 32 ACP, 6-shot magazine. **Barrel:** 2.8". **Weight:** 22 oz. **Length:** 5.4" overall. **Stocks:** Laminated wood. **Sights:** Fixed. **Features:** Choice of black Teflon or chrome finish. Announced 1986. Made in U.S. by Davis Industries.

Price: **$107.00**

DESERT EAGLE MARK XIX PISTOL

Caliber: 357 Mag., 9-shot; 44 Mag., 8-shot; 50 Magnum, 7-shot. **Barrel:** 6", 10", interchangeable. **Weight:** 357 Mag.—62 oz.; 44 Mag.—69 oz.; 50 Mag.— 72 oz. **Length:** 10-1/4" overall (6" bbl.). **Stocks:** Rubber. **Sights:** Blade on ramp front, combat-style rear. Adjustable available. **Features:** Interchangeable barrels; rotating three-lug bolt; ambidextrous safety; adjustable trigger. Military epoxy finish. Satin, bright nickel, hard chrome, polished and blued finishes available. 10" barrel extra. Imported from Israel by Magnum Research, Inc.

Price: 357, 6" bbl., standard pistol **$1,199.00**

Price: 44 Mag., 6", standard pistol **$1,199.00**

Price: 50 Magnum, 6" bbl., standard pistol **$1,199.00**

Price: 440 Cor-Bon, 6" bbl. **$1,389.00**

Desert Eagle Baby Eagle

E.A.A. Witness

Entréprise Elite P500

Entréprise Boxer P500

DESERT EAGLE BABY EAGLE PISTOLS

Caliber: 9mm Para., 40 S&W, 45 ACP, 10-round magazine. **Barrel:** 3.5", 3.7", 4.72". **Weight:** NA. **Length:** 7.25" to 8.25" overall. **Grips:** Polymer. **Sights:** Drift-adjustable rear, blade front. **Features:** Steel frame and slide; polygonal rifling to reduce barrel wear; slide safety; decocker. Reintroduced in 1999. Imported from Israel by Magnum Research Inc.

Price: Standard (9mm or 40 cal.; 4.72" barrel, 8.25" overall) . . . **$499.00**
Price: Semi-Compact (9mm, 40 or 45 cal.; 3.7" barrel, 7.75" overall) . . . **$499.00**
Price: Compact (9mm or 40 cal.; 3.5" barrel, 7.25" overall) . . . **$499.00**
Price: Polymer (9mm or 40 cal; polymer frame; 3.25" barrel, 7.25" overall) . . . **$499.00**

E.A.A. WITNESS DA AUTO PISTOL

Caliber: 9mm Para., 10-shot magazine; 38 Super, 40 S&W, 10-shot magazine; 45 ACP, 10-shot magazine. **Barrel:** 4.50". **Weight:** 35.33 oz. **Length:** 8.10" overall. **Stocks:** Checkered rubber. **Sights:** Undercut blade front, open rear adjustable for windage. **Features:** Double-action trigger system; round trigger guard; frame-mounted safety. Introduced 1991. Imported from Italy by European American Armory.

Price: 9mm, blue . . . **$351.00**
Price: 9mm, Wonder finish . . . **$366.00**
Price: 9mm Compact, blue, 10-shot . . . **$351.00**
Price: As above, Wonder finish . . . **$366.60**
Price: 40 S&W, blue . . . **$366.60**
Price: As above, Wonder finish . . . **$366.60**
Price: 40 S&W Compact, 9-shot, blue . . . **$366.60**
Price: As above, Wonder finish . . . **$366.60**
Price: 45 ACP, blue . . . **$351.00**
Price: As above, Wonder finish . . . **$366.60**
Price: 45 ACP Compact, 8-shot, blue . . . **$351.00**
Price: As above, Wonder finish . . . **$366.60**

E.A.A. EUROPEAN MODEL AUTO PISTOLS

Caliber: 32 ACP or 380 ACP, 7-shot magazine. **Barrel:** 3.88". **Weight:** 26 oz. **Length:** 7-3/8" overall. **Stocks:** European hardwood. **Sights:** Fixed blade front, rear drift-adjustable for windage. **Features:** Chrome or blue finish; magazine, thumb and firing pin safeties; external hammer; safety-lever takedown. Imported from Italy by European American Armory.

Price: Blue . . . **$132.60**
Price: Wonder finish . . . **$163.80**

ENTRÉPRISE ELITE P500 AUTO PISTOL

Caliber: 45 ACP, 10-shot magazine. **Barrel:** 5". **Weight:** 40 oz. **Length:** 8.5" overall. **Stocks:** Black ultra-slim, double diamond, checkered synthetic. **Sights:** Dovetailed blade front, rear adjustable for windage; three-dot system. **Features:** Reinforced dust cover; lowered and flared ejection port; squared trigger guard; adjustable match trigger; bolstered front strap; high grip cut; high ride beavertail grip safety; steel flat mainspring housing; extended thumb lock; skeletonized hammer, match grade sear, disconnector; Wolff springs. Introduced 1998. Made in U.S. by Entréprise Arms.

Price: . . . **$739.90**

Entréprise Boxer P500 Auto Pistol

Similar to the Medalist model except has adjustable Competizione "melded" rear sight with dovetailed Patridge front; high mass chiseled slide with sweep cut; machined slide parallel rails; polished breech face and barrel channel. Introduced 1998. Made in U.S. by Entréprise Arms.

Price: . . . **$1,399.00**

Entréprise Medalist P500 Auto Pistol

Similar to the Elite model except has adjustable Competizione "melded" rear sight with dovetailed Patridge front; machined slide parallel rails with polished breech face and barrel channel; front and rear slide serrations; lowered and flared ejection port; full-length one-piece guide rod with plug; National Match barrel and bushing; stainless firing pin; tuned match extractor; oversize firing pin stop; throated barrel and polished ramp; slide lapped to frame. Introduced 1998. Made in U.S. by Entréprise Arms.

Price: 45 ACP . . . **$979.00**
Price: 40 S&W . . . **$1,099.00**

Entréprise Tactical 500

Felk MTF 450

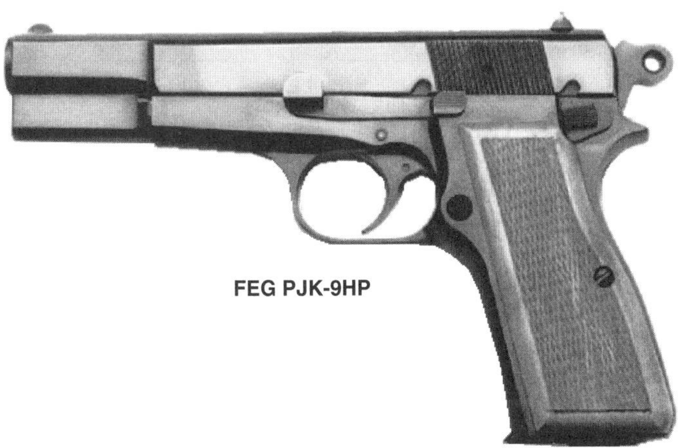

FEG PJK-9HP

Glock 17C

Entréprise Tactical P500 Auto Pistol

Similar to the Elite model except has Tactical2 Ghost Ring sight or Novak lo-mount sight; ambidextrous thumb safety; front and rear slide serrations; full-length guide rod; throated barrel, polished ramp; tuned match extractor; fitted barrel and bushing; stainless firing pin; slide lapped to frame; dehorned. Introduced 1998. Made in U.S. by Entréprise Arms.

Price: **$979.90**

Price: Tactical Plus (full-size frame, Officer's slide) **$1,049.00**

ERMA KGP68 AUTO PISTOL

Caliber: 32 ACP, 6-shot, 380 ACP, 5-shot. **Barrel:** 4". **Weight:** 22-1/2 oz. **Length:** 7-3/8" overall. **Stocks:** Checkered plastic. **Sights:** Fixed. **Features:** Toggle action similar to original "Luger" pistol. Action stays open after last shot. Has magazine and sear disconnect safety systems.

Price: **$499.95**

FEG PJK-9HP AUTO PISTOL

Caliber: 9mm Para., 10-shot magazine. **Barrel:** 4.75". **Weight:** 32 oz. **Length:** 8" overall. **Stocks:** Hand-checkered walnut. **Sights:** Blade front, rear adjustable for windage; three dot system. **Features:** Single action; polished blue or hard chrome finish; rounded combat-style serrated hammer. Comes with two magazines and cleaning rod. Imported from Hungary by K.B.I., Inc.

Price: Blue **$259.95**

Price: Hard chrome. **$259.95**

FEG SMC-380 AUTO PISTOL

Caliber: 380 ACP, 6-shot magazine. **Barrel:** 3.5". **Weight:** 18.5 oz. **Length:** 6.1" overall. **Stocks:** Checkered composition with thumbrest. **Sights:** Blade front, rear adjustable for windage. **Features:** Patterned after the PPK pistol. Alloy frame, steel slide; double action. Blue finish. Comes with two magazines, cleaning rod. Imported from Hungary by K.B.I., Inc.

Price: **$224.95**

FELK MTF 450 AUTO PISTOL

Caliber: 9mm Para. (10-shot); 40 S&W (8-shot); 45 ACP (9-shot magazine). **Barrel:** 3.5". **Weight:** 19.9 oz. **Length:** 6.4" overall. **Stocks:** Checkered. **Sights:** Blade front; adjustable rear. **Features:** Double-action-only trigger, striker fired; polymer frame; trigger safety, firing pin safety, trigger bar safety; adjustable trigger weight; fully interchangeable slide/barrel to change calibers. Introduced 1998. Imported by Felk Inc.

Price: **$395.00**

Price: 45 ACP pistol with 9mm and 40 S&W slide/barrel assemblies **$999.00**

GLOCK 17 AUTO PISTOL

Caliber: 9mm Para., 10-shot magazine. **Barrel:** 4.49". **Weight:** 22.04 oz. (without magazine). **Length:** 7.32" overall. **Stocks:** Black polymer. **Sights:** Dot on front blade, white outline rear adjustable for windage. **Features:** Polymer frame, steel slide; double-action trigger with "Safe Action" system; mechanical firing pin safety, drop safety; simple takedown without tools; locked breech, recoil operated action. Adopted by Austrian armed forces 1983. NATO approved 1984. Imported from Austria by Glock, Inc.

Price: Fixed sight, with extra magazine, magazine loader, cleaning kit **$641.00**

Price: Adjustable sight **$671.00**

Price: Model 17L (6" barrel) **$800.00**

Price: Model 17C, ported barrel (compensated) **$646.00**

Glock 22

Glock 26

Glock 19 Auto Pistol

Similar to the Glock 17 except has a 4" barrel, giving an overall length of 6.85" and weight of 20.99 oz. Magazine capacity is 10 rounds. Fixed or adjustable rear sight. Introduced 1988.

Price: Fixed sight **$641.00**
Price: Adjustable sight **$671.00**
Price: Model 19C, ported barrel **$646.00**

Glock 20 10mm Auto Pistol

Similar to the Glock Model 17 except chambered for 10mm Automatic cartridge. Barrel length is 4.60", overall length is 7.59", and weight is 26.3 oz. (without magazine). Magazine capacity is 10 rounds. Fixed or adjustable rear sight. Comes with an extra magazine, magazine loader, cleaning rod and brush. Introduced 1990. Imported from Austria by Glock, Inc.

Price: Fixed sight **$700.00**
Price: Adjustable sight **$730.00**

Glock 21 Auto Pistol

Similar to the Glock 17 except chambered for 45 ACP, 10-shot magazine. Overall length is 7.59", weight is 25.2 oz. (without magazine). Fixed or adjustable rear sight. Introduced 1991.

Price: Fixed sight **$700.00**
Price: Adjustable sight **$730.00**

Glock 22 Auto Pistol

Similar to the Glock 17 except chambered for 40 S&W, 10-shot magazine. Overall length is 7.28", weight is 22.3 oz. (without magazine). Fixed or adjustable rear sight. Introduced 1990.

Price: Fixed sight **$641.00**
Price: Adjustable sight **$671.00**
Price: Model 22C, ported barrel **$646.00**

Glock 30

Glock 31

Glock 23 Auto Pistol

Similar to the Glock 19 except chambered for 40 S&W, 10-shot magazine. Overall length is 6.85", weight is 20.6 oz. (without magazine). Fixed or adjustable rear sight. Introduced 1990.

Price: Fixed sight **$641.00**
Price: Model 23C, ported barrel **$646.00**
Price: Adjustable sight **$671.00**

GLOCK 26, 27 AUTO PISTOLS

Caliber: 9mm Para. (M26), 10-shot magazine; 40 S&W (M27), 9-shot magazine. **Barrel:** 3.46". **Weight:** 21.75 oz. **Length:** 6.29" overall. **Stocks:** Integral. Stippled polymer. **Sights:** Dot on front blade, fixed or fully adjustable white outline rear. **Features:** Subcompact size. Polymer frame, steel slide; double-action trigger with "Safe Action" system, three safeties. Matte black Tenifer finish. Hammer-forged barrel. Imported from Austria by Glock, Inc. Introduced 1996.

Price: Fixed sight **$641.00**
Price: Adjustable sight **$671.00**

GLOCK 29, 30 AUTO PISTOLS

Caliber: 10mm (M29), 45 ACP (M30), 10-shot magazine. **Barrel:** 3.78". **Weight:** 24 oz. **Length:** 6.7" overall. **Stocks:** Integral. Stippled polymer. **Sights:** Dot on front, fixed or fully adjustable white outline rear. **Features:** Compact size. Polymer frame steel slide; double-recoil spring reduces recoil; Safe Action system with three safeties; Tenifer finish. Two magazines supplied. Introduced 1997. Imported from Austria by Glock, Inc.

Price: Fixed sight **$700.00**
Price: Adjustable sight **$730.00**

Glock 31/31C Auto Pistols

Similar to the Glock 17 except chambered for 357 Auto cartridge; 10-shot magazine. Overall length is 7.32", weight is 23.28 oz. (without magazine). Fixed or adjustable sight. Imported from Austria by Glock, Inc.

Price: Fixed sight **$641.00**
Price: Adjustable sight **$671.00**
Price: Model 31C, ported barrel **$646.00**

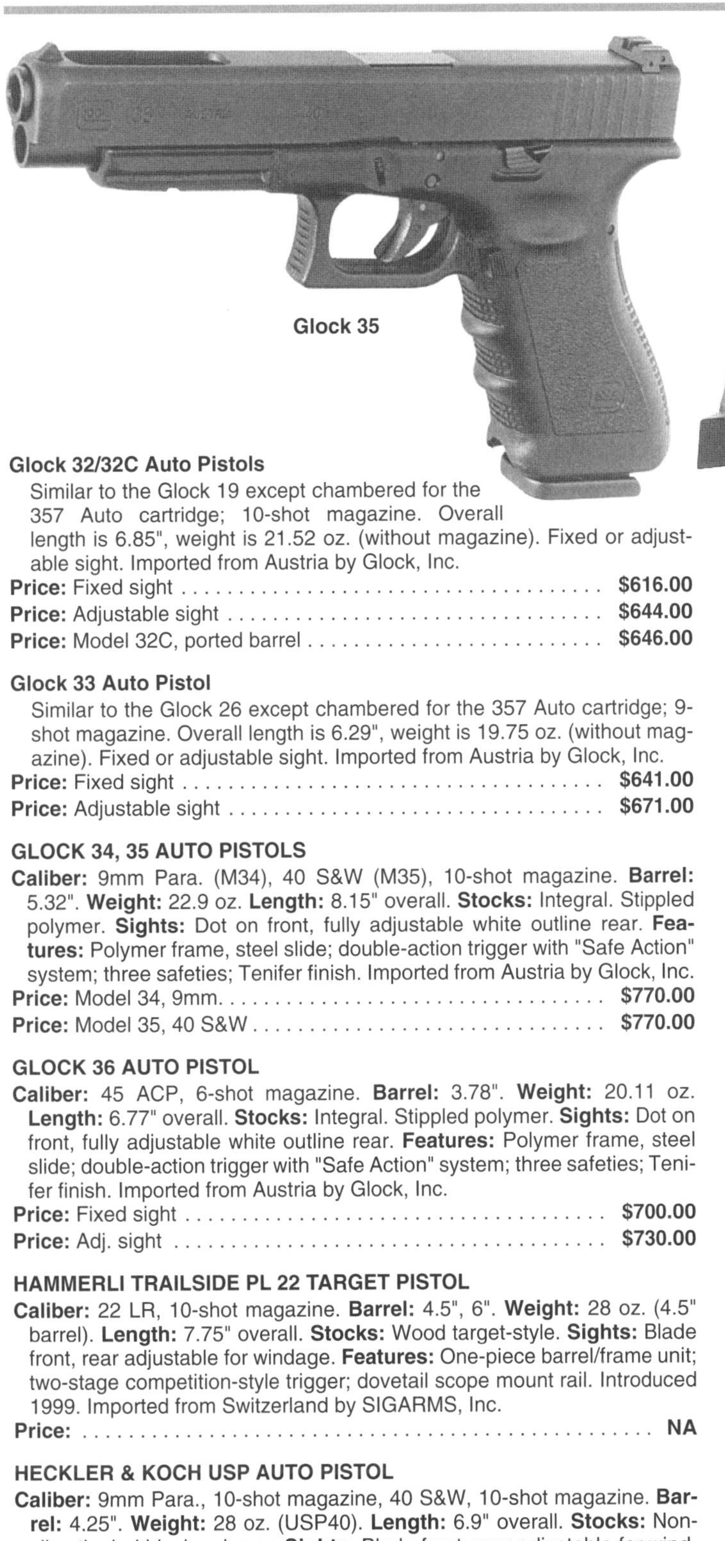
Glock 35

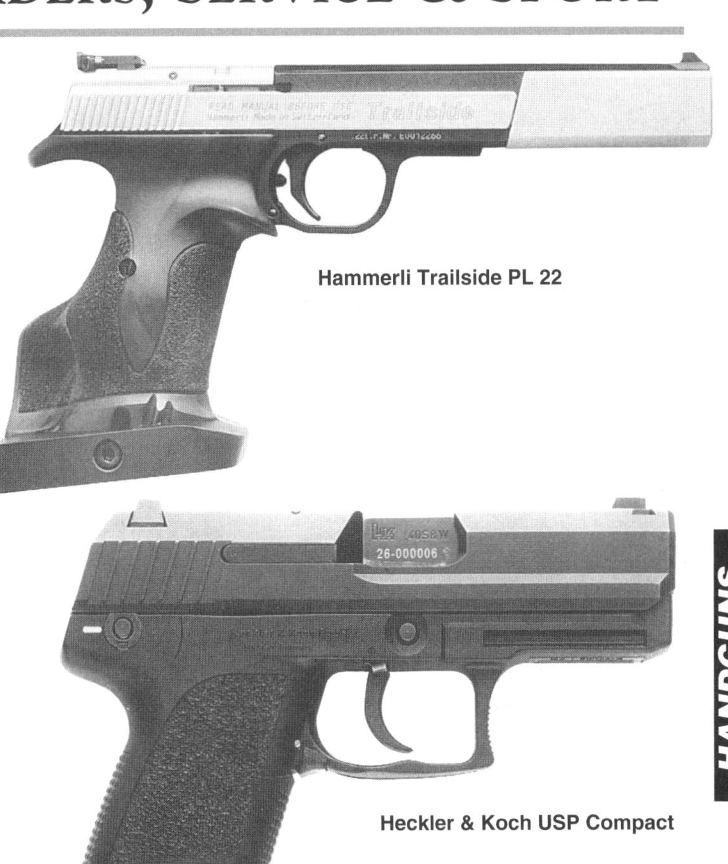
Hammerli Trailside PL 22

Glock 32/32C Auto Pistols

Similar to the Glock 19 except chambered for the 357 Auto cartridge; 10-shot magazine. Overall length is 6.85", weight is 21.52 oz. (without magazine). Fixed or adjustable sight. Imported from Austria by Glock, Inc.

Price: Fixed sight **$616.00**
Price: Adjustable sight **$644.00**
Price: Model 32C, ported barrel **$646.00**

Glock 33 Auto Pistol

Similar to the Glock 26 except chambered for the 357 Auto cartridge; 9-shot magazine. Overall length is 6.29", weight is 19.75 oz. (without magazine). Fixed or adjustable sight. Imported from Austria by Glock, Inc.

Price: Fixed sight **$641.00**
Price: Adjustable sight **$671.00**

GLOCK 34, 35 AUTO PISTOLS

Caliber: 9mm Para. (M34), 40 S&W (M35), 10-shot magazine. **Barrel:** 5.32". **Weight:** 22.9 oz. **Length:** 8.15" overall. **Stocks:** Integral. Stippled polymer. **Sights:** Dot on front, fully adjustable white outline rear. **Features:** Polymer frame, steel slide; double-action trigger with "Safe Action" system; three safeties; Tenifer finish. Imported from Austria by Glock, Inc.

Price: Model 34, 9mm.................... **$770.00**
Price: Model 35, 40 S&W **$770.00**

GLOCK 36 AUTO PISTOL

Caliber: 45 ACP, 6-shot magazine. **Barrel:** 3.78". **Weight:** 20.11 oz. **Length:** 6.77" overall. **Stocks:** Integral. Stippled polymer. **Sights:** Dot on front, fully adjustable white outline rear. **Features:** Polymer frame, steel slide; double-action trigger with "Safe Action" system; three safeties; Tenifer finish. Imported from Austria by Glock, Inc.

Price: Fixed sight **$700.00**
Price: Adj. sight **$730.00**

HAMMERLI TRAILSIDE PL 22 TARGET PISTOL

Caliber: 22 LR, 10-shot magazine. **Barrel:** 4.5", 6". **Weight:** 28 oz. (4.5" barrel). **Length:** 7.75" overall. **Stocks:** Wood target-style. **Sights:** Blade front, rear adjustable for windage. **Features:** One-piece barrel/frame unit; two-stage competition-style trigger; dovetail scope mount rail. Introduced 1999. Imported from Switzerland by SIGARMS, Inc.

Price: .... **NA**

HECKLER & KOCH USP AUTO PISTOL

Caliber: 9mm Para., 10-shot magazine, 40 S&W, 10-shot magazine. **Barrel:** 4.25". **Weight:** 28 oz. (USP40). **Length:** 6.9" overall. **Stocks:** Non-slip stippled black polymer. **Sights:** Blade front, rear adjustable for windage. **Features:** New HK design with polymer frame, modified Browning action with recoil reduction system, single control lever. Special "hostile environment" finish on all metal parts. Available in SA/DA, DAO, left- and right-hand versions. Introduced 1993. Imported from Germany by Heckler & Koch, Inc.

Price: Right-hand **$699.00**
Price: Left-hand **$714.00**
Price: Stainless steel, right-hand **$749.00**
Price: Stainless steel, left-hand **$799.00**

Heckler & Koch USP Compact

Heckler & Koch USP45

Heckler & Koch USP Compact Auto Pistol

Similar to the USP except has 3.58" barrel, measures 6.81" overall, and weighs 1.60 lbs. (9mm). Available in 9mm Para. 357 SIG or 40 S&W with 10-shot magazine. Introduced 1996. Imported from Germany by Heckler & Koch, Inc.

Price: Blue **$759.00**
Price: Blue with control lever on right.... **$784.00**
Price: Stainless steel **$849.00**
Price: Stainless steel with control lever on right.................... **$874.00**

Heckler & Koch USP45 Auto Pistol

Similar to the 9mm and 40 S&W USP except chambered for 45 ACP, 10-shot magazine. Has 4.13" barrel, overall length of 7.87" and weighs 30.4 oz. Has adjustable three-dot sight system. Available in SA/DA, DAO, left- and right-hand versions. Introduced 1995. Imported from Germany by Heckler & Koch, Inc.

Price: Right-hand **$799.00**
Price: Left-hand **$824.00**
Price: Stainless steel right-hand.................... **$859.00**
Price: Stainless steel left-hand.................... **$884.00**

Heckler & Koch USP45 Tactical

Heckler & Koch USP Expert

Heckler & Koch P7M8

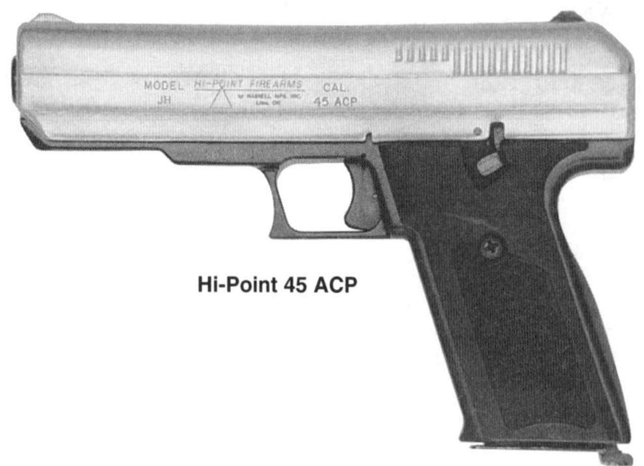

Hi-Point 45 ACP

Heckler & Koch USP45 Compact

Similar to the USP45 except has stainless slide; 8-shot magazine; modified and contoured slide and frame; extended slide release; 3.80" barrel, 7.09" overall length, weighs 1.75 lbs.; adjustable three-dot sights. Introduced 1998. Imported from Germany by Heckler & Koch, Inc.

Price: With control lever on left, stainless. **$879.00**
Price: As above, blue **$879.00**
Price: With control lever on right, stainless. **$904.00**
Price: As above, blue **$854.00**

HECKLER & KOCH USP45 TACTICAL PISTOL

Caliber: 45 ACP, 10-shot magazine. **Barrel:** 4.92". **Weight:** 2.24 lbs. **Length:** 8.64" overall. **Stocks:** Non-slip stippled polymer. **Sights:** Blade front, fully adjustable target rear. **Features:** Has extended threaded barrel with rubber O-ring; adjustable trigger; extended magazine floorplate; adjustable trigger stop; polymer frame. Introduced 1998. Imported from Germany by Heckler & Koch, Inc.

Price: **$1,069.00**

HECKLER & KOCH MARK 23 SPECIAL OPERATIONS PISTOL

Caliber: 45 ACP, 10-shot magazine. **Barrel:** 5.87". **Weight:** 43 oz. **Length:** 9.65" overall. **Stocks:** Integral with frame; black polymer. **Sights:** Blade front, rear drift adjustable for windage; three-dot. **Features:** Polymer frame; double action; exposed hammer; short recoil, modified Browning action. Civilian version of the SOCOM pistol. Introduced 1996. Imported from Germany by Heckler & Koch, Inc.

Price: **$2,289.00**

Heckler & Koch USP Expert Pistol

Combines features of the USP Tactical and HK Mark 23 pistols with a new slide design. Chambered for 45 ACP; 10-shot magazine. Has adjustable target sights, 5.20" barrel, 8.74" overall length, weighs 1.87 lbs. Match-grade single- and double-action trigger pull with adjustable stop; ambidextrous control levers; elongated target slide; barrel O-ring that seals and centers barrel. Suited to IPSC competition. Introduced 1999. Imported from Germany by Heckler & Koch, Inc.

Price: **$1,449.00**

HECKLER & KOCH P7M8 AUTO PISTOL

Caliber: 9mm Para., 8-shot magazine. **Barrel:** 4.13". **Weight:** 29 oz. **Length:** 6.73" overall. **Stocks:** Stippled black plastic. **Sights:** Blade front, adjustable rear; three dot system. **Features:** Unique "squeeze cocker" in frontstrap cocks the action. Gas-retarded action. Squared combat-type trigger guard. Blue finish. Compact size. Imported from Germany by Heckler & Koch, Inc.

Price: P7M8, blued **$1,369.00**

HI-POINT FIREARMS 40 S&W AUTO

Caliber: 40 S&W, 8-shot magazine. **Barrel:** 4.5". **Weight:** 39 oz. **Length:** 7.72" overall. **Stocks:** Checkered acetal resin. **Sights:** Adjustable; low profile. **Features:** Internal drop-safe mechanism; alloy frame. Introduced 1991. From MKS Supply, Inc.

Price: Matte black. **$159.00**

HI-POINT FIREARMS 45 CALIBER PISTOL

Caliber: 45 ACP, 7-shot magazine. **Barrel:** 4.5". **Weight:** 39 oz. **Length:** 7.95" overall. **Stocks:** Checkered acetal resin. **Sights:** Adjustable; low profile. **Features:** Internal drop-safe mechanism; alloy frame. Introduced 1991. From MKS Supply, Inc.

Price: Matte black. **$159.00**
Price: Chrome slide, black frame **$169.00**

Hi-Point 9MM Comp

HI-POINT FIREARMS 9MM COMP PISTOL

Caliber: 9mm, Para., 10-shot magazine. **Barrel:** 4". **Weight:** 39 oz. **Length:** 7.72" overall. **Stocks:** Textured acetal plastic. **Sights:** Adjustable; low profile. **Features:** Single-action design. Scratch-resistant, non-glare blue finish, alloy frame. Muzzle brake/compensator. Compensator is slotted for laser or flashlight mounting. Introduced 1998. From MKS Supply, Inc.

Price: Matte black **$159.00**

HI-POINT FIREARMS MODEL 9MM COMPACT PISTOL

Caliber: 9mm Para., 8-shot magazine. **Barrel:** 3.5". **Weight:** 29 oz. **Length:** 6.7" overall. **Stocks:** Textured acetal plastic. **Sights:** Combat-style adjustable three-dot system; low profile. **Features:** Single-action design; frame-mounted magazine release; polymer or alloy frame. Scratch-resistant matte finish. Introduced 1993. Made in U.S. by MKS Supply, Inc.

Price: Black, alloy frame **$137.00**

Price: With polymer frame (29 oz.), non-slip grips **$137.00**

Price: Aluminum with polymer frame **$137.00**

Hi-Point Firearms Model 380 Polymer Pistol

Similar to the 9mm Compact model except chambered for 380 ACP, 8-shot magazine, adjustable three-dot sights. Weighs 29 oz. Polymer frame. Introduced 1998. Made in U.S. by MKS Supply.

Price: **$99.95**

NEW! **Hi-Point Firearms 380 Comp Pistol**

Similar to the 380 Polymer Pistol except has a 4" barrel with muzzle compensator; action locks open after last shot. Includes a 10-shot and an 8-shot magazine; trigger lock. Introduced 2001. Made in U.S. by MKS Supply Inc.

Price: **$125.00**

Price: With laser sight **$190.00**

HS AMERICA HS 2000 PISTOL

Caliber: 9mm Para., 357 SIG, 40 S&W, 10-shot magazine. **Barrel:** 4.08". **Weight:** 22.88 oz. **Length:** 7.2" overall. **Grips:** Integral black polymer. **Sights:** Drift-adjustable white dot rear, white dot blade front. **Features:** Incorporates trigger, firing pin, grip and out-of-battery safeties; firing-pin status and loaded chamber indicators; ambidextrous magazine release; dual-tension recoil spring with stand-off device; polymer frame; black finish with chrome-plated magazine. Imported from Croatia by HS America.

Price: **$419.00**

IAI M-3000 AUTO PISTOL

Caliber: 9mm Para., 7-shot magazine. **Barrel:** 3-1/2". **Weight:** 32 oz. **Length:** 6-1/2" overall. **Grips:** Plastic. **Sights:** High-contrast fixed. **Features:** Double-action; all-steel construction; automatic firing-pin safety; field strips without tools; slide stays open after last shot. Imported by IAI Inc.

Price: **$373.70**

IAI M-4000 AUTO PISTOL

Similar to IAI M-3000 Pistol above, except chambered in 40 S&W. All-steel construction; 7-shot magazine.

Price: **$373.70**

Kahr K9

Kahr MK40

IAI M-5000 AUTO PISTOL

Caliber: 45 ACP, 8-shot magazine. **Barrel:** 4.25". **Weight:** 36 oz. **Length:** 6" overall. **Grips:** Plastic. **Sights:** Fixed. **Features:** 1911-style; blued steel frame and slide; beavertail grip safety; extended slide stop, safety and magazine release; beveled feed ramp; combat-style hammer; beveled magazine well; ambidexterous safety. Imported from the Philippines by IAI Inc.

Price: **$447.40**

IAI M-6000 AUTO PISTOL

Caliber: 45 ACP, 8-shot magazine. **Barrel:** 5". **Weight:** 36 oz. **Length:** 8-1/2" overall. **Grips:** Plastic. **Sights:** Fixed. **Features:** 1911-style; blued steel frame and slide; beavertail grip safety; extended slide stop, safety and magazine release; beveled feed ramp and magazine well; combat-style hammer; ambidexterous safety. Imported from the Philippines by IAI Inc.

Price: **$447.40**

KAHR K9, K40 DA AUTO PISTOLS

Caliber: 9mm Para., 7-shot, 40 S&W, 6-shot magazine. **Barrel:** 3.5". **Weight:** 25 oz. **Length:** 6" overall. **Stocks:** Wrap-around textured soft polymer. **Sights:** Blade front, rear drift adjustable for windage; bar-dot combat style. **Features:** Trigger-cocking double-action mechanism with passive firing pin block. Made of 4140 ordnance steel with matte black finish. Contact maker for complete price list. Introduced 1994. Made in U.S. by Kahr Arms.

Price: E9, black matte finish **$399.00**

Price: Matte black, night sights 9mm **$640.00**

Price: Matte stainless steel, 9mm **$580.00**

Price: 40 S&W, matte black **$550.00**

Price: 40 S&W, matte black, night sights **$640.00**

Price: 40 S&W, matte stainless **$580.00**

Price: K9 Elite 98 (high-polish stainless slide flats, Kahr combat trigger), from **$631.00**

Price: As above, MK9 Elite 98, from **$631.00**

Price: As above, K40 Elite 98, from **$631.00**

Kel-Tec P-11

Kimber Custom 45

Kel-Tec P-32

Kimber Compact Custom

Kahr K9 9mm Compact Polymer Pistol

Similar to K9 steel frame pistol except has polymer frame, matte stainless steel slide. Barrel length 3.5"; overall length 6"; weighs 17.9 oz. Includes two 7-shot magazines, hard polymer case, trigger lock. Introduced 2000. Made in U.S. by Kahr Arms.

Price: **$527.00**

Kahr MK9/MK40 Micro Pistol

Similar to the K9/K40 except is 5.5" overall, 4" high, has a 3" barrel. Weighs 22 oz. Has snag-free bar-dot sights, polished feed ramp, dual recoil spring system, DA-only trigger. Comes with 6- and 7-shot magazines. Introduced 1998. Made in U.S. by Kahr Arms.

Price: Matte stainless **$580.00**
Price: Elite 98, polished stainless, tritium night sights **$721.00**

KEL-TEC P-11 AUTO PISTOL

Caliber: 9mm Para., 10-shot magazine. **Barrel:** 3.1". **Weight:** 14 oz. **Length:** 5.6" overall. **Stocks:** Checkered black polymer. **Sights:** Blade front, rear adjustable for windage. **Features:** Ordnance steel slide, aluminum frame. Double-action-only trigger mechanism. Introduced 1995. Made in U.S. by Kel-Tec CNC Industries, Inc.

Price: Blue **$309.00**
Price: Hard chrome. **$363.00**
Price: Parkerized **$350.00**

KEL-TEC P-32 AUTO PISTOL

Caliber: 32 ACP, 7-shot magazine. **Barrel:** 2.68". **Weight:** 6.6 oz. **Length:** 5.07" overall. **Stocks:** Checkered composite. **Sights:** Fixed. **Features:** Double-action-only mechanism with 6-lb. pull; internal slide stop. Textured composite grip/frame. Made in U.S. by Kel-Tec CNC Industries, Inc.

Price: **$295.00**

KIMBER CUSTOM AUTO PISTOL

Caliber: 45 ACP, 7-shot magazine. **Barrel:** 5", match grade. **Weight:** 38 oz. **Length:** 8.7" overall. **Stocks:** Checkered black rubber (standard), or rosewood. **Sights:** McCormick dovetailed front, low combat rear. **Features:** Slide, frame and barrel machined from steel forgings; match-grade barrel, chamber, trigger; extended thumb safety; beveled magazine well; beveled front and rear slide serrations; high-ride beavertail safety; checkered flat mainspring housing; kidney cut under trigger guard; high cut grip design; match-grade stainless barrel bushing; Commander-style hammer; lowered and flared ejection port; Wolff springs; bead blasted black oxide finish. Made in U.S. by Kimber Mfg., Inc.

Price: Custom. **$730.00**
Price: Custom Walnut (double-diamond walnut grips) **$752.00**
Price: Custom Stainless **$832.00**
Price: Custom Stainless 40 S&W **$870.00**
Price: Custom Stainless Target 45 ACP (stainless, adj. sight) **$944.00**
Price: Custom Stainless Target 40 S&W **$974.00**

Kimber Compact Auto Pistol

Similar to the Custom model except has 4" bull barrel fitted directly to the slide without a bushing; full-length guide rod; grip is .400" shorter than full-size gun; no front serrations. Steel frame models weigh 34 oz., aluminum 28 oz. Introduced 1998. Made in U.S. by Kimber Mfg., Inc.

Price: 45 ACP, matte black. **$764.00**
Price: Compact Stainless 45 ACP **$871.00**
Price: Compact Stainless 40 S&W. **$902.00**
Price: Compact Aluminum Stainless 45 ACP (aluminum frame, stainless slide) **$837.00**
Price: Compact Aluminum Stainless 40 S&W **$873.00**

Kimber Ultra Carry

Kimber Pro CDP

Kimber High Capacity Polymer

Kimber Pro Carry Auto Pistol

Similar to the Compact model except has aluminum frame with full-length grip. Has 4" bull barrel fitted directly to the slide without bushing. Introduced 1998. Made in U.S. by Kimber Mfg., Inc.

Price: 45 ACP $773.00
Price: 40 S&W $808.00
Price: Pro Carry Stainless 45 ACP $845.00
Price: Pro Carry Stainless 40 S&W $881.00

Kimber Ultra Carry Auto Pistol

Similar to the Compact Aluminum model except has 3" balljoint spherical bushingless cone barrel; aluminum frame; beveling at front and rear of ejection port; relieved breech face; tuned ejector; special slide stop; dual captured low-effort spring system. Weighs 25 oz. Introduced 1999. made in U.S. by Kimber Mfg., Inc.

Price: 45 ACP $808.00
Price: 40 S&W $847.00
Price: Stainless, 45 ACP $886.00
Price: Stainless, 40 S&W $931.00

KIMBER HIGH CAPACITY POLYMER PISTOL

Caliber: 45 ACP, 10- and 14-shot magazine. **Barrel:** 5". **Weight:** 34 oz. **Length:** 8.7" overall. **Stocks:** Integral; checkered black polymer. **Sights:** McCormick low profile front and rear. **Features:** Polymer frame with steel insert. Comes with 10-shot magazine. Checkered front strap and mainspring housing; polymer trigger; stainless high ride beavertail grip safety; hooked trigger guard. Introduced 1997. Made in U.S. by Kimber Mfg., Inc.

Price: Polymer Custom, matte black finish $795.00
Price: Polymer Stainless (satin-finish stainless slide) $856.00
Price: Polymer Pro Carry (compact slide, 4" bull barrel) $814.00
Price: Polymer Pro Carry Stainless $874.00
New! **Price:** Polymer Ultra Ten II (polymer/stainless) $896.00

Kimber Gold Match Auto Pistol

Similar to the Custom model except has Kimber adjustable sight with rounded and blended edges; stainless steel match-grade barrel hand-fitted to spherical barrel bushing; premium aluminum trigger; extended ambidextrous thumb safety; hand-checkered double diamond rosewood grips. Hand-fitted by Kimber Custom Shop. Made in U.S. by Kimber Mfg., Inc.

Price: Gold Match 45 ACP $1,169.00
Price: Gold Match Stainless 45 ACP (highly polished flats) $1,315.00
Price: Gold Match Stainless 40 S&W $1,345.00

Kimber Polymer Gold Match Auto Pistol

Similar to the Polymer model except has Kimber adjustable sight with rounded and blended edges; stainless steel match-grade barrel hand-fitted to spherical barrel bushing; premium aluminum trigger; extended ambidextrous thumb safety. Hand-fitted by Kimber Custom Shop. Introduced 1999. Made in U.S. by Kimber Mfg., Inc.

Price: $1,041.00
Price: Polymer Stainless Gold Match (polished stainless slide) . $1,177.00

Kimber Gold Combat Auto Pistol

Similar to the Gold Match except designed for concealed carry. Has two-piece extended and beveled magazine well, tritium night sights; premium aluminum trigger; 30 lpi front strap checkering; special Custom Shop markings; Kim Pro black finish. Introduced 1999. Made in U.S. by Kimber Mfg., Inc.

Price: 45 ACP $1,682.00
Price: Gold Combat Stainless (satin-finished stainless frame and slide, special Custom Shop markings) $1,623.00

KIMBER PRO CDP AUTO PISTOL

Caliber: 45 ACP, 7-shot magazine. **Barrel:** 4". **Weight:** 28 oz. **Length:** 7.7" overall. **Grips:** Hand-checkered. double diamond rosewood. **Sights:** Tritium three-dot. **Features:** Matte black, machined aluminum frame; satin stainless steel slide; match-grade barrel and chamber; beveled magazine well; extended ejector; high-ride beavertail grip safety; match-grade trigger group; ambidextrous safety; checkered frontstrap; meltdown treatment. Introduced 2000. Made in U.S. by Kimber.

Price: $1,142.00

KIMBER ULTRA CDP AUTO PISTOL

Caliber: 45 ACP, 6-shot magazine. **Barrel:** 3". **Weight:** 25 oz. **Length:** 6.8" overall. **Grips:** Hand-checkered. double diamond rosewood. **Sights:** Tritium three-dot. **Features:** Matte black, machined aluminum frame; satin stainless steel slide; match-grade barrel and chamber; beveled magazine well and ejection port; dual recoil spring system for reliability and ease of manual slide operation; match-grade barrel, chamber and trigger; ambidextrous safety; checkered frontstrap; meltdown treatment. Introduced 2000. Made in U.S. by Kimber.

Price: $1,142.00

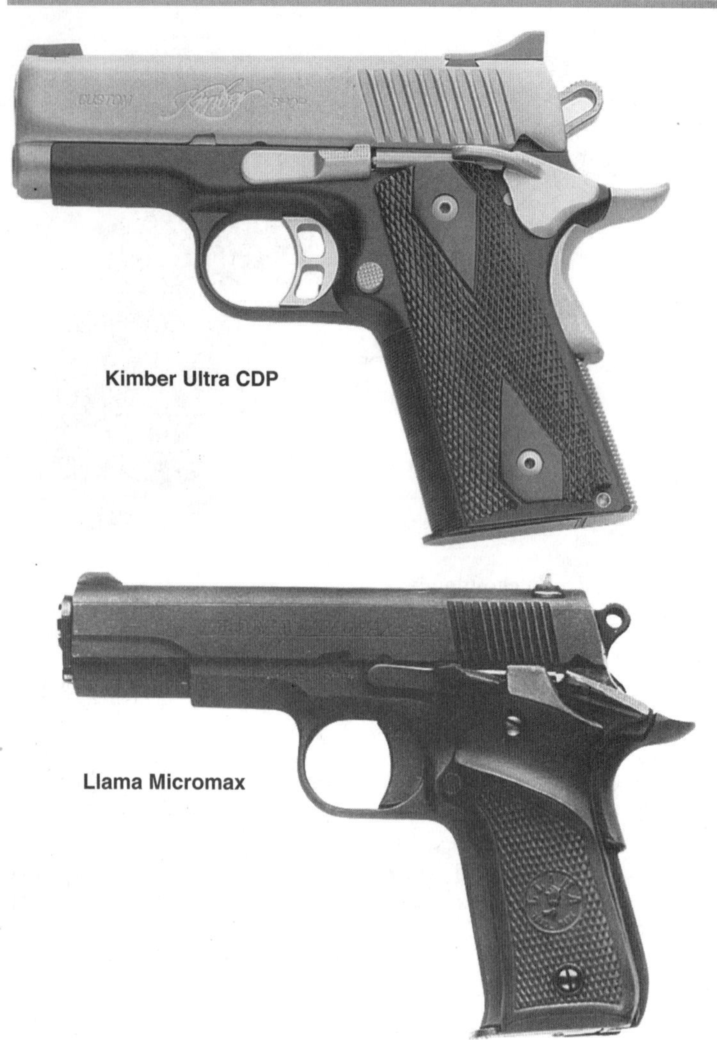

Kimber Ultra CDP

Llama Micromax

Llama Minimax

Llama Max-1

LLAMA MICROMAX 380 AUTO PISTOL

Caliber: 32 ACP, 8-shot, 380 ACP, 7-shot magazine. **Barrel:** 3-11/16". **Weight:** 23 oz. **Length:** 6-1/2" overall. **Stocks:** Checkered high impact polymer. **Sights:** 3-dot combat. **Features:** Single-action design. Mini custom extended slide release; mini custom extended beavertail grip safety; combat-style hammer. Introduced 1997. Imported from Spain by Import Sports, Inc.

Price: Matte blue. **$281.95**

Price: Satin chrome (380 only) **$298.95**

LLAMA MINIMAX SERIES

Caliber: 9mm Para., 8-shot; 40 S&W, 7-shot; 45 ACP, 6-shot magazine. **Barrel:** 3-1/2". **Weight:** 35 oz. **Length:** 7-1/3" overall. **Stocks:** Checkered rubber. **Sights:** Three-dot combat. **Features:** Single action, skeletonized combat-style hammer, extended slide release, cone-style barrel, flared ejection port. Introduced 1996. Imported from Spain by Import Sports, Inc.

Price: Blue **$316.95**

Price: Duo-Tone finish (45 only) **$324.95**

Price: Satin chrome **$333.95**

Llama Minimax Sub-Compact Auto Pistol

Similar to the Minimax except has 3.14" barrel, weighs 31 oz.; 6.8" overall length; has 10-shot magazine with finger extension; beavertail grip safety. Introduced 1999. Imported from Spain by Import Sports, Inc.

Price: 45 ACP, matte blue. **$331.95**

Price: As above, satin chrome **$349.95**

Price: Duo-Tone finish (45 only) **$341.95**

LLAMA MAX-I AUTO PISTOLS

Caliber: 45 ACP, 7-shot. **Barrel:** 5-1/8". **Weight:** 36 oz. **Length:** 8-1/2" overall. **Stocks:** Black rubber. **Sights:** Blade front, rear adjustable for windage; three-dot system. **Features:** Single-action trigger; skeletonized combat-style hammer; steel frame; extended manual and grip safeties. Introduced 1995. Imported from Spain by Import Sports, Inc.

Price: 45 ACP, 7-shot, Government model. **$310.95**

NORTH AMERICAN ARMS GUARDIAN PISTOL

Caliber: 32 ACP, 6-shot magazine. **Barrel:** 2.1". **Weight:** 13.5 oz. **Length:** 4.36" overall. **Stocks:** Black polymer. **Sights:** Fixed. **Features:** Double-action-only mechanism. All stainless steel construction; snag-free. Introduced 1998. Made in U.S. by North American Arms.

Price: **$359.00**

OLYMPIC ARMS OA-96 AR PISTOL

Caliber: 223. **Barrel:** 6", 8", 4140 chrome-moly steel. **Weight:** 5 lbs. **Length:** 15-3/4" overall. **Stocks:** A2 stowaway pistol grip; no buttstock or receiver tube. **Sights:** Flat-top upper receiver, cut-down front sight base. **Features:** AR-15-type receivers with special bolt carrier; short aluminum hand guard; Vortex flash hider. Introduced 1996. Made in U.S. by Olympic Arms, Inc.

Price: **$858.00**

Olympic Arms OA-98 AR Pistol

Similar to the OA-93 except has removable 7-shot magazine, weighs 3 lbs. Introduced 1999. Made in U.S. by Olympic Arms, Inc.

Price: **$990.00**

North American Arms Guardian

One Pro .45

ONE PRO .45 AUTO PISTOL

Caliber: 45 ACP or 400 Cor-Bon, 10-shot magazine. **Barrel:** 3.75" **Weight:** 31.1 oz. **Length:** 7.04" overall. **Stocks:** Textured composition. **Sights:** Blade front, drift-adjustable rear; three-dot system. **Features:** All-steel construction; decocking lever and automatic firing pin lock; DA or DAO operation. Introduced 1997. Imported from Switzerland by Magnum Research, Inc.

Price: **$649.00**

Price: Conversion kit, 45 ACP/400, 400/45 ACP **$249.00**

ONE PRO 9 AUTO PISTOL

Caliber: 9mm Para., 10-shot magazine. **Barrel:** 3.01". **Weight:** 25.1 oz. **Length:** 6.06" overall. **Stocks:** Smooth wood. **Sights:** Blade front, rear adjustable for windage. **Features:** Rotating barrel; short slide; double recoil springs; double-action mechanism; decocking lever. Introduced 1998. Imported from Switzerland by Magnum Research.

Price: **$649.00**

PARA-ORDNANCE P-SERIES AUTO PISTOLS

Caliber: 9mm Para., 40 S&W, 45 ACP, 10-shot magazine. **Barrel:** 3", 3-1/2", 4-1/4", 5". **Weight:** From 24 oz. (alloy frame). **Length:** 8.5" overall. **Stocks:** Textured composition. **Sights:** Blade front, rear adjustable for windage. High visibility three-dot system. **Features:** Available with alloy, steel or stainless steel frame with black finish (silver or stainless gun). Steel and stainless steel frame guns weigh 40 oz. (P14.45), 36 oz. (P13.45), 34 oz. (P12.45). Grooved match trigger, rounded combat-style hammer. Beveled magazine well. Manual thumb, grip and firing pin lock safeties. Solid barrel bushing. Contact maker for full details. Introduced 1990. Made in Canada by Para-Ordnance.

Price: P14.45ER (steel frame) **$750.00**

Price: P14.45RR (alloy frame) **$740.00**

Price: P12.45RR (3-1/2" bbl., 24 oz., alloy) **$740.00**

Price: P13.45RR (4-1/4" barrel, 28 oz., alloy) **$740.00**

Price: P12.45ER (steel frame) **$750.00**

Price: P16.40ER (steel frame) **$750.00**

Price: P10-9RR (9mm, alloy frame) **$740.00**

Price: Stainless receiver (40, 45) **$799.00**

Price: Stainless receiver (9mm) **$850.00**

Para-Ordnance Limited Pistols

Similar to the P-Series pistols except with full-length recoil guide system; fully adjustable rear sight; tuned trigger with overtravel stop; beavertail grip safety; competition hammer; front and rear slide serrations; ambidextrous safety; lowered ejection port; ramped match-grade barrel; dovetailed front sight. Introduced 1998. Made in Canada by Para-Ordnance.

Price: 9mm, 40 S&W, 45 ACP . . . . **$865.00 to $899.00**

Para-Ordnance P12.45

Para-Ordnance LDA

Peters Stahl High Capacity

Phoenix Arms HP22

Peters Stahl Trophy Master

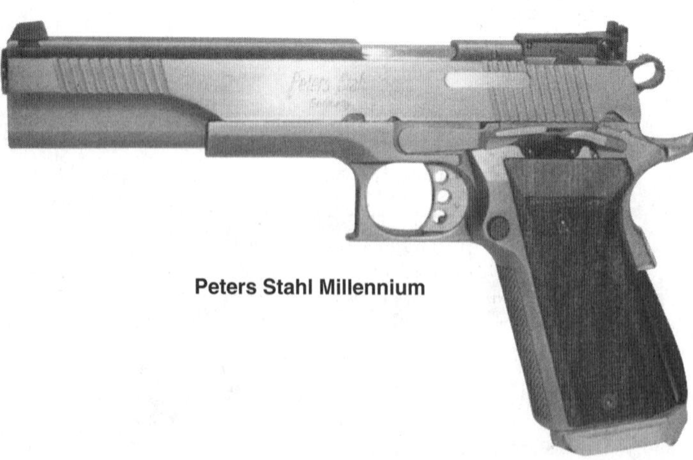
Peters Stahl Millennium

Para-Ordnance LDA Auto Pistols

Similar to the P-series except has double-action trigger mechanism. Steel frame with matte black finish, checkered composition grips. Available in 9mm Para., 40 S&W, 45 ACP. Introduced 1999. Made in Canada by Para-Ordnance.

Price: **$775.00**

Para-Ordnance LDA Limited Pistols

Similar to the LDA except has ambidextrous safety, adjustable rear sight, front slide serrations and full-length recoil guide system. Made in Canada by Para-Ordnance.

Price: Black finish. **$899.00**
Price: Stainless. **$929.00**

PETERS STAHL AUTOLOADING PISTOLS

Caliber: 9mm Para., 45 ACP. **Barrel:** 5" or 6". **Weight:** NA. **Length:** NA. **Grips:** Walnut or walnut with rubber wrap. **Sights:** Fully adjustable rear, blade front. **Features:** Stainless steel extended slide stop, safety and extended magazine release button; speed trigger with stop and approx. 3-lb. pull; polished ramp. Introduced 2000. Imported from Germany by Phillips & Rogers.

Price: High Capacity (accepts 15-shot magazines in 45 cal.; includes 10-shot magazine) **$1,695.00**
Price: Trophy Master (blued or stainless, 7-shot in 45, 8-shot in 9mm) **$1,995.00**
Price: Millennium Model (titanium coating on receiver and slide) **$2,195.00**

PHOENIX ARMS HP22, HP25 AUTO PISTOLS

Caliber: 22 LR, 10-shot (HP22), 25 ACP, 10-shot (HP25). **Barrel:** 3". **Weight:** 20 oz. **Length:** 5-1/2" overall. **Stocks:** Checkered composition. **Sights:** Blade front, adjustable rear. **Features:** Single action, exposed hammer; manual hold-open; button magazine release. Available in satin nickel, polished blue finish. Introduced 1993. Made in U.S. by Phoenix Arms.

Price: With gun lock and cable lanyard **$128.00**
Price: HP Rangemaster kit with 5" bbl., locking case and assessories **$169.00**
Price: HP Deluxe Rangemaster kit with 3" and 5" bbls., 2 mags., case **$199.00**

PSA-25 AUTO POCKET PISTOL

Caliber: 25 ACP, 6-shot magazine. **Barrel:** 2-1/8". **Weight:** 9.5 oz. **Length:** 4-1/8" overall. **Stocks:** Checkered black polymer, ivory, checkered transparent carbon fiber-filled polymer. **Sights:** Fixed. **Features:** All steel construction; striker fired; single action only; magazine disconnector; cocking indicator. Introduced 1987. Made in U.S. by Precision Small Arms, Inc.

Price: Traditional (polished black oxide). **$269.00**
Price: Nouveau-Satin (brushed nickel). **$269.00**
Price: Nouveau-Mirror (highly polished nickel). **$309.00**
Price: Featherweight (aluminum frame, nickel slide) **$405.00**
Price: Diplomat (black oxide with gold highlights, ivory grips) **$625.00**
Price: Montreaux (gold plated, ivory grips). **$692.00**
Price: Renaissance (hand engraved nickel, ivory grips) **$1,115.00**
Price: Imperiale (inlaid gold filigree over blue, scrimshawed ivory grips) **$3,600.00**

PSA-25 Auto

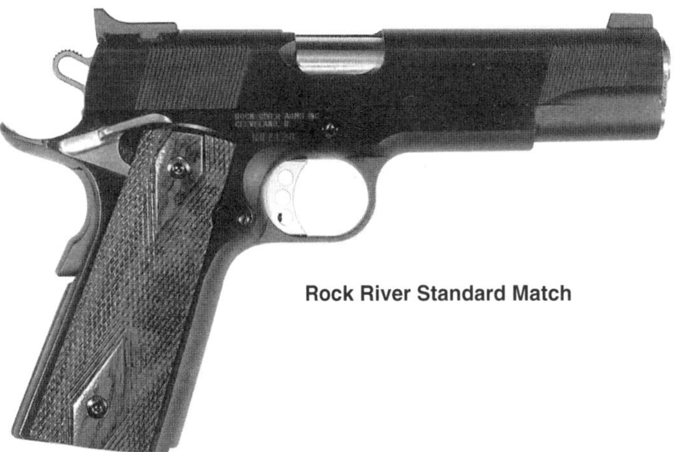

Rock River Standard Match

Republic Patriot

Ruger P89

REPUBLIC PATRIOT PISTOL

Caliber: 45 ACP, 6-shot magazine. **Barrel:** 3". **Weight:** 20 oz. **Length:** 6" overall. **Stocks:** Checkered. **Sights:** Blade front, drift-adjustable rear. **Features:** Black polymer frame, stainless steel slide; double-action-only trigger system; squared trigger guard. Introduced 1997. Made in U.S. by Republic Arms, Inc.

Price: About **$325.00**

ROCK RIVER ARMS STANDARD MATCH AUTO PISTOL

Caliber: 45 ACP. **Barrel:** NA. **Weight:** NA. **Length:** NA. **Grips:** Cocobolo, checkered. **Sights:** Heine fixed rear, blade front. **Features:** Chrome-moly steel frame and slide; beavertail grip safety with raised pad; checkered slide stop; ambidextrous safety; polished feed ramp and extractor; aluminum speed trigger with 3.5 lb. pull. Made in U.S. From Rock River Arms.

Price: **$1,025.00**

ROCKY MOUNTAIN ARMS PATRIOT PISTOL

Caliber: 223, 10-shot magazine. **Barrel:** 7", with muzzle brake. **Weight:** 5 lbs. **Length:** 20.5" overall. **Stocks:** Black composition. **Sights:** None furnished. **Features:** Milled upper receiver with enhanced Weaver base; milled lower receiver from billet plate; machined aluminum National Match handguard. Finished in DuPont Teflon-S matte black or NATO green. Comes with black nylon case, one magazine. Introduced 1993. From Rocky Mountain Arms, Inc.

Price: With A-2 handle top . . . . **$2,500.00 to $2,800.00**

Price: Flat top model. . . . . **$3,000.00 to $3,500.00**

RUGER P89 AUTOLOADING PISTOL

Caliber: 9mm Para., 10-shot magazine. **Barrel:** 4.50". **Weight:** 32 oz. **Length:** 7.84" overall. **Stocks:** Grooved black Xenoy composition. **Sights:** Square post front, square notch rear adjustable for windage, both with white dot inserts. **Features:** Double action with ambidextrous slide-mounted safety-levers. Slide is 4140 chrome-moly steel or 400-series stainless steel, frame is a lightweight aluminum alloy. Ambidextrous magazine release. Blue or stainless steel. Introduced 1986; stainless introduced 1990.

Price: P89, blue, with extra magazine and magazine loading tool, plastic case with lock **$452.00**

Price: KP89, stainless, with extra magazine and magazine loading tool, plastic case with lock **$499.00**

Ruger P89D Decocker Autoloading Pistol

Similar to the standard P89 except has ambidextrous decocking levers in place of the regular slide-mounted safety. The decocking levers move the firing pin inside the slide where the hammer can not reach it, while simultaneously blocking the firing pin from forward movement—allows shooter to decock a cocked pistol without manipulating the trigger. Conventional thumb decocking procedures are therefore unnecessary. Blue or stainless steel. Introduced 1990.

Price: P89D, blue with extra magazine and loader, plastic case with lock **$452.00**

Price: KP89D, stainless, with extra magazine, plastic case with lock **$499.00**

Ruger P89 Double-Action-Only Autoloading Pistol

Same as the KP89 except operates only in the double-action mode. Has a spurless hammer, gripping grooves on each side of the rear of the slide; no external safety or decocking lever. An internal safety prevents forward movement of the firing pin unless the trigger is pulled. Available in 9mm Para., stainless steel only. Introduced 1991.

Price: With lockable case, extra magazine, magazine loading tool **$499.00**

Ruger P90

Ruger KP95DAO

Ruger P93D

RUGER P90 MANUAL SAFETY MODEL AUTOLOADING PISTOL

Caliber: 45 ACP, 7-shot magazine. **Barrel:** 4.50". **Weight:** 33.5 oz. **Length:** 7.87" overall. **Stocks:** Grooved black Xenoy composition. **Sights:** Square post front, square notch rear adjustable for windage, both with white dot inserts. **Features:** Double action with ambidextrous slide-mounted safety-levers which move the firing pin inside the slide where the hammer can not reach it, while simultaneously blocking the firing pin from forward movement. Stainless steel only. Introduced 1991.

Price: KP90 with extra magazine, loader, plastic case with lock $539.00

Price: P90 (blue) $499.00

Ruger KP90 Decocker Autoloading Pistol

Similar to the P90 except has a manual decocking system. The ambidextrous decocking levers move the firing pin inside the slide where the hammer can not reach it, while simultaneously blocking the firing pin from forward movement—allows shooter to decock a cocked pistol without manipulating the trigger. Available only in stainless steel. Overall length 7.87", weighs 34 oz. Introduced 1991.

Price: KP90D with lockable case, extra magazine, and magazine loading tool $539.00

RUGER P93 COMPACT AUTOLOADING PISTOL

Caliber: 9mm Para., 10-shot magazine. **Barrel:** 3.9". **Weight:** 31 oz. **Length:** 7.3" overall. **Stocks:** Grooved black Xenoy composition. **Sights:** Square post front, square notch rear adjustable for windage. **Features:** Front of slide is crowned with a convex curve; slide has seven finger grooves; trigger guard bow is higher for a better grip; 400-series stainless slide, lightweight alloy frame; also in blue. Decocker-only or DAO-only. Includes hard case with lock. Introduced 1993. Made in U.S. by Sturm, Ruger & Co.

Price: KP93DAO, double-action-only $546.00

Price: KP93D ambidextrous decocker, stainless $546.00

Price: P93D, ambidextrous decocker, blue $467.00

Ruger KP94 Autoloading Pistol

Sized midway between the full-size P-Series and the compact P93. Has 4.25" barrel, 7.5" overall length and weighs about 33 oz. KP94 is manual safety model; KP94DAO is double-action-only (both 9mm Para., 10-shot magazine); KP94D is decocker-only in 40-caliber with 10-shot magazine. Slide gripping grooves roll over top of slide. KP94 has ambidextrous safety-levers; KP94DAO has no external safety, full-cock hammer position or decocking lever; KP94D has ambidextrous decocking levers. Matte finish stainless slide, barrel, alloy frame. Also available in blue. Includes hard case and lock. Introduced 1994. Made in U.S. by Sturm, Ruger & Co.

Price: P94, P944, blue (manual safety) $467.00

Price: KP94 (9mm), KP944 (40-caliber) (manual safety-stainless) $546.00

Price: KP94DAO (9mm), KP944DAO (40-caliber) $546.00

Price: KP94D (9mm), KP944D (40-caliber)-decock only $546.00

RUGER P95 AUTOLOADING PISTOL

Caliber: 9mm Para., 10-shot magazine. **Barrel:** 3.9". **Weight:** 27 oz. **Length:** 7.3" overall. **Stocks:** Grooved; integral with frame. **Sights:** Blade front, rear drift adjustable for windage; three-dot system. **Features:** Moulded polymer grip frame, stainless steel or chrome-moly slide. Suitable for +P+ ammunition. Safety model, decocker or DAO. Introduced 1996. Made in U.S. by Sturm, Ruger & Co. Comes with lockable plastic case, spare magazine, loading tool.

Price: P95 DAO double-action-only $407.00

Price: P95D decocker only $407.00

Price: KP95 stainless steel $453.00

Price: KP95DAO double-action only, stainless steel $453.00

Price: KP95 safety model, stainless steel $453.00

Price: P95 safety model, blued finish $407.00

RUGER P97 AUTOLOADING PISTOL

Caliber: 45ACP 8-shot magazine. **Barrel:** 4-1/8". **Weight:** 30-1/2 oz. **Length:** 7-1/4" overall. Grooved: Integral with frame. **Sights:** Blade front, rear drift adjustable for windage; three dot system. **Features:** Moulded polymer grip frame, stainless steel slide. Decocker or DAO. Introduced 1997. Made in U.S. by Sturm, Ruger & Co. Comes with lockable plastic case, spare magaline, loading tool. .

Price: (KP97D decock-only) $483.00

Price: (KP97DAO double-action only) $483.00

Ruger KMK-4

Ruger 22/45-P4

RUGER MARK II STANDARD AUTOLOADING PISTOL

Caliber: 22 LR, 10-shot magazine. **Barrel:** 4-3/4" or 6". **Weight:** 25 oz. (4-3/4" bbl.). **Length:** 8-5/16" (4-3/4" bbl.). **Stocks:** Checkered plastic. **Sights:** Fixed, wide blade front, fixed rear. **Features:** Updated design of the original Standard Auto. Has new bolt hold-open latch. 10-shot magazine, magazine catch, safety, trigger and new receiver contours. Introduced 1982.

Price: Blued (MK 4, MK 6) **$278.00**
Price: In stainless steel (KMK 4, KMK 6) **$364.00**

Ruger 22/45 Mark II Pistol

Similar to the other 22 Mark II autos except has grip frame of Zytel that matches the angle and magazine latch of the Model 1911 45 ACP pistol. Available in 4" bull, 4-3/4" standard and 5-1/2" bull barrels. Comes with extra magazine, plastic case, lock. Introduced 1992.

Price: P4, 4" bull barrel, adjustable sights **$275.00**
Price: KP 4 (4-3/4" barrel), stainless steel, fixed sights **$305.00**
Price: KP512 (5-1/2" bull barrel), stainless steel, adj. sights **$359.00**
Price: P512 (5-1/2" bull barrel, all blue), adj. sights **$275.00**

SAFARI ARMS ENFORCER PISTOL

Caliber: 45 ACP, 6-shot magazine. **Barrel:** 3.8", stainless. **Weight:** 36 oz. **Length:** 7.3" overall. **Stocks:** Smooth walnut with etched black widow spider logo. **Sights:** Ramped blade front, LPA adjustable rear. **Features:** Extended safety, extended slide release; Commander-style hammer; beavertail grip safety; throated, polished, tuned. Parkerized matte black or satin stainless steel finishes. Made in U.S. by Safari Arms.

Price: **$630.00**

SAFARI ARMS GI SAFARI PISTOL

Caliber: 45 ACP, 7-shot magazine. **Barrel:** 5", 416 stainless. **Weight:** 39.9 oz. **Length:** 8.5" overall. **Stocks:** Checkered walnut. **Sights:** G.I.-style blade front, drift-adjustable rear. **Features:** Beavertail grip safety; extended thumb safety and slide release; Commander-style hammer. Parkerized finish. Reintroduced 1996.

Price: **$439.00**

Ruger KP512

SAFARI ARMS CARRIER PISTOL

Caliber: 45 ACP, 7-shot magazine. **Barrel:** 6", 416 stainless steel. **Weight:** 30 oz. **Length:** 9.5" overall. **Stocks:** Wood. **Sights:** Ramped blade front, LPA adjustable rear. **Features:** Beavertail grip safety; extended controls; full-length recoil spring guide; Commander-style hammer. Throated, polished and tuned. Satin stainless steel finish. Introduced 1999. Made in U.S. by Safari Arms, Inc.

Price: **$714.00**

SAFARI ARMS COHORT PISTOL

Caliber: 45 ACP, 7-shot magazine. **Barrel:** 3.8", 416 stainless. **Weight:** 37 oz. **Length:** 8.5" overall. **Stocks:** Smooth walnut with laser-etched black widow logo. **Sights:** Ramped blade front, LPA adjustable rear. **Features:** Combines the Enforcer model, slide and MatchMaster frame. Beavertail grip safety; extended thumb safety and slide release; Commander-style hammer. Throated, polished and tuned. Satin stainless finish. Introduced 1996. Made in U.S. by Safari Arms, Inc.

Price: **$654.00**

SAFARI ARMS MATCHMASTER PISTOL

Caliber: 45 ACP, 7-shot. **Barrel:** 5" or 6", 416 stainless steel. **Weight:** 38 oz. (5" barrel). **Length:** 8.5" overall. **Stocks:** Smooth walnut. **Sights:** Ramped blade, LPA adjustable rear. **Features:** Beavertail grip safety; extended controls; Commander-style hammer; throated, polished, tuned. Parkerized matte-black or satin stainless steel. Made in U.S. by Olympic Arms, Inc.

Price: 5" barrel **$594.00**
Price: 6" barrel **$654.00**

Safari Arms Carry Comp Pistol

Similar to the Matchmaster except has Wil Schueman-designed hybrid compensator system. Made in U.S. by Olympic Arms, Inc.

Price: **$1,067.00**

SEECAMP LWS 32 STAINLESS DA AUTO

Caliber: 32 ACP Win. Silvertip, 6-shot magazine. **Barrel:** 2", integral with frame. **Weight:** 10.5 oz. **Length:** 4-1/8" overall. **Stocks:** Glass-filled nylon. **Sights:** Smooth, no-snag, contoured slide and barrel top. **Features:** Aircraft quality 17-4 PH stainless steel. Inertia-operated firing pin. Hammer fired double-action-only. Hammer automatically follows slide down to safety rest position after each shot—no manual safety needed. Magazine safety disconnector. Polished stainless. Introduced 1985. From L.W. Seecamp.

Price: **$425.00**

SIG SAUER P220 SERVICE AUTO PISTOL

Caliber: 45 ACP, (7- or 8-shot magazine). **Barrel:** 4-3/8". **Weight:** 27.8 oz. **Length:** 7.8" overall. **Stocks:** Checkered black plastic. **Sights:** Blade front, drift adjustable rear for windage. Optional Siglite nightsights. **Features:** Double action. Decocking lever permits lowering hammer onto locked firing pin. Squared combat-type trigger guard. Slide stays open after last shot. Imported from Germany by SIGARMS, Inc.

Price: Blue SA/DA or DAO **$790.00**
Price: Blue, Siglite night sights **$880.00**
Price: K-Kote or nickel slide **$830.00**
Price: K-Kote or nickel slide with Siglite night sights **$930.00**

HANDGUNS — AUTOLOADERS, SERVICE & SPORT

SIG Sauer P220

SIG Arms Pro 2009

SIG Arms P245 Compact

SIG Sauer P229S

HANDGUNS

SIG Sauer P220 Sport Auto Pistol

Similar to the P220 except has 4.9" barrel, ported compensator, all-stainless steel frame and slide, factory-tuned trigger, adjustable sights, extended competition controls. Overall length is 9.9", weighs 43.5 oz. Introduced 1999. From SIGARMS, Inc.

Price: $1,320.00

SIG Sauer P245 Compact Auto Pistol

Similar to the P220 except has 3.9" barrel, shorter grip, 6-shot magazine, 7.28" overall length, and weighs 27.5 oz. Introduced 1999. From SIGARMS, Inc.

Price: Blue $780.00
Price: Blue, with Siglite sights. $850.00
Price: Two-tone. $830.00
Price: Two-tone with Siglite sights $930.00
Price: With K-Kote finish. $830.00
Price: K-Kote with Siglite sights $930.00

SIG Sauer P229 DA Auto Pistol

Similar to the P228 except chambered for 9mm Para., 40 S&W, 357 SIG. Has 3.86" barrel, 7.08" overall length and 3.35" height. Weight is 30.5 oz. Introduced 1991. Frame made in Germany, stainless steel slide assembly made in U.S.; pistol assembled in U.S. From SIGARMS, Inc.

Price: $795.00
Price: With nickel slide $890.00
Price: Nickel slide Siglite night sights. $935.00

SIG PRO AUTO PISTOL

Caliber: 9mm Para., 40 S&W, 10-shot magazine. **Barrel:** 3.86". **Weight:** 27.2 oz. **Length:** 7.36" overall. **Stocks:** Composite and rubberized one-piece. **Sights:** Blade front, rear adjustable for windage. Optional Siglite night sights. **Features:** Polymer frame, stainless steel slide; integral frame accessory rail; replaceable steel frame rails; left- or right-handed magazine release. Introduced 1999. From SIGARMS, Inc.

Price: SP2340 (40 S&W) $596.00
Price: SP2009 (9mm Para.) $596.00
Price: As above with Siglite night sights. $655.00

SIG Sauer P226 Service Pistol

Similar to the P220 pistol except has 4.4" barrel, and weighs 28.3 oz. 357 SIG or 40 S&W. Imported from Germany by SIGARMS, Inc.

Price: Blue SA/DA or DAO $830.00
Price: With Siglite night sights $930.00
Price: Blue, SA/DA or DAO 357 SIG $830.00
Price: With Siglite night sights $930.00
Price: K-Kote finish, 40 S&W only or nickel slide $830.00
Price: K-Kote or nickel slide Siglite night sights $930.00
Price: Nickel slide 357 SIG. $875.00
Price: Nickel slide, Siglite night sights $930.00

SIG Sauer P229 Sport Auto Pistol

Similar to the P229 except available in 357 SIG only; 4.8" heavy barrel; 8.6" overall length; weighs 40.6 oz.; vented compensator; adjustable target sights; rubber grips; extended slide latch and magazine release. Made of stainless steel. Introduced 1998. From SIGARMS, Inc.

Price: $1,320.00

SIG SAUER P232 PERSONAL SIZE PISTOL

Caliber: 380 ACP, 7-shot. **Barrel:** 3-3/4". **Weight:** 16 oz. **Length:** 6-1/2" overall. **Stocks:** Checkered black composite. **Sights:** Blade front, rear adjustable for windage. **Features:** Double action/single action or DAO. Blowback operation, stationary barrel. Introduced 1997. Imported from Germany by SIGARMS, Inc.

Price: Blue SA/DA or DAO $505.00
Price: In stainless steel. $545.00
Price: With stainless steel slide, blue frame $525.00
Price: Stainless steel, Siglite night sights, Hogue grips $585.00

SIG Sauer P232

Smith & Wesson 4013 TSW

Smith & Wesson 457

SIG SAUER P239 PISTOL

Caliber: 9mm Para., 8-shot, 357 SIG 40 S&W, 7-shot magazine. **Barrel:** 3.6". **Weight:** 25.2 oz. **Length:** 6.6" overall. **Stocks:** Checkered black composite. **Sights:** Blade front, rear adjustable for windage. Optional Siglite night sights. **Features:** SA/DA or DAO; blackened stainless steel slide, aluminum alloy frame. Introduced 1996. Made in U.S. by SIGARMS, Inc.

Price: SA/DA or DAO **$620.00**
Price: SA/DA or DAO with Siglite night sights **$720.00**
Price: Two-tone finish **$665.00**
Price: Two-tone finish, Siglite sights **$765.00**

SMITH & WESSON MODEL 22A SPORT PISTOL

Caliber: 22 LR, 10-shot magazine. **Barrel:** 4", 5-1/2", 7". **Weight:** 29 oz. **Length:** 8" overall. **Stocks:** Two-piece polymer. **Sights:** Patridge front, fully adjustable rear. **Features:** Comes with a sight bridge with Weaver-style integral optics mount; alloy frame; .312" serrated trigger; stainless steel slide and barrel with matte blue finish. Introduced 1997. Made in U.S. by Smith & Wesson.

Price: 4" **$230.00**
Price: 5-1/2" **$255.00**
Price: 7" **$289.00**

SMITH & WESSON MODEL 457 TDA AUTO PISTOL

Caliber: 45 ACP, 7-shot magazine. **Barrel:** 3-3/4". **Weight:** 29 oz. **Length:** 7-1/4" overall. **Stocks:** One-piece Xenoy, wrap-around with straight backstrap. **Sights:** Post front, fixed rear, three-dot system. **Features:** Aluminum alloy frame, matte blue carbon steel slide; bobbed hammer; smooth trigger. Introduced 1996. Made in U.S. by Smith & Wesson.

Price: **$563.00**

SMITH & WESSON MODEL 908 AUTO PISTOL

Caliber: 9mm Para., 8-shot magazine. **Barrel:** 3-1/2". **Weight:** 26 oz. **Length:** 6-13/16". **Stocks:** One-piece Xenoy, wrap-around with straight backstrap. **Sights:** Post front, fixed rear, three-dot system. **Features:** Aluminum alloy frame, matte blue carbon steel slide; bobbed hammer; smooth trigger. Introduced 1996. Made in U.S. by Smith & Wesson.

Price: **$509.00**

SMITH & WESSON 9mm RECON AUTO PISTOL MODEL

Caliber: 9mm Para. **Barrel:** 3-1/2". **Weight:** 27 oz. **Length:** 7" overall. **Stocks:** Hogue wrap-around, finger-groove rubber. **Sights:** Three-dot Novak Low Mount, drift adjustable. **Features:** Traditional double-action mechanism. Tuned action, hand-crowned muzzle, polished feed ramp, hand-lapped slide, spherical barrel bushing. Checkered frontstrap. Introduced 1999. Made by U.S. by Smith & Wesson.

Price: **$1,150.00**

SMITH & WESSON MODEL 2213, 2214 SPORTSMAN AUTOS

Caliber: 22 LR, 8-shot magazine. **Barrel:** 3". **Weight:** 18 oz. **Length:** 6-1/8" overall. **Stocks:** Checkered black polymer. **Sights:** Patridge front, fixed rear; three-dot system. **Features:** Internal hammer; serrated trigger; single action. Model 2213 is stainless with alloy frame, Model 2214 is blued carbon steel with alloy frame. Introduced 1990. Made in U.S. by Smith & Wesson.

Price: Model 2213 . . . . **$340.00**
Price: Model 2214 . . . . **$292.00**

SMITH & WESSON MODEL 4013, 4053 TSW AUTOS

Caliber: 40 S&W, 9-shot magazine. **Barrel:** 3-1/2". **Weight:** 26.4 oz. **Length:** 6-7/8" overall. **Stocks:** Xenoy one-piece wrap-around. **Sights:** Novak three-dot system. **Features:** Traditional double-action system; stainless slide, alloy frame; fixed barrel bushing; ambidextrous decocker; reversible magazine catch. Introduced 1997. Made in U.S. by Smith & Wesson.

Price: Model 4013 TSW **$844.00**
Price: Model 4053 TSW, double-action-only **$844.00**

Smith & Wesson Model 22S Sport Pistols

Similar to the Model 22A Sport except with stainless steel frame. Available only with 5-1/2" or 7" barrel. Introduced 1997. Made in U.S. by Smith & Wesson.

Price: 5-1/2" standard barrel. **$312.00**
Price: 5-1/2" bull barrel, wood target stocks with thumbrest. **$379.00**
Price: 7" standard barrel. **$344.00**
Price: 5-1/2" bull barrel, two-piece target stocks with thumbrest . . **$353.00**

SMITH & WESSON MODEL 410 DA AUTO PISTOL

Caliber: 40 S&W, 10-shot magazine. **Barrel:** 4". **Weight:** 28.5 oz. **Length:** 7.5 oz. **Stocks:** One-piece Xenoy, wrap-around with straight backstrap. **Sights:** Post front, fixed rear; three-dot system. **Features:** Aluminum alloy frame; blued carbon steel slide; traditional double action with left-side slide-mounted decocking lever. Introduced 1996. Made in U.S. by Smith & Wesson.

Price: **$563.00**

Smith & Wesson 3913 TSW

Smith & Wesson 3913 LadySmith

SMITH & WESSON MODEL 910 DA AUTO PISTOL

Caliber: 9mm Para., 10-shot magazine. **Barrel:** 4". **Weight:** 28 oz. **Length:** 7-3/8" overall. **Stocks:** One-piece Xenoy, wrap-around with straight backstrap. **Sights:** Post front with white dot, fixed two-dot rear. **Features:** Alloy frame, blue carbon steel slide. Slide-mounted decocking lever. Introduced 1995.

Price: Model 910. . . . . **$509.00**

SMITH & WESSON MODEL 3913 TRADITIONAL DOUBLE ACTION

Caliber: 9mm Para., 8-shot magazine. **Barrel:** 3-1/2". **Weight:** 26 oz. **Length:** 6-13/16" overall. **Stocks:** One-piece Delrin wrap-around, textured surface. **Sights:** Post front with white dot, Novak LoMount Carry with two dots, adjustable for windage. **Features:** Aluminum alloy frame, stainless slide (M3913) or blue steel slide (M3914). Bobbed hammer with no half-cock notch; smooth .304" trigger with rounded edges. Straight backstrap. Extra magazine included. Introduced 1989.

Price: **$662.00**

Smith & Wesson Model 3913-LS LadySmith Auto

Similar to the standard Model 3913 except has frame that is upswept at the front, rounded trigger guard. Comes in frosted stainless steel with matching gray grips. Grips are ergonomically correct for a woman's hand. Novak LoMount Carry rear sight adjustable for windage, smooth edges for snag resistance. Extra magazine included. Introduced 1990.

Price: **$744.00**

Smith & Wesson Model 3953 DAO Pistol

Same as the Model 3913 except double-action-only. Model 3953 has stainless slide with alloy frame. Overall length 7"; weighs 25.5 oz. Extra magazine included. Introduced 1990.

Price: **$724.00**

Smith & Wesson 4506

Smith & Wesson Model 3913TSW/3953TSW Auto Pistols

Similar to the Model 3913 and 3953 except TSW guns have tighter tolerances, ambidextrous manual safety/decocking lever, flush-fit magazine, delayed-unlock firing system; magazine disconnector. Compact alloy frame, stainless steel slide. Straight backstrap. Introduced 1998. Made in U.S. by Smith & Wesson.

Price: Single action/double action **$724.00**
Price: Double action only **$724.00**

SMITH & WESSON MODEL 4006 TDA AUTO

Caliber: 40 S&W, 10-shot magazine. **Barrel:** 4". **Weight:** 38.5 oz. **Length:** 7-7/8" overall. **Stocks:** Xenoy wrap-around with checkered panels. **Sights:** Replaceable post front with white dot, Novak LoMount Carry fixed rear with two white dots, or micro. click adjustable rear with two white dots. **Features:** Stainless steel construction with non-reflective finish. Straight back-strap. Extra magazine included. Introduced 1990.

Price: With adjustable sights **$899.00**
Price: With fixed sight. **$864.00**
Price: With fixed night sights **$991.00**

Smith & Wesson Model 4043, 4046 DA Pistols

Similar to the Model 4006 except is double-action-only. Has a semi-bobbed hammer, smooth trigger, 4" barrel; Novak LoMount Carry rear sight, post front with white dot. Overall length is 7-1/2", weighs 28 oz. Model 4043 has alloy frame. Extra magazine included. Introduced 1991.

Price: Model 4043 (alloy frame) **$844.00**
Price: Model 4046 (stainless frame). **$864.00**
Price: Model 4046 with fixed night sights **$991.00**

SMITH & WESSON MODEL 4500 SERIES AUTOS

Caliber: 45 ACP, 8-shot magazine. **Barrel:** 5" (M4506). **Weight:** 41 oz. (4506). **Length:** 8-1/2" overall. **Stocks:** Xenoy one-piece wrap-around, arched or straight backstrap. **Sights:** Post front with white dot, adjustable or fixed Novak LoMount Carry on M4506. **Features:** M4506 has serrated hammer spur. All have two magazines. Contact Smith & Wesson for complete data. Introduced 1989.

Price: Model 4506, fixed sight **$822.00**
Price: Model 4506, adjustable sight **$855.00**
Price: Model 4566 (stainless, 4-1/4", traditional DA, ambidextrous safety, fixed sight) **$897.00**
Price: Model 4586 (stainless, 4-1/4", DA only) **$897.00**

SMITH & WESSON MODEL 4513TSW/4553TSW PISTOLS

Caliber: 45 ACP, 6-shot magazine. **Barrel:** 3-3/4". **Weight:** 28 oz. (M4513TSW). **Length:** 6-7/8 overall. **Stocks:** Checkered Xenoy; straight backstrap. **Sights:** White dot front, Novak Lo Mount Carry 2-Dot rear. **Features:** Model 4513TSW is traditional double action, Model 4553TSW is double action only. TSW series has tighter tolerances, ambidextrous manual safety/decocking lever, flush-fit magazine, delayed-unlock firing system; magazine disconnector. Compact alloy frame, stainless steel slide. Introduced 1998. Made in U.S. by Smith & Wesson.

Price: Model 4513TSW **$880.00**
Price: Model 4553TSW **$837.00**

Smith & Wesson 4553 TSW

Springfield 1911A1 Standard

Springfield Full-Size 1911A1

Smith & Wesson Sigma SW40V

SMITH & WESSON MODEL 5900 SERIES AUTO PISTOLS

Caliber: 9mm Para., 10-shot magazine. **Barrel:** 4". **Weight:** 28-1/2 to 37-1/2 oz. (fixed sight); 38 oz. (adjustable sight). **Length:** 7-1/2" overall. **Stocks:** Xenoy wrap-around with curved backstrap. **Sights:** Post front with white dot, fixed or fully adjustable with two white dots. **Features:** All stainless, stainless and alloy or carbon steel and alloy construction. Smooth .304" trigger, .260" serrated hammer. Introduced 1989.

Price: Model 5906 (stainless, traditional DA, adjustable sight, ambidextrous safety) $861.00
Price: As above, fixed sight $822.00
Price: With fixed night sights $948.00
Price: Model 5946 DAO (as above, stainless frame and slide) . . $822.00

SMITH & WESSON ENHANCED SIGMA SERIES PISTOLS

Caliber: 9mm Para., 40 S&W, 10-shot magazine. **Barrel:** 4". **Weight:** 26 oz. **Length:** 7.4" overall. **Stocks:** Integral. **Sights:** White dot front, fixed rear; three-dot system. Tritium night sights available. **Features:** Ergonomic polymer frame; low barrel centerline; internal striker firing system; corrosion-resistant slide; Teflon-filled, electroless-nickel coated magazine. Introduced 1994. Made in U.S. by Smith & Wesson.

Price: SW9E, 9mm, 4" barrel, black finish, fixed sights $657.00
Price: SW9V, 9mm, 4" barrel, satin stainless, fixed night sights. . $447.00
Price: SW40E, 40 S&W, 4" barrel, black finish, fixed sights. $657.00
Price: SW40V, 40 S&W, 4" barrel, black polymer, fixed sights . . . $447.00

SMITH & WESSON SIGMA SW380 AUTO

Caliber: 380 ACP, 6-shot magazine. **Barrel:** 3". **Weight:** 14 oz. **Length:** 5.8" overall. **Stocks:** Integral. **Sights:** Fixed groove in the slide. **Features:** Polymer frame; double-action-only trigger mechanism; grooved/serrated front and rear straps; two passive safeties. Introduced 1995. Made in U.S. by Smith & Wesson.

Price: $328.00

Smith & Wesson Model 6906 Double-Action Auto

Similar to the Model 5906 except with 3-1/2" barrel, 10-shot magazine, fixed rear sight, .260" bobbed hammer. Extra magazine included. Introduced 1989.

Price: Model 6906, stainless $720.00
Price: Model 6906 with fixed night sights $836.00
Price: Model 6946 (stainless, DA only, fixed sights). $720.00

SMITH & WESSON MODEL CS9 CHIEFS SPECIAL AUTO

Caliber: 9mm Para., 7-shot magazine. **Barrel:** 3". **Weight:** 20.8 oz. **Length:** 6-1/4" overall. **Stocks:** Hogue wrap-around rubber. **Sights:** White dot front, fixed two-dot rear. **Features:** Traditional double-action trigger mechanism. Alloy frame, stainless or blued slide. Introduced 1999. Made in U.S. by Smith & Wesson.

Price: Blue or stainless. $648.00

Smith & Wesson Model CS40 Chiefs Special Auto

Similar to the CS9 except chambered for 40 S&W (7-shot magazine), has 3-1/4" barrel, weighs 24.2 oz., and measures 6-1/2" overall. Introduced 1999. Made in U.S. by Smith & Wesson.

Price: Blue or stainless. $683.00

Smith & Wesson Model CS45 Chiefs Special Auto

Similar to the CS40 except chambered for 45 ACP, 6-shot magazine, weighs 23.9 oz. Introduced 1999. Made in U.S. by Smith & Wesson.

Price: Blue or stainless. $683.00

SPRINGFIELD, INC. FULL-SIZE 1911A1 AUTO PISTOL

Caliber: 9mm Para., 9-shot; 38 Super, 9-shot; 40 S&W, 9-shot; 45 ACP, 8-shot. **Barrel:** 5". **Weight:** 35.6 oz. **Length:** 8-5/8" overall. **Stocks:** Checkered plastic or walnut. **Sights:** Fixed three-dot system. **Features:** Beveled magazine well; lowered and flared ejection port. All forged parts, including frame, barrel, slide. All new production. Introduced 1990. From Springfield, Inc.

Price: Mil-Spec 45 ACP, Parkerized $559.00
Price: Standard, 45 ACP, blued $770.00
Price: Standard, 45 ACP, stainless. $828.00
Price: Lightweight 45 ACP (28.6 oz., matte finish, night sights). . $832.00
Price: 40 S&W, stainless $812.00
Price: 9mm, stainless $837.00

Springfield TRP

Stoeger American Eagle Luger

Springfield V10 Ultra Compact

Springfield, Inc. TRP Pistols

Similar to the 1911A1 except 45 ACP only; has checkered front strap and mainspring housing; Novak Night Sight combat rear sight and matching dovetailed front sight; tuned, polished extractor; oversize barrel link; lightweight speed trigger and combat action job; match barrel and bushing; extended ambidextrous thumb safety and fitted beavertail grip safety; Carry bevel on entire pistol; checkered cocobolo wood grips; comes with two Wilson 8-shot magazines. Frame is engraved "Tactical," both sides of frame with "TRP." Introduced 1998. From Springfield, Inc.

Price: Standard with Armory Kote finish **$1,395.00**
Price: Standard, stainless steel **$1,265.00**
Price: Champion, Armory Kote, adj. sights................. **$1,407.00**

Springfield, Inc. 1911A1 High Capacity Pistol

Similar to the Standard 1911A1 except available in 45 ACP with 10-shot magazine. Has Commander-style hammer, walnut grips, beveled magazine well, plastic carrying case. Introduced 1993. From Springfield, Inc.

Price: Mil-Spec 45 ACP **$807.00**
Price: 45 ACP Ultra Compact (3-1/2" bbl.) **$812.00**
Price: As above, stainless steel **$884.00**

Springfield, Inc. 1911A1 V-Series Ported Pistols

Similar to the standard 1911A1 except comes with scalloped slides with 10, 12 or 16 matching barrel ports to redirect powder gasses and reduce recoil and muzzle flip. Adjustable rear sight, extended thumb safety, Videki speed trigger, and beveled magazine well. Checkered walnut grips standard. Available in 45 ACP, stainless or bi-tone. Introduced 1992.

Price: V-16 Long Slide, stainless **$1,080.00**
Price: Target V-12, stainless............................. **$878.00**
Price: V-10 (Ultra-Compact, bi-tone) **$853.00**
Price: V-10 stainless.. **NA**

Springfield, Inc. 1911A1 Champion Pistol

Similar to the standard 1911A1 except slide is 4.025". Novak Night Sights. Comes with Delta hammer and cocobolo grips. Available in 45 ACP only; Parkerized or stainless. Introduced 1989.

Price: Parkerized **$817.00**
Price: Stainless....................................... **$870.00**
Price: Lightweight, matte finish........................... **$867.00**

Springfield Inc. Ultra Compact Pistol

Similar to the 1911A1 Compact except has shorter slide, 3.5" barrel, beavertail grip safety, beveled magazine well, Novak Low Mount or Novak Night Sights, Videki speed trigger, flared ejection port, stainless steel frame, blued slide, match grade barrel, rubber grips. Introduced 1996. From Springfield, Inc.

Price: Parkerized 45 ACP, Night Sights **$817.00**
Price: Stainless 45 ACP, Night Sights **$884.00**
Price: Lightweight, matte finish........................... **$867.00**
Price: Lightweight, 9mm, stainless......................... **$853.00**

Springfield Inc. Long Slide 1911 A1 Pistol

Similar to the Full Size model except has a 6" barrel and slide for increased sight radius and higher velocity, fully adjustable sights, muzzle-forward weight distribution for reduced recoil and quicker shot-to-shot recovery. From Springfield Inc.

Price: Target, 45 ACP, stainless with Night Sights **$1,002.00**
Price: Trophy Match, stainless with adj. sights.............. **$1,399.00**

STEYR M & S SERIES AUTO PISTOLS

Caliber: 9mm Para., 40 S&W, 357 SIG; 10-shot magazine. **Barrel:** 4" (3.58" for Model S). **Weight:** 28 oz. (22.5 oz. for Model S). **Length:** 7.05" overall (6.53" for Model S). **Grips:** Ultra-rigid polymer. **Sights:** Drift-adjustable, white-outline rear; white-triangle blade front. **Features:** Polymer frame; trigger-drop firing pin, manual and key-lock safeties; loaded chamber indicator; 5.5-lb. trigger pull; 111-degree grip angle enhances natural pointing. Introduced 2000. Imported from Austria by GSI Inc.

Price: Model M (full-sized frame with 4" barrel) **$609.95**
Price: Model S (compact frame with 3.58" barrel) **$609.95**
Price: Extra 10-shot magazines (Model M or S) **$39.00**

STOEGER AMERICAN EAGLE LUGER

Caliber: 9mm Para., 7-shot magazine. **Barrel:** 4", 6". **Weight:** 32 oz. **Length:** 9.6" overall. **Stocks:** Checkered walnut. **Sights:** Blade front, fixed rear. **Features:** Recreation of the American Eagle Luger pistol in stainless steel. Chamber loaded indicator. Introduced 1994. From Stoeger Industries.

Price: 4", or 6" Navy Model **$720.00**
Price: With matte black finish............................ **$798.00**

Taurus PT 22

Taurus PT92B

TAURUS MODEL PT 22/PT 25 AUTO PISTOLS

Caliber: 22 LR, 8-shot (PT 22); 25 ACP, 9-shot (PT 25). **Barrel:** 2.75". **Weight:** 12.3 oz. **Length:** 5.25" overall. **Stocks:** Smooth rosewood or mother-of-pearl. **Sights:** Blade front, fixed rear. **Features:** Double action. Tip-up barrel for loading, cleaning. Blue, nickel, duotone or blue with gold accents. Introduced 1992. Made in U.S. by Taurus International.

Price: 22 LR or 25 ACP, blue, nickel or with duo-tone finish with rosewood grips **$215.00**

Price: 22 LR or 25 ACP, blue with gold trim, rosewood grips **$230.00**

Price: 22 LR or 25 ACP, blue, nickel or duotone finish with checkered wood grips. . . . **$190.00**

Price: 22 LR or 25 ACP, blue with gold trim, mother of pearl grips **$230.00**

TAURUS MODEL PT92B AUTO PISTOL

Caliber: 9mm Para., 15-shot magazine. **Barrel:** 5". **Weight:** 34 oz. **Length:** 8.5" overall. **Stocks:** Black rubber. **Sights:** Fixed notch rear. Three-dot sight system. Also offered with micrometer-click adjustable night sights. **Features:** Double action, exposed hammer, chamber loaded indicator, ambidextrous safety, inertia firing pin. Imported by Taurus International.

Price: Blue **$575.00**

Price: Stainless steel **$595.00**

Price: Blue with gold trim, rosewood grips **$625.00**

Price: Blue with gold trim, mother-of-pearl grips. . . . **$645.00**

Price: Stainless steel with gold trim, rosewood grips **$645.00**

Price: Stainless steel with gold trim, mother-of-pearl grips. . . . **$655.00**

Price: Blue with checkered rubber grips, night sights. . . . **$655.00**

Price: Stainless steel with checkered rubber grips, night sights. . . **$670.00**

Taurus Model PT99 Auto Pistol

Similar to the PT92 except has fully adjustable rear sight, smooth Brazilian walnut stocks and is available in stainless steel or polished blue. Introduced 1983.

Price: Blue **$595.00**

Price: Stainless steel **$610.00**

Price: 22 Conversion kit for PT 92 and PT99 (includes barrel and slide) **$266.00**

TAURUS MODEL PT-100B AUTO PISTOL

NEW!

Caliber: 40 S&W, 10-shot magazine. **Barrel:** 5". **Weight:** 34 oz. **Length:** 8-1/2". **Grips:** Checkered rubber, rosewood or mother-of-pearl. **Sights:** 3-dot fixed or adjustable; night sights available. **Features:** Single/double action with three-position safety/decocker. Re-introduced in 2001. Imported by Taurus International.

Price: Blued finish. . . . **$575.00**

Price: Stainless steel **$595.00**

Price: Blue with gold accents, rosewood grips. . . . **$625.00**

Price: Blue with gold accents, mother-of-pearl grips **$645.00**

Price: Stainless w/gold accents, mother-of-pearl grips **$655.00**

TAURUS MODEL PT-111 MILLENNIUM AUTO PISTOL

Caliber: 9mm Para., 10-shot magazine. **Barrel:** 3.25". **Weight:** 18.7 oz. **Length:** 6.0" overall. **Stocks:** Polymer. **Sights:** 3-dot fixed; night sights available. Low profile, three-dot combat. **Features:** Double action only. Firing pin lock; polymer frame; striker fired; push-button magazine release. Introduced 1998. Imported by Taurus International.

Price: Blue **$425.00**

Price: Stainless. . . . **$435.00**

Price: With night sights, blue slide **$500.00**

Price: With night sights, stainless slide **$520.00**

Taurus Model PT-111 Millennium Titanium Pistol

Similar to the PT-111 except with titanium slide, night sights.

Price: **$585.00**

TAURUS PT-132 MILLENIUM AUTO PISTOL

Caliber: 32 ACP, 10-shot magazine. **Barrel:** 3.25". **Weight:** 18.7 oz. **Length:** NA. **Grips:** Polymer. **Sights:** 3-dot fixed; night sights available. **Features:** Double-action only; polymer frame; matte stainless or blue steel slide; manual safety; integral key-lock action. Introduced 2001.

Price: . . . . **$422.00 to $438.00**

Taurus Model PT-138 Auto Pistol

Similar to the PT-111 except chambered for 380 ACP, with 10-shot magazine. Double-action-only mechanism. Has black polymer frame with blue or stainless slide. Introduced 1999. Imported by Taurus International.

Price: Blue . . . . **$425.00** (**$500.00** with night sights)

Price: Stainless. . . . **$435.00** (**$520.00** with night sights)

TAURUS PT-140 MILLENIUM AUTO PISTOL

Caliber: 40 S&W, 10-shot magazine. **Barrel:** 3.25". **Weight:** 18.7 oz. **Length:** NA. **Grips:** Checkered polymer. **Sights:** 3-dot fixed; night sights available. **Features:** Double-action only; matte stainless or blue steel slide; black polymer frame; manual safety; integral key-lock action. From Taurus International.

Price: . . . . **$455.00 to $555.00**

TAURUS PT-145 MILLENIUM AUTO PISTOL

Caliber: 45 ACP, 10-shot magazine. **Barrel:** 3.27". **Weight:** 23 oz. **Length:** NA. **Stock:** Checkered polymer. **Sights:** 3-dot fixed; night sights available. **Features:** Double-action only; matte stainless or blue steel slide; black polymer frame; manual safety; integral key-lock action. From Taurus International.

Price: . . . . **$490.00 to $575.00**

TAURUS MODEL PT-911 AUTO PISTOL

Caliber: 9mm Para., 10-shot magazine. **Barrel:** 4". **Weight:** 28.2 oz. **Length:** 7" overall. **Stocks:** Black rubber. **Sights:** Fixed. Low profile, three-dot combat. **Features:** Double action, exposed hammer; ambidextrous hammer drop; chamber loaded indicator. Introduced 1997. Imported by Taurus International.

Taurus PT-911

Taurus PT-938

Price: Blue **$505.00**
Price: Stainless....................................... **$525.00**
Price: Blue with gold accents, rosewood grips **$555.00**
Price: Stainless with gold accents, rosewood grips **$570.00**
Price: Blue/gold accents, mother-of-pearl grips **$570.00**
Price: Stainless/gold accents, mother-of-pearl grips **$585.00**
Price: Blue finish, night sights............................. **$585.00**
Price: Stainless finish, night sights......................... **$600.00**

TAURUS MODEL PT-938 AUTO PISTOL

Caliber: 380 ACP, 10-shot magazine. **Barrel:** 3.72". **Weight:** 27 oz. **Length:** 6.5" overall. **Grips:** Black rubber. **Sights:** Fixed. Low profile, three-dot combat. **Features:** Double-action only. Chamber loaded indicator; firing pin block; ambidextrous hammer drop. Introduced 1997. Imported by Taurus International.

Price: Blue **$500.00**
Price: Stainless....................................... **$530.00**

TAURUS MODEL PT-940 AUTO PISTOL

Caliber: 40 S&W, 10-shot magazine. **Barrel:** 3.35". **Weight:** 28.2 oz. **Length:** 7.05" overall. **Grips:** Checkered rubber, rosewood or mother-of-pearl. **Sights:** Drift-adjustable front and rear; three-dot combat. **Features:** Single/double action, exposed hammer; manual ambidextrous hammer-drop; inertia firing pin; chamber loaded indicator. Introduced 1996. Imported by Taurus International.

Price: Blue **$525.00**
Price: Stainless steel **$535.00**
Price: Blue with gold accents, rosewood grips **$570.00**
Price: Stainless with gold accents, rosewood grips **$600.00**

TAURUS MODEL PT-945 AUTO PISTOL

Caliber: 45 ACP, 8-shot magazine. **Barrel:** 4.25". **Weight:** 29.5 oz. **Length:** 7.48" overall. **Grips:** Checkered black rubber, rosewood or mother-of-pearl. **Sights:** Drift-adjustable front and rear; three-dot system. **Features:** Single/double-action mechanism. Has manual ambidextrous hammer drop safety, intercept notch, firing pin block, chamber loaded indicator, integral key-lock, last-shot hold-open. Introduced 1995. Imported by Taurus International.

Taurus PT-940

Taurus PT-945

Taurus PT-957

Price: Blue **$560.00**
Price: Stainless....................................... **$580.00**
Price: Blue, ported **$600.00**
Price: Stainless, ported **$620.00**
Price: Blue with gold accents, rosewood grips................ **$610.00**
Price: Blue with gold accents, mother-of-pearl grips **$625.00**
Price: Stainless w/gold accents, mother-of-pearl grips **$645.00**

TAURUS MODEL PT-957 AUTO PISTOL

Caliber: 357 SIG, 10-shot magazine. **Barrel:** 3-5/8". **Weight:** 28 oz. **Length:** 7" overall. **Stocks:** Checkered rubber. **Sights:** Fixed, low profile, three-dot combat; night sights optional. **Features:** Single/double action mechanism; blue, stainless steel, blue with gold accents or stainless with gold accents; exposed hammer; ported barrel/slide; three-position safety with decocking lever and ambidextrous safety. Introduced 1999. Imported by Taurus International.

Price: Blue **$560.00**
Price: Stainless....................................... **$575.00**
Price: Blue with gold accents, rosewood grips **$610.00**
Price: Stainless with gold accents, rosewood grips **$625.00**

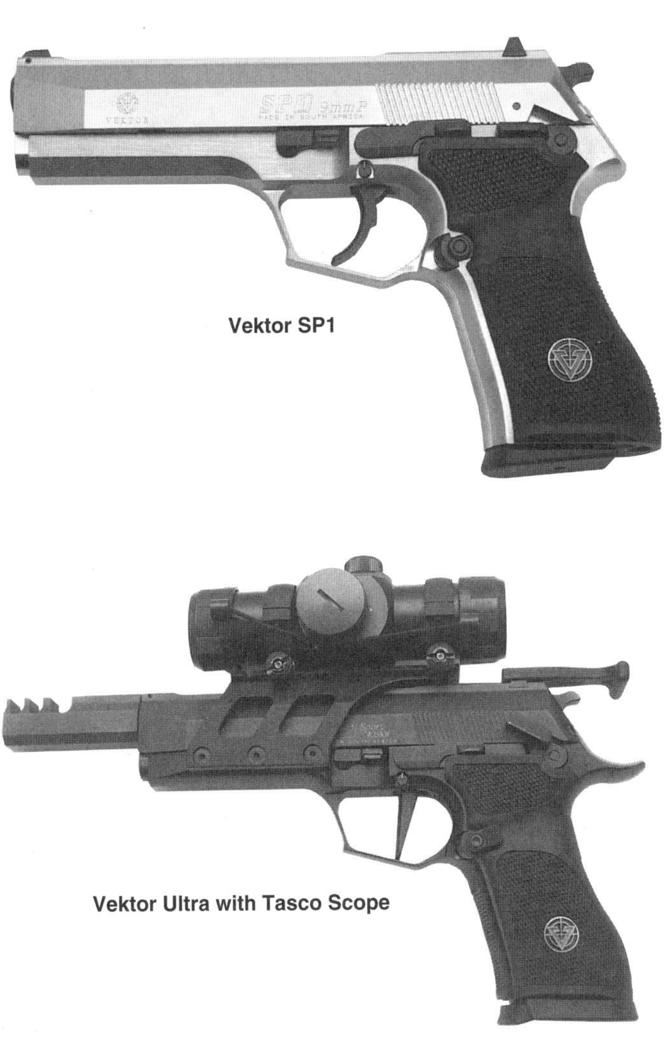

Vektor SP1

Walther PP

Walther PPK/S

Vektor Ultra with Tasco Scope

VEKTOR SP1 SPORT PISTOL

Caliber: 9mm Para., 10-shot magazine. **Barrel:** 5 ".**Weight:** 38 oz. **Length:** 9-3/8" overall. **Stocks:** Checkered black composition. **Sights:** Combat-type blade front, adjustable rear. **Features:** Single action only with adjustable trigger stop; three-chamber compensator; extended magazine release. Introduced 1999. Imported from South Africa by Vektor USA.

Price: **$829.95**

Vektor SP1 Tuned Sport Pistol

Similar to the Vektor Sport except has fully adjustable straight trigger, LPA three-dot sight system, and hard nickel finish. Introduced 1999. Imported from South Africa by Vektor USA.

Price: **$1,199.95**

Vektor SP1 Target Pistol

Similar to the Vektor Sport except has 5-7/8" barrel without compensator; weighs 40-1/2 oz.; has fully adjustable straight match trigger; black slide, bright frame. Introduced 1999. Imported from South Africa by Vektor USA.

Price: **$1,299.95**

Vektor SP1, SP2 Ultra Sport Pistols

Similar to the Vektor Target except has three-chamber compensator with three jet ports; strengthened frame with integral beavertail; lightweight polymer scope mount (Weaver rail). Overall length is 11", weighs 41-1/2 oz. Model SP2 is in 40 S&W. Introduced 1999. Imported from South Africa by Vektor USA.

Price: SP1 (9mm) **$2,149.95**

Price: SP2 (40 S&W) **$2,149.95**

VEKTOR SP1 AUTO PISTOL

Caliber: 9mm Para., 40 S&W (SP2), 10-shot magazine. **Barrel:** 4-5/8". **Weight:** 35 oz. **Length:** 8-1/4" overall. **Stocks:** Checkered black composition. **Sights:** Combat-type fixed. **Features:** Alloy frame, steel slide; traditional double-action mechanism; matte black finish. Introduced 1999. Imported from South Africa by Vektor USA.

Price: SP1 (9mm) **$599.95**

Price: SP1 with nickel finish **$629.95**

Price: SP2 (40 S&W) **$649.95**

Vektor SP1, SP2 Compact General's Model Pistol

Similar to the 9mm Para. Vektor SP1 except has 4" barrel, weighs 31-1/2 oz., and is 7-1/2" overall. Recoil operated. Traditional double-action mechanism. SP2 model is chambered for 40 S&W. Introduced 1999. Imported from South Africa by Vektor USA.

Price: SP1 (9mm Para.) **$649.95**

Price: SP2 (40 S&W) **$649.95**

VEKTOR CP-1 COMPACT PISTOL

Caliber: 9mm Para., 10-shot magazine. **Barrel:** 4". **Weight:** 25.4 oz. **Length:** 7" overall. **Stocks:** Textured polymer. **Sights:** Blade front adjustable for windage, fixed rear; adjustable sight optional. **Features:** Ergonomic grip frame shape; stainless steel barrel; delayed gas-buffered blowback action. Introduced 1999. Imported from South Africa by Vektor USA.

Price: With black slide **$479.95**

Price: With nickel slide **$499.95**

Price: With black slide, adjustable sight **$509.95**

Price: With nickel slide, adjustable sight **$529.95**

WALTHER PP AUTO PISTOL

Caliber: 380 ACP, 7-shot magazine. **Barrel:** 3.86". **Weight:** 23-1/2 oz. **Length:** 6.7" overall. **Stocks:** Checkered plastic. **Sights:** Fixed, white markings. **Features:** Double action; manual safety blocks firing pin and drops hammer; chamber loaded indicator on 32 and 380; extra finger rest magazine provided. Imported from Germany by Carl Walther USA.

Price: 380 . . . . **$999.00**

Walther PPK/S American Auto Pistol

Similar to Walther PP except made entirely in the United States. Has 3.27" barrel with 6.1" length overall. Introduced 1980.

Price: 380 ACP only, blue **$540.00**

Price: As above, 32 ACP or 380 ACP, stainless **$540.00**

Walther PPK

Walther P99

Walther TPH

Dan Wesson Pointman Major

Walther PPK American Auto Pistol

Similar to Walther PPK/S except weighs 21 oz., has 6-shot capacity. Made in the U.S. Introduced 1986.

Price: Stainless, 32 ACP or 380 ACP. **$540.00**
Price: Blue, 380 ACP only **$540.00**

WALTHER MODEL TPH AUTO PISTOL

Caliber: 22 LR, 25 ACP, 6-shot magazine. **Barrel:** 2-1/4". **Weight:** 14 oz. **Length:** 5-3/8" overall. **Stocks:** Checkered black composition. **Sights:** Blade front, rear drift-adjustable for windage. **Features:** Made of stainless steel. Scaled-down version of the Walther PP/PPK series. Made in U.S. Introduced 1987. From Carl Walther USA.

Price: Blue or stainless steel, 22 or 25 . . . . **$440.00**

WALTHER P88 COMPACT PISTOL

Caliber: 9mm Para., 10-shot magazine. **Barrel:** 3.93". **Weight:** 28 oz. **Length:** NA. **Stocks:** Checkered black polymer. **Sights:** Blade front, drift adjustable rear. **Features:** Double action with ambidextrous decocking lever and magazine release; alloy frame; loaded chamber indicator; matte blue finish. Imported from Germany by Carl Walther USA.

Price: **$900.00**

WALTHER P99 AUTO PISTOL

Caliber: 9mm Para., 9x21, 40 S&W,10-shot magazine. **Barrel:** 4". **Weight:** 25 oz. **Length:** 7" overall. **Stocks:** Textured polymer. **Sights:** Blade front (comes with three interchangeable blades for elevation adjustment), micrometer rear adjustable for windage. **Features:** Double-action mechanism with trigger safety, decock safety, internal striker safety; chamber loaded indicator; ambidextrous magazine release levers; polymer frame with interchangeable backstrap inserts. Comes with two magazines. Introduced 1997. Imported from Germany by Carl Walther USA.

Price: **$799.00**

Walther P990 Auto Pistol

Similar to the P99 except is double action only. Available in blue or silver tenifer finish. Introduced 1999. Imported from Germany by Carl Walther USA.

Price: **$749.00**

WALTHER P-5 AUTO PISTOL

Caliber: 9mm Para., 8-shot magazine. **Barrel:** 3.62". **Weight:** 28 oz. **Length:** 7.10" overall. **Stocks:** Checkered plastic. **Sights:** Blade front, adjustable rear. **Features:** Uses the basic Walther P-38 double-action mechanism. Blue finish. Imported from Germany by Carl Walther USA.

Price: **$900.00**

DAN WESSON POINTMAN MAJOR AUTO PISTOL

Caliber: 45 ACP. **Barrel:** 5". **Weight:** NA. **Length:** NA. **Grips:** Rosewood checkered. **Sights: Features:** Blued or stainless steel frame and serrated slide; Chip McCormick match-grade trigger group, sear and disconnect; match-grade barrel; high-ride beavertail safety; checkered slide release; high rib; interchangeable sight system; laser engraved. Introduced 2000. Made in U.S. by Dan Wesson Firearms.

Price: Model PM1-B (blued) **$789.00**
Price: Model PM1-S (stainless) **$799.00**

Dan Wesson Pointman Minor Auto Pistol

Similar to Pointman Major except has blued frame and slide with fixed rear sight. Introduced 2000. Made in U.S. by Dan Wesson Firearms.

Price: Model PM2-P **$579.00**

Dan Wesson Pointman Seven

Dan Wesson Pointman Guardian

Dan Wesson Pointman Seven Auto Pistols

Similar to Pointman Major except has dovetail adjustable target rear sight and dovetail target front sight. Available in blued or stainless finish. Introduced 2000. Made in U.S. by Dan Wesson Firearms.

Price: PM7 (blued frame and slide) **$999.00**
Price: PM7S (stainless finish). **$1,099.00**

Dan Wesson Pointman Guardian Auto Pistols

Similar to Pointman Major except has a more compact frame with 4.25" barrel. Avaiable in blued or stainless finish with fixed or adjustable sights. Introduced 2000. Made in U.S. by Dan Wesson Firearms.

Price: PMG-FS (blued frame and slide, fixed sights) **$769.00**
Price: PMG-AS (blued frame and slide, adjustable sights). **$779.00**
Price: PMGD-FS Guardian Duce (stainless frame and blued slide, fixed sights). **$829.00**
Price: PMGD-AS Guardian Duce (stainless frame and blued slide, adj. sights). **$839.00**

NEW! **Dan Wesson Pointman Hi-Cap Auto Pistol**

Similar to Pointman Minor except has full-size high-capacity (10-shot) magazine with 5" chromed barrel, blued finish and dovetail fixed rear sight. Match adjustable trigger, ambidextrous extended thumb safety, beavertail safety. Introduced 2001. From Dan Wesson Firearms.

Price: PMHC (Pointman High-Cap) **$669.00**

NEW! **Dan Wesson Pointman Dave Pruitt Signature Series**

Similar to other full-sized Pointman models except customized by Master Pistolsmith and IDPA Grand Master Dave Pruitt. Alloy carbon-steel from with black oxide bluing and bead-blast matte finish. Front and rear chevron cocking serrations; dovetail-mount fixed Novak style sights; match trigger group, sear and hammer; exotic hardwood grips. Introduced 2001. From Dan Wesson Firearms.

Price: PMDP (Pointman Dave Pruitt) **$899.00**

Wilkinson Sherry

WILKINSON SHERRY AUTO PISTOL

Caliber: 22 LR, 8-shot magazine. **Barrel:** 2-1/8". **Weight:** 9-1/4 oz. **Length:** 4-3/8" overall. **Stocks:** Checkered black plastic. **Sights:** Fixed, groove. **Features:** Cross-bolt safety locks the sear into the hammer. Available in all blue finish or blue slide and trigger with gold frame. Introduced 1985.

Price: **$195.00**

WILKINSON LINDA AUTO PISTOL

Caliber: 9mm Para. **Barrel:** 8-5/16". **Weight:** 4 lbs., 13 oz. **Length:** 12-1/4" overall. **Stocks:** Checkered black plastic pistol grip, walnut forend. **Sights:** Protected blade front, aperture rear. **Features:** Fires from closed bolt. Semi-auto only. Straight blowback action. Cross-bolt safety. Removable barrel. From Wilkinson Arms.

Price: **$533.33**

HANDGUNS — COMPETITION HANDGUNS

Includes models suitable for several forms of competition and other sporting purposes.

Baer 1911 Ultimate Master

Baer 1911 Bullseye Wadcutter

Beretta Model 89

Beretta Model 96 Combat

BAER 1911 ULTIMATE MASTER COMBAT PISTOL

Caliber: 9x23, 38 Super, 400 Cor-Bon 45 ACP (others available), 10-shot magazine. **Barrel:** 5", 6"; Baer NM. **Weight:** 37 oz. **Length:** 8.5" overall. **Stocks:** Checkered rosewood. **Sights:** Baer dovetail front, low-mount Bo-Mar rear with hidden leaf. **Features:** Full-house competition gun. Baer forged NM blued steel frame and double serrated slide; Baer triple port, tapered cone compensator; fitted slide to frame; lowered, flared ejection port; Baer reverse recoil plug; full-length guide rod; recoil buff; beveled magazine well; Baer Commander hammer, sear; Baer extended ambidextrous safety, extended ejector, checkered slide stop, beavertail grip safety with pad, extended magazine release button; Baer speed trigger. Made in U.S. by Les Baer Custom, Inc.

Price: Compensated, open sights. **$2,476.00**
Price: 6" Model 400 Cor-Bon **$2,541.00**

BAER 1911 NATIONAL MATCH HARDBALL PISTOL

Caliber: 45 ACP, 7-shot magazine. **Barrel:** 5". **Weight:** 37 oz. **Length:** 8.5" overall. **Stocks:** Checkered walnut. **Sights:** Baer dovetail front with undercut post, low-mount Bo-Mar rear with hidden leaf. **Features:** Baer NM forged steel frame, double serrated slide and barrel with stainless bushing; slide fitted to frame; Baer match trigger with 4-lb. pull; polished feed ramp, throated barrel; checkered front strap, arched mainspring housing; Baer beveled magazine well; lowered, flared ejection port; tuned extractor; Baer extended ejector, checkered slide stop; recoil buff. Made in U.S. by Les Baer Custom, Inc.

Price: **$1,335.00**

Baer 1911 Bullseye Wadcutter Pistol

Similar to the National Match Hardball except designed for wadcutter loads only. Has polished feed ramp and barrel throat; Bo-Mar rib on slide; full-length recoil rod; Baer speed trigger with 3-1/2-lb. pull; Baer deluxe hammer and sear; Baer beavertail grip safety with pad; flat mainspring housing checkered 20 lpi. Blue finish; checkered walnut grips. Made in U.S. by Les Baer Custom, Inc.

Price: From. **$1,495.00**
Price: With 6" barrel, from **$1,690.00**

BENELLI MP90S WORLD CUP PISTOL

Caliber: 22 Long Rifle, 6- or 9-shot magazine. **Barrel:** 4.4"**Weight:** 2.5 lbs. **Length:** 11.75". Grip: Walnut. **Sights:** Blade front, fully adjustable rear. **Features:** Single-action target pistol with fully adjustable trigger and adjustable heel rest; integral scope rail mount; attachment system for optional external weights.

Price: **$1,190.00**

Benelli MP95E Atlanta Pistol

Similar to MP90S World Cup Pistol, but available in blue finish with walnut grip or chrome finish with laminate grip. Overall length 11.25". Trigger overtravel adjustment only.

Price: (blue finish, walnut grip) **$740.00**
Price: (chrome finish, laminate grip) **$810.00**

BERETTA MODEL 89 GOLD STANDARD PISTOL

Caliber: 22 LR, 8-shot magazine. **Barrel:** 6". **Weight:** 41 oz. **Length:** 9.5" overall. **Stocks:** Target-type walnut with thumbrest. **Sights:** Interchangeable blade front, fully adjustable rear. **Features:** Single action target pistol. Matte black, Bruniton finish. Imported from Italy by Beretta U.S.A.

Price: **$802.00**

BERETTA MODEL 96 COMBAT PISTOL

Caliber: 40 S&W, 10-shot magazine. **Barrel:** 4.9" (5.9" with weight). **Weight:** 34.4 oz. **Length:** 8.5" overall. **Stocks:** Checkered black plastic. **Sights:** Blade front, fully adjustable target rear. **Features:** Uses heavier Brigadier slide with front and rear serrations; extended frame-mounted safety; extended, reversible magazine release; single-action-only with competition-tuned trigger with extra-short let-off and over-travel adjustment. Comes with tool kit. Introduced 1997. Imported from Italy by Beretta U.S.A.

Price: **$1,593.00**
Price: 4.9" barrel. **$1,341.00**
Price: 5.9" barrel. **$1,634.00**
Price: Combo **$1,599.00**

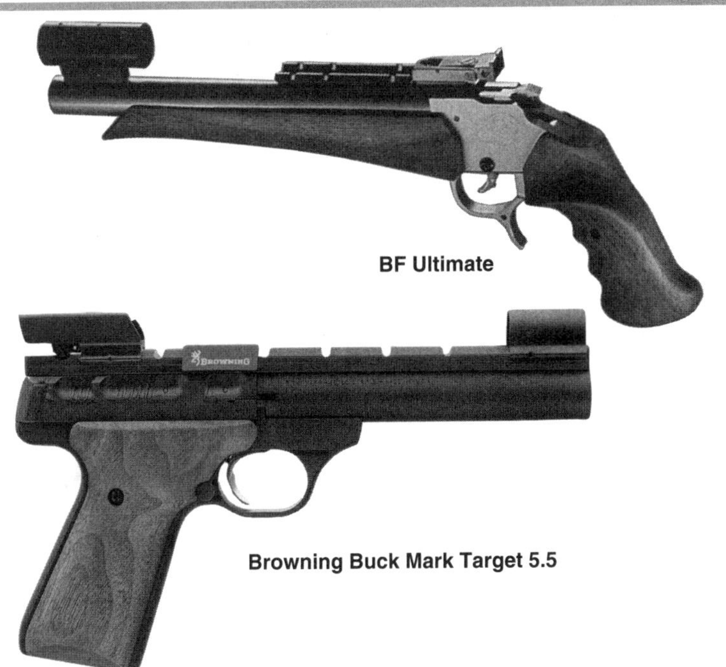

BF Ultimate

Browning Buck Mark Target 5.5

Browning Buck Mark Bullseye

Colt Gold Cup Trophy

Beretta Model 96 Stock Pistol

Similar to the Model 96 Combat except is single/double action, with half-cock notch. Has front and rear slide serrations, rubber magazine bumper, replaceable accurizing barrel bushing, ultra-thin fine-checkered grips (aluminum optional), checkered front and back straps, radiused back strap, fitted case. Weighs 35 oz., 8.5" overall. Introduced 1997. Imported from Italy by Beretta U.S.A.

Price: $1,700.00

BF ULTIMATE SILHOUETTE HB SINGLE SHOT PISTOL

Caliber: 7mm U.S., 22 LR Match and 100 other chamberings. **Barrel:** 10.75" Heavy Match Grade with 11-degree target crown. **Weight:** 3 lbs., 15 oz. **Length:** 16" overall. **Stocks:** Thumbrest target style. **Sights:** Bo-Mar/Bond ScopeRib I Combo with hooded post front adjustable for height and width, rear notch available in .032", .062", .080" and .100" widths; 1/2-MOA clicks. **Features:** Designed to meet maximum rules for IHMSA Production Gun. Falling block action gives rigid barrel-receiver mating. Hand fitted and headspaced. Etched receiver; gold-colored trigger. Introduced 1988. Made in U.S. by E. Arthur Brown Co. Inc.

Price: $669.00

Classic BF Hunting Pistol

Similar to BF Ultimate Silhouette HB Single Shot Pistol, except no sights; drilled and tapped for scope mount. Barrels from 8 to 15". Variety of options offered. Made in U.S. by E. Arthur Brown Co. Inc.

Price: $599.00

BROWNING BUCK MARK SILHOUETTE

Caliber: 22 LR, 10-shot magazine. **Barrel:** 9-7/8". **Weight:** 53 oz. **Length:** 14" overall. **Stocks:** Smooth walnut stocks and forend, or finger-groove walnut. **Sights:** Post-type hooded front adjustable for blade width and height; Pro Target rear fully adjustable for windage and elevation. **Features:** Heavy barrel with .900" diameter; 12-1/2" sight radius. Special sighting plane forms scope base. Introduced 1987. Made in U.S. From Browning.

Price: $448.00

Browning Buck Mark Target 5.5

Same as the Buck Mark Silhouette except has a 5-1/2" barrel with .900" diameter. Has hooded sights mounted on a scope base that accepts an optical or reflex sight. Rear sight is a Browning fully adjustable Pro Target, front sight is an adjustable post that customizes to different widths, and can be adjusted for height. Contoured walnut grips with thumbrest, or finger-groove walnut. Matte blue finish. Overall length is 9-5/8", weighs 35-1/2 oz. Has 10-shot magazine. Introduced 1990. From Browning.

Price: $425.00

Price: Target 5.5 Gold (as above with gold anodized frame and top rib) $477.00

Price: Target 5.5 Nickel (as above with nickel frame and top rib). $477.00

Browning Buck Mark Field 5.5

Same as the Target 5.5 except has hoodless ramp-style front sight and low profile rear sight. Matte blue finish, contoured or finger-groove walnut stocks. Introduced 1991.

Price: $425.00

Browning Buck Mark Bullseye

Similar to the Buck Mark Silhouette except has 7-1/4" heavy barrel with three flutes per side; trigger is adjustable from 2-1/2 to 5 lbs.; specially designed rosewood target or three-finger-groove stocks with competition-style heel rest, or with contoured rubber grip. Overall length is 11-5/16", weighs 36 oz. Introduced 1996. Made in U.S. From Browning.

Price: With ambidextrous moulded composite stocks $389.00

Price: With rosewood stocks, or wrap-around finger groove $500.00

COLT GOLD CUP MODEL O PISTOL

Caliber: 45 ACP, 8-shot magazine. **Barrel:** 5", with new design bushing. **Weight:** 39 oz. **Length:** 8-1/2". **Stocks:** Checkered rubber composite with silver-plated medallion. **Sights:** Patridge-style front, Bomar-style rear adjustable for windage and elevation, sight radius 6-3/4". **Features:** Arched or flat housing; wide, grooved trigger with adjustable stop; ribbed-top slide, hand fitted, with improved ejection port.

Price: Blue $1,050.00

Price: Stainless.......... $1,116.00

COMPETITOR SINGLE SHOT PISTOL

Caliber: 22 LR through 50 Action Express, including belted magnums. **Barrel:** 14" standard; 10.5" silhouette; 16" optional. **Weight:** About 59 oz. (14" bbl.). **Length:** 15.12" overall. **Stocks:** Ambidextrous; synthetic (standard) or laminated or natural wood. **Sights:** Ramp front, adjustable rear. **Features:** Rotary canon-type action cocks on opening; cammed ejector; interchangeable barrels, ejectors. Adjustable single stage trigger, sliding thumb safety and trigger safety. Matte blue finish. Introduced 1988. From Competitor Corp., Inc.

Price: 14", standard calibers, synthetic grip $414.95

Price: Extra barrels, from $159.95

Competitor Single Shot

E.A.A. Witness Gold Team

Freedom Arms 252 Silhouette

Hammerli SP 20

CZ 75 CHAMPION COMPETITION PISTOL

Caliber: 9mm Para., 9x21, 40 S&W, 10-shot magazine. **Barrel:** 4.49". **Weight:** 35 oz. **Length:** 9.44" overall. **Stocks:** Black rubber. **Sights:** Blade front, fully adjustable rear. **Features:** Single-action trigger mechanism; three-port compensator (40 S&W, 9mm have two port) full-length guide rod; extended magazine release; ambidextrous safety; flared magazine well; fully adjustable match trigger. Introduced 1999. Imported from the Czech Republic by CZ USA.

Price: 9mm Para., 9x21, 40 S&W, dual-tone finish. **$1,484.00**

CZ 75 ST IPSC AUTO PISTOL

Caliber: 40 S&W, 10-shot magazine. **Barrel:** 5.12". **Weight:** 2.9 lbs. **Length:** 8.86" overall. **Stocks:** Checkered walnut. **Sights:** Fully adjustable rear. **Features:** Single-action mechanism; extended slide release and ambidextrous safety; full-length slide rail; double slide serrations. Introduced 1999. Imported from the Czech Republic by CZ-USA.

Price: Dual-tone finish **$1,038.00**

EAA/BAIKAL IZH35 AUTO PISTOL

Caliber: 22 LR, 5-shot magazine. **Barrel:** 6". **Weight:** NA. **Length:** NA. **Grips:** Walnut; fully adjustable right-hand target-style. **Sights:** Fully adjustable rear, blade front; detachable scope mount. **Features:** Hammer-forged target barrel; machined steel receiver; adjustable trigger; manual slide hold back, grip and manual trigger-bar disconnect safeties; cocking indicator. Introduced 2000. Imported from Russia by European American Armory.

Price: Blued finish. **$519.00**

E.A.A. WITNESS GOLD TEAM AUTO

Caliber: 9mm Para., 9x21, 38 Super, 40 S&W, 45 ACP. **Barrel:** 5.1". **Weight:** 41.6 oz. **Length:** 9.6" overall. **Stocks:** Checkered walnut, competition style. **Sights:** Square post front, fully adjustable rear. **Features:** Triple-chamber cone compensator; competition SA trigger; extended safety and magazine release; competition hammer; beveled magazine well; beavertail grip. Hand-fitted major components. Hard chrome finish. Match-grade barrel. From E.A.A. Custom Shop. Introduced 1992. From European American Armory.

Price: **$2,150.00**

E.A.A. Witness Silver Team Auto

Similar to the Witness Gold Team except has double-chamber compensator, oval magazine release, black rubber grips, double-dip blue finish. Comes with Super Sight and drilled and tapped for scope mount. Built for the intermediate competition shooter. Introduced 1992. From European American Armory Custom Shop.

Price: 9mm Para., 9x21, 38 Super, 40 S&W, 45 ACP **$968.00**

ENTRÉPRISE TOURNAMENT SHOOTER MODEL I

Caliber: 45 ACP, 10-shot magazine. **Barrel:** 6". **Weight:** 40 oz. **Length:** 8.5" overall. **Stocks:** Black ultra-slim double diamond checkered synthetic. **Sights:** Dovetailed Patridge front, adjustable Competizione "melded" rear. **Features:** Oversized magazine release button; flared magazine well; fully machined parallel slide rails; front and rear slide serrations; serrated top of slide; stainless ramped bull barrel with fully supported chamber; full-length guide rod with plug; stainless firing pin; match extractor; polished ramp; tuned match extractor; black oxide. Introduced 1998. Made in U.S. by Entréprise Arms.

Price: **$2,300.00**

Price: TSMIII (Satin chrome finish, two-piece guide rod) **$2,700.00**

Excel Industries CP-45 Auto Pistol NEW

Caliber: 45 ACP, 6-shot magazine. **Barrel:** 3-1/4 inches. **Weight:** 31 oz. **Length:** 6-3/8 inches overall. **Grips:** Checkered black nylon. **Sights:** Fully adjustable rear, three-dot; blade front. **Features:** Stainless steel frame and slide; single action with external hammer and firing pin block, manual thumb safety; last-shot hold open. Includes gun lock and cleaning kit. Introduced 2001. Made in U.S. by Excel Industries Inc.

Price: **$425.00**

FREEDOM ARMS MODEL 83 FIELD GRADE SILHOUETTE CLASS

Caliber: 22 LR, 5-shot cylinder. **Barrel:** 10". **Weight:** 63 oz. **Length:** 15.5" overall. **Stocks:** Black Micarta. **Sights:** Removable patridge front blade; Iron Sight Gun Works silhouette rear, click adjustable for windage and elevation (optional adj. front sight and hood). **Features:** Stainless steel, matte finish, manual sliding-bar safety system; dual firing pins, lightened hammer for fast lock time, pre-set trigger stop. Introduced 1991. Made in U.S. by Freedom Arms.

Price: Silhouette Class **$1,765.00**

Price: Extra fitted 22 WMR cylinder **$264.00**

GAUCHER GP SILHOUETTE PISTOL

Caliber: 22 LR, single shot. **Barrel:** 10". **Weight:** 42.3 oz. **Length:** 15.5" overall. **Stocks:** Stained hardwood. **Sights:** Hooded post on ramp front, open rear adjustable for windage and elevation. **Features:** Matte chrome barrel, blued bolt and sights. Other barrel lengths available on special order. Introduced 1991. Imported by Mandall Shooting Supplies.

Price: **$425.00**

HAMMERLI SP 20 TARGET PISTOL

Caliber: 22 LR, 32 S&W. **Barrel:** 4.6". **Weight:** 34.6-41.8 oz. **Length:** 11.8" overall. **Stocks:** Anatomically shaped synthetic Hi-Grip available in five sizes. **Sights:** Integral front in three widths, adjustable rear with changeable notch widths. **Features:** Extremely low-level sight line; anatomically shaped trigger; adjustable JPS buffer system for different recoil characteristics. Receiver available in red, blue, gold, violet or black. Introduced 1998. Imported from Switzerland by SIGARMS, Inc and Hammerli Pistols USA.

Price: . . . . **NA**

High Standard Trophy

High Standard Victor

HARRIS GUNWORKS SIGNATURE JR. LONG RANGE PISTOL

Caliber: Any suitable caliber. **Barrel:** To customer specs. **Weight:** 5 lbs. **Stock:** Gunworks fiberglass. **Sights:** None furnished; comes with scope rings. **Features:** Right- or left-hand benchrest action of titanium or stainless steel; single shot or repeater. Comes with bipod. Introduced 1992. Made in U.S. by Harris Gunworks, Inc.

Price: **$2,700.00**

HIGH STANDARD TROPHY TARGET PISTOL

Caliber: 22 LR, 10-shot magazine. **Barrel:** 5-1/2" bull or 7-1/4" fluted. **Weight:** 44 oz. **Length:** 9.5" overall. **Stock:** Checkered hardwood with thumbrest. **Sights:** Undercut ramp front, frame-mounted micro-click rear adjustable for windage and elevation; drilled and tapped for scope mounting. **Features:** Gold-plated trigger, slide lock, safety-lever and magazine release; stippled front grip and backstrap; adjustable trigger and sear. Barrel weights optional. From High Standard Manufacturing Co., Inc.

Price: 5-1/2", scope base **$510.00**
Price: 7.25" **$650.00**
Price: 7.25", scope base **$591.00**

HIGH STANDARD VICTOR TARGET PISTOL

Caliber: 22 LR, 10-shot magazine. **Barrel:** 4-1/2" or 5-1/2"; push-button takedown. **Weight:** 46 oz. **Length:** 9.5" overall. **Stock:** Checkered hardwood with thumbrest. **Sights:** Undercut ramp front, micro-click rear adjustable for windage and elevation. Also available with scope mount, rings, no sights. **Features:** Stainless steel construction. Full-length vent rib. Gold-plated trigger, slide lock, safety-lever and magazine release; stippled front grip and backstrap; polished slide; adjustable trigger and sear. Comes with barrel weight. From High Standard Manufacturing Co., Inc.

Price: **$591.00**
Price: With Weaver rib **$532.00**

KIMBER SUPER MATCH AUTO PISTOL

Caliber: 45 ACP, 7-shot magazine. **Barrel:** 5". **Weight:** 38 oz. **Length:** 18.7" overall. **Sights:** Blade front, Kimber fully adjustable rear. **Features:** Guaranteed to have shot 3" group at 50 yards. Stainless steel frame, black KimPro slide; two-piece magazine well; premium aluminum match-grade trigger; 30 lpi front strap checkering; stainless match-grade barrel; ambidextrous safety; special Custom Shop markings. Introduced 1999. Made in U.S. by Kimber Mfg., Inc.

Price: **$1,927.00**

MORINI MODEL 84E FREE PISTOL

Caliber: 22 LR, single shot. **Barrel:** 11.4". **Weight:** 43.7 oz. **Length:** 19.4" overall. **Stocks:** Adjustable match type with stippled surfaces. **Sights:** Interchangeable blade front, match-type fully adjustable rear. **Features:** Fully adjustable electronic trigger. Introduced 1995. Imported from Switzerland by Nygord Precision Products.

Price: **$1,450.00**

PARDINI MODEL SP, HP TARGET PISTOLS

Caliber: 22 LR, 32 S&W, 5-shot magazine. **Barrel:** 4.7". **Weight:** 38.9 oz. **Length:** 11.6" overall. **Stocks:** Adjustable; stippled walnut; match type. **Sights:** Interchangeable blade front, interchangeable, fully adjustable rear. **Features:** Fully adjustable match trigger. Introduced 1995. Imported from Italy by Nygord Precision Products.

Price: Model SP (22 LR) **$950.00**
Price: Model HP (32 S&W) **$1,050.00**

PARDINI GP RAPID FIRE MATCH PISTOL

Caliber: 22 Short, 5-shot magazine. **Barrel:** 4.6". **Weight:** 43.3 oz. **Length:** 11.6" overall. **Stocks:** Wrap-around stippled walnut. **Sights:** Interchangeable post front, fully adjustable match rear. **Features:** Model GP Schuman has extended rear sight for longer sight radius. Introduced 1995. Imported from Italy by Nygord Precision Products.

Price: Model GP **$1,095.00**
Price: Model GP Schuman **$1,595.00**

PARDINI K22 FREE PISTOL

Caliber: 22 LR, single shot. **Barrel:** 9.8". **Weight:** 34.6 oz. **Length:** 18.7" overall. **Stocks:** Wrap-around walnut; adjustable match type. **Sights:** Interchangeable post front, fully adjustable match open rear. **Features:** Removable, adjustable match trigger. Barrel weights mount above the barrel. New model introduced in 1999. Imported from Italy by Nygord Precision Products.

Price: **$1,295.00**

RUGER MARK II TARGET MODEL AUTOLOADING PISTOL

Caliber: 22 LR, 10-shot magazine. **Barrel:** 6-7/8". **Weight:** 42 oz. **Length:** 11-1/8" overall. **Stocks:** Checkered hard plastic. **Sights:** .125" blade front, micro-click rear, adjustable for windage and elevation. Sight radius 9-3/8". Comes with lockable plastic case with lock.
Features: Introduced 1982.

Price: Blued (MK-678) **$336.00**
Price: Stainless (KMK-678) **$420.00**

Ruger Mark II Government Target Model

Same gun as the Mark II Target Model except has 6-7/8" barrel, higher sights and is roll marked "Government Target Model" on the right side of the receiver below the rear sight. Identical in all aspects to the military model used for training U.S. Armed Forces except for markings. Comes with factory test target. Comes with lockable plastic case and lock. Introduced 1987.

Price: Blued (MK-678G) **$405.00**
Price: Stainless (KMK-678G) **$485.00**

Ruger Stainless Competition Model Pistol

Similar to the Mark II Government Target Model stainless pistol except has 6-7/8" slab-sided barrel; the receiver top is fitted with a Ruger scope base of blued, chrome moly steel; comes with Ruger 1" stainless scope rings for mounting a variety of optical sights; has checkered laminated grip panels with right-hand thumbrest. Has blued open sights with 9-1/4" radius. Overall length is 11-1/8", weight 45 oz. Comes with lockable plastic case and lock. Introduced 1991.

Price: KMK-678GC **$499.00**

Ruger Mark II Bull Barrel

Same gun as the Target Model except has 5-1/2" or 10" heavy barrel (10" meets all IHMSA regulations). Weight with 5-1/2" barrel is 42 oz., with 10" barrel, 51 oz. Comes with lockable plastic case with lock.

Price: Blued (MK-512) **$336.00**
Price: Blued (MK-10) **$340.00**
Price: Stainless (KMK-10) **$425.00**
Price: Stainless (KMK-512) **$420.00**

Ruger Mark II Bull Barrel - MK10

Safari Arms Big Deuce

Smith & Wesson Model 41

Springfield 1911A1 Trophy Match

SAFARI ARMS BIG DEUCE PISTOL

Caliber: 45 ACP, 7-shot magazine. **Barrel:** 6", 416 stainless steel. **Weight:** 40.3 oz. **Length:** 9.5" overall. **Stocks:** Smooth walnut. **Sights:** Ramped blade front, LPA adjustable rear. **Features:** Beavertail grip safety; extended thumb safety and slide release; Commander-style hammer. Throated, polished and tuned. Parkerized matte black slide with satin stainless steel frame. Introduced 1995. Made in U.S. by Safari Arms, Inc.

Price: **$714.00**

SMITH & WESSON MODEL 41 TARGET

Caliber: 22 LR, 10-shot clip. **Barrel:** 5-1/2", 7". **Weight:** 44 oz. (5-1/2" barrel). **Length:** 9" overall (5-1/2" barrel). **Stocks:** Checkered walnut with modified thumbrest, usable with either hand. **Sights:** 1/8" Patridge on ramp base; micro-click rear adjustable for windage and elevation. **Features:** 3/8" wide, grooved trigger; adjustable trigger stop.

Price: S&W Bright Blue, either barrel **$801.00**

SMITH & WESSON MODEL 22A TARGET PISTOL

Caliber: 22 LR, 10-shot magazine. **Barrel:** 5-1/2" bull. **Weight:** 38.5 oz. **Length:** 9-1/2" overall. **Stocks:** Dymondwood with ambidextrous thumbrests and flared bottom or rubber soft touch with thumbrest. **Sights:** Patridge front, fully adjustable rear. **Features:** Sight bridge with Weaver-style integral optics mount; alloy frame, stainless barrel and slide; matte black finish. Introduced 1997. Made in U.S. by Smith & Wesson.

Price: **$320.00**

Smith & Wesson Model 22S Target Pistol

Similar to the Model 22A except has stainless steel frame. Introduced 1997. Made in U.S. by Smith & Wesson.

Price: **$379.00**

Springfield, Inc. 1911A1 Trophy Match Pistol

Similar to the 1911A1 except factory accurized, Videki speed trigger, skeletonized hammer; has 4- to 5-1/2-lb. trigger pull, click adjustable rear sight, match-grade barrel and bushing. Comes with cocobolo grips. Introduced 1994. From Springfield, Inc.

Price: Blue **$1,089.00**

Price: Stainless steel **$1,149.00**

Price: High Capacity (stainless steel, 10-shot magazine, front slide serrations, checkered slide serrations) **$1,118.00**

Springfield, Inc. Expert Pistol

Similar to the Competition Pistol except has triple-chamber tapered cone compensator on match barrel with dovetailed front sight; lowered and flared ejection port; fully tuned for reliability; fitted slide to frame; extended ambidextrous thumb safety, extended magazine release button; beavertail grip safety; Pachmayr wrap-around grips. Comes with two magazines, plastic carrying case. Introduced 1992. From Springfield, Inc.

Price: 45 ACP, Duotone finish **$1,724.00**

Price: Expert Ltd. (non-compensated) **$1,624.00**

Springfield, Inc. Distinguished Pistol

Has all the features of the 1911A1 Expert except is full-house pistol with deluxe Bo-Mar low-mounted adjustable rear sight; full-length recoil spring guide rod and recoil spring retainer; checkered frontstrap; S&A magazine well; walnut grips. Hard chrome finish. Comes with two magazines with slam pads, plastic carrying case. From Springfield, Inc.

Price: 45 ACP. **$2,445.00**

Price: Distinguished Limited (non-compensated). **$2,345.00**

SPRINGFIELD, INC. 1911A1 BULLSEYE WADCUTTER PISTOL

Caliber: 38 Super, 45 ACP. **Barrel:** 5". **Weight:** 45 oz. **Length:** 8.59" overall (5" barrel). **Stocks:** Checkered walnut. **Sights:** Bo-Mar rib with undercut blade front, fully adjustable rear. **Features:** Built for wadcutter loads only. Has full-length recoil spring guide rod, fitted Videki speed trigger with 3.5-lb. pull; match Commander hammer and sear; beavertail grip safety; lowered and flared ejection port; tuned extractor; fitted slide to frame; recoil buffer system; beveled and polished magazine well; checkered front strap and steel mainspring housing (flat housing standard); polished and throated National Match barrel and bushing. Comes with two magazines with slam pads, plastic carrying case, test target. Introduced 1992. From Springfield, Inc.

Price: **$1,499.00**

Springfield, Inc. Basic Competition Pistol

Has low-mounted Bo-Mar adjustable rear sight, undercut blade front; match throated barrel and bushing; polished feed ramp; lowered and flared ejection port; fitted Videki speed trigger with tuned 3.5-lb. pull; fitted slide to frame; recoil buffer system; checkered walnut grips; serrated, arched mainspring housing. Comes with two magazines with slam pads, plastic carrying case. Introduced 1992. From Springfield, Inc.

Price: 45 ACP, blue, 5" only **$1,295.00**

Springfield, Inc. 1911A1 N.M. Hardball Pistol

Has Bo-Mar adjustable rear sight with undercut front blade; fitted match Videki trigger with 4-lb. pull; fitted slide to frame; throated National Match barrel and bushing, polished feed ramp; recoil buffer system; tuned extractor; Herrett walnut grips. Comes with two magazines, plastic carrying case, test target. Introduced 1992. From Springfield, Inc.

Price: 45 ACP, blue **$1,336.00**

Thompson/Center Super 14 Contender

Unique D.E.S. 69U

STI EAGLE 5.0 PISTOL

Caliber: 9mm Para., 38 Super, 40 S&W, 45 ACP, 10-ACP, 10-shot magazine. **Barrel:**5", bull. **Weight:** 34 oz. **Length:** 8.62" overall. **Stocks:** Checkered polymer. **Sights:** Bo-Mar blade front, Bo-Mar fully adjustable rear. **Features:** Modular frame design; adjustable match trigger; skeletonized hammer; extended grip safety with locator pad; match-grade fit of all parts. Many options available. Introduced 1994. Made in U.S. by STI International.

Price: $1,792.00

THOMPSON/CENTER SUPER 14 CONTENDER

Caliber: 22 LR, 222 Rem., 223 Rem., 7-30 Waters, 30-30 Win., 357 Rem. Maximum, 44 Mag., single shot. **Barrel:** 14". **Weight:** 45 oz. **Length:** 17-1/4" overall. **Stocks:** T/C "Competitor Grip" (walnut and rubber). **Sights:** Fully adjustable target-type. **Features:** Break-open action with auto safety. Interchangeable barrels for both rimfire and centerfire calibers. Introduced 1978.

Price: Blued $520.24
Price: Stainless steel $578.40
Price: Extra barrels, blued $251.06
Price: Extra barrels, stainless steel $278.68

Thompson/Center Super 16 Contender

Same as the T/C Super 14 Contender except has 16-1/4" barrel. Rear sight can be mounted at mid-barrel position (10-3/4" radius) or moved to the rear (using scope mount position) for 14-3/4" radius. Overall length is 20-1/4". Comes with T/C Competitor Grip of walnut and rubber. Available in, 223 Rem., 45-70 Gov't. Also available with 16" vent rib barrel with internal choke, caliber 45 Colt/410 shotshell.

Price: Blue $525.95
Price: 45-70 Gov't., blue $531.52
Price: Super 16 Vent Rib, blued $559.70
Price: Extra 16" barrel, blued $245.61
Price: Extra 45-70 barrel, blued $251.08
Price: Extra Super 16 vent rib barrel, blue $278.73

UNIQUE D.E.S. 32U TARGET PISTOL

Caliber: 32 S&W Long wadcutter. **Barrel:** 5.9". **Weight:** 40.2 oz. **Stocks:** Anatomically shaped, adjustable stippled French walnut. **Sights:** Blade front, micrometer click rear. **Features:** Trigger adjustable for weight and position; dry firing mechanism; slide stop catch. Optional sleeve weights. Introduced 1990. Imported from France by Nygord Precision Products.

Price: Right-hand, about $1,350.00
Price: Left-hand, about $1,380.00

UNIQUE D.E.S. 69U TARGET PISTOL

Caliber: 22 LR, 5-shot magazine. **Barrel:** 5.91". **Weight:** 35.3 oz. **Length:** 10.5" overall. **Stocks:** French walnut target-style with thumbrest and adjustable shelf; hand-checkered panels. **Sights:** Ramp front, micro. adjustable rear mounted on frame; 8.66" sight radius. **Features:** Meets U.I.T. standards. Comes with 260-gram barrel weight; 100, 150, 350-gram weights available. Fully adjustable match trigger; dry-firing safety device. Imported from France by Nygord Precision Products.

Price: Right-hand, about $1,250.00
Price: Left-hand, about $1,290.00

UNIQUE MODEL 96U TARGET PISTOL

Caliber:22 LR, 5- or 6-shot magazine. **Barrel:** 5.9". **Weight:** 40.2 oz. **Length:** 11.2" overall. **Stocks:** French walnut. Target style with thumbrest and adjustable shelf. **Sights:** Blade front, micrometer rear mounted on frame. **Features:** Designed for Sport Pistol and Standard U.I.T. shooting. External hammer; fully adjustable and movable trigger; dry-firing device. Introduced 1997. Imported from France by Nygord Precision Products.

Price: $1,350.00

WALTHER GSP MATCH PISTOL

Caliber: 22 LR, 32 S&W Long (GSP-C), 5-shot magazine. **Barrel:** 4.22". **Weight:** 44.8 oz. (22 LR), 49.4 oz. (32). **Length:** 11.8" overall. **Stocks:** Walnut. **Sights:** Post front, match rear adjustable for windage and elevation. **Features:** Available with either 2.2-lb. (1000 gm) or 3-lb. (1360 gm) trigger. Spare magazine, barrel weight, tools supplied. Imported from Germany by Nygord Precision Products.

Price: GSP, with case $1,495.00
Price: GSP-C, with case $1,595.00

Handguns — Double Action Revolvers, Service & Sport

Includes models suitable for hunting and competitive courses of fire, both police and international.

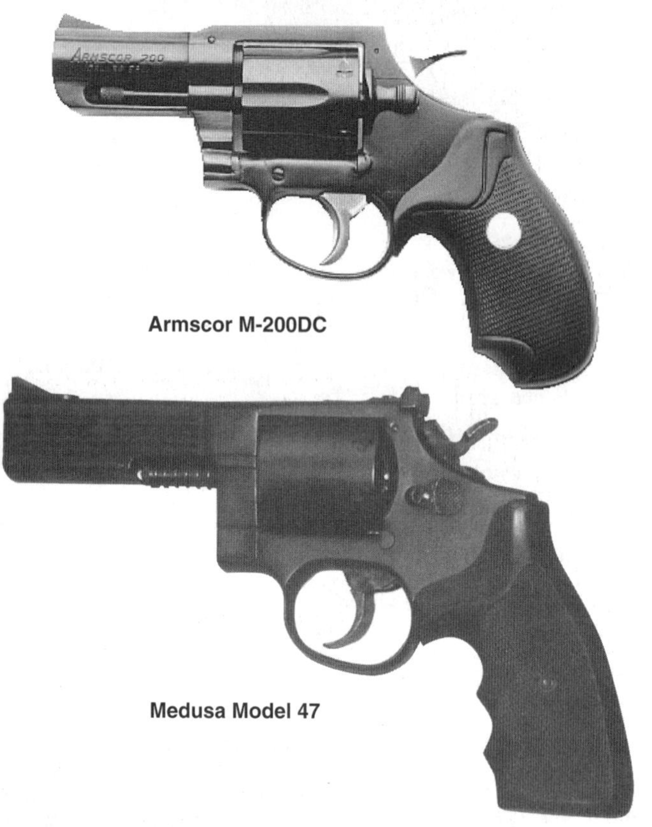

Armscor M-200DC

Medusa Model 47

Ruger GP161

ARMSCOR M-200DC REVOLVER

Caliber: 38 Spec., 6-shot cylinder. **Barrel:** 2-1/2", 4". **Weight:** 22 oz. (2-1/2" barrel). **Length:** 7-3/8" overall (2-1/2" barrel). **Stocks:** Checkered rubber. **Sights:** Blade front, fixed notch rear. **Features:** All-steel construction; floating firing pin, transfer bar ignition; shrouded ejector rod; blue finish. Reintroduced 1996. Imported from the Philippines by K.B.I., Inc.

Price: 2-1/2" **$199.99**
Price: 4" **$205.00**

ARMSPORT MODEL 4540 REVOLVER

Caliber: 38 Special. **Barrel:** 4". **Weight:** 32 oz **Length:** 9" overall. **Sights:** Fixed rear, blade front. **Features:** Ventilated rib; blued finish. Imported from Argentina by Armsport Inc.

Price: **$140.00**

E.A.A. STANDARD GRADE REVOLVERS

Caliber: 38 Spec., 6-shot; 357 magnum, 6-shot. **Barrel:** 2", 4". **Weight:** 38 oz. (22 rimfire, 4"). **Length:** 8.8" overall (4" bbl.). **Stocks:** Rubber with finger grooves. **Sights:** Blade front, fixed or adjustable on rimfires; fixed only on 32, 38. **Features:** Swing-out cylinder; hammer block safety; blue finish. Introduced 1991. Imported from Germany by European American Armory.

Price: 38 Special 2" **$180.00**
Price: 38 Special, 4" **$199.00**
Price: 357 Magnum, 2" **$199.00**
Price: 357 Magnum, 4" **$233.00**

MEDUSA MODEL 47 REVOLVER

Caliber: Most 9mm, 38 and 357 caliber cartridges; 6-shot cylinder. **Barrel:** 2-1/2", 3", 4", 5", 6"; fluted. **Weight:** 39 oz. **Length:** 10" overall (4" barrel). **Stocks:** Gripper-style rubber. **Sights:** Changeable front blades, fully adjustable rear. **Features:** Patented extractor allows gun to chamber, fire and extract over 25 different cartridges in the .355 to .357 range, without half-moon clips. Steel frame and cylinder; match quality barrel. Matte blue finish. Introduced 1996. Made in U.S. by Phillips & Rogers, Inc.

Price: **$899.00**

ROSSI MODEL 351/352 REVOLVERS

Caliber: 38 Special, 5-shot. **Barrel:** 2". **Weight:** 24 oz. **Length:** 6-1/2" overall. **Grips:** Rubber. **Sights:** Blade front, fixed rear. **Features:** Patented key-lock Taurus Security System; forged steel frame handles +P ammunition. Introduced 2001. Imported by BrazTech/Taurus.

Price: Model 351 (blued finish) **$298.00**
Price: Model 352 (stainless finish) **$345.00**

ROSSI MODEL 461/462 REVOLVERS

Caliber: 357 Magnum, 6-shot. **Barrel:** 2". **Weight:** 26 oz. **Length:** 6-1/2" overall. **Grips:** Rubber. **Sights:** Blade front, low-profile fixed rear. **Features:** Patented key-lock Taurus Security System; forged steel frame handles +P ammunition. Introduced 2001. Imported by BrazTech/Taurus.

Price: Model 461 (blued finish) **$298.00**
Price: Model 462 (stainless finish) **$345.00**

ROSSI MODEL 971/972 REVOLVERS

Caliber: 357 Magnum, 6-shot. **Barrel:** 4" or 6". **Weight:** NA. **Length:** 8-1/2" or 10-1/2" overall. **Grips:** Rubber. **Sights:** Red ramp front, adjustable rear. **Features:** Patented key-lock Taurus Security System; forged steel frame handles +P ammunition. Introduced 2001. Imported by BrazTech/Taurus.

Price: Model 971 (blued finish, 4" barrel) **$345.00**
Price: Model 972 (stainless steel finish, 6" barrel) **$391.00**

Rossi Model 851

Similar to the Model 971/972 except chambered for 38 Special. Blued finish, 4" barrel. Introduced 2001. From BrazTech/Taurus.

Price: **$298.00**

RUGER GP-100 REVOLVERS

Caliber: 38 Spec., 357 Mag., 6-shot. **Barrel:** 3", 3" full shroud, 4", 4" full shroud, 6", 6" full shroud. **Weight:** 3" barrel—35 oz., 3" full shroud—36 oz., 4" barrel—37 oz., 4" full shroud—38 oz. **Sights:** Fixed; adjustable on 4" full shroud and all 6" barrels. **Stocks:** Ruger Santoprene Cushioned Grip with Goncalo Alves inserts. **Features:** Uses action and frame incorporating improvements and features of both the Security-Six and Redhawk revolvers. Full length and short ejector shroud. Satin blue and stainless steel.

Price: GP-141 (357, 4" full shroud, adj. sights, blue) **$475.00**
Price: GP-160 (357, 6", adj. sights, blue) **$475.00**
Price: GP-161 (357, 6" full shroud, adj. sights, blue), 46 oz. **$475.00**
Price: GPF-331 (357, 3" full shroud) **$465.00**
Price: GPF-340 (357, 4") **$465.00**
Price: GPF-341 (357, 4" full shroud) **$465.00**
Price: KGP-141 (357, 4" full shroud, adj. sights, stainless) **$515.00**
Price: KGP-160 (357, 6", adj. sights, stainless), 43 oz. **$515.00**
Price: KGP-161 (357, 6" full shroud, adj. sights, stainless) 46 oz. **$515.00**
Price: KGPF-330 (357, 3", stainless) **$499.00**
Price: KGPF-331 (357, 3" full shroud, stainless) **$499.00**
Price: KGPF-340 (357, 4", stainless), KGPF-840 (38 Spec.) **$499.00**
Price: KGPF-341 (357, 4" full shroud, stainless) **$499.00**

HANDGUNS — DOUBLE ACTION REVOLVERS, SERVICE & SPORT

Ruger KSP-821

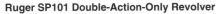

Ruger KSRH-7

Smith & Wesson Model 10

Smith & Wesson Model 14

Ruger SP101 Double-Action-Only Revolver

Similar to the standard SP101 except is double-action-only with no single-action sear notch. Has spurless hammer for snag-free handling, floating firing pin and Ruger's patented transfer bar safety system. Available with 2-1/4" barrel in 357 Magnum. Weighs 25-1/2 oz., overall length 7.06". Natural brushed satin or high-polish stainless steel. Introduced 1993.

Price: KSP321XL (357 Mag.) **$458.00**

RUGER SP101 REVOLVERS

Caliber: 22 LR, 32 H&R Mag., 6-shot; 38 Spec. +P, 357 Mag., 5-shot. **Barrel:** 2-1/4", 3-1/16", 4". **Weight:** (38 & 357 mag models) 2-1/4"—25 oz.; 3-1/16"—27 oz. **Sights:** Adjustable on 22, 32, fixed on others. **Stocks:** Ruger Santoprene Cushioned Grip with Xenoy inserts. **Features:** Incorporates improvements and features found in the GP-100 revolvers into a compact, small frame, double-action revolver. Full-length ejector shroud. Stainless steel only. Introduced 1988.

Price: KSP-821X (2-1/2", 38 Spec.) **$458.00**
Price: KSP-831X (3-1/16", 38 Spec.) **$458.00**
Price: KSP-221X (2-1/4", 22 LR), 32 oz. **$458.00**
Price: KSP-240X (4", 22 LR), 33 oz. **$458.00**
Price: KSP-241X (4" heavy bbl., 22 LR), 34 oz. **$458.00**
Price: KSP-3231X (3-1/16", 32 H&R), 30 oz. **$458.00**
Price: KSP-321X (2-1/4", 357 Mag.). **$458.00**
Price: KSP331X (3-1/16", 357 Mag.) **$458.00**

RUGER REDHAWK

Caliber: 44 Rem. Mag., 45 Colt, 6-shot. **Barrel:** 5-1/2", 7-1/2". **Weight:** About 54 oz. (7-1/2" bbl.). **Length:** 13" overall (7-1/2" barrel). **Stocks:** Square butt Goncalo Alves. **Sights:** Interchangeable Patridge-type front, rear adjustable for windage and elevation. **Features:** Stainless steel, brushed satin finish, or blued ordnance steel. Has a 9-1/2" sight radius. Introduced 1979.

Price: Blued, 44 Mag., 5-1/2" RH-445, 7-1/2" RH-44 . . . . **$560.00**
Price: Blued, 44 Mag., 7-1/2" RH44R, with scope mount, rings . . **$595.00**
Price: Stainless, 44 Mag., 5-1/2", 7-1/2" KRH-445. . . . . **$615.00**
Price: Stainless, 44 Mag., 7-1/2", with scope mount, rings KRH-44. . . . . **$615.00**
Price: Stainless, 45 Colt, 5-1/2", 7-1/2" KRH-455 . . . . **$615.00**
Price: Stainless, 45 Colt, 7-1/2", with scope mount KRH-45 . . . . **$615.00**

Ruger Super Redhawk Revolver

Similar to the standard Redhawk except has a heavy extended frame with the Ruger Integral Scope Mounting System on the wide topstrap. Also available in 454 Casull and new 480 Ruger. The wide hammer spur has been lowered for better scope clearance. Incorporates the mechanical design features and improvements of the GP-100. Choice of 7-1/2" or 9-1/2" barrel, both with ramp front sight base with Redhawk-style Interchangeable Insert sight blades, adjustable rear sight. Comes with Ruger "Cushioned Grip" panels of Santoprene with Goncalo Alves wood panels. Satin stainless steel. Introduced 1987.

Price: KSRH-7 (7-1/2"), KSRH-9 (9-1/2"). **$650.00**
Price: KSRH-7454 (7-1/2") 454 Casull. **$745.00**
New! **Price:** KSRH-7480 (7-1/2") 480 Ruger **$745.00**
New! **Price:** KSRH-9480 (9-1/2") 480 Ruger **$745.00**

Ruger Super Redhawk 454 Casull Revolver

Similar to the Ruger Super Redhawk except chambered for 454 Casull (also accepts 45 Colt cartridges). Unfluted cylinder, 7" barrel, weighs 53 ounces. Comes with 1" stainless scope rings. Introduced 2000.

Price: (Target gray stainless steel finish) **$745.00**

SMITH & WESSON MODEL 10 M&P HB REVOLVER

Caliber: 38 Spec., 6-shot. **Barrel:** 4". **Weight:** 33.5 oz. **Length:** 9-5/16" overall. **Stocks:** Uncle Mike's Combat soft rubber; square butt. **Sights:** Fixed; ramp front, square notch rear.

Price: Blue **$458.00**

SMITH & WESSON MODEL 14 FULL LUG REVOLVER

Caliber: 38 Spec., 6-shot. **Barrel:** 6", full lug. **Weight:** 47 oz. **Length:** 11-1/8" overall. **Stocks:** Hogue soft rubber. **Sights:** Pinned Patridge front, adjustable micrometer click rear. **Features:** Has .500" target hammer, .312" smooth combat trigger. Polished blue finish. Reintroduced 1991. Limited production.

Price: **$498.00**

Smith & Wesson Model 19

Smith & Wesson Model 36LS

Smith & Wesson Model 629 Classic DX

Smith & Wesson Model 65LS

SMITH & WESSON MODEL 15 COMBAT MASTERPIECE

Caliber: 38 Spec., 6-shot. **Barrel:** 4". **Weight:** 32 oz. **Length:** 9-5/16" (4" bbl.). **Stocks:** Uncle Mike's Combat soft rubber. **Sights:** Serrated ramp front, micro-click rear adjustable for windage and elevation.

Price: Blued **$450.00**

SMITH & WESSON MODEL 19 COMBAT MAGNUM

Caliber: 357 Mag. and 38 Spec., 6-shot. **Barrel:** 4". **Weight:** 36 oz. **Length:** 9-9/16" (4" bbl.). **Stocks:** Uncle Mike's Combat soft rubber; wood optional. **Sights:** Red ramp front, micro-click rear adjustable for windage and elevation.

Price: 4" **$457.00**

SMITH & WESSON MODEL 629 REVOLVERS

Caliber: 44 Magnum, 6-shot. **Barrel:** 5", 6", 8-3/8". **Weight:** 47 oz. (6" bbl.). **Length:** 11-3/8" overall (6" bbl.). **Stocks:** Soft rubber; wood optional. **Sights:** 1/8" red ramp front, micro-click rear, adjustable for windage and elevation.

Price: Model 629 (stainless steel), 5" **$625.00**

Price: Model 629, 6" **$631.00**

Price: Model 629, 8-3/8" barrel **$646.00**

Smith & Wesson Model 629 Classic Revolver

Similar to the standard Model 629 except has full-lug 5", 6-1/2" or 8-3/8" barrel; chamfered front of cylinder; interchangeable red ramp front sight with adjustable white outline rear; Hogue grips with S&W monogram; the frame is drilled and tapped for scope mounting. Factory accurizing and endurance packages. Overall length with 5" barrel is 10-1/2"; weighs 51 oz. Introduced 1990.

Price: Model 629 Classic (stainless), 5", 6-1/2" **$670.00**

Price: As above, 8-3/8" **$691.00**

Smith & Wesson Model 629 Classic DX Revolver

Similar to the Model 629 Classic except offered only with 6-1/2" or 8-3/8" full-lug barrel; comes with five front **sights:** red ramp; black Patridge; black Patridge with gold bead; black ramp; and black Patridge with white dot. Comes with Hogue combat-style and wood round butt grip. Introduced 1991.

Price: Model 629 Classic DX, 6-1/2" **$860.00**

Price: As above, 8-3/8" **$888.00**

SMITH & WESSON MODEL 36, 37 CHIEF'S SPECIAL & AIRWEIGHT

Caliber: 38 Spec.+P, 5-shot. **Barrel:** 1-7/8". **Weight:** 19-1/2 oz. (2" bbl.); 13-1/2 oz. (Airweight). **Length:** 6-1/2" (round butt). **Stocks:** Round butt soft rubber. **Sights:** Fixed, serrated ramp front, square notch rear.

Price: Blue, standard Model 36 . . . . **$406.00**

Price: Blue, Airweight Model 37 . . . . **$483.00**

Smith & Wesson Model 36LS, 60LS LadySmith

Similar to the standard Model 36. Available with 1-7/8" barrel, 38 Special. Comes with smooth, contoured rosewood grips with the S&W monogram. Has a speedloader cutout. Comes in a fitted carry/storage case. Introduced 1989.

Price: Model 36LS **$478.00**

Price: Model 60LS, as above except in stainless, 357 Magnum . **$539.00**

SMITH & WESSON MODEL 60 357 MAGNUM

Caliber: 357 Magnum, 5-shot. **Barrel:** 2-1/8" or 3". **Weight:** 24 oz. **Length:** 7-1/2 overall (3" barrel). **Stocks:** Uncle Mike's Combat. **Sights:** Fixed, serrated ramp front, square notch rear. **Features:** Stainless steel construction. Made in U.S. by Smith & Wesson.

Price: 2-1/8" barrel **$505.00**

Price: 3" barrel **$536.00**

SMITH & WESSON MODEL 65

Caliber: 357 Mag. and 38 Spec., 6-shot. **Barrel:** 3", 4". **Weight:** 34 oz. **Length:** 9-5/16" overall (4" bbl.). **Stocks:** Uncle Mike's Combat. **Sights:** 1/8" serrated ramp front, fixed square notch rear. **Features:** Heavy barrel. Stainless steel construction.

Price: **$501.00**

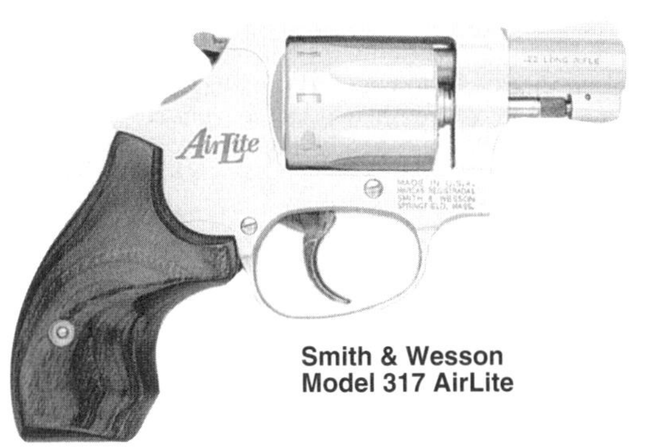

Smith & Wesson Model 317 AirLite

Smith & Wesson Model 625

Smith & Wesson Model 586, 686 Distinguished Combat

SMITH & WESSON MODEL 317 AIRLITE, 317 LADYSMITH REVOLVERS

Caliber: 22 LR, 8-shot. **Barrel:** 1-7/8" 3". **Weight:** 9.9 oz. **Length:** 6-3/16" overall. **Stocks:** Dymondwood Boot or Uncle Mike's Boot. **Sights:** Serrated ramp front, fixed notch rear. **Features:** Aluminum alloy, carbon and stainless steels, and titanium construction. Short spur hammer, smooth combat trigger. Clear Cote finish. Introduced 1997. Made in U.S. by Smith & Wesson.

Price: With Uncle Mike's Boot grip **$508.00**
Price: With DymondWood Boot grip, 3" barrel **$537.00**
Price: Model 317 LadySmith (DymondWood only, comes with display case) **$568.00**

Smith & Wesson Model 637 Airweight Revolver

Similar to the Model 37 Airweight except has alloy frame, stainless steel barrel, cylinder and yoke; rated for 38 Spec. +P; Uncle Mike's Boot Grip. Weighs 15 oz. Introduced 1996. Made in U.S. by Smith & Wesson.

Price: **$459.00**

SMITH & WESSON MODEL 64 STAINLESS M&P

Caliber: 38 Spec., 6-shot. **Barrel:** 2", 3", 4". **Weight:** 34 oz. **Length:** 9-5/16" overall. **Stocks:** Soft rubber. **Sights:** Fixed, 1/8" serrated ramp front, square notch rear. **Features:** Satin finished stainless steel, square butt.

Price: 2" **$487.00**
Price: 3", 4". **$496.00**

SMITH & WESSON MODEL 65LS LADYSMITH

Caliber: 357 Magnum, 6-shot. **Barrel:** 3". **Weight:** 31 oz. **Length:** 7.94" overall. **Stocks:** Rosewood, round butt. **Sights:** Serrated ramp front, fixed notch rear. **Features:** Stainless steel with frosted finish. Smooth combat trigger, service hammer, shrouded ejector rod. Comes with case. Introduced 1992.

Price: **$539.00**

SMITH & WESSON MODEL 66 STAINLESS COMBAT MAGNUM

Caliber: 357 Mag. and 38 Spec., 6-shot. **Barrel:** 2-1/2", 4", 6". **Weight:** 36 oz. (4" barrel). **Length:** 9-9/16" overall. **Stocks:** Soft rubber. **Sights:** Red ramp front, micro-click rear adjustable for windage and elevation. **Features:** Satin finish stainless steel.

Price: 2-1/2" **$545.00**
Price: 4", 6". **$551.00**

SMITH & WESSON MODEL 67 COMBAT MASTERPIECE

Caliber: 38 Special, 6-shot. **Barrel:** 4". **Weight:** 32 oz. **Length:** 9-5/16" overall. **Stocks:** Soft rubber. **Sights:** Red ramp front, micro-click rear adjustable for windage and elevation. **Features:** Stainless steel with satin finish. Smooth combat trigger, semi-target hammer. Introduced 1994.

Price: **$546.00**

SMITH & WESSON MODEL 242 AIRLITE Ti REVOLVER

Caliber: 38 Special, 7-shot. **Barrel:** 2-1/2". **Weight:** 18.9 oz. **Length:** 7-3/8" overall. **Stocks:** Uncle Mike's Boot grip. **Sights:** Serrated ramp front, fixed notch rear. **Features:** Alloy frame, yoke and barrel shroud; titanium cylinder; stainless barrel insert. Medium L-frame size. Introduced 1999. Made in U.S. by Smith & Wesson.

Price: **$658.00**

SMITH & WESSON MODEL 296 AIRLITE Ti REVOLVER

Caliber: 44 Spec. **Barrel:** 2-1/2". **Weight:** 18.9 oz. **Length:** 7-3/8" overall. **Stocks:** Uncle Mike's Boot grip. **Sights:** Serrated ramp front, fixed notch rear. **Features:** Alloy frame, yoke and barrel shroud; titanium cylinder; stainless steel barrel insert. Medium, L-frame size. Introduced 1999. Made in U.S. by Smith & Wesson.

Price: **$718.00**

SMITH & WESSON MODEL 586, 686 DISTINGUISHED COMBAT MAGNUMS

Caliber: 357 Magnum. **Barrel:** 4", 6" (M 586); 2-1/2", 4", 6", 8-3/8" (M 686). **Weight:** 46 oz. (6"), 41 oz. (4"). **Stocks:** Soft rubber. **Sights:** Red ramp front, S&W micrometer click rear. Drilled and tapped for scope mount. **Features:** Uses L-frame, but takes all K-frame grips. Full-length ejector rod shroud. Smooth combat-type trigger, semi-target type hammer. Also available in stainless as Model 686. Introduced 1981.

Price: Model 586, blue, 4", from **$494.00**
Price: Model 586, blue, 6" **$499.00**
Price: Model 686, 6", ported barrel. **$564.00**
Price: Model 686, 8-3/8". **$550.00**
Price: Model 686, 2-1/2". **$514.00**

Smith & Wesson Model 686 Magnum PLUS Revolver

Similar to the Model 686 except has 7-shot cylinder, 2-1/2", 4" or 6" barrel. Weighs 34-1/2 oz., overall length 7-1/2" (2-1/2" barrel). Hogue rubber grips. Introduced 1996. Made in U.S. by Smith & Wesson.

Price: 2-1/2" barrel **$534.00**
Price: 4" barrel **$542.00**
Price: 6" barrel **$550.00**

SMITH & WESSON MODEL 625 REVOLVER

Caliber: 45 ACP, 6-shot. **Barrel:** 5". **Weight:** 46 oz. **Length:** 11.375" overall. **Stocks:** Soft rubber; wood optional. **Sights:** Patridge front on ramp, S&W micrometer click rear adjustable for windage and elevation. **Features:** Stainless steel construction with .400" semi-target hammer, .312" smooth combat trigger; full lug barrel. Introduced 1989.

Price: **$636.00**

Smith & Wesson Model 442

Smith & Wesson Model 649

SMITH & WESSON MODEL 640 CENTENNIAL

Caliber: 357 Mag., 5-shot. **Barrel:** 2-1/8". **Weight:** 25 oz. **Length:** 6-3/4" overall. **Stocks:** Uncle Mike's Boot Grip. **Sights:** Serrated ramp front, fixed notch rear. **Features:** Stainless steel. Fully concealed hammer, snag-proof smooth edges. Introduced 1995 in 357 Magnum.

Price: **$502.00**

SMITH & WESSON MODEL 617 FULL LUG REVOLVER

Caliber: 22 LR, 6- or 10-shot. **Barrel:** 4", 6", 8-3/8". **Weight:** 42 oz. (4" barrel). **Length:** NA. **Stocks:** Soft rubber. **Sights:** Patridge front, adjustable rear. Drilled and tapped for scope mount. **Features:** Stainless steel with satin finish; 4" has .312" smooth trigger, .375" semi-target hammer; 6" has either .312" combat or .400" serrated trigger, .375" semi-target or .500" target hammer; 8-3/8" with .400" serrated trigger, .500" target hammer. Introduced 1990.

Price: 4" **$534.00**
Price: 6", target hammer, target trigger **$524.00**
Price: 6", 10-shot **$566.00**
Price: 8-3/8", 10 shot **$578.00**

SMITH & WESSON MODEL 610 CLASSIC HUNTER REVOLVER

Caliber: 10mm, 6-shot cylinder. **Barrel:** 6-1/2" full lug. **Weight:** 52 oz. **Length:** 12" overall. **Stocks:** Hogue rubber combat. **Sights:** Interchangeable blade front, micro-click rear adjustable for windage and elevation. **Features:** Stainless steel construction; target hammer, target trigger; unfluted cylinder; drilled and tapped for scope mounting. Introduced 1998.

Price: **$684.00**

SMITH & WESSON MODEL 331, 332 AIRLITE Ti REVOLVERS

Caliber: 32 H&R Mag., 6-shot. **Barrel:** 1-7/8". **Weight:** 11.2 oz. (with wood grip). **Length:** 6-15/16" overall. **Stocks:** Uncle Mike's Boot or Dymondwood Boot. **Sights:** Black serrated ramp front, fixed notch rear. **Features:** Aluminum alloy frame, barrel shroud and yoke; titanium cylinder; stainless steel barrel liner. Matte finish. Introduced 1999. Made in U.S. by Smith & Wesson.

Price: Model 331 Chiefs **$682.00**
Price: Model 332 .... **$699.00**

SMITH & WESSON MODEL 337 CHIEFS SPECIAL AIRLITE Ti

Caliber: 38 Spec., 5-shot. **Barrel:** 1-7/8". **Weight:** 11.2 oz. (Dymondwood grips). **Length:** 6-5/16" overall. **Stocks:** Uncle Mike's Boot or Dymondwood Boot. **Sights:** Black serrated front, fixed notch rear. **Features:** Aluminum alloy frame, barrel shroud and yoke; titanium cylinder; stainless steel barrel liner. Matte finish. Introduced 1999. Made in U.S. by Smith & Wesson.

Price: **$682.00**

SMITH & WESSON MODEL 342 CENTENNIAL AIRLITE Ti

Caliber: 38 Spec., 5-shot. **Barrel:** 1-7/8". **Weight:** 11.3 oz. (Dymondwood stocks). **Length:** 6-15/16" overall. **Stocks:** Uncle Mike's Boot or Dymondwood Boot. **Sights:** Black serrated ramp front, fixed notch rear. **Features:** Aluminum alloy frame, barrel shroud and yoke; titanium cylinder; stainless steel barrel liner. Shrouded hammer. Matte finish. Introduced 1999. Made in U.S. by Smith & Wesson.

Price: **$699.00**

Smith & Wesson Model 442 Centennial Airweight

Similar to the Model 640 Centennial except has alloy frame giving weight of 15.8 oz. Chambered for 38 Special, 1-7/8" carbon steel barrel; carbon steel cylinder; concealed hammer; Uncle Mike's Boot grip. Fixed square notch rear sight, serrated ramp front. Introduced 1993.

Price: Blue **$459.00**

SMITH & WESSON MODEL 638 AIRWEIGHT BODYGUARD

Caliber: 38 Spec., 5-shot. **Barrel:** 1-7/8". **Weight:** 15 oz. **Length:** 6-15/16" overall. **Stocks:** Uncle Mike's Boot grip. **Sights:** Serrated ramp front, fixed notch rear. **Features:** Alloy frame, stainless cylinder and barrel; shrouded hammer. Introduced 1997. Made in U.S. by Smith & Wesson.

Price: With Uncle Mike's Boot grip **$492.00**

Smith & Wesson Model 642 Airweight Revolver

Similar to the Model 442 Centennial Airweight except has stainless steel barrel, cylinder and yoke with matte finish; Uncle Mike's Boot Grip; weighs 15.8 oz. Introduced 1996. Made in U.S. by Smith & Wesson.

Price: **$474.00**

Smith & Wesson Model 642LS LadySmith Revolver

Same as the Model 642 except has smooth combat wood grips, and comes with case; aluminum alloy frame, stainless cylinder, barrel and yoke; frosted matte finish. Weighs 15.8 oz. Introduced 1996. Made in U.S. by Smith & Wesson.

Price: **$505.00**

SMITH & WESSON MODEL 649 BODYGUARD REVOLVER

Caliber: 357 Mag., 5-shot. **Barrel:** 2-1/8". **Weight:** 20 oz. **Length:** 6-5/16" overall. **Stocks:** Uncle Mike's Combat. **Sights:** Black pinned ramp front, fixed notch rear. **Features:** Stainless steel construction; shrouded hammer; smooth combat trigger. Made in U.S. by Smith & Wesson.

Price: **$502.00**

SMITH & WESSON MODEL 657 REVOLVER

Caliber: 41 Mag., 6-shot. **Barrel:** 6". **Weight:** 48 oz. **Length:** 11-3/8" overall. **Stocks:** Soft rubber. **Sights:** Pinned 1/8" red ramp front, micro-click rear adjustable for windage and elevation. **Features:** Stainless steel construction.

Price: **$564.00**

SMITH & WESSON MODEL 696 REVOLVER

Caliber: 44 Spec., 5-shot. **Barrel:** 3". **Weight:** 35.5 oz. **Length:** 8-1/4" overall. **Stocks:** Uncle Mike's Combat. **Sights:** Red ramp front, click adjustable white outline rear. **Features:** Stainless steel construction; round butt frame; satin finish. Introduced 1997. Made in U.S. by Smith & Wesson.

Price: **$525.00**

TAURUS MODEL 65 REVOLVER

Caliber: 357 Mag., 6-shot. **Barrel:** 4". **Weight:** 38 oz. **Length:** 10-1/2" overall. **Stocks:** Soft rubber. **Sights:** Serrated front, notch rear. **Features:** Solid rib barrel; +P rated. Integral key-lock action. Imported by Taurus International.

Price: Blue **$345.00**
Price: Stainless....................................... **$395.00**

Smith & Wesson Model 696

Taurus Model 85

Taurus Model 85Ti/731Ti

Taurus Model 85CH

Taurus Model 82

Taurus Model 66 Revolver

Same to the Model 65 except with 4" or 6" barrel, 7-shot cylinder, adjustable rear sight. Integral key-lock action. Imported by Taurus International.

Price: Blue **$395.00**
Price: Stainless. **$435.00**

NEW! **Taurus Model 66 Silhouette Revolver**

Similar to the Model 66 except has a 12" barrel with scope mount, 7-shot cylinder, adjustable rear sight. Integral key-lock action, blue or matte stainless steel finish and rubber grips. Introduced 2001. Imported by Taurus International.

Price: . . . . **$414.00 to $461.00**

TAURUS MODEL 82 HEAVY BARREL REVOLVER

Caliber: 38 Spec., 6-shot. **Barrel:** 4", heavy. **Weight:** 34 oz. (4" bbl.). **Length:** 9-1/4" overall (4" bbl.). **Stocks:** Soft black rubber. **Sights:** Serrated ramp front, square notch rear. **Features:** Imported by Taurus International.

Price: Blue **$325.00**
Price: Polished, stainless **$375.00**

TAURUS MODEL 85 REVOLVER

Caliber: 38 Spec., 5-shot. **Barrel:** 2", 3". **Weight:** 21 oz. **Stocks:** Rubber, rosewood or mother-of-pearl. **Sights:** Ramp front, square notch rear. **Features:** Blue, matte, polished stainless steel, blue with gold accents, pearl and blue with gold accents; heavy barrel; rated for +P ammo. Introduced 1980. Imported by Taurus International.

Price: Blue, 2", 3" **$345.00**
Price: Stainless steel **$395.00**
Price: Blue, 2", ported barrel **$360.00**
Price: Stainless, 2", ported barrel. **$405.00**
Price: Blue, Ultra-Lite (17 oz.), 2". **$375.00**
Price: Stainless, Ultra-Lite (17 oz.), 2", ported barrel **$425.00**
Price: Blue with gold trim, ported, rosewood grips **$380.00**

Taurus Model 85UL/Ti Revolver

Similar to the Model 85 except has titanium cylinder, aluminum alloy frame, and ported aluminum barrel with stainless steel sleeve. Weight is 13.5 oz. International.

Price: **$515.00**

Taurus Model 85Ti Revolver

Similar to the 2" Model 85 except has titanium frame, cylinder and ported barrel with stainless steel liner; yoke detent and extended ejector rod. Weight is 15.4 oz. Comes with soft, ridged Ribber grips. Available in Bright and Matte Spectrum blue, Matte Spectrum gold, and Shadow Gray colors. Introduced 1999. Imported by Taurus International.

Price: Model 85Ti **$530.00**

Taurus Model 85CH Revolver

Same as the Model 85 except has 2" barrel only and concealed hammer. Double aciton only. Soft rubber boot grip. Introduced 1991. Imported by Taurus International.

Price: Blue **$345.00**
Price: Stainless. **$395.00**
Price: Blue, ported barrel **$360.00**
Price: Stainless, ported barrel **$405.00**

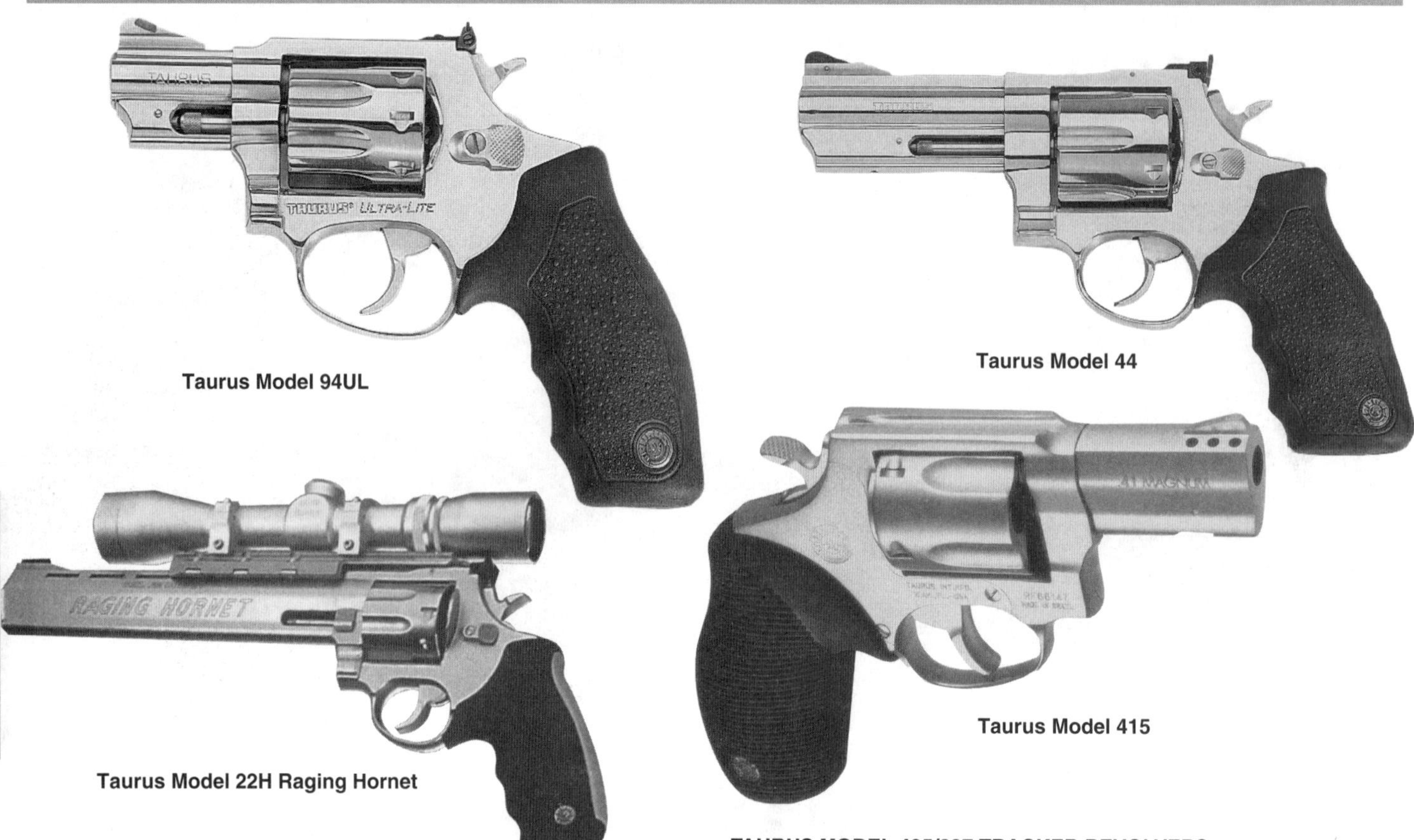

Taurus Model 94UL

Taurus Model 44

Taurus Model 415

Taurus Model 22H Raging Hornet

TAURUS MODEL 94 REVOLVER

Caliber: 22 LR, 9-shot cylinder. **Barrel:** 2", 4", 5". **Weight:** 25 oz. **Stocks:** Soft black rubber. **Sights:** Serrated ramp front, click-adjustable rear for windage and elevation. **Features:** Floating firing pin, color case-hardened hammer and trigger. Introduced 1989. Imported by Taurus International.

Price: Blue **$325.00**
Price: Stainless. **$375.00**
Price: Model 94 UL, blue, 2", fixed sight, weighs 14 oz. **$365.00**
Price: As above, stainless **$410.00**

TAURUS MODEL 22H RAGING HORNET REVOLVER

Caliber: 22 Hornet, 8-shot cylinder. **Barrel:** 10". **Weight:** 50 oz. **Length:** 6.5" overall. **Stocks:** Soft black rubber. **Sights:** Patridge front, micrometer click adjustable rear. **Features:** Ventilated rib; 1:10: twist rifling; comes with scope base; stainless steel construction with matte finish. Introduced 1999. Imported by Taurus International.

Price: **$898.00**

TAURUS MODEL 44 REVOLVER

Caliber: 44 Mag., 6-shot. **Barrel:** 4", 6-1/2", 8-3/8". **Weight:** 44-3/4 oz. (4" barrel). **Length:** NA. **Stocks:** Soft black rubber. **Sights:** Serrated ramp front, micro-click rear adjustable for windage and elevation. **Features:** Heavy solid rib on 4", vent rib on 6-1/2", 8-3/8". Compensated barrel. Blued model has color case-hardened hammer and trigger, integral key-lock action. Introduced 1994. Imported by Taurus International.

Price: Blue, 4". **$500.00**
Price: Blue, 6-1/2", 8-3/8" **$525.00**
Price: Stainless, 4" **$565.00**
Price: Stainless, 6-1/2", 8-3/8" **$573.00**

TAURUS MODEL 415 REVOLVER

Caliber: 41 Mag., 5-shot. **Barrel:** 2-1/2". **Weight:** 30 oz. **Length:** 7-1/8" overall. **Stocks:** Soft, ridged Ribber. **Sights:** Serrated front, notch rear. **Features:** Stainless steel construction; matte finish; ported barrel. Introduced 1999. Imported by Taurus International.

Price: **$475.00**

TAURUS MODEL 425/627 TRACKER REVOLVERS

Caliber: 357 Mag., 7-shot; 41 Mag., 5-shot. **Barrel:** 4" and 6". **Weight:** 24.3 oz. (titanium) to 40.0 oz. (6"). **Length:** 8-3/4" and 10-3/4" overall. **Grips:** Soft, ridged Ribber. **Sights:** Blade front, adjustable rear. **Features:** Stainless steel, Shadow Gray or Total Titanium; vent rib (steel models only); integral key-lock action. Imported by Taurus International.

Price: **$500.00**
Price: (Total Titanium). **$690.00**

TAURUS MODEL 445, 445CH REVOLVERS

Caliber: 44 Special, 5-shot. **Barrel:** 2". **Weight:** 28.25 oz. **Length:** 6-3/4" overall. **Stocks:** Soft black rubber. **Sights:** Serrated ramp front, notch rear. **Features:** Blue or stainless steel. Standard or concealed hammer. Introduced 1997. Imported by Taurus International.

Price: Blue **$345.00**
Price: Blue, ported **$360.00**
Price: Stainless. **$395.00**
Price: Stainless, ported **$400.00**
Price: M445CH, concealed hammer, blue, DAO **$345.00**
Price: M445CH, blue, ported **$360.00**
Price: M445CH, stainless. **$395.00**
Price: M445CH, stainless, ported. **$400.00**
Price: M445CH, Ultra-Lite, stainless, ported **$500.00**

TAURUS MODEL 605 REVOLVER

Caliber: 357 Mag., 5-shot. **Barrel:** 2-1/4", 3". **Weight:** 24.5 oz. **Length:** NA. **Stocks:** Soft black rubber. **Sights:** Serrated ramp front, fixed notch rear. **Features:** Heavy, solid rib barrel; floating firing pin. Blue or stainless. Introduced 1995. Imported by Taurus International.

Price: Blue **$345.00**
Price: Stainless. **$395.00**
Price: Model 605CH (concealed hammer) 2-1/4", blue, DAO . . . **$345.00**
Price: Model 605CH, stainless, 2-1/4" **$395.00**
Price: Blue, 2-1/4", ported barrel **$360.00**
Price: Stainless, 2-1/4", ported barrel. **$405.00**
Price: Blue, 2-1/4", ported barrel, concealed hammer, DAO **$360.00**
Price: Stainless, 2-1/4", ported barrel, concealed hammer, DAO. **$405.00**

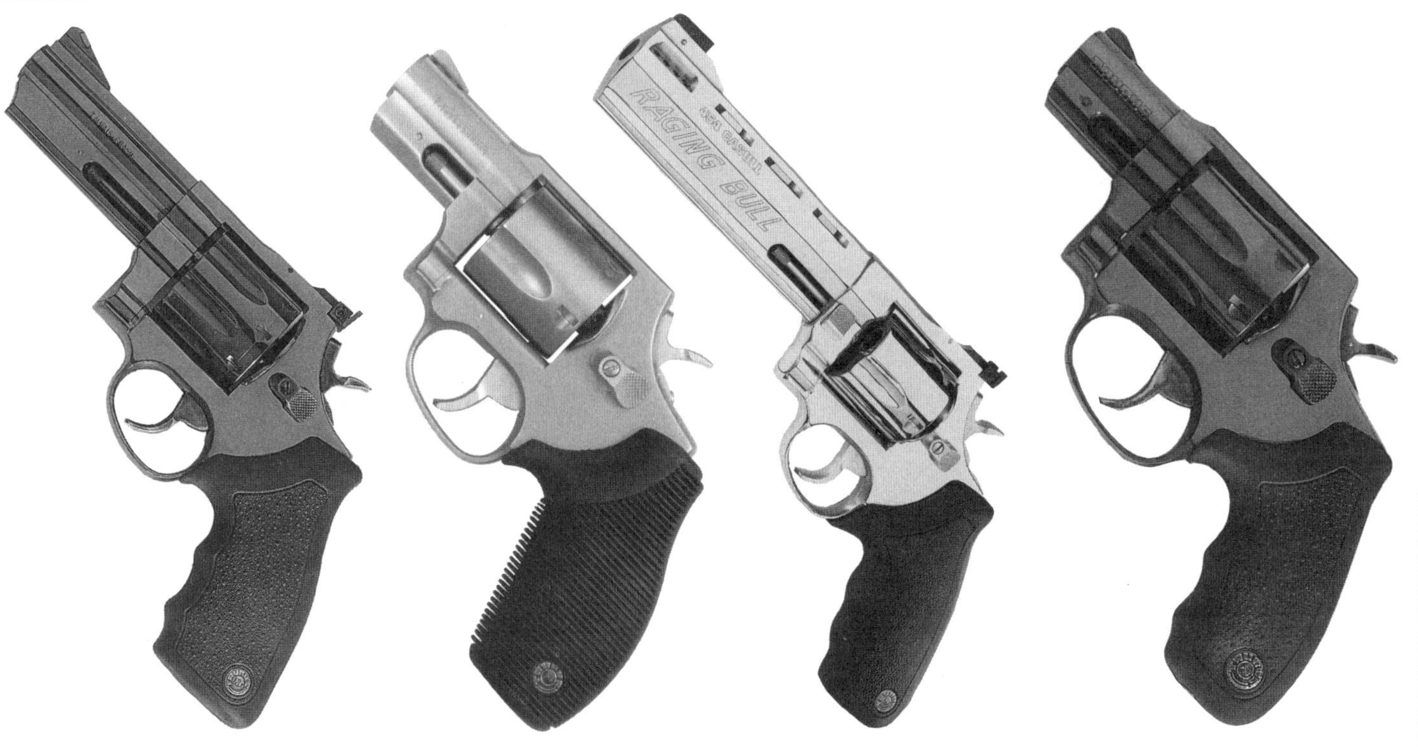

Taurus Model 608 | Taurus Model 450 | Taurus Model 454 Raging Bull | Taurus Model 817

TAURUS MODEL 608 REVOLVER

Caliber: 357 Mag., 8-shot. **Barrel:** 4", 6-1/2", 8-3/8". **Weight:** 44 oz. **Length:** 9-3/8" overall. **Grips:** Soft black rubber. **Sights:** Serrated ramp front, fully adjustable rear. **Features:** Built-in compensator, integral key-lock action. Available in blue or stainless. Introduced 1995. Imported by Taurus International.

Price: Blue, 4", solid rib **$445.00**
Price: Blue, 6-1/2", 8-3/8", vent rib **$465.00**
Price: Stainless, 4", solid rib **$510.00**
Price: Stainless, 6-1/2", 8-3/8", vent rib **$525.00**

TAURUS MODEL 650CIA REVOLVER

Caliber: 357 Magnum, 5-shot. **Barrel:** 2". **Weight:** NA. **Length:** NA. **Grips:** Rubber. **Sights:** Ramp front, square notch rear. **Features:** Double-action only; blue or matte stainless steel; rated for +P ammo; integral key-lock action. Introduced 2001. From Taurus International.

Price: . . . . . **$375.00 to $422.00**

TAURUS MODEL 450 REVOLVER

Caliber: 45 Colt, 5-shot cylinder. **Barrel:** 2". **Weight:** 28 oz. **Length:** 6-5/8" overall. **Stocks:** Soft, ridged rubber. **Sights:** Serrated front, notch rear. **Features:** Stainless steel construction; ported barrel. Introduced 1999. Imported by Taurus International.

Price: **$470.00**
Price: Ultra-Lite (alloy frame) **$525.00**

TAURUS MODEL 444/454/480 RAGING BULL REVOLVERS

Caliber: 454 Casull, 5-shot (also fires 45 Colt). **Barrel:** 5", 6-1/2", 8-3/8". **Weight:** 53 oz. (6-1/2" barrel). **Length:** 12" overall (6-1/2" barrel). **Stocks:** Soft black rubber. **Sights:** Patridge front, micrometer click adjustable rear. **Features:** Ventilated rib; integral compensating system. Introduced 1997. Imported by Taurus International.

Price: 6-1/2", 8-3/8", blue **$785.00**
Price: 6-1/2", polished, stainless **$855.00**
Price: 5", 6-1/2", 8-3/8", matte stainless **$855.00**
Price: Model 444 (44 Mag.), blue, 6-1/2", 8-3/8", 6-shot **$575.00**
Price: Model 444, matte, stainless, 6-1/2", 8-3/8" **$630.00**
New! **Price:** Model 480 (480 Ruger), 5-shot **$855.00**

TAURUS MODEL 617 REVOLVER

Caliber: 357 Magnum, 7-shot. **Barrel:** 2". **Weight:** 29 oz. **Length:** 6-3/4" overall. **Stocks:** Soft black rubber. **Sights:** Serrated ramp front, notch rear. **Features:** Heavy, solid barrel rib, ejector shroud. Available with porting, concealed hammer. Introduced 1998. Imported by Taurus International.

Price: Blue, regular or concealed hammer **$375.00**
Price: Stainless, regular or concealed hammer **$420.00**
Price: Blue, ported **$395.00**
Price: Stainless, ported **$440.00**
Price: Blue, concealed hammer, ported **$395.00**
Price: Stainless, concealed hammer, ported **$440.00**

Taurus Model 415Ti, 445Ti, 450Ti, 617Ti Revolvers

Similar to the Model 617 except has titanium frame, cylinder, and ported barrel with stainless steel liner; yoke detent and extended ejector rod; +P rated; ridged Ribber grips. Available in Bright and Matte Spectrum Blue, Matte Spectrum Gold, and Shadow Gray. Introduced 1999. Imported by Taurus International.

Price: Model 617Ti, (357 Mag., 7-shot, 19.9 oz.) **$600.00**
Price: Model 415Ti (41 Mag., 5-shot, 20.9 oz.) **$600.00**
Price: Model 450Ti (45 Colt, 5-shot, 19.2 oz.) **$600.00**
Price: Model 445Ti (44 Spec., 5-shot, 19.8 oz.) **$600.00**

Taurus Model 617ULT Revolver

Similar to the Model 617 except has aluminum alloy and titanium components, matte stainless finish, integral key-lock action. Rated for +P ammo. Available ported or non-ported. Introduced 2001. Imported by Taurus International.

Price: (5-shot cylinder) . . . . . **$530.00 to $545.00**

TAURUS MODEL 817 ULTRA-LITE REVOLVER

Caliber: 38 Spec., 7-shot. **Barrel:** 2". **Weight:** 21 oz. **Length:** 6-1/2" overall. **Grips:** Soft rubber. **Sights:** Serrated front, notch rear. **Features:** Compact alloy frame. Introduced 1999. Imported by Taurus International.

Price: Blue **$375.00**
Price: Blue, ported **$395.00**
Price: Matte, stainless **$420.00**
Price: Matte, stainless, ported **$440.00**

Taurus Model 941

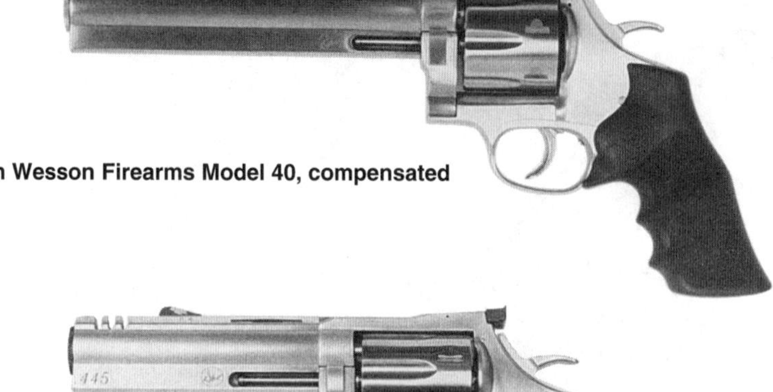

Dan Wesson Firearms Model 40, compensated

Dan Wesson Firearms Model 445 Supermag

TAURUS MODEL 850CIA REVOLVER

NEW! **Caliber:** 38 Special, 5-shot. **Barrel:** 2". **Weight:** NA. **Length:** NA. **Grips:** Rubber. **Sights:** Ramp front, square notch rear. **Features:** Double-action only; blue or matte stainless steel; rated for +P ammo; integral key-lock action. Introduced 2001. From Taurus International.

Price: .... **$375.00 to $422.00**
Price: Total Titanium model **$563.00**

TAURUS MODEL 941 REVOLVER

Caliber: 22 WMR, 8-shot. **Barrel:** 2", 4", 5". **Weight:** 27.5 oz. (4" barrel). **Length:** NA. **Grips:** Soft black rubber. **Sights:** Serrated ramp front, rear adjustable for windage and elevation. **Features:** Solid rib heavy barrel with full-length ejector rod shroud. Blue or stainless steel. Introduced 1992. Imported by Taurus International.

Price: Blue **$345.00**
Price: Stainless...................................... **$395.00**
Price: Model 941 Ultra Lite, blue, 2", fixed sight, weighs 8.5 oz. . . **$375.00**
Price: As above, stainless **$419.00**

TAURUS MODEL 970/971 TRACKER REVOLVERS

NEW! **Caliber:** 22 LR (Model 970), 22 WMR (Model 971); 7-shot. **Barrel:** 6". **Weight:** NA. **Length:** NA. **Grips:** Soft, black rubber. **Sights:** Blade front, adjustable rear. **Features:** Heavy barrel with ventilated rib; matte stainless finish. Introduced 2001. From Taurus International.

Price: **$855.00**

TAURUS MODEL 980/981 SILHOUETTE REVOLVERS

NEW! **Caliber:** 22 LR (Model 980), 22 WMR (Model 981); 7-shot. **Barrel:** 12". **Weight:** NA. **Length:** NA. **Grips:** Soft, black rubber. **Sights:** Blade front, adjustable rear. **Features:** Heavy barrel with ventilated rib and scope mount, matte stainless finish. Introduced 2001. From Taurus International.

Price: (Model 980) **$397.00**
Price: (Model 981) **$414.00**

DAN WESSON FIREARMS MODEL 722 SILHOUETTE REVOLVER

Caliber: 22 LR, 6-shot. **Barrel:** 10", vent heavy. **Weight:** 53 oz. **Stocks:** Combat style. **Sights:** Patridge-style front, .080" narrow notch rear. **Features:** Single action only. Satin brushed stainless finish. Reintroduced 1997. Made in U.S. by Dan Wesson Firearms.

Price: 722 VH10 (vent heavy 10" bbl.) **$888.00**
Price: 722 VH10 SRS1 (Super Ram Silhouette , Bo-Mar sights, front hood, trigger job)... **$1,164.00**

DAN WESSON FIREARMS MODEL 3220/73220 TARGET REVOLVER

Caliber: 32-20, 6-shot. **Barrel:** 2.5", 4", 6", 8", 10" standard vent, vent heavy. **Weight:** 47 oz. (6" VH). **Length:** 11.25" overall. **Stocks:** Hogue Gripper rubber (walnut, exotic hardwoods optional). **Sights:** Red ramp interchangeable front, fully adjustable rear. **Features:** Bright blue (3220) or stainless (73220). Reintroduced 1997. Made in U.S. by Dan Wesson Firearms.

Price: 3220 VH2.5 (blued, 2.5" vent heavy bbl.)............... **$643.00**
Price: 73220 VH10 (stainless 10" vent heavy bbl.)............ **$873.00**

DAN WESSON FIREARMS MODEL 40/740 REVOLVERS

Caliber: 357 Maximum, 6-shot. **Barrel:** 4", 6", 8", 10". **Weight:** 72 oz. (8" bbl.). **Length:** 14.3" overall (8" bbl.). **Stocks:** Hogue Gripper rubber (walnut or exotic hardwood optional). **Sights:** 1/8" serrated front, fully adjustable rear. **Features:** Blue or stainless steel. Made in U.S. by Dan Wesson Firearms.

Price: Blue, 4"....................................... **$702.00**
Price: Blue, 6"....................................... **$749.00**
Price: Blue, 8"....................................... **$795.00**
Price: Blue, 10"...................................... **$858.00**
Price: Stainless, 4" **$834.00**
Price: Stainless, 6" **$892.00**
Price: Stainless, 8" slotted **$1,024.00**
Price: Stainless, 10" **$998.00**
Price: 4", 6", 8" Compensated, blue .... **$749.00 to $885.00**
Price: As above, stainless .... **$893.00 to $1,061.00**

DAN WESSON FIREARMS MODEL 22/722 REVOLVERS

Caliber: 22 LR, 22 WMR, 6-shot. **Barrel:** 2-1/2", 4", 6", 8" or 10"; interchangeable. **Weight:** 36 oz. (2-1/2"), 44 oz. (6"). **Length:** 9-1/4" overall (4" barrel). **Stocks:** Hogue Gripper rubber (walnut, exotic woods optional). **Sights:** 1/8" serrated, interchangeable front, white outline rear adjustable for windage and elevation. **Features:** Built on the same frame as the Wesson 357; smooth, wide trigger with over-travel adjustment, wide spur hammer, with short double-action travel. Available in blue or stainless steel. Reintroduced 1997. Contact Dan Wesson Firearms for complete price list.

Price: 22 VH2.5/722 VH2.5 (blued or stainless 2-1/2" bbl.) **$551.00**
Price: 22VH10/722 VH10 (blued or stainless 10" bbl.)......... **$750.00**

Dan Wesson 722M Small Frame Revolver

Similar to Model 22/722 except chambered for 22 WMR. Blued or stainless finish, 2-1/2", 4", 6", 8" or 10" barrels.

Price: Blued or stainless finish .... **$643.00 to $873.00**

Dan Wesson Firearms Model 414/7414 and 445/7445 SuperMag Revolvers

Similar size and weight as the Model 40 revolvers. Chambered for the 414 SuperMag or 445 SuperMag cartridge. Barrel lengths of 4", 6", 8", 10". Contact maker for complete price list. Reintroduced 1997. Made in the U.S. by Dan Wesson Firearms.

Price: 4", vent heavy, blue or stainless..................... **$904.00**
Price: 8", vent heavy, blue or stainless.................. **$1,026.00**
Price: 10", vent heavy, blue or stainless................. **$1,103.00**
Price: Compensated models .... **$965.00 to $1,149.00**

Dan Wesson Firearms Silhouette

Dan Wesson Firearms Super Ram Silhouette

DAN WESSON FIREARMS MODEL 15/715 and 32/732 REVOLVERS

Caliber: 32-20, 32 H&R Mag. (Model 32), 357 Mag. (Model 15). **Barrel:** 2-1/2", 4", 6", 8" (M32), 2-1/2", 4", 6", 8", 10" (M15); vent heavy. **Weight:** 36 oz. (2-1/2" barrel). **Length:** 9-1/4" overall (4" barrel). **Stocks:** Checkered, interchangeable. **Sights:** 1/8" serrated front, fully adjustable rear. **Features:** New Generation Series. Interchangeable barrels; wide, smooth trigger, wide hammer spur; short double-action travel. Available in blue or stainless. Reintroduced 1997. Made in U.S. by Dan Wesson Firearms. Contact maker for full list of models.

Price: Model 15/715, 2-1/2" (blue or stainless) **$551.00**
Price: Model 15/715, 8" (blue or stainless) **$612.00**
Price: Model 15/715, compensated . . . . **$704.00 to $827.00**
Price: Model 32/732, 4" (blue or stainless) **$674.00**
Price: Model 32/732, 8" (blue or stainless) **$766.00**

DAN WESSON FIREARMS MODEL 41/741, 44/744 and 45/745 REVOLVERS

Caliber: 41 Mag., 44 Mag., 45 Colt, 6-shot. **Barrel:** 4", 6", 8", 10"; interchangeable; 4", 6", 8" Compensated. **Weight:** 48 oz. (4"). **Length:** 12" overall (6" bbl.) **Stocks:** Smooth. **Sights:** 1/8" serrated front, white outline rear adjustable for windage and elevation. **Features:** Available in blue or stainless steel. Smooth, wide trigger with adjustable over-travel; wide hammer spur. Available in Pistol Pac set also. Reintroduced 1997. Contact Dan Wesson Firearms for complete price list.

Price: 41 Mag., 4", vent heavy (blue or stainless) **$643.00**
Price: 44 Mag., 6", vent heavy (blue or stainless) **$689.00**
Price: 45 Colt, 8", vent heavy (blue or stainless) **$766.00**
Price: Compensated models (all calibers) . . . . **$812.00 to $934.00**

DAN WESSON FIREARMS MODEL 360/7360 REVOLVERS

Caliber: 357 Mag. **Barrel:** 4", 6", 8", 10"; vent heavy. **Weight:** 64 oz. (8" barrel). **Length:** NA. **Stocks:** Hogue rubber finger groove. **Sights:** Interchangeable ramp or Patridge front, fully adjustable rear. **Features:** New Generation Large Frame Series. Interchangeable barrels and grips; smooth trigger, wide hammer spur. Blue (360) or stainless (7360). Introduced 1999. Made in U.S. by Dan Wesson Firearms.

Price: 4" bbl., blue or stainless **$735.00**
Price: 10" bbl., blue or stainless **$873.00**
Price: Compensated models . . . . **$858.00 to $980.00**

DAN WESSON FIREARMS MODEL 460/7460 REVOLVERS

Caliber: 45 ACP, 45 Auto Rim, 45 Super, 45 Winchester Magnum and 460 Rowland. **Barrel:** 4", 6", 8", 10"; vent heavy. **Weight:** 49 oz. (4" barrel). **Length:** NA. **Stocks:** Hogue rubber finger groove; interchangeable. **Sights:** Interchangeable ramp or Patridge front, fully adjustable rear. **Features:** New Generation Large Frame Series. Shoots five cartridges (45 ACP, 45 Auto Rim, 45 Super, 45 Winchester Magnum and 460 Rowland; six half-moon clips for auto cartridges included). Interchangeable barrels and grips. Available with non-fluted cylinder and Slotted Lightweight barrel shroud. Introduced 1999. Made in U.S. by Dan Wesson Firearms.

Price: 4" bbl., blue or stainless **$735.00**
Price: 10" bbl., blue or stainless **$888.00**
Price: Compensated models . . . . **$919.00 to $1,042.00**

DAN WESSON FIREARMS STANDARD SILHOUETTE REVOLVERS

Caliber: 357 SuperMag/Maxi, 41 Mag., 414 SuperMag, 445 SuperMag. **Barrel:** 8", 10" **Weight:** 64 oz. (8" barrel). **Length:** 14.3" overall (8" barrel). **Stocks:** Hogue rubber finger groove; interchangeable. **Sights:** Patridge front, fully adjustable rear. **Features:** Interchangeable barrels and grips; fluted or non-fluted cylinder; satin brushed stainless finish. Introduced 1999. Made in U.S. by Dan Wesson Firearms.

Price: 357 SuperMag/Maxi, 8" **$1,057.00**
Price: 41 Mag., 10" **$888.00**
Price: 414 SuperMag., 8" **$1,057.00**
Price: 445 SuperMag., 8" **$1,057.00**

Dan Wesson Firearms Super Ram Silhouette Revolver

Similar to the Standard Silhouette except has 10 land and groove Laser Coat barrel, Bo-Mar target sights with hooded front, and special laser engraving. Fluted or non-fluted cylinder. Introduced 1999. Made in U.S. by Dan Wesson Firearms.

Price: 357 SuperMag/Maxi, 414 SuperMag., 445 SuperMag., 8", blue or stainless **$1,364.00**
Price: 41 Magnum, 44 Magnum, 8", blue or stainless **$1,241.00**
Price: 41 Magnum, 44 Magnum, 10", blue or stainless **$1,333.00**

HANDGUNS — SINGLE ACTION REVOLVERS

Both classic six-shooters and modern adaptations for hunting and sport.

American Frontier 1871-1872 Open-Top

American Frontier 1851 Mason

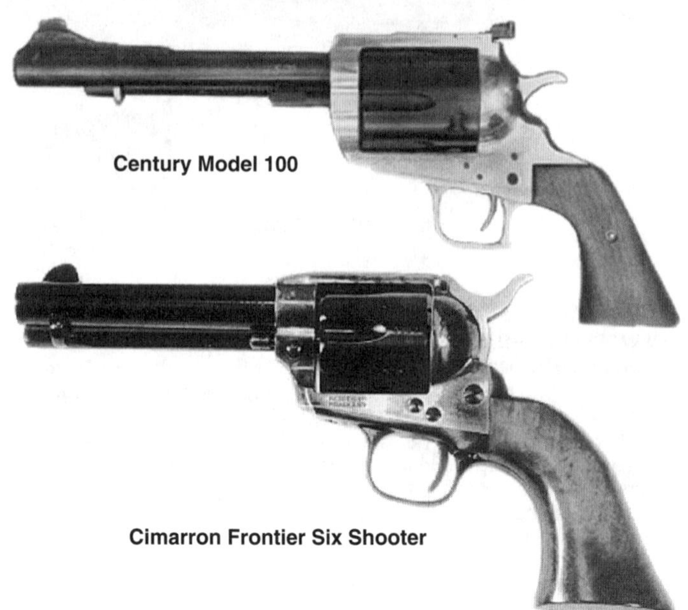

Century Model 100

Cimarron Frontier Six Shooter

HANDGUNS

AMERICAN FRONTIER 1851 NAVY CONVERSION

Caliber: 38, 44. **Barrel:** 5-1/2", 7-1/2", octagon. **Weight:** NA. **Length:** NA. **Stocks:** Varnished walnut, Navy size. **Sights:** Blade front, fixed rear. **Features:** Shoots metallic cartridge ammunition. Non-rebated cylinder; blued steel backstrap and trigger guard; color case-hardened hammer, trigger, ramrod, plunger; no ejector rod assembly. Introduced 1996.

Price: **$795.00**

AMERICAN FRONTIER 1871-1872 OPEN-TOP REVOLVERS

Caliber: 38, 44. **Barrel:** 5-1/2", 7-1/2", 8" round. **Weight:** NA. **Length:** NA. **Stocks:** Varnished walnut. **Sights:** Blade front, fixed rear. **Features:** Reproduction of the early cartridge conversions from percussion. Made for metallic cartridges. High polish blued steel, silver-plated brass backstrap and trigger guard, color case-hardened hammer; straight non-rebated cylinder with naval engagement engraving; stamped with original patent dates. Does not have conversion breechplate.

Price: **$795.00**

AMERICAN FRONTIER RICHARDS 1860 ARMY

Caliber: 38, 44. **Barrel:** 5-1/2", 7-1/2", round. **Weight:** NA. **Length:** NA. **Stocks:** Varnished walnut, Army size. **Sights:** Blade front, fixed rear. **Features:** Shoots metallic cartridge ammunition. Rebated cylinder; available with or without ejector assembly; high-polish blue including backstrap; silver-plated trigger guard; color case-hardened hammer and trigger. Introduced 1996.

Price: **$795.00**

American Frontier 1851 Navy Richards & Mason Conversion

Similar to the 1851 Navy Conversion except has Mason ejector assembly. Introduced 1996. Imported from Italy by American Frontier Firearms Mfg.

Price: **$695.00**

NEW!

CABELA'S MILLENNIUM REVOLVER

Caliber: 45 Colt. **Barrel:** 4-3/4". **Weight:** NA. **Length:** 10" overall. **Grips:** Hardwood. **Sights:** Blade front, hammer notch rear. **Features:** Matte black finish; unpolished brass accents. Introduced 2001. From Cabela's.

Price: **$199.99**

CENTURY GUN DIST. MODEL 100 SINGLE-ACTION

Caliber: 30-30, 375 Win., 444 Marlin, 45-70, 50-70. **Barrel:** 6-1/2" (standard), 8", 10". **Weight:** 6 lbs. (loaded). **Length:** 15" overall (8" bbl.). **Stocks:** Smooth walnut. **Sights:** Ramp front, Millett adjustable square notch rear. **Features:** Highly polished high tensile strength manganese bronze frame, blue cylinder and barrel; coil spring trigger mechanism. Contact maker for full price information. Introduced 1975. Made in U.S. From Century Gun Dist., Inc.

Price: 6-1/2" barrel, 45-70 . . . . **$2,000.00**

NEW!

CIMARRON LIGHTNING SA

Caliber: 38 Special. **Barrel:** 3-1/2", 4-3/4" or 5-1/2". **Weight:** NA. **Length:** NA. **Grips:** Checkered walnut. **Sights:** Blade front. **Features:** Replica of the Colt 1877 Lightning DA. Similar to Cimarron Thunderer™, except smaller grip frame to fit smaller hands. Blue finish with color-case hardened frame. Introduced 2001. From Cimarron F.A. Co.

Price: **$389.00**

NEW

CIMARRON MODEL "P" JR.

Caliber: 38 Special. **Barrel:** 3-1/2" and 4-1/2". **Weight:** NA. **Length:** NA. **Grips:** Checkered walnut. **Sights:** Blade front. **Features:** Styled after 1873 Colt Peacemaker, except 20 percent smaller. Blue finish with color-case hardened frame; Cowboy Comp® action. Introduced 2001. From Cimarron F.A. Co.

Price: **$389.00**

CIMARRON U.S. CAVALRY MODEL SINGLE-ACTION

Caliber: 45 Colt. **Barrel:** 7-1/2". **Weight:** 42 oz. **Length:** 13-1/2" overall. **Stocks:** Walnut. **Sights:** Fixed. **Features:** Has "A.P. Casey" markings; "U.S." plus patent dates on frame, serial number on backstrap, trigger guard, frame and cylinder, "APC" cartouche on left grip; color case-hardened frame and hammer, rest charcoal blue. Exact copy of the original. Imported by Cimarron F.A. Co.

Price: **$499.00**

Cimarron Rough Rider Artillery Model Single-Action

Similar to the U.S. Cavalry model except has 5-1/2" barrel, weighs 39 oz., and is 11-1/2" overall. U.S. markings and cartouche, case-hardened frame and hammer; 45 Colt only.

Price: **$499.00**

NEW

CIMARRON 1872 OPEN TOP REVOLVER

Caliber: 38, 44 Special, 45 S&W Schofield. **Barrel:** 5-1/2" and 7-1/2". **Weight:** NA. **Length:** NA. **Grips:** Walnut. **Sights:** Blade front, fixed rear. **Features:** Replica of first cartridge-firing revolver. Blue, charcoal blue, nickel or Original® finish; Navy-style brass or steel Army-style frame. Introduced 2001 by Cimarron F.A. Co.

Price: **$469.00**

CIMARRON 1873 FRONTIER SIX SHOOTER

Caliber: 38 WCF, 357 Mag., 44 WCF, 44 Spec., 45 Colt. **Barrel:** 4-3/4", 5-1/2", 7-1/2". **Weight:** 39 oz. **Length:** 10" overall (4" barrel). **Stocks:** Walnut. **Sights:** Blade front, fixed or adjustable rear. **Features:** Uses "old model" blackpowder frame with "Bullseye" ejector or New Model frame. Imported by Cimarron F.A. Co.

Price: 4-3/4" barrel **$469.00**
Price: 5-1/2" barrel **$469.00**
Price: 7-1/2" barrel **$469.00**

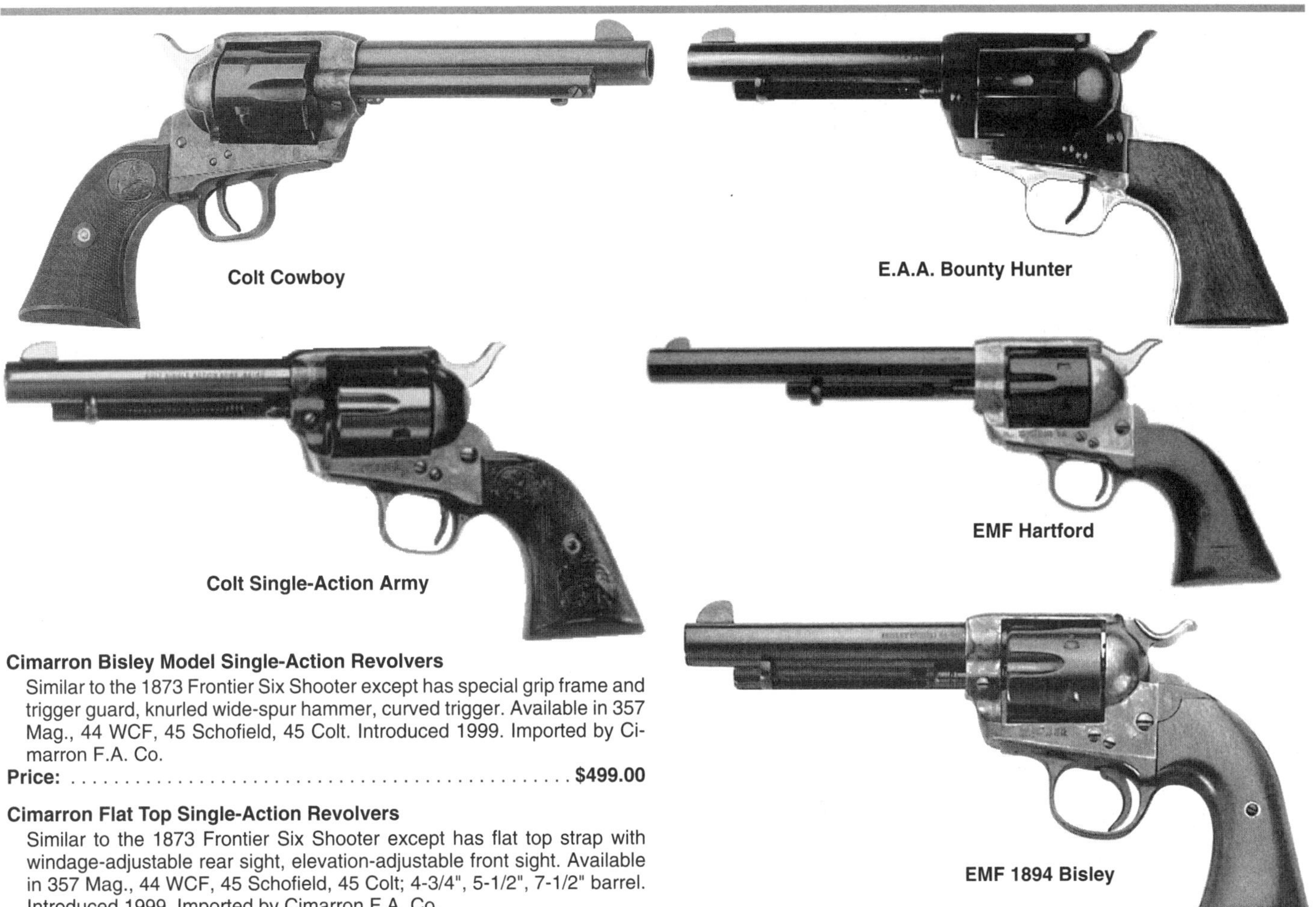
Colt Cowboy

E.A.A. Bounty Hunter

Colt Single-Action Army

EMF Hartford

EMF 1894 Bisley

Cimarron Bisley Model Single-Action Revolvers

Similar to the 1873 Frontier Six Shooter except has special grip frame and trigger guard, knurled wide-spur hammer, curved trigger. Available in 357 Mag., 44 WCF, 45 Schofield, 45 Colt. Introduced 1999. Imported by Cimarron F.A. Co.

Price: **$499.00**

Cimarron Flat Top Single-Action Revolvers

Similar to the 1873 Frontier Six Shooter except has flat top strap with windage-adjustable rear sight, elevation-adjustable front sight. Available in 357 Mag., 44 WCF, 45 Schofield, 45 Colt; 4-3/4", 5-1/2", 7-1/2" barrel. Introduced 1999. Imported by Cimarron F.A. Co.

Price: **$479.00**

Cimarron Bisley Flat Top Revolver

Similar to the Flat Top revolver except has special grip frame and trigger guard, wide spur hammer, curved trigger. Introduced 1999. Imported by Cimarron F.A. Co.

Price: **$509.00**

CIMARRON THUNDERER REVOLVER

Caliber: 357 Mag., 44 WCF, 44 Spec., 45 Colt, 6-shot. **Barrel:** 3-1/2", 4-3/4", 5-1/2", 7-1/2", with ejector. **Weight:** 38 oz. (3-1/2" barrel). **Length:** NA. **Stocks:** Smooth walnut. **Sights:** Blade front, notch rear. **Features:** Thunderer grip; color case-hardened frame with balance blued. Introduced 1993. Imported by Cimarron F.A. Co.

Price: 3-1/2", 4-3/4", smooth grips **$489.00**
Price: As above, checkered grips.... **$524.00**
Price: 5-1/2", 7-1/2", smooth grips **$529.00**
Price: As above, checkered grips.... **$564.00**

CIMARRON 1872 OPEN-TOP REVOLVER

Caliber: 38 Spec., 38 Colt, 44 Spec., 44 Colt, 44 Russian, 45 Schofield. **Barrel:** 7-1/2". **Weight:** NA. **Length:** NA. **Stocks:** Smooth walnut. **Sights:** Blade front, fixed rear. **Features:** Replica of the original production. Color case-hardened frame, rest blued, including grip frame. Introduced 1999. Imported from Italy by Cimarron F.A. Co.

Price: **$579.00**

COLT COWBOY SINGLE-ACTION REVOLVER

Caliber: 45 Colt, 6-shot. **Barrel:** 5-1/2". **Weight:** 42 oz. **Stocks:** Black composition, first generation style. **Sights:** Blade front, notch rear. **Features:** Dimensional replica of Colt's original Peacemaker with medium-size color case-hardened frame; transfer bar safety system; half-cock loading. Introduced 1998. Made in U.S. by Colt's Mfg. Co.

Price: About **$670.00**

COLT SINGLE-ACTION ARMY REVOLVER

Caliber: 44-40, 45 Colt, 6-shot. **Barrel:** 4-3/4", 5-1/2", 7-1/2". **Weight:** 40 oz. (4-3/4" barrel). **Length:** 10-1/4" overall (4-3/4" barrel). **Stocks:** Black Eagle composite. **Sights:** Blade front, notch rear. **Features:** Available in full nickel finish with nickel grip medallions, or Royal Blue with color case-hardened frame, gold grip medallions. Reintroduced 1992.

Price: **$1,938.00**

E.A.A. BOUNTY HUNTER SA REVOLVERS

Caliber: 22 LR/22 WMR, 357 Mag., 44 Mag., 45 Colt, 6-shot. **Barrel:** 4-1/2", 7-1/2". **Weight:** 2.5 lbs. **Length:** 11" overall (4-5/8" barrel). **Stocks:** Smooth walnut. **Sights:** Blade front, grooved topstrap rear. **Features:** Transfer bar safety; three position hammer; hammer forged barrel. Introduced 1992. Imported by European American Armory.

Price: Blue or case-hardened.... **$280.00**
Price: Nickel.... **$298.00**
Price: 22LR/22WMR, blue **$187.20**
Price: As above, nickel.... **$204.36**

EMF HARTFORD SINGLE-ACTION REVOLVERS

Caliber: 357 Mag., 32-20, 38-40, 44-40, 44 Spec., 45 Colt. **Barrel:** 4-3/4", 5-1/2", 7-1/2". **Weight:** 45 oz. **Length:** 13" overall (7-1/2" barrel). **Stocks:** Smooth walnut. **Sights:** Blade front, fixed rear. **Features:** Identical to the original Colts with inspector cartouche on left grip, original patent dates and U.S. markings. All major parts serial numbered using original Colt-style lettering, numbering. Bullseye ejector head and color case-hardening on frame and hammer. Introduced 1990. From E.M.F.

Price: **$500.00**
Price: Cavalry or Artillery **$390.00**
Price: Nickel plated, add.... **$125.00**
Price: Casehardened New Model frame **$365.00**

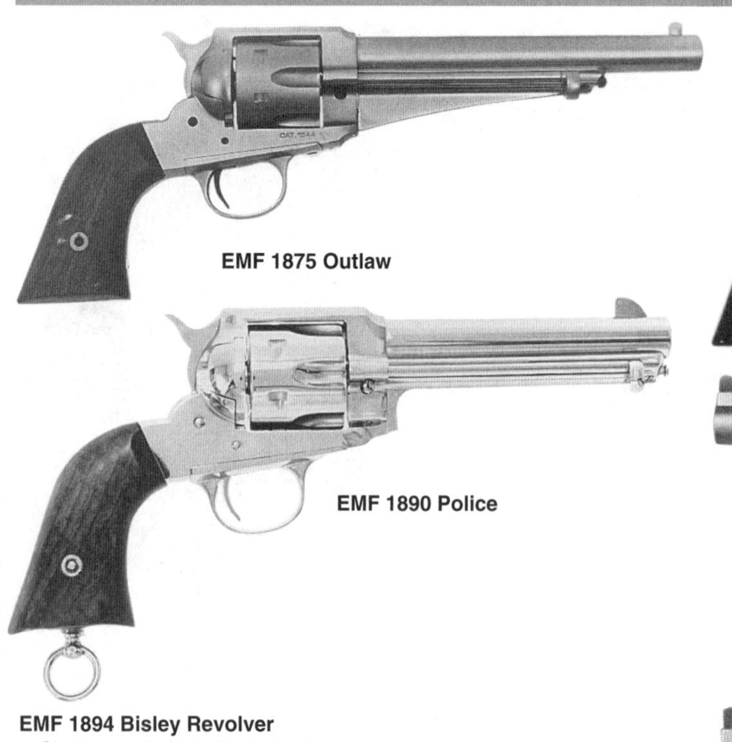

EMF 1875 Outlaw

EMF 1890 Police

EMF 1894 Bisley Revolver

Similar to the Hartford single-action revolver except has special grip frame and trigger guard, wide spur hammer; available in 38-40 or 45 Colt, 4-3/4", 5-1/2" or 7-1/2" barrel. Introduced 1995. Imported by E.M.F.

Price: Casehardened/blue **$400.00**
Price: Nickel **$525.00**

EMF Hartford Pinkerton Single-Action Revolver

Same as the regular Hartford except has 4" barrel with ejector tube and birds head grip. Calibers: 357 Mag., 45 Colt. Introduced 1997. Imported by E.M.F.

Price: **$375.00**

EMF Hartford Express Single-Action Revolver

Same as the regular Hartford model except uses grip of the Colt Lightning revolver. Barrel lengths of 4", 4-3/4", 5-1/2". Introduced 1997. Imported by E.M.F.

Price: **$375.00**

EMF 1875 OUTLAW REVOLVER

Caliber: 357 Mag., 44-40, 45 Colt. **Barrel:** 7-1/2". **Weight:** 46 oz. **Length:** 13-1/2" overall. **Stocks:** Smooth walnut. **Sights:** Blade front, fixed groove rear. **Features:** Authentic copy of 1875 Remington with firing pin in hammer; color case-hardened frame, blue cylinder, barrel, steel backstrap and brass trigger guard. Also available in nickel, factory engraved. Imported by E.M.F.

Price: All calibers **$575.00**
Price: Nickel **$735.00**

EMF 1890 Police Revolver

Similar to the 1875 Outlaw except has 5-1/2" barrel, weighs 40 oz., with 12-1/2" overall length. Has lanyard ring in butt. No web under barrel. Calibers 357, 44-40, 45 Colt. Imported by E.M.F.

Price: All calibers **$590.00**
Price: Nickel **$750.00**

FREEDOM ARMS MODEL 83 PREMIER GRADE REVOLVER

Caliber: 357 Mag., 41 Rem. Mag., 44 Rem. Mag., 454 Casull, 475 Linebaugh, 50 AE, 5-shot. **Barrel:** 4-3/4", 6", 7-1/2", 9" (357 Mag. only), 10" (except 475 Linebaugh). **Weight:** 52 oz. **Length:** 14" overall (7-1/2" bbl.). **Stocks:** Impregnated hardwood (Premier grade), or Pachmayr (Field Grade). **Sights:** Blade front, notch or adjustable rear. **Features:** All stainless steel construction; sliding bar safety system. Lifetime warranty. Made in U.S. by Freedom Arms, Inc.

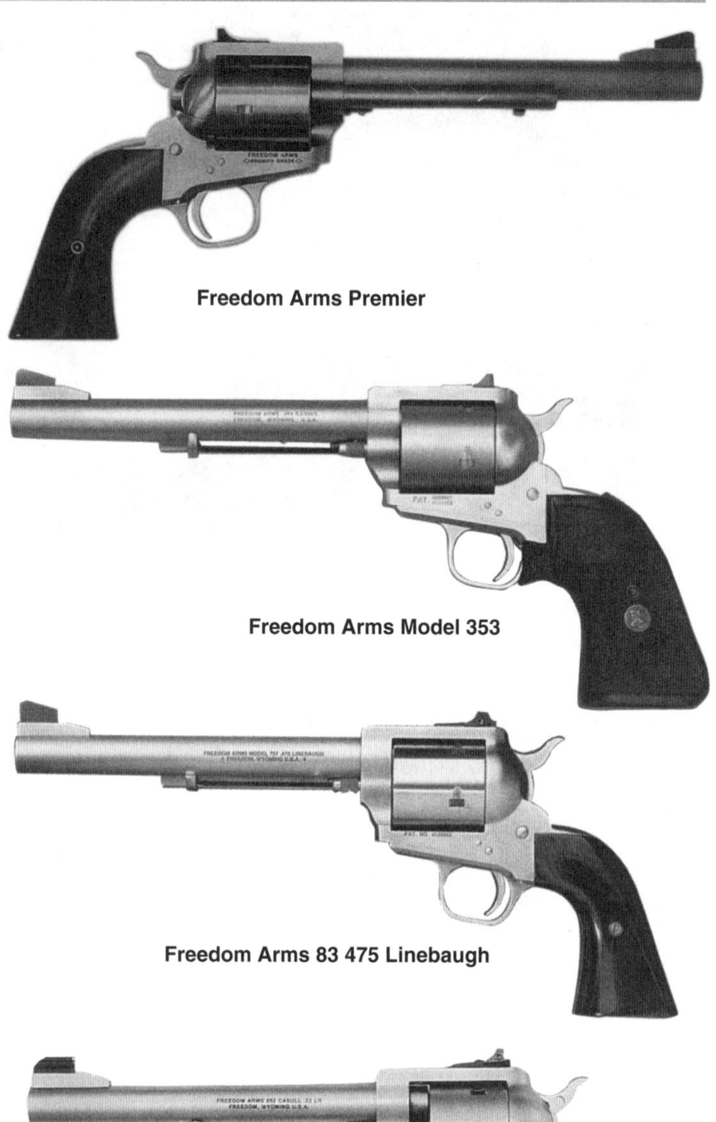

Freedom Arms Premier

Freedom Arms Model 353

Freedom Arms 83 475 Linebaugh

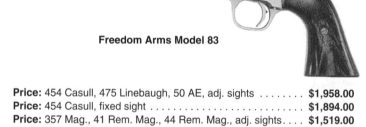

Freedom Arms Model 83

Price: 454 Casull, 475 Linebaugh, 50 AE, adj. sights **$1,958.00**
Price: 454 Casull, fixed sight **$1,894.00**
Price: 357 Mag., 41 Rem. Mag., 44 Rem. Mag., adj. sights. . . . **$1,519.00**
Price: 44 Rem. Mag., fixed sight **$1,816.00**
Price: Extra cylinder **$264.00**

Freedom Arms Model 83 Field Grade Revolver

Made on the Model 83 frame. Weighs 52 oz. Field grade model has adjustable rear sight with replaceable front blade, matte finish, Pachmayr grips. All stainless steel. Introduced 1992. Made in U.S. by Freedom Arms Inc.

Price: 454 Casull, 475 Linebaugh, 50 AE, adj. sights **$1,519.00**
Price: 454 Casull, fixed sights **$1,484.00**
Price: 357 Mag., 41 Rem. Mag., 44 Rem. Mag., adj. sights. . . . **$1,442.00**
Price: Extra cylinder **$264.00**

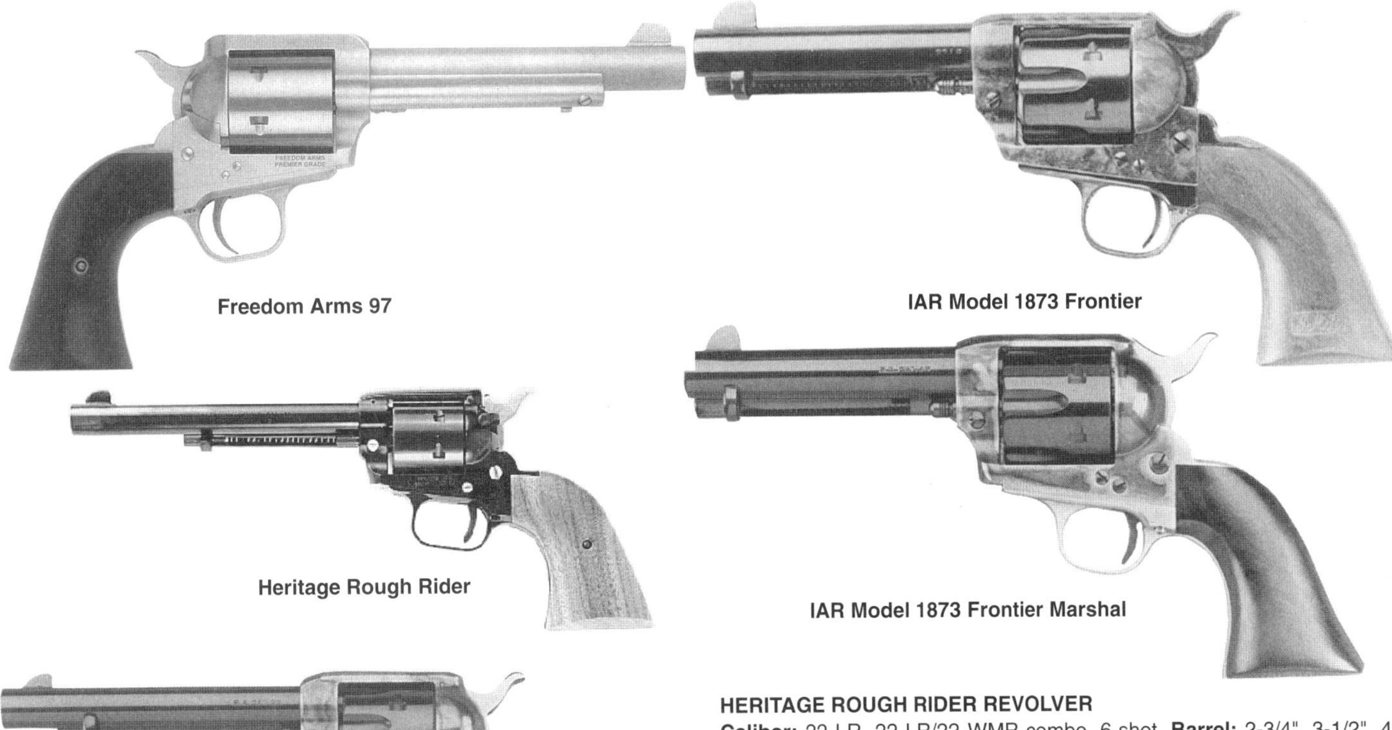

Freedom Arms 97

IAR Model 1873 Frontier

Heritage Rough Rider

IAR Model 1873 Frontier Marshal

IAR Model 1873 Six Shooter

Freedom Arms Model 83 Field Grade Varmint Class Revolver

Made on the Model 83 frame. Chambered for 22 LR with 5-shot cylinder; 5-1/8" or 7-1/2" barrel. Weighs 58 oz. (7-1/2" barrel). Brass bead front, adjustable rear express with shallow "V." All-stainless construction with matte finish, manual sliding-bar safety system, dual firing pins, lightened hammer, pre-set trigger stop. Made in U.S. by Freedom Arms.

Price: Varmint Class **$1,714.00**
Price: Extra fitted 22 WMR cylinder **$264.00**

FREEDOM ARMS MODEL 97 MID-FRAME REVOLVER

Caliber: 357 Mag., 6-shot cylinder; 45 Colt, 41 Rem. Mag., 5-shot. **Barrel:** 4-1/4", 5-1/2", 7-1/2". **Weight:** 41 oz. (5-1/2" barrel). **Length:** 10-3/4" overall (5-1/2" barrel). **Grips:** Impregnated hardwood or black Micarta optional. **Sights:** Blade on ramp front, fixed or fully adjustable rear. **Features:** Made of stainless steel; brushed finish; automatic transfer bar safety system. Introduced 1997. Made in U.S. by Freedom Arms.

Price: Adjustable sight **$1,576.00**
Price: 357 Mag., 45 Colt, fixed sight **$1,500.00**
Price: Extra cylinder **$264.00**

FREEDOM ARMS MODEL 252 VARMINT CLASS REVOLVER

Caliber: 22 LR, 5-shot. **Barrel:** 5.125", 7.5". **Weight:** 58 oz. (7.5" barrel). **Length:** NA. **Stocks:** Black and green laminated hardwood. **Sights:** Brass bead express front, express rear with shallow V-notch. **Features:** All stainless steel construction. Dual firing pins; lightened hammer; pre-set trigger stop. Built on Model 83 frame and accepts Model 83 Freedom Arms sights and/or scope mounts. Introduced 1991. Made in U.S. by Freedom Arms.

Price: **$1,527.00**
Price: Extra fitted 22 WMR cylinder **$264.00**

HERITAGE ROUGH RIDER REVOLVER

Caliber: 22 LR, 22 LR/22 WMR combo, 6-shot. **Barrel:** 2-3/4", 3-1/2", 4-3/4", 6-1/2", 9". **Weight:** 31 to 38 oz. **Length:** NA. **Grips:** Exotic hardwood, laminated wood or mother of pearl; bird's head models offered. **Sights:** Blade front, fixed rear. Adjustable sight on 6-1/2" only. **Features:** Hammer block safety. High polish blue or nickel finish. Introduced 1993. Made in U.S. by Heritage Mfg., Inc.

Price: . . . . **$184.95 to $239.95**

IAR MODEL 1873 SIX SHOOTER

Caliber: 22 LR/22 WMR combo. **Barrel:** 5-1/2". **Weight:** 36-1/2" oz. **Length:** 11-3/8" overall. **Stocks:** One-piece walnut. **Sights:** Blade front, notch rear. **Features:** A 3/4-scale reproduction. Color case-hardened frame, blued barrel. All-steel construction. Made by Uberti. Imported from Italy by IAR, Inc.

Price: **$360.00**

IAR MODEL 1873 FRONTIER REVOLVER

Caliber: 22 RL, 22 LR/22 WMR. **Barrel:** 4-3/4". **Weight:** 45 oz. **Length:** 10-1/2" overall. **Stocks:** One-piece walnut with inspector's cartouche. **Sights:** Blade front, notch rear. **Features:** Color case-hardened frame, blued barrel, black nickel-plated brass trigger guard and backstrap. Bright nickel and engraved versions available. Introduced 1997. Imported from Italy by IAR, Inc.

Price: **$395.00**
Price: Nickel-plated **$485.00**
Price: 22 LR/22WMR combo **$425.00**

IAR MODEL 1873 FRONTIER MARSHAL

Caliber: 357 Mag., 45 Colt. **Barrel:** 4-3/4", 5-1/2, 7-1/2". **Weight:** 39 oz. **Length:** 10-1/2" overall. **Stocks:** One-piece walnut. **Sights:** Blade front, notch rear. **Features:** Bright brass trigger guard and backstrap, color case-hardened frame, blued barrel and cylinder. Introduced 1998. Imported from Italy by IAR, Inc.

Price: **$395.00**

MAGNUM RESEARCH BFR SINGLE-ACTION REVOLVER

Caliber: 22 Hornet, 45 Colt +P, 454 Casull (Little Max, standard cylinder). **Barrel:** 7-1/2", 10". **Weight:** 4 lbs. **Length:** 11" overall with 7-1/2" barrel. **Stocks:** Checkered rubber. **Sights:** Orange blade on ramp front, fully adjustable rear. **Features:** Stainless steel construction. Optional exotic wood finger-groove grips available. Introduced 1997. Made in U.S. From Magnum Research, Inc.

Price: **$999.00**

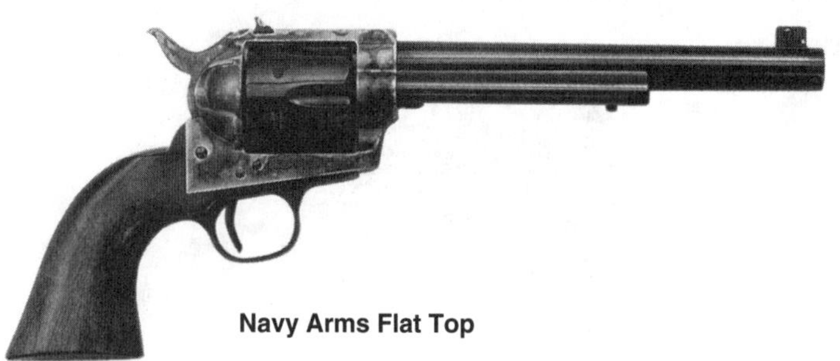
Navy Arms Flat Top

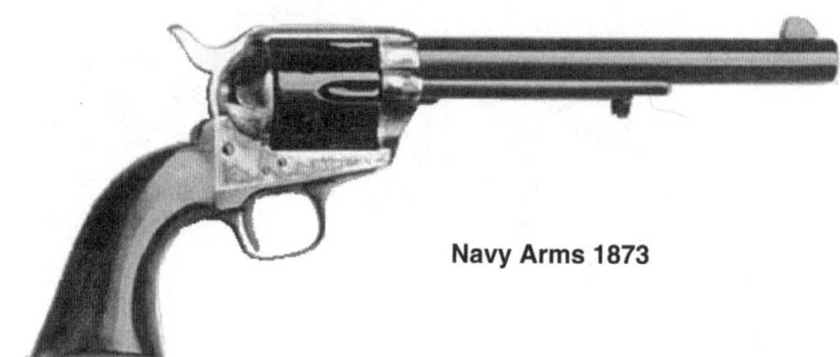
Navy Arms 1873

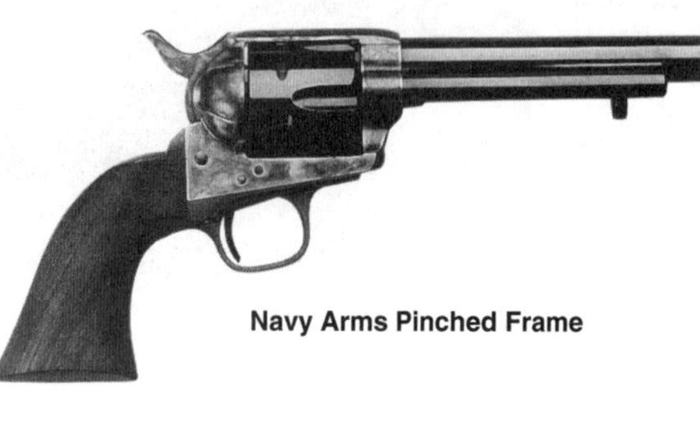
Navy Arms Pinched Frame

Navy Arms Schofield

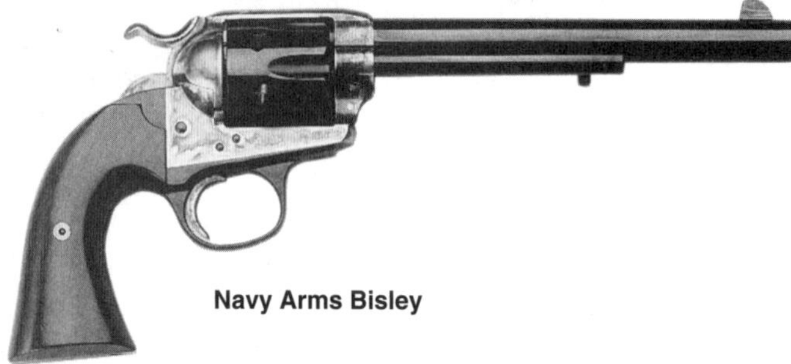
Navy Arms Bisley

MAGNUM RESEARCH LITTLE MAX REVOLVER

Caliber: 22 Hornet, 45 Colt, 454 Casull, 50 A.E. **Barrel:** 6-1/2", 7-1/2", 10". **Weight:** 45 oz. **Length:** 13" overall (7-1/2" barrel). **Stocks:** Rubber. **Sights:** Ramp front, adjustable rear. **Features:** Single action; stainless steel construction. Announced 1998. Made in U.S. From Magnum Research.

Price: **$999.00**

Price: Maxine model (7-1/2", 10", 45 Colt/410, 45-70, 444 Marlin) **$999.00**

NAVY ARMS FLAT TOP TARGET MODEL REVOLVER

Caliber: 45 Colt, 6-shot cylinder. **Barrel:** 7-1/2". **Weight:** 40 oz. **Length:** 13-1/4" overall. **Stocks:** Smooth walnut. **Sights:** Spring-loaded German silver front, rear adjustable for windage. **Features:** Replica of Colt's Flat Top Frontier target revolver made from 1888 to 1896. Blue with color case-hardened frame. Introduced 1997. Imported by Navy Arms.

Price: **$435.00**

NAVY ARMS "PINCHED FRAME" SINGLE-ACTION REVOLVER

Caliber: 45 Colt, 6-shot. **Barrel:** 7-1/2". **Weight:** 37 oz. **Length:** 13" overall. **Stocks:** Smooth walnut **Sights:** German silver blade, notch rear. **Features:** Replica of Colt's original Peacemaker. Color case-hardened frame, hammer, rest charcoal blued. Introduced 1997. Imported by Navy Arms.

Price: **$415.00**

NAVY ARMS BISLEY MODEL SINGLE-ACTION REVOLVER

Caliber: 44-40 or 45 Colt, 6-shot cylinder. **Barrel:** 4-3/4", 5-1/2", 7-1/2". **Weight:** 40 oz. **Length:** 12-1/2" overall (7-1/2" barrel). **Stocks:** Smooth walnut. **Sights:** Blade front, notch rear. **Features:** Replica of Colt's Bisley Model. Polished blue finish, color case-hardened frame. Introduced 1997. Imported by Navy Arms.

Price: **$415.00**

NAVY ARMS 1872 OPEN TOP REVOLVER

Caliber: 38 Spec., 6-shot. **Barrel:** 5-1/2" or 7-1/2". **Weight:** 2 lbs., 12 oz. **Length:** 11" or 13". **Stocks:** Smooth walnut. **Sights:** Blade front, notch rear. **Features:** Replica of Colt's first production cartridge "six shooter." Polished blue finish with color case hardened frame, silver plated trigger guard and backstrap Introduced 2000. Imported by Navy Arms.

Price: **$390.00**

NAVY ARMS 1873 SINGLE-ACTION REVOLVER

Caliber: 357 Mag., 44-40, 45 Colt, 6-shot cylinder. **Barrel:** 4-3/4", 5-1/2", 7-1/2". **Weight:** 36 oz. **Length:** 10-3/4" overall (5-1/2" barrel). **Stocks:** Smooth walnut. **Sights:** Blade front, notch rear. **Features:** Blue with color case-hardened frame. Introduced 1991. Imported by Navy Arms.

Price: **$395.00**

Price: 1873 U.S. Cavalry Model (7-1/2", 45 Colt, arsenal markings) **$465.00**

Price: 1895 U.S. Artillery Model (as above, 5-1/2" barrel) **$465.00**

NAVY ARMS 1875 SCHOFIELD REVOLVER

Caliber: 44-40, 45 Colt, 6-shot cylinder. **Barrel:** 3-1/2", 5", 7". **Weight:** 39 oz. **Length:** 10-3/4" overall (5" barrel). **Stocks:** Smooth walnut. **Sights:** Blade front, notch rear. **Features:** Replica of Smith & Wesson Model 3 Schofield. Single-action, top-break with automatic ejection. Polished blue finish. Introduced 1994. Imported by Navy Arms.

Price: Hideout Model, 3-1/2" barrel **$695.00**

Price: Wells Fargo, 5" barrel. **$695.00**

Price: U.S. Cavalry model, 7" barrel, military markings **$695.00**

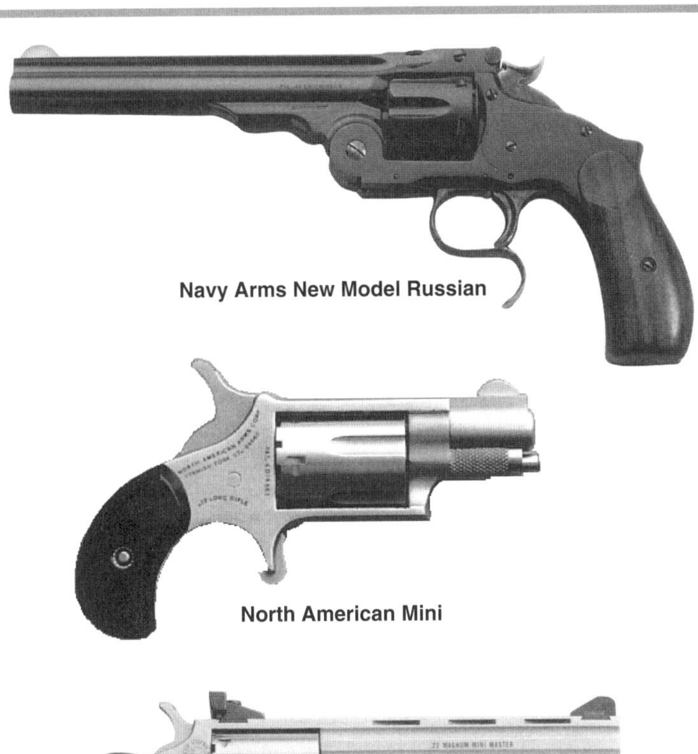
Navy Arms New Model Russian

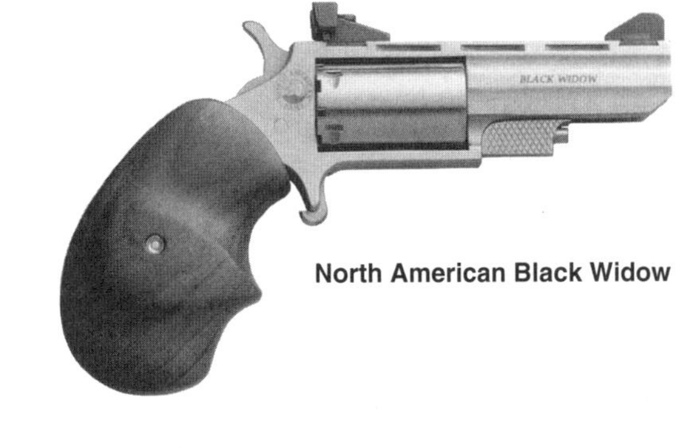

North American Black Widow

North American Mini

Ruger Blackhawk

North American Mini-Master

NAVY ARMS NEW MODEL RUSSIAN REVOLVER

Caliber: 44 Russian, 6-shot cylinder. **Barrel:** 6-1/2". **Weight:** 40 oz. **Length:** 12" overall. **Stocks:** Smooth walnut. **Sights:** Blade front, notch rear. **Features:** Replica of the S&W Model 3 Russian Third Model revolver. Spur trigger guard, polished blue finish. Introduced 1999. Imported by Navy Arms.

Price: **$745.00**

NAVY ARMS 1851 NAVY CONVERSION REVOLVER

Caliber: 38 Spec., 38 Long Colt. **Barrel:** 5-1/2", 7-1/2". **Weight:** 44 oz. **Length:** 14" overall (7-1/2" barrel). **Stocks:** Smooth walnut. **Sights:** Bead front, notch rear. **Features:** Replica of Colt's cartridge conversion revolver. Polished blue finish with color case-hardened frame, silver plated trigger guard and backstrap. Introduced 1999. Imported by Navy Arms.

Price: **$365.00**

NAVY ARMS 1860 ARMY CONVERSION REVOLVER

Caliber: 38 Spec., 38 Long Colt. **Barrel:** 5-1/2", 7-1/2". **Weight:** 44 oz. **Length:** 13-1/2" overall (7-1/2" barrel). **Stocks:** Smooth walnut. **Sights:** Blade front, notch rear. **Features:** Replica of Colt's conversion revolver. Polished blue finish with color case-hardened frame, full-size 1860 Army grip with blued steel backstrap. Introduced 1999. Imported by Navy Arms.

Price: **$365.00**

NAVY ARMS 1861 NAVY CONVERSION REVOLVER

Caliber: 38 Spec., 38 Long Colt. **Barrel:** 5-1/2", 7-1/2". **Weight:** 44 oz. **Length:** 13-1/2" overall (7-1/2" barrel). **Stocks:** Smooth walnut. **Sights:** Blade front, notch rear. **Features:** Replica of Colt's cartridge conversion. Polished blue finish with color case-hardened frame, silver plated trigger guard and backstrap. Introduced 1999. Imported by Navy Arms.

Price: **$365.00**

NORTH AMERICAN MINI-REVOLVERS

Caliber: 22 Short, 22 LR, 22 WMR, 5-shot. **Barrel:** 1-1/8", 1-5/8". **Weight:** 4 to 6.6 oz. **Length:** 3-5/8" to 6-1/8" overall. **Stocks:** Laminated wood. **Sights:** Blade front, notch fixed rear. **Features:** All stainless steel construction. Polished satin and matte finish. Engraved models available. From North American Arms.

Price: 22 Short, 22 LR **$176.00**
Price: 22 WMR, 1-5/8" bbl. **$194.00**
Price: 22 WMR, 1-1/8" or 1-5/8" bbl. with extra 22 LR cylinder . . **$231.00**

NORTH AMERICAN MINI-MASTER

Caliber: 22 LR, 22 WMR, 5-shot cylinder. **Barrel:** 4". **Weight:** 10.7 oz. **Length:** 7.75" overall. **Stocks:** Checkered hard black rubber. **Sights:** Blade front, white outline rear adjustable for elevation, or fixed. **Features:** Heavy vent barrel; full-size grips. Non-fluted cylinder. Introduced 1989.

Price: Adjustable sight, 22 WMR or 22 LR. **$299.00**
Price: As above with extra WMR/LR cylinder. **$336.00**
Price: Fixed sight, 22 WMR or 22 LR. **$281.00**
Price: As above with extra WMR/LR cylinder. **$318.00**

North American Black Widow Revolver

Similar to the Mini-Master except has 2" heavy vent barrel. Built on the 22 WMR frame. Non-fluted cylinder, black rubber grips. Available with either Millett Low Profile fixed sights or Millett sight adjustable for elevation only. Overall length 5-7/8", weighs 8.8 oz. From North American Arms.

Price: Adjustable sight, 22 LR or 22 WMR. **$269.00**
Price: As above with extra WMR/LR cylinder. **$306.00**
Price: Fixed sight, 22 LR or 22 WMR. **$251.00**
Price: As above with extra WMR/LR cylinder. **$288.00**

RUGER NEW MODEL BLACKHAWK REVOLVER

Caliber: 30 Carbine, 357 Mag./38 Spec., 41 Mag., 45 Colt, 6-shot. **Barrel:** 4-5/8" or 5-1/2", either caliber; 7-1/2" (30 Carbine and 45 Colt). **Weight:** 42 oz. (6-1/2" bbl.). **Length:** 12-1/4" overall (5-1/2" bbl.). **Stocks:** American walnut. **Sights:** 1/8" ramp front, micro-click rear adjustable for windage and elevation. **Features:** Ruger transfer bar safety system, independent firing pin, hardened chrome-moly steel frame, music wire springs throughout. Comes with plastic lockable case and lock.

HANDGUNS — SINGLE ACTION REVOLVERS

Ruger Bisley Vaquero

Ruger Bisley Single-Action

Ruger New Bearcat

Ruger Super Single-Six

Price: Blue 30 Carbine, 7-1/2" (BN31) **$415.00**
Price: Blue, 357 Mag., 4-5/8", 6-1/2" (BN34, BN36). **$415.00**
Price: As above, stainless (KBN34, KBN36) **$505.00**
Price: Blue, 357 Mag./9mm Convertible, 4-5/8", 6-1/2" (BN34X, BN36X) **$465.00**
Price: Blue, 41 Mag., 4-5/8", 6-1/2" (BN41, BN42). **$415.00**
Price: Blue, 45 Colt, 4-5/8", 5-1/2", 7-1/2" (BN44, BN455, BN45) **$415.00**
Price: Stainless, 45 Colt, 4-5/8", 7-1/2" (KBN44, KBN45) **$505.00**
Price: Blue, 45 Colt/45 ACP Convertible, 4-5/8", 5-1/2" (BN44X, BN455X). **$465.00**

RUGER NEW MODEL SUPER BLACKHAWK

Caliber: 44 Mag., 6-shot. Also fires 44 Spec. **Barrel:** 4-5/8", 5-1/2", 7-1/2", 10-1/2" bull. **Weight:** 48 oz. (7-1/2" bbl.), 51 oz. (10-1/2" bbl.). **Length:** 13-3/8" overall (7-1/2" bbl.). **Stocks:** American walnut. **Sights:** 1/8" ramp front, micro-click rear adjustable for windage and elevation. **Features:** Ruger transfer bar safety system, fluted or un-fluted cylinder, steel grip and cylinder frame, round or square back trigger guard, wide serrated trigger and wide spur hammer. Comes with plastic lockable case and lock.
Price: Blue, 4-5/8", 5-1/2", 7-1/2" (S458N, S45N, S47N) **$489.00**
Price: Blue, 10-1/2" bull barrel (S411N) **$499.00**
Price: Stainless, 4-5/8", 5-1/2", 7-1/2" (KS458N, KS45N, KS47N) **$510.00**
Price: Stainless, 10-1/2" bull barrel (KS411N) **$519.00**

RUGER VAQUERO SINGLE-ACTION REVOLVER

Caliber: 357 Mag., 44-40, 44 Mag., 45 Colt, 6-shot. **Barrel:** 4-5/8", 5-1/2", 7-1/2". **Weight:** 41 oz. **Length:** 13-1/8" overall (7-1/2" barrel). **Stocks:** Smooth rosewood with Ruger medallion. **Sights:** Blade front, fixed notch rear. **Features:** Uses Ruger's patented transfer bar safety system and loading gate interlock with classic styling. Blued model has color case-hardened finish on the frame, the rest polished and blued. Stainless model has high-gloss polish. Introduced 1993. From Sturm, Ruger & Co.
Price: 357 Mag. BNV34 (4-5/8"), BNV35 (5-1/2"). **$510.00**
Price: 357 Mag. KBNV34 (4-5/8"), KBNV35 (5-1/2") stainless. . . **$510.00**
Price: BNV44 (4-5/8"), BNV445 (5-1/2"), BNV45 (7-1/2"), blue . . **$510.00**
Price: KBNV44 (4-5/8"), KBNV455 (5-1/2"), KBNV45 (7-1/2"), stainless **$510.00**
Price: 45 Colt BNV455, all blue finish, 4-5/8" or 5-1/2" **$510.00**
Price: 45 Colt KBNV455, stainless, 5-1/2" **$510.00**

Ruger Bisley-Vaquero Single-Action Revolver

Similar to the Vaquero except has Bisley-style hammer, grip and trigger and is available in 357 Magnum, 44 Magnum and 45 Colt only, with 4-5/8" or 5-1/2" barrel. Has smooth rosewood grips with Ruger medallion. Roll-engraved, unfluted cylinder. Introduced 1997. From Sturm, Ruger & Co.
Price: Color case-hardened frame, blue grip frame, barrel and cylinder, RBNV-475, RBNV-455 . . . . **$510.00**
Price: High-gloss stainless steel, KRBNV-475, KRBNV-455 . . . . . **$529.00**
Price: For simulated ivory grips add **$36.00**
Price: 44-40 BNV40 (4-5/8"), BNV405 (5-1/2"), BNV407 (7-1/2") . **$510.00**
Price: 44-40 KBNV40 (4-5/8"), KBNV405 (5-1/2"), KBNV407 (7-1/2") stainless **$510.00**

RUGER NEW BEARCAT SINGLE-ACTION

Caliber: 22 LR, 6-shot. **Barrel:** 4". **Weight:** 24 oz. **Length:** 8-7/8" overall. **Stocks:** Smooth rosewood with Ruger medallion. **Sights:** Blade front, fixed notch rear. **Features:** Reintroduction of the Ruger Bearcat with slightly lengthened frame, Ruger patented transfer bar safety system. Available in blue only. Introduced 1993. Comes with plastic lockable case and lock. From Sturm, Ruger & Co.
Price: SBC4, blue **$359.00**

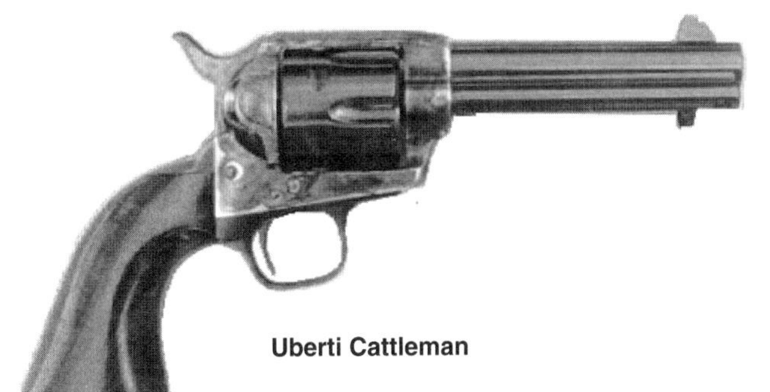
Uberti Cattleman

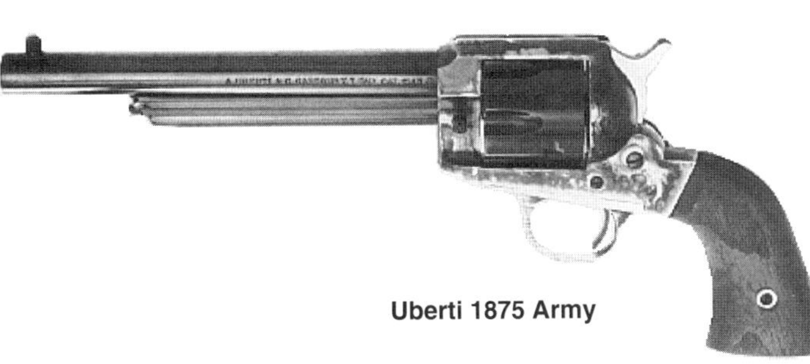
Uberti 1875 Army

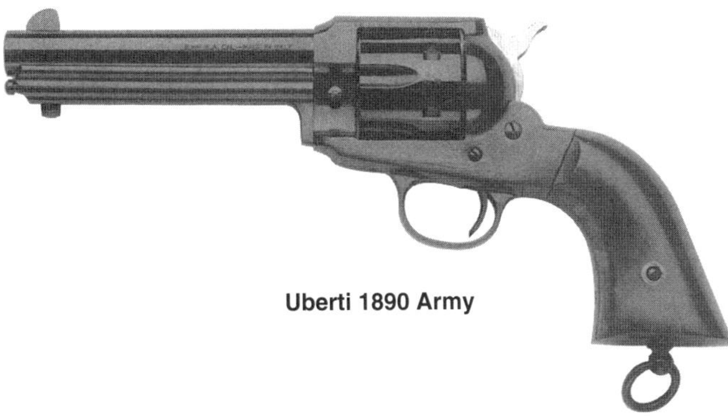
Uberti 1890 Army

RUGER SINGLE-SIX AND SUPER SINGLE-SIX CONVERTIBLE

Caliber: 22 LR, 6-shot; 22 WMR in extra cylinder. **Barrel:** 4-5/8", 5-1/2", 6-1/2", 9-1/2" (6-groove). **Weight:** 35 oz. (6-1/2" bbl.). **Length:** 11-13/16" overall (6-1/2" bbl.). **Stocks:** Smooth American walnut. **Sights:** Improved Patridge front on ramp, fully adjustable rear protected by integral frame ribs (super single-six); or fixed sight single six). **Features:** Ruger transfer bar safety system, loading gate interlock, hardened chrome-moly steel frame, wide trigger, music wire springs throughout, independent firing pin.

Price: 4-5/8", 5-1/2", 6-1/2", 9-1/2" barrel, blue, adjustable sight NR4, NR6, NR9, NR5 . . . . **$369.00**

Price: 5-1/2", 6-1/2" bbl. only, stainless steel, adjustable sight KNR5, KNR6. . . . . **$449.00**

Price: 5-1/2", 6-1/2" barrel, blue fixed sights **$369.00**

Ruger Bisley Small Frame Revolver

Similar to the Single-Six except frame is styled after the classic Bisley "flat-top." Most mechanical parts are unchanged. Hammer is lower and smoothly curved with a deeply checkered spur. Trigger is strongly curved with a wide smooth surface. Longer grip frame designed with a hand-filling shape, and the trigger guard is a large oval. Adjustable dovetail rear sight; front sight base accepts interchangeable square blades of various heights and styles. Has an unfluted cylinder and roll engraving. Weighs 41 oz. Chambered for 22 LR, 6-1/2" barrel only. Comes with plastic lockable case and lock. Introduced 1985.

Price: RB-22AW **$402.00**

Uberti Russian

Ruger Bisley Single-Action Revolver

Similar to standard Blackhawk except the hammer is lower with a smoothly curved, deeply checkered wide spur. The trigger is strongly curved with a wide smooth surface. Longer grip frame has a hand-filling shape. Adjustable rear sight, ramp-style front. Has an unfluted cylinder and roll engraving, adjustable sights. Chambered for 357, 44 Mags. and 45 Colt; 7-1/2" barrel; overall length of 13"; weighs 48 oz. Comes with plastic lockable case and lock. Introduced 1985.

Price: RB-35W, 357Mag, R3-44W, 44Mag, RB-45W, 45 Colt . . . **$510.00**

TRISTAR/UBERTI REGULATOR REVOLVER

Caliber: 45 Colt. **Barrel:** 4-3/4", 5-1/2", 7-1/2". **Weight:** 32-38 oz. **Length:** 8-1/4" overall (4-3/4" bbl.) **Grips:** One-piece walnut. **Sights:** Blade front, notch rear. **Features:** Uberti replica of 1873 Colt Model "P" revolver. Color-case hardened steel frame, brass backstrap and trigger guard, hammer-block safety. Imported from Italy by Tristar Sporting Arms.

Price: Regulator **$335.00**

Price: Regulator Deluxe (blued backstrap, trigger guard) **$367.00**

UBERTI 1873 CATTLEMAN SINGLE-ACTION

Caliber: 22 LR/22 WMR, 38 Spec., 357 Mag., 44 Spec., 44-40, 45 Colt/45 ACP, 6-shot. **Barrel:** 4-3/4", 5-1/2", 7-1/2"; 44-40, 45 Colt also with 3", 3-1/2", 4". **Weight:** 38 oz. (5-1/2" bbl.). **Length:** 10-3/4" overall (5-1/2" bbl.). **Stocks:** One-piece smooth walnut. **Sights:** Blade front, groove rear; fully adjustable rear available. **Features:** Steel or brass backstrap, trigger guard; color case-hardened frame, blued barrel, cylinder. Imported from Italy by Uberti U.S.A.

Price: Steel backstrap, trigger guard, fixed sights **$435.00**

Price: Brass backstrap, trigger guard, fixed sights. **$365.00**

Price: Bisley model. **$435.00**

Uberti 1873 Buckhorn Single-Action

A slightly larger version of the Cattleman revolver. Available in 44 Magnum or 44 Magnum/44-40 convertible, otherwise has same specs.

Price: Steel backstrap, trigger guard, fixed sights **$410.00**

Price: Convertible (two cylinders). **$475.00**

UBERTI 1875 SA ARMY OUTLAW REVOLVER

Caliber: 357 Mag., 44-40, 45 Colt, 45 Colt/45 ACP convertible, 6-shot. **Barrel:** 5-1/2", 7-1/2". **Weight:** 44 oz. **Length:** 13-3/4" overall. **Stocks:** Smooth walnut. **Sights:** Blade front, notch rear. **Features:** Replica of the 1875 Remington S.A. Army revolver. Brass trigger guard, color case-hardened frame, rest blued. Imported by Uberti U.S.A.

Price: **$435.00**

Price: 45 Colt/45 ACP convertible **$475.00**

UBERTI 1890 ARMY OUTLAW REVOLVER

Caliber: 357 Mag., 44-40, 45 Colt, 45 Colt/45 ACP convertible, 6-shot. **Barrel:** 5-1/2", 7-1/2". **Weight:** 37 oz. **Length:** 12-1/2" overall. **Stocks:** American walnut. **Sights:** Blade front, groove rear. **Features:** Replica of the 1890 Remington single-action. Brass trigger guard, rest is blued. Imported by Uberti U.S.A.

Price: **$435.00**

Price: 45 Colt/45 ACP convertible **$475.00**

UBERTI NEW MODEL RUSSIAN REVOLVER

Caliber: 44 Russian, 6-shot cylinder. **Barrel:** 6-1/2". **Weight:** 40 oz. **Length:** 12" overall. **Stocks:** Smooth walnut. **Sights:** Blade front, notch rear. **Features:** Repica of the S&W Model 3 Russian Third Model revolver. Spur trigger guard, polished blue finish. Introduced 1999. Imported by Uberti USA.

Price: **$775.00**

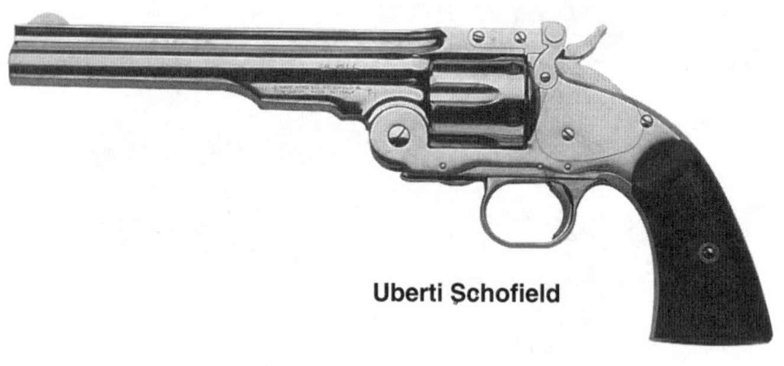
Uberti Schofield

Uberti Bisley Flat Top

Uberti Bisley

UBERTI 1875 SCHOFIELD REVOLVER

Caliber: 44-40, 45 Colt, 6-shot cylinder. **Barrel:** 5", 7". **Weight:** 39 oz. **Length:** 10-3/4" overall (5" barrel). **Stocks:** Smooth walnut. **Sights:** Blade front, notch rear. **Features:** Replica of Smith & Wesson Model 3 Schofield. Single-action, top-break with automatic ejection. Polished blue finish. Introduced 1994. Imported by Uberti USA.

Price: **$700.00**

UBERTI BISLEY MODEL SINGLE-ACTION REVOLVER

Caliber: 38-40, 357 Mag., 44 Spec., 44-40 or 45 Colt, 6-shot cylinder. **Barrel:** 4-3/4", 5-1/2", 7-1/2". **Weight:** 40 oz. **Length:** 12-1/2" overall (7-1/2" barrel). **Stocks:** Smooth walnut. **Sights:** Blade front, notch rear. **Features:** Replica of Colt's Bisley Model. Polished blue finish, color case-hardened frame. Introduced 1997. Imported by Uberti USA.

Price: **$435.00**

Uberti Bisley Model Flat Top Target Revolver

Similar to the standard Bisley model except with flat top strap, 7-1/2" barrel only, and a spring-loaded German silver front sight blade, standing leaf rear sight adjustable for windage. Polished blue finish, color case-hardened frame. Introduced 1998. Imported by Uberti USA.

Price: **$455.00**

U.S. FIRE-ARMS SINGLE ACTION ARMY REVOLVER

Caliber: 44 Russian, 38-40, 44-40, 45 Colt, 6-shot cylinder. **Barrel:** 4", 4-3/4", 5-1/2", 7-1/2", 10". **Weight:** 37 oz. **Length:** NA. **Grips:** Hard rubber. **Sights:** Blade front, notch rear. **Features:** Recreation of original guns; 3" and 4" have no ejector. Available with all-blue, blue with color case-hardening, or full nickel-plate finish. Made in U.S. by United States Fire-Arms Mfg. Co.

Price: 4" blue **$1,099.00**
Price: 4-3/4", blue/cased-colors **$1,199.00**
Price: 7-1/2", carbonal blue/case-colors **$1,425.00**
Price: 7-1/2" nickel **$1,349.00**

U.S. Fire-Arms Nettleton Cavalry Revolver

Similar to the Single Action Army, except in 45 Colt only, with 7-1/2" barrel, color case-hardened/blue finish, and has old-style hand numbering, exact cartouche branding and correct inspector hand-stamp markings. Made in U.S. by United States Fire-Arms Mfg. Co.

Price: **$1,225.00**
Price: Artillery Model, 5-1/2" barrel **$1,225.00**

U.S. Fire-Arms Bird Head Model Revolver

Similar to the Single Action Army except has bird's-head grip and comes with 3-1/2", 4" or 4-3/4" barrel. Made in U.S. by United States Fire-Arms Mfg. Co.

Price: 3-1/2" or 4" blue/color-case hardening **$1,199.00**
Price: 4-3/4", nickel-plated **$1,299.00**

U.S. Fire-Arms Flattop Target Revolver

Similar to the Single Action Army except 4-3/4", 5-1/2" or 7-1/2" barrel, two-piece hard rubber stocks, flat top frame, adjustable rear sight. Made in U.S. by United States Fire-Arms Mfg. Co.

Price: 4-3/4", blue, polished hammer **$1,150.00**
Price: 4-3/4", blue, case-colored hammer **$1,150.00**
Price: 5-1/2", blue, case-colored hammer **$1,150.00**
Price: 5-1/2", nickel-plated **$1,299.00**
Price: 7-1/2", blue, polished hammer **$1,150.00**
Price: 7-1/2", blue, case-colored hammer **$1,150.00**

U.S. FIRE-ARMS BISLEY MODEL REVOLVER

Caliber: 4 Colt, 6-shot cylinder. **Barrel:** 4-3/4", 5-1/2", 7-1/2", 10". **Weight:** 38 oz. (5-1/2" barrel). **Length:** NA. **Grips:** Two-piece hard rubber. **Sights:** Blade front, notch rear. **Features:** Available in all-blue, blue with color case-hardening, or full nickel plate finish. Made in U.S. by United States Patent Fire-Arms Mfg. Co.

Price: 5-1/2", blue/case-colors **$1,350.00**
Price: 7-1/2", blue/case-colors **$1,350.00**
Price: 10", nickel **$1,435.00**

U.S. Fire-Arms "China Camp" Cowboy Action Revolver

Similar to Single Action Army revolver except available in Silver Steel finish only. Offered in 4-3/4", 5-1/2", 7-1/2" and 10" barrels. Made in U.S. by United States Fire-Arms Mfg. Co.

Price: **$995.00**

U.S. Fire-Arms "Buntline Special"

Similar to Single Action Army revolver except has 16" barrel, flip-up rear peep sight, 45 Colt only. Bone case frame, armory blue or nickel finish. Made in U.S. by United States Fire-Arms Mfg. Co.

Price: **$2,199.00**

U.S. Fire-Arms Omni-Potent Six Shooter

Similar to Single Action Army revolver except has bird's head grip with lanyard ring and hump in backstrap. Offered in 4-3/4", 5-1/2" and 7-1/2" barrels. Made in U.S. by United States Fire-Arms Mfg. Co.

Price: 3-1/2", 4" blue/color case hardening **$1,340.00**
Price: 4-3/4", nickel plated **$1,439.00**

HANDGUNS — MISCELLANEOUS

Specially adapted single-shot and multi-barrel arms.

American Derringer Model 1

Bond Arms C2K Defender

AMERICAN DERRINGER MODEL 1

Caliber: 22 LR, 22 WMR, 30 Carbine, 30 Luger, 30-30 Win., 32 H&R Mag., 32-20, 380 ACP, 38 Super, 38 Spec., 38 Spec. shotshell, 38 Spec. +P, 9mm Para., 357 Mag., 357 Mag./45/410, 357 Maximum, 10mm, 40 S&W, 41 Mag., 38-40, 44-40 Win., 44 Spec., 44 Mag., 45 Colt, 45 Win. Mag., 45 ACP, 45 Colt/410, 45-70 single shot. **Barrel:** 3". **Weight:** 15-1/2 oz. (38 Spec.). **Length:** 4.82" overall. **Stocks:** Rosewood, Zebra wood. **Sights:** Blade front. **Features:** Made of stainless steel with high-polish or satin finish. Two-shot capacity. Manual hammer block safety. Introduced 1980. Available in almost any pistol caliber. Contact the factory for complete list of available calibers and prices. From American Derringer Corp.

Price: 22 LR **$320.00**
Price: 38 Spec. **$320.00**
Price: 357 Maximum **$345.00**
Price: 357 Mag. **$335.00**
Price: 9mm, 380 . . . . . **$320.00**
Price: 40 S&W **$335.00**
Price: 44 Spec. **$398.00**
Price: 44-40 Win. **$398.00**
Price: 45 Colt **$385.00**
Price: 30-30, 45 Win. Mag. **$460.00**
Price: 41, 44 Mags. **$470.00**
Price: 45-70, single shot **$387.00**
Price: 45 Colt, 410, 2-1/2" **$385.00**
Price: 45 ACP, 10mm Auto **$340.00**

American Derringer Model 4

Similar to the Model 1 except has 4.1" barrel, overall length of 6", and weighs 16-1/2 oz.; chambered for 357 Mag., 357 Maximum, 45-70, 3" 410-bore shotshells or 45 Colt or 44 Mag. Made of stainless steel. Manual hammer block safety. Introduced 1985.

Price: 3" 410/45 Colt **$425.00**
Price: 45-70 . . . . . **$560.00**
Price: 44 Mag. with oversize grips **$515.00**
Price: Alaskan Survival model (45-70 upper barrel, 410 or 45 Colt lower) **$475.00**

American Derringer Model 6

Similar to the Model 1 except has 6" barrel chambered for 3" 410 shotshells or 22 WMR, 357 Mag., 45 ACP, 45 Colt; rosewood stocks; 8.2" o.a.l. and weighs 21 oz. Shoots either round for each barrel. Manual hammer block safety. Introduced 1986.

Price: 22 WMR **$440.00**
Price: 357 Mag. **$440.00**
Price: 45 Colt/410 . . . . . **$450.00**
Price: 45 ACP **$440.00**

American Derringer Model 7 Ultra Lightweight

Similar to Model 1 except made of high strength aircraft aluminum. Weighs 7-1/2 oz., 4.82" o.a.l., rosewood stocks. Available in 22 LR, 22 WMR, 32 H&R Mag., 380 ACP, 38 Spec., 44 Spec. Introduced 1986.

Price: 22 LR, WMR **$325.00**
Price: 38 Spec. **$325.00**
Price: 380 ACP **$325.00**
Price: 32 H&R Mag/32 S&W Long **$325.00**
Price: 44 Spec. **$565.00**

American Derringer Model 10 Lightweight

Similar to the Model 1 except frame is of aluminum, giving weight of 10 oz. Stainless barrels. Available in 38 Spec., 45 Colt or 45 ACP only. Matte gray finish. Introduced 1989.

Price: 45 Colt **$385.00**
Price: 45 ACP **$330.00**
Price: 38 Spec. **$305.00**

American Derringer Lady Derringer

Same as the Model 1 except has tuned action, is fitted with scrimshawed synthetic ivory grips; chambered for 32 H&R Mag. and 38 Spec.; 357 Mag., 45 Colt, 45/410. Deluxe Grade is highly polished; Deluxe Engraved is engraved in a pattern similar to that used on 1880s derringers. All come in a French fitted jewelry box. Introduced 1991.

Price: 32 H&R Mag. **$375.00**
Price: 357 Mag. **$405.00**
Price: 38 Spec. **$360.00**
Price: 45 Colt, 45/410 . . . . . **$435.00**

American Derringer Texas Commemorative

A Model 1 Derringer with solid brass frame, stainless steel barrel and rosewood grips. Available in 38 Spec., 44-40 Win., or 45 Colt. Introduced 1987.

Price: 38 Spec. **$365.00**
Price: 44-40 . . . . . **$420.00**
Price: Brass frame, 45 Colt **$450.00**

AMERICAN DERRINGER DA 38 MODEL

Caliber: 22 LR, 9mm Para., 38 Spec., 357 Mag., 40 S&W. **Barrel:** 3". **Weight:** 14.5 oz. **Length:** 4.8" overall. **Stocks:** Rosewood, walnut or other hardwoods. **Sights:** Fixed. **Features:** Double-action only; two-shots. Manual safety. Made of satin-finished stainless steel and aluminum. Introduced 1989. From American Derringer Corp.

Price: 22 LR **$435.00**
Price: 38 Spec. **$460.00**
Price: 9mm Para. **$445.00**
Price: 357 Mag. **$450.00**
Price: 40 S&W **$475.00**

ANSCHUTZ MODEL 64P SPORT/TARGET PISTOL

Caliber: 22 LR, 22 WMR, 5-shot magazine. **Barrel:** 10". **Weight:** 3 lbs., 8 oz. **Length:** 18-1/2" overall. **Stock:** Choate Rynite. **Sights:** None furnished; grooved for scope mounting. **Features:** Right-hand bolt; polished blue finish. Introduced 1998. Imported from Germany by AcuSport.

Price: 22 LR **$455.95**
Price: 22 WMR **$479.95**

BOND ARMS TEXAS DEFENDER DERRINGER

Caliber: 9mm Para, 38 Spec./357 Mag., 40 S&W, 44 Spec./44 Mag., 45 Colt/410 shotshell. **Barrel:** 3", 3-1/2". **Weight:** 21 oz. **Length:** 5" overall. **Stocks:** Laminated black ash or rosewood. **Sights:** Blade front, fixed rear.

Davis Big Bore

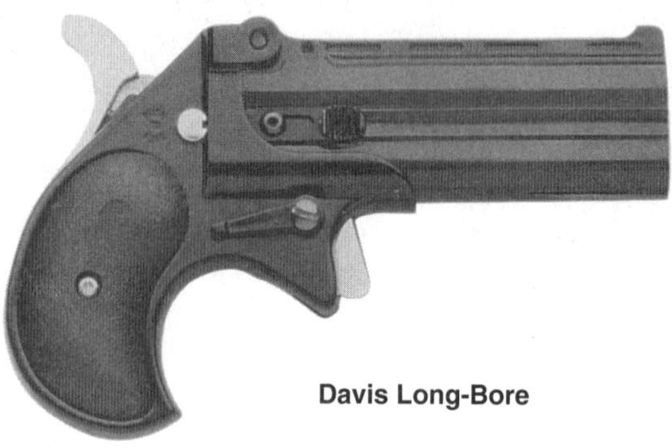
Davis Long-Bore

Features: Interchangeable barrels; retracting firing pins; rebounding firing pins; cross-bolt safety; removable trigger guard; automatic extractor for rimmed calibers. Stainless steel construction with blasted/polished and ground combination finish. Introduced 1997. Made in U.S. by Bond Arms, Inc.
Price: **$349.00**
Price: Century 2000 Defender (410-bore, 3-1/2" barrels). **$369.00**

BROWN CLASSIC SINGLE SHOT PISTOL

Caliber: 17 Ackley Hornet through 45-70 Govt. **Barrel:** 15" airgauged match grade. **Weight:** About 3 lbs., 7 oz. **Stocks:** Walnut; thumbrest target style. **Sights:** None furnished; drilled and tapped for scope mounting. **Features:** Falling block action gives rigid barrel-receiver mating; hand-fitted and headspaced. Introduced 1998. Made in U.S. by E.A. Brown Mfg.
Price: **$499.00**

DAVIS BIG BORE DERRINGERS

Caliber: 22 WMR, 38 Spec., 9mm Para. **Barrel:** 2.75". **Weight:** 11.5 oz. **Length:** 4.65" overall. **Stocks:** Textured black synthetic. **Sights:** Blade front, fixed notch rear. **Features:** Alloy frame, steel-lined barrels, steel breech block. Plunger-type safety with integral hammer block. Chrome or black Teflon finish. Introduced 1992. Made in U.S. by Davis Industries.
Price: **$98.00**
Price: 9mm Para. **$104.00**

DAVIS LONG-BORE DERRINGERS

Caliber: 22 WMR, 38 Spec., 9mm Para. **Barrel:** 3.5". **Weight:** 13 oz. **Length:** 5.65" overall. **Stocks:** Textured black synthetic. **Sights:** Fixed. **Features:** Chrome or black Teflon finish. Larger than Davis D-Series models. Introduced 1995. Made in U.S. by Davis Industries.
Price: **$104.00**
Price: 9mm Para. **$110.00**
Price: Big-Bore models (same calibers, 3/4" shorter barrels). **$98.00**

DAVIS D-SERIES DERRINGERS

Caliber: 22 LR, 22 WMR, 25 ACP, 32 ACP. **Barrel:** 2.4". **Weight:** 9.5 oz. **Length:** 4" overall. **Stocks:** Laminated wood or pearl. **Sights:** Blade front, fixed notch rear. **Features:** Choice of black Teflon or chrome finish; spur trigger. Introduced 1986. Made in U.S. by Davis Industries.
Price: **$99.50**

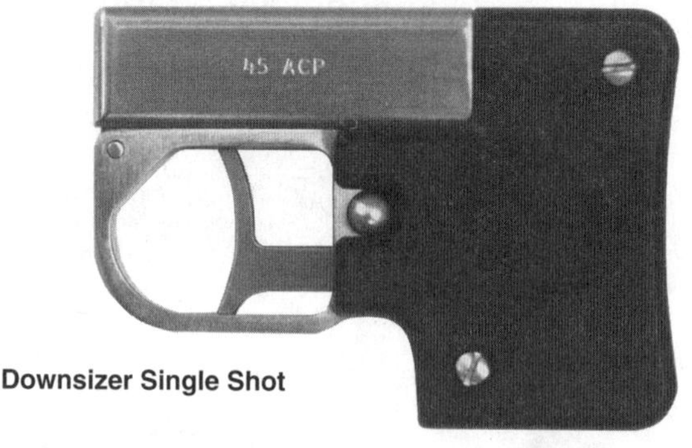

Downsizer Single Shot

Gaucher GN1 Silhouette

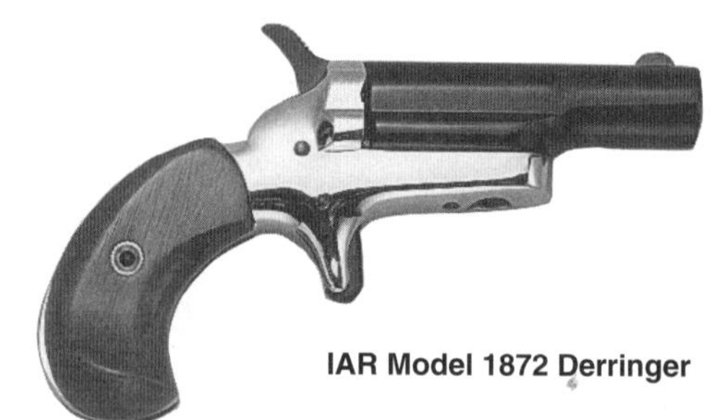
IAR Model 1872 Derringer

DOWNSIZER WSP SINGLE SHOT PISTOL

Caliber: 357 Magnum, 45 ACP. **Barrel:** 2.10". **Weight:** 11 oz. **Length:** 3.25" overall. **Stocks:** Black polymer. **Sights:** None. **Features:** Single shot, tip-up barrel. Double action only. Stainless steel construction. Measures .900" thick. Introduced 1997. From Downsizer Corp.
Price: **$459.00**

GAUCHER GN1 SILHOUETTE PISTOL

Caliber: 22 LR, single shot. **Barrel:** 10". **Weight:** 2.4 lbs. **Length:** 15.5" overall. **Stocks:** European hardwood. **Sights:** Blade front, open adjustable rear. **Features:** Bolt action, adjustable trigger. Introduced 1990. Imported from France by Mandall Shooting Supplies.
Price: About **$525.00**
Price: Model GP Silhouette **$425.00**

IAR MODEL 1872 DERRINGER

Caliber: 22 Short. **Barrel:** 2-3/8". **Weight:** 7 oz. **Length:** 5-1/8" overall. **Stocks:** Smooth walnut. **Sights:** Blade front, notch rear. **Features:** Gold or nickel frame with blue barrel. Reintroduced 1996 using original Colt designs and tooling for the Colt Model 4 Derringer. Made in U.S. by IAR, Inc.
Price: **$99.00**
Price: Single cased gun **$125.00**
Price: Double cased set **$215.00**

IAR MODEL 1888 DOUBLE DERRINGER

Caliber: 38 Special. **Barrel:** 2-3/4". **Weight:** 16 oz. **Length:** NA. **Stocks:** Smooth walnut. **Sights:** Blade front, notch rear. **Features:** All steel construction. Blue barrel, color case-hardened frame. Uses original designs and tooling for the Uberti New Maverick Derringer. Introduced 1999. Made in U.S. by IAR, Inc.
Price: **$395.00**

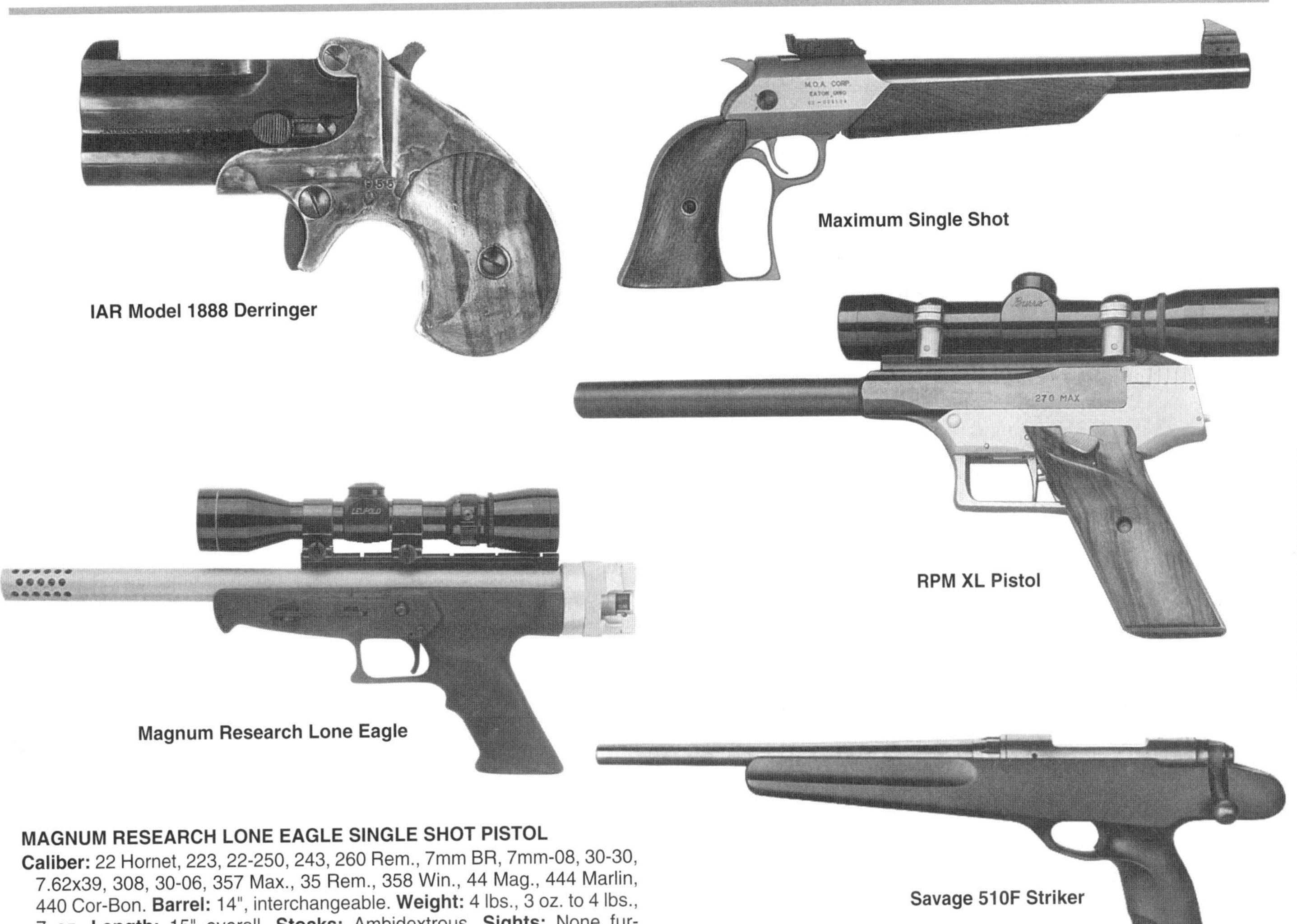

IAR Model 1888 Derringer

Maximum Single Shot

RPM XL Pistol

Magnum Research Lone Eagle

Savage 510F Striker

MAGNUM RESEARCH LONE EAGLE SINGLE SHOT PISTOL

Caliber: 22 Hornet, 223, 22-250, 243, 260 Rem., 7mm BR, 7mm-08, 30-30, 7.62x39, 308, 30-06, 357 Max., 35 Rem., 358 Win., 44 Mag., 444 Marlin, 440 Cor-Bon. **Barrel:** 14", interchangeable. **Weight:** 4 lbs., 3 oz. to 4 lbs., 7 oz. **Length:** 15" overall. **Stocks:** Ambidextrous. **Sights:** None furnished; drilled and tapped for scope mounting and open sights. Open sights optional. **Features:** Cannon-type rotating breech with spring-activated ejector. Ordnance steel with matte blue finish. Cross-bolt safety. External cocking lever on left side of gun. Muzzle brake optional. Introduced 1991. Available from Magnum Research, Inc.

Price: Complete pistol, black **$438.00**
Price: Barreled action only, black **$319.00**
Price: Complete pistol, chrome. **$478.00**
Price: Barreled action, chrome **$359.00**
Price: Scope base **$14.00**
Price: Adjustable open sights **$35.00**

MAXIMUM SINGLE SHOT PISTOL

Caliber: 22 LR, 22 Hornet, 22 BR, 22 PPC, 223 Rem., 22-250, 6mm BR, 6mm PPC, 243, 250 Savage, 6.5mm-35M, 270 MAX, 270 Win., 7mm TCU, 7mm BR, 7mm-35, 7mm INT-R, 7mm-08, 7mm Rocket, 7mm Super-Mag., 30 Herrett, 30 Carbine, 30-30, 308 Win., 30x39, 32-20, 350 Rem. Mag., 357 Mag., 357 Maximum, 358 Win., 375 H&H, 44 Mag., 454 Casull. **Barrel:** 8-3/4", 10-1/2", 14". **Weight:** 61 oz. (10-1/2" bbl.); 78 oz. (14" bbl.). **Length:** 15", 18-1/2" overall (with 10-1/2" and 14" bbl., respectively). **Stocks:** Smooth walnut stocks and forend. Also available with 17" finger groove grip. **Sights:** Ramp front, fully adjustable open rear. **Features:** Falling block action; drilled and tapped for M.O.A. scope mounts; integral grip frame/receiver; adjustable trigger; Douglas barrel (interchangeable). Introduced 1983. Made in U.S. by M.O.A. Corp.

Price: Stainless receiver, blue barrel **$799.00**
Price: Stainless receiver, stainless barrel. **$883.00**
Price: Extra blued barrel. **$254.00**
Price: Extra stainless barrel **$317.00**
Price: Scope mount **$60.00**

RPM XL SINGLE SHOT PISTOL

Caliber: 22 LR through 45-70. **Barrel:** 8", 10-3/4", 12", 14". **Weight:** About 60 oz. **Length:** NA. **Stocks:** Smooth Goncalo Alves with thumb and heel rests. **Sights:** Hooded front with interchangeable post, or Patridge; ISGW rear adjustable for windage and elevation. **Features:** Barrel drilled and tapped for scope mount. Visible cocking indicator. Spring-loaded barrel lock, positive hammer-block safety. Trigger adjustable for weight of pull and over-travel. Contact maker for complete price list. Made in U.S. by RPM.

Price: Hunter model (stainless frame, 5/16" underlug, latch lever and positive extractor) **$1,295.00**
Price: Extra barrel, 8" through 10-3/4" **$387.50**
Price: Extra barrel with positive extractor, add **$100.00**
Price: Muzzle brake **$100.00**

SAVAGE STRIKER BOLT-ACTION HUNTING HANDGUN

Caliber: 223, 22-250, 243, 206, 7mm-08, 308, 2-shot magazine. **Barrel:** 14". **Weight:** About 5 lbs. **Length:** 22-1/2" overall. **Stock:** Black composite ambidextrous mid-grip; grooved forend; "Dual Pillar" bedding. **Sights:** None furnished; drilled and tapped for scope mounting. **Features:** Short left-hand bolt with right-hand ejection; free-floated barrel; uses Savage Model 110 rifle scope rings/bases. Introduced 1998. Made in U.S. by Savage Arms, Inc.

Price: Model 510F (blued barrel and action) **$425.00**
Price: Model 516FSS (stainless barrel and action) **$462.00**
Price: Model 516FSAK (stainless, adjustable muzzle brake). **$512.00**
Price: Super Striker **$512.00**

HANDGUNS — MISCELLANEOUS

T/C Encore

Weatherby Mark V CFP

T/C Stainless Contender

Savage Sport Striker Bolt-Action Hunting Handgun

Similar to the Striker, but chambered in 22 LR and 22 WMR. Detachable, 10-shot magazine (5-shot magazine for 22 WMR). Overall length 19", weighs 4 lbs. Ambidextrous fiberglass/graphite composite rear grip. Drilled and tapped, scope mount installed. Introduced 2000. Made in U.S. by Savage Arms Inc.

Price: Model 501F (blue finish, 22LR) **$201.00**
Price: Model 502F (blue finish, 22 WMR). **$221.00**

THOMPSON/CENTER ENCORE PISTOL

Caliber: 22-250, 223, 260 Rem., 7mm-08, 243, 308, 270, 30-06, 44 Mag., 454 Casull, 444 Marlin single shot. **Barrel:** 12", 15", tapered round. **Weight:** NA. **Length:** 21" overall with 12" barrel. **Stocks:** American walnut with finger grooves, walnut forend. **Sights:** Blade on ramp front, adjustable rear, or none. **Features:** Interchangeable barrels; action opens by squeezing the trigger guard; drilled and tapped for scope mounting; blue finish. Announced 1996. Made in U.S. by Thompson/Center Arms.

Price: **$554.06**
Price: Extra 12" barrels. **$240.68**
Price: Extra 15" barrels. **$248.14**
Price: 45 Colt/410 barrel, 12" **$263.24**
Price: 45 Colt/410 barrel, 15" **$280.39**

Thompson/Center Stainless Encore Pistol

Similar to the blued Encore except made of stainless steel and available wtih 15" barrel in 223, 22-250 7mm-08, 308. Comes with black rubber grip and forend. Made in U.S. by Thompson/Center Arms.

Price: **$620.99**

Thompson/Center Stainless Super 14

Same as the standard Super 14 and Super 16 except they are made of stainless steel with blued sights. Both models have black Rynite forend and finger-groove, ambidextrous grip with a built-in rubber recoil cushion that has a sealed-in air pocket. Receiver has a different cougar etching. Available in 22 LR Match, .223 Rem., 30-30 Win., 35 Rem. (Super 14), 45 Colt/410. Introduced 1993.

Price: **$578.40**
Price: 45 Colt/410, 14" **$613.94**

Thompson/Center Contender Shooter's Package

Package contains a 14" barrel without iron sights (10" for the 22 LR Match); Weaver-style base and rings; 2.5x-7x Recoil Proof pistol scope; and a soft carrying case. Calibers 22 LR, 223, 7-30 Waters, 30-30. Frame and barrel are blued; grip and forend are black composite. Introduced 1998. Made in U.S. by Thompson/Center Arms.

Price **$735.00**

THOMPSON/CENTER CONTENDER

Caliber: 7mm TCU, 30-30 Win., 22 LR, 22 WMR, 22 Hornet, 223 Rem., 270 Rem., 7-30 Waters, 32-20 Win., 357 Mag., 357 Rem. Max., 44 Mag., 10mm Auto, 445 SuperMag., 45/410, single shot. **Barrel:** 10", bull barrel and vent. rib. **Weight:** 43 oz. (10" bbl.). **Length:** 13-1/4" (10" bbl.). **Stock:** T/C "Competitor Grip." Right or left hand. **Sights:** Under-cut blade ramp front, rear adjustable for windage and elevation. **Features:** Break-open action with automatic safety. Single-action only. Interchangeable bbls., both caliber (rim & centerfire), and length. Drilled and tapped for scope. Engraved frame. See T/C catalog for exact barrel/caliber availability.

Price: Blued (rimfire cals.) **$509.03**
Price: Blued (centerfire cals.) **$509.03**
Price: Extra bbls. **$229.02**
Price: 45/410, internal choke bbl. **$235.11**

Thompson/Center Stainless Contender

Same as the standard Contender except made of stainless steel with blued sights, black Rynite forend and ambidextrous finger-groove grip with a built-in rubber recoil cushion that has a sealed-in air pocket. Receiver has a different cougar etching. Available with 10" bull barrel in 22 LR, 22 LR Match, 22 Hornet, 223 Rem., 30-30 Win., 357 Mag., 44 Mag., 45 Colt/410. Introduced 1993.

Price: **$566.59**
Price: 45 Colt/410. . . . . **$590.44**
Price: With 22 LR match chamber **$578.40**

UBERTI ROLLING BLOCK TARGET PISTOL

Caliber: 22 LR, 22 WMR, 22 Hornet, 357 Mag., 45 Colt, single shot. **Barrel:** 9-7/8", half-round, half-octagon. **Weight:** 44 oz. **Length:** 14" overall. **Stock:** Walnut grip and forend. **Sights:** Blade front, fully adjustable rear. **Features:** Replica of the 1871 rolling block target pistol. Brass trigger guard, color case-hardened frame, blue barrel. Imported by Uberti U.S.A.

Price: **$410.00**

WEATHERBY MARK V CFP PISTOL

Caliber: 22-250, 243, 7mm-08, 308. **Barrel:** 15" fluted stainless. **Weight:** NA. **Length:** NA. **Stock:** Brown laminate with ambidextrous rear grip. **Sights:** None furnished; drilled and tapped for scope mounting. **Features:** Uses Mark V lightweight receiver of chrome-moly steel, matte blue finish. Introduced 1998. Made in U.S. From Weatherby.

Price: **$1,049.00**

WEATHERBY MARK V ACCUMARK CFP PISTOL

Caliber: 223, 22-250, 243, 7mm-08, 308; 3-shot magazine. **Barrel:** 15"; 1:12" twist (223). **Weight:** 5 lbs. **Length:** 26-1/2" overall. **Stock:** Kevlar-fiberglass composite. **Sights:** None; drilled and tapped for scope mounting. **Features:** Molded-in aluminum bedding plate; fluted stainless steel barrel; fully adjustable trigger. Introduced 2000. From Weatherby.

Price: . . . . **NA**

BLACKPOWDER SINGLE SHOT PISTOLS — FLINT & PERCUSSION

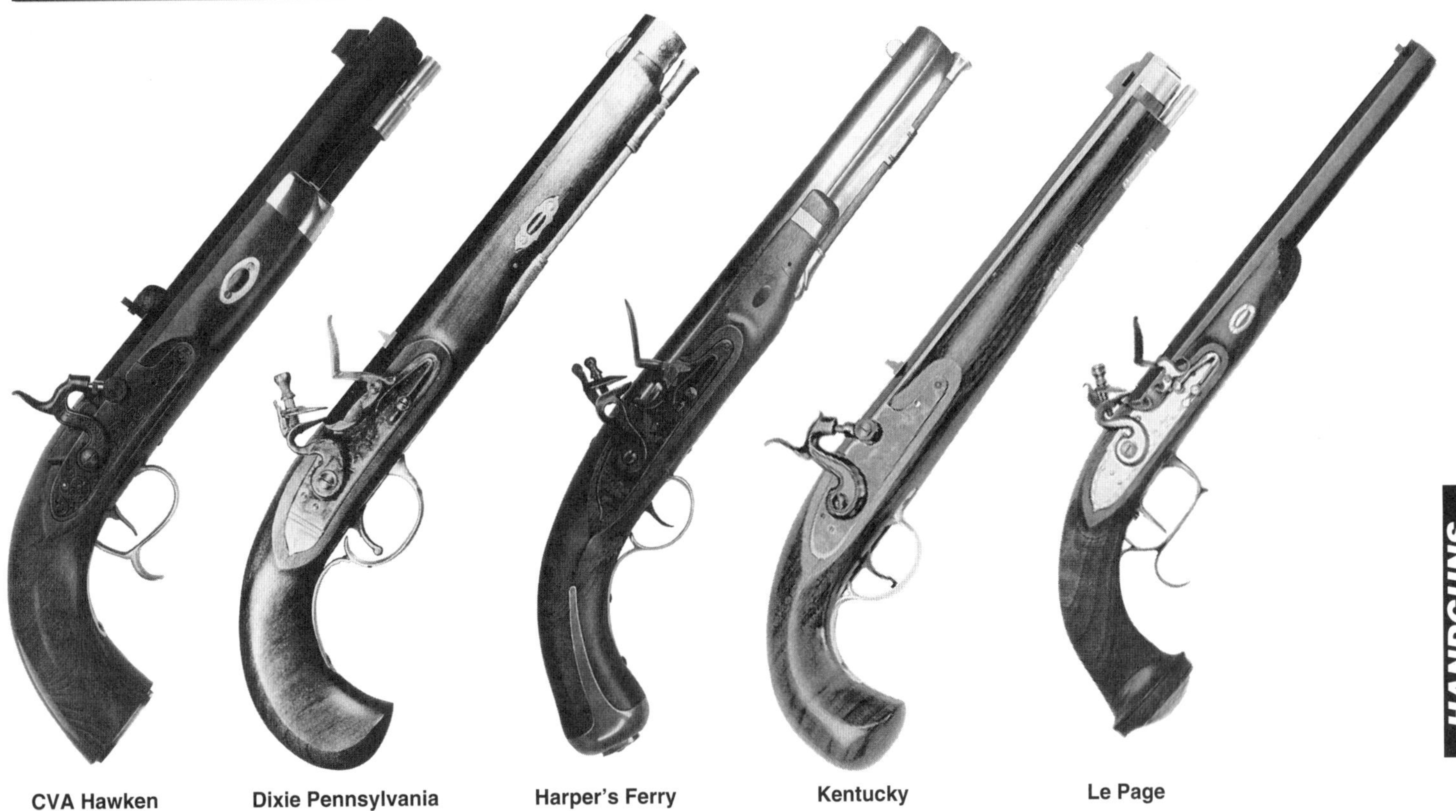

CVA Hawken   Dixie Pennsylvania   Harper's Ferry   Kentucky   Le Page

HANDGUNS

CVA HAWKEN PISTOL

Caliber: 50. **Barrel:** 9-3/4"; 15/16" flats. **Weight:** 50 oz. **Length:** 16-1/2" overall. **Stocks:** Select hardwood. **Sights:** Beaded blade front, fully adjustable open rear. **Features:** Color case-hardened lock, polished brass wedge plate, instep, ramrod thimble, trigger guard, grip cap. Imported by CVA.

Price: **$167.95**

Price: Kit **$127.95**

DIXIE PENNSYLVANIA PISTOL

Caliber: 44 (.430" round ball). **Barrel:** 10", (7/8" octagon). **Weight:** 2-1/2 labs. **Stocks:** Walnut-stained hardwood. **Sights:** Blade front, open rear drift-adjustable for windage; brass. **Features:** Available in flint only. Brass trigger guard, thimbles, instep, wedge plates; high-luster blue barrel. Imported from Italy by Dixie Gun Works.

Price: Finished **$195.00**

Price: Kit **$185.00**

FRENCH-STYLE DUELING PISTOL

Caliber: 44. **Barrel:** 10". **Weight:** 35 oz. **Length:** 15-3/4" overall. **Stocks:** Carved walnut. **Sights:** Fixed. **Features:** Comes with velvet-lined case and accessories. Imported by Mandall Shooting Supplies.

Price: **$295.00**

HARPER'S FERRY 1806 PISTOL

Caliber: 58 (.570" round ball). **Barrel:** 10". **Weight:** 40 oz. **Length:** 16" overall. **Stocks:** Walnut. **Sights:** Fixed. **Features:** Case-hardened lock, brass-mounted browned barrel. Replica of the first U.S. Gov't.-made flintlock pistol. Imported by Navy Arms, Dixie Gun Works.

Price: . . . . **$275.00 to $405.00**

Price: Kit (Dixie) **$249.00**

KENTUCKY FLINTLOCK PISTOL

Caliber: 44, 45. **Barrel:** 10-1/8". **Weight:** 32 oz. **Length:** 15-1/2" overall. **Stocks:** Walnut. **Sights:** Fixed. **Features:** Specifications, including caliber, weight and length may vary with importer. Case-hardened lock, blued barrel; available also as brass barrel flint Model 1821. Imported by Navy Arms, The Armoury.

Price: . . . . **$145.00 to $235.00**

Price: In kit form, from . . . . **$90.00 to $112.00**

Price: Single cased set (Navy Arms) **$360.00**

Price: Double cased set (Navy Arms) **$590.00**

Kentucky Percussion Pistol

Similar to flint version but percussion lock. Imported by The Armoury, Navy Arms, CVA (50-cal.).

Price: . . . . **$129.95 to $225.00**

Price: Blued steel barrel (CVA) **$167.95**

Price: Kit form (CVA) **$119.95**

Price: Steel barrel (Armoury) **$179.00**

Price: Single cased set (Navy Arms) **$355.00**

Price: Double cased set (Navy Arms) **$600.00**

LE PAGE PERCUSSION DUELING PISTOL

Caliber: 44. **Barrel:** 10", rifled. **Weight:** 40 oz. **Length:** 16" overall. **Stocks:** Walnut, fluted butt. **Sights:** Blade front, notch rear. **Features:** Double-set triggers. Blued barrel; trigger guard and buttcap are polished silver. Imported by Dixie Gun Works.

Price: **$259.95**

LYMAN PLAINS PISTOL

Caliber: 50 or 54. **Barrel:** 8"; 1:30" twist, both calibers. **Weight:** 50 oz. **Length:** 15" overall. **Stocks:** Walnut half-stock. **Sights:** Blade front, square notch rear adjustable for windage. **Features:** Polished brass trigger guard and ramrod tip, color case-hardened coil spring lock, spring-loaded trigger, stainless steel nipple, blackened iron furniture. Hooked patent breech, detachable belt hook. Introduced 1981. From Lyman Products.

Price: Finished **$229.95**

Price: Kit **$184.95**

PEDERSOLI MANG TARGET PISTOL

Caliber: 38. **Barrel:** 10.5", octagonal; 1:15" twist, **Weight:** 2.5 lbs. **Length:** 17.25" overall. **Stocks:** Walnut with fluted grip. **Sights:** Blade front, open rear adjustable for windage. **Features:** Browned barrel, polished breech plug, rest color case-hardened. Imported from Italy by Dixie Gun Works.

Price: **$786.00**

BLACKPOWDER SINGLE SHOT PISTOLS — FLINT & PERCUSSION

Lyman Plains Pistol · Pedersoli Mang · Queen Anne · Traditions Pioneer · Traditions William Parker

QUEEN ANNE FLINTLOCK PISTOL

Caliber: 50 (.490" round ball). **Barrel:** 7-1/2", smoothbore. **Stocks:** Walnut. **Sights:** None. **Features:** Browned steel barrel, fluted brass trigger guard, brass mask on butt. Lockplate left in the white. Made by Pedersoli in Italy. Introduced 1983. Imported by Dixie Gun Works.

Price: $225.00
Price: Kit $175.00

THOMPSON/CENTER ENCORE 209x50 MAGNUM PISTOL

Caliber: 50. **Barrel:** 15"; 1:20" twist. **Weight:** About 4 lbs. Grips: American walnut grip and forend. **Sights:** Click-adjustable, steel rear, ramp front. **Features:** Uses 209 shotgun primer for closed-breech ignition; accepts charges up to 110 grains of FFg black powder or two, 50-grain Pyrodex pellets. Introduced 2000.

Price: $569.47

TRADITIONS BUCKHUNTER PRO IN-LINE PISTOL

Caliber: 50. **Barrel:** 9-1/2", round. **Weight:** 48 oz. **Length:** 14" overall. **Stocks:** Smooth walnut or black epoxy-coated hardwood grip and forend. **Sights:** Beaded blade front, folding adjustable rear. **Features:** Thumb safety; removable stainless steel breech plug; adjustable trigger, barrel drilled and tapped for scope mounting. From Traditions.

Price: With walnut grip $229.00
Price: Nickel with black grip $239.00
Price: With walnut grip and 12-1/2" barrel $239.00
Price: Nickel with black grip, muzzle brake and 14-3/4" fluted barrel $284.00

TRADITIONS KENTUCKY PISTOL

Caliber: 50. **Barrel:** 10"; octagon with 7/8" flats; 1:20" twist. **Weight:** 40 oz. **Length:** 15" overall. **Stocks:** Stained beech. **Sights:** Blade front, fixed rear. **Features:** Birds-head grip; brass thimbles; color case-hardened lock. Percussion only. Introduced 1995. From Traditions.

Price: Finished $139.00
Price: Kit $109.00

TRADITIONS PIONEER PISTOL

Caliber: 45. **Barrel:** 9-5/8"; 13/16" flats, 1:16" twist. **Weight:** 31 oz. **Length:** 15" overall. **Stocks:** Beech. **Sights:** Blade front, fixed rear. **Features:** V-type mainspring. Single trigger. German silver furniture, blackened hardware. From Traditions.

Traditions Buckhunter Pro

Price: $139.00
Price: Kit $119.00

TRADITIONS TRAPPER PISTOL

Caliber: 50. **Barrel:** 9-3/4"; 7/8" flats; 1:20" twist. **Weight:** 2-3/4 lbs. **Length:** 16" overall. **Stocks:** Beech. **Sights:** Blade front, adjustable rear. **Features:** Double-set triggers; brass buttcap, trigger guard, wedge plate, forend tip, thimble. From Traditions.

Price: Percussion $189.00
Price: Flintlock $209.00
Price: Kit $149.00

TRADITIONS VEST-POCKET DERRINGER

Caliber: 31. **Barrel:** 2-1/4"; brass. **Weight:** 8 oz. **Length:** 4-3/4" overall. **Stocks:** Simulated ivory. **Sights:** Beed front. **Features:** Replica of riverboat gamblers' derringer; authentic spur trigger. From Traditions.

Price: $109.00

TRADITIONS WILLIAM PARKER PISTOL

Caliber: 50. **Barrel:** 10-3/8"; 15/16" flats; polished steel. **Weight:** 37 oz. **Length:** 17-1/2" overall. **Stocks:** Walnut with checkered grip. **Sights:** Brass blade front, fixed rear. **Features:** Replica dueling pistol with 1:20" twist, hooked breech. Brass wedge plate, trigger guard, cap guard; separate ramrod. Double-set triggers. Polished steel barrel, lock. Imported by Traditions.

Price: $269.00

BLACKPOWDER REVOLVERS

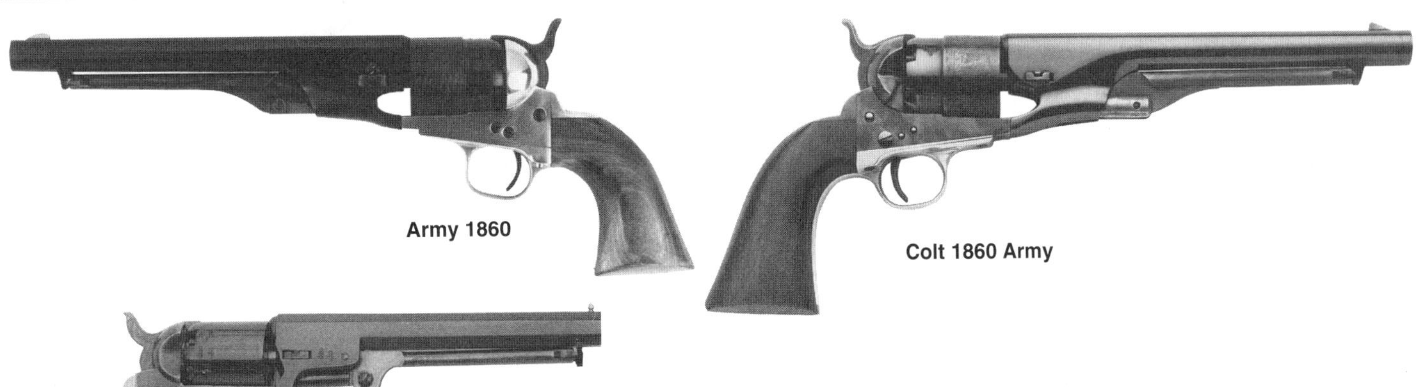

Army 1860

Colt 1860 Army

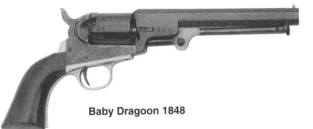

Baby Dragoon 1848

ARMY 1851 PERCUSSION REVOLVER

Caliber: 44, 6-shot. **Barrel:** 7-1/2". **Weight:** 45 oz. **Length:** 13" overall. **Stocks:** Walnut finish. **Sights:** Fixed. **Features:** 44-caliber version of the 1851 Navy. Imported by The Armoury, Armsport.

Price: **$129.00**

ARMY 1860 PERCUSSION REVOLVER

Caliber: 44, 6-shot. **Barrel:** 8". **Weight:** 40 oz. **Length:** 13-5/8" overall. **Stocks:** Walnut. **Sights:** Fixed. **Features:** Engraved Navy scene on cylinder; brass trigger guard; case-hardened frame, loading lever and hammer. Some importers supply pistol cut for detachable shoulder stock, have accessory stock available. Imported by Cabela's (1860 Lawman), E.M.F., Navy Arms, The Armoury, Cimarron, Dixie Gun Works (half-fluted cylinder, not roll engraved), Euroarms of America (brass or steel model), Armsport, Traditions (brass or steel), Uberti U.S.A. Inc., United States Patent Fire-Arms.

Price: About .... **$92.95 to $395.00**

Price: Hartford model, steel frame, German silver trim, cartouches (E.M.F.) **$215.00**

Price: Single cased set (Navy Arms) **$300.00**

Price: Double cased set (Navy Arms)...................... **$490.00**

Price: 1861 Navy: Same as Army except 36-cal., 7-1/2" bbl., weighs 41 oz., cut for shoulder stock; round cylinder (fluted available), from Cabela's, CVA (brass frame, 44-cal.), United States Patent Fire-Arms ....**$99.95 to $385.00**

Price: Steel frame kit (E.M.F., Euroarms).......... **$125.00 to $216.25**

Price: Colt Army Police, fluted cyl., 5-1/2", 36-cal. (Cabela's) ... **$124.95**

Price: With nickeled frame, barrel and backstrap, gold-tone fluted cylinder, trigger and hammer, simulated ivory grips (Traditions) **$199.00**

BABY DRAGOON 1848, 1849 POCKET, WELLS FARGO

Caliber: 31. **Barrel:** 3", 4", 5", 6"; seven-groove; RH twist. **Weight:** About 21 oz. **Stocks:** Varnished walnut. **Sights:** Brass pin front, hammer notch rear. **Features:** No loading lever on Baby Dragoon or Wells Fargo models. Unfluted cylinder with stagecoach holdup scene; cupped cylinder pin; no grease grooves; one safety pin on cylinder and slot in hammer face; straight (flat) mainspring. From Armsport, Cimarron F.A. Co., Dixie Gun Works, Uberti U.S.A. Inc.

Price: 6" barrel, with loading lever (Dixie Gun Works) **$254.95**

Price: 4" (Uberti USA Inc.) **$335.00**

CABELA'S STARR PERCUSSION REVOLVERS

Caliber: 44. **Barrel:** 6", 8". **Weight:** N/A. **Length:** N/A. Grips: Walnut. **Sights:** Blade front. **Features:** Replicas of government-contract revolvers made by Ebenezer T. Starr. Knurled knob allows quick removal and replacement of cylinder. Introduced 2000. From Cabela's.

Price: Starr 1858 Army double action, 6" barrel. **$349.99**

Price: Starr 1863 Army single action, 8" barrel **$349.99**

COLT 1860 ARMY PERCUSSION REVOLVER

Caliber: 44. **Barrel:** 8", 7-groove, left-hand twist. **Weight:** 42 oz. **Stocks:** One-piece walnut. **Sights:** German silver front sight, hammer notch rear. **Features:** Steel backstrap cut for shoulder stock; brass trigger guard. Cylinder has Navy scene. Color case-hardened frame, hammer, loading lever. Reproduction of original gun with all original markings. From Colt Blackpowder Arms Co.

Price: **$449.95**

COLT 1848 BABY DRAGOON REVOLVER

Caliber: 31, 5-shot. **Barrel:** 4". **Weight:** About 21 oz. **Stocks:** Smooth walnut. **Sights:** Brass pin front, hammer notch rear. **Features:** Color case-hardened frame; no loading lever; square-back trigger guard; round bolt cuts; octagonal barrel; engraved cylinder scene. Imported by Colt Blackpowder Arms Co.

Price: **$429.95**

Colt 1860 "Cavalry Model" Percussion Revolver

Similar to the 1860 Army except has fluted cylinder. Color case-hardened frame, hammer, loading lever and plunger; blued barrel, backstrap and cylinder, brass trigger guard. Has four-screw frame cut for optional shoulder stock. From Colt Blackpowder Arms Co.

Price: **$399.95**

COLT 1851 NAVY PERCUSSION REVOLVER

Caliber: 36. **Barrel:** 7-1/2", octagonal; 7-groove left-hand twist. **Weight:** 40-1/2 oz. **Stocks:** One-piece oiled American walnut. **Sights:** Brass pin front, hammer notch rear. **Features:** Faithful reproduction of the original gun. Color case-hardened frame, loading lever, plunger, hammer and latch. Blue cylinder, trigger, barrel, screws, wedge. Silver-plated brass backstrap and square-back trigger guard. From Colt Blackpowder Arms Co.

Price: **$449.95**

COLT 1861 NAVY PERCUSSION REVOLVER

Caliber: 36. **Barrel:** 7-1/2". **Weight:** 42 oz. **Length:** 13-1/8" overall. **Stocks:** One-piece walnut. **Sights:** Blade front, hammer notch rear. **Features:** Color case-hardened frame, loading lever, plunger; blued barrel, backstrap, trigger guard; roll-engraved cylinder and barrel. From Colt Blackpowder Arms Co.

Price: **$449.95**

COLT 1849 POCKET DRAGOON REVOLVER

Caliber: 31. **Barrel:** 4". **Weight:** 24 oz. **Length:** 9-1/2" overall. **Stocks:** One-piece walnut. **Sights:** Fixed. Brass pin front, hammer notch rear. **Features:** Color case-hardened frame. No loading lever. Unfluted cylinder with engraved scene. Exact reproduction of original. From Colt Blackpowder Arms Co.

Price: **$429.95**

COLT 1862 POCKET POLICE "TRAPPER MODEL" REVOLVER

Caliber: 36. **Barrel:** 3-1/2". **Weight:** 20 oz. **Length:** 8-1/2" overall. **Stocks:** One-piece walnut. **Sights:** Blade front, hammer notch rear. **Features:** Has separate 4-5/8" brass ramrod. Color case-hardened frame and hammer; silver-plated backstrap and trigger guard; blued semi-fluted cylinder, blued barrel. From Colt Blackpowder Arms Co.

Price: **$429.95**

BLACKPOWDER REVOLVERS

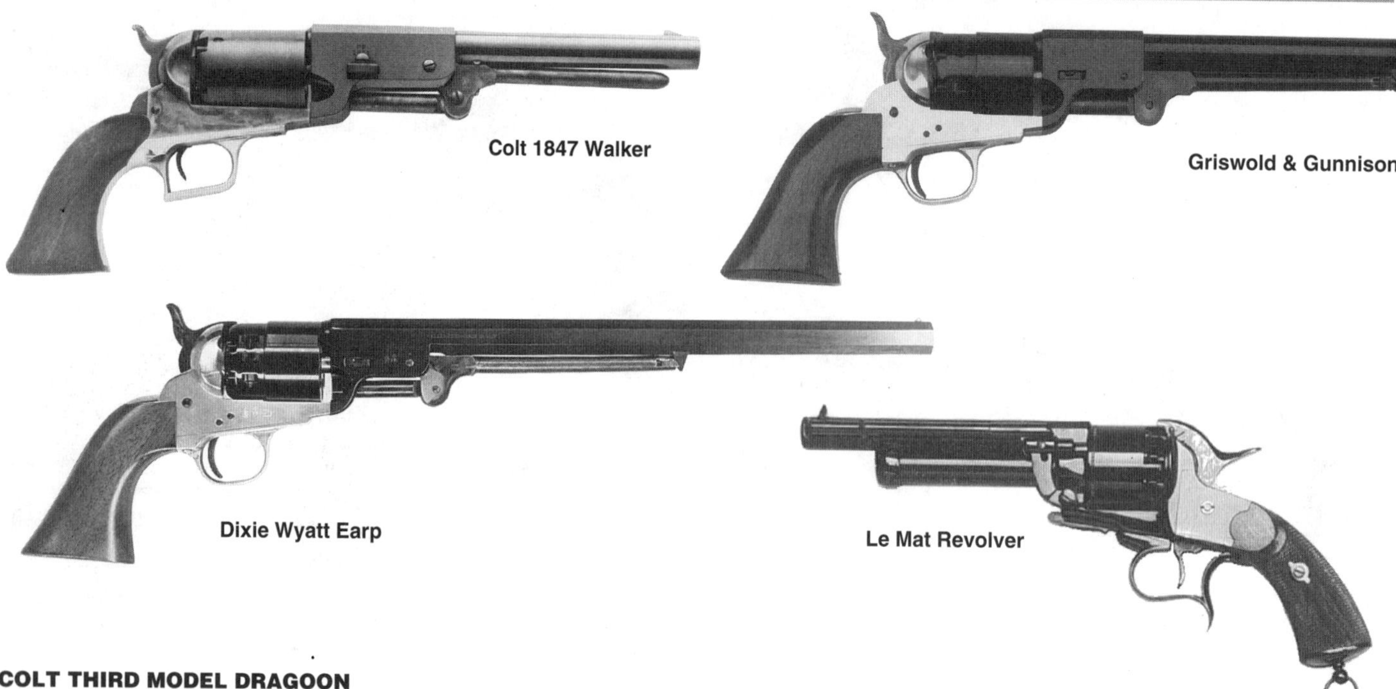

Colt 1847 Walker

Griswold & Gunnison

Dixie Wyatt Earp

Le Mat Revolver

HANDGUNS

COLT THIRD MODEL DRAGOON

Caliber: 44. **Barrel:** 7-1/2". **Weight:** 66 oz. **Length:** 13-3/4" overall. **Stocks:** One-piece walnut. **Sights:** Blade front, hammer notch rear. **Features:** Color case-hardened frame, hammer, lever and plunger; round trigger guard; flat mainspring; hammer roller; rectangular bolt cuts. From Colt Blackpowder Arms Co.

Price: Three-screw frame with brass grip straps **$499.95**

Price: First Dragoon (oval bolt cuts in cylinder, square-back trigger guard) **$499.95**

Price: Second Dragoon (rectangular bolt cuts in cylinder, square-back trigger guard) **$499.95**

Colt Walker 150th Anniversary Revolver

Similar to the standard Walker except has original-type "A Company No. 1" markings embellished in gold. Serial numbers begin with 221, a continuation of A Company numbers. Imported by Colt Blackpowder Arms Co.

Price: **$699.95**

COLT 1847 WALKER PERCUSSION REVOLVER

Caliber: 44. **Barrel:** 9", 7-groove; right-hand twist. **Weight:** 73 oz. **Stocks:** One-piece walnut. **Sights:** German silver front sight, hammer notch rear. **Features:** Made in U.S. Faithful reproduction of the original gun, including markings. Color case-hardened frame, hammer, loading lever and plunger. Blue steel backstrap, brass square-back trigger guard. Blue barrel, cylinder, trigger and wedge. From Colt Blackpowder Arms Co.

Price: **$499.95**

DIXIE WYATT EARP REVOLVER

Caliber: 44. **Barrel:** 12", octagon. **Weight:** 46 oz. **Length:** 18" overall. **Stocks:** Two-piece walnut. **Sights:** Fixed. **Features:** Highly polished brass frame, backstrap and trigger guard; blued barrel and cylinder; case-hardened hammer, trigger and loading lever. Navy-size shoulder stock ($45) will fit with minor fitting. From Dixie Gun Works.

Price: **$150.00**

GRISWOLD & GUNNISON PERCUSSION REVOLVER

Caliber: 36 or 44, 6-shot. **Barrel:** 7-1/2". **Weight:** 44 oz. (36-cal.). **Length:** 13" overall. **Stocks:** Walnut. **Sights:** Fixed. **Features:** Replica of famous Confederate pistol. Brass frame, backstrap and trigger guard; case-hardened loading lever; rebated cylinder (44-cal. only). Rounded Dragoon-type barrel. Imported by Navy Arms as Reb Model 1860.

Price: **$115.00**

Price: Kit.. **$90.00**

Price: Single cased set................................ **$235.00**

Price: Double cased set **$365.00**

LE MAT REVOLVER

Caliber: 44/65. **Barrel:** 6-3/4" (revolver); 4-7/8" (single shot). **Weight:** 3 lbs., 7 oz. **Stocks:** Hand-checkered walnut. **Sights:** Post front, hammer notch rear. **Features:** Exact reproduction with all-steel construction; 44-cal. 9-shot cylinder, 65-cal. single barrel; color case-hardened hammer with selector; spur trigger guard; ring at butt; lever-type barrel release. From Navy Arms.

Price: Cavalry model (lanyard ring, spur trigger guard) **$595.00**

Price: Army model (round trigger guard, pin-type barrel release) **$595.00**

Price: Naval-style (thumb selector on hammer).............. **$595.00**

Price: Engraved 18th Georgia cased set **$795.00**

Price: Engraved Beauregard cased set **$1,000.00**

NAVY ARMS NEW MODEL POCKET REVOLVER

Caliber: 31, 5-shot. **Barrel:** 3-1/2", octagon. **Weight:** 15 oz. **Length:** 7-3/4". **Stocks:** Two-piece walnut. **Sights:** Fixed. **Features:** Replica of the Remington New Model Pocket. Available with polisehd brass frame or nickel plated finish. Introduced 2000. Imported by Navy Arms.

Price: Brass frame **$165.00**

Price: Nickel plated **$175.00**

NAVY ARMS DELUXE 1858 REMINGTON-STYLE REVOLVER

Caliber: 44. **Barrel:** 6". **Weight:** 3 lbs. **Length:** 11-3/4". **Stocks:** Smooth walnut. **Sights:** Blade front, notch rear. **Features:** Replica of the famous percussion double action revolver. Polished blue finish. Introduced 1999. Imported by Navy Arms.

Price: **$355.00**

NAVY ARMS STARR SINGLE ACTION MODEL 1863 ARMY REVOLVER

Caliber: 44. **Barrel:** 8". **Weight:** 3 lbs. **Length:** 13-3/4". **Stocks:** Smooth walnut. **Sights:** Blade front, notch rear. **Features:** Replica of the third most popular revolver used by Union forces during the Civil War. Polished blue finish. Introduced 1999. Imported by Navy Arms.

Price: **$355.00**

NAVY ARMS STARR DOUBLE ACTION MODEL 1858 ARMY REVOLVER

Caliber: 44. **Barrel:** 8". **Weight:** 2 lbs., 13 oz. **Stocks:** Smooth walnut. **Sights:** Dovetailed blade front. **Features:** First exact reproduction—correct in size and weight to the original, with progressive rifling; highly polished with blue finish. From Navy Arms.

Price: Deluxe model.................................... **$415.00**

Uberti 1858

Ruger Old Army

North American Companion

Pocket Police 1862

Rogers & Spencer

NAVY MODEL 1851 PERCUSSION REVOLVER

Caliber: 36, 44, 6-shot. **Barrel:** 7-1/2". **Weight:** 44 oz. **Length:** 13" overall. **Stocks:** Walnut finish. **Sights:** Post front, hammer notch rear. **Features:** Brass backstrap and trigger guard; some have 1st Model squareback trigger guard, engraved cylinder with navy battle scene; case-hardened frame, hammer, loading lever. Imported by The Armoury, Cabela's, Cimarron F.A. Co., Navy Arms, E.M.F., Dixie Gun Works, Euroarms of America, Armsport, CVA (44-cal. only), Traditions (44 only), Uberti U.S.A. Inc., United States Patent Fire-Arms.

Price: Brass frame ... **$99.95 to $385.00**
Price: Steel frame ... **$130.00 to $285.00**
Price: Kit form ... **$110.00 to $123.95**
Price: Engraved model (Dixie Gun Works) ... **$159.95**
Price: Single cased set, steel frame (Navy Arms) ... **$280.00**
Price: Double cased set, steel frame (Navy Arms) ... **$455.00**
Price: Confederate Navy (Cabela's) ... **$89.99**
Price: Hartford model, steel frame, German silver trim, cartouche (E.M.F.) ... **$190.00**

NEW MODEL 1858 ARMY PERCUSSION REVOLVER

Caliber: 36 or 44, 6-shot. **Barrel:** 6-1/2" or 8". **Weight:** 38 oz. **Length:** 13-1/2" overall. **Stocks:** Walnut. **Sights:** Blade front, groove-in-frame rear. **Features:** Replica of Remington Model 1858. Also available from some importers as Army Model Belt Revolver in 36-cal., a shortened and lightened version of the 44. Target Model (Uberti U.S.A. Inc., Navy Arms) has fully adjustable target rear sight, target front, 36 or 44. Imported by Cabela's, Cimarron F.A. Co., CVA (as 1858 Army, brass frame, 44 only), Dixie Gun Works, Navy Arms, The Armoury, E.M.F., Euroarms of America (engraved, stainless and plain), Armsport, Traditions (44 only), Uberti U.S.A. Inc.

Price: Steel frame, about ... **$99.95 to $280.00**
Price: Steel frame kit (Euroarms, Navy Arms) ... **$115.95 to $150.00**
Price: Single cased set (Navy Arms) ... **$290.00**
Price: Double cased set (Navy Arms) ... **$480.00**
Price: Stainless steel Model 1858 (Euroarms, Uberti U.S.A. Inc., Cabela's, Navy Arms, Armsport, Traditions) ... **$169.95 to $380.00**
Price: Target Model, adjustable rear sight (Cabela's, Euroarms, Uberti U.S.A. Inc., Stone Mountain Arms) ... **$95.95 to $399.00**
Price: Brass frame (CVA, Cabela's, Traditions, Navy Arms) ... **$79.95 to $159.95**
Price: As above, kit (Dixie Gun Works, Navy Arms) ... **$145.00 to $188.95**
Price: Buffalo model, 44-cal. (Cabela's) ... **$119.99**
Price: Hartford model, steel frame, German silver trim, cartouche (E.M.F.) ... **$215.00**

NORTH AMERICAN COMPANION PERCUSSION REVOLVER

Caliber: 22. **Barrel:** 1-1/8". **Weight:** 5.1 oz. **Length:** 4-5/10" overall. **Stocks:** Laminated wood. **Sights:** Blade front, notch fixed rear. **Features:** All stainless steel construction. Uses standard #11 percussion caps. Comes with bullets, powder measure, bullet seater, leather clip holster, gun rug. Long Rifle or Magnum frame size. Introduced 1996. Made in U.S. by North American Arms.

Price: Long Rifle frame ... **$191.00**

North American Magnum Companion Percussion Revolver

Similar to the Companion except has larger frame. Weighs 7.2 oz., has 1-5/8" barrel, measures 5-7/16" overall. Comes with bullets, powder measure, bullet seater, leather clip holster, gun rag. Introduced 1996. Made in U.S. by North American Arms.

Price: ... **$209.00**

POCKET POLICE 1862 PERCUSSION REVOLVER

Caliber: 36, 5-shot. **Barrel:** 4-1/2", 5-1/2", 6-1/2", 7-1/2". **Weight:** 26 oz. **Length:** 12" overall (6-1/2" bbl.). **Stocks:** Walnut. **Sights:** Fixed. **Features:** Round tapered barrel; half-fluted and rebated cylinder; case-hardened frame, loading lever and hammer; silver or brass trigger guard and backstrap. Imported by Dixie Gun Works, Navy Arms (5-1/2" only), Uberti U.S.A. Inc. (5-1/2", 6-1/2" only), United States Patent Fire-Arms and Cimarron F.A. Co.

Price: About ... **$139.95 to $335.00**
Price: Single cased set with accessories (Navy Arms) ... **$365.00**
Price: Hartford model, steel frame, German silver trim, cartouche (E.M.F.) ... **$215.00**

ROGERS & SPENCER PERCUSSION REVOLVER

Caliber: 44. **Barrel:** 7-1/2". **Weight:** 47 oz. **Length:** 13-3/4" overall. **Stocks:** Walnut. **Sights:** Cone front, integral groove in frame for rear. **Features:** Accurate reproduction of a Civil War design. Solid frame; extra large nipple cut-out on rear of cylinder; loading lever and cylinder easily removed for cleaning. From Dixie Gun Works, Euroarms of America (standard blue, engraved, burnished, target models), Navy Arms.

Price: ... **$160.00 to $299.95**
Price: Nickel-plated ... **$215.00**
Price: Engraved (Euroarms) ... **$287.00**

BLACKPOWDER REVOLVERS

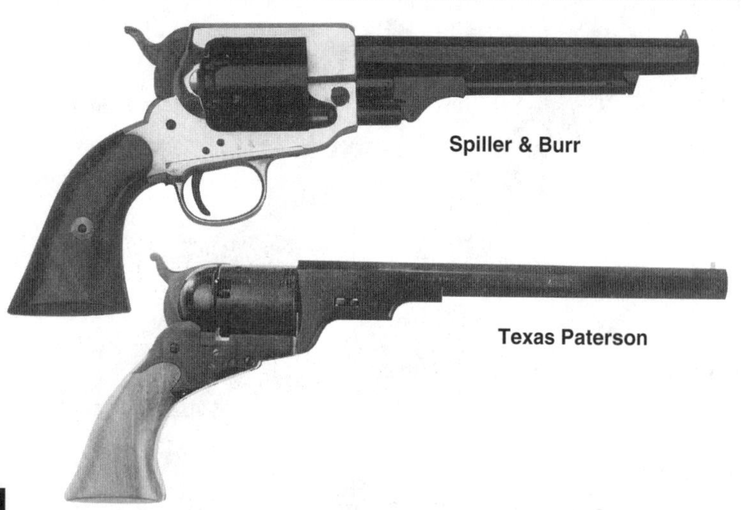

Spiller & Burr

Texas Paterson

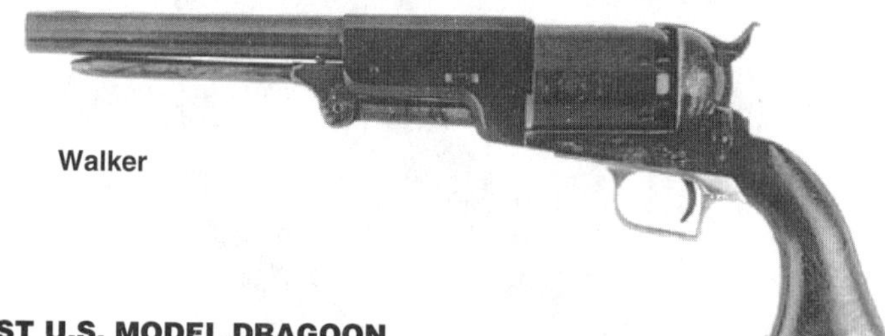

Walker

Price: Kit version. . . . . **$245.00 to $252.00**
Price: Target version (Euroarms) . . . . **$239.00 to $270.00**
Price: Burnished London Gray (Euroarms) . . . . **$245.00 to $270.00**

RUGER OLD ARMY PERCUSSION REVOLVER

Caliber: 45, 6-shot. Uses .457" dia. lead bullets. **Barrel:** 7-1/2" (6-groove; 16" twist). **Weight:** 46 oz. **Length:** 13-3/4" overall. **Stocks:** Smooth walnut. **Sights:** Ramp front, rear adjustable for windage and elevation; or fixed (groove). **Features:** Stainless steel; standard size nipples, chrome-moly steel cylinder and frame, same lockwork as in original Super Blackhawk. Also available in stainless steel. Includes hard case and lock. Made in USA. From Sturm, Ruger & Co.

Price: Stainless steel (Model KBP-7) **$510.00**
Price: Blued steel (Model BP-7) **$478.00**
Price: Blued steel, fixed sight (BP-7F) **$478.00**
Price: Stainless steel, fixed sight (KBP-7F) **$510.00**

SHERIFF MODEL 1851 PERCUSSION REVOLVER

Caliber: 36, 44, 6-shot. **Barrel:** 5". **Weight:** 40 oz. **Length:** 10-1/2" overall. **Stocks:** Walnut. **Sights:** Fixed. **Features:** Brass backstrap and trigger guard; engraved navy scene; case-hardened frame, hammer, loading lever. Imported by E.M.F.

Price: Steel frame. **$172.00**
Price: Brass frame **$140.00**

SPILLER & BURR REVOLVER

Caliber: 36 (.375" round ball). **Barrel:** 7", octagon. **Weight:** 2-1/2 lbs. **Length:** 12-1/2" overall. **Stocks:** Two-piece walnut. **Sights:** Fixed. **Features:** Reproduction of the C.S.A. revolver. Brass frame and trigger guard. Also available as a kit. From Dixie Gun Works, Navy Arms.

Price: **$145.00**
Price: Kit form (Dixie) **$149.95**
Price: Single cased set (Navy Arms) **$270.00**
Price: Double cased set (Navy Arms). **$430.00**

TEXAS PATERSON 1836 REVOLVER

Caliber: 36 (.375" round ball). **Barrel:** 7-1/2". **Weight:** 42 oz. **Stocks:** One-piece walnut. **Sights:** Fixed. **Features:** Copy of Sam Colt's first commercially-made revolving pistol. Has no loading lever but comes with loading tool. From Cimarron F.A. Co., Dixie Gun Works, Navy Arms, Uberti U.S.A. Inc.

Price: About . . . . **$310.00 to $395.00**
Price: With loading lever (Uberti U.S.A. Inc.) **$450.00**
Price: Engraved (Navy Arms). **$485.00**

Uberti 1861 Navy Percussion Revolver

Similar to Colt 1851 Navy except has round 7-1/2" barrel, rounded trigger guard, German silver blade front sight, "creeping" loading lever. Available with fluted or round cylinder. Imported by Uberti U.S.A. Inc.

Price: Steel backstrap, trigger guard, cut for stock. **$300.00**

1ST U.S. MODEL DRAGOON

Caliber: 44. **Barrel:** 7-1/2", part round, part octagon. **Weight:** 64 oz. **Stocks:** One-piece walnut. **Sights:** German silver blade front, hammer notch rear. **Features:** First model has oval bolt cuts in cylinder, square-back flared trigger guard, V-type mainspring, short trigger. Ranger and Indian scene roll-engraved on cylinder. Color case-hardened frame, loading lever, plunger and hammer; blue barrel, cylinder, trigger and wedge. Available with old-time charcoal blue or standard blue-black finish. Polished brass backstrap and trigger guard. From Cimarron F.A. Co., Uberti U.S.A. Inc., United States Patent Fire-Arms, Navy Arms.

Price: . . . . **$325.00 to $435.00**

2nd U.S. Model Dragoon Revolver

Similar to the 1st Model except distinguished by rectangular bolt cuts in the cylinder. From Cimarron F.A. Co., Uberti U.S.A. Inc., United States Patent Fire-Arms, Navy Arms.

Price: . . . . **$325.00 to $435.00**

3rd U.S. Model Dragoon Revolver

Similar to the 2nd Model except for oval trigger guard, long trigger, modifications to the loading lever and latch. Imported by Cimarron F.A. Co., Uberti U.S.A. Inc., United States Patent Fire-Arms.

Price: Military model (frame cut for shoulder stock, steel backstrap) . . . .**$330.00 to $435.00**
Price: Civilian (brass backstrap, trigger guard) **$325.00**

1862 POCKET NAVY PERCUSSION REVOLVER

Caliber: 36, 5-shot. **Barrel:** 5-1/2", 6-1/2", octagonal, 7-groove, LH twist. **Weight:** 27 oz. (5-1/2" barrel). **Length:** 10-1/2" overall (5-1/2" bbl.). **Stocks:** One-piece varnished walnut. **Sights:** Brass pin front, hammer notch rear. **Features:** Rebated cylinder, hinged loading lever, brass or silver-plated backstrap and trigger guard, color-cased frame, hammer, loading lever, plunger and latch, rest blued. Has original-type markings. From Cimarron F.A. Co. and Uberti U.S.A. Inc.

Price: With brass backstrap, trigger guard **$310.00**

1861 Navy Percussion Revolver

Similar to Colt 1851 Navy except has round 7-1/2" barrel, rounded trigger guard, German silver blade front sight, "creeping" loading lever. Fluted or round cylinder. Imported by Cimarron F.A. Co., Uberti U.S.A. Inc.

Price: Steel backstrap, trigger guard, cut for stock. **$300.00**

U.S. PATENT FIRE-ARMS 1862 POCKET NAVY

Caliber: 36. **Barrel:** 4-1/2", 5-1/2", 6-1/2". **Weight:** 27 oz. (5-1/2" barrel). **Length:** 10-1/2" overall (5-1/2" barrel). **Stocks:** Smooth walnut. **Sights:** Brass pin front, hammer notch rear. **Features:** Blued barrel and cylinder, color case-hardened frame, hammer, lever; silver-plated backstrap and trigger guard. Imported from Italy; available from United States Patent Fire-Arms Mfg. Co.

Price: **$335.00**

WALKER 1847 PERCUSSION REVOLVER

Caliber: 44, 6-shot. **Barrel:** 9". **Weight:** 84 oz. **Length:** 15-1/2" overall. **Stocks:** Walnut. **Sights:** Fixed. **Features:** Case-hardened frame, loading lever and hammer; iron backstrap; brass trigger guard; engraved cylinder. Imported by Cabela's, Cimarron F.A. Co., Navy Arms, Dixie Gun Works, Uberti U.S.A. Inc., E.M.F., Cimarron, Traditions, United States Patent Fire-Arms.

Price: About . . . . **$225.00 to $445.00**
Price: Single cased set (Navy Arms) **$405.00**
Price: Deluxe Walker with French fitted case (Navy Arms) **$540.00**
Price: Hartford model, steel frame, German silver trim, cartouche (E.M.F.) **$295.00**

Beeman P1

Beeman/FWB P30

Beeman/FWB C55

Beeman/Feinwerkbau 103

Benjamin Sheridan CO2

BEEMAN P1 MAGNUM AIR PISTOL

Caliber: 177, 5mm, single shot. **Barrel:** 8.4". **Weight:** 2.5 lbs. **Length:** 11" overall. **Power:** Top lever cocking; spring-piston. **Stocks:** Checkered walnut. **Sights:** Blade front, square notch rear with click micrometer adjustments for windage and elevation. Grooved for scope mounting. **Features:** Dual power for 177 and 20-cal.: low setting gives 350-400 fps; high setting 500-600 fps. Rearward expanding mainspring simulates firearm recoil. All Colt 45 auto grips fit gun. Dry-firing feature for practice. Optional wooden shoulder stock. Introduced 1985. Imported by Beeman.

Price: 177, 5mm **$415.00**

Beeman P2 Match Air Pistol

Similar to the Beeman P1 Magnum except shoots only 177 pellets; completely recoilless single-stroke pnuematic action. Weighs 2.2 lbs. Choice of thumbrest match grips or standard style. Introduced 1990.

Price: 177, 5mm, standard grip **$385.00**

Price: 177, match grip **$455.00**

BEEMAN P3 AIR PISTOL

Caliber: 177 pellet, single shot. **Barrel:** N/A. **Weight:** 1.7 lbs. **Length:** 9.6" overall. **Power:** Single-stroke pneumatic; overlever barrel cocking. **Grips:** Reinforced polymer. **Sights:** Adjustable rear, blade front. **Features:** Velocity 410 fps. Polymer frame; automatic safety; two-stage trigger; built-in muzzle brake. Introduced 1999 by Beeman.

Price: **$159.00**

BEEMAN/FEINWERKBAU 65 MKII AIR PISTOL

Caliber: 177, single shot. **Barrel:** 6.1", removable bbl. wgt. available. **Weight:** 42 oz. **Length:** 13.3" overall. **Power:** Spring, sidelever cocking. **Stocks:** Walnut, stippled thumbrest; adjustable or fixed. **Sights:** Front, interchangeable post element system, open rear, click adjustable for windage and elevation and for sighting notch width. Scope mount available. **Features:** New shorter barrel for better balance and control. Cocking effort 9 lbs. Two-stage trigger, four adjustments. Quiet firing, 525 fps. Programs instantly for recoil or recoilless operation. Permanently lubricated. Steel piston ring. Imported by Beeman.

Price: Right-hand **$1,070.00**

BEEMAN/FEINWERKBAU 103 PISTOL

Caliber: 177, single shot. **Barrel:** 10.1", 12-groove rifling. **Weight:** 2.5 lbs. **Length:** 16.5" overall. **Power:** Single-stroke pneumatic, underlever cocking. **Stocks:** Stippled walnut with adjustable palm shelf. **Sights:** Blade front, open rear adjustable for windage and elevation. Notch size adjustable for width. Interchangeable front blades. **Features:** Velocity 510 fps. Fully adjustable trigger. Cocking effort of 2 lbs. Imported by Beeman.

Price: Right-hand **$1,195.00**

Price: Left-hand **$1,235.00**

BEEMAN/FWB P30 MATCH AIR PISTOL

Caliber: 177, single shot. **Barrel:** 10-5/16", with muzzlebrake. **Weight:** 2.4 lbs. **Length:** 16.5" overall. **Power:** Pre-charged pneumatic. **Stocks:** Stippled walnut; adjustable match type. **Sights:** Undercut blade front, fully adjustable match rear. **Features:** Velocity to 525 fps; up to 200 shots per CO_2 cartridge. Fully adjustable trigger; built-in muzzlebrake. Introduced 1995. Imported from Germany by Beeman.

Price: Right-hand **$1,275.00**

Price: Left-hand **$1,350.00**

BEEMAN/FWB C55 CO_2 RAPID FIRE PISTOL

Caliber: 177, single shot or 5-shot magazine. **Barrel:** 7.3". **Weight:** 2.5 lbs. **Length:** 15" overall. **Power:** Special CO_2 cylinder. **Stocks:** Anatomical, adjustable. **Sights:** Interchangeable front, fully adjustable open micro-click rear with adjustable notch size. **Features:** Velocity 510 fps. Has 11.75" sight radius. Built-in muzzlebrake. Introduced 1993. Imported by Beeman Precision Airguns.

Price: Right-hand **$1,460.00**

Price: Left-hand **$1,520.00**

BEEMAN HW70A AIR PISTOL

Caliber: 177, single shot. **Barrel:** 6-1/4", rifled. **Weight:** 38 oz. **Length:** 12-3/4" overall. **Power:** Spring, barrel cocking. **Stocks:** Plastic, with thumbrest. **Sights:** Hooded post front, square notch rear adjustable for windage and elevation. Comes with scope base. **Features:** Adjustable trigger, 31-lb. cocking effort, 440 fps MV; automatic barrel safety. Imported by Beeman.

Price: **$185.00**

Price: HW70S, black grip, silver finish **$210.00**

BEEMAN/WEBLEY TEMPEST AIR PISTOL

Caliber: 177, 22, single shot. **Barrel:** 6-7/8". **Weight:** 32 oz. **Length:** 8.9" overall. **Power:** Spring-piston, break barrel. **Stocks:** Checkered black plastic with thumbrest. **Sights:** Blade front, adjustable rear. **Features:** Velocity to 500 fps (177), 400 fps (22). Aluminum frame; black epoxy finish; manual safety. Imported from England by Beeman.

Price: **$180.00**

Beeman/Webley Hurricane Air Pistol

Similar to the Tempest except has extended frame in the rear for a click-adjustable rear sight; hooded front sight; comes with scope mount. Imported from England by Beeman.

Price: **$225.00**

BENJAMIN SHERIDAN CO_2 PELLET PISTOLS

Caliber: 177, 20, 22, single shot. **Barrel:** 6-3/8", rifled brass. **Weight:** 29 oz. **Length:** 9.8" overall. **Power:** 12-gram CO_2 cylinder. **Stocks:** Walnut. **Sights:** High ramp front, fully adjustable notch rear. **Features:** Velocity to 500 fps. Turn-bolt action with cross-bolt safety. Gives about 40 shots per CO_2 cylinder. Black or nickel finish. Made in U.S. by Benjamin Sheridan Co.

Price: Black finish, EB17 (177), EB20 (20), about **$115.23**

BRNO TAU-7

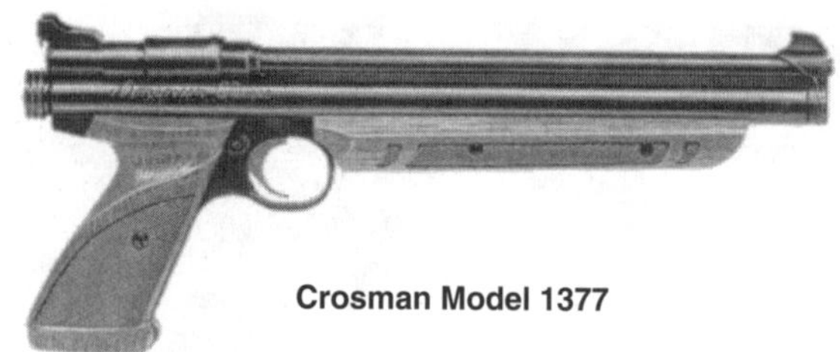
Crosman Model 1377

Crosman Auto Air II

Crosman Model 1008

BENJAMIN SHERIDAN PNEUMATIC PELLET PISTOLS

Caliber: 177, 20, 22, single shot. **Barrel:** 9-3/8", rifled brass. **Weight:** 38 oz. **Length:**13-1/8" overall. **Power:** Underlever pnuematic, hand pumped. **Stocks:** Walnut stocks and pump handle. **Sights:** High ramp front, fully adjustable notch rear. **Features:** Velocity to 525 fps (variable). Bolt action with cross-bolt safety. Choice of black or nickel finish. Made in U.S. by Benjamin Sheridan Co.

Price: Black finish, HB17 (177), HB20 (20), HB22 (22), about............ **$129.50**

BERETTA 92 FS/CO_2 AIR PISTOLS

Caliber: 177 pellet, 8-shot magazine. **Barrel:** 4.9". **Weight:** 44.4 oz. **Length:** 8.2" (10.2" with compensator). Power: CO2 cartridge. **Grips:** Plastic or wood. **Sights:** Adjustable rear, blade front. **Features:** Velocity 375 fps. Replica of Beretta 92 FS pistol. Single- and double-action trigger; ambidextrous safety; black or nickel-plated finish. Made by Umarex for Beretta USA.

Price: Starting at **$200.00**

BRNO TAU-7 CO_2 MATCH PISTOL

Caliber: 177. **Barrel:** 10.24". **Weight:** 37 oz. **Length:** 15.75" overall. **Power:** 12.5-gram CO_2 cartridge. **Stocks:** Stippled hardwood with adjustable palm rest. **Sights:** Blade front, open fully adjustable rear. **Features:** Comes with extra seals and counterweight. Blue finish. Imported by Great Lakes Airguns.

Price: About.. **$299.50**

BSA 240 MAGNUM AIR PISTOL

Caliber: 177, 22, single shot. **Barrel:** 6". **Weight:** 2 lbs. **Length:** 9" overall. **Power:** Spring-air, top-lever cocking. **Stocks:** Walnut. **Sights:** Blade front, micrometer adjustable rear. **Features:** Velocity 510 fps (177), 420 fps (22); crossbolt safety. Combat autoloader styling. Imported from U.K. by Precision Sales International, Inc.

Price: **$259.99**

COLT GOVERNMENT 1911 A1 AIR PISTOL

Caliber: 177, 8-shot cylinder magazine. **Barrel:** 5", rifled. **Weight:** 38 oz. **Length:** 8-1/2" overall. **Power:** CO_2 cylinder. **Stocks:** Checkered black plastic or smooth wood. **Sights:** Post front, adjustable rear. **Features:** Velocity to 393 fps. Quick-loading cylinder magazine; single and double action; black or silver finish. Introduced 1998. Imported by Colt's Mfg. Co., Inc.

Price: Black finish.. **$199.00**
Price: Silver finish... **$209.00**

CROSMAN BLACK VENOM PISTOL

Caliber: 177 pellets, BB, 17-shot magazine; darts, single shot. **Barrel:** 4.75" smoothbore. **Weight:** 16 oz. **Length:** 10.8" overall. **Power:** Spring. **Stocks:** Checkered. **Sights:** Blade front, adjustable rear. **Features:** Velocity to 270 fps (BBs), 250 fps (pellets). Spring-fed magazine; cross-bolt safety. Introduced 1996. Made in U.S. by Crosman Corp.

Price: About.. **$20.00**

CROSMAN BLACK FANG PISTOL

Caliber: 177 BB, 17-shot magazine. **Barrel:** 4.75" smoothbore. **Weight:** 10 oz. **Length:** 10.8" overall. **Power:** Spring. **Stocks:** Checkered. **Sights:** Blade front, fixed notch rear. **Features:** Velocity to 250 fps. Spring-fed magazine; cross-bolt safety. Introduced 1996. Made in U.S. by Crosman Corp.

Price: About.. **$16.00**

CROSMAN MODEL 1322, 1377 AIR PISTOLS

Caliber: 177 (M1377), 22 (M1322), single shot. **Barrel:** 8", rifled steel. **Weight:** 39 oz. **Length:** 13-5/8". **Power:** Hand pumped. **Sights:** Blade front, rear adjustable for windage and elevation. **Features:** Bolt action moulded plastic grip, hand size pump forearm. Cross-bolt safety. From Crosman.

Price: About.. **$60.00**

CROSMAN AUTO AIR II PISTOL

Caliber: BB, 17-shot magazine, 177 pellet, single shot. **Barrel:** 8-5/8" steel, smoothbore. **Weight:** 13 oz. **Length:** 10-3/4" overall. **Power:** CO_2 Powerlet. **Stocks:** Grooved plastic. **Sights:** Blade front, adjustable rear; highlighted system. **Features:** Velocity to 480 fps (BBs), 430 fps (pellets). Semi-automatic action with BBs, single shot with pellets. Silvered finish. Introduced 1991. From Crosman.

Price: About.. **$38.00**

CROSMAN MODEL 357 SERIES AIR PISTOL

Caliber: 177 10-shot pellet clips. **Barrel:** 4" (Model 3574GT), 6" (Model 3576GT). **Weight:** 32 oz. (6"). **Length:** 11-3/8" overall (357-6). **Power:** CO_2 Powerlet. **Stocks:** Grip, wrap-around style. **Sights:** Ramp front, fully adjustable rear. **Features:** Average 430 fps (Model 3574GT). Break-open barrel for easy loading. Single or double action. Vent. rib barrel. Wide, smooth trigger. Two cylinders come with each gun. Black finish. From Crosman.

Price: 4" or 6", about.. **$65.00**

CROSMAN MODEL 1008 REPEAT AIR

Caliber: 177, 8-shot pellet clip. **Barrel:** 4.25", rifled steel. **Weight:** 17 oz. **Length:** 8.625" overall. **Power:** CO_2 Powerlet. **Stocks:** Checkered black plastic. **Sights:** Post front, adjustable rear. **Features:** Velocity about 430 fps. Break-open barrel for easy loading; single or double semi-automatic action; two 8-shot clips included. Optional carrying case available. Introduced 1992. From Crosman.

Price: About.. **$60.00**
Price: With case, about....................................... **$70.00**
Price: Model 1008SB (silver and black finish), about.......... **$60.00**

DAISY MODEL 2003 PELLET PISTOL

Caliber: 177 pellet, 35-shot clip. **Barrel:** Rifled steel. **Weight:** 2.2 lbs. **Length:** 11.7" overall. **Power:** CO_2. **Stocks:** Checkered plastic. **Sights:** Blade front, open rear. **Features:** Velocity to 400 fps. Crossbolt trigger-block safety. Made in U.S. by Daisy Mfg. Co.

Price: About.. **$67.95**

DAISY MODEL 454 AIR PISTOL

Caliber: 177 BB, 20-shot clip. **Barrel:** Smoothbore steel. **Weight:** 1.6 lbs. **Length:** 10.4" overall. **Power:** CO_2. **Stocks:** Moulded black, ribbed composition. **Sights:** Blade front, fixed rear. **Features:** Velocity to 420 fps. Semi-automatic action; cross-bolt safety; black finish. Introduced 1998. Made in U.S. by Dairy Mfg. Co.

Price: **$61.95**

Daisy/Power Line 717

Daisy/PowerLine 1270

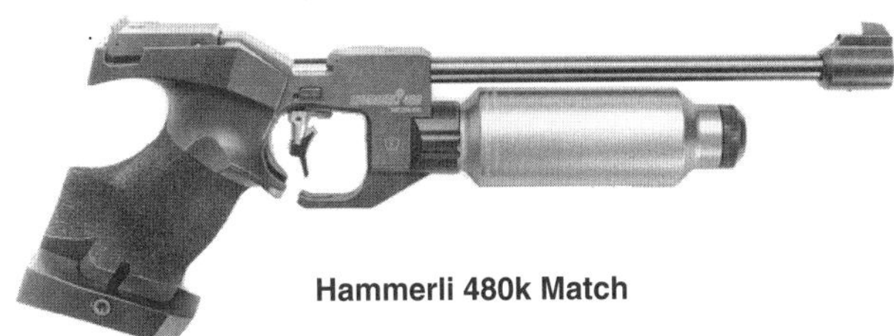
Hammerli 480k Match

DAISY/POWERLINE 717 PELLET PISTOL
Caliber: 177, single shot. **Barrel:** 9.61". **Weight:** 2.25 lbs. **Length:** 13-1/2" overall. **Stocks:** Moulded wood-grain plastic, with thumbrest. **Sights:** Blade and ramp front, micro-adjustable notch rear. **Features:** Single pump pneumatic pistol. Rifled steel barrel. Cross-bolt trigger block. Muzzle velocity 385 fps. From Daisy Mfg. Co. Introduced 1979.
Price: About **$71.95**

Daisy/PowerLine 747 Pistol
Similar to the 717 pistol except has a 12-groove rifled steel barrel by Lothar Walther, and adjustable trigger pull weight. Velocity of 360 fps. Manual cross-bolt safety.
Price: About **$140.00**

DAISY/POWERLINE 1140 PELLET PISTOL
Caliber: 177, single shot. **Barrel:** Rifled steel. **Weight:** 1.3 lbs. **Length:** 11.7" overall. **Power:** Single-stroke barrel cocking. **Stocks:** Checkered resin. **Sights:** Hooded post front, open adjustable rear. **Features:** Velocity to 325 fps. Made of black lightweight engineering resin. Introduced 1995. From Daisy.
Price: About **$38.95**

DAISY/POWERLINE 44 REVOLVER
Caliber: 177 pellets, 6-shot. **Barrel:** 6", rifled steel; interchangeable 4" and 8". **Weight:** 2.7 lbs. **Length:** 13.1" overall. **Power:** CO_2. **Stocks:** Moulded plastic with checkering. **Sights:** Blade on ramp front, fully adjustable notch rear. **Features:** Velocity up to 400 fps. Replica of 44 Magnum revolver. Has swingout cylinder and interchangeable barrels. Introduced 1987. From Daisy Mfg. Co.
Price: **$59.95**

DAISY/POWERLINE 1270 CO_2 AIR PISTOL
Caliber: BB, 60-shot magazine. **Barrel:** Smoothbore steel. **Weight:** 17 oz. **Length:** 11.1" overall. **Power:** CO_2 pump action. **Stocks:** Moulded black polymer. **Sights:** Blade on ramp front, adjustable rear. **Features:** Velocity to 420 fps. Crossbolt trigger block safety; plated finish. Introduced 1997. Made in U.S. by Daisy Mfg. Co.
Price: About **$39.95**

EAA/BAIKAL IZH-46 TARGET AIR PISTOL
Caliber: 177, single shot. **Barrel:** 11.02". **Weight:** 2.87 lbs. **Length:** 16.54" overall. **Power:** Underlever single-stroke pneumatic. **Grips:** Adjustable wooden target.

Marksman 2005 Laserhawk

Sights: Micrometer fully adjustable rear, blade front. **Features:** Velocity about 420 fps. Hammer-forged, rifled barrel. Imported from Russia by European American Armory.
Price: **$275.00**

EAA/BAIKAL MP-654K AIR PISTOL
Caliber: 177 BB, detachable 13-shot magazine. **Barrel:** 3.75". **Weight:** 1.6 lbs. **Length:** 6.34". **Power:** CO2 cartridge. **Grips:** Black checkered plastic. **Sights:** Notch rear, blade front. **Features:** Velocity about 380 fps. Double-action trigger; slide safety; metal slide and frame. Replica of Makarov pistol. Imported from Russia by European American Armory.
Price: **$110.00**

EAA/BAIKAL MP-651K AIR PISTOL/RIFLE
Caliber: 177 pellet (8-shot magazine); 177 BB (23-shot). **Barrel:** 5.9" (17.25" with rifle attachment). **Weight:** 1.54 lbs. (3.3 lbs. with rifle attachment). **Length:** 9.4" (31.3" with rifle attachment) **Power:** CO2 cartridge, semi-automatic. **Stock:** Plastic. **Sights:** Notch rear/blade front (pistol); periscopic sighting system (rifle). **Features:** Velocity 328 fps. Unique pistol/rifle combination allows the pistol to be inserted into the rifle shell. Imported from Russia by European American Armory.
Price: **$95.00**

"GAT" AIR PISTOL
Caliber: 177, single shot. **Barrel:** 7-1/2" cocked, 9-1/2" extended. **Weight:** 22 oz. **Power:** Spring-piston. **Stocks:** Cast checkered metal. **Sights:** Fixed. **Features:** Shoots pellets, corks or darts. Matte black finish. Imported from England by Stone Enterprises, Inc.
Price: **$24.95**

HAMMERLI 480 MATCH AIR PISTOL
Caliber: 177, single shot. **Barrel:** 9.8". **Weight:** 37 oz. **Length:** 16.5" overall. **Power:** Air or CO_2. **Stocks:** Walnut with 7-degree rake adjustment. Stippled grip area. **Sights:** Undercut blade front, fully adjustable open match rear. **Features:** Underbarrel cannister charges with air or CO_2 for power supply; gives 320 shots per filling. Trigger adjustable for position. Introduced 1994. Imported from Switzerland by Hammerli Pistols U.S.A.
Price: **$1,325.00**

Hammerli 480K2 Match Air Pistol
Similar to the 480 except has a short, detachable aluminum air cylinder for use only with compressed air; can be filled while on the gun or off; special adjustable barrel weights. Muzzle velocity of 470 fps, gives about 180 shots. Has stippled black composition grip with adjustable palm shelf and rake angle. Comes with air pressure gauge. Introduced 1996. Imported from Switzerland by SIGARMS, Inc.
Price: **$1,112.50**

MARKSMAN 1010 REPEATER PISTOL
Caliber: 177, 18-shot BB repeater. **Barrel:** 2-1/2", smoothbore. **Weight:** 24 oz. **Length:** 8-1/4" overall. **Power:** Spring. **Features:** Velocity to 200 fps. Thumb safety. Black finish. Uses BBs, darts, bolts or pellets. Repeats with BBs only. From Marksman Products.
Price: Matte black finish **$26.00**
Price: Model 2000 (as above except silver-chrome finish)................ **$27.00**

MARKSMAN 2005 LASERHAWK SPECIAL EDITION AIR PISTOL
Caliber: 177, 24-shot magazine. **Barrel:** 3.8", smoothbore. **Weight:** 22 oz. **Length:** 10.3" overall. **Power:** Spring-air. **Stocks:** Checkered. **Sights:** Fixed fiber optic front sight. **Features:** Velocity to 300 fps with Hyper-Velocity pellets. Square trigger guard with skeletonized trigger; extended barrel for greater velocity and accuracy. Shoots BBs, pellets, darts or bolts. Made in the U.S. From Marksman Products.
Price: **$32.00**

MORINI 162E MATCH AIR PISTOL
Caliber: 177, single shot. **Barrel:** 9.4". **Weight:** 32 oz. **Length:** 16.1" overall. **Power:** Scuba air. **Stocks:** Adjustable match type. **Sights:** Interchangeable blade front, fully adjustable match-type rear. **Features:** Power mechanism shuts down when pres-

sure drops to a pre-set level. Adjustable electronic trigger. Introduced 1995. Imported from Switzerland by Nygord Precision Products.
Price: $995.00

PARDINI K58 MATCH AIR PISTOL
Caliber: 177, single shot. **Barrel:** 9.0". **Weight:** 37.7 oz. **Length:** 15.5" overall. **Power:** Pre-charged compressed air; single-stroke cocking. **Stocks:** Adjustable match type; stippled walnut. **Sights:** Interchangeable post front, fully adjustable match rear. **Features:** Fully adjustable trigger. Introduced 1995. Imported from Italy by Nygord Precision Products.
Price: $750.00
Price: K2 model, precharged air pistol, introduced in 1998 .... $895.00

NEW!
RWS 9B/9N AIR PISTOLS
Caliber: 177, single shot. **Barrel:** N/A. **Weight:** N/A. **Length:** N/A. **Grips:** Plastic with thumbrest. **Sights:** Adjustable. **Features:** Spring-piston powered; 550 fps. Black or nickel finish. Introduced 2001. Imported from Germany by Dynamit Nobel-RWS.
Price: .... NA

RWS C-225 AIR PISTOLS
Caliber: 177, 8-shot rotary magazine. **Barrel:** 4", 6". **Weight:** NA. **Length:** NA. **Power:** CO2. Stocks: Checkered black plastic. **Sights:** Post front, rear adjustable for windage. **Features:** Velocity to 385 fps. Semi-automatic fire; decocking lever. Imported from Germany by Dynamit Nobel-RWS.
Price: 4", blue.. $210.00
Price: 4", nickel.. $220.00
Price: 6", blue.. $220.00

STEYR LP 5CP MATCH AIR PISTOL
Caliber: 177, 5-shot magazine. **Barrel:** NA. **Weight:** 40.7 oz. **Length:** 15.2" overall. **Power:** Pre-charged air cylinder. **Stocks:** Adjustable match type. **Sights:** Interchangeable blade front, fully adjustable match rear. **Features:** Adjustable sight radius; fully adjustable trigger. Has barrel compensator. Introduced 1995. Imported from Austria by Nygord Precision Products.
Price: $1,150.00

STEYR LP10P MATCH PISTOL
Caliber: 177, single shot. **Barrel:** 9". **Weight:** 38.7 oz. **Length:** 15.3" overall. **Power:** Scuba air. **Stocks:** Fully adjustable Morini match with palm shelf; stippled walnut. **Sights:** Interchangeable blade in 4mm, 4.5mm or 5mm widths, fully adjustable open rear with interchangeable 3.5mm or 4mm leaves. **Features:** Velocity about 500 fps. Adjustable trigger, adjustable sight radius from 12.4" to 13.2". With compensator. Imported from Austria by Nygord Precision Products.
Price: $1,195.00

TECH FORCE SS2 OLYMPIC COMPETITION AIR PISTOL
Caliber: 177 pellet, single shot. **Barrel:** 7.4". **Weight:** 2.8 lbs. **Length:** 16.5" overall. **Power:** Spring piston, sidelever. **Grips:** Hardwood. **Sights:** Extended adjustable rear, blade front accepts inserts. **Features:** Velocity 520 fps. Recoilless design; adjustments allow duplication of a firearm's feel. Match-grade, adjustable trigger; includes carrying case. Imported from China by Compasseco Inc.
Price: $295.00

TECH FORCE 35 AIR PISTOL
Caliber: 177 pellet, single shot. **Barrel:** N/A. **Weight:** 2.86 lbs. **Length:** 14.9" overall. **Power:** Spring piston, underlever. **Grips:** Hardwood. **Sights:** Micrometer adjustable rear, blade front. **Features:** Velocity 400 fps. Grooved for scope mount; trigger safety. Imported from China by Compasseco Inc.
Price: $49.95

Tech Force 8 Air Pistol
Similar to Tech Force 35, but with break-barrel action, ambidextrous polymer grips. From Compasseco Inc.
Price: $59.95

Tech Force S2-1 Air Pistol
Similar to Tech Force 8, but more basic grips and sights for plinking. From Compasseco Inc.
Price: $29.95

Walther CP88

WALTHER CP88 PELLET PISTOL
Caliber: 177, 8-shot rotary magazine. **Barrel:** 4", 6". **Weight:** 37 oz. (4" barrel) **Length:** 7" (4" barrel). **Power:** CO_2. **Stocks:** Checkered plastic. **Sights:** Blade front, fully adjustable rear. **Features:** Faithfully replicates size, weight and trigger pull of the 9mm Walther P88 compact pistol. Has SA/DA trigger mechanism; ambidextrous safety, levers. Comes with two magazines, 500 pellets, one CO2 cartridge. Introduced 1997. Imported from Germany by Interarms.
Price: Blue $179.00
Price: Nickel $189.00

WALTHER LP20I MATCH PISTOL
Caliber: 177, single shot. **Barrel:** 8.66". **Weight:** NA. **Length:** 15.1" overall. **Power:** Scuba air. **Stocks:** Orthopaedic target type. **Sights:** Undercut blade front, open match rear fully adjustable for windage and elevation. **Features:** Adjustable velocity; matte finish. Introduced 1995. Imported from Germany by Nygord Precision Products.
Price: $1,095.00

Walther CP88 Competition Pellet Pistol
Similar to the standard CP88 except has 6" match-grade barrel, muzzle weight, wood or plastic stocks. Weighs 41 oz., has overall length of 9". Introduced 1997. Imported from Germany by Interarms.
Price: Blue, plastic grips.................................. $170.00
Price: Nickel, plastic grips $195.00
Price: Blue, wood grips..................................... $205.00
Price: Nickel, wood grips $232.00

WALTHER CP99 AIR PISTOL
Caliber: 177 pellet, 8-shot rotary magazine. **Barrel:** 3". **Weight:** 26 oz. **Length:** 7.1" overall. **Power:** CO2 cartridge. **Grip:** Polymer. **Sights:** Drift-adjustable rear, blade front. **Features:** Velocity 320 fps. Replica of Walther P99 pistol. Trigger allows single and double action; ambidextrous magazine release; interchangeable backstraps to fit variety of hand sizes. Introduced 2000. From Walther USA.
Price: .... NA

WALTHER PPK/S AIR PISTOL
Caliber: 177 BB. **Barrel:** N/A. **Weight:** 20 oz. **Length:** 6.3" overall. **Power:** CO2 cartridge. **Grip:** Plastic. **Sights:** Fixed rear, blade front. **Features:** Replica of Walther PPK pistol. Blow back system moves slide when fired; trigger allows single and double action. Introduced 2000. From Walther USA.
Price: .... NA

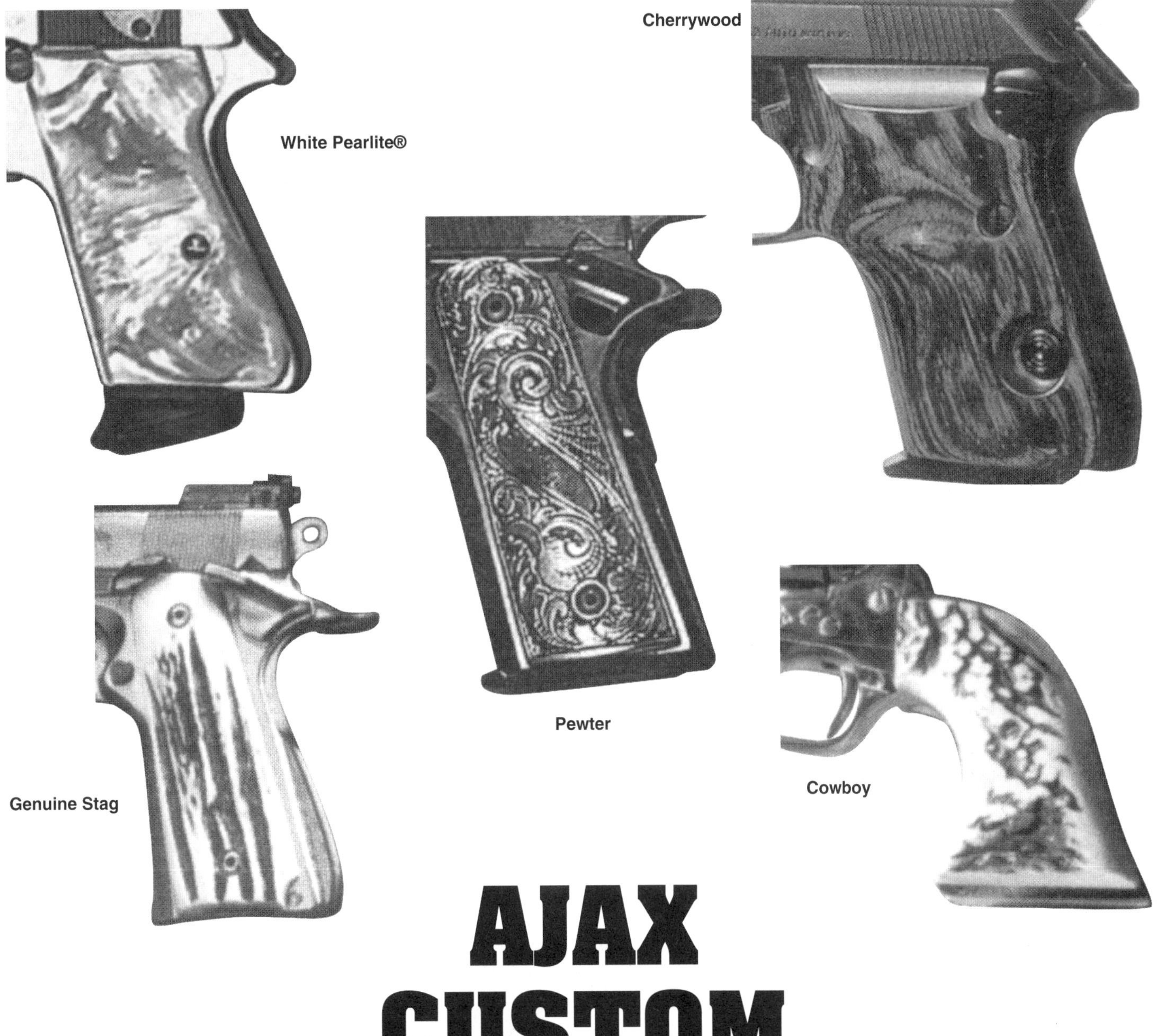

AJAX CUSTOM GRIPS

Grip materials include ivory polymer, ivory, white and black Pearlite, Indian Sambar stag, walnut, cherrywood, black silverwood, simulated buffalo horn and pewter. Smooth, fingergroove and checkered designs offered for some models. Available for most single- and double-action revolvers and automatics. Made in U.S. by Ajax Custom Grips Inc.

Prices: $35 to $145 (ivory is by special order only)

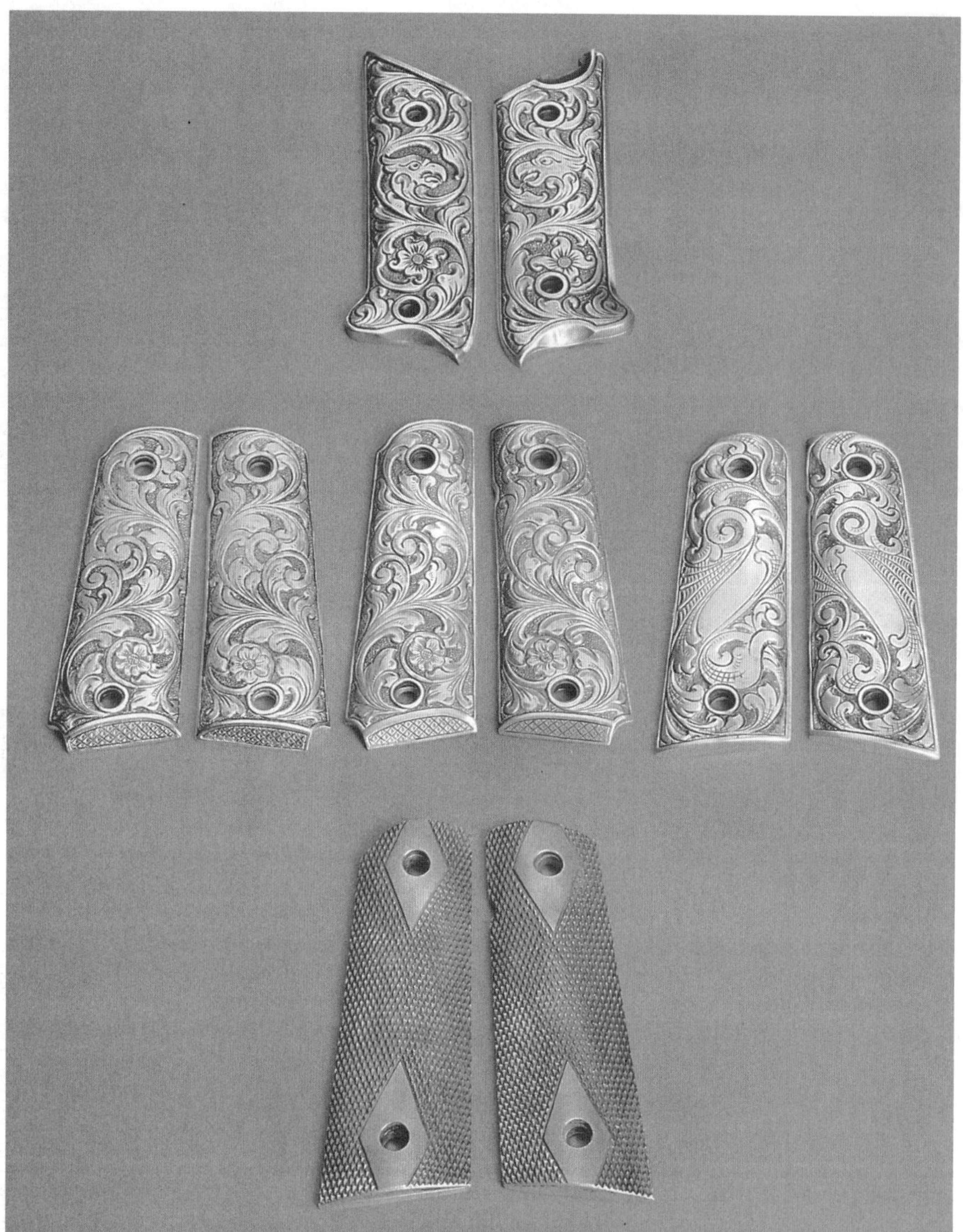

ALL AMERICA SALES

All America Sales offers pewter grips in a variety of patterns, including scrollwork, checkering, "the right to keep and bear arms" eagle and others. Some models feature a gold finish. Grips available for Colt Government, Gold Cup and Commander models; Ruger Mark II pistol; and some single-action revolvers. From All America Sales Inc.

Prices: $49.95 to $59.95

ALL AMERICA SALES *(continued)*

Colt Government Model Landing Eagle

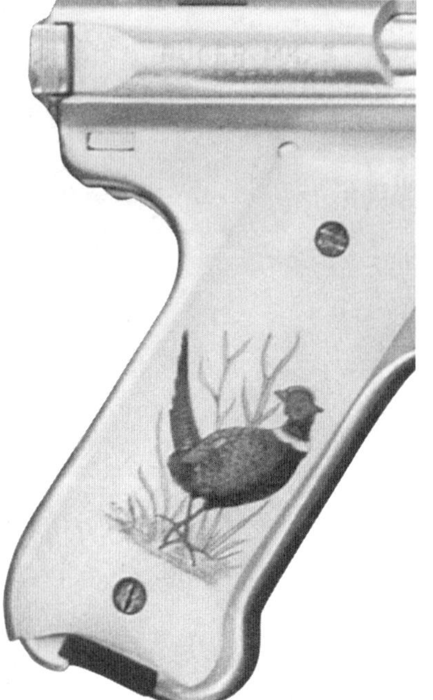

Ruger Pheasant

Colt Single Action Army Classic Panel

ALTAMONT CUSTOM GRIPS

Colt Government Model Facing Buck

Beretta Super Rosewood

Grip materials include bonded ivory, laminated rosewood, fancy walnut, laminated walnut, laminated silver-black hardwood, black ebony, bocote, rosewood, hard black epoxy, imitation pearl, Asian Sambar stag and ivory. Scrimshaw designs, inlays, carvings and personalization available. Smooth, fingergroove and checkered designs offered. Grips made for most single- and double-action revolvers and automatics. Made in U.S. by Altamont.

Prices: $21 to $85 (ivory and other exotics at additional cost)

Slip-on Grips for Autoloaders

Boot Grips for Revolvers

Grips for Pistols

BUTLER CREEK (UNCLE MIKE'S)

CUSTOM GRADE SYNTHETIC MOLDED GRIPS

These Uncle Mike's polymer grips are designed by custom handgun grip maker Craig Spegel. They are designed to fill the hand without a spongy feel. Double-action revolver grips feature finger grooves for improved control. From Butler Creek.

Price: Revolver Grips (for most Ruger, Smith & Wesson and Taurus single- and double-action revolvers) **$19.95**
Price: Revolver Boot Grips (for small-frame Ruger, Smith & Wesson and Taurus double-action revolvers) **$19.95**
Price: Slip-on Grips (for most small, medium, compact large-frame and full-size large frame automatics that do not have grip safeties) . . . **$19.95**
Price: Pistol Grips (for most Ruger, Smith & Wesson Beretta, Colt, Sig-Sauer, Taurus and CZ-75 autos) **$19.95**

GRIPS

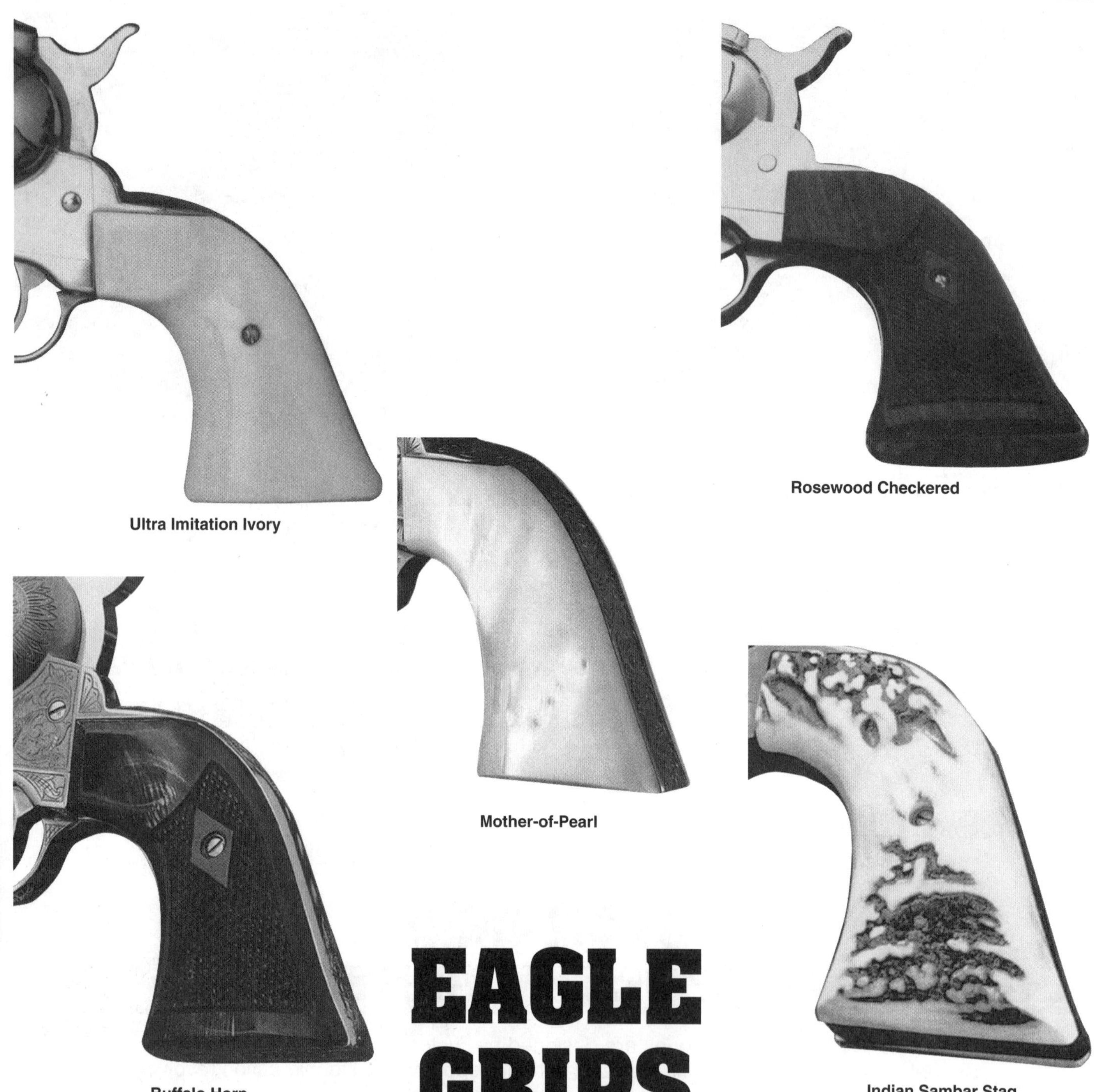

Ultra Imitation Ivory

Rosewood Checkered

Mother-of-Pearl

Buffalo Horn

Indian Sambar Stag

ACCESSORIES

Grip materials include imitation ivory, rosewood, buffalo horn, ebony, mother of pearl and Indian Sambar stag. Smooth, fingergroove and checkered designs offered. Grips made for most single- and double-action revolvers and automatics. Made in U.S. by Eagle Grips.

Prices: $39.95 to $195.00 (checkering at additional cost)

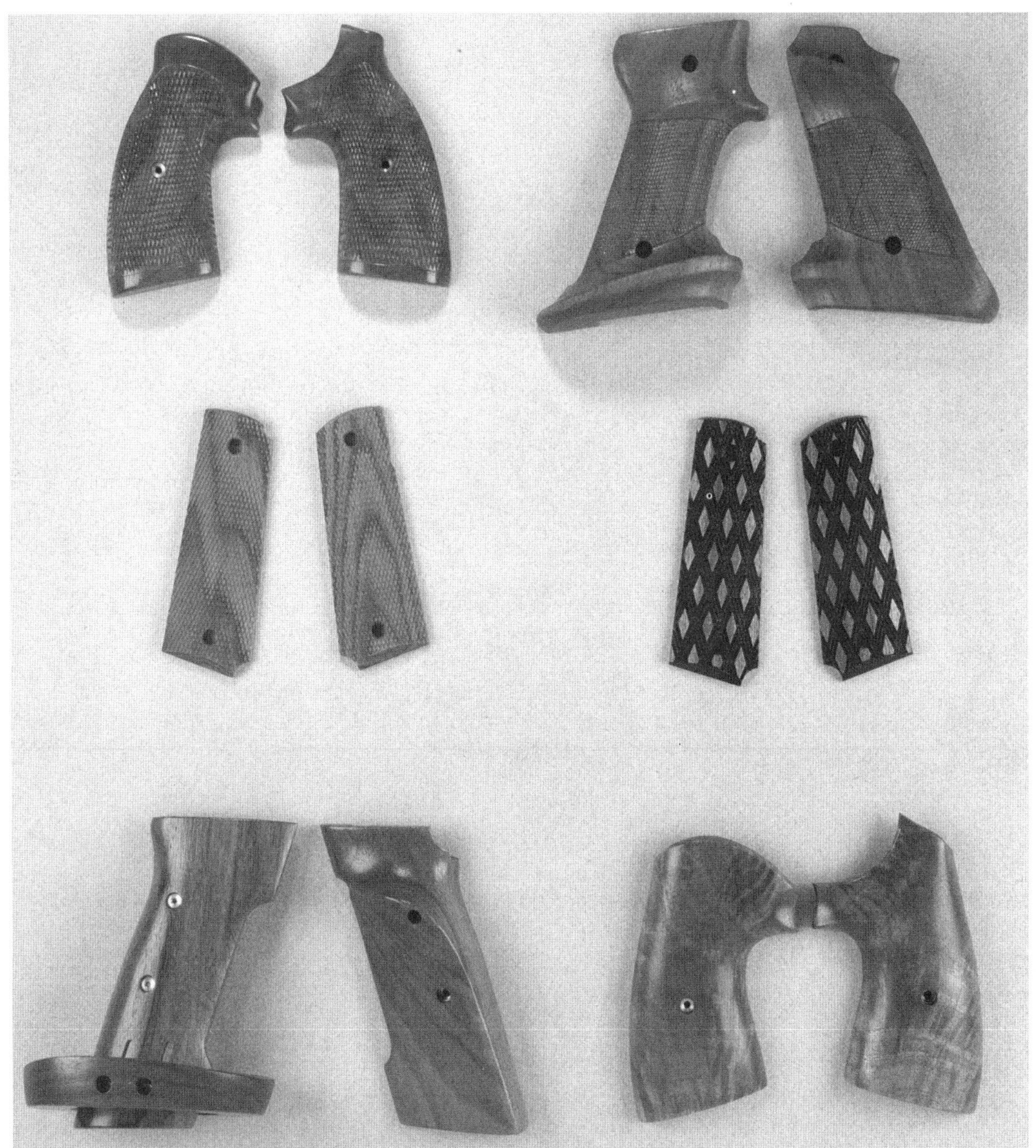

HERRETT STOCKS INC.

Herrett Stocks Inc. of Twin Falls, Idaho, has been producing high-quality handgun grips (and rifle stocks) for more than 40 years. Models are available to fit nearly every pistol and revolver in production — and even a few that are no longer made. The company specializes in American walnut grips, but also offers cocobolo, bubinga and other exotic woods. Grips are available with a variety of options, including smooth, checkered or finger grooved; double-diamond pattern; black lacquer finish for contrast of the diamond pattern; and many models custom-fitted to the shooter's hand, including the famous Shooting Star design. Herrett grips are made in the U.S.

Prices: $19.95 to $329.95

From left to right: 1911-style in camiteo; 1911-style in tulipwood; 1911-style in red raspberry Dymondwood; 1911-style in zebrawood; and 1911-style in cocobolo

KIM AHRENDS CUSTOM FIREARMS INC.

Kim Ahrends Custom Firearms Inc. specializes in grips for Colt and Browning pistols, but also offers grips for Beretta, Smith & Wesson, Walther and many other handguns. Woods available include bubinga, cocobolo, Gaboon ebony, kingwood, Madagascar rosewood, Moradillo, tulipwood, cordia, camiteo, padauk, Iowa black walnut, African blackwood, thuya burl and others. Laminated Dymondwood is offered in 10 colors, including winewood, red raspberry, indigo royal blue, French green, charcoal ruby and apple jack. Offered in smooth, fully checkered, tactical and diamond patterns. Made in U.S. by Kim Ahrends Custom Firearms Inc..

Prices: $36.00 to $86.00
(skip checkering and other options offered at additional cost)

KIM AHRENDS CUSTOM FIREARMS INC. *(continued)*

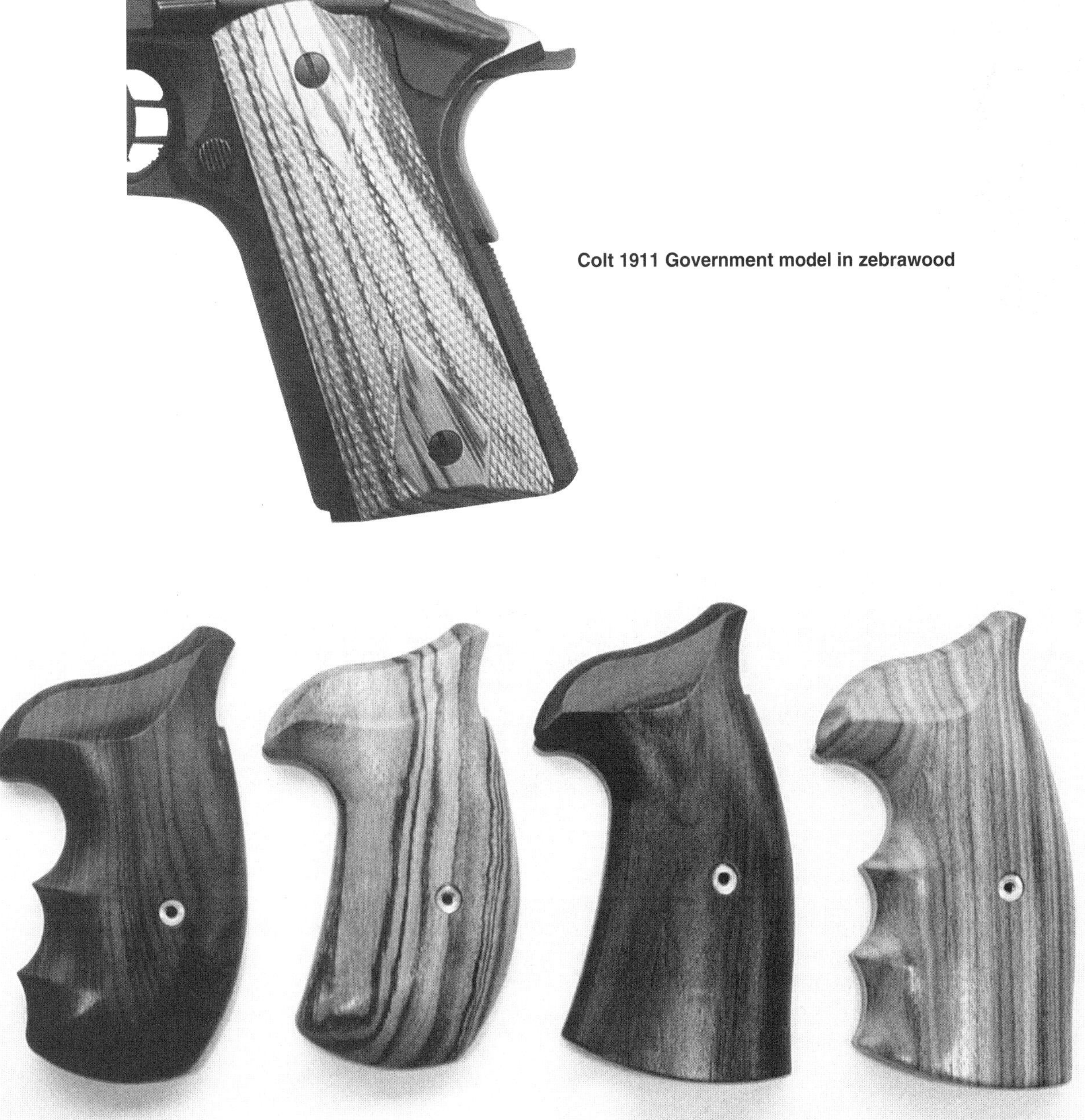

Colt 1911 Government model in zebrawood

From left to right: S&W revolver in cocobolo; S&W revolver in cordia; S&W revolver in cocobolo; and S&W revolver in moradillo

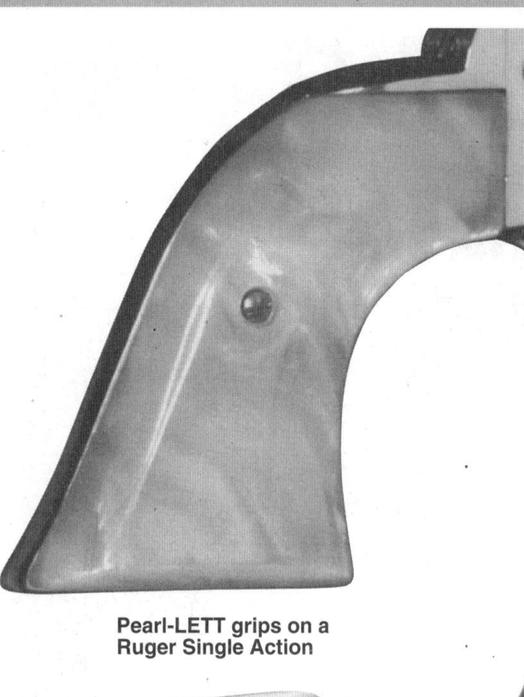

Pearl-LETT grips on a Ruger Single Action

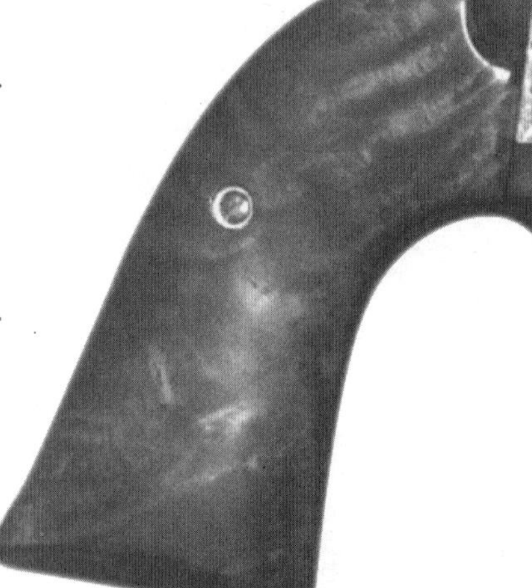

Fancy walnut on a Ruger Bisley

Genuine India stag on a Ruger Single Action

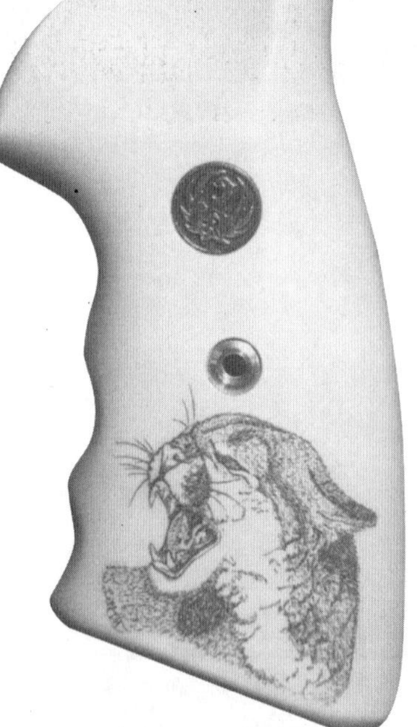

Scrimshaw on micarta for Ruger Double Action

LETT CUSTOM GRIPS

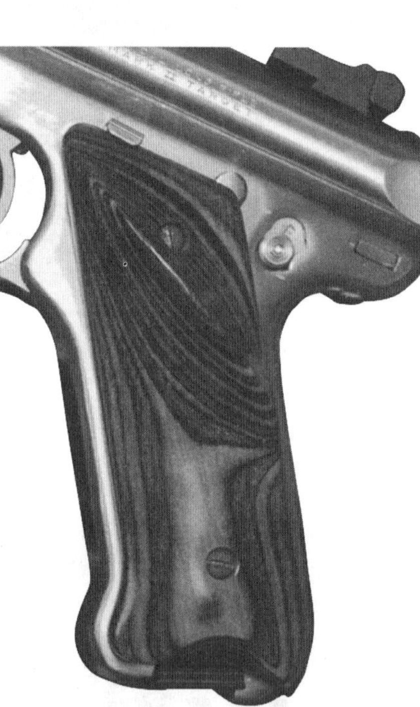

Wood laminate on Ruger MK II

Grip materials offered include imitation ivory, Pearl-Lett (imitation mother of pearl), Bolivian rosewood, zebrawood, fancy walnut, goncalo alves, charcoal burgundy laminate, silver black laminate, charcoal ruby laminate, hawkeye laminate, winewood laminate, camouflage laminate, ivory micarta and black micarta. Checkering and scrimshaw designs, as well as custom scrimshaw, available. Grips made for most single- and double-action revolvers and automatics. Made in U.S. by W.F. Lett Mfg. Inc.

Prices: $26 to $98.50

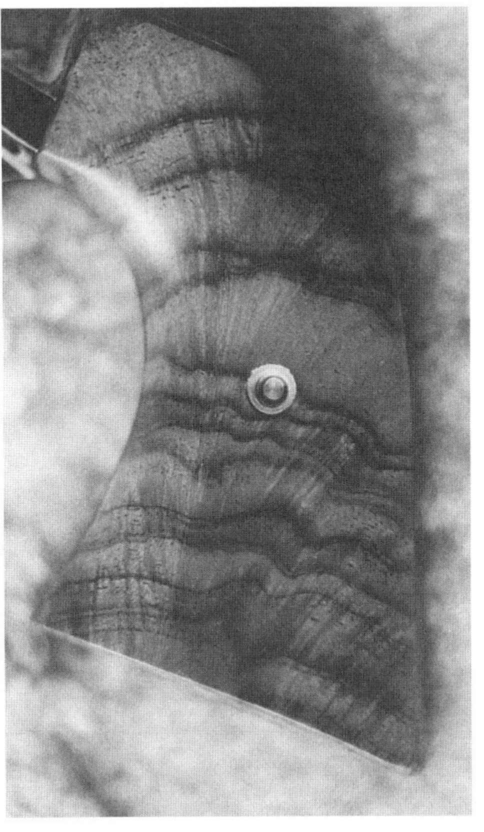

Hi-Grade French Walnut

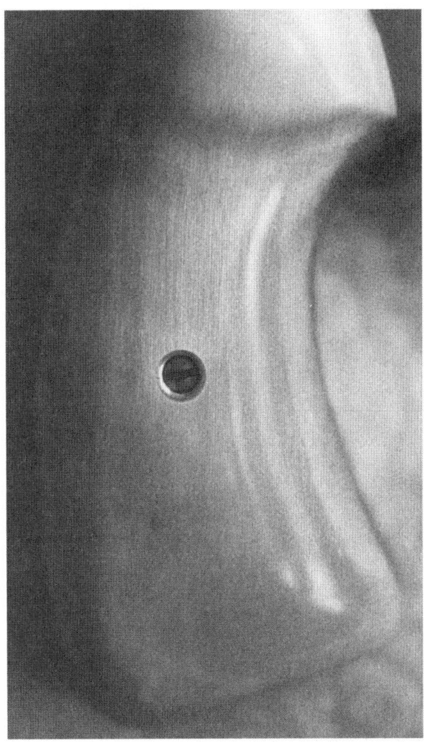

Alaskan Dall Ram's Horn

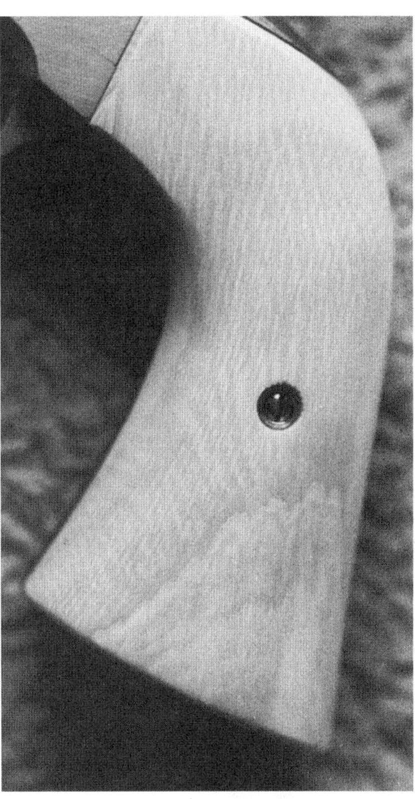

Elephant Ivory

ROY'S CUSTOM GRIPS

This Lynchburg Va., company offers handgun grips in more than 40 materials, including cocobolo, ebony, flamewood, curly koa, pau ferro, rosewood, snakewood, tulipwood, walnut, bubinga, briar burl, zebrawood, Alaskan Dall ram horn, European red stag and genuine ivory. Several finishes are offered. Each set of grips is handmade and fitted to the individual firearm. Made in U.S. by Roy's Custom Grips.

Prices: $150.00 to $700.00

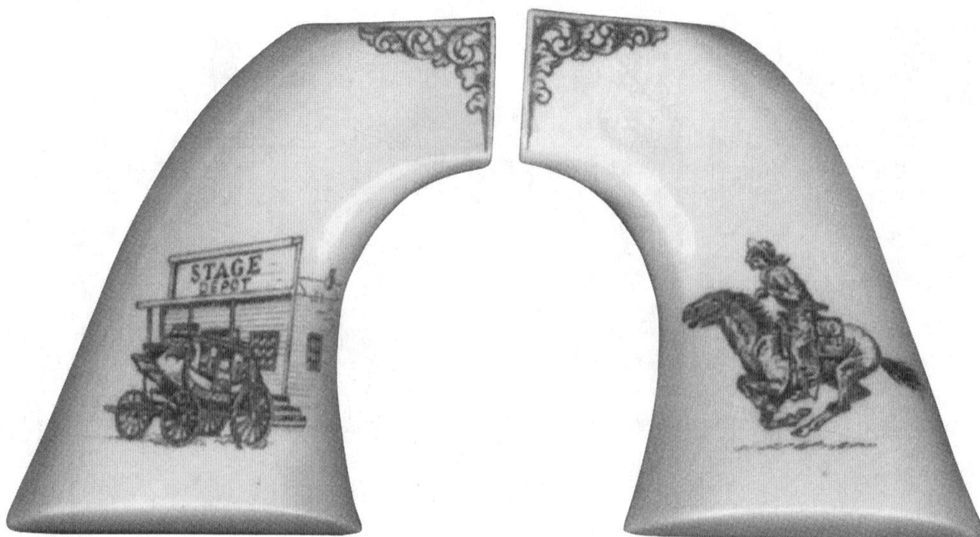

Double Scrimshaw with border

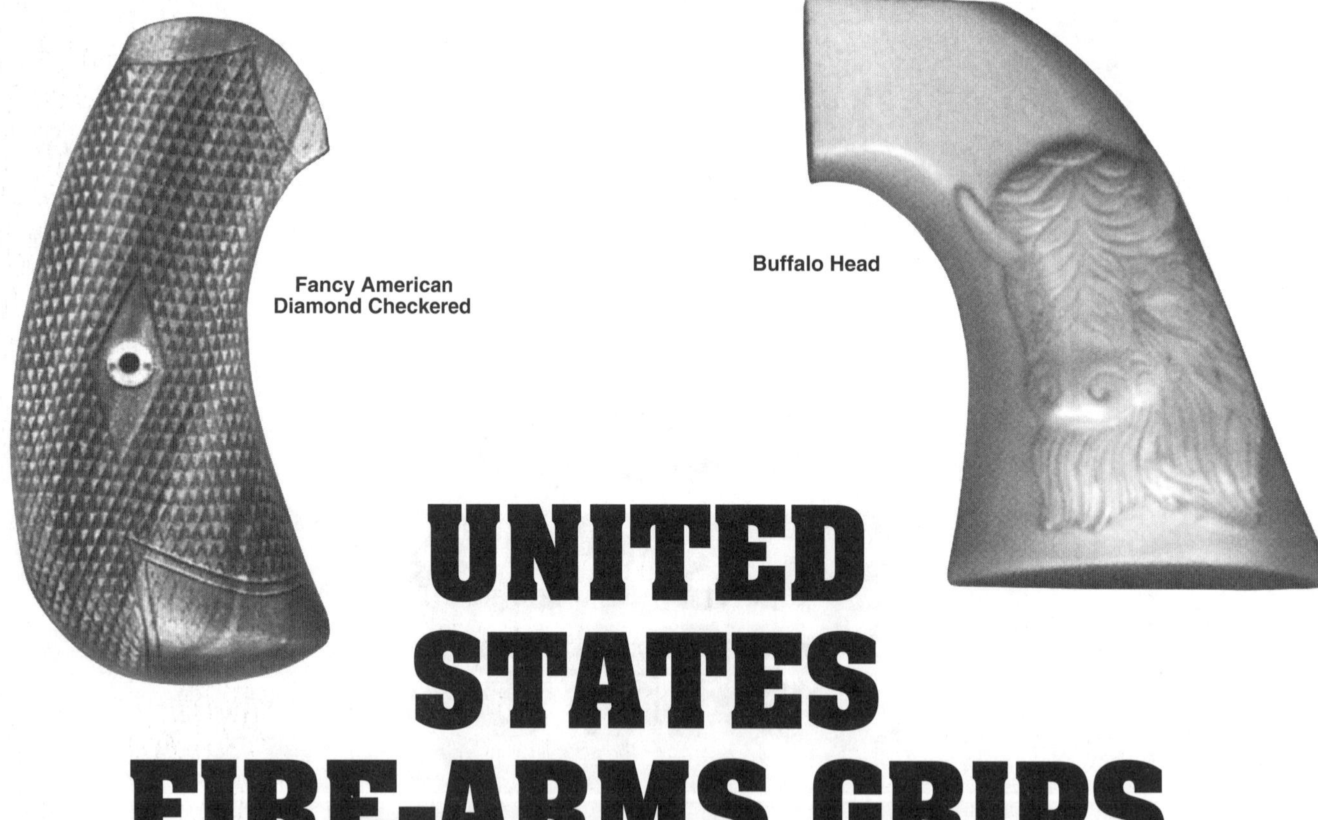

Fancy American
Diamond Checkered

Buffalo Head

UNITED STATES FIRE-ARMS GRIPS

Grip materials include hard rubber, American walnut, Turkish burl, bastone burl, English burl, African rosewood, stag, pearl, bone, ivory micarta and ivory. Checkering, scrimshaw and carved figuring also available. Grips available for single-action revolvers. Made in U.S. by United States Fire-Arms Manu. Co. Inc.

Prices: $75 to $550

CH4D Heavyduty Champion

Frame: Cast iron
Frame Type: O-frame
Die Thread: 7/8-14 or 1-14
Avg. Rounds Per Hour: NA
Ram Stroke: 3-1/4"
Weight: 26 lbs.
Features: 1.185" diameter ram with 16 square inches of bearing surface; ram drilled to allow passage of spent primers; solid steel handle; toggle that slightly breaks over the top dead center. Includes universal primer arm with large and small punches. From CH Tool & Die/4D Custom Die.
Price: **$220.00**

CH4D No. 444 4-Station "H" Press

Frame: Aluminum alloy
Frame Type: H-frame
Die Thread: 7/8-14
Avg. Rounds Per Hour: 200
Ram Stroke: 3-3/4"
Weight: 12 lbs.
Features: Two 7/8" solid steel shaft "H" supports; platen rides on permanently lubed bronze bushings; loads smallest pistol to largest magnum rifle cases and has strength to full-length resize. Includes four rams, large and small primer arm and primer catcher. From CH Tool & Die/4D Custom Die, Co.
Price: **$195.00**

CH4D No. 444-X Pistol Champ

Frame: Aluminum alloy
Frame Type: H-frame
Die Thread: 7/8-14
Avg. Rounds Per Hour: 200
Ram Stroke: 3-3/4"
Weight: 12 lbs.
Features: Tungsten carbide sizing die; Speed Seater seating die with tapered entrance to automatically align bullet on case mouth; automatic primer feed for large or small primers; push-button powder measure with easily changed bushings for 215 powder/load combinations; taper crimp die. Conversion kit for caliber changeover available. From CH Tool & Die/4D Custom Die, Co.
Price: .... **$292.00-$316.50**

FORSTER Co-Ax Press B-2

Frame: Cast iron
Frame Type: Modified O-frame
Die Thread: 7/8-14
Avg. Rounds Per Hour: 120
Ram Stroke: 4"
Weight: 18 lbs.
Features: Snap in/snap out die change; spent primer catcher with drop tube threaded into carrier below shellholder; automatic, handle-activated, cammed shellholder with opposing spring-loaded jaws to contact extractor groove; floating guide rods for alignment and reduced friction; no torque on the head due to design of linkage and pivots; shellholder jaws that float with die permitting case to center in the die; right- or left-hand operation; priming device for seating to factory specifications. "S" shellholder jaws included. From Forster Products.
Price: **$298.00**
Price: Extra shellholder jaws **$26.00**

HOLLYWOOD Senior Press

Frame: Ductile iron
Frame Type: O-frame
Die Thread: 7/8-14
Avg. Rounds Per Hour: 50-100
Ram Stroke: 6-1/2"
Weight: 50 lbs.
Features: Leverage and bearing surfaces ample for reloading cartridges or swaging bullets. Precision ground one-piece 2-1/2" pillar with base; operating

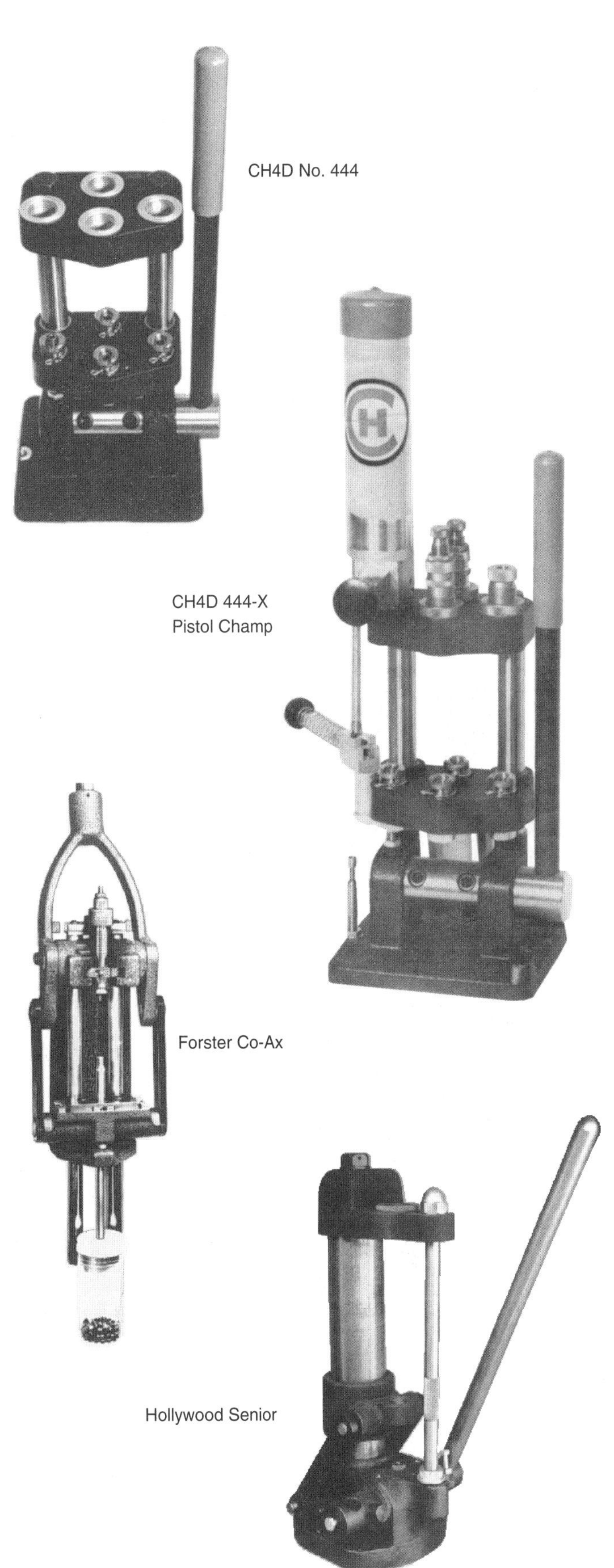

CH4D No. 444

CH4D 444-X Pistol Champ

Forster Co-Ax

Hollywood Senior

ACCESSORIES

Hollywood Senior Turret

Lee Hand Press

Hornady Lock-N-Load Classic

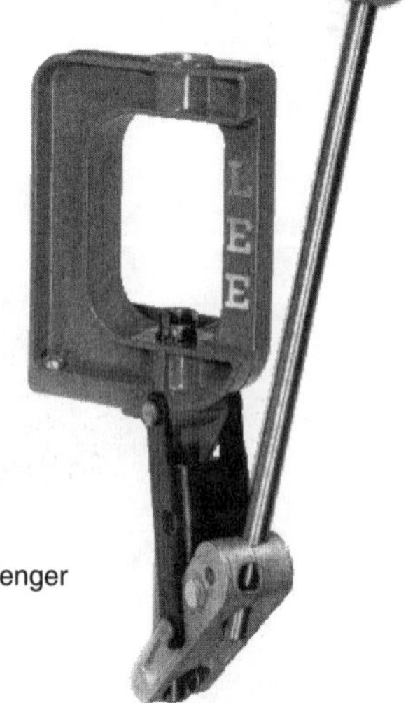
Lee Challenger

handle of 3/4" steel and 15" long; 5/8" steel tie-down rod fro added strength when swaging; heavy steel toggle and camming arms held by 1/2" steel pins in reamed holes. The 1-1/2" steel die bushing takes standard threaded dies; removed, it allows use of Hollywood shotshell dies. From Hollywood Engineering.

Price: $500.00

HOLLYWOOD Senior Turret Press

Frame: Ductile iron
Frame Type: H-frame
Die Thread: 7/8-14
Avg. Rounds Per Hour: 50-100
Ram Stroke: 6-1/2"
Weight: 50 lbs.
Features: Same features as Senior press except has three-position turret head; holes in turret may be tapped 1-1/2" or 7/8" or four of each. Height, 15". Comes complete with one turret indexing handle; one 1-1/2" to 7/8" die hole bushing; one 5/8" tie down bar for swaging. From Hollywood Engineering.
Price: $600.00

HORNADY Lock-N-Load Classic

Frame: Die cast heat-treated aluminum alloy
Frame Type: O-frame
Die Thread: 7/8-14
Avg. Rounds Per Hour: NA
Ram Stroke: 3-5/8"
Weight: 14 lbs.
Features: Features Lock-N-Load bushing system that allows instant die changeovers. Solid steel linkage arms that rotate on steel pins; 30˚ angled frame design for improved visibility and accessibility; primer arm automatically moves in and out of ram for primer pickup and solid seating; two primer arms for large and small primers; long offset handle for increased leverage and unobstructed reloading; lifetime warranty. Comes as a package with primer catcher, PPS automatic primer feed and three Lock-N-Load die bushings. Dies and shellholder available separately or as a kit with primer catcher, positive priming system, automatic primer feed, three die bushings and reloading accessories. From Hornady Mfg. Co.
Price: Press and Three Die Bushings $99.95
Price: Classic Reloading Kit. $259.95

LEE Hand Press

Frame: ASTM 380 aluminum
Frame Type: NA
Die Thread: 7/8-14
Avg. Rounds Per Hour: 100
Ram Stroke: 3-1/4"
Weight: 1 lb., 8 oz.
Features: Small and lightweight for portability; compound linkage for handling up to 375 H&H and case forming. Dies and shellholder not included. From Lee Precision, Inc.
Price: $22.98

LEE Challenger Press

Frame: ASTM 380 aluminum
Frame Type: O-frame
Die Thread: 7/8-14
Avg. Rounds Per Hour: 100
Ram Stroke: 3-1/2"
Weight: 4 lbs., 1 oz.
Features: Larger than average opening with 30˚ offset for maximum hand clearance; steel connecting pins; spent primer catcher; handle adjustable for start and stop positions; handle repositions for left- or right-hand use; shortened handle travel to prevent springing the frame from alignment. Dies and shellholders not included. From Lee Precision, Inc.
Price: $45.00

Metallic Cartridge Presses

LEE Loader

Kit consists of reloading dies to be used with mallet or soft hammer. Neck sizes only. Comes with powder charge cup. From Lee Precision, Inc.

Price: $19.98

LEE Reloader Press

Frame: ASTM 380 aluminum
Frame Type: C-frame
Die Thread: 7/8-14
Avg. Rounds Per Hour: 100
Ram Stroke: 3"
Weight: 1 lb., 12 oz.
Features: Balanced lever to prevent pinching fingers; unlimited hand clearance; left- or right-hand use. Dies and shellholders not included. From Lee Precision, Inc.
Price: $24.98

Lee Reloader

LEE Turret Press

Frame: ASTM 380 aluminum
Frame Type: O-frame
Die Thread: 7/8-14
Avg. Rounds Per Hour: 300
Ram Stroke: 3"
Weight: 7 lbs., 2 oz.
Features: Replaceable turret lifts out by rotating 30°; T-primer arm reverses for large or small primers; built-in primer catcher; adjustable handle for right- or left-hand use or changing angle of down stroke; accessory mounting hole for Lee Auto-Disk powder measure. Optional Auto-Index rotates die turret to next station for semi-progressive use. Safety override prevents overstressing should turret not turn. From Lee Precision, Inc.
Price: $69.98
Price: With Auto-Index $83.98
Price: Four-Hole Turret with Auto-Index $85.98

Lee Turret

LYMAN 310 Tool

Frame: Stainless steel
Frame Type: NA
Die Thread: 7/8-14
Avg. Rounds Per Hour: NA
Ram Stroke: NA
Weight: 10 oz.
Features: Compact, portable reloading tool for pistol or rifle cartridges. Adapter allows loading rimmed or rimless cases. Die set includes neck resizing/decapping die, primer seating chamber; neck expanding die; bullet seating die; and case head adapter. From Lyman Products Corp.
Price: Dies $34.95
Price: Press $34.95
Price: Carrying pouch...................................... $9.95

LYMAN AccuPress

Frame: Die cast
Frame Type: C-frame
Die Thread: 7/8-14
Avg. Rounds Per Hour: 75
Ram Stroke: 3.4"
Weight: 4 lbs.
Features: Reversible, contoured handle for bench mount or hand-held use; for rifle or pistol; compound leverage; Delta frame design. Accepts all standard powder measures. From Lyman Products Corp.
Price: $32.00

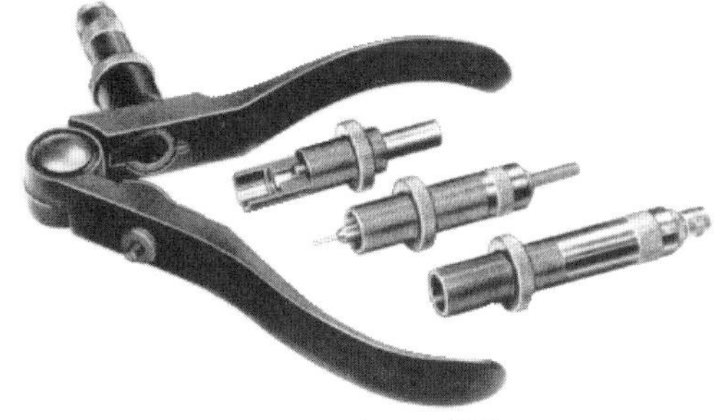

Lyman 310

Metallic Cartridge Presses

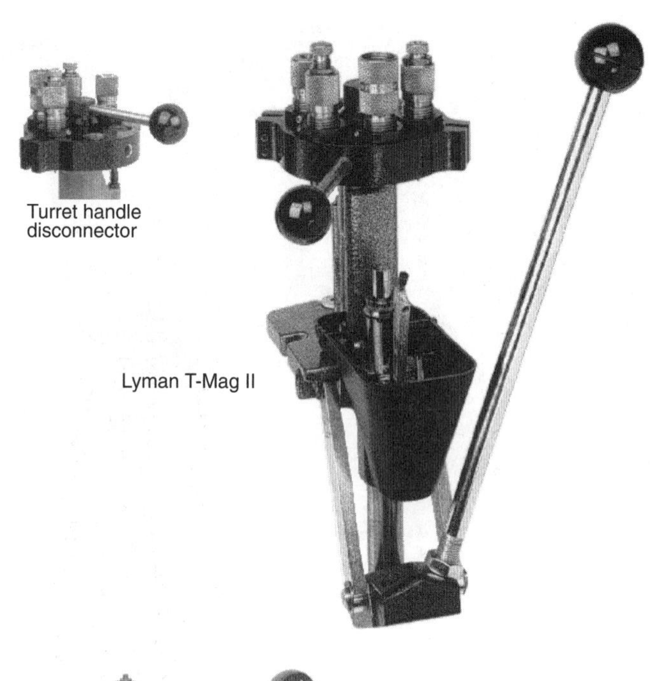

Turret handle disconnector

Lyman T-Mag II

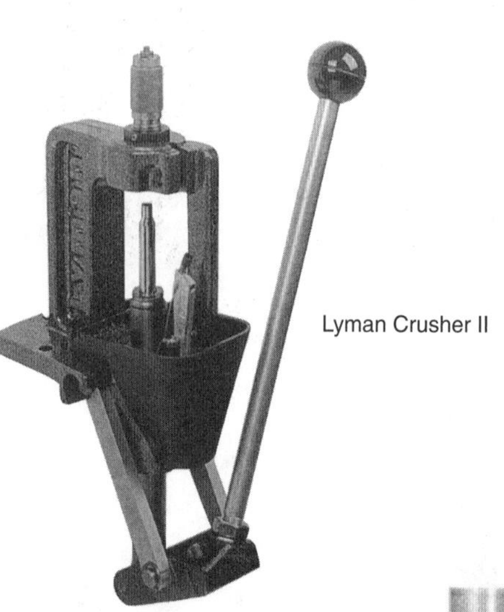

Lyman Crusher II

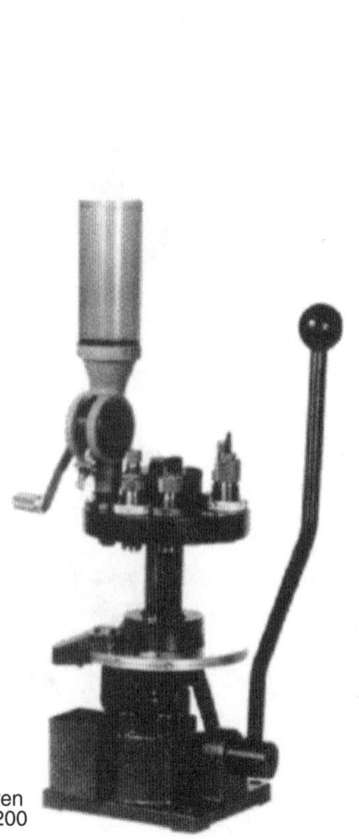

Ponsness/Warren Metal-Matic P-200

LYMAN Crusher II

Frame: Cast iron
Frame Type: O-frame
Die Thread: 7/8-14
Avg. Rounds Per Hour: 75
Ram Stroke: 3-7/8"
Weight: 19 lbs.
Features: Reloads both pistol and rifle cartridges; 1" diameter ram; 4-1/2" press opening for loading magnum cartridges; direct torque design; right- or left-hand use. New base design with 14 square inches of flat mounting surface with three bolt holes. Comes with priming arm and primer catcher. Dies and shellholders not included. From Lyman Products Corp.
Price: **$108.00**

LYMAN T-Mag II

Frame: Cast iron with silver metalflake powder finish
Frame Type: Turret
Die Thread: 7/8-14
Avg. Rounds Per Hour: 125
Ram Stroke: 3-13/16"
Weight: 18 lbs.
Features: Reengineered and upgraded with new turret system for ease of indexing and tool-free turret removal for caliber changeover; new flat machined base for bench mounting; new nickel-plated non-rust handle and links; and new silver hammertone powder coat finish for durability. Right- or left-hand operation; handles all rifle or pistol dies. Comes with priming arm and primer catcher. Dies and shellholders not included. From Lyman Products Corp.
Price: **$149.95**
Price: Extra turret **$34.95**

PONSNESS/WARREN Metal-Matic P-200

Frame: Die cast aluminum
Frame Type: Unconventional
Die Thread: 7/8-14
Avg. Rounds Per Hour: 200+
Weight: 18 lbs.
Features: Designed for straight-wall cartridges; die head with 10 tapped holes for holding dies and accessories for two calibers at one time; removable spent primer box; pivoting arm moves case from station to station. Comes with large and small primer tool. Optional accessories include primer feed, extra die head, primer speed feeder, powder measure extension and dust cover. Dies, powder measure and shellholder not included. From Ponsness/Warren.
Price: **$215.00**
Price: Extra die head **$44.95**
Price: Powder measure extension **$29.95**
Price: Primer feed **$44.95**
Price: Primer speed feed **$14.50**
Price: Dust cover **$21.95**

RCBS Partner

Frame: Aluminum
Frame Type: O-frame
Die Thread: 7/8-14
Avg. Rounds Per Hour: 50-60
Ram Stroke: 3-5/8"
Weight: 5 lbs.
Features: Designed for the beginning reloader. Comes with primer arm equipped with interchangeable primer plugs and sleeves for seating large and small primers. Shellholder and dies not included. Available in kit form (see Metallic Presses—Accessories). From RCBS.
Price: **$61.95**

METALLIC CARTRIDGE PRESSES

RCBS AmmoMaster Single

Frame: Aluminum base; cast iron top plate connected by three steel posts.
Frame Type: NA
Die Thread: 1-1/4"-12 bushing; 7/8-14 threads
Avg. Rounds Per Hour: 50-60
Ram Stroke: 5-1/4"
Weight: 19 lbs.
Features: Single-stage press convertible to progressive. Will form cases or swage bullets. Case detection system to disengage powder measure when no case is present in powder charging station; five-station shellplate; Uniflow Powder measure with clear powder measure adaptor to make bridged powders visible and correctable. 50-cal. conversion kit allows reloading 50 BMG. Kit includes top plate to accommodate either 1-3/8" x 12 or 1-1/2" x 12 reloading dies. Piggyback die plate for quick caliber change-overs available. Reloading dies not included. From RCBS.
Price: **$206.95**
Price: 50 conversion kit **$96.95**
Price: Piggyback/AmmoMaster die plate **$25.95**
Price: Piggyback/AmmoMaster shellplate **$25.95**
Price: Press cover **$10.95**

RCBS Reloader Special-5

Frame: Aluminum
Frame Type: 30° offset O-frame
Die Thread: 1-1/4"-12 bushing; 7/8-14 threads
Avg. Rounds Per Hour: 50-60
Ram Stroke: 3-1/16"
Weight: 7.5 lbs.
Features: Single-stage press convertible to progressive with RCBS Piggyback II. Primes cases during resizing operation. Will accept RCBS shotshell dies. From RCBS.
Price: **$112.95**

RCBS Rock Chucker

Frame: Cast iron
Frame Type: O-frame
Die Thread: 1-1/4"-12 bushing; 7/8-14 threads
Avg. Rounds Per Hour: 50-60
Ram Stroke: 3-1/16"
Weight: 17 lbs.
Features: Designed for heavy-duty reloading, case forming and bullet swaging. Provides 4" of ram-bearing surface to support 1" ram and ensure alignment; ductile iron toggle blocks; hardened steel pins. Comes standard with Universal Primer Arm and primer catcher. Can be converted from single-stage to progressive with Piggyback II conversion unit. From RCBS.
Price: **$141.95**

REDDING Turret Press

Frame: Cast iron
Frame Type: Turret
Die Thread: 7/8-14
Avg. Rounds Per Hour: NA
Ram Stroke: 3.4"
Weight: 23 lbs., 2 oz.
Features: Strength to reload pistol and magnum rifle, case form and bullet swage; linkage pins heat-treated, precision ground and in double shear; hollow ram to collect spent primers; removable turret head for caliber changes; progressive linkage for increased power as ram nears die; slight frame tilt for comfortable operation; rear turret support for stability and precise alignment; six-station turret head; priming arm for both large and small primers. Also available in kit form with shellholder, primer catcher and one die set. From Redding Reloading Equipment.
Price: **$298.50**
Price: Kit **$336.00**

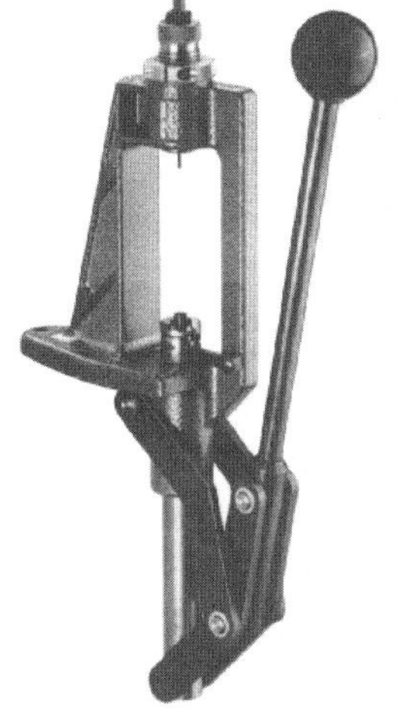

RCBS Partner

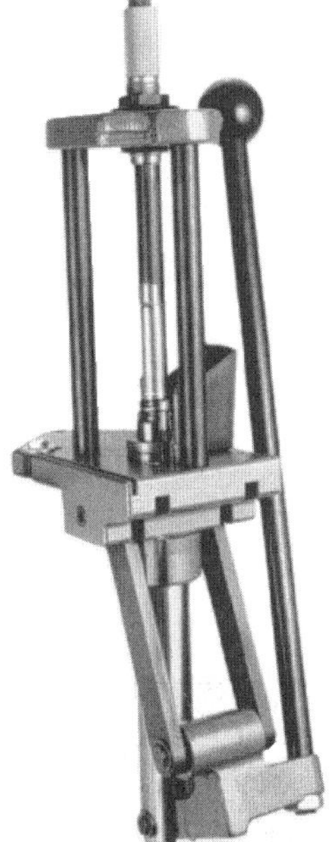

RCBS AmmoMaster Single

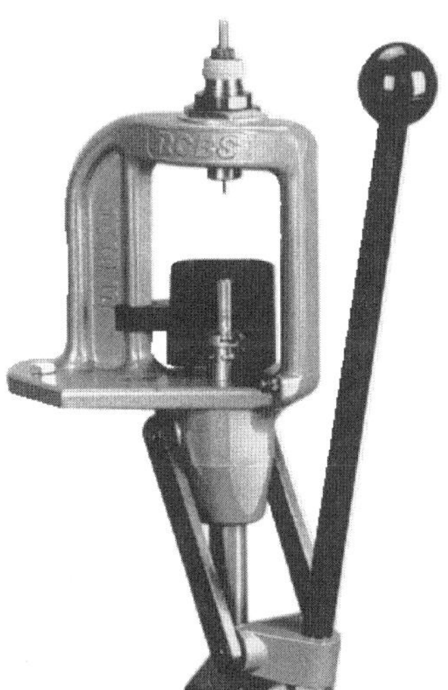

RCBS Reloader Special-5

RCBS Rock Chucker

METALLIC CARTRIDGE PRESSES

Redding Model 25

Redding Boss

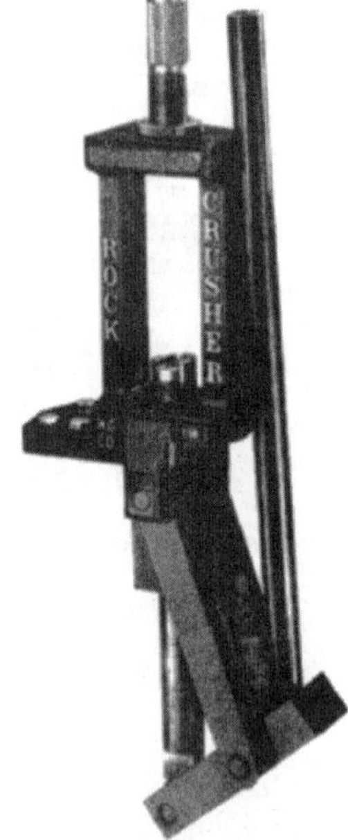

Rock Crusher

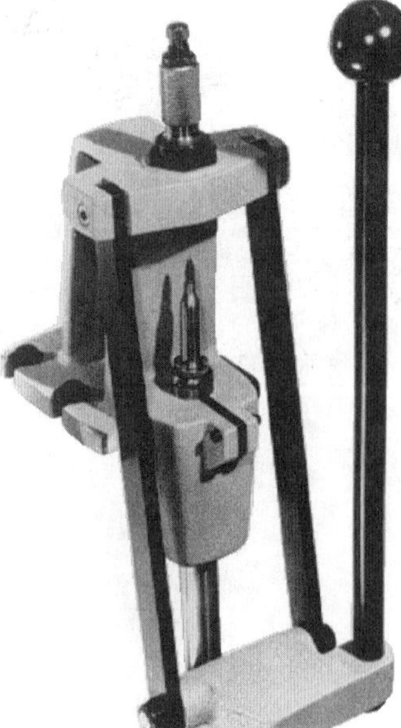

Redding Ultramag

REDDING Boss

Frame: Cast iron
Frame Type: O-frame
Die Thread: 7/8-14
Avg. Rounds Per Hour: NA
Ram Stroke: 3.4"
Weight: 11 lbs., 8 oz.
Features: 36° frame offset for visibility and accessibility; primer arm positioned at bottom ram travel; positive ram travel stop machined to hit exactly top-dead-center. Also available in kit form with shellholder and set of Redding A dies. From Redding Reloading Equipment.
Price: $135.00
Price: Kit $172.00

REDDING Ultramag

Frame: Cast iron
Frame Type: Non-conventional
Die Thread: 7/8-14
Avg. Rounds Per Hour: NA
Ram Stroke: 4-1/8"
Weight: 23 lbs., 6 oz.
Features: Unique compound leverage system connected to top of press for tons of ram pressure; large 4-3/4" frame opening for loading outsized cartridges; hollow ram for spent primers. Kit available with shellholder and one set Redding A dies. From Redding Reloading Equipment.
Price: $298.50
Price: Kit $336.00

ROCK CRUSHER Press

Frame: Cast iron
Frame Type: O-frame
Die Thread: 2-3/4"-12 with bushing reduced to 1-1/2"-12
Avg. Rounds Per Hour: 50
Ram Stroke: 6"
Weight: 67 lbs.
Features: Designed to load and form ammunition from 50 BMG up to 23x115 Soviet. Frame opening of 8-1/2"x3-1/2"; 1-1/2"x12"; bushing can be removed and bushings of any size substituted; ram pressure can exceed 10,000 lbs. with normal body weight; 40mm diameter ram. Angle block for bench mounting and reduction bushing for RCBS dies available. Accessories for Rock Crusher include powder measure, dies, shellholder, bullet puller, priming tool, case gauge and other accessories found elsewhere in this catalog. From The Old Western Scrounger.
Price: $795.00
Price: Angle block $57.95
Price: Reduction bushing $21.00
Price: Shellholder $47.25
Price: Priming tool, 50 BMG, 20 Lahti $65.10

PROGRESSIVE PRESSES

DILLON AT 500

Frame: Aluminum alloy
Frame Type: NA
Die Thread: 7/8-14
Avg. Rounds Per Hour: 200-300
Ram Stroke: 3-7/8"
Weight: NA
Features: Four stations; removable tool head to hold dies in alignment and allow caliber changes without die adjustment; manual indexing; capacity to be upgraded to progressive RL 550B. Comes with universal shellplate to accept 223, 22-250, 243, 30-06, 9mm, 38/357, 40 S&W, 45 ACP. Dies not included. From Dillon Precision Products.
Price: $193.95

METALLIC CARTRIDGE PRESSES

DILLON RL 550B

Frame: Aluminum alloy
Frame Type: NA
Die Thread: 7/8-14
Avg. Rounds Per Hour: 500-600
Ram Stroke: 3-7/8"
Weight: 25 lbs.
Features: Four stations; removable tool head to hold dies in alignment and allow caliber changes without die adjustment; auto priming system that emits audible warning when primer tube is low; a 100-primer capacity magazine contained in DOM steel tube for protection; new auto powder measure system with simple mechanical connection between measure and loading platform for positive powder bar return; a separate station for crimping with star-indexing system; 220 ejected-round capacity bin; 3/4-lb. capacity powder measure. Height above bench, 35"; requires 3/4" bench overhang. Will reload 120 different rifle and pistol calibers. Comes with one caliber conversion kit. Dies not included. From Dillon Precision Products, Inc.
Price: **$325.95**

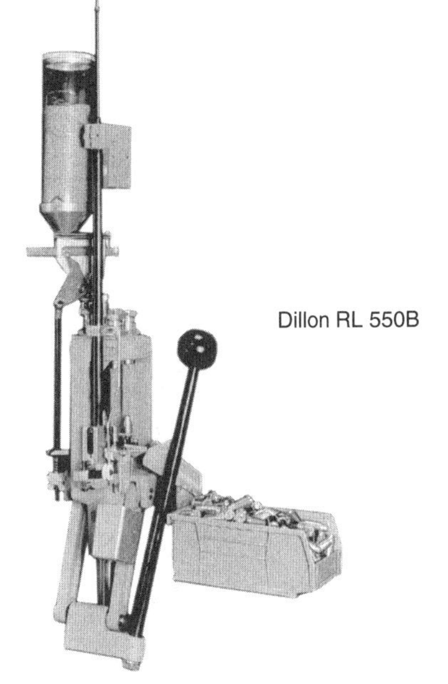

Dillon RL 550B

DILLON RL 1050

Frame: Ductile iron
Frame Type: Platform type
Die Thread: 7/8-14
Avg. Rounds Per Hour: 1000-1200
Ram Stroke: 2-5/16"
Weight: 62 lbs.
Features: Eight stations; auto case feed; primer pocket swager for military cartridge cases; auto indexing; removable tool head; auto prime system with 100-primer capacity; low primer supply alarm; positive powder bar return; auto powder measure; 515 ejected round bin capacity; 500-600 case feed capacity; 3/4-lb. capacity powder measure. Loads all pistol rounds as well as 30 M1 Carbine, 223, and 7.62x39 rifle rounds. Height above the bench, 43". Dies not included. From Dillon Precision Products, Inc.
Price: **$1,199.95**

DILLON Super 1050

Similar to RL1050, but has lengthened frame and short-stroke crank to accommodate long calibers.
Price: **$1,299.95**

DILLON Square Deal B

Frame: Zinc alloy
Frame Type: NA
Die Thread: None (unique Dillon design)
Avg. Rounds Per Hour: 400-500
Ram Stroke: 2-5/16"
Weight: 17 lbs.
Features: Four stations; auto indexing; removable tool head; auto prime system with 100-primer capacity; low primer supply alarm; auto powder measure; positive powder bar return; 170 ejected round capacity bin; 3/4-lb. capacity powder measure. Height above the bench, 34". Comes complete with factory adjusted carbide die set. From Dillon Precision Products, Inc.
Price: **$252.95**

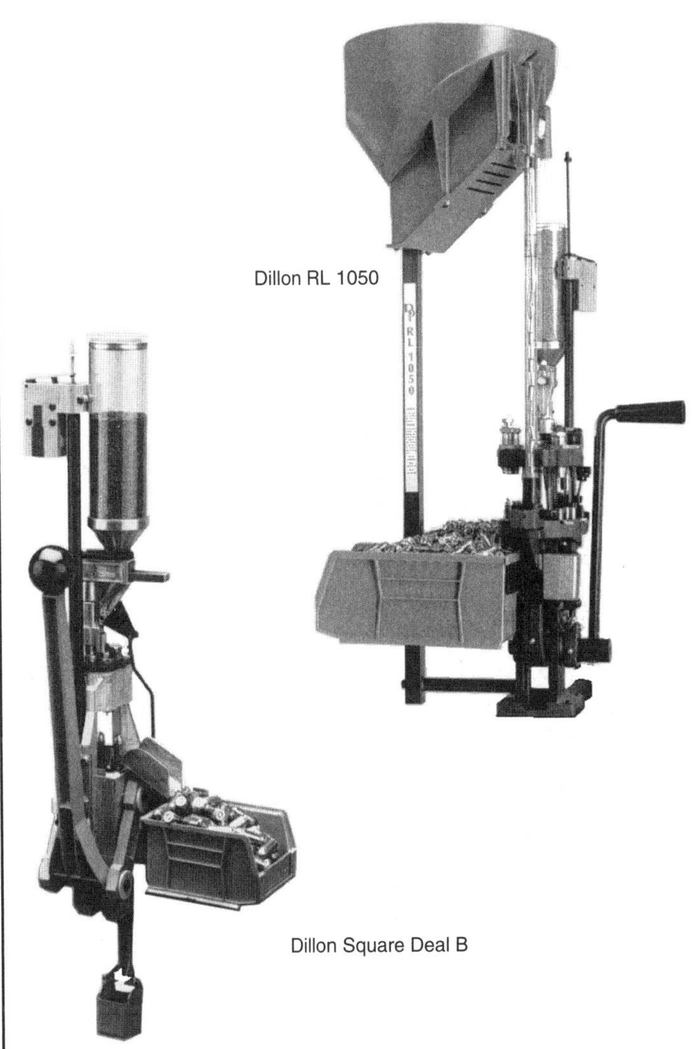

Dillon RL 1050

Dillon Square Deal B

DILLON XL 650

Frame: Aluminum alloy
Frame Type: NA
Die Thread: 7/8-14
Avg. Rounds Per Hour: 800-1000
Ram Stroke: 4-9/16"
Weight: 46 lbs.
Features: Five stations; auto indexing; auto case feed; removable tool head;

ACCESSORIES

METALLIC CARTRIDGE PRESSES

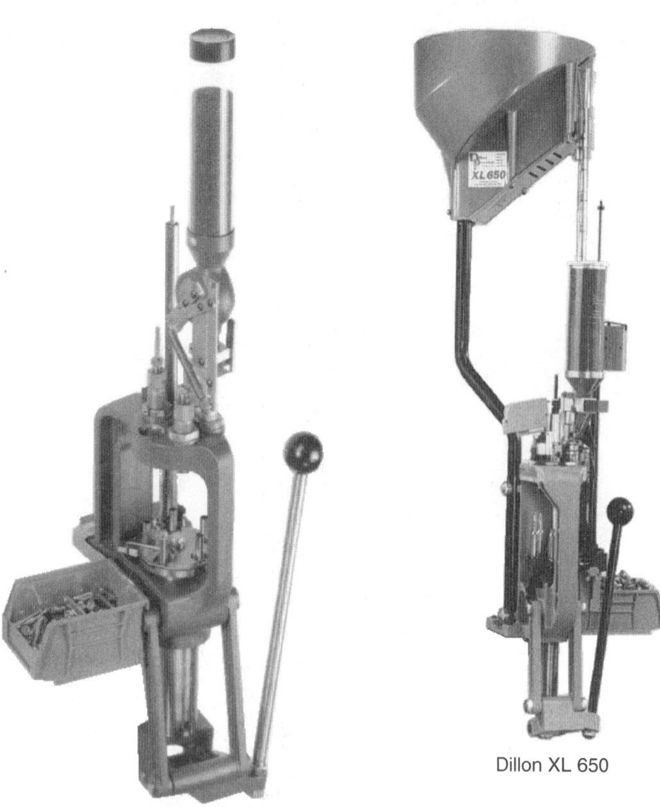
Hornady Lock-N-Load AP

Dillon XL 650

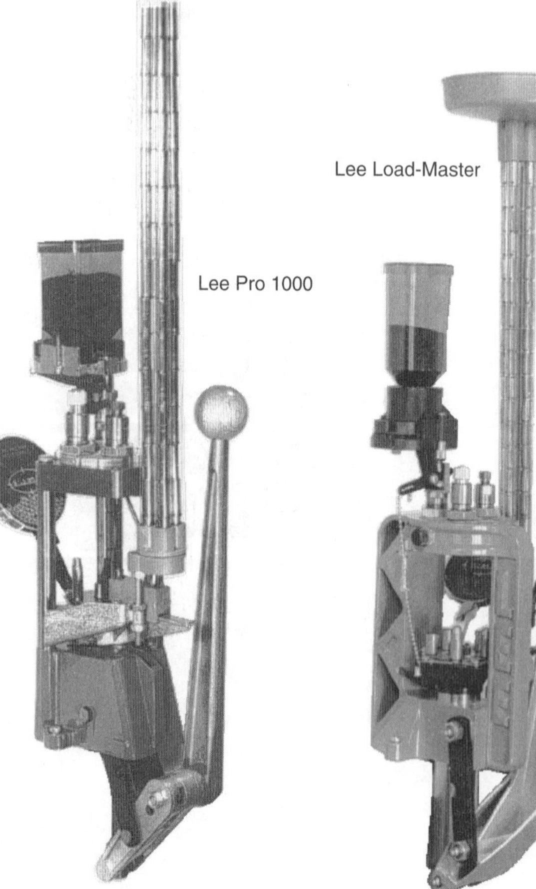
Lee Pro 1000

Lee Load-Master

auto prime system with 100-primer capacity; low primer supply alarm; auto powder measure; positive powder bar return; 220 ejected round capacity bin; 3/4-lb. capacity powder measure. 500-600 case feed capacity with optional auto case feed. Loads all pistol/rifle calibers less than 3-1/2" in length. Height above the bench, 44"; 3/4" bench overhang required. From Dillon Precision Products, Inc.
Price: Less dies **$443.95**

HORNADY Lock-N-Load AP

Frame: Die cast heat-treated aluminum alloy
Frame Type: O-frame
Die Thread: 7/8-14
Avg. Rounds Per Hour: NA
Ram Stroke: 3-3/4"
Weight: 26 lbs.
Features: Features Lock-N-Load bushing system that allows instant die changeovers; five-station die platform with option of seating and crimping separately or adding taper-crimp die; auto prime with large and small primer tubes with 100-primer capacity and protective housing; brass kicker to eject loaded rounds into 80-round capacity cartridge catcher; offset operating handle for leverage and unobstructed operation; 2" diameter ram driven by heavy-duty cast linkage arms rotating on steel pins. Comes with five Lock-N-Load die bushings, shellplate, deluxe powder measure, auto powder drop, and auto primer feed and shut-off, brass kicker and primer catcher. Lifetime warranty. From Hornady Mfg. Co.
Price: **$367.65**

LEE Load-Master

Frame: ASTM 380 aluminum
Frame Type: O-frame
Die Thread: 7/8-14
Avg. Rounds Per Hour: 600
Ram Stroke: 3-1/4"
Weight: 8 lbs., 4 oz.
Features: Available in kit form only. A 1-3/4" diameter hard chrome ram for handling largest magnum cases; loads rifle or pistol rounds; five station press to factory crimp and post size; auto indexing with wedge lock mechanism to hold one ton; auto priming; removable turrets; four-tube case feeder with optional case collator and bullet feeder (late 1995); loaded round ejector with chute to optional loaded round catcher; quick change shellplate; primer catcher. Dies and shellholder for one caliber included. From Lee Precision, Inc.
Price: Rifle **$320.00**
Price: Pistol **$330.00**
Price: Extra turret **$10.98**
Price: Adjustable charge bar **$9.98**

LEE Pro 1000

Frame: ASTM 380 aluminum and steel
Frame Type: O-frame
Die Thread: 7/8-14
Avg. Rounds Per Hour: 600
Ram Stroke: 3-1/4"
Weight: 8 lbs., 7 oz.
Features: Optional transparent large/small or rifle case feeder; deluxe auto-disk case-activated powder measure; case sensor for primer feed. Comes complete with carbide die set (steel dies for rifle) for one caliber. Optional accessories include: case feeder for large/small pistol cases or rifle cases; shell plate carrier with auto prime, case ejector, auto-index and spare parts; case collator for case feeder. From Lee Precision, Inc.
Price: **$199.98**

PONSNESS/WARREN Metallic II

Frame: Die cast aluminum
Frame Type: H-frame
Die Thread: 7/8-14
Avg. Rounds Per Hour: 150+
Ram Stroke: NA

Weight: 32 lbs.
Features: Die head with five tapped 7/8-14 holes for dies, powder measure or other accessories; pivoting die arm moves case from station to station; depriming tube for removal of spent primers; auto primer feed; interchangeable die head. Optional accessories include additional die heads, powder measure extension tube to accommodate any standard powder measure, primer speed feeder to feed press primer tube without disassembly. Comes with small and large primer seating tools. Dies, powder measure and shellholder not included. From Ponsness/Warren.
Price: **$375.00**
Price: Extra die head **$56.95**
Price: Primer speed feeder **$14.50**
Price: Powder measure extension **$29.95**
Price: Dust cover **$27.95**

RCBS AmmoMaster-Auto

Frame: Aluminum base; cast iron top plate connected by three steel posts
Frame Type: NA
Die Thread: 1-1/4-12 bushing; 7/8-14 threads
Avg. Rounds Per Hour: 400-500
Ram Stroke: 5-1/4"
Weight: 19 lbs.
Features: Progressive press convertible to single-stage. Features include: 1-1/2" solid ram; automatic indexing, priming, powder charging and loaded round ejection. Case detection system disengages powder measure when no case is present in powder charging station. Comes with five-station shellplate and Uniflow powder measure with clear powder measure adaptor to make bridged powders visible and correctable. Piggyback die plate for quick caliber change-over available. Reloading dies not included. From RCBS.
Price: **$394.95**
Price: Piggyback/AmmoMaster die plate **$22.95**
Price: Piggyback/AmmoMaster shellplate **$27.95**
Price: Press cover **$10.95**

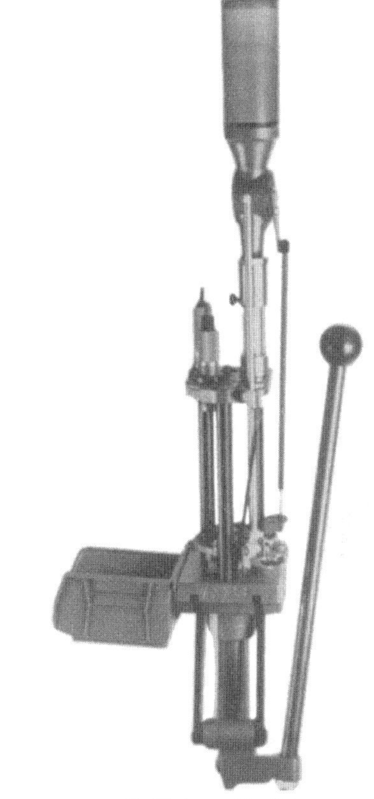

RCBS AmmoMaster

RCBS Pro 2000™

Frame: Cast iron
Frame Type: H-Frame
Die Thread: 7/8 x 14
Avg. Rounds Per Hour: NA
Ram Stroke: NA
Weight: NA
Features: Five-station manual indexing; full-length sizing; removable die plate; fast caliber conversion. Uses APS Priming System. From RCBS.
Price: **$468.95**

STAR Universal Pistol Press

Frame: Cast iron with aluminum base
Frame Type: Unconventional
Die Thread: 11/16-24 or 7/8-14
Avg. Rounds Per Hour: 300
Ram Stroke: NA
Weight: 27 lbs.
Features: Four or five-station press depending on need to taper crimp; handles all popular handgun calibers from 32 Long to 45 Colt. Comes completely assembled and adjusted with carbide dies (except 30 Carbine) and shellholder to load one caliber. Prices slightly higher for 9mm and 30 Carbine. From Star Machine Works.
Price: With taper crimp **$1,055.00**
Price: Without taper crimp **$1,025.00**
Price: Extra tool head, taper crimp **$425.00**
Price: Extra tool head, w/o taper crimp **$395.00**

Fully-automated Star Universal

ACCESSORIES

Misc. Handgun Sights

MILLETT SCOPE-SITE Open, adjustable or fixed rear sights dovetail into a base integral with the top scope-mounting ring. Blaze orange front ramp sight is integral with the front ring half. Rear sights have white outline aperture. Provides fast, short-radius, Patridge-type open sights on the top of the scope. Can be used with all Millett rings, Weaver-style bases, Ruger 77 (also fits Redhawk), Ruger Ranch Rifle, No. 1, No. 3, Rem. 870, 1100; Burris, Leupold and Redfield bases.
Price: Scope-Site top only, windage only **$31.15**
Price: As above, fully adjustable. **$66.10**
Price: Scope-Site Hi-Turret, fully adjustable, low, medium, high . . . **$66.10**

WICHITA MULTI RANGE SIGHT SYSTEM Designed for silhouette shooting. System allows you to adjust the rear sight to four repeatable range settings, once it is pre-set. Sight clicks to any of the settings by turning a serrated wheel. Front sight is adjustable for weather and light conditions with one adjustment. Specify gun when ordering.
Price: Rear sight. **$120.00**
Price: Front sight **$90.00**

WILLIAMS DOVETAIL OPEN SIGHT (WDOS) Open rear sight with windage and elevation adjustment. Furnished with "U" notch or choice of blades. Slips into dovetail and locks with gib lock. Heights from .281″ to .531″.
Price: With blade **$15.86**
Price: Less Blade **$9.92**

EAW RECEIVER SIGHT A fully adjustable aperture sight that locks securely into the EAW quick-detachable scope mount rear base. Made by New England Custom Gun Service.
Price: **$95.00**

G.G.&G. MAD IRIS Multiple Aperture Device is a four sight, rotating aperture disk with small and large apertures on the same plane. Mounts on M-16/AR-15 flat top receiver. Fully adjustable.
Price: **$141.95**
Price: A2 IRIS, two apertures, full windage adjustments **$124.95**

Front Sights

ERA FRONT SIGHTS European-type front sights inserted from the front. Various heights available. From New England Custom Gun Service.
Price: 1/16″ silver bead. **$11.50**
Price: 3/32″ silver bead. **$16.00**
Price: Sourdough bead. **$14.50**
Price: Tritium night sight. **$44.00**
Price: Folding night sight with ivory bead. **$39.50**

Globe Target Front Sights

LYMAN 20 MJT TARGET FRONT Has 7/8″ diameter, one-piece steel globe with 3/8″ dovetail base. Height is .700″ from bottom of dovetail to center of aperture; height on 20 LJT is .750″. Comes with seven Anschutz-size steel inserts—two posts and five apertures .126″ through .177″.
Price: 20 MJT or 20 LJT. **$31.50**

LYMAN No. 17A TARGET Includes seven interchangeable inserts: four apertures, one transparent amber and two posts .50″ and .100″ in width.
Price: **$26.00**
Price: Insert set. **$9.00**

Lyman 17AEU

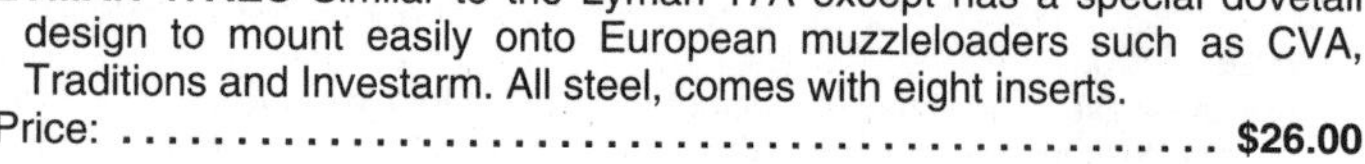

LYMAN 17AEU Similar to the Lyman 17A except has a special dovetail design to mount easily onto European muzzleloaders such as CVA, Traditions and Investarm. All steel, comes with eight inserts.
Price: **$26.00**

Handgun Sights

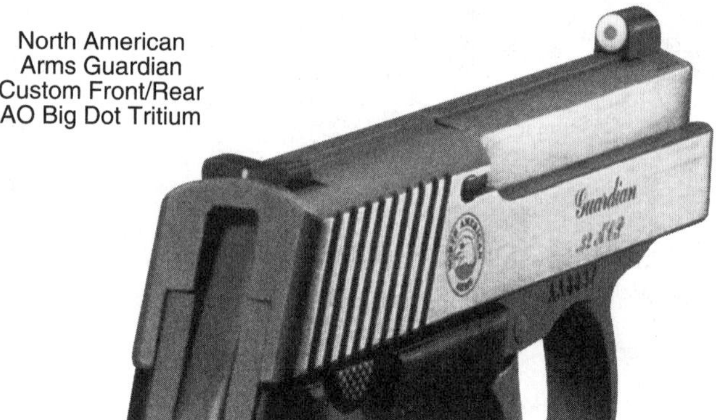

North American Arms Guardian Custom Front/Rear AO Big Dot Tritium

Springfield V10 Compact Small Custom Express AO Big Dot Tritium

AO Express Big Dot

METALLIC SIGHTS

AO EXPRESS SIGHTS Low-profile, snag-free express-type sights. Shallow V rear with white vertical line, white dot front. All-steel, matte black finish. Rear is available in different heights. Made for most pistols, many with double set-screws. From AO Sight Systems, Inc.
Price: Standard Set, front and rear **$60.00**
Price: Big Dot Set, front and rear **$60.00**
Price: Tritium Set, Standard or Big Dot **$90.00**

AO Pro Express

AO PRO EXPRESS SIGHTS Big Dot Tritium or Standard Dot Tritium Front Sight incorporating a new vertical Tritium Bar within the Rear Express Sight. Provides enhanced low-light sight acquisition with speed of Express Sight Principle. Rear sights available in fitted or double set-screw style for easier installation. From AO Sight Systems.
Price: Pro Express Big Dot Tritium **$120.00**
Price: Pro Express Standard Dot Tritium **$120.00**

AO Adjustable

AO ADJUSTABLE EXPRESS SIGHT SETS Incorporates Adjustable Rear Express Sight with a white stripe rear, or Pro Express Rear with a Vertical Tritium Bar, fits either a Bomar style cut, LPA style cut, or a Kimber Tgt cut rear sight. Affords same Express Sight principles as fixed sight models.
Price: Adjustable Express w/White Stripe Rear and Big Dot Front or Standard Dot Front **$90.00**
Price: Adjustable Express w/White Stripe Rear and Big Dot Tritium or Standard Dot Tritium Front **$120.00**
Price: Adjustable Pro Express w/Tritium Rear and Big Dot Tritium or Standard Dot Tritium Front **$150.00**

BO-MAR DELUXE BMCS Gives 3/8″ windage and elevation adjustment at 50 yards on Colt Gov't 45; sight radius under 7″. For GM and Commander models only. Uses existing dovetail slot. Has shield-type rear blade.
Price: **$65.95**
Price: BMCS-2 (for GM and 9mm) **$68.95**
Price: Flat bottom **$65.95**
Price: BMGC (for Colt Gold Cup), angled serrated blade, rear **$68.95**
Price: BMGC front sight **$12.95**
Price: BMCZ-75 (for CZ-75,TZ-75, P-9 and most clones). Works with factory front **$68.95**

BO-MAR FRONT SIGHTS Dovetail style for S&W 4506, 4516, 1076; undercut style (.250″, .280″, 5/16″ high); Fast Draw style (.210″, .250″, .230″ high).
Price **$12.95**

BO-MAR BMU XP-100/T/C CONTENDER No gunsmithing required; has .080″ notch.
Price: **$77.00**

BO-MAR BMML For muzzleloaders; has .062″ notch, flat bottom.
Price: **$65.95**
Price: With 3/8″ dovetail **$65.95**

BO-MAR RUGER "P" ADJUSTABLE SIGHT Replaces factory front and rear sights.
Price: Rear sight **$65.95**
Price: Front sight **$12.00**

BO-MAR BMR Fully adjustable rear sight for Ruger MKI, MKII Bull barrel autos.
Price: Rear **$65.95**
Price: Undercut front sight **$12.00**

BO-MAR GLOCK Fully adjustable, all-steel replacement sights. Sight fits factory dovetail. Longer sight radius. Uses Novak Glock .275″ high, .135″ wide front, or similar.
Price: Rear sight **$68.95**
Price: Front sight **$20.95**

BO-MAR LOW PROFILE RIB & ACCURACY TUNER Streamlined rib with front and rear sights; 7 1/8″ sight radius. Brings sight line closer to the bore than standard or extended sight and ramp. Weight 5 oz. Made for Colt Gov't 45, Super 38, and Gold Cup 45 and 38.
Price: **$140.00**

BO-MAR COMBAT RIB For S&W Model 19 revolver with 4″ barrel. Sight radius 5 3/4″, weight 5 1/2 oz.
Price: **$127.00**

BO-MAR WINGED RIB For S&W 4″ and 6″ length barrels—K-38, M10, HB 14 and 19. Weight for the 6″ model is about 7 1/4 oz.
Price: **$140.00**

BO-MAR COVER-UP RIB Adjustable rear sight, winged front guards. Fits right over revolver's original front sight. For S&W 4″ M-10HB, M-13, M-58, M-64 & 65, Ruger 4″ models SDA-34, SDA-84, SS-34, SS-84, GF-34, GF-84.
Price: **$130.00**

C-MORE SIGHTS Replacement front sight blades offered in two types and five styles. Made of Du Pont Acetal, they come in a set of five high-contrast colors: blue, green, pink, red and yellow. Easy to install. Patridge style for Colt Python (all barrels), Ruger Super Blackhawk (7 1/2″), Ruger Blackhawk (4 5/8″); ramp style for Python (all barrels), Blackhawk (4 5/8″), Super Blackhawk (7 1/2″ and 10 1/2″). From C-More Systems.
Price: Per set **$19.95**

G.G. & G. GHOST RINGS Replaces the factory rear sight without gunsmithing. Black phosphate finish. Available for Colt M1911 and Commander, Beretta M92F, Glock, S&W, SIG Sauer.
Price: **$65.00**

JP GHOST RING Replacement bead front, ghost ring rear for Glock and M1911 pistols. From JP Enterprises.
Price: **$79.95**
Price: Bo-Mar replacement leaf with JP dovetail front bead **$99.95**

MMC TACTICAL ADJUSTABLE SIGHTS Low-profile, snag free design. Twenty-two click positions for elevation, drift adjustable for windage. Machined from 4140 steel and heat treated to 40 RC. Tritium and non-tritium. Ten different configurations and colors. Three different finishes. For 1911s, all Glock, HK USP, S&W, Browning Hi-Power.
Price: Sight set, tritium **$144.92**
Price: Sight set, white outline or white dot **$99.90**
Price: Sight set, black **$93.90**

MEPROLIGHT TRITIUM NIGHT SIGHTS Replacement sight assemblies for use in low-light conditions. Available for rifles, shotguns, handguns and bows. **TRU-DOT** models carry a 12-year warranty on the useable illumination, while non-**TRU-DOT** have a 5-year warranty. Contact Hesco, Inc. for complete list of available models.
Price: Kahr K9, K40, fixed, **TRU-DOT** **$100.00**
Price: Ruger P85, P89, P94, adjustable, **TRU-DOT** **$156.00**
Price: Ruger Mini-14R sights **$140.00**
Price: SIG Sauer P220, P225, P226, P228, adjustable, **TRU-DOT** **$156.00**
Price: Smith&Wesson autos, fixed or adjustable, **TRU-DOT** **$100.00**
Price: Taurus PT92, PT100, adjustable, **TRU-DOT** **$156.00**
Price: Walther P-99, fixed, **TRU-DOT** **$100.00**
Price: Shotgun bead **$32.00**
Price: Beretta M92, Cougar, Brigadier, fixed, **TRU-DOT** **$100.00**
Price: Browning Hi-Power, adjustable, **TRU-DOT** **$156.00**
Price: Colt M1911 Govt., adjustable, **TRU-DOT** **$156.00**

METALLIC SIGHTS

Meprolight Night Sights

Glock Pistol

Beretta Pistol

Colt 1911 Govt. Commander Pistol

Ruger P85, P85MKII & P89 Pistol

H&K USP

Taurus Model 44 & 608 Revolvers

Millett Series 100

Millett Glock Series 100 Sight

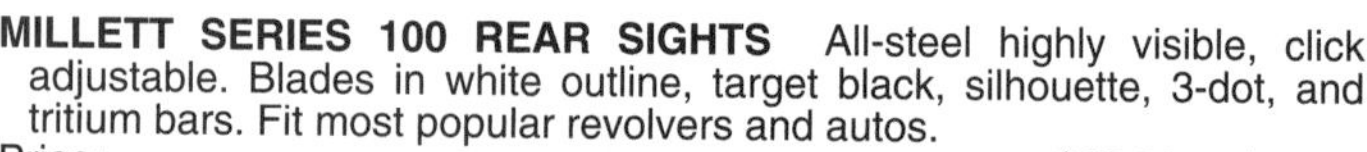

MILLETT SERIES 100 REAR SIGHTS All-steel highly visible, click adjustable. Blades in white outline, target black, silhouette, 3-dot, and tritium bars. Fit most popular revolvers and autos.
Price: .... **$49.30** to **$80.00**

MILLETT BAR-DOT-BAR TRITIUM NIGHT SIGHTS Replacement front and rear combos fit most automatics. Horizontal tritium bars on rear, dot front sight.
Price: **$145.00**

MILLETT 3-DOT SYSTEM SIGHTS The 3-Dot System sights use a single white dot on the front blade and two dots flanking the rear notch. Fronts available in Dual-Crimp and Wide Stake-On styles, as well as special applications. Adjustable rear sight available for most popular auto pistols and revolvers.
Price: Front, from **$16.00**
Price: Adjustable rear **$55.60**

MILLETT REVOLVER FRONT SIGHTS All-steel replacement front sights with either white or orange bar. Easy to install. For Ruger GP-100, Redhawk, Security-Six, Police-Six, Speed-Six, Colt Trooper, Diamondback, King Cobra, Peacemaker, Python, Dan Wesson 22 and 15-2.
Price: .... **$13.60** to **$16.00**

MILLETT DUAL-CRIMP FRONT SIGHT Replacement front sight for automatic pistols. Dual-Crimp uses an all-steel two-point hollow rivet system. Available in eight heights and four styles. Has a skirted base that covers the front sight pad. Easily installed with the Millett Installation Tool Set. Available in Blaze Orange Bar, White Bar, Serrated Ramp, Plain Post.
Price: **$16.00**

MILLETT STAKE-ON FRONT SIGHT Replacement front sight for automatic pistols. Stake-On sights have skirted base that covers the front sight pad. Easily installed with the Millet Installation Tool Set. Available in seven heights and four styles—Blaze Orange Bar, White Bar, Serrated Ramp, Plain Post.
Price: **$16.00**

OMEGA OUTLINE SIGHT BLADES Replacement rear sight blades for Colt and Ruger single action guns and the Interarms Virginian Dragoon. Standard Outline available in gold or white notch outline on blue metal. From Omega Sales, Inc.
Price: **$8.95**

OMEGA MAVERICK SIGHT BLADES Replacement "peep-sight" blades for Colt, Ruger SAs, Virginian Dragoon. Three models available—No. 1, Plain; No. 2, Single Bar; No. 3, Double Bar Rangefinder. From Omega Sales, Inc.
Price: Each **$6.95**

METALLIC SIGHTS

Pachmayr Accu-Set

PACHMAYR ACCU-SET Low-profile, fully adjustable rear sight to be used with existing front sight. Available with target, white outline or 3-dot blade. Blue finish. Uses factory dovetail and locking screw. For Browning, Colt, Glock, SIG Sauer, S&W and Ruger autos. From Pachmayr.
Price: .... **NA**

P-T TRITIUM NIGHT SIGHTS Self-luminous tritium sights for most popular handguns, Colt AR-15, H&K rifles and shotguns. Replacement handgun sight sets available in 3-Dot style (green/green, green/yellow, green/orange) with bold outlines around inserts; Bar-Dot available in green/green with or without white outline rear sight. Functional life exceeds 15 years. From Innovative Weaponry, Inc.
Price: Handgun sight sets **$99.95**
Price: Rifle sight sets...................................... **$99.95**
Price: Rifle, front only **$49.95**
Price: Shotgun, front only **$49.95**

Trijicon Night Sights

TRIJICON NIGHT SIGHTS Three-dot night sight system uses tritium lamps in the front and rear sights. Tritium "lamps" are mounted in silicone rubber inside a metal cylinder. A polished crystal sapphire provides protection and clarity. Inlaid white outlines provide 3-dot aiming in daylight also. Available for most popular handguns. From Trijicon, Inc.
Price:...................................... **$50.00 to $175.00**

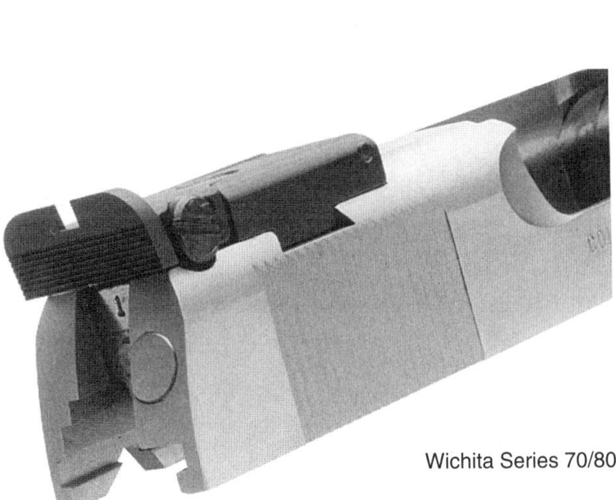

Wichita Series 70/80

WICHITA SERIES 70/80 SIGHT Provides click windage and elevation adjustments with precise repeatability of settings. Sight blade is grooved and angled back at the top to reduce glare. Available in Low Mount Combat or Low Mount Target styles for Colt 45s and their copies, S&W 645, Hi-Power, CZ 75 and others.
Price: Rear sight, target or combat.......................... **$75.00**
Price: Front sight, Patridge or ramp **$15.00**

WICHITA GRAND MASTER DELUXE RIBS Ventilated rib has wings machined into it for better sight acquisition and is relieved for Mag-Na-Porting. Milled to accept Weaver see-thru-style rings. Made of stainless or blued steel; front and rear sights blued. Has Wichita Multi-Range rear sight system, adjustable front sight. Made for revolvers with 6″ barrel.
Price: Model 301S, 301B (adj. sight K frames with custom bbl. of 1″ to 1.032″ dia. L and N frame with 1.062″ to 1.100″ dia. bbl.)...... **$189.00**
Price: Model 303S, 303B (adj. sight K, L, N frames with factory barrel) . . . **$189.00**

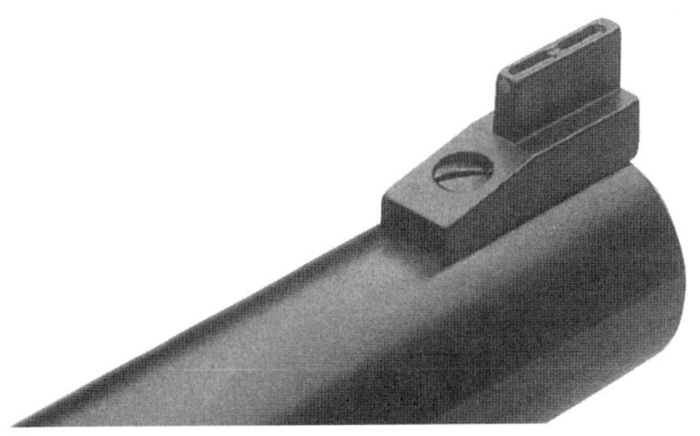

Williams Fire Sight Ruger MKII Sights

Williams Fire Sight Set

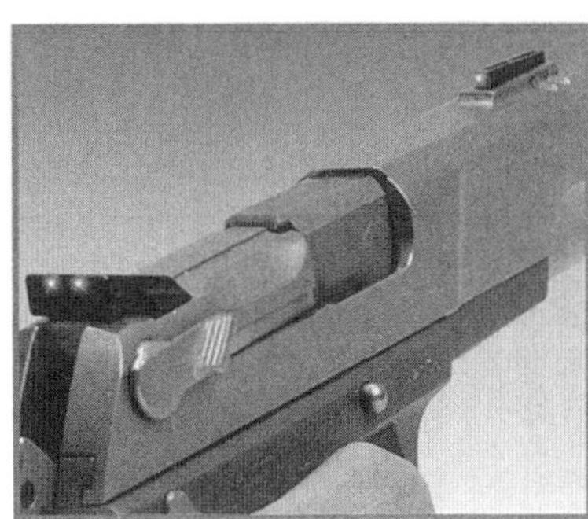

WILLIAMS FIRE SIGHT SETS Red fiber optic metallic sight replaces the original. Rear sight has two green fiber optic elements. Made of CNC-machined aluminum. Fits all Glocks, Ruger P-Series (except P-85), S&W 910, Colt Gov't. Model Series 80, Ruger GP 100 and Redhawk, and SIG Sauer (front only).
Price: Front and rear set **$39.95**
Price: SIG Sauer front...................................... **$19.95**

ACCESSORIES

METALLIC SIGHTS

Sight Attachments

MERIT ADJUSTABLE APERTURES Eleven clicks give 12 different apertures. No. 3 Disc and Master, primarily target types, 0.22″ to .125″; No. 4, 1/2″ dia. hunting type, .025″ to .155″. Available for all popular sights. The Master, with flexible rubber light shield, is particularly adapted to extension, scope height, and tang sights. All models have internal click springs; are hand fitted to minimum tolerance.
Price: No. 3 Master Disk **$66.00**
Price: No. 3 Target Disc (Plain Face) **$56.00**
Price: No. 4 Hunting Disc **$48.00**

MERIT LENS DISC Similar to Merit Iris Shutter (Model 3 or Master) but incorporates provision for mounting prescription lens integrally. Lens may be obtained locally from your optician. Sight disc is 7/16″ wide (Model 3), or 3/4″ wide (Master).
Price: No. 3 Target Lens Disk **$68.00**
Price: No. 3 Master Lens Disk. **$78.00**

MERIT OPTICAL ATTACHMENT For iron sight shooting with handgun or rifle. Instantly attached by rubber suction cup to prescription or shooting glasses. Swings aside. Aperture adjustable from .020" to .156".
Price: **$65.00**

WILLIAMS APERTURES Standard thread, fits most sights. Regular series 3/8″ to 1/2″ O.D., .050″ to .125″ hole. "Twilight" series has white reflector ring.
Price: Regular series. **$4.97**
Price: Twilight series **$6.79**
Price: Wide open 5/16″ aperture for shotguns fits 5-D or Foolproof sights (specify model). **$8.77**

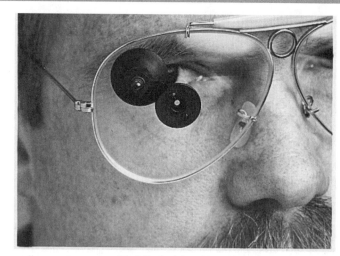

Merit Optical Attachment

MUZZLE BRAKES

Gentry Quiet Muzzle Brake

Developed by gunmaker David Gentry, the "Quiet Muzzle Brake" is said to reduce recoil by up to 85 percent with no loss of accuracy or velocity. There is no increase in noise level because the noise and gases are directed away from the shooter. The barrel is threaded for installation and the unit is blued to match the barrel finish. Price, installed, is **$150.00**. Add **$15.00** for stainless steel, **$45.00** for knurled cap to protect threads. Shipping extra.

JP Muzzle Brake

Designed for single shot handguns, AR-15, Ruger Mini-14, Ruger Mini Thirty and other sporting rifles, the JP Muzzle Brake redirects high pressure gases against a large frontal surface which applies forward thrust to the gun. All gases are directed up, rearward and to the sides. Priced at **$79.95** (AR-15 or sporting rifles), **$89.95** (bull barrel and SKS, AK models), **$89.95** (Ruger Minis), Dual Chamber model **$79.95.** From JP Enterprises, Inc.

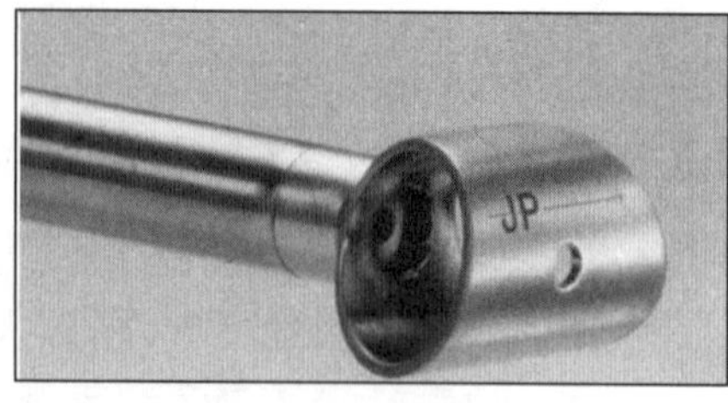

JP Muzzle Brake

KDF Slim Line Muzzle Brake

This threaded muzzle brake has 30 pressure ports that direct combustion gases in all directions to reduce felt recoil up to a claimed 80 percent without affecting accuracy or ballistics. It is said to reduce felt recoil of a 30-06 to that of a 243. Price, installed, is **$179.00**. From KDF, Inc.

Mag-Na-Port

Electrical Discharge Machining works on any firearm except those having non-conductive shrouded barrels. EDM is a metal erosion technique using carbon electrodes that control the area to be processed. The Mag-Na-Port venting process utilizes small trapezoidal openings to direct powder gases upward and outward to reduce recoil. No effect is had on bluing or nickeling outside the Mag-Na-Port area so no refinishing is needed. Rifle-style porting on single shot or large caliber handguns with barrels 7 1/2″ or longer is **$110.00**; Dual Trapezoidal porting on most handguns with minimum barrel length of 3″, **$100.00**; standard revolver porting, **$78.50**; porting through the slide and barrel for semi-autos, **$115.00**; traditional rifle porting, **$125.00**. Prices do not include shipping, handling and insurance. From Mag-Na-Port International.

Mag-Na-Brake

A screw-on brake under 2″ long with progressive integrated exhaust chambers to neutralize expanding gases. Gases dissipate with an opposite twist to prevent the brake from unscrewing, and with a 5-degree forward angle to minimize sound pressure level. Available in blue, satin blue, bright or satin stainless. Standard and Light Contour installation cost **$179.00** for bolt-action rifles, many single action and single shot handguns. A knurled thread protector supplied at extra cost. Also available in Varmint style with exhaust chambers covering 220 degrees for prone-position shooters. From Mag-Na-Port International.

SSK Arrestor Brake

This is a true muzzle brake with an expansion chamber. It takes up about 1″ of barrel and reduces velocity accordingly. Some Arrestors are added to a barrel, increasing its length. Said to reduce the felt recoil of a 458 to that approaching a 30-06. Can be set up to give zero muzzle rise in any caliber, and can be added to most guns. For handgun or rifle. Prices start at **$95.00**. Contact SSK Industries for full data.

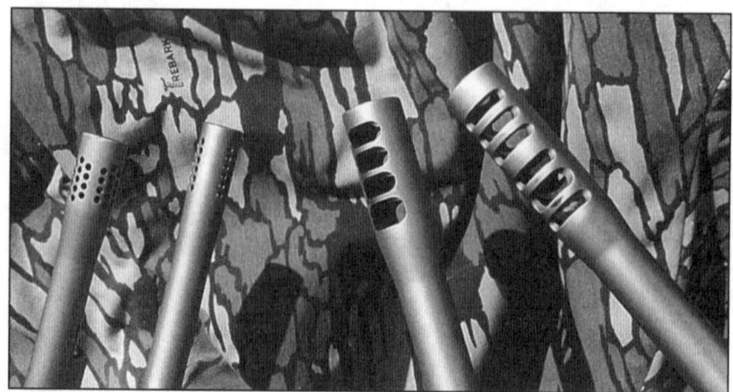

SSK Arrestor Muzzle Brakes

SCOPES / HUNTING, TARGET & VARMINT

Maker and Model	Magn.	Field at 100 Yds. (feet)	Eye Relief (in.)	Length (in.)	Tube Dia. (in.)	W & E Adjustments	Weight (ozs.)	Price
ADCO								
Magnum 50 mm[5]	0	—	—	4.1	45 mm	Int.	6.8	**$269.00**
MIRAGE Ranger 1"	0	—	—	5.2	1	Int.	3.9	**159.00**
MIRAGE Ranger 30mm	0	—	—	5.5	30mm	Int.	5	**159.00**
MIRAGE Competitor	0	—	—	5.5	30mm	Int.	5.5	**229.00**
IMP Sight[2]	0	—	—	4.5	—	Int.	1.3	**17.95**
Square Shooter 2[3]	0	—	—	5	—	Int.	5	**99.00**
MIRAGE Eclipse[1]	0	—	—	5.5	30mm	Int.	5.5	**229.00**
Champ Red Dot	0	—	—	4.5	—	Int.	2	**33.95**
Vantage 1"	0	—	—	3.9	1	Int.	3.9	**129.00**
Vantage 30mm	0	—	—	4.2	30mm	Int.	4.9	**132.00**
Vision 2000[6]	0	60	—	4.7	—	Int.	6.2	**79.00**
e-dot ESB[1]	0	—	—	4.12	1	Int.	3.7	**139.00**

ADCO — Other Data: [1]Multi-Color Dot system changes from red to green. [2]For airguns, paintball, rimfires. Uses common lithium water battery. [3]Comes with standard dovetail mount. [4].75" dovetail mount; poly body; adj. intensity diode. [5]10 MOA dot; black or nickel. [6]Square format; with mount battery. From ADCO Sales.

Maker and Model	Magn.	Field at 100 Yds. (feet)	Eye Relief (in.)	Length (in.)	Tube Dia. (in.)	W & E Adjustments	Weight (ozs.)	Price
AIMPOINT								
Comp	0	—	—	4.6	30mm	Int.	4.3	**331.00**
Comp M[4]	0	—	—	5	30mm	Int.	6.1	**409.00**
Series 5000[3]	0	—	—	6	30mm	Int.	6	**297.00**
Series 3000 Universal[2]	0	—	—	6.25	1	Int.	6	**232.00**
Series 5000/2x[1]	2	—	—	7	30mm	Int.	9	**388.00**

AIMPOINT — Other Data: Illuminates red dot in field of view. Noparallax (dot does not need to be centered). Unlimited field of view and eye relief. On/off, adj. intensity. Dot covers 3" @100 yds. [1]Comes with 30mm rings, battery, lense cloth. [2] Requires 1" rings. Black finish. AP Comp avail. in black, blue, SS, camo. [3]Black finish (AP 5000-B) ; avail. with regular 3-min. or 10-min. Mag Dot as B2 or S2. [4]Band pass reflection coating for compatibility with night vision equipment; U.S. Army contract model; with anti-reflex coated lenses (Comp ML), **$359.00**. From Aimpoint U.S.A.

Maker and Model	Magn.	Field at 100 Yds. (feet)	Eye Relief (in.)	Length (in.)	Tube Dia. (in.)	W & E Adjustments	Weight (ozs.)	Price
ARMSON O.E.G.								
Standard	0	—	—	5.125	1	Int.	4.3	**202.00**

ARMSON O.E.G. — Other Data: Shown red dot aiming point. No batteries needed. Standard model fits 1" ring mounts (not incl.). From Trijicon, Inc.

Maker and Model	Magn.	Field at 100 Yds. (feet)	Eye Relief (in.)	Length (in.)	Tube Dia. (in.)	W & E Adjustments	Weight (ozs.)	Price
BEEMAN								
Pistol Scopes								
5021	2	19	10-24	9.1	1	Int.	7.4	**85.50**
5020	1.5	14	11-16	8.3	.75	Int.	3.6	**NA**

BEEMAN — Other Data: All scopes have 5 point reticle, all glass fully coated lenses. Imported by Beeman.

Maker and Model	Magn.	Field at 100 Yds. (feet)	Eye Relief (in.)	Length (in.)	Tube Dia. (in.)	W & E Adjustments	Weight (ozs.)	Price
BSA								
Pistol								
P52x20	2	N/A	N/A	N/A	N/A	Int.	N/A	**79.95**
P54x28	4	N/A	N/A	N/A	N/A	Int.	N/A	**89.95**
Red Dot								
RD30[1]	1	88	unlimited	3.8	30mm	Int.	5	**59.95**

BSA — Other Data: Imported by BSA. [1]Red dot sights also available in 42mm and 50mm versions.

Maker and Model	Magn.	Field at 100 Yds. (feet)	Eye Relief (in.)	Length (in.)	Tube Dia. (in.)	W & E Adjustments	Weight (ozs.)	Price
BURRIS								
Speeddot 135[13]								
Red Dot	1	—	—	4.85	35mm	Int.	5	**291.00**
Handgun								
1.50-4x LER[1,5,10]	1.6-3.	16-11	11-25	10.25	1	Int.	11	**363.00**
2-7x LER[2,3,5,10]	2-6.5	21-7	7-27	9.5	1	Int.	12.6	**401.00**
3-9x LER[3,5,10]	3.4-8.4	12-5	22-14	11	1	Int.	14	**453.00**
2x LER[3,5,6]	1.7	21	10-24	8.75	1	Int.	6.8	**265.00**
4x LER[1,3,5,6,10]	3.7	11	10-22	9.625	1	Int.	9	**296.00**
10x LER[1,4,6]	9.5	4	8-12	13.5	1	Int.	14	**460.00**
Scout Scope								
1xXER[2,9]	1.5	32	4-24	9	1	Int.	7.0	**290.00**
2.75x[2,9]	2.7	15	7-14	9.375	1	Int.	7.0	**319.00**

BURRIS — Other Data: [1]Dot reticle on some models. [2]Matte satin finish. [3]Available with parallax adjustment (standard on 10x, 12x, 4-12x, 6-12x, 6-18x, 6x HBR and 3-12x Signature). [5]Silver matte finish extra. [6]Target knobs extra, standard on silhouette models. LER and XER with P.A., 6x HBR. [9]Available with Heavy Plex reticle. [10]Available with Posi-Lock. [13]Selected models available with camo finish.
Signature Series: LER=Long Eye Relief; XER=Extra Eye Relief.
Speeddot 135: [13]Waterproof, fogproof, coated lenses, 11 brightness settings;3-MOA or 11-MOA dot size; includes Weaver-style rings and battery. **Partial listing shown.** Contact Burris for complete details.

Plex

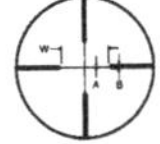
Fine Plex

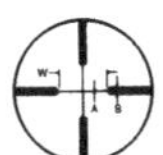
Heavy Plex & Electro-Dot Plex

Peep Plex

Ballistic Mil-Dot

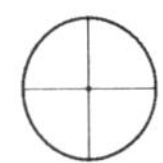
Target Dot

Mil-Dot

SCOPES / HUNTING, TARGET & VARMINT

Maker and Model	Magn.	Field at 100 Yds. (feet)	Eye Relief (in.)	Length (in.)	Tube Dia. (in.)	W & E Adjustments	Weight (ozs.)	Price	Other Data
BUSHNELL									
Elite 3200 Handgun									[1]Also in matte and silver finish. [2]Only in matte finish. [3]Also in silver finish. **Partial listings shown. Contact Bushnell Sports Optics for details.** [4]Variable intensity; **$111.95**
32-2632M[3]	2-6	10-4	20	9	1	Int.	10	**444.95**	
32-2632G	2-6	10-4	20	9	1	Int.	10	**444.95**	
HOLOsight Model[4]	1	—	—	6	—	Int.	8.7	**444.95**	
Trophy Handgun									
73-0232[1]	2	20	9-26	8.7	1	Int.	7.7	**218.95**	
73-2632[2]	2-6	21-7	9-26	9.1	1	Int.	10.9	**287.95**	
Red Dots									
73-0131	1	68	unlim.	5.5	28mm	Int.	6	**102.95**	

HOLOSIGHT RETICLES

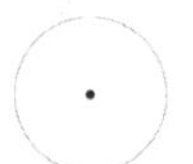

MOA Dot

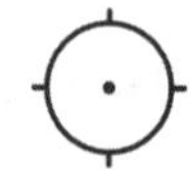

Standard

SCOPE RETICLES

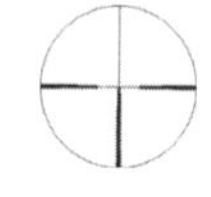

CP2

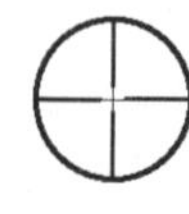

Multi

Euro

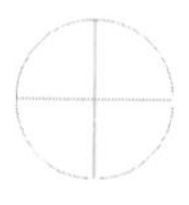

Circle-X

Maker and Model	Magn.	Field at 100 Yds. (feet)	Eye Relief (in.)	Length (in.)	Tube Dia. (in.)	W & E Adjustments	Weight (ozs.)	Price	Other Data
C-MORE SYSTEMS									
Red Dots									[1]All Weaver and Picatinny-style rail mounts. [2]Most popular auto pistols. [3]Mounts to any flat surface, custom mounts, shotgun ribs; Glock adapter plate for direct slide mounting. From C-More Systems, Inc.
Railway[1]	1	—	—	4.8	—	Int.	5	**249.00**	
Serendipity[2]	1	—	—	5.3	—	Int.	3.75	**299.00**	
Slide Ride[3]	1	—	—	4.8	—	Int.	3	**249.00**	
KILHAM									
Hutson Handgunner II	1.7	8	—	5.5	.875	Int.	5.1	**119.95**	Unlimited eye relief; internal click adjustments; crosshair reticle. Fits Thompson/Center rail mounts, for S&W K, N, Ruger Blackhawk, Super, Super Single-Six, Contender.
Hutson Handgunner	3	8	10-12	6	.875	Int.	5.3	**119.95**	
LEUPOLD									
M8-2X EER[1]	1.7	21.2	12-24	7.9	1	Int.	6	**312.50**	Constantly centered reticles, choice of Duplex, tapered CPC, Leupold Dot, Crosshair and Dot. CPC and Dot reticles extra. [1]2x and 4x scopes have from 12"-24" of eye relief and are suitable for handguns, top ejection arms and muzzleloaders. [2]3x9 Compact, 6x Compact, 12x, 3x9, and 6.5x20 come with adjustable objective. Sunshade available for all adjustable objective scopes, **$23.20-$41.10**. [3]Silver finish about **$25.00** extra. [4]Long Range scopes have side focus parallax adjustment, additional windage and elevation travel. Partial listing shown. **Contact Leupold for complete details.** *Models available with illuminated reticle for additional cost.
M8-2X EER Silver[1]	1.7	21.2	12-24	7.9	1	Int.	6	**337.50**	
M8-4X EER[1]	3.7	9	12-24	8.4	1	Int.	7	**425.00**	
M8-4X EER Silver[1]	3.7	9	12-24	8.4	1	Int.	7	**425.00**	
Vari-X 2.5-8 EER	2.5-8	13-4.3	11.7-12	9.7	1	Int.	10.9	**608.90**	

Duplex

CPC

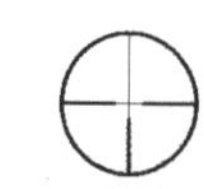

Post & Duplex

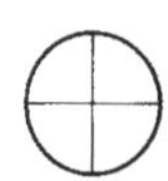

Leupold Dot

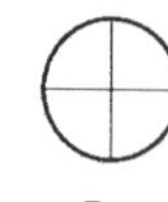

Dot

Maker and Model	Magn.	Field at 100 Yds. (feet)	Eye Relief (in.)	Length (in.)	Tube Dia. (in.)	W & E Adjustments	Weight (ozs.)	Price	Other Data
MEPROLIGHT									
Meprolight Reflex Sights 14-21 5.5 MOA 1x30[1]	1	—	—	4.4	30mm	Int.	5.2	**335.00**	[1]Also available with 4.2 MOA dot. Uses tritium and fiber optics-no batteries required. From Kimber of America.
MILLETT									
SP-1 Compact[1] Red Dot	1	36.65	—	4.1	1	Int.	3.2	**149.95**	[1]3-MOA dot. [2]5-MOA dot. [3]3-, 5-, 8-, 10-MOA dots. [4]10-MOA dot. All have click adjustments; waterproof, shockproof; 11 dot intensity settings. All avail. in matte/black or silver finish. From Millett Sights.
SP-2 Compact[2] Red Dot	1	58	—	4.5	30mm	Int.	4.3	**149.95**	
MultiDot SP[3]	1	50	—	4.8	30mm	Int.	5.3	**289.95**	
30mm Wide View[4]	1	60	—	5.5	30mm	Int.	5	**289.95**	
NIKON									
Monarch UCC									Super multi-coated lenses and blackening of all internal metal parts for maximum light gathering capability; positive .25-MOA; fogproof; waterproof; shockproof; luster and matte finish. From Nikon, Inc.
2x20 EER	2	22	26.4	8.1	1	Int.	6.3	**248.95**	

SCOPES / HUNTING, TARGET & VARMINT

Maker and Model	Magn.	Field at 100 Yds. (feet)	Eye Relief (in.)	Length (in.)	Tube Dia. (in.)	W & E Adjustments	Weight (ozs.)	Price	Other Data
SIGHTRON									
Pistol									
SII 1x28P	1	30	9-24	9.49	1	Int.	8.46	**135.95**	
SII 2x28P	2	16-10	9-24	9.49	1	Int.	8.28	**135.95**	
SIMMONS									
Prohunter Handgun									[1]Black matte finish; also available in silver. [2]With dovetail rings. [3]With 3V lithium battery, extension tube, polarizing filter, Weaver rings. Contact Simmons Outdoor Corp. for complete details.
7732[1]	2	22	9-17	8.75	1	Int.	7	**139.99**	
7738[1]	4	15	11.8-17.6	8.5	1	Int.	8	**149.99**	
Red Dot									
51004[2]	1	—	—	4.8	25mm	Int.	4.7	**59.99**	
51112[3]	1	—	—	5.25	30mm	Int.	6	**99.99**	
SWIFT									All Swift scopes have Quadraplex reticles and are fogproof and waterproof. Available in regular matte black or silver finish. [2]Comes with ring mounts, wrench, lens caps, extension tubes, filter, battery.
667 Fire-Fly[2]	1	40	—	5.4	30mm	Int.	5	**220.00**	
Pistol									
679M 1.25-4x28	1.25-4	23-9	23-15	9.3	1	Int.	8.2	**250.00**	
661 4x32	4	90	10-22	9.2	1	Int.	9.5	**130.00**	
663 2x20[1]	2	18.3	9-21	7.2	1	Int.	8.4	**130.00**	
TASCO									
PDP2[2, 3]	1	40	Unltd.	5	30mm	Int.	5	**109.99**	[1]Fits most popular auto pistols, MP5, AR-15/M16. [2]Also matte aluminum finish. [3]Available with 5-min., or 10-min. dot. [4]20mm; black matte; also stainless steel; also 32mm. [5]Has 4, 8, 12, 16MOA dots (switchable). **Contact Tasco for details on complete line.**
PDP3[2, 3]	1	52	Unltd.	5	30mm	Int.	5	**129.99**	
PDP3CMP	1	68	Unltd.	4.75	33mm	Int.	—	**144.99**	
PDP5CMP	1	82	Unltd.	4	47mm	Int.	8	**204.99**	
Optima 2000									
OPP2000-3.5[1, 4]	1	—	—	1.5	—	Int.	1/2	**249.99**	
OPP2000-7[1, 4]	1	—	—	1.5	—	Int.	1.2	**249.99**	
Pistol Scopes									
PX20[2]	2	21	10-23	8	1	Int.	6.5	**69.99**	
P1.254x28[2]	1.25-4	23-9	15-23	9.25	1	Int.	8.2	**109.99**	
PDP2[2, 3]	1	40	Unltd.	5	30mm	Int.	5	**109.99**	
THOMPSON/CENTER RECOIL PROOF SERIES									
Pistol Scopes									[1]Black; lighted reticle. From Thompson/Center Arms.
8315[1]	2.5-7	15-5	8-21, 8-11	9.25	1	Int.	9.2	**308.99**	
8326	2.5-7	15-5	8-21, 8-11	9.25	1	Int.	10.5	**360.49**	
TRIJICON									
ReflexII 1x24	1	—	—	4.25	1	Int.	4.6	**379.00**	
ULTRA DOT									
Ultra-Dot Sights[1]									[1]Ultra Dot sights include rings, battery, polarized filter, and 5-year warranty. All models available in black or satin finish. [2]Illuminated red dot has eleven brightness settings. Shockproof aluminum tube. From Ultra Dot Distribution.
Ultra-Dot 25[2]	1	—	—	5.1	1	Int.	3.9	**159.00**	
Ultra-Dot 30[2]	1	—	—	5.1	30mm	Int.	4	**179.00**	
WEAVER									
Handgun									[1]Gloss black, [2]Matte black, [3]Silver. All scopes are shockproof, waterproof, and fogproof. From Weaver Products.
H2[1-3]	2	21	4-29	8.5	1	Int.	6.7	**212.99-224.99**	
H4[1-3]	4	18	11.5-18	8.5	1	Int.	6.7	**234.99**	
VH4[1-3]	1.5-4	13.6-5.8	11-17	8.6	1	Int.	8.1	**289.99**	
VH8[1-2-3]	2.5-8	8.5-3.7	12.16	9.3	1	Int.	8.3	**299.99**	

Hunting scopes in general are furnished with a choice of reticle—crosshairs, post with crosshairs, tapered or blunt post, or dot crosshairs, etc. W—Windage E—Elevation MOA—Minute of Angle or 1" (approx.) at 100 yards, etc.

LASER SIGHTS

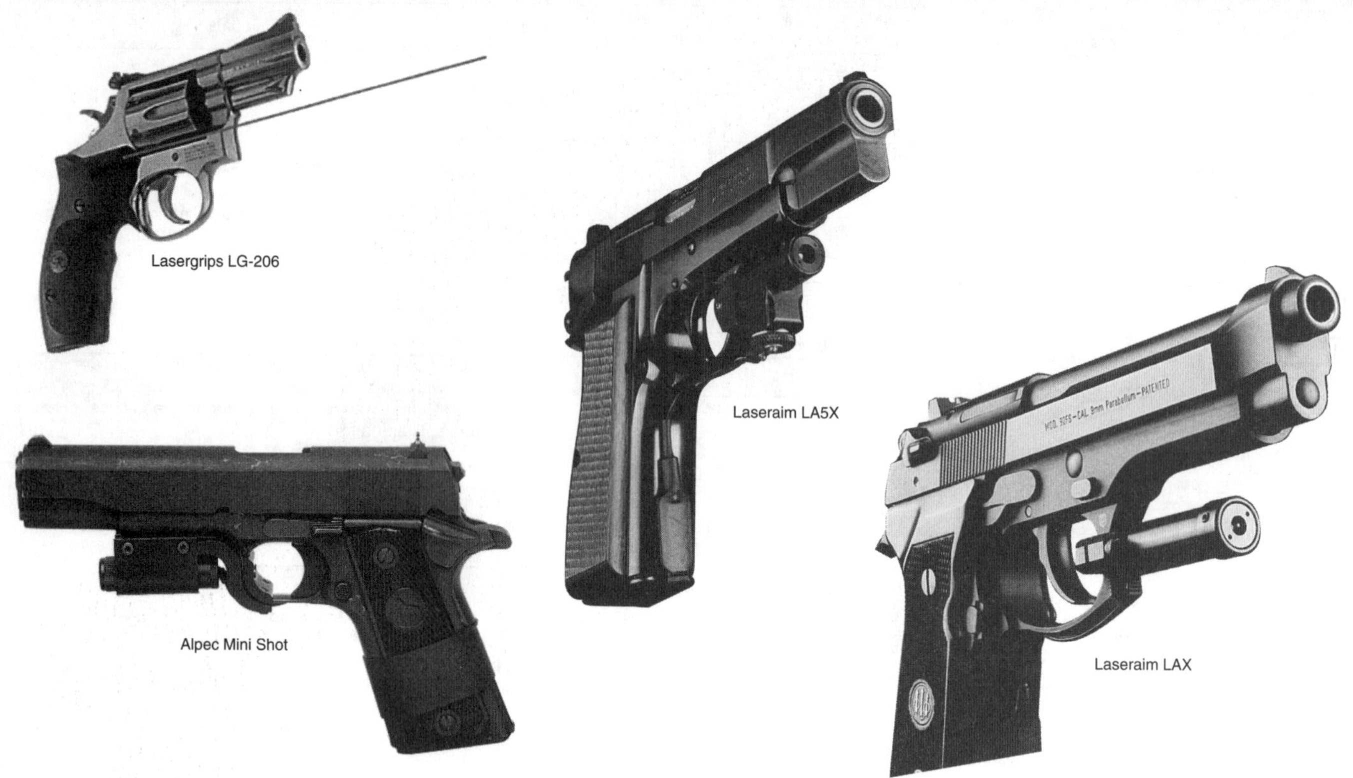
Lasergrips LG-206

Laseraim LA5X

Alpec Mini Shot

Laseraim LAX

Maker and Model	Wavelength (nm)	Beam Color	Lens	Operating Temp. (degrees F.)	Weight (ozs.)	Price	Other Data
ALPEC							[1]Range 1000 yards. [2]Range 300 yards. Mini Shot II range 500 yards, output 650mm, **$129.95**. [3]Range 300 yards; Laser Shot II 500 yards; Super Laser Shot 1000 yards. Black or stainless finish aluminum; removable pressure or push-button switch. Mounts for most handguns, many rifles and shotguns. From Alpec Team, Inc.
Power Shot[1]	635	Red	Glass	NA	2.5	**$199.95**	
Mini Shot[2]	670	Red	Glass	NA	2.5	**99.95**	
Laser Shot[3]	670	Red	Glass	NA	3.0	**99.95**	
BEAMSHOT							[1]Black or silver finish; adj. for windage and elevation; 300-yd. range; also M1000/S (500-yd. range), M1000/u (800-yd.). [2]Black finish; 300-, 500-, 800-yd. models. All come with removable touch pad switch, 5" cable. Mounts to fit virtually any firearm. From Quarton USA Co.
1000[1]	670	Red	Glass	—	3.8	**NA**	
3000[2]	635/670	Red	Glass	—	2	**NA**	
1001/u	635	Red	Glass	—	3.8	**NA**	
780	780	Red	Glass	—	3.8	**NA**	
BSA							[1]Comes with mounts for 22/air rifle and Weaver-style bases.
LS650[1]	N/A	Red	N/A	N/A	N/A	**69.95**	
LASERAIM							[1]1.5-mile range; 1" dot at 100 yds.; 20+ hrs. batt. life. [2]Laser projects 2" dot at 100 yds.: with rotary switch; with Hotdot **$237.00**; with Hotdot touch switch **$357.00**. [3]For Glock 17-27; G1 Hotdot **$299.00**; price installed. All have w&e adj.; black or satin silver finish. From Laseraim Technologies, Inc.
LA5X Handgun Sight[1]	—	Red	—	—	1 oz.	**129.95**	
LAX[1]	—	Red	—	—	2 oz.	**79.00**	
LA10 Hotdot[1]	—	—	—	—	NA	**199.00**	
MA-35RB Mini Aimer[2]	—	—	—	—	1.0	**129.00**	
G1 Laser[3]	—	—	—	—	2.0	**229.00**	
LASER DEVICES							[1]For S&W P99 semi-auto pistols; also BA-2, 5 oz., **$339.00**. [2]For revolvers. [3]For HK, Walther P99. [4]For semi-autos. [5]For rifles; also FA-4/ULS, 2.5 oz., **$325.00**. [6]For HK sub guns. [7]For military rifles. [8]For shotguns. [9]For SIG-Pro pistol. [10]Universal, semi-autos. [11]For AR-15 variants. All avail. with Magnum Power Point (650nM) or daytime-visible Super Power Point (632nM) diode. Infrared diodes avail. for law enforcement. From Laser Devices, Inc.
BA-1[1]	632	Red	Glass	—	2.4	**372.00**	
BA-3[2]	632	Red	Glass	—	3.3	**332.50**	
BA-5[3]	632	Red	Glass	—	3.2	**372.00**	
Duty-Grade[4]	632	Red	Glass	—	3.5	**372.00**	
FA-4[5]	632	Red	Glass	—	2.6	**358.00**	

LASER SIGHTS

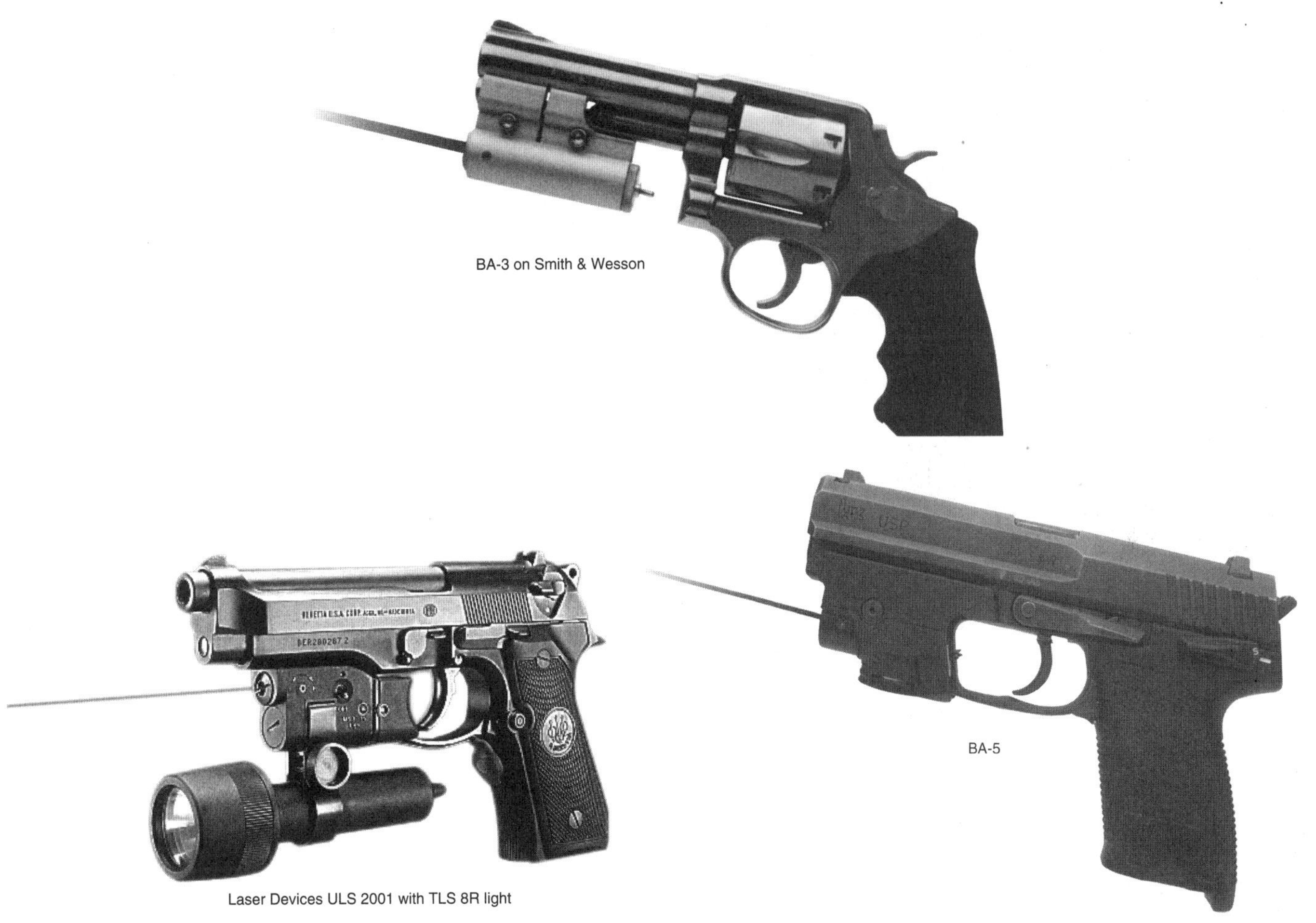

BA-3 on Smith & Wesson

Laser Devices ULS 2001 with TLS 8R light

BA-5

Maker and Model	Wavelength (nm)	Beam Color	Lens	Operating Temp. (degrees F.)	Weight (ozs.)	Price	Other Data
LASER DEVICES (cont.)							
LasTac[1]	632	Red	Glass	—	5.5	**298.00 to 477.00**	
MP-5[6]	632	Red	Glass	—	2.2	**495.00**	
MR-2[7]	632	Red	Glass	—	6.3	**485.00**	
SA-2[8]	632	Red	Glass	—	3.0	**360.00**	
SIG-Pro[9]	632	Red	Glass	—	2.6	**372.00**	
ULS-2001[10]	632	Red	Glass	—	4.5	**210.95**	
Universal AR-2A	632	Red	Glass	—	4.5	**445.00**	
LASERGRIPS							Replaces existing grips with built-in laser high in the right grip panel. Integrated pressure sensitive pad in grip activates the laser. Also has master on/off switch. [1]For Beretta 92, 96, Colt 1911/Commander, Ruger MkII, S&W J-frames, SIG Sauer P228, P229. [2]For all Glock models. Option on/off switch. Requires factory installation. [3]For S&W K, L, N frames, round or square butt (LG-207); [4]For Taurus small-frame revolvers. [5]For Ruger SP-101. [6]For SIG Sauer P226. From Crimson Trace Corp.
LG-201[1]	633	Red-Orange	Glass	NA	—	**349.00**	
LG-206[3]	633	Red-Orange	Glass	NA	—	**289.00**	
LG-085[4]	633	Red-Orange	Glass	NA	—	**279.00**	
LG-101[5]	633	Red-Orange	Glass	NA	—	**289.00**	
LG-226[6]	633	Red-Orange	Glass	NA	—	**379.00**	
GLS-630[2]	633	Red-Orange	Glass	NA	—	**595.00**	

ACCESSORIES

Laser Sights

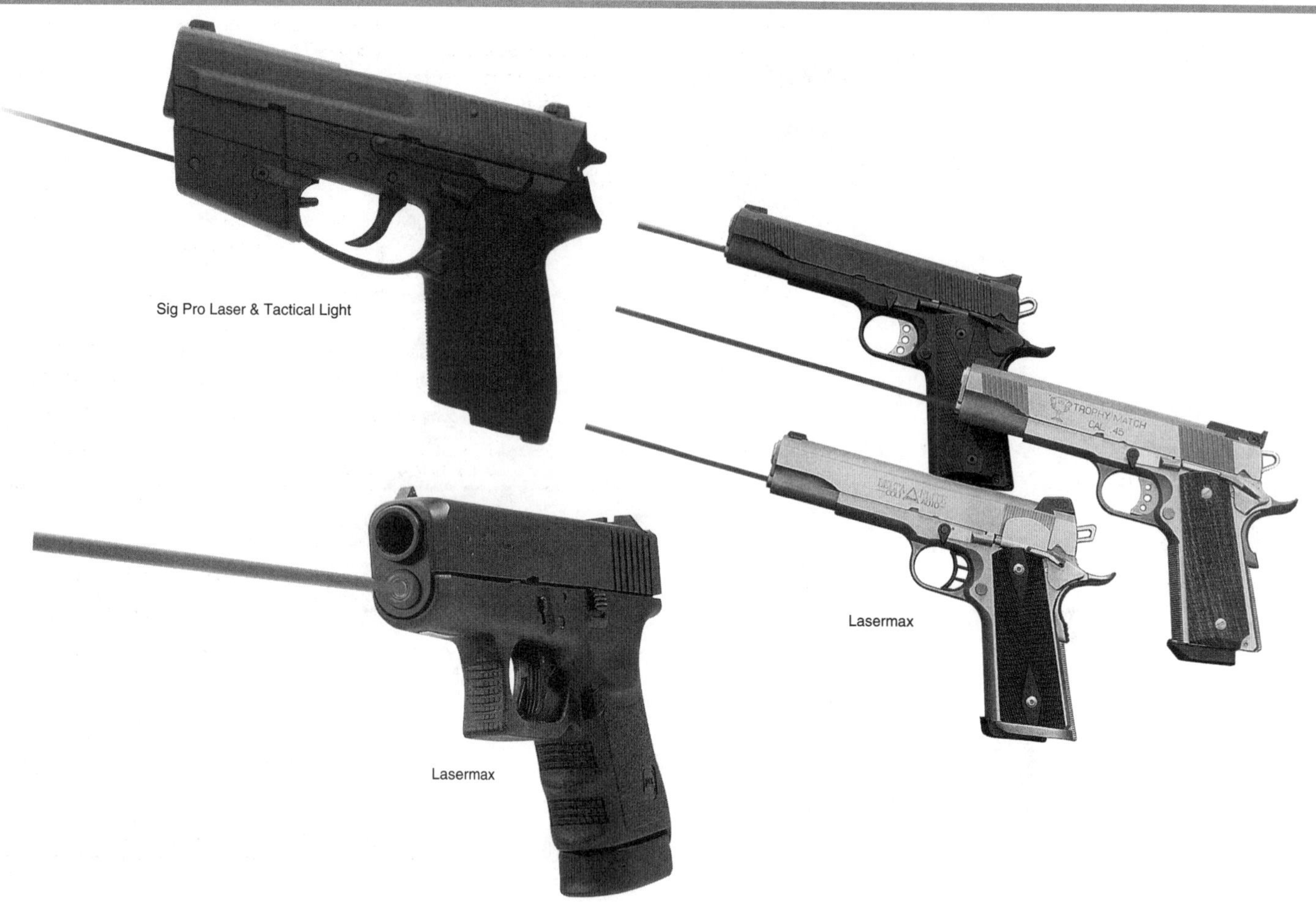

Sig Pro Laser & Tactical Light

Lasermax

Lasermax

Maker and Model	Wavelength (nm)	Beam Color	Lens	Operating Temp. (degrees F.)	Weight (ozs.)	Price	Other Data
LASERLYTE							[1]Dot/circle or dot/crosshair projection; black or stainless. [2]Also 635/645mm model. From TacStar Laserlyte.
LLX-0006-140/090[1]	635/645	Red	—	—	1.4	**159.95**	
WPL-0004-140/090[2]	670	Red	—	—	1.2	**109.95**	
TPL-0004-140/090[2]	670	Red	—	—	1.2	**109.95**	
T7S-0004-140[2]	670	Red	—	—	0.8	**109.95**	
LASERMAX							
LMS-1000 Internal Guide Rod	635	Red-Orange	Glass	40-120	.25	**From 394.95**	Replaces the recoil spring guide rod; includes a customized takedown lever that serves as the laser's instant on/off switch. For Glock, Smith & Wesson, Sigarms, Beretta and select Taurus models. Installs in most pistols without gunsmithing. Battery life 1/2 hour to 2 hours in continuous use. From LaserMax.
NIGHT STALKER							
S0 Smart	635	Red	NA	NA	2.46	**515.00**	Waterproof; LCD panel displays power remaining; programmable blink rate; constant or memory on. From Wilcox Industries Corp.

SCOPE MOUNTS

Maker, Model, Type	Adjust.	Scopes	Price
AIMTECH			
Handguns			
AMT Auto Mag II .22 Mag.	No	Weaver rail	**$56.99**
Astra .44 Mag Revolver	No	Weaver rail	**63.25**
Beretta/Taurus 92/99	No	Weaver rail	**63.25**
Browning Buckmark/Challenger II	No	Weaver rail	**56.99**
Browning Hi-Power	No	Weaver rail	**63.25**
Glock 17, 17L, 19, 23, 24 etc. no rail	No	Weaver rail	**63.25**
Glock 20, 21 no rail	No	Weaver rail	**63.25**
Glock 9mm and .40 with access. rail	No	Weaver rail	**74.95**
Govt. 45 Auto/.38 Super	No	Weaver rail	**63.25**
Hi-Standard (Mitchell version) 107	No	Weaver rail	**63.25**
H&K USP 9mm/40 rail mount	No	Weaver rail	**74.95**
Rossi 85/851/951 Revolvers	No	Weaver rail	**63.25**
Ruger Mk I, Mk II	No	Weaver rail	**49.95**
Ruger P85/P89	No	Weaver rail	**63.25**
S&W K, L, N frames	No	Weaver rail	**63.25**
S&W K. L, N with tapped top strap*	No	Weaver rail	**69.95**
S&W Model 41 Target 22	No	Weaver rail	**63.25**
S&W Model 52 Target 38	No	Weaver rail	**63.25**
S&W Model 99 Walther frame rail mount	No	Weaver rail	**74.95**
S&W 2nd Gen. 59/459/659 etc.	No	Weaver rail	**56.99**
S&W 3rd Gen. full size 5906 etc.	No	Weaver rail	**69.95**
S&W 422, 622, 2206	No	Weaver rail	**56.99**
S&W 645/745	No	Weaver rail	**56.99**
S&W Sigma	No	Weaver rail	**64.95**
Taurus PT908	No	Weaver rail	**63.25**
Taurus 44 6.5" bbl.	No	Weaver rail	**69.95**
Walther 99	No	Weaver rail	**74.95**

All mounts no-gunsmithing, see-through/iron sight usable. All mounts accommodate standard split rings of all makes. From Aimtech, L&S Technologies, Inc. *3-blade sight and mount combination.

Maker, Model, Type	Adjust.	Scopes	Price
B-SQUARE			
Pistols (centerfire)			
Beretta 92, 96/Taurus 99	No	Weaver rail	**66.95**
Colt M1911	E only	Weaver rail	**66.95**
Desert Eagle	No	Weaver rail	**66.95**
Glock	No	Weaver rail	**66.95**
H&K USP, 9mm and 40 S&W	No	Weaver rail	**66.95**
Ruger P85/89	E only	Weaver rail	**66.95**
SIG Sauer P226	E only	Weaver rail	**66.95**
Pistols (rimfire)			
Browning Buck Mark	No	Weaver rail	**29.95**
Colt 22	No	Weaver rail	**33.95**
Ruger Mk I/II, bull or taper	No	Weaver rail	**29.95-49.95**
Smith & Wesson 41, 2206	No	Weaver rail	**36.95-49.95**
Revolvers			
Colt Anaconda/Python	No	Weaver rail	**29.95-74.95**
B-SQUARE (cont.)			
Ruger Single-Six	No	Weaver rail	**64.95**
Ruger GP-100	No	Weaver rail	**64.95**
Ruger Blackhawk, Super	No	Weaver rail	**64.95**
Ruger Redhawk, Super	No	Weaver rail	**64.95**
Smith & Wesson K, L, N	No	Weaver rail	**36.95-74.95**
Taurus 66, 669, 607, 608	No	Weaver rail	**64.95**

Maker, Model, Type	Adjust.	Scopes	Price
BURRIS			
L.E.R. (LU) Mount Bases[1]	W only	1" split rings	**24.00-52.00**
L.E.R. No Drill-No Tap Bases[1,2,3]	W only	1" split rings	**48.00-52.00**

[1]Universal dovetail; accepts Burris, Universal, Redfield, Leupold rings. For Dan Wesson, S&W, Virginian, Ruger Blackhawk, Win. 94. [2]Selected rings and bases available with matte Safari or silver finish. [3]For S&W K, L, N frames, Colt Python, Dan Wesson with 6" or longer barrels.

Maker, Model, Type	Adjust.	Scopes	Price
CONETROL			
Pistol Bases, 2-or 3-ring[1]	W only	—	**NA**

[1]For XP-100, T/C Contender, Colt SAA, Ruger Blackhawk, S&W and others. Three-ring mount for T/C Contender and other pistols in Conetrol's three grades. Any Conetrol mount available in stainless or Teflon for double regular cost of grade.

Maker, Model, Type	Adjust.	Scopes	Price
KRIS MOUNTS			
One Piece (T)[1]	No	1", 26mm split rings	**12.98**

[1]Blackhawk revolver. Mounts have oval hole to permit use of iron sights.

Maker, Model, Type	Adjust.	Scopes	Price
LASER AIM	No	Laser Aim	**19.99-69.00**

Mounts Laser Aim above or below barrel. Avail. for most popular handguns, rifles, shotguns, including militaries. From Laser Aim Technologies, Inc.

Maker, Model, Type	Adjust.	Scopes	Price
LEUPOLD			
STD Bases[1]	W only	One- or two-piece bases	**24.20**
STD Rings[2]	—	1" super low, low, medium, high	**32.40**

[1]Base and two rings; Casull, Ruger, S&W, T/C; add $5.00 for silver finish. [2]Rem. 700, Win. 70-type actions.

Maker, Model, Type	Adjust.	Scopes	Price
MILLETT			
One-Piece Bases[2]	Yes	1"	**23.95**
Handgun Bases, Rings[1]	—	1"	**34.60-69.15**
30mm Rings[3]	—	30mm	**37.75-42.95**

[1]Two- and three-ring sets for Colt Python, Trooper, Diamondback, Peacekeeper, Dan Wesson, Ruger Redhawk, Super Redhawk. [2]Turn-in bases and Weaver-style for most popular rifles and T/C Contender, XP-100 pistols. [3]Both Weaver and turn-in styles; three heights. From Millett Sights.

Maker, Model, Type	Adjust.	Scopes	Price
SSK INDUSTRIES			
T'SOB	No	1"	**65.00-145.00**
Quick Detachable	No	1"	**From 160.00**

Custom installation using from two to four rings (included). For T/C Contender, most 22 auto pistols, Ruger and other S.A. revolvers, Ruger, Dan Wesson, S&W, Colt DA revolvers. Black or white finish. Uses Kimber rings in two- or three-ring sets. In blue or SSK chrome. For T/C Contender or most popular revolvers. Standard, non-detachable model also available, from **$65.00.**

Maker, Model, Type	Adjust.	Scopes	Price
TASCO			
World Class			
Aluminum Ringsets	Yes	1", 30mm	**12.00-17.00**

From Tasco.

Scope Mounts

Maker, Model, Type	Adjust.	Scopes	Price
THOMPSON/CENTER			
Duo-Ring Mount[1]	No	1"	**61.99-62.99**
Weaver-Style Bases	No	—	**10.28-33.36**
Weaver-Style Rings[3]	No	1"	**27.74-42.13**

[1]Attaches directly to T/C Contender bbl., no drilling/tapping; also for T/C M/L rifles, needs base adapter; blue or stainless. [3]Medium and high; blue or silver finish. From Thompson/Center.

Maker, Model, Type	Adjust.	Scopes	Price
WARNE			
Premier Series (all steel)			
T.P.A. (Permanently Attached)	No	1", 4 heights 30mm, 2 heights	**87.75** **98.55**
Premier Series Rings fit Premier Series Bases			
Premier Series (all-steel Q.D. rings)			
Premier Series (all steel) Quick detachable lever	No	1", 4 heights 26mm, 2 heights 30mm, 3 heights	**125.00** **129.95** **136.70**
All-Steel One-Piece Base, ea.			**38.50**
All-Steel Two-Piece Base, ea.			**14.00**
Maxima Series (fits all Weaver-style bases)			
Permanently Attached[1]	No	1", 3 heights 30mm, 3 heights	**34.55** **50.00**

Vertically split rings with dovetail clamp, precise return to zero. Fit most popular rifles, handguns. Regular blue, matte blue, silver finish. [1]All-Steel, non-Q.D. rings. [2]All-steel, Q.D. rings. From Warne Mfg. Co.

Maker, Model, Type	Adjust.	Scopes	Price
WEAVER			
Complete Mount Systems			
Pistol	No	1"	**75.00-105.00**

Detachable rings in standard, See-Thru, and extension styles, in Low, Medium, High or X-High heights; gloss (blued), silver and matte finishes to match scopes. Extension rings are only available in 1" High style and See-Thru X-tensions only in gloss finish. No Drill & Tap Pistol systems in gloss or silver for: Colt Python, Trooper, 357, Officer's Model; Ruger Single-Six, Security-Six (gloss finish only), Blackhawk, Super Blackhawk, Blackhawk SRM 357, Redhawk, Ruger 22 Auto Pistols, Mark II; Smith & Wesson I- and current K-frames with adj. rear sights. From Weaver.

Maker, Model, Type	Adjust.	Scopes	Price
WEIGAND			
Browning Buck Mark[1]	No	—	**29.95**
Colt 22 Automatic[1]	No	—	**19.95**
Integra Mounts[2]	No	—	**39.95-69.00**
S&W Revolver[3]	No	—	**29.95**
Ruger 10/22[4]	No	—	**14.95-39.95**
Ruger Revolver[5]	No	—	**29.95**
Taurus Revolver[4]	No	—	**29.95-65.00**
T/C Encore Monster Mount	No	—	**69.00**
T/C Contender Monster Mount	No	—	**69.00**
Lightweight Rings	No	1", 30mm	**29.95-39.95**
1911, P-9 Scopemounts			
SM3[6]	No	Weaver rail	**99.95**
SRS 1911-2[7]	No	30mm	**59.95**
APCMNT[8]	No	—	**69.95**

[1]No gunsmithing. [2] S&W K, L, N frames; Taurus vent rib models; Colt Anaconda/Python; Ruger Redhawk; Ruger 10/22. [3]K, L, N frames. [4]Three models. [5] Redhawk, Blackhawk, GP-100. [6]3rd Gen.; drill and tap; without slots **$59.95**. [7]Ringless design, silver only. [8]For Aimpoint Comp. Red Dot scope, silver only. From Weigand Combat Handguns, Inc.

Maker, Model, Type	Adjust.	Scopes	Price
WIDEVIEW			
Desert Eagle Pistol Mount	No	1", 30mm	**34.95-44.95**

[1]For Weaver-type base. From Wideview Scope Mount Corp.

SPOTTING SCOPES

BAUSCH & LOMB DISCOVERER 15x to 60x zoom, 60mm objective. Constant focus throughout range. Field at 1000 yds. 38 ft (60x), 150 ft. (15x). Comes with lens caps. Length 17 1/2″; weight 48.5 oz.

Price: **$391.95**

BAUSCH & LOMB ELITE 15x to 45x zoom, 60mm objective. Field at 1000 yds., 125-65 ft. Length is 12.2″; weight, 26.5 oz. Waterproof, armored. Tripod mount. Comes with black case.

Price: **$766.95**

BAUSCH & LOMB ELITE ZOOM 20x-60x, 70mm objective. Roof prism. Field at 1000 yds. 90-50 ft. Length is 16"; weight 40 oz. Waterproof, armored. Tripod mount. Comes with black case.

Price: **$921.95**

BAUSCH & LOMB 80MM ELITE 20x-60x zoom, 80mm objective. Field of view at 1000 yds. 108-62 ft. (zoom). Weight 51 oz. (20x, 30x), 54 oz. (zoom); length 16.8″. Interchangeable bayonet-style eyepieces. Built-in peep sight.

Price: With EDPrime Glass. **$1,212.95**

BSA CE12-36x50

BSA SPS 20x40 RD

BSA Spotting Scopes Offset 45-degree or straight body; offered in 40mm, 50mm and 60mm objective lenses and 20x, 12-36x, 20-40x, 15-45x and 20-60x. Field of view at 100 yards: 16.9 feet (12-36x). Length 11"; weight 24 oz. (12-36x).

Price: 20x40m with red dot viewfinder **$59.95**

Price: 20-40x40mm with red dot viewfinder **$69.95**

Price: 15-45x50mm Zoom **$79.95**

Price: 20-60x60mm Zoom **$89.95**

Price: 12-36x50mm Zoom **$119.95**

Price: 10-30 x50mm Zoom **$139.95**

Price: 20-60x60mm Zoom **$169.95**

BURRIS 18-45x SIGNATURE SPOTTER 60mm objective, 18x-45x, constant focus, Field at 1000 yds. 112-63 ft.; weighs 29oz.; length 12.6". Camera adapters available.

Price: **$819.00**

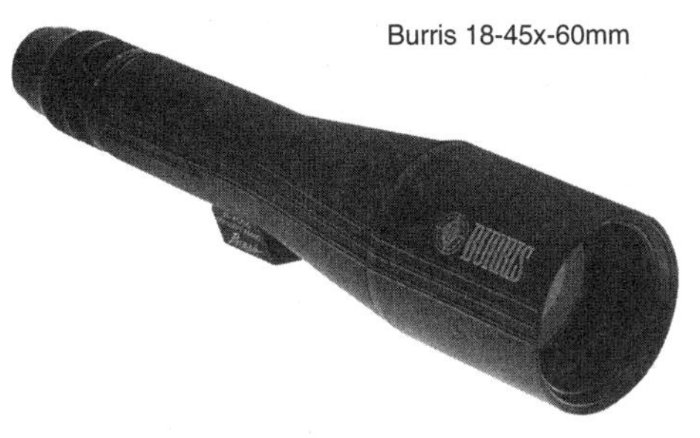

Burris 18-45x-60mm

Burris 15-45x-60mm

BURRIS LANDMARK SPOTTER 15-45x, 60mm objective. Straight type. Field at 100 yds. 146-72 ft. Length 12.7″; weight 24 oz. Rubber armor coating, multi-coated lenses, 22mm eye relief. Recessed focus adjustment. Nitrogen filled.

Price: 30x 60mm **$644.00**

BUSHNELL TROPHY 63mm objective, 20x-60x zoom. Field at 1000 yds. 90ft. (20x), 45 ft. (60x). Length 12.7"; weight 20 oz. Black rubber armored, waterproof. Case included.

Price: **$421.95**

BUSHNELL COMPACT TROPHY 50mm objective, 20x-50x zoom. Field at 1000 yds. 92 ft. (20x), 52 ft. (50x). Length 12.2″; weight 17 oz. Black rubber armored, waterproof. Case included.

Price: **$337.95**

Bushnell Banner Sentry

BUSHNELL BANNER SENTRY 18x-36x zoom, 50mm objective. Field at 1000 yds. 115-78 ft. Length 14.5″, weight 27 oz. Black rubber armored. Built-in peep sight. Comes with tripod and hardcase.

Price: **$180.95**

Price: With 45 field eyepiece, includes tripod **$202.95**

SPOTTING SCOPES

BUSHNELL SPACEMASTER 20x-45x zoom. Long eye relief. Rubber armored, prismatic. 60mm objective. Field at 1000 yds. 98-58 ft. Minimum focus 20 ft. Length 12.7″; weight 43 oz.
Price: With tripod, carrying case and 20x-45x LER eyepiece. **$560.95**

BUSHNELL SPORTVIEW 12x-36x 200m, 50mm objective. Field at 100 yds. 160 ft. (12x), 90 ft. (36x). Length 14.6″; weight 25 oz.
Price: With tripod and carrying case. **$159.95**

HERMES 1 70mm objective, 16x, 25x, 40x. Field at 1000 meters 160 ft. (16x), 75ft. (40x). Length 12.2"; weight 33 oz. From CZ-USA.
Price: Body **$359.00**
Price: 25x eyepiece **$86.00**
Price: 40x eyepiece **$128.00**

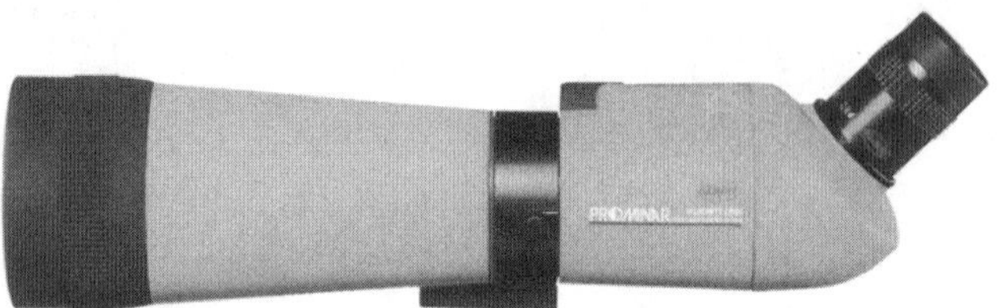

Kowa TSN-823

KOWA TSN SERIES Offset 45 or straight body. 77mm objective, 20x WA, 25x, 25x LER, 30x WA, 40x, 60x, 77x and 20-60x zoom. Field at 1000 yds. 179 ft. (20xWA), 52 ft. (60x). Available with flourite lens.
Price: TSN-1 (without eyepiece) 45 offset scope. **$696.00**
Price: TSN-2 (without eyepiece) Straight scope. **$660.00**
Price: 20x W.A. (wide angle) eyepiece. **$230.00**
Price: 25x eyepiece **$143.00**
Price: 25x LER (long eye relief) eyepiece **$214.00**
Price: 30x W.A. (wide angle) eyepiece. **$266.00**
Price: 40x eyepiece **$159.00**
Price: 60x W.A. (wide angle) eyepiece. **$230.00**
Price: 77x eyepiece **$235.00**
Price: 20-60x zoom eyepiece **$302.00**

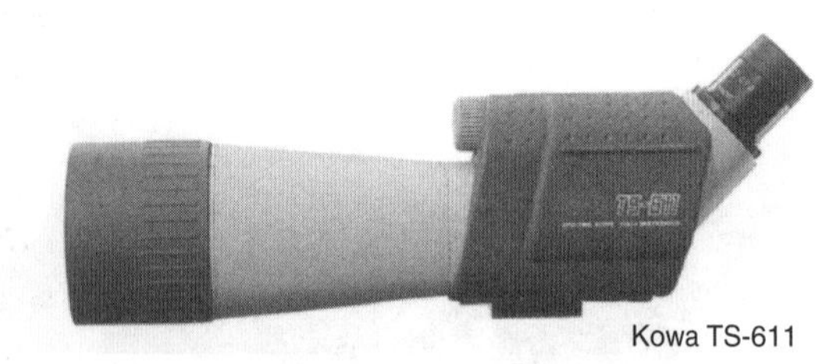

Kowa TS-611

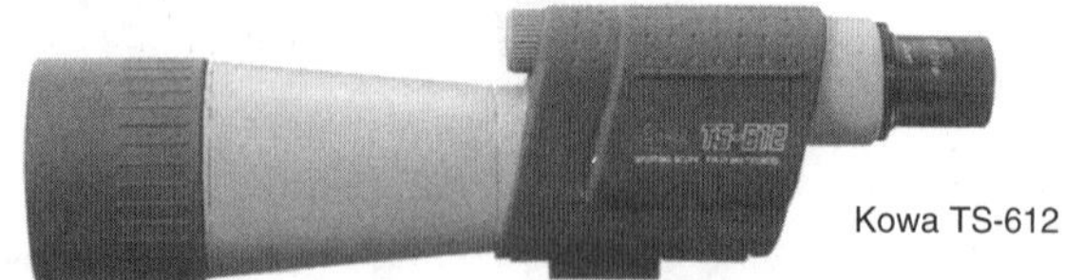

Kowa TS-612

KOWA TS-610 SERIES Offset 45 or straight body. 60mm objective, 20x WA, 25x, 25x LER, 27x WA, 40x and 20x-60x zoom. Field at 1000 yds. 162 ft. (20x WA), 51 ft. (60x). Available with ED lens.
Price: TS-611 (without eyepiece) 45 offset scope. **$510.00**
Price: TS-612 (without eyepiece) Straight scope **$462.00**
Price: 20x W.A. (wide angle) eyepiece. **$111.00**
Price: 25x eyepiece **$95.00**
Price: 25x LER (long eye relief) eyepiece **$214.00**
Price: 27x W.A. (wide angle) eyepiece. **$166.00**
Price: 40x eyepiece **$98.00**
Price: 20-60x zoom eyepiece **$207.00**

KOWA TS-9 SERIES Offset 45 ,straight or rubber armored (straight only). 50mm objective, 15x, 20x and 11-33x zoom. Field at 1000 yds. 188 ft. (15x), 99 ft. (33x).
Price: TS-9B (without eyepiece) 45 offset scope. **$223.00**
Price: TS-9C (without eyepiece) straight scope **$176.00**
Price: TS-9R (without eyepiece) straight rubber armored scope/black **$197.00**
Price: 15x eyepiece **$38.00**
Price: 20x eyepiece **$36.00**
Price: 11-33x zoom eyepiece **$122.00**

Leupold 12-40x60mm

LEUPOLD 12-40x60 VARIABLE 60mm objective, 12-40x. Field at 100 yds. 17.5-5.3 ft.; eye relief 1.2″ (20x). Overall length 11.5″, weight 32 oz. Rubber armored.
Price: **$1,217.90**

LEUPOLD 25x50 COMPACT 50mm objective, 25x. Field at 100 yds. 8.3 ft.; eye relief 1″; length overall 9.4″; weight 20.5 oz.
Price: Armored model. **$848.20**
Price: Packer Tripod. **$96.40**

MIRADOR TTB SERIES Draw tube armored spotting scopes. Available with 75mm or 80mm objective. Zoom model (28x-62x, 80mm) is 11 7/8″ (closed), weighs 50 oz. Field at 1000 yds. 70-42 ft. Comes with lens covers.
Price: 28-62x80mm **$1,133.95**
Price: 32x80mm **$971.95**
Price: 26-58x75mm **$989.95**
Price: 30x75mm **$827.95**

MIRADOR SSD SPOTTING SCOPES 60mm objective, 15x, 20x, 22x, 25x, 40x, 60x, 20-60x; field at 1000 yds. 37 ft.; length 10 1/4″; weight 33 oz.
Price: 25x **$575.95**
Price: 22x Wide Angle **$593.95**
Price: 20-60x Zoom **$746.95**
Price: As above, with tripod, case **$944.95**

MIRADOR SIA SPOTTING SCOPES Similar to the SSD scopes except with 45° eyepiece. Length 12 1/4″; weight 39 oz.
Price: 25x **$809.95**
Price: 22x Wide Angle **$827.95**
Price: 20-60x Zoom **$980.95**

MIRADOR SSR SPOTTING SCOPES 50mm or 60mm objective. Similar to SSD except rubber armored in black or camouflage. Length 11 1/8″; weight 31 oz.
Price: Black, 20x. **$521.95**
Price: Black, 18x Wide Angle **$539.95**
Price: Black, 16-48x Zoom **$692.95**
Price: Black, 20x, 60mm, EER **$692.95**
Price: Black, 22x Wide Angle, 60mm **$701.95**
Price: Black, 20-60x Zoom **$854.95**

Spotting Scopes

MIRADOR SSF FIELD SCOPES Fixed or variable power, choice of 50mm, 60mm, 75mm objective lens. Length 9 3/4″; weight 20 oz. (15-32x50).

Price: 20x50mm **$359.95**
Price: 25x60mm **$440.95**
Price: 30x75mm **$584.95**
Price: 15-32x50mm Zoom **$548.95**
Price: 18-40x60mm Zoom **$629.95**
Price: 22-47x75mm Zoom **$773.95**

MIRADOR SRA MULTI ANGLE SCOPES Similar to SSF Series except eyepiece head rotates for viewing from any angle.

Price: 20x50mm **$503.95**
Price: 25x60mm **$647.95**
Price: 30x75mm **$764.95**
Price: 15-32x50mm Zoom **$692.95**
Price: 18-40x60mm Zoom **$836.95**
Price: 22-47x75mm Zoom **$953.95**

MIRADOR SIB FIELD SCOPES Short-tube, 45° scopes with porro prism design. 50mm and 60mm objective. Length 10 1/4″; weight 18.5 oz. (15-32x50mm); field at 1000 yds. 129-81 ft.

Price: 20x50mm **$386.95**
Price: 25x60mm **$449.95**
Price: 15-32x50mm Zoom **$575.95**
Price: 18-40x60mm Zoom **$638.95**

Nikon Fieldscope 78mm

NIKON FIELDSCOPES 60mm and 78mm lens. Field at 1000 yds. 105 ft. (60mm, 20x), 126 ft. (78mm, 25x). Length 12.8″ (straight 60mm), 12.6″ (straight 78mm); weight 34.5-47.5 oz. Eyepieces available separately.

Price: 60mm straight body **$690.95**
Price: 60mm angled body **$796.95**
Price: 60mm straight ED body **$1,200.95**
Price: 60mm angled ED body **$1,314.95**
Price: 78mm straight ED body **$2,038.95**
Price: 78mm angled ED body **$2,170.95**
Price: Eyepieces (15x to 60x) . . . . . . **$146.95** to **$324.95**
Price: 20-45x eyepiece (25-56x for 78mm) **$318.95**

NIKON SPOTTING SCOPE 60mm objective, 20x fixed power or 15-45x zoom. Field at 1000 yds. 145 ft. (20x). Gray rubber armored. Straight or angled eyepiece. Weighs 44.2 oz., length 12.1″ (20x).

Price: 20x60 fixed (with eyepiece) **$368.95**
Price: 15-45x zoom (with case, tripod, eyepiece) **$578.95**

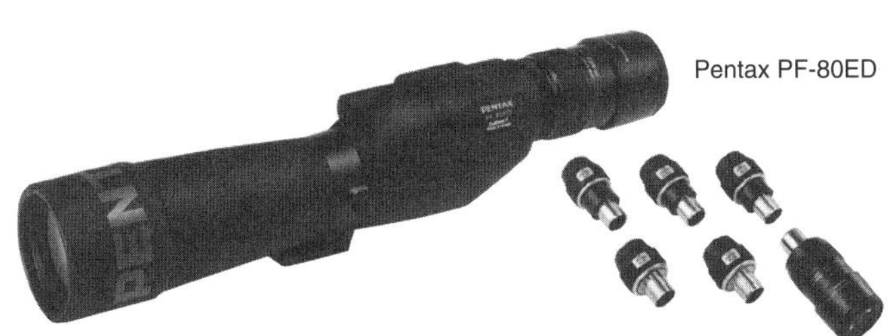

Pentax PF-80ED

PENTAX PF-80ED spotting scope 80mm objective lens available in 18x, 24x, 36x, 48x, 72x and 20-60x. Length 15.6", weight 11.9 to 19.2 oz.

Price: **$1,320.00**

SIGHTRON SII 2050X63 63mm objective lens, 20x-50x zoom. Field at 1000 yds 91.9 ft. (20x), 52.5 ft. (50x). Length 14"; weight 30.8 oz. Black rubber finish. Also available with 80mm objective lens.

Price: 63mm or 80mm **$339.95**

SIMMONS 1280 50mm objective, 15-45x zoom. Black matte finish. Ocular focus. Peep finder sight. Waterproof. FOV 95-51 ft. @ 1000 yards. Wgt. 33.5 oz., length 12″.

Price: With tripod **$267.99**

SIMMONS 1281 60mm objective, 20-60x zoom. Black matte finish. Ocular focus. Peep finder sight. Waterproof. FOV 78-43 ft. @ 1000 yards. Wgt. 34.5 oz. Length 12″.

Price: With tripod **$295.99**

SIMMONS 77206 PROHUNTER 50mm objectives, 25x fixed power. Field at 1000 yds. 113 ft.; length 10.25"; weighs 33.25 oz. Black rubber armored.

Price: With tripod case **$160.60**

SIMMONS 41200 REDLINE 50mm objective, 15x-45x zoom. Field at 1000 yds. 104-41 ft.; length 16.75"; weighs 32.75 oz.

Price: With hard case and tripod **$99.99**
Price: 20-60x, Model 41201 . . . . . . **$129.99**

STEINER FIELD TELESCOPE 24x, 80mm objective. Field at 1000 yds. 105 ft. Weight 44 oz. Tripod mounts. Rubber armored.

Price: **$1,299.00**

SWAROVSKI CT EXTENDIBLE SCOPES 75mm or 85mm objective, 20-60x zoom, or fixed 15x, 22x, 30x, 32x eyepieces. Field at 1000 yds. 135 ft. (15x), 99 ft. (32x); 99 ft. (20x), 5.2 ft. (60x) for zoom. Length 12.4″ (closed), 17.2″ (open) for the CT75; 9.7″/17.2″ for CT85. Weight 40.6 oz. (CT75), 49.4 oz. (CT85). Green rubber armored.

Price: CT75 body **$765.56**
Price: CT85 body **$1,094.44**
Price: 20-60x eyepiece **$343.33**
Price: 15x, 22x eyepiece **$232.22**
Price: 30x eyepiece **$265.55**

SWAROVSKI AT-80/ST-80 SPOTTING SCOPES 80mm objective, 20-60x zoom, or fixed 15x, 22x, 30x, 32x eyepieces. Field at 1000 yds. 135 ft. (15x), 99 ft. (32x); 99 ft. (20x), 52.5 ft. (60x) for zoom. Length 16″ (AT-80), 15.6″ (ST-80); weight 51.8 oz. Available with HD (high density) glass.

Price: AT-80 (angled) body **$1,094.44**
Price: ST-80 (straight) body **$1,094.44**
Price: With HD glass **$1,555.00**
Price: 20-60x eyepiece **$343.33**
Price: 15x, 22x eyepiece **$232.22**
Price: 30x eyepiece **$265.55**

SWIFT LYNX M836 15x-45x zoom, 60mm objective. Weight 7 lbs., length 14″. Has 45° eyepiece, sunshade.

Price: **$315.00**

SWIFT NIGHTHAWK M849U 80mm objective, 20x-60x zoom, or fixed 19, 25x, 31x, 50x, 75x eyepieces. Has rubber armored body, 1.8x optical finder, retractable lens hood, 45° eyepiece. Field at 1000 yds. 60 ft. (28x), 41 ft. (75x). Length 13.4 oz.; weight 39 oz.

Price: Body only **$870.00**
Price: 20-68x eyepiece **$370.00**
Price: Fixed eyepieces . . . . . . **$130.00** to **$240.00**
Price: Model 849 (straight) body **$795.00**

SWIFT NIGHTHAWK M850U 65mm objective, 16x-48x zoom, or fixed 19x, 20x, 25x, 40x, 60x eyepieces. Rubber armored with a 1.8x optical finder, retractable lens hood. Field at 1000 yds. 83 ft. (22x), 52 ft. (60x). Length 12.3"; weight 30 oz. Has 45° eyepiece.

Price: Body only **$650.00**
Price: 16x-48x eyepiece **$370.00**
Price: Fixed eyepieces . . . . . . **$130.00** to **$240.00**
Price: Model 850 (straight) body **$575.00**

SWIFT LEOPARD M837 50mm objective, 25x. Length 9 11/16″ to 10 1/2″. Weight with tripod 28 oz. Rubber armored. Comes with tripod.

Price: **$160.00**

SPOTTING SCOPES

SWIFT TELEMASTER M841 60mm objective. 15x to 60x variable power. Field at 1000 yds. 160 feet (15x) to 40 feet (60x). Weight 3.25 lbs.; length 18″ overall.
Price: **$399.50**

SWIFT PANTHER M844 15x-45x zoom or 22x WA, 15x, 20x, 40x. 60mm objective. Field at 1000 yds. 141 ft. (15x), 68 ft. (40x), 95-58 ft. (20x-45x).
Price: Body only **$380.00**
Price: 15x-45x zoom eyepiece **$120.00**
Price: 20x-45x zoom (long eye relief) eyepiece **$140.00**
Price: 15x, 20x, 40x eyepiece.................... **$65.00**
Price: 22x WA eyepiece **$80.00**

Swift M700T Scout

SWIFT M700T 12x-36x, 50mm objective. Field of view at 100 yds. 16 ft. (12x), 9 ft. (36x). Length 14″; weight with tripod 3.22 lbs.
Price: **$225.00**

SWIFT SEARCHER M839 60mm objective, 20x, 40x. Field at 1000 yds. 118 ft. (30x), 59 ft. (40x). Length 12.6″; weight 3 lbs. Rotating eyepiece head for straight or 45° viewing.
Price: **$580.00**
Price: 30x, 50x eyepieces, each.................... **$67.00**

TASCO 29TZBWP WATERPROOF SPOTTER 60mm objective lens, 20x-60x zoom. Field at 100 yds. 7 ft., 4 in. to 3 ft., 8 in. Black rubber armored. Comes with tripod, hard case.
Price: **$356.50**

TASCO WC28TZ WORLD CLASS SPOTTING SCOPE 50mm objective, 12-36x zoom. Field at 100 yds. World Class. 13-3.8 ft. Comes with tripod and case.
Price: **$220.00**

TASCO CW5001 COMPACT ZOOM 50mm objective, 12x-36x zoom. Field at 100 yds. 16 ft., 9 in. Includes photo adapter tube, tripod with panhead lever, case.
Price: **$280.00**

TASCO 3700WP WATERPROOF SPOTTER 50mm objective, 18x-36x zoom. Field at 100 yds. 12ft., 6 in. to 7 ft., 9 in. Black rubber armored. Comes with tripod, hard case.
Price: **$288.60**

TASCO 3700, 3701 SPOTTING SCOPE 50mm objective. 18x-36x zoom. Field at 100 yds. 12 ft., 6 in. to 7 ft., 9 in. Black rubber armored.
Price: Model 3700 (black, with tripod, case).................... **$237.00**
Price: Model 3701 (as above, brown camo).................... **$237.00**

TASCO 21EB ZOOM 50mm objective lens, 15x-45x zoom. Field at 100 yds. 11 ft. (15x). Weight 22 oz.; length 18.3″ overall. Comes with panhead lever tripod.
Price: **$119.00**

TASCO 22EB ZOOM 60mm objective lens, 20x-60x zoom. Field at 100 yds. 7 ft., 2 in. (20x). Weight 28 oz.; length 21.5″ overall. Comes with micro-adjustable tripod.
Price: **$183.00**

UNERTL "FORTY-FIVE" 54mm objective. 20x (single fixed power). Field at 100 yds. 10',10″; eye relief 1″; focusing range infinity to 33 ft. Weight about 32 oz.; overall length 153/4″. With lens covers.
Price: With multi-layer lens coating **$662.00**
Price: With mono-layer magnesium coating.................... **$572.00**

UNERTL STRAIGHT PRISMATIC 63.5mm objective, 24x. Field at 100 yds., 7 ft. Relative brightness, 6.96. Eye relief 1/2″. Weight 40 oz.; length closed 19″. Push-pull and screw-focus eyepiece. 16x and 32x eyepieces **$125.00** each.
Price: **$515.00**

UNERTL 20x STRAIGHT PRISMATIC 54mm objective, 20x. Field at 100 yds. 8.5 ft. Relative brightness 6.1. Eye relief 1/2″. Weight 36 oz.; length closed 13 1/2″. Complete with lens covers.
Price: **$477.00**

UNERTL TEAM SCOPE 100mm objective. 15x, 24x, 32x eyepieces. Field at 100 yds. 13 to 7.5 ft. Relative brightness, 39.06 to 9.79. Eye relief 2″ to 11/2″. Weight 13 lbs.; length 29 7/8″ overall. Metal tripod, yoke and wood carrying case furnished (total weight 80 lbs.).
Price: **$2,810.00**

WEAVER 20x50 50mm objective. Field of view 124 ft. at 100 yds. Eye relief .85″; weighs 21 oz.; overall length 10″. Waterproof, armored.
Price: **$368.99**

WEAVER 15-40x60 ZOOM 60mm objective. 15x-40x zoom. Field at 100 yds. 119 ft. (15x), 66 ft. (60x). Overall length 12.5″, weighs 26 oz. Waterproof, armored.
Price: **$551.99**

Compendium of State Laws Governing Firearms

The following chart lists the main provisions of state firearms laws as of the date of publication. In addition to the state provisions, the purchase, sale, and, in certain circumstances, the possession and interstate transportation of firearms are regulated by the Federal Gun Control Act of 1968 as amended by the Firearms Owners' Protection Act of 1986. Also, cities and localities may have their own gun ordinances in addition to federal and state restrictions. Details may be obtained by contacting local law enforcement authorities or by consulting your state's firearms law digest compiled by the NRA Institute for Legislative Action.

STATE	GUN BAN	EXEMPTIONS TO NICS[2]	STATE WAITING PERIOD - NUMBER OF DAYS		LICENSE OR PERMIT TO PURCHASE		REGISTRATION		RECORD OF SALE REPORTED TO STATE OR LOCAL GOVT.
			HANDGUNS	LONG GUNS	HANDGUNS	LONG GUNS	HANDGUNS	LONG GUNS	
Alabama	—	—	—	—	—	—	—	—	X
Alaska	—	RTC	—	—	—	—	—	—	—
Arizona	—	RTC	—	—	—	—	—	—	—
Arkansas	—	RTC	—	—	—	—	—	—	—
California	X[20]	—	10	10	—	—	X	—	X
Colorado	—	—	—	—	—	—	—	—	—
Connecticut	X[20]	GRTC	14[14, 15]	14[14, 15]	X[16]	—	—	—	X
Delaware	—	GRTC	—	—	—	—	—	—	—
Florida	—	GRTC	3[14, 15]	—	—	—	—	—	—
Georgia	—	RTC	—	—	—	—	—	—	—
Hawaii	X[20]	L, RTC	—	—	X[16]	X[16]	X[12]	X[12]	X
Idaho	—	RTC	—	—	—	—	—	—	—
Illinois	[20]	L	3	1	X[16]	X[16]	—[4]	—[4]	X
Indiana	—	RTC, O[3]	—	—	—	—	—	—	X
Iowa	—	L, RTC	—	—	X[16]	—	—	—	X
Kansas	—	—	[1]	—	[1]	—	—[1]	—	[1]
Kentucky	—	RTC	—	—	—	—	—	—	—
Louisiana	—	GRTC	—	—	—	—	—	—	—
Maine	—	—	—	—	—	—	—	—	—
Maryland	X[20]	GRTC	7	7[9]	[8]	—	—	—	X
Massachusetts	X[20]	L, RTC	7	—	X[16]	X[16]	—	—	X
Michigan	—	L	—	—	X[16]	—	X	—	X
Minnesota	—	L, GRTC	7[16]	[16]	X[16]	X[16]	—	—	X
Mississippi	—	RTC[3]	—	—	—	—	—	—	—
Missouri	—	—	7	—	X[16]	—	—	—	X
Montana	—	RTC	—	—	—	—	—	—	—
Nebraska	—	L	—	—	X	—	—	—	—
Nevada	—	RTC	[1]	—	—	—	[1]	—	—
New Hampshire	—	—	—	—	—	—	—	—	X
New Jersey	X[20]	—	—	—	X[16]	X[16]	—	—	X
New Mexico	—	—	—	—	—	—	—	—	—
New York	X[20]	L, RTC	—	—	X[16]	[16]	X	[7]	X
North Carolina	—	L, RTC	—	—	X[16]	—	—	—	X
North Dakota	—	RTC	—	—	—	—	—	—	X
Ohio	X[20]	—	[1]	—	[16]	—	[1]	—	[1]
Oklahoma	—	RTC	—	—	—	—	—	—	—
Oregon	—	—	—	—	—	—	—	—	X
Pennsylvania	—	—	—	—	—	—	—	—	X
Rhode Island	—	—	7	7	—	—	—	—	X
South Carolina	—	RTC	[8]	—	[8]	—	—	—	X
South Dakota	—	GRTC	2	—	—	—	—	—	X
Tennessee	—	RTC	—	—	—	—	—	—	X
Texas	—	RTC[3]	—	—	—	—	—	—	—
Utah	—	RTC	—	—	—	—	—	—	—
Vermont	—	—	—	—	—	—	—	—	—
Virginia	X[20]	—	[1, 8]	—	[1,8]	—	—	—	[1]
Washington	—	RTC	5[10]	—	—	—	—	—	X
West Virginia	—	—	—	—	—	—	—	—	—
Wisconsin	—	—	2	—	—	—	—	—	X
Wyoming	—	RTC	—	—	—	—	—	—	—
District of Columbia	X[20]	L	—	—	X[16]	X[16]	X[16]	X	X

COMPENDIUM OF STATE LAWS GOVERNING FIREARMS

Since state laws are subject to frequent change, this chart is not to be considered legal advice or a restatement of the law. All fifty states have sportsmen's protections laws to halt harrassment.

Compiled by
NRA INSTITUTE FOR LEGISLATIVE ACTION
11250 WAPLES MILL ROAD
FAIRFAX, VIRGINIA 22030
www.nraila.org

STATE	STATE PROVISION FOR RIGHT-TO-CARRY CONCEALED[15]	CARRYING OPENLY PROHIBITED	OWNER ID CARDS OR LICENSING	FIREARM RIGHTS CONSTITUTIONAL PROVISION	STATE FIREARMS PREEMPTION LAWS	RANGE PROTECTION LAW
Alabama	R	X[11]	—	X	X	—
Alaska	R	—	—	X	—	X
Arizona	R	—	—	X	X	—
Arkansas	R	X[5]	—	X	X	X
California	L	X[6]	—	—	X	X
Colorado	L	1	—	X	—	X
Connecticut	R	X	—	X	X[17]	X
Delaware	L	—	—	X	X	X
Florida	R	X	—	X	X	X
Georgia	R	X	—	X	X	X
Hawaii	L	X	X	X	—	—
Idaho	R	—	—	X	X	X
Illinois	D	X	X	X	—	X
Indiana	R	X	—	X	X[18]	X
Iowa	L	X	—	—	X	X
Kansas	D	1	—	X	—	—
Kentucky	R	—	—	X	X	X
Louisiana	R	—	—	X	X	X
Maine	R	—	—	X	X	X
Maryland	L	X	—	—	X	X
Massachusetts	L	X	X	X	X[17]	X
Michigan	L	X[11]	—	X	X	X
Minnesota	L	X	—	—	X	—
Mississippi	R	—	—	X	X	—
Missouri	D	—	—	X	X	X
Montana	R	—	—	X	X	X
Nebraska	D	—	—	X	—	—
Nevada	R	—	—	X	X	X
New Hampshire	R	—	—	X	—	X
New Jersey	L	X	X	—	X[17]	X
New Mexico	D	—	—	X	X	—
New York	L	X	X	—	X[22]	X
North Carolina	R	—	—	X	X	X
North Dakota	R	X[6]	—	X	X	X
Ohio	D	1	16	X	—	X
Oklahoma	R	X[6]	—	X	X	X
Oregon	R	—	—	X	X	X
Pennsylvania	R	X[11]	—	X	X	X
Rhode Island	L	X	—	X	X	X
South Carolina	R	X	—	X	X	—
South Dakota	R	—	—	X	X	X
Tennessee	R	X[5]	—	X	X	X
Texas	R	X	—	X	X	—
Utah	R	X[6]	—	X	X	X
Vermont	R[19]	X[5]	—	X	X	X
Virginia	R	—	—	X	X	X
Washington	R	X[21]	—	X	X	—
West Virginia	R	—	—	X	X	X
Wisconsin	D	—	—	X	X	X
Wyoming	R	—	—	X	X	X
District of Columbia	L	X	X	NA	—	—

With over 20,000 "gun control" laws on the books in America, there are two challenges facing every gun owner. First, you owe it to yourself to become familiar with the federal laws on gun ownership. Only by knowing the laws can you avoid innocently breaking one.

Second, while federal legislation receives much more media attention, state legislatures and city councils make many more decisions regarding your right to own and carry firearms. NRA members and all gun owners must take extra care to be aware of anti-gun laws and ordinances at the state and local levels.

Notes:

1. In certain cities or counties.
2. **National Instant Check System (NICS) exemption codes:**
   RTC-Carry Permit Holders Exempt From NICS
   GRTC-Holders of RTC Permits issued before November 30, 1998 exempt from NICS. Holders of more recent permits are not exempt.
   L-Holders of state licenses to possess or purchase or firearms ID cards exempt from NICS.
   O-Other, See Note 3.
3. **NICS exemptions notes: Indiana:** Personal protection and hunting and target permits; **Mississippi:** Permit issued to security guards does **not** qualify.; **Texas:** Texas Peace Officer license, TCLEOSE Card, is grandfathered only.
4. Chicago only. No handgun not already registered may be possessed.
5. **Arkansas** prohibits carrying a firearm "with a purpose to employ it as a weapon against a person." **Tennessee** prohibits carrying "with the intent to go armed." **Vermont** prohibits carrying a firearm "with the intent or purpose of injuring another."
6. Loaded.
7. New York City only.
8. A permit is required to acquire another handgun before 30 days have elapsed following the acquisition of a handgun.
9. **Maryland** subjects purchases of "assault weapons" to a 7-day waiting period.
10. May be extended by police to 30 days in some circumstances. An individual not holding a driver's license must wait 90 days.
11. Carrying a handgun openly in a motor vehicle requires a license.
12. Every person arriving in **Hawaii** is required to register any firearm(s) brought into the State within 3 days of arrival of the person or firearm(s), whichever occurs later. Handguns purchased from licensed dealers must be registered within 5 days.
13. Concealed carry laws vary significantly between the states. Ratings reflect the real effect a state's particular laws have on the ability of citizens to carry firearms for self-defense.
14. Purchases from licensed dealers only.
15. The state waiting period does not apply to a person holding a valid permit or license to carry a firearm. In **Connecticut,** a hunting license also exempts the holder, for long gun purchases. In **Indiana,** only persons with unlimited carry permits are exempt.
16. **Connecticut:** A permit to purchase or a carry permit is required to obtain a handgun and a carry permit is required to transport a handgun outside your home. **District of Columbia:** No handgun may be possessed unless it was registered prior to Sept. 23, 1976 and re-registered by Feb. 5, 1977. A permit to purchase is required for a rifle or shotgun. **Hawaii:** Purchase permits, required for all firearms, may not be issued until 14 days after application. A handgun purchase permit is valid for 10 days, for one handgun; a long gun permit is valid for one year, for multiple long guns. **Illinois:** A Firearm Owner's Identification Card (FOI) is required to possess or purchase a firearm, must be issued to qualified applicants within 30 days, and is valid for 5 years. **Iowa:** A purchase permit is required for handguns, and is valid for one year, beginning three days after issuance. **Massachusetts:** Firearms and feeding devices for firearms are divided into classes. Depending on the class, a firearm identification card (FID) or class A license or class B license is required to possess, purchase, or carry a firearm, ammunition therefore, or firearm feeding device, or "large capacity feeding device." **Michigan:** A handgun purchaser must obtain a license to purchase from local law enforcement, and within 10 days present the license and handgun to obtain a certificate of inspection. **Minnesota:** A handgun transfer or carrying permit, or a 7-day waiting period and handgun transfer report, is required to purchase handguns or "assault weapons" from a dealer. A permit or transfer report must be issued to qualified applicants within 7 days. A permit is valid for one year, a transfer report for 30 days. **Missouri:** A purchase permit is required for a handgun, must be issued to qualified applicants within 7 days, and is valid for 30 days. **New Jersey:** Firearm owners must possess an FID, which must be issued to qualified applicants within 30 days. To purchase a handgun, an FID and a purchase permit, which must be issued within 30 days to qualified applicants, is valid for 90 days, are required. An FID is required to purchase long guns. **New York:** Purchase, possession and/or carrying of a handgun require a single license, which includes any restrictions made upon the bearer. New York City also requires a license for long guns. **North Carolina:** To purchase a handgun, a license or permit is required, which must be issued to qualified applicants within 30 days. **Ohio**: Some cities require a permit-to-purchase or firearm owner ID card.
17. Preemption through judicial ruling. Local regulation may be instituted in **Massachusetts** if ratified by the legislature.
18. Except Gary and East Chicago and local laws enacted before January, 1994.
19. **Vermont** law respects your right to carry without a permit.
20. **California prohibits** "assault weapons" and commencing January 1, 2001, any "unsafe handgun." **Connecticut, New Jersey, New York City,** and other local jurisdictions in **New York,** and some local jurisdictions in **Ohio** prohibit "assault weapons." **Hawaii** prohibits "assault pistols." **Illinois:** Chicago, Evanston, Oak Park, Morton Grove, Winnetka, Wilmette, and Highland Park prohibit handguns; some cities prohibit other kinds of firearms. **Maryland** prohibits several small, low-caliber, inexpensive handguns and "assault pistols." **Massachusetts:** It is unlawful to sell, transfer or possess "any assault weapon or large capacity feeding device" [more than 10 rounds] that was not legally possessed on September 13, 1994. **Ohio:** some cities prohibit handguns of certain magazine capacities." **Virginia** prohibits "Street Sweeper" shotguns. The **District of Columbia** prohibits new acquisition of handguns and any semi-automatic firearm capable of using a detachable ammunition magazine of more than 12 rounds capacity. (With respect to some of these laws and ordinances, individuals may retain prohibited firearms owned previously, with certain restrictions.)
21. Local jurisdictions may opt out of prohibition.
22. Preemption only applies to handguns.

Concealed carry codes:

R: Right-to-Carry: "shall issue" or less restrictive discretionary permit system (Ala., Conn.) (See also note #21.)
L: Right-to-Carry Limited by local authority's discretion over permit issuance.
D: Right-to-Carry Denied, no permit system exists; concealed carry is prohibited.

REFERENCE

NL 00930

Rev.3/2001 5m

NRA - Right-To-Carry Reciprocity Guide

- **The right to self-defense neither begins nor ends at a state border.**
- **A law-abiding citizen does not suffer a character change by crossing a state line.**
- **An "unalienable right" is not determined by geographical bundaries.**
- **A patchwork of state laws regarding the carrying of firearms can make criminals out of honest folks, especially those who frequently must travel the states to earn a living.**
- **Using data for all 3,054 U.S. counties from 1977 to 1994, University of Chicago Prof. John Lott finds that for each additional year a concealed handgun law is in effect the murder rate declines by 3%, robberies by over 2%, and the rape rate by 2%.**

In spite of the truth of these statements and the fact that nearly half of all Americans live in states that allow a law-abiding citizen to carry a firearm concealed for personal protection, it has not been commonplace that these same citizens could carry their firearm across states lines. NRA-ILA is working to pass right-to-carry reciprocity laws granting permit holders the ability to carry their firearms legally while visiting or traveling beyond their home state.

In order to assist NRA Members in determining which states recognize their permits, NRA-ILA has created this guide. **This guide is not to be considered as legal advice or a restatement of the law. It is important to remember that state carry laws vary considerably. Be sure to check with state and local authorities outside your home state for a complete listing of restrictions on carrying concealed in that state.** Many states restrict carrying in bars, restaurants (where alcohol is served), establishments where packaged alcohol is sold, schools, colleges, universities, churches, parks, sporting events, correctional facilities, courthouses, federal and state government offices/buildings, banks, airport terminals, police stations, polling places, any posted private property restricting the carrying of concealed firearms, etc. In addition to state restrictions, federal law prohibits carrying on military bases, in national parks and the sterile area of airports. National Forests usually follow laws of the state wherein the forest is located.

NOTE: Vermont does not issue permits, but allows carrying of concealed firearms if there is no intent to commit a crime. Vermont residents traveling to other states must first obtain a non-resident permit from that state—if available—prior to carrying concealed.

•• Last Revised 12/2000 ••

NRA - Right-To-Carry Reciprocity Guide

Alabama

Right-to-Carry Law Type
Right-to-Carry

Issuing Authority:
County Sheriff
These states also recognize your permit:
Idaho, Indiana, Michigan, Utah, Vermont, Wyoming
Contact agency for non-resident permits if granted:
Permits not granted.
www.legislature.state.al.us/codeofalabama/1975/coatoc.htm

Alaska

Right-to-Carry Law Type
Right-to-Carry

Issuing Authority:
State Trooper
These states also recognize your permit:
Idaho, Indiana, Michigan, Montana, Texas, Vermont, Wyoming
Contact agency for non-resident permits if granted:
Permits not granted.
www.dps.state.ak.us/ast/achp/

Arizona

Right-to-Carry Law Type
Right-to-Carry

Issuing Authority:
Department of Public Safety
These states also recognize your permit:
Arkansas, Idaho, Indiana, Kentucky, Michigan, Montana, Texas, Utah, Vermont, Wyoming
Contact agency for non-resident permits if granted:
Permits not granted.
www.dps.state.az.us/ccw/welcome.htm

Arkansas

Right-to-Carry Law Type
Right-to-Carry

Issuing Authority:
State Police
These states also recognize your permit:
Arizona, Florida, Idaho, Indiana, Kentucky, Michigan, Montana, Oklahoma, South Carolina, Tennessee, Texas, Utah, Vermont, Wyoming
Contact agency for non-resident permits if granted:
Permits not granted.
www.state.ar.us/asp/handgun.html

California

Right-to-Carry Law Type
Limited Issue

Issuing Authority:
County Sheriff
These states also recognize your permit:
Idaho, Indiana, Michigan, Montana, Vermont, Wyoming
Contact agency for non-resident permits if granted:
Permits not granted.
caag.state.ca.us/firearms/

Colorado

Right-to-Carry Law Type
Limited Issue

Issuing Authority:
Chief of Police/County Sheriff
These states also recognize your permit:
Idaho, Indiana, Michigan, Montana, Vermont, Wyoming
Contact agency for non-resident permits if granted:
Permits not granted.
www.state.co.us/gov_dir/cdps/firearms.htm

Connecticut

Right-to-Carry Law Type
Right-to-Carry

Issuing Authority:
Commissioner of State Police
These states also recognize your permit:
Idaho, Indiana, Michigan, Montana, Utah, Vermont, Wyoming
Contact agency for non-resident permits if granted:
State Police Special Licensing Division; (860) 685-8290
www.bfpe.state.ct.us/

Delaware

Right-to-Carry Law Type
Limited Issue

Issuing Authority:
Prothonotary of Superior Court
These states also recognize your permit:
Idaho, Indiana, Michigan, Vermont, Wyoming
Contact agency for non-resident permits if granted:
Permits not granted.
www.lexislawpublishing.com/resources/

Florida

Right-to-Carry Law Type
Right-to-Carry

Issuing Authority:
Department of State
These states also recognize your permit:
Arkansas, Georgia, Idaho, Indiana, Kentucky, Louisiana, Michigan, Mississippi, Montana, New Hampshire, North Dakota, Tennessee, Texas, Utah, Vermont, Wyoming
Contact agency for non-resident permits if granted:
Dept. of State, Division of Licensing; (904) 488-5381
licweb.dos.state.fl.us/weapons/index

Georgia

Right-to-Carry Law Type
Right-to-Carry

Issuing Authority:
County Probate Judge
These states also recognize your permit:
Florida, Idaho, Indiana, Kentucky, Michigan, Montana, New Hampshire, Tennessee, Vermont, Wyoming
Contact agency for non-resident permits if granted:
Permits not granted.
www.ganet.or/cgi-bin/pub/ocode/ocresearch?number=16-11-128

NRA - Right-To-Carry Reciprocity Guide

Hawaii

Right-to-Carry Law Type
Limited Issue

Issuing Authority:
Chief of Police
These states also recognize your permit:
Idaho, Indiana, Michigan, Vermont, Wyoming
Contact agency for non-resident permits if granted:
Permits not granted.
www.capitol.hawaii.gov/site1/docs/docs.asp?press1=docs

Idaho

Right-to-Carry Law Type
Right-to-Carry

Issuing Authority:
County Sheriff
These states also recognize your permit:
Florida, Georgia, Indiana, Kentucky, Michigan, Montana, Vermont, Wyoming
Contact agency for non-resident permits if granted:
Any Sheriffs' Department
www3./state.id.us/newidst?sctid=180330002.k

Illinois

Right-to-Carry Law Type
None

Issuing Authority:
n/a
These states also recognize your permit:

Contact agency for non-resident permits if granted:
Permits not granted.
www.legis.state.il.us/ilcs/ch720act5articles/ch720act5sub34.htm

Indiana

Right-to-Carry Law Type
Right-to-Carry

Issuing Authority:
Chief Law Enforcement Officer of Municipality
These states also recognize your permit:
Florida, Georgia, Idaho, Kentucky, Michigan, Montana, Vermont, Wyoming
Contact agency for non-resident permits if granted:
Permits not granted.
www.ai.org/legislative/ic/code/title35/ar47/ch2.htm

Iowa

Right-to-Carry Law Type
Limited Issue

Issuing Authority:
(resident) Sheriff (non-resident) Commissioner of Public Safety
These states also recognize your permit:
Idaho, Indiana, Michigan, Montana, Vermont, Wyoming
Contact agency for non-resident permits if granted:
Commissioner of Public Safety; (515) 281-7610
www.state.ia.us/government/dps/asd/wp/index.htm

Kansas

Right-to-Carry Law Type
None

Issuing Authority:
n/a
These states also recognize your permit:

Contact agency for non-resident permits if granted:
Permits not granted.
www.ink.org/public/legislative/statutes/statutes.cgi

Kentucky

Right-to-Carry Law Type
Right-to-Carry

Issuing Authority:
State Police
These states also recognize your permit:
Arizona, Arkansas, Florida, Georgia, Idaho, Indiana, Louisiana, Michigan, Mississippi, Montana, Tennessee, Texas, Utah, West Virginia, Vermont, Wyoming
Contact agency for non-resident permits if granted:
Permits not granted.
www.state.ky.us/agencies/ksp/ccdw/ccdfr.htm

Louisiana

Right-to-Carry Law Type
Right-to-Carry

Issuing Authority:
Deputy Secretary of the Department of Public Safety & Corrections.
These states also recognize your permit:
Florida, Idaho, Indiana, Kentucky, Michigan, Montana, Tennessee, Texas, Utah, Vermont, Wyoming
Contact agency for non-resident permits if granted:
Permits not granted.
www.dps.state.la.us/lsp/chips.html

Maine

Right-to-Carry Law Type
Right-to-Carry

Issuing Authority:
County Sheriff/Chief of Police
These states also recognize your permit:
Idaho, Indiana, Michigan, Vermont, Wyoming
Contact agency for non-resident permits if granted:
Chief of State Police; (207) 624-8775
janus.state.me.us/legis/ros/meconlaw.htm

Maryland

Right-to-Carry Law Type
Limited Issue

Issuing Authority:
Superintendent of State Police
These states also recognize your permit:
Idaho, Indiana, Michigan, Montana, Vermont, Wyoming
Contact agency for non-resident permits if granted:
Permits not granted.
www.inform.umd.edu/ums+state/md_resources/mdsp/license.htm

NRA - Right-To-Carry Reciprocity Guide

Massachusetts

Right-to-Carry Law Type
Limited Issue

Issuing Authority:
Chief of Police
These states also recognize your permit:
Idaho, Indiana, Michigan, Montana, Utah, Vermont, Wyoming
Contact agency for non-resident permits if granted:
Permits not granted.
www.state.ma.us/msp/firearms/index.htm

Michigan

Right-to-Carry Law Type
Limited Issue

Issuing Authority:
County Gun Board/Sheriff
These states also recognize your permit:
Florida, Georgia, Idaho, Indiana, Kentucky, Montana, Vermont, Wyoming
Contact agency for non-resident permits if granted:
Permits not granted.
www.msp.state.mi.us/reports/ccw/ccwtoc.htm

Minnesota

Right-to-Carry Law Type
Limited Issue

Issuing Authority:
Chief of Police/County Sheriff
These states also recognize your permit:
Idaho, Indiana, Michigan, Montana, Vermont, Wyoming
Contact agency for non-resident permits if granted:
Permits not granted.
www.revisor.leg.state.mn.us/

Mississippi

Right-to-Carry Law Type
Right-to-Carry

Issuing Authority:
Department of Public Safety
These states also recognize your permit:
Florida, Idaho, Indiana, Kentucky, Michigan, Montana, Tennessee, Vermont, Wyoming
Contact agency for non-resident permits if granted:
Permits not granted.
www.mscode.com/free/statutes/45/009/0101.htm

Missouri

Right-to-Carry Law Type
None

Issuing Authority:
n/a
These states also recognize your permit:

Contact agency for non-resident permits if granted:
Permits not granted.
www.moga.state.mo.us/statutes/c500-599/5710030.htm

Montana

Right-to-Carry Law Type
Right-to-Carry

Issuing Authority:
County Sheriff
These states also recognize your permit:
Florida, Idaho, Indiana, Michigan, North Dakota, Vermont, Wyoming
Contact agency for non-resident permits if granted:
Permits not granted.
www.doj.state.mt.us/ls/weaponslist.htm

Nebraska

Right-to-Carry Law Type
None

Issuing Authority:
n/a
These states also recognize your permit:

Contact agency for non-resident permits if granted:
Permits not granted.
www.unicam.state.ne.us/statutes.htm

Nevada

Right-to-Carry Law Type
Right-to-Carry

Issuing Authority:
County Sheriff
These states also recognize your permit:
Idaho, Indiana, Michigan, Montana, Utah, Vermont, Wyoming
Contact agency for non-resident permits if granted:
Permits not granted.
www.leg.state.nv.us/law1.htm

New Hampshire

Right-to-Carry Law Type
Right-to-Carry

Issuing Authority:
Selectman/Mayor or Chief of Police
These states also recognize your permit:
Florida, Georgia, Idaho, Indiana, Kentucky, Michigan, North Dakota, Vermont, Wyoming
Contact agency for non-resident permits if granted:
Director of State Police; (603) 271-3575
199.192.9.6/rsa/12/159-6-d.htm

New Jersey

Right-to-Carry Law Type
Limited Issue

Issuing Authority:
Chief of Police/Superintendent of State Police
These states also recognize your permit:
Idaho, Indiana, Michigan, Montana, Vermont, Wyoming
Contact agency for non-resident permits if granted:
Superintendent of State Police; (609) 882-2000 ext. 2664
www.njleg.state.nj.us/html.statutes.htm

NRA - Right-To-Carry Reciprocity Guide

New Mexico

Right-to-Carry Law Type
None

Issuing Authority:
n/a
These states also recognize your permit:

Contact agency for non-resident permits if granted:
Permits not granted.
www.dps.nm.org/faq/concealcarry.htm

New York

Right-to-Carry Law Type
Limited Issue

Issuing Authority:
Varies by county
These states also recognize your permit:
Idaho, Indiana, Michigan, Montana, Vermont, Wyoming
Contact agency for non-resident permits if granted:
Permits not granted.
leginfo.state.ny.us:82/index1.html

North Carolina

Right-to-Carry Law Type
Right-to-Carry

Issuing Authority:
County Sheriff
These states also recognize your permit:
Idaho, Indiana, Michigan, Montana, Utah, Vermont, Wyoming
Contact agency for non-resident permits if granted:
Permits not granted.
www.jus.state.nc.us/ncja/guns.htm

North Dakota

Right-to-Carry Law Type
Right-to-Carry

Issuing Authority:
Chief of the Bureau of Criminal Investigation
These states also recognize your permit:
Florida, Idaho, Indiana, Michigan, Montana, Vermont, Wyoming
Contact agency for non-resident permits if granted:
Permits not granted.
expedition.bismarck.ag.state.nd.us/ndag/manuals/weapons.html

Ohio

Right-to-Carry Law Type
None

Issuing Authority:
n/a
These states also recognize your permit:

Contact agency for non-resident permits if granted:
Permits not granted.
orc.avv.com

Oklahoma

Right-to-Carry Law Type
Right-to-Carry

Issuing Authority:
State Bureau of Investigation
These states also recognize your permit:
Arkansas, Idaho, Indiana, Michigan, Montana, Texas, Utah, Vermont, Wyoming
Contact agency for non-resident permits if granted:
Permits not granted.
www.osbi.state.ok.us/sda/sda.html

Oregon

Right-to-Carry Law Type
Right-to-Carry

Issuing Authority:
County Sheriff
These states also recognize your permit:
Idaho, Indiana, Michigan, Montana, Utah, Vermont, Wyoming
Contact agency for non-resident permits if granted:
Permits not granted.
www.leg.state.or.us/ors/166.html

Pennsylvania

Right-to-Carry Law Type
Right-to-Carry

Issuing Authority:
County Sheriff
These states also recognize your permit:
Idaho, Indiana, Michigan, Montana, Vermont, Wyoming
Contact agency for non-resident permits if granted:
Any Sheriff's Department
www.pacode.com

Rhode Island

Right-to-Carry Law Type
Limited Issue

Issuing Authority:
Attorney General
These states also recognize your permit:
Idaho, Indiana, Michigan, Vermont, Wyoming
Contact agency for non-resident permits if granted:
Attorney General by mail only (no phone calls) send self-addressed stamped envelope to: Dept. of Attorney General 150 South Main Street Providence, RI 02903 Attn: Bureau of Criminal Identification
www.rilin.state.ri.us/statutes/title11/11-47/s00014.htm

South Carolina

Right-to-Carry Law Type
Right-to-Carry

Issuing Authority:
S.C. Law Enforcement Division
These states also recognize your permit:
Arkansas, Idaho, Indiana, Michigan, Montana, Tennessee, Utah, Vermont, Wyoming
Contact agency for non-resident permits if granted:
Permits not granted.
www.lpitr.state.sc.us/code/statmast.htm

NRA - Right-To-Carry Reciprocity Guide

South Dakota

Right-to-Carry Law Type
Right-to-Carry

Issuing Authority:
Chief of Police/County Sheriff
These states also recognize your permit:
Idaho, Indiana, Michigan, Vermont, Wyoming
Contact agency for non-resident permits if granted:
Permits not granted.
legis.state.sd.us/statutes/index.cfm

Tennessee

Right-to-Carry Law Type
Right-to-Carry

Issuing Authority:
Department of Public Safety
These states also recognize your permit:
Arkansas, Florida, Idaho, Indiana, Kentucky, Louisiana, Michigan, Mississippi, Montana, South Carolina, Texas, Utah, Virginia, Vermont, Wyoming
Contact agency for non-resident permits if granted:
Permits not granted.
www.state.tn.us/safety/handguns.html

Texas

Right-to-Carry Law Type
Right-to-Carry

Issuing Authority:
Department of Public Safety
These states also recognize your permit:
Alaska, Arizona, Arkansas, Idaho, Indiana, Louisiana, Michigan, Montana, Oklahoma, Tennessee, Utah, Vermont, Wyoming
Contact agency for non-resident permits if granted:
Permits granted by DPS to qualified non-residents from states with no concealed carry permit system. Call (800) 224-5744 or (512) 424-7293.
www.txdps.state.tx.us./administration/crime_records/chl/chlsindex.htm

Utah

Right-to-Carry Law Type
Right-to-Carry

Issuing Authority:
Department of Public Safety
These states also recognize your permit:
Arizona, Arkansas, Idaho, Indiana, Michigan, Montana, Oklahoma, South Carolina, Vermont, Wyoming
Contact agency for non-resident permits if granted:
Department of Public Safety; (801) 965-4484
www.le.state.ut.us/ÿ7Ecode/title 76/htm/76-oco45.htm

Vermont

Right-to-Carry Law Type
Right-to-Carry

Issuing Authority:
Vermont allows concealed carry without a permit and issues no official permit.
These states also recognize your permit:
N/A
Contact agency for non-resident permits if granted:
No permit required.
www.leg.state.vt.us/statutes/title13/chap085.htm

Virginia

Right-to-Carry Law Type
Right-to-Carry

Issuing Authority:
Clerk of Circuit Court
These states also recognize your permit:
Idaho, Indiana, Michigan, Montana, Tennessee, West Virginia, Vermont, Wyoming
Contact agency for non-resident permits if granted:
Permits not granted.
www.vsp.state.va.us/basrcwp.html

Washington

Right-to-Carry Law Type
Right-to-Carry

Issuing Authority:
Chief of Police/Sheriff
These states also recognize your permit:
Idaho, Indiana, Michigan, Montana, Vermont, Wyoming
Contact agency for non-resident permits if granted:
Any Sheriff's Department
www.leg.wa.gov/wsladm/rcw.htm

West Virginia

Right-to-Carry Law Type
Right-to-Carry

Issuing Authority:
Sheriff
These states also recognize your permit:
Idaho, Indiana, Kentucky, Michigan, Montana, Virginia, Vermont, Wyoming
Contact agency for non-resident permits if granted:
Permits not granted.
www.wvstatepolice.com/legal/legal.shtml

Wisconsin

Right-to-Carry Law Type
None

Issuing Authority:
n/a
These states also recognize your permit:

Contact agency for non-resident permits if granted:
Permits not granted.
www.legis.state.wi.us/rsb/stats.html

Wyoming

Right-to-Carry Law Type
Right-to-Carry

Issuing Authority:
Attorney General
These states also recognize your permit:
Florida, Idaho, Indiana, Kentucky, Michigan, Mississippi, Montana, North Dakota, Oklahoma, South Carolina, Vermont
Contact agency for non-resident permits if granted:
Permits not granted.
www.state.wy.us/~ag/dci/cw.html

ARMS ASSOCIATIONS

UNITED STATES

ALABAMA

Alabama Gun Collectors Assn.
Secretary, P.O. Box 70965, Tuscaloosa, AL 35407

ALASKA

Alaska Gun Collectors Assn., Inc.
C.W. Floyd, Pres., 5240 Little Tree, Anchorage, AK 99507

ARIZONA

Arizona Arms Assn.
Don DeBusk, President, 4837 Bryce Ave., Glendale, AZ 85301

CALIFORNIA

California Cartridge Collectors Assn.
Rick Montgomery, 1729 Christina, Stockton, CA 95204/209-463-7216 evs.

California Waterfowl Assn.
4630 Northgate Blvd., #150, Sacramento, CA 95834

Greater Calif. Arms & Collectors Assn.
Donald L. Bullock, 8291 Carburton St., Long Beach, CA 90808-3302

Los Angeles Gun Ctg. Collectors Assn.
F.H. Ruffra, 20810 Amie Ave., Apt. #9, Torrance, CA 90503

Stock Gun Players Assn.
6038 Appian Way, Long Beach, CA, 90803

COLORADO

Colorado Gun Collectors Assn.
L.E.(Bud) Greenwald, 2553 S. Quitman St., Denver, CO 80219/303-935-3850

Rocky Mountain Cartridge Collectors Assn.
John Roth, P.O. Box 757, Conifer, CO 80433

CONNECTICUT

Ye Connecticut Gun Guild, Inc.
Dick Fraser, P.O. Box 425, Windsor, CT 06095

FLORIDA

Unified Sportsmen of Florida
P.O. Box 6565, Tallahassee, FL 32314

GEORGIA

Georgia Arms Collectors Assn., Inc.
Michael Kindberg, President, P.O. Box 277, Alpharetta, GA 30239-0277

ILLINOIS

Illinois State Rifle Assn.
P.O. Box 637, Chatsworth, IL 60921

Mississippi Valley Gun & Cartridge Coll. Assn.
Bob Filbert, P.O. Box 61, Port Byron, IL 61275/309-523-2593

Sauk Trail Gun Collectors
Gordell M. Matson, P.O. Box 1113, Milan, IL 61264

Wabash Valley Gun Collectors Assn., Inc.
Roger L. Dorsett, 2601 Willow Rd., Urbana, IL 61801/217-384-7302

INDIANA

Indiana State Rifle & Pistol Assn.
Thos. Glancy, P.O. Box 552, Chesterton, IN 46304

Southern Indiana Gun Collectors Assn., Inc.
Sheila McClary, 309 W. Monroe St., Boonville, IN 47601/812-897-3742

IOWA

Beaver Creek Plainsmen Inc.
Steve Murphy, Secy., P.O. Box 298, Bondurant, IA 50035

Central States Gun Collectors Assn.
Dennis Greischar, Box 841, Mason City, IA 50402-0841

KANSAS

Kansas Cartridge Collectors Assn.
Bob Linder, Box 84, Plainville, KS 67663

KENTUCKY

Kentuckiana Arms Collectors Assn.
Charles Billips, President, Box 1776, Louisville, KY 40201

Kentucky Gun Collectors Assn., Inc.
Ruth Johnson, Box 64, Owensboro, KY 42302/502-729-4197

LOUISIANA

Washitaw River Renegades
Sandra Rushing, P.O. Box 256, Main St., Grayson, LA 71435

MARYLAND

Baltimore Antique Arms Assn.
Mr. Cillo, 1034 Main St., Darlington, MD 21304

MASSACHUSETTS

Bay Colony Weapons Collectors, Inc.
John Brandt, Box 111, Hingham, MA 02043

Massachusetts Arms Collectors
Bruce E. Skinner, P.O. Box 31, No. Carver, MA 02355/508-866-5259

MICHIGAN

Association for the Study and Research of .22 Caliber Rimfire Cartridges
George Kass, 4512 Nakoma Dr., Okemos, MI 48864

MINNESOTA

Sioux Empire Cartridge Collectors Assn.
Bob Cameron, 14597 Glendale Ave. SE, Prior Lake, MN 55372

MISSISSIPPI

Mississippi Gun Collectors Assn.
Jack E. Swinney, P.O. Box 16323, Hattiesburg, MS 39402

MISSOURI

Greater St. Louis Cartridge Collectors Assn.
Don MacChesney, 634 Scottsdale Rd., Kirkwood, MO 63122-1109

Mineral Belt Gun Collectors Assn.
D.F. Saunders, 1110 Cleveland Ave., Monett, MO 65708

Missouri Valley Arms Collectors Assn., Inc.
L.P Brammer II, Membership Secy., P.O. Box 33033, Kansas City, MO 64114

MONTANA

Montana Arms Collectors Assn.
Dean E. Yearout, Sr., Exec. Secy., 1516 21st Ave. S., Great Falls, MT 59405

Weapons Collectors Society of Montana
R.G. Schipf, Ex. Secy., 3100 Bancroft St., Missoula, MT 59801/406-728-2995

NEBRASKA

Nebraska Cartridge Collectors Club
Gary Muckel, P.O. Box 84442, Lincoln, NE 68501

NEW HAMPSHIRE

New Hampshire Arms Collectors, Inc.
James Stamatelos, Secy., P.O. Box 5, Cambridge, MA 02139

NEW JERSEY

Englishtown Benchrest Shooters Assn.
Michael Toth, 64 Cooke Ave., Carteret, NJ 07008

Jersey Shore Antique Arms Collectors
Joe Sisia, P.O. Box 100, Bayville, NJ 08721-0100

New Jersey Arms Collectors Club, Inc.
Angus Laidlaw, Vice President, 230 Valley Rd., Montclair, NJ 07042/201-746-0939; e-mail: acclaidlaw@juno.com

NEW YORK

Iroquois Arms Collectors Assn.
Bonnie Robinson, Show Secy., P.O. Box 142, Ransomville, NY 14131/716-791-4096

Mid-State Arms Coll. & Shooters Club
Jack Ackerman, 24 S. Mountain Terr., Binghamton, NY 13903

NORTH CAROLINA

North Carolina Gun Collectors Assn.
Jerry Ledford, 3231-7th St. Dr. NE, Hickory, NC 28601

OHIO

Ohio Gun Collectors Assn.
P.O. Box 9007, Maumee, OH 43537-9007/419-897-0861; Fax:419-897-0860

Shotshell Historical and Collectors Society
Madeline Bruemmer, 3886 Dawley Rd., Ravenna, OH 44266

The Stark Gun Collectors, Inc.
William I. Gann, 5666 Waynesburg Dr., Waynesburg, OH 44688

OREGON

Oregon Arms Collectors Assn., Inc.
Phil Bailey, P.O. Box 13000-A, Portland, OR 97213-0017/503-281-6864; off.:503-281-0918

Oregon Cartridge Collectors Assn.
Boyd Northrup, P.O. Box 285, Rhododendron, OR 97049

PENNSYLVANIA

Presque Isle Gun Collectors Assn.
James Welch, 156 E. 37 St., Erie, PA 16504

SOUTH CAROLINA

Belton Gun Club, Inc.
Attn. Secretary, P.O. Box 126, Belton, SC 29627/864-369-6767

Gun Owners of South Carolina
Membership Div.: William Strozier, Secretary, P.O. Box 70, Johns Island, SC 29457-0070/803-762-3240; Fax:803-795-0711; e-mail:76053.222@compuserve.com

SOUTH DAKOTA

Dakota Territory Gun Coll. Assn., Inc.
Curt Carter, Castlewood, SD 57223

TENNESSEE

Smoky Mountain Gun Coll. Assn., Inc.
Hugh W. Yabro, President, P.O. Box 23225, Knoxville, TN 37933

Tennessee Gun Collectors Assn., Inc.
M.H. Parks, 3556 Pleasant Valley Rd., Nashville, TN 37204-3419

TEXAS

Houston Gun Collectors Assn., Inc.
P.O. Box 741429, Houston, TX 77274-1429

Texas Cartridge Collectors Assn., Inc.
Robert Mellichamp, Memb. Contact, 907 Shirkmere, Houston, TX 77008/713-869-0558

Texas Gun Collectors Assn.
Bob Eder, Pres., P.O. Box 12067, El Paso, TX 79913/915-584-8183

Texas State Rifle Assn.
1131 Rockingham Dr., Suite 101, Richardson, TX 75080-4326

VIRGINIA

Virginia Gun Collectors Assn., Inc.
Addison Hurst, Secy., 38802 Charlestown Height, Waterford, VA 20197/540-882-3543

WASHINGTON

Association of Cartridge Collectors on the Pacific Northwest
Robert Jardin, 14214 Meadowlark Drive KPN, Gig Harbor, WA 98329

Washington Arms Collectors, Inc.
Joyce Boss, P.O. Box 389, Renton, WA, 98057-0389/206-255-8410

WISCONSIN

Great Lakes Arms Collectors Assn., Inc.
Edward C. Warnke, 2913 Woodridge Lane, Waukesha, WI 53188

Wisconsin Gun Collectors Assn., Inc.
Lulita Zellmer, P.O. Box 181, Sussex, WI 53089

WYOMING

Wyoming Weapons Collectors
P.O. Box 284, Laramie, WY 82073/307-745-4652 or 745-9530

NATIONAL ORGANIZATIONS

Amateur Trapshooting Assn.
David D. Bopp, Exec. Director, 601 W. National Rd., Vandalia, OH 45377/937-898-4638; Fax:937-898-5472

American Airgun Field Target Assn.
5911 Cherokee Ave., Tampa, FL 33604

American Coon Hunters Assn.
Opal Johnston, P.O. Cadet, Route 1, Box 492, Old Mines, MO 63630

American Custom Gunmakers Guild
Jan Billeb, Exec. Director, P.O. Box 812, Burlington, IA 52601-0812/319-752-6114 (Phone or Fax)

American Defense Preparedness Assn.
Two Colonial Place, 2101 Wilson Blvd., Suite 400, Arlington, VA 22201-3061

American Paintball League
P.O. Box 3561, Johnson City, TN 37602/800-541-9169

American Pistolsmiths Guild
Alex B. Hamilton, Pres., 1449 Blue Crest Lane, San Antonio, TX 78232/210-494-3063

American Police Pistol & Rifle Assn.
3801 Biscayne Blvd., Miami, FL 33137

American Single Shot Rifle Assn.
Gary Staup, Secy., 709 Carolyn Dr., Delphos, OH 45833/419-692-3866. Website: www.assra.com

American Society of Arms Collectors
George E. Weatherly, P.O. Box 2567, Waxahachie, TX 75165

American Tactical Shooting Assn.(A.T.S.A.)
c/o Skip Gochenour, 2600 N. Third St., Harrisburg, PA 17110/717-233-0402; Fax:717-233-5340

Association of Firearm and Tool Mark Examiners
Lannie G. Emanuel, Secy., Southwest Institute of Forensic Sciences, P.O. Box 35728, Dallas, TX 75235/214-920-5979; Fax:214-920-5928; Membership Secy., Ann D. Jones, VA Div. of Forensic Science, P.O. Box 999, Richmond, VA 23208/804-786-4706; Fax:804-371-8328

Boone & Crockett Club
250 Station Dr., Missoula, MT 59801-2753

Browning Collectors Assn.
Secretary:Scherrie L. Brennac, 2749 Keith Dr., Villa Ridge, MO 63089/314-742-0571

The Cast Bullet Assn., Inc.
Ralland J. Fortier, Editor, 4103 Foxcraft Dr., Traverse City, MI 49684

Citizens Committee for the Right to Keep and Bear Arms
Natl. Hq., Liberty Park, 12500 NE Tenth Pl., Bellevue, WA 98005

Colt Collectors Assn.
25000 Highland Way, Los Gatos, CA 95030/408-353-2658.

Ducks Unlimited, Inc.
Natl. Headquarters, One Waterfowl Way, Memphis, TN 38120/901-758-3937

Fifty Caliber Shooters Assn.
PO Box 111, Monroe UT 84754-0111

Firearms Coalition/Neal Knox Associates
Box 6537, Silver Spring, MD 20906/301-871-3006

Firearms Engravers Guild of America
Rex C. Pedersen, Secy., 511 N. Rath Ave., Lundington, MI 49431/616-845-7695(Phone and Fax)

Foundation for North American Wild Sheep
720 Allen Ave., Cody, WY 82414-3402/web site: http://iigi.com/os/non/fnaws/fnaws.htm; e-mail: fnaws@wyoming.com

Freedom Arms Collectors Assn.
P.O. Box 160302, Miami, FL 33116-0302

REFERENCE

Arms Association

Garand Collectors Assn.
P.O. Box 181, Richmond, KY 40475

Golden Eagle Collectors Assn. (G.E.C.A.)
Chris Showler, 11144 Slate Creek Rd., Grass Valley, CA 95945

Gun Owners of America
8001 Forbes Place, Suite 102, Springfield, VA 22151/703-321-8585

Handgun Hunters International
J.D. Jones, Director, P.O. Box 357 MAG, Bloomingdale, OH 43910

Harrington & Richardson Gun Coll. Assn.
George L. Cardet, 330 S.W. 27th Ave., Suite 603, Miami, FL 33135

High Standard Collectors' Assn.
John J. Stimson, Jr., Pres., 540 W. 92nd St., Indianapolis, IN 46260

Hopkins & Allen Arms & Memorabilia Society (HAAMS)
P.O. Box 187, 1309 Pamela Circle, Delphos, OH 45833

International Ammunition Association, Inc.
C.R. Punnett, Secy., 8 Hillock Lane, Chadds Ford, PA 19317/610-358-1285;Fax:610-358-1560

International Benchrest Shooters
Joan Borden, RR1, Box 250BB, Springville, PA 18844/717-965-2366

International Blackpowder Hunting Assn.
P.O. Box 1180, Glenrock, WY 82637/307-436-9817

IHMSA (Intl. Handgun Metallic Silhouette Assn.)
PO Box 368, Burlington, IA 52601 Website: www.ihmsa.cor

International Society of Mauser Arms Collectors
Michael Kindberg, Pres., P.O. Box 277, Alpharetta, GA 30239-0277

Jews for the Preservation of Firearms Ownership (JPFO) 501(c)(3)
2872 S. Wentworth Ave., Milwaukee, WI 53207/414-769-0760; Fax:414-483-8435

The Mannlicher Collectors Assn.
Membership Office: P.O. Box1249, The Dalles, Oregon 97058

Marlin Firearms Collectors Assn., Ltd.
Dick Paterson, Secy., 407 Lincoln Bldg., 44 Main St., Champaign, IL 61820

Merwin Hulbert Association,
2503 Kentwood Ct., High Point, NC 27265

Miniature Arms Collectors/Makers Society, Ltd.
Ralph Koebbeman, Pres., 4910 Kilburn Ave., Rockford, IL 61101/815-964-2569

M1 Carbine Collectors Assn. (M1-CCA)
623 Apaloosa Ln., Gardnerville, NV 89410-7840

National Association of Buckskinners (NAB)
Territorial Dispatch—1800s Historical Publication, 4701 Marion St., Suite 324, Livestock Exchange Bldg., Denver, CO 80216/303-297-9671

The National Association of Derringer Collectors
P.O. Box 20572, San Jose, CA 95160

National Assn. of Federally Licensed Firearms Dealers
Andrew Molchan, 2455 E. Sunrise, Ft. Lauderdale, FL 33304

National Association to Keep and Bear Arms
P.O. Box 78336, Seattle, WA 98178

National Automatic Pistol Collectors Assn.
Tom Knox, P.O. Box 15738, Tower Grove Station, St. Louis, MO 63163

National Bench Rest Shooters Assn., Inc.
Pat Ferrell, 2835 Guilford Lane, Oklahoma City, OK 73120-4404/405-842-9585; Fax: 405-842-9575

National Muzzle Loading Rifle Assn.
Box 67, Friendship, IN 47021 / 812-667-5131. Website: www.nmlra@nmlra.org

National Professional Paintball League (NPPL)
540 Main St., Mount Kisco, NY 10549/914-241-7400

National Reloading Manufacturers Assn.
One Centerpointe Dr., Suite 300, Lake Oswego, OR 97035

National Rifle Assn. of America
11250 Waples Mill Rd., Fairfax, VA 22030 / 703-267-1000. Website: www.nra.org

National Shooting Sports Foundation, Inc.
Robert T. Delfay, President, Flintlock Ridge Office Center, 11 Mile Hill Rd., Newtown, CT 06470-2359/203-426-1320; FAX: 203-426-1087

National Skeet Shooting Assn.
Dan Snyuder, Director, 5931 Roft Road, San Antonio, TX 78253-9261/800-877-5338. Website: nssa-nsca.com

National Sporting Clays Association
Ann Myers, Director, 5931 Roft Road, San Antonio, TX 78253-9261/800-877-5338. Website: nssa-nsca.com

National Wild Turkey Federation, Inc.
P.O. Box 530, 770 Augusta Rd., Edgefield, SC 29824

North American Hunting Club
P.O. Box 3401, Minnetonka, MN 55343/612-936-9333; Fax: 612-936-9755

North American Paintball Referees Association (NAPRA)
584 Cestaric Dr., Milpitas, CA 95035

North-South Skirmish Assn., Inc.
Stevan F. Meserve, Exec. Secretary, 507 N. Brighton Court, Sterling, VA 20164-3919

Remington Society of America
Gordon Fosburg, Secretary, 11900 North Brinton Road, Lake, MI 48623

Rocky Mountain Elk Foundation
P.O. Box 8249, Missoula, MT 59807-8249/406-523-4500;Fax: 406-523-4581
Website: www.rmef.org

Ruger Collector's Assn., Inc.
P.O. Box 240, Greens Farms, CT 06436

Safari Club International
4800 W. Gates Pass Rd., Tucson, AZ 85745/520-620-1220

Sako Collectors Assn., Inc.
Jim Lutes, 202 N. Locust, Whitewater, KS 67154

Second Amendment Foundation
James Madison Building, 12500 NE 10th Pl., Bellevue, WA 98005

Single Action Shooting Society (SASS)
23255-A La Palma Avenue, Yorba Linda, CA 92887/714-6941800; FAX: 714-694-1815/email: sasseot@aol.com Website: www.sassnet.com

Smith & Wesson Collectors Assn.
Cally Pletl, Admin. Asst.,PO Box 444, Afton, NY 13730

The Society of American Bayonet Collectors
P.O. Box 234, East Islip, NY 11730-0234

Southern California Schuetzen Society
Dean Lillard, 34657 Ave. E., Yucaipa, CA 92399

Sporting Arms and Ammunition Manufacturers' Institute (SAAMI)
Flintlock Ridge Office Center, 11 Mile Hill Rd., Newtown, CT 06470-2359/203-426-4358; FAX: 203-426-1087

Sporting Clays of America (SCA)
Ron L. Blosser, Pres., 9257 Buckeye Rd., Sugar Grove, OH 43155-9632/614-746-8334; Fax: 614-746-8605

The Thompson/Center Assn.
Joe Wright, President, Box 792, Northboro, MA 01532/508-845-6960

U.S. Practical Shooting Assn./IPSC
Dave Thomas, P.O. Box 811, Sedro Woolley, WA 98284/360-855-2245

U.S. Revolver Assn.
Brian J. Barer, 40 Larchmont Ave., Taunton, MA 02780/508-824-4836

U.S. Shooting Team
U.S. Olympic Shooting Center, One Olympic Plaza, Colorado Springs, CO 80909/719-578-4670

The Varmint Hunters Assn., Inc.
Box 759, Pierre, SD 57501/Member Services 800-528-4868

Weatherby Collectors Assn., Inc.
P.O. Box 888, Ozark, MO 65721

The Wildcatters
P.O. Box 170, Greenville, WI 54942

Winchester Arms Collectors Assn.
P.O. Box 230, Brownsboro, TX 75756/903-852-4027

The Women's Shooting Sports Foundation (WSSF)
4620 Edison Avenue, Ste. C, Colorado Springs, CO 80915/719-638-1299; FAX: 719-638-1271/email: wssf@worldnet.att.net

ARGENTINA

Asociacion Argentina de Coleccionistas de Armes y Municiones
Castilla de Correos No. 28, Succursal I B, 1401 Buenos Aires, Republica Argentina

AUSTRALIA

Antique & Historical Arms Collectors of Australia
P.O. Box 5654, GCMC Queensland 9726, Australia

The Arms Collector's Guild of Queensland Inc.
Ian Skennerton, P.O. Box 433, Ashmore City 4214, Queensland, Australia

Australian Cartridge Collectors Assn., Inc.
Bob Bennett, 126 Landscape Dr., E. Doncaster 3109, Victoria, Ausrtalia

Sporting Shooters Assn. of Australia, Inc.
P.O. Box 2066, Kent Town, SA 5071, Australia

CANADA

ALBERTA

Canadian Historical Arms Society
P.O. Box 901, Edmonton, Alb., Canada T5J 2L8

National Firearms Assn.
Natl. Hq: P.O. Box 1779, Edmonton, Alb., Canada T5J 2P1

BRITISH COLUMBIA

The Historical Arms Collectors of B.C. (Canada)
Harry Moon, Pres., P.O. Box 50117, South Slope RPO, Burnaby, BC V5J 5G3, Canada/604-438-0950; Fax:604-277-3646

ONTARIO

Association of Canadian Cartridge Collectors
Monica Wright, RR 1, Millgrove, ON, L0R IV0, Canada

Tri-County Antique Arms Fair
P.O. Box 122, RR #1, North Lancaster, Ont., Canada K0C 1Z0

EUROPE

BELGIUM

European Catridge Research Assn.
Graham Irving, 21 Rue Schaltin, 4900 Spa, Belgium/32.87.77.43.40; Fax:32.87.77.27.51

CZECHOSLOVAKIA

Spolecnost Pro Studium Naboju (Czech Cartridge Research Assn.)
JUDr. Jaroslav Bubak, Pod Homolko 1439, 26601 Beroun 2, Czech Republic

DENMARK

Aquila Dansk Jagtpatron Historic Forening (Danish Historical Cartridge Collectors Club)
Steen Elgaard Møller, Ulriksdalsvej 7, 4840 Nr. Alslev, Denmark 10045-53846218;Fax:00455384 6209

ENGLAND

Arms and Armour Society
Hon. Secretary A. Dove, P.O. Box 10232, London, 5W19 2ZD, England

Dutch Paintball Federation
Aceville Publ., Castle House 97 High Street, Colchester, Essex C01 1TH, England/011-44-206-564840

European Paintball Sports Foundation
c/o Aceville Publ., Castle House 97 High St., Colchester, Essex, C01 1TH, England

Historical Breechloading Smallarms Assn.
D.J. Penn M.A., Secy., P.O. Box 12778, London SE1 6BX, England. Journal and newsletter are $23 a yr., including airmail.

National Rifle Assn.
(Great Britain) Bisley Camp, Brookwood, Woking Surrey GU24 OPB, England/01483.797777; Fax: 014730686275

United Kingdom Cartridge Club
Ian Southgate, 20 Millfield, Elmley Castle, Nr. Pershore, Worcestershire, WR10 3HR, England

FRANCE

STAC-Western Co.
3 Ave. Paul Doumer (N.311); 78360 Montesson, France/01.30.53-43-65; Fax: 01.30.53.19.10

GERMANY

Bund Deutscher Sportschützen e.v. (BDS)
Borsigallee 10, 53125 Bonn 1, Germany

Deutscher Schützenbund
Lahnstrasse 120, 65195 Wiesbaden, Germany

SPAIN

Asociacion Espanola de Coleccionistas de Cartuchos (A.E.C.C.)
Secretary: Apdo. Correos No. 1086, 2880-Alcala de Henares (Madrid), Spain. President: Apdo. Correos No. 682, 50080 Zaragoza, Spain

SWEDEN

Scandinavian Ammunition Research Assn.
Box 107, 77622 Hedemora, Sweden

NEW ZEALAND

New Zealand Cartridge Collectors Club
Terry Castle, 70 Tiraumea Dr., Pakuranga, Auckland, New Zealand

New Zealand Deerstalkers Assn.
P.O. Box 6514 TE ARO, Wellington, New Zealand

SOUTH AFRICA

Historical Firearms Soc. of South Africa
P.O. Box 145, 7725 Newlands, Republic of South Africa

Republic of South Africa Cartridge Collectors Assn.
Arno Klee, 20 Eugene St., Malanshof Randburg, Gauteng 2194, Republic of South Africa

S.A.A.C.A. (Southern Africa Arms and Ammunition Assn.)
Gauteng Office:
P.O. Box 7597, Weltevreden Park, 1715, Republic of South Africa/011-679-1151; Fax: 011-679-1131;
e-mail: saaaca@iafrica.com.

Kwa-Zulu Natal office:
P.O. Box 4065, Northway, Kwazulu-Natal 4065, Republic of South Africa

SAGA (S.A. Gunowners' Assn.)
P.O. Box 35203, Northway, Kwazulu-Natal 4065, Republic of South Africa

PERIODICAL PUBLICATIONS

AAFTA News (M)
5911 Cherokee Ave., Tampa, FL 33604. Official newsletter of the American Airgun Field Target Assn.

Action Pursuit Games Magazine (M)
CFW Enterprises, Inc., 4201 W. Vanowen Pl., Burbank, CA 91505 818-845-2656. $4.99 single copy U.S., $5.50 Canada. Editor: Dan Reeves. World's leading magazine of paintball sports.

Air Gunner Magazine
4 The Courtyard, Denmark St., Wokingham, Berkshire RG11 2AZ, England/011-44-734-771677. $U.S. $44 for 1 yr. Leading monthly airgun magazine in U.K.

Airgun Ads
Box 33, Hamilton, MT 59840/406-363-3805; Fax: 406-363-4117. $35 1 yr. (for first mailing; $20 for second mailing; $35 for Canada and foreign orders.) Monthly tabloid with extensive For Sale and Wanted airgun listings.

The Airgun Letter
Gapp, Inc., 4614 Woodland Rd., Ellicott City, MD 21042-6329/410-730-5496; Fax: 410-730-9544; e-mail: staff@airgnltr.net; http://www.airgunletter.com. $21 U.S., $24 Canada, $27 Mexico and $33 other foreign orders, 1 yr. Monthly newsletter for airgun users and collectors.

Airgun World
4 The Courtyard, Denmark St., Wokingham, Berkshire RG40 2AZ, England/011-44-734-771677. Call for subscription rates. Oldest monthly airgun magazine in the U.K., now a sister publication to *Air Gunner*.

Alaska Magazine
Morris Communications, 735 Broad Street, Augusta, GA 30901/706-722-6060. Hunting, Fishing and Life on the Last Frontier articles of Alaska and western Canada.

American Firearms Industry
Nat'l. Assn. of Federally Licensed Firearms Dealers, 2455 E. Sunrise Blvd., Suite 916, Ft. Lauderdale, FL 33304. $35.00 yr. For firearms retailers, distributors and manufacturers.

American Guardian
NRA, 11250 Waples Mill Rd., Fairfax, VA 22030. Publications division. $15.00 1 yr. Magazine features personal protection; home-self-defense; family recreation shooting; women's issues; etc.

American Gunsmith
Belvoir Publications, Inc., 75 Holly Hill Lane, Greenwich, CT 06836-2626/203-661-6111. $49.00 (12 issues). Technical journal of firearms repair and maintenance.

American Handgunner*
Publisher's Development Corp., 591 Camino de la Reina, Suite 200, San Diego, CA 92108/800-537-3006 $16.95 yr. Articles for handgun enthusiasts, competitors, police and hunters.

American Hunter (M)
National Rifle Assn., 11250 Waples Mill Rd., Fairfax, VA 22030 (Same address for both.) Publications Div. $35.00 yr. Wide scope of hunting articles.

American Rifleman (M)
National Rifle Assn., 11250 Waples Mill Rd., Fairfax, VA 22030 (Same address for both). Publications Div. $35.00 yr. Firearms articles of all kinds.

American Single Shot Rifle News* (M)
Membership Secy. Tim Mather, 1180 Easthill SE, N. Canton, Ohio. Annual dues $20 for 6 issues. Official journal of the American Single Shot Rifle Assn.

American Survival Guide
McMullen Angus Publishing, Inc., 774 S. Placentia Ave., Placentia, CA 92670-6846. 12 issues $19.95/714-572-2255; FAX: 714-572-1864.

Arms Collecting (Q)
Museum Restoration Service, P.O. Box 70, Alexandria Bay, NY 13607-0070. $22.00 yr.; $62.00 3 yrs.; $112.00 5 yrs.

Australian Shooters Journal
Sporting Shooters' Assn. of Australia, Inc., P.O. Box 2066, Kent Town SA 5071, Australia. $45.00 yr. locally; $55.00 yr. overseas surface mail only. Hunting and shooting articles.

The Backwoodsman Magazine
P.O. Box 627, Westcliffe, CO 81252. $16.00 for 6 issues per yr.; $30.00 for 2 yrs.; sample copy $2.75. Subjects include muzzle-loading, woodslore, primitive survival, trapping, homesteading, blackpowder cartridge guns, 19th century how-to.

Black Powder Cartridge News (Q)
SPG, Inc., P.O. Box 761, Livingston, MT 59047/Phone/Fax: 406-222-8416. $17 yr. (4 issues) ($6 extra 1st class mailing). For the blackpowder cartridge enthusiast.

Blackpowder Hunting (M)
Intl. Blackpowder Hunting Assn., P.O. Box 1180Z, Glenrock, WY 82637/307-436-9817. $20.00 1 yr., $36.00 2 yrs. How-to and where-to features by experts on hunting; shooting; ballistics; traditional and modern blackpowder rifles, shotguns, pistols and cartridges.

Black Powder Times
P.O. Box 234, Lake Stevens, WA 98258. $20.00 yr.; add $5 per year for Canada, $10 per year other foreign. Tabloid newspaper for blackpowder activities; test reports.

Blade Magazine
Krause Publications, 700 East State St., Iola, WI 54990-0001. $25.98 for 12 issues. Foreign price (including Canada-Mexico) $50.00. A magazine for all enthusiasts of handmade, factory and antique knives.

Caliber
GFI-Verlag, Theodor-Heuss Ring 62, 50668 K"ln, Germany. For hunters, target shooters and reloaders.

The Caller (Q) (M)
National Wild Turkey Federation, P.O. Box 530, Edgefield, SC 29824. Tabloid newspaper for members; 4 issues per yr. (membership fee $25.00)

Cartridge Journal (M)
Robert Mellichamp, 907 Shirkmere, Houston, TX 77008/713-869-0558. Dues $12 for U.S. and Canadian members (includes the newsletter); 6 issues.

The Cast Bullet*(M)
Official journal of The Cast Bullet Assn. Director of Membership, 203 E. 2nd St., Muscatine, IA 52761. Annual membership dues $14, includes 6 issues.

COLTELLI, che Passione (Q)
Casella postale N.519, 20101 Milano, Italy/Fax:02-48402857. $15 1 yr., $27 2 yrs. Covers all types of knives—collecting, combat, historical. Italian text.

Combat Handguns*
Harris Publications, Inc., 1115 Broadway, New York, NY 10010.

Deer & Deer Hunting Magazine
Krause Publications, 700 E. State St., Iola, WI 54990-0001. $19.95 yr. (9 issues). For the serious deer hunter. Website: www.krause.com

The Derringer Peanut (M)
The National Association of Derringer Collectors, P.O. Box 20572, San Jose, CA 95160. A newsletter dedicated to developing the best derringer information. Write for details.

Deutsches Waffen Journal
Journal-Verlag Schwend GmbH, Postfach 100340, D-74503 Schwäbisch Hall, Germany/0791-404-500; FAX:0791-404-505 and 404-424. DM102 p. yr. (interior); DM125.30 (abroad), postage included. Antique and modern arms and equipment. German text.

Double Gun Journal
P.O. Box 550, East Jordan, MI 49727/800-447-1658. $35 for 4 issues.

Ducks Unlimited, Inc. (M)
1 Waterfowl Way, Memphis, TN 38120

The Engraver (M) (Q)
P.O. Box 4365, Estes Park, CO 80517/970-586-2388; Fax: 970-586-0394. Mike Dubber, editor. The journal of firearms engraving.

PERIODICAL PUBLICATIONS

The Field
King's Reach Tower, Stamford St., London SE1 9LS England. £36.40 U.K. 1 yr.; 49.90 (overseas, surface mail) yr.; £82.00 (overseas, air mail) yr. Hunting and shooting articles, and all country sports.

Field & Stream
Times Mirror Magazines, Two Park Ave., New York, NY 10016/212-779-5000. Monthly shooting column. Articles on hunting and fishing. Website: www.timesmirror.com

Field Tests
Belvoir Publications, Inc., 75 Holly Hill Lane; P.O. Box 2626, Greenwich, CT 06836-2626/203-661-6111; 800-829-3361 (subscription line). U.S. & Canada $29 1 yr., $58 2 yrs.; all other countries $45 1 yr., $90 2 yrs. (air).

Fur-Fish-Game
A.R. Harding Pub. Co., 2878 E. Main St., Columbus, OH 43209. $15.95 yr. Practical guidance regarding trapping, fishing and hunting.

The Gottlieb-Tartaro Report
Second Amendment Foundation, James Madison Bldg., 12500 NE 10th Pl., Bellevue, WA 98005/206-454-7012;Fax:206-451-3959. $30 for 12 issues. An insiders guide for gun owners.

Gray's Sporting Journal
Gray's Sporting Journal, P.O. Box 1207, Augusta, GA 30903. $36.95 per yr. for 6 issues. Hunting and fishing journals. Expeditions and Guides Book (Annual Travel Guide).

Gun List†
700 E. State St., Iola, WI 54990. $36.98 yr. (26 issues); $65.98 2 yrs. (52 issues). Indexed market publication for firearms collectors and active shooters; guns, supplies and services. Website: www.krause.com

Gun News Digest (Q)
Second Amendment Fdn., P.O. Box 488, Station C, Buffalo, NY 14209/716-885-6408;Fax:716-884-4471. $10 U.S.; $20 foreign.

The Gun Report
World Wide Gun Report, Inc., Box 38, Aledo, IL 61231-0038. $33.00 yr. For the antique and collectable gun dealer and collector.

Gunmaker (M) (Q)
ACGG, P.O. Box 812, Burlington, IA 52601-0812. The journal of custom gunmaking.

The Gunrunner
Div. of Kexco Publ. Co. Ltd., Box 565G, Lethbridge, Alb., Canada T1J 3Z4. $23.00 yr., sample $2.00. Monthly newspaper, listing everything from antiques to artillery.

Gun Show Calendar (Q)
700 E. State St., Iola, WI 54990. $14.95 yr. (4 issues). Gun shows listed; chronologically and by state. Website: www.krause.com

Gun Tests
11 Commerce Blvd., Palm Coast, FL 32142. The consumer resource for the serious shooter. Write for information.

Gun Trade News
Bruce Publishing Ltd., P.O. Box 82, Wantage, Ozon OX12 7A8, England/44-1-235-771770; Fax: 44-1-235-771848. Britain's only "trade only" magazine exclusive to the gun trade.

Gun Week†
Second Amendment Foundation, P.O. Box 488, Station C, Buffalo, NY 14209. $35.00 yr. U.S. and possessions; $45.00 yr. other countries. Tabloid paper on guns, hunting, shooting and collecting (36 issues).

Gun World
Y-Visionary Publishing, LP 265 South Anita Drive, Ste. 120, Orange, CA 92868. $21.97 yr.; $34.97 2 yrs. For the hunting, reloading and shooting enthusiast.

Guns & Ammo
EMAP USA, 6420 Wilshire Blvd., Los Angeles, CA 90048/213-782-2780. $23.94 yr. Guns, shooting, and technical articles.

Guns
Publishers Development Corporation, P.O. Box 85201, San Diego, CA 92138/800-537-3006. $19.95 yr. In-depth articles on a wide range of guns, shooting equipment and related accessories for gun collectors, hunters and shooters.

Guns Review
Ravenhill Publishing Co. Ltd., Box 35, Standard House, Bonhill St., London EC 2A 4DA, England. £20.00 sterling (approx. U.S. $38 USA & Canada) yr. For collectors and shooters.

H.A.C.S. Newsletter (M)
Harry Moon, Pres., P.O. Box 50117, South Slope RPO, Burnaby BC, V5J 5G3, Canada/604-438-0950;Fax:604-277-364 6. $25 p. yr. U.S. and Canada. Official newsletter of The Historical Arms Collectors of B.C. (Canada).

Handgunner*
Richard A.J. Munday, Seychelles house, Brightlingsen, Essex CO7 ONN, England/012063-305201. £ 18.00 (sterling).

Handguns
EMAP USA, 6420 Wilshire Blvd., Los Angeles, CA 90048/323-782-2868. $23/94 yr. For the handgunning and shooting enthusiast. Website: www.petersenco.com

Handloader*
Wolfe Publishing Co., 6471 Airpark Dr., Prescott, AZ 86301/520-445-7810;Fax:520-778-5124. $22.00 yr. The journal of ammunition reloading.

INSIGHTS*
NRA, 11250 Waples Mill Rd., Fairfax, VA 22030. Editor, John E. Robbins. $15.00 yr., which includes NRA junior membership; $10.00 for adult subscriptions (12 issues). Plenty of details for the young hunter and target shooter; emphasizes gun safety, marksmanship training, hunting skills.

International Arms & Militaria Collector (Q)
Arms & Militaria Press, P.O. Box 80, Labrador, Qld. 4215, Australia. A$39.50 yr. (U.S. & Canada), 2 yrs. A$77.50; A$37.50 (others), 1 yr., 2 yrs. $73.50 all air express mail; surface mail is less. Editor: Ian D. Skennerton.

International Shooting Sport*/UIT Journal
International Shooting Union (UIT), Bavariaring 21, D-80336 Munich, Germany. Europe: (Deutsche Mark) DM44.00 yr., 2 yrs. DM83.00; outside Europe: DM50.00 yr., 2 yrs. DM95.00 (air mail postage included.) For international sport shooting.

Internationales Waffen-Magazin
Habegger-Verlag Zürich, Postfach 9230, CH-8036 Zürich, Switzerland. SF 105.00 (approx. U.S. $73.00) surface mail for 10 issues. Modern and antique arms, self-defense. German text; English summary of contents.

The Journal of the Arms & Armour Society (M)
A. Dove, P.O. Box 10232, London, SW19 2ZD England. £15.00 surface mail; £20.00 airmail sterling only yr. Articles for the historian and collector.

Journal of the Historical Breechloading Smallarms Assn.
Published annually. P.O. Box 12778, London, SE1 6XB, England. $21.00 yr. Articles for the collector plus mailings of short articles on specific arms, reprints, newsletters, etc.

Knife World
Knife World Publications, P.O. Box 3395, Knoxville, TN 37927. $15.00 yr.; $25.00 2 yrs. Published monthly for knife enthusiasts and collectors. Articles on custom and factory knives; other knife-related interests, monthly column on knife identification, military knives.

Man At Arms*
P.O. Box 460, Lincoln, RI 02865. $27.00 yr., $52.00 2 yrs. plus $8.00 for foreign subscribers. The N.R.A. magazine of arms collecting-investing, with excellent articles for the collector of antique arms and militaria.

PERIODICAL PUBLICATIONS

The Mannlicher Collector (Q)(M)
Mannlicher Collectors Assn., Inc., P.O. Box 7144, Salem Oregon 97303. $20/ yr. subscription included in membership.

MAN/MAGNUM
S.A. Man (Pty) Ltd., P.O. Box 35204, Northway, Durban 4065, Republic of South Africa. SA Rand 200.00 for 12 issues. Africa's only publication on hunting, shooting, firearms, bushcraft, knives, etc.

The Marlin Collector (M)
R.W. Paterson, 407 Lincoln Bldg., 44 Main St., Champaign, IL 61820.

Muzzle Blasts (M)
National Muzzle Loading Rifle Assn., P.O. Box 67, Friendship, IN 47021/812-667-5131. $35.00 yr. annual membership. For the blackpowder shooter.

Muzzleloader Magazine*
Scurlock Publishing Co., Inc., Dept. Gun, Route 5, Box 347-M, Texarkana, TX 75501. $18.00 U.S.; $22.50 U.S./yr. for foreign subscribers. The publication for blackpowder shooters.

National Defense (M)*
American Defense Preparedness Assn., Two Colonial Place, Suite 400, 2101 Wilson Blvd., Arlington, VA 22201-3061/703-522-1820; FAX: 703-522-1885. $35.00 yr. Articles on both military and civil defense field, including weapons, materials technology, management.

National Knife Magazine (M)
Natl. Knife Coll. Assn., 7201 Shallowford Rd., P.O. Box 21070, Chattanooga, TN 37424-0070. Membership $35 yr.; $65.00 International yr.

National Rifle Assn. Journal (British) (Q)
Natl. Rifle Assn. (BR.), Bisley Camp, Brookwood, Woking, Surrey, England. GU24, OPB. £24.00 Sterling including postage.

National Wildlife*
Natl. Wildlife Fed., 1400 16th St. NW, Washington, DC 20036, $16.00 yr. (6 issues); *International Wildlife*, 6 issues, $16.00 yr. Both, $22.00 yr., includes all membership benefits. Write attn.: Membership Services Dept., for more information.

New Zealand GUNS*
Waitekauri Publishing, P.O. 45, Waikino 3060, New Zealand. $NZ90.00 (6 issues) yr. Covers the hunting and firearms scene in New Zealand.

New Zealand Wildlife (Q)
New Zealand Deerstalkers Assoc., Inc., P.O. Box 6514, Wellington, N.Z. $30.00 (N.Z.). Hunting, shooting and firearms/game research articles.

North American Hunter* (M)
P.O. Box 3401, Minnetonka, MN 55343/612-936-9333; e-mail: huntingclub@pclink.com. $18.00 yr. (7 issues). Articles on all types of North American hunting.

Outdoor Life
Times Mirror Magazines, Two Park Ave., New York, NY 10016. $16.95/yr. Extensive coverage of hunting and shooting. Shooting column by Jim Carmichel. Website: www.timesmirror.com

La Passion des Courteaux (Q)
Phenix Editions, 25 rue Mademoiselle, 75015 Paris, France. French text.

Paintball Games International Magazine
Aceville Publications, Castle House, 97 High St., Colchester, Essex, England CO1 1TH/011-44-206-564840. Write for subscription rates. Leading magazine in the U.K. covering competitive paintball activities.

Paintball News
PBN Publishing, P.O. Box 1608, 24 Henniker St., Hillsboro, NH 03244/603-464-6080. $35 U.S. 1 yr. Bi-weekly. Newspaper covering the sport of paintball, new product reviews and industry features.

Paintball Sports (Q)
Paintball Publications, Inc., 540 Main St., Mount Kisco, NY 10549/941-241-7400. $24.75 U.S. 1 yr., $32.75 foreign. Covering the competitive paintball scene.

Performance Shooter
Belvoir Publications, Inc., 75 Holly Hill Lane, Greenwich, CT 06836-2626/203-661-6111. $45.00 yr. (12 issues). Techniques and technology for improved rifle and pistol accuracy.

Petersen's HUNTING Magazine
EMAP USA, 6420 Wilshire Blvd., Los Angeles, CA 90048. $19.94 yr.; Canada $29.34 yr.; foreign countries $29.94 yr. Hunting articles for all game; test reports.

P.I. Magazine
America's Private Investigation Journal, 755 Bronx Dr., Toledo, OH 43609. Chuck Klein, firearms editor with column about handguns.

Pirsch
BLV Verlagsgesellschaft mbH, Postfach 400320, 80703 Munich, Germany/089-12704-0;Fax:089-12705-354. German text.

Point Blank
Citizens Committee for the Right to Keep and Bear Arms (sent to contributors), Liberty Park, 12500 NE 10th Pl., Bellevue, WA 98005

POINTBLANK (M)
Natl. Firearms Assn., Box 4384 Stn. C, Calgary, AB T2T 5N2, Canada. Official publication of the NFA.

The Police Marksman*
6000 E. Shirley Lane, Montgomery, AL 36117. $17.95 yr. For law enforcement personnel.

Police Times (M)
3801 Biscayne Blvd., Miami, FL 33137/305-573-0070.

Popular Mechanics
Hearst Corp., 224 W. 57th St., New York, NY 10019. Firearms, camping, outdoor oriented articles.

Precision Shooting
Precision Shooting, Inc., 222 McKee St., Manchester, CT 06040. $32.00 yr. U.S. Journal of the International Benchrest Shooters, and target shooting in general. Also considerable coverage of varmint shooting, as well as big bore, small bore, schuetzen, lead bullet, wildcats and precision reloading.

Rifle*
Wolfe Publishing Co., 6471 Airpark Dr., Prescott, AZ 86301/520-445-7810; Fax: 520-778-5124. $19.00 yr. The sporting firearms journal.

Rifle's Hunting Annual
Wolfe Publishing Co., 6471 Airpark Dr., Prescott, AZ 86301/520-445-7810; Fax: 520-778-5124. $4.99 Annual. Dedicated to the finest pursuit of the hunt.

Rod & Rifle Magazine
Lithographic Serv. Ltd., P.O. Box 38-138, Wellington, New Zealand. $50.00 yr. (6 issues). Hunting, shooting and fishing articles.

Safari* (M)
Safari Magazine, 4800 W. Gates Pass Rd., Tucson, AZ 85745/602-620-1220. $55.00 (6 times). The journal of big game hunting, published by Safari Club International. Also publish *Safari Times*, a monthly newspaper, included in price of $55.00 national membership.

Second Amendment Reporter
Second Amendment Foundation, James Madison Bldg., 12500 NE 10th Pl., Bellevue, WA 98005. $15.00 yr. (non-contributors).

Shooter's News
23146 Lorain Rd., Box 349, North Olmsted, OH 44070/216-979-5258;Fax:216-979-5259. $29 U.S. 1 yr., $54 2 yrs.; $52 foreign surface. A journal dedicated to precision riflery.

Shooting Industry
Publisher's Dev. Corp., 591 Camino de la Reina, Suite 200, San Diego, CA 92108. $50.00 yr. To the trade. $25.00.

Periodical Publications

Shooting Sports USA
National Rifle Assn. of America, 11250 Waples Mill Road, Fairfax, VA 22030. Annual subscriptions for NRA members are $5 for classified shooters and $10 for non-classified shooters. Non-NRA member subscriptions are $15. Covering events, techniques and personalities in competitive shooting.

Shooting Sportsman*
P.O. Box 11282, Des Moines, IA 50340/800-666-4955 (for subscriptions). Editorial: P.O. Box 1357, Camden, ME 04843. $19.95 for six issues. The magazine of wingshooting and fine guns.

The Shooting Times & Country Magazine (England)†
IPC Magazines Ltd., King's Reach Tower, Stamford St, 1 London SE1 9LS, England/0171-261-6180;Fax:0171-261-7179. £65 (approx. $98.00) yr.; £79 yr. overseas (52 issues). Game shooting, wild fowling, hunting, game fishing and firearms articles. Britain's best selling field sports magazine.

Shooting Times
Primedia, News Plaza, P.O. Box 1790, Peoria, IL 61656/309-682-6626. $16.97 yr. Guns, shooting, reloading; articles on every gun activity.

The Shotgun News‡
Primedia, News Plaza, P.O. Box 1790, Peoria, IL 61656/800-495-8362. $28.95 yr.; foreign subscription call for rates. Sample copy $4.00. Gun ads of all kinds.

SHOT Business
Flintlock Ridge Office Center, 11 Mile Hill Rd., Newtown, CT 06470-2359/203-426-1320; FAX: 203-426-1087. For the shooting, hunting and outdoor trade retailer.

Shotgun Sports
P.O. Box 6810, Auburn, CA 95604/916-889-2220; FAX:916-889-9106. $31.00 yr. Trapshooting how-to's, shotshell reloading, shotgun patterning, shotgun tests and evaluations, Sporting Clays action, waterfowl/upland hunting. Call 1-800-676-8920 for a free sample copy.

The Sixgunner (M)
Handgun Hunters International, P.O. Box 357, MAG, Bloomingdale, OH 43910

The Skeet Shooting Review
National Skeet Shooting Assn., 5931 Roft Rd., San Antonio, TX 78253. $20.00 yr. (Assn. membership includes mag.) Competition results, personality profiles of top Skeet shooters, how-to articles, technical, reloading information.

Soldier of Fortune
Subscription Dept., P.O. Box 348, Mt. Morris, IL 61054. $29.95 yr.; $39.95 Canada; $50.95 foreign.

Sporting Clays Magazine
Patch Communications, 5211 South Washington Ave., Titusville, FL 32780/407-268-5010; FAX: 407-267-7216. $29.95 yr. (12 issues). Official publication of the National Sporting Clays Association.

Sporting Goods Business
Miller Freeman, Inc., One Penn Plaza, 10th Fl., New York, NY 10119-0004. Trade journal.

Sporting Goods Dealer
Two Park Ave., New York, NY 10016. $100.00 yr. Sporting goods trade journal.

Sporting Gun
Bretton Court, Bretton, Peterborough PE3 8DZ, England. £27.00 (approx. U.S. $36.00), airmail £35.50 yr. For the game and clay enthusiasts.

Sports Afield
11650 Riverside Drive, North Hollywood, CA 91602-1066/818-904-9981.

The Squirrel Hunter
P.O. Box 368, Chireno, TX 75937. $14.00 yr. Articles about squirrel hunting.

Stott's Creek Calendar
Stott's Creek Printers, 2526 S 475 W, Morgantown, IN 46160/317-878-5489. 1 yr (3 issues) $11.50; 2 yrs. (6 issues) $20.00. Lists all gun shows everywhere in convenient calendar form; call for information.

Super Outdoors
2695 Aiken Road, Shelbyville, KY 40065/502-722-9463; 800-404-6064; Fax: 502-722-8093. Mark Edwards, publisher. Contact for details.

TACARMI
Via E. De Amicis, 25; 20123 Milano, Italy. $100.00 yr. approx. Antique and modern guns. (Italian text.)

Territorial Dispatch—1800s Historical Publication (M)
National Assn. of Buckskinners, 4701 Marion St., Suite 324, Livestock Exchange Bldg., Denver, CO 80216. Michael A. Nester & Barbara Wyckoff, editors. 303-297-9671.

Trap & Field
1000 Waterway Blvd., Indianapolis, IN 46202. $25.00 yr. Official publ. Amateur Trapshooting Assn. Scores, averages, trapshooting articles.

Turkey Call* (M)
Natl. Wild Turkey Federation, Inc., P.O. Box 530, Edgefield, SC 29824. $25.00 with membership (6 issues per yr.)

Turkey & Turkey Hunting*
Krause Publications, 700 E. State St., Iola, WI 54990-0001. $13.95 (6 issue p. yr.). Magazine with leading-edge articles on all aspects of wild turkey behavior, biology and the successful ways to hunt better with that info. Learn the proper techniques to calling, the right equipment, and more.

The U.S. Handgunner* (M)
U.S. Revolver Assn., 40 Larchmont Ave., Taunton, MA 02780. $10.00 yr. General handgun and competition articles. Bi-monthly sent to members.

U.S. Airgun Magazine
P.O. Box 2021, Benton, AR 72018/800-247-4867; Fax: 501-316-8549. 10 issues a yr. Cover the sport from hunting, 10-meter, field target and collecting. Write for details.

The Varmint Hunter Magazine (Q)
The Varmint Hunters Assn., Box 759, Pierre, SD 57501/800-528-4868. $24.00 yr.

Waffenmarkt-Intern
GFI-Verlag, Theodor-Heuss Ring 62, 50668 K"ln, Germany. Only for gunsmiths, licensed firearms dealers and their suppliers in Germany, Austria and Switzerland.

Wild Sheep (M) (Q)
Foundation for North American Wild Sheep, 720 Allen Ave., Cody, WY 82414. Website: http://iigi.com/os/non/fnaws/fnaws.htm; e-mail: fnaws@wyoming.com. Official journal of the foundation.

Wisconsin Outdoor Journal
Krause Publications, 700 E. State St., Iola, WI 54990-0001. $17.97 yr. (8 issues). For Wisconsin's avid hunters and fishermen, with features from all over that state with regional reports, legislative updates, etc. Website: www.krause.com

Women & Guns
P.O. Box 488, Sta. C, Buffalo, NY 14209. $24.00 yr. U.S.; $72.00 foreign (12 issues). Only magazine edited by and for women gun owners.

World War II*
Cowles History Group, 741 Miller Dr. SE, Suite D-2, Leesburg, VA 20175-8920. Annual subscriptions $19.95 U.S.; $25.95 Canada; 43.95 foreign. The title says it—WWII; good articles, ads, etc.

---

*Published bi-monthly
† Published weekly
‡Published three times per month. All others are published monthly.

THE ARMS LIBRARY

FOR COLLECTOR ◆ HUNTER ◆ SHOOTER ◆ OUTDOORSMAN

IMPORTANT NOTICE TO BOOK BUYERS

Books listed here may be bought from Ray Riling Arms Books Co., 6844 Gorsten St., P.O. Box 18925, Philadelphia, PA 19119, Phone 215/438-2456; FAX: 215-438-5395. E-Mail: sales@rayrilingarmsbooks.com. Joe Riling is the researcher and compiler of "The Arms Library" and a seller of gun books for over 32 years. The Riling stock includes books classic and modern, many hard-to-find items, and many not obtainable elsewhere. These pages list a portion of the current stock. They offer prompt, complete service, with delayed shipments occurring only on out-of-print or out-of-stock books.

Visit our web site at **www.rayrilingarmsbooks.com** and order all of your favorite titles on line from our secure site.

NOTICE FOR ALL CUSTOMERS: Remittance in U.S. funds must accompany all orders. For your convenience we now accept VISA, MasterCard & American Express. For shipments in the U.S. add $7.00 for the 1st book and $2.00 for each additional book for postage and insurance. Minimum order $10.00. International Orders add $13.00 for the 1st book and $5.00 for each additional book. All International orders are shipped at the buyer's risk unless an additional $5 for insurance is included. USPS does not offer insurance to all countries unless shipped Air-Mail please e-mail or call for pricing.

Payments in excess of order or for "Backorders" are credited or fully refunded at request. Books "As-Ordered" are not returnable except by permission and a handling charge on these of 10% or $2.00 per book which ever is greater is deducted from refund or credit. Only Pennsylvania customers must include current sales tax.

A full variety of arms books also available from Rutgers Book Center, 127 Raritan Ave., Highland Park, NJ 08904/908-545-4344; FAX: 908-545-6686 or I.D.S.A. Books, 1324 Stratford Drive, Piqua, OH 45356/937-773-4203; FAX: 937-778-1922.

BALLISTICS AND HANDLOADING

ABC's of Reloading, 6th Edition, by C. Rodney James and the editors of Handloader's Digest, DBI Books, a division of Krause Publications, Iola, WI, 1997. 288 pp., illus. Paper covers. $21.95
The definitive guide to every facet of cartridge and shotshell reloading.

Accurate Arms Loading Guide Number 2, by Accurate Arms. McEwen, TN: Accurate Arms Company, Inc., 2000. Paper Covers. $18.95
Includes new data on smokeless powders XMR4064 and XMP5744 as well as a special section on Cowboy Action Shooting. The new manual includes 50 new pages of data. An appendix includes nominal rotor charge weights, bullet diameters.

The American Cartridge, by Charles Suydam, Borden Publishing Co. Alhambra, CA, 1986. 184 pp., illus. $24.95
An illustrated study of the rimfire cartridge in the United States.

Ammo and Ballistics, by Robert W. Forker, Safari Press, Inc., Huntington Beach, CA., 1999. 252 pp., illustrated. Paper covers. $18.95
Ballistic data on 125 calibers and 1,400 loads out to 500 yards.

Ammunition: Grenades and Projectile Munitions, by Ian V. Hogg, Stackpole Books, Mechanicsburg, PA, 1998. 144 pp., illus. $22.95
Concise guide to modern ammunition. International coverage with detailed specifications and illustrations.

Barnes Reloading Manual #2, Barnes Bullets, American Fork, UT, 1999. 668 pp., illus. $24.95
Features data and trajectories on the new weight X, XBT and Solids in calibers from .22 to .50 BMG.

Big Bore Rifles And Cartridges, Wolfe Publishing Co., Prescott, AZ, 1991. Paper covers. $26.00
This book covers cartridges from 8mm to .600 Nitro with loading tables.

Black Powder Guide, 2nd Edition, by George C. Nonte, Jr., Stoeger Publishing Co., So. Hackensack, NJ, 1991. 288 pp., illus. Paper covers. $14.95
How-to instructions for selection, repair and maintenance of muzzleloaders, making your own bullets, restoring and refinishing, shooting techniques.

Blackpowder Loading Manual, 3rd Edition, by Sam Fadala, DBI Books, a division of Krause Publications, Iola, WI, 1995. 368 pp., illus. Paper covers. $20.95
Revised and expanded edition of this landmark blackpowder loading book. Covers hundreds of loads for most of the popular blackpowder rifles, handguns and shotguns.

Cartridges of the World, 9th Edition, by Frank Barnes, Krause Publications, Iola, WI, 2000. 512 pp., illus. Paper covers. $27.95
Completely revised edition of the general purpose reference work for which collectors, police, scientists and laymen reach first for answers to cartridge identification questions.

Cartridge Reloading Tools of the Past, by R.H. Chamberlain and Tom Quigley, Tom Quigley, Castle Rock, WA, 1998. 167 pp., illustrated. Paper covers. $25.00
A detailed treatment of the extensive Winchester and Ideal line of handloading tools and bullet molds, plus Remington, Marlin, Ballard, Browning, Maynard, and many others.

Cast Bullets for the Black Powder Rifle, by Paul A. Matthews, Wolfe Publishing Co., Prescott, AZ, 1996. 133 pp., illus. Paper covers. $22.50
The tools and techniques used to make your cast bullet shooting a success.

Complete Blackpowder Handbook, 3rd Edition, by Sam Fadala, DBI Books, a division of Krause Publications, Iola, WI, 1997. 400 pp., illus. Paper covers. $21.95
Expanded and completely rewritten edition of the definitive book on the subject of blackpowder.

Complete Reloading Guide, by Robert & John Traister, Stoeger Publishing Co., Wayne, NJ, 1997. 608 pp., illus. Paper covers. $34.95
Perhaps the finest, most comprehensive work ever published on the subject of reloading.

Complete Reloading Manual, One Book / One Caliber. California: Load Books USA, 2000. $7.95 Each
Containing unabridged information from U. S. Bullet and Powder Makers. With thousands of proven and tested loads, plus dozens of various bullet designs and different powders. Spiral bound. Available in all Calibers.

Early Loading Tools & Bullet Molds, Pioneer Press, 1988. 88 pages, illustrated. Softcover. $7.50

European Sporting Cartridges: Volume 1, by Brad Dixon, Seattle, WA: Armory Publications, 1997. 1st edition. 250 pp., Illus. $60.00
Photographs and drawings of over 550 centerfire cartridge case types in 1,300 illustrations produced in Germany and Austria from 1875-1995.

European Sporting Cartridges: Volume 2, by Brad Dixon, Seattle, WA: Armory Publications, 2000. 1st edition. 240 pages. $60.00
An illustrated history of centerfire hunting and target cartridges produced in Czechoslovakia, Switzerland, Norway, Sweden, Finland, Russia, Italy, Denmark, Belguim from 1875 to 1998. Adds 50 specimens to volume 1, Germany-Austria. Also, illustrates 40 small arms magazine experiments during the late 19th Century, and includes the English-Language export ammunition catalogue of Kovo (Povaszke Strojarne), Prague, Czeck. from the 1930's.

Game Loads and Practical Ballistics for the American Hunter, by Bob Hagel, Wolfe Publishing Co., Prescott, AZ, 1992. 310 pp., illus. $27.90
Hagel's knowledge gained as a hunter, guide and gun enthusiast is gathered in this informative text.

German 7.9MM Military Ammunition 1888-1945, by Daniel Kent, Ann Arbor, MI: Kent, 1990. 153 pp., plus appendix. illus., b&w photos. $35.00

Handbook for Shooters and Reloaders, by P.O. Ackley, Salt Lake City, UT, 1998, (Vol. I), 567 pp., illus. Includes a separate exterior ballistics chart. $21.95 (Vol. II), a new printing with specific new material. 495 pp., illus. $20.95

Handgun Muzzle Flash Tests: How Police Cartridges Compare, by Robert Olsen, Paladin Press, Boulder, CO.Fully illustrated. 133 pages. Softcover. $20.00
Tests dozens of pistols and revolvers for the brightness of muzzle flash, a critical factor in the safety of law enforcement personnel.

Handgun Stopping Power; The Definitive Study, by Marshall & Sandow. Boulder, CO: Paladin Press, 1992. 240 pages. $45.00
Offers accurate predictions of the stopping power of specific loads in calibers from .380 Auto to .45 ACP, as well as such specialty rounds as the Glaser Safety Slug, Federal Hydra-Shok, MagSafe, etc. This is the definitive methodology for predicting the stopping power of handgun loads, the first to take into account what really happens when a bullet meets a man.

Handloader's Digest, 17th Edition, edited by Bob Bell. DBI Books, a division of Krause Publications, Iola, WI, 1997. 480 pp., illustrated. Paper covers. $27.95
Top writers in the field contribute helpful information on techniques and components. Greatly expanded and fully indexed catalog of all currently available tools, accessories and components for metallic, blackpowder cartridge, shotgun reloading and swaging.

Handloader's Manual of Cartridge Conversions, by John J. Donnelly, Stoeger Publishing Co., So. Hackensack, NJ, 1986. Unpaginated. $39.95
From 14 Jones to 70-150 Winchester in English and American cartridges, and from 4.85 U.K. to 15.2x28R Gevelot in metric cartridges. Over 900 cartridges described in detail.

Hatcher's Notebook, by S. Julian Hatcher, Stackpole Books, Harrisburg, PA, 1992. 488 pp., illus. $39.95
A reference work for shooters, gunsmiths, ballisticians, historians, hunters and collectors.

The Arms Library

History and Development of Small Arms Ammunition; Volume 2 Centerfire: Primitive, and Martial Long Arms. by George A. Hoyem. Oceanside, CA: Armory Publications, 1991. 303 pages, illustrated. $60.00

Covers the blackpowder military centerfire rifle, carbine, machine gun and volley gun ammunition used in 28 nations and dominions, together with the firearms that chambered them.

History and Development of Small Arms Ammunition; Volume 4, American Military Rifle Cartridges. Oceanside, CA: Armory Publications, 1998. 244pp., illus. $60.00

Carries on what Vol. 2 began with American military rifle cartridges. Now the sporting rifle cartridges are at last organized by their originators-235 individual case types designed by eight makers of single shot rifles and four of magazine rifles from .50-140 Winchester Express to .22-15-60 Stevens. plus experimentals from .70-150 to .32-80. American Civil War enthusiasts and European collectors will find over 150 primitives in Appendix A to add to those in Volumes One and Two. There are 16 pages in full color of 54 box labels for Sharps, Remington and Ballard cartridges. There are large photographs with descriptions of 15 Maynard, Sharps, Winchester, Browning, Freund, Remington-Hepburn, Farrow and other single shot rifles, some of them rare one of a kind specimens.

Hodgdon Powder Data Manual #27, Hodgdon Powder Co., Shawnee Mission, KS, 1999. 800 pp. $27.95

Reloading data for rifle and pistol loads.

Hodgdon Shotshell Data Manual, Hodgdon Powder Co., Shawnee Mission, KS, 1999. 208 pp. $19.95

Contains hundreds of loads for lead shot, buck shot, slugs, bismuth shot and steel shot plus articles on ballistics, patterning, special reloads and much more.

Home Guide to Cartridge Conversions, by Maj. George C. Nonte Jr., The Gun Room Press, Highland Park, NJ, 1976. 404 pp., illus. $24.95

Revised and updated version of Nonte's definitive work on the alteration of cartridge cases for use in guns for which they were not intended.

Hornady Handbook of Cartridge Reloading, 5th Edition, Vol. I and II, Edited by Larry Steadman, Hornady Mfg. Co., Grand Island, NE, 2000., illus. $49.95

2 Volumes; Volume 1, 773 pp.; Volume 2, 717 pp. New edition of this famous reloading handbook covers rifle and handgun reloading data and ballistic tables. Latest loads, ballistic information, etc.

How-To's for the Black Powder Cartridge Rifle Shooter, by Paul A. Matthews, Wolfe Publishing Co., Prescott, AZ, 1995. 45 pp. Paper covers. $22.50

Covers lube recipes, good bore cleaners and over-powder wads. Tips include compressing powder charges, combating wind resistance, improving ignition and much more.

The Illustrated Reference of Cartridge Dimensions, edited by Dave Scovill, Wolfe Publishing Co., Prescott, AZ, 1994. 343 pp., illus. Paper covers. $19.00

A comprehensive volume with over 300 cartridges. Standard and metric dimensions have been taken from SAAMI drawings and/or fired cartridges.

Kynock, by Dale J. Hedlund, Armory Publications, Seattle, WA, 2000. 130 pages, illus. 9" x 12" with four color dust jacket. $59.95

A comprehensive review of Kynoch shotgun cartridges covering over 50 brand names and case types, and over 250 Kynoch shotgun cartridge headstamps. Additional information on Kynoch metallic ammunition including the identity of the mysterious .434 Seelun.

Lee Modern Reloading, by Richard Lee, 350 pp. of charts and data and 85 illustrations. 512 pp. $24.95

Bullet casting, lubricating and author's formula for calculating proper charges for cast bullets. Includes virtually all current load data published by the powder suppliers. Exclusive source of volume measured loads.

Loading the Black Powder Rifle Cartridge, by Paul A Matthews, Wolfe Publishing Co., Prescott, AZ, 1993. 121 pp., illus. Paper covers. $22.50

Author Matthews brings the blackpowder cartridge shooter valuable information on the basics, including cartridge care, lubes and moulds, powder charges and developing and testing loads in his usual authoritative style.

Loading the Peacemaker—Colt's Model P, by Dave Scovill, Wolfe Publishing Co., Prescott, AZ, 1996. 227 pp., illus. $24.95

A comprehensive work about the history, maintenance and repair of the most famous revolver ever made, including the most extensive load data ever published.

Lyman Cast Bullet Handbook, 3rd Edition, edited by C. Kenneth Ramage, Lyman Publications, Middlefield, CT, 1980. 416 pp., illus. Paper covers. $19.95

Information on more than 5000 tested cast bullet loads and 19 pages of trajectory and wind drift tables for cast bullets.

Lyman Black Powder Handbook, edited by C. Kenneth Ramage, Lyman Products for Shooters, Middlefield, CT, 1975. 239 pp., illus. Paper covers. $14.95

Comprehensive load information for the modern blackpowder shooter.

Lyman Pistol & Revolver Handbook, 2nd Edition, edited by Thomas J. Griffin, Lyman Products Co., Middlefield, CT, 1996. 287 pp., illus. Paper covers. $18.95

The most up-to-date loading data available including the hottest new calibers, like 40 S&W, 9x21, 9mm Makarov, 9x25 Dillon and 454 Casull.

Lyman Reloading Handbook No. 47, edited by Edward A. Matunas, Lyman Publications, Middlefield, CT, 1992. 480 pp., illus. Paper covers. $24.95

A comprehensive reloading manual complete with "How to Reload" information. Expanded data section with all the newest rifle and pistol calibers.

Lyman Shotshell Handbook, 4th Edition, edited by Edward A. Matunas, Lyman Products Co., Middlefield, CT, 1996. 330 pp., illus. Paper covers. $24.95

Has 9000 loads, including slugs and buckshot, plus feature articles and a full color I.D. section.

Lyman's Guide to Big Game Cartridges & Rifles, by Edward Matunas, Lyman Publishing Corporation, Middlefield, CT, 1994. 287 pp., illus. Paper covers. $17.95

A selection guide to cartridges and rifles for big game—antelope to elephant.

Making Loading Dies and Bullet Molds, by Harold Hoffman, H & P Publishing, San Angelo, TX, 1993. 230 pp., illus. Paper covers. $24.95

A good book for learning tool and die making.

Metallic Cartridge Reloading, 3rd Edition, by M.L. McPherson, DBI Books, a division of Krause Publications, Iola, WI., 1996. 352 pp., illus. Paper covers. $21.95

A true reloading manual with over 10,000 loads for all popular metallic cartridges and a wealth of invaluable technical data provided by a recognized expert.

Military Rifle and Machine Gun Cartridges, by Jean Huon, Alexandria, VA: Ironside International, 1995. 1st edition. 378 pages, over 1,000 photos. $34.95

Superb reference text.

Modern Combat Ammunition, by Duncan Long, Paladin Press, Boulder, CO, 1997, soft cover, photos, illus., 216 pp. $34.00

Now, Paladin's leading weapons author presents his exhaustive evaluation of the stopping power of modern rifle, pistol, shotgun and machine gun rounds based on actual case studies of shooting incidents. He looks at the hot new cartridges that promise to dominate well into the next century .40 S&W, 10mm auto, sub-sonic 9mm's - as well as the trusted standbys. Find out how to make your own exotic tracers, fléchette and sabot rounds, caseless ammo and fragmenting bullets.

Modern Exterior Ballistics, by Robert L. McCoy, Schiffer Publishing Co., Atglen, PA, 1999. 128 pp. $95.00

Advanced students of exterior ballistics and flight dynamics will find this comprehensive textbook on the subject a useful addition to their libraries.

Modern Handloading, by Maj. Geo. C. Nonte, Winchester Press, Piscataway, NJ, 1972. 416 pp., illus. $15.00

Covers all aspects of metallic and shotshell ammunition loading, plus more loads than any book in print.

Modern Reloading, by Richard Lee, Inland Press, 1996. 510 pp., illus. $24.98

The how-to's of rifle, pistol and shotgun reloading plus load data for rifle and pistol calibers.

Modern Sporting Rifle Cartridges, by Wayne van Zwoll, Stoeger Publishing Co., Wayne, NJ, 1998. 310 pp., illustrated. Paper covers. $21.95

Illustrated with hundreds of photos and backed up by dozens of tables and schematic drawings, this four-part book tells the story of how rifle bullets and cartridges were developed and, in some cases, discarded.

Modern Practical Ballistics, by Art Pejsa, Pejsa Ballistics, Minneapolis, MN, 1990. 150 pp., illus. $29.95

Covers all aspects of ballistics and new, simplified methods. Clear examples illustrate new, easy but very accurate formulas.

Mr. Single Shot's Cartridge Handbook, by Frank de Haas, Mark de Haas, Orange City, IA, 1996. 116 pp., illus. Paper covers. $21.50

This book covers most of the cartridges, both commercial and wildcat, that the author has known and used.

Nick Harvey's Practical Reloading Manual, by Nick Harvey, Australian Print Group, Maryborough, Victoria, Australia, 1995. 235 pp., illus. Paper covers. $24.95

Contains data for rifle and handgun including many popular wildcat and improved cartridges. Tools, powders, components and techniques for assembling optimum reloads with particular application to North America.

Nosler Reloading Manual #4, edited by Gail Root, Nosler Bullets, Inc., Bend, OR, 1996. 516 pp., illus. $26.99

Combines information on their Ballistic Tip, Partition and Handgun bullets with traditional powders and new powders never before used, plus trajectory information from 100 to 500 yards.

The Paper Jacket, by Paul Matthews, Wolfe Publishing Co., Prescott, AZ, 1991. Paper covers. $13.50

Up-to-date and accurate information about paper-patched bullets.

Reloading Tools, Sights and Telescopes for S/S Rifles, by Gerald O. Kelver, Brighton, CO, 1982. 163 pp., illus. Softcover. $15.00

A listing of most of the famous makers of reloading tools, sights and telescopes with a brief description of the products they manufactured.

Reloading for Shotgunners, 4th Edition, by Kurt D. Fackler and M.L. McPherson, DBI Books, a division of Krause Publications, Iola, WI, 1997. 320 pp., illus. Paper covers. $19.95

Expanded reloading tables with over 11,000 loads. Bushing charts for every major press and component maker. All new presentation on all aspects of shotshell reloading by two of the top experts in the field.

The Rimfire Cartridge in the United States and Canada, Illustrated history of rimfire cartridges, manufacturers, and the products made from 1857-1984. by John L. Barber, Thomas Publications, Gettysburg, PA 2000. 1st edition. Profusely illustrated. 221 pages. $50.00

The author has written an encyclopedia of rimfire cartridges from the .22 to the massive 1.00 in. Gatling. Fourteen chapters, six appendices and an excellent bibliography make up a reference volume that all cartridge collectors should aquire.

Sierra 50th Anniversary, 4th Edition Rifle Manual, edited by Ken Ramage, Sierra Bullets, Santa Fe Springs, CA, 1997. 800 pp., illus. $26.99

New cartridge introductions, etc.

Sierra 50th Anniversary, 4th Edition Handgun Manual, edited by Ken Ramage, Sierra Bullets, Santa Fe, CA, 1997. 700 pp., illus. $21.99

Histories, reloading recommendations, bullets, powders and sections on the reloading process, etc.

THE ARMS LIBRARY

Sixgun Cartridges and Loads, by Elmer Keith, The Gun Room Press, Highland Park, NJ, 1986. 151 pp., illus. $24.95

A manual covering the selection, uses and loading of the most suitable and popular revolver cartridges. Originally published in 1936. Reprint.

Speer Reloading Manual No. 13, edited by members of the Speer research staff, Omark Industries, Lewiston, ID, 1999. 621 pp., illustrated. $24.95

With thirteen new sections containing the latest technical information and reloading trends for both novice and expert in this latest edition. More than 9,300 loads are listed, including new propellant powders from Accurate Arms, Alliant, Hodgdon and Vihtavuori.

Street Stoppers, The Latest Handgun Stopping Power Street Results, by Marshall & Lanow. Boulder, CO, Paladin Press, 1996. 374 pages, illus. Softcover. $42.95

Street Stoppers is the long-awaited sequel to Handgun Stopping Power. It provides the latest results of real-life shootings in all of the major handgun calibers, plus more than 25 thought-provoking chapters that are vital to anyone interested in firearms, would ballistics, and combat shooting. This book also covers the street results of the hottest new caliber to hit the shooting world in years, the .40 Smith & Wesson. Updated street results of the latest exotic ammunition including Remington Golden Saber and CCI-Speer Gold Dot, plus the venerable offerings from MagSafe, Glaser, Cor-Bon and others. A fascinating look at the development of Hydra-Shok ammunition is included.

Understanding Ballistics, Revised 2nd Edition by Robert A. Rinker, Mulberry House Publishing Co., Corydon, IN, 2000. 430 pp., illus Paper covers. New, Revised and Expanded. 2nd Edition. $24.95

Explains basic to advanced firearm ballistics in understandable terms.

Why Not Load Your Own?, by Col. T. Whelen, Gun Room Press, Highland Park, NJ 1996, 4th ed., rev. 237 pp., illus. $20.00

A basic reference on handloading, describing each step, materials and equipment. Includes loads for popular cartridges.

Wildcat Cartridges Volumes 1 & 2 Combination, by the editors of Handloaders magazine, Wolfe Publishing Co., Prescott, AZ, 1997. 350 pp., illus. Paper covers. $39.95

A profile of the most popular information on wildcat cartridges that appeared in the Handloader magazine.

COLLECTORS

A Glossary of the Construction, Decoration and Use of Arms and Armor in All Countries and in All Times. By George Cameron Stone., Dover Publishing, New York 1999. Softcover. $39.95

An exhaustive study of arms and armor in all countries through recorded history - from the stone age up to the second world war. With over 4500 Black & White Illustrations. This Dover edition is an unabridged republication of the work originally published in 1934 by the Southworth Press, Portland MA. A new Introduction has been specially prepared for this edition.

Accoutrements of the United States Infantry, Riflemen, and Dragoons 1834-1839. by R.T. Huntington, Historical Arms Series No. 20. Canada: Museum Restoration. 58 pp. illus. Softcover. $8.95

Although the 1841 edition of the U.S. Ordnance Manual provides ample information on the equipment that was in use during the 1840s, it is evident that the patterns of equipment that it describes were not introduced until 1838 or 1839. This guide is intended to fill this gap in our knowledge by providing an overview of what we now know about the accoutrements that were issued to the regular infantryman, rifleman, and dragoon, in the 1830's with excursions into earlier and later years.

Age of the Gunfighter; Men and Weapons on the Frontier 1840-1900, by Joseph G. Rosa, University of Oklahoma Press, Norman, OK, 1999. 192 pp., illustrated. Paper covers. $21.95

Stories of gunfighters and their encounters and detailed descriptions of virtually every firearm used in the old West.

Air Guns, by Eldon G. Wolff, Duckett's Publishing Co., Tempe, AZ, 1997. 204 pp., illus Paper covers. $35.00

Historical reference covering many makers, European and American guns, canes and more.

Allied and Enemy Aircraft: May 1918; Not to be Taken from the Front Lines, Historical Arms Series No. 27. Canada: Museum Restoration. Softcover. $8.95

The basis for this title is a very rare identification manual published by the French government in 1918 that illustrated 60 aircraft with three or more views: French, English American, German, Italian, and Belgian, which might have been seen over the trenches ofFrance. Each is describe in a text translated from the original French. This is probably the most complete collection of illustrations of WW1 aircraft which has survived.

American Beauty; The Prewar Colt National Match Government Model Pistol, by Timothy J. Mullin, Collector Grade Publications, Cobourg, Ontario, Canada. 72 pp., illustrated. $34.95

Includes over 150 serial numbers, and 20 spectacular color photos of factory engraved guns and other authenticated upgrades, including rare "double-carved" ivory grips.

The American Military Saddle, 1776-1945, by R. Stephen Dorsey & Kenneth L. McPheeters, Collector's Library, Eugene, OR, 1999. 400 pp., illustrated. $59.95

The most complete coverage of the subject ever writeen on the American Military Saddle. Nearly 1000 actual photos and official drawings, from the major public and private collections in the U.S. and Great Britain.

American Police Collectibles; Dark Lanterns and Other Curious Devices, by Matthew G. Forte, Turn of the Century Publishers, Upper Montclair, NJ, 1999. 248 pp., illustrated. $24.95

For collectors of police memorabilia (handcuffs, police dark lanterns, mechanical and chain nippers, rattles, billy clubs and nightsticks) and police historians.

Ammunition; Small Arms, Grenades, and Projected Munitions, by Greenhill Publishing. 144 pp., Illustrated. $22.95 The best concise guide to modern ammunition available today. Covers ammo for small arms, grenades, and projected munitions. 144 pp., Illustrated. As NEW – Hardcover.

Antique Guns, the Collector's Guide, 2nd Edition, edited by John Traister, Stoeger Publishing Co., So. Hackensack, NJ, 1994. 320 pp., illus. Paper covers. $19.95

Covers a vast spectrum of pre-1900 firearms: those manufactured by U.S. gunmakers as well as Canadian, French, German, Belgian, Spanish and other foreign firms.

Arming the Glorious Cause; Weapons of the Second War for Independence, by James B. Whisker, Daniel D. Hartzler and Larry W. Tantz, Old Bedford Village Press, Bedford, PA., 1998. 175 pp., illustrated. $45.00

A photographic study of Confederate weapons.

Arms & Accoutrements of the Mounted Police 1873-1973, by Roger F. Phillips and Donald J. Klancher, Museum Restoration Service, Ont., Canada, 1982. 224 pp., illus. $49.95

A definitive history of the revolvers, rifles, machine guns, cannons, ammunition, swords, etc. used by the NWMP, the RNWMP and the RCMP during the first 100 years of the Force.

Arms and Armor In Antiquity and The Middle Ages. By Charles Boutell, Combined Books Inc., PA 1996. 296 pp., w/ b/w illus. Also a descriptive Notice of Modern Weapons. Translated from the French of M.P. Lacombe, and with a preface, notes, and one additional chapter on Arms and Armour in England. $14.95

Arms and Armor in the Art Institute of Chicago. By Waltler J. Karcheski, Bulfinch, New York 1999. 128 pp., 103 color photos, 12 black & white illustrations. $50.00

The George F. Harding Collection of arms and armor is the most visited installation at the Art Institute of Chicago - a testament to the enduring appeal of swords, muskets and the other paraphernalia of medieval and early modern war. Organized both chronologically and by type of weapon, this book captures the best of this astonishing collection in 115 striking photographs - most in color - accompanied by illuminating text. Here are intricately filigreed breastplates and ivory-handled crossbows, samurai katana and Toledo-steel scimitars, elaborately decorated maces and beautifully carved flintlocks - a treat for anyone who has ever been beguiled by arms, armor and the age of chivalry.

Arms and Armor in Colonial America 1526-1783. by Harold Peterson, Dover Publishing, New York, 2000. 350 pages with over 300 illustrations, index, bibliography & appendix. Softcover. $29.95

Over 200 years of firearms, ammunition, equipment & edged weapons.

Arms and Armor: The Cleveland Museum of Art. By Stephen N. Fliegel, Abrams, New York, 1998. 172 color photos, 17 halftones. 181 pages. $49.50

Intense look at the culture of the warrior and hunter, with an intriguing discussion of the decorative arts found on weapons and armor, set against the background of political and social history. Also provides information on the evolution of armor, together with manufacture and decoration, and weapons as technology and art.

Arms and Equipment of the Civil War, by Jack Coggins, Barnes & Noble, Rockleight, N.J., 1999. 160 pp., illustrated. $12.98

This unique encyclopedia provides a new perspective on the war. It provides lively explanations of how ingenious new weapons spelled victory or defeat for both sides. Aided by more than 500 illustrations and on-the-scene comments by Union and Confederate soldiers.

Arms Makers of Colonial America, by James B. Whisker, Selinsgrove, PA:, 1992: Susquehanna University Press. 1st edition. 217 pages, illustrated. $45.00

A comprehensively documented historial survey of the broad spectrum of arms makers in America who were active before 1783.

Arms Makers of Maryland, by Daniel D. Hartzler, George Shumway, York, PA, 1975. 200 pp., illus. $50.00

A thorough study of the gunsmiths of Maryland who worked during the late 18th and early 19th centuries.

Arms Makers of Pennsylvania, by James B. Whisker, Selinsgrove, PA, Susquehanna Univ. Press, 1990. 1st edition. 218 pages, illustrated in black and white and color. $45.00

Concentrates primarily on the cottage industry gunsmiths & gun makers who worked in the Keystone State from it's early years through 1900.

Arms Makers of Western Pennsylvania, by James B. Whisker, Old Bedford Village Press. 1st edition. This deluxe hard bound edition has 176 pages, $45.00

Printed on fine coated paper, with many large photographs, and detailed text describing the period, lives, tools, and artistry of the Arms Makers of Western Pennsylvania.

Arsenal Of Freedom: The Springfield Armory 1890-1948, by Lt. Col. William Brophy, Andrew Mowbray, Inc., Lincoln, RI,1997. 20 pgs. of photos. 400 pages. As new - Softcover. $29.95

A year by year account drawn from offical records. Packed with reports, charts, tables, line drawings, and 20 page photo section.

Artistic Ingredients of the Longrifle, by George Shumway Publisher, 1989 102 pp., with 94 illus. $20.00

After a brief review of Pennsylvania-German folk art and architecture, to establish the artistic enviroment in which the longrifle was made, the author demonstrates that the sophisticated rococo decoration on the many of the finer longrifles is comparable to the best rococo work of Philadelphia cabinet makers and silversmiths.

The Art of Gun Engraving, by Claude Gaier and Pietro Sabatti, Knickerbocker Press, N.Y., 1999. 160 pp., illustrated. $34.95

The richness and detail lavished on early firearms represents a craftmanship nearly vanished. Beginning with crossbows in the 100's, hunting scenes, portraits, or mythological themes are intricately depicted within a few square inches of etched metal. The full-color photos contained herein recaptures this lost art with exquisite detail.

Astra Automatic Pistols, by Leonardo M. Antaris, FIRAC Publishing Co., Sterling, CO, 1989. 248 pp., illus. $55.00

Charts, tables, serial ranges, etc. The definitive work on Astra pistols.

Basic Documents on U.S. Martial Arms, commentary by Col. B. R. Lewis, reissue by Ray Riling, Phila., PA, 1956 and 1960. *Rifle Musket Model 1855.*

The first issue rifle of musket caliber, a muzzle loader equipped with the Maynard Primer, 32 pp. *Rifle Musket Model 1863.* The typical Union muzzle-loader of the Civil War, 26 pp. *Breech-Loading Rifle Musket Model 1866.* The first of our 50-caliber breechloading rifles, 12 pp. *Remington Navy Rifle Model 1870.* A commercial type breech-loader made at Springfield, 16 pp. *Lee Straight Pull Navy Rifle Model 1895.* A magazine cartridge arm of 6mm caliber. 23 pp. *Breech-Loading Arms* (five models) 27 pp. *Ward-Burton Rifle Musket 1871*-16 pp. Each $10.00.

Battle Weapons of the American Revolution, by George C. Neuman, Scurlock Publishing Co., Texarkana, TX, 2001. 400 pp. Illus. Softcovers. $34.95

The most extensive photographic collection of Revolutionary War weapons ever in one volume. More than 1,600 photos of over 500 muskets, rifles, swords, bayonets, knives and other arms used by both sides in America's War for Independence.

The Bedford County Rifle and Its Makers, by George Shumway. 40pp. illustrated, Softcover. $10.00

The authors study of the graceful and distinctive muzzle-loading rifles made in Bedford County, Pennsylvania. Stands as a milestone on the long path to the understanding of America's longrifles.

Behold the Longrifle Again, by James B. Whisker, Old Bedford Village Press, Bedford, PA, 1997. 176 pp., illus. $45.00

Excellent reference work for the collector profusely illustrated with photographs of some of the finest Kentucky rifles showing front and back profiles and overall view.

The Belgian Rattlesnake; The Lewis Automatic Machine Gun, by William M. Easterly, Collector Grade Publications, Cobourg, Ontario, Canada, 1998. 584 pp., illustrated. $79.95

The most complete account ever published on the life and times of Colonel Isaac Newton Lewis and his crowning invention, the Lewis Automatic machine gun.

Beretta Automatic Pistols, by J.B. Wood, Stackpole Books, Harrisburg, PA, 1985. 192 pp., illus. $24.95

Only English-language book devoted to the Beretta line. Includes all important models.

The Big Guns, Civil War Siege, Seacoast, and Naval Cannon, by Edwin Olmstead, Wayne E. Stark, and Spencer C. Tucker, Museum Restoration Service, Bloomfield, Ontario, Canada, 1997. 360 pp., illustrated. $80.00

This book is designed to identify and record the heavy guns available to both sides by the end of the Civil War.

Birmingham Gunmakers, by Douglas Tate, Safari Press, Inc., Huntington Beach, CA, 1997. 300 pp., illus. $50.00

An invaluable work for anybody interested in the fine sporting arms crafted in this famous British gunmakers' city.

Blue Book of Gun Values, 22nd Edition, edited by S.P. Fjestad, Blue Book Publications, Inc. Minneapolis, MN 2001. $34.95

This new 22nd Edition simply contains more firearms values and information than any other single publication. Expanded to over 1,600 pages featuring over 100,000 firearms prices, the new Blue Book of Gun Values also contains over million words of text – no other book is even close! Most of the information contained in this publication is simply not available anywhere else, for any price!

Blue Book of Modern Black Powder Values, by Dennis Adler, Blue Book Publications, Inc. Minneapolis, MN 2000. 200 pp., illustrated. 41 color photos. Softcover. $14.95

This new title contains more up-to-date black powder values and related information than any other single publication. With 120 pages, this new book will keep you up to date on modern black powder models and prices, including most makes & models introduced this year! .

The Blunderbuss 1500-1900, by James D. Forman, Historical Arms Series No. 32. Canada: Museum Restoration, 1994. An excellent and authoritative booklet giving tons of information on the Blunderbuss, a very neglected subject. 40 pages, illustrated. Softcover. $8.95

Boarders Away I: With Steel-Edged Weapons & Polearms, by William Gilkerson, Andrew Mowbray, Inc. Publishers, Lincoln, RI, 1993. 331 pages. $48.00

Contains the essential 24 page chapter 'War at Sea' which sets the historical and practical context for the arms discussed. Includeds chapters on, Early Naval Weapons, Boarding Axes, Cutlasses, Officers Fighting Swords and Dirks, and weapons at hand of Random Mayhem.

Boarders Away, Volume II: Firearms of the Age of Fighting Sail, by William Gilkerson, Andrew Mowbray, Inc. Publishers, Lincoln, RI, 1993. 331 pp., illus. $65.00

Covers the pistols, muskets, combustibles and small cannon used aboard American and European fighting ships, 1626-1826.

The Book of Colt Firearms, by R. L. Wilson, Blue Book Publications, Inc, Minneapolis, MN, 1993. 616 pp., illus. $158.00

A complete Colt library in a single volume. In over 1,250.000 words, over 1,250 black and white and 67 color photographs, this mammoth work tells the Colt story from 1832 throught the present.

Boothroyd's Revised Directory Of British Gunmakers, by Geoffrey Boothroyd, Long Beach, CA: Safari Press, 2000. Revised edition. 412pp, photos. $39.95

Over a 30 year period Geoffrey Boothroyd has accumulated information on just about every sporting gun maker that ever has existed in the British Isles from 1850 onward. In this magnificent reference work he has placed all the gun makers he has found over the years (over 1000 entries) in an alphabetical listing with as much information as he has been able to unearth. One of the best reference sources on all British makers (including Wales, Scotland and Ireland) in which you can find data on the most obscure as well as the most famous. Contains starting date of the business, addresses, proprietors, what they made and how long they operated with other interesting details for the collector of fine British guns.

Boston's Gun Bible, by Boston T. Party, Ignacio, CO: Javelin Press, August 2000. Expanded Edition.Softcover. $28.00

This mammoth guide for gun owners everywhere is a completely updated and expanded edition (more than 500 new pages!) of Boston T. Party's classic Boston on Guns and Courage. Pulling no punches, Boston gives new advice on which shoulder weapons and handguns to buy and why before exploring such topics as why you should consider not getting a concealed carry permit, what guns and gear will likely be outlawed next, how to spend within your budget, why you should go to a quality defensive shooting academy now, which guns and gadgets are inferior and why, how to stay off illegal government gun registration lists, how to spot an undercover agent trying to entrap law-abiding gun owners and much more.

Breech-Loading Carbines of the United States Civil War Period, by Brig. Gen. John Pitman, Armory Publications, Tacoma, WA, 1987. 94 pp., illus. $29.95

The first in a series of previously unpublished manuscripts originated by the late Brigadier General John Putnam. Exploded drawings showing parts actual size follow each sectioned illustration.

The Breech-Loading Single-Shot Rifle, by Major Ned H. Roberts and Kenneth L. Waters, Wolfe Publishing Co., Prescott, AZ, 1995. 333 pp., illus. $28.50

A comprehensive and complete history of the evolution of the Schutzen and single-shot rifle.

The Bren Gun Saga, by Thomas B. Dugelby, Collector Grade Publications, Cobourg, Ontario, Canada, 1999, revised and expanded edition. 406 pp., illustrated. $65.95

A modern, definitive book on the Bren in this revised expanded edition, which in terms of numbers of pages and illustrations is nearly twice the size of the original.

British Board of Ordnance Small Arms Contractors 1689-1840, by De Witt Bailey, Rhyl, England: W. S. Curtis, 2000. 150 pp. $18.00

Thirty years of research in the Archives of the Ordnance Board in London has identified more than 600 of these suppliers. The names of many can be found marking the regulation firearms of the period. In the study, the contractors are identified both alphabetically and under a combination of their date period together with their specialist trade.

The British Enfield Rifles, Volume 1, The SMLE Mk I and Mk III Rifles, by Charles R. Stratton, North Cape Pub. Tustin, CA, 1997. 150 pp., illus. Paper covers. $16.95

A systematic and thorough examination on a part-by-part basis of the famous British battle rifle that endured for nearly 70 years as the British Army's number one battle rifle.

British Enfield Rifles, Volume 2, No.4 and No.5 Rifles, by Charles R. Stratton, North Cape Publications, Tustin, CA, 1999. 150 pp., illustrated. Paper covers. $16.95

The historical background for the development of both rifles describing each variation and an explanation of all the "marks", "numbers" and codes found on most parts.

British Enfield Rifles, Volume 4, The Pattern 1914 and U. S. Model 1917 Rifles, by Charles R. Stratton, North Cape Publications, Tustin, CA, 2000. Paper covers. $16.95

One of the lease know American and British collectible military rifles is analyzed on a part by part basis. All markings and codes, refurbishment procedures and WW 2 upgrade are included as are the varios sniper rifle versions.

The British Falling Block Breechloading Rifle from 1865, by Jonathan Kirton, Tom Rowe Books, Maynardsville, TN, 2nd edition, 1997. 380 pp., illus. $70.00

Expanded 2nd edition of a comprehensive work on the British falling block rifle.

British Gun Engraving, by Douglas Tate, Safari Press, Inc., Huntington Beach, CA, 1999. 240 pp., illustrated. Limited, signed and numbered edition, in a slipcase. $80.00

A historic and photographic record of the last two centuries.

British Service Rifles and Carbines 1888-1900, by Alan M. Petrillo, Excaliber Publications, Latham, NY, 1994. 72 pp., illus, Paper covers. $11.95

A complete review of the Lee-Metford and Lee-Enfield rifles and carbines.

British Single Shot Rifles, Volume 1, Alexander Henry, by Wal Winfer, Tom Rowe, Maynardsville, TN, 1998, 200 pp., illus. $50.00

Detailed Study of the single shot rifles made by Henry. Illustrated with hundreds of photographs and drawings.

British Single Shot Rifles Volume 2, George Gibbs, by Wal Winfer, Tom Rowe, Maynardsville, TN, 1998. 177 pp., illus. $50.00

Detailed study of the Farquharson as made by Gibbs. Hundreds of photos.

THE ARMS LIBRARY

British Single Shot Rifles, Volume 3, Jeffery, by Wal Winfer, Rowe Publications, Rochester, N.Y., 1999. 260 pp., illustrated. $60.00

The Farquharsen as made by Jeffery and his competitors, Holland & Holland, Bland, Westley, Manton, etc. Large section on the development of nitro cartridges including the .600.

British Single Shot Rifles, Vol. 4; Westley Richards, by Wal Winfer, Rowe Publications, Rochester, N.Y., 2000. 265 pages, illustrated, photos. $60.00

In his 4th volume Winfer covers a detailed study of the Westley Richards single shot rifles, including Monkey Tails, Improved Martini, 1872,1873, 1878,1881, 1897 Falling Blocks. He also covers Westley Richards Cartridges, History and Reloading information.

British Small Arms Ammunition, 1864-1938 (Other than .303 inch), by Peter Labbett, Armory Publications, Seattle, WA. 1993, 358 pages, illus. Four-color dust jacket. $79.00

A study of British military rifle, handgun, machine gun, and aiming tube ammunition through 1 inch from 1864 to 1938. Photo-illustrated including the firearms that chambered the cartridges.

The British Soldier's Firearms from Smoothbore to Rifled Arms, 1850-1864, by Dr. C.H. Roads, R&R Books, Livonia, NY, 1994. 332 pp., illus. $49.00

A reprint of the classic text covering the development of British military hand and shoulder firearms in the crucial years between 1850 and 1864.

British Sporting Guns & Rifles, compiled by George Hoyem, Armory Publications, Coeur d'Alene, ID, 1997. 1024 pp., illus. In two volumes. $250.00

Eighteen old sporting firearms trade catalogs and a rare book reproduced with their color covers in a limited, signed and numbered edition.

Browning Dates of Manufacture, compiled by George Madis, Art and Reference House, Brownsboro, TX, 1989. 48 pp. $10.00

Gives the date codes and product codes for all models from 1824 to the present.

Browning Sporting Arms of Distinction 1903-1992, by Matt Eastman, Matt Eastman Publications, Fitzgerald, GA, 1995. 450 pp., illus. $49.95

The most recognized publication on Browning sporting arms; covers all models.

Buffalo Bill's Wild West: An American Legend, by R.L. Wilson and Greg Martine, Random House, N.Y., 1999. 3,167 pp., illustrated. $60.00

Over 225 color plates and 160 black-and-white illustrations, with in-depth text and captions, the colorful arms, posters, photos, costumes, saddles, accoutrement are brought to life.

Bullard Arms, by G. Scott Jamieson, The Boston Mills Press, Ontario, Canada, 1989. 244 pp., illus. $35.00

The story of a mechanical genius whose rifles and cartridges were the equal to any made in America in the 1880s.

Burning Powder, compiled by Major D.B. Wesson, Wolfe Publishing Company, Prescott, AZ, 1992. 110 pp. Soft cover. $10.95

A rare booklet from 1932 for Smith & Wesson collectors.

The Burnside Breech Loading Carbines, by Edward A. Hull, Andrew Mowbray, Inc., Lincoln, RI, 1986. 95 pp., illus. $16.00

No. 1 in the "Man at Arms Monograph Series." A model-by-model historical/technical examination of one of the most widely used cavalry weapons of the American Civil War based upon important and previously unpublished research.

Camouflage Uniforms of European and NATO Armies; 1945 to the Present, by J. F. Borsarello, Atglen, PA: Schiffer Publications. Over 290 color and b/w photographs, 120 pages. Softcover. $29.95

This full-color book covers nearly all of the NATO, and other European armies' camouflaged uniforms, and not only shows and explains the many patterns, but also their efficacy of design. Described and illustrated are the variety of materials tested in over forty different armies, and includes the history of obsolete trial tests from 1945 to the present time. More than two hundred patterns have been manufactured since World War II using various landscapes and seasonal colors for their look. The Vietnam and Gulf Wars, African or South American events, as well as recent Yugoslavian independence wars have been used as experimental terrains to test a variety of patterns. This book provides a superb reference for the historian, reenactor, designer, and modeler.

Camouflage Uniforms of the Waffen-SS A Photographic Reference, by Michael Beaver, Schiffer Publishing, Atglen, PA. Over 1,000 color and b/w photographs and illustrations, 296 pages. $69.95

Finally a book that unveils the shroud of mystery surrounding Waffen-SS camouflage clothing. Illustrated here, both in full color and in contemporary black and white photographs, this unparalleled look at Waffen-SS combat troops and their camouflage clothing will benefit both the historian and collector.

Canadian Gunsmiths from 1608: A Checklist of Tradesmen, by John Belton, Historical Arms Series No. 29. Canada: Museum Restoration, 1992. 40 pp., 17 illustrations. Softcover. $8.95

This Checklist is a greatly expanded version of HAS No. 14, listing the names, occupation, location, and dates of more than 1,500 men and women who worked as gunmakers, gunsmiths, armorers, gun merchants, gun patent holders, and a few other gun related trades. A collection of contemporary gunsmiths' letterhead have been provided to add color and depth to the study.

Cap Guns, by James Dundas, Schiffer Publishing, Atglen, PA, 1996. 160 pp., illus. Paper covers. $29.95

Over 600 full-color photos of cap guns and gun accessories with a current value guide.

Carbines of the Civil War, by John D. McAulay, Pioneer Press, Union City, TN, 1981. 123 pp., illus. Paper covers. $12.95

A guide for the student and collector of the colorful arms used by the Federal cavalry.

Carbines of the U.S. Cavalry 1861-1905, by John D. McAulay, Andrew Mowbray Publishers, Lincoln, RI, 1996. $35.00

Covers the crucial use of carbines from the beginning of the Civil War to the end of the cavalry carbine era in 1905.

Cartridge Carbines of the British Army, by Alan M. Petrillo, Excalibur Publications, Latham, NY, 1998. 72 pp., illustrated. Paper covers. $11.95

Begins with the Snider-Enfield which was the first regulation cartridge carbine introduced in 1866 and ends with the .303 caliber No.5, Mark 1 Enfield.

Cartridge Catalogues, compiled by George Hoyem, Armory Publications, Coeur d'Alene, ID., 1997. 504 pp., illus. $125.00

Fourteen old ammunition makers' and designers' catalogs reproduced with their color covers in a limited, signed and numbered edition. Completely revised edition of the general purpose reference work for which collectors, police, scientists and laymen reach first for answers to cartridge identification questions. Available October, 1996.

Cartridge Reloading Tools of the Past, by R.H. Chamberlain and Tom Quigley, Tom Quigley, Castle Rock, WA, 1998. 167 pp., illustrated. Paper covers. $25.00

A detailed treatment of the extensive Winchester and Ideal lines of handloading tools and bulletmolds plus Remington, Marlin, Ballard, Browning and many others.

Cartridges for Collectors, by Fred Datig, Pioneer Press, Union City, TN, 1999. In three volumes of 176 pp. each. Vol.1 (Centerfire); Vol.2 (Rimfire and Misc.) types; Vol.3 (Additional Rimfire, Centerfire, and Plastic.). All illustrations are shown in full-scale drawings. Volume 1, softcover only, $19.95. Volumes 2 & 3, Hardcover $19.95

Civil War Arms Makers and Their Contracts, edited by Stuart C. Mowbray and Jennifer Heroux, Andrew Mowbray Publishing, Lincoln, RI, 1998. 595 pp. $39.50

A facsimile reprint of the Report by the Commissioner of Ordnance and Ordnance Stores, 1862.

Civil War Arms Purchases and Deliveries, edited by Stuart C. Mowbray, Andrew Mowbray Publishing, Lincoln, RI, 1998. 300pp., illus. $39.50

A facsimile reprint of the master list of Civil War weapons purchases and deliveries including Small Arms, Cannon, Ordnance and Projectiles.

Civil War Breech Loading Rifles, by John D. McAulay, Andrew Mowbray, Inc., Lincoln, RI, 1991. 144 pp., illus. Paper covers. $15.00

All the major breech-loading rifles of the Civil War and most, if not all, of the obscure types are detailed, illustrated and set in their historical context.

Civil War Cartridge Boxes of the Union Infantryman, by Paul Johnson, Andrew Mowbray, Inc., Lincoln, RI, 1998. 352 pp., illustrated. $45.00

There were four patterns of infantry cartridge boxes used by Union forces during the Civil War. The author describes the development and subsequent pattern changes to these cartridge boxes.

Civil War Commanders, by Dean Thomas, Thomas Publications, Gettysburg, PA. 1998. 72 pages, illustrated, photos. Paper Covers. $9.95

138 photographs and capsule biographies of Union and Confederate officers. A convenient personalities reference guide.

Civil War Firearms, by Joseph G. Bilby, Combined Books, Conshohocken, PA, 1996. 252 pp., illus. $34.95

A unique work combining background data on each firearm including its battlefield use, and a guide to collecting and firing surviving relics and modern reproductions.

Civil War Guns, by William B. Edwards, Thomas Publications, Gettysburg, PA, 1997. 444 pp., illus. $40.00

The complete story of Federal and Confederate small arms; design, manufacture, identifications, procurement issue, employment, effectiveness, and postwar disposal by the recognized expert.

Civil War Infantryman: In Camp, On the March, And in Battle, by Dean Thomas, Thomas Publications, Gettysburg, PA. 1998. 72 pages, illustrated, Softcovers. $12.95

Uses first-hand accounts to shed some light on the "common soldier" of the Civil War from enlistment to muster-out, including camp, marching, rations, equipment, fighting, and more.

Civil War Pistols, by John D. McAulay, Andrew Mowbray Inc., Lincoln, RI, 1992. 166 pp., illus. $38.50

A survey of the handguns used during the American Civil War.

Civil War Sharps Carbines and Rifles, by Earl J. Coates and John D. McAulay, Thomas Publications, Gettysburg, PA, 1996. 108 pp., illus. Paper covers. $12.95

Traces the history and development of the firearms including short histories of specific serial numbers and the soldiers who received them.

Civil War Small Arms of the U.S. Navy and Marine Corps, by John D. McAulay, Mowbray Publishing, Lincoln, RI, 1999. 186 pp., illustrated. $39.00

The first reliable and comprehensive guide to the firearms and edged weapons of the Civil War Navy and Marine Corps.

The W.F. Cody Buffalo Bill Collector's Guide with Values, by James W. Wojtowicz, Collector Books, Paducah, KY, 1998. 271 pp., illustrated. $24.95

A profusion of colorful collectibles including lithographs, programs, photographs, books, medals, sheet music, guns, etc. and today's values.

Col. Burton's Spiller & Burr Revolver, by Matthew W. Norman, Mercer University Press, Macon, GA, 1997. 152 pp., illus. $22.95

A remarkable archival research project on the arm together with a comprehensive story of the establishment and running of the factory.

Collector's Guide to Colt .45 Service Pistols Models of 1911 and 1911A1, Enlarged and revised edition. Clawson Publications, Fort Wayne, IN, 1998. 130 pp., illustrated. $45.00

From 1911 to the end of production in 1945 with complete military identification including all contractors.

THE ARMS LIBRARY

A Collector's Guide to United States Combat Shotguns, by Bruce N. Canfield, Andrew Mowbray Inc., Lincoln, RI, 1992. 184 pp., illus. Paper covers. $24.00

This book provides full coverage of combat shotguns, from the earliest examples right up to the Gulf War and beyond.

A Collector's Guide to Winchester in the Service, by Bruce N. Canfield, Andrew Mowbray, Inc., Lincoln, RI, 1991. 192 pp., illus. Paper covers. $22.00

The firearms produced by Winchester for the national defense. From Hotchkiss to the M14, each firearm is examined and illustrated.

A Collector's Guide to the '03 Springfield, by Bruce N. Canfield, Andrew Mowbray Inc., Lincoln, RI, 1989. 160 pp., illus. Paper covers. $22.00

A comprehensive guide follows the '03 through its unparalleled tenure of service. Covers all of the interesting variations, modifications and accessories of this highly collectible military rifle.

Collector's Illustrated Encyclopedia of the American Revolution, by George C. Neumann and Frank J. Kravic, Rebel Publishing Co., Inc., Texarkana, TX, 1989. 286 pp., illus. $36.95

A showcase of more than 2,300 artifacts made, worn, and used by those who fought in the War for Independence.

Colonial Frontier Guns, by T.M. Hamilton, Pioneer Press, Union City, TN, 1988. 176 pp., illus. Paper covers. $17.50

A complete study of early flint muskets of this country.

Colt: An American Legend, by R.L. Wilson, Artabras, New York, 1997. 406 pages, fully illustrated, most in color. $60.00

A reprint of the commemorative album celebrates 150 years of the guns of Samuel Colt and the manufacturing empire he built, with expert discussion of every model ever produced, the innovations of each model and variants, updated model and serial number charts and magnificent photographic showcases of the weapons.

The Colt Armory, by Ellsworth Grant, Man-at-Arms Bookshelf, Lincoln, RI, 1996. 232 pp., illus. $35.00

A history of Colt's Manufacturing Company.

Colt Blackpowder Reproductions & Replica: A Collector's and Shooter's Guide, by Dennis Miller, Blue Book Publications, Minneapolis, MN, 1999. 288 pp., illustrated. Paper covers. $29.95

The first book on this important subject, and a must for the investor, collector, and shooter.

Colt Heritage, by R.L. Wilson, Simon & Schuster, 1979. 358 pp., illus. $75.00

The official history of Colt firearms 1836 to the present.

Colt Memorabilia Price Guide, by John Ogle, Krause Publications, Iola, WI, 1998. 256 pp., illus. Paper covers. $29.95

The first book ever compiled about the vast array of non-gun merchandise produced by Sam Colt's companies, and other companies using the Colt name.

The Colt Model 1905 Automatic Pistol, by John Potocki, Andrew Mowbray Publishing, Lincoln, RI, 1998. 191 pp., illus. $28.00

Covers all aspects of the Colt Model 1905 Automatic Pistol, from its invention by the legendary John Browning to its numerous production variations.

Colt Peacemaker British Model, by Keith Cochran, Cochran Publishing Co., Rapid City, SD, 1989. 160 pp., illus. $35.00

Covers those revolvers Colt squeezed in while completing a large order of revolvers for the U.S. Cavalry in early 1874, to those magnificent cased target revolvers used in the pistol competitions at Bisley Commons in the 1890s.

Colt Peacemaker Encyclopedia, by Keith Cochran, Keith Cochran, Rapid City, SD, 1986. 434 pp., illus. $65.00

A must book for the Peacemaker collector.

Colt Peacemaker Encyclopedia, Volume 2, by Keith Cochran, Cochran Publishing Co., SD, 1992. 416 pp., illus. $60.00

Included in this volume are extensive notes on engraved, inscribed, historical and noted revolvers, as well as those revolvers used by outlaws, lawmen, movie and television stars.

Colt Percussion Accoutrements 1834-1873, by Robin Rapley, Robin Rapley, Newport Beach, CA, 1994. 432 pp., illus. Paper covers. $39.95

The complete collector's guide to the identification of Colt percussion accoutrements; including Colt conversions and their values.

Colt Pocket Hammerless Pistols, by Dr. John W. Brunner, Phillips Publications, Williamstown, NJ, 1998. 212 pp., illustrated. $59.95

You will never again have to question a .25, .32 or .380 with this well illustrated, definitive reference guide at hand.

Colt Revolvers and the Tower of London, by Joseph G. Rosa, Royal Armouries of the Tower of London, London, England, 1988. 72 pp., illus. Soft covers. $15.00

Details the story of Colt in London through the early cartridge period.

Colt Rifles and Muskets from 1847-1870, by Herbert Houze, Krause Publications, Iola, WI, 1996. 192 pp., illus. $34.95

Discover previously unknown Colt models along with an extensive list of production figures for all models.

Colt's SAA Post War Models, by George Garton, The Gun Room Press, Highland Park, NJ, 1995. 166 pp., illus. $39.95

Complete facts on the post-war Single Action Army revolvers. Information on calibers, production numbers and variations taken from factory records.

Colt Single Action Army Revolvers: The Legend, the Romance and the Rivals, by "Doc" O'Meara, Krause Publications, Iola, WI, 2000. 160 pp., illustrated with 250 photos in b&w and a 16 page color section. $34.95

Production figures, serial numbers by year, and rarities.

Colt Single Action Army Revolvers and Alterations, by C. Kenneth Moore, Mowbray Publishers, Lincoln, RI, 1999. 112 pp., illustrated. $35.00

A comprehensive history of the revolvers that collectors call "Artillery Models." These are the most historical of all S.A.A. Colts, and this new book covers all the details.

Colt Single Action Army Revolvers and the London Agency, by C. Kenneth Moore, Andrew Mowbray Publishers, Lincoln, RI, 1990. 144 pp., illus. $35.00

Drawing on vast documentary sources, this work chronicles the relationship between the London Agency and the Hartford home office.

The Colt U.S. General Officers' Pistols, by Horace Greeley IV, Andrew Mowbray Inc., Lincoln, RI, 1990. 199 pp., illus. $38.00

These unique weapons, issued as a badge of rank to General Officers in the U.S. Army from WWII onward, remain highly personal artifacts of the military leaders who carried them. Includes serial numbers and dates of issue.

Colts from the William M. Locke Collection, by Frank Sellers, Andrew Mowbray Publishers, Lincoln, RI, 1996. 192 pp., illus. $55.00

This important book illustrates all of the famous Locke Colts, with captions by arms authority Frank Sellers.

Colt's Dates of Manufacture 1837-1978, by R.L. Wilson, published by Maurie Albert, Coburg, Australia; N.A. distributor I.D.S.A. Books, Hamilton, OH, 1983. 61 pp. $6.00

An invaluable pocket guide to the dates of manufacture of Colt firearms up to 1978.

Colt's 100th Anniversary Firearms Manual 1836-1936: A Century of Achievement, Wolfe Publishing Co., Prescott, AZ, 1992. 100 pp., illus. Paper covers. $12.95

Originally published by the Colt Patent Firearms Co., this booklet covers the history, manufacturing procedures and the guns of the first 100 years of the genius of Samuel Colt.

Colt's Pocket '49: Its Evolution Including the Baby Dragoon and Wells Fargo, by Robert Jordan and Darrow Watt, privately printed, Loma Mar, CA 2000. 304 pages, with 984 color photos, illus. Beautifully bound in a deep blue leather like case. $125.00

Detailed information on all models and covers engaving, cases, accoutrements, holsters, fakes, and much more. Included is a summary booklet containing information such as serial numbers, production ranges & identifing photos. This book is a masterpiece on its subject.

Complete Guide to all United States Military Medals 1939 to Present, by Colonel Frank C. Foster, Medals of America Press, Fountain Inn, SC, 2000. 121 pp,.illustrated, photos. $29.95

Complete criteria for every Army, Navy, Marines, Air Force, Coast Guard, and Merchant Marine awards since 1939. All decorations, service medals, and ribbons shown in full-color and accompanied by dates and campaigns as well as detailed descriptions on proper wear and display.

Complete Guide to the M1 Garand and the M1 Carbine, by Bruce N. Canfield, 2nd printing, Andrew Mowbray Inc., Lincoln, RI, 1999. 296 pp., illus. $39.50

Expanded and updated coverage of both the M1 Garand and the M1 Carbine, with more than twice as much information as the author's previous book on this topic.

The Complete Guide to U.S. Infantry Weapons of the First War, by Bruce Canfield, Andrew Mowbray, Publisher, Lincoln, RI, 2000. 304 pp., illus. $39.95

The definitive study of the U.S. Infantry weapons used in WW1.

The Complete Guide to U.S. Infantry Weapons of World War Two, by Bruce Canfield, Andrew Mowbray, Publisher, Lincoln, RI, 1995. 303 pp., illus. $39.95

A definitive work on the weapons used by the United States Armed Forces in WWII.

A Concise Guide to the Artillery at Gettysburg, by Gregory Coco, Thomas Publications, Gettysburg, PA, 1998. 96 pp., illus. Paper Covers. $10.00

Coco's tenth book on Gettysburg is a beginner's guide to artillery and its use at the battle. It covers the artillery batteries describing the types of cannons, shells, fuses, etc.using interesting narrative and human interest stories.

Cooey Firearms, Made in Canada 1919-1979, by John A. Belton, Museum Restoration, Canada, 1998. 36pp., with 46 illus. Paper Covers. $8.95

More than 6 million rifles and at least 67 models, were made by this small Canadian riflemaker. They have been identified from the first 'Cooey Canuck' through the last variations made by the 'Winchester-Cooey'. Each is descibed and most are illustrated in this first book on The Cooey.

Cowboy Collectibles and Western Memorabilia, by Bob Bell and Edward Vebell, Schiffer Publishing, Atglen, PA, 1992. 160 pp., illus. Paper covers. $29.95

The exciting era of the cowboy and the wild west collectibles including rifles, pistols, gun rigs, etc.

Cowboy Culture: The Last Frontier of American Antiques, by Michael Friedman, Schiffer Publishing, Ltd., West Chester, PA, 1992. 300 pp., illustrated.

Covers the artful aspects of the old west, the antiques and collectibles. Illustrated with clear color plates of over 1,000 items such as spurs, boots, guns, saddles etc.

Cowboy and Gunfighter Collectible, by Bill Mackin, Mountain Press Publishing Co., Missoula, MT, 1995. 178 pp., illus. Paper covers. $25.00

A photographic encyclopedia with price guide and makers' index.

Cowboys and the Trappings of the Old West, by William Manns and Elizabeth Clair Flood, Zon International Publishing Co., Santa Fe, NM, 1997, 1st edition. 224 pp., illustrated. $45.00

A pictorial celebration of the cowboys dress and trappings.

THE ARMS LIBRARY

Cowboy Hero Cap Pistols, by Rudy D'Angelo, Antique Trader Books, Dubuque, IA, 1998. 196 pp., illus. Paper covers. $34.95

Aimed at collectors of cap pistols created and named for famous film and television cowboy heros, this in-depth guide hits all the marks. Current values are given.

Custom Firearms Engraving, by Tom Turpin, Krause Publications, Iola, WI, 1999. 208 pp., illustrated. $49.95

Over 200 four-color photos with more than 75 master engravers profiled. Engravers Directory with addresses in the U.S. and abroad.

The Decorations, Medals, Ribbons, Badges and Insignia of the United States Army; World War 2 to Present, by Col. Frank C. Foster, Medals of America Press, Fountain Inn, SC. 2001. 145 pages, illustrated. $29.95

The most complete guide to United States Army medals, ribbons, rank, insignia nad patches from WWII to the present day. Each medal and insignia shown in full color. Includes listing of respective criteria and campaigns.

The Decorations, Medals, Ribbons, Badges and Insignia of the United States Navy; World War 2 to Present, by James G. Thompson, Medals of America Press, Fountain Inn, SC. 2000. 123 pages, illustrated. $29.95

The most complete guide to United States Army medals, ribbons, rank, insignia nad patches from WWII to the present day. Each medal and insignia shown in full color. Includes listing of respective criteria and campaigns.

The Derringer in America, Volume 1, The Percussion Period, by R.L. Wilson and L.D. Eberhart, Andrew Mowbray Inc., Lincoln, RI, 1985. 271 pp., illus. $48.00

A long awaited book on the American percussion deringer.

The Derringer in America, Volume 2, The Cartridge Period, by L.D. Eberhart and R.L. Wilson, Andrew Mowbray Inc., Publishers, Lincoln, RI, 1993. 284 pp., illus. $65.00

Comprehensive coverage of cartridge deringers organized alphabetically by maker. Includes all types of deringers known by the authors to have been offered to the American market.

The Devil's Paintbrush: Sir Hiram Maxim's Gun, by Dolf Goldsmith, 3rd Edition, expanded and revised, Collector Grade Publications, Toronto, Canada, 2000. 384 pp., illus. $79.95

The classic work on the world's first true automatic machine gun.

Dr. Josephus Requa Civil War Dentist and the Billinghurst-Requa Volley Gun, by John M. Hyson, Jr., & Margaret Requa DeFrancisco, Museum Restoration Service, Bloomfield, Ont., Canada, 1999. 36 pp., illus. Paper covers. $8.95

The story of the inventor of the first practical rapid-fire gun to be used during the American Civil War.

The Duck Stamp Story, by Eric Jay Dolin and Bob Dumaine, Krause Publications, Iola, WI, 2000. 208 pp., illustrated with color throughout. Paper covers. $29.95; Hardbound. $49.95.

Detailed information on the value and rarity of every federal duck stamp. Outstanding art and illustrations.

The Dutch Luger (Parabellum) A Complete History, by Bas J. Martens and Guus de Vries, Ironside International Publishers, Inc., Alexandria, VA, 1995. 268 pp., illus. $49.95.

The history of the Luger in the Netherlands. An extensive description of the Dutch pistol and trials and the different models of the Luger in the Dutch service.

The Eagle on U.S. Firearms, by John W. Jordan, Pioneer Press, Union City, TN, 1992. 140 pp., illus. Paper covers. $17.50.

Stylized eagles have been stamped on government owned or manufactured firearms in the U.S. since the beginning of our country. This book lists and illustrates these various eagles in an informative and refreshing manner.

Encyclopedia of Rifles & Handguns; A Comprehensive Guide to Firearms, edited by Sean Connolly, Chartwell Books, Inc., Edison, NJ., 1996. 160 pp., illustrated. $26.00.

A lavishly illustrated book providing a comprehensive history of military and civilian personal firepower.

Eprouvettes: A Comprehensive Study of Early Devices for the Testing of Gunpowder, by R.T.W. Kempers, Royal Armouries Museum, Leeds, England, 1999. 352 pp., illustrated with 240 black & white and 28 color plates. $125.00.

The first comprehensive study of eprouvettes ever attempted in a single volume.

European Firearms in Swedish Castles, by Kaa Wennberg, Bohuslaningens Boktryckeri AB, Uddevalla, Sweden, 1986. 156 pp., illus. $50.00.

The famous collection of Count Keller, the Ettersburg Castle collection, and others. English text.

European Sporting Cartridges, Part 1, by W.B. Dixon, Armory Publications, Inc., Coeur d'Alene, ID, 1997. 250 pp., illus. $63.00

Photographs and drawings of over 550 centerfire cartridge case types in 1,300 illustrations produced in German and Austria from 1875 to 1995.

European Sporting Cartridges, Part 2, by W.B. Dixon, Armory Publications, Inc., Coeur d'Alene, ID, 2000. 240 pp., illus. $63.00

An illustrated history of centerfire hunting and target cartridges produced in Czechoslovakia, Switzerland, Norway, Sweden, Finland, Russia, Italy, Denmark, Belguim from 1875 to 1998. Adds 50 specimens to volume 1 (Germany-Austria). Also, illustrates 40 small arms magazine experiments during the late 19th Century, and includes the English-Language export ammunition catalogue of Kovo (Povaszke Strojarne), Prague, Czeck. from the, 1930's.

Fifteen Years in the Hawken Lode, by John D. Baird, The Gun Room Press, Highland Park, NJ, 1976. 120 pp., illus. $24.95.

A collection of thoughts and observations gained from many years of intensive study of the guns from the shop of the Hawken brothers.

'51 Colt Navies, by Nathan L. Swayze, The Gun Room Press, Highland Park, NJ, 1993. 243 pp., illus. $59.95.

The Model 1851 Colt Navy, its variations and markings.

Fighting Iron, by Art Gogan, Andrew Mowbray, Inc., Lincoln, R.I., 1999. 176 pp., illustrated. $28.00.

It doesn't matter whether you collect guns, swords, bayonets or accountrement—sooner or later you realize that it all comes down to the metal. If you don't understand the metal you don't understand your collection.

Fine Colts, The Dr. Joseph A. Murphy Collection, by R.L. Wilson, Sheffield Marketing Associates, Inc., Doylestown, PA, 1999. 258 pp., illustrated. Limited edition signed and numbered. $99.00.

This lavish new work covers exquisite, deluxe and rare Colt arms from Paterson and other percussion revolvers to the cartridge period and up through modern times.

Firearms, by Derek Avery, Desert Publications, El Dorado, AR, 1999. 95 pp., illustrated. $9.95.

The firearms included in this book are by necessity only a selection, but nevertheless one that represents the best and most famous weapons seen since the Second World War.

Firearms and Tackle Memorabilia, by John Delph, Schiffer Publishing, Ltd., West Chester, PA, 1991. 124 pp., illus. $39.95.

A collector's guide to signs and posters, calendars, trade cards, boxes, envelopes, and other highly sought after memorabilia. With a value guide.

Firearms of the American West 1803-1865, Volume 1, by Louis A. Garavaglia and Charles Worman, University of Colorado Press, Niwot, CO, 1998. 402 pp., illustrated. $59.95.

Traces the development and uses of firearms on the frontier during this period.

Firearms of the American West 1866-1894, by Louis A. Garavaglia and Charles G. Worman, University of Colorado Press, Niwot, CO, 1998. 416 pp., illus. $59.95.

A monumental work that offers both technical information on all of the important firearms used in the West during this period and a highly entertaining history of how they were used, who used them, and why.

Firearms from Europe, by David Noe, Larry W. Yantz, Dr. James B. Whisker, Rowe Publications, Rochester, N.Y., 1999. 192 pp., illustrated. $45.00.

A history and description of firearms imported during the American Civil War by the United States of America and the Confederate States of America.

Firepower from Abroad, by Wiley Sword, Andrew Mowbray Publishing, Lincoln, R.I., 2000. 120 pp., illustrated. $23.00.

The Confederate Enfield and the LeMat revolver and how they reached the Confederate market.

Flayderman's Guide to Antique American Firearms and Their Values, 7th Edition, edited by Norm Flayderman, DBI books, a division of Krause Publications, Iola, WI, 1998. 656 pp., illus. Paper covers. $32.95.

A completely updated and new edition with more than 3,600 models and variants extensively described with all marks and specifications necessary for quick identification.

The FN-FAL Rifle, et al, by Duncan Long, Paladin Press, Boulder, CO, 1999. 144 pp., illustrated. Paper covers. $18.95.

Detailed descriptions of the basic models produced by Fabrique Nationale and the myriad variants that evolved as a result of the firearms universal acceptance.

The .45-70 Springfield, by Joe Poyer and Craig Riesch, North Cape Publications, Tustin, CA, 1996. 150 pp., illus. Paper covers. $16.95.

A revised and expanded second edition of a best-selling reference work organized by serial number and date of production to aid the collector in identifying popular "Trapdoor" rifles and carbines.

The French 1935 Pistols, by Eugene Medlin and Colin Doane, Eugene Medlin, El Paso, TX, 1995. 172 pp., illus. Paper covers. $25.95.

The development and identification of successive models, fakes and variants, holsters and accessories, and serial numbers by dates of production.

Freund & Bro. Pioneer Gunmakers to the West, by F.J. Pablo Balentine, Graphic Publishers, Newport Beach, CA, 1997. 380 pp., illustrated $69.95.

The story of Frank W. and George Freund, skilled German gunsmiths who plied their trade on the Western American frontier during the final three decades of the nineteenth century.

From the Kingdom of Lilliput: The Miniature Firearms of David Kucer, by K. Corey Keeble and **The Making of Miniatures,** by David Kucer, Museum Restoration Service, Ontario, Canada, 1994. 51 pp., illus, $25.00.

An overview of the subject of miniatures in general combined with an outline by the artist himself on the way he makes a miniature firearm.

Frontier Pistols and Revolvers, by Dominique Venner, Book Sales Inc., Edison, N.J., 1998. 144 pp., illus. $19.95.

Colt, Smith & Wesson, Remington and other early-brand revolvers which tamed the American frontier are shown amid vintage photographs, etchings and paintings to evoke the wild West.

The Fusil de Tulole in New France, 1691-1741, by Russel Bouchard, Museum Restorations Service, Bloomfield, Ontario, Canada, 1997. 36 pp., illus. Paper covers. $8.95

The development of the company and the identification of their arms.

Game Guns & Rifles: Percussion to Hammerless Ejector in Britain, by Richard Akehurst, Trafalgar Square, N. Pomfret, VT, 1993. 192 pp., illus. $39.95.

Long considered a classic this important reprint covers the period of British gunmaking between 1830-1900.

The Gas Trap Garand, by Billy Pyle, Collector Grade Publications, Cobourg, Ontario, Canada, 1999 316 pp., illustrated. $59.95.

The in-depth story of the rarest Garands of them all, the initial 80 Model Shop rifles made under the personal supervision of John Garand himself in 1934 and

REFERENCE

1935, and the first 50,000 plus production "gas trap" M1's manufactured at Springfield Armory between August, 1937 and August, 1940.

George Schreyer, Sr. and Jr., Gunmakers of Hanover, Pennsylvania, by George Shumway, George Shumway Publishers, York, PA, 1990. 160pp., illus. $50.00.

This monograph is a detailed photographic study of almost all known surviving long rifles and smoothbore guns made by highly regarded gunsmiths George Schreyer, Sr. and Jr.

The German Assault Rifle 1935-1945, by Peter R. Senich, Paladin Press, Boulder, CO, 1987. 328 pp., illus. $60.00.

A complete review of machine carbines, machine pistols and assault rifles employed by Hitler's Wehrmacht during WWII.

The German K98k Rifle, 1934-1945: The Backbone of the Wehrmacht, by Richard D. Law, Collector Grade Publications, Toronto, Canada, 1993. 336 pp., illus. $69.95.

The most comprehensive study ever published on the 14,000,000 bolt-action K98k rifles produced in Germany between 1934 and 1945.

German Machine Guns, by Daniel D. Musgrave, revised edition, Ironside International Publishers, Inc. Alexandria, VA, 1992. 586 pp., 650 illus. $49.95.

The most definitive book ever written on German machineguns. Covers the introduction and development of machineguns in Germany from 1899 to the rearmament period after WWII.

German Military Rifles and Machine Pistols, 1871-1945, by Hans Dieter Gotz, Schiffer Publishing Co., West Chester, PA, 1990. 245 pp., illus. $35.00.

This book portrays in words and pictures the development of the modern German weapons and their ammunition including the scarcely known experimental types.

The German MP40 Maschinenpistole, by Frank Iannamico, Moose Lake Publishing, Harmony, ME, 1999. 185 pp., illustrated. Paper covers. $19.95.

The history, development and use of this famous gun of World War 2.

German 7.9mm Military Ammunition, by Daniel W. Kent, Daniel W. Kent, Ann Arbor, MI, 1991. 244 pp., illus. $35.00.

The long-awaited revised edition of a classic among books devoted to ammunition.

The Golden Age of Remington, by Robert W.D. Ball, Krause publications, Iola, WI, 1995. 194 pp., illus. $29.95.

For Remington collectors or firearms historians, this book provides a pictorial history of Remington through World War I. Includes value guide.

The Government Models, by William H.D. Goddard, Andrew Mowbray Publishing, Lincoln, RI, 1998. 296 pp., illustrated. $58.50.

The most authoritative source on the development of the Colt model of 1911.

Grasshoppers and Butterflies, by Adrian B. Caruana, Museum Restoration Service, Alexandria, Bay, N.Y., 1999. 32 pp., illustrated. Paper covers. $8.95.

No.39 in the Historical Arms Series. The light 3 pounders of Pattison and Townsend.

The Greener Story, by Graham Greener, Quiller Press, London, England, 2000. 256 pp., illustrated with 32 pages of color photos. $64.50.

W.W. Greener, his family history, inventions, guns, patents, and more.

A Guide to American Trade Catalogs 1744-1900, by Lawrence B. Romaine, Dover Publications, New York, NY. 422 pp., illus. Paper covers. $12.95

A Guide to Ballard Breechloaders, by George J. Layman, Pioneer Press, Union City, TN, 1997. 261 pp., illus. Paper covers. $19.95

Documents the saga of this fine rifle from the first models made by Ball & Williams of Worchester, to its production by the Marlin Firearms Co, to the cessation of 19th century manufacture in 1891, and finally to the modern reproductions made in the 1990's.

A Guide to the Maynard Breechloader, by George J. Layman, George J. Layman, Ayer, MA, 1993. 125 pp., illus. Paper covers. $11.95.

The first book dedicated entirely to the Maynard family of breech-loading firearms. Coverage of the arms is given from the 1850s through the 1880s.

A Guide to U. S. Army Dress Helmets 1872-1904, by Kasal and Moore, North Cape Publications, 2000. 88 pp., illus. Paper covers. $15.95

This thorough study provides a complete description of the Model 1872 & 1881 dress helmets worn by the U.S. Army. Including all componets from bodies to plates to plumes & shoulder cords and tells how to differentiate the originals from reproductions. Extensively illustrated with photographs, '8 pages in full color' of complete helmets and their components.

Gun Collecting, by Geoffrey Boothroyd, Sportsman's Press, London, 1989. 208 pp., illus. $29.95.

The most comprehensive list of 19th century British gunmakers and gunsmiths ever published.

Gunmakers of London 1350-1850, by Howard L. Blackmore, George Shumway Publisher, York, PA, 1986. 222 pp., illus. $35.00.

A listing of all the known workmen of gun making in the first 500 years, plus a history of the guilds, cutlers, armourers, founders, blacksmiths, etc. 260 gunmarks are illustrated.

Gunmakers of London Supplement 1350-1850, by Howard L. Blackmore, Museum Restoration Service, Alexandria Bay, NY, 1999. 156 pp., illustrated. $60.00.

Begins with an introductory chapter on "foreighn" gunmakers followed by records of all the new information found about previously unidentified armourers, gunmakers and gunsmiths.

The Guns that Won the West: Firearms of the American Frontier, 1865-1898, by John Walter, Stackpole Books, Inc., Mechanicsburg, PA.,1999. 256 pp., illustrated. $34.95.

Here is the story of the wide range of firearms from pistols to rifles used by plainsmen and settlers, gamblers, native Americans and the U.S. Army.

Gunsmiths of Illinois, by Curtis L. Johnson, George Shumway Publishers, York, PA, 1995. 160 pp., illus. $50.00.

Genealogical information is provided for nearly one thousand gunsmiths. Contains hundreds of illustrations of rifles and other guns, of handmade origin, from Illinois.

The Gunsmiths of Manhattan, 1625-1900: A Checklist of Tradesmen, by Michael H. Lewis, Museum Restoration Service, Bloomfield, Ont., Canada, 1991. 40 pp., illus. Paper covers. $8.95.

This listing of more than 700 men in the arms trade in New York City prior to about the end of the 19th century will provide a guide for identification and further research.

The Guns of Dagenham: Lanchester, Patchett, Sterling, by Peter Laidler and David Howroyd, Collector Grade Publications, Inc., Cobourg, Ont., Canada, 1995. 310 pp., illus. $39.95.

An in-depth history of the small arms made by the Sterling Company of Dagenham, Essex, England, from 1940 until Sterling was purchased by British Aerospace in 1989 and closed.

Guns of the Western Indian War, by R. Stephen Dorsey, Collector's Library, Eugene, OR, 1997. 220 pp., illus. Paper covers. $30.00.

The full story of the guns and ammunition that made western history in the turbulent period of 1865-1890.

Gun Powder Cans & Kegs, by Ted & David Bacyk and Tom Rowe, Rowe Publications, Rochester, NY, 1999. 150 pp., illus. $65.00.

The first book devoted to powder tins and kegs. All cans and kegs in full color. With a price guide and rarity scale.

The Guns of Remington: Historic Firearms Spanning Two Centuries, compiled by Howard M. Madaus, Biplane Productions, Publisher, in cooperation with Buffalo Bill Historical Center, Cody, WY, 1998. 352 pp., illustrated with over 800 color photos. $79.95.

A complete catalog of the firearms in the exhibition, "It Never Failed Me: The Arms & Art of Remington Arms Company" at the Buffalo Bill Historical Center, Cody, Wyoming.

Gun Tools, Their History and Identification by James B. Shaffer, Lee A. Rutledge and R. Stephen Dorsey, Collector's Library, Eugene, OR, 1992. 375 pp., illus. $30.00.

Written history of foreign and domestic gun tools from the flintlock period to WWII.

Gun Tools, Their History and Identifications, Volume 2, by Stephen Dorsey and James B. Shaffer, Collectors' Library, Eugene, OR, 1997. 396 pp., illus. Paper covers. $30.00.

Gun tools from the Royal Armouries Museum in England, Pattern Room, Royal Ordnance Reference Collection in Nottingham and from major private collections.

Gunsmiths of the Carolinas 1660-1870, by Daniel D. Hartzler and James B. Whisker, Old Bedford Village Press, Bedford, PA, 1998. 176 pp., illustrated. $40.00.

This deluxe hard bound edition of 176 pages is printed on fine coated paper, with about 90 pages of large photographs of fine longrifles from the Carolinas, and about 90 pages of detailed research on the gunsmiths who created the highly prized and highly collectable longrifles. Dedicated to serious students of original Kentucky rifles, who may seldom encounter fine longrifles from the Carolinas.

Gunsmiths of Maryland, by Daniel D. Hartzler and James B. Whisker, Old Bedford Village Press, Bedford, PA, 1998. 208 pp., illustrated. $45.00.

Covers firelock Colonial period through the breech-loading patent models. Featuring longrifles.

Gunsmiths of Virginia, by Daniel D. Hartzler and James B. Whisker, Old Bedford Village Press, Bedford, PA, 1992. 206 pp., illustrated. $45.00.

A photographic study of American longrifles.

Gunsmiths of West Virginia, by Daniel D. Hartzler and James B. Whisker, Old Bedford Village Press, Bedford, PA, 1998. 176 pp., illustrated. $40.00.

A photographic study of American longrifles.

Gunsmiths of York County, Pennsylvania, by Daniel D. Hartzler and James B. Whisker, Old Bedford Village Press, Bedford, PA, 1998. 160 pp., illustrated. $40.00.

160 pages of photographs and research notes on the longrifles and gunsmiths of York County, Pennsylvania. Many longrifle collectors and gun builders have noticed that York County style rifles tend to be more formal in artistic decoration than some other schools of style. Patriotic themes, and folk art were popular design elements.

Hall's Military Breechloaders, by Peter A. Schmidt, Andrew Mowbray Publishers, Lincoln, RI, 1996. 232 pp., illus. $55.00.

The whole story behind these bold and innovative firearms.

The Handgun, by Geoffrey Boothroyd, David and Charles, North Pomfret, VT, 1989. 566 pp., illus. $60.00.

Every chapter deals with an important period in handgun history from the 14th century to the present.

Handgun of Military Rifle Marks 1866-1950, by Richard A. Hoffman and Noel P. Schott, Mapleleaf Militaria Publishing, St. Louis, MO, 1999, second edition. 60 pp., illustrated. Paper covers. $20.00.

An illustrated guide to identifying military rifle and marks.

Handguns & Rifles: The Finest Weapons from Around the World, by Ian Hogg, Random House Value Publishing, Inc., N.Y., 1999. 128 pp., illustrated. $18.98.

The serious gun collector will welcome this fully illustrated examination of international handguns and rifles. Each entry covers the history of the weapon, what purpose it serves, and its advantages and disadvantages.

THE ARMS LIBRARY

The Hawken Rifle: Its Place in History, by Charles E. Hanson, Jr., The Fur Press, Chadron, NE, 1979. 104 pp., illus. Paper covers. $15.00.
A definitive work on this famous rifle.

Hawken Rifles, The Mountain Man's Choice, by John D. Baird, The Gun Room Press, Highland Park, NJ, 1976. 95 pp., illus. $29.95.
Covers the rifles developed for the Western fur trade. Numerous specimens are described and shown in photographs.

High Standard: A Collector's Guide to the Hamden & Hartford Target Pistols, by Tom Dance, Andrew Mowbray, Inc., Lincoln, RI, 1991. 192 pp., illus. Paper covers. $24.00.
From Citation to Supermatic, all of the production models and specials made from 1951 to 1984 are covered according to model number or series.

Historic Pistols: The American Martial Flintlock 1760-1845, by Samuel E. Smith & Edwin W. Bitter, The Gun Room Press, Highland Park, NJ, 1986. 353 pp., illus. $45.00.
Covers over 70 makers and 163 models of American martial arms.

Historical Hartford Hardware, by William W. Dalrymple, Colt Collector Press, Rapid City, SD, 1976. 42 pp., illus. Paper covers. $10.00.
Historically associated Colt revolvers.

The History and Development of Small Arms Ammunition, Volume 2, by George A. Hoyem, Armory Publications, Oceanside, CA, 1991. 303 pp., illus. $65.00.
Covers the blackpowder military centerfire rifle, carbine, machine gun and volley gun ammunition used in 28 nations and dominions, together with the firearms that chambered them.

The History and Development of Small Arms Ammunition, Volume 4, by George A. Hoyem, Armory Publications, Seattle, WA, 1998. 200 pp., illustrated $65.00.
A comprehensive book on American black powder and early smokeless rifle cartridges.

The History of Colt Firearms, by Dean Boorman, Lyons Press, New York, NY, 2001. 144 pp., illus. $29.95
Discover the fascinating story of the world's most famous revolver, complete with more than 150 stunning full-color photographs.

History of Modern U.S. Military Small Arms Ammunition. Volume 1, 1880-1939, revised by F.W. Hackley, W.H. Woodin and E.L. Scranton, Thomas Publications, Gettysburg, PA, 1998. 328 pp., illus. $49.95.
This revised edition incorporates all publicly available information concerning military small arms ammunition for the period 1880 through 1939 in a single volume.

History of Modern U.S. Military Small Arms Ammunition. Volume 2, 1940-1945 by F.W. Hackley, W.H. Woodin and E.L. Scranton. Gun Room Press, Highland Park, NJ. 300 + pages, illustrated. $39.95
Based on decades of original research conducted at the National Archives, numerous military, public and private museums and libraries, as well as individual collections, this edition incorporates all publicly available information concerning military small arms ammunition for the period 1940 through 1945.

The History of Winchester Rifles, by Dean Boorman, Lyons Press, New York, NY, 2001. 144 pp., illus. $29.95
A captivating and wonderfully photographed history of one of the most legendary names in gun lore. 150 full-color photos.

The History of Winchester Firearms 1866-1992, sixth edition, updated, expanded, and revised by Thomas Henshaw, New Win Publishing, Clinton, NJ, 1993. 280 pp., illus. $27.95.
This classic is the standard reference for all collectors and others seeking the facts about any Winchester firearm, old or new.

History of Winchester Repeating Arms Company, by Herbert G. Houze, Krause Publications, Iola, WI, 1994. 800 pp., illus. $50.00.
The complete Winchester history from 1856-1981.

Honour Bound: The Chauchat Machine Rifle, by Gerard Demaison and Yves Buffetaut, Collector Grade Publications, Inc., Cobourg, Ont., Canada, 1995. $39.95.
The story of the CSRG (Chauchat) machine rifle, the most manufactured automatic weapon of World War One.

Hopkins & Allen Revolvers & Pistols, by Charles E. Carder, Avil Onze Publishing, Delphos, OH, 1998, illustrated. Paper covers. $24.95.
Covers over 165 photos, graphics and patent drawings.

How to Buy and Sell Used Guns, by John Traister, Stoeger Publishing Co., So. Hackensack, NJ, 1984. 192 pp., illus. Paper covers. $10.95.
A new guide to buying and selling guns.

Hunting Weapons From the Middle Ages to the Twentieth Century, by Howard L. Blackmore, Dover Publications, Meneola, NY, 2000. 480 pp., illustrated. Paper covers. $16.95.
Dealing mainly with the different classes of weapons used in sport—swords, spears, crossbows, guns, and rifles—from the Middle Ages until the present day.

Identification Manual on the .303 British Service Cartridge, No. 1-Ball Ammunition, by B.A. Temple, I.D.S.A. Books, Piqua, OH, 1986. 84 pp., 57 illus. $12.50

Identification Manual on the .303 British Service Cartridge, No. 2-Blank Ammunition, by B.A. Temple, I.D.S.A. Books, Piqua, OH, 1986. 95 pp., 59 illus. $12.50

Identification Manual on the .303 British Service Cartridge, No. 3-Special Purpose Ammunition, by B.A. Temple, I.D.S.A. Books, Piqua, OH, 1987. 82 pp., 49 illus. $12.50

Identification Manual on the .303 British Service Cartridge, No. 4-Dummy Cartridges Henry 1869-c.1900, by B.A. Temple, I.D.S.A. Books, Piqua, OH, 1988. 84 pp., 70 illus. $12.50

Identification Manual on the .303 British Service Cartridge, No. 5-Dummy Cartridges (2), by B.A. Temple, I.D.S.A. Books, Piqua, OH, 1994. 78 pp. $12.50

The Illustrated Book of Guns, by David Miller, Salamander Books, N.Y., N.Y., 2000. 304 pp., illustrated in color. $34.95.
An illustrated directory of over 1,000 military and sporting firearms.

The Illustrated Encyclopedia of Civil War Collectibles, by Chuck Lawliss, Henry Holt and Co., New York, NY, 1997. 316 pp., illus. Paper covers. $22.95.
A comprehensive guide to Union and Confederate arms, equipment, uniforms, and other memorabilia.

Illustrations of United States Military Arms 1776-1903 and Their Inspector's Marks, compiled by Turner Kirkland, Pioneer Press, Union City, TN, 1988. 37 pp., illus. Paper covers. $7.00.
Reprinted from the 1949 Bannerman catalog. Valuable information for both the advanced and beginning collector.

Indian War Cartridge Pouches, Boxes and Carbine Boots, by R. Stephen Dorsey, Collector's Library, Eugene, OR, 1993. 156 pp., illus. Paper Covers. $20.00.
The key reference work to the cartridge pouches, boxes, carbine sockets and boots of the Indian War period 1865-1890.

An Introduction to the Civil War Small Arms, by Earl J. Coates and Dean S. Thomas, Thomas Publishing Co., Gettysburg, PA, 1990. 96 pp., illus. Paper covers. $10.00.
The small arms carried by the individual soldier during the Civil War.

Japanese Rifles of World War Two, by Duncan O. McCollum, Excalibur Publications, Latham, NY, 1996. 64 pp., illus. Paper covers. $18.95.
A sweeping view of the rifles and carbines that made up Japan's arsenal during the conflict.

Kalashnikov Arms, compiled by Alexei Nedelin, Design Military Parade, Ltd., Moscow, Russia, 1997. 240 pp., illus. $49.95.
Weapons versions stored in the St. Petersburg Military Historical Museum of Artillery, Engineer Troops and Communications and in the Izhmash JSC.

Kalashnikov "Machine Pistols, Assault Rifles, and Machine Guns, 1945 to the Present", by John Walter, Paladin Press, Boulder, CO, 1999, hardcover, photos, illus., 146 pp. $22.95
This exhaustive work published by Greenhill Military Manuals features a gun-by-gun directory of Kalashnikov variants. Technical specifications and illustrations are provided throughout, along with details of sights, bayonets, markings and ammunition. A must for the serious collector and historian.

The Kentucky Pistol, by Roy Chandler and James Whisker, Old Bedford Village Press, Bedford, PA, 1997. 225 pp., illus. $60.00
A photographic study of Kentucky pistols from famous collections.

The Kentucky Rifle, by Captain John G.W. Dillin, George Shumway Publisher, York, PA, 1993. 221 pp., illus. $50.00.
This well-known book was the first attempt to tell the story of the American longrifle. This edition retains the original text and illustrations with supplemental footnotes provided by Dr. George Shumway.

Know Your Broomhandle Mausers, by R.J. Berger, Blacksmith Corp., Southport, CT, 1985. 96 pp., illus. Paper covers. $12.95.
An interesting story on the big Mauser pistol and its variations.

Krag Rifles, by William S. Brophy, The Gun Room Press, Highland Park, NJ, 1980. 200 pp., illus. $35.00.
The first comprehensive work detailing the evolution and various models, both military and civilian.

The Krieghoff Parabellum, by Randall Gibson, Midland, TX, 1988. 279 pp., illus. $40.00.
A comprehensive text pertaining to the Lugers manufactured by H. Krieghoff Waffenfabrik.

Las Pistolas Espanolas Tipo "Mauser," by Artemio Mortera Perez, Quiron Ediciones, Valladolid, Spain, 1998. 71 pp., illustrated. Paper covers. $34.95.
This book covers in detail Spanish machine pistols and C96 copies made in Spain. Covers all Astra "Mauser" pistol series and the complete line of Beistegui C96 type pistols. Spanish text.

Law Enforcement Memorabilia Price and Identification Guide, by Monty McCord, DBI Books a division of Krause Publications, Inc. Iola, WI, 1999. 208 pp., illustrated. Paper covers. $19.95.
An invaluable reference to the growing wave of law enforcement collectors. Hundreds of items are covered from miniature vehicles to clothes, patches, and restraints.

Legendary Sporting Guns, by Eric Joly, Abbeville Press, New York, N.Y., 1999. 228 pp., illustrated. $65.00.
A survey of hunting through the ages and relates how many different types of firearms were created and refined for use afield.

Legends and Reality of the AK, by Val Shilin and Charlie Cutshaw, Paladen Press, Boulder, CO, 2000. 192 pp., illustrated. Paper covers. $35.00.
A behind-the-scenes look at history, design and impact of the Kalashnikov family of weapons.

LeMat, the Man, the Gun, by Valmore J. Forgett and Alain F. and Marie-Antoinette Serpette, Navy Arms Co., Ridgefield, NJ, 1996. 218 pp., illus. $49.95.
The first definitive study of the Confederate revolvers invention, development and delivery by Francois Alexandre LeMat.

Les Pistolets Automatiques Francaise 1890-1990, by Jean Huon, Combined Books, Inc., Conshohocken, PA, 1997. 160 pp., illus. French text. $34.95
French automatic pistols from the earliest experiments through the World Wars and Indo-China to modern security forces.

Levine's Guide to Knives And Their Values, 4th Edition, by Bernard Levine, DBI Books, a division of Krause Publications, Iola, WI, 1997. 512 pp., illus. Paper covers. $27.95
All the basic tools for identifying, valuing and collecting folding and fixed blade knives.

THE ARMS LIBRARY

The Light 6-Pounder Battalion Gun of 1776, by Adrian Caruana, Museum Restoration Service, Bloomfield, Ontario, Canada, 2001. 76 pp., illus. Paper covers. $8.95

The London Gun Trade, 1850-1920, by Joyce E. Gooding, Museum Restoration Service, Bloomfield, Ontario, Canada, 2001. 48 pp., illus. Paper covers. $8.95

Names, dates and locations of London gunmakers working between 1850 and 1920 are listed. Compiled from the original Kelly's Post Office Directories of the City of London.

The London Gunmakers and the English Duelling Pistol, 1770-1830, by Keith R. Dill, Museum Restoration Service, Bloomfield, Ontario, Canada, 1997. 36 pp., illus. Paper covers. $8.95

Ten gunmakers made London one of the major gunmaking centers of the world. This book examines how the design and construction of their pistols contributed to that reputation and how these characteristics may be used to date flintlock arms.

Longrifles of North Carolina, by John Bivens, George Shumway Publisher, York, PA, 1988. 256 pp., illus. $50.00.

Covers art and evolution of the rifle, immigration and trade movements. Committee of Safety gunsmiths, characteristics of the North Carolina rifle.

Longrifles of Pennsylvania, Volume 1, Jefferson, Clarion & Elk Counties, by Russel H. Harringer, George Shumway Publisher, York, PA, 1984. 200 pp., illus. $50.00.

First in series that will treat in great detail the longrifles and gunsmiths of Pennsylvania.

The Luger Handbook, by Aarron Davis, Krause Publications, Iola, WI, 1997. 112 pp., illus. Paper covers. $9.95.

Quick reference to classify Luger models and variations with complete details including proofmarks.

Lugers at Random, by Charles Kenyon, Jr., Handgun Press, Glenview, IL, 1990. 420 pp., illus. $59.95.

A new printing of this classic, comprehensive reference for all Luger collectors.

The Luger Story, by John Walter, Stackpole Books, Mechanicsburg, PA, 2001. 256 pp., illus. Paper Covers $29.95.

The standard history of the world's most famous handgun.

M1 Carbine, by Larry Ruth, Gun room Press, Highland Park, NJ, 1987. 291 pp., illus. Paper $19.95.

The origin, development, manufacture and use of this famous carbine of World War II.

The M1 Carbine: Owner's Guide, by Scott A. Duff, Scott A. Duff, Export, PA, 1997. 126 pp., illus. Paper covers. $19.95.

This book answers the questions M1 owners most often ask concerning maintenance activities not encounted by military users.

The M1 Garand: Owner's Guide, by Scott A. Duff, Scott A. Duff, Export, PA, 1998. 132 pp., illus. Paper covers. $19.95.

This book answers the questions M1 owners most often ask concerning maintenance activities not encounted by military users.

The M1 Garand Serial Numbers and Data Sheets, by Scott A. Duff, Export, PA, 1995. 101 pp., illus. Paper covers. $11.95.

Provides the reader with serial numbers related to dates of manufacture and a large sampling of data sheets to aid in identification or restoration.

The M1 Garand 1936 to 1957, by Joe Poyer and Craig Riesch, North Cape Publications, Tustin, CA, 1996. 216 pp., illus. Paper covers. $19.95.

Describes the entire range of M1 Garand production in text and quick-scan charts.

The M1 Garand: Post World War, by Scott A. Duff, Scott A. Duff, Export, PA, 1990. 139 pp., illus. Soft covers. $19.95.

A detailed account of the activities at Springfield Armory through this period. International Harvester, H&R, Korean War production and quantities delivered. Serial numbers.

The M1 Garand: World War 2, by Scott A. Duff, Scott A. Duff, Export, PA, 1993. 210 pp., illus. Paper covers. $39.95.

The most comprehensive study available to the collector and historian on the M1 Garand of World War II.

Maine Made Guns and Their Makers, by Dwight B. Demeritt Jr., Maine State Museum, Augusta, ME, 1998. 209 pp., illustrated. $55.00.

An authoritative, biographical study of Maine gunsmiths.

Marlin Firearms: A History of the Guns and the Company That Made Them, by Lt. Col. William S. Brophy, USAR, Ret., Stackpole Books, Harrisburg, PA, 1989. 672 pp., illus. $75.00.

The definitive book on the Marlin Firearms Co. and their products.

Martini-Henry .450 Rifles & Carbines, by Dennis Lewis, Excalibur Publications, Latham, NY, 1996. 72 pp., illus. Paper covers. $11.95.

The stories of the rifles and carbines that were the mainstay of the British soldier through the Victorian wars.

Mauser Bolt Rifles, by Ludwig Olson, F. Brownell & Son, Inc., Montezuma, IA, 1999. 364 pp., illus. $59.95.

The most complete, detailed, authoritative and comprehensive work ever done on Mauser bolt rifles. Completely revised deluxe 3rd edition.

Mauser Military Rifles of the World, 2nd Edition, by Robert Ball, Krause Publications, Iola, WI, 2000. 304 pp., illustrated with 1,000 b&w photos and a 48 page color section. $44.95.

This 2nd edition brings more than 100 new photos of these historic rifles and the wars in which they were carried.

Mauser Smallbores Sporting, Target and Training Rifles, by Jon Speed, Collector Grade Publications, Cobourg, Ontario, Canada 1998. 349 pp., illustrated. $67.50.

A history of all the smallbore sporting, target and training rifles produced by the legendary Mauser-Werke of Obendorf Am Neckar.

Military Holsters of World War 2, by Eugene J. Bender, Rowe Publications, Rochester, NY, 1998. 200 pp., illustrated. $45.00.

A revised edition with a new price guide of the most definitive book on this subject.

Military Pistols of Japan, by Fred L. Honeycutt, Jr., Julin Books, Palm Beach Gardens, FL, 1997. 168 pp., illus. $42.00.

Covers every aspect of military pistol production in Japan through WWII.

The Military Remington Rolling Block Rifle, by George Layman, Pioneer Press, TN, 1998. 146 pp., illus. Paper covers. $24.95.

A standard reference for those with an interest in the Remington rolling block family of firearms.

Military Rifles of Japan, 5th Edition, by F.L. Honeycutt, Julin Books, Lake Park, FL, 1999. 208 pp., illus. $42.00.

A new revised and updated edition. Includes the early Murata-period markings, etc.

Military Small Arms Data Book, by Ian V. Hogg, Stackpole Books, Mechanicsburg, PA, 1999. $44.95. 336 pp., illustrated.

Data on more than 1,500 weapons. Covers a vast range of weapons from pistols to anti-tank rifles. Essential data, 1870-2000, in one volume.

Modern Beretta Firearms, by Gene Gangarosa, Jr., Stoeger Publishing Co., So. Hackensack, NJ, 1994. 288 pp., illus. Paper covers. $16.95.

Traces all models of modern Beretta pistols, rifles, machine guns and combat shotguns.

Modern Gun Values, The Gun Digest Book of, 10th Edition, by the Editors of Gun Digest, DBI Books, a division of Krause Publications, Iola, WI., 1996. 560 pp. illus. Paper covers. $21.95.

Greatly updated and expanded edition describing and valuing over 7,000 firearms manufactured from 1900 to 1996. The standard for valuing modern firearms.

Modern Gun Identification & Value Guide, 13th Edition, by Russell and Steve Quertermous, Collector Books, Paducah, KY, 1998. 504 pp., illus. Paper covers. $14.95.

Features current values for over 2,500 models of rifles, shotguns and handguns, with over 1,800 illustrations.

More Single Shot Rifles, by James C. Grant, The Gun Room Press, Highland Park, NJ, 1976. 324 pp., illus. $35.00.

Details the guns made by Frank Wesson, Milt Farrow, Holden, Borchardt, Stevens, Remington, Winchester, Ballard and Peabody-Martini.

Mortimer, the Gunmakers, 1753-1923, by H. Lee Munson, Andrew Mowbray Inc., Lincoln, RI, 1992. 320 pp., illus. $65.00.

Seen through a single, dominant, English gunmaking dynasty this fascinating study provides a window into the classical era of firearms artistry.

The Mosin-Nagant Rifle, by Terence W. Lapin, North Cape Publications, Tustin, CA, 1998. 30 pp., illustrated. Paper covers. $19.95.

The first ever complete book on the Mosin-Nagant rifle written in English. Covers every variation.

The Navy Luger, by Joachim Gortz and John Walter, Handgun Press, Glenview, IL, 1988. 128 pp., illus. $24.95.

The 9mm Pistole 1904 and the Imperial German Navy. A concise illustrated history.

The New World of Russian Small Arms and Ammunition, by Charlie Cutshaw, Paladin Press, Boulder, CO, 1998. 160 pp., illustrated. $42.95.

Detailed descriptions, specifications and first-class illustrations of the AN-94, PSS silent pistol, Bizon SMG, Saifa-12 tactical shotgun, the GP-25 grenade launcher and more cutting edge Russian weapons.

The Number 5 Jungle Carbine, by Alan M. Petrillo, Excalibur Publications, Latham, NY, 1994. 32 pp., illus. Paper covers. $7.95.

A comprehensive treatment of the rifle that collectors have come to call the "Jungle Carbine"—the Lee-Enfield Number 5, Mark 1.

The '03 Era: When Smokeless Revolutionized U.S. Riflery, by Clark S. Campbell, Collector Grade Publications, Inc., Ontario, Canada, 1994. 334 pp., illus. $44.50.

A much-expanded version of Campbell's *The '03 Springfields*, representing forty years of in-depth research into "all things '03."

Observations on Colt's Second Contract, November 2, 1847, by G. Maxwell Longfield and David T. Basnett, Museum Restoration Service, Bloomfield, Ontario, Canada, 1997. 36 pp., illus. Paper covers. $6.95.

This study traces the history and the construction of the Second Model Colt Dragoon supplied in 1848 to the U.S. Cavalry.

Official Guide to Gunmarks, 3rd Edition, by Robert H. Balderson, House of Collectibles, New York, NY, 1996. 367 pp., illus. Paper covers. $15.00.

Identifies manufacturers' marks that appear on American and foreign pistols, rifles and shotguns.

Official Price Guide to Gun Collecting, by R.L. Wilson, Ballantine/House of Collectibles, New York, NY, 1998. 450 pp., illus. Paper covers. $21.50.

Covers more than 30,000 prices from Colt revolvers to Winchester rifles and shotguns to German Lugers and British sporting rifles and game guns.

Official Price Guide to Military Collectibles, 6th Edition, by Richard J. Austin, Random House, Inc., New York, NY, 1998. 200 pp., illus. Paper cover. $20.00.

Covers weapons and other collectibles from wars of the distant and recent past. More than 4,000 prices are listed. Illustrated with 400 black & white photos plus a full-color insert.

THE ARMS LIBRARY

The Official Soviet SVD Manual, by Major James F. Gebhardt (Ret.) Paladin Press, Boulder, CO, 1999. 112 pp., illustrated. Paper covers. $15.00.
Operating instructions for the 7.62mm Dragunov, the first Russian rifle developed from scratch specifically for sniping.

Old Gunsights: A Collector's Guide, 1850 to 2000, by Nicholas Stroebel, Krause Publications, Iola, WI, 1998. 320 pp., illus. Paper covers. $29.95
An in-depth and comprehensive examination of old gunsights and the rifles on which they were used to get accurate feel for prices in this expanding market.

Old Rifle scopes, by Nicholas Stroebel, Krause Publications, Iola, WI, 2000. 400 pp., illustrated. Paper covers. $31.95.
This comprehensive collector's guide takes aim at more than 120 scope makers and 60 mount makers and features photos and current market values for 300 scopes and mounts manufactured from 1950-1985.

The P-08 Parabellum Luger Automatic Pistol, edited by J. David McFarland, Desert Publications, Cornville, AZ, 1982. 20 pp., illus. Paper covers. $11.95.
Covers every facet of the Luger, plus a listing of all known Luger models.

Packing Iron, by Richard C. Rattenbury, Zon International Publishing, Millwood, NY, 1993. 216 pp., illus. $45.00.
The best book yet produced on pistol holsters and rifle scabbards. Over 300 variations of holster and scabbards are illustrated in large, clear plates.

Parabellum: A Technical History of Swiss Lugers, by Vittorio Bobba, Priuli & Verlucca, Editori, Torino, Italy, 1996. Italian and English text. Illustrated. $100.00.

Patents for Inventions, Class 119 (Small Arms), 1855-1930. British Patent Office, Armory Publications, Oceanside, CA, 1993. 7 volume set. $250.00.
Contains 7980 abridged patent descriptions and their sectioned line drawings, plus a 37-page alphabetical index of the patentees.

Pattern Dates for British Ordnance Small Arms, 1718-1783, by DeWitt Bailey, Thomas Publications, Gettysburg, PA, 1997. 116 pp., illus. Paper covers. $20.00
The weapons discussed in this work are those carried by troops sent to North America between 1737 and 1783, or shipped to them as replacement arms while in America.

The Pitman Notes on U.S. Martial Small Arms and Ammunition, 1776-1933, Volume 2, Revolvers and Automatic Pistols, by Brig. Gen. John Pitman, Thomas Publications, Gettysburg, PA, 1990. 192 pp., illus. $29.95.
A most important primary source of information on United States military small arms and ammunition.

The Plains Rifle, by Charles Hanson, Gun Room Press, Highland Park, NJ, 1989. 169 pp., illus. $35.00.
All rifles that were made with the plainsman in mind, including pistols.

Powder and Ball Small Arms, by Martin Pegler, Windrow & Green, London, 1998. 128 pp., illus. $39.95.
Part of the new "Live Firing Classic Weapons" series featuring full color photos of experienced shooters dressed in authentic costumes handling, loading and firing historic weapons.

The Powder Flask Book, by Ray Riling, R&R Books, Livonia, NY, 1993. 514 pp., illus. $69.95.
The complete book on flasks of the 19th century. Exactly scaled pictures of 1,600 flasks are illustrated.

Proud Promise: French Autoloading Rifles, 1898-1979,by Jean Huon, Collector Grade Publications, Inc., Cobourg, Ont., Canada, 1995. 216 pp., illus. $39.95.
The author has finally set the record straight about the importance of French contributions to modern arms design.

E. C. Prudhomme's Gun Engraving Review, by E. C. Prudhomme, R&R Books, Livonia, NY, 1994. 164 pp., illus. $60.00.
As a source for engravers and collectors, this book is an indispensable guide to styles and techniques of the world's foremost engravers.

Purdey Gun and Rifle Makers: The Definitive History, by Donald Dallas, Quiller Press, London, 2000. 245 pp., illus. Color throughout. $100.00
A limited edition of 3,000 copies. Signed and Numbered. With a PURDEY book plate.

Reloading Tools, Sights and Telescopes for Single Shot Rifles, by Gerald O. Kelver, Brighton, CO, 1982. 163 pp., illus. Paper covers. $13.95.
A listing of most of the famous makers of reloading tools, sights and telescopes with a brief description of the products they manufactured.

The Remington-Lee Rifle, by Eugene F. Myszkowski, Excalibur Publications, Latham, NY, 1995. 100 pp., illus. Paper covers. $22.50.
Features detailed descriptions, including serial number ranges, of each model from the first Lee Magazine Rifle produced for the U.S. Navy to the last Remington-Lee Small Bores shipped to the Cuban Rural Guard.

Revolvers of the British Services 1854-1954, by W.H.J. Chamberlain and A.W.F. Taylerson, Museum Restoration Service, Ottawa, Canada, 1989. 80 pp., illus. $27.50.
Covers the types issued among many of the United Kingdom's naval, land or air services.

Rhode Island Arms Makers & Gunsmiths, by William O. Archibald, Andrew Mowbray, Inc., Lincoln, RI, 1990. 108 pp., illus. $16.50.
A serious and informative study of an important area of American arms making.

Rifles of the World, by Oliver Achard, Chartwell Books, Inc., Edison, NJ, 141 pp., illus. $24.95.
A unique insight into the world of long guns, not just rifles, but also shotguns, carbines and all the usual multi-barreled guns that once were so popular with European hunters, especially in Germany and Austria.

The Rock Island '03, by C.S. Ferris, C.S. Ferris, Arvada, CO, 1993. 58 pp., illus. Paper covers. $12.50.
A monograph of interest to the collector or historian concentrating on the U.S. M1903 rifle made by the less publicized of our two producing facilities.

Round Ball to Rimfire, Vol. 1, by Dean Thomas, Thomas Publications, Gettysburg, PA, 1997. 144 pp., illus. $40.00.
The first of a two-volume set of the most complete history and guide for all small arms ammunition used in the Civil War. The information includes data from research and development to the arsenals that created it.

Ruger and his Guns, by R.L. Wilson, Simon & Schuster, New York, NY, 1996. 358 pp., illus. $65.00.
A history of the man, the company and their firearms.

Russell M. Catron and His Pistols, by Warren H. Buxton, Ucross Books, Los Alamos, NM, 1998. 224 pp., illustrated. Paper covers. $49.50.
An unknown American firearms inventor and manufacturer of the mid twentieth century. Military, commerical, ammunition.

The SAFN-49 and The FAL, by Joe Poyer and Dr. Richard Feirman, North Cape Publications, Tustin, CA, 1998. 160 pp., illus. Paper covers. $14.95.
The first complete overview of the SAFN-49 battle rifle, from its pre-World War 2 beginnings to its military service in countries as diverse as the Belgian Congo and Argentina. The FAL was "light" version of the SAFN-49 and it became the Free World's most adopted battle rifle.

Sam Colt's Own Record 1847, by John Parsons, Wolfe Publishing Co., Prescott, AZ, 1992. 167 pp., illus. $24.50.
Chronologically presented, the correspondence published here completes the account of the manufacture, in 1847, of the Walker Model Colt revolver.

J. P. Sauer & Sohn, Sauer "Dein Waffenkamerad" Volume 2, by Cate & Krause, Walsworth Publishing, Chattanooga, TN, 2000. 440 pp., illus. $79.00.
A historical study of Sauer automatic pistols. This new volume includes a great deal of new knowledge that has surfaced about the firm J.P. Sauer. You will find new photos, documentation, serial number ranges and historial facts which will expand the knowledge and interest in the oldest and best of the German firearms companies.

Scottish Firearms, by Claude Blair and Robert Woosnam-Savage, Museum Restoration Service, Bloomfield, Ont., Canada, 1995. 52 pp., illus. Paper covers. $8.95.
This revision of the first book devoted entirely to Scottish firearms is supplemented by a register of surviving Scottish long guns.

The Scottish Pistol, by Martin Kelvin. Fairleigh Dickinson University Press, Dist. By Associated University Presses, Cranbury, NJ, 1997. 256 pp., illus. $49.50.
The Scottish pistol, its history, manufacture and design.

Sharps Firearms, by Frank Seller, Frank M. Seller, Denver, CO, 1998. 358 pp., illus. $55.00.
Traces the development of Sharps firearms with full range of guns made including all martial variations.

Simeon North: First Official Pistol Maker of the United States, by S. North and R. North, The Gun Room Press, Highland Park, NJ, 1972. 207 pp., illus. $15.95.
Reprint of the rare first edition.

The SKS Carbine, by Steve Kehaya and Joe Poyer, North Cape Publications, Tustin, CA, 1997. 150 pp., illus. Paper covers. $16.95.
The first comprehensive examination of a major historical firearm used through the Vietnam conflict to the diamond fields of Angola.

The SKS Type 45 Carbines, by Duncan Long, Desert Publications, El Dorado, AZ, 1992. 110 pp., illus. Paper covers. $19.95
Covers the history and practical aspects of operating, maintaining and modifying this abundantly available rifle.

Smith & Wesson 1857-1945, by Robert J. Neal and Roy G. Jinks, R&R Books, Livonia, NY, 1996. 434 pp., illus. $50.00.
The bible for all existing and aspiring Smith & Wesson collectors.

Sniper Variations of the German K98k Rifle, by Richard D. Law, Collector Grade Publications, Ontario, Canada, 1997. 240 pp., illus. $47.50.
Volume 2 of "Backbone of the Wehrmacht" the author's in-depth study of the German K98k rifle. This volume concentrates on the telescopic-sighted rifle of choice for most German snipers during World War 2.

Southern Derringers of the Mississippi Valley, by Turner Kirkland, Pioneer Press, Tenn., 1971. 80 pp., illus., paper covers. $4.00.
A guide for the collector, and a much-needed study.

Soviet Russian Postwar Military Pistols and Cartridges, by Fred A. Datig, Handgun Press, Glenview, IL, 1988. 152 pp., illus. $29.95.
Thoroughly researched, this definitive sourcebook covers the development and adoption of the Makarov, Stechkin and the new PSM pistols. Also included in this source book is coverage on Russian clandestine weapons and pistol cartridges.

Soviet Russian Tokarev "TT" Pistols and Cartridges 1929-1953, by Fred Datig, Graphic Publishers, Santa Ana, CA, 1993. 168 pp., illus. $39.95.
Details of rare arms and their accessories are shown in hundreds of photos. It also contains a complete bibliography and index.

Soviet Small-Arms and Ammunition, by David Bolotin, Handgun Press, Glenview, IL, 1996. 264 pp., illus. $49.95.
An authoritative and complete book on Soviet small arms.

Sporting Collectibles, by Jim and Vivian Karsnitz, Schiffer Publishing Ltd., West Chester, PA, 1992. 160 pp., illus. Paper covers. $29.95.
The fascinating world of hunting related collectibles presented in an informative text.

The Springfield 1903 Rifles, by Lt. Col. William S. Brophy, USAR, Ret., Stackpole Books Inc., Harrisburg, PA, 1985. 608 pp., illus. $75.00.
The illustrated, documented story of the design, development, and production of all the models, appendages, and accessories.

THE ARMS LIBRARY

Springfield Armory Shoulder Weapons 1795-1968, by Robert W.D. Ball, Antique Trader Books, Dubuque, IA, 1998. 264 pp., illus. $34.95.

This book documents the 255 basic models of rifles, including test and trial rifles, produced by the Springfield Armory. It features the entire history of rifles and carbines manufactured at the Armory, the development of each weapon with specific operating characteristics and procedures.

Springfield Model 1903 Service Rifle Production and Alteration, 1905-1910, by C.S. Ferris and John Beard, Arvada, CO, 1995. 66 pp., illus. Paper covers. $12.50.

A highly recommended work for any serious student of the Springfield Model 1903 rifle.

Springfield Shoulder Arms 1795-1865, by Claud E. Fuller, S. & S. Firearms, Glendale, NY, 1996. 76 pp., illus. Paper covers. $17.95.

Exact reprint of the scarce 1930 edition of one of the most definitive works on Springfield flintlock and percussion muskets ever published.

Standard Catalog of Firearms, 11th Edition, by Ned Schwing, Krause Publications, Iola, WI, 2001.1328 Pages, illustrated. 6,000+ b&w photos plus a 16-page color section. Paper covers. $32.95.

This is the largest, most comprehensive and best-selling firearm book of all time! And this year's edition is a blockbuster for both shooters and firearm collectors. More than 12,000 firearms are listed and priced in up to six grades of condition. That's almost 80,000 prices! Gun enthusiasts will love the new full-color section of photos highlighting the finest firearms sold at auction this past year –including the new record for an American historical firearm: $684,000!

Standard Catalog of Winchester, 1st Edition, edited by David D. Kowalski, Krause Publications, Iola, WI, 2000. 704 pp., illustrated with 2,000 B&W photos and 75 color photos. Paper covers. $39.95.

This book identifies and values more than 5,000 collectibles, including firearms, cartridges shotshells, fishing tackle, sporting goods and tools manufactured by Winchester Repeating Arms Co.

Steel Canvas: The Art of American Arms, by R.L. Wilson, Random House, NY, 1995, 384 pp., illus. $65.00.

Presented here for the first time is the breathtaking panorama of America's extraordinary engravers and embellishers of arms, from the 1700s to modern times.

Stevens Pistols & Pocket Rifles, by K.L. Cope, Museum Restoration Service, Alexandria Bay, NY, 1992. 114 pp., illus. $24.50.

This is the story of the guns and the man who designed them and the company which he founded to make them.

A Study of Colt Conversions and Other Percussion Revolvers, by R. Bruce McDowell, Krause Publications, Iola, WI, 1997. 464 pp., illus. $39.95.

The ultimate reference detailing Colt revolvers that have been converted from percussion to cartridge.

The Sumptuous Flaske, by Herbert G. Houze, Andrew Mowbray, Inc., Lincoln, RI, 1989. 158 pp., illus. Soft covers. $35.00.

Catalog of a recent show at the Buffalo Bill Historical Center bringing together some of the finest European and American powder flasks of the 16th to 19th centuries.

The Swedish Mauser Rifles, by Steve Kehaya and Joe Poyer, North Cape Publications, Tustin, CA, 1999. 267 pp., illustrated. Paper covers. $19.95.

Every known variation of the Swedish Mauser carbine and rifle is described including all match and target rifles and all sniper fersions. Includes serial number and production data.

Televisions Cowboys, Gunfighters & Cap Pistols, by Rudy A. D'Angelo, Antique Trader Books, Norfolk, VA, 1999. 287 pp., illustrated in color and black and white. Paper covers. $31.95.

Over 850 beautifully photographed color and black and white images of cap guns, actors, and the characters they portrayed in the "Golden Age of TV Westerns. With accurate descriptions and current values.

Thompson: The American Legend, by Tracie L. Hill, Collector Grade Publications, Ontario, Canada, 1996. 584 pp., illus. $85.00.

The story of the first American submachine gun. All models are featured and discussed.

Toys That Shoot and Other Neat Stuff, by James Dundas, Schiffer Books, Atglen, PA, 1999. 112 pp., illustrated. Paper covers. $24.95.

Shooting toys from the twentieth century, especially 1920's to 1960's, in over 420 color photographs of BB guns, cap shooters, marble shooters, squirt guns and more. Complete with a price guide.

The Trapdoor Springfield, by M.D. Waite and B.D. Ernst, The Gun Room Press, Highland Park, NJ, 1983. 250 pp., illus. $39.95.

The first comprehensive book on the famous standard military rifle of the 1873-92 period.

Treasures of the Moscow Kremlin: Arsenal of the Russian Tsars, A Royal Armories and the Moscow Kremlin exhibition. HM Tower of London 13, June 1998 to 11 September, 1998. BAS Printers, Over Wallop, Hampshire, England. xxii plus 192 pp. over 180 color illustrations. Text in English and Russian. $65.00.

For this exchibition catalog each of the 94 objects on display are photographed and described in detail to provide a most informative record of this important exhibition.

U.S. Breech-Loading Rifles and Carbines, Cal. 45, by Gen. John Pitman, Thomas Publications, Gettysburg, PA, 1992. 192 pp., illus. $29.95.

The third volume in the Pitman Notes on U.S. Martial Small Arms and Ammunition, 1776-1933. This book centers on the "Trapdoor Springfield" models.

U.S. Handguns of World War 2: The Secondary Pistols and Revolvers, by Charles W. Pate, Andrew Mowbray, Inc., Lincoln, RI, 1998. 515 pp., illus. $39.00.

This indispensable new book covers all of the American military handguns of World War 2 except for the M1911A1 Colt automatic.

United States Martial Flintlocks, by Robert M. Reilly, Mowbray Publishing Co., Lincoln, RI, 1997. 264 pp., illus. $40.00.

A comprehensive history of American flintlock longarms and handguns (mostly military) c. 1775 to c. 1840.

U.S. Martial Single Shot Pistols, by Daniel D. Hartzler and James B. Whisker, Old Bedford Village Pess, Bedford, PA, 1998. 128 pp., illus. $45.00.

A photographic chronicle of military and semi-martial pistols supplied to the U.S. Government and the several States.

U.S. Military Arms Dates of Manufacture from 1795, by George Madis, David Madis, Dallas, TX, 1989. 64 pp. Soft covers. $6.00.

Lists all U.S. military arms of collector interest alphabetically, covering about 250 models.

U.S. Military Small Arms 1816-1865, by Robert M. Reilly, The Gun Room Press, Highland Park, NJ, 1983. 270 pp., illus. $39.95.

Covers every known type of primary and secondary martial firearms used by Federal forces.

U.S. M1 Carbines: Wartime Production, by Craig Riesch, North Cape Publications, Tustin, CA, 1994. 72 pp., illus. Paper covers. $16.95.

Presents only verifiable and accurate information. Each part of the M1 Carbine is discussed fully in its own section; including markings and finishes.

U.S. Naval Handguns, 1808-1911, by Fredrick R. Winter, Andrew Mowbray Publishers, Lincoln, RI, 1990. 128 pp., illus. $26.00.

The story of U.S. Naval Handguns spans an entire century—included are sections on each of the important naval handguns within the period.

Walther: A German Legend, by Manfred Kersten, Safari Press, Inc., Huntington Beach, CA, 2000. 400 pp., illustrated. $85.00.

This comprehensive book covers, in rich detail, all aspects of the company and its guns, including an illustrious and rich history, the WW2 years, all the pistols (models 1 through 9), the P-38, P-88, the long guns, .22 rifles, centerfires, Wehrmacht guns, and even a gun that could shoot around a corner.

Walther Pistols: Models 1 Through P99, Factory Variations and Copies, by Dieter H. Marschall, Ucross Books, Los Alamos, NM. 2000. 140 pages, with 140 b & w illustrations, index. Paper Covers. $19.95.

This is the English translation, revised and updated, of the highly successful and widely acclaimed German language edition. This book provides the collector with a reference guide and overview of the entire line of the Walther military, police, and self-defense pistols from the very first to the very latest. Models 1-9, PP, PPK, MP, AP, HP, P.38, P1, P4, P38K, P5, P88, P99 and the Manurhin models. Variations, where issued, serial ranges, calibers, marks, proofs, logos, and design aspects in an astonishing quantity and variety are crammed into this very well researched and highly regarded work.

The Walther Handgun Story: A Collector's and Shooter's Guide, by Gene Gangarosa, Steiger Publications, 1999. 300., illustrated. Paper covers. $21.95.

Covers the entire history of the Walther empire. Illustrated with over 250 photos.

Walther P-38 Pistol, by Maj. George Nonte, Desert Publications, Cornville, AZ, 1982. 100 pp., illus. Paper covers. $11.95.

Complete volume on one of the most famous handguns to come out of WWII. All models covered.

Walther Models PP & PPK, 1929-1945 – Volume 1, by James L. Rankin, Coral Gables, FL, 1974. 142 pp., illus. $40.00

Complete coverage on the subject as to finish, proofmarks and Nazi Party inscriptions.

Walther Volume II, Engraved, Presentation and Standard Models, by James L. Rankin, J.L. Rankin, Coral Gables, FL, 1977. 112 pp., illus. $40.00.

The new Walther book on embellished versions and standard models. Has 88 photographs, including many color plates.

Walther, Volume III, 1908-1980, by James L. Rankin, Coral Gables, FL, 1981. 226 pp., illus. $40.00.

Covers all models of Walther handguns from 1908 to date, includes holsters, grips and magazines.

Winchester: An American Legend, by R.L. Wilson, Random House, New York, NY, 1991. 403 pp., illus. $65.00.

The official history of Winchester firearms from 1849 to the present.

Winchester Bolt Action Military & Sporting Rifles 1877 to 1937, by Herbert G. Houze, Andrew Mowbray Publishing, Lincoln, RI, 1998. 295 pp., illus. $45.00.

Winchester was the first American arms maker to commercially manufacture a bolt action repeating rifle, and this book tells the exciting story of these Winchester bolt actions.

The Winchester Book, by George Madis, David Madis Gun Book Distributor, Dallas, TX, 1986. 650 pp., illus. $49.50.

A new, revised 25th anniversary edition of this classic book on Winchester firearms. Complete serial ranges have been added.

Winchester Dates of Manufacture 1849-1984, by George Madis, Art & Reference House, Brownsboro, TX, 1984. 59 pp. $9.95.

A most useful work, compiled from records of the Winchester factory.

Winchester Engraving, by R.L. Wilson, Beinfeld Books, Springs, CA, 1989. 500 pp., illus. $135.00.

A classic reference work of value to all arms collectors.

The Winchester Handbook, by George Madis, Art & Reference House, Lancaster, TX, 1982. 287 pp., illus. $24.95.

The complete line of Winchester guns, with dates of manufacture, serial numbers, etc.

THE ARMS LIBRARY

The Winchester-Lee Rifle, by Eugene Myszkowski, Excalibur Publications, Tucson, AZ 2000. 96 pp., illustrated. Paper Covers. $22.95

The development of the Lee Straight Pull, the cartridge and the approval for military use. Covers details of the inventor and memorabilia of Winchester-Lee related material.

Winchester Lever Action Repeating Firearms, Vol. 1, The Models of 1866, 1873 and 1876, by Arthur Pirkle, North Cape Publications, Tustin, CA, 1995. 112 pp., illus. Paper covers. $19.95.

Complete, part-by-part description, including dimensions, finishes, markings and variations throughout the production run of these fine, collectible guns.

Winchester Lever Action Repeating Rifles, Vol. 2, The Models of 1886 and 1892, by Arthur Pirkle, North Cape Publications, Tustin, CA, 1996. 150 pp., illus. Paper covers. $19.95.

Describes each model on a part-by-part basis by serial number range complete with finishes, markings and changes.

Winchester Lever Action Repeating Rifles, Volume 3, The Model of 1894, by Arthur Pirkle, North Cape Publications, Tustin, CA, 1998. 150 pp., illus. Paper covers. $19.95.

The first book ever to provide a detailed description of the Model 1894 rifle and carbine.

The Winchester Lever Legacy, by Clyde "Snooky" Williamson, Buffalo Press, Zachary, LA, 1988. 664 pp., illustrated. $75.00

A book on reloading for the different calibers of the Winchester lever action rifle.

The Winchester Model 94: The First 100 Years, by Robert C. Renneberg, Krause Publications, Iola, WI, 1991. 208 pp., illus. $34.95.

Covers the design and evolution from the early years up to the many different editions that exist today.

Winchester Rarities, by Webster, Krause Publications, Iola, WI, 2000. 208 pp., with over 800 color photos, illus. $49.95.

This book details the rarest of the rare; the one-of-a-kind items and the advertising pieces from years gone by. With nearly 800 full color photos and detailed pricing provided by experts in the field, this book gives collectors and enthusiasts everything they need.

Winchester Shotguns and Shotshells, by Ronald W. Stadt, Krause Publications, Iola, WI, 1995. 256 pp., illus. $34.95.

The definitive book on collectible Winchester shotguns and shotshells manufactured through 1961.

The Winchester Single-Shot- Volume 1; A History and Analysis, by John Campbell, Andrew Mowbray, Inc., Lincoln RI, 1995. 272 pp., illus. $55.00.

Covers every important aspect of this highly-collectible firearm.

The Winchester Single-Shot- Volume 2; Old Secrets and New Discoveries, by John Campbell, Andrew Mowbray, Inc., Lincoln RI, 2000. 280 pp., illus. $55.00.

An exciting follow-up to the classic first volume.

Winchester Slide-Action Rifles, Volume 1: Model 1890 & 1906, by Ned Schwing, Krause Publications, Iola, WI, 1992. 352 pp., illus. $39.95.

First book length treatment of models 1890 & 1906 with over 50 charts and tables showing significant new information about caliber style and rarity.

Winchester Slide-Action Rifles, Volume 2: Model 61 & Model 62, by Ned Schwing, Krause Publications, Iola, WI, 1993. 256 pp., illus. $34.95.

A complete historic look into the Model 61 and the Model 62. These favorite slide-action guns receive a thorough presentation which takes you to the factory to explore receivers, barrels, markings, stocks, stampings and engraving in complete detail.

Winchester's North West Mounted Police Carbines and other Model 1876 Data, by Lewis E. Yearout, The author, Great Falls, MT, 1999. 224 pp., illustrated. Paper covers. $38.00

An impressive accumulation of the facts on the Model 1876, with particular empasis on those purchased for the North West Mounted Police.

Worldwide Webley and the Harrington and Richardson Connection, by Stephen Cuthbertson, Ballista Publishing and Distributing Ltd., Gabriola Island, Canada, 1999. 259 pp., illus. $50.00

A masterpiece of scholarship. Over 350 photographs plus 75 original documents, patent drawings, and advertisements accompany the text.

GENERAL

Action Shooting: Cowboy Style, by John Taffin, Krause Publications, Iola, WI, 1999. 320 pp., illustrated. $39.95.

Details on the guns and ammunition. Explanations of the rules used for many events. The essential cowboy wardrobe.

Advanced Muzzleloader's Guide, by Toby Bridges, Stoeger Publishing Co., So. Hackensack, NJ, 1985. 256 pp., illus. Paper covers. $14.95.

The complete guide to muzzle-loading rifles, pistols and shotguns—flintlock and percussion.

Aids to Musketry for Officers & NCOs, by Capt. B.J. Friend, Excalibur Publications, Latham, NY, 1996. 40 pp., illus. Paper covers. $7.95.

A facsimile edition of a pre-WWI British manual filled with useful information for training the common soldier.

Air Gun Digest, 3rd Edition, by J.I. Galan, DBI Books, a division of Krause Publications, Iola, WI, 1995. 258 pp., illus. Paper covers. $19.95

Everything from A to Z on air gun history, trends and technology.

American and Imported Arms, Ammunition and Shooting Accessories, Catalog No. 18 of the Shooter's Bible, Stoeger, Inc., reprinted by Fayette Arsenal, Fayetteville, NC, 1988. 142 pp., illus. Paper covers. $10.95.

A facsimile reprint of the 1932 Stoeger's Shooter's Bible.

America's Great Gunmakers, by Wayne van Zwoll, Stoeger Publishing Co., So. Hackensack, NJ, 1992. 288 pp., illus. Paper covers. $16.95.

This book traces in great detail the evolution of guns and ammunition in America and the men who formed the companies that produced them.

Ammunition: Small Arms, Grenades and Projected Munitions, by Ian V. Hogg, Greenhill Books, London, England, 1998. 144 pp., illustrated. $22.95.

The best concise guide to modern ammunition. Wide-ranging and international coverage. Detailed specifications and illustrations.

Armed and Female, by Paxton Quigley, E.P. Dutton, New York, NY, 1989. 237 pp., illus. $16.95.

The first complete book on one of the hottest subjects in the media today, the arming of the American woman.

Arming the Glorious Cause: Weapons of the Second War for Independence, by James B. Whisker, Daniel D. Hartzler and Larry W. Yantz, R & R Books, Livonia, NY, 1998. 175 pp., illustrated. $45.00.

A photographic study of Confederate weapons.

Arms and Armour in Antiquity and the Middle Ages, by Charles Boutell, Stackpole Books, Mechanicsburg, PA, 1996. 352 pp., illus. $22.95.

Detailed descriptions of arms and armor, the development of tactics and the outcome of specific battles.

Arms & Armor in the Art Institute of Chicago, by Walter J. Karcheski, Jr., Bulfinch Press, Boston, MA, 1995. 128 pp., illus. $35.00.

Now, for the first time, the Art Institute of Chicago's arms and armor collection is presented in the visual delight of 103 color illustrations.

Arms for the Nation: Springfield Longarms, edited by David C. Clark, Scott A. Duff, Export, PA, 1994. 73 pp., illus. Paper covers. $9.95.

A brief history of the Springfield Armory and the arms made there.

Arsenal of Freedom, The Springfield Armory, 1890-1948: A Year-by-Year Account Drawn from Official Records, compiled and edited by Lt. Col. William S. Brophy, USAR Ret., Andrew Mowbray, Inc., Lincoln, RI, 1991. 400 pp., illus. Soft covers. $29.95.

A "must buy" for all students of American military weapons, equipment and accoutrements.

Assault Pistols, Rifles and Submachine Guns, by Duncan Long, Paladin Press, Boulder, CO, 1997, 8 1/2 x 11, soft cover, photos, illus. 152 pp. $21.95

This book offers up-to-date, practical information on how to operate and field-strip modern military, police and civilian combat weapons. Covers new developments and trends such as the use of fiber optics, liquid-recoil systems and lessening of barrel length are covered. Troubleshooting procedures, ballistic tables and a list of manufacturers and distributors are also included.

Assault Weapons, 5th Edition, The Gun Digest Book of, edited by Jack Lewis and David E. Steele, DBI Books, a division of Krause Publications, Iola, WI, 2000. 256 pp., illustrated. Paper covers. $21.95.

This is the latest word on true assault weaponry in use today by international military and law enforcement organizations.

The Belgian Rattlesnake: The Lewis Automatic Machine Gun, by William M. Easterly, Collector Grade Publications, Inc., Cobourg, Ont. Canada, 1998. 542 pp., illus. $79.95.

A social and technical biography of the Lewis automatic machine gun and its inventors.

The Big Guns: Civil War Siege, Seacoast, and Naval Cannon, by Edwin Olmstead, Wayne E. Stark and Spencer C. Tucker, Museum Restoration Service, Bloomfield, Ontario, Canada, 1997. 360 pp., illus. $80.00.

This book is designed to identify and record the heavy guns available to both sides during the Civil War.

Blackpowder Loading Manual, 3rd Edition, by Sam Fadala, DBI Books, a division of Krause Publications, Iola, WI, 1995. 368 pp., illus. Paper covers. $20.95.

Revised and expanded edition of this landmark blackpowder loading book. Covers hundreds of loads for most of the popular blackpowder rifles, handguns and shotguns.

Bolt Action Rifles, 3rd Edition, by Frank de Haas, DBI Books, a division of Krause Publications, Iola, WI, 1995. 528 pp., illus. Paper covers. $24.95.

A revised edition of the most definitive work on all major bolt-action rifle designs.

The Book of the Crossbow, by Sir Ralph Payne-Gallwey, Dover Publications, Mineola, NY, 1996. 416 pp., illus. Paper covers. $14.95.

Unabridged republication of the scarce 1907 London edition of the book on one of the most devastating hand weapons of the Middle Ages.

Bows and Arrows of the Native Americans, by Jim Hamm, Lyons & Burford Publishers, New York, NY, 1991. 156 pp., illus. $19.95.

A complete step-by-step guide to wooden bows, sinew-backed bows, composite bows, strings, arrows and quivers.

British Small Arms of World War 2, by Ian D. Skennerton, I.D.S.A. Books, Piqua, OH, 1988. 110 pp., 37 illus. $25.00.

"Carbine," the Story of David Marshall Williams, by Ross E. Beard, Jr. Phillips Publications, Williamstown, NJ, 1999. 225 pp., illus. $29.95.

The story of the firearms genius, David Marshall "Carbine" Williams. From prison to the pinnacles of fame, the tale of this North Carolinian is inspiring. The author details many of Williams' firearms inventions and developments.

Combat Handgunnery, 4th Edition, The Gun Digest Book of, by Chuck Taylor, DBI Books, a division of Krause Publications, Iola, WI, 1997. 256 pp., illus. Paper covers. $18.95.

This edition looks at real world combat handgunnery from three different perspectives—military, police and civilian.

THE ARMS LIBRARY

The Complete Blackpowder Handbook, 3rd Edition, by Sam Fadala, DBI Books, a division of Krause Publications, Iola, WI, 1997. 400 pp., illus. Paper covers. $21.95.

Expanded and completely rewritten edition of the definitive book on the subject of blackpowder.

The Complete Guide to Game Care and Cookery, 3rd Edition, by Sam Fadala, DBI Books, a division of Krause Publications, Iola, WI, 1994. 320 pp., illus. Paper covers. $18.95.

Over 500 photos illustrating the care of wild game in the field and at home with a separate recipe section providing over 400 tested recipes.

The Complete .50-caliber Sniper Course, by Dean Michaelis, Paladin Press, Boulder, CO, 2000. 576 pp, illustrated, $60.00

The history from German Mauser T-Gewehr of World War 1 to the Soviet PTRD and beyond. Includes the author's Program of Instruction for Special Operations Hard-Target Interdiction Course.

Complete Guide to Guns & Shooting, by John Malloy, DBI Books, a division of Krause Publications, Iola, WI, 1995. 256 pp., illus. Paper covers. $18.95.

What every shooter and gun owner should know about firearms, ammunition, shooting techniques, safety, collecting and much more.

Cowboy Action Shooting, by Charly Gullett, Wolfe Publishing Co., Prescott, AZ, 1995. 400 pp., illus. Paper covers. $24.50.

The fast growing of the shooting sports is comprehensively covered in this text—the guns, loads, tactics and the fun and flavor of this Old West era competition.

Crossbows, edited by Roger Combs, DBI Books, a division of Krause Publications, Iola, WI, 1986. 192 pp., illus. Paper covers. $15.95.

Complete, up-to-date coverage of the hottest bow going—and the most controversial.

Custom Firearms Engraving, by Tom Turpin, Krause Publications, Iola, WI, 1999. 208 pp., illustrated. $49.95.

Provides a broad and comprehensive look at the world of firearms engraving. The exquisite styles of more than 75 master engravers are shown on beautiful examples of handguns, rifles, shotguns, and other firearms, as well as knives.

Dead On, by Tony Noblitt and Warren Gabrilska, Paladin Press, Boulder, CO, 1998. 176 pp., illustrated. Paper covers. $22.00

The long-range marksman's guide to extreme accuracy.

Death from Above: The German FG42 Paratrooper Rifle, by Thomas B. Dugelby and R. Blake Stevens, Collector Grade Publications, Toronto, Canada, 1990. 147 pp., illus. $39.95.

The first comprehensive study of all seven models of the FG42.

Early American Flintlocks, by Daniel D. Hartzler and James B. Whisker, Bedford Valley Press, Bedford, PA 2000. 192 pp., Illustrated.

Covers early Colonial Guns, New England Guns, Pennsylvania Guns and Souther Guns.

Encyclopedia of Modern Firearms, Vol. 1, compiled and publ. by Bob Brownell, Montezuma, IA, 1959. 1057 pp. plus index, illus. $70.00. Dist. By Bob Brownell, Montezuma, IA 50171.

Massive accumulation of basic information of nearly all modern arms pertaining to "parts and assembly." Replete with arms photographs, exploded drawings, manufacturers' lists of parts, etc.

Encyclopedia of Native American Bows, Arrows and Quivers, by Steve Allely and Jim Hamm, The Lyons Press, N.Y., 1999. 160 pp., illustrated. $29.95.

A landmark book for anyone interested in archery history, or Native Americans.

The Exercise of Armes, by Jacob de Gheyn, edited and with an introduction by Bas Kist, Dover Publications, Inc., Mineola, NY, 1999. 144 pp., illustrated. Paper covers. $12.95.

Republications of all 117 engravings from the 1607 classic military manual. A meticulously accurate portrait of uniforms and weapons of the 17th century Netherlands.

Exploded Long Gun Drawings, The Gun Digest Book of, edited by Harold A. Murtz, DBI Books, a division of Krause Publications, Iola, WI, 512 pp., illus. Paper covers. $20.95.

Containing almost 500 rifle and shotgun exploded drawings.

Fighting Iron; A Metals Handbook for Arms Collectors, by Art Gogan, Mowbray Publishers, Inc., Lincoln, RI, 1999. 176 pp., illustrated. $28.00.

A guide that is easy to use, explains things in simple English and covers all of the different historical periods that we are interested in.

The Fighting Submachine Gun, Machine Pistol, and Shotgun, a Hands-On Evaluation, by Timothy J. Mullin, Paladin Press, Boulder, CO, 1999. 224 pp., illustrated. Paper covers. $35.00.

An invaluable reference for military, police and civilian shooters who may someday need to know how a specific weapon actually performs when the targets are shooting back and the margin of errors is measured in lives lost.

Fireworks: A Gunsight Anthology, by Jeff Cooper, Paladin Press, Boulder, CO, 1998. 192 pp., illus. Paper cover. $27.00

A collection of wild, hilarious, shocking and always meaningful tales from the remarkable life of an American firearms legend.

Frank Pachmayr: The Story of America's Master Gunsmith and his Guns, by John Lachuk, Safari Press, Huntington Beach, CA, 1996. 254 pp., illus. First edition, limited, signed and slipcased. $85.00; Second printing trade edition. $50.00.

The colorful and historically significant biography of Frank A. Pachmayr, America's own gunsmith emeritus.

From a Stranger's Doorstep to the Kremlin Gate, by Mikhail Kalashnikov, Ironside International Publishers, Inc., Alexandria, VA, 1999. 460 pp., illustrated. $34.95.

A biography of the most influential rifle designer of the 20th century. His AK-47 assault rifle has become the most widely used (and copied) assault rifle of this century.

The Frontier Rifleman, by H.B. LaCrosse Jr., Pioneer Press, Union City, TN, 1989. 183 pp., illus. Soft covers. $17.50.

The Frontier rifleman's clothing and equipment during the era of the American Revolution, 1760-1800.

The Gatling Gun: 19th Century Machine Gun to 21st Century Vulcan, by Joseph Berk, Paladin Press, Boulder, CO, 1991. 136 pp., illus. $34.95.

Here is the fascinating on-going story of a truly timeless weapon, from its beginnings during the Civil War to its current role as a state-of-the-art modern combat system.

German Artillery of World War Two, by Ian V. Hogg, Stackpole Books, Mechanicsburg, PA, 1997. 304 pp., illus. $44.95.

Complete details of German artillery use in WWII.

Grand Old Lady of No Man's Land: The Vickers Machine Gun, by Dolf L. Goldsmith, Collector Grade Publications, Cobourg, Canada, 1994. 600 pp., illus. $79.95.

Goldsmith brings his years of experience as a U.S. Army armourer, machine gun collector and shooter to bear on the Vickers, in a book sure to become a classic in its field.

The Grenade Recognition Manual, Volume 1, U.S. Grenades & Accessories, by Darryl W. Lynn, Service Publications, Ottawa, Canada, 1998. 112 pp., illus. Paper covers. $29.95.

This new book examines the hand grenades of the United States beginning with the hand grenades of the U.S. Civil War and continues through to the present.

The Grenade Recognition Manual, Vol. 2, British and Commonwealth Grenades and Accessories, by Darryl W. Lynn, Printed by the Author, Ottawa, Canada, 2001. 201 pp., illustrated with over 200 photos and drawings. Paper covers. $29.95.

Covers British, Australian, and Canadian Grenades. It has the complete British Numbered series, most of the L series as well as the Australian and Canadian grenades in use. Also covers Launchers, fuzes and lighters, launching cartridges, fillings, and markings.

Gun Digest Treasury, 7th Edition, edited by Harold A. Murtz, DBI Books, a division of Krause Publications, Iola, WI, 1994. 320 pp., illus. Paper covers. $17.95.

A collection of some of the most interesting articles which have appeared in Gun Digest over its first 45 years.

Gun Digest 2002, 56th Edition, edited by Ken Ramage, DBI Books a division of Krause Publications, Iola, WI, 2001. 544 pp., illustrated. Paper covers. $24.95.

This all new 56th edition continues the editorial excellence, quality, content and comprehensive cataloguing that firearms enthusiasts have come to know and expect. The most read gun book in the world for the last half century.

Gun Engraving, by C. Austyn, Safari Press Publication, Huntington Beach, CA, 1998. 128 pp., plus 24 pages of color photos. $50.00.

A well-illustrated book on fine English and European gun engravers. Includes a fantastic pictorial section that lists types of engravings and prices.

Gun Notes, Volume 1, by Elmer Keith, Safari Press, Huntington Beach, CA, 1995. 219 pp., illustrated Limited Edition, Slipcased. $75.00

A collection of Elmer Keith's most interesting columns and feature stories that appeared in "Guns & Ammo" magazine from 1961 to the late 1970's.

Gun Notes, Volume 2, by Elmer Keith, Safari Press, Huntington Beach, CA, 1997. 292 pp., illus. Limited 1st edition, numbered and signed by Keith's son. Slipcased. $75.00. Trade edition. $35.00.

Covers articles from Keith's monthly column in "Guns & Ammo" magazine during the period from 1971 through Keith's passing in 1982.

Gun Talk, edited by Dave Moreton, Winchester Press, Piscataway, NJ, 1973. 256 pp., illus. $9.95.

A treasury of original writing by the top gun writers and editors in America. Practical advice about every aspect of the shooting sports.

The Gun That Made the Twenties Roar, by Wm. J. Helmer, rev. and enlarged by George C. Nonte, Jr., The Gun Room Press, Highland Park, NJ, 1977. Over 300 pp., illus. $24.95.

Historical account of John T. Thompson and his invention, the infamous "Tommy Gun."

Gun Trader's Guide, 23rd Edition, published by Stoeger Publishing Co., Wayne, NJ, 1999. 592 pp., illus. Paper covers. $23.95.

Complete specifications and current prices for used guns. Prices of over 5,000 handguns, rifles and shotguns both foreign and domestic.

Gun Writers of Yesteryear, compiled by James Foral, Wolfe Publishing Co., Prescott, AZ, 1993. 449 pp. $35.00.

Here, from the pre-American rifleman days of 1898-1920, are collected some 80 articles by 34 writers from eight magazines.

The Gunfighter, Man or Myth? by Joseph G. Rosa, Oklahoma Press, Norman, OK, 1969. 229 pp., illus. (including weapons). Paper covers. $14.95.

A well-documented work on gunfights and gunfighters of the West and elsewhere. Great treat for all gunfighter buffs.

Gunfitting: The Quest for Perfection, by Michael Yardley, Safari Press, Huntington Beach, CA, 1995. 128 pp., illus. $24.95.

The author, a very experienced shooting instructor, examines gun stocks and gunfitting in depth.

THE ARMS LIBRARY

Guns Illustrated 2002, 3rd Edition, edited by Ken Ramage, DBI Books a division of Krause Publications, Iola, WI, 1999. 352 pp., illustrated. Paper covers. $22.95.

Highly informative, technical articles on a wide range of shooting topics by some of the top writers in the industry. A catalog section lists more than 3,000 firearms currently manufactured in or imported to the U.S.

Guns & Shooting: A Selected Bibliography, by Ray Riling, Ray Riling Arms Books Co., Phila., PA, 1982. 434 pp., illus. Limited, numbered edition. $75.

A limited edition of this superb bibliographical work, the only modern listing of books devoted to guns and shooting.

Guns, Bullets, and Gunfighters, by Jim Cirillo, Paladin Press, Boulder, CO, 1996. 119 pp., illus. Paper covers. $16.00.

Lessons and tales from a modern-day gunfighter.

Guns, Loads, and Hunting Tips, by Bob Hagel, Wolfe Publishing Co., Prescott, AZ, 1986. 509 pp., illus. $19.95.

A large hardcover book packed with shooting, hunting and handloading wisdom.

Handgun Digest, 3rd Edition, edited by Chris Christian, DBI Books, a division of Krause Publications, Iola, WI, 1995. 256 pp., illus. Paper covers. $18.95.

Full coverage of all aspects of handguns and handgunning from a highly readable and knowledgeable author.

Hidden in Plain Sight, "A Practical Guide to Concealed Handgun Carry" (Revised 2nd Edition), by Trey Bloodworth and Mike Raley, Paladin Press, Boulder, CO, 1997, 5 1/2 x 8 1/2, softcover, photos, 176 pp. $20.00

Concerned with how to comfortably, discreetly and safely exercise the privileges granted by a CCW permit? This invaluable guide offers the latest advice on what to look for when choosing a CCW, how to dress for comfortable, effective concealed carry, traditional and more unconventional carry modes, accessory holsters, customized clothing and accessories, accessibility data based on draw-time comparisons and new holsters on the market. Includes 40 new manufacturer listings.

HK Assault Rifle Systems, by Duncan Long, Paladin Press, Boulder, CO, 1995. 110 pp., illus. Paper covers. $27.95.

The little known history behind this fascinating family of weapons tracing its beginnings from the ashes of World War Two to the present time.

The Hunter's Table, by Terry Libby/Recipes of Chef Richard Blondin, Countrysport Press, Selma, AL, 1999. 230 pp. $30.00.

The Countrysport book of wild game guisine.

I Remember Skeeter, compiled by Sally Jim Skelton, Wolfe Publishing Co., Prescott, AZ, 1998. 401 pp., illus. Paper covers. $19.95.

A collection of some of the beloved storyteller's famous works interspersed with anecdotes and tales from the people who knew best.

In The Line of Fire, "A Working Cop's Guide to Pistol Craft", by Michael E. Conti, Paladin Press, Boulder, CO, 1997, soft cover, photos, illus., 184 pp. $30.00

As a working cop, you want to end your patrol in the same condition you began: alive and uninjured. Improve your odds by reading and mastering the information in this book on pistol selection, stopping power, combat reloading, stoppages, carrying devices, stances, grips and Conti's "secrets" to accurate shooting.

Joe Rychertinik Reflects on Guns, Hunting, and Days Gone By, by Joe Rychertinik, Precision Shooting, Inc., Manchester, CT, 1999. 281 pp., illustrated. Paper covers. $16.95.

Thirty articles by a master story-teller.

Kill or Get Killed, by Col. Rex Applegate, Paladin Press, Boulder, CO, 1996. 400 pp., illus. $39.95.

The best and longest-selling book on close combat in history.

Larrey: Surgeon to Napoleon's Imperial Guard, by Robert G. Richardson, Quiller Press, London, 2000. 269 pp., illus. B & W photos, maps and drawings. $23.95

Not a book for the squeamish, but one full of interest, splendidly researched, bringing both the character of the Napoleonic wars and Larrey himself vividly to life. Authenticity of detail is preserved throughout.

The Long-Range War: Sniping in Vietnam, by Peter R. Senich, Paladin Press, Boulder, CO, 1994. 280 pp., illus. $49.95.

The most complete report on Vietnam-era sniping ever documented.

Manual for H&R Reising Submachine Gun and Semi-Auto Rifle, edited by George P. Dillman, Desert Publications, El Dorado, AZ, 1994. 81 pp., illus. Paper covers. $12.95.

A reprint of the Harrington & Richardson 1943 factory manual and the rare military manual on the H&R submachine gun and semi-auto rifle.

The Manufacture of Gunflints, by Sydney B.J. Skertchly, facsimile reprint with new introduction by Seymour de Lotbiniere, Museum Restoration Service, Ontario, Canada, 1984. 90 pp., illus. $24.50.

Limited edition reprinting of the very scarce London edition of 1879.

Master Tips, by J. Winokur, Potshot Press, Pacific Palisades, CA, 1985. 96 pp., illus. Paper covers. $11.95.

Basics of practical shooting.

The Military and Police Sniper, by Mike R. Lau, Precision Shooting, Inc., Manchester, CT, 1998. 352 pp., illustrated. Paper covers. $44.95.

Advanced precision shooting for combat and law enforcement.

Military Rifle & Machine Gun Cartridges, by Jean Huon, Paladin Press, Boulder, CO, 1990. 392 pp., illus. $34.95.

Describes the primary types of military cartridges and their principal loadings, as well as their characteristics, origin and use.

Military Small Arms of the 20th Century, 7th Edition, by Ian V. Hogg and John Weeks, DBI Books, a division of Krause Publications, Iola, WI, 2000. 416 pp., illustrated. Paper covers. $24.95.

Cover small arms of 46 countries. Over 800 photographs and illustrations.

Modern Custom Guns, Walnut, Steel, and Uncommon Artistry, by Tom Turpin, Krause Publications, Iola, WI, 1997. 206 pp., illus. $49.95.

From exquisite engraving to breathtaking exotic woods, the mystique of today's custom guns is expertly detailed in word and awe-inspiring color photos of rifles, shotguns and handguns.

Modern Guns Identification & Values, 13th Edition, by Russell & Steve Quertermous, Collector Books, Paducah, KY, 1999. 516 pp., illus. Paper covers. $12.95.

A standard reference for over 20 years. Over 1,800 illustrations of over 2,500 models with their current values.

Modern Law Enforcement Weapons & Tactics, 2nd Edition, by Tom Ferguson, DBI Books, a division of Krause Publications, Iola, WI, 1991. 256 pp., illus. Paper covers. $18.95.

An in-depth look at the weapons and equipment used by law enforcement agencies of today.

Modern Machine Guns, by John Walter, Stackpole Books, Inc. Mechanicsburg, PA, 2000. 144 pp., with 146 illustrations. $22.95.

A compact and authoritative guide to post-war machine-guns. A gun-by-gun directory identifying individual variants and types including detailed evaluations and technical data.

Modern Sporting Guns, by Christopher Austyn, Safari Press, Huntington Beach, CA, 1994. 128 pp., illus. $40.00.

A discussion of the "best" English guns; round action, over-and-under, boxlocks, hammer guns, bolt action and double rifles as well as accessories.

The More Complete Cannoneer, by M.C. Switlik, Museum & Collectors Specialties Co., Monroe, MI, 1990. 199 pp., illus. $19.95.

Compiled agreeably to the regulations for the U.S. War Department, 1861, and containing current observations on the use of antique cannons.

The MP-40 Machine Gun, Desert Publications, El Dorado, AZ, 1995. 32 pp., illus. Paper covers. $11.95.

A reprint of the hard-to-find operating and maintenance manual for one of the most famous machine guns of World War II.

Naval Percussion Locks and Primers, by Lt. J. A. Dahlgren, Museum Restoration Service, Bloomfield, Canada, 1996. 140 pp., illus. $35.00

First published as an Ordnance Memoranda in 1853, this is the finest existing study of percussion locks and primers origin and development.

The Official Soviet AKM Manual, translated by Maj. James F. Gebhardt (Ret.), Paladin Press, Boulder, CO, 1999. 120 pp., illustrated. Paper covers. $18.00.

This official military manual, available in English for the first time, was originally published by the Soviet Ministry of Defence. Covers the history, function, maintenance, assembly and disassembly, etc. of the 7.62mm AKM assault rifle.

The One-Round War: U.S.M.C. Scout-Snipers in Vietnam, by Peter Senich, Paladin Press, Boulder, CO, 1996. 384 pp., illus. Paper covers $59.95.

Sniping in Vietnam focusing specifically on the Marine Corps program.

Pin Shooting: A Complete Guide, by Mitchell A. Ota, Wolfe Publishing Co., Prescott, AZ, 1992. 145 pp., illus. Paper covers. $14.95.

Traces the sport from its humble origins to today's thoroughly enjoyable social event, including the mammoth eight-day Second Chance Pin Shoot in Michigan.

Powder and Ball Small Arms, by Martin Pegler, Windrow & Greene Publishing, London, 1998. 128 pp., illustrated with 200 color photos. $39.95.

Part of the new "Live Firing Classic Weapons" series. Full-color photos of experienced shooters dressed in authentic costumes handling, loading and firing historic weapons.

Principles of Personal Defense, by Jeff Cooper, Paladin Press, Boulder, CO, 1999. 56 pp., illustrated. Paper covers. $14.00.

This revised edition of Jeff Cooper's classic on personal defense offers great new illustrations and a new preface while retaining the timeliness theory of individual defense behavior presented in the original book.

E.C. Prudhomme, Master Gun Engraver, A Retrospective Exhibition: 1946-1973, intro. by John T. Amber, The R. W. Norton Art Gallery, Shreveport, LA, 1973. 32 pp., illus. Paper covers. $9.95.

Examples of master gun engravings by Jack Prudhomme.

The Quotable Hunter, edited by Jay Cassell and Peter Fiduccia, The lyons Press, N.Y., 1999. 224 pp., illustrated. $20.00.

This collection of more than three hundred memorable quotes from hunters through the ages captures the essence of the sport, with all its joys idiosyncrasies, and challenges.

A Rifleman Went to War, by H. W. McBride, Lancer Militaria, Mt. Ida, AR, 1987. 398 pp., illus. $29.95.

The classic account of practical marksmanship on the battlefields of World War I.

Sharpshooting for Sport and War, by W.W. Greener, Wolfe Publishing Co., Prescott, AZ, 1995. 192 pp., illus. $30.00.

This classic reprint explores the *first* expanding bullet; service rifles; shooting positions; trajectories; recoil; external ballistics; and other valuable information.

The Shooter's Bible 2002, No. 93, edited by William S. Jarrett, Stoeger Publishing Co., Wayne, NJ, 2001. 576 pp., illustrated. Paper covers. $23.95.

Over 3,000 firearms currently offered by major American and foreign gunmakers. Represented are handguns, rifles, shotguns and black powder arms with complete specifications and retail prices.

Shooting To Live, by Capt. W. E. Fairbairn & Capt. E. A. Sykes, Paladin Press, Boulder, CO, 1997, 4 1/2 x 7, soft cover, illus., 112 pp. $14.00

Shooting to Live is the product of Fairbairn's and Sykes' practical experience with the handgun. Hundreds of incidents provided the basis for the first true book on life-or-death shootouts with the pistol. Shooting to Live teaches all concepts, considerations and applications of combat pistol craft.

THE ARMS LIBRARY

Shooting Sixguns of the Old West, by Mike Venturino, MLV Enterprises, Livingston, MT, 1997. 221 pp., illus. Paper covers. $26.50.

A comprehensive look at the guns of the early West: Colts, Smith & Wesson and Remingtons, plus blackpowder and reloading specs.

Sniper Training, FM 23-10, Reprint of the U.S. Army field manual of August, 1994, Paladin Press, Boulder, CO, 1995. 352pp., illus. Paper covers. $30.00

The most up-to-date U.S. military sniping information and doctrine.

Sniping in France, by Major H. Hesketh-Prichard, Lancer Militaria, Mt. Ida, AR, 1993. 224 pp., illus. $24.95.

The author was a well-known British adventurer and big game hunter. He was called upon in the early days of "The Great War" to develop a program to offset an initial German advantage in sniping. How the British forces came to overcome this advantage.

Special Warfare: Special Weapons, by Kevin Dockery, Emperor's Press, Chicago, IL, 1997. 192 pp., illus. $29.95.

The arms and equipment of the UDT and SEALS from 1943 to the present.

Sporting Collectibles, by Dr. Stephen R. Irwin, Stoeger Publishing Co., Wayne, NJ, 1997. 256 pp., illus. Paper covers. $19.95.

A must book for serious collectors and admirers of sporting collectibles.

The Sporting Craftsmen: A Complete Guide to Contemporary Makers of Custom-Built Sporting Equipment, by Art Carter, Countrysport Press, Traverse City, MI, 1994. 240 pp., illus. $35.00.

Profiles leading makers of centerfire rifles; muzzleloading rifles; bamboo fly rods; fly reels; flies; waterfowl calls; decoys; handmade knives; and traditional longbows and recurves.

Sporting Rifle Takedown & Reassembly Guide, 2nd Edition, by J.B. Wood, DBI Books, a division of Krause Publications, Iola, WI, 1997. 480 pp., illus. $19.95.

An updated edition of the reference guide for anyone who wants to properly care for their sporting rifle. (Available September 1997)

2001 Standard Catalog of Firearms, the Collector's Price & Reference Guide, 11th Edition, by Ned Schwing, Krause Publications, Iola, WI, 2000. 1,248 pp., illus. Paper covers. $32.95.

Packed with more than 80,000 real world prices with more than 5,000 photos. Easy to use master index listing every firearm model.

The Street Smart Gun Book, by John Farnam, Police Bookshelf, Concord, NH, 1986. 45 pp., illus. Paper covers. $11.95.

Weapon selection, defensive shooting techniques, and gunfight-winning tactics from one of the world's leading authorities.

Stress Fire, Vol. 1: Stress Fighting for Police, by Massad Ayoob, Police Bookshelf, Concord, NH, 1984. 149 pp., illus. Paper covers. $9.95.

Gunfighting for police, advanced tactics and techniques.

Survival Guns, by Mel Tappan, Desert Publications, El Dorado, AZ, 1993. 456 pp., illus. Paper covers. $21.95.

Discusses in a frank and forthright manner which handguns, rifles and shotguns to buy for personal defense and securing food, and the ones to avoid.

The Tactical Advantage, by Gabriel Suarez, Paladin Press, Boulder, CO, 1998. 216 pp., illustrated. Paper covers. $22.00.

Learn combat tactics that have been tested in the world's toughest schools.

Tactical Marksman, by Dave M. Lauch, Paladin Press, Boulder, CO, 1996. 165 pp., illus. Paper covers. $35.00.

A complete training manual for police and practical shooters.

Thompson Guns 1921-1945, Anubis Press, Houston, TX, 1980. 215 pp., illus. Paper covers. $15.95.

Facsimile reprinting of five complete manuals on the Thompson submachine gun.

To Ride, Shoot Straight, and Speak the Truth, by Jeff Cooper, Paladin Press, Boulder, CO, 1997, 5 1/2 x 8 1/2, soft-cover, illus., 384 pp. $32.00

Combat mind-set, proper sighting, tactical residential architecture, nuclear war - these are some of the many subjects explored by Jeff Cooper in this illustrated anthology. The author discusses various arms, fighting skills and the importance of knowing how to defend oneself, and one's honor, in our rapidly changing world.

Trailriders Guide to Cowboy Action Shooting, by James W. Barnard, Pioneer Press, Union City, TN, 1998. 134 pp., plus 91 photos, drawings and charts. Paper covers. $24.95.

Covers the complete spectrum of this shooting discipline, from how to dress to authentic leather goods, which guns are legal, calibers, loads and ballistics.

The Ultimate Sniper, by Major John L. Plaster, Paladin Press, Boulder, CO, 1994. 464 pp., illus. Paper covers. $42.95.

An advanced training manual for military and police snipers.

Unrepentant Sinner, by Col. Charles Askins, Paladin Press, Boulder, CO, 2000. 322 pp., illustrated. $29.95.

The autobiography of Colonel Charles Askins.

U.S. Marine Corp Rifle and Pistol Marksmanship, 1935, reprinting of a government publication, Lancer Militaria, Mt. Ida, AR, 1991. 99 pp., illus. Paper covers. $11.95.

The old corps method of precision shooting.

U.S. Marine Corps Scout/Sniper Training Manual, Lancer Militaria, Mt. Ida, AR, 1989. Soft covers. $19.95.

Reprint of the original sniper training manual used by the Marksmanship Training Unit of the Marine Corps Development and Education Command in Quantico, Virginia.

U.S. Marine Corps Scout-Sniper, World War II and Korea, by Peter R. Senich, Paladin Press, Boulder, CO, 1994. 236 pp., illus. $44.95.

The most thorough and accurate account ever printed on the training, equipment and combat experiences of the U.S. Marine Corps Scout-Snipers.

U.S. Marine Corps Sniping, Lancer Militaria, Mt. Ida, AR, 1989. Irregular pagination. Soft covers. $17.95.

A reprint of the official Marine Corps FMFM1-3B.

Weapons of the Waffen-SS, by Bruce Quarrie, Sterling Publishing Co., Inc., 1991. 168 pp., illus. $24.95.

An in-depth look at the weapons that made Hitler's Waffen-SS the fearsome fighting machine it was.

Weatherby: The Man, The Gun, The Legend, by Grits and Tom Gresham, Cane River Publishing Co., Natchitoches, LA, 1992. 290 pp., illus. $24.95.

A fascinating look at the life of the man who changed the course of firearms development in America.

The Winchester Era, by David Madis, Art & Reference House, Brownsville, TX, 1984. 100 pp., illus. $19.95.

Story of the Winchester company, management, employees, etc.

Winchester Repeating Arms Company by Herbert Houze, Krause Publications, Iola, WI. 512 pp., illus. $50.00.

With British Snipers to the Reich, by Capt. C. Shore, Lander Militaria, Mt. Ida, AR, 1988. 420 pp., illus. $29.95.

One of the greatest books ever written on the art of combat sniping.

The World's Machine Pistols and Submachine Guns - Vol. 2a 1964 to 1980, by Nelson & Musgrave, Ironside International, Alexandria, VA, 2000. 673 pages, illustrated. $59.95

Containing data, history and photographs of over 200 weapons. With a special section covering shoulder stocked automatic pistols, 100 additional photos.

The World's Submachine Guns - Vol. 1 1918 to 1963, by Nelson & Musgrave, Ironside International, Alexandria, VA, 2001. 673 pages, illustrated. $59.95.

A revised edition covering much new material that has come to light since the book was originally printed in 1963.

The World's Sniping Rifles, by Ian V. Hogg, Paladin Press, Boulder, CO, 1998. 144 pp., illustrated. $22.95.

A detailed manual with descriptions and illustrations of more than 50 high-precision rifles from 14 countries and a complete analysis of sights and systems.

GUNSMITHING

Accurizing the Factory Rifle, by M.L. McPhereson, Precision Shooting, Inc., Manchester, CT, 1999. 335 pp., illustrated. Paper covers. $44.95.

A long-awaiting book, which bridges the gap between the rudimentary (mounting sling swivels, scope blocks and that general level of accomplishment) and the advanced (precision chambering, barrel fluting, and that general level of accomplishment) books that are currently available today.

Advanced Rebarreling of the Sporting Rifle, by Willis H. Fowler, Jr., Willis H. Fowler, Jr., Anchorage, AK, 1994. 127 pp., illus. Paper covers. $32.50.

A manual outlining a superior method of fitting barrels and doing chamber work on the sporting rifle.

The Art of Engraving, by James B. Meek, F. Brownell & Son, Montezuma, IA, 1973. 196 pp., illus. $38.95.

A complete, authoritative, imaginative and detailed study in training for gun engraving. The first book of its kind—and a great one.

Artistry in Arms, The R. W. Norton Gallery, Shreveport, LA, 1970. 42 pp., illus. Paper covers. $9.95.

The art of gunsmithing and engraving.

Barrels & Actions, by Harold Hoffman, H&P Publishers, San Angelo, TX, 1990. 309 pp., illus. Spiral bound. $29.95.

A manual on barrel making.

Black Powder Hobby Gunsmithing, by Sam Fadala and Dale Storey, DBI Books, a division of Krause Publications, Iola, WI., 1994. 256 pp., illus. Paper covers. $18.95.

A how-to guide for gunsmithing blackpowder pistols, rifles and shotguns from two men at the top of their respective fields.

Checkering and Carving of Gun Stocks, by Monte Kennedy, Stackpole Books, Harrisburg, PA, 1962. 175 pp., illus. $39.95.

Revised, enlarged cloth-bound edition of a much sought-after, dependable work.

The Complete Metal Finishing Book, by Harold Hoffman, H&P Publishers, San Angelo, TX, 1992. 364 pp., illus. Paper covers. $29.95.

Instructions for the different metal finishing operations that the normal craftsman or shop will use. Primarily firearm related.

Exploded Handgun Drawings, The Gun Digest Book of, edited by Harold A. Murtz, DBI Books, a division of Krause Publications, Iola, WI. 1992. 512 pp., illus. Paper covers. $20.95.

Exploded or isometric drawings for 494 of the most popular handguns.

Exploded Long Gun Drawings, The Gun Digest Book of, edited by Harold A. Murtz, DBI Books, a division of Krause Publications, Iola, WI. 512 pp., illus. Paper covers. $20.95.

Containing almost 500 rifle and shotgun exploded drawings. An invaluable aid to both professionals and hobbyists.

The Finishing of Gun Stocks, by Harold Hoffman, H&P Publishers, San Angelo, TX, 1994. 98 pp., illus. Paper covers. $17.95.

Covers different types of finishing methods and finishes.

THE ARMS LIBRARY

Firearms Assembly/Disassembly, Part I: Automatic Pistols, 2nd Revised Edition, The Gun Digest Book of, by J.B. Wood, DBI Books, a division of Krause Publications, Iola, WI, 1999. 480 pp., illus. Paper covers. $24.95.

Covers 58 popular autoloading pistols plus nearly 200 variants of those models integrated into the text and completely cross-referenced in the index.

Firearms Assembly/Disassembly Part II: Revolvers, Revised Edition, The Gun Digest Book of, by J.B. Wood, DBI Books, a division of Krause Publications, Iola, WI, 1990. 480 pp., illus. Paper covers. $19.95.

Covers 49 popular revolvers plus 130 variants. The most comprehensive and professional presentation available to either hobbyist or gunsmith.

Firearms Assembly/Disassembly Part III: Rimfire Rifles, Revised Edition, The Gun Digest Book of, by J. B. Wood, DBI Books, a division of Krause Publications, Iola, WI., 1994. 480 pp., illus. Paper covers. $19.95.

Greatly expanded edition covering 65 popular rimfire rifles plus over 100 variants all completely cross-referenced in the index.

Firearms Assembly/Disassembly Part IV: Centerfire Rifles, Revised Edition, The Gun Digest Book of, by J.B. Wood, DBI Books, a division of Krause Publications, Iola, WI, 1991. 480 pp., illus. Paper covers. $19.95.

Covers 54 popular centerfire rifles plus 300 variants. The most comprehensive and professional presentation available to either hobbyist or gunsmith.

Firearms Assembly/Disassembly, Part V: Shotguns, Revised Edition, The Gun Digest Book of, by J.B. Wood, DBI Books, a division of Krause Publications, Iola, WI, 1992. 480 pp., illus. Paper covers. $19.95.

Covers 46 popular shotguns plus over 250 variants with step-by-step instructions on how to dismantle and reassemble each. The most comprehensive and professional presentation available to either hobbyist or gunsmith.

Firearms Assembly/Disassembly Part VI: Law Enforcement Weapons, The Gun Digest Book of, by J.B. Wood, DBI Books, a division of Krause Publications, Iola, WI, 1981. 288 pp., illus. Paper covers. $16.95.

Step-by-step instructions on how to completely dismantle and reassemble the most commonly used firearms found in law enforcement arsenals.

Firearms Assembly 3: The NRA Guide to Rifle and Shotguns, NRA Books, Wash., DC, 1980. 264 pp., illus. Paper covers. $13.95.

Text and illustrations explaining the takedown of 125 rifles and shotguns, domestic and foreign.

Firearms Assembly 4: The NRA Guide to Pistols and Revolvers, NRA Books, Wash., DC, 1980. 253 pp., illus. Paper covers. $13.95.

Text and illustrations explaining the takedown of 124 pistol and revolver models, domestic and foreign.

Firearms Bluing and Browning, By R.H. Angier, Stackpole Books, Harrisburg, PA. 151 pp., illus. $19.95.

A world master gunsmith reveals his secrets of building, repairing and renewing a gun, quite literally, lock, stock and barrel. A useful, concise text on chemical coloring methods for the gunsmith and mechanic.

Firearms Disassembly—With Exploded Views, by John A. Karns & John E. Traister, Stoeger Publishing Co., S. Hackensack, NJ, 1995. 320 pp., illus. Paper covers. $19.95.

Provides the do's and don'ts of firearms disassembly. Enables owners and gunsmiths to disassemble firearms in a professional manner.

Guns and Gunmaking Tools of Southern Appalachia, by John Rice Irwin, Schiffer Publishing Ltd., 1983. 118 pp., illus. Paper covers. $9.95.

The story of the Kentucky rifle.

Gunsmithing: Pistols & Revolvers, by Patrick Sweeney, DBI Books, a division of Krause Publications, Iola, WI, 1998. 352 pp., illus. Paper covers. $24.95.

Do-it-Yourself projects, diagnosis and repair for pistols and revolvers.

Gunsmithing: Rifles, by Patrick Sweeney, Krause Publications, Iola, WI, 1999. 352 pp., illustrated. Paper covers. $24.95.

Tips for lever-action rifles. Building a custom Ruger 10/22. Building a better hunting rifle.

Gunsmithing Tips and Projects, a collection of the best articles from the *Handloader* and *Rifle* magazines, by various authors, Wolfe Publishing Co., Prescott, AZ, 1992. 443 pp., illus. Paper covers. $25.00.

Includes such subjects as shop, stocks, actions, tuning, triggers, barrels, customizing, etc.

Gunsmith Kinks, by F.R. (Bob) Brownell, F. Brownell & Son, Montezuma, IA, 1st ed., 1969. 496 pp., well illus. $22.98.

A widely useful accumulation of shop kinks, short cuts, techniques and pertinent comments by practicing gunsmiths from all over the world.

Gunsmith Kinks 2, by Bob Brownell, F. Brownell & Son, Publishers, Montezuma, IA, 1983. 496 pp., illus. $22.95.

A collection of gunsmithing knowledge, shop kinks, new and old techniques, shortcuts and general know-how straight from those who do them best—the gunsmiths.

Gunsmith Kinks 3, edited by Frank Brownell, Brownells Inc., Montezuma, IA, 1993. 504 pp., illus. $24.95.

Tricks, knacks and "kinks" by professional gunsmiths and gun tinkerers. Hundreds of valuable ideas are given in this volume.

Gunsmith Kinks 4, edited by Frank Brownell, Brownells Inc., Montezuma, IA, 2001. 564 pp., illus. $27.75

332 detailed illustrations. 560+ pages with 706 separate subject headings and over 5000 cross-indexed entries. An incredible gold mine of information.

Gunsmithing, by Roy F. Dunlap, Stackpole Books, Harrisburg, PA, 1990. 742 pp., illus. $34.95.

A manual of firearm design, construction, alteration and remodeling. For amateur and professional gunsmiths and users of modern firearms.

Gunsmithing at Home: Lock, Stock and Barrel, by John Traister, Stoeger Publishing Co., Wayne, NJ, 1997. 320 pp., illus. Paper covers. $19.95.

A complete step-by-step fully illustrated guide to the art of gunsmithing.

The Gunsmith's Manual, by J.P. Stelle and Wm. B. Harrison, The Gun Room Press, Highland Park, NJ, 1982. 376 pp., illus. $19.95.

For the gunsmith in all branches of the trade.

Home Gunsmithing the Colt Single Action Revolvers, by Loren W. Smith, Ray Riling Arms Books, Co., Phila., PA, 2001. 119 pp., illus. $29.95.

Affords the Colt Single Action owner detailed, pertinent information on the operating and servicing of this famous and historic handgun.

How to Convert Military Rifles, Williams Gun Sight Co., Davision, MI, new and enlarged seventh edition, 1997. 76 pp., illus. Paper covers. $13.95.

This latest edition updated the changes that have occured over the past thirty years. Tips, instructions and illustratons on how to convert popular military rifles as the Enfield, Mauser 96 nad SKS just to name a few are presented.

Mauser M98 & M96, by R.A. Walsh, Wolfe Publishing Co., Prescott, AR, 1998. 123 pp., illustrated. Paper covers. $32.50.

How to build your own favorite custom Mauser rifle from two of the best bolt action rifle designs ever produced—the military Mauser Model 1898 and Model 1896 bolt rifles.

Mr. Single Shot's Gunsmithing-Idea-Book, by Frank de Haas, Mark de Haas, Orange City, IA, 1996. 168 pp., illus. Paper covers. $21.50.

Offers easy to follow, step-by-step instructions for a wide variety of gunsmithing procedures all reinforced by plenty of photos.

Pistolsmithing, by George C. Nonte, Jr., Stackpole Books, Harrisburg, PA, 1974. 560 pp., illus. $34.95.

A single source reference to handgun maintenance, repair, and modification at home, unequaled in value.

Practical Gunsmithing, by the editors of American Gunsmith, DBI Books, a division of Krause Publications, Iola, WI, 1996. 256 pp., illus. Paper covers. $19.95.

A book intended primarily for home gunsmithing, but one that will be extremely helpful to professionals as well.

Professional Stockmaking, by D. Wesbrook, Wolfe Publishing Co., Prescott AZ, 1995. 308 pp., illus. $54.00.

A step-by-step how-to with complete photographic support for every detail of the art of working wood into riflestocks.

Recreating the American Longrifle, by William Buchele, et al, George Shumway Publisher, York, Pa, 5th edition, 1999. 175 pp., illustrated. $40.00.

Includes full size plans for building a Kentucky rifle.

Riflesmithing, The Gun Digest Book of, by Jack Mitchell, DBI Books, a division of Krause Publications, Iola, WI, 1982. 256 pp., illus. Paper covers. $16.95.

The art and science of rifle gunsmithing. Covers tools, techniques, designs, finishing wood and metal, custom alterations.

Shotgun Gunsmithing, The Gun Digest Book of, by Ralph Walker, DBI Books, a division of Krause Publications, Iola, WI, 1983. 256 pp., illus. Paper covers. $16.95.

The principles and practices of repairing, individualizing and accurizing modern shotguns by one of the world's premier shotgun gunsmiths.

Sporting Rifle Take Down & Reassembly Guide, 2nd Edition, by J.B. Wood, Krause Publications, Iola, WI, 1997. 480 pp., illus. Paper covers. $19.95.

Hunters and shooting enthusiasts must have this reference featuring 52 of the most popular and widely used sporting centerfire and rimfire rifles.

The Story of Pope's Barrels, by Ray M. Smith, R&R Books, Livonia, NY, 1993. 203 pp., illus. $39.00.

A reissue of a 1960 book whose author knew Pope personally. It will be of special interest to Schuetzen rifle fans, since Pope's greatest days were at the height of the Schuetzen-era before WWI.

Survival Gunsmithing, by J.B. Wood, Desert Publications, Cornville, AZ, 1986. 92 pp., illus. Paper covers. $11.95.

A guide to repair and maintenance of the most popular rifles, shotguns and handguns.

The Tactical 1911, by Dave Lauck, Paladin Press, Boulder, CO, 1998. 137 pp., illus. Paper covers. $20.00.

Here is the only book you will ever need to teach you how to select, modify, employ and maintain your Colt.

HANDGUNS

Advanced Master Handgunning, by Charles Stephens, Paladin Press, Boulder, CO., 1994. 72 pp., illus. Paper covers. $14.00.

Secrets and surefire techniques for winning handgun competitions.

American Beauty: The Prewar Colt National Match Government Model Pistol, by Timothy Mullin, Collector Grade Publications, Canada, 1999. 72 pp., 69 illus. $34.95

69 illustrations, 20 in full color photos of factory engraved guns and other authenticated upgrades, including rare 'double-carved' ivory grips.

Axis Pistols: WORLD WAR TWO 50 YEARS COMMEMORATIVE ISSUE, by Jan C. Stills, Walsworth Publishing, 1989. 360 pages, illus. $59.95

The Ayoob Files: The Book, by Massad Ayoob, Police Bookshelf, Concord, NH, 1995. 223 pp., illus. Paper covers. $14.95.

The best of Massad Ayoob's acclaimed series in American Handgunner magazine.

REFERENCE

THE ARMS LIBRARY

Big Bore Sixguns, by John Taffin, Krause Publications, Iola, WI, 1997. 336 pp., illus. $39.95.
The author takes aim on the entire range of big bores from .357 Magnums to .500 Maximums, single actions and cap-and-ball sixguns to custom touches for big bores..

The Browning High Power Automatic Pistol (Expanded Edition), by Blake R. Stevens, Collector Grade Publications, Canada, 1996. 310 pages, with 313 illus. $49.95
An in-depth chronicle of seventy years of High Power history, from John M Browning's original 16-shot prototypes to the present. Profusely illustrated with rare original photos and drawings from the FN Archive to describe virtually every sporting and military version of the High Power. The numerous modifications made to the basic design over the years are, for the first time, accurately arranged in chronological order, thus permitting the dating of any High Power to within a few years of its production. Full details on the WWII Canadian-made Inglis Browning High Power pistol. The Expanded Edition contains 30 new pages on the interesting Argentine full-auto High Power, the latest FN 'MK3' and BDA9 pistols, plus FN's revolutionary P90 5.7x28mm Personal Defence Weapon, and more!

Browning Hi-Power Pistols, Desert Publications, Cornville, AZ, 1982. 20 pp., illus. Paper covers. $11.95.
Covers all facets of the various military and civilian models of the Browning Hi-Power pistol.

Canadian Military Handguns 1855-1985, by Clive M. Law, Museum Restoration Service, Bloomfield, Ont. Canada, 1994. 130pp., illus. $40.00.
A long-awaited and important history for arms historians and pistol collectors.

The Colt .45 Auto Pistol, compiled from U.S. War Dept. Technical Manuals, and reprinted by Desert Publications, Cornville, AZ, 1978. 80 pp., illus. Paper covers. $11.95.
Covers every facet of this famous pistol from mechanical training, manual of arms, disassembly, repair and replacement of parts.

Colt Automatic Pistols, by Donald B. Bady, Pioneer Press, Union City, TN, 1999. 368 pp., illustrated. Softcover. $19.95.
A revised and enlarged edition of a key work on a fascinating subject. Complete information on every Colt automatic pistol.

Combat Handgunnery, 4th Edition, by Chuck Taylor, DBI Books, a division of Krause Publications, Iola, WI, 1997. 256 pp., illus. Paper covers. $18.95.
This all-new edition looks at real world combat handgunnery from three different perspectives—military, police and civilian. Available, October, 1996.

Combat Revolvers, by Duncan Long, Paladin Press, Boulder, CO, 1999, 8 1/2 x 11, soft cover, 115 photos, 152 pp. $21.95
This is an uncompromising look at modern combat revolvers. All the major foreign and domestic guns are covered: the Colt Python, S&W Model 29, Ruger GP 100 and hundreds more. Know the gun that you may one day stake your life on.

The Complete Book of Combat Handgunning, by Chuck Taylor, Desert Publications, Cornville, AZ, 1982. 168 pp., illus. Paper covers. $20.00.
Covers virtually every aspect of combat handgunning.

Complete Guide to Compact Handguns, by Gene Gangarosa, Jr., Stoeger Publishing Co., Wayne, NJ, 1997. 228 pp., illus. Paper covers. $22.95.
Includes hundreds of compact firearms, along with text results conducted by the author.

Complete Guide to Service Handguns, by Gene Gangarosa, Jr., Stoeger Publishing Co., Wayne, NJ, 1998. 320 pp., illus. Paper covers. $22.95.
The author explores the revolvers and pistols that are used around the globe by military, law enforcement and civilians.

The Custom Government Model Pistol, by Layne Simpson, Wolfe Publishing Co., Prescott, AZ, 1994. 639 pp., illus. Paper covers. $24.50.
The book about one of the world's greatest firearms and the things pistolsmiths do to make it even greater.

The CZ-75 Family: The Ultimate Combat Handgun, by J.M. Ramos, Paladin Press, Boulder, CO, 1990. 100 pp., illus. Soft covers. $25.00.
An in-depth discussion of the early-and-late model CZ-75s, as well as the many newest additions to the Czech pistol family.

Encyclopedia of Pistols & Revolvers, by A.E. Hartnik, Knickerbocker Press, New York, NY, 1997. 272 pp., illus. $19.95.
A comprehensive encyclopedia specially written for collectors and owners of pistols and revolvers.

Experiments of a Handgunner, by Walter Roper, Wolfe Publishing Co., Prescott, AZ, 1989. 202 pp., illus. $37.00.
A limited edition reprint. A listing of experiments with functioning parts of handguns, with targets, stocks, rests, handloading, etc.

The Farnam Method of Defensive Handgunning, by John S. Farnam, Police Bookshelf, 1999. 191 pp., illus. Paper covers. $25.00
A book intended to not only educate the new shooter, but also to serve as a guide and textbook for his and his instructor's training courses.

Fast and Fancy Revolver Shooting, by Ed. McGivern, Anniversary Edition, Winchester Press, Piscataway, NJ, 1984. 484 pp., illus. $18.95.
A fascinating volume, packed with handgun lore and solid information by the acknowledged dean of revolver shooters.

.45 ACP Super Guns, by J.M. Ramos, Paladin Press, Boulder, CO, 1991. 144 pp., illus. Paper covers. $24.00.
Modified .45 automatic pistols for competition, hunting and personal defense.

The .45, The Gun Digest Book of, by Dean A. Grennell, DBI Books, a division of Krause Publications, Iola, WI, 1989. 256 pp., illus. Paper covers. $17.95.
Definitive work on one of America's favorite calibers.

Glock: The New Wave in Combat Handguns, by Peter Alan Kasler, Paladin Press, Boulder, CO, 1993. 304 pp., illus. $27.00.
Kasler debunks the myths that surround what is the most innovative handgun to be introduced in some time.

Glock's Handguns, by Duncan Long, Desert Publications, El Dorado, AR, 1996. 180 pp., illus. Paper covers. $18.95.
An outstanding volume on one of the world's newest and most successful firearms of the century.

Hand Cannons: The World's Most Powerful Handguns, by Duncan Long, Paladin Press, Boulder, CO, 1995. 208 pp., illus. Paper covers. $22.00.
Long describes and evaluates each powerful gun according to their features.

The Handgun, by Geoffrey Boothroyd, Safari Press, Inc., Huntington Beach, CA, 1999. 566 pp., illustrated. $50.00.
A very detailed history of the handgun. Now revised and a completely new chapter written to take account of developments since the 1970 edition.

Handguns 2002, 13th Edition, edited by Harold A. Murtz, DBI Books a division of Krause Publications, Iola, WI, 1999. 352 pp., illustrated. Paper covers. $22.95.
Top writers in the handgun industry give you a complete report on new handgun developments, testfire reports on the newest introductions and previews on what's ahead.

Handgun Digest, 3rd Edition, edited by Chris Christian, DBI Books, a division of Krause Publications, Iola, WI, 1995. 256 pp., illus. Paper covers. $18.95.
Full coverage of all aspects of handguns and handgunning from a highly readable and knowledgeable author.

Handgun Reloading, The Gun Digest Book of, by Dean A. Grennell and Wiley M. Clapp, DBI Books, a division of Krause Publications, Iola, WI, 1987. 256 pp., illus. Paper covers. $16.95.
Detailed discussions of all aspects of reloading for handguns, from basic to complex. New loading data.

Handgun Stopping Power "The Definitive Study", by Evan P. Marshall & Edwin J. Sanow, Paladin Press, Boulder, CO, 1997, soft cover, photos, 240 pp. $45.00
Dramatic first-hand accounts of the results of handgun rounds fired into criminals by cops, storeowners, cabbies and others are the heart and soul of this long-awaited book. This is the definitive methodology for predicting the stopping power of handgun loads, the first to take into account what really happens when a bullet meets a man.

Heckler & Koch's Handguns, by Duncan Long, Desert Publications, El Dorado, AR, 1996. 142 pp., illus. Paper covers. $19.95.
Traces the history and the evolution of H&K's pistols from the company's beginning at the end of WWII to the present.

Hidden in Plain Sight, by Trey Bloodworth & Mike Raley, Professional Press, Chapel Hill, NC, 1995. Paper covers. $19.95.
A practical guide to concealed handgun carry.

High Standard Automatic Pistols 1932-1950, by Charles E. Petty, The Gunroom Press, Highland Park, NJ, 1989. 124 pp., illus. $19.95.
A definitive source of information for the collector of High Standard arms.

Hi-Standard Pistols and Revolvers, 1951-1984, by James Spacek, James Spacek, Chesire, CT, 1998. 128 pp., illustrated. Paper covers. $12.50.
Technical details, marketing features and instruction/parts manual of every model High Standard pistol and revolver made between 1951 and 1984. Most accurate serial number information available.

The Hi-Standard Pistol Guide, by Burr Leyson, Duckett's Sporting Books, Tempe AZ, 1995. 128 pp., illus. Paper covers. $22.00.
Complete information on selection, care and repair, ammunition, parts, and accessories.

How to Become a Master Handgunner: The Mechanics of X-Count Shooting, by Charles Stephens, Paladin Press, Boulder, CO, 1993. 64 pp., illus. Paper covers. $14.00.
Offers a simple formula for success to the handgunner who strives to master the technique of shooting accurately.

Hunting for Handgunners, by Larry Kelly and J.D. Jones, DBI Books, a division of Krause Publications, Iola, WI, 1990. 256 pp., illus. Paper covers. $16.95.
Covers the entire spectrum of hunting with handguns in an amusing, easy-flowing manner that combines entertainment with solid information.

Illustrated Encyclopedia of Handguns, by A.B. Zhuk, Stackpole Books, Mechanicsburg, PA, 1994. 256 pp., illus. Cloth cover, $49.95
Identifies more than 2,000 military and commercial pistols and revolvers with details of more than 100 popular handgun cartridges.

The Inglis Diamond: The Canadian High Power Pistol, by Clive M. Law, Collector Grade Publications, Canada, 2001. 312 pp., illustrated. $49.95
This definitive work on Canada's first and indeed only mass produced handgun, in production for a very brief span of time and consequently made in relatively few numbers, the venerable Inglis-made Browning High Power covers the pistol's initial history, the story of Chinese and British adoption, use post-war by Holland, Australia, Greece, Belgium, New Zealand, Peru, Brasil and other countries. All new information on the famous light-weights and the Inglis Diamond variations. Completely researched through official archives in a dozen countries. Many of the bewildering variety of markings have never been satisfactorily explained until now. Also included are many photos of holsters and accessories.

Instinct Combat Shooting, by Chuck Klein, The Goose Creek, IN, 1989. 49 pp., illus. Paper covers. $12.00.
Defensive handgunning for police.

Know Your Czechoslovakian Pistols, by R.J. Berger, Blacksmith Corp., Chino Valley, AZ, 1989. 96 pp., illus. Soft covers. $12.95.
A comprehensive reference which presents the fascinating story of Czech pistols.

THE ARMS LIBRARY

Know Your 45 Auto Pistols—Models 1911 & A1, by E.J. Hoffschmidt, Blacksmith Corp., Southport, CT, 1974. 58 pp., illus. Paper covers. $12.95.
A concise history of the gun with a wide variety of types and copies.

Know Your Walther P38 Pistols, by E.J. Hoffschmidt, Blacksmith Corp., Southport, CT, 1974. 77 pp., illus. Paper covers. $12.95.
Covers the Walther models Armee, M.P., H.P., P.38—history and variations.

Know Your Walther PP & PPK Pistols, by E.J. Hoffschmidt, Blacksmith Corp., Southport, CT, 1975. 87 pp., illus. Paper covers. $12.95.
A concise history of the guns with a guide to the variety and types.

La Connaissance du Luger, Tome 1, by Gerard Henrotin, H & L Publishing, Belguim, 1996. 144 pages, illustrated. $45.00.
(The Knowledge of Luger, Volume 1, translated.) B&W and Color photo's. French text.

The Luger Handbook, by Aarron Davis, Krause Publications, Iola, WI, 1997. 112 pp., illus. Paper covers. $9.95.
Now you can identify any of the legendary Luger variations using a simple decision tree. Each model and variation includes pricing information, proof marks and detailed attributes in a handy, user-friendly format. Plus, it's fully indexed. Instantly identify that Luger!

Lugers of Ralph Shattuck, by Ralph Shattuck, Peoria, AZ, 2000. 49 pages, illus. Hardcover. $29.95.
49 pages, illustrated with maps and full color photos of here to now never before shown photos of some of the rarest lugers ever. Written by one of the world's renowned collectors. A MUST have book for any Luger collector.

Lugers at Random (Revised Format Edition), by Charles Kenyon, Jr., Handgun Press, Glenview, IL, 2000. 420 pp., illus. $59.95.
A new printing of this classic, comprehensive reference for all Luger collectors.

The Luger Story, by John Walter, Stackpole Books, Mechanicsburg, PA, 2001. 256 pp., illus. Paper Covers. $29.95.
The standard history of the world's most famous handgun.

The Mauser Self-Loading Pistol, by Belford & Dunlap, Borden Publ. Co., Alhambra, CA. Over 200 pp., 300 illus., large format. $29.95.
The long-awaited book on the "Broom Handles," covering their inception in 1894 to the end of production. Complete and in detail: pocket pistols, Chinese and Spanish copies, etc.

9mm Handguns, 2nd Edition, The Gun Digest Book of, edited by Steve Comus, DBI Books, a division of Krause Publications, Iola, WI, 1993. 256 pp., illus. Paper covers. $18.95.
Covers the 9mm cartridge and the guns that have been made for it in greater depth than any other work available.

9mm Parabellum; The History & Development of the World's 9mm Pistols & Ammunition, by Klaus-Peter Konig and Martin Hugo, Schiffer Publishing Ltd., Atglen, PA, 1993. 304 pp., illus. $39.95.
Detailed history of 9mm weapons from Belguim, Italy, Germany, Israel, France, USA, Czechoslovakia, Hungary, Poland, Brazil, Finland and Spain.

The Official 9mm Markarov Pistol Manual, translated into English by Major James Gebhardt, U.S. Army (Ret.), Desert Publications, El Dorado, AR, 1996. 84 pp., illus. Paper covers. $12.95.
The information found in this book will be of enormous benefit and interest to the owner or a prospective owner of one of these pistols.

The Official Soviet 7.62mm Handgun Manual, by Translation by Maj. James F. Gebhardt Ret.), Paladin Press, Boulder, CO, 1997, soft cover, illus., 104 pp. $20.00
This Soviet military manual, now available in English for the first time, covers instructions for use and maintenance of two side arms, the Nagant 7.62mm revolver, used by the Russian tsarist armed forces and later the Soviet armed forces, and the Tokarev7.62mm semi-auto pistol, which replaced the Nagant.

P-38 Automatic Pistol, by Gene Gangarosa, Jr., Stoeger Publishing Co., S. Hackensack, NJ, 1993. 272 pp., illus. Paper covers. $16.95
This book traces the origins and development of the P-38, including the momentous political forces of the World War II era that caused its near demise and, later, its rebirth.

The P-38 Pistol: The Walther Pistols, 1930-1945. Volume 1. by Warren Buxton, Ucross Books, Los Alamos, MN 1999. $68.50
A limited run reprint of this scarce and sought-after work on the P-38 Pistol. 328 pp. with 160 illustrations.

The P-38 Pistol: The Contract Pistols, 1940-1945. Volume 2. by Warren Buxton, Ucross Books, Los Alamos, MN 1999. 256 pp. with 237 illustrations. $68.50

The P-38 Pistol: Postwar Distributions, 1945-1990. Volume 3. by Warren Buxton, Ucross Books, Los Alamos, MN 1999. $68.50
Plus an addendum to Volumes 1 & 2. 272 pp. with 342 illustrations.

PARABELLUM - A Technical History of Swiss Lugers, by V. Bobba, Italy.1998. 224pp, profuse color photos, large format. $100.00.
The is the most beautifully illustrated and well-documented book on the Swiss Lugers yet produced. This splendidly produced book features magnificent images while giving an incredible amount of detail on the Swiss Luger. In-depth coverage of key issues include: the production process, pistol accessories, charts with serial numbers, production figures, variations, markings, patent drawings, etc. Covers the Swiss Luger story from 1894 when the first Bergmann-Schmeisser models were tested till the commercial model 1965. Shows every imaginable production variation in amazing detail and full color! A must for all Luger collectors. This work has been produced in an extremely attractive package using quality materials throughout and housed in a protective slipcase.

Pistols and Revolvers, by Jean-Noel Mouret, Barns and Noble, Rockleigh, N.J., 1999. 141 pp., illustrated. $12.98.
Here in glorious display is the master guidebook to flintlocks, minatures, the Sig P-210 limited edition, the Springfield Trophy Master with Aimpoint 5000 telescopic sight, every major classic and contemporary handgun, complete with their technical data.

Report of Board on Tests of Revolvers and Automatic Pistols, From the Annual Report of the Chief of Ordnance, 1907. Reprinted by J.C. Tillinghast, Marlow, NH, 1969. 34 pp., 7 plates, paper covers. $9.95.
A comparison of handguns, including Luger, Savage, Colt, Webley-Fosbery and other makes.

Ruger Automatic Pistols and Single Action Revolvers, by Hugo A. Lueders, edited by Don Findley, Blacksmith Corp., Chino Valley, AZ, 1993. 79 pp., illus. Paper covers. $14.95.
The definitive work on Ruger automatic pistols and single action revolvers.

The Ruger "P" Family of Handguns, by Duncan Long, Desert Publications, El Dorado, AZ, 1993. 128 pp., illus. Paper covers. $14.95.
A full-fledged documentary on a remarkable series of Sturm Ruger handguns.

The Ruger .22 Automatic Pistol, Standard/Mark I/Mark II Series, by Duncan Long, Paladin Press, Boulder, CO, 1989. 168 pp., illus. Paper covers. $16.00.
The definitive book about the pistol that has served more than 1 million owners so well.

The Semiautomatic Pistols in Police Service and Self Defense, by Massad Ayoob, Police Bookshelf, Concord, NH, 1990. 25 pp., illus. Soft covers. $9.95.
First quantitative, documented look at actual police experience with 9mm and 45 police service automatics.

The Sharpshooter—How to Stand and Shoot Handgun Metallic Silhouettes, by Charles Stephens, Yucca Tree Press, Las Cruces, NM, 1993. 86 pp., illus. Paper covers. $10.00.
A narration of some of the author's early experiences in silhouette shooting, plus how-to information.

Shooting Colt Single Actions, by Mike Venturino, Livingston, MT, 1997. 205 pp., illus. Paper covers. $25.00
A definitive work on the famous Colt SAA and the ammunition it shoots.

Sig/Sauer Handguns, by Duncan Long, Desert Publications, El Dorado, AZ, 1995. 150 pp., illus. Paper covers. $16.95.
The history of Sig/Sauer handguns, including Sig, Sig-Hammerli and Sig/Sauer variants.

Sixgun Cartridges and Loads, by Elmer Keith, reprint edition by The Gun Room Press, Highland Park, NJ, 1984. 151 pp., illus. $24.95.
A manual covering the selection, use and loading of the most suitable and popular revolver cartridges.

Sixguns, by Elmer Keith, Wolfe Publishing Company, Prescott, AZ, 1992. 336 pp. Paper covers. $29.95. Hardcover $35.00
The history, selection, repair, care, loading, and use of this historic frontiersman's friend—the one-hand firearm.

Smith & Wesson's Automatics, by Larry Combs, Desert Publications, El Dorado, AZ, 1994. 143 pp., illus. Paper covers. $19.95.
A must for every S&W auto owner or prospective owner.

Spanish Handguns: The History of Spanish Pistols and Revolvers, by Gene Gangarosa, Jr., Stoeger Publishing Co., Accokeek, MD, 2001. 320 pp., illustrated. B & W photos. Paper covers. $21.95

Street Stoppers: The Latest Handgun Stopping Power Street Results, by Evan P. Marshall & Edwin J. Sandow, Paladin Press, Boulder, CO, 1997. 392 pp., illus. Paper covers. $42.95.
Compilation of the results of real-life shooting incidents involving every major handgun caliber.

The Tactical 1911, by Dave Lauck, Paladin Press, Boulder, CO, 1999. 152 pp., illustrated. Paper covers. $22.00.
The cop's and SWAT operator's guide to employment and maintenance.

The Tactical Pistol, by Gabriel Suarez with a foreword by Jeff Cooper, Paladin Press, Boulder, CO, 1996. 216 pp., illus. Paper covers. $25.00.
Advanced gunfighting concepts and techniques.

The Thompson/Center Contender Pistol, by Charles Tephens, Paladin Press, Boulder, CO, 1997. 58 pp., illus. Paper covers. $14.00.
How to tune and time, load and shoot accurately with the Contender pistol.

The .380 Enfield No. 2 Revolver, by Mark Stamps and Ian Skennerton, I.D.S.A. Books, Piqua, OH, 1993. 124 pp., 80 illus. Paper covers. $19.95.

The Truth AboUt Handguns, by Duane Thomas, Paladin Press, Boulder, CO, 1997. 136 pp., illus. Paper covers. $18.00.
Exploding the myths, hype, and misinformation about handguns.

Walther Pistols: Models 1 Through P99, Factory Variations and Copies, by Dieter H. Marschall, Ucross Books, Los Alamos, NM. 2000. 140 pages, with 140 b & w illustrations, index. Paper Covers. $19.95.
This is the English translation, revised and updated, of the highly successful and widely acclaimed German language edition. This book provides the collector with a reference guide and overview of the entire line of the Walther military, police, and self-defense pistols from the very first to the very latest. Models 1-9, PP, PPK, MP, AP, HP, P.38, P1, P4, P38K, P5, P88, P99 and the Manurhin models. Variations, where issued, serial ranges, calibers, marks, proofs, logos, and design aspects in an astonishing quantity and variety are crammed into this very well researched and highly regarded work.

U.S. Handguns of World War 2, The Secondary Pistols and Revolvers, by Charles W. Pate, Mowbray Publishers, Lincoln, RI, 1997. 368 pp., illus. $39.00.
This indispensable new book covers all of the American military handguns of W.W.2 except for the M1911A1.

DIRECTORY OF THE HANDGUNNING TRADE

HANDGUNS 2002

REFERENCE

PRODUCT & SERVICE DIRECTORY

AMMUNITION, COMMERCIAL

American Ammunition
Arizona Ammunition, Inc.
Atlantic Rose, Inc.
Bergman & Williams
Big Bear Arms & Sporting Goods, Inc.
Black Hills Ammunition, Inc.
Blammo Ammo
Blount, Inc., Sporting Equipment Div.
Brown Dog Ent.
Buffalo Bullet Co., Inc.
BulletMakers Workshop, The
Bull-X, Inc.
California Magnum
CBC
Colorado Sutlers Arsenal
Cor-Bon Bullet & Ammo Co.
Cumberland States Arsenal
Daisy Mfg. Co.
Dead Eye's Sport Center
Delta Frangible Ammunition, LLC
Denver Bullets, Inc.
Dynamit Nobel-RWS, Inc.
Eldorado Cartridge Corp.
Eley Ltd.
Elite Ammunition
Estate Cartridge, Inc.
Federal Cartridge Co.
4W Ammunition
Hunters Supply
GOEX, Inc.
Goldcoast Reloaders, Inc.
Hansen & Co.
Hansen Cartridge Co.
Hart & Son, Inc., Robert W.
Hirtenberger Aktiengesellschaft
Hornady Mfg. Co.
ICI-America
IMI
Israel Military Industries Ltd.
Jones, J.D.
Keng's Firearms Specialty, Inc.
Kent Cartridge Mfg. Co. Ltd.
Lapua Ltd.
M&D Munitions Ltd.
MagSafe Ammo Co.
Markell, Inc.
Mathews & Son, Inc., George E.
Men—Metallwerk Elisenhuette, GmbH
Mullins Ammunition
NECO
New England Ammunition Co.
Oklahoma Ammunition Co.
Old Western Scrounger, Inc.
Omark Industries
Pacific Cartridge, Inc.
PMC/Eldorado Cartridge Corp.
Pony Express Reloaders
Precision Delta Corp.
Pro Load Ammunition, Inc.
Remington Arms Co., Inc.
Rucker Dist. Inc.
RWS
Spence, George W.
SSK Industries
Talon Mfg. Co., Inc.
Taylor & Robbins
Thompson Bullet Lube Co.
3-D Ammunition & Bullets
3-Ten Corp.
USAC
Valor Corp.
Victory USA
Vihtavuori Oy/Kaltron-Pettibone
Voere-KGH m.b.H.
Widener's Reloading & Shooting
Supply, Inc.
Winchester Div., Olin Corp.
Zero Ammunition Co., Inc.

AMMUNITION, CUSTOM

Accuracy Unlimited (Littleton, CO)
AFSCO Ammunition
American Derringer Corp.
Arizona Ammunition, Inc.
Arms Corporation of the Philippines
Atlantic Rose, Inc.
Black Hills Ammunition, Inc.
Bruno Shooters Supply
Brynin, Milton
Buckskin Bullet Co.
BulletMakers Workshop, The
CBC
Country Armourer, The
Custom Tackle and Ammo
Dead Eye's Sport Center
Delta Frangible Ammunition, LLC
DKT, Inc.
Elite Ammunition
Estate Cartridge, Inc.
4W Ammunition
Freedom Arms, Inc.
GDL Enterprises
Glaser Safety Slug, Inc.
GOEX, Inc.
"Gramps" Antique Cartridges
Granite Custom Bullets
Gun Accessories
Heidenstrom Bullets
Hirtenberger Aktiengesellschaft
Hoelscher, Virgil
Horizons Unlimited
Hornady Mfg. Co.
Hunters Supply
IMI
Israel Military Industries Ltd.
Kaswer Custom, Inc.
Keeler, R.H.
Kent Cartridge Mfg. Co. Ltd.
KJM Fabritek, Inc.
Lindsley Arms Cartridge Co.
MagSafe Ammo Co.
MAST Technology
McMurdo, Lynn
Men-Metallwerk Elisenhuette, GmbH
Milstor Corp.
Mullins Ammunition
Naval Ordnance Works
NECO
Northern Precision Custom Swaged Bullets
Old Western Scrounger, Inc.
Oklahoma Ammunition Company
Precision Delta Corp.
Precision Munitions, Inc.
Precision Reloading, Inc.
Professional Hunter Supplies
Sanders Custom Gun Service
Sandia Die & Cartridge Co.
SOS Products Co.
Specialty Gunsmithing
Spence, George W.
Spencer's Custom Guns
Star Custom Bullets
State Arms Gun Co.
Stewart's Gunsmithing
Talon Mfg. Co., Inc.
3-D Ammunition & Bullets
3-Ten Corp.
Unmussig Bullets, D.L.
Vulpes Ventures, Inc.
Warren Muzzleloading Co., Inc.
Weaver Arms Corp. Gun Shop
Worthy Products, Inc.
Yukon Arms Classic Ammunition

AMMUNITION, FOREIGN

AFSCO Ammunition
Armscorp USA, Inc.
Atlantic Rose, Inc.
BulletMakers Workshop, The
CBC
Dead Eye's Sport Center
Diana
DKT, Inc.
Dynamit Nobel-RWS, Inc.
First, Inc., Jack
Fisher Enterprises, Inc.
Fisher, R. Kermit
FN Herstal
Forgett Jr., Valmore J.
GOEX, Inc.
Hansen & Co.
Hansen Cartridge Co.
Heidenstrom Bullets
Hirtenberger Aktiengesellschaft
Hornady Mfg. Co.
IMI
IMI Services USA, Inc.
Israel Military Industries Ltd.
JägerSport, Ltd.
K.B.I., Inc.
Keng's Firearms Specialty, Inc.
Magnum Research, Inc.
MagSafe Ammo Co.
MagTech Recreational Products, Inc.
Maionchi-L.M.I.
MAST Technology
Merkuria Ltd.
Mullins Ammunition
Oklahoma Ammunition Co.
Old Western Scrounger, Inc.
Petro-Explo, Inc.
Precision Delta Corp.
R.E.T. Enterprises
RWS
Sentinel Arms
Southern Ammunition Co., Inc.
Spence, George W.
Stratco, Inc.
SwaroSports, Inc.
T.F.C. S.p.A.
Vihtavuori Oy/Kaltron-Pettibone
Yukon Arms Classic Ammunition

AMMUNITION COMPONENTS—BULLETS, POWDER

PRIMERS, CASES
Acadian Ballistic Specialties
Accuracy Unlimited (Littleton, CO)
Accurate Arms Co., Inc.
Accurate Bullet Co.
Action Bullets, Inc.
Alaska Bullet Works, Inc.
Alliant Techsystems
Allred Bullet Co.
American Products Inc.
Arco Powder
Atlantic Rose, Inc.
Baer's Hollows
Ballard Built
Barnes Bullets, Inc.
Beartooth Bullets
Beeline Custom Bullets Limited
Bell Reloading, Inc.
Belt MTN Arms
Berger Bullets, Ltd.
Bergman & Williams
Berry's Mfg., Inc.
Bertram Bullet Co.
Big Bore Bullets of Alaska
Big Bore Express
Bitterroot Bullet Co.
Black Belt Bullets
Black Hills Shooters Supply
Black Powder Products
Blount, Inc., Sporting Equipment Div.
Briese Bullet Co., Inc.
Brown Co., E. Arthur
Brown Dog Ent.
Brownells, Inc.
BRP, Inc.
Bruno Shooters Supply
Buck Stix
Buckeye Custom Bullets
Buckskin Bullet Co.
Buffalo Arms Co.
Buffalo Rock Shooters Supply
Bullet, Inc.
Bullseye Bullets
Bull-X, Inc.
Butler Enterprises
Canyon Cartridge Corp.
Carnahan Bullets
Cascade Bullet Co., Inc.
Cast Performance Bullet Company
CCI
Champion's Choice, Inc.
Cheddite France, S.A.
CheVron Bullets
C.J. Ballistics, Inc.
Colorado Sutlers Arsenal
Competitor Corp., Inc.
Cook Engineering Service
Copperhead Bullets, Inc.
Cor-Bon Bullet & Ammo Co.
Cumberland States Arsenal
Cummings Bullets
Curtis Cast Bullets
Custom Bullets by Hoffman
Cutsinger Bench Rest Bullets
D&J Bullet Co. & Custom Gun Shop, Inc.
Dixie Gun Works, Inc.
DKT, Inc.
Dohring Bullets
Double A Ltd.
Eichelberger Bullets, Wm.
Eldorado Cartridge Corp.
Elkhorn Bullets
Epps, Ellwood
Federal Cartridge Co.
Forkin, Ben
4W Ammunition
Fowler, Bob
Fowler Bullets
Foy Custom Bullets
Freedom Arms, Inc.
Fusilier Bullets
G&C Bullet Co., Inc.
Gander Mountain, Inc.
Gehmann, Walter
GOEX, Inc.
Golden Bear Bullets
Gotz Bullets
"Gramps" Antique Cartridges
Granite Custom Bullets
Grayback Wildcats
Green Mountain Rifle Barrel Co., Inc.
Grier's Hard Cast Bullets
Group Tight Bullets
Gun City
Hammets VLD Bullets
Hardin Specialty Dist.
Harris Enterprises
Harrison Bullets
Hart & Son, Inc., Robert W.
Hawk, Inc.
Haydon Shooters' Supply, Russ
Heidenstrom Bullets
Hi-Performance Ammunition Company
Hirtenberger Aktiengesellschaft
Hobson Precision Mfg. Co.
Hodgdon Powder Co.
Hornady Mfg. Co.
HT Bullets
Huntington Die Specialties
Hunters Supply
IMI Services USA, Inc.
IMR Powder Co.
J-4, Inc.
J&D Components
J&L Superior Bullets
Jensen Bullets
Jensen's Firearms Academy
Jericho Tool & Die Co. Inc.
Jester Bullets
JLK Bullets
JRP Custom Bullets
Ka Pu Kapili
Kasmarsik Bullets
Kaswer Custom, Inc.
Keith's Bullets
Ken's Kustom Kartridge
Keng's Firearms Specialty, Inc.
Kent Cartridge Mfg. Co. Ltd.
KJM Fabritek, Inc.
KLA Enterprises
Kodiak Custom Bullets
Lapua Ltd.
Legend Products Corp.
Liberty Shooting Supplies
Lightning Performance Innovations, Inc.
Lindsley Arms Cartridge Co.
Lomont Precision Bullets
M&D Munitions Ltd.
Magnus Bullets
Maine Custom Bullets
Maionchi-L.M.I.
Marchmon Bullets
Markesbery Muzzle Loaders, Inc.
Marple & Associates, Dick
MAST Technology
Mathews & Son, Inc., George E.

REFERENCE

AMMUNITION COMPONENTS—BULLETS, POWDER (*continued*)

McMurdo, Lynn
Meister Bullets
Men—Metallwerk Elisenhuette, GmbH
Merkuria Ltd.
Mitchell Bullets, R.F.
MI-TE Bullets
Modern Muzzleloading, Inc.
MoLoc Bullets
Montana Armory, Inc.
Montana Precision Swaging
Mountain State Muzzleloading Supplies, Inc.
Mt. Baldy Bullet Co.
Mulhern, Rick
Mushroom Express Bullet Co.
Nagel's Bullets
National Bullet Co.
Navy Arms Co.
Necromancer Industries, Inc.
Norma
North American Shooting Systems
North Devon Firearms Services
Northern Precision Custom Swaged Bullets
Nosler, Inc.
Oklahoma Ammunition Co.
Old Wagon Bullets
Old Western Scrounger, Inc.
Omark Industries
Ordnance Works, The
Oregon Trail Bullet Company
Pacific Cartridge, Inc.
Page Custom Bullets
Patrick Bullets
Pease Accuracy, Bob
Petro-Explo, Inc.
Phillippi Custom Bullets, Justin
Pinetree Bullets
PMC/Eldorado Cartridge Corp.
Pomeroy, Robert
Precision Components
Precision Components and Guns
Precision Delta Corp.
Precision Munitions, Inc.
Prescott Projectile Co.
Price Bullets, Patrick W.
PRL Bullets
Professional Hunter Supplies
Rainier Ballistics Corp.
Ranger Products
Red Cedar Precision Mfg.
Redwood Bullet Works
Remington Arms Co., Inc.
Rhino
Rifle Works & Armory
R.I.S. Co., Inc.
R.M. Precision, Inc.
Robinson H.V. Bullets
Rolston, Inc., Fred W.
Rubright Bullets
SAECO
Scharch Mfg., Inc.
Schmidtman Custom Ammunition
Schneider Bullets
Schroeder Bullets
Scot Powder
Seebeck Assoc., R.E.
Shappy Bullets
Sierra Bullets
Silhouette, The
SOS Products Co.
Specialty Gunsmithing
Speer Products
Spencer's Custom Guns
Stanley Bullets
Star Ammunition, Inc.
Star Custom Bullets
Stark's Bullet Mfg.
Starke Bullet Company
Stewart's Gunsmithing
Talon Mfg. Co., Inc.
TCSR
T.F.C. S.p.A.
Thompson Precision
3-D Ammunition & Bullets
TMI Products
Traditions, Inc.
Trophy Bonded Bullets, Inc.
True Flight Bullet Co.
Tucson Mold, Inc.
Unmussig Bullets, D.L.
USAC
Vann Custom Bullets
Vihtavuori Oy/Kaltron-Pettibone
Vincent's Shop
Viper Bullet and Brass Works
Warren Muzzleloading Co., Inc.
Watson Trophy Match Bullets
Western Nevada West Coast Bullets
Widener's Reloading & Shooting Supply
Williams Bullet Co., J.R.
Winchester Div., Olin Corp.
Winkle Bullets
Worthy Products, Inc.
Wyant Bullets
Wyoming Custom Bullets
Yukon Arms Classic Ammunition
Zero Ammunition Co., Inc.

ANTIQUE ARMS DEALERS

Ackerman & Co.
Ad Hominem
Antique American Firearms
Antique Arms Co.
Aplan Antiques & Art, James O.
Armoury, Inc., The
Bear Mountain Gun & Tool
Bob's Tactical Indoor Shooting Range & Gun Shop
British Antiques
Buckskin Machine Works
Buffalo Arms Co.
Cape Outfitters
Carlson, Douglas R.
Chadick's Ltd.
Chambers Flintlocks Ltd., Jim
Champlin Firearms, Inc.
Chuck's Gun Shop
Classic Guns, Inc.
Clements' Custom Leathercraft, Chas
Cole's Gun Works
Colonial Arms, Inc.
D&D Gunsmiths, Ltd.
Dixie Gun Works, Inc.
Dixon Muzzleloading Shop, Inc.
Duffy, Charles E.
Dyson & Son Ltd., Peter
Ed's Gun House
Enguix Import-Export
Fagan & Co., William
Fish Mfg. Gunsmith Sptg. Co., Marshall F.
Flayderman & Co., N.
Forgett Jr., Valmore J.
Frielich Police Equipment
Fulmer's Antique Firearms, Chet
Getz Barrel Co.
Glass, Herb
Goergen's Gun Shop, Inc.
Golden Age Arms Co.
Gun Room, The
Gun Room Press, The
Guncraft Sports, Inc.
Gun Works, The
Guns Antique & Modern DBA/Charles E. Duffy
Hallowell & Co.
HandiCrafts Unltd.
Hansen & Co.
Hunkeler, A.
Johns Master Engraver, Bill
Kelley's
Ledbetter Airguns, Riley
LeFever Arms Co., Inc.
Lever Arms Service Ltd.
Lock's Philadelphia Gun Exchange
Log Cabin Sport Shop
Mandall Shooting Supplies, Inc.
Martin's Gun Shop
Montana Outfitters
Museum of Historical Arms, Inc.
Muzzleloaders Etcetera, Inc.
New England Arms Co.
Pony Express Sport Shop, Inc.
Retting, Inc., Martin B.
R.G.-G., Inc.
Scott Fine Guns, Inc., Thad
Shootin' Shack, Inc.
Steves House of Guns
Stott's Creek Armory, Inc.
Strawbridge, Victor W.
Vic's Gun Refinishing
Vintage Arms, Inc.
Westley Richards & Co.
Wiest, M.C.
Winchester Sutler, Inc., The
Wood, Frank
Yearout, Lewis E.

APPRAISERS—GUNS, ETC.

Antique Arms Co.
Armoury, Inc., The
Arundel Arms & Ammunition, Inc., A.
Barsotti, Bruce
Beitzinger, George
Blue Book Publications, Inc.
Bob's Tactical Indoor Shooting Range & Gun Shop
British Antiques
Bustani, Leo
Butterfield & Butterfield
Camilli, Lou
Cannon's, Andy Cannons
Cape Outfitters
Chadick's Ltd.
Champlin Firearms, Inc.
Christie's East
Clark Firearms Engraving
Classic Guns, Inc.
Clements' Custom Leathercraft, Chas
Cole's Gun Works
Colonial Arms, Inc.
Colonial Repair
Corry, John
Custom Tackle and Ammo
D&D Gunsmiths, Ltd.
DGR Custom Rifles
Dixon Muzzleloading Shop, Inc.
Duane's Gun Repair
Ed's Gun House
Epps, Ellwood
Eversull Co., Inc., K.
Fagan & Co., William
Ferris Firearms
Fish Mfg. Gunsmith Sptg. Co, Marshall F.
Flayderman & Co., Inc., N.
Forgett, Valmore J., Jr.
Forty Five Ranch Enterprises
Francotte & Cie S.A., Auguste
Frontier Arms Co., Inc.
Getz Barrel Co.
Gillmann, Edwin
Golden Age Arms Co.
Gonzalez Guns, Ramon B.
Griffin & Howe, Inc.
Gun City
Gun Hunter Trading Co.
Gun Room Press, The
Gun Shop, The
Guncraft Sports, Inc.
Guns
Hallowell & Co.
Hammans, Charles E.
HandiCrafts Unltd.
Hank's Gun Shop
Hansen & Co.
Hughes, Steven Dodd
Irwin, Campbell H.
Island Pond Gun Shop
Jackalope Gun Shop
Jaeger, Inc., Paul/Dunn's
Jensen's Custom Ammunition
Kelley's
LaRocca Gun Works, Inc.
Ledbetter Airguns, Riley
LeFever Arms Co., Inc.
L.L. Bean, Inc.
Lock's Philadelphia Gun Exchange
Mac's .45 Shop
Madis, George
Mandall Shooting Supplies, Inc.
Martin's Gun Shop
McCann's Muzzle-Gun Works
Montana Outfitters
Museum of Historical Arms, Inc.
Muzzleloaders Etcetera, Inc.
Navy Arms Co.
New England Arms Co.
Nitex, Inc.
Orvis Co., The
Pasadena Gun Center
Pentheny de Pentheny
Perazzi USA, Inc.
Peterson Gun Shop, Inc., A.W.
Pettinger Books, Gerald
Pony Express Sport Shop, Inc.
R.E.T. Enterprises
Retting, Inc., Martin B.
Richards, John
Safari Outfitters Ltd.
Scott Fine Guns, Inc., Thad
Shootin' Shack, Inc.
Steger, James R.
Stratco, Inc.
Strawbridge, Victor W.
Swampfire Shop, The
Thurston Sports, Inc.
Vic's Gun Refinishing
Wayne Firearms for Collectors and Investors, James
Wells Custom Gunsmith, R.A.
Whildin & Sons Ltd., E.H.
Wiest, M.C.
Williams Shootin' Iron Service
Winchester Sutler, Inc., The
Wood, Frank
Yearout, Lewis E.
Yee, Mike

BOOKS (Publishers and Dealers)

Action Direct, Inc.
American Handgunner Magazine
Armory Publications, Inc.
Arms & Armour Press
Barnes Bullets, Inc.
Blackhawk West
Blacksmith Corp.
Blacktail Mountain Books
Blue Book Publications, Inc.
Blue Ridge Machinery & Tools, Inc.
Brown Co., E. Arthur
Brownell Checkering Tools, W.E.
Brownell's, Inc.
Bullet'n Press
Calibre Press, Inc.
Cape Outfitters
Colonial Repair
Colorado Sutlers Arsenal
Corbin Mfg. & Supply, Inc.
Cumberland States Arsenal
DBI Books
Flores Publications, Inc., J.
Forgett Jr., Valmore J.
Golden Age Arms Co.
Gun City
Gun Hunter Books
Gun Hunter Trading Co.
Gun List
Gun Parts Corp., The
Gun Room Press, The
Gun Works, The
Guncraft Books
Guncraft Sports, Inc.
Gunnerman Books
GUNS Magazine
H&P Publishing
Handgun Press
Harris Publications
Hawk Laboratories, Inc.
Heritage/VSP Gun Books
Hodgdon Powder Co., Inc.
Home Shop Machinist, The
Hornady Mfg. Co.
Hungry Horse Books
I.D.S.A. Books
Info-Arm
Ironside International Publishers, Inc.
Koval Knives
Krause Publications, Inc.
Lane Publishing

REFERENCE

PRODUCT & SERVICE DIRECTORY

BOOKS (Publishers and Dealers) (*continued*)

Lapua Ltd.
Lethal Force Institute
Liberty Shooting Supplies
Lyman Products Corp.
Madis Books
Martin Bookseller, J.
McKee Publications
MI-TE Bullets
Montana Armory, Inc.
Mountain South
New Win Publishing, Inc.
NgraveR Co., The
OK Weber, Inc.
Outdoorsman's Bookstore, The
Paintball Games International
Magazine (Aceville Publications)
Paintball Sports Magazine
Pejsa Ballistics
Petersen Publishing Co.
Pettinger Books, Gerald
Police Bookshelf
PWL Gunleather
R.G.-G., Inc.
Riling Arms Books Co., Ray
Rocky Mountain Wildlife Products
Rutgers Book Center
S&S Firearms
Safari Press, Inc.
Saunders Gun & Machine Shop
Semmer, Charles
Shootin' Accessories, Ltd.
Sierra Bullets
SPG, Inc.
Stackpole Books
Stewart Game Calls, Inc., Johnny
Stoeger Publishing Co.
"Su-Press-On," Inc.
Thomas, Charles C.
Track of the Wolf, Inc.
Trafalgar Square
Trotman, Ken
Vintage Industries, Inc.
VSP Publishers
WAMCO—New Mexico
Wiest, M.C.
Wilderness Sound Products Ltd.
Williams Gun Sight Co.
Winchester Press
Wolfe Publishing Co.
Wolf's Western Traders

BULLET AND CASE LUBRICANTS

Blackhawk West
Brown Co., E. Arthur
Camp-Cap Products
Chem-Pak, Inc.
C-H Tool & Die Corp.
Cooper-Woodward
CVA
Elkhorn Bullets
E-Z-Way Systems
Forster Products
4-D Custom Die Co.
Guardsman Products
HEBB Resources
Hollywood Engineering
Hornady Mfg. Co.
Le Clear Industries
Lee Precision, Inc.
Lestrom Laboratories, Inc.
Lithi Bee Bullet Lube
M&N Bullet Lube
Michaels of Oregon Co.
MI-TE Bullets
NECO
Paco's
RCBS
Reardon Products
Rooster Laboratories
Shay's Gunsmithing
Small Custom Mould & Bullet Co.
Tamarack Products, Inc.
Uncle Mike's
Warren Muzzleloading Co., Inc.
Widener's Reloading & Shooting
Supply, Inc.
Young Country Arms

BULLET SWAGE DIES AND TOOLS

Brynin, Milton
Bullet Swaging Supply, Inc.
Camdex, Inc.
Corbin Mfg. & Supply, Inc.
Cumberland Arms
Eagan, Donald V.
Heidenstrom Bullets
Holland's
Hollywood Engineering
Necromancer Industries, Inc.
Niemi Engineering, W.B.
North Devon Firearms Services
Rorschach Precision Products
Sport Flite Manufacturing Co.

CARTRIDGES FOR COLLECTORS

Ad Hominem
Buck Stix—SOS Products Co.
Cameron's
Campbell, Dick
Cartridge Transfer Group
Cole's Gun Works
Colonial Repair
Country Armourer, The
de Coux, Pete
DGR Custom Rifles
Duane's Gun Repair
Ed's Gun House
Enguix Import-Export
Epps, Ellwood
First, Inc., Jack
Fitz Pistol Grip Co.
Forty Five Ranch Enterprises
Goergen's Gun Shop, Inc.
"Gramps" Antique Cartridges
Gun City
Gun Parts Corp., The
Gun Room Press, The
Mandall Shooting Supplies, Inc.
MAST Technology
Michael's Antiques
Montana Outfitters
Mountain Bear Rifle Works, Inc.
Pasadena Gun Center
San Francisco Gun Exchange
Samco Global Arms, Inc.
Scott Fine Guns, Inc., Thad
SOS Products Co.
Stone Enterprises, Ltd.
Ward & Van Valkenburg
Yearout, Lewis E.

CASES, CABINETS, RACKS AND SAFES—GUN

Abel Safe & File, Inc.
Alco Carrying Cases
All Rite Products, Inc.
Allen Co., Bob
Allen Co., Inc.
Alumna Sport by Dee Zee
American Display Co.
American Security Products Co.
Americase
Ansen Enterprises
Arizona Custom Case
Arkfeld Mfg. & Dist. Co., Inc.
Art Jewel Enterprises Ltd.
Bagmaster Mfg., Inc.
Barramundi Corp.
BEC, Inc.
Berry's Mfg., Inc.
Big Sky Racks, Inc.
Big Spring Enterprises "Bore Stores"
Bill's Custom Cases
Bison Studios
Black Sheep Brand
Boyt
Brauer Bros. Mfg. Co.
Brown, H.R.
Browning Arms Co.
Bucheimer, J.M.
Bushmaster Hunting & Fishing
Cannon Safe, Inc.
Chipmunk
Cobalt Mfg., Inc.
CONKKO
Connecticut Shotgun Mfg. Co.
D&L Industries
Dara-Nes, Inc.
Deepeeka Exports Pvt. Ltd.
D.J. Marketing
Doskocil Mfg. Co., Inc.
DTM International, Inc.
Elk River, Inc.
English, Inc., A.G.
Enhanced Presentations, Inc.
Eutaw Co., Inc.,, The
Eversull Co., Inc. K.
Fort Knox Security Products
Frontier Safe Co.
Galati Internationl
GALCO International Ltd.
Granite Custom Bullets
Gun Locker
Gun-Ho Sports Cases
Gusdorf Corp.
Hafner Creations, Inc.
Hall Plastics, Inc., John
Harrison-Hurtz Enterprises, Inc.
Hastings Barrels
Homak
Hoppe's Div.
Huey Gun Cases
Hugger Hooks Co.
Hunter Co., Inc.
Impact Case Co.
Johanssons Vapentillbehor, Bert
Johnston Bros.
Jumbo Sports Products
Kalispel Case Line
Kane Products, Inc.
KK Air International
Knock on Wood Antiques
Kolpin Mfg., Inc.
Lakewood Products, LLC
Liberty Safe
Marsh, Mike
Maximum Security Corp.
McWelco Products
Morton Booth Co.
MPC
MTM Molded Products Co., Inc.
Nalpak
National Security Safe Co., Inc.
Necessary Concepts, Inc.
Nesci Enterprises, Inc.
Oregon Arms, Inc.
Outa-Site Gun Carriers
Outdoor Connection, Inc., The
Pachmayr Ltd.
Palmer Security Products
Penguin Industries, Inc.
Pflumm Mfg. Co.
Poburka, Philip
Powell & Son (Gunmakers) Ltd., William
Protecto Plastics
Prototech Industries, Inc.
Quality Arms, Inc.
Rogue Rifle Co., Inc.
Schulz Industries
Silhouette Leathers
Southern Security
Sportsman's Communicators
Sun Welding Safe Co.
Surecase Co., The
Sweet Home, Inc.
Tinks & Ben Lee Hunting Products
Waller & Son, Inc., W.
WAMCO, Inc.
Wilson Case, Inc.
Woodstream
Zanotti Armor, Inc.
Ziegel Engineering

CHRONOGRAPHS AND PRESSURE TOOLS

Brown Co., E. Arthur
Canons Delcour
Competition Electronics, Inc.
Custom Chronograph, Inc.
D&H Precision Tooling
Hege Jagd-u. Sporthandels, GmbH
Hornady Mfg. Co.
Kent Cartridge Mfg. Co. Ltd.
Oehler Research, Inc.
P.A.C.T., Inc.
Shooting Chrony, Inc.
SKAN A.R.
Stratco, Inc.
Tepeco

CLEANING AND REFINISHING SUPPLIES

AC Dyna-tite Corp.
Acculube II, Inc.
Accupro Gun Care
American Gas & Chemical Co., Ltd.
Answer Products Co.
Armite Laboratories
Atlantic Mills, Inc.
Atsko/Sno-Seal, Inc.
Barnes Bullets, Inc.
Birchwood Casey
Blackhawk East
Blount, Inc., Sporting Equipment Div.
Blue and Gray Products, Inc.
Break-Free, Inc.
Bridgers Best
Brown Co., E. Arthur
Camp-Cap Products
Cape Outfitters
Chem-Pak, Inc.
CONKKO
Crane & Crane Ltd.
Creedmoor Sports, Inc.
CRR, Inc./Marble's Inc.
Custom Products
D&H Prods. Co., Inc.
Dara-Nes, Inc.
Decker Shooting Products
Deepeeka Exports Pvt. Ltd.
Dewey Mfg. Co., Inc., J.
Du-Lite Corp.
Dutchman's Firearms, Inc., The
Dykstra, Doug
E&L Mfg., Inc.
Eezox, Inc.
Ekol Leather Care
Faith Associates, Inc.
Flitz International Ltd.
Fluoramics, Inc.
Frontier Products Co.
G96 Products Co., Inc.
Goddard, Allen
Golden Age Arms Co.
Gozon Corp., U.S.A.
Great Lakes Airguns
Guardsman Products
Half Moon Rifle Shop
Heatbath Corp.

CLEANING AND REFINISHING SUPPLIES (*continued*)

Hoppe's Div.
Hornady Mfg. Co.
Hydrosorbent Products
Iosso Products
Johnston Bros.
Kellogg's Professional Products
Kent Cartridge Mfg. Co. Ltd.
Kesselring Gun Shop
Kleen-Bore, Inc.
Laurel Mountain Forge
Lee Supplies, Mark
LEM Gun Specialties, Inc.
Lewis Lead Remover, The
List Precision Engineering
LPS Laboratories, Inc.
Marble Arms
Micro Sight Co.
Minute Man High Tech Industries
Mountain View Sports, Inc.
MTM Molded Products Co., Inc.
Muscle Products Corp.
Nesci Enterprises, Inc.
Northern Precision Custom Swaged Bullets
Now Products, Inc.
Old World Oil Products
Omark Industries
Original Mink Oil, Inc.
Outers Laboratories, Div. of Blount
Ox-Yoke Originals, Inc.
P&M Sales and Service
Pachmayr Ltd.
PanaVise Products, Inc.
Parker Gun Finishes
Pendleton Royal
Penguin Industries, Inc.
Precision Reloading, Inc.
Prolix® Lubricants
Pro-Shot Products, Inc.
R&S Industries Corp.
Radiator Specialty Co.
Rickard, Inc., Pete
RIG Products Co.
Rod Guide Co.
Rooster Laboratories
Rusteprufe Laboratories
Rusty Duck Premium Gun Care Products
Saunders Gun & Machine Shop
Shiloh Creek
Shooter's Choice
Shootin' Accessories, Ltd.
Silencio/Safety Direct
Sno-Seal, Inc.
Spencer's Custom Guns
Stoney Point Products, Inc.
Svon Corp.
Tag Distributors
TDP Industries, Inc.
Tetra Gun Lubricants
Texas Platers Supply Co.
T.F.C. S.p.A.
Thompson Bullet Lube Co.
Thompson/Center Arms
Track of the Wolf, Inc.
United States Products Co.
Van Gorden & Son, Inc., C.S.
Venco Industries, Inc.
VibraShine, Inc.
Warren Muzzleloading Co., Inc.
WD-40 Co.
Wick, David E.
Willow Bend
Young Country Arms
Z-Coat Industrial Coatings, Inc.

COMPUTER SOFTWARE—BALLISTICS

ADC, Inc.
Action Target, Inc.
AmBr Software Group Ltd.
Arms, Programming Solutions
Arms Software
Ballistic Engineering & Software, Inc.
Ballistic Program Co., Inc., The
Barnes Bullets, Inc.
Beartooth Bullets
Blackwell, W.
Canons Delcour
Corbin Mfg. & Supply, Inc.
Country Armourer, The
Data Tech Software Systems
Exe, Inc.
FlashTek, Inc.
Hodgdon Powder Co., Inc.
Hutton Rifle Ranch
Jensen Bullets
J.I.T. Ltd.
JWH: Software
Kent Cartridge Mfg. Co. Ltd.
Load From A Disk
Maionchi-L.M.I.
Oehler Research, Inc.
P.A.C.T., Inc.
PC Bullet/ADC, Inc.
Pejsa Ballistics
Powley Computer
RCBS
Sierra Bullets
Tioga Engineering Co., Inc.
Vancini, Carl
W. Square Enterprises

CUSTOM METALSMITHS

Ahlman Guns
Aldis Gunsmithing & Shooting Supply
Amrine's Gun Shop
Answer Products Co.
Arnold Arms Co., Inc.
Arundel Arms & Ammunition, Inc., A.
Baer Custom, Inc., Les
Bansner's Gunsmithing Specialties
Baron Technology
Barsotti, Bruce
Bear Mountain Gun & Tool
Behlert Precision, Inc.
Beitzinger, George
Bell, Sid
Benchmark Guns
Bengtson Arms Co., L.
Biesen, Al
Billeb, Stephen L.
Billingsley & Brownell
Brace, Larry D.
Briganti, A.J.
Brown Precision, Inc.
Buckhorn Gun Works
Bullberry Barrel Works, Ltd.
Campbell, Dick
Carter's Gun Shop
Champlin Firearms, Inc.
Checkmate Refinishing
Chicasaw Gun Works
Christman Jr., Gunmaker, David
Classic Guns, Inc.
Cochran, Oliver
Colonial Repair
Colorado Gunsmithing Academy
Craftguard
Crandall Tool & Machine Co.
Cullity Restoration, Daniel
Custom Gun Products
Custom Gunsmiths
Custom Shop, The
D&D Gunsmiths, Ltd.
D&H Precision Tooling
DAMASCUS-U.S.A.
Delorge, Ed
DGS, Inc.
Dietz Gun Shop & Range, Inc.
Duane's Gun Repair
Duncan's Gunworks, Inc.
Eversull Co., Inc., K.
Eyster Heritage Gunsmiths, Inc., Ken
Ferris Firearms
Forster, Larry L.
Forthofer's Gunsmithing & Knifemaking
Francesca, Inc.
Frank Custom Classic Arms, Ron
Fullmer, Geo. M.
Gilkes, Anthony W.
Gordie's Gun Shop
Grace, Charles E.
Graybill's Gun Shop
Green, Roger M.
Gun Shop, The
Guns
Hamilton, Alex B.
Hartmann & Weiss GmbH
Harwood, Jack O.
Hecht, Hubert J.
Heilmann, Stephen
Heritage Wildlife Carvings
Highline Machine Co.
Hiptmayer, Armurier
Hiptmayer, Klaus
Hoag, James W.
Hoelscher, Virgil
Holland's
Hollis Gun Shop
Hyper-Single, Inc.
Island Pond Gun Shop
Ivanoff, Thomas G.
J&S Heat Treat
Jaeger, Inc., Paul/Dunn's
Jamison's Forge Works
Jeffredo Gunsight
Johnston, James
KDF, Inc.
Ken's Gun Specialties
Kilham & Co.
Klein Custom Guns, Don
Kleinendorst, K.W.
Kopp, Terry K.
Lampert, Ron
Lawson Co., Harry
List Precision Engineering
Mac's .45 Shop
Makinson, Nicholas
McCament, Jay
McCann's Machine & Gun Shop
McFarland, Stan
Morrow, Bud
Mullis Guncraft
Nelson, Stephen
Nettestad Gun Works
New England Custom Gun Service
Nicholson Custom
Nitex, Inc.
Noreen, Peter H.
North Fork Custom Gunsmithing
Nu-Line Guns, Inc.
Olson, Vic
Ozark Gun Works
P&S Gun Service
Pagel Gun Works, Inc.
Parker Gun Finishes
Pasadena Gun Center
Penrod Precision
Precision Metal Finishing
Precise Metalsmithing Enterprises
Precision Metal Finishing, John Westrom
Precision Specialties
Rice, Keith
Rifles Inc.
Robar Co.'s, Inc., The
Rocky Mountain Arms, Inc.
Score High Gunsmithing
Simmons Gun Repair, Inc.
Sipes Gun Shop
Skeoch, Brian R.
Smith, Art
Snapp's Gunshop
Spencer's Custom Guns
Sportsmen's Exchange & Western Gun Traders, Inc.
Starnes Gunmaker, Ken
Steffens, Ron
Steger, James R.
Stiles Custom Guns
Storey, Dale A.
Strawbridge, Victor W.
Ten-Ring Precision, Inc.
Thompson, Randall
Tom's Gun Repair
Tooley Custom Rifles
Van Horn, Gil
Van Patten, J.W.
Von Minden Gunsmithing Services
Waldron, Herman
Weber & Markin Custom Gunsmiths
Wells, Fred F.
Wells Custom Gunsmith, R.A.
Welsh, Bud
Werth, T.W.
Wessinger Custom Guns & Engraving
West, Robert G.
Westrom, John
White Rock Tool & Die
Wiebe, Duane
Williams Gun Sight Co.
Williams Shootin' Iron Service
Williamson Precision Gunsmithing
Wise Guns, Dale
Wood, Frank
Zufall, Joseph F.

ENGRAVERS, ENGRAVING TOOLS

Ackerman & Co.
Adair Custom Shop, Bill
Adams, John J. & Son Engravers
Adams Jr., John J.
Ahlman Guns
Alfano, Sam
Allard, Gary
Allen Firearm Engraving
Altamont Co.
American Pioneer Video
Anthony and George Ltd.
Baron Technology
Barraclough, John K.
Bates Engraving, Billy
Bell, Sid
Blair Engraving, J.R.
Bleile, C. Roger
Boessler, Erich
Bone Engraving, Ralph
Bratcher, Dan
Brgoch, Frank
Brooker, Dennis
Brownell Checkering Tools, W.E.
Burgess, Byron
CAM Enterprises
Churchill, Winston
Clark Firearms Engraving
Collings, Ronald
Creek Side Metal & Woodcrafters
Cullity Restoration, Daniel
Cupp, Custom Engraver, Alana
Custom Gun Engraving
DAMASCUS-U.S.A.
Davidson, Jere
Dayton Traister
Delorge, Ed
Desquesnes, Gerald
Dixon Muzzleloading Shop, Inc.
Dolbare, Elizabeth
Drain, Mark
Dubber, Michael W.
Engraving Artistry
Evans Engraving, Robert
Eversull Co., Inc., K.
Eyster Heritage Gunsmiths, Inc., Ken
Fanzoj GmbH
Firearms Engraver's Guild of America
Flannery Engraving Co., Jeff W.
Forty Five Ranch Enterprises
Fountain Products
Francotte & Cie S.A., Auguste
Frank Knives
French, Artistic Engraving, J.R.
Gene's Custom Guns
George, Tim
Glimm, Jerome C.
Golden Age Arms Co.
Gournet, Geoffroy
Grant, Howard V.
Griffin & Howe, Inc.
GRS Corp., Glendo
Gun Room, The
Guns
Gurney, F.R.
Gwinnell, Bryson J.
Hale/Engraver, Peter
Half Moon Rifle Shop
Hands Engraving, Barry Lee
Harris Gunworks
Harris Hand Engraving, Paul A.
Harwood, Jack O.
Hawken Shop, The
Hendricks, Frank E.

REFERENCE

PRODUCT & SERVICE DIRECTORY

ENGRAVERS, ENGRAVING TOOLS (*continued*)

Heritage Wildlife Carvings
Hiptmayer, Armurier
Hiptmayer, Heidemarie
Horst, Alan K.
Ingle, Engraver, Ralph W.
Jaeger, Inc., Paul/Dunn's
Jantz Supply
Johns Master Engraver, Bill
Kamyk Engraving Co., Steve
Kane, Edward
Kehr, Roger
Kelly, Lance
Klingler Woodcarving
Koevenig's Engraving Service
Kudlas, John M.
LeFever Arms Co., Inc.
Leibowitz, Leonard
Lindsay, Steve
Little Trees Ramble
Lutz Engraving, Ron
Master Engravers, Inc.
McCombs, Leo
McDonald, Dennis
McKenzie, Lynton
Mele, Frank
Metals Hand Engraver
Mittermeier, Inc., Frank
Montgomery Community College
Moschetti, Mitchell R.
Mountain States Engraving
Nelson, Gary K.
New England Custom Gun Service
New Orleans Jewelers Supply Co.
NgraveR Co., The
Oker's Engraving
P&S Gun Service
Pedersen, C.R.
Pedersen, Rex C.
Pilgrim Pewter, Inc.
Pilkington, Scott
Piquette, Paul R.
Potts, Wayne E.
Rabeno, Martin
Reed, Dave
Reno, Wayne
Riggs, Jim
Roberts, J.J.
Rohner, Hans
Rohner, John
Rosser, Bob
Rundell's Gun Shop
Runge, Robert P.
Sampson, Roger
Schiffman, Mike
Sherwood, George
Singletary, Kent
Smith, Mark A.
Smith, Ron
Smokey Valley Rifles
Theis, Terry
Thiewes, George W.
Thirion Gun Engraving, Denise
Thompson/Center Arms
Valade Engraving, Robert
Vest, John
Viramontez, Ray
Vorhes, David
Wagoner, Vernon G.
Wallace, Terry
Warenski, Julie
Warren, Kenneth W.
Weber & Markin Custom Gunsmiths
Welch, Sam
Wells, Rachel
Wessinger Custom Guns & Engraving
Wood, Mel
Yee, Mike

GUN PARTS, U.S. AND FOREIGN

Accuracy Gun Shop
Actions by "T"
Ahlman Guns
Amherst Arms
Aro-Tek, Ltd.
Auto-Ordnance Corp.
Badger Shooters Supply, Inc.
Bear Mountain Gun & Tool
Billings Gunsmiths, Inc.
Bob's Gun Shop
Bowen Classic Arms Corp.
Briese Bullet Co., Inc.
British Antiques
Buffer Technologies
Bushmaster Firearms
Bustani, Leo
Cape Outfitters
Caspian Arms Ltd.
Chicasaw Gun Works
Clark Custom Guns, Inc.
Cochran, Oliver
Cole's Gun Works
Colonial Repair
Cylinder & Slide, Inc.
Dayton Traister
Delta Arms Ltd.
DGR Custom Rifles
Dibble, Derek A.
Duane's Gun Repair
Duffy, Charles E.
Dyson & Son Ltd., Peter
E&L Mfg., Inc.
EGW Evolution Gun Works
Elliott Inc., G.W.
EMF Co., Inc.
Enguix Import-Export
Fleming Firearms
Forrest, Inc., TomGalati International
Glimm, Jerome C.
Goodwin, Fred
Greider Precision
Groenewold, John
Gun Parts Corp., The
Gun Shop, The
Guns Antique & Modern DBA/Charles E. Duffy
Gunsmithing, Inc.
Gun-Tec
Hastings Barrels
Hawken Shop, The
High Performance International
Irwin, Campbell H.
I.S.S.
Jaeger, Inc., Paul/Dunn's
Jamison's Forge Works
Johnson's Gunsmithing, Inc., Neal G
J.R. Distributing (Wolf competiition guns)
K&T Co.
Kimber of America, Inc.
K.K. Arms Co.
Krico Jagd-und Sportwaffen GmbH
Laughridge, William R.
List Precision Engineering
Lodewick, Walter H.
Long, George F.
Lothar Walther Precision Tool, Inc.
Mac's .45 Shop
Mandall Shooting Supplies, Inc.
Markell, Inc.
Martin's Gun Shop
Martz, John V.
McCormick Corp., Chip
MCS, Inc.
Merkuria Ltd.
Mid-America Recreation, Inc.
Mo's Competitor Supplies
Morrow, Bud
NCP Products, Inc.
North Star West
Nu-Line Guns, Inc.
Olympic Arms
Pachmayr Ltd.
Parts & Surplus
Pennsylvania Gun Parts
Perazone, Brian
Performance Specialists
Peterson Gun Shop, Inc., A.W.
P.S.M.G. Gun Co.
Quality Firearms of Idaho, Inc.
Quality Parts Co.
Randco UK
Ravell Ltd.
Retting, Inc., Martin B.
R.G.-G., Inc.
Ruger
S&S Firearms
Sabatti S.R.L.
Sarco, Inc.
Scherer
Shockley, Harold H.
Shootin' Shack, Inc.
Silver Ridge Gun Shop
Simmons Gun Repair, Inc.
Sipes Gun Shop
Smires, C.L.
Smith & Wesson
Southern Ammunition Co., Inc.
Southern Armory, The
Sportsmen's Exchange & Western Gun Traders, Inc.
Springfield, Inc.
Springfield Sporters, Inc.
Starr Trading Co., Jedediah
Steyr Mannlicher AG & CO KG
Sturm, Ruger & Co., Inc.
"Su-Press-On," Inc.
Swampfire Shop, The
Tank's Rifle Shop
Tarnhelm Supply Co., Inc.
Triple-K Mfg. Co., Inc.
Twin Pine Armory
USA Sporting Inc.
Vintage Arms, Inc.
Volquartsen Custom Ltd.
Walker Arms Co., Inc.
Waller & Son, Inc. W.
Weaver Arms Corp. Gun Shop
Wescombe, Bill
Westfield Engineering
Whitestone Lumber Corp.
Williams Mfg. of Oregon
Winchester Sutler, Inc., The
Wise Guns, Dale
Wolff Co., W.C.

GUNS, AIR

Airrow
Beeman Precision Airguns
Benjamin/Sheridan Co.
Brass Eagle, Inc.
Brocock Ltd.
BSA Guns Ltd.
Crosman Airguns
Crosman Products of Canada Ltd.
Daisy Mfg. Co.
Diana
Dynamit Nobel-RWS, Inc.
FAS
Frankonia Jagd
FWB
Gamo USA, Inc.
Gaucher Armes, S.A.
Great Lakes Airguns
Hebard Guns, Gil
Hofmann & Co.
Interarms
Labanu, Inc.
List Precision Engineering
Mac-1 Distributors
Marksman Products
Maryland Paintball Supply
Merkuria Ltd.
Pardini Armi Srl
Penguin Industries, Inc.
Precision Airgun Sales, Inc.
Precision Sales Int'l., Inc.
Ripley Rifles
Robinson, Don
RWS
S.G.S. Sporting Guns Srl
SKAN A.R.
Smart Parts
Steyr Mannlicher AG & CO KG
Stone Enterprises Ltd.
Swivel Machine Works, Inc.
Theoben Engineering
Tippman Pneumatics, Inc.
Tristar Sporting Arms, Ltd.
Trooper Walsh
UltraSport Arms, Inc.
Valor Corp.
Vortek Products
Walther GmbH, Carl
Webley and Scott Ltd.
Weihrauch KG, Hermann
Whiscombe
World Class Airguns

GUNS, FOREIGN—IMPORTERS (Manufacturers)

Accuracy International (Anschutz GmbH target rifles)
AcuSport Corporation (Anschutz GmbH)
Air Rifle Specialists (airguns)
American Arms, Inc. (Fausti Cav. Stefano & Figlie snc; Franchi S.p.A.; Grulla Armes; Uberti, Aldo; Zabala Hermanos S.A.; blackpowder arms)
American Frontier Firearms Mfg. Inc. (single-action revolvers)
Amtec 2000, Inc. (Erma Werke GmbH)
Anics Firm, Inc. (Anics)
Arms United Corp. (Gamo)
Armsport, Inc. (Bernardelli S.p.A., Vincenzo)
Aspen Outfitting Co. (Ugartechea S.A., Ignacio)
Auto-Ordnance Corp. (Techno Arms)
Autumn Sales, Inc. (Blaser Jagdwaffen GmbH)
Beauchamp & Son, Inc. (Pedersoli and Co., Davide)
Beeman Precision Airguns (Beeman Precision Airguns, Inc.; FWB; Webley & Scott Ltd.; Weihrauch KG, Hermann)
Beretta U.S.A. Corp. (Beretta S.p.A., Pietro)
Big Bear Arms & Sporting Goods, Inc. (Russian/Big Bear Arms)
Bohemia Arms Co. (BRNO)
British Sporting Arms
Browning Arms Co. (Browning Arms Co.)
Cabela's (Pedersoli and Co., Davide; Uberti, Aldo; blackpowder arms)
Cape Outfitters (Armi Sport; Pedersoli and Co., Davide; San Marco; Societa Armi Bresciane Srl.; blackpowder arms)
Century International Arms, Inc. (FEG)
Champion Shooters' Supply (Anschutz GmbH)
Champion's Choice (Anschutz GmbH; Walther GmbH, Carl; target rifles)
Chapuis USA (Chapuis Armes)
Champlin Firearms, Inc. (Chapuis Armes; M.Thys)
Christopher Firearms Co., Inc., E.
Cimarron Arms (Uberti, Aldo; Armi San Marco; Pedersoli)
CVA (blackpowder arms)
CZ USA
Daisy Mfg. Co. (Daisy Mfg. Co.; Gamo)
Dixie Gun Works, Inc. (Pedersoli and Co., Davide; Uberti, Aldo; blackpowder arms)
Dynamit Nobel-RWS, Inc. (Brenneke KG, Wilhelm; Diana; Gamo; Norma Precision AB; RWS)
E.A.A. Corp. (Astra-Sport, S.A.; Sabatti S.r.l.; Tanfoglio Fratelli S.r.l.; Weihrauch KG, Hermann; Star Bonifacio Echeverria S.A.)
Eagle Imports, Inc. (Bersa S.A.)
EMF Co., Inc. (Dakota; Hartford; Pedersoli and Co., Davide; San Marco; Uberti, Aldo; blackpowder arms)
Euroarms of America, Inc. (blackpowder arms)
Eversull Co., Inc., K.
Fiocchi of America, Inc. (Fiocchi Munizioni S.p.A.)
Forgett Jr., Valmore J. (Navy Arms Co.; Uberti, Aldo)

GUNS, FOREIGN—IMPORTERS (Manufacturers) (*continued*)

Franzen International, Inc. (Peters Stahl GmbH)
Gamba, USA (Societa Armi Bresciane Srl.)
Gamo USA, Inc. (Gamo airguns)
Giacomo Sporting, Inc.
Glock, Inc. (Glock GmbH)
Great Lakes Airguns (air pistols & rifles)
Groenewold, John (BSA Guns Ltd.; Webley & Scott Ltd.)
GSI, Inc. (Mauser Werke Oberndorf; Merkel Freres; Steyr-Mannlicher AG)
Gun Shop, The (Ugartechea S.A., Ignacio)
Hammerli USA (Hammerli Ltd.)
Hanus Birdguns, Bill (Ugartechea S.A., Ignacio)
Heckler & Koch, Inc. (Benelli Armi S.p.A.; Heckler & Koch, GmbH)
IAR, Inc. (Uberti, Kimar, Armi San Marco, S.I.A.C.E.)
Import Sports Inc. (Llama Gabilondo Y Cia)
Israel Arms International, Inc. (KSN Industries, Ltd.)
Ithaca Gun Co., LLC (Fabarm S.p.A.)
JägerSport, Ltd. (Voere-KGH m.b.H.)
J.R. Distributing (Wolf competition guns)
K.B.I., Inc. (FEG; Miroku, B.C./Daly, Charles)
Kemen American (Armas Kemen S.A.)
Keng's Firearms Specialty, Inc. (Lapua Ltd.; Ultralux)
Kongsberg America L.L.C. (Kongsberg)
K-Sports Imports, Inc.
Lion Country Supply (Ugartechea S.A., Ignacio)
London Guns Ltd. (London Guns Ltd.)
Mac-1 Distributors
Magnum Research, Inc.
MagTech Recreational Products, Inc. (MagTech)
Mandall Shooting Supplies, Inc. (Arizaga; Atamec-Bretton; Cabanas; Crucelegui, Hermanos; Erma Werke GmbH; Firearms Co. Ltd./Alpine; Hammerli Ltd.; Korth; Krico Jagd-und Sportwaffen GmbH; Morini; SIG; Tanner; Zanoletti, Pietro; blackpowder arms)
Marx, Harry (FERLIB)
MCS, Inc. (Pardini)
MEC-Gar U.S.A., Inc. (MEC-Gar S.R.L.)
Moore & Co., Wm. Larkin (Garbi; Piotti; Rizzini, Battista; Rizzini F.lli)
Nationwide Sports Distributors, Inc. (Daewoo Precision Industries Ltd.)
Navy Arms Co. (Navy Arms Co.)
Pedersoli and Co., Davide; Pietta; Uberti, Aldo; blackpowder and cartridge arms)
Nevada Cartridge Co. (Effebi SNC-Dr. Franco Beretta)
Nygord Precision Products (FAS; Morini; Pardini Armi Srl; Steyr-Mannlicher AG; TOZ; Unique/M.A.P.F.)
Pachmayr Ltd.
Para-Ordnance, Inc. (Para-Ordnance Mfg., Inc.)
Powell Agency, William, The (William Powell & Son [Gunmakers] Ltd.)
P.S.M.G. Gun Co. (Astra Sport, S.A.; Interarms; Star Bonifacio Echeverria S.A.; Walther GmbH, Carl)
Sarco, Inc.
Schuetzen Pistol Works (Peters Stahl GmbH)
Sigarms, Inc. (Hammerli Ltd.; Sauer rifles; SIG-Sauer)
Specialty Shooters Supply, Inc. (JSL Ltd.)
Sphinx USA Inc. (Sphinx Engineering SA)
Springfield, Inc. (Springfield, Inc.)
Stoeger Industries (IGA; Sako Ltd.; Tikka; target pistols)
Stone Enterprises Ltd. (airguns)
Swarovski Optik North America Ltd.
Taurus Firearms, Inc. (Taurus International Firearms)
Taylor's & Co., Inc. (Armi San Marco; Armi Sport; I.A.B.; Pedersoli and Co., Davide; Pietta; Uberti, Aldo)
Tradewinds, Inc. (blackpowder arms)
Tristar Sporting Arms, Ltd. (Turkish, German, Italian and Spanish made firearms)
Trooper Walsh
Turkish Firearms Corp. (Turkish Firearms Corp.)
Uberti USA, Inc. (Uberti, Aldo; blackpowder arms)
USA Sporting Inc. (Armas Kemen S.A.)
Vintage Arms, Inc.
Whitestone Lumber Corp. (Heckler & Koch; Bennelli Armi S.p.A.)
World Class Airguns (Air Arms)

GUNS, FOREIGN—MANUFACTURERS (Importers)

Accuracy International Precision Rifles (Gunsite Custom Shop; Gunsite Training Center)
Air Arms (World Class Airguns)
Anics (Anics Firm, Inc.)
Anschutz GmbH (Accuracy International; AcuSport Corporation; Champion Shooters' Supply; Champion's Choice; Gunsmithing, Inc.)
Astra Sport, S.A. (E.A.A. Corp.; P.S.M.G. Gun Co.)
Atamec-Bretton (Mandall Shooting Supplies, Inc.)
BEC Scopes (BEC, Inc.)
Beeman Precision Airguns, Inc. (Beeman Precision Airguns)
Benelli Armi S.p.A. (Heckler & Koch, Inc.; Whitestone Lumber Co.)
Beretta S.p.A., Pietro (Beretta U.S.A. Corp.)
Bersa S.A. (Eagle Imports, Inc.)
Bondini Paolo (blackpowder arms)
Borovnik KG, Ludwig
BRNO (Bohemia Arms Co.)
Brocock Ltd.
Browning Arms Co. (Browning Arms Co.)
BSA Guns Ltd. (Groenewold, John; Precision Sales International, Inc.)
CBC
Daisy Mfg. Co. (Daisy Mfg. Co.)
Diana (Dynamit Nobel-RWS, Inc.)
Erma Werke GmbH (Amtec 2000, Inc.; Mandall Shooting Supplies, Inc.)
F.A.I.R. Techni-Mec s.n.c.
FAS (Nygord Precision Products)
FEG (Century International Arms, Inc.; K.B.I., Inc.)
Firearms Co. Ltd./Alpine (Mandall Shooting Supplies, Inc.)
FN Herstal
FWB (Beeman Precision Airguns)
Gamba S.p.A.-Societa Armi Bresciane Srl., Renato (Gamba, USA)
Gamo (Arms United Corp.; Daisy Mfg. Co.; Dynamit Nobel-RWS, Inc.; Gamo USA, Inc.)
Gaucher Armes S.A.
Glock GmbH (Glock, Inc.)
Hammerli Ltd. (Hammerli USA; Mandall Shooting Supplies, Inc.; Sigarms, Inc.)
Hartford (EMF Co., Inc.)
Hartmann & Weiss GmbH
Heckler & Koch, GmbH (Heckler & Koch, Inc.)
Hege Jagd-u. Sporthandels, GmbH
Helwan (Interarms)
I.A.B. (Taylor's & Co., Inc.)
IGA (Stoeger Industries)
IMI
Interarms (Interarms; P.S.M.G. Gun Co.)
JSL Ltd. (Specialty Shooters Supply, Inc.)
Kimar (IAR, Inc.)
Kongsberg (Kongsberg America L.L.C.)
Korth (Interarms; Mandall Shooting Supplies, Inc.)
KSN Industries, Ltd. (Israel Arms International, Inc.)
Lapua Ltd. (Keng's Firearms Specialty, Inc.)
Llama Gabilondo Y Cia (Import Sports Inc.)
MagTech (MagTech Recreational Products, Inc.)
Mauser Werke Oberndorf (GSI, Inc.)
MEC-Gar S.R.L. (MEC-Gar U.S.A., Inc.)
Navy Arms Co. (Forgett Jr., Valmore J.; Navy Arms Co.)
Norinco (Century International Arms, Inc.; Interarms)
Norma Precision AB (Dynamit Nobel-RWS Inc.; The Paul Co., Inc.)
Para-Ordnance Mfg., Inc. (Para-Ordnance, Inc.)
Pardini Armi Srl. (Nygord Precision Products; MCS, Inc.)
Powell & Son Ltd., William (Powell Agency, The, William)
RWS (Dynamit Nobel-RWS, Inc.)
SIG (Mandall Shooting Supplies, Inc.)
SIG-Sauer (Sigarms, Inc.)
Sphinx Engineering SA (Sphinx USA Inc.)
Springfield, Inc. (Springfield, Inc.)
Star Bonifacio Echeverria S.A. (E.A.A. Corp.; Interarms; P.S.M.G. Gun Co.)
Steyr-Mannlicher AG (GSI, Inc.; Nygord Precision Products)
Tanner (Mandall Shooting Supplies, Inc.)
Taurus International Firearms (Taurus Firearms, Inc.)
Taurus S.A., Forjas
Techno Arms (Auto-Ordnance Corp.)
T.F.C. S.p.A.
Turkish Firearms Corp. (Turkish Firearms Corp.)
Uberti, Aldo (American Arms, Inc.; Cabela's; Cimarron Arms; Dixie Gun Works, Inc.; EMF Co., Inc.; Forgett Jr., Valmore J.; IAR, Inc.; Navy Arms Co.; Taylor's & Co., Inc.; Uberti USA, Inc.)
Ultralux (Keng's Firearms Specialty, Inc.)
Unique/M.A.P.F. (Nygord Precision Products)
Walther GmbH, Carl (Champion's Choice; Interarms; P.S.M.G. Gun Co.)
Webley & Scott Ltd. (Beeman Precision Airguns; Groenewold, John)
Weihrauch KG, Hermann (Beeman Precision Airguns; E.A.A. Corp.)

GUNS, U.S.-MADE

A.A. Arms, Inc.
Accu-Tek
Airrow
American Arms, Inc.
American Derringer Corp.
American Frontier Firearms Co.
A.M.T.
Auto-Ordnance Corp.
Baer Custom, Inc., Les
Beretta S.p.A., Pietro
Beretta U.S.A. Corp.
Bond Arms, Inc.
Braverman Corp., R.J.
Brolin Arms
Brown Co., E. Arthur
Brown Products, Inc., Ed
Browning Arms Co. (Parts & Service)
Calico Light Weapon Systems
Casull Arms Corp.
Century Gun Dist., Inc.
Champlin Firearms, Inc.
Colt's Mfg. Co., Inc.
Competitor Corp., Inc.
Connecticut Valley Classics
Coonan Arms
Cumberland Arms
Cumberland Mountain Arms
CVA
CVC
Davis Industries
Dayton Traister
Dixie Gun Works, Inc.
Downsizer Corp.
Eagle Arms, Inc.
Emerging Technologies, Inc.
FN Herstal
Forgett Jr., Valmore J.
Fort Worth Firearms
Frank Custom Classic Arms, Ron
Freedom Arms, Inc.
Fullmer, Geo. M.
Gonic Arms, Inc.
Gunsite Custom Shop
Gunsite Gunsmithy
H&R 1871, Inc.
Harris Gunworks
Harrington & Richardson
Heritage Firearms
Heritage Manufacturing, Inc.
Hesco-Meprolight
High Standard Mfg. Co., Inc.
Hi-Point Firearms
HJS Arms, Inc.
Holston Ent. Inc.
IAR, Inc.
Imperial Russian Armory
Intratec
Jones, J.D.
J.P. Enterprises, Inc.
JS Worldwide DBA
Kahr Arms
Kel-Tec CNC Industries, Inc.
Kimber of America, Inc.
K.K. Arms Co.
Knight's Mfg. Co.
L.A.R. Mfg., Inc.
Laseraim, Inc.
Lever Arms Service Ltd.
Ljutic Industries, Inc.
Lorcin Engineering Co., Inc.
Mag-Na-Port International, Inc.
Magnum Research, Inc.
MKS Supply, Inc.
M.O.A. Corp.
Montana Armory, Inc.
NCP Products, Inc.
North American Arms, Inc.
North Star West
Nowlin Mfg. Co.
Olympic Arms, Inc.

PRODUCT & SERVICE DIRECTORY

GUNS, U.S.-MADE (*continued*)

Oregon Arms, Inc.
Phillips & Rogers, Inc.
Phoenix Arms
Precision Small Arms
Professional Ordnance, Inc.
Raptor Arms Co., Inc.
Recoilless Technologies, Inc.
Remington Arms Co., Inc.
Republic Arms, Inc.
Rocky Mountain Arms, Inc.
Ruger
Scattergun Technologies, Inc.
Seecamp Co., Inc., L.W.
Shepherd & Turpin Dist. Company
Small Arms Specialties
Smith & Wesson
Springfield, Inc.
SSK Industries
STI International
Stoeger Industries
Sturm, Ruger & Co., Inc.
Sundance Industries, Inc.
Sunny Hill Enterprizes, Inc.
Survival Arms, Inc.
Swivel Machine Works, Inc.
Texas Armory
Taurus Firearms, Inc.
Taylor & Robbins
Texas Longhorn Arms, Inc.
Thompson/Center Arms
Time Precision, Inc.
Tristar Sporting Arms, Ltd.
Ultra Light Arms, Inc.
UFA, Inc.
Wells, Fred F.
Wescombe, Bill
Wesson Firearms Co., Inc.
Wesson Firearms, Dan
Wildey, Inc.
Wilkinson Arms
Z-M Weapons

GUNS AND GUN PARTS, REPLICA AND ANTIQUE

Armi San Paolo
Auto-Ordnance Corp.
Bear Mountain Gun & Tool
Beauchamp & Son, Inc.
Billings Gunsmiths, Inc.
Bob's Gun Shop
British Antiques
Buckskin Machine Works
Buffalo Arms Co.
Burgess & Son Gunsmiths, R.W.
Cache La Poudre Rifleworks
Cape Outfitters
Chambers Flintlocks Ltd., Jim
Chicasaw Gun Works
Cochran, Oliver
Cogar's Gunsmithing
Cole's Gun Works
Colonial Arms, Inc.
Colonial Repair
Custom Riflestocks, Inc.
Dangler, Homer L.
Day & Sons, Inc., Leonard
Delhi Gun House
Delta Arms Ltd.
Dilliott Gunsmithing, Inc.
Dixon Muzzleloading Shop, Inc.
Dyson & Son., Ltd. Peter
Ed's Gun House
Flintlocks, Etc.
Forgett, Valmore J., Jr.
Getz Barrel Co.
Golden Age Arms Co.
Goodwin, Fred
Groenewold, John
Gun Parts Corp., The
Gun Works, The
Guns
Gun-Tec
Hastings Barrels
Hunkeler, A.
IAR, Inc.
Kokolus, Michael
Liberty Antique Gunworks
List Precision Engineering
L&R Lock Co.
Lucas, Edw. E.
Mandall Shooting Supplies, Inc.
Martin's Gun Shop
McKee Publications
McKinney, R.P.
Mountain Bear Rifle Works, Inc.
Mountain State Muzzleloading Supplies, Inc.
Munsch Gunsmithing, Tommy
Museum of Historical Arms, Inc.
Navy Arms Co.
Neumann GmbH
North Star West
October Country
Pasadena Gun Center
Pecatonica River Longrifle
PEM's Mfg. Co.
Pony Express Sport Shop, Inc.
Precise Metalsmithing Enterprises
Quality Firearms of Idaho, Inc.
Ranch Products
Randco UK
Ravell Ltd.
Retting, Inc., Martin B.
R.G.-G., Inc.
S&S Firearms
Sarco, Inc.
Shootin' Shack, Inc.
Silver Ridge Gun Shop
Simmons Gun Repair, Inc.
Southern Ammunition Co., Inc.
Starnes Gunmaker, Ken
Stott's Creek Armory, Inc.
Taylor's & Co., Inc.
Tennessee Valley Mfg.
Triple-K Mfg. Co., Inc.
Uberti USA, Inc.
Vintage Industries, Inc.
Vortek Products, Inc.
Walker Arms Co., Inc.
Weisz Parts
Wescombe, Bill
Winchester Sutler, Inc., The

GUNS, SURPLUS—PARTS AND AMMUNITION

Ad Hominem
Alpha 1 Drop Zone
Armscorp USA, Inc.
Arundel Arms & Ammunition, Inc., A.
Ballistica Maximus North
Bohemia Arms Co.
Bondini Paolo
Century International Arms, Inc.
Chuck's Gun Shop
Cole's Gun Works
Combat Military Ordnance Ltd.
Delta Arms Ltd.
Ed's Gun House
First, Inc., Jack
Flaig's
Fleming Firearms
Forgett, Valmore J., Jr.
Forrest, Inc., Tom
Frankonia Jagd
Fulton Armory
Garcia National Gun Traders, Inc.
Goodwin, Fred
Gun City
Gun Parts Corp., The
Hart & Son, Inc., Robert W.
Hege Jagd-u. Sporthandels, GmbH
Hofmann & Co.
Interarms
Jackalope Gun Shop
LaRocca Gun Works, Inc.
Lever Arms Service Ltd.
Lomont Precision Bullets
Mandall Shooting Supplies, Inc.
Navy Arms Co.
Nevada Pistol Academy Inc.
Oil Rod and Gun Shop
Paragon Sales & Services, Inc.
Parts & Surplus
Pasadena Gun Center
Perazone, Brian
Quality Firearms of Idaho, Inc.
Raptor Arms. Inc., Co.
Ravell Ltd.
Retting, Inc., Martin B.
Samco Global Arms, Inc.
San Francisco Gun Exchange
Sanders Custom Gun Service
Sarco, Inc.
Shootin' Shack, Inc.
Silver Ridge Gun Shop
Simmons Gun Repair, Inc.
Sportsmen's Exchange & Western Gun Traders, Inc.
Springfield Sporters, Inc.
Starnes Gunmaker, Ken
Tarnhelm Supply Co., Inc.
T.F.C. S.p.A.
Thurston Sports, Inc.
Westfield Engineering
Williams Shootin' Iron Service
Whitestone Lumber Corp.

GUNSMITH SCHOOLS

Bull Mountain Rifle Co.
Colorado Gunsmithing Academy
Colorado School of Trades
Cylinder & Slide, Inc.
Lassen Community College, Gunsmithing Dept.
Laughridge, William R.
Modern Gun Repair School
Montgomery Community College
Murray State College
North American Correspondence Schools
Nowlin Mfg. Co.
NRI Gunsmith School
Pennsylvania Gunsmith School
Piedmont Community College
Pine Technical College
Professional Gunsmiths of America
Southeastern Community College
Smith & Wesson
Spencer's Custom Guns
Trinidad State Junior College
Gunsmithing Dept.
Wright's Hardwood Gunstock Blanks
Yavapai College

HANDGUN ACCESSORIES

A.A. Arms, Inc.
Ace Custom 45's, Inc.
Action Direct, Inc.
ADCO Sales, Inc.
Adventurer's Outpost
African Import Co.
Aimpoint U.S.A.
Aimtech Mount Systems
Ajax Custom Grips, Inc.
Alpha Gunsmith Division
American Derringer Corp.
American Frontier Firearms Co.
Arms Corporation of the Philippines
Aro-Tek, Ltd.
Astra Sport, S.A.
Baer Custom, Inc., Les
Bar-Sto Precision Machine
BEC, Inc.
Behlert Precision, Inc.
Blue and Gray Products, Inc.
Bond Custom Firearms
Bowen Classic Arms Corp.
Broken Gun Ranch
Brown Products, Inc., Ed
Brownells, Inc.
Bucheimer, J.M.
Bushmaster Firearms
Bushmaster Hunting & Fishing
Butler Creek Corp.
C3 Systems
Centaur Systems, Inc.
Central Specialties Ltd.
Clark Custom Guns, Inc.
Conetrol Scope Mounts
Craig Custom Ltd.
CRR, Inc./Marble's Inc.
D&L Industries
Dade Screw Machine Products
Dayson Arms Ltd.
Delhi Gun House
D.J. Marketing
Doskocil Mfg. Co., Inc
E&L Mfg., Inc.
E.A.A. Corp.
Eagle International Sporting Goods, Inc.
European American Armory Corp.
Faith Associates, Inc.
Feminine Protection, Inc.
Fisher Custom Firearms
Flashette Co.
Fleming Firearms
Flores Publications, Inc., J.
Frielich Police Equipment
FWB
Gage Manufacturing
Galati International
GALCO International Ltd.
G.G. & G.
Glock, Inc.
Greider Precision
Gremmel Enterprises
Gun Parts Corp., The
Gun-Alert
Gun-Ho Sports Cases
Hebard Guns, Gil
Heinie Specialty Products
Henigson & Associates
Hill Speed Leather, Ernie
H.K.S. Products
Hoppe's Div.
Hunter Co., Inc.
Impact Case Co.
Jarvis, Inc.
JB Custom
Jeffredo Gunsight
Jones, J.D.
J.P. Enterprises, Inc.
Jumbo Sports Products
KeeCo Impressions
KK Air International
Keller Co., The
King's Gun Works
K.K. Arms Co.
L&S Technologies, Inc.
Lee's Red Ramps Lem Sports, Inc.
Loch Leven Industries
Lohman Mfg. Co., Inc.
Mac's .45 Shop
Mag-Na-Port International, Inc.
Magnolia Sports, Inc.
Marble Arms
Markell, Inc.
Maxi-Mount
MCA Sports
McCormick Corp., Chip
MEC-Gar S.R.L.
Merkuria Ltd.
Mid-America Guns and Ammo
Middlebrooks Custom Shop
Millett Sights
MTM Molded Products Co., Inc.
MCA Sports
Noble Co., Jim
No-Sho Mfg. Co.
Omega Sales
Ox-Yoke Originals, Inc.
PAST Sporting Goods, Inc.
Pearce Grip, Inc.
Penguin Industries, Inc.
Phoenix Arms
Power Custom, Inc.
Practical Tools, Inc.
Protector Mfg. Co., Inc., The
Quality Parts Co.
Ram-Line Blount, Inc.

REFERENCE

HANDGUN ACCESSORIES (*continued*)

Ranch Products
Ransom International Corp.
Recoilless Technologies, Inc.
Redfield, Inc.
Robar Co.'s, Inc., The
Round Edge, Inc.
RPM
Simmons Gun Repair, Inc.
Slings 'N Things, Inc.
Southwind Sanctions
SSK Industries
STI International
TacStar Industries, Inc.
TacTell, Inc.
Tanfoglio Fratelli S.r.l.
T.F.C. S.p.A.
Thompson/Center Arms
Trigger Lock Division
Trijicon, Inc.
Triple-K Mfg. Co., Inc.
Tyler Manufacturing & Distributing
Valor Corp.
Volquartsen Custom Ltd.
Waller & Son, Inc., W.
Weigand Combat Handguns, Inc.
Wessinger Custom Guns & Engraving
Western Design
Wichita Arms, Inc.
Wilson Gun Shop

HANDGUN GRIPS

A.A. Arms, Inc.
Ahrends, Kim
Ajax Custom Grips, Inc.
Altamont Co.
American Derringer Corp.
American Frontier Firearms Co.
American Gripcraft
Arms Corporation of the Philippines
Art Jewel Enterprises Ltd.
Baelder, Harry
Baer Custom, Inc., Les
Barami Corp.
Bear Hug Grips, Inc.
Big Bear Arms & Sporting Goods, Inc.
Boone's Custom Ivory Grips, Inc.
Boyds' Gunstock Industries, Inc.
Brooks Tactical Systems
Brown Products, Inc., Ed
CAM Enterprises
Cole-Grip
Colonial Repair
Custom Firearms
Dayson Arms Ltd.
E.A.A. Corp.
EMF Co., Inc.
Essex Arms
European American Armory Corp.
Eyears Insurance
Fisher Custom Firearms
Fitz Pistol Grip Co.
Forrest, Inc., Tom
FWB
Harrison-Hurtz Enterprises, Inc.
Herrett's Stocks, Inc.
Hogue Grips
Huebner, Corey O.
KeeCo Impressions
Knight's Mfg. Co.
Korth
Lee's Red Ramps
Lett Custom Grips
Linebaugh Custom Sixgun & Rifle Works
Mac's .45 Shop
Masen Co., Inc., John
Michaels of Oregon Co.
Mid-America Guns and Ammo
Millett Sights
N.C. Ordnance Co.
Newell, Robert H.
Nickels, Paul R.
Pacific Rifle Co.
Pardini Armi Srl
Phoenix Arms
Pilgrim Pewter, Inc.
Radical Concepts
Recoilless Technologies, Inc.
Rosenberg & Sons, Jack A.
Roy's Custom Grips
Sile Distributors, Inc.
Smith & Wesson
Speedfeed, Inc.
Spegel, Craig
Stoeger Industries
Taurus Firearms, Inc.
Tyler Manufacturing & Distributing
Uncle Mike's
Vintage Industries, Inc.
Volquartsen Custom Ltd.
Western Gunstock Mfg. Co.

HEARING PROTECTORS

Aero Peltor
Ajax Custom Grips, Inc.
Autauga Arms, Inc.
Brown Co., E. Arthur
Brown Products, Inc., Ed
Browning Arms Co.
Clark Co., Inc., David
E-A-R, Inc.
Electronic Shooters Protection, Inc.
Faith Associates, Inc.
Flents Products Co., Inc.
Gentex Corp.
Hoppe's Div.
Kesselring Gun Shop
North Specialty Products
Paterson Gunsmithing
Peltor, Inc.
Penguin Industries, Inc.
R.E.T. Enterprises
Rucker Dist. Inc.
Silencio/Safety Direct
Willson Safety Prods. Div.

HOLSTERS AND LEATHER GOODS

A&B Industries, Inc.
Action Direct, Inc.
Action Products, Inc.
Aker Leather Products
Alessi Holsters, Inc.
American Sales & Kirkpatrick
Arratoonian, Andy
Bagmaster Mfg., Inc.
Baker's Leather Goods, Roy
Bandcor Industries
Bang-Bang Boutique
Barami Corp.
Bear Hug Grips, Inc.
Beretta S.p.A., Pietro
Bianchi International, Inc.
Bill's Custom Cases
Blocker Holsters, Inc., Ted
Brauer Bros. Mfg. Co.
Brown, H.R.
Browning Arms Co.
Bucheimer, J.M.
Bull-X, Inc.
Bushwacker Backpack & Supply Co.
Carvajal Belts & Holsters
Cathey Enterprises, Inc.
Chace Leather Products
Churchill Glove Co., James
Cimarron Arms
Clements' Custom Leathercraft, Chas
Cobra Sport
Colonial Repair
Counter Assault
Creedmoor Sports, Inc.
Davis Leather Co., G. Wm.
Delhi Gun House
DeSantis Holster & Leather Goods, Inc.
Dixie Gun Works, Inc.
D-Max, Inc.
Easy Pull Outlaw Products
Ekol Leather Care
El Dorado Leather (c/o Dill)
El Paso Saddlery Co.
EMF Co., Inc.
Eutaw Co., Inc., The
F&A Inc.
Faust, Inc., T.G.
Feminine Protection, Inc.
Ferdinand, Inc.
Flores Publications, Inc., J.
Fobus International Ltd.
Forgett Jr., Valmore J.
Frankonia Jagd
Gage Manufacturing
GALCO International Ltd.
GML Products, Inc.
Gould & Goodrich
Gun Leather Limited
Gunfitters, The
Gun Works, The
Gusty Winds Corp.
Hafner Creations, Inc.
HandiCrafts Unltd.
Hank's Gun Shop
Hebard Guns, Gil
Heinie Specialty Products
Hellweg Ltd.
Henigson & Associates, Steve
Hill Speed Leather, Ernie
Hofmann & Co.
Holster Shop, The
Horseshoe Leather Products
Hoyt Holster Co., Inc.
Hume, Don
Hunter Co., Inc.
John's Custom Leather
Jumbo Sports Products
Kane Products, Inc.
Keller Co., The
Kirkpatrick Leather Co.
Kolpin Mfg., Inc.
Korth
Kramer Handgun Leather, Inc.
L.A.R. Mfg., Inc.
Law Concealment Systems, Inc.
Lawrence Leather Co.
Leather Arsenal
Lone Star Gunleather
Magnolia Sports, Inc.
Markell, Inc.
Michaels of Oregon Co.
Minute Man High Tech Industries
Mixson Corp.
Noble Co., Jim
No-Sho Mfg. Co.
Null Holsters Ltd., K.L.
October Country
Ojala Holsters, Arvo
Oklahoma Leather Products, Inc.
Old West Reproductions, Inc.
Pathfinder Sports Leather
PWL Gunleather
Recoilless Technologies, Inc.
Renegade
Ringler Custom Leather Co.
Rybka Custom Leather Equipment, Thad
Safariland Ltd., Inc.
Safety Speed Holster, Inc.
Schulz Industries
Second Chance Body Armor
Shoemaker & Sons, Inc., Tex
ShurKatch Corporation
Silhouette Leathers
Smith Saddlery, Jesse W.
Southwind Sanctions
Sparks, Milt
Stalker, Inc.
Starr Trading Co., Jedediah
Strong Holster Co.
Stuart, V. Pat
Tabler Marketing
Texas Longhorn Arms, Inc.
Top-Line USA Inc.
Torel, Inc.
Triple-K Mfg. Co., Inc.
Tristar Sporting Arms, Ltd.
Tyler
Tyler Manufacturing & Distributing
Uncle Mike's
Valor Corp.
Venus Industries
Viking Leathercraft, Inc.
Walt's Custom Leather
Westley Richards & Co.
Whinnery, Walt
Wild Bill's Originals
Wilson Gun Shop

LABELS, BOXES, CARTRIDGE HOLDERS

Ballistic Products, Inc.
Berry's Mfg., Inc.
Brown Co., E. Arthur
Cabinet Mountain Outfitters Scents & Lures
Cape Outfitters
Crane & Crane Ltd.
Del Rey Products
DeSantis Holster & Leather Goods, Inc.
Fitz Pistol Grip Co.
Flambeau Products Corp.
J&J Products Co.
Kolpin Mfg., Inc.
Liberty Shooting Supplies
Midway Arms, Inc.
MTM Molded Products Co., Inc.
Pendleton Royal

LOAD TESTING AND PRODUCT TESTING (Chronographing, Ballistic Studies)

Ballistic Research
Bartlett, Don
Briese Bullet Co., Inc.
Buck Stix—SOS Products Co.
Clearview Products
Clerke Co., J.A.
D&H Precision Tooling
Defense Training International, Inc.
DGR Custom Rifles
Duane's Gun Repair
Henigson & Associates, Steve
Hensler, Jerry
Hoelscher, Virgil
Jackalope Gun Shop
Jensen Bullets
Lomont Precision Bullets
Maionchi-L.M.I.
MAST Technology
McMurdo, Lynn
Middlebrooks Custom Shop
Multiplex International
Oil Rod and Gun Shop
Rupert's Gun Shop
SOS Products Co.
Spencer's Custom Guns
Vancini, Carl
Vulpes Ventures, Inc.
Wells Custom Gunsmith, R.A.
White Laboratory, Inc., H.P.
X-Spand Target Systems

Product & Service Directory

MUZZLE-LOADING GUNS, BARRELS AND EQUIPMENT

Accuracy Unlimited (Littleton, CO)
Adkins, Luther
Aimtech Mount Systems
Allen Manufacturing
Anderson Manufacturing Co., Inc.
Armi San Paolo
Armoury, Inc., The
Bauska Barrels
Beauchamp & Son, Inc.
Beaver Lodge
Bentley, John
Big Bore Bullets
Birdsong & Associates, W.E.
Blackhawk West
Black Powder Products
Blue and Gray Products, Inc.
Bridgers Best
Buckskin Bullet Co.
Buckskin Machine Works
Burgess & Son Gunsmiths, R.W.
Butler Creek Corp.
Cache La Poudre Rifleworks
California Sights
Cash Manufacturing Co., Inc.
CenterMark
Chambers Flintlocks, Ltd., Jim
Chopie Mfg., Inc.
Cimarron Arms
Cogar's Gunsmithing
Colonial Repair
Colt Blackpowder Arms Co.
Conetrol Scope Mounts
Cousin Bob's Mountain Products
Cumberland Arms
Cumberland Mountain Arms
Cumberland Knife & Gun Works
Curly Maple Stock Blanks
CVA
Dangler, Homer L.
Day & Sons, Inc., Leonard
Dayton Traister
deHaas Barrels
Delhi Gun House
Dixie Gun Works, Inc.
Dyson & Son Ltd., Peter
EMF Co., Inc.
Euroarms of America, Inc.
Eutaw Co., Inc., The
Fautheree, Andy
Feken, Dennis
Fellowes, Ted
Fire'n Five
Flintlocks, Etc.
Forgett Jr., Valmore J.
Fort Hill Gunstocks
Fowler, Bob
Frankonia Jagd
Frontier
Gain Twist Barrel Co.
Getz Barrel Co.
Golden Age Arms Co.
Gonic Arms, Inc.
Green Mountain Rifle Barrel Co., Inc.
Gun Works, The
Hastings Barrels
Hawken Shop, The
Hege Jagd-u. Sporthandels, GmbH
Hofmann & Co.
Hodgdon Powder Co., Inc.
Hoppe's Div.
Hornady Mfg. Co.
House of Muskets, Inc., The
Hunkeler, A.
Impact Case Co.
Jamison's Forge Works
Jones Co., Dale
K&M Industries, Inc.
Kennedy Firearms
Knight Rifles
Knight's Mfg. Co.
Kwik-Site Co.
L&R Lock Co.
L&S Technologies, Inc.
Legend Products Corp.
Lestrom Laboratories, Inc.
Log Cabin Sport Shop
Lone Star Rifle Company
Lothar Walther Precision Tool, Inc.
Lyons Gunworks, Larry
Lyman
Marlin Firearms Co.
Mathews & Son, Inc., George E.
McCann's Muzzle-Gun Works
Michaels of Oregon Co.
MMP
Modern MuzzleLoading, Inc.
Montana Precision Swaging
Mountain State Muzzle-loading Supplies, Inc.
Mowrey Gun Works
MSC Industrial Supply Co.
Mt. Alto Outdoor Products
Mushroom Express Bullet Co.
Muzzleloaders Etcetera, Inc.
Naval Ordnance Works
North Star West
October Country
Oklahoma Leather Products, Inc.
Olson, Myron
Orion Rifle Barrel Co.
Ox-Yoke Originals, Inc.
Pacific Rifle Co.
Parker Gun Finishes
Pecatonica River Longrifle
Pedersoli and Co., Davide
Penguin Industries, Inc.
Pioneer Arms Co.
Prairie River Arms
R.E. Davis
Rusty Duck Premium Gun Care Products
R.V.I.
S&B Industries
S&S Firearms
Selsi Co., Inc.
Shiloh Creek
Shooter's Choice
Sile Distributors
Simmons Gun Repair, Inc.
Sklany's Machine Shop
Slings 'N Things, Inc.
Smokey Valley Rifles
South Bend Replicas, Inc.
Southern Bloomer Mfg. Co.
Starr Trading Co., Jedediah
Stone Mountain Arms
Taylor's & Co., Inc.
Tennessee Valley Mfg.
Thompson Bullet Lube Co.
Thompson/Center Arms
Thunder Mountain Arms
Tiger-Hunt
Track of the Wolf, Inc.
Traditions, Inc.
Treso, Inc.
UFA, Inc.
Uberti, Aldo
Uncle Mike's
Upper Missouri Trading Co.
Venco Industries, Inc.
Voere-KGH m.b.H.
Walters, John
Warren Muzzleloading Co., Inc.
Wescombe, Bill
White Owl Enterprises
White Muzzleloading Systems
White Shooting Systems, Inc.
Williams Gun Sight Co.
Woodworker's Supply
Wright's Hardwood Gunstock Blanks
Young Country Arms

PISTOLSMITHS

Acadian Ballistic Specialties
Accuracy Gun Shop
Accuracy Unlimited (Glendale, AZ)
Actions by "T"
Adair Custom Shop, Bill
Ahlman Guns
Ahrends, Kim
Aldis Gunsmithing & Shooting Supply
Alpha Precision, Inc.
Alpine's Precision Gunsmithing & Indoor Shooting Range
Armament Gunsmithing Co., Inc.
Arundel Arms & Ammunition, Inc., A.
Baer Custom, Inc., Les
Bain & Davis, Inc.
Baity's Custom Gunworks
Banks, Ed
Bear Arms
Behlert Precision, Inc.
Bellm Contenders
Belt MTN Arms
Bengtson Arms Co., L.
Bowen Classic Arms Corp.
Broken Gun Ranch
Campbell, Dick
Cannon's, Andy Cannon
Caraville Manufacturing
Carter's Gun Shop
Chicasaw Gun Works
Clark Custom Guns, Inc.
Cochran, Oliver
Colonial Repair
Colorado School of Trades
Corkys Gun Clinic
Craig Custom Ltd.
Curtis Custom Shop
Custom Firearms
Custom Gunsmiths
D&D Gunsmiths, Ltd.
D&L Sports
Davis Service Center, Bill
Dayton Traister
Dilliott Gunsmithing, Inc.
EGW Evolution Gun Works
Ellicott Arms, Inc./Woods Pistolsmithing
Ferris Firearms
Fisher Custom Firearms
Forkin, Ben
Francesca, Inc.
Frielich Police Equipment
Garthwaite, Pistolsmith, Inc., Jim
G.G. & G.
Gonzalez Guns, Ramon B.
Greider Precision
Gun Room Press, The
Guncraft Sports, Inc.
Gunsite Custom Shop
Gunsite Gunsmithy
Gunsite Training Center
Hamilton, Alex B.
Hamilton, Keith
Hammond Custom Guns Ltd.
Hank's Gun Shop
Hanson's Gun Center, Dick
Harwood, Jack O.
Harris Gunworks
Hawken Shop, The
Hebard Guns, Gil
Heinie Specialty Products
High Bridge Arms, Inc.
Highline Machine Co.
Hoag, James W.
Irwin, Campbell H.
Island Pond Gun Shop
Ivanoff, Thomas G.
J&S Heat Treat
Jacobson, Teddy
Jarvis, Inc.
Jensen's Custom Ammunition
Johnston, James
Jones, J.D.
Jungkind, Reeves C.
K-D, Inc.
Kaswer Custom, Inc.
Ken's Gun Specialties
Kilham & Co.
Kimball, Gary
Kopp, Terry K.
La Clinique du .45
LaFrance Specialties
LaRocca Gun Works, Inc.
Lathrop's, Inc.
Lawson, John G.
Lee's Red Ramps
Leckie Professional Gunsmithing
Liberty Antique Gunworks
Linebaugh Custom Sixguns & Rifle Works
List Precision Engineering
Long, George F.
Mac's .45 Shop
Mag-Na-Port International, Inc.
Mahony, Philip Bruce
Mandall Shooting Supplies, Inc.
Marent, Rudolf
Marvel, Alan
Maxi-Mount
McCann's Machine & Gun Shop
MCS, Inc.
Middlebrooks Custom Shop
Miller Custom
Mitchell's Accuracy Shop
MJK Gunsmithing, Inc.
Mo's Competitor Supplies
Mountain Bear Rifle Works, Inc.
Mowrey's Guns & Gunsmithing
Mullis Guncraft
Nastoff's 45 Shop, Inc., Steve
NCP Products, Inc.
Novak's Inc.
Nowlin Custom Mfg.
Nygord Precision Products
Oglesby & Oglesby Gunmakers, Inc.
Paris, Frank J.
Pace Marketing, Inc.
Pasadena Gun Center
Peacemaker Specialists
PEM's Mfg. Co.
Performance Specialists
Pierce Pistols
Plaxco, J. Michael
Precision Specialties
Randco UK
Ries, Chuck
Rim Pac Sports, Inc.
Robar Co.'s, Inc., The
RPM
Score High Gunsmithing
Scott, McDougall & Associates
Seecamp Co., Inc., L.W.
Shooter Shop, The
Shooters Supply
Shootin' Shack, Inc.
Sight Shop, The
Singletary, Kent
Sipes Gun Shop
Spokhandguns, Inc.
Springfield, Inc.
SSK Industries
Starnes Gunmaker, Ken
Steger, James R.
Swenson's 45 Shop, A.D.
Swift River Gunworks
Ten-Ring Precision, Inc.
Thompson, Randall
300 Gunsmith Service, Inc.
Thurston Sports, Inc.
Tom's Gun Repair
Vic's Gun Refinishing
Volquartsen Custom Ltd.
Walker Arms Co., Inc.
Walters Industries
Wardell Precision Handguns Ltd.
Weigand Combat Handguns, Inc.
Wessinger Custom Guns & Engraving
Williams Gun Sight Co.
Williamson Precision Gunsmithing
Wilson Gun Shop
Wichita Arms, Inc.

REBORING AND RERIFLING

A.M.T.
Arundel Arms & Ammunition, Inc., A.
BlackStar AccuMax Barrels
BlackStar Barrel Accurizing
Chicasaw Gun Works
Cochran, Oliver
Ed's Gun House
Flaig's
Gun Works, The
IAI
H&S Liner Service
Ivanoff, Thomas G.
Jackalope Gun Shop
K-D, Inc.
Kopp, Terry K.
LaBounty Precision Reboring
Matco, Inc.
NCP Products, Inc.
Pence Precision Barrels
Pro-Port Ltd.
Ranch Products
Redman's Rifling & Reboring
Rice, Keith
Ridgetop Sporting Goods
Shaw, Inc., E.R.
Siegrist Gun Shop
Simmons Gun Repair, Inc.
Stratco, Inc.
300 Gunsmith Service, Inc.
Time Precision, Inc.
Tom's Gun Repair
Van Patten, J.W.
West, Robert G.
White Rock Tool & Die
Zufall, Joseph F.

PRODUCT & SERVICE DIRECTORY

RELOADING TOOLS AND ACCESSORIES

Action Bullets, Inc.
Advance Car Mover Co., Rowell Div.
Alaska Bullet Works, Inc.
American Products Inc.
Ames Metal Products
Ammo Load, Inc.
Anderson Manufacturing Co., Inc.
Armite Laboratories
Arms Corporation of the Philippines
Atlantic Rose, Inc.
Atsko/Sno-Seal, Inc.
Bald Eagle Precision Machine Co.
Ballistic Products, Inc.
Ballisti-Cast, Inc.
Belltown, Ltd.
Ben's Machines
Berger Bullets, Ltd.
Berry's Mfg., Inc.
Birchwood Casey
Blount, Inc., Sporting Equipment Div.
Blue Ridge Machinery & Tools, Inc.
Bonanza
Break-Free, Inc.
Brobst, Jim
Brown Co., E. Arthur
Bruno Shooters Supply
Brynin, Milton
B-Square Co., Inc.
Buck Stix—SOS Products Co.
Bull Mountain Rifle Co.
Bullet Swaging Supply, Inc.
Bullseye Bullets
C&D Special Products
Camdex, Inc.
Camp-Cap Products
Canyon Cartridge Corp.
Carbide Die & Mfg. Co., Inc.
Case Sorting System
CFVentures
C-H Tool & Die Corp.
Chem-Pak, Inc.
CheVron Case Master
Claybuster Wads & Harvester Bullets
Cleanzoil Corp.
Clearview Products
Clymer Manufacturing Co., Inc.
Coats, Mrs. Lester
Colorado Shooter's Supply
CONKKO
Cook Engineering Service
Cooper-Woodward
Crouse's Country Cover
Cumberland Arms
Custom Products, Neil A. Jones
CVA
Davis, Don
Davis Products, Mike
D.C.C. Enterprises
Denver Bullets, Inc.
Denver Instrument Co.
Dever Co., Jack
Dewey Mfg. Co., Inc., J.
Dillon Precision Products, Inc.
Dropkick
Dutchman's Firearms, Inc., The
E&L Mfg., Inc.
Eagan, Donald V.
Eezox, Inc.
Eichelberger Bullets, Wm.
Elkhorn Bullets
Engineered Accessories
Enguix Import-Export
Estate Cartridge, Inc.
E-Z-Way Systems
F&A Inc.
Federal Cartridge Co.
Federated-Fry
Feken, Dennis
Ferguson, Bill
First, Inc., Jack
Fisher Custom Firearms
Fitz Pistol Grip Co.
Flambeau Products Corp.
Flitz International Ltd.
Forgett Jr., Valmore J.
Forgreens Tool Mfg., Inc.
Forster Products
4-D Custom Die Co.
4W Ammunition
Fremont Tool Works
Fry Metals
Fusilier Bullets
G&C Bullet Co., Inc.
GAR
Gehmann, Walter
Goddard, Allen
Gozon Corp., U.S.A.
Graf & Sons
"Gramps" Antique Cartridges
Graphics Direct
Graves Co.
Green, Arthur S.
Greenwood Precision
Gun Works, The
Hanned Line, The
Hanned Precision
Harrell's Precision
Harris Enterprises
Harrison Bullets
Haselbauer Products, Jerry
Haydon Shooters' Supply, Russ
Heidenstrom Bullets
Hensley & Gibbs
Hirtenberger Aktiengesellschaft
Hobson Precision Mfg. Co.
Hoch Custom Bullet Moulds
Hodgdon Powder Co., Inc.
Hoehn Sales, Inc.
Hoelscher, Virgil
Holland's Gunsmithing
Hollywood Engineering
Hondo Industries
Hornady Mfg. Co.
Howell Machine
Hunters Supply
Huntington Die Specialties
Image Ind. Inc.
IMI Services USA, Inc.
Imperial
Imperial Magnum Corp.
INTEC International, Inc.
Iosso Products
Javelina Lube Products
JGS Precision Tool Mfg.
J&L Superior Bullets
JLK Bullets
Jonad Corp.
Jones Custom Products, Neil A.
Jones Moulds, Paul
K&M Services
K&S Mfg. Inc.
Kapro Mfg. Co., Inc.
King & Co.
Kleen-Bore, Inc.
Korzinek Riflesmith, J.
Lane Bullets, Inc.
Lapua Ltd.
LBT
Le Clear Industries
Lee Precision, Inc.
Legend Products Corp.
Liberty Metals
Liberty Shooting Supplies
Lightning Performance Innovations, Inc.
Lithi Bee Bullet Lube
Littleton, J.F.
Lortone, Inc.
Loweth Firearms, Richard H.R.
Luch Metal Merchants, Barbara
Lyman Instant Targets, Inc.
Lyman Products Corp.
M&D Munitions Ltd.
MA Systems
Magma Engineering Co.
MarMik, Inc.
Marquart Precision Co.
MAST Technology
Match Prep—Doyle Gracey
Mayville Engineering Co.
McKillen & Heyer, Inc.
MCRW Associates Shooting Supplies
MCS, Inc.
MEC, Inc.
Midway Arms, Inc.
Miller Engineering
MI-TE Bullets
MMP
Mo's Competitor Supplies
Montana Armory, Inc.
Mountain State Muzzleloading Supplies, Inc.
Mt. Baldy Bullet Co.
MTM Molded Products Co., Inc.
Multi-Scale Charge Ltd.
MWG Company
Necromancer Industries, Inc.
NEI Handtools, Inc.
Niemi Engineering, W.B.
North Devon Firearms Services
Northern Precision Custom Swaged Bullets
October Country
Old West Bullet Moulds
Omark Industries
Original Box, Inc.
Paco's
Pattern Control
Pease Accuracy, Bob
Pedersoli and Co., Davide
Peerless Alloy, Inc.
Pend Oreille Sport Shop
Pinetree Bullets
Plum City Ballistic Range
Pomeroy, Robert
Ponsness/Warren
Prairie River Arms
Precision Castings & Equipment, Inc.
Precision Reloading, Inc.
Prime Reloading
Professional Hunter Supplies
Prolix® Lubricants
Pro-Shot Products, Inc.
Protector Mfg. Co., Inc., The
Quinetics Corp.
R&D Engineering & Manufacturing
Rapine Bullet Mould Mfg. Co.
Raytech
RCBS
R.D.P. Tool Co., Inc.
Redding Reloading Equipment
R.E.I.
Reloading Specialties, Inc.
Rice, Keith
Riebe Co., W.J.
RIG Products
R.I.S. Co., Inc.
Roberts Products
Rochester Lead Works, Inc.
Rolston, Inc., Fred. W.
Rooster Laboratories
Rorschach Precision Products
Rosenthal, Brad and Sallie
SAECO
Sandia Die & Cartridge Co.
Saunders Gun & Machine Shop
Saville Iron Co.
Scharch Mfg., Inc.
Scot Powder Co. of Ohio, Inc.
Scott, Dwight
Seebeck Assoc., R.E.
Sharp Shooter Supply
Sharps Arms Co. Inc., C.
Shiloh Creek
Shiloh Rifle Mfg.
Shooter's Choice
ShurKatch Corporation
Sierra Specialty Prod. Co.
Silhouette, The
Silver Eagle Machining
Simmons, Jerry
Sinclair International, Inc.
Skip's Machine
S.L.A.P. Industries
Small Custom Mould & Bullet Co.
Sno-Seal
SOS Products Co.
Spence, George W.
Spencer's Custom Guns
SPG, Inc.
Sport Flite Manufacturing Co.
Sportsman Supply Co.
Stalwart Corp.
Star Custom Bullets
Star Machine Works
Starr Trading Co., Jedediah
Stillwell, Robert
Stoney Point Products, Inc.
Stratco, Inc.
Taracorp Industries
TCCI
TCSR
TDP Industries, Inc.
Tetra Gun Lubricants
Thompson Bullet Lube Co.
Thompson/Center Arms
Timber Heirloom Products
Time Precision, Inc.
TMI Products
TR Metals Corp.
Trammco, Inc.
Tru-Square Metal Prods., Inc.
TTM
Varner's Service
Vega Tool Co.
Venco Industries, Inc.
VibraShine, Inc.
Vibra-Tek Co.
Vihtavuori Oy/Kaltron-Pettibone
Vitt/Boos
Von Minden Gunsmithing Services
Walters, John
Webster Scale Mfg. Co.
WD-40 Co.
Welsh, Bud
Wells Custom Gunsmith, R.A.
Werner, Carl
Westfield Engineering
White Rock Tool & Die
Whitetail Design & Engineering Ltd.
Widener's Reloading & Shooting Supply
William's Gun Shop, Ben
Wilson, Inc., L.E.
Wise Guns, Dale
Wolf's Western Traders
Woodleigh
WTA Manufacturing, Bill Wood
Yesteryear Armory & Supply
Young Country Arms

RESTS—BENCH, PORTABLE—AND ACCESSORIES

Accuright
Adventure 16, Inc.
Armor Metal Products
Bald Eagle Precision Machine Co.
Bartlett Engineering
Borden's Accuracy
Browning Arms Co.
B-Square Co., Inc.
Bull Mountain Rifle Co.
Canons Delcour
Chem-Pak, Inc.
Clift Mfg., L.R.
Clift Welding Supply
Cravener's Gun Shop
Decker Shooting Products
Desert Mountain Mfg.
Erickson's Mfg., Inc., C.W.
F&A Inc.
Greenwood Precision
Harris Engineering, Inc.
Hidalgo, Tony
Hoehn Sales, Inc.
Hoelscher, Virgil
Hoppe's Div.
Kolpin Mfg., Inc.
Kramer Designs
Midway Arms, Inc.
Millett Sights
MJM Manufacturing
Outdoor Connection, Inc., The
PAST Sporting Goods, Inc.
Penguin Industries, Inc.
Portus, Robert
Protektor Model
Ransom International Corp
Saville Iron Co.
ShurKatch Corporation
Stoney Point Products, Inc.
Thompson Target Technology
T.H.U. Enterprises, Inc.
Tonoloway Tack Drivers
Varner's Service
Wichita Arms, Inc.
Zanotti Armor, Inc.

PRODUCT & SERVICE DIRECTORY

SCOPES, MOUNTS, ACCESSORIES, OPTICAL EQUIPMENT

ADCO Sales, Inc.
Aimpoint U.S.A.
Aimtech Mount Systems
Anderson Manufacturing Co., Inc.
Apel GmbH, Ernst
Baer Custom, Inc., Les
Barrett Firearms Mfg., Inc.
Bausch & Lomb Sports Optics Div.
Blount, Inc., Sporting Equipment Div.
Brown Co., E. Arthur
Brownells, Inc.
Brunton U.S.A.
B-Square Co., Inc.
Burris
Bushnell Sports Optics Worldwide
Butler Creek Corp.
Celestron International
Center Lock Scope Rings
Combat Military Ordnance Ltd.
Compass Industries, Inc.
Concept Development Corp.
Conetrol Scope Mounts
CRDC Laser Systems Group
Custom Quality Products, Inc.
Doctor Optic Technologies, Inc.
Emerging Technologies, Inc.
Excalibur Enterprises
Fotar Optics
Fujinon, Inc.
Great Lakes Airguns
Hammerli USA
Ironsighter Co.
Jeffredo Gunsight
Kahles, A Swarovski Company
KDF, Inc.
Knight's Mfg. Co.
Kowa Optimed, Inc.
Kris Mounts
KVH Industries, Inc.
Kwik Mount Corp.
Kwik-Site Co.
L&S Technologies, Inc.
L.A.R. Mfg., Inc.
Laser Devices, Inc.
Laseraim
LaserMax, Inc.
Leica USA, Inc.
Leupold & Stevens, Inc.
Lightforce U.S.A. Inc.
Lyte Optronics
Mac's .45 Shop
Mag-Na-Port International, Inc.
Masen Co., Inc., John
Maxi-Mount
MCS, Inc.
Merit Corp.
Michaels of Oregon Co.
Military Armament Corp.
Millett Sights
Mirador Optical Corp.
Mitchell Optics Inc.
Nightforce
Nikon, Inc.
Norincoptics
Olympic Optical Co.
Optical Services Co.
Outdoor Connection, Inc., The
Parsons Optical Mfg. Co.
PECAR Herbert Schwarz, GmbH
Pentax Corp.
Precision Sport Optics
Quarton USA, Ltd. Co.
Ram-Line Blount, Inc.
Ranch Products
Randolph Engineering, Inc.
Ranging, Inc.
Redfield, Inc.
Rocky Mountain High Sports Glasses
RPM
S&K Mfg. Co.
Saunders Gun & Machine Shop
Schmidt & Bender, Inc.
Scope Control Inc.
ScopLevel
Score High Gunsmithing
Seattle Binocular & Scope Repair Co.
Segway Industries
Selsi Co., Inc.
Sightron, Inc.
Simmons Enterprises, Ernie
Simmons Outdoor Corp.
Springfield, Inc.
Stoeger Industries
SwaroSports, Inc.
Swarovski Optik North America Ltd.
Swift Instruments, Inc.
TacStar Industires, Inc.
Tasco Sales, Inc.
Tele-Optics
Thompson/Center Arms
Trijicon, Inc.
Ultra Dot Distribution
Uncle Mike's
Unertl Optical Co., Inc., John
United Binocular Co.
United States Optics Tech., Inc.
Voere-KGH m.b.H.
Warne Manufacturing Co.
Warren Muzzleloading Co., Inc.
WASP Shooting Systems
Weaver Products
Weaver Scope Repair Service
Weigand Combat Handguns, Inc.
Westfield Engineering
White Muzzleloading Systems
White Shooting Systems, Inc.
White Rock Tool & Die
Wideview Scope Mount Corp.
Williams Gun Sight Co.
York M-1 Conversions
Zanotti Armor, Inc.
Zeiss Optical, Carl

SHOOTING/TRAINING SCHOOLS

Accuracy Gun Shop
Alpine Precision Gunsmithing & Indoor Shooting Range
American Small Arms Academy
Auto Arms
Barsotti, Bruce
Bob's Tactical Indoor Shooting Range & Gun Shop
Cannon's, Andy Cannon
Chapman Academy of Practical Shooting
Chelsea Gun Club of New York City, Inc.
CQB Training
Daisy Mfg. Co.
Defense Training International, Inc.
Dowtin Gunworks
Executive Protection Institute
Feminine Protection, Inc.
Ferris Firearms
Firearm Training Center, The
Firearms Academy of Seattle
G.H. Enterprises Ltd.
Front Sight Firearms Training Institute
Gunsite Training Center
Guncraft Sports, Inc.
Henigson & Associates, Steve
International Shootists, Inc.
Jensen's Custom Ammunition
Jensen's Firearms Acadamy
L.L. Bean, Inc.
McMurdo, Lynn
Mendez, John A.
Montgomery Community College
NCP Products, Inc.
Nevada Pistol Academy Inc.
North American Shooting Systems
North Mountain Pine Training Center
Performance Specialists
Quigley's Personal Protection Strategies, Paxton
SAFE
Shooter's World
Shooting Gallery, The
Smith & Wesson
Specialty Gunsmithing
Starlight Training Center, Inc.
Steger, James R.
Tactical Defense Institute
Thunder Ranch
300 Gunsmith Service, Inc.
Western Missouri Shooters Alliance
Yankee Gunsmith
Yavapai Firearms Academy Ltd.

SIGHTS, METALLIC

Alpec Team, Inc.
Anschutz GmbH
Baer Custom, Inc., Les
BEC, Inc.
Bo-Mar Tool & Mfg. Co.
Bowen Classic Arms Corp.
Brown Co., E. Arthur
Brown Products, Inc., Ed
Center Lock Scope Rings
C-More Systems
CRR, Inc./Marble's Inc.
Eagle International Sporting Goods, Inc.
Engineered Accessories
Forgett Jr., Valmore J.
Gun Works, The
Heinie Specialty Products
Hesco-Meprolight
Innovative Weaponry, Inc.
J.P. Enterprises, Inc.
Kris Mounts
Lee's Red Ramps
List Precision Engineering
London Guns Ltd.
L.P.A. Snc
Lyman Products Corp.
Mac's .45 Shop
Marble Arms
MCS, Inc.
MEC-Gar S.R.L.
Meier Works
Meprolight
Merit Corp.
Millett Sights
MMC
Novak's Inc.
Oakshore Electronic Sights, Inc.
P.M. Enterprises, Inc.
Quarton USA, Ltd. Co.
RPM
STI International
Talley, Dave
T.F.C. S.p.A.
Thompson/Center Arms
Trijicon, Inc.
Wichita Arms, Inc.
Wild West Guns, Inc.
Williams Gun Sight Co.
Wilson Gun Shop

TARGETS, BULLET AND CLAYBIRD TRAPS

Action Target, Inc.
American Target
American Whitetail Target Systems
A-Tech Corp.
Autauga Arms, Inc.
Beomat of America Inc.
Birchwood Casey
Blount, Inc., Sporting Equipment Div.
Blue and Gray Products, Inc.
Brown Manufacturing
Bull-X, Inc.
Camp-Cap Products
Caswell International Corp.
Champion Target Co.
Cunningham Co., Eaton
Dapkus Co., Inc., J.G.
Datumtech Corp.
Dayson Arms Ltd.
D.C.C. Enterprises
Detroit-Armor Corp.
Diamond Mfg. Co.
Estate Cartridge, Inc.
Federal Champion Target Co.
Freeman Animal Targets
G.H. Enterprises Ltd.
Gun Parts Corp., The
Hiti-Schuch, Atelier Wilma
H-S Precision, Inc.
Hunterjohn
Innovision Enterprises
JWH: Software
Kennebec Journal
Kleen-Bore, Inc.
Lakefield Arms Ltd.
Littler Sales Co.
Lyman Instant Targets, Inc.
Lyman Products Corp.
M&D Munitions Ltd.
Mendez, John A.
MSR Targets
National Target Co.
N.B.B., Inc.
North American Shooting Systems
Nu-Teck
Outers Laboratories, Div. of Blount
Ox-Yoke Originals, Inc.
Passive Bullet Traps, Inc.
PlumFire Press, Inc.
Remington Arms Co., Inc.
Rockwood Corp., Speedwell Div.
Rocky Mountain Target Co.
Savage Arms (Canada), Inc.
Savage Range Systems, Inc.
Schaefer Shooting Sports
Seligman Shooting Products
Shooters Supply
Shoot-N-C Targets
Thompson Target Technology
Trius Products, Inc.
World of Targets
X-Spand Target Systems
Z's Metal Targets & Frames
Zriny's Metal Targets

TAXIDERMY

African Import Co.
Jonas Appraisers—Taxidermy
Animals, Jack
Kulis Freeze Dry Taxidermy
Montgomery Community College
Parker, Mark D.
World Trek, Inc.

MANUFACTURER'S DIRECTORY

A

A Zone Bullets, 2039 Walter Rd., Billings, MT 59105 / 800-252-3111; FAX: 406-248-1961
A&B Industries,Inc (See Top-Line USA Inc)
A&M Waterfowl,Inc., P.O. Box 102, Ripley, TN 38063 / 901-635-4003; FAX: 901-635-2320
A&W Repair, 2930 Schneider Dr., Arnold, MO 63010 / 314-287-3725
A-Square Co.,Inc., One Industrial Park, Bedford, KY 40006-9667 / 502-255-7456; FAX: 502-255-7657
A-Tech Corp., P.O. Box 1281, Cottage Grove, OR 97424
A.A. Arms, Inc., 4811 Persimmont Ct., Monroe, NC 28110 / 704-289-5356 or 800-935-1119; FAX: 704-289-5859
A.B.S. III, 9238 St. Morritz Dr., Fern Creek, KY 40291
A.G. Russell Knives,Inc., 1705 Hwy. 71B North, Springdale, AR 72764 / 501-751-7341
A.R.M.S., Inc., 230 W. Center St., West Bridgewater, MA 02379-1620 / 508-584-7816; FAX: 508-588-8045
A.W. Peterson Gun Shop, Inc., 4255 W. Old U.S. 441, Mt. Dora, FL 32757-3299 / 352-383-4258; FAX: 352-735-1001
ABO (USA) Inc, 615 SW 2nd Avenue, Miami, FL 33130 / 305-859-2010 FAX: 305-859-2099
AC Dyna-tite Corp., 155 Kelly St., P.O. Box 0984, Elk Grove Village, IL 60007 / 847-593-5566; FAX: 847-593-1304
Acadian Ballistic Specialties, P.O. Box 787, folsom, LA 70437 / 504-796-0078 gunsmith@neasolft.com
Accu-Tek, 4510 Carter Ct, Chino, CA 91710
Accupro Gun Care, 15512-109 Ave., Surrey, BC U3R 7E8 CANADA / 604-583-7807
Accura-Site (See All's, The Jim Tembelis Co., Inc.)
Accuracy Innovations, Inc., P.O. Box 376, New Paris, PA 15554 / 814-839-4517; FAX: 814-839-2601
Accuracy Int'l. North America, Inc., PO Box 5267, Oak Ridge, TN 37831 / 423-482-0330; FAX: 423-482-0336
Accuracy International, 9115 Trooper Trail, P.O. Box 2019, Bozeman, MT 59715 / 406-587-7922; FAX: 406-585-9434
Accuracy Internationl Precision Rifles (See U.S. Importer-Gunsite Custom Shop; Gunsite Training Center)
Accuracy Unlimited, 16036 N. 49 Ave., Glendale, AZ 85306 / 602-978-9089; FAX: 602-978-9089
Accuracy Unlimited, 7479 S. DePew St., Littleton, CO 80123
Accurate Arms Co., Inc., 5891 Hwy. 230 West, McEwen, TN 37101 / 800-416-3006 FAX: 931-729-4211
Accuright, RR 2 Box 397, Sebeka, MN 56477 / 218-472-3383
Ace Custom 45's, Inc., 1880 1/2 Upper Turtle Creek Rd., Kerrville, TX 78028 / 830-257-4290; FAX: 830-257-5724
Ace Sportswear, Inc., 700 Quality Rd., Fayetteville, NC 28306 / 919-323-1223; FAX: 919-323-5392
Ackerman & Co., Box 133 US Highway Rt. 7, Pownal, VT 05261 / 802-823-9874 muskets@togsther.net
Ackerman, Bill (See Optical Services Co)
Acra-Bond Laminates, 134 Zimmerman Rd., Kalispell, MT 59901 / 406-257-9003; FAX: 406-257-9003
Action Bullets & Alloy Inc, RR 1, P.O. Box 189, Quinter, KS 67752 / 913-754-3609; FAX: 913-754-3629
Action Direct, Inc., P.O. Box 830760, Miami, FL 33283 / 305-559-4652; FAX: 305-559-4652 action-direct.com
Action Products, Inc., 22 N. Mulberry St., Hagerstown, MD 21740 / 301-797-1414; FAX: 301-733-2073
Action Target, Inc., P.O. Box 636, Provo, UT 84603 / 801-377-8033; FAX: 801-377-8096
Actions by "T" Teddy Jacobson, 16315 Redwood Forest Ct., Sugar Land, TX 77478 / 281-277-4008
AcuSport Corporation, 1 Hunter Place, Bellefontaine, OH 43311-3001 / 513-593-7010 FAX: 513-592-5625
Ad Hominem, 3130 Gun Club Lane, RR, Orillia, ON L3V 6H3 CANADA / 705-689-5303; FAX: 705-689-5303
Adair Custom Shop, Bill, 2886 Westridge, Carrollton, TX 75006
Adams & Son Engravers, John J, 87 Acorn Rd, Dennis, MA 02638 / 508-385-7971
Adams Jr., John J., 87 Acorn Rd., Dennis, MA 02638 / 508-385-7971
ADCO Sales, Inc., 4 Draper St. #A, Woburn, MA 01801 / 781-935-1799; FAX: 781-935-1011
Adkins, Luther, 1292 E. McKay Rd., Shelbyville, IN 46176-8706 / 317-392-3795
Advance Car Mover Co., Rowell Div., P.O. Box 1, 240 N. Depot St., Juneau, WI 53039 / 414-386-4464; FAX: 414-386-4416
Adventure 16, Inc., 4620 Alvarado Canyon Rd., San Diego, CA 92120 / 619-283-6314
Adventure Game Calls, R.D. 1, Leonard Rd., Spencer, NY 14883 / 607-589-4611
Adventurer's Outpost, P.O. Box 547, Cottonwood, AZ 86326-0547 / 800-762-7471; FAX: 602-634-8781
Aero Peltor, 90 Mechanic St, Southbridge, MA 01550 / 508-764-5500; FAX: 508-764-0188
African Import Co., 22 Goodwin Rd, Plymouth, MA 02360 / 508-746-8552 FAX: 508-746-0404
AFSCO Ammunition, 731 W. Third St., P.O. Box L, Owen, WI 54460 / 715-229-2516
Ahlman Guns, 9525 W. 230th St., Morristown, MN 55052 / 507-685-4243; FAX: 507-685-4280
Ahrends, Kim (See Custom Firearms, Inc), Box 203, Clarion, IA 50525 / 515-532-3449; FAX: 515-532-3926
Aimpoint c/o Springfield, Inc., 420 W. Main St, Geneseo, IL 61254 / 309-944-1702
Aimtech Mount Systems, P.O. Box 223, Thomasville, GA 31799-1638 / 912-226-4313; FAX: 912-227-0222 aimtech@surfsouth.com www.aimtech-mounts.com
Air Arms, Hailsham Industrial Park, Diplocks Way, Hailsham, E. Sussex, BN27 3JF ENGLAND / 011-0323-845853
Air Rifle Specialists, P.O. Box 138, 130 Holden Rd., Pine City, NY 14871-0138 / 607-734-7340; FAX: 607-733-3261
Air Venture Airguns, 9752 E. Flower St., Bellflower, CA 90706 / 310-867-6355
Airgun Repair Centre, 3227 Garden Meadows, Lawrenceburg, IN 47025 / 812-637-1463; FAX: 812-637-1463
Airrow, 11 Monitor Hill Rd, Newtown, CT 06470 / 203-270-6343
Aitor-Cuchilleria Del Norte S.A., Izelaieta, 17, 48260, Ermua, S SPAIN / 43-17-08-50
Ajax Custom Grips, Inc., 9130 Viscount Row, Dallas, TX 75247 / 214-630-8893; FAX: 214-630-4942
Aker International, Inc., 2248 Main St., Suite 6, Chula Vista, CA 91911 / 619-423-5182; FAX: 619-423-1363
Al Lind Custom Guns, 7821 76th Ave. SW, Tacoma, WA 98498 / 206-584-6361
Alana Cupp Custom Engraver, P.O. Box 207, Annabella, UT 84711 / 801-896-4834
Alaska Bullet Works, Inc., 9978 Crazy Horse Drive, Juneau, AK 99801 / 907-789-3834; FAX: 907-789-3433
Alco Carrying Cases, 601 W. 26th St., New York, NY 10001 / 212-675-5820; FAX: 212-691-5935
Aldis Gunsmithing & Shooting Supply, 502 S. Montezuma St., Prescott, AZ 86303 / 602-445-6723; FAX: 602-445-6763
Alessi Holsters, Inc., 2465 Niagara Falls Blvd., Amherst, NY 14228-3527 / 716-691-5615
Alex, Inc., Box 3034, Bozeman, MT 59772 / 406-282-7396; FAX: 406-282-7396
Alfano, Sam, 36180 Henry Gaines Rd., Pearl River, LA 70452 / 504-863-3364; FAX: 504-863-7715
All American Lead Shot Corp., P.O. Box 224566, Dallas, TX 75062
All Rite Products, Inc., 5752 N. Silverstone Circle, Mountain Green, UT 84050 / 801-876-3330; FAX: 801-876-2216
All's, The Jim J. Tembelis Co., Inc., 216 Loper Ct., Neenah, WI 54956 / 920-725-5251; FAX: 920-725-5251
Allard, Gary/Creek Side Metal & Woodcrafters, Fishers Hill, VA 22626 / 703-465-3903
Allen Co., Bob, 214 SW Jackson, P.O. Box 477, Des Moines, IA 50315 / 515-283-2191 or 800-685-7020; FAX: 515-283-0779
Allen Co., Inc., 525 Burbank St., Broomfield, CO 80020 / 303-469-1857 or 800-876-8600; FAX: 303-466-7437
Allen Firearm Engraving, 339 Grove Ave., Prescott, AZ 86301 / 520-778-1237
Allen Mfg., 6449 Hodgson Rd., Circle Pines, MN 55014 / 612-429-8231
Allen Sportswear, Bob (See Allen Co., Bob)
Alley Supply Co., P.O. Box 848, Gardnerville, NV 89410 / 702-782-3800
Alliant Techsystems Smokeless Powder Group, 200 Valley Rd., Suite 305, Mt. Arlington, NJ 07856 / 800-276-9337; FAX: 201-770-2528
Allred Bullet Co., 932 Evergreen Drive, Logan, UT 84321 / 435-752-6983; FAX: 435-752-6983
Alpec Team, Inc., 201 Ricken Backer Cir., Livermore, CA 94550 / 510-606-8245; FAX: 510-606-4279
Alpha 1 Drop Zone, 2121 N. Tyler, Wichita, KS 67212 / 316-729-0800
Alpha Gunsmith Division, 1629 Via Monserate, Fallbrook, CA 92028 / 619-723-9279 or 619-728-2663
Alpha LaFranck Enterprises, P.O. Box 81072, Lincoln, NE 68501 / 402-466-3193
Alpha Precision, Inc., 2765-B Preston Rd. NE, Good Hope, GA 30641 / 770-267-6163
Alpine Indoor Shooting Range, 2401 Government Way, Coeur d'Alene, ID 83814 / 208-676-8824 FAX: 208-676-8824
Altamont Co., 901 N. Church St., P.O. Box 309, Thomasboro, IL 61878 / 217-643-3125 or 800-626-5774; FAX: 217-643-7973
Alumna Sport by Dee Zee, 1572 NE 58th Ave., P.O. Box 3090, Des Moines, IA 50316 / 800-798-9899
Amadeo Rossi S.A., Rua: Amadeo Rossi, 143, Sao Leopoldo, RS 93030-220 BRAZIL / 051-592-5566
AmBr Software Group Ltd., P.O. Box 301, Reistertown, MD 21136-0301 / 800-888-1917; FAX: 410-526-7212
American Ammunition, 3545 NW 71st St., Miami, FL 33147 / 305-835-7400; FAX: 305-694-0037
American Arms Inc., 2604 NE Industrial Dr, N. Kansas City, MO 64116 / 816-474-3161; FAX: 816-474-1225
American Bullet, 1512 W Chester Pike #298, West Chester, PA 19382-7754 / 610-399-6584
American Custom Gunmakers Guild, PO Box 812, Burlington, IA 52601 / 318-752-6114; FAX: 319-752-6114 acgg@acgg.org acgg.org
American Derringer Corp., 127 N. Lacy Dr., Waco, TX 76705 / 800-642-7817 or 817-799-9111; FAX: 817-799-7935
American Display Co., 55 Cromwell St., Providence, RI 02907 / 401-331-2464; FAX: 401-421-1264
American Frontier Firearms Mfg., Inc, PO Box 744, Aguanga, CA 92536 / 909-763-0014; FAX: 909-763-0014
American Gas & Chemical Co., Ltd, 220 Pegasus Ave, Northvale, NJ 07647 / 201-767-7300
American Gripcraft, 3230 S Dodge 2, Tucson, AZ 85713 / 602-790-1222
American Gunsmithing Institute, 1325 Imola Ave #504, Napa, CA 94559 / 707-253-0462; FAX: 707-253-7149
American Handgunner Magazine, 591 Camino de la Reina, Ste 200, San Diego, CA 92108 / 619-297-5350; FAX: 619-297-5353
American Pioneer Video, PO Box 50049, Bowling Green, KY 42102-2649 / 800-743-4675
American Products, Inc., 14729 Spring Valley Road, Morrison, IL 61270 / 815-772-3336; FAX: 815-772-8046
American Safe Arms, Inc., 1240 Riverview Dr., Garland, UT 84312 / 801-257-7472; FAX: 801-785-8156
American Sales & Kirkpatrick Mfg. Co., P.O. Box 677, Laredo, TX 78042 / 210-723-6893; FAX: 210-725-0672
American Sales & Mfg. Co., PO Box 677, Laredo, TX 78042 / 956-723-6893; FAX: 956-725-0672 holsters@kirkpatrickleather.com http://kirkpatrickleather.com
American Security Products Co., 11925 Pacific Ave., Fontana, CA 92337 / 909-685-9680 or 800-421-6142; FAX: 909-685-9685
American Small Arms Academy, P.O. Box 12111, Prescott, AZ 86304 / 602-778-5623
American Target, 1328 S. Jason St., Denver, CO 80223 / 303-733-0433; FAX: 303-777-0311
American Target Knives, 1030 Brownwood NW, Grand Rapids, MI 49504 / 616-453-1998
American Western Arms, Inc., 1450 S.W. 10th St., Suite 3B, Delray Beach, FL 33444 / 877-292-4867; FAX: 561-330-0881
American Whitetail Target Systems, P.O. Box 41, 106 S. Church St., Tennyson, IN 47637 / 812-567-4527
Americase, P.O. Box 271, 1610 E. Main, Waxahachie, TX 75165 / 800-880-3629; FAX: 214-937-8373
Ames Metal Products, 4323 S. Western Blvd., Chicago, IL 60609 / 773-523-3230; or 800-255-6937 FAX: 773-523-3854
Amherst Arms, P.O. Box 1457, Englewood, FL 34295 / 941-475-2020; FAX: 941-473-1212
Ammo Load, Inc., 1560 E. Edinger, Suite G, Santa Ana, CA 92705 / 714-558-8858; FAX: 714-569-0319
Amrine's Gun Shop, 937 La Luna, Ojai, CA 93023 / 805-646-2376
Amsec, 11925 Pacific Ave., Fontana, CA 92337
Amtec 2000, Inc., 84 Industrial Rowe, Gardner, MA 01440 / 508-632-9608; FAX: 508-632-2300
Analog Devices, Box 9106, Norwood, MA 02062
Andela Tool & Machine, Inc., RD3, Box 246, Richfield Springs, NY 13439
Anderson Manufacturing Co., Inc., 22602 53rd Ave. SE, Bothell, WA 98021 / 206-481-1858; FAX: 206-481-7839
Andres & Dworsky, Bergstrasse 18, A-3822 Karlstein, Thaya, AUSTRIA / 0 28 44-285
Angel Arms, Inc., 1825 Addison Way, Haywood, CA 94545 / 510-783-7122
Angelo & Little Custom Gun Stock Blanks, P.O. Box 240046, Dell, MT 59724-0046
Anics Firm Inc3 Commerce Park Square, 23200 Chagrin Blvd., Suite 240, Beechwood, OH 44122 / 800-556-1582; FAX: 216-292-2588
Anschutz GmbH, Postfach 1128, D-89001 Ulm, Donau, GERMANY / 731-40120
Answer Products Co., 1519 Westbury Drive, Davison, MI 48423 / 810-653-2911
Anthony and George Ltd., Rt. 1, P.O. Box 45, Evington, VA 24550 / 804-821-8117

MANUFACTURER'S DIRECTORY

Antique American Firearms, P.O. Box 71035, Dept. GD, Des Moines, IA 50325 / 515-224-6552
Antique Arms Co., 1110 Cleveland Ave., Monett, MO 65708 / 417-235-6501
Apel GmbH, Ernst, Am Kirschberg 3, D-97218, Gerbrunn, GERMANY / 0 (931) 707192
Aplan Antiques & Art, James O., James O., HC 80, Box 793-25, Piedmont, SD 57769 / 605-347-5016
AR-7 Industries, LLC, 998 N. Colony Rd., Meriden, CT 06450 / 203-630-3536; FAX: 203-630-3637
Arco Powder, HC-Rt. 1 P.O. Box 102, County Rd. 357, Mayo, FL 32066 / 904-294-3882; FAX: 904-294-1498
Arizona Ammunition, Inc., 21421 No. 14th Ave., Suite E, Phoenix, AZ 85027 / 623-516-9004; FAX: 623-516-9012 azammo.com
Arkansas Mallard Duck Calls, Rt. Box 182, England, AR 72046 / 501-842-3597
ArmaLite, Inc., P.O. Box 299, Geneseo, IL 61254 / 309-944-6939; FAX: 309-944-6949
Armament Gunsmithing Co., Inc., 525 Rt. 22, Hillside, NJ 07205 / 908-686-0960 FAX: 718-738-5019
Armas Kemen S. A. (See U.S. Importers)
Armas Urki Garbi, 12-14 20.600, Eibar (Guipuzcoa), / 43-11 38 73
Armfield Custom Bullets, 4775 Caroline Drive, San Diego, CA 92115 / 619-582-7188; FAX: 619-287-3238
Armi Perazzi S.p.A., Via Fontanelle 1/3, 1-25080, Botticino Mattina, / 030-2692591; FAX: 030 2692594+
Armi San Marco (See U.S. Importers-Taylor's & Co I
Armi San Paolo, 172-A, I-25062, via Europa, ITALY / 030-2751725
Armi Sport (See U.S. Importers-Cape Outfitters)
Armite Laboratories, 1845 Randolph St., Los Angeles, CA 90001 / 213-587-7768; FAX: 213-587-5075
Armoloy Co. of Ft. Worth, 204 E. Daggett St., Fort Worth, TX 76104 / 817-332-5604; FAX: 817-335-6517
Armor (See Buck Stop Lure Co., Inc.)
Armor Metal Products, P.O. Box 4609, Helena, MT 59604 / 406-442-5560; FAX: 406-442-5650
Armory Publications, 17171 Bothall Way NE, #276, Seattle, WA 98155 / 208-664-5061; FAX: 208-664-9906 armorypub@aol.com www.grocities.com/armorypub
Arms & Armour Press, Wellington House, 125 Strand, London, WC2R 0BB ENGLAND / 0171-420-5555; FAX: 0171-240-7265
Arms Corporation of the Philippines, Bo. Parang Marikina, Metro Manila, PHILIPPINES / 632-941-6243 or 632-941-6244; FAX: 632-942-0682
Arms Craft Gunsmithing, 1106 Linda Dr., Arroyo Grande, CA 93420 / 805-481-2830
Arms Ingenuity Co., P.O. Box 1, 51 Canal St., Weatogue, CT 06089 / 203-658-5624
Arms Software, P.O. Box 1526, Lake Oswego, OR 97035 / 800-366-5559 or 503-697-0533; FAX: 503-697-3337
Arms, Programming Solutions (See Arms Software)
Armscorp USA, Inc., 4424 John Ave., Baltimore, MD 21227 / 410-247-6200; FAX: 410-247-6205 armscorp_md@yahoo.com
Armsport, Inc., 3950 NW 49th St., Miami, FL 33142 / 305-635-7850; FAX: 305-633-2877
Arnold Arms Co., Inc., P.O. Box 1011, Arlington, WA 98223 / 800-371-1011 or 360-435-1011; FAX: 360-435-7304
Aro-Tek Ltd., 206 Frontage Rd. North, Suite C, Pacific, WA 98047 / 206-351-2984; FAX: 206-833-4483
Arratoonian, Andy (See Horseshoe Leather Products)
Arrieta S.L., Morkaiko 5, 20870, Elgoibar, SPAIN / 34-43-743150; FAX: 34-43-743154+
Art Jewel Enterprises Ltd., Eagle Business Ctr., 460 Randy Rd., Carol Stream, IL 60188 / 708-260-0400
Art's Gun & Sport Shop, Inc., 6008 Hwy. Y, Hillsboro, MO 63050
Artistry in Wood, 134 Zimmerman Rd., Kalispell, MT 59901 / 406-257-9003
Arundel Arms & Ammunition, Inc., A., 24A Defense St., Annapolis, MD 21401 / 410-224-8683
Arvo Ojala Holsters, P.O. Box 98, N. Hollywood, CA 91603 / 818-222-9700; FAX: 818-222-0401
Ashby Turkey Calls, P.O. Box 1466, Ava, MO 65608-1466 / 417-967-3787
Ashley Outdoors, Inc, 2401 Ludelle St, Fort Worth, TX 76105 / 888-744-4880; FAX: 800-734-7939
Aspen Outfitting Co, Jon Hollinger, 9 Dean St, Aspen, CO 81611 / 970-925-3406
Astra Sport, S.A., Apartado 3, 48300 Guernica, Espagne, SPAIN / 34-4-6250100; FAX: 34-4-6255186+
Atamec-Bretton, 19 rue Victor Grignard, F-42026, St.-Etienne (Cedex 1, / 77-93-54-69; FAX: 33-77-93-57-98+
Atlanta Cutlery Corp., 2143 Gees Mill Rd., Box 839 CIS, Conyers, GA 30207 / 800-883-0300; FAX: 404-388-0246
Atlantic Mills, Inc., 1295 Towbin Ave., Lakewood, NJ 08701-5934 / 800-242-7374
Atlantic Rose, Inc., P.O. Box 10717, Bradenton, FL 34282-0717
Atsko/Sno-Seal, Inc., 2664 Russell St., Orangeburg, SC 29115 / 803-531-1820; FAX: 803-531-2139
Auguste Francotte & Cie S.A., rue du Trois Juin 109, 4400 Herstal-Liege, BELGIUM / 32-4-248-13-18; FAX: 32-4-948-11-79
Austin & Halleck, 1099 Welt, Weston, MO 64098 / 816-386-2176; FAX: 816-386-2177
Austin Sheridan USA, Inc., P.O. Box 577, 36 Haddam Quarter Rd., Durham, CT 06422 / 860-349-1772; FAX: 860-349-1771 swalzer@palm.net
Autauga Arms, Inc., Pratt Plaza Mall No. 13, Prattville, AL 36067 / 800-262-9563; FAX: 334-361-2961
Auto Arms, 738 Clearview, San Antonio, TX 78228 / 512-434-5450
Auto-Ordnance Corp., PO Box 220, Blauvelt, NY 10913 / 914-353-7770
Automatic Equipment Sales, 627 E. Railroad Ave., Salesburg, MD 21801
Autumn Sales, Inc. (Blaser), 1320 Lake St., Fort Worth, TX 76102 / 817-335-1634; FAX: 817-338-0119
Avnda Otaola Norica, 16 Apartado 68, 20600, Eibar,
AWC Systems Technology, P.O. Box 41938, Phoenix, AZ 85080-1938 / 602-780-1050 FAX: 602-780-2967
AYA (See U.S. Importer-New England Custom Gun Service)

B

B & P America, 12321 Brittany Cir, Dallas, TX 75230 / 972-726-9069
B&D Trading Co., Inc., 3935 Fair Hill Rd., Fair Oaks, CA 95628 / 800-334-3790 or 916-967-9366; FAX: 916-967-4873
B-Square Company, Inc., ;, P.O. Box 11281, 2708 St. Louis Ave., Ft. Worth, TX 76110 / 817-923-0964 or 800-433-2909 FAX: 817-926-7012
B-West Imports, Inc., 2425 N. Huachuca Dr., Tucson, AZ 85745-1201 / 602-628-1990; FAX: 602-628-3602
B.B. Walker Co., PO Box 1167, 414 E Dixie Dr, Asheboro, NC 27203 / 910-625-1380; FAX: 910-625-8125
B.C. Outdoors, Larry McGhee, PO Box 61497, Boulder City, NV 89006 / 702-294-0025
B.M.F. Activator, Inc., 12145 Mill Creek Run, Plantersville, TX 77363 / 936-894-2397 or 800-527-2881 FAX: 936-894-2397
Badger Shooters Supply, Inc., P.O. Box 397, Owen, WI 54460 / 800-424-9069; FAX: 715-229-2332
Baekgaard Ltd., 1855 Janke Dr., Northbrook, IL 60062 / 708-498-3040; FAX: 708-493-3106
Baelder, Harry, Alte Goennebeker Strasse 5, 24635, Rickling, GERMANY / 04328-722732; FAX: 04328-722733
Baer Custom, Inc, Les, 29601 34th Ave, Hillsdale, IL 61257 / 309-658-2716; FAX: 309-658-2610
Baer's Hollows, P.O. Box 284, Eads, CO 81036 / 719-438-5718
Bagmaster Mfg., Inc., 2731 Sutton Ave., St. Louis, MO 63143 / 314-781-8002; FAX: 314-781-3363
Bain & Davis, Inc., 307 E. Valley Blvd., San Gabriel, CA 91776-3522 / 818-573-4241 or 213-283-7449 caindavis@aol.com
Baker, Stan, 10000 Lake City Way, Seattle, WA 98125 / 206-522-4575
Baker's Leather Goods, Roy, PO Box 893, Magnolia, AR 71753 / 501-234-0344
Balance Co., 340-39 Ave., S.E., Box 505, Calgary, AB T2G 1X6 CANADA
Bald Eagle Precision Machine Co., 101-A Allison St., Lock Haven, PA 17745 / 570-748-6772; FAX: 570-748-4443
Balickie, Joe, 408 Trelawney Lane, Apex, NC 27502 / 919-362-5185
Ballard Industries, 10271 Lockwood Dr., Suite B, Cupertino, CA 95014 / 408-996-0957; FAX: 408-257-6828
Ballard Rifle & Cartridge Co., LLC, 113 W Yellowstone Ave, Cody, WY 82414 / 307-587-4914; FAX: 307-527-6097
Ballisti-Cast, Inc., 6347 49th St. NW, Plaza, ND 58771 / 701-497-3333; FAX: 701-497-3335
Ballistic Engineering & Software, Inc., 185 N. Park Blvd., Suite 330, Lake Orion, MI 48362 / 313-391-1074
Ballistic Product, Inc., 20015 75th Ave. North, Corcoran, MN 55340-9456 / 612-494-9237; FAX: 612-494-9236 info@ballisticproducts.com www.ballisticproducts.com
Ballistic Research, 1108 W. May Ave., McHenry, IL 60050 / 815-385-0037
Bandcor Industries, Div. of Man-Sew Corp., 6108 Sherwin Dr., Port Richey, FL 34668 / 813-848-0432
Bang-Bang Boutique (See Holster Shop, The)
Banks, Ed, 2762 Hwy. 41 N., Ft. Valley, GA 31030 / 912-987-4665
Bansner's Gunsmithing Specialties, 261 East Main St. Box VH, Adamstown, PA 19501 / 800-368-2379; FAX: 717-484-0523
Bar-Sto Precision Machine, 73377 Sullivan Rd., P.O. Box 1838, Twentynine Palms, CA 92277 / 760-367-2747; FAX: 760-367-2407
Barbour, Inc., 55 Meadowbrook Dr., Milford, NH 03055 / 603-673-1313; FAX: 603-673-6510
Barnes, 110 Borner St S, Prescott, WI 54021-1149 / 608-897-8416
Barnes Bullets, Inc., P.O. Box 215, American Fork, UT 84003 / 801-756-4222 or 800-574-9200; FAX: 801-756-2465 email@barnesbullets.com barnesbullets.com
Baron Technology, 62 Spring Hill Rd., Trumbull, CT 06611 / 203-452-0515; FAX: 203-452-0663
Barraclough, John K., 55 Merit Park Dr., Gardena, CA 90247 / 310-324-2574
Barramundi Corp., P.O. Drawer 4259, Homosassa Springs, FL 32687 / 904-628-0200
Barrett Firearms Manufacturer, Inc., P.O. Box 1077, Murfreesboro, TN 37133 / 615-896-2938; FAX: 615-896-7313
Barry Lee Hands Engraving, 26192 E. Shore Route, Bigfork, MT 59911 / 406-837-0035
Barta's Gunsmithing, 10231 US Hwy. 10, Cato, WI 54206 / 920-732-4472
Barteaux Machete, 1916 SE 50th Ave., Portland, OR 97215-3238 / 503-233-5880
Bartlett Engineering, 40 South 200 East, Smithfield, UT 84335-1645 / 801-563-5910
Basics Information Systems, Inc., 1141 Georgia Ave., Suite 515, Wheaton, MD 20902 / 301-949-1070; FAX: 301-949-5326
Bates Engraving, Billy, 2302 Winthrop Dr, Decatur, AL 35603 / 256-355-3690
Bauer, Eddie, 15010 NE 36th St., Redmond, WA 98052
Baumgartner Bullets, 3011 S. Alane St., W. Valley City, UT 84120
Bauska Barrels, 105 9th Ave. W., Kalispell, MT 59901 / 406-752-7706
Bear Archery, RR 4, 4600 Southwest 41st Blvd., Gainesville, FL 32601 / 904-376-2327
Bear Arms, 121 Rhodes St., Jackson, SC 29831 / 803-471-9859
Bear Hug Grip, Inc., P.O. Box 16649, Colorado Springs, CO 80935-6649 / 800-232-7710
Bear Mountain Gun & Tool, 120 N. Plymouth, New Plymouth, ID 83655 / 208-278-5221; FAX: 208-278-5221
Beartooth Bullets, P.O. Box 491, Dept. HLD, Dover, ID 83825-0491 / 208-448-1865 beartooth@trasport.com
Beaver Lodge (See Fellowes, Ted)
Beaver Park Product, Inc., 840 J St., Penrose, CO 81240 / 719-372-6744
BEC, Inc., 1227 W. Valley Blvd., Suite 204, Alhambra, CA 91803 / 626-281-5751; FAX: 626-293-7073
Beeline Custom Bullets Limited, P.O. Box 85, Yarmouth, NS B5A 4B1 CANADA / 902-648-3494; FAX: 902-648-0253
Beeman Precision Airguns, 5454 Argosy Dr., Huntington Beach, CA 92649 / 714-890-4800; FAX: 714-890-4808
Behlert Precision, Inc., P.O. Box 288, 7067 Easton Rd., Pipersville, PA 18947 / 215-766-8681 or 215-766-7301; FAX: 215-766-8681
Beitzinger, George, 116-20 Atlantic Ave, Richmond Hill, NY 11419 / 718-847-7661
Belding's Custom Gun Shop, 10691 Sayers Rd., Munith, MI 49259 / 517-596-2388
Bell & Carlson, Inc., Dodge City Industrial Park, 101 Allen Rd., Dodge City, KS 67801 / 800-634-8586 or 316-225-6688; FAX: 316-225-9095
Bell Reloading, Inc., 1725 Harlin Lane Rd., Villa Rica, GA 30180
Bell's Gun & Sport Shop, 3309-19 Mannheim Rd, Franklin Park, IL 60131
Bell's Legendary Country Wear, 22 Circle Dr., Bellmore, NY 11710 / 516-679-1158
Bellm Contenders, P.O. Box 459, Cleveland, UT 84518 / 801-653-2530
Belltown Ltd., 11 Camps Rd., Kent, CT 06757 / 860-354-5750 FAX: 860-354-6764
Ben William's Gun Shop, 1151 S. Cedar Ridge, Duncanville, TX 75137 / 214-780-1807
Ben's Machines, 1151 S. Cedar Ridge, Duncanville, TX 75137 / 214-780-1807 FAX: 214-780-0316
Benchmark Guns, 12593 S. Ave. 5 East, Yuma, AZ 85365
Benchmark Knives (See Gerber Legendary Blades)
Benelli Armi S.p.A., Via della Stazione, 61029, Urbino, ITALY / 39-722-307-1; FAX: 39-722-327427+
Benelli USA Corp, 17603 Indian Head Hwy, Accokeek, MD 20607 / 301-283-6981; FAX: 301-283-6988 benelliusa.com

REFERENCE

MANUFACTURER'S DIRECTORY

Bengtson Arms Co., L., 6345-B E. Akron St., Mesa, AZ 85205 / 602-981-6375
Benjamin/Sheridan Co., Crossman, Rts. 5 and 20, E. Bloomfield, NY 14443 / 716-657-6161; FAX: 716-657-5405
Bentley, John, 128-D Watson Dr., Turtle Creek, PA 15145
Beomat of America, Inc., 300 Railway Ave., Campbell, CA 95008 / 408-379-4829
Beretta S.p.A., Pietro, Via Beretta, 18-25063, Gardone V.T., ITALY / 39-30-8341-1 FAX: 39-30-8341-421
Beretta U.S.A. Corp., 17601 Beretta Drive, Accokeek, MD 20607 / 301-283-2191; FAX: 301-283-0435
Berger Bullets Ltd., 5342 W. Camelback Rd., Suite 200, Glendale, AZ 85301 / 602-842-4001; FAX: 602-934-9083
Bernardelli S.p.A., Vincenzo, 125 Via Matteotti, PO Box 74, Brescia, ITALY / 39-30-8912851-2-3; FAX: 39-30-8910249
Berry's Mfg., Inc., 401 North 3050 East St., St. George, UT 84770 / 435-634-1682; FAX: 435-634-1683 sales@berrysmfg.com www.berrysmfg.com
Bersa S.A., Gonzales Castillo 312, 1704, Ramos Mejia, ARGENTINA / 541-656-2377; FAX: 541-656-2093+
Bert Johanssons Vapentillbehor, S-430 20 Veddige, SWEDEN,
Bertuzzi (See U.S. Importer-New England Arms Co)
Better Concepts Co., 663 New Castle Rd., Butler, PA 16001 / 412-285-9000
Beverly, Mary, 3201 Horseshoe Trail, Tallahassee, FL 32312
Bianchi International, Inc., 100 Calle Cortez, Temecula, CA 92590 / 909-676-5621; FAX: 909-676-6777
Biesen, Al, 5021 Rosewood, Spokane, WA 99208 / 509-328-9340
Biesen, Roger, 5021 W. Rosewood, Spokane, WA 99208 / 509-328-9340
Big Bear Arms & Sporting Goods, Inc., 1112 Milam Way, Carrollton, TX 75006 / 972-416-8051 or 800-400-BEAR; FAX: 972-416-0771
Big Bore Bullets of Alaska, P.O. Box 872785, Wasilla, AK 99687 / 907-373-2673; FAX: 907-373-2673 doug@mt-aonline.net ww.awloo.com/bbb/index.
Big Bore Express, 7154 W. State St., Boise, ID 83703 / 800-376-4010; FAX: 208-376-4020
Big Sky Racks, Inc., P.O. Box 729, Bozeman, MT 59771-0729 / 406-586-9393; FAX: 406-585-7378
Big Spring Enterprises "Bore Stores", P.O. Box 1115, Big Spring Rd., Yellville, AR 72687 / 870-449-5297; FAX: 870-449-4446
Bilal, Mustafa, 908 NW 50th St., Seattle, WA 98107-3634 / 206-782-4164
Bilinski, Bryan. See: FIELDSPORT LTD
Bill Austin's Calls, Box 284, Kaycee, WY 82639 / 307-738-2552
Bill Adair Custom Shop, 2886 Westridge, Carrollton, TX 75006 / 972-418-0950
Bill Hanus Birdguns LLC, P.O. Box 533, Newport, OR 97365 / 541-265-7433; FAX: 541-265-7400
Bill Johns Master Engraver, 7927 Ranch Roach 965, Fredericksburg, TX 78624-9545 / 830-997-6795
Bill Wiseman and Co., P.O. Box 3427, Bryan, TX 77805 / 409-690-3456; FAX: 409-690-0156
Bill's Custom Cases, P.O. Box 2, Dunsmuir, CA 96025 / 530-235-0177; FAX: 530-235-4959
Bill's Gun Repair, 1007 Burlington St., Mendota, IL 61342 / 815-539-5786
Billeb, Stephen L., 1101 N. 7th St., Burlington, IA 52601 / 319-753-2110
Billings Gunsmiths Inc., 1841 Grand Ave., Billings, MT 59102 / 406-256-8390
Billingsley & Brownell, P.O. Box 25, Dayton, WY 82836 / 307-655-9344
Billy Bates Engraving, 2302 Winthrop Dr., Decatur, AL 35603 / 205-355-3690
Birchwood Casey, 7900 Fuller Rd., Eden Prairie, MN 55344 / 800-328-6156 or 612-937-7933; FAX: 612-937-7979
Birdsong & Assoc, W. E., 1435 Monterey Rd, Florence, MS 39073-9748 / 601-366-8270
Bismuth Cartridge Co., 3500 Maple Ave., Suite 1650, Dallas, TX 75219 / 214-521-5880; FAX: 214-521-9035
Bison Studios, 1409 South Commerce St., Las Vegas, NV 89102 / 702-388-2891; FAX: 702-383-9967
Bitterroot Bullet Co., PO Box 412, Lewiston, ID 83501-0412 / 208-743-5635 FAX: 208-743-5635
BKL Technologies, PO Box 5237, Brownsville, TX 78523
Black Belt Bullets (See Big Bore Express)
Black Hills Ammunition, Inc., P.O. Box 3090, Rapid City, SD 57709-3090 / 605-348-5150; FAX: 605-348-9827
Black Hills Shooters Supply, P.O. Box 4220, Rapid City, SD 57709 / 800-289-2506
Black Powder Products, 67 Township Rd. 1411, Chesapeake, OH 45619 / 614-867-8047
Black Sheep Brand, 3220 W. Gentry Parkway, Tyler, TX 75702 / 903-592-3853; FAX: 903-592-0527
Blackhawk East, Box 2274, Loves Park, IL 61131
Blacksmith Corp., PO Box 280, North Hampton, OH 45349 / 800-531-2665; FAX: 937-969-8399 bcbooks@glass-city.net
BlackStar AccuMax Barrels, 11501 Brittmoore Park Drive, Houston, TX 77041 / 281-721-6040; FAX: 281-721-6041
BlackStar Barrel Accurizing (See BlackStar AccuMax Barrels)
Blacktail Mountain Books, 42 First Ave. W., Kalispell, MT 59901 / 406-257-5573
Blair Engraving, J. R., PO Box 64, Glenrock, WY 82637 / 307-436-8115
Blammo Ammo, P.O. Box 1677, Seneca, SC 29679 / 803-882-1768
Blaser Jagdwaffen GmbH, D-88316, Isny Im Allgau, GERMANY
Bleile, C. Roger, 5040 Ralph Ave., Cincinnati, OH 45238 / 513-251-0249
Blount, Inc., Sporting Equipment Div., 2299 Snake River Ave., P.O. Box 856, Lewiston, ID 83501 / 800-627-3640 or 208-746-2351; FAX: 208-799-3904
Blue and Gray Products Inc (See Ox-Yoke Originals, Inc.,)
Blue Book Publications, Inc., One Appletree Square, 8009 34th Ave. S. Suite 175, Minneapolis, MN 55425 / 800-877-4867 or 612-854-5229; FAX: 612-853-1486
Blue Mountain Bullets, HCR 77, P.O. Box 231, John Day, OR 97845 / 541-820-4594
Blue Ridge Machinery & Tools, Inc., P.O. Box 536-GD, Hurricane, WV 25526 / 800-872-6500; FAX: 304-562-5311
BMC Supply, Inc., 26051 - 179th Ave. S.E., Kent, WA 98042
Bo-Mar Tool & Mfg. Co., Rt. 8, Box 405, Longview, TX 75604 / 903-759-4784; FAX: 903-759-9141
Bob Allen Co.214 SW Jackson, P.O. Box 477, Des Moines, IA 50315 / 800-685-7020 FAX: 515-283-0779
Bob Rogers Gunsmithing, P.O. Box 305, 344 S. Walnut St., Franklin Grove, IL 61031 / 815-456-2685; FAX: 815-288-7142
Bob Schrimsher's Custom Knifemaker's Supply, P.O. Box 308, Emory, TX 75440 / 903-473-3330; FAX: 903-473-2235
Bob's Gun Shop, P.O. Box 200, Royal, AR 71968 / 501-767-1970; FAX: 501-767-1970
Bob's Tactical Indoor Shooting Range & Gun Shop, 90 Lafayette Rd., Salisbury, MA 01952 / 508-465-5561
Boessler, Erich, Am Vogeltal 3, 97702, Munnerstadt, GERMANY
Bohemia Arms Co., 17101 Los Modelos St., Fountain Valley, CA 92708 / 619-442-7005; FAX: 619-442-7005
Boker USA, Inc., 1550 Balsam Street, Lakewood, CO 80215 / 303-462-0662; FAX: 303-462-0668 bokerusa@worldnet.att.net bokerusa.com
Boltin, John M., P.O. Box 644, Estill, SC 29918 / 803-625-2185
Bonanza (See Forster Products), 310 E Lanark Ave, Lanark, IL 61046 / 815-493-6360; FAX: 815-493-2371
Bond Arms, Inc., P.O. Box 1296, Granbury, TX 76048 / 817-573-4445; FAX: 817-573-5636
Bond Custom Firearms, 8954 N. Lewis Ln., Bloomington, IN 47408 / 812-332-4519
Bondini Paolo, Via Sorrento 345, San Carlo di Cesena, ITALY / 0547-663-240; FAX: 0547-663-780
Bone Engraving, Ralph, 718 N Atlanta, Owasso, OK 74055 / 918-272-9745
Boone Trading Co., Inc., P.O. Box BB, Brinnan, WA 98320
Boone's Custom Ivory Grips, Inc., 562 Coyote Rd., Brinnon, WA 98320 / 206-796-4330
Boonie Packer Products, P.O. Box 12204, Salem, OR 97309 / 800-477-3244 or 503-581-3244; FAX: 503-581-3191
Borden Ridges Rimrock Stocks, RR 1 Box 250 BC, Springville, PA 18844 / 570-965-2505 FAX: 570-965-2328
Borden Rifles Inc, RD 1, Box 250BC, Springville, PA 18844 / 717-965-2505; FAX: 717-965-2328
Border Barrels Ltd., Riccarton Farm, Newcastleton, SCOTLAND UK
Borovnik KG, Ludwig, 9170 Ferlach, Bahnhofstrasse 7, AUSTRIA / 042 27 24 42; FAX: 042 26 43 49
Bosis (See U.S. Importer-New England Arms Co.)
Boss Manufacturing Co., 221 W. First St., Kewanee, IL 61443 / 309-852-2131 or 800-447-4581; FAX: 309-852-0848
Bostick Wildlife Calls, Inc., P.O. Box 728, Estill, SC 29918 / 803-625-2210 or 803-625-4512
Bowen Classic Arms Corp., P.O. Box 67, Louisville, TN 37777 / 865-984-3583 bowsarms.com
Bowen Knife Co., Inc., P.O. Box 590, Blackshear, GA 31516 / 912-449-4794
Bowerly, Kent, 710 Golden Pheasant Dr, Redmond, OR 97756 / 541-595-6028
Boyds' Gunstock Industries, Inc., 25376 403RD AVE, MITCHELL, SD 57301 / 605-996-5011; FAX: 605-996-9878
Brace, Larry D., 771 Blackfoot Ave., Eugene, OR 97404 / 541-688-1278; FAX: 541-607-5833
Bradley Gunsight Co., P.O. Box 340, Plymouth, VT 05056 / 860-589-0531; FAX: 860-582-6294
Brass Eagle, Inc., 7050A Bramalea Rd., Unit 19, Mississauga,, ON L4Z 1C7 CANADA / 416-848-4844
Bratcher, Dan, 311 Belle Air Pl., Carthage, MO 64836 / 417-358-1518
Brauer Bros. Mfg. Co., 2020 Delman Blvd., St. Louis, MO 63103 / 314-231-2864; FAX: 314-249-4952
Break-Free, Inc., P.O. Box 25020, Santa Ana, CA 92799 / 714-953-1900; FAX: 714-953-0402
Brenneke KG, Wilhelm, Ilmenauweg 2, 30851 Langenhagen, GERMANY / 0511-97262-0; FAX: 0511-97262-62
Brian Perazone-Gunsmith, Cold Spring Rd., Roxbury, NY 12474 / 607-326-4088; FAX: 607-326-3140
Bridgeman Products, Harry Jaffin, 153 B Cross Slope Court, Englishtown, NJ 07726 / 732-536-3604; FAX: 732-972-1004
Bridgers Best, P.O. Box 1410, Berthoud, CO 80513
Briese Bullet Co., Inc., RR1, Box 108, Tappen, ND 58487 / 701-327-4578; FAX: 701-327-4579
Brigade Quartermasters, 1025 Cobb International Blvd., Dept. VH, Kennesaw, GA 30144-4300 / 404-428-1248 or 800-241-3125; FAX: 404-426-7726
Briganti, A.J., 512 Rt. 32, Highland Mills, NY 10930 / 914-928-9573
Briley Mfg. Inc., 1230 Lumpkin, Houston, TX 77043 / 800-331-5718 or 713-932-6995; FAX: 713-932-1043
British Antiques, P.O. Box 35369, Tucson, AZ 85740 / 520-575-9063 britishantiques@hotmail.com
British Sporting Arms, RR1, Box 130, Millbrook, NY 12545 / 914-677-8303
BRNO (See U.S. Importers-Bohemia Arms Co.)
Broad Creek Rifle Works, Ltd., 120 Horsey Ave., Laurel, DE 19956 / 302-875-5446; FAX: 302-875-1449 bcqw4guns@aol.com
Brockman's Custom Gunsmithing, P.O. Box 357, Gooding, ID 83330 / 208-934-5050
Brocock Ltd., 43 River Street, Digbeth, Birmingham, B5 5SA ENGLAND / 011-021-773-1200
Broken Gun Ranch, 10739 126 Rd., Spearville, KS 67876 / 316-385-2587; FAX: 316-385-2597
Brolin Arms, 2755 Thompson Creek Rd., Pomona, CA 91767 / 909-392-7822; FAX: 909-392-7824
Brooker, Dennis, Rt. 1, Box 12A, Derby, IA 50068 / 515-533-2103
Brooks Tactical Systems, 279-C Shorewood Ct., Fox Island, WA 98333 / 253-549-2866 FAX: 253-549-2703 brooks@brookstactical.com www.brookstactical.com
Brown, H. R. (See Silhouette Leathers)
Brown Co, E. Arthur, 3404 Pawnee Dr, Alexandria, MN 56308 / 320-762-8847
Brown Dog Ent., 2200 Calle Camelia, 1000 Oaks, CA 91360 / 805-497-2318; FAX: 805-497-1618
Brown Manufacturing, P.O. Box 9219, Akron, OH 44305 / 800-837-GUNS
Brown Precision,Inc., 7786 Molinos Ave., Los Molinos, CA 96055 FAX: 916-384-1638
Brown Products, Inc., Ed, 43825 Muldrow Trail, Perry, MO 63462 / 573-565-3261; FAX: 573-565-2791
Brownells, Inc., 200 S. Front St., Montezuma, IA 50171 / 515-623-5401; FAX: 515-623-3896
Browning Arms Co., One Browning Place, Morgan, UT 84050 / 801-876-2711; FAX: 801-876-3331
Browning Arms Co. (Parts & Service), 3005 Arnold Tenbrook Rd., Arnold, MO 63010 / 314-287-6800; FAX: 314-287-9751
BRP, Inc. High Performance Cast Bullets, 1210 Alexander Rd., Colorado Springs, CO 80909 / 719-633-0658
Brunton U.S.A., 620 E. Monroe Ave., Riverton, WY 82501 / 307-856-6559; FAX: 307-856-1840
Bryan & Assoc, R D Sauls, PO Box 5772, Anderson, SC 29623-5772 / 864-261-6810
Brynin, Milton, P.O. Box 383, Yonkers, NY 10710 / 914-779-4333
BSA Guns Ltd., Armoury Rd. Small Heath, Birmingham, ENGLAND / 011-021-772-8543; FAX: 011-021-773-084
BSA Optics, 3911 SW 47th Ave #914, Ft Lauderdale, FL 33314 / 954-581-2144 FAX: 954-581-3165
Bucheimer, J. (See JUMBO SPORTS PRODUCTS)
Bucheimer, J. M. (See Jumbo Sports Products), 721 N 20th St, St Louis, MO 63103 / 314-241-1020
Buck Knives, Inc., 1900 Weld Blvd., P.O. Box 1267, El Cajon, CA 92020 / 619-449-1100 or 800-326-2825; FAX: 619-562-5774 8

MANUFACTURER'S DIRECTORY

Buck Stix--SOS Products Co., Box 3, Neenah, WI 54956
Buck Stop Lure Co., Inc., 3600 Grow Rd. NW, P.O. Box 636, Stanton, MI 48888 / 517-762-5091; FAX: 517-762-5124
Buckeye Custom Bullets, 6490 Stewart Rd., Elida, OH 45807 / 419-641-4463
Buckhorn Gun Works, 8109 Woodland Dr., Black Hawk, SD 57718 / 605-787-6472
Buckskin Bullet Co., P.O. Box 1893, Cedar City, UT 84721 / 435-586-3286
Buckskin Machine Works, A. Hunkeler, 3235 S. 358th St., Auburn, WA 98001 / 206-927-5412
Budin, Dave, Main St., Margaretville, NY 12455 / 914-568-4103; FAX: 914-586-4105
Buenger Enterprises/Goldenrod Dehumidifier, 3600 S. Harbor Blvd., Oxnard, CA 93035 / 800-451-6797 or 805-985-5828; FAX: 805-985-1534
Buffalo Arms Co., 99 Raven Ridge, Samuels, ID 83864 / 208-263-6953; FAX: 208-265-2096
Buffalo Bullet Co., Inc.., 12637 Los Nietos Rd., Unit A., Santa Fe Springs, CA 90670 FAX: 562-944-5054
Buffalo Rock Shooters Supply, R.R. 1, Ottawa, IL 61350 / 815-433-2471
Buffer Technologies, P.O. Box 104930, Jefferson City, MO 65110 / 573-634-8529; FAX: 573-634-8522
Bull Mountain Rifle Co., 6327 Golden West Terrace, Billings, MT 59106 / 406-656-0778
Bull-X, Inc., 520 N. Main, Farmer City, IL 61842 / 309-928-2574 or 800-248-3845; FAX: 309-928-2130
Bullberry Barrel Works, Ltd., 2430 W. Bullberry Ln. 67-5, Hurricane, UT 84737 / 435-635-9866; FAX: 435-635-0348
Bullet Metals, P.O. Box 1238, Sierra Vista, AZ 85636 / 520-458-5321; FAX: 520-458-1421 alloymetalsmith@theriver.com
Bullet Swaging Supply Inc., P.O. Box 1056, 303 McMillan Rd, West Monroe, LA 71291 / 318-387-3266; FAX: 318-387-7779
Bullet'n Press, 19 Key St., Eastport, ME 04631 / 207-853-4116 www.nemaine.com/bnpress
Bullet, Inc., 3745 Hiram Alworth Rd., Dallas, GA 30132
Bullseye Bullets, 8100 E Broadway Ave #A, Tampa, FL 33619-2223 / 813-630-9186 bbullets8100@aol.com
Burgess, Byron, PO Box 6853, Los Osos, CA 93412 / 805-528-1005
Burkhart Gunsmithing, Don, P.O. Box 852, Rawlins, WY 82301 / 307-324-6007
Burnham Bros., P.O. Box 1148, Menard, TX 78659 / 915-396-4572; FAX: 915-396-4574
Burris Co., Inc., P.O. Box 1747, 331 E. 8th St., Greeley, CO 80631 / 970-356-1670; FAX: 970-356-8702
Bushmann Hunters & Safaris, P.O. Box 293088, Lewisville, TX 75029 / 214-317-0768
Bushmaster Firearms (See Quality Parts Co/Bushmaster Firearms)
Bushmaster Hunting & Fishing, 451 Alliance Ave., Toronto, ON M6N 2J1 Canada / 416-763-4040; FAX: 416-763-0623
Bushnell Sports Optics Worldwide, 9200 Cody, Overland Park, KS 66214 / 913-752-3400 or 800-423-3537; FAX: 913-752-3550
Bushwacker Backpack & Supply Co (See Counter Assault)
Bustani, Leo, P.O. Box 8125, W. Palm Beach, FL 33410 / 305-622-2710
Buster's Custom Knives, P.O. Box 214, Richfield, UT 84701 / 801-896-5319
Butler Creek Corp., 290 Arden Dr., Belgrade, MT 59714 / 800-423-8327 or 406-388-1356; FAX: 406-388-7204
Butler Enterprises, 834 Oberting Rd., Lawrenceburg, IN 47025 / 812-537-3584
Butterfield & Butterfield, 220 San Bruno Ave., San Francisco, CA 94103 / 415-861-7500
Buzztail Brass (See Grayback Wildcats)
Byron Burgess, P.O. Box 6853, Los Osos, CA 93412 / 805-528-1005

C

C&D Special Products (See Claybuster Wads & Harvester Bullets)
C&H Research, 115 Sunnyside Dr., Box 351, Lewis, KS 67552 / 316-324-5445 www.09.net(chr)
C-More Systems, P.O. Box 1750, 7553 Gary Rd., Manassas, VA 20108 / 703-361-2663; FAX: 703-361-5881
C. Palmer Manufacturing Co., Inc., P.O. Box 220, West Newton, PA 15089 / 412-872-8200; FAX: 412-872-8302
C. Sharps Arms Co. Inc., 100 Centennial, Box 885, Big Timber, MT 59011 / 406-932-4353; FAX: 406-932-4443
C.S. Van Gorden & Son, Inc., 1815 Main St., Bloomer, WI 54724 / 715-568-2612
C.W. Erickson's Mfg. Inc., 530 Garrison Ave NE, PO Box 522, Buffalo, MN 55313 / 612-682-3665; FAX: 612-682-4328
Cabanas (See U.S. Importer-Mandall Shooting Supplies, Inc.)
Cabela's, 812-13th Ave., Sidney, NE 69160 / 308-254-6644 or 800-237-4444; FAX: 308-254-6745
Cabinet Mtn. Outfitters Scents & Lures, P.O. Box 766, Plains, MT 59859 / 406-826-3970
Cache La Poudre Rifleworks, 140 N. College, Ft. Collins, CO 80524 / 303-482-6913
Cali'co Hardwoods, Inc., 3580 Westwind Blvd., Santa Rosa, CA 95403 / 707-546-4045; FAX: 707-546-4027 calicohardwoods@msn.com
Calibre Press, Inc., 666 Dundee Rd., Suite 1607, Northbrook, IL 60062 / 800-323-0037; FAX: 708-498-6869
Calico Light Weapon Systems, 1489 Greg St., Sparks, NV 89431
California Sights (See Fautheree, Andy)
Cambos Outdoorsman, 532 E. Idaho Ave., Ontario, OR 97914 / 541-889-3138 FAX: 541-889-2633
Camdex, Inc., 2330 Alger, Troy, ML 48083 / 810-528-2300; FAX: 810-528-0989
Cameron's, 16690 W. 11th Ave., Golden, CO 80401 / 303-279-7365; FAX: 303-628-5413
Camilli, Lou, 600 Sandtree Dr., Suite 212, Lake Park, FL 33403
Camillus Cutlery Co., 54 Main St., Camillus, NY 13031 / 315-672-8111; FAX: 315-672-8832
Camp-Cap Products, P.O. Box 3805, Chesterfield, MO 63006 / 314-532-4340; FAX: 314-532-4340
Campbell, Dick, 20000 Silver Ranch Rd., Conifer, CO 80433 / 303-697-0150; FAX: 303-697-0150
Cannon, Andy. (See CANNON'S)
Cannon Safe, Inc., 9358 Stephens St., Pico Rivera, CA 90660 / 310-692-0636 or 800-242-1055; FAX: 310-692-7252
Cannon's, Andy Cannon, Box 1026, 320 Main St., Polson, MT 59860 / 406-887-2048
Canons Delcour, Rue J.B. Cools, B-4040, Herstal, BELGIUM / +32.(0)42.40.61.40; FAX: +32(0)42.40.22.88
Canyon Cartridge Corp., P.O. Box 152, Albertson, NY 11507 FAX: 516-294-8946
Cape Outfitters, 599 County Rd. 206, Cape Girardeau, MO 63701 / 573-335-4103; FAX: 573-335-1555
Caraville Manufacturing, P.O. Box 4545, Thousand Oaks, CA 91359 / 805-499-1234
Carbide Checkering Tools (See J&R Engineering)
Carbide Die & Mfg. Co., Inc., 15615 E. Arrow Hwy., Irwindale, CA 91706 / 626-337-2518
Carhartt,Inc., P.O. Box 600, 3 Parklane Blvd., Dearborn, MI 48121 / 800-358-3825 or 313-271-8460; FAX: 313-271-3455
Carl Walther GmbH, B.P. 4325, D-89033, Ulm, GERMANY
Carl Walther USA, PO Box 208, Ten Prince St, Alexandria, VA 22313 / 703-548-1400; FAX: 703-549-7826
Carl Zeiss Inc, 13017 N Kingston Ave, Chester, VA 23836-2743 / 804-861-0033 or 800-388-2984; FAX: 804-733-4024
Carlson, Douglas R, Antique American Firearms, PO Box 71035, Dept GD, Des Moines, IA 50325 / 515-224-6552
Carnahan Bullets, 17645 110th Ave. SE, Renton, WA 98055
Carolina Precision Rifles, 1200 Old Jackson Hwy., Jackson, SC 29831 / 803-827-2069
Carrell's Precision Firearms, 643 Clark Ave., Billings, MT 59101-1614 / 406-962-3593
Carry-Lite, Inc., 5203 W. Clinton Ave., Milwaukee, WI 53223 / 414-355-3520; FAX: 414-355-4775
Carter's Gun Shop, 225 G St., Penrose, CO 81240 / 719-372-6240
Cartridge Transfer Group, Pete de Coux, 235 Oak St., Butler, PA 16001 / 412-282-3426
Cascade Bullet Co., Inc., 2355 South 6th St., Klamath Falls, OR 97601 / 503-884-9316
Cascade Shooters, 2155 N.W. 12th St., Redwood, OR 97756
Case & Sons Cutlery Co., W R, Owens Way, Bradford, PA 16701 / 814-368-4123 or 800-523-6350; FAX: 814-768-5369
Case Sorting System, 12695 Cobblestone Creek Rd., Poway, CA 92064 / 619-486-9340
Cash Mfg. Co., Inc., P.O. Box 130, 201 S. Klein Dr., Waunakee, WI 53597-0130 / 608-849-5664; FAX: 608-849-5664
Caspian Arms, Ltd., 14 North Main St., Hardwick, VT 05843 / 802-472-6454; FAX: 802-472-6709
Cast Performance Bullet Company, 113 Riggs Rd, Shoshoni, WY 82649 / 307-856-4347
Casull Arms Corp., P.O. Box 1629, Afton, WY 83110 / 307-886-0200
Caswell Detroit Armor Companies, 1221 Marshall St. NE, Minneapolis, MN 55413-1055 / 612-379-2000; FAX: 612-379-2367
Catco-Ambush, Inc., P.O.Box 300, Corte Madera, CA 94926
Cathey Enterprises, Inc., P.O. Box 2202, Brownwood, TX 76804 / 915-643-2553; FAX: 915-643-3653
Cation, 2341 Alger St., Troy, MI 48083 / 810-689-0658; FAX: 810-689-7558
Caywood, Shane J., P.O. Box 321, Minocqua, WI 54548 / 715-277-3866
CBC, Avenida Humberto de Campos 3220, 09400-000, Ribeirao Pires, SP, BRAZIL / 55-11-742-7500; FAX: 55-11-459-7385
CBC-BRAZIL, 3 Cuckoo Lane, Honley, Yorkshire HD7 2BR, ENGLAND / 44-1484-661062; FAX: 44-1484-663709
CCG Enterprises, 5217 E. Belknap St., Halton City, TX 76117 / 800-819-7464
CCI Div. of Blount, Inc., Sporting Equipment Div.2299 Sn, P.O. Box 856, Lewiston, ID 83501 / 800-627-3640 or 208-746-2351; FAX: 208-746-2915
CCL Security Products, 199 Whiting St, New Britain, CT 06051 / 800-733-8588
Cedar Hill Game Calls Inc., 238 Vic Allen Rd, Downsville, LA 71234 / 318-982-5632; FAX: 318-368-2245
Celestron International, P.O. Box 3578, 2835 Columbia St., Torrance, CA 90503 / 310-328-9560; FAX: 310-212-5835
Centaur Systems, Inc., 1602 Foothill Rd., Kalispell, MT 59901 / 406-755-8609; FAX: 406-755-8609
Center Lock Scope Rings, 9901 France Ct., Lakeville, MN 55044 / 612-461-2114
Central Specialties Ltd (See Trigger Lock Division/Central Specialties Ltd.,)
Century Gun Dist. Inc., 1467 Jason Rd., Greenfield, IN 46140 / 317-462-4524
Century International Arms, Inc., 1161 Holland Dr, Boca Raton, FL 33487
CFVentures, 509 Harvey Dr., Bloomington, IN 47403-1715
CH Tool & Die Co (See 4-D Custom Die Co), 711 N Sandusky St, PO Box 889, Mt Vernon, OH 43050-0889 / 740-397-7214; FAX: 740-397-6600
Chace Leather Products, 507 Alden St., Fall River, MA 02722 / 508-678-7556; FAX: 508-675-9666
Chadick's Ltd., P.O. Box 100, Terrell, TX 75160 / 214-563-7577
Chambers Flintlocks Ltd., Jim, 116 Sams Branch Rd, Candler, NC 28715 / 828-667-8361 FAX: 828-665-0852
Champion Shooters' Supply, P.O. Box 303, New Albany, OH 43054 / 614-855-1603; FAX: 614-855-1209
Champion Target Co., 232 Industrial Parkway, Richmond, IN 47374 / 800-441-4971
Champion's Choice, Inc., 201 International Blvd., LaVergne, TN 37086 / 615-793-4066; FAX: 615-793-4070
Champlin Firearms, Inc., P.O. Box 3191, Woodring Airport, Enid, OK 73701 / 580-237-7388; FAX: 580-242-6922
Chapman Academy of Practical Shooting, 4350 Academy Rd., Hallsville, MO 65255 / 573-696-5544 or 573-696-2266
Chapman, J Ken. (See OLD WEST BULLET MOULDS J ken Champman)
Chapman Manufacturing Co., 471 New Haven Rd., P.O. Box 250, Durham, CT 06422 / 860-349-9228; FAX: 860-349-0084
Chapuis Armes, 21 La Gravoux, BP15, 42380, St. Bonnet-le-Chatea, FRANCE / (33)77.50.06.96+
Chapuis USA, 416 Business Park, Bedford, KY 40006
Charter 2000, 273 Canal St, Shelton, CT 06484 / 203-922-1652
Checkmate Refinishing, 370 Champion Dr., Brooksville, FL 34601 / 352-799-5774 FAX: 352-799-2986
Cheddite France S.A., 99 Route de Lyon, F-26501, Bourg-les-Valence, FRANCE / 33-75-56-4545; FAX: 33-75-56-3587
Chelsea Gun Club of New York City Inc., 237 Ovington Ave., Apt. D53, Brooklyn, NY 11209 / 718-836-9422 or 718-833-2704
Chem-Pak Inc., PO Box 2058, Winchester, VA 22604-1258 / 800-336-9828 or 703-667-1341 FAX: 703-722-3993
Cherry Creek State Park Shooting Center, 12500 E. Belleview Ave., Englewood, CO 80111 / 303-693-1765
Chet Fulmer's Antique Firearms, P.O. Box 792, Rt. 2 Buffalo Lake, Detroit Lakes, MN 56501 / 218-847-7712
CheVron Bullets, RR1, Ottawa, IL 61350 / 815-433-2471
Cheyenne Pioneer Products, PO Box 28425, Kansas City, MO 64188 / 816-413-9196 FAX: 816-455-2859 cheyennepp@aol.com www.cartridgeboxes.com
Chicago Cutlery Co., 1536 Beech St., Terre Haute, IN 47804 / 800-457-2665

Chicasaw Gun Works, 4 Mi. Mkr., Pluto Rd. Box 868, Shady Spring, WV 25918-0868 / 304-763-2848 FAX: 304-763-3725
Chipmunk (See Oregon Arms, Inc.)
Choate Machine & Tool Co., Inc., P.O. Box 218, 116 Lovers Ln., Bald Knob, AR 72010 / 501-724-6193 or 800-972-6390; FAX: 501-724-5873
Chopie Mfg.,Inc., 700 Copeland Ave., LaCrosse, WI 54603 / 608-784-0926
Christensen Arms, 385 N. 3050 E., St. George, UT 84790 / 435-624-9535; FAX: 435-674-9293
Christie's East, 219 E. 67th St., New York, NY 10021 / 212-606-0400
Chu Tani Ind., Inc., P.O. Box 2064, Cody, WY 82414-2064
Chuck's Gun Shop, P.O. Box 597, Waldo, FL 32694 / 904-468-2264
Churchill (See U.S. Importer-Ellett Bros)
Churchill, Winston, Twenty Mile Stream Rd., RFD P.O. Box 29B, Proctorsville, VT 05153 / 802-226-7772
Churchill Glove Co., James, PO Box 298, Centralia, WA 98531 / 360-736-2816 FAX: 360-330-0151
CIDCO, 21480 Pacific Blvd., Sterling, VA 22170 / 703-444-5353
Ciener Inc., Jonathan Arthur, 8700 Commerce St., Cape Canaveral, FL 32920 / 407-868-2200; FAX: 407-868-2201
Cimarron F.A. Co., P.O. Box 906, Fredericksburg, TX 78624-0906 / 210-997-9090; FAX: 210-997-0802
Cincinnati Swaging, 2605 Marlington Ave., Cincinnati, OH 45208
Clark Custom Guns, Inc., 336 Shootout Lane, Princeton, LA 71067 / 318-949-9884; FAX: 318-949-9829
Clark Firearms Engraving, P.O. Box 80746, San Marino, CA 91118 / 818-287-1652
Clarkfield Enterprises, Inc., 1032 10th Ave., Clarkfield, MN 56223 / 612-669-7140
Claro Walnut Gunstock Co., 1235 Stanley Ave., Chico, CA 95928 / 530-342-5188; FAX: 530-342-5199
Classic Arms Company, Rt 1 Box 120F, Burnet, TX 78611 / 512-756-4001
Classic Arms Corp., P.O. Box 106, Dunsmuir, CA 96025-0106 / 530-235-2000
Classic Guns, Inc., Frank S. Wood, 3230 Medlock Bridge Rd., Suite 110, Norcross, GA 30092 / 404-242-7944
Classic Old West Styles, 1060 Doniphan Park Circle C, El Paso, TX 79936 / 915-587-0684
Claybuster Wads & Harvester Bullets, 309 Sequoya Dr., Hopkinsville, KY 42240 / 800-922-6287 or 800-284-1746; FAX: 502-885-8088 50
Clean Shot Technologies, 21218 St. Andrews Blvd. Ste 504, Boca Raton, FL 33433 / 888-866-2532
Clear Creek Outdoors, Pat LaBoone, 2550 Hwy 23, Wrenshall, MN 55797 / 218-384-3670
Clearview Mfg. Co., Inc., 413 S. Oakley St., Fordyce, AR 71742 / 501-352-8557; FAX: 501-352-7120
Clearview Products, 3021 N. Portland, Oklahoma City, OK 73107
Cleland's Outdoor World, Inc, 10306 Airport Hwy, Swanton, OH 43558 / 419-865-4713; FAX: 419-865-5865
Clements' Custom Leathercraft, Chas, 1741 Dallas St., Aurora, CO 80010-2018 / 303-364-0403; FAX: 303-739-9824
Clenzoil Corp., P.O. Box 80226, Sta. C, Canton, OH 44708-0226 / 330-833-9758; FAX: 330-833-4724
Clift Mfg., L. R., 3821 hammonton Rd, Marysville, CA 95901 / 916-755-3390; FAX: 916-755-3393
Clift Welding Supply & Cases, 1332-A Colusa Hwy., Yuba City, CA 95993 / 916-755-3390 FAX: 916-755-3393
Cloward's Gun Shop, 4023 Aurora Ave. N, Seattle, WA 98103 / 206-632-2072
Clymer Manufacturing Co. Inc., 1645 W. Hamlin Rd., Rochester Hills, MI 48309-3312 / 248-853-5555; FAX: 248-853-1530
Cobalt Mfg., Inc., 4020 Mcewen Rd Ste 180, Dallas, TX 75244-5090 / 817-382-8986 FAX: 817-383-4281
Cobra Sport S.r.l., Via Caduti Nei Lager No. 1, 56020 San Romano, Montopoli v/Arno (Pi, ITALY / 0039-571-450490; FAX: 0039-571-450492
Coffin, Charles H., 3719 Scarlet Ave., Odessa, TX 79762 / 915-366-4729 FAX: 915-366-4729
Coffin, Jim (See Working Guns)
Coffin, Jim. See: WORKING GUNS
Cogar's Gunsmithing, P.O. Box 755, Houghton Lake, MI 48629 / 517-422-4591
Coghlan's Ltd., 121 Irene St., Winnipeg, MB R3T 4C7 CANADA / 204-284-9550; FAX: 204-475-4127
Cold Steel Inc., 2128-D Knoll Dr., Ventura, CA 93003 / 800-255-4716 or 800-624-2363 FAX: 805-642-9727
Cole's Gun Works, Old Bank Building, Rt. 4 Box 250, Moyock, NC 27958 / 919-435-2345
Cole-Grip, 16135 Cohasset St., Van Nuys, CA 91406 / 818-782-4424
Coleman Co., Inc., 250 N. St. Francis, Wichita, KS 67201
Coleman's Custom Repair, 4035 N. 20th Rd., Arlington, VA 22207 / 703-528-4486
Collectors Firearms Etc, P.O. Box 62, Minnesota City, MN 55959 / 507-689-2925
Collings, Ronald, 1006 Cielta Linda, Vista, CA 92083
Colonial Arms, Inc., P.O. Box 636, Selma, AL 36702-0636 / 334-872-9455; FAX: 334-872-9540 colonialarms@mindspring.com www.colonialarms.com
Colonial Knife Co., Inc., P.O. Box 3327, Providence, RI 02909 / 401-421-1600; FAX: 401-421-2047
Colonial Repair, 47 NAVARRE ST, ROSLINDALE, MA 02131-4725 / 617-469-4951
Colorado Gunsmithing Academy, 27533 Highway 287 South, Lamar, CO 81052 / 719-336-4099 or 800-754-2046; FAX: 719-336-9642
Colorado School of Trades, 1575 Hoyt St., Lakewood, CO 80215 / 800-234-4594; FAX: 303-233-4723
Colorado Sutlers Arsenal (See Cumberland States Arsenal)
Colt Blackpowder Arms Co., 110 8th Street, Brooklyn, NY 11215 / 212-925-2159; FAX: 212-966-4986
Colt's Mfg. Co., Inc., P.O. Box 1868, Hartford, CT 06144-1868 / 800-962-COLT or 860-236-6311; FAX: 860-244-1449
Compass Industries, Inc., 104 East 25th St., New York, NY 10010 / 212-473-2614 or 800-221-9904; FAX: 212-353-0826
Compasseco, Ltd., 151 Atkinson Hill Ave., Bardtown, KY 40004 / 502-349-0910
Competition Electronics, Inc., 3469 Precision Dr., Rockford, IL 61109 / 815-874-8001; FAX: 815-874-8181
Competitor Corp. Inc., Appleton Business Center, 30 Tricnit Road Unit 16, New Ipswich, NH 03071 / 603-878-3891; FAX: 603-878-3950
Component Concepts, Inc., 530 S Springbrook Dr, Newberg, OR 97132-7056 / 503-554-8095 FAX: 503-554-9370
Concept Development Corp., 14715 N. 78th Way, Suite 300, Scottsdale, AZ 85260 / 800-472-4405; FAX: 602-948-7560
Conetrol Scope Mounts, 10225 Hwy. 123 S., Seguin, TX 78155 / 210-379-3030 or 800-CONETROL; FAX: 210-379-3030
CONKKO, P.O. Box 40, Broomall, PA 19008 / 215-356-0711
Connecticut Shotgun Mfg. Co., P.O. Box 1692, 35 Woodland St., New Britain, CT 06051 / 860-225-6581; FAX: 860-832-8707
Connecticut Valley Classics (See CVC)
Conrad, C. A., 3964 Ebert St., Winston-Salem, NC 27127 / 919-788-5469
Cook Engineering Service, 891 Highbury Rd., Vict, 3133 AUSTRALIA
Coonan Arms (JS Worldwide DBA), 1745 Hwy. 36 E., Maplewood, MN 55109 / 612-777-3156; FAX: 612-777-3683
Cooper Arms, P.O. Box 114, Stevensville, MT 59870 / 406-777-5534; FAX: 406-777-5228
Cooper-Woodward, 3800 Pelican Rd., Helena, MT 59602 / 406-458-3800
Cor-Bon Bullet & Ammo Co., 1311 Industry Rd., Sturgis, SD 57785 / 800-626-7266; FAX: 800-923-2666
Corbin Mfg. & Supply, Inc., 600 Industrial Circle, P.O. Box 2659, White City, OR 97503 / 541-826-5211; FAX: 541-826-8669
Corkys Gun Clinic, 4401 Hot Springs Dr., Greeley, CO 80634-9226 / 970-330-0516
Corry, John, 861 Princeton Ct., Neshanic Station, NJ 08853 / 908-369-8019
Cosmi Americo & Figlio s.n.c., Via Flaminia 307, Ancona, ITALY / 071-888208; FAX: 39-071-887008+
Coulston Products, Inc., P.O. Box 30, 201 Ferry St. Suite 212, Easton, PA 18044-0030 / 215-253-0167 or 800-445-9927; FAX: 215-252-1511
Counter Assault, Box 4721, Missoula, MT 59806 / 406-728-6241 FAX: 406-728-8800
Cousin Bob's Mountain Products, 7119 Ohio River Blvd., Ben Avon, PA 15202 / 412-766-5114 FAX: 412-766-5114
Cox, Ed. C., RD 2, Box 192, Prosperity, PA 15329 / 412-228-4984
CP Bullets, 1310 Industrial Hwy #5-6, South Hampton, PA 18966 / 215-953-7264; FAX: 215-953-7275
CQB Training, P.O. Box 1739, Manchester, MO 63011
Craftguard, 3624 Logan Ave., Waterloo, IA 50703 / 319-232-2959 FAX: 319-234-0804
Craig, Spegel, P.O. Box 3108, Bay City, OR 97107 / 503-377-2697
Craig Custom Ltd., Research & Development, 629 E. 10th, Hutchinson, KS 67501 / 316-669-0601
Crandall Tool & Machine Co., 19163 21 Mile Rd., Tustin, MI 49688 / 616-829-4430
Creative Concepts USA, Inc., P.O. Box 1705, Dickson, TN 37056 / 615-446-8346 or 800-874-6965 FAX: 615-446-0646
Creedmoor Sports, Inc., P.O. Box 1040, Oceanside, CA 92051 / 619-757-5529
Creek Side Metal & Woodcrafters, Fishers Hill, VA 22626 / 703-465-3903
Creekside Gun Shop Inc., Main St., Holcomb, NY 14469 / 716-657-6338 FAX: 716-657-7900
Creighton Audette, 19 Highland Circle, Springfield, VT 05156 / 802-885-2331
Crimson Trace Lasers, 1433 N.W. Quimby, Portland, OR 97209 / 503-295-2406; FAX: 503-295-2225
Crit'R Call (See Rocky Mountain Wildlife Products)
Crosman Airguns, Rts. 5 and 20, E. Bloomfield, NY 14443 / 716-657-6161 FAX: 716-657-5405
Crosman Blades (See Coleman Co., Inc.)
Crosman Products of Canada Ltd., 1173 N. Service Rd. West, Oakville, ON L6M 2V9 CANADA / 905-827-1822
Crossfire, L.L.C., 2169 Greenville Rd., La Grange, GA 30241 / 706-882-8070 FAX: 706-882-9050
Crouse's Country Cover, P.O. Box 160, Storrs, CT 06268 / 860-423-8736
CRR, Inc./Marble's Inc., 420 Industrial Park, P.O. Box 111, Gladstone, MI 49837 / 906-428-3710; FAX: 906-428-3711
Crucelegui, Hermanos (See U.S. Importer-Mandall Shooting Supplies Inc.,)
Cryo-Accurizing, 2250 N. 1500 West, Ogden, UT 84404 801-395-2796 or 888-279-6266
Cubic Shot Shell Co., Inc., 98 Fatima Dr., Campbell, OH 44405 / 330-755-0349
Cullity Restoration, 209 Old Country Rd., East Sandwich, MA 02537 / 508-888-1147
Cumberland Arms, 514 Shafer Road, Manchester, TN 37355 / 800-797-8414
Cumberland Mountain Arms, P.O. Box 710, Winchester, TN 37398 / 615-967-8414; FAX: 615-967-9199
Cumberland States Arsenal, 1124 Palmyra Road, Clarksville, TN 37040
Cummings Bullets, 1417 Esperanza Way, Escondido, CA 92027
Cupp, Alana, Custom Engraver, PO Box 207, Annabella, UT 84711 / 801-896-4834
Curly Maple Stock Blanks (See Tiger-Hunt)
Curtis Cast Bullets, 527 W. Babcock St., Bozeman, MT 59715 / 406-587-8117; FAX: 406-587-8117
Curtis Custom Shop, RR1, Box 193A, Wallingford, KY 41093 / 703-659-4265
Curtis Gun Shop (See Curtis Cast Bullets)
Custom Bullets by Hoffman, 2604 Peconic Ave., Seaford, NY 11783
Custom Calls, 607 N. 5th St., Burlington, IA 52601 / 319-752-4465
Custom Checkering Service, Kathy Forster, 2124 SE Yamhill St., Portland, OR 97214 / 503-236-5874
Custom Chronograph, Inc., 5305 Reese Hill Rd., Sumas, WA 98295 / 360-988-7801
Custom Firearms (See Ahrends, Kim)
Custom Gun Products, 5021 W. Rosewood, Spokane, WA 99208 / 509-328-9340
Custom Gun Stocks, 3062 Turners Bend Rd, McMinnville, TN 37110 / 615-668-3912
Custom Products (See Jones Custom Products)
Custom Quality Products, Inc., 345 W. Girard Ave., P.O. Box 71129, Madison Heights, MI 48071 / 810-585-1616; FAX: 810-585-0644
Custom Riflestocks, Inc., Michael M. Kokolus, 7005 Herber Rd., New Tripoli, PA 18066 / 610-298-3013
Custom Tackle and Ammo, P.O. Box 1886, Farmington, NM 87499 / 505-632-3539
Cutco Cutlery, P.O. Box 810, Olean, NY 14760 / 716-372-3111
CVA, 5988 Peachtree Corners East, Norcross, GA 30071 / 800-251-9412; FAX: 404-242-8546
CVC, 5988 Peachtree Crns East, Norcross, GA 30071
Cylinder & Slide, Inc., William R. Laughridge, 245 E. 4th St., Fremont, NE 68025 / 402-721-4277; FAX: 402-721-0263
CZ USA, PO Box 171073, Kansas City, KS 66117 / 913-321-1811; FAX: 913-321-4901

D

D&D Gunsmiths, Ltd., 363 E. Elmwood, Troy, MI 48083 / 810-583-1512; FAX: 810-583-1524
D&G Precision Duplicators (See Greene Precision Du
D&H Precision Tooling, 7522 Barnard Mill Rd., Ringwood, IL 60072 / 815-653-4011
D&H Prods. Co., Inc., 465 Denny Rd., Valencia, PA 16059 / 412-898-2840 or 800-776-0281; FAX: 412-898-2013

MANUFACTURER'S DIRECTORY

D&J Bullet Co. & Custom Gun Shop, Inc., 426 Ferry St., Russell, KY 41169 / 606-836-2663; FAX: 606-836-2663
D&L Industries (See D.J. Marketing)
D&L Sports, P.O. Box 651, Gillette, WY 82717 / 307-686-4008
D&R Distributing, 308 S.E. Valley St., Myrtle Creek, OR 97457 / 503-863-6850
D-Boone Ent., Inc., 5900 Colwyn Dr., Harrisburg, PA 17109
D.C.C. Enterprises, 259 Wynburn Ave., Athens, GA 30601
D.D. Custom Stocks, R.H. "Dick" Devereaux, 5240 Mule Deer Dr., Colorado Springs, CO 80919 / 719-548-8468
D.J. Marketing, 10602 Horton Ave., Downey, CA 90241 / 310-806-0891; FAX: 310-806-6231
Da-Mar Gunsmith's Inc., 102 1st St., Solvay, NY 13209
Dade Screw Machine Products, 2319 NW 7th Ave., Miami, FL 33127 / 305-573-5050
Daewoo Precision Industries Ltd., 34-3 Yeoeuido-Dong, Yeongdeungoo-GU 15th Fl., Seoul, KOREA
Daisy Mfg. Co., PO Box 220, Rogers, AR 72757 / 501-621-4210; FAX: 501-636-0573
Dakota (See U.S. Importer-EMF Co., Inc.)
Dakota Arms, Inc., HC 55, Box 326, Sturgis, SD 57785 / 605-347-4686; FAX: 605-347-4459
Dakota Corp., 77 Wales St., P.O. Box 543, Rutland, VT 05701 / 802-775-6062 or 800-451-4167; FAX: 802-773-3919
DAMASCUS-U.S.A., 149 Deans Farm Rd., Tyner, NC 27980 / 252-221-2010; FAX: 252-221-2009
DAN WESSON FIREARMS, 119 Kemper Lane, Norwich, NY 13815 / 607-336-1174; FAX: FAX:607-336-2730
Dan's Whetstone Co., Inc., 130 Timbs Place, Hot Springs, AR 71913 / 501-767-1616; FAX: 501-767-9598
Danforth, Mikael. (See VEKTOR USA, Mikael Danforth)
Dangler, Homer L., Box 254, Addison, MI 49220 / 517-547-6745
Danner Shoe Mfg. Co., 12722 NE Airport Way, Portland, OR 97230 / 503-251-1100 or 800-345-0430; FAX: 503-251-1119
Danuser Machine Co., 550 E. Third St., P.O. Box 368, Fulton, MO 65251 / 573-642-2246; FAX: 573-642-2240
Dara-Nes, Inc. (See Nesci Enterprises, Inc.)
Darlington Gun Works, Inc., P.O. Box 698, 516 S. 52 By-pass, Darlington, SC 29532 / 803-393-3931
Darwin Hensley Gunmaker, P.O. Box 329, Brightwood, OR 97011 / 503-622-5411
Data Tech Software Systems, 19312 East Eldorado Drive, Aurora, CO 80013
Datumtech Corp., 2275 Wehrle Dr., Buffalo, NY 14221
Dave Norin Schrank's Smoke & Gun, 2010 Washington St., Waukegan, IL 60085 / 708-662-4034
Dave's Gun Shop, 555 Wood Street, Powell, WY 82435 / 307-754-9724
David Clark Co., Inc., PO Box 15054, Worcester, MA 01615-0054 / 508-756-6216; FAX: 508-753-5827
David Condon, Inc., 109 E. Washington St., Middleburg, VA 22117 / 703-687-5642
David Miller Co., 3131 E Greenlee Rd, Tucson, AZ 85716 / 520-326-3117
David R. Chicoine, 19 Key St., Eastport, ME 04631 / 207-853-4116 gnpress@nemaine.com
David W. Schwartz Custom Guns, 2505 Waller St, Eau Claire, WI 54703 / 715-832-1735
Davide Pedersoli and Co., Via Artigiani 57, Gardone VT, Brescia 25063, ITALY / 030-8912402; FAX: 030-8911019
Davidson, Jere, Rt. 1, Box 132, Rustburg, VA 24588 / 804-821-3637
Davis, Don, 1619 Heights, Katy, TX 77493 / 713-391-3090
Davis Industries, 15150 Sierra Bonita Ln., Chino, CA 91710 / 909-597-4726; FAX: 909-393-9771
Davis Products, Mike, 643 Loop Dr., Moses Lake, WA 98837 / 509-765-6178 or 509-766-7281
Daystate Ltd., Birch House Lanee, Cotes Heath Staffs, ST15.022, ENGLAND / 01782-791755; FAX: 01782-791617
Dayton Traister, 4778 N. Monkey Hill Rd., P.O. Box 593, Oak Harbor, WA 98277 / 360-679-4657; FAX: 360-675-1114
DBI Books Division of Krause Publications 700 E State St, Iola, WI 54990-0001 / 630-759-1229
de Coux, Pete (See Cartridge Transfer Group)
Dead Eye's Sport Center, RD 1, 76 Baer Rd, Shickshinny, PA 18655 / 570-256-7432
Decker Shooting Products, 1729 Laguna Ave., Schofield, WI 54476 / 715-359-5873
Deepeeka Exports Pvt. Ltd., D-78, Saket, Meerut-250-006, INDIA / 011-91-121-512889 or 011-91-121-545363; FAX: 011-91-121-542988
Deer Me Products Co., Box 34, 1208 Park St., Anoka, MN 55303 / 612-421-8971; FAX: 612-422-0526
Defense Training International, Inc., 749 S. Lemay, Ste. A3-337, Ft. Collins, CO 80524 / 303-482-2520; FAX: 303-482-0548
Degen Inc. (See Aristocrat Knives)
deHaas Barrels, RR 3, Box 77, Ridgeway, MO 64481 / 816-872-6308
Del Rey Products, P.O. Box 5134, Playa Del Rey, CA 90296-5134 / 213-823-0494
Del-Sports, Inc., Box 685, Main St., Margaretville, NY 12455 / 914-586-4103; FAX: 914-586-4105
Delhi Gun House, 1374 Kashmere Gate, Delhi, 0110 006 INDIA FAX: 91-11-2917344
Delorge, Ed, 6734 W. Main, Houma, LA 70360 / 504-223-0206
Delta Arms Ltd., P.O. Box 1000, Delta, VT 84624-1000
Delta Enterprises, 284 Hagemann Drive, Livermore, CA 94550
Delta Frangible Ammunition LLC, P.O. Box 2350, Stafford, VA 22555-2350 / 540-720-5778 or 800-339-1933; FAX: 540-720-5667
Dem-Bart Checkering Tools, Inc., 6807 Bickford Ave., Old Hwy. 2, Snohomish, WA 98290 / 360-568-7356; FAX: 360-568-1798
Denver Instrument Co., 6542 Fig St., Arvada, CO 80004 / 800-321-1135 or 303-431-7255; FAX: 303-423-4831
DeSantis Holster & Leather Goods, Inc., P.O. Box 2039, 149 Denton Ave., New Hyde Park, NY 11040-0701 / 516-354-8000; FAX: 516-354-7501
Desert Mountain Mfg., P.O. Box 130184, Coram, MT 59913 / 800-477-0762 or 406-387-5361; FAX: 406-387-5361
Detroit-Armor Corp., 720 Industrial Dr. No. 112, Cary, IL 60013 / 708-639-7666; FAX: 708-639-7694
Dever Co, Jack, 8590 NW 90, Oklahoma City, OK 73132 / 405-721-6393
Devereaux, R.H. "Dick" (See D.D. Custom Stocks, R.H. "Dick Devereaux)
Dewey Mfg. Co., Inc., J., P.O. Box 2014, Southbury, CT 06488 / 203-264-3064; FAX: 203-262-6907 deweyrods@worldnet.att.net www.deweyrods.com
DGR Custom Rifles, 4191 37th Ave SE, Tappen, ND 58487 / 701-327-8135
DGS, Inc., Dale A. Storey, 1117 E. 12th, Casper, WY 82601 / 307-237-2414 FAX: 307-237-2414 dalest@trib.com www.dgsrifle.com
DHB Products, P.O. Box 3092, Alexandria, VA 22302 / 703-836-2648
Diamond Machining Technology, Inc. (See DMT)
Diamond Mfg. Co., P.O. Box 174, Wyoming, PA 18644 / 800-233-9601
Diana (See U.S. Importer - Dynamit Nobel-RWS, Inc., 81 Ruckman Rd., Closter, NJ 07624 / 201-767-7971; (FAX: 201-767-1589)
Dibble, Derek A., 555 John Downey Dr., New Britain, CT 06051 / 203-224-2630
Dick Marple & Associates, 21 Dartmouth St, Hooksett, NH 03106 / 603-627-1837; FAX: 603-627-1837
Dietz Gun Shop & Range, Inc., 421 Range Rd., New Braunfels, TX 78132 / 210-885-4662
Dilliott Gunsmithing, Inc., 657 Scarlett Rd., Dandridge, TN 37725 / 865-397-9204 gunsmithd@aol.com dilliott-gunsmithing.com
Dillon, Ed, 1035 War Eagle Dr. N., Colorado Springs, CO 80919 / 719-598-4929; FAX: 719-598-4929
Dillon Precision Products, Inc., 8009 East Dillon's Way, Scottsdale, AZ 85260 / 602-948-8009 or 800-762-3845; FAX: 602-998-2786
Dina Arms Corporation, P.O. Box 46, Royersford, PA 19468 / 610-287-0266; FAX: 610-287-0266
Division Lead Co., 7742 W. 61st Pl., Summit, IL 60502
Dixie Gun Works, Inc., Hwy. 51 South, Union City, TN 38261 / order 800-238-6785;
Dixon Muzzleloading Shop, Inc., 9952 Kunkels Mill Rd., Kempton, PA 19529 / 610-756-6271
DKT, Inc., 14623 Vera Drive, Union, MI 49130-9744 / 800-741-7083 orders; FAX: 616-641-2015
DLO Mfg., 10807 SE Foster Ave., Arcadia, FL 33821-7304
DMT--Diamond Machining Technology Inc., 85 Hayes Memorial Dr., Marlborough, MA 01752 FAX: 508-485-3924
Doctor Optic Technologies, Inc., 4685 Boulder Highway, Suite A, Las Vegas, NV 89121 / 800-290-3634 or 702-898-7161; FAX: 702-898-3737
Dohring Bullets, 100 W. 8 Mile Rd., Ferndale, MI 48220
Dolbare, Elizabeth, P.O. Box 222, Sunburst, MT 59482-0222
Domino, PO Box 108, 20019 Settimo Milanese, Milano, ITALY / 1-39-2-33512040; FAX: 1-39-2-33511587
Donnelly, C. P., 405 Kubli Rd., Grants Pass, OR 97527 / 541-846-6604
Doskocil Mfg. Co., Inc., P.O. Box 1246, 4209 Barnett, Arlington, TX 76017 / 817-467-5116; FAX: 817-472-9810
Double A Ltd., P.O. Box 11306, Minneapolis, MN 55411 / 612-522-0306
Douglas Barrels Inc., 5504 Big Tyler Rd., Charleston, WV 25313-1398 / 304-776-1341; FAX: 304-776-8560
Downsizer Corp., P.O. Box 710316, Santee, CA 92072-0316 / 619-448-5510; FAX: 619-448-5780 www.downsizer.com
Dr. O's Products Ltd., P.O. Box 111, Niverville, NY 12130 / 518-784-3333; FAX: 518-784-2800
Drain, Mark, SE 3211 Kamilche Point Rd., Shelton, WA 98584 / 206-426-5452
Dremel Mfg. Co., 4915-21st St., Racine, WI 53406
Dressel Jr., Paul G., 209 N. 92nd Ave., Yakima, WA 98908 / 509-966-9233; FAX: 509-966-3365
Dri-Slide, Inc., 411 N. Darling, Fremont, MI 49412 / 616-924-3950
Dropkick, 1460 Washington Blvd., Williamsport, PA 17701 / 717-326-6561; FAX: 717-326-4950
DTM International, Inc., 40 Joslyn Rd., P.O. Box 5, Lake Orion, MI 48362 / 313-693-6670
Du-Lite Corp., 171 River Rd., Middletown, CT 06457 / 203-347-2505; FAX: 203-347-9404
Duane A. Hobbie Gunsmithing, 2412 Pattie Ave, Wichita, KS 67216 / 316-264-8266
Duane's Gun Repair (See DGR Custom Rifles)
Dubber, Michael W., P.O. Box 312, Evansville, IN 47702 / 812-424-9000; FAX: 812-424-6551
Duck Call Specialists, P.O. Box 124, Jerseyville, IL 62052 / 618-498-9855
Duffy, Charles E (See Guns Antique & Modern DBA), Williams Lane, PO Box 2, West Hurley, NY 12491 / 914-679-2997
Dumoulin, Ernest, Rue Florent Boclinville 8-10, 13-4041, Votten, BELGIUM / 41 27 78 92
Duncan's Gun Works, Inc., 1619 Grand Ave., San Marcos, CA 92069 / 619-727-0515
Dunham Boots, 1 Keuka business Park #300, Penn Yan, NY 14527-8995 / 802-254-2316
Duofold, Inc., RD 3 Rt. 309, Valley Square Mall, Tamaqua, PA 18252 / 717-386-2666; FAX: 717-386-3652
Dybala Gun Shop, P.O. Box 1024, FM 3156, Bay City, TX 77414 / 409-245-0866
Dykstra, Doug, 411 N. Darling, Fremont, MI 49412 / 616-924-3950
Dynalite Products, Inc., 215 S. Washington St., Greenfield, OH 45123 / 513-981-2124
Dynamit Nobel-RWS, Inc., 81 Ruckman Rd., Closter, NJ 07624 / 201-767-7971; FAX: 201-767-1589

E

E&L Mfg., Inc., 4177 Riddle By Pass Rd., Riddle, OR 97469 / 541-874-2137; FAX: 541-874-3107
E-A-R, Inc., Div. of Cabot Safety Corp., 5457 W. 79th St., Indianapolis, IN 46268 / 800-327-3431; FAX: 800-488-8007
E-Z-Way Systems, P.O. Box 4310, Newark, OH 43058-4310 / 614-345-6645 or 800-848-2072; FAX: 614-345-6600
E. Arthur Brown Co., 3404 Pawnee Dr., Alexandria, MN 56308 / 320-762-8847
E.A.A. Corp., P.O. Box 1299, Sharpes, FL 32959 / 407-639-4842 or 800-536-4442; FAX: 407-639-7006
Eagan, Donald V., P.O. Box 196, Benton, PA 17814 / 717-925-6134
Eagle Arms, Inc. (See ArmaLite, Inc.)
Eagle Grips, Eagle Business Center, 460 Randy Rd., Carol Stream, IL 60188 / 800-323-6144 or 708-260-0400; FAX: 708-260-0486
Eagle Imports, Inc., 1750 Brielle Ave., Unit B1, Wanamassa, NJ 07712 / 908-493-0333
EAW (See U.S. Importer-New England Custom Gun Service)
Echols & Co., D'Arcy, 164 W. 580 S., Providence, UT 84332 / 801-753-2367
Eckelman Gunsmithing, 3125 133rd St. SW, Fort Ripley, MN 56449 / 218-829-3176
Eclectic Technologies, Inc., 45 Grandview Dr., Suite A, Farmington, CT 06034
Ed~ Brown Products, Inc., 43825 Muldrow Trail, Perry, MO 63462 / 573-565-3261; FAX: 573-565-2791
Eddie Salter Calls, Inc., Hwy. 31 South-Brewton Industrial, Park, Brewton, AL 36426 / 205-867-2584; FAX: 206-867-9005
Edenpine, Inc. c/o Six Enterprises, Inc., 320 D Turtle Creek Ct., San Jose, CA 95125 / 408-999-0201; FAX: 408-999-0216
EdgeCraft Corp., S. Weiner, 825 Southwood Road, Avondale, PA 19311 / 610-268-0500 or 800-342-3255; FAX: 610-268-3545 www.chefschoice.com
Edmisten Co., P.O. Box 1293, Boone, NC 28607
Edmund Scientific Co., 101 E. Gloucester Pike, Barrington, NJ 08033 / 609-543-6250

REFERENCE

MANUFACTURER'S DIRECTORY

Ednar, Inc., 2-4-8 Kayabacho, Nihonbashi Chuo-ku, Tokyo, JAPAN / 81(Japan)-3-3667-1651; FAX: 81-3-3661-8113
Eezox, Inc., P.O. Box 772, Waterford, CT 06385-0772 / 800-462-3331; FAX: 860-447-3484
Effebi SNC-Dr. Franco Beretta, via Rossa, 4, 25062, ITALY / 030-2751955; FAX: 030-2180414
Efficient Machinery Co, 12878 NE 15th Pl, Bellevue, WA 98005
Eggleston, Jere D., 400 Saluda Ave., Columbia, SC 29205 / 803-799-3402
EGW Evolution Gun Works, 4050 B-8 Skyron Dr., Doylestown, PA 18901 / 215-348-9892; FAX: 215-348-1056
Eichelberger Bullets, Wm, 158 Crossfield Rd., King Of Prussia, PA 19406
Ekol Leather Care, P.O. Box 2652, West Lafayette, IN 47906 / 317-463-2250; FAX: 317-463-7004
El Dorado Leather (c/o Dill), P.O. Box 566, Benson, AZ 85602 / 520-586-4791; FAX: 520-586-4791
El Paso Saddlery Co., P.O. Box 27194, El Paso, TX 79926 / 915-544-2233; FAX: 915-544-2535
Eldorado Cartridge Corp (See PMC/Eldorado Cartridge Corp.)
Electro Prismatic Collimators, Inc., 1441 Manatt St., Lincoln, NE 68521
Electronic Shooters Protection, Inc., 11997 West 85th Place, Arvada, CO 80005 / 800-797-7791; FAX: 303-456-7179
Electronic Trigger Systems, Inc., P.O. Box 13, 230 Main St. S., Hector, MN 55342 / 320-848-2760; FAX: 320-848-2760
Eley Ltd., P.O. Box 705, Witton, Birmingham, B6 7UT ENGLAND / 021-356-8899; FAX: 021-331-4173
Elite Ammunition, P.O. Box 3251, Oakbrook, IL 60522 / 708-366-9006
Elk River, Inc., 1225 Paonia St., Colorado Springs, CO 80915 / 719-574-4407
Elkhorn Bullets, P.O. Box 5293, Central Point, OR 97502 / 541-826-7440
Ellett Bros., 267 Columbia Ave., P.O. Box 128, Chapin, SC 29036 / 803-345-3751 or 800-845-3711; FAX: 803-345-1820
Ellicott Arms, Inc./Woods Pistolsmithing, 3840 Dahlgren Ct., Ellicott City, MD 21042 / 410-465-7979
Elliott Inc., G. W., 514 Burnside Ave, East Hartford, CT 06108 / 203-289-5741; FAX: 203-289-3137
Elsen Inc., Pete, 1523 S 113th St, West Allis, WI 53214
Emerging Technologies, Inc. (See Laseraim Technologies, Inc.)
Emap USA, 6420 Wilshire Blvd., Los Angeles, CA 90048 / 213-782-2000; FAX: 213-782-2867
EMF Co., Inc., 1900 E. Warner Ave., Suite 1-D, Santa Ana, CA 92705 / 714-261-6611; FAX: 714-756-0133
Empire Cutlery Corp., 12 Kruger Ct., Clifton, NJ 07013 / 201-472-5155; FAX: 201-779-0759
English, Inc., A.G., 708 S. 12th St., Broken Arrow, OK 74012 / 918-251-3399
Engraving Artistry, 36 Alto Rd., RFD 2, Burlington, CT 06013 / 203-673-6837
Enguix Import-Export, Alpujarras 58, Alzira, Valencia, SPAIN / (96) 241 43 95; FAX: (96) (241 43 95
Enhanced Presentations, Inc., 5929 Market St., Wilmington, NC 28405 / 910-799-1622; FAX: 910-799-5004
Enlow, Charles, 895 Box, Beaver, OK 73932 / 405-625-4487
Entre'prise Arms, Inc., 15861 Business Center Dr., Irwindale, CA 91706
EPC, 1441 Manatt St., Lincoln, NE 68521 / 402-476-3946
Epps, Ellwood (See "Gramps" Antique, Box 341, Washago, ON L0K 2B0 CANADA / 705-689-5348
Erhardt, Dennis, 3280 Green Meadow Dr., Helena, MT 59601 / 406-442-4533
Erma Werke GmbH, Johan Ziegler St., 13/15/FeldiglSt., D-8060 Dachau, GERMANY
Eskridge Rifles, Steven Eskridge, 218 N. Emerson, Mart, TX 76664 / 817-876-3544
Eskridge, Steven. (See ESKRIDGE RIFLES)
Essex Arms, P.O. Box 363, Island Pond, VT 05846 / 802-723-6203 FAX: 802-723-6203
Essex Metals, 1000 Brighton St., Union, NJ 07083 / 800-282-8369
Estate Cartridge, Inc., 12161 FM 830, Willis, TX 77378 / 409-856-7277; FAX: 409-856-5486
Euber Bullets, No. Orwell Rd., Orwell, VT 05760 / 802-948-2621
Euro-Imports, 905 West Main St Ste E, El Cajon, CA 92020 / 619-442-7005; FAX: 619-442-7005
Euroarms of America, Inc., P.O. Box 3277, Winchester, VA 22604 / 540-662-1863; FAX: 540-662-4464
European American Armory Corp (See E.A.A. Corp)
Evans, Andrew, 2325 NW Squire St., Albany, OR 97321 / 541-928-3190; FAX: 541-928-4128
Evans Engraving, Robert, 332 Vine St, Oregon City, OR 97045 / 503-656-5693
Evans Gunsmithing (See Evans, Andrew)
Eversull Co., Inc., K., 1 Tracemont, Boyce, LA 71409 / 318-793-8728; FAX: 318-793-5483
Excalibur Electro Optics Inc, P.O. Box 400, Fogelsville, PA 18051-0400 / 610-391-9105; FAX: 610-391-9220
Excel Industries Inc., 4510 Carter Ct., Chino, CA 91710 / 909-627-2404; FAX: 909-627-7817
Executive Protection Institute, PO Box 802, Berryville, VA 22611 / 540-955-1128
Eyster Heritage Gunsmiths, Inc., Ken, 6441 Bishop Rd., Centerburg, OH 43011 / 614-625-6131
Eze-Lap Diamond Prods., P.O. Box 2229, 15164 West State St., Westminster, CA 92683 / 714-847-1555; FAX: 714-897-0280

F

F&A Inc. (See ShurKatch Corporation)
F.A.I.R. Techni-Mec s.n.c. di Isidoro Rizzini & C., Via Gitti, 41 Zona Industrial, 25060 Marcheno (Bres, ITALY / 030/861162-8610344; FAX: 030/8610179
Fabarm S.p.A., Via Averolda 31, 25039 Travagliato, Brescia, ITALY / 030-6863629; FAX: 030-6863684
Fagan & Co.Inc, 22952 15 Mile Rd, Clinton Township, MI 48035 / 810-465-4637; FAX: 810-792-6996
Fair Game International, P.O. Box 77234-34053, Houston, TX 77234 / 713-941-6269
Faith Associates, Inc., PO Box 549, Flat Rock, NC 28731-0549 / 828-692-1916; FAX: 828-697-6827
Fanzoj GmbH, Griesgasse 1, 9170 Ferlach, 9170 AUSTRIA / (43) 04227-2283; FAX: (43) 04227-2867
Far North Outfitters, Box 1252, Bethel, AK 99559
Farm Form Decoys, Inc., 1602 Biovu, P.O. Box 748, Galveston, TX 77553 / 409-744-0762 or 409-765-6361; FAX: 409-765-8513
Farmer-Dressel, Sharon, 209 N. 92nd Ave., Yakima, WA 98908 / 509-966-9233; FAX: 509-966-3365
Farr Studio,Inc., 1231 Robinhood Rd., Greeneville, TN 37743 / 615-638-8825
Farrar Tool Co., Inc., 12150 Bloomfield Ave., Suite E, Santa Fe Springs, CA 90670 / 310-863-4367; FAX: 310-863-5123
Faulhaber Wildlocker, Dipl.-Ing. Norbert Wittasek, Seilergasse 2, A-1010 Wien, AUSTRIA / OM-43-1-5137001; FAX: OM-43-1-5137001
Faulk's Game Call Co., Inc., 616 18th St., Lake Charles, LA 70601 / 318-436-9726 FAX: 318-494-7205
Faust Inc., T. G., 544 minor St, Reading, PA 19602 / 610-375-8549; FAX: 610-375-4488
Fausti Cav. Stefano & Figlie snc, Via Martiri Dell Indipendenza, 70, Marcheno, 25060 ITALY
Fautheree, Andy, P.O. Box 4607, Pagosa Springs, CO 81157 / 970-731-5003; FAX: 970-731-5009
Feather, Flex Decoys, 1655 Swan Lake Rd., Bossier City, LA 71111 / 318-746-8596; FAX: 318-742-4815
Federal Arms Corp. of America, 7928 University Ave, Fridley, MN 55432 / 612-780-8780; FAX: 612-780-8780
Federal Cartridge Co., 900 Ehlen Dr., Anoka, MN 55303 / 612-323-2300; FAX: 612-323-2506
Federal Champion Target Co., 232 Industrial Parkway, Richmond, IN 47374 / 800-441-4971; FAX: 317-966-7747
Federated-Fry (See Fry Metals)
FEG, Budapest, Soroksariut 158, H-1095, HUNGARY
Feken, Dennis, Rt. 2, Box 124, Perry, OK 73077 / 405-336-5611
Felk, Inc., 2121 Castlebridge Rd., Midlothian, VA 23113 / 804-794-3744
Fellowes, Ted, Beaver Lodge, 9245 16th Ave. SW, Seattle, WA 98106 / 206-763-1698
Feminine Protection, Inc., 949 W. Kearney Ste. 100, Mesquite, TX 75149 / 972-289-8997 FAX: 972-289-4410
Ferguson, Bill, P.O. Box 1238, Sierra Vista, AZ 85636 / 520-458-5321; FAX: 520-458-9125
FERLIB, Via Costa 46, 25063, Gardone V.T., ITALY / 30-89-12-586; FAX: 30-89-12-586
Ferris Firearms, 7110 F.M. 1863, Bulverde, TX 78163 / 210-980-4424
Fibron Products, Inc., P.O. Box 430, Buffalo, NY 14209-0430 / 716-886-2378; FAX: 716-886-2394
Fieldsport Ltd, Bryan Bilinski, 3313 W South Airport Rd, Traverse Vity, MI 49684 / 616-933-0767
Fiocchi Munizioni S.p.A. (See U.S. Importer-Fiocchi of America, Inc.,)
Fiocchi of America Inc., 5030 Fremont Rd., Ozark, MO 65721 / 417-725-4118 or 800-721-2666 FAX: 417-725-1039
Firearms Co Ltd/Alpine (See U.S. Importer-Mandall Shooting Supplies, Inc.)
Firearms Engraver's Guild of America, 332 Vine St., Oregon City, OR 97045 / 503-656-5693
Firearms International, 5709 Hartsdale, Houston, TX 77036 / 713-460-2447
First Inc, Jack, 1201 Turbine Dr., Rapid City, SD 57701 / 605-343-9544; FAX: 605-343-9420
Fish Mfg. Gunsmith Sptg. Co., Marshall F, Rd. Box 2439, Rt. 22 N, Westport, NY 12993 / 518-962-4897 FAX: 518-962-4897
Fisher, Jerry A., 553 Crane Mt. Rd., Big Fork, MT 59911 / 406-837-2722
Fisher Custom Firearms, 2199 S. Kittredge Way, Aurora, CO 80013 / 303-755-3710
Fisher Enterprises, Inc., 1071 4th Ave. S., Suite 303, Edmonds, WA 98020-4143 / 206-771-5382
Fisher, R. Kermit (See Fisher Enterprises, Inc), 1071 4th Ave S Ste 303, Edmonds, WA 98020-4143 / 206-771-5382
Fitz Pistol Grip Co., P.O. Box 744, LEWISTON, CA 96052-0744 / 916-778-0240
Flambeau Products Corp., 15981 Valplast Rd., Middlefield, OH 44062 / 216-632-1631; FAX: 216-632-1581
Flannery Engraving Co., Jeff W, 11034 Riddles Run Rd, Union, KY 41091 / 606-384-3127
Flashette Co., 4725 S. Kolin Ave., Chicago, IL 60632 FAX: 773-927-3083
Flayderman & Co., Inc., PO Box 2446, Ft Lauderdale, FL 33303 / 954-761-8855
Fleming Firearms, 7720 E 126th St. N, Collinsville, OK 74021-7016 / 918-665-3624
Flents Products Co., Inc., P.O. Box 2109, Norwalk, CT 06852 / 203-866-2581; FAX: 203-854-9322
Flintlocks Etc., 160 Rositter Rd, Richmond, MA 01254 / 413-698-3822
Flintlocks, Etc, 160 Rossiter Rd., P.O. Box 181, Richmond, MA 01254 / 413-698-3822; FAX: 413-698-3866 flintetc@vgernet.net pedersoli
Flitz International Ltd., 821 Mohr Ave., Waterford, WI 53185 / 414-534-5898; FAX: 414-534-2991
Flores Publications Inc, J (See Action Direct Inc), PO Box 830760, Miami, FL 33283 / 305-559-4652; FAX: 305-559-4652
Fluoramics, Inc., 18 Industrial Ave., Mahwah, NJ 07430 / 800-922-0075; FAX: 201-825-7035
Flynn's Custom Guns, P.O. Box 7461, Alexandria, LA 71306 / 318-455-7130
FN Herstal, Voie de Liege 33, Herstal, 4040 Belgium / (32)41.40.82.83; FAX: (32)41.40.86.79
Fobus International Ltd., P.O. Box 64, Kfar Hess, 40692 ISRAEL / 972-9-7964170; FAX: 972-9-7964169
Folks, Donald E., 205 W. Lincoln St., Pontiac, IL 61764 / 815-844-7901
Foothills Video Productions, Inc., P.O. Box 651, Spartanburg, SC 29304 / 803-573-7023 or 800-782-5358
Foredom Electric Co., Rt. 6, 16 Stony Hill Rd., Bethel, CT 06801 / 203-792-8622
Forgett Jr., Valmore J., 689 Bergen Blvd., Ridgefield, NJ 07657 / 201-945-2500; FAX: 201-945-6859
Forgreens Tool Mfg., Inc., P.O. Box 990, 723 Austin St., Robert Lee, TX 76945 / 915-453-2800; FAX: 915-453-2460
Forkin, Ben (See Belt MTN Arms)
Forkin Arms, 205 10th Ave SW, White Sulphur Spring, MT 59645 / 406-547-2344; FAX: 406-547-2456
Forrest Inc., Tom, PO Box 326, Lakeside, CA 92040 / 619-561-5800; FAX: 619-561-0227
Forrest Tool Co., P.O. Box 768, 44380 Gordon Lane, Mendocino, CA 95460 / 707-937-2141; FAX: 717-937-1817
Forster, Kathy (See Custom Checkering Service, Kathy Forster)
Forster, Larry L., P.O. Box 212, 220 First St. NE, Gwinner, ND 58040-0212 / 701-678-2475
Forster Products, 310 E Lanark Ave, Lanark, IL 61046 / 815-493-6360; FAX: 815-493-2371
Fort Hill Gunstocks, 12807 Fort Hill Rd., Hillsboro, OH 45133 / 513-466-2763
Fort Knox Security Products, 1051 N. Industrial Park Rd., Orem, UT 84057 / 801-224-7233 or 800-821-5216; FAX: 801-226-5493
Fort Worth Firearms, 2006-B, Martin Luther King Fwy., Ft. Worth, TX 76104-6303 / 817-536-0718; FAX: 817-535-0290
Forthofer's Gunsmithing & Knifemaking, 5535 U.S. Hwy 93S, Whitefish, MT 59937-8411 / 406-862-2674
Fortune Products, Inc., HC04, Box 303, Marble Falls, TX 78654 / 210-693-6111; FAX: 210-693-6394
Forty Five Ranch Enterprises, Box 1080, Miami, OK 74355-1080 / 918-542-5875
Fountain Products, 492 Prospect Ave., West Springfield, MA 01089 / 413-781-4651; FAX: 413-733-8217
4-D Custom Die Co., 711 N. Sandusky St., P.O. Box 889, Mt. Vernon, OH 43050-0889 / 740-397-7214; FAX: 740-397-6600

Fowler Bullets, 806 Dogwood Dr., Gastonia, NC 28054 / 704-867-3259
Fowler, Bob (See Black Powder Products)
Fox River Mills, Inc., P.O. Box 298, 227 Poplar St., Osage, IA 50461 / 515-732-3798; FAX: 515-732-5128
Foy Custom Bullets, 104 Wells Ave., Daleville, AL 36322
Francesca, Inc., 3115 Old Ranch Rd., San Antonio, TX 78217 / 512-826-2584; FAX: 512-826-8211
Franchi S.p.A., Via del Serpente 12, 25131, Brescia, ITALY / 030-3581833; FAX: 030-3581554
Francotte & Cie S.A. Auguste, rue de Trois Juin 109, 4400 Herstal-Liege, BELGIUM / 32-4-248-13-18; FAX: 32-4-948-11-79
Frank Custom Classic Arms, Ron, 7131 Richland Rd, Ft Worth, TX 76118 / 817-284-9300; FAX: 817-284-9300
Frank E. Hendricks Master Engravers, Inc., HC03, Box 434, Dripping Springs, TX 78620 / 512-858-7828
Frank Knives, 13868 NW Keleka Pl., Seal Rock, OR 97376 / 541-563-3041; FAX: 541-563-3041
Frank Mittermeier, Inc., P.O. Box 2G, 3577 E. Tremont Ave., Bronx, NY 10465 / 718-828-3843
Frankonia Jagd Hofmann & Co., D-97064 Wurzburg, Wurzburg, GERMANY / 09302-200; FAX: 09302-20200
Franzen International,Inc (U.S. Importer for Peters Stahl GmbH)
Fred F. Wells/Wells Sport Store, 110 N Summit St, Prescott, AZ 86301 / 520-445-3655
Freedom Arms, Inc., P.O. Box 150, Freedom, WY 83120 / 307-883-2468 or 800-833-4432; FAX: 307-883-2005
Freeman Animal Targets, 5519 East County Road, 100 South, Plainsfield, IN 46168 / 317-272-2663; FAX: 317-272-2674
Fremont Tool Works, 1214 Prairie, Ford, KS 67842 / 316-369-2327
French, Artistic Engraving, J. R., 1712 Creek Ridge Ct, Irving, TX 75060 / 214-254-2654
Frielich Police Equipment, 211 East 21st St., New York, NY 10010 / 212-254-3045
Front Sight Firearms Training Institute, P.O. Box 2619, Aptos, CA 95001 / 800-987-7719; FAX: 408-684-2137
Frontier, 2910 San Bernardo, Laredo, TX 78040 / 956-723-5409; FAX: 956-723-1774
Frontier Arms Co.,Inc., 401 W. Rio Santa Cruz, Green Valley, AZ 85614-3932
Frontier Products Co., 2401 Walker Rd, Roswell, NM 88201-8950 / 614-262-9357
Frontier Safe Co., 3201 S. Clinton St., Fort Wayne, IN 46806 / 219-744-7233; FAX: 219-744-6678
Frost Cutlery Co., P.O. Box 22636, Chattanooga, TN 37422 / 615-894-6079; FAX: 615-894-9576
Fry Metals, 4100 6th Ave., Altoona, PA 16602 / 814-946-1611
Fujinon, Inc., 10 High Point Dr., Wayne, NJ 07470 / 201-633-5600; FAX: 201-633-5216
Fullmer, Geo. M., 2499 Mavis St., Oakland, CA 94601 / 510-533-4193
Fulmer's Antique Firearms, Chet, PO Box 792, Rt 2 Buffalo Lake, Detroit Lakes, MN 56501 / 218-847-7712
Fulton Armory, 8725 Bollman Place No. 1, Savage, MD 20763 / 301-490-9485; FAX: 301-490-9547
Furr Arms, 91 N. 970 W., Orem, UT 84057 / 801-226-3877; FAX: 801-226-3877
Fusilier Bullets, 10010 N. 6000 W., Highland, UT 84003 / 801-756-6813
FWB, Neckarstrasse 43, 78727, Oberndorf a. N., GERMANY / 07423-814-0; FAX: 07423-814-89

G

G&H Decoys,Inc., P.O. Box 1208, Hwy. 75 North, Henryetta, OK 74437 / 918-652-3314; FAX: 918-652-3400
G.C.C.T., 4455 Torrance Blvd., Ste. 453, Torrance, CA 90503-4398
G.G. & G., 3602 E. 42nd Stravenue, Tucson, AZ 85713 / 520-748-7167; FAX: 520-748-7583
G.H. Enterprises Ltd., Bag 10, Okotoks, AB T0L 1T0 CANADA / 403-938-6070
G.U. Inc (See U.S. Importer for New SKB Arms Co)
G.W. Elliott, Inc., 514 Burnside Ave., East Hartford, CT 06108 / 203-289-5741; FAX: 203-289-3137
G96 Products Co., Inc., 85 5th Ave, Bldg #6, Paterson, NJ 07544 / 973-684-4050 FAX: 973-684-4050
Gage Manufacturing, 663 W. 7th St., A, San Pedro, CA 90731 / 310-832-3546
Gaillard Barrels, P.O. Box 21, Pathlow, SK S0K 3B0 CANADA / 306-752-3769; FAX: 306-752-5969
Gain Twist Barrel Co. Rifle Works and Armory, 707 12th Street, Cody, WY 82414 / 307-587-4919; FAX: 307-527-6097
Galati International, PO Box 10, Wesco, MO 65586 / 314-257-4837; FAX: 314-257-2268
Galaxy Imports Ltd.,Inc., P.O. Box 3361, Victoria, TX 77903 / 361-573-4867; FAX: 361-576-9622 galaxy@tisd.net
GALCO International Ltd., 2019 W. Quail Ave., Phoenix, AZ 85027 / 602-258-8295 or 800-874-2526; FAX: 602-582-6854
Galena Industries AMT, 3551 Mayer Ave., Sturgis, SD 57785 / 605-423-4105
Gamba S.p.A. Societa Armi Bresciane Srl, Renato, Via Artigiani 93, ITALY / 30-8911640; FAX: 30-8911648
Gamba, USA, P.O. Box 60452, Colorado Springs, CO 80960 / 719-578-1145; FAX: 719-444-0731
Game Haven Gunstocks, 13750 Shire Rd., Wolverine, MI 49799 / 616-525-8257
Game Winner, Inc., 2625 Cumberland Parkway, Suite 220, Atlanta, GA 30339 / 770-434-9210; FAX: 770-434-9215
Gamebore Division, Polywad Inc, PO Box 7916, Macon, GA 31209 / 912-477-0669
Gamo (See U.S. Importers-Arms United Corp, Daisy Mfg. Co.,)
Gamo USA, Inc., 3911 SW 47th Ave., Suite 914, Ft. Lauderdale, FL 33314 / 954-581-5822; FAX: 954-581-3165
Gander Mountain, Inc., 12400 Fox River Rd., Wilmont, WI 53192 / 414-862-6848
GAR, 590 McBride Avenue, West Paterson, NJ 07424 / 973-754-1114; FAX: 973-754-1114
Garbi, Armas Urki, 12-14 20.600 Eibar, Guipuzcoa, SPAIN
Garcia National Gun Traders, Inc., 225 SW 22nd Ave., Miami, FL 33135 / 305-642-2355
Garrett Cartridges Inc., P.O. Box 178, Chehalis, WA 98532 / 360-736-0702
Garthwaite Pistolsmith, Inc., Jim, Rt 2 Box 310, Watsontown, PA 17777 / 570-538-1566; FAX: 570-538-2965
Gary Goudy Classic Stocks, 263 Hedge Rd., Menlo Park, CA 94025-1711 / 415-322-1338
Gary Reeder Custom Guns, 2710 N Steves Blvd. #22, Flagstaff, AZ 86004 / 520-526-3313; FAX: 520-527-0840 gary@reedercustomguns.com www.reedercustomguns.com
Gary Schneider Rifle Barrels Inc., 12202 N. 62nd Pl., Scottsdale, AZ 85254 / 602-948-2525
Gator Guns & Repair, 6255 Spur Hwy., Kenai, AK 99611 / 907-283-7947
Gaucher Armes, S.A., 46 rue Desjoyaux, 42000, Saint-Etienne, FRANCE / 04-77-33-38-92; FAX: 04-77-61-95-72
GDL Enterprises, 409 Le Gardeur, Slidell, LA 70460 / 504-649-0693
Gehmann, Walter (See Huntington Die Specialties)
Genco, P.O. Box 5704, Asheville, NC 28803
Gene's Custom Guns, P.O. Box 10534, White Bear Lake, MN 55110 / 612-429-5105
Genecco Gun Works, K, 10512 Lower Sacramento Rd., Stockton, CA 95210 / 209-951-0706 FAX: 209-931-3872
Gentex Corp., 5 Tinkham Ave., Derry, NH 03038 / 603-434-0311; FAX: 603-434-3002 sales@derry.gentexcorp.com www.derry.gentexcorp.com
Gentner Bullets, 109 Woodlawn Ave., Upper Darby, PA 19082 / 610-352-9396
Gentry Custom Gunmaker, David, 314 N Hoffman, Belgrade, MT 59714 / 406-388-GUNS
George & Roy's, PO Box 2125, Sisters, OR 97759-2125 / 503-228-5424 or 800-553-3022; FAX: 503-225-9409
George, Tim, Rt. 1, P.O. Box 45, Evington, VA 24550 / 804-821-8117
George E. Mathews & Son, Inc., 10224 S. Paramount Blvd., Downey, CA 90241 / 562-862-6719; FAX: 562-862-6719
George Ibberson (Sheffield) Ltd., 25-31 Allen St., Sheffield, S3 7AW ENGLAND / 0114-2766123; FAX: 0114-2738465
Gerald Pettinger Books, see Pettinger Books, G, Rt. 2, Box 125, Russell, IA 50238 / 515-535-2239
Gerber Legendary Blades, 14200 SW 72nd Ave., Portland, OR 97223 / 503-639-6161 or 800-950-6161; FAX: 503-684-7008
Gervais, Mike, 3804 S. Cruise Dr., Salt Lake City, UT 84109 / 801-277-7729
Getz Barrel Co., P.O. Box 88, Beavertown, PA 17813 / 717-658-7263
Giacomo Sporting USA, 6234 Stokes Lee Center Rd., Lee Center, NY 13363
Gibbs Rifle Co., Inc., 211 Lawn St, Martinsburg, WV 25401 / 304-262-1651; FAX: 304-262-1658
Gil Hebard Guns, 125-129 Public Square, Knoxville, IL 61448 / 309-289-2700 FAX: 309-289-2233
Gilbert Equipment Co., Inc., 960 Downtowner Rd., Mobile, AL 36609 / 205-344-3322
Gilkes, Anthony W., 26574 HILLMAN HWY, MEADOWVIEW, VA 24361-3142 / 303-657-1873; FAX: 303-657-1885
Gillmann, Edwin, 33 Valley View Dr., Hanover, PA 17331 / 717-632-1662
Gilman-Mayfield, Inc., 3279 E. Shields, Fresno, CA 93703 / 209-221-9415; FAX: 209-221-9419
Gilmore Sports Concepts, 5949 S. Garnett, Tulsa, OK 74146 / 918-250-3810; FAX: 918-250-3845 gilmore@webzone.net www.gilmoresports.com
Giron, Robert E., 1328 Pocono St., Pittsburgh, PA 15218 / 412-731-6041
Glacier Glove, 4890 Aircenter Circle, Suite 210, Reno, NV 89502 / 702-825-8225; FAX: 702-825-6544
Glaser Safety Slug, Inc., P.O. Box 8223, Foster City, CA 94404 / 800-221-3489; FAX: 510-785-6685 safetyslug.com
Glass, Herb, P.O. Box 25, Bullville, NY 10915 / 914-361-3021
Glimm, Jerome C., 19 S. Maryland, Conrad, MT 59425 / 406-278-3574
Glock GmbH, P.O. Box 50, A-2232, Deutsch Wagram, AUSTRIA
Glock, Inc., PO Box 369, Smyrna, GA 30081 / 770-432-1202; FAX: 770-433-8719
Glynn Scobey Duck & Goose Calls, Rt. 3, Box 37, Newbern, TN 38059 / 901-643-6241
GML Products, Inc., 394 Laredo Dr., Birmingham, AL 35226 / 205-979-4867
Gner's Hard Cast Bullets, 1107 11th St., LaGrande, OR 97850 / 503-963-8796
Goens, Dale W., P.O. Box 224, Cedar Crest, NM 87008 / 505-281-5419
Goergen's Gun Shop, Inc., 17985 538th Ave, Austin, MN 55912 / 507-433-9280 FAX: 507-433-9280
GOEX Inc., PO Box 659, Doyline, LA 71023-0659 / 318-382-9300; FAX: 318-382-9303
Golden Age Arms Co., 115 E. High St., Ashley, OH 43003 / 614-747-2488
Golden Bear Bullets, 3065 Fairfax Ave., San Jose, CA 95148 / 408-238-9515
Gonic Arms/North American Arm, 134 Flagg Rd., Gonic, NH 03839 / 603-332-8456 or 603-332-8457
Gonzalez Guns, Ramon B, PO Box 370, 93 St. Joseph's Hill Rd, Monticello, NY 12701 / 914-794-4515
Goodling's Gunsmithing, R.D. 1, Box 1097, Spring Grove, PA 17362 / 717-225-3350
Goodwin, Fred, Silver Ridge Gun Shop, Sherman Mills, ME 04776 / 207-365-4451
Gordie's Gun Shop, 1401 Fulton St., Streator, IL 61364 / 815-672-7202
Gordon Wm. Davis Leather Co., P.O. Box 2270, Walnut, CA 91788 / 909-598-5620
Gotz Bullets, 7313 Rogers St., Rockford, IL 61111
Gould & Goodrich, 709 E. McNeil, Lillington, NC 27546 / 910-893-2071; FAX: 910-893-4742
Gournet, Geoffroy, 820 Paxinosa Ave., Easton, PA 18042 / 610-559-0710
Gozon Corp. U.S.A., P.O. Box 6278, Folson, CA 95763 / 916-983-2026; FAX: 916-983-9500
Grace, Charles E., 1305 Arizona Ave., Trinidad, CO 81082 / 719-846-9435
Grace Metal Products, P.O. Box 67, Elk Rapids, MI 49629 / 616-264-8133
Graf & Sons, 4050 S Clark St, Mexico, MO 65265 / 573-581-2266 FAX: 573-581-2875
"Gramps" Antique Cartridges, Box 341, Washago, ON L0K 2B0 CANADA / 705-689-5348
Granite Mountain Arms, Inc, 3145 W Hidden Acres Trail, Prescott, AZ 86305 / 520-541-9758; FAX: 520-445-6826
Grant, Howard V., Hiawatha 15, Woodruff, WI 54568 / 715-356-7146
Graphics Direct, P.O. Box 372421, Reseda, CA 91337-2421 / 818-344-9002
Graves Co., 1800 Andrews Ave., Pompano Beach, FL 33069 / 800-327-9103; FAX: 305-960-0301
Grayback Wildcats, 5306 Bryant Ave., Klamath Falls, OR 97603 / 541-884-1072
Graybill's Gun Shop, 1035 Ironville Pike, Columbia, PA 17512 / 717-684-2739
GrE-Tan Rifles, 29742 W.C.R. 50, Kersey, CO 80644 / 970-353-6176; FAX: 970-356-9133
Great American Gunstock Co., 3420 Industrial Drive, Yuba City, CA 95993 / 530-671-4570; FAX: 530-671-3906
Great Lakes Airguns, 6175 S. Park Ave, New York, NY 14075 / 716-648-6666; FAX: 716-648-5279
Green, Arthur S., 485 S. Robertson Blvd., Beverly Hills, CA 90211 / 310-274-1283
Green, Roger M., P.O. Box 984, 435 E. Birch, Glenrock, WY 82637 / 307-436-9804
Green Genie, Box 114, Cusseta, GA 31805

Green Head Game Call Co., RR 1, Box 33, Lacon, IL 61540 / 309-246-2155
Green Mountain Rifle Barrel Co., Inc., P.O. Box 2670, 153 West Main St., Conway, NH 03818 / 603-447-1095; FAX: 603-447-1099
Greenwood Precision, P.O. Box 468, Nixa, MO 65714-0468 / 417-725-2330
Greg Gunsmithing Repair, 3732 26th Ave. North, Robbinsdale, MN 55422 / 612-529-8103
Greg's Superior Products, P.O. Box 46219, Seattle, WA 98146
Greider Precision, 431 Santa Marina Ct., Escondido, CA 92029 / 619-480-8892; FAX: 619-480-9800
Gremmel Enterprises, 2111 Carriage Drive, Eugene, OR 97408-7537 / 541-302-3000
Grier's Hard Cast Bullets, 1107 11th St., LaGrande, OR 97850 / 503-963-8796
Griffin & Howe, Inc., 36 W. 44th St., Suite 1011, New York, NY 10036 / 212-921-0980
Griffin & Howe, Inc., 33 Claremont Rd., Bernardsville, NJ 07924 / 908-766-2287
Grifon, Inc., 58 Guinam St., Waltham, MS 02154
Groenewold, John, P.O. Box 830, Mundelein, IL 60060 / 847-566-2365
GRS Corp., Glendo, P.O. Box 1153, 900 Overlander St., Emporia, KS 66801 / 316-343-1084 or 800-835-3519
Grulla Armes, Apartado 453, Avda Otaloa 12, Eiber, SPAIN
Gruning Precision Inc, 7101 Jurupa Ave., No. 12, Riverside, CA 92504 / 909-689-6692 FAX: 909-689-7791
GSI, Inc., 7661 Commerce Ln., Trussville, AL 35173 / 205-655-8299
GTB, 482 Comerwood Court, San Francisco, CA 94080 / 650-583-1550
Guarasi, Robert. (See WILCOX INDUSTRIES CORP)
Guardsman Products, 411 N. Darling, Fremont, MI 49412 / 616-924-3950
Gun Accessories (See Glaser Safety Slug, Inc.), PO Box 8223, Foster City, CA 94404 / 800-221-3489; FAX: 510-785-6685
Gun City, 212 W. Main Ave., Bismarck, ND 58501 / 701-223-2304
Gun Hunter Books (See Gun Hunter Trading Co), 5075 Heisig St, Beaumont, TX 77705 / 409-835-3006
Gun Hunter Trading Co., 5075 Heisig St., Beaumont, TX 77705 / 409-835-3006
Gun Leather Limited, 116 Lipscomb, Ft. Worth, TX 76104 / 817-334-0225; FAX: 800-247-0609
Gun List (See Krause Publications), 700 E State St, Iola, WI 54945 / 715-445-2214; FAX: 715-445-4087
Gun Locker Div. of Airmold W.R. Grace & Co.-Conn., Becker Farms Ind. Park, P.O. Box 610, Roanoke Rapids, NC 27870 / 800-344-5716; FAX: 919-536-2201
Gun South, Inc. (See GSI, Inc.)
Gun Vault, 7339 E Acoma Dr., Ste. 7, Scottsdale, AZ 85260 / 602-951-6855
Gun-Alert, 1010 N. Maclay Ave., San Fernando, CA 91340 / 818-365-0864; FAX: 818-365-1308
Gun-Ho Sports Cases, 110 E. 10th St., St. Paul, MN 55101 / 612-224-9491
Guncraft Books (See Guncraft Sports Inc), 10737 Dutchtown Rd, Knoxville, TN 37932 / 423-966-4545; FAX: 423-966-4500
Guncraft Sports Inc., 10737 Dutchtown Rd., Knoxville, TN 37932 / 423-966-4545; FAX: 423-966-4500
Gunfitters, P.O. 426, Cambridge, WI 53523-0426 / 608-764-8128 gunfitters@aol.com www.gunfitters.com
Gunline Tools, 2950 Saturn St., "O", Brea, CA 92821 / 714-993-5100; FAX: 714-572-4128
Gunnerman Books, P.O. Box 217, Owosso, MI 48867 / 517-729-7018; FAX: 517-725-9391
Guns, 81 E. Streetsboro St., Hudson, OH 44236 / 330-650-4563
Guns Antique & Modern DBA/Charles E. Duffy, Williams Lane, West Hurley, NY 12491 / 914-679-2997
Guns Div. of D.C. Engineering, Inc., 8633 Southfield Fwy., Detroit, MI 48228 / 313-271-7111 or 800-886-7623; FAX: 313-271-7112
GUNS Magazine, 591 Camino de la Reina, Suite 200, San Diego, CA 92108 / 619-297-5350 FAX: 619-297-5353
Gunsite Custom Shop, P.O. Box 451, Paulden, AZ 86334 / 520-636-4104; FAX: 520-636-1236
Gunsite Gunsmithy (See Gunsite Custom Shop)
Gunsite Training Center, P.O. Box 700, Paulden, AZ 86334 / 520-636-4565; FAX: 520-636-1236
Gunsmithing Ltd., 57 Unquowa Rd., Fairfield, CT 06430 / 203-254-0436; FAX: 203-254-1535
Gunsmithing, Inc., 208 West Buchanan St., Colorado Springs, CO 80907 / 719-632-3795; FAX: 719-632-3493
Gurney, F. R., Box 13, Sooke, BC V0S 1N0 CANADA / 604-642-5282; FAX: 604-642-7859
Gwinnell, Bryson J., P.O. Box 248C, Maple Hill Rd., Rochester, VT 05767 / 802-767-3664

H

H&B Forge Co., Rt. 2, Geisinger Rd., Shiloh, OH 44878 / 419-895-1856
H&P Publishing, 7174 Hoffman Rd., San Angelo, TX 76905 / 915-655-5953
H&R 1871, Inc., 60 Industrial Rowe, Gardner, MA 01440 / 978-632-9393; FAX: 978-632-2300
H&S Liner Service, 515 E. 8th, Odessa, TX 79761 / 915-332-1021
H-S Precision, Inc., 1301 Turbine Dr., Rapid City, SD 57701 / 605-341-3006; FAX: 605-342-8964
H. Krieghoff Gun Co., Boschstrasse 22, D-89079, Ulm, GERMANY / 731-401820; FAX: 731-4018270
H.K.S. Products, 7841 Founion Dr., Florence, KY 41042 / 606-342-7841 or 800-354-9814; FAX: 606-342-5865
H.P. White Laboratory, Inc., 3114 Scarboro Rd., Street, MD 21154 / 410-838-6550; FAX: 410-838-2802
Hafner World Wide, Inc., P.O. Box 1987, Lake City, FL 32055 / 904-755-6481; FAX: 904-755-6595
Hagn Rifles & Actions, Martin, PO Box 444, Cranbrook, BC V1C 4H9 CANADA / 604-489-4861
Hakko Co. Ltd., 1-13-12, Narimasu, Itabashiku Tokyo, JAPAN / 03-5997-7870/2; FAX: 81-3-5997-7840
Hale, Engraver, Peter, 800 E Canyon Rd., Spanish Fork, UT 84660 / 801-798-8215
Half Moon Rifle Shop, 490 Halfmoon Rd., Columbia Falls, MT 59912 / 406-892-4409
Hall Manufacturing, 142 CR 406, Clanton, AL 35045 / 205-755-4094
Hall Plastics, Inc., John, P.O. Box 1526, Alvin, TX 77512 / 713-489-8709
Hallberg Gunsmith, Fritz, 532 E. Idaho Ave, Ontario, OR 97914 / 541-889-3135; FAX: 541-889-2633
Hallowell & Co., PO Box 1445, Livingston, MT 59047 / 406-222-4770 FAX: 406-222-4792 morris@hallowellco.com hallowellco.com
Hally Caller, 443 Wells Rd., Doylestown, PA 18901 / 215-345-6354
Halstead, Rick, 313 TURF ST, CARL JUNCTION, MO 64834-9658 / 918-540-0933
Hamilton, Jim, Rte. 5, Box 278, Guthrie, OK 73044 / 405-282-3634
Hamilton, Alex B (See Ten-Ring Precision, Inc)
Hammans, Charles E., P.O. Box 788, 2022 McCracken, Stuttgart, AR 72106 / 870-673-1388
Hammerli Ltd., Seonerstrasse 37, CH-5600, SWITZERLAND / 064-50 11 44; FAX: 064-51 38 27
Hammerli USA, 19296 Oak Grove Circle, Groveland, CA 95321 FAX: 209-962-5311
Hammets VLD Bullets, P.O. Box 479, Rayville, LA 71269 / 318-728-2019
Hammond Custom Guns Ltd., 619 S. Pandora, Gilbert, AZ 85234 / 602-892-3437
Hammonds Rifles, RD 4, Box 504, Red Lion, PA 17356 / 717-244-7879
HandCrafts Unltd (See Clements' Custom Leathercraft, Chas,), 1741 Dallas St, Aurora, CO 80010-2018 / 303-364-0403; FAX: 303-739-9824
Handgun Press, P.O. Box 406, Glenview, IL 60025 / 847-657-6500; FAX: 847-724-8831 jschroed@inter-access.com
Hands Engraving, Barry Lee, 26192 E Shore Route, Bigfork, MT 59911 / 406-837-0035
Hank's Gun Shop, Box 370, 50 West 100 South, Monroe, UT 84754 / 801-527-4456
Hanned Precision (See Hanned Line, The)
Hansen & Co. (See Hansen Cartridge Co.), 244-246 Old Post Rd, Southport, CT 06490 / 203-259-6222; FAX: 203-254-3832
Hanson's Gun Center, Dick, 233 Everett Dr, Colorado Springs, CO 80911
Hanus Birdguns Bill, PO Box 533, Newport, OR 97365 / 541-265-7433; FAX: 541-265-7400
Hanusin, John, 3306 Commercial, Northbrook, IL 60062 / 708-564-2706
Hardin Specialty Dist., P.O. Box 338, Radcliff, KY 40159-0338 / 502-351-6649
Harford (See U.S. Importer-EMF Co. Inc.)
Harper's Custom Stocks, 928 Lombrano St., San Antonio, TX 78207 / 210-732-5780
Harrell's Precision, 5756 Hickory Dr., Salem, VA 24133 / 703-380-2683
Harrington & Richardson (See H&R 1871, Inc.)
Harris Engineering Inc., Dept GD54, Barlow, KY 42024 / 502-334-3633 FAX: 502-334-3000
Harris Enterprises, P.O. Box 105, Bly, OR 97622 / 503-353-2625
Harris Gunworks, 20813 N. 19th Ave., PO Box 9249, Phoenix, AZ 85027 / 602-582-9627; FAX: 602-582-5178
Harris Hand Engraving, Paul A., 113 Rusty Ln, Boerne, TX 78006-5746 / 512-391-5121
Harris Publications, 1115 Broadway, New York, NY 10010 / 212-807-7100 FAX: 212-627-4678
Harrison Bullets, 6437 E. Hobart St., Mesa, AZ 85205
Harry Lawson Co., 3328 N. Richey Blvd., Tucson, AZ 85716 / 520-326-1117
Hart & Son, Inc., Robert W., 401 Montgomery St, Nescopeck, PA 18635 / 717-752-3655; FAX: 717-752-1088
Hart Rifle Barrels,Inc., P.O. Box 182, 1690 Apulia Rd., Lafayette, NY 13084 / 315-677-9841; FAX: 315-677-9610 hartrb@aol.com hartbarrels.com
Hartford (See U.S. Importer-EMF Co. Inc.)
Hartmann & Weiss GmbH, Rahlstedter Bahnhofstr. 47, 22143, Hamburg, GERMANY / (40) 677 55 85; FAX: (40) 677 55 92
Harvey, Frank, 218 Nightfall, Terrace, NV 89015 / 702-558-6998
Harwood, Jack O., 1191 S. Pendlebury Lane, Blackfoot, ID 83221 / 208-785-5368
Hastings Barrels, 320 Court St., Clay Center, KS 67432 / 913-632-3169; FAX: 913-632-6554
Hatfield Gun, 224 N. 4th St., St. Joseph, MO 64501
Hawk Laboratories, Inc. (See Hawk, Inc.), 849 Hawks Bridge Rd, Salem, NJ 08079 / 609-299-2700; FAX: 609-299-2800
Hawk, Inc., 849 Hawks Bridge Rd., Salem, NJ 08079 / 609-299-2700; FAX: 609-299-2800
Hawken Shop, The (See Dayton Traister)
Haydel's Game Calls, Inc., 5018 Hazel Jones Rd., Bossier City, LA 71111 / 800-HAYDELS; FAX: 318-746-3711
Haydon Shooters Supply, Russ, 15018 Goodrich Dr NW, Gig Harbor, WA 98329-9738 / 253-857-7557; FAX: 253-857-7884
Heatbath Corp., P.O. Box 2978, Springfield, MA 01101 / 413-543-3381
Hebard Guns, Gil, 125-129 Public Square, Knoxville, IL 61448
HEBB Resources, P.O. Box 999, Mead, WA 99021-0999 / 509-466-1292
Hecht, Hubert J, Waffen-Hecht, PO Box 2635, Fair Oaks, CA 95628 / 916-966-1020
Heckler & Koch GmbH, P.O. Box 1329, 78722 Oberndorf, Neckar, GERMANY / 49-7423179-0; FAX: 49-7423179-2406
Heckler & Koch, Inc., 21480 Pacific Blvd., Sterling, VA 20166-8900 / 703-450-1900; FAX: 703-450-8160
Hege Jagd-u. Sporthandels GmbH, P.O. Box 101461, W-7770, Ueberlingen a. Boden, GERMANY
Heidenstrom Bullets, Urdngt 1, 3937 Heroya, NORWAY
Heilmann, Stephen, P.O. Box 657, Grass Valley, CA 95945 / 530-272-8758
Heinie Specialty Products, 301 Oak St., Quincy, IL 62301-2500 / 217-228-9500; FAX: 217-228-9502 rheinie@heinie.com www.heinie.com
Hellweg Ltd., 40356 Oak Park Way, Suite W, Oakhurst, CA 93644 / 209-683-3030; FAX: 209-683-3422
Helwan (See U.S. Importer-Interarms)
Hendricks, Frank E. Inc., Master Engravers, HC 03, Box 434, Dripping Springs, TX 78620 / 512-858-7828
Henigson & Associates, Steve, PO Box 2726, Culver City, CA 90231 / 310-305-8288; FAX: 310-305-1905
Henriksen Tool Co., Inc., 8515 Wagner Creek Rd., Talent, OR 97540 / 541-535-2309 FAX: 541-535-2309
Henry Repeating Arms Co., 110 8th St., Brooklyn, NY 11215 / 718-499-5600
Hensley, Gunmaker, Darwin, PO Box 329, Brightwood, OR 97011 / 503-622-5411
Heppler, Keith. (See KEITH'S CUSTOM GUNSTOCKS)
Heppler's Machining, 2240 Calle Del Mundo, Santa Clara, CA 95054 / 408-748-9166; FAX: 408-988-7711
Heppler, Keith M, Keith's Custom Gunstocks, 540 Banyan Cir, Walnut Creek, CA 94598 / 510-934-3509; FAX: 510-934-3143
Hercules, Inc. (See Alliant Techsystems, Smokeless Powder Group)
Heritage Firearms (See Heritage Mfg., Inc.)
Heritage Manufacturing, Inc., 4600 NW 135th St., Opa Locka, FL 33054 or 305-685-5966; FAX: 305-687-6721
Heritage Wildlife Carvings, 2145 Wagner Hollow Rd., Fort Plain, NY 13339 / 518-993-3983
Heritage/VSP Gun Books, P.O. Box 887, McCall, ID 83638 / 208-634-4104; FAX: 208-634-3101
Herrett's Stocks, Inc., P.O. Box 741, Twin Falls, ID 83303 / 208-733-1498
Hertel & Reuss, Werk fr Optik und Feinmechanik GmbH, Quellhofstrasse 67, 34 127, GERMANY / 0561-83006; FAX: 0561-893308

MANUFACTURER'S DIRECTORY

Herter's Manufacturing, Inc., 111 E. Burnett St., P.O. Box 518, Beaver Dam, WI 53916 / 414-887-1765; FAX: 414-887-8444
Hesco-Meprolight, 2139 Greenville Rd., LaGrange, GA 30241 / 706-884-7967; FAX: 706-882-4683
Heydenberk, Warren R., 1059 W. Sawmill Rd., Quakertown, PA 18951 / 215-538-2682
Hi-Grade Imports, 8655 Monterey Rd., Gilroy, CA 95021 / 408-842-9301; FAX: 408-842-2374
Hi-Performance Ammunition Company, 484 State Route 366, Apollo, PA 15613 / 412-327-8100
Hi-Point Firearms, 5990 Philadelphia Dr., Dayton, OH 45415 / 513-275-4991; FAX: 513-522-8330
Hickman, Jaclyn, Box 1900, Glenrock, WY 82637
Hidalgo, Tony, 12701 SW 9th Pl., Davie, FL 33325 / 954-476-7645
High Bridge Arms, Inc, 3185 Mission St., San Francisco, CA 94110 / 415-282-8358
High North Products, Inc., P.O. Box 2, Antigo, WI 54409 / 715-627-2331 FAX: 715-623-5451
High Performance International, 5734 W. Florist Ave., Milwaukee, WI 53218 / 414-466-9040
High Standard Mfg. Co., Inc., 10606 Hempstead Hwy., Suite 116, Houston, TX 77092 / 713-462-4200, 800-467-2228
High Tech Specialties, Inc., P.O. Box 387R, Adamstown, PA 19501 / 215-484-0405 or 800-231-9385
Highline Machine Co., Randall Thompson, 654 Lela Place, Grand Junction, CO 81504 / 970-434-4971
Hill, Loring F., 304 Cedar Rd., Elkins Park, PA 19027
Hill Speed Leather, Ernie, 4507 N 195th Ave, Litchfield Park, AZ 85340 / 602-853-9222; FAX: 602-853-9235
Hines Co, S C, PO Box 423, Tijeras, NM 87059 / 505-281-3783
Hinman Outfitters, Bob, 107 N Sanderson Ave, Bartonville, IL 61607-1839 / 309-691-8132
HIP-GRIP Barami Corp., 6689 Orchard Lake Rd. No. 148, West Bloomfield, MI 48322 / 248-738-0462; FAX: 248-738-2542
Hiptmayer, Armurier, RR 112 750, P.O. Box 136, Eastman, PQ J0E 1P0 CANADA / 514-297-2492
Hiptmayer, Heidemarie, RR 112 750, P.O. Box 136, Eastman, PQ J0E 1P0 CANADA / 514-297-2492
Hiptmayer, Klaus, RR 112 750, P.O. Box 136, Eastman, PQ J0E 1P0 CANADA / 514-297-2492
Hirtenberger Aktiengesellschaft, Leobersdorferstrasse 31, A-2552, Hirtenberg, / 43(0)2256 81184; FAX: 43(0)2256 81807
HiTek International, 484 El Camino Real, Redwood City, CA 94063 / 415-363-1404 or 800-54-NIGHT FAX: 415-363-1408
Hiti-Schuch, Atelier Wilma, A-8863 Predlitz, Pirming, Y1 AUSTRIA / 0353418278
HJS Arms,Inc., P.O. Box 3711, Brownsville, TX 78523-3711 / 800-453-2767; FAX: 210-542-2767
Hoag, James W., 8523 Canoga Ave., Suite C, Canoga Park, CA 91304 / 818-998-1510
Hobson Precision Mfg. Co., 210 Big Oak Ln, Brent, AL 35034 / 205-926-4662 FAX: 205-926-3193 cahobbob@dbtech.net
Hoch Custom Bullet Moulds (See Colorado Shooter's
Hodgdon Powder Co., 6231 Robinson, Shawnee Mission, KS 66202 / 913-362-9455; FAX: 913-362-1307
Hodgman, Inc., 1750 Orchard Rd., Montgomery, IL 60538 / 708-897-7555; FAX: 708-897-7558
Hodgson, Richard, 9081 Tahoe Lane, Boulder, CO 80301
Hoehn Sales, Inc., 2045 Kohn Road, Wright City, MO 63390 / 636-745-8144; FAX: 636-745-7868 hoehnsal@usmo.com benchrestcentral.com
Hoelscher, Virgil, 8230 Hillrose St., Sunland, CA 91040-2404 / 310-631-8545
Hoenig & Rodman, 6521 Morton Dr., Boise, ID 83704 / 208-375-1116
Hofer Jagdwaffen, P., Buchsenmachermeister, Kirchgasse 24, A-9170 Ferlach, AUSTRIA
Hoffman New Ideas, 821 Northmoor Rd., Lake Forest, IL 60045 / 312-234-4075
Hogue Grips, P.O. Box 1138, Paso Robles, CA 93447 / 800-438-4747 or 805-239-1440; FAX: 805-239-2553
Holland & Holland Ltd., 33 Bruton St., London, ENGLAND / 44-171-499-4411; FAX: 44-171-408-7962
Holland's Gunsmithing, P.O. Box 69, Powers, OR 97466 / 541-439-5155; FAX: 541-439-5155
Hollinger, Jon. (See ASPEN OUTFITTING CO)
Hollis Gun Shop, 917 Rex St., Carlsbad, NM 88220 / 505-885-3782
Hollywood Engineering, 10642 Arminta St., Sun Valley, CA 91352 / 818-842-8376
Homak, 5151 W. 73rd St., Chicago, IL 60638-6613 / 312-523-3100; FAX: 312-523-9455
Home Shop Machinist The Village Press Publications, P.O. Box 1810, Traverse City, MI 49685 / 800-447-7367; FAX: 616-946-3289
Hondo Ind., 510 S. 52nd St., I04, Tempe, AZ 85281
Hoover, Harvey, 5750 Pearl Dr., Paradise, CA 95969-4829
Hoppe's Div. Penguin Industries, Inc., Airport Industrial Mall, Coatesville, PA 19320 / 610-384-6000
Horizons Unlimited, P.O. Box 426, Warm Springs, GA 31830 / 706-655-3603; FAX: 706-655-3603
Hornady Mfg. Co., P.O. Box 1848, Grand Island, NE 68802 / 800-338-3220 or 308-382-1390; FAX: 308-382-5761
Horseshoe Leather Products, Andy Arratoonian, The Cottage Sharow, Ripon, ENGLAND / 44-1765-605858
Houtz & Barwick, P.O. Box 435, W. Church St., Elizabeth City, NC 27909 / 800-775-0337 or 919-335-4191; FAX: 919-335-1152
Howa Machinery, Ltd., Sukaguchi, Shinkawa-cho Nishikasugai-gun, Aichi 452, JAPAN
Howell Machine, 815 1/2 D St., Lewiston, ID 83501 / 208-743-7418
Hoyt Holster Co., Inc., P.O. Box 69, Coupeville, WA 98239-0069 / 360-678-6640; FAX: 360-678-6549
HT Bullets, 244 Belleville Rd., New Bedford, MA 02745 / 508-999-3338
Hubert J. Hecht Waffen-Hecht, P.O. Box 2635, Fair Oaks, CA 95628 / 916-966-1020
Hubertus Schneidwarenfabrik, P.O. Box 180 106, D-42626, Solingen, GERMANY / 01149-212-59-19-94; FAX: 01149-212-59-19-92
Huebner, Corey O., P.O. Box 2074, Missoula, MT 59806-2074 / 406-721-7168
Huey Gun Cases, P.O. Box 22456, Kansas City, MO 64113 / 816-444-1637; FAX: 816-444-1637
Hugger Hooks Co., 3900 Easley Way, Golden, CO 80403 / 303-279-0600
Hughes, Steven Dodd, P.O. Box 545, Livingston, MT 59047 / 406-222-9377; FAX: 406-222-9377
Hume, Don, P.O. Box 351, Miami, OK 74355 / 800-331-2686 FAX: 918-542-4340
Hungry Horse Books, 4605 Hwy. 93 South, Whitefish, MT 59937 / 406-862-7997
Hunkeler, A (See Buckskin Machine Works, A. Hunkeler) 3235 S 358th St., Auburn, WA 98001 / 206-927-5412
Hunter Co., Inc., 3300 W. 71st Ave., Westminster, CO 80030 / 303-427-4626; FAX: 303-428-3980
Hunter's Specialties Inc., 6000 Huntington Ct. NE, Cedar Rapids, IA 52402-1268 / 319-395-0321; FAX: 319-395-0326
Hunterjohn, P.O. Box 771457, St. Louis, MO 63177 / 314-531-7250
Hunters Supply, Inc., PO Box 313, Tioga, TX 76271 / 940-437-2458; FAX: 940-437-2228 hunterssupply@hotmail.com hunterssupply.net
Hunting Classics Ltd., P.O. Box 2089, Gastonia, NC 28053 / 704-867-1307; FAX: 704-867-0491
Huntington Die Specialties, 601 Oro Dam Blvd., Oroville, CA 95965 / 530-534-1210; FAX: 530-534-1212
Hutton Rifle Ranch, P.O. Box 45236, Boise, ID 83711 / 208-345-8781
Hydrosorbent Products, P.O. Box 437, Ashley Falls, MA 01222 / 413-229-2967; or 800-229-8743 FAX: 413-229-8743 orders@dehumidify.com www.dehumidify.com
Hyper-Single, Inc., 520 E. Beaver, Jenks, OK 74037 / 918-299-2391

I

I.A.B. (See U.S. Importer-Taylor's & Co. Inc.)
I.D.S.A. Books, 1324 Stratford Drive, Piqua, OH 45356 / 937-773-4203; FAX: 937-778-1922
I.N.C. Inc (See Kick Eez)
I.S.S., P.O. Box 185234, Ft. Worth, TX 76181 / 817-595-2090
I.S.W., 106 E. Cairo Dr., Tempe, AZ 85282
IAR Inc., 33171 Camino Capistrano, San Juan Capistrano, CA 92675 / 949-443-3642; FAX: 949-443-3647
IGA (See U.S. Importer-Stoeger Industries)
Ignacio Ugartechea S.A., Chonta 26, Eibar, 20600 SPAIN / 43-121257; FAX: 43-121669
Illinois Lead Shop, 7742 W. 61st Place, Summit, IL 60501
Image Ind. Inc., 382 Balm Court, Wood Dale, IL 60191 / 630-766-2402; FAX: 630-766-7373
IMI, P.O. Box 1044, Ramat Hasharon, 47100 ISRAEL / 972-3-5485617; FAX: 972-3-5406908
IMI Services USA, Inc., 2 Wisconsin Circle, Suite 420, Chevy Chase, MD 20815 / 301-215-4800; FAX: 301-657-1446
Impact Case Co., P.O. Box 9912, Spokane, WA 99209-0912 / 800-262-3322 or 509-467-3303; FAX: 509-326-5436 kkair.com
Imperial (See E-Z-Way Systems), PO Box 4310, Newark, OH 43058-4310 / 614-345-6645; FAX: 614-345-6600
Imperial Magnum Corp., P.O. Box 249, Oroville, WA 98844 / 604-495-3131; FAX: 604-495-2816
Imperial Miniature Armory, 10547 S. Post Oak, Houston, TX 77035 / 713-729-8428 FAX: 713-729-2274
Imperial Schrade Corp., 7 Schrade Ct., Box 7000, Ellenville, NY 12428 / 914-647-7601; FAX: 914-647-8701
Import Sports Inc., 1750 Brielle Ave., Unit B1, Wanamassa, NJ 07712 / 908-493-0302; FAX: 908-493-0301
IMR Powder Co., 1080 Military Turnpike, Suite 2, Plattsburgh, NY 12901 / 518-563-2253; FAX: 518-563-6916
Info-Arm, P.O. Box 1262, Champlain, NY 12919 / 514-955-0355; FAX: 514-955-0357
Ingle, Ralph W., Engraver, 112 Manchester Ct., Centerville, GA 31028 / 912-953-5824
Innovative Weaponry Inc., 2513 E. Loop 820 N., Fort Worth, TX 76118 / 817-284-0099; or 800-334-3573
Innovision Enterprises, 728 Skinner Dr., Kalamazoo, MI 49001 / 616-382-1681 FAX: 616-382-1830
INTEC International, Inc., P.O. Box 5708, Scottsdale, AZ 85261 / 602-483-1708
Inter Ordnance of America LP, 3305 Westwood Industrial Dr, Monroe, NC 28110-5204 / 704-821-8337; FAX: 704-821-8523
Intercontinental Distributors, Ltd., PO Box 815, Beulah, ND 58523
Intrac Arms International, 5005 Chapman Hwy., Knoxville, TN 37920
Intratec, 12405 SW 130th St., Miami, FL 33186-6224 / 305-232-1821; FAX: 305-253-7207
Ion Industries, Inc, 3508 E Allerton Ave, Cudahy, WI 53110 / 414-486-2007; FAX: 414-486-2017
Iosso Products, 1485 Lively Blvd., Elk Grove Village, IL 60007 / 847-437-8400; FAX: 847-437-8478
Iron Bench, 12619 Bailey Rd., Redding, CA 96003 / 916-241-4623
Ironside International Publishers, Inc., P.O. Box 55, 800 Slaters Lane, Alexandria, VA 22313 / 703-684-6111; FAX: 703-683-5486
Ironsighter Co., P.O. Box 85070, Westland, MI 48185 / 734-326-8731; FAX: 734-326-3378
Irwin, Campbell H., 140 Hartland Blvd., East Hartland, CT 06027 / 203-653-3901
Island Pond Gun Shop, Cross St., Island Pond, VT 05846 / 802-723-4546
Israel Arms International, Inc., 5709 Hartsdale, Houston, TX 77036 / 713-789-0745; FAX: 713-789-7513
Israel Military Industries Ltd. (See IMI), PO Box 1044, Ramat Hasharon, ISRAEL / 972-3-5485617; FAX: 972-3-5406908
Ithaca Classic Doubles, Stephen Lamboy, PO Box 665, Mendon, NY 14506 / 706-569-6760; FAX: 706-561-9248
Ithaca Gun Co. LLC, 891 Route 34-B, King Ferry, NY 13081 / 888-9ITHACA; FAX: 315-364-5134
Ivanoff, Thomas G (See Tom's Gun Repair)

J

J J Roberts Firearm Engraver, 7808 Lake Dr, Manassas, VA 20111 / 703-330-0448 FAX: 703-264-8600
J Martin Inc, PO Drawer AP, Beckley, WV 25802 / 304-255-4073; FAX: 304-255-4077
J&D Components, 75 East 350 North, Orem, UT 84057-4719 / 801-225-7007
J&J Products, Inc., 9240 Whitmore, El Monte, CA 91731 / 818-571-5228; FAX: 800-927-8361
J&J Sales, 1501 21st Ave. S., Great Falls, MT 59405 / 406-453-7549
J&L Superior Bullets (See Huntington Die Specialties)
J&R Engineering, P.O. Box 77, 200 Lyons Hill Rd., Athol, MA 01331 / 508-249-9241
J&R Enterprises, 4550 Scotts Valley Rd., Lakeport, CA 95453
J&S Heat Treat, 803 S. 16th St., Blue Springs, MO 64015 / 816-229-2149; FAX: 816-228-1135
J-4 Inc., 1700 Via Burton, Anaheim, CA 92806 / 714-254-8315; FAX: 714-956-4421
J-Gar Co., 183 Turnpike Rd., Dept. 3, Petersham, MA 01366-9604
J. Dewey Mfg. Co., Inc., P.O. Box 2014, Southbury, CT 06488 / 203-264-3064; FAX: 203-262-6907
J. Korzinek Riflesmith, RD 2, Box 73D, Canton, PA 17724 / 717-673-8512
J.A. Blades, Inc. (See Christopher Firearms Co.,)
J.A. Henckels Zwillingswerk Inc., 9 Skyline Dr., Hawthorne, NY 10532 / 914-592-7370
J.G. Dapkus Co., Inc., Commerce Circle, P.O. Box 293, Durham, CT 06422
J.I.T. Ltd., P.O. Box 230, Freedom, WY 83120 / 708-494-0937
J.J. Roberts/Engraver, 7808 Lake Dr., Manassas, VA 22111 / 703-330-0448

MANUFACTURER'S DIRECTORY

J.M. Bucheimer Jumbo Sports Products, 721 N. 20th St., St. Louis, MO 63103 / 314-241-1020
J.P. Enterprises Inc., P.O. Box 26324, Shoreview, MN 55126 / 612-486-9064; FAX: 612-482-0970
J.P. Gunstocks, Inc., 4508 San Miguel Ave., North Las Vegas, NV 89030 / 702-645-0718
J.R. Blair Engraving, P.O. Box 64, Glenrock, WY 82637 / 307-436-8115
J.R. Williams Bullet Co., 2008 Tucker Rd., Perry, GA 31069 / 912-987-0274
J.W. Morrison Custom Rifles, 4015 W. Sharon, Phoenix, AZ 85029 / 602-978-3754
J/B Adventures & Safaris Inc., 2275 E. Arapahoe Rd., Ste. 109, Littleton, CO 80122-1521 / 303-771-0977
Jack Dever Co., 8590 NW 90, Oklahoma City, OK 73132 / 405-721-6393
Jack A. Rosenberg & Sons, 12229 Cox Ln., Dallas, TX 75234 / 214-241-6302
Jack First, Inc., 1201 Turbine Dr., Rapid City, SD 57701 / 605-343-9544; FAX: 605-343-9420
Jackalope Gun Shop, 1048 S. 5th St., Douglas, WY 82633 / 307-358-3441
Jaffin, Harry. (See BRIDGEMAN PRODUCTS)
Jagdwaffen, P. Hofer, Buchsenmachermeister, Kirchgasse 24 A-9170, Ferlach, AUSTRIA / 04227-3683
James Calhoon Varmint Bullets, Shambo Rt., 304, Havre, MT 59501 / 406-395-4079
James Churchill Glove Co., P.O. Box 298, Centralia, WA 98531
James Calhoon Mfg., Rt. 304, Havre, MT 59501 / 406-395-4079
James Wayne Firearms for Collectors and Investors, 2608 N. Laurent, Victoria, TX 77901 / 512-578-1258; FAX: 512-578-3559
Jamison's Forge Works, 4527 Rd. 6.5 NE, Moses Lake, WA 98837 / 509-762-2659
Jantz Supply, P.O. Box 584-GD, Davis, OK 73030-0584 / 580-369-2316; FAX: 580-369-3082
Jarrett Rifles, Inc., 383 Brown Rd., Jackson, SC 29831 / 803-471-3616
Jarvis, Inc., 1123 Cherry Orchard Lane, Hamilton, MT 59840 / 406-961-4392
JAS, Inc., P.O. Box 0, Rosemount, MN 55068 / 612-890-7631
Javelina Lube Products, P.O. Box 337, San Bernardino, CA 92402 / 714-882-5847; FAX: 714-434-6937
JB Custom, P.O. Box 6912, Leawood, KS 66206 / 913-381-2329
Jeff W. Flannery Engraving Co., 11034 Riddles Run Rd., Union, KY 41091 / 606-384-3127
Jeffredo Gunsight, P.O. Box 669, San Marcos, CA 92079 / 619-728-2695
Jena Eur, PO Box 319, Dunmore, PA 18512
Jenco Sales, Inc., P.O. Box 1000, Manchaca, TX 78652 / 800-531-5301 FAX: 800-266-2373
Jenkins Recoil Pads, Inc., 5438 E. Frontage Ln., Olney, IL 62450 / 618-395-3416
Jensen Bullets, 86 North, 400 West, Blackfoot, ID 83221 / 208-785-5590
Jensen's Custom Ammunition, 5146 E. Pima, Tucson, AZ 85712 / 602-325-3346 FAX: 602-322-5704
Jensen's Firearms Academy, 1280 W. Prince, Tucson, AZ 85705 / 602-293-8516
Jericho Tool & Die Co., Inc., RD 3 Box 70, Route 7, Bainbridge, NY 13733-9496 / 607-563-8222; FAX: 607-563-8560
Jerry Phillips Optics, P.O. Box L632, Langhorne, PA 19047 / 215-757-5037 FAX: 215-757-7097
Jesse W. Smith Saddlery, 16909 E. Jackson Road, Elk, WA 99009-9600 / 509-325-0622
Jester Bullets, Rt. 1 Box 27, Orienta, OK 73737
Jewell Triggers, Inc., 3620 Hwy. 123, San Marcos, TX 78666 / 512-353-2999
JGS Precision Tool Mfg., 100 Main Sumner, Coos Bay, OR 97420 / 541-267-4331 FAX: 541-267-5996
Jim Chambers Flintlocks Ltd., Rt. 1, Box 513-A, Candler, NC 28715 / 704-667-8361
Jim Garthwaite Pistolsmith, Inc., Rt. 2 Box 310, Watsontown, PA 17777 / 717-538-1566
Jim Noble Co., 1305 Columbia St, Vancouver, WA 98660 / 360-695-1309; FAX: 360-695-6835 jnoble-co@aol.com
Jim Norman Custom Gunstocks, 14281 Cane Rd, Valley Center, CA 92082 / 619-749-6252
Jim's Gun Shop (See Spradlin's)
Jim's Precision, Jim Ketchum, 1725 Moclips Dr., Petaluma, CA 94952 / 707-762-3014
JLK Bullets, 414 Turner Rd., Dover, AR 72837 / 501-331-4194
Johanssons Vapentillbehor, Bert, S-430 20, Veddige, SWEDEN
John Hall Plastics, Inc., Inc., P.O. Box 1526, Alvin, TX 77512 / 713-489-8709
John J. Adams & Son Engravers, PO Box 66, Vershire, VT 05079 / 802-685-0019
John Masen Co. Inc., 1305 Jelmak, Grand Prairie, TX 75050 / 817-430-8732; FAX: 817-430-1715
John Norrell Arms, 2608 Grist Mill Rd, Little Rock, AR 72207 / 501-225-7864
John Partridge Sales Ltd., Trent Meadows Rugeley, Staffordshire, WS15 2HS ENGLAND
John Rigby & Co., 1317 Spring St., Paso Robles, CA 93446 / 805-227-4236; FAX: 805-227-4723
John Unertl Optical Co., Inc., 308-310 Clay Ave., Mars, PA 16046-0818 / 724-625-3810
John's Custom Leather, 523 S. Liberty St., Blairsville, PA 15717 / 412-459-6802
Johnny Stewart Game Calls, Inc., P.O. Box 7954, 5100 Fort Ave., Waco, TX 76714 / 817-772-3261; FAX: 817-772-3670
Johnson Wood Products, 34968 Crystal Road, Strawberry Point, IA 52076 / 319-933-4930
Johnson's Gunsmithing, Inc, Neal, 208 W Buchanan St, Ste B, Colorado Springs, CO 80907 / 800-284-8671; FAX: 719-632-3493
Johnston Bros. (See C&T Corp. TA Johnson Brothers)
Johnston, James (See North Fork Custom Gunsmithing, James Johnston)
Jonad Corp., 2091 Lakeland Ave., Lakewood, OH 44107 / 216-226-3161
Jonathan Arthur Ciener, Inc., 8700 Commerce St., Cape Canaveral, FL 32920 / 407-868-2200; FAX: 407-868-2201
Jones Co., Dale, 680 Hoffman Draw, Kila, MT 59920 / 406-755-4684
Jones Custom Products, Neil A., 17217 Brookhouser Rd., Saegertown, PA 16433 / 814-763-2769; FAX: 814-763-4228
Jones Moulds, Paul, 4901 Telegraph Rd, Los Angeles, CA 90022 / 213-262-1510
Jones, J.D./SSK Industries, 590 Woodvue Ln., Wintersville, OH 43953 / 740-264-0176; FAX: 740-264-2257
JP Sales, Box 307, Anderson, TX 77830
JRP Custom Bullets, RR2 2233 Carlton Rd., Whitehall, NY 12887 / 518-282-0084 or 802-438-5548
JS Worldwide DBA (See Coonan Arms)
JSL Ltd (See U.S. Importer-Specialty Shooters Supply, Inc.)
Juenke, Vern, 25 Bitterbush Rd., Reno, NV 89523 / 702-345-0225
Jumbo Sports Products, J. M. Bucheimer, 721 N. 20th St., St. Louis, MO 63103 / 314-241-1020
Jungkind, Reeves C., 5001 Buckskin Pass, Austin, TX 78745-2841 / 512-442-1094
Jurras, L. E., P.O. Box 680, Washington, IN 47501 / 812-254-7698
Justin Phillippi Custom Bullets, P.O. Box 773, Ligonier, PA 15658 / 412-238-9671

K

K&M Industries, Inc., Box 66, 510 S. Main, Troy, ID 83871 / 208-835-2281; FAX: 208-835-5211
K&M Services, 5430 Salmon Run Rd., Dover, PA 17315 / 717-292-3175; FAX: 717-292-3175
K-D, Inc., Box 459, 585 N. Hwy. 155, Cleveland, UT 84518 / 801-653-2530
K-Sports Imports Inc., 2755 Thompson Creek Rd., Pomona, CA 91767 / 909-392-2345 FAX: 909-392-2354
K. Eversull Co., Inc., 1 Tracemont, Boyce, LA 71409 / 318-793-8728
K.B.I. Inc, PO Box 6625, Harrisburg, PA 17112 / 717-540-8518; FAX: 717-540-8567
K.K. Arms Co., Star Route Box 671, Kerrville, TX 78028 / 210-257-4718 FAX: 210-257-4891
K.L. Null Holsters Ltd., 161 School St. NW, Hill City Station, Resaca, GA 30735 / 706-625-5643; FAX: 706-625-9392
Ka Pu Kapili, P.O. Box 745, Honokaa, HI 96727 / 808-776-1644; FAX: 808-776-1731
KA-BAR Knives, 1116 E. State St., Olean, NY 14760 / 800-282-0130; FAX: 716-373-6245
Kahles A Swarovski Company, 1 Wholesale Way, Cranston, RI 02920-5540 / 401-946-2220; FAX: 401-946-2587
Kahr Arms, P.O. Box 220, 630 Route 303, Blauvelt, NY 10913 / 914-353-5996; FAX: 914-353-7833
Kalispel Case Line, P.O. Box 267, Cusick, WA 99119 / 509-445-1121
Kamik Outdoor Footwear, 554 Montee de Liesse, Montreal, PQ H4T 1P1 CANADA / 514-341-3950; FAX: 514-341-1861
Kamyk Engraving Co., Steve, 9 Grandview Dr, Westfield, MA 01085-1810 / 413-568-0457
Kane, Edward, P.O. Box 385, Ukiah, CA 95482 / 707-462-2937
Kane Products, Inc., 5572 Brecksville Rd., Cleveland, OH 44131 / 216-524-9962
Kapro Mfg.Co. Inc. (See R.E.I.)
Kasenit Co., Inc., 13 Park Ave., Highland Mills, NY 10930 / 914-928-9595; FAX: 914-928-7292
Kasmarsik Bullets, 4016 7th Ave. SW, Puyallup, WA 98373
Kaswer Custom, Inc., 13 Surrey Drive, Brookfield, CT 06804 / 203-775-0564; FAX: 203-775-6872
KDF, Inc., 2485 Hwy. 46 N., Seguin, TX 78155 / 210-379-8141; FAX: 210-379-5420
KeeCo Impressions, Inc., 346 Wood Ave., North Brunswick, NJ 08902 / 800-468-0546
Keeler, R. H., 817 "N" St., Port Angeles, WA 98362 / 206-457-4702
Kehr, Roger, 2131 Agate Ct. SE, Lacy, WA 98503 / 360-456-0831
Keith's Bullets, 942 Twisted Oak, Algonquin, IL 60102 / 708-658-3520
Keith's Custom Gunstocks (See Heppler, Keith M)
Keith's Custom Gunstocks, Keith M Heppler, 540 Banyan Circle, Walnut Creek, CA 94598 / 925-934-3509; FAX: 925-934-3143
Kel-Tec CNC Industries, Inc., P.O. Box 3427, Cocoa, FL 32924 / 407-631-0068; FAX: 407-631-1169
Kelbly, Inc., 7222 Dalton Fox Lake Rd., North Lawrence, OH 44666 / 216-683-4674; FAX: 216-683-7349
Kelley's, P.O. Box 125, Woburn, MA 01801 / 617-935-3389
Kellogg's Professional Products, 325 Pearl St., Sandusky, OH 44870 / 419-625-6551; FAX: 419-625-6167
Kelly, Lance, 1723 Willow Oak Dr., Edgewater, FL 32132 / 904-423-4933
Kemen America, 2550 Hwy. 23, Wrenshall, MN 55797
Ken Eyster Heritage Gunsmiths, Inc., 6441 Bishop Rd., Centerburg, OH 43011 / 614-625-6131
Ken Starnes Gunmaker, 15940 SW Holly Hill Rd, Hillsboro, OR 97123-9033 / 503-628-0705; FAX: 503-628-6005
Ken's Gun Specialties, Rt. 1, Box 147, Lakeview, AR 72642 / 501-431-5606
Ken's Kustom Kartridges, 331 Jacobs Rd., Hubbard, OH 44425 / 216-534-4595
Ken's Rifle Blanks, Ken McCullough, Rt. 2, P.O. Box 85B, Weston, OR 97886 / 503-566-3879
Keng's Firearms Specialty, Inc./US Tactical Systems, 875 Wharton Dr., P.O. Box 44405, Atlanta, GA 30336-1405 / 404-691-7611; FAX: 404-505-8445
Kennebec Journal, 274 Western Ave., Augusta, ME 04330 / 207-622-6288
Kennedy Firearms, 10 N. Market St., Muncy, PA 17756 / 717-546-6695
Kenneth W. Warren Engraver, P.O. Box 2842, Wenatchee, WA 98807 / 509-663-6123 FAX: 509-665-6123
KenPatable Ent., Inc., P.O. Box 19422, Louisville, KY 40259 / 502-239-5447
Kent Cartridge America, Inc, PO Box 849, 1000 Zigor Rd, Kearneysville, WV 25430
Kent Cartridge Mfg. Co. Ltd., Unit 16 Branbridges Industrial Esta, Tonbridge, Kent, ENGLAND / 622-872255; FAX: 622-872645
Keowee Game Calls, 608 Hwy. 25 North, Travelers Rest, SC 29690 / 864-834-7204; FAX: 864-834-7831
Kershaw Knives, 25300 SW Parkway Ave., Wilsonville, OR 97070 / 503-682-1966 or 800-325-2891; FAX: 503-682-7168
Kesselring Gun Shop, 400 Hwy. 99 North, Burlington, WA 98233 / 206-724-3113; FAX: 206-724-7003
Ketchum, Jim (See Jim's Precision)
Kickeez Inc, 301 Industrial Dr, Carl Junction, MO 64834-8806 / 419-649-2100; FAX: 417-649-2200 kickey@ipa.net
Kilham & Co., Main St., P.O. Box 37, Lyme, NH 03768 / 603-795-4112
Kim Ahrends Custom Firearms, Inc., Box 203, Clarion, IA 50525 / 515-532-3449; FAX: 515-532-3926
Kimar (See U.S. Importer-IAR,Inc)
Kimball, Gary, 1526 N. Circle Dr., Colorado Springs, CO 80909 / 719-634-1274
Kimber of America, Inc., 1 Lawton St., Yonkers, NY 10705 / 800-880-2418; FAX: 914-964-9340
King & Co., P.O. Box 1242, Bloomington, IL 61702 / 309-473-2161
King's Gun Works, 1837 W. Glenoaks Blvd., Glendale, CA 91201 / 818-956-6010; FAX: 818-548-8606
Kingyon, Paul L. (See Custom Calls)
Kirkpatrick Leather Co., PO Box 677, Laredo, TX 78040 / 956-723-6631; FAX: 956-725-0672
KK Air International (See Impact Case Co.)
KLA Enterprises, P.O. Box 2028, Eaton Park, FL 33840 / 941-682-2829 FAX: 941-682-2829

MANUFACTURER'S DIRECTORY

Kleen-Bore,Inc., 16 Industrial Pkwy., Easthampton, MA 01027 / 413-527-0300; FAX: 413-527-2522 info@kleen-bore.com www.kleen-bore.com
Klein Custom Guns, Don, 433 Murray Park Dr, Ripon, WI 54971 / 920-748-2931
Kleinendorst, K. W., RR 1, Box 1500, Hop Bottom, PA 18824 / 717-289-4687
Klingler Woodcarving, P.O. Box 141, Thistle Hill, Cabot, VT 05647 / 802-426-3811
Kmount, P.O. Box 19422, Louisville, KY 40259 / 502-239-5447
Kneiper, James, P.O. Box 1516, Basalt, CO 81621-1516 / 303-963-9880
Knife Importers, Inc., P.O. Box 1000, Manchaca, TX 78652 / 512-282-6860
Knight & Hale Game Calls, Box 468, Industrial Park, Cadiz, KY 42211 / 502-924-1755; FAX: 502-924-1763
Knight Rifles, 21852 hwy j46, P.O. Box 130, Centerville, IA 52544 / 515-856-2626; FAX: 515-856-2628
Knight Rifles (See Modern Muzzle Loading, Inc.)
Knight's Mfg. Co., 7750 9th St. SW, Vero Beach, FL 32968 / 561-562-5697; FAX: 561-569-2955
Knippel, Richard, 500 Gayle Ave Apt 213, Modesto, CA 95350-4241 / 209-869-1469
Knock on Wood Antiques, 355 Post Rd., Darien, CT 06820 / 203-655-9031
Knoell, Doug, 9737 McCardle Way, Santee, CA 92071
Koevenig's Engraving Service, Box 55 Rabbit Gulch, Hill City, SD 57745 / 605-574-2239
KOGOT, 410 College, Trinidad, CO 81082 / 719-846-9406 FAX: 719-846-9406
Kokolus, Michael M. (See Custom Riflestocks, Inc., Michael M. Kokolus)
Kolar, 1925 Roosevelt Ave, Racine, WI 53406 / 414-554-0800; FAX: 414-554-9093
Kolpin Mfg., Inc., P.O. Box 107, 205 Depot St., Fox Lake, WI 53933 / 414-928-3118; FAX: 414-928-3687
Korth, Robert-Bosch-Str. 4, P.O. Box 1320, 23909 Ratzeburg, GERMANY / 451-4991497; FAX: 451-4993230
Korzinek Riflesmith, J, RD 2 Box 73D, Canton, PA 17724 / 717-673-8512
Koval Knives, 5819 Zarley St., Suite A, New Albany, OH 43054 / 614-855-0777; FAX: 614-855-0945
Kowa Optimed, Inc., 20001 S. Vermont Ave., Torrance, CA 90502 / 310-327-1913; FAX: 310-327-4177
Kramer Designs, P.O. Box 129, Clancy, MT 59634 / 406-933-8658; FAX: 406-933-8658
Kramer Handgun Leather, P.O. Box 112154, Tacoma, WA 98411 / 206-564-6652; FAX: 206-564-1214
Krause Publications, Inc., 700 E. State St., Iola, WI 54990 / 715-445-2214; FAX: 715-445-4087
Krico Jagd-und Sportwaffen GmbH, Nurnbergerstrasse 6, D-90602, Pyrbaum, GERMANY / 09180-2780; FAX: 09180-2661
Krieger Barrels, Inc., N114 W18697 Clinton Dr., Germantown, WI 53022 / 414-255-9593; FAX: 414-255-9586
Krieghoff Gun Co., H., Boschstrasse 22, D-89079 Elm, GERMANY or 731-4018270
Krieghoff International,Inc., 7528 Easton Rd., Ottsville, PA 18942 / 610-847-5173; FAX: 610-847-8691
Kris Mounts, 108 Lehigh St., Johnstown, PA 15905 / 814-539-9751
KSN Industries Ltd (See U.S. Importer-Israel Arms International, Inc.,)
Kudlas, John M., 622 14th St. SE, Rochester, MN 55904 / 507-288-5579
Kulis Freeze Dry Taxidermy, 725 Broadway Ave., Bedford, OH 44146 / 216-232-8352; FAX: 216-232-7305 jkulis@kastaway.com
KVH Industries, Inc., 110 Enterprise Center, Middletown, RI 02842 / 401-847-3327; FAX: 401-849-0045
Kwik Mount Corp., P.O. Box 19422, Louisville, KY 40259 / 502-239-5447
Kwik-Site Co., 5555 Treadwell, Wayne, MI 48184 / 734-326-1500; FAX: 734-326-4120

L

L&R Lock Co., 1137 Pocalla Rd., Sumter, SC 29150 / 803-775-6127 FAX: 803-775-5171
L&S Technologies Inc (See Aimtech Mount Systems)
L. Bengtson Arms Co., 6345-B E. Akron St., Mesa, AZ 85205 / 602-981-6375
L.A.R. Mfg., Inc., 4133 W. Farm Rd., West Jordan, UT 84088 / 801-280-3505; FAX: 801-280-1972
L.E. Wilson, Inc., Box 324, 404 Pioneer Ave., Cashmere, WA 98815 / 509-782-1328; FAX: 509-782-7200
L.L. Bean, Inc., Freeport, ME 04032 / 207-865-4761; FAX: 207-552-2802
L.P.A. Snc, Via Alfieri 26, Gardone V.T., Brescia, ITALY / 30-891-14-81; FAX: 30-891-09-51
L.R. Clift Mfg., 3821 Hammonton Rd., Marysville, CA 95901 / 916-755-3390; FAX: 916-755-3393
L.S. Starrett Co., 121 Crescent St., Athol, MA 01331 / 617-249-3551
L.W. Seecamp Co., Inc., P.O. Box 255, New Haven, CT 06502 / 203-877-3429
La Clinique du .45, 1432 Rougemont, Chambly,, PQ J3L 2L8 CANADA / 514-658-1144
Labanu, Inc., 2201-F Fifth Ave., Ronkonkoma, NY 11779 / 516-467-6197; FAX: 516-981-4112
LaBoone, Pat. (See CLEAR CREEK OUTDOORS)
LaBounty Precision Reboring, Inc, 7968 Silver Lake Rd., PO Box 186, Maple Falls, WA 98266 / 360-599-2047 FAX: 360-599-3018
LaCrosse Footwear, Inc., P.O. Box 1328, La Crosse, WI 54602 / 608-782-3020 or 800-323-2668; FAX: 800-658-9444
LaFrance Specialties, P.O. Box 87933, San Diego, CA 92138-7933 / 619-293-3373; FAX: 619-293-7087
Lage Uniwad, P.O. Box 2302, Davenport, IA 52809 / 319-388-LAGE; FAX: 319-388-LAGE
Lair, Sam, 520 E. Beaver, Jenks, OK 74037 / 918-299-2391
Lake Center, P.O. Box 38, St. Charles, MO 63302 / 314-946-7500
Lakefield Arms Ltd (See Savage Arms Inc)
Lakewood Products LLC, 275 June St., Berlin, WI 54923 / 800-872-8458; FAX: 920-361-7719
Lamboy, Stephen. (See ITHACA CLASSIC DOUBLES)
Lampert, Ron, Rt. 1, Box 177, Guthrie, MN 56461 / 218-854-7345
Lamson & Goodnow Mfg. Co., 45 Conway St., Shelburne Falls, MA 03170 / 413-625-6564; or 800-872-6564 FAX: 413-625-9816 www.lamsonsharp.com
Lanber Armas, S.A., Zubiaurre 5, Zaldibar, 48250 SPAIN / 34-4-6827702; FAX: 34-4-6827999
Langenberg Hat Co., P.O. Box 1860, Washington, MO 63090 / 800-428-1860; FAX: 314-239-3151
Lanphert, Paul, P.O. Box 1985, Wenatchee, WA 98807
Lansky Levine, Arthur. (See LANSKY SHARPENERS)
Lansky Sharpeners, Arthur Lansky Levine, PO Box 50830, Las Vegas, NV 89016 / 702-361-7511; FAX: 702-896-9511
Lapua Ltd., P.O. Box 5, Lapua, FINLAND / 6-310111; FAX: 6-4388991
LaRocca Gun Works, 51 Union Place, Worcester, MA 01608 / 508-754-2887; FAX: 508-754-2887
Larry Lyons Gunworks, 110 Hamilton St., Dowagiac, MI 49047 / 616-782-9478
Laser Devices, Inc., 2 Harris Ct. A-4, Monterey, CA 93940 / 408-373-0701; FAX: 408-373-0903
Laseraim Technologies, Inc., P.O. Box 3548, Little Rock, AR 72203 / 501-375-2227
LaserMax, Inc., 3495 Winton Place, Bldg. B, Rochester, NY 14623-2807 / 800-527-3703 FAX: 716-272-5427
Lassen Community College, Gunsmithing Dept., P.O. Box 3000, Hwy. 139, Susanville, CA 96130 / 916-251-8800; FAX: 916-251-8838
Lathrop's, Inc., Inc., 5146 E. Pima, Tucson, AZ 85712 / 520-881-0266 or 800-875-4867; FAX: 520-322-5704
Laughridge, William R (See Cylinder & Slide Inc)
Laurel Mountain Forge, P.O. Box 52, Crown Point, IN 48065 / 219-548-2950; FAX: 219-548-2950
Laurona Armas Eibar, S.A.L., Avenida de Otaola 25, P.O. Box 260, Eibar 20600, SPAIN / 34-43-700600; FAX: 34-43-700616
Lawrence Brand Shot (See Precision Reloading, Inc.)
Lawrence Leather Co., P.O. Box 1479, Lillington, NC 27546 / 910-893-2071; FAX: 910-893-4742
Lawson Co., Harry, 3328 N Richey Blvd., Tucson, AZ 85716 / 520-326-1117 FAX: 520-326-1117
Lawson, John. (See THE SIGHT SHOP)
Lawson, John G (See Sight Shop, The)
Lazzeroni Arms Co., PO Box 26696, Tucson, AZ 85726 / 888-492-7247; FAX: 520-624-4250
LBT, HCR 62, Box 145, Moyie Springs, ID 83845 / 208-267-3588
Le Clear Industries (See E-Z-Way Systems), PO Box 4310, Newark, OH 43058-4310 / 614-345-6645; FAX: 614-345-6600
Lea Mfg. Co., 237 E. Aurora St., Waterbury, CT 06720 / 203-753-5116
Leapers, Inc., 7675 Five Mile Rd., Northville, MI 48167 / 248-486-1231; FAX: 248-486-1430
Leatherman Tool Group, Inc., 12106 NE Ainsworth Cir., P.O. Box 20595, Portland, OR 97294 / 503-253-7826; FAX: 503-253-7830
Lebeau-Courally, Rue St. Gilles, 386 4000, Liege, BELGIUM / 042-52-48-43; FAX: 32-042-52-20-08
Leckie Professional Gunsmithing, 546 Quarry Rd., Ottsville, PA 18942 / 215-847-8594
Lectro Science, Inc., 6410 W. Ridge Rd., Erie, PA 16506 / 814-833-6487; FAX: 814-833-0447
Ledbetter Airguns, Riley, 1804 E Sprague St, Winston Salem, NC 27107-3521 / 919-784-0676
Lee Co., T. K., 1282 Branchwater Ln, Birmingham, AL 35216 / 205-913-5222
Lee Precision, Inc., 4275 Hwy. U, Hartford, WI 53027 / 414-673-3075; FAX: 414-673-9273 leeprecision.com
Lee Supplies, Mark, 9901 France Ct., Lakeville, MN 55044 / 612-461-2114
Lee's Red Ramps, 4 Kristine Ln., Silver City, NM 88061 / 505-538-8529
LeFever Arms Co., Inc., 6234 Stokes, Lee Center Rd., Lee Center, NY 13363 / 315-337-6722; FAX: 315-337-1543
Legacy Sports International, 10 Prince St., Alexandria, VA 22314 / 703-548-4837
Legend Products Corp., 21218 Saint Andrews Blvd., Boca Raton, FL 33433-2435
Leibowitz, Leonard, 1205 Murrayhill Ave., Pittsburgh, PA 15217 / 412-361-5455
Leica USA, Inc., 156 Ludlow Ave., Northvale, NJ 07647 / 201-767-7500; FAX: 201-767-8666
LEM Gun Specialties Inc. The Lewis Lead Remover, P.O. Box 2855, Peachtree City, GA 30269-2024
Leonard Day, 6 Linseed Rd Box 1, West Hatfield, MA 01088-7505 / 413-337-8369
Les Baer Custom,Inc., 29601 34th Ave., Hillsdale, IL 61257 / 309-658-2716; FAX: 309-658-2610
Lestrom Laboratories, Inc., P.O. Box 628, Mexico, NY 13114-0628 / 315-343-3076; FAX: 315-592-3370
Lethal Force Institute (See Police Bookshelf), PO Box 122, Concord, NH 03301 / 603-224-6814; FAX: 603-226-3554
Lett Custom Grips, 672 Currier Rd., Hopkinton, NH 03229-2652 / 800-421-5388 FAX: 603-226-4580
Leupold & Stevens, Inc., 14400 NW Greenbrier Pky., Beaverton, OR 97006 / 503-646-9171; FAX: 503-526-1455
Lever Arms Service Ltd., 2131 Burrard St., Vancouver, BC V6J 3H7 CANADA / 604-736-2711; FAX: 604-738-3503
Lew Horton Dist. Co., Inc., 15 Walkup Dr., Westboro, MA 01581 / 508-366-7400; FAX: 508-366-5332
Liberty Metals, 2233 East 16th St., Los Angeles, CA 90021 / 213-581-9171; FAX: 213-581-9351
Liberty Safe, 1060 N. Spring Creek Pl., Springville, UT 84663 / 800-247-5625; FAX: 801-489-6409
Liberty Shooting Supplies, P.O. Box 357, Hillsboro, OR 97123 / 503-640-5518; FAX: 503-640-5518
Liberty Trouser Co., 3500 6 Ave S., Birmingham, AL 35222-2406 / 205-251-9143
Lightfield Ammunition Corp. (See Slug Group, Inc.), PO Box 376, New Paris, PA 15554 / 814-839-4517; FAX: 814-839-2601
Lightforce U.S.A. Inc., 19226 66th Ave. So., L-103, Kent, WA 98032 / 206-656-1577; FAX: 206-656-1578
Lightning Performance Innovations, Inc., RD1 Box 555, Mohawk, NY 13407 / 800-242-5873; FAX: 315-866-1578
Lilja Precision Rifle Barrels, P.O. Box 372, Plains, MT 59859 / 406-826-3084; FAX: 406-826-3083 lilja@riflebarrels.com www.riflebarrel.com
Lincoln, Dean, Box 1886, Farmington, NM 87401
Lind Custom Guns, Al, 7821 76th Ave SW, Tacoma, WA 98498 / 253-584-6361 lindcustguns@worldnot.att.net
Linder Solingen Knives, 4401 Sentry Dr., Tucker, GA 30084 / 770-939-6915; FAX: 770-939-6738
Lindsay, Steve, RR 2 Cedar Hills, Kearney, NE 68847 / 308-236-7885
Lindsley Arms Cartridge Co., P.O. Box 757, 20 College Hill Rd., Henniker, NH 03242 / 603-428-3127
Linebaugh Custom Sixguns, Route 2, Box 100, Maryville, MO 64468 / 660-562-3031 sixgunner.com
Lion Country Supply, P.O. Box 480, Port Matilda, PA 16870
List Precision Engineering, Unit 1 Ingley Works, 13 River Road, Barking, ENGLAND / 011-081-594-1686
Lithi Bee Bullet Lube, 1728 Carr Rd., Muskegon, MI 49442 / 616-788-4479
"Little John's" Antique Arms, 1740 W. Laveta, Orange, CA 92668
Little Trees Ramble (See Scott Pilkington, Little
Littler Sales Co., 20815 W. Chicago, Detroit, MI 48228 / 313-273-6888; FAX: 313-273-1099
Littleton, J. F., 275 Pinedale Ave., Oroville, CA 95966 / 916-533-6084
Ljutic Industries, Inc., 732 N. 16th Ave., Suite 22, Yakima, WA 98907 / 509-248-0476; FAX: 509-576-8233
Llama Gabilondo Y Cia, Apartado 290, E-01080, Victoria, spain, SPAIN
Loch Leven Industries, P.O. Box 2751, Santa Rosa, CA 95405 / 707-573-8735; FAX: 707-573-0369
Lock's Philadelphia Gun Exchange, 6700 Rowland Ave., Philadelphia, PA 19149 / 215-332-6225; FAX: 215-332-4800

MANUFACTURER'S DIRECTORY

Lodewick, Walter H., 2816 NE Halsey St., Portland, OR 97232 / 503-284-2554
Log Cabin Sport Shop, 8010 Lafayette Rd., Lodi, OH 44254 / 330-948-1082; FAX: 330-948-4307
Logan, Harry M., Box 745, Honokaa, HI 96727 / 808-776-1644
Lohman Mfg. Co., Inc., 4500 Doniphan Dr., P.O. Box 220, Neosho, MO 64850 / 417-451-4438; FAX: 417-451-2576
Lomont Precision Bullets, RR 1, Box 34, Salmon, ID 83467 / 208-756-6819; FAX: 208-756-6824
London Guns Ltd., Box 3750, Santa Barbara, CA 93130 / 805-683-4141; FAX: 805-683-1712
Lone Star Gunleather, 1301 Brushy Bend Dr., Round Rock, TX 78681 / 512-255-1805
Lone Star Rifle Company, 11231 Rose Road, Conroe, TX 77303 / 409-856-3363
Long, George F., 1500 Rogue River Hwy., Ste. F, Grants Pass, OR 97527 / 541-476-7552
Lortone Inc., 2856 NW Market St., Seattle, WA 98107
Lothar Walther Precision Tool Inc., 3425 Hutchinson Rd., Cumming, GA 30040 / 770-889-9998; FAX: 770-889-4918 lotharwalther@mindspring.com www.lothar-walther.com
Loweth, Richard H.R., 29 Hedgegrow Lane, Kirby Muxloe, Leics, LE9 2BN ENGLAND / (0) 116 238 6295
LPS Laboratories, Inc., 4647 Hugh Howell Rd., P.O. Box 3050, Tucker, GA 30084 / 404-934-7800
Lucas, Edward E, 32 Garfield Ave., East Brunswick, NJ 08816 / 201-251-5526
Lucas, Mike, 1631 Jessamine Rd., Lexington, SC 29073
Lupton, Keith. (See PAWLING MOUNTAIN CLUB)
Lutz Engraving, Ron E., E1998 Smokey Valley Rd, Scandinavia, WI 54977 / 715-467-2674
Lyman Instant Targets, Inc. (See Lyman Products, Corp.)
Lyman Products Corp., 475 Smith Street, Middletown, CT 06457-1541 / 860-632-2020 or 800-22-LYMAN FAX: 860-632-1699
Lyman Products Corporation, 475 Smith Street, Middletown, CT 06457-1529 / 800-22-LYMAN or 860-632-2020; FAX: 860-632-1699
Lyte Optronics (See TracStar Industries Inc)

M

M. Thys (See U.S. Importer-Champlin Firearms Inc)
M.H. Canjar Co., 500 E. 45th Ave., Denver, CO 80216 / 303-295-2638; FAX: 303-295-2638
M.O.A. Corp., 2451 Old Camden Pike, Eaton, OH 45320 / 937-456-3669
MA Systems, P.O. Box 1143, Chouteau, OK 74337 / 918-479-6378
Mac-1 Airgun Distributors, 13974 Van Ness Ave., Gardena, CA 90249 / 310-327-3581; FAX: 310-327-0238 mac1@concentric.net mac1airgun.com
Macbean, Stan, 754 North 1200 West, Orem, UT 84057 / 801-224-6446
Madis, George, P.O. Box 545, Brownsboro, TX 75756 / 903-852-6480
Madis Books, 2453 West Five Mile Pkwy., Dallas, TX 75233 / 214-330-7168
MAG Instrument, Inc., 1635 S. Sacramento Ave., Ontario, CA 91761 / 909-947-1006; FAX: 909-947-3116
Mag-Na-Port International, Inc., 41302 Executive Dr., Harrison Twp., MI 48045-1306 / 810-469-6727; FAX: 810-469-0425
Mag-Pack Corp., P.O. Box 846, Chesterland, OH 44026
Magma Engineering Co., P.O. Box 161, 20955 E. Ocotillo Rd., Queen Creek, AZ 85242 / 602-987-9008 FAX: 602-987-0148
Magnolia Sports,Inc., 211 W. Main, Magnolia, AR 71753 / 501-234-8410 or 800-530-7816; FAX: 501-234-8117
Magnum Power Products, Inc., P.O. Box 17768, Fountain Hills, AZ 85268
Magnum Research, Inc., 7110 University Ave. NE, Minneapolis, MN 55432 / 800-772-6168 or 612-574-1868; FAX: 612-574-0109 magnumresearch.com
Magnus Bullets, P.O. Box 239, Toney, AL 35773 / 256-420-8359; FAX: 256-420-8360
MagSafe Ammo Co., 4700 S US Highway 17/92, Casselberry, FL 32707-3814 / 407-834-9966; FAX: 407-834-8185
Magtech Ammunition Co. Inc., 837 Boston Rd #12, Madison, CT 06443 / 203-245-8983; FAX: 203-245-2883 rfinemtek@aol.com
Mahony, Philip Bruce, 67 White Hollow Rd., Lime Rock, CT 06039-2418 / 203-435-9341
Mahovsky's Metalife, R.D. 1, Box 149a Eureka Road, Grand Valley, PA 16420 / 814-436-7747
Maine Custom Bullets, RFD 1, Box 1755, Brooks, ME 04921
Maionchi-L.M.I., Via Di Coselli-Zona, Industriale Di Guamo 55060, Lucca, ITALY / 011 39-583 94291
Makinson, Nicholas, RR 3, Komoka, ON N0L 1R0 CANADA / 519-471-5462
Malcolm Enterprises, 1023 E. Prien Lake Rd., Lake Charles, LA 70601
Mallardtone Game Calls, 2901 16th St., Moline, IL 61265 / 309-762-8089
Mandall Shooting Supplies Inc., 3616 N. Scottsdale Rd., Scottsdale, AZ 85252 / 480-945-2553; FAX: 480-949-0734
Marathon Rubber Prods. Co., Inc., 1009 3rd St, Wausau, WI 54403-4765 / 715-845-6255
Marble Arms (See CRR, Inc./Marble's Inc.)
Marchmon Bullets, 8191 Woodland Shore Dr., Brighton, MI 48116
Marent, Rudolf, 9711 Tiltree St., Houston, TX 77075 / 713-946-7028
Mark Lee Supplies, 9901 France Ct., Lakeville, MN 55044 / 612-461-2114
Markell,Inc., 422 Larkfield Center 235, Santa Rosa, CA 95403 / 707-573-0792; FAX: 707-573-9867
Markesbery Muzzle Loaders, Inc., 7785 Foundation Dr., Ste. 6, Florence, KY 41042 / 606-342-5553; or 606-342-2380
Marksman Products, 5482 Argosy Dr., Huntington Beach, CA 92649 / 714-898-7535 or 800-822-8005; FAX: 714-891-0782
Marlin Firearms Co., 100 Kenna Dr., North Haven, CT 06473 / 203-239-5621; FAX: 203-234-7991
MarMik, Inc., 2116 S. Woodland Ave., Michigan City, IN 46360 / 219-872-7231; FAX: 219-872-7231
Marocchi F.lli S.p.A, Via Galileo Galilei 8, I-25068 Zanano, ITALY
Marquart Precision Co., (See Morrison Precision)
Marsh, Johnny, 1007 Drummond Dr., Nashville, TN 37211 / 615-833-3259
Marsh, Mike, Croft Cottage, Main St., Derbyshire, DE4 2BY ENGLAND / 01629 650 669
Marshall Enterprises, 792 Canyon Rd., Redwood City, CA 94062
Marshall F. Fish Mfg. Gunsmith Sptg. Co., Rd. Box 2439, Rt. 22 North, Westport, NY 12993 / 518-962-4897 FAX: 518-962-4897
Martin B. Retting Inc., 11029 Washington, Culver City, CA 90232 / 213-837-2412
Martin Hagn Rifles & Actions, P.O. Box 444, Cranbrook, BC V1C 4H9 CANADA / 604-489-4861
Martin's Gun Shop, 937 S. Sheridan Blvd., Lakewood, CO 80226 / 303-922-2184
Martz, John V., 8060 Lakeview Lane, Lincoln, CA 95648 FAX: 916-645-3815
Marvel, Alan, 3922 Madonna Rd., Jarretsville, MD 21084 / 301-557-6545
Marx, Harry (See U.S. Importer for FERLIB)
Maryland Paintball Supply, 8507 Harford Rd., Parkville, MD 21234 / 410-882-5607
MAST Technology, 4350 S. Arville, Suite 3, Las Vegas, NV 89103 / 702-362-5043; FAX: 702-362-9554
Master Engravers, Inc. (See Hendricks, Frank E)
Master Lock Co., 2600 N. 32nd St., Milwaukee, WI 53245 / 414-444-2800
Match Prep--Doyle Gracey, P.O. Box 155, Tehachapi, CA 93581 / 661-822-5383; FAX: 661-823-8680
Matco, Inc., 1003-2nd St., N. Manchester, IN 46962 / 219-982-8282
Mathews & Son, Inc., George E., 10224 S Paramount Blvd, Downey, CA 90241 / 562-862-6719; FAX: 562-862-6719
Matthews Cutlery, 4401 Sentry Dr., Tucker, GA 30084 / 770-939-6915
Mauser Werke Oberndorf Waffensysteme GmbH, Postfach 1349, 78722, Oberndorf/N., GERMANY
Maverick Arms, Inc., 7 Grasso Ave., P.O. Box 497, North Haven, CT 06473 / 203-230-5300; FAX: 203-230-5420
Maxi-Mount, P.O. Box 291, Willoughby Hills, OH 44094-0291 / 216-944-9456; FAX: 216-944-9456
Maximum Security Corp., 32841 Calle Perfecto, San Juan Capistrano, CA 92675 / 714-493-3684; FAX: 714-496-7733
Mayville Engineering Co. (See MEC, Inc.)
Mazur Restoration, Pete, 13083 Drummer Way, Grass Valley, CA 95949 / 530-268-2412
McBros Rifle Co., P.O. Box 86549, Phoenix, AZ 85080 / 602-582-3713; FAX: 602-581-3825
McCament, Jay, 1730-134th St. Ct. S., Tacoma, WA 98444 / 253-531-8832
McCann Industries, P.O. Box 641, Spanaway, WA 98387 / 253-537-6919; FAX: 253-537-6919 mccann.machine@worldnet.att.net www.mccannindustries.com
McCann's Machine & Gun Shop, P.O. Box 641, Spanaway, WA 98387 / 253-537-6919; FAX: 253-537-6993 mccann.machine@worldnet.att.net www.mccannindustries.com
McCann's Muzzle-Gun Works, 14 Walton Dr., New Hope, PA 18938 / 215-862-2728
McCluskey Precision Rifles, 10502 14th Ave. NW, Seattle, WA 98177 / 206-781-2776
McCombs, Leo, 1862 White Cemetery Rd., Patriot, OH 45658 / 614-256-1714
McCormick Corp., Chip, 1825 Fortview Rd Ste 115, Austin, TX 78704 / 800-328-CHIP; FAX: 512-462-0009
McCullough, Ken. (See KEN'S RIFLE BLANKS)
McDonald, Dennis, 8359 Brady St., Peosta, IA 52068 / 319-556-7940
McFarland, Stan, 2221 Idella Ct., Grand Junction, CO 81505 / 970-243-4704
McGhee, Larry. (See B.C. OUTDOORS)
McGowen Rifle Barrels, 5961 Spruce Lane, St. Anne, IL 60964 / 815-937-9816; FAX: 815-937-4024
McGuire, Bill, 1600 N. Eastmont Ave., East Wenatchee, WA 98802 / 509-884-6021
Mchalik, Gary. (See ROSSI FIREARMS, BRAZTECH)
McKenzie, Lynton, 6940 N. Alvernon Way, Tucson, AZ 85718 / 520-299-5090
McKillen & Heyer, Inc., 35535 Euclid Ave., Suite 11, Willoughby, OH 44094 / 216-942-2044
McKinney, R.P. (See Schuetzen Gun Co.)
McMillan Fiberglass Stocks, Inc., 21421 N. 14th Ave., Suite B, Phoenix, AZ 85027 / 602-582-9635; FAX: 602-581-3825
McMillan Optical Gunsight Co., 28638 N. 42nd St., Cave Creek, AZ 85331 / 602-585-7868; FAX: 602-585-7872
McMillan Rifle Barrels, P.O. Box 3427, Bryan, TX 77805 / 409-690-3456; FAX: 409-690-0156
McMurdo, Lynn (See Specialty Gunsmithing), PO Box 404, Afton, WY 83110 / 307-886-5535
MCRW Associates Shooting Supplies, R.R. 1, Box 1425, Sweet Valley, PA 18656 / 717-864-3967; FAX: 717-864-2669
MCS, Inc., 34 Delmar Dr., Brookfield, CT 06804 / 203-775-1013; FAX: 203-775-9462
McWelco Products, 6730 Santa Fe Ave., Hesperia, CA 92345 / 619-244-8876; FAX: 619-244-9398
MDS, P.O. Box 1441, Brandon, FL 33509-1441 / 813-653-1180; FAX: 813-684-5953
Meadow Industries, 24 Club Lane, Palmyra, VA 22963 / 804-589-7672; FAX: 804-589-7672
Measurement Group Inc., Box 27777, Raleigh, NC 27611
Measures, Leon. (See SHOOT WHERE YOU LOOK)
MEC, Inc., 715 South St., Mayville, WI 53050 / 414-387-4500; FAX: 414-387-5802 reloaders@mayul.com www.mayvl.com
MEC-Gar S.r.l., Via Madonnina 64, Gardone V.T. Brescia, ITALY / 39-30-8912687; FAX: 39-30-8910065
MEC-Gar U.S.A., Inc., Box 112, 500B Monroe Turnpike, Monroe, CT 06468 / 203-635-8662; FAX: 203-635-8662
Mech-Tech Systems, Inc., 1602 Foothill Rd., Kalispell, MT 59901 / 406-755-8055
Meister Bullets (See Gander Mountain)
Mele, Frank, 201 S. Wellow Ave., Cookeville, TN 38501 / 615-526-4860
Melton Shirt Co., Inc., 56 Harvester Ave., Batavia, NY 14020 / 716-343-8750; FAX: 716-343-6887
Men-Metallwerk Elisenhuette GmbH, P.O. Box 1263, Nassau/Lahn, D-56372 GERMANY / 2604-7819
Menck, Gunsmith Inc., T.W., 5703 S 77th St, Ralston, NE 68127
Mendez, John A., P.O. Box 620984, Orlando, FL 32862 / 407-344-2791
Meprolight (See Hesco-Meprolight)
Mercer Custom Stocks, R. M., 216 S Whitewater Ave, Jefferson, WI 53549 / 920-674-3839
Merit Corp., Box 9044, Schenectady, NY 12309 / 518-346-1420
Merkel Freres, Strasse 7 October, 10, Suhl, GERMANY
Merkuria Ltd., Argentinska 38, 17005, Praha 7 CZECH, REPUBLIC / 422-875117; FAX: 422-809152
Metal Merchants, PO Box 186, Walled Lake, MI 48390-0186
Metalife Industries (See Mahovsky's Metalife)
Metaloy, Inc., Rt. 5, Box 595, Berryville, AR 72616 / 501-545-3611
Metals Hand Engraver/European Hand Engraving, Ste. 216, 12 South First St., San Jose, CA 95113 / 408-293-6559
MI-TE Bullets, 1396 Ave. K, Ellsworth, KS 67439 / 785-472-4575; FAX: 785-472-5579
Michael's Antiques, Box 591, Waldoboro, ME 04572
Michaels Of Oregon, 1710 Red Soils Ct., Oregon City, OR 97045
Micro Sight Co., 242 Harbor Blvd., Belmont, CA 94002 / 415-591-0769; FAX: 415-591-7531
Microfusion Alfa S.A., Paseo San Andres N8, P.O. Box 271, Eibar, 20600 SPAIN / 34-43-11-89-16; FAX: 34-43-11-40-38

MANUFACTURER'S DIRECTORY

Mid-America Guns and Ammo, 1205 W. Jefferson, Suite E, Effingham, IL 62401 / 800-820-5177
Mid-America Recreation, Inc., 1328 5th Ave., Moline, IL 61265 / 309-764-5089; FAX: 309-764-2722
Middlebrooks Custom Shop, 7366 Colonial Trail East, Surry, VA 23883 / 757-357-0881; FAX: 757-365-0442
Midway Arms, Inc., 5875 W. Van Horn Tavern Rd., Columbia, MO 65203 / 800-243-3220 or 573-445-6363; FAX: 573-446-1018
Midwest Gun Sport, 1108 Herbert Dr., Zebulon, NC 27597 / 919-269-5570
Midwest Sport Distributors, Box 129, Fayette, MO 65248
Mike Davis Products, 643 Loop Dr., Moses Lake, WA 98837 / 509-765-6178 or 509-766-7281
Milberry House Publishing, PO Box 575, Corydon, IN 47112 / 888-738-1567; FAX: 888-738-1567
Military Armament Corp., P.O. Box 120, Mt. Zion Rd., Lingleville, TX 76461 / 817-965-3253
Millennium Designed Muzzleloaders, PO Box 536, Routes 11 & 25, Limington, ME 04049 / 207-637-2316
Miller Arms, Inc., P.O. Box 260 Purl St., St. Onge, SD 57779 / 605-642-5160; FAX: 605-642-5160
Miller Custom, 210 E. Julia, Clinton, IL 61727 / 217-935-9362
Miller Single Trigger Mfg. Co., Rt. 209, Box 1275, Millersburg, PA 17061 / 717-692-3704
Millett Sights, 7275 Murdy Circle, Adm. Office, Huntington Beach, CA 92647 / 714-842-5575 or 800-645-5388; FAX: 714-843-5707
Mills Jr., Hugh B., 3615 Canterbury Rd., New Bern, NC 28560 / 919-637-4631
Milstor Corp., 80-975 Indio Blvd., Indio, CA 92201 / 760-775-9998; FAX: 760-775-5229 milstor@webtv.net
Miltex, Inc, 700 S Lee St, Alexandria, VA 22314-4332 / 888-642-9123; FAX: 301-645-1430
Minute Man High Tech Industries, 10611 Canyon Rd. E., Suite 151, Puyallup, WA 98373 / 800-233-2734
Mirador Optical Corp., P.O. Box 11614, Marina Del Rey, CA 90295-7614 / 310-821-5587; FAX: 310-305-0386
Miroku, B C/Daly, Charles (See U.S. Importer-Bell's)
Mitchell, Jack, c/o Geoff Gaebe, Addieville East Farm, 200 Pheasant Dr, Mapleville, RI 02839 / 401-568-3185
Mitchell Bullets, R.F., 430 Walnut St, Westernport, MD 21562
Mitchell Optics, Inc., 2072 CR 1100 N, Sidney, IL 61877 / 217-688-2219 or 217-621-3018; FAX: 217-688-2505
Mitchell's Accuracy Shop, 68 Greenridge Dr., Stafford, VA 22554 / 703-659-0165
Mittermeier, Inc., Frank, PO Box 2G, 3577 E Tremont Ave, Bronx, NY 10465 / 718-828-3843
Mixson Corp., 7635 W. 28th Ave., Hialeah, FL 33016 / 305-821-5190 or 800-327-0078; FAX: 305-558-9318
MJK Gunsmithing, Inc., 417 N. Huber Ct., E. Wenatchee, WA 98802 / 509-884-7683
MJM Mfg., 3283 Rocky Water Ln., Suite B, San Jose, CA 95148 / 408-270-4207
MKS Supply, Inc. (See Hi-Point Firearms)
MMC, 2513 East Loop 820 North, Ft. Worth, TX 76118 / 817-595-0404; FAX: 817-595-3074
MMP, Rt. 6, Box 384, Harrison, AR 72601 / 501-741-5019; FAX: 501-741-3104
Mo's Competitor Supplies (See MCS Inc)
Modern Gun Repair School, P.O. Box 92577, Southlake, TX 76092 / 800-493-4114; FAX: 800-556-5112
Modern Muzzleloading, Inc, PO Box 130, Centerville, IA 52544 / 515-856-2626
Moeller, Steve, 1213 4th St., Fulton, IL 61252 / 815-589-2300
Molin Industries, Tru-Nord Division, P.O. Box 365, 204 North 9th St., Brainerd, MN 56401 / 218-829-2870
Monell Custom Guns, 228 Red Mills Rd., Pine Bush, NY 12566 / 914-744-3021
Moneymaker Guncraft Corp., 1420 Military Ave., Omaha, NE 68131 / 402-556-0226
Montana Armory, Inc (See C. Sharps Arms Co. Inc.), 100 Centennial, Box 885, Big Timber, MT 59011 / 406-932-4353
Montana Outfitters, Lewis E. Yearout, 308 Riverview Dr. E., Great Falls, MT 59404 / 406-761-0859
Montana Precision Swaging, P.O. Box 4746, Butte, MT 59702 / 406-782-7502
Montana Vintage Arms, 2354 Bear Canyon Rd., Bozeman, MT 59715
Montgomery Community College, P.O. Box 787-GD, Troy, NC 27371 / 910-576-6222 or 800-839-6222; FAX: 910-576-2176
Morini (See U.S. Importers-Mandall Shooting Supplies, Inc.,)
Morrison Custom Rifles, J. W., 4015 W Sharon, Phoenix, AZ 85029 / 602-978-3754
Morrison Precision, 6719 Calle Mango, Hereford, AZ 85615 / 520-378-6207 / morprec@c2i2.com (e-mail)
Morrow, Bud, 11 Hillside Lane, Sheridan, WY 82801-9729 / 307-674-8360
Morton Booth Co., P.O. Box 123, Joplin, MO 64802 / 417-673-1962; FAX: 417-673-3642
Moss Double Tone, Inc., P.O. Box 1112, 2101 S. Kentucky, Sedalia, MO 65301 / 816-827-0827
Mountain Hollow Game Calls, Box 121, Cascade, MD 21719 / 301-241-3282
Mountain Plains, Inc., 244 Glass Hollow Rd., Alton, VA 22920 / 800-687-3000
Mountain Rifles, Inc., P.O. Box 2789, Palmer, AK 99645 / 907-373-4194; FAX: 907-373-4195
Mountain South, P.O. Box 381, Barnwell, SC 29812 / FAX: 803-259-3227
Mountain State Muzzleloading Supplies, Inc., Box 154-1, Rt. 2, Williamstown, WV 26187 / 304-375-7842; FAX: 304-375-3737
Mountain View Sports, Inc., Box 188, Troy, NH 03465 / 603-357-9690; FAX: 603-357-9691
Mowrey Gun Works, P.O. Box 246, Waldron, IN 46182 / 317-525-6181; FAX: 317-525-9595
Mowrey's Guns & Gunsmithing, 119 Fredericks St., Canajoharie, NY 13317 / 518-673-3483
MPC, P.O. Box 450, McMinnville, TN 37110-0450 / 615-473-5513; FAX: 615-473-5516
MPI Stocks, PO Box 83266, Portland, OR 97283 / 503-226-1215; FAX: 503-226-2661
MSC Industrial Supply Co., 151 Sunnyside Blvd., Plainview, NY 11803-9915 / 516-349-0330
MSR Targets, P.O. Box 1042, West Covina, CA 91793 / 818-331-7840
Mt. Alto Outdoor Products, Rt. 735, Howardsville, VA 24562
Mt. Baldy Bullet Co., 12981 Old Hill City Rd., Keystone, SD 57751-6623 / 605-666-4725
MTM Molded Products Co., Inc., 3370 Obco Ct., Dayton, OH 45414 / 937-890-7461; FAX: 937-890-1747
Mulhern, Rick, Rt. 5, Box 152, Rayville, LA 71269 / 318-728-2688
Mullins Ammunition, Rt. 2, Box 304K, Clintwood, VA 24228 / 540-926-6772; FAX: 540-926-6092
Mullis Guncraft, 3523 Lawyers Road E., Monroe, NC 28110 / 704-283-6683
Multi-Scale Charge Ltd., 3269 Niagara Falls Blvd., N. Tonawanda, NY 14120 / 905-566-1255; FAX: 905-276-6295
Multiplex International, 26 S. Main St., Concord, NH 03301 / FAX: 603-796-2223
Multipropulseurs, La Bertrandiere, 42580, FRANCE / 77 74 01 30; FAX: 77 93 19 34
Mundy, Thomas A., 69 Robbins Road, Somerville, NJ 08876 / 201-722-2199
Murmur Corp., 2823 N. Westmoreland Ave., Dallas, TX 75222 / 214-630-5400
Murray State College, 1 Murray Campus St., Tishomingo, OK 73460 / 508-371-2371
Muscle Products Corp., 112 Fennell Dr., Butler, PA 16001 / 800-227-7049 or 412-283-0567; FAX: 412-283-8310
Museum of Historical Arms, Inc., 2750 Coral Way, Suite 204, Miami, FL 33145 / 305-444-9199
Mushroom Express Bullet Co., 601 W. 6th St., Greenfield, IN 46140-1728 / 317-462-6332
Muzzleloaders Etcetera, Inc., 9901 Lyndale Ave. S., Bloomington, MN 55420 / 612-884-1161 muzzleloaders-etcetera.com
Muzzleloading Technologies, Inc, 25 E. Hwy. 40, Suite 330-12, Roosevelt, UT 84066 / 801-722-5996; FAX: 801-722-5909
MWG Co., P.O. Box 971202, Miami, FL 33197 / 800-428-9394 or 305-253-8393; FAX: 305-232-1247

N

N&J Sales, Lime Kiln Rd., Northford, CT 06472 / 203-484-0247
N.B.B., Inc., 24 Elliot Rd., Sterling, MA 01564 / 508-422-7538 or 800-942-9444
N.C. Ordnance Co., P.O. Box 3254, Wilson, NC 27895 / 919-237-2440; FAX: 919-243-9845
Nagel's Custom Bullets, 100 Scott St., Baytown, TX 77520-2849
Nalpak, 1937-C Friendship Drive, El Cajon, CA 92020 / 619-258-1200
Nastoff's 45 Shop, Inc., Steve, 12288 Mahoning Ave, PO Box 446, North Jackson, OH 44451 / 330-538-2977
National Bullet Co., 1585 E. 361 St., Eastlake, OH 44095 / 216-951-1854; FAX: 216-951-7761
National Target Co., 4690 Wyaconda Rd., Rockville, MD 20852 / 800-827-7060 or 301-770-7060; FAX: 301-770-7892
Naval Ordnance Works, Rt. 2, Box 919, Sheperdstown, WV 25443 / 304-876-0998
Navy Arms Co., 689 Bergen Blvd., Ridgefield, NJ 07657 / 201-945-2500; FAX: 201-945-6859
NCP Products, Inc., 3500 12th St. N.W., Canton, OH 44708 / 330-456-5130; FAX: 330-456-5234
Neal Johnson's Gunsmithing, Inc., 208 W. Buchanan St., Suite B, Colorado Springs, CO 80907 / 800-284-8671; FAX: 719-632-3493
Necessary Concepts, Inc., P.O. Box 571, Deer Park, NY 11729 / 516-667-8509; FAX: 516-667-8588
Necromancer Industries, Inc., 14 Communications Way, West Newton, PA 15089 / 412-872-8722
NEI Handtools, Inc., 51583 Columbia River Hwy., Scappoose, OR 97056 / 503-543-6776; FAX: 503-543-6799
Neil A. Jones Custom Products, 17217 Brookhouser Road, Saegertown, PA 16433 / 814-763-2769; FAX: 814-763-4228
Nelson, Gary K., 975 Terrace Dr., Oakdale, CA 95361 / 209-847-4590
Nelson, Stephen, 7365 NW Spring Creek Dr., Corvallis, OR 97330 / 541-745-5232
Nelson/Weather-Rite, Inc., 14760 Santa Fe Trail Dr., Lenexa, KS 66215 / 913-492-3200; FAX: 913-492-8749
Nesci Enterprises Inc., P.O. Box 119, Summit St., East Hampton, CT 06424 / 203-267-2588
Nesika Bay Precision, 22239 Big Valley Rd., Poulsbo, WA 98370 / 206-697-3830
Nettestad Gun Works, RR 1, Box 160, Pelican Rapids, MN 56572 / 218-863-4301
Neumann GmbH, Am Galgenberg 6, 90575, GERMANY / 09101/8258; FAX: 09101/6356
Nevada Pistol Academy, Inc., 4610 Blue Diamond Rd., Las Vegas, NV 89139 / 702-897-1100
New England Ammunition Co., 1771 Post Rd. East, Suite 223, Westport, CT 06880 / 203-254-8048
New England Arms Co., Box 278, Lawrence Lane, Kittery Point, ME 03905 / 207-439-0593; FAX: 207-439-0525 info@newenglandarms.com www.newenglandarms.com
New England Custom Gun Service, 438 Willow Brook Rd., Plainfield, NH 03781 / 603-469-3450; FAX: 603-469-3471
New England Firearms, 60 Industrial Rowe, Gardner, MA 01440 / 508-632-9393; FAX: 508-632-2300
New Orleans Jewelers Supply Co., 206 Charters St., New Orleans, LA 70130 / 504-523-3839; FAX: 504-523-3836
New SKB Arms Co., C.P.O. Box 1401, Tokyo, JAPAN / 81-3-3943-9550; FAX: 81-3-3943-0695
New Win Publishing, Inc., 186 Center St., Clinton, NJ 08809 / 908-735-9701; FAX: 908-735-9703
Newark Electronics, 4801 N. Ravenswood Ave., Chicago, IL 60640
Newell, Robert H., 55 Coyote, Los Alamos, NM 87544 / 505-662-7135
Newman Gunshop, 119 Miller Rd., Agency, IA 52530 / 515-937-5775
Nicholson Custom, 17285 Thornlay Road, Hughesville, MO 65334 / 816-826-8746
Nickels, Paul R., 4789 Summerhill Rd., Las Vegas, NV 89121 / 702-435-5318
Nicklas, Ted, 5504 Hegel Rd., Goodrich, MI 48438 / 810-797-4493
Niemi Engineering, W. B., Box 126 Center Rd, Greensboro, VT 05841 / 802-533-7180; FAX: 802-533-7141
Nightforce (See Lightforce USA Inc)
Nikolai leather, 15451 Electronic ln, Huntington Beach, CA 92649 / 714-373-2721 FAX: 714-373-2723
Nikon, Inc., 1300 Walt Whitman Rd., Melville, NY 11747 / 516-547-8623; FAX: 516-547-0309
Nitex, Inc., P.O. Box 1706, Uvalde, TX 78801 / 888-543-8843
No-Sho Mfg. Co., 10727 Glenfield Ct., Houston, TX 77096 / 713-723-5332
Noreen, Peter H., 5075 Buena Vista Dr., Belgrade, MT 59714 / 406-586-7383
Norica, Avnda Otaola, 16 Apartado 68, Eibar, SPAIN
Norinco, 7A Yun Tan N, Beijing, CHINA
Norincoptics (See BEC, Inc.)
Norma Precision AB (See U.S. Importers-Dynamit Nobel-RWS, Inc.,)
Normark Corp., 10395 Yellow Circle Dr., Minnetonka, MN 55343-9101 / 612-933-7060 FAX: 612-933-0046
North American Arms, Inc., 2150 South 950 East, Provo, UT 84606-6285 / 800-821-5783 or 801-374-9990; FAX: 801-374-9998
North American Correspondence Schools The Gun Pro, Oak & Pawney St., Scranton, PA 18515 / 717-342-7701
North American Shooting Systems, P.O. Box 306, Osoyoos, BC V0H 1V0 CANADA / 604-495-3131; FAX: 604-495-2816

MANUFACTURER'S DIRECTORY

North Devon Firearms Services, 3 North St., Braunton, EX33 1AJ ENGLAND / 01271 813624; FAX: 01271 813624
North Fork Custom Gunsmithing, James Johnston, 428 Del Rio Rd., Roseburg, OR 97470 / 503-673-4467
North Mountain Pine Training Center (See Executive Protection Institute)
North Pass, 425 South Bowen St., Ste. 6, Longmount, CO 80501 / 303-682-4315; FAX: 303-678-7109
North Specialty Products, 2664-B Saturn St., Brea, CA 92621 / 714-524-1665
North Star West, P.O. Box 488, Glencoe, CA 95232 / 209-293-7010
North Wind Decoy Co., 1005 N. Tower Rd., Fergus Falls, MN 56537 / 218-736-4378; FAX: 218-736-7060
Northern Precision Custom Swaged Bullets, 329 S. James St., Carthage, NY 13619 / 315-493-1711
Northlake Outdoor Footwear, P.O. Box 10, Franklin, TN 37065-0010 / 615-794-1556; FAX: 615-790-8005
Northside Gun Shop, 2725 NW 109th, Oklahoma City, OK 73120 / 405-840-2353
Northwest Arms, 26884 Pearl Rd., Parma, ID 83660 / 208-722-6771; FAX: 208-722-1062
Nosler, Inc., P.O. Box 671, Bend, OR 97709 / 800-285-3701 or 541-382-3921; FAX: 541-388-4667
Novak's, Inc., 1206 1/2 30th St., P.O. Box 4045, Parkersburg, WV 26101 / 304-485-9295; FAX: 304-428-6722
Now Products, Inc., PO Box 27608, Tempe, AZ 85285 / 800-662-6063: FAX: 480-966-0890
Nowlin Mfg. Co., 20622 S 4092 Rd, Claremore, OK 74017 / 918-342-0689; FAX: 918-342-0624
NRI Gunsmith School, 4401 Connecticut Ave. NW, Washington, DC 20008
Nu-Line Guns,Inc., 1053 Caulks Hill Rd., Harvester, MO 63304 / 314-441-4500 or 314-447-4501; FAX: 314-447-5018
Null Holsters Ltd. K.L., 161 School St NW, Resaca, GA 30735 / 706-625-5643; FAX: 706-625-9392
Numrich Arms Corp., 203 Broadway, W. Hurley, NY 12491
NW Sinker and Tackle, 380 Valley Dr., Myrtle Creek, OR 97457-9717
Nygord Precision Products, P.O. Box 12578, Prescott, AZ 86304 / 520-717-2315; FAX: 520-717-2198

O

O.F. Mossberg & Sons,Inc., 7 Grasso Ave., North Haven, CT 06473 / 203-230-5300; FAX: 203-230-5420
Oakland Custom Arms,Inc., 4690 W. Walton Blvd., Waterford, MI 48329 / 810-674-8261
Oakman Turkey Calls, RD 1, Box 825, Harrisonville, PA 17228 / 717-485-4620
Obermeyer Rifled Barrels, 23122 60th St., Bristol, WI 53104 / 262-843-3537; FAX: 262-843-2129
October Country Muzzleloading, P.O. Box 969, Dept. GD, Hayden, ID 83835 / 208-772-2068; FAX: 208-772-9230 octobercountry.com
Oehler Research,Inc., P.O. Box 9135, Austin, TX 78766 / 512-327-6900 or 800-531-5125; FAX: 512-327-6903
Oil Rod and Gun Shop, 69 Oak St., East Douglas, MA 01516 / 508-476-3687
Ojala Holsters, Arvo, PO Box 98, N Hollywood, CA 91603 / 503-669-1404
OK Weber,Inc., P.O. Box 7485, Eugene, OR 97401 / 541-747-0458; FAX: 541-747-5927
Oker's Engraving, 365 Bell Rd., P.O. Box 126, Shawnee, CO 80475 / 303-838-6042
Oklahoma Ammunition Co., 3701A S. Harvard Ave., No. 367, Tulsa, OK 74135-2265 / 918-396-3187; FAX: 918-396-4270
Oklahoma Leather Products,Inc., 500 26th NW, Miami, OK 74354 / 918-542-6651; FAX: 918-542-6653
Old Wagon Bullets, 32 Old Wagon Rd., Wilton, CT 06897
Old West Bullet Moulds, J Ken Chapman, P.O. Box 519, Flora Vista, NM 87415 / 505-334-6970
Old West Reproductions,Inc. R.M. Bachman, 446 Florence S. Loop, Florence, MT 59833 / 406-273-2615; FAX: 406-273-2615
Old Western Scrounger,Inc., 12924 Hwy. A-l2, Montague, CA 96064 / 916-459-5445; FAX: 916-459-3944
Old World Gunsmithing, 2901 SE 122nd St., Portland, OR 97236 / 503-760-7681
Old World Oil Products, 3827 Queen Ave. N., Minneapolis, MN 55412 / 612-522-5037
Ole Frontier Gunsmith Shop, 2617 Hwy. 29 S., Cantonment, FL 32533 / 904-477-8074
Olson, Myron, 989 W. Kemp, Watertown, SD 57201 / 605-886-9787
Olson, Vic, 5002 Countryside Dr., Imperial, MO 63052 / 314-296-8086
Olympic Arms Inc., 620-626 Old Pacific Hwy. SE, Olympia, WA 98513 / 360-491-3447; FAX: 360-491-3447
Olympic Optical Co., P.O. Box 752377, Memphis, TN 38175-2377 / 901-794-3890 or 800-238-7120; FAX: 901-794-0676 80
Omark Industries,Div. of Blount,Inc., 2299 Snake River Ave., P.O. Box 856, Lewiston, ID 83501 / 800-627-3640 or 208-746-2351
Omega Sales, P.O. Box 1066, Mt. Clemens, MI 48043 / 810-469-7323; FAX: 810-469-0425
One Of A Kind, 15610 Purple Sage, San Antonio, TX 78255 / 512-695-3364
Op-Tec, P.O. Box L632, Langhorn, PA 19047 / 215-757-5037
Optical Services Co., P.O. Box 1174, Santa Teresa, NM 88008-1174 / 505-589-3833
Orchard Park Enterprise, P.O. Box 563, Orchard Park, NY 14227 / 616-656-0356
Oregon Arms, Inc. (See Rogue Rifle Co., Inc.)
Oregon Trail Bullet Company, P.O. Box 529, Dept. P, Baker City, OR 97814 / 800-811-0548; FAX: 514-523-1803
Original Box, nc., 700 Linden Ave., York, PA 17404 / 717-854-2897; FAX: 717-845-4276
Original Mink Oil,Inc., 10652 NE Holman, Portland, OR 97220 / 503-255-2814 or 800-547-5895; FAX: 503-255-2487
Orion Rifle Barrel Co., RR2, 137 Cobler Village, Kalispell, MT 59901 / 406-257-5649
Otis Technology, Inc, RR 1 Box 84, Boonville, NY 13309 / 315-942-3320
Ottmar, Maurice, Box 657, 113 E. Fir, Coulee City, WA 99115 / 509-632-5717
Outa-Site Gun Carriers, 219 Market St., Laredo, TX 78040 / 210-722-4678 or 800-880-9715; FAX: 210-726-4858
Outdoor Edge Cutlery Corp., 2888 Bluff St., Suite 130, Boulder, CO 80301 / 303-652-8212; FAX: 303-652-8238
Outdoor Enthusiast, 3784 W. Woodland, Springfield, MO 65807 / 417-883-9841
Outdoor Sports Headquarters,Inc., 967 Watertower Ln., West Carrollton, OH 45449 / 513-865-5855; FAX: 513-865-5962
Outers Laboratories Div. of Blount, Inc.Sporting E, Route 2, P.O. Box 39, Onalaska, WI 54650 / 608-781-5800; FAX: 608-781-0368
Ox-Yoke Originals, Inc., 34 Main St., Milo, ME 04463 / 800-231-8313 or 207-943-7351; FAX: 207-943-2416
Ozark Gun Works, 11830 Cemetery Rd., Rogers, AR 72756 / 501-631-6944; FAX: 501-631-6944 ogw@hotmail.com http://members.tripod.com~ozarkw1

P

P&M Sales and Service, 5724 Gainsborough Pl., Oak Forest, IL 60452 / 708-687-7149
P.A.C.T., Inc., P.O. Box 531525, Grand Prairie, TX 75053 / 214-641-0049
P.M. Enterprises, Inc., 146 Curtis Hill Rd., Chehalis, WA 98532 / 360-748-3743; FAX: 360-748-1802
P.S.M.G. Gun Co., 10 Park Ave., Arlington, MA 02174 / 617-646-8845; FAX: 617-646-2133
Pac-Nor Barreling, 99299 Overlook Rd., P.O. Box 6188, Brookings, OR 97415 / 503-469-7330; FAX: 503-469-7331
Pace Marketing, Inc., P.O. Box 2039, Stuart, FL 34995 / 561-871-9682; FAX: 561-871-6552
Pachmayr Div. Lyman Products, 1875 S. Mountain Ave., Monrovia, CA 91016 / 626-357-7771
Pacific Cartridge, Inc., 2425 Salashan Loop Road, Ferndale, WA 98248 / 360-366-4444; FAX: 360-366-4445
Pacific Research Laboratories, Inc. (See Rimrock R
Pacific Rifle Co., PO Box 1473, Lake Oswego, OR 97035 / 503-538-7437
Paco's (See Small Custom Mould & Bullet Co)
Page Custom Bullets, P.O. Box 25, Port Moresby, NEW GUINEA
Pagel Gun Works, Inc., 1407 4th St. NW, Grand Rapids, MN 55744 / 218-326-3003
Pager Pal, 200 W Pleasantview, Hurst, TX 76054 / 800-561-1603 FAX: 817-285-8769 www.pagerpal.com
Paintball Games International Magazine (Aceville Publications, Castle House) 97 High St., Essex, ENGLAND / 011-44-206-564840
Palmer Security Products, 2930 N. Campbell Ave., Chicago, IL 60618 / 800-788-7725; FAX: 773-267-8080
Palsa Outdoor Products, P.O. Box 81336, Lincoln, NE 68501 / 402-488-5288; FAX: 402-488-2321
Para-Ordnance Mfg., Inc., 980 Tapscott Rd., Scarborough, ON M1X 1E7 CANADA / 416-297-7855; FAX: 416-297-1289
Para-Ordnance, Inc., 1919 NE 45th St., Ste 215, Ft. Lauderdale, FL 33308
Paragon Sales & Services, Inc., 2501 Theodore St, Crest Hill, IL 60435-1613 / 815-725-9212; FAX: 815-725-8974
Pardini Armi Srl, Via Italica 154, 55043, Lido Di Camaiore Lu, ITALY / 584-90121; FAX: 584-90122
Paris, Frank J., 17417 Pershing St., Livonia, MI 48152-3822
Parker & Sons Shooting Supply, 9337 Smoky Row Rd, Straw Plains, TN 97871-1257
Parker Gun Finishes, 9337 Smokey Row Rd., Strawberry Plains, TN 37871 / 423-933-3286
Parker Reproductions, 124 River Rd., Middlesex, NJ 08846 / 908-469-0100 FAX: 908-469-9692
Parsons Optical Mfg. Co., P.O. Box 192, Ross, OH 45061 / 513-867-0820; FAX: 513-867-8380
Partridge Sales Ltd., John, Trent Meadows, Rugeley, ENGLAND
Parts & Surplus, P.O. Box 22074, Memphis, TN 38122 / 901-683-4007
Pasadena Gun Center, 206 E. Shaw, Pasadena, TX 77506 / 713-472-0417; FAX: 713-472-1322
Passive Bullet Traps, Inc. (See Savage Range Systems, Inc.,)
PAST Sporting Goods,Inc., P.O. Box 1035, Columbia, MO 65205 / 314-445-9200; FAX: 314-446-6606
Paterson Gunsmithing, 438 Main St., Paterson, NJ 07502 / 201-345-4100
Pathfinder Sports Leather, 2920 E. Chambers St., Phoenix, AZ 85040 / 602-276-0016
Patrick Bullets, P.O. Box 172, Warwick, QSLD, 4370 AUSTRALIA
Patrick W. Price Bullets, 16520 Worthley Drive, San Lorenzo, CA 94580 / 510-278-1547
Pattern Control, 114 N. Third St., P.O. Box 462105, Garland, TX 75046 / 214-494-3551; FAX: 214-272-8447
Paul A. Harris Hand Engraving, 113 Rusty Lane, Boerne, TX 78006-5746 / 512-391-5121
Paul D. Hillmer Custom Gunstocks, 7251 Hudson Heights, Hudson, IA 50643 / 319-988-3941
Paul Jones Moulds, 4901 Telegraph Rd., Los Angeles, CA 90022 / 213-262-1510
Paulsen Gunstocks, Rt. 71, Box 11, Chinook, MT 59523 / 406-357-3403
Pawling Mountain Club, Keith Lupton, PO Box 573, Pawling, NY 12564 / 914-855-3825
Paxton Quigley's Personal Protection Strategies, 9903 Santa Monica Blvd., 300, Beverly Hills, CA 90212 / 310-281-1762 www.defend-net.com/paxton
Payne Photography, Robert, Robert, P.O. Box 141471, Austin, TX 78714 / 512-272-4554
PC Co., 5942 Secor Rd., Toledo, OH 43623 / 419-472-6222
Peacemaker Specialists, P.O. Box 157, Whitmore, CA 96096 / 916-472-3438
Pearce Grip, Inc., P.O. Box 187, Bothell, WA 98041-0187 / 206-485-5488; FAX: 206-488-9497
Pease Accuracy, Bob, P.O. Box 310787, New Braunfels, TX 78131 / 210-625-1342
Pease International, 53 Durham St, Portsmouth, NH 03801 / 603-431-1331; FAX: 603-431-1221
PECAR Herbert Schwarz GmbH, Kreuzbergstrasse 6, 10965, Berlin, GERMANY / 004930-785-7383; FAX: 004930-785-1934
Pecatonica River Longrifle, 5205 Nottingham Dr., Rockford, IL 61111 / 815-968-1995 FAX: 815-968-1996
Pedersen, C. R., 2717 S. Pere Marquette Hwy., Ludington, MI 49431 / 616-843-2061
Pedersen, Rex C., 2717 S. Pere Marquette Hwy., Ludington, MI 49431 / 616-843-2061
Peerless Alloy, Inc., 1445 Osage St., Denver, CO 80204-2439 / 303-825-6394 or 800-253-1278
Peet Shoe Dryer, Inc., 130 S. 5th St., P.O. Box 618, St. Maries, ID 83861 / 208-245-2095 or 800-222-PEET; FAX: 208-245-5441
Peifer Rifle Co., P.O. Box 192, Nokomis, IL 62075-0192 / 217-563-7050; FAX: 217-563-7060
Pejsa Ballistics, 2120 Kenwood Pkwy., Minneapolis, MN 55405 / 612-374-3337; FAX: 612-374-5383
Pelaire Products, 5346 Bonky Ct., W. Palm Beach, FL 33415 / 561-439-0691; FAX: 561-967-0052
Pell, John T. (See KOGOT)
Peltor, Inc. (See Aero Peltor)
PEM's Mfg. Co., 5063 Waterloo Rd., Atwater, OH 44201 / 216-947-3721
Pence Precision Barrels, 7567 E. 900 S., S. Whitley, IN 46787 / 219-839-4745
Pendleton Royal, c/o Swingler Buckland Ltd., 4/7 Highgate St., Birmingham, ENGLAND / 44 121 440 3060 or 44 121 446 5898; FAX: 44 121 446 4165
Pendleton Woolen Mills, P.O. Box 3030, 220 N.W. Broadway, Portland, OR 97208 / 503-226-4801
Penn Bullets, P.O. Box 756, Indianola, PA 15051

MANUFACTURER'S DIRECTORY

Penn's Woods Products, Inc., 19 W. Pittsburgh St., Delmont, PA 15626 / 412-468-8311; FAX: 412-468-8975
Pennsylvania Gun Parts Inc, PO Box 665, 300 Third St, East Berlin, PA 17316-0665 / 717-259-8010; FAX: 717-259-0057
Pennsylvania Gunsmith School, 812 Ohio River Blvd., Avalon, Pittsburgh, PA 15202 / 412-766-1812 FAX: 412-766-0855 pgs@pagunsmith.com www.pagunsmith.com
Penrod Precision, 312 College Ave., P.O. Box 307, N. Manchester, IN 46962 / 219-982-8385
Pentax Corp., 35 Inverness Dr. E., Englewood, CO 80112 / 303-799-8000; FAX: 303-790-1131
Pentheny de Pentheny, 108 Petaluma Ave #202, Sebastopol, CA 95472-4220 / 707-573-1390; FAX: 707-573-1390
Perazone-Gunsmith, Brian, Cold Spring Rd, Roxbury, NY 12474 / 607-326-4088; FAX: 607-326-3140
Perazzi USA, Inc., 1207 S. Shamrock Ave., Monrovia, CA 91016 / 626-303-0068; FAX: 626-303-2081
Performance Specialists, 308 Eanes School Rd., Austin, TX 78746 / 512-327-0119
Perugini Visini & Co. S.r.l., Via Camprelle, 126, 25080 Nuvolera, ITALY / 30-6897535; FAX: 30-6897821
Pete Elsen, Inc., 1529 S. 113th St., West Allis, WI 53214
Pete Mazur Restoration, 13083 Drummer Way, Grass Valley, CA 95949 / 916-268-2412
Pete Rickard, Inc., 115 Roy Walsh Rd, Cobleskill, NY 12043 / 518-234-2731: FAX: 518-234-2454 rickard@telenet.net peterickard.com
Peter Dyson & Son Ltd., 3 Cuckoo Lane, Honley Huddersfield, Yorkshire, HD7 2BR ENGLAND / 44-1484-661062; FAX: 44-1484-663709
Peter Hale/Engraver, 800 E. Canyon Rd., Spanish Fork, UT 84660 / 801-798-8215
Peters Stahl GmbH, Stettiner Strasse 42, D-33106, Paderborn, / 05251-750025; FAX: 05251-75611
Petersen Publishing Co., (See Emap USA)
Peterson Gun Shop, Inc., A.W., 4255 W. Old U.S. 441, Mt. Dora, FL 32757-3299 / 352-383-4258; FAX: 352-735-1001
Petro-Explo Inc., 7650 U.S. Hwy. 287, Suite 100, Arlington, TX 76017 / 817-478-8888
Pettinger Books, Gerald, Rt. 2, Box 125, Russell, IA 50238 / 515-535-2239
Pflumm Mfg. Co., 10662 Widmer Rd., Lenexa, KS 66215 / 800-888-4867; FAX: 913-451-7857
PFRB Co., P.O. Box 1242, Bloomington, IL 61702 / 309-473-3964; FAX: 309-473-2161
Philip S. Olt Co., P.O. Box 550, 12662 Fifth St., Pekin, IL 61554 / 309-348-3633; FAX: 309-348-3300
Phillippi Custom Bullets, Justin, P.O. Box 773, Ligonier, PA 15658 / 724-238-2962; FAX: 724-238-9671 jrp@wpa.net http://www.wpa.net~jrphil
Phillips & Rogers, Inc., 100 Hilbig #C, Conroe, TX 77301 / 409-435-0011
Phoenix Arms, 1420 S. Archibald Ave., Ontario, CA 91761 / 909-947-4843; FAX: 909-947-6798
Photronic Systems Engineering Company, 6731 Via De La Reina, Bonsall, CA 92003 / 619-758-8000
Piedmont Community College, P.O. Box 1197, Roxboro, NC 27573 / 336-599-1181 FAX: 336-597-3817 www.piedmont.cc.nc.us
Pierce Pistols, 55 Sorrellwood Lane, Sharpsburg, GA 30277-9523 / 404-253-8192
Pietta (See U.S. Importers-Navy Arms Co, Taylor's & Co.,)
Pilgrim Pewter,Inc. (See Bell Originals Inc. Sid)
Pilkington, Scott (See Little Trees Ramble)
Pine Technical College, 1100 4th St., Pine City, MN 55063 / 800-521-7463; FAX: 612-629-6766
Pinetree Bullets, 133 Skeena St., Kitimat, BC V8C 1Z1 CANADA / 604-632-3768; FAX: 604-632-3768
Pioneer Arms Co., 355 Lawrence Rd., Broomall, PA 19008 / 215-356-5203
Piotti (See U.S. Importer-Moore & Co, Wm. Larkin)
Piquette, Paul R., 80 Bradford Dr., Feeding Hills, MA 01030 / 413-786-8118; or 413-789-4582
Plaxco, J. Michael, Rt. 1, P.O. Box 203, Roland, AR 72135 / 501-868-9787
Plaza Cutlery, Inc., 3333 Bristol, 161 South Coast Plaza, Costa Mesa, CA 92626 / 714-549-3932
Plum City Ballistic Range, N2162 80th St., Plum City, WI 54761 / 715-647-2539
PlumFire Press, Inc., 30-A Grove Ave., Patchogue, NY 11772-4112 / 800-695-7246; FAX: 516-758-4071
PMC/Eldorado Cartridge Corp., P.O. Box 62508, 12801 U.S. Hwy. 95 S., Boulder City, NV 89005 / 702-294-0025; FAX: 702-294-0121
Poburka, Philip (See Bison Studios)
Pohl, Henry A. (See Great American Gun Co.
Pointing Dog Journal, Village Press Publications, P.O. Box 968, Dept. PGD, Traverse City, MI 49685 / 800-272-3246; FAX: 616-946-3289
Police Bookshelf, P.O. Box 122, Concord, NH 03301 / 603-224-6814; FAX: 603-226-3554
Polywad, Inc., P.O. Box 7916, Macon, GA 31209 / 912-477-0669 polywadmpb@aol.com www.polywad.com
Pomeroy, Robert, RR1, Box 50, E. Corinth, ME 04427 / 207-285-7721
Ponsness/Warren, P.O. Box 8, Rathdrum, ID 83858 / 208-687-2231; FAX: 208-687-2233
Pony Express Reloaders, 608 E. Co. Rd. D, Suite 3, St. Paul, MN 55117 / 612-483-9406; FAX: 612-483-9884
Pony Express Sport Shop, 16606 Schoenborn St., North Hills, CA 91343 / 818-895-1231
Potts, Wayne E., 912 Poplar St., Denver, CO 80220 / 303-355-5462
Powder Horn Antiques, P.O. Box 4196, Ft. Lauderdale, FL 33338 / 305-565-6060
Powell & Son (Gunmakers) Ltd., William, 35-37 Carrs Lane, Birmingham, B4 7SX ENGLAND / 121-643-0689; FAX: 121-631-3504
Powell Agency, William, 22 Circle Dr., Bellmore, NY 11710 / 516-679-1158
Power Custom, Inc., 29739 Hwy. J, Gravois Mills, MO 65037 / 513-372-5684; FAX: 573-372-5799 pwpowers@laurie.net www.powercustom.com
Power Plus Enterprises, Inc., PO Box 38, Warm Springs, GA 31830 / 706-655-2132
Powley Computer (See Hutton Rifle Ranch)
Practical Tools, Inc., 7067 Easton Rd., P.O. Box 133, Pipersville, PA 18947 / 215-766-7301; FAX: 215-766-8681
Prairie Gun Works, 1-761 Marion St., Winnipeq, MB R2J 0K6 Canada / 204-231-2976; FAX: 204-231-8566
Prairie River Arms, 1220 N. Sixth St., Princeton, IL 61356 / 815-875-1616 or 800-445-1541; FAX: 815-875-1402
Pranger, Ed G., 1414 7th St., Anacortes, WA 98221 / 206-293-3488
Pre-Winchester 92-90-62 Parts Co., P.O. Box 8125, W. Palm Beach, FL 33407
Precise Metalsmithing Enterprises, 146 Curtis Hill Rd., Chehalis, WA 98532 / 206-748-3743; FAX: 206-748-8102
Precision Airgun Sales, Inc., 5247 Warrensville Ctr Rd, Maple Hts., OH 44137 / 216-587-5005 FAX: 216-587-5005
Precision Cartridge, 176 Eastside Rd., Deer Lodge, MT 59722 / 800-397-3901 or 406-846-3900
Precision Cast Bullets, 101 Mud Creek Lane, Ronan, MT 59864 / 406-676-5135
Precision Castings & Equipment, P.O. Box 326, Jasper, IN 47547-0135 / 812-634-9167
Precision Components, 3177 Sunrise Lake, Milford, PA 18337 / 570-686-4414
Precision Components and Guns, Rt. 55, P.O. Box 337, Pawling, NY 12564 / 914-855-3040
Precision Delta Corp., P.O. Box 128, Ruleville, MS 38771 / 601-756-2810; FAX: 601-756-2590
Precision Gun Works, 104 Sierra Rd Dept. GD, Kerrville, TX 78028 / 830-367-4587
Precision Munitions, Inc., P.O. Box 326, Jasper, IN 47547
Precision Reloading, Inc., P.O. Box 122, Stafford Springs, CT 06076 / 860-684-5680 FAX: 860-684-6788
Precision Sales International, Inc., P.O. Box 1776, Westfield, MA 01086 / 413-562-5055; FAX: 413-562-5056
Precision Shooting,Inc., 222 McKee St., Manchester, CT 06040 / 860-645-8776; FAX: 860-643-8215
Precision Small Arms, 9777 Wilshire Blvd., Suite 1005, Beverly Hills, CA 90212 / 310-859-4867; FAX: 310-859-2868
Precision Small Arms Inc, 9272 Jeronimo Rd, Ste 121, Irvine, CA 92618 / 800-554-5515; FAX: 949-768-4808 www.tcbebe.com
Precision Specialties, 131 Hendom Dr., Feeding Hills, MA 01030 / 413-786-3365; FAX: 413-786-3365
Precision Sport Optics, 15571 Producer Lane, Unit G, Huntington Beach, CA 92649 / 714-891-1309; FAX: 714-892-6920
Premier Reticles, 920 Breckinridge Lane, Winchester, VA 22601-6707 / 540-722-0601; FAX: 540-722-3522
Prescott Projectile Co., 1808 Meadowbrook Road, Prescott, AZ 86303
Preslik's Gunstocks, 4245 Keith Ln., Chico, CA 95926 / 916-891-8236
Price Bullets, Patrick W., 16520 Worthley Dr., San Lorenzo, CA 94580 / 510-278-1547
Prime Reloading, 30 Chiswick End, Meldreth, ROYSTON UK / 0763-260636
Primos, Inc., P.O. Box 12785, Jackson, MS 39236-2785 / 601-366-1288; FAX: 601-362-3274
PRL Bullets, c/o Blackburn Enterprises, 114 Stuart Rd., Ste. 110, Cleveland, TN 37312 / 423-559-0340
Pro Load Ammunition, Inc., 5180 E. Seltice Way, Post Falls, ID 83854 / 208-773-9444; FAX: 208-773-9441
Pro-Mark Div. of Wells Lamont, 6640 W. Touhy, Chicago, IL 60648 / 312-647-8200
Pro-Port Ltd., 41302 Executive Dr., Harrison Twp., MI 48045-1306 / 810-469-6727 FAX: 810-469-0425
Pro-Shot Products, Inc., P.O. Box 763, Taylorville, IL 62568 / 217-824-9133; FAX: 217-824-8861
Professional Gunsmiths of America,Inc., Route 1, Box 224F, Lexington, MO 64067 / 816-259-2636
Professional Hunter Supplies (See Star Custom Bullets,) PO Box 608, 468 Main St, Ferndale, CA 95536 / 707-786-9140; FAX: 707-786-9117
Professional Ordnance, Inc., 1215 E. Airport Dr., Box 182, Ontario, CA 91761 / 909-923-5559; FAX: 909-923-0899
Prolixrr Lubricants, P.O. Box 1348, Victorville, CA 92393 / 800-248-5823 or 760-243-3129; FAX: 760-241-0148
Proofmark Corp., P.O. Box 610, Burgess, VA 22432 / 804-453-4337; FAX: 804-453-4337 proofmark@rivnet.net
Protektor Model, 1-11 Bridge St., Galeton, PA 16922 / 814-435-2442
Prototech Industries, Inc., Rt. 1, Box 81, Delia, KS 66418 / 913-771-3571; FAX: 913-771-2531
ProWare, Inc., 15847 NE Hancock St., Portland, OR 97230 / 503-239-0159
PWL Gunleather, P.O. Box 450432, Atlanta, GA 31145 / 770-822-1640; FAX: 770-822-1704 covert@pwlusa.com www.pwlusa.com
Pyromid, Inc., 3292 S. Highway 97, Redmond, OR 97756 / 503-548-1041; FAX: 503-923-1004

Q

Quack Decoy & Sporting Clays, 4 Ann & Hope Way, P.O. Box 98, Cumberland, RI 02864 / 401-723-8202; FAX: 401-722-5910
Quaker Boy, Inc., 5455 Webster Rd., Orchard Parks, NY 14127 / 716-662-3979; FAX: 716-662-9426
Quality Arms, Inc., Box 19477, Dept. GD, Houston, TX 77224 / 281-870-8377; FAX: 281-870-8524 arrieta2@excite.com www.gunshop.com
Quality Firearms of Idaho, Inc., 659 Harmon Way, Middleton, ID 83644-3065 / 208-466-1631
Quality Parts Co./Bushmaster Firearms, 999 Roosevelt Trail Bldg. 3, Windham, ME 04062 / 207-892-2005; FAX: 207-892-8068
Quarton USA, Ltd. Co., 7042 Alamo Downs Pkwy., Suite 370, San Antonio, TX 78238-4518 / 800-520-8435 or 210-520-8430; FAX: 210-520-8433
Que Industries, Inc., P.O. Box 2471, Everett, WA 98203 / 800-769-6930 or 206-347-9843; FAX: 206-514-3266
Queen Cutlery Co., P.O. Box 500, Franklinville, NY 14737 / 800-222-5233; FAX: 800-299-2618

R

R&C Knives & Such, 2136 CANDY CANE WALK, Manteca, CA 95336-9501 / 209-239-3722; FAX: 209-825-6947
R&D Gun Repair, Kenny Howell, RR1 Box 283, Beloit, WI 53511
R&J Gun Shop, 337 S Humbolt St, Canyon City, OR 97820 / 541-575-2130 rjgunshop@highdestertnet.com
R&S Industries Corp., 8255 Brentwood Industrial Dr., St. Louis, MO 63144 / 314-781-5400 polishingcloth.com
R. Murphy Co., Inc., 13 Groton-Harvard Rd., P.O. Box 376, Ayer, MA 01432 / 617-772-3481
R.A. Wells Custom Gunsmith, 3452 1st Ave., Racine, WI 53402 / 414-639-5223
R.E. Seebeck Assoc., P.O. Box 59752, Dallas, TX 75229
R.E.I., P.O. Box 88, Tallevast, FL 34270 / 813-755-0085
R.E.T. Enterprises, 2608 S. Chestnut, Broken Arrow, OK 74012 / 918-251-GUNS; FAX: 918-251-0587
R.F. Mitchell Bullets, 430 Walnut St., Westernport, MD 21562
R.I.S. Co., Inc., 718 Timberlake Circle, Richardson, TX 75080 / 214-235-0933
R.M. Precision, P.O. Box 210, LaVerkin, UT 84745 / 801-635-4656; FAX: 801-635-4430
R.T. Eastman Products, P.O. Box 1531, Jackson, WY 83001 / 307-733-3217 or 800-624-4311
Rabeno, Martin, 92 Spook Hole Rd., Ellenville, NY 12428 / 914-647-4567; FAX: 914-647-2129
Radack Photography, Lauren, 21140 Jib Court L-12, Aventura, FL 33180 / 305-931-3110
Radiator Specialty Co., 1900 Wilkinson Blvd., P.O. Box 34689, Charlotte, NC 28234 / 800-438-6947; FAX: 800-421-9525
Radical Concepts, P.O. Box 1473, Lake Grove, OR 97035 / 503-538-7437
Rainier Ballistics Corp., 4500 15th St. East, Tacoma, WA 98424 / 800-638-8722 or 206-922-7589; FAX: 206-922-7854

REFERENCE

Manufacturer's Directory

Ralph Bone Engraving, 718 N. Atlanta, Owasso, OK 74055 / 918-272-9745
Ram-Line Blount, Inc., P.O. Box 39, Onalaska, WI 54650
Ramon B. Gonzalez Guns, P.O. Box 370, 93 St. Joseph's Hill Road, Monticello, NY 12701 / 914-794-4515
Rampart International, 2781 W. MacArthur Blvd., B-283, Santa Ana, CA 92704 / 800-976-7240 or 714-557-6405
Ranch Products, P.O. Box 145, Malinta, OH 43535 / 313-277-3118; FAX: 313-565-8536
Randall-Made Knives, P.O. Box 1988, Orlando, FL 32802 / 407-855-8075
Randco UK, 286 Gipsy Rd., Welling, DA16 1JJ ENGLAND / 44 81 303 4118
Randolph Engineering, Inc., 26 Thomas Patten Dr., Randolph, MA 02368 / 800-541-1405; FAX: 800-875-4200
Randy Duane Custom Stocks, 110 W. North Ave., Winchester, VA 22601 / 703-667-9461; FAX: 703-722-3993
Range Brass Products Company, P.O. Box 218, Rockport, TX 78381
Ranger Products, 2623 Grand Blvd., Suite 209, Holiday, FL 34609 / 813-942-4652 or 800-407-7007; FAX: 813-942-6221
Ranger Shooting Glasses, 26 Thomas Patten Dr., Randolph, MA 02368 / 800-541-1405; FAX: 617-986-0337
Ranging, Inc., Routes 5 & 20, East Bloomfield, NY 14443 / 716-657-6161; FAX: 716-657-5405
Ransom International Corp., 1027 Spire Dr, Prescott, AZ 86302 / 520-778-7899; FAX: 520-778-7993 ransom@primenet.com www.ransom-intl.com
Rapine Bullet Mould Mfg. Co., 9503 Landis Lane, East Greenville, PA 18041 / 215-679-5413; FAX: 215-679-9795
Raptor Arms Co., Inc., 273 Canal St, #179, Shelton, CT 06484 / 203-924-7618; FAX: 203-924-7624
Ravell Ltd., 289 Diputacion St., 08009, Barcelona, SPAIN / 34(3) 4874486; FAX: 34(3) 4881394
Ray Riling Arms Books Co., 6844 Gorsten St., P.O. Box 18925, Philadelphia, PA 19119 / 215-438-2456; FAX: 215-438-5395
Ray's Gunsmith Shop, 3199 Elm Ave., Grand Junction, CO 81504 / 970-434-6162; FAX: 970-434-6162
Raytech Div. of Lyman Products Corp., 475 Smith Street, Middletown, CT 06457-1541 / 860-632-2020; FAX: 860-632-1699
RCBS Div. of Blount, 605 Oro Dam Blvd., Oroville, CA 95965 / 800-533-5000 or 916-533-5191; FAX: 916-533-1647 www.rcbs.com
Reagent Chemical & Research, Inc. (See Calico Hardwoods, Inc.)
Reardon Products, P.O. Box 126, Morrison, IL 61270 / 815-772-3155
Red Diamond Dist. Co., 1304 Snowdon Dr., Knoxville, TN 37912
Redding Reloading Equipment, 1089 Starr Rd., Cortland, NY 13045 / 607-753-3331; FAX: 607-756-8445
Redfield Media Resource Center, 4607 N.E. Cedar Creek Rd., Woodland, WA 98674 / 360-225-5000 FAX: 360-225-7616
Redfield, Inc, 5800 E Jewell Ave, Denver, CO 80224 / 303-757-6411; FAX: 303-756-2338
Redfield/Blount, PO Box 39, Onalaska, WI 54650 / 800-635-7656
Redman's Rifling & Reboring, 189 Nichols Rd., Omak, WA 98841 / 509-826-5512
Redwood Bullet Works, 3559 Bay Rd., Redwood City, CA 94063 / 415-367-6741
Reed, Dave, Rt. 1, Box 374, Minnesota City, MN 55959 / 507-689-2944
Reiswig, Wallace E. (See Claro Walnut Gunstock Co.,)
Reloaders Equipment Co., 4680 High St., Ecorse, ML 48229
Reloading Specialties, Inc., Box 1130, Pine Island, MN 55463 / 507-356-8500; FAX: 507-356-8800
Remington Arms Co., Inc., 870 Remington Drive, P.O. Box 700, Madison, NC 27025-0700 / 800-243-9700; FAX: 910-548-8700
Remington Double Shotguns, 7885 Cyd Dr., Denver, CO 80221 / 303-429-6947
Renato Gamba S.p.A.-Societa Armi Bresciane Srl., Via Artigiani 93, 25063 Gardone, Val Trompia (BS), ITALY / 30-8911640; FAX: 30-8911648
Renegade, P.O. Box 31546, Phoenix, AZ 85046 / 602-482-6777; FAX: 602-482-1952
Renfrew Guns & Supplies, R.R. 4, Renfrew, ON K7V 3Z7 CANADA / 613-432-7080
Reno, Wayne, 2808 Stagestop Rd, Jefferson, CO 80456 / 719-836-3452
Republic Arms, Inc., 15167 Sierra Bonita Lane, Chino, CA 91710 / 909-597-3873; FAX: 909-597-2612
Retting, Inc., Martin B, 11029 Washington, Culver City, CA 90232 / 213-837-2412
RG-G, Inc., PO Box 935, Trinidad, CO 81082 / 719-845-1436
Rhino, P.O. Box 787, Locust, NC 28097 / 704-753-2198
Rhodeside, Inc., 1704 Commerce Dr., Piqua, OH 45356 / 513-773-5781
Rice, Keith (See White Rock Tool & Die)
Richard H.R. Loweth (Firearms), 29 Hedgegrow Lane, Kirby Muxloe, Leics. LE9 2BN, ENGLAND
Richards Micro-Fit Stocks, 8331 N. San Fernando Ave., Sun Valley, CA 91352 / 818-767-6097; FAX: 818-767-7121
Rickard, Inc., Pete, RD 1, Box 292, Cobleskill, NY 12043 / 800-282-5663; FAX: 518-234-2454
Ridgeline, Inc, Bruce Sheldon, PO Box 930, Dewey, AZ 86327-0930 / 800-632-5900; FAX: 520-632-5900
Ridgetop Sporting Goods, P.O. Box 306, 42907 Hilligoss Ln. East, Eatonville, WA 98328 / 360-832-6422; FAX: 360-832-6422
Ries, Chuck, 415 Ridgecrest Dr., Grants Pass, OR 97527 / 503-476-5623
Rifles, Inc., 873 W. 5400 N., Cedar City, UT 84720 / 801-586-5996; FAX: 801-586-5996
Rigby & Co., John, 66 Great Suffolk St, London, ENGLAND / 0171-620-0690; FAX: 0171-928-9205
Riggs, Jim, 206 Azalea, Boerne, TX 78006 / 210-249-8567
Riley Ledbetter Airguns, 1804 E. Sprague St., Winston Salem, NC 27107-3521 / 919-784-0676
Riling Arms Books Co., Ray, 6844 Gorsten St, PO Box 18925, Philadelphia, PA 19119 / 215-438-2456; FAX: 215-438-5395
Rim Pac Sports, Inc., 1034 N. Soldano Ave., Azusa, CA 91702-2135
Ringler Custom Leather Co., 31 Shining Mtn. Rd., Powell, WY 82435 / 307-645-3255
Ripley Rifles, 42 Fletcher Street, Ripley, Derbyshire, DE5 3LP ENGLAND / 011-0773-748353
River Road Sporting Clays, Bruce Barsotti, P.O. Box 3016, Gonzales, CA 93926 / 408-675-2473
Rizzini F.lli (See U.S. Importers-Moore & C England)
Rizzini SNC, Via 2 Giugno, 7/7Bis-25060, Marcheno (Brescia), ITALY
RLCM Enterprises, 110 Hill Crest Drive, Burleson, TX 76028
RMS Custom Gunsmithing, 4120 N. Bitterwell, Prescott Valley, AZ 86314 / 520-772-7626
Robert Evans Engraving, 332 Vine St., Oregon City, OR 97045 / 503-656-5693
Robert Valade Engraving, 931 3rd Ave., Seaside, OR 97138 / 503-738-7672
Roberts Products, 25328 SE Iss. Beaver Lk. Rd., Issaquah, WA 98029 / 206-392-8172
Robinett, R. G., P.O. Box 72, Madrid, IA 50156 / 515-795-2906
Robinson, Don, Pennsylvaia Hse, 36 Fairfax Crescent, W Yorkshire, ENGLAND / 0422-364458
Robinson Firearms Mfg. Ltd., 1699 Blondeaux Crescent, Kelowna, BC V1Y 4J8 CANADA / 604-868-9596
Robinson H.V. Bullets, 3145 Church St., Zachary, LA 70791 / 504-654-4029
Rochester Lead Works, 76 Anderson Ave., Rochester, NY 14607 / 716-442-8500; FAX: 716-442-4712
Rock River Arms, 101 Noble St., Cleveland, IL 61241
Rockwood Corp., Speedwell Division, 136 Lincoln Blvd., Middlesex, NJ 08846 / 800-243-8274; FAX: 980-560-7475
Rocky Mountain Arms, Inc., 1813 Sunset Pl, Unit D, Longmont, CO 80501 / 800-375-0846; FAX: 303-678-8766
Rocky Mountain High Sports Glasses, 8121 N. Central Park Ave., Skokie, IL 60076 / 847-679-1012 or 800-323-1418; FAX: 847-679-0184
Rocky Mountain Rifle Works Ltd., 1707 14th St., Boulder, CO 80302 / 303-443-9189
Rocky Mountain Target Co., 3 Aloe Way, Leesburg, FL 34788 / 352-365-9598
Rocky Mountain Wildlife Products, P.O. Box 999, La Porte, CO 80535 / 970-484-2768; FAX: 970-484-0807
Rocky Shoes & Boots, 294 Harper St., Nelsonville, OH 45764 / 800-848-9452 or 614-753-1951; FAX: 614-753-4024
Rodgers & Sons Ltd., Joseph (See George Ibberson (Sheffield) Ltd.,)
Rogue Rifle Co., Inc., P.O. Box 20, Prospect, OR 97536 / 541-560-4040; FAX: 541-560-4041
Rogue River Rifleworks, 1317 Spring St., Paso Robles, CA 93446 / 805-227-4706; FAX: FAX:805-227-4723
Rohner, Hans, 1148 Twin Sisters Ranch Rd., Nederland, CO 80466-9600
Rohner, John, 186 Virginia Ave, Asheville, NC 28806 / 303-444-3841
Romain's Custom Guns, Inc., RD 1, Whetstone Rd., Brockport, PA 15823 / 814-265-1948
Ron Frank Custom Classic Arms, 7131 Richland Rd., Ft. Worth, TX 76118 / 817-284-9300; FAX: 817-284-9300
Ron Lutz Engraving, E. 1998 Smokey Valley Rd., Scandinavia, WI 54977 / 715-467-2674
Rooster Laboratories, P.O. Box 412514, Kansas City, MO 64141 / 816-474-1622; FAX: 816-474-1307
Rorschach Precision Products, P.O. Box 151613, Irving, TX 75015 / 214-790-3487
Rosenberg & Son, Jack A, 12229 Cox Ln, Dallas, TX 75234 / 214-241-6302
Rosenthal, Brad and Sallie, 19303 Ossenfort Ct., St. Louis, MO 63038 / 314-273-5159; FAX: 314-273-5149
Ross, Don, 12813 West 83 Terrace, Lenexa, KS 66215 / 913-492-6982
Rosser, Bob, 1824 29th Ave., Suite 214, Birmingham, AL 35209 / 205-870-4422; FAX: 205-870-4421
Rossi Firearms, Braztech, Gary Mchalik, 16175 NW 49th Ave, Miami, FL 33014-6314 / 305-474-0401
Roto Carve, 2754 Garden Ave., Janesville, IA 50647
Rottweil Compe, 1330 Glassell, Orange, CA 92667
Round Edge, Inc., P.O. Box 723, Lansdale, PA 19446 / 215-361-0859
Roy Baker's Leather Goods, P.O. Box 893, Magnolia, AR 71753 / 501-234-0344
Roy's Custom Grips, 793 Mt. Olivet Church Road, Lynchburg, VA 24504-9715 / 804-993-3470
Royal Arms Gunstocks, 919 8th Ave. NW, Great Falls, MT 59404 / 406-453-1149 FAX: 406-453-1194 royalarms@lmt.net lmt.net/~royalarms
RPM, 15481 N. Twin Lakes Dr., Tucson, AZ 85739 / 520-825-1233; FAX: 520-825-3333
Rubright Bullets, 1008 S. Quince Rd., Walnutport, PA 18088 / 215-767-1339
Rucker Dist. Inc., P.O. Box 479, Terrell, TX 75160 / 214-563-2094
Ruger (See Sturm, Ruger & Co., Inc.)
Rumanya Inc., 11513 Piney Lodge Rd, Gaithersburg, MD 20878-2443 / 281-345-2077; FAX: 281-345-2005
Rundell's Gun Shop, 6198 Frances Rd., Clio, MI 48420 / 313-687-0559
Runge, Robert P., 94 Grove St., Ilion, NY 13357 / 315-894-3036
Rupert's Gun Shop, 2202 Dick Rd., Suite B, Fenwick, MI 48834 / 517-248-3252
Russ Haydon Shooters' Supply, 15018 Goodrich Dr. NW, Gig Harbor, WA 98329 / 253-857-7557; FAX: 253-857-7884
Russ Trading Post, William A. Russ, 23 William St., Addison, NY 14801-1326 / 607-359-3896
Russ, William. (See RUSS TRADING POST)
Rusteprufe Laboratories, 1319 Jefferson Ave., Sparta, WI 54656 / 608-269-4144
Rusty Duck Premium Gun Care Products, 7785 Foundation Dr., Suite 6, Florence, KY 41042 / 606-342-5553; FAX: 606-342-5556
Rutgers Book Center, 127 Raritan Ave., Highland Park, NJ 08904 / 732-545-4344 FAX: 732-545-6686
Rutten (See U.S. Importer-Labanu Inc)
RWS (See US Importer-Dynamit Nobel-RWS, Inc.), 81 Ruckman Rd, Closter, NJ 07624 / 201-767-7971; FAX: 201-767-1589
Ryan, Chad L., RR 3, Box 72, Cresco, IA 52136 / 319-547-4384

S

S&B Industries, 11238 McKinley Rd., Montrose, MI 48457 / 810-639-5491
S&K Mfg. Co., P.O. Box 247, Pittsfield, PA 16340 / 814-563-7808; FAX: 814-563-4067
S&S Firearms, 74-11 Myrtle Ave., Glendale, NY 11385 / 718-497-1100; FAX: 718-497-1105
S.A.R.L. G. Granger, 66 cours Fauriel, 42100, Saint Etienne, FRANCE / 04 77 25 14 73; FAX: 04 77 38 66 99
S.C.R.C., P.O. Box 660, Katy, TX 77492-0660 FAX: 713-578-2124
S.D. Meacham, 1070 Angel Ridge, Peck, ID 83545
S.G.S. Sporting Guns Srl., Via Della Resistenza, 37 20090, Buccinasco, ITALY / 2-45702446; FAX: 2-45702464
S.I.A.C.E. (See U.S. Importer-IAR Inc)
S.L.A.P. Industries, P.O. Box 1121, Parklands, 02121 SOUTH AFRICA / 27-11-788-0030; FAX: 27-11-788-0030
Sabatti S.r.l., via Alessandro Volta 90, 25063 Gardone V.T., Brescia, ITALY / 030-8912207-831312; FAX: 030-8912059
SAECO (See Redding Reloading Equipment)
Saf-T-Lok, 5713 Corporate Way, Suite 100, W. Palm Beach, FL 33407
Safari Outfitters Ltd., 71 Ethan Allan Hwy., Ridgefield, CT 06877 / 203-544-9505
Safari Press, Inc., 15621 Chemical Lane B, Huntington Beach, CA 92649 / 714-894-9080; FAX: 714-894-4949

MANUFACTURER'S DIRECTORY

Safariland Ltd., Inc., 3120 E. Mission Blvd., P.O. Box 51478, Ontario, CA 91761 / 909-923-7300; FAX: 909-923-7400
SAFE, P.O. Box 864, Post Falls, ID 83854 / 208-773-3624 FAX: 208-773-6819 staysafe@safe-llc.com www.safe-llc.com
Safety Speed Holster, Inc., 910 S. Vail Ave., Montebello, CA 90640 / 323-723-4140; FAX: 323-726-6973
Sako Ltd (See U.S. Importer-Stoeger Industries)
Samco Global Arms, Inc., 6995 NW 43rd St., Miami, FL 33166 / 305-593-9782 FAX: 305-593-1014
Sampson, Roger, 2316 Mahogany St., Mora, MN 55051 / 612-679-4868
San Francisco Gun Exchange, 124 Second St., San Francisco, CA 94105 / 415-982-6097
San Marco (See U.S. Importers-Cape Outfitters-EMF)
Sanders Custom Gun Service, 2358 Tyler Lane, Louisville, KY 40205 / 502-454-3338; FAX: 502-451-8857
Sanders Gun and Machine Shop, 145 Delhi Road, Manchester, IA 52057
Sandia Die & Cartridge Co., 37 Atancacio Rd. NE, Auquerque, NM 87123 / 505-298-5729
Sarco, Inc., 323 Union St., Stirling, NJ 07980 / 908-647-3800; FAX: 908-647-9413
Sauer (See U.S. Importers-Paul Co., The, Sigarms Inc.,)
Sauls, R. (See BRYAN & ASSOC)
Saunders Gun & Machine Shop, R.R. 2, Delhi Road, Manchester, IA 52057
Savage Arms (Canada), Inc., 248 Water St., P.O. Box 1240, Lakefield, ON K0L 2H0 CANADA / 705-652-8000; FAX: 705-652-8431
Savage Arms, Inc., 100 Springdale Rd., Westfield, MA 01085 / 413-568-7001; FAX: 413-562-7764
Savage Range Systems, Inc., 100 Springdale RD., Westfield, MA 01085 / 413-568-7001; FAX: 413-562-1152
Saville Iron Co. (See Greenwood Precision)
Savino, Barbara J., P.O. Box 51, West Burke, VT 05871-0051
Scanco Environmental Systems, 5000 Highlands Parkway, Suite 180, Atlanta, GA 30082 / 770-431-0025; FAX: 770-431-0028
Scansport, Inc., P.O. Box 700, Enfield, NH 03748 / 603-632-7654
Scattergun Technologies, Inc., 620 8th Ave. South, Nashville, TN 37203 / 615-254-1441; FAX: 615-254-1449
Sceery Game Calls, P.O. Box 6520, Sante Fe, NM 87502 / 505-471-9110; FAX: 505-471-3476
Schaefer Shooting Sports, P.O. Box 1515, Melville, NY 11747-0515 / 516-643-5466 FAX: 516-643-2426 rschaefe@optonline.net www.schaefershooting.com
Scharch Mfg., Inc., 10325 CR 120, Salida, CO 81201 / 719-539-7242 or 800-836-4683; FAX: 719-539-3021
Scherer, Box 250, Ewing, VA 24240 / 615-733-2615; FAX: 615-733-2073
Schiffman, Curt, 3017 Kevin Cr., Idaho Falls, ID 83402 / 208-524-4684
Schiffman, Mike, 8233 S. Crystal Springs, McCammon, ID 83250 / 208-254-9114
Schiffman, Norman, 3017 Kevin Cr., Idaho Falls, ID 83402 / 208-524-4684
Schmidt & Bender, Inc., 438 Willow Brook Rd., Meriden, NH 03770 / 800-468-3450 or 800-468-3450; FAX: 603-469-3471
Schmidtke Group, 17050 W. Salentine Dr., New Berlin, WI 53151-7349
Schmidtman Custom Ammunition, 6 Gilbert Court, Cotati, CA 94931
Schneider Bullets, 3655 West 214th St., Fairview Park, OH 44126
Schneider Rifle Barrels, Inc, Gary, 12202 N 62nd Pl, Scottsdale, AZ 85254 / 602-948-2525
Schroeder Bullets, 1421 Thermal Ave., San Diego, CA 92154 / 619-423-3523; FAX: 619-423-8124
Schuetzen Pistol Works, 620-626 Old Pacific Hwy. SE, Olympia, WA 98513 / 360-459-3471; FAX: 360-491-3447
Schulz Industries, 16247 Minnesota Ave., Paramount, CA 90723 / 213-439-5903
Schumakers Gun Shop, 512 Prouty Corner Lp. A, Colville, WA 99114 / 509-684-4848
Scope Control, Inc., 5775 Co. Rd. 23 SE, Alexandria, MN 56308 / 612-762-7295
ScopLevel, 151 Lindbergh Ave., Suite C, Livermore, CA 94550 / 925-449-5052; FAX: 925-373-0861
Score High Gunsmithing, 9812-A, Cochiti SE, Albuquerque, NM 087123 / 800-326-5632 or 505-292-5532; FAX: 505-292-2592
Scot Powder, Rt.1 Box 167, McEwen, TN 37101 / 800-416-3006; FAX: 615-729-4211
Scot Powder Co. of Ohio, Inc., Box GD96, Only, TN 37140 / 615-729-4207 or 800-416-3006; FAX: 615-729-4217
Scott, Dwight, 23089 Englehardt St., Clair Shores, MI 48080 / 313-779-4735
Scott Fine Guns Inc., Thad, PO Box 412, Indianola, MS 38751 / 601-887-5929
Scott McDougall & Associates, 7950 Redwood Dr., Suite 13, Cotati, CA 94931 / 707-546-2264; FAX: 707-795-1911 www.colt380.com
Searcy Enterprises, PO Box 584, Boron, CA 93596 / 760-762-6771 FAX: 760-762-0191
Second Chance Body Armor, P.O. Box 578, Central Lake, MI 49622 / 616-544-5721; FAX: 616-544-9824
Seebeck Assoc., R.E., P. O. Box 59752, Dallas, TX 75229
Seecamp Co. Inc., L. W., PO Box 255, New Haven, CT 06502 / 203-877-3429
Segway Industries, P.O. Box 783, Suffern, NY 10901-0783 / 914-357-5510
Seligman Shooting Products, Box 133, Seligman, AZ 86337 / 602-422-3607
Sellier & Bellot, USA Inc, PO Box 27006, Shawnee Mission, KS 66225 / 913-685-0916; FAX: 913-685-0917
Selsi Co., Inc., P.O. Box 10, Midland Park, NJ 07432-0010 / 201-935-0388; FAX: 201-935-5851
Semmer, Charles (See Remington Double Shotguns), 7885 Cyd Dr, Denver, CO 80221 / 303-429-6947
Sentinel Arms, P.O. Box 57, Detroit, MI 48231 / 313-331-1951; FAX: 313-331-1456
Service Armament, 689 Bergen Blvd., Ridgefield, NJ 07657
Servus Footwear Co., 1136 2nd St., Rock Island, IL 61204 / 309-786-7741; FAX: 309-786-9808
Shappy Bullets, 76 Milldale Ave., Plantsville, CT 06479 / 203-621-3704
Sharp Shooter Supply, 4970 Lehman Road, Delphos, OH 45833 / 419-695-3179
Sharps Arms Co., Inc., C., 100 Centennial, Box 885, Big Timber, MT 59011 / 406-932-4353
Shaw, Inc., E. R. (See Small Arms Mfg. Co.)
Shay's Gunsmithing, 931 Marvin Ave., Lebanon, PA 17042
Sheffield Knifemakers Supply, Inc., P.O. Box 741107, Orange City, FL 32774-1107 / 904-775-6453; FAX: 904-774-5754
Sheldon, Bruce. (See RIDGELINE, INC)
Shepherd Enterprises, Inc., Box 189, Waterloo, NE 68069 / 402-779-2424; FAX: 402-779-4010 sshepherd@shepherdscopes.com www.shepherdscopes.com
Sherwood, George, 46 N. River Dr., Roseburg, OR 97470 / 541-672-3159
Shilen, Inc., 205 Metro Park Blvd., Ennis, TX 75119 / 972-875-5318; FAX: 972-875-5402
Shiloh Creek, Box 357, Cottleville, MO 63338 / 314-925-1842; FAX: 314-925-1842
Shiloh Rifle Mfg., 201 Centennial Dr., Big Timber, MT 59011 / 406-932-4454; FAX: 406-932-5627
Shockley, Harold H., 204 E. Farmington Rd., Hanna City, IL 61536 / 309-565-4524
Shoemaker & Sons Inc., Tex, 714 W Cienega Ave, San Dimas, CA 91773 / 909-592-2071; FAX: 909-592-2378
Shoot Where You Look, Leon Measures, Dept GD, 408 Fair, Livingston, TX 77351
Shoot-N-C Targets (See Birchwood Casey)
Shooter's Choice, 16770 Hilltop Park Place, Chagrin Falls, OH 44023 / 216-543-8808; FAX: 216-543-8811
Shooter's Edge Inc., P.O.Box 769, Trinidad, CO 81082
Shooter's World, 3828 N. 28th Ave., Phoenix, AZ 85017 / 602-266-0170
Shooters Supply, 1120 Tieton Dr., Yakima, WA 98902 / 509-452-1181
Shootin' Accessories, Ltd., P.O. Box 6810, Auburn, CA 95604 / 916-889-2220
Shootin' Shack, Inc., 1065 Silver Beach Rd., Riviera Beach, FL 33403 / 561-842-0990
Shooting Chrony, Inc., 3269 Niagara Falls Blvd., N. Tonawanda, NY 14120 / 905-276-6292; FAX: 416-276-6295
Shooting Specialties (See Titus, Daniel)
Shooting Star, 1715 FM 1626 Ste 105, Manchaca, TX 78652 / 512-462-0009
Shotgun Sports, PO Box 6810, Auburn, CA 95604 / 530-889-2220; FAX: 530-889-9106
Shotguns Unlimited, 2307 Fon Du Lac Rd., Richmond, VA 23229 / 804-752-7115
ShurKatch Corporation, PO Box 850, Richfield Springs, NY 13439 / 315-858-1470; FAX: 315-858-2969
Siegrist Gun Shop, 8752 Turtle Road, Whittemore, MI 48770
Sierra Bullets, 1400 W. Henry St., Sedalia, MO 65301 / 816-827-6300; FAX: 816-827-6300
Sierra Specialty Prod. Co., 1344 Oakhurst Ave., Los Altos, CA 94024 FAX: 415-965-1536
SIG, CH-8212 Neuhausen, SWITZERLAND
SIG-Sauer (See U.S. Importer-Sigarms Inc.)
Sigarms, Inc., Corporate Park, Exeter, NH 03833 / 603-772-2302; FAX: 603-772-9082
Sightron, Inc., 1672B Hwy. 96, Franklinton, NC 27525 / 919-528-8783; FAX: 919-528-0995
Signet Metal Corp., 551 Stewart Ave., Brooklyn, NY 11222 / 718-384-5400; FAX: 718-388-7488
Sile Distributors, Inc., 7 Centre Market Pl., New York, NY 10013 / 212-925-4111; FAX: 212-925-3149
Silencio/Safety Direct, 56 Coney Island Dr., Sparks, NV 89431 / 800-648-1812 or 702-354-4451; FAX: 702-359-1074
Silent Hunter, 1100 Newton Ave., W. Collingswood, NJ 08107 / 609-854-3276
Silhouette Leathers, P.O. Box 1161, Gunnison, CO 81230 / 303-641-6639
Silver Eagle Machining, 18007 N. 69th Ave., Glendale, AZ 85308
Silver Ridge Gun Shop (See Goodwin, Fred)
Simmons, Jerry, 715 Middlebury St., Goshen, IN 46526 / 219-533-8546
Simmons Gun Repair, Inc., 700 S. Rogers Rd., Olathe, KS 66062 / 913-782-3131; FAX: 913-782-4189
Simmons Outdoor Corp., PO Box 217, Heflin, AL 36264
Sinclair International, Inc., 2330 Wayne Haven St., Fort Wayne, IN 46803 / 219-493-1858; FAX: 219-493-2530
Singletary, Kent, 2915 W. Ross, Phoenix, AZ 85027 / 602-582-4900
Sipes Gun Shop, 7415 Asher Ave., Little Rock, AR 72204 / 501-565-8480
Siskiyou Gun Works (See Donnelly, C. P.)
Six Enterprises, 320-D Turtle Creek Ct., San Jose, CA 95125 / 408-999-0201; FAX: 408-999-0216
SKAN A.R., 4 St. Catherines Road, Long Melford, Suffolk, O10 9JU ENGLAND / 011-0787-312942
SKB Shotguns, 4325 S. 120th St., Omaha, NE 68137 / 800-752-2767; FAX: 402-330-8029
Skeoch, Brian R., P.O. Box 279, Glenrock, WY 82637 / 307-436-9655 FAX: 307-436-9034
Skip's Machine, 364 29 Road, Grand Junction, CO 81501 / 303-245-5417
Sklany's Machine Shop, 566 Birch Grove Dr., Kalispell, MT 59901 / 406-755-4257
Slezak, Jerome F., 1290 Marlowe, Lakewood (Cleveland), OH 44107 / 216-221-1668
Slug Group, Inc., P.O. Box 376, New Paris, PA 15554 / 814-839-4517; FAX: 814-839-2601
Slug Site, Ozark Wilds, 21300 Hwy. 5, Versailles, MO 65084 / 573-378-6430 john.ebeling.com
Small Arms Mfg. Co., 5312 Thoms Run Rd., Bridgeville, PA 15017 / 412-221-4343; FAX: 412-221-4303
Small Arms Specialists, 443 Firchburg Rd, Mason, NH 03048 / 603-878-0427 FAX: 603-878-3905 miniguns@empire.net miniguns.com
Small Custom Mould & Bullet Co., Box 17211, Tucson, AZ 85731
Smart Parts, 1203 Spring St., Latrobe, PA 15650 / 412-539-2660; FAX: 412-539-2298
Smires, C. L., 5222 Windmill Lane, Columbia, MD 21044-1328
Smith & Wesson, 2100 Roosevelt Ave., Springfield, MA 01104 / 413-781-8300; FAX: 413-731-8980
Smith, Art, 230 Main St. S., Hector, MN 55342 / 320-848-2760; FAX: 320-848-2760
Smith, Mark A., P.O. Box 182, Sinclair, WY 82334 / 307-324-7929
Smith, Michael, 620 Nye Circle, Chattanooga, TN 37405 / 615-267-8341
Smith, Ron, 5869 Straley, Ft. Worth, TX 76114 / 817-732-6768
Smith, Sharmon, 4545 Speas Rd., Fruitland, ID 83619 / 208-452-6329
Smith Abrasives, Inc., 1700 Sleepy Valley Rd., P.O. Box 5095, Hot Springs, AR 71902-5095 / 501-321-2244; FAX: 501-321-9232
Smith Saddlery, Jesse W., 16909 E Jackson Rd, Elk, WA 99009-9600 / 509-325-0622
Smokey Valley Rifles (See Lutz Engraving, Ron E)
Snapp's Gunshop, 6911 E. Washington Rd., Clare, MI 48617 / 517-386-9226
Sno-Seal, Inc. (See Atsko/Sno-Seal)
Societa Armi Bresciane Srl (See U.S. Importer-Cape Outfitters)
SOS Products Co. (See Buck Stix-SOS Products Co.), Box 3, Neenah, WI 54956
Sotheby's, 1334 York Ave. at 72nd St., New York, NY 10021 / 212-606-7260
Sound Technology, Box 391, Pelham, AL 35124 / 205-664-5860 or 907-486-2825
South Bend Replicas, Inc., 61650 Oak Rd.., South Bend, IN 46614 / 219-289-4500
Southeastern Community College, 1015 S. Gear Ave., West Burlington, IA 52655 / 319-752-2731
Southern Ammunition Co., Inc., 4232 Meadow St., Loris, SC 29569-3124 / 803-756-3262; FAX: 803-756-3583

REFERENCE

MANUFACTURER'S DIRECTORY

Southern Bloomer Mfg. Co., P.O. Box 1621, Bristol, TN 37620 / 615-878-6660; FAX: 615-878-8761
Southern Security, 1700 Oak Hills Dr., Kingston, TN 37763 / 423-376-6297; FAX: 800-251-9992
Southwind Sanctions, P.O. Box 445, Aledo, TX 76008 / 817-441-8917
Sparks, Milt, 605 E. 44th St. No. 2, Boise, ID 83714-4800
Spartan-Realtree Products, Inc., 1390 Box Circle, Columbus, GA 31907 / 706-569-9101; FAX: 706-569-0042
Specialty Gunsmithing, Lynn McMurdo, P.O. Box 404, Afton, WY 83110 / 307-886-5535
Specialty Shooters Supply, Inc., 3325 Griffin Rd., Suite 9mm, Fort Lauderdale, FL 33317
Speedfeed Inc., PO Box 1146, Rocklin, CA 95677 / 916-630-7720; FAX: 916-630-7719
Speer Products Div. of Blount Inc. Sporting Equipm, P.O. Box 856, Lewiston, ID 83501 / 208-746-2351; FAX: 208-746-2915
Spegel, Craig, PO Box 387, Nehalem, OR 97131 / 503-368-5653
Speiser, Fred D., 2229 Dearborn, Missoula, MT 59801 / 406-549-8133
Spencer Reblue Service, 1820 Tupelo Trail, Holt, MI 48842 / 517-694-7474
Spencer's Custom Guns, 4107 Jacobs Creek Dr, Scottsville, VA 24590 / 804-293-6836 FAX: 804-293-6836
SPG LLC, P.O. Box 1625, Cody, WY 82414 / 307-587-7621; FAX: 307-587-7695
Sphinx Engineering SA, Ch. des Grandex-Vies 2, CH-2900, Porrentruy, SWITZERLAND FAX: 41 66 66 30 90
Spokhandguns, Inc., 1206 Fig St., Benton City, WA 99320 / 509-588-5255
Sport Flite Manufacturing Co., P.O. Box 1082, Bloomfield Hills, MI 48303 / 248-647-3747
Sporting Arms Mfg., Inc., 801 Hall Ave., Littlefield, TX 79339 / 806-385-5665; FAX: 806-385-3394
Sporting Clays Of America, 9257 Bluckeye Rd, Sugar Grove, OH 43155-9632 / 740-746-8334; FAX: 740-746-8605
Sports Innovations Inc., P.O. Box 5181, 8505 Jacksboro Hwy., Wichita Falls, TX 76307 / 817-723-6015
Sportsman Safe Mfg. Co., 6309-6311 Paramount Blvd., Long Beach, CA 90805 / 800-266-7150 or 310-984-5445
Sportsman Supply Co., 714 E. Eastwood, P.O. Box 650, Marshall, MO 65340 / 816-886-9393
Sportsman's Communicators, 588 Radcliffe Ave., Pacific Palisades, CA 90272 / 800-538-3752
Sportsmatch U.K. Ltd., 16 Summer St., Leighton Buzzard, Bedfordshire, LU7 8HT ENGLAND / 01525-381638; FAX: 01525-851236
Sportsmen's Exchange & Western Gun Traders, Inc., 560 S. C St., Oxnard, CA 93030 / 805-483-1917
Spradlin's, 457 Shannon Rd, Texos Creek, CO 81223 / 719-275-7105 FAX: 719-275-3852 spradlins@prodigt.net jimspradlin.com
Springfield Sporters, Inc., RD 1, Penn Run, PA 15765 / 412-254-2626; FAX: 412-254-9173
Springfield, Inc., 420 W. Main St., Geneseo, IL 61254 / 309-944-5631; FAX: 309-944-3676
Spyderco, Inc., 4565 N. Hwy. 93, P.O. Box 800, Golden, CO 80403 / 303-279-8383 or 800-525-7770; FAX: 303-278-2229
SSK Industries, 590 Woodvue Lane, Wintersville, OH 43953 / 740-264-0176; FAX: 740-264-2257
Stackpole Books, 5067 Ritter Rd., Mechanicsburg, PA 17055-6921 / 717-796-0411; FAX: 717-796-0412
Stalker, Inc., P.O. Box 21, Fishermans Wharf Rd., Malakoff, TX 75148 / 903-489-1010
Stalwart Corporation, 76 Imperial, Unit A, Evanston, WY 82930 / 307-789-7687; FAX: 307-789-7688
Stan De Treville & Co., 4129 Normal St., San Diego, CA 92103 / 619-298-3393
Stanley Bullets, 2085 Heatheridge Ln., Reno, NV 89509
Stanley Scruggs' Game Calls, Rt. 1, Hwy. 661, Cullen, VA 23934 / 804-542-4241 or 800-323-4828
Star Ammunition, Inc., 5520 Rock Hampton Ct., Indianapolis, IN 46268 / 800-221-5927; FAX: 317-872-5847
Star Bonifacio Echeverria S.A., Torrekva 3, Eibar, 20600 SPAIN / 43-107340; FAX: 43-101524
Star Custom Bullets, P.O. Box 608, 468 Main St., Ferndale, CA 95536 / 707-786-9140; FAX: 707-786-9117
Star Machine Works, PO Box 1872, Pioneer, CA 95666 / 209-295-5000
Stark's Bullet Mfg., 2580 Monroe St., Eugene, OR 97405
Starke Bullet Company, P.O. Box 400, 605 6th St. NW, Cooperstown, ND 58425 / 888-797-3431
Starkey Labs, 6700 Washington Ave. S., Eden Prairie, MN 55344
Starkey's Gun Shop, 9430 McCombs, El Paso, TX 79924 / 915-751-3030
Starlight Training Center, Inc., Rt. 1, P.O. Box 88, Bronaugh, MO 64728 / 417-843-3555
Starline, Inc., 1300 W. Henry St., Sedalia, MO 65301 / 660-827-6640 FAX: 660-827-6650 bjhayden@starlinebra.com http://www.starlinebrass.com
Starr Trading Co., Jedediah, P.O. Box 2007, Farmington Hills, MI 48333 / 810-683-4343; FAX: 810-683-3282
Starrett Co., L. S., 121 Crescent St, Athol, MA 01331 / 978-249-3551 FAX: 978-249-8495
State Arms Gun Co., 815 S. Division St., Waunakee, WI 53597 / 608-849-5800
Steelman's Gun Shop, 10465 Beers Rd., Swartz Creek, MI 48473 / 810-735-4884
Steffens, Ron, 18396 Mariposa Creek Rd., Willits, CA 95490 / 707-485-0873
Stegall, James B., 26 Forest Rd., Wallkill, NY 12589
Steger, James R., 1131 Dorsey Pl., Plainfield, NJ 07062
Steve Henigson & Associates, P.O. Box 2726, Culver City, CA 90231 / 310-305-8288; FAX: 310-305-1905
Steve Kamyk Engraver, 9 Grandview Dr., Westfield, MA 01085-1810 / 413-568-0457
Steve Nastoff's 45 Shop, Inc., 12288 Mahoning Ave., P.O. Box 446, North Jackson, OH 44451 / 330-538-2977
Steves House of Guns, Rt. 1, Minnesota City, MN 55959 / 507-689-2573
Stewart Game Calls, Inc., Johnny, PO Box 7954, 5100 Fort Ave, Waco, TX 76714 / 817-772-3261; FAX: 817-772-3670
Stewart's Gunsmithing, P.O. Box 5854, Pietersburg North 0750, Transvaal, SOUTH AFRICA / 01521-89401
Steyr Mannlicher AG & CO KG, Mannlicherstrasse 1, A-4400, Steyr, AUSTRIA / 0043-7252-78621; FAX: 0043-7252-68621
STI International, 114 Halmar Cove, Georgetown, TX 78628 / 800-959-8201; FAX: 512-819-0465
Stiles Custom Guns, 76 Cherry Run Rd, Box 1605, Homer City, PA 15748 / 712-479-9945
Stillwell, Robert, 421 Judith Ann Dr., Schertz, TX 78154
Stoeger Industries, 5 Mansard Ct., Wayne, NJ 07470 / 201-872-9500 or 800-631-0722; FAX: 201-872-2230
Stoeger Publishing Co. (See Stoeger Industries)
Stone Enterprises Ltd., Rt. 609, P.O. Box 335, Wicomico Church, VA 22579 / 804-580-5114; FAX: 804-580-8421
Stone Mountain Arms, 5988 Peachtree Corners E., Norcross, GA 30071 / 800-251-9412
Stoney Point Products, Inc., PO Box 234, 1822 N Minnesota St, New Ulm, MN 56073-0234 / 507-354-3360; FAX: 507-354-7236 stoney@newulmtel.net www.stoneypoint.com
Storage Tech, 1254 Morris Ave., N. Huntingdon, PA 15642 / 800-437-9393
Storey, Dale A. (See DGS Inc.)
Storm, Gary, P.O. Box 5211, Richardson, TX 75083 / 214-385-0862
Stott's Creek Armory, Inc., 2526 S. 475W, Morgantown, IN 46160 / 317-878-5489; FAX: 317-878-9489 www.sccalendar.com
Stratco, Inc., P.O. Box 2270, Kalispell, MT 59901 / 406-755-1221; FAX: 406-755-1226
Strawbridge, Victor W., 6 Pineview Dr., Dover, NH 03820 / 603-742-0013
Strayer, Sandy. (See STRAYER-VOIGT, INC)
Strayer-Voigt, Inc, Sandy Strayer, 3435 Ray Orr Blvd, Grand Prairie, TX 75050 / 972-513-0575
Streamlight, Inc., 1030 W. Germantown Pike, Norristown, PA 19403 / 215-631-0600; FAX: 610-631-0712
Strong Holster Co., 39 Grove St., Gloucester, MA 01930 / 508-281-3300; FAX: 508-281-6321
Strutz Rifle Barrels, Inc., W. C., PO Box 611, Eagle River, WI 54521 / 715-479-4766
Stuart, V. Pat, Rt.1, Box 447-S, Greenville, VA 24440 / 804-556-3845
Sturgeon Valley Sporters, K. Ide, P.O. Box 283, Vanderbilt, MI 49795 / 517-983-4338
Sturm Ruger & Co. Inc., 200 Ruger Rd., Prescott, AZ 86301 / 520-541-8820; FAX: 520-541-8850
Sullivan, David S .(See Westwind Rifles Inc.)
Summit Specialties, Inc., P.O. Box 786, Decatur, AL 35602 / 205-353-0634; FAX: 205-353-9818
Sun Welding Safe Co., 290 Easy St. No.3, Simi Valley, CA 93065 / 805-584-6678 or 800-729-SAFE FAX: 805-584-6169
Sunny Hill Enterprises, Inc., W1790 Cty. HHH, Malone, WI 53049 / 920-795-4722 FAX: 920-795-4822
"Su-Press-On",Inc., P.O. Box 09161, Detroit, MI 48209 / 313-842-4222
Sure-Shot Game Calls, Inc., P.O. Box 816, 6835 Capitol, Groves, TX 77619 / 409-962-1636; FAX: 409-962-5465
Survival Arms, Inc., 273 Canal St., Shelton, CT 06484-3173 / 203-924-6533; FAX: 203-924-2581
Svon Corp., 280 Eliot St., Ashland, MA 01721 / 508-881-8852
Swann, D. J., 5 Orsova Close, Eltham North Vic., 3095 AUSTRALIA / 03-431-0323
Swanndri New Zealand, 152 Elm Ave., Burlingame, CA 94010 / 415-347-6158
SwaroSports, Inc. (See JagerSport Ltd, One Wholesale Way, Cranston, RI 02920 / 800-962-4867; FAX: 401-946-2587
Swarovski Optik North America Ltd., 2 Slater Rd., Cranston, RI 02920 / 401-946-2220 or 800-426-3089 FAX: 401-946-2587
Sweet Home, Inc., P.O. Box 900, Orrville, OH 44667-0900
Swenson's 45 Shop, A. D., 3839 Ladera Vista Rd, Fallbrook, CA 92028-9431
Swift Bullet Co., P.O. Box 27, 201 Main St., Quinter, KS 67752 / 913-754-3959; FAX: 913-754-2359
Swift Instruments, Inc., 952 Dorchester Ave., Boston, MA 02125 / 617-436-2960; FAX: 617-436-3232
Swift River Gunworks, 450 State St., Belchertown, MA 01007 / 413-323-4052
Szweda, Robert (See RMS Custom Gunsmithing)

T

T&S Industries, Inc., 1027 Skyview Dr., W. Carrollton, OH 45449 / 513-859-8414
T.F.C. S.p.A., Via G. Marconi 118, B, Villa Carcina 25069, ITALY / 030-881271; FAX: 030-881826
T.G. Faust, Inc., 544 Minor St., Reading, PA 19602 / 610-375-8549; FAX: 610-375-4488
T.H.U. Enterprises, Inc., P.O. Box 418, Lederach, PA 19450 / 215-256-1665; FAX: 215-256-9718
T.K. Lee Co., 1282 Branchwater Ln., Birmingham, AL 35216 / 205-913-5222
T.W. Menck Gunsmith Inc., 5703 S. 77th St., Ralston, NE 68127
Tabler Marketing, 2554 Lincoln Blvd., Suite 555, Marina Del Rey, CA 90291 / 818-755-4565; FAX: 818-755-0972
Taconic Firearms Ltd., Perry Lane, PO Box 553, Cambridge, NY 12816 / 518-677-2704; FAX: 518-677-5974
TacStar, PO Box 547, Cottonwood, AZ 86326-0547 / 602-639-0072; FAX: 602-634-8781
TacTell, Inc., P.O. Box 5654, Maryville, TN 37802 / 615-982-7855; FAX: 615-558-8294
Tactical Defense Institute, 574 Miami Bluff Ct., Loveland, OH 45140 / 513-677-8229 FAX: 513-677-0447
Talley, Dave, P.O. Box 821, Glenrock, WY 82637 / 307-436-8724 or 307-436-9315
Talmage, William G., 10208 N. County Rd. 425 W., Brazil, IN 47834 / 812-442-0804
Talon Mfg. Co., Inc., 621 W. King St., Martinsburg, WV 25401 / 304-264-9714; FAX: 304-264-9725
Tamarack Products, Inc., P.O. Box 625, Wauconda, IL 60084 / 708-526-9333; FAX: 708-526-9353
Tanfoglio Fratelli S.r.l., via Valtrompia 39, 41, Brescia, ITALY / 30-8910361; FAX: 30-8910183
Tanglefree Industries, 1261 Heavenly Dr., Martinez, CA 94553 / 800-982-4868; FAX: 510-825-3874
Tank's Rifle Shop, P.O. Box 474, Fremont, NE 68026-0474 / 402-727-1317; FAX: 402-721-2573
Tanner (See U.S. Importer-Mandall Shooting Supplies Inc.,)
Tar-Hunt Custom Rifles, Inc., RR3, P.O. Box 572, Bloomsburg, PA 17815-9351 / 717-784-6368; FAX: 717-784-6368
Taracorp Industries, Inc., 1200 Sixteenth St., Granite City, IL 62040 / 618-451-4400
Target Shooting, Inc., PO Box 773, Watertown, SD 57201 / 605-882-6955; FAX: 605-882-8840
Tarnhelm Supply Co., Inc., 431 High St., Boscawen, NH 03303 / 603-796-2551; FAX: 603-796-2918
Tasco Sales, Inc., 2889 Commerce Pky., Miramar, FL 33025
Taurus International Firearms, Inc., 16175 NW 49th Ave., Miami, FL 33014 / 305-624-1115; FAX: 305-623-7506
Taurus S.A. Forjas, Avenida Do Forte 511, Porto Alegre, RS BRAZIL 91360 / 55-51-347-4050; FAX: 55-51-347-3065
Taylor & Robbins, P.O. Box 164, Rixford, PA 16745 / 814-966-3233
Taylor's & Co., Inc., 304 Lenoir Dr., Winchester, VA 22603 / 540-722-2017; FAX: 540-722-2018
TCCI, P.O. Box 302, Phoenix, AZ 85001 / 602-237-3823; FAX: 602-237-3858
TCSR, 3998 Hoffman Rd., White Bear Lake, MN 55110-4626 / 800-328-5323; FAX: 612-429-0526
TDP Industries, Inc., 606 Airport Blvd., Doylestown, PA 18901 / 215-345-8687; FAX: 215-345-6057
Techno Arms (See U.S. Importer- Auto-Ordnance Corp.)
Tecnolegno S.p.A., Via A. Locatelli, 6 10, 24019 Zogno, I ITALY / 0345-55111; FAX: 0345-55155

MANUFACTURER'S DIRECTORY

Ted Blocker Holsters, Inc., Clackamas Business Park Bldg A, 14787 SE 82nd Dr, Clackamas, OR 97015 / 503-557-7757; FAX: 503-557-3771
Tele-Optics, 630 E. Rockland Rd., PO Box 6313, Libertyville, IL 60048 / 847-362-7757
Ten-Ring Precision, Inc., Alex B. Hamilton, 1449 Blue Crest Lane, San Antonio, TX 78232 / 210-494-3063; FAX: 210-494-3066
TEN-X Products Group, 1905 N Main St, Suite 133, Cleburne, TX 76031-1305 / 972-243-4016 or 800-433-2225; FAX: 972-243-4112
Tennessee Valley Mfg., P.O. Box 1175, Corinth, MS 38834 / 601-286-5014
Tepeco, P.O. Box 342, Friendswood, TX 77546 / 713-482-2702
Terry K. Kopp Professional Gunsmithing, Rt 1 Box 224F, Lexington, MO 64067 / 816-259-2636
Testing Systems, Inc., 220 Pegasus Ave., Northvale, NJ 07647
Teton Arms, Inc., P.O. Box 411, Wilson, WY 83014 / 307-733-3395
Tetra Gun Lubricants (See FTI, Inc.)
Tex Shoemaker & Sons, Inc., 714 W. Cienega Ave., San Dimas, CA 91773 / 909-592-2071; FAX: 909-592-2378
Texas Armory (See Bond Arms, Inc.)
Texas Platers Supply Co., 2453 W. Five Mile Parkway, Dallas, TX 75233 / 214-330-7168
Thad Rybka Custom Leather Equipment, 134 Havilah Hill, Odenville, AL 35120
Thad Scott Fine Guns, Inc., P.O. Box 412, Indianola, MS 38751 / 601-887-5929
The Accuracy Den, 25 Bitterbrush Rd., Reno, NV 89523 / 702-345-0225
The Armoury, Inc., Rt. 202, Box 2340, New Preston, CT 06777 / 860-868-0001; FAX: 860-868-2919
The Ballistic Program Co., Inc., 2417 N. Patterson St., Thomasville, GA 31792 / 912-228-5739 or 800-368-0835
The BulletMakers Workshop, RFD 1 Box 1755, Brooks, ME 04921
The Competitive Pistol Shop, 5233 Palmer Dr., Ft. Worth, TX 76117-2433 / 817-834-8479
The Country Armourer, P.O. Box 308, Ashby, MA 01431-0308 / 508-827-6797; FAX: 508-827-4845
The Creative Craftsman, Inc., 95 Highway 29 North, P.O. Box 331, Lawrenceville, GA 30246 / 404-963-2112; FAX: 404-513-9488
The Custom Shop, 890 Cochrane Crescent, Peterborough, ON K9H 5N3 CANADA / 705-742-6693
The Dutchman's Firearms, Inc., 4143 Taylor Blvd., Louisville, KY 40215 / 502-366-0555
The Ensign-Bickford Co., 660 Hopmeadow St., Simsbury, CT 06070
The Eutaw Co., Inc., P.O. Box 608, U.S. Hwy. 176 West, Holly Hill, SC 29059 / 803-496-3341
The Firearm Training Center, 9555 Blandville Rd., West Paducah, KY 42086 / 502-554-5886
The Fouling Shot, 6465 Parfet St., Arvada, CO 80004
The Gun Doctor, 435 East Maple, Roselle, IL 60172 / 708-894-0668
The Gun Doctor, P.O. Box 39242, Downey, CA 90242 / 310-862-3158
The Gun Parts Corp., 226 Williams Lane, West Hurley, NY 12491 / 914-679-2417; FAX: 914-679-5849
The Gun Room, 1121 Burlington, Muncie, IN 47302 / 765-282-9073; FAX: 765-282-5270 bshstleguns@aol.com
The Gun Room Press, 127 Raritan Ave., Highland Park, NJ 08904 / 732-545-4344; FAX: 732-545-4344
The Gun Shop, 62778 Spring Creek Rd., Montrose, CO 81401
The Gun Shop, 5550 S. 900 East, Salt Lake City, UT 84117 / 801-263-3633
The Gun Shop, 716-A South Rogers Road, Olathe, KS 66062
The Gun Works, 247 S. 2nd, Springfield, OR 97477 / 541-741-4118; FAX: 541-988-1097 gunworks@worldnet.att.net www.thegunworks.com
The Gunsight, 1712 North Placentia Ave., Fullerton, CA 92631
The Gunsmith in Elk River, 14021 Victoria Lane, Elk River, MN 55330 / 612-441-7761
The Hanned Line, P.O. Box 2387, Cupertino, CA 95015-2387 smith@hanned.com www.hanned.com
The Holster Shop, 720 N. Flagler Dr., Ft. Lauderdale, FL 33304 / 305-463-7910; FAX: 305-761-1483
The House of Muskets, Inc., P.O. Box 4640, Pagosa Springs, CO 81157 / 970-731-2295
The Keller Co., 4215 McEwen Rd., Dallas, TX 75244 / 214-770-8585
The Lewis Lead Remover (See LEM Gun Specialties Inc.)
The NgraveR Co., 67 Wawecus Hill Rd., Bozrah, CT 06334 / 860-823-1533
The Ordnance Works, 2969 Pidgeon Point Road, Eureka, CA 95501 / 707-443-3252
The Orvis Co., Rt. 7, Manchester, VT 05254 / 802-362-3622; FAX: 802-362-3525
The Outdoor Connection,Inc., 201 Cotton Dr., P.O. Box 7751, Waco, TX 76714-7751 / 800-533-6076 or 817-772-5575; FAX: 817-776-3553
The Outdoorsman's Bookstore, Llangorse, Brecon, LD3 7UE U.K. / 44-1874-658-660; FAX: 44-1874-658-650
The Park Rifle Co., Ltd., Unit 6a Dartford Trade Park, Power Mill Lane, Dartford DA7 7NX, ENGLAND / 011-0322-222512
The Paul Co., 27385 Pressonville Rd., Wellsville, KS 66092 / 785-883-4444; FAX: 785-883-2525
The Powder Horn, Inc., P.O. Box 114 Patty Drive, Cusseta, GA 31805 / 404-989-3257
The Protector Mfg. Co., Inc., 443 Ashwood Place, Boca Raton, FL 33431 / 407-394-6011
The Robar Co.'s, Inc., 21438 N. 7th Ave., Suite B, Phoenix, AZ 85027 / 602-581-2648; FAX: 602-582-0059
The School of Gunsmithing, 6065 Roswell Rd., Atlanta, GA 30328 / 800-223-4542
The Shooting Gallery, 8070 Southern Blvd., Boardman, OH 44512 / 216-726-7788
The Sight Shop, John G. Lawson, 1802 E. Columbia Ave., Tacoma, WA 98404 / 206-474-5465
The Southern Armory, 25 Millstone Road, Woodlawn, VA 24381 / 703-238-1343; FAX: 703-238-1453
The Surecase Co., 233 Wilshire Blvd., Ste. 900, Santa Monica, CA 90401 / 800-92ARMLOC
The Swampfire Shop (See Peterson Gun Shop, Inc.)
The Walnut Factory, 235 West Rd. No. 1, Portsmouth, NH 03801 / 603-436-2225; FAX: 603-433-7003
The Wilson Arms Co., 63 Leetes Island Rd., Branford, CT 06405 / 203-488-7297; FAX: 203-488-0135
Theis, Terry, HC 63 Box 213, Harper, TX 78631 / 830-864-4438
Theoben Engineering, Stephenson Road, St. Ives Huntingdon, Cambs., PE17 4WJ ENGLAND / 011-0480-461718
Thiewes, George W., 14329 W. Parada Dr., Sun City West, AZ 85375
Things Unlimited, 235 N. Kimbau, Casper, WY 82601 / 307-234-5277
Thirion Gun Engraving, Denise, PO Box 408, Graton, CA 95444 / 707-829-1876
Thomas, Charles C., 2600 S. First St., Springfield, IL 62794 / 217-789-8980; FAX: 217-789-9130
Thompson, Norm, 18905 NW Thurman St., Portland, OR 97209
Thompson Bullet Lube Co., P.O. Box 472343, Garland, TX 75047-2343 / 972-271-8063; FAX: 972-840-6743 thomlube@flash.net www.thompsonbulletlube.com
Thompson Precision, 110 Mary St., P.O. Box 251, Warren, IL 61087 / 815-745-3625
Thompson, Randall. (See HIGHLINE MACHINE CO.)
Thompson Target Technology, 618 Roslyn Ave., SW, Canton, OH 44710 / 216-453-7707; FAX: 216-478-4723
Thompson, Randall (See Highline Machine Co.)
Thompson/Center Arms, P.O. Box 5002, Rochester, NH 03867 / 603-332-2394; FAX: 603-332-5133
3-D Ammunition & Bullets, PO Box 433, Doniphan, NE 68832 / 402-845-2285 or 800-255-6712; FAX: 402-845-6546
3-Ten Corp., P.O. Box 269, Feeding Hills, MA 01030 / 413-789-2086; FAX: 413-789-1549
300 Below Services (See Cryo-Accurizing)
Thunden Ranch, HCR 1, Box 53, Mt. Home, TX 78058 / 830-640-3138
Thunder Mountain Arms, P.O. Box 593, Oak Harbor, WA 98277 / 206-679-4657; FAX: 206-675-1114
Thurston Sports, Inc., RD 3 Donovan Rd., Auburn, NY 13021 / 315-253-0966
Tiger-Hunt Gunstocks, Box 379, Beaverdale, PA 15921 / 814-472-5161 tigerhunt4@aol.com www.gunstockwood.com
Tikka (See U.S. Importer-Stoeger Industries)
Timber Heirloom Products, 618 Roslyn Ave. SW, Canton, OH 44710 / 216-453-7707; FAX: 216-478-4723
Time Precision, Inc., 640 Federal Rd., Brookfield, CT 06804 / 203-775-8343
Tink's Safariland Hunting Corp., P.O. Box 244, 1140 Monticello Rd., Madison, GA 30650 / 706-342-4915; FAX: 706-342-7568
Tinks & Ben Lee Hunting Products (See Wellington Outdoors)
Tioga Engineering Co., Inc., P.O. Box 913, 13 Cone St., Wellsboro, PA 16901 / 717-724-3533; FAX: 717-662-3347
Tippman Pneumatics, Inc., 3518 Adams Center Rd., Fort Wayne, IN 46806 / 219-749-6022; FAX: 219-749-6619
Tirelli, Snc Di Tirelli Primo E.C., Via Matteotti No. 359, Gardone V.T. Brescia, I ITALY / 030-8912819; FAX: 030-832240
TM Stockworks, 6355 Maplecrest Rd., Fort Wayne, IN 46835 / 219-485-5389
TMI Products (See Haselbauer Products, Jerry)
Tom Forrest, Inc., P.O. Box 326, Lakeside, CA 92040 / 619-561-5800; FAX: 619-561-0227
Tom's Gun Repair, Thomas G. Ivanoff, 76-6 Rt. Southfork Rd., Cody, WY 82414 / 307-587-6949
Tom's Gunshop, 3601 Central Ave., Hot Springs, AR 71913 / 501-624-3856
Tombstone Smoke'n' Deals, 3218 East Bell Road, Phoenix, AZ 85032 / 602-905-7013; FAX: 602-443-1998
Tonoloway Tack Drives, HCR 81, Box 100, Needmore, PA 17238
Tooley Custom Rifles, 516 Creek Meadow Dr., Gastonia, NC 28054 / 704-864-7525
Top-Line USA, Inc., 7920-28 Hamilton Ave., Cincinnati, OH 45231 / 513-522-2992 or 800-346-6699; FAX: 513-522-0916
Torel, Inc., 1708 N. South St., P.O. Box 592, Yoakum, TX 77995 / 512-293-2341; FAX: 512-293-3413
TOZ (See U.S. Importer-Nygord Precision Products)
Track of the Wolf, Inc., P.O. Box 6, Osseo, MN 55369-0006 / 612-424-2500; FAX: 612-424-9860
TracStar Industries, Inc., 218 Justin Dr., Cottonwood, AZ 86326 / 520-639-0072; FAX: 520-634-8781
Tradewinds, Inc., P.O. Box 1191, 2339-41 Tacoma Ave. S., Tacoma, WA 98401 / 206-272-4887
Traditions Performance Firearms, P.O. Box 776, 1375 Boston Post Rd., Old Saybrook, CT 06475 / 860-388-4656; FAX: 860-388-4657 trad@ctz.nai.net www.traditionsmuzzle.com
Trafalgar Square, P.O. Box 257, N. Pomfret, VT 05053 / 802-457-1911
Traft Gunshop, P.O. Box 1078, Buena Vista, CO 81211
Trail Visions, 5800 N. Ames Terrace, Glendale, WI 53209 / 414-228-1328
Trammco, 839 Gold Run Rd., Boulder, CO 80302
Trax America, Inc., P.O. Box 898, 1150 Eldridge, Forrest City, AR 72335 / 870-633-0410 or 800-232-2327; FAX: 870-633-4788
Treadlok Gun Safe, Inc., 1764 Granby St. NE, Roanoke, VA 24012 / 800-729-8732 or 703-982-6881; FAX: 703-982-1059
Treemaster, P.O. Box 247, Guntersville, AL 35976 / 205-878-3597
Treso, Inc., P.O. Box 4640, Pagosa Springs, CO 81157 / 303-731-2295
Trevallion Gunstocks, 9 Old Mountain Rd., Cape Neddick, ME 03902 / 207-361-1130
Trico Plastics, 590 S. Vincent Ave., Azusa, CA 91702
Trigger Lock Division/Central Specialties Ltd., 1122 Silver Lake Road, Cary, IL 60013 / 847-639-3900; FAX: 847-639-3972
Trijicon, Inc., 49385 Shafer Ave., P.O. Box 930059, Wixom, MI 48393-0059 / 810-960-7700; FAX: 810-960-7725
Trilux, Inc., P.O. Box 24608, Winston-Salem, NC 27114 / 910-659-9438; FAX: 910-768-7720
Trinidad St. Jr Col Gunsmith Dept, 600 Prospect St., Trinidad, CO 81082 / 719-846-5631; FAX: 719-846-5667
Triple-K Mfg. Co., Inc., 2222 Commercial St., San Diego, CA 92113 / 619-232-2066; FAX: 619-232-7675
Tristar Sporting Arms, Ltd., 1814-16 Linn St., P.O. Box 7496, N. Kansas City, MO 64116 / 816-421-1400; FAX: 816-421-4182
Trius Traps, Inc., P.O. Box 471, 221 S. Miami Ave., Cleves, OH 45002 / 513-941-5682; FAX: 513-941-7970
Trooper Walsh, 2393 N Edgewood St, Arlington, VA 22207
Trophy Bonded Bullets, Inc., 900 S. Loop W., Suite 190, Houston, TX 77054 / 713-645-4499 or 888-308-3006; FAX: 713-741-6393
Trotman, Ken, 135 Ditton Walk, Unit 11, Cambridge, CB5 8PY ENGLAND / 01223-211030; FAX: 01223-212317
Tru-Balance Knife Co., P.O. Box 140555, Grand Rapids, MI 49514 / 616-453-3679
Tru-Square Metal Prods., Inc., 640 First St. SW, P.O. Box 585, Auburn, WA 98071 / 206-833-2310; FAX: 206-833-2349
True Flight Bullet Co., 5581 Roosevelt St., Whitehall, PA 18052 / 610-262-7630; FAX: 610-262-7806
Truglo, Inc, PO Box 1612, McKinna, TX 75070 / 972-774-0300 FAX: 972-774-0323 www.truglosights.com
Trulock Tool, Broad St., Whigham, GA 31797 / 912-762-4678
TTM, 1550 Solomon Rd., Santa Maria, CA 93455 / 805-934-1281
Tucker, James C., P.O. Box 1212, Paso Robles, CA 93447-1212

MANUFACTURER'S DIRECTORY

Tucson Mold, Inc., 930 S. Plumer Ave., Tucson, AZ 85719 / 520-792-1075; FAX: 520-792-1075

Turkish Firearms Corp., 522 W. Maple St., Allentown, PA 18101 / 610-821-8660; FAX: 610-821-9049

Turnbull Restoration, Doug, 6680 Rt 58 & 20 Dept. SM 2000, PO Box 471, Bloomfield, NY 14469 / 716-657-6338

Tuttle, Dale, 4046 Russell Rd., Muskegon, MI 49445 / 616-766-2250

Tyler Manufacturing & Distributing, 3804 S. Eastern, Oklahoma City, OK 73129 / 405-677-1487 or 800-654-8415

U

U.S. Fire-Arms Mfg. Co. Inc., 55 Van Dyke Ave., Hartford, CT 06106 / 877-227-6901; FAX: 860-724-6809 sales @ usfirearms.com; www.usfirearms.com

U.S. Importer-Wm. Larkin Moore, 8430 E. Raintree Ste. B-7, Scottsdale, AZ 85260

U.S. Repeating Arms Co., Inc., 275 Winchester Ave., Morgan, UT 84050-9333 / 801-876-3440; FAX: 801-876-3737

U.S. Tactical Systems (See Keng's Firearms Specialty)

U.S.A. Magazines, Inc., P.O. Box 39115, Downey, CA 90241 / 800-872-2577

Uberti, Aldo, Casella Postale 43, I-25063 Gardone V.T., ITALY

Uberti USA, Inc., P.O. Box 469, Lakeville, CT 06039 / 860-435-8068; FAX: 860-435-8146

UFA, Inc., 6927 E. Grandview Dr., Scottsdale, AZ 85254 / 800-616-2776

Ugartechea S. A., Ignacio, Chonta 26, Eibar, SPAIN / 43-121257; FAX: 43-121669

Ultimate Accuracy, 121 John Shelton Rd., Jacksonville, AR 72076 / 501-985-2530

Ultra Dot Distribution, 2316 N.E. 8th Rd., Ocala, FL 34470

Ultra Light Arms, Inc., P.O. Box 1270, 214 Price St., Granville, WV 26505 / 304-599-5687; FAX: 304-599-5687

Ultralux (See U.S. Importer-Keng's Firearms Specia

UltraSport Arms, Inc., 1955 Norwood Ct., Racine, WI 53403 / 414-554-3237; FAX: 414-554-9731

Uncle Bud's, HCR 81, Box 100, Needmore, PA 17238 / 717-294-6000; FAX: 717-294-6005

Uncle Mike's (See Michaels of Oregon Co)

Unertl Optical Co. Inc., John, 308 Clay Ave, PO Box 818, Mars, PA 16046-0818 / 412-625-3810

Unique/M.A.P.F., 10 Les Allees, 64700, Hendaye, FRANCE / 33-59 20 71 93

UniTec, 1250 Bedford SW, Canton, OH 44710 / 216-452-4017

United Binocular Co., 9043 S. Western Ave., Chicago, IL 60620

United Cutlery Corp., 1425 United Blvd., Sevierville, TN 37876 / 865-428-2532 or 800-548-0835 FAX: 865-428-2267

United States Optics Technologies, Inc., 5900 Dale St., Buena Park, CA 90621 / 714-994-4901; FAX: 714-994-4904

United States Products Co., 518 Melwood Ave., Pittsburgh, PA 15213 / 412-621-2130; FAX: 412-621-8740

Universal Sports, P.O. Box 532, Vincennes, IN 47591 / 812-882-8680; FAX: 812-882-8680

Unmussig Bullets, D. L., 7862 Brentford Dr., Richmond, VA 23225 / 804-320-1165

Upper Missouri Trading Co., 304 Harold St., Crofton, NE 68730 / 402-388-4844

USAC, 4500-15th St. East, Tacoma, WA 98424 / 206-922-7589

Utica Cutlery Co., 820 Noyes St., Utica, NY 13503 / 315-733-4663; FAX: 315-733-6602

V

V.H. Blackinton & Co., Inc., 221 John L. Dietsch, Attleboro Falls, MA 02763-0300 / 508-699-4436; FAX: 508-695-5349

Valade Engraving, Robert, 931 3rd Ave, Seaside, OR 97138 / 503-738-7672

Valor Corp., 5555 NW 36th Ave., Miami, FL 33142 / 305-633-0127; FAX: 305-634-4536

Valtro USA, Inc, 1281 Andersen Dr., San Rafael, CA 94901 / 415-256-2575; FAX: 415-256-2576

VAM Distribution Co LLC, 1141-B Mechanicsburg Rd, Wooster, OH 44691 www.rex10.com

Van Gorden & Son Inc., C. S., 1815 Main St., Bloomer, WI 54724 / 715-568-2612

Van Horn, Gil, P.O. Box 207, Llano, CA 93544

Van Patten, J. W., P.O. Box 145, Foster Hill, Milford, PA 18337 / 717-296-7069

Van's Gunsmith Service, 224 Route 69-A, Parish, NY 13131 / 315-625-7251

Vancini, Carl (See Bestload, Inc.)

Vann Custom Bullets, 330 Grandview Ave., Novato, CA 94947

Varmint Masters, LLC, Rick Vecqueray, PO Box 6724, Bend, OR 97708 / 541-318-7306; FAX: 541-318-7306 varmintmasters@bendnet.com

Vecqueray, Rick. (See VARMINT MASTERS, LLC)

Vega Tool Co., c/o T.R. Ross, 4865 Tanglewood Ct., Boulder, CO 80301 / 303-530-0174

Vektor USA, Mikael Danforth, 5139 Stanart St, Norfolk, VA 23502 / 888-740-0837; or 757-455-8895; FAX: 757-461-9155

Venco Industries, Inc. (See Shooter's Choice)

Venus Industries, P.O. Box 246, Sialkot-1, PAKISTAN FAX: 92 432 85579

Verney-Carron, B.P. 72, 54 Boulevard Thiers, 42002, FRANCE / 33-477791500; FAX: 33-477790702

Vest, John, P.O. Box 1552, Susanville, CA 96130 / 916-257-7228

Vibra-Tek Co., 1844 Arroya Rd., Colorado Springs, CO 80906 / 719-634-8611; FAX: 719-634-6886

VibraShine, Inc., P.O. Box 577, Taylorsville, MS 39168 / 601-785-9854; FAX: 601-785-9874

Vic's Gun Refinishing, 6 Pineview Dr., Dover, NH 03820-6422 / 603-742-0013

Victory Ammunition, PO Box 1022, Milford, PA 18337 / 717-296-5768; FAX: 717-296-9298

Victory USA, P.O. Box 1021, Pine Bush, NY 12566 / 914-744-2060; FAX: 914-744-5181

Vihtavuori Oy, FIN-41330 Vihtavuori, FINLAND, / 358-41-3779211; FAX: 358-41-3771643

Vihtavuori Oy/Kaltron-Pettibone, 1241 Ellis St., Bensenville, IL 60106 / 708-350-1116; FAX: 708-350-1606

Viking Video Productions, P.O. Box 251, Roseburg, OR 97470

Vincent's Shop, 210 Antoinette, Fairbanks, AK 99701

Vincenzo Bernardelli S.p.A., 125 Via Matteotti, P.O. Box 74, Gardone V.T., Bresci, 25063 ITALY / 39-30-8912851-2-3; FAX: 39-30-8910249+

Vintage Arms, Inc., 6003 Saddle Horse, Fairfax, VA 22030 / 703-968-0779; FAX: 703-968-0780

Vintage Industries, Inc., 781 Big Tree Dr., Longwood, FL 32750 / 407-831-8949; FAX: 407-831-5346

Viper Bullet and Brass Works, 11 Brock St., Box 582, Norwich, ON N0J 1P0 CANADA

Viramontez, Ray, 601 Springfield Dr., Albany, GA 31707 / 912-432-9683

Virgin Valley Custom Guns, 450 E 800 N #20, Hurricane, UT 84737 / 435-635-8941; FAX: 435-635-8943 vvcguns@infowest.com www.virginvalleyguns.com

Visible Impact Targets, Rts. 5 & 20, E. Bloomfield, NY 14443 / 716-657-6161; FAX: 716-657-5405

Vitt/Boos, 2178 Nichols Ave., Stratford, CT 06614 / 203-375-6859

Voere-KGH m.b.H., P.O. Box 416, A-6333 Kufstein, Tirol, AUSTRIA / 0043-5372-62547; FAX: 0043-5372-65752

Volquartsen Custom Ltd., 24276 240th Street, P.O. Box 397, Carroll, IA 51401 / 712-792-4238; FAX: 712-792-2542

Vom Hoffe (See Old Western Scrounger, Inc., The), 12924 Hwy A-12, Montague, CA 96064 / 916-459-5445; FAX: 916-459-3944

Vorhes, David, 3042 Beecham St., Napa, CA 94558 / 707-226-9116

Vortek Products, Inc., P.O. Box 871181, Canton, MI 48187-6181 / 313-397-5656; FAX: 313-397-5656

VSP Publishers (See Heritage/VSP Gun Books), PO Box 887, McCall, ID 83638 / 208-634-4104; FAX: 208-634-3101

Vulpes Ventures, Inc. Fox Cartridge Division, P.O. Box 1363, Bolingbrook, IL 60440-7363 / 630-759-1229; FAX: 815-439-3945

W

W. Square Enterprises, 9826 Sagedale, Houston, TX 77089 / 713-484-0935; FAX: 281-484-0935

W. Square Enterprises, Load From A Disk, 9826 Sagedale, Houston, TX 77089 / 713-484-0935; FAX: 281-484-0935

W. Waller & Son, Inc., 2221 Stoney Brook Rd., Grantham, NH 03753-7706 / 603-863-4177

W.B. Niemi Engineering, Box 126 Center Road, Greensboro, VT 05841 / 802-533-7180 or 802-533-7141

W.C. Strutz Rifle Barrels, Inc., P.O. Box 611, Eagle River, WI 54521 / 715-479-4766

W.C. Wolff Co., PO Box 458, Newtown Square, PA 19073 / 610-359-9600; FAX: 610-359-9496

W.E. Birdsong & Assoc., 1435 Monterey Rd., Florence, MS 39073-9748 / 601-366-8270

W.E. Brownell Checkering Tools, 9390 Twin Mountain Cir, San Diego, CA 92126 / 619-695-2479; FAX: 619-695-2479

W.J. Riebe Co., 3434 Tucker Rd., Boise, ID 83703

W.R. Case & Sons Cutlery Co., Owens Way, Bradford, PA 16701 / 814-368-4123 or 800-523-6350; FAX: 814-768-5369

Wagoner, Vernon G., 2325 E. Encanto, Mesa, AZ 85213 / 602-835-1307

Wakina by Pic, 24813 Alderbrook Dr., Santa Clarita, CA 91321 / 800-295-8194

Waldron, Herman, Box 475, 80 N. 17th St., Pomeroy, WA 99347 / 509-843-1404

Walker Arms Co., Inc., 499 County Rd. 820, Selma, AL 36701 / 334-872-6231; FAX: 334-872-6262

Walker Mfg., Inc., 8296 S. Channel, Harsen's Island, ML 48028

Wallace, Terry, 385 San Marino, Vallejo, CA 94589 / 707-642-7041

Walls Industries, Inc., P.O. Box 98, 1905 N. Main, Cleburne, TX 76031 / 817-645-4366; FAX: 817-645-7946

Walt's Custom Leather, Walt Whinnery, 1947 Meadow Creek Dr., Louisville, KY 40218 / 502-458-4361

Walters, John, 500 N. Avery Dr., Moore, OK 73160 / 405-799-0376

Walters Industries, 6226 Park Lane, Dallas, TX 75225 / 214-691-6973

Walther GmbH, Carl, B.P. 4325, D-89033 Ulm, GERMANY

WAMCO, Inc., Mingo Loop, P.O. Box 337, Oquossoc, ME 04964-0337 / 207-864-3344

WAMCO--New Mexico, P.O. Box 205, Peralta, NM 87042-0205 / 505-869-0826

Ward & Van Valkenburg, 114 32nd Ave. N., Fargo, ND 58102 / 701-232-2351

Ward Machine, 5620 Lexington Rd., Corpus Christi, TX 78412 / 512-992-1221

Wardell Precision Handguns Ltd., 48851 N. Fig Springs Rd., New River, AZ 85027-8513 / 602-465-7995

Warenski, Julie, 590 E. 500 N., Richfield, UT 84701 / 801-896-5319; FAX: 801-896-5319

Warne Manufacturing Co., 9039 SE Jannsen Rd., Clackamas, OR 97015 / 503-657-5590 or 800-683-5590; FAX: 503-657-5695

Warren & Sweat Mfg. Co., P.O. Box 350440, Grand Island, FL 32784 / 904-669-3166; FAX: 904-669-7272

Warren Muzzleloading Co., Inc., Hwy. 21 North, P.O. Box 100, Ozone, AR 72854 / 501-292-3268

Warren, Kenneth W. (See Mountain States Engraving)

Washita Mountain Whetstone Co., P.O. Box 378, Lake Hamilton, AR 71951 / 501-525-3914

Wasmundt, Jim, P.O. Box 511, Fossil, OR 97830

WASP Shooting Systems, Rt. 1, Box 147, Lakeview, AR 72642 / 501-431-5606

Waterfield Sports, Inc., 13611 Country Lane, Burnsville, MN 55337 / 612-435-8339

Watson Bros., 39 Redcross Way, London Bridge, LONDON U.K. FAX: 44-171-403-336

Watson Trophy Match Bullets, 2404 Wade Hampton Blvd., Greenville, SC 29615 / 864-244-7948 or 941-635-7948

Wayne E. Schwartz Custom Guns, 970 E. Britton Rd., Morrice, MI 48857 / 517-625-4079

Wayne Firearms for Collectors and Investors, James, 2608 N. Laurent, Victoria, TX 77901 / 512-578-1258; FAX: 512-578-3559

Wayne Reno, 2808 Stagestop Rd., Jefferson, CO 80456 / 719-836-3452

Wayne Specialty Services, 260 Waterford Drive, Florissant, MO 63033 / 413-831-7083

WD-40 Co., 1061 Cudahy Pl., San Diego, CA 92110 / 619-275-1400; FAX: 619-275-5823

Weatherby, Inc., 3100 El Camino Real, Atascadero, CA 93422 / 805-466-1767 or 800-227-2016; FAX: 805-466-2527

Weaver Arms Corp. Gun Shop, RR 3, P.O. Box 266, Bloomfield, MO 63825-9528

Weaver Products, P.O. Box 39, Onalaska, WI 54650 / 800-648-9624 or 608-781-5800; FAX: 608-781-0368

Weaver Scope Repair Service, 1121 Larry Mahan Dr., Suite B, El Paso, TX 79925 / 915-593-1005

Webb, Bill, 6504 North Bellefontaine, Kansas City, MO 64119 / 816-453-7431

Weber & Markin Custom Gunsmiths, 4-1691 Powick Rd., Kelowna, BC V1X 4L1 CANADA / 250-762-7575; FAX: 250-861-3655

Weber Jr., Rudolf, P.O. Box 160106, D-5650, GERMANY / 0212-592136

Webley and Scott Ltd., Frankley Industrial Park, Tay Rd., Birmingham, B45 0PA ENGLAND / 011-021-453-1864; FAX: 021-457-7846

Webster Scale Mfg. Co., P.O. Box 188, Sebring, FL 33870 / 813-385-6362

Weems, Cecil, 510 W Hubbard St, Mineral Wells, TX 76067-4847 / 817-325-1462

MANUFACTURER'S DIRECTORY

Weigand Combat Handguns, Inc., 685 South Main Rd., Mountain Top, PA 18707 / 570-868-8358; FAX: 570-868-5218 sales@jackweigand.com www.jackweigand.com

Weihrauch KG, Hermann, Industriestrasse 11, 8744 Mellrichstadt, Mellrichstadt, GERMANY

Weisz Parts, P.O. Box 20038, Columbus, OH 43220-0038 / 614-45-70-500; FAX: 614-846-8585

Welch, Sam, CVSR 2110, Moab, UT 84532 / 801-259-8131

Wellington Outdoors, P.O. Box 244, 1140 Monticello Rd., Madison, GA 30650 / 706-342-4915; FAX: 706-342-7568

Wells, Rachel, 110 N. Summit St., Prescott, AZ 86301 / 520-445-3655

Wells Creek Knife & Gun Works, 32956 State Hwy. 38, Scottsburg, OR 97473 / 541-587-4202; FAX: 541-587-4223

Welsh, Bud, 80 New Road, E. Amherst, NY 14051 / 716-688-6344

Wenger North America/Precise Int'l, 15 Corporate Dr., Orangeburg, NY 10962 / 800-431-2996 FAX: 914-425-4700

Wenig Custom Gunstocks, 103 N. Market St., P.O. Box 249, Lincoln, MO 65338 / 816-547-3334; FAX: 816-547-2881 gunstock@wenig.com www.wenig.com

Werth, T. W., 1203 Woodlawn Rd., Lincoln, IL 62656 / 217-732-1300

Wescombe, Bill (See North Star West)

Wessinger Custom Guns & Engraving, 268 Limestone Rd., Chapin, SC 29036 / 803-345-5677

West, Jack L., 1220 W. Fifth, P.O. Box 427, Arlington, OR 97812

Western Cutlery (See Camillus Cutlery Co.)

Western Design (See Alpha Gunsmith Division)

Western Gunstock Mfg. Co., 550 Valencia School Rd., Aptos, CA 95003 / 408-688-5884

Western Missouri Shooters Alliance, P.O. Box 11144, Kansas City, MO 64119 / 816-597-3950; FAX: 816-229-7350

Western Nevada West Coast Bullets, PO BOX 2270, DAYTON, NV 89403-2270 / 702-246-3941; FAX: 702-246-0836

Westley Richards & Co., 40 Grange Rd., Birmingham, ENGLAND / 010-214722953

Westley Richards Agency USA (See U.S. Importer for Westley Richards & Co.,)

Westrom, John (See Precision Metal Finishing)

Westwind Rifles, Inc., David S. Sullivan, P.O. Box 261, 640 Briggs St., Erie, CO 80516 / 303-828-3823

Weyer International, 2740 Nebraska Ave., Toledo, OH 43607 / 419-534-2020; FAX: 419-534-2697

Whildin & Sons Ltd, E.H., RR 2 Box 119, Tamaqua, PA 18252 / 717-668-6743; FAX: 717-668-6745

Whinnery, Walt (See Walt's Custom Leather)

Whiscombe (See U.S. Importer-Pelaire Products)

White Barn Workshop, 431 County Road, Broadlands, IL 61816

White Flyer Targets, 124 River Road, Middlesex, NJ 08846 / 908-469-0100 or 602-972-7528 FAX: 908-469-9692

White Owl Enterprises, 2583 Flag Rd., Abilene, KS 67410 / 913-263-2613; FAX: 913-263-2613

White Pine Photographic Services, Hwy. 60, General Delivery, Wilno, ON K0J 2N0 CANADA / 613-756-3452

White Rock Tool & Die, 6400 N. Brighton Ave., Kansas City, MO 64119 / 816-454-0478

White Shooting Systems, Inc. (See White Muzzleloading)

Whitestone Lumber Corp., 148-02 14th Ave., Whitestone, NY 11357 / 718-746-4400; FAX: 718-767-1748

Whitetail Design & Engineering Ltd., 9421 E. Mannsiding Rd., Clare, MI 48617 / 517-386-3932

Wichita Arms, Inc., 923 E. Gilbert, P.O. Box 11371, Wichita, KS 67211 / 316-265-0661; FAX: 316-265-0760

Wick, David E., 1504 Michigan Ave., Columbus, IN 47201 / 812-376-6960

Widener's Reloading & Shooting Supply, Inc., P.O. Box 3009 CRS, Johnson City, TN 37602 / 615-282-6786; FAX: 615-282-6651

Wideview Scope Mount Corp., 13535 S. Hwy. 16, Rapid City, SD 57701 / 605-341-3220; FAX: 605-341-9142 wvdon@rapidnet.com

Wiebe, Duane, 846 Holly WYA, Placerville, CA 95667-3415

Wiest, M. C., 10737 Dutchtown Rd., Knoxville, TN 37932 / 423-966-4545

Wilcox All-Pro Tools & Supply, 4880 147th St., Montezuma, IA 50171 / 515-623-3138; FAX: 515-623-3104

Wilcox Industries Corp, Robert F Guarasi, 53 Durham St, Portsmouth, NH 03801 / 603-431-1331; FAX: 603-431-1221

Wild Bill's Originals, P.O. Box 13037, Burton, WA 98013 / 206-463-5738; FAX: 206-465-5925

Wild West Guns, 7521 Old Seward Hwy, Unit A, Anchorage, AK 99518 / 800-992-4570 or 907-344-4500; FAX: 907-344-4005

Wilderness Sound Products Ltd., 4015 Main St. A, Springfield, OR 97478 / 503-741-0263 or 800-437-0006; FAX: 503-741-7648

Wildey, Inc., 45 Angevine Rd, Warren, CT 06754-1818 / 203-355-9000; FAX: 203-354-7759

Wildlife Research Center, Inc., 1050 McKinley St., Anoka, MN 55303 / 612-427-3350 or 800-USE-LURE; FAX: 612-427-8354

Wilhelm Brenneke KG, Ilmenauweg 2, 30851, Langenhagen, GERMANY / 0511/97262-0; FAX: 0511/97262-62

Will-Burt Co., 169 S. Main, Orrville, OH 44667

William Fagan & Co., 22952 15 Mile Rd., Clinton Township, MI 48035 / 810-465-4637; FAX: 810-792-6996

William Powell & Son (Gunmakers) Ltd., 35-37 Carrs Lane, Birmingham, B4 7SX ENGLAND / 121-643-0689; FAX: 121-631-3504

William Powell Agency, 22 Circle Dr., Bellmore, NY 11710 / 516-679-1158

Williams Gun Sight Co., 7389 Lapeer Rd., Box 329, Davison, MI 48423 / 810-653-2131 or 800-530-9028; FAX: 810-658-2140 williamsgunsight.com

Williams Mfg. of Oregon, 110 East B St., Drain, OR 97435 / 503-836-7461; FAX: 503-836-7245

Williams Shootin' Iron Service, The Lynx-Line, Rt 2 Box 223A, Mountain Grove, MO 65711 / 417-948-0902 FAX: 417-948-0902

Williamson Precision Gunsmithing, 117 W. Pipeline, Hurst, TX 76053 / 817-285-0064; FAX: 817-280-0044

Willow Bend, P.O. Box 203, Chelmsford, MA 01824 / 978-256-8508; FAX: 978-256-8508

Willson Safety Prods. Div., PO Box 622, Reading, PA 19603-0622 / 610-376-6161; FAX: 610-371-7725

Wilson Case, Inc., P.O. Box 1106, Hastings, NE 68902-1106 / 800-322-5493; FAX: 402-463-5276 sales@wilsoncase.com www.wilsoncase.com

Wilson Gun Shop, 2234 County Road 719, Berryville, AR 72616 / 870-545-3618; FAX: 870-545-3310

Winchester Div. Olin Corp., 427 N. Shamrock, E. Alton, IL 62024 / 618-258-3566; FAX: 618-258-3599

Winchester Press (See New Win Publishing, Inc.), 186 Center St, Clinton, NJ 08809 / 908-735-9701; FAX: 908-735-9703

Winchester Sutler, Inc., The, 270 Shadow Brook Lane, Winchester, VA 22603 / 540-888-3595; FAX: 540-888-4632

Windish, Jim, 2510 Dawn Dr., Alexandria, VA 22306 / 703-765-1994

Windjammer Tournament Wads Inc., 750 W. Hampden Ave., Suite 170, Englewood, CO 80110 / 303-781-6329

Wingshooting Adventures, 0-1845 W. Leonard, Grand Rapids, MI 49544 / 616-677-1980; FAX: 616-677-1986

Winkle Bullets, R.R. 1, Box 316, Heyworth, IL 61745

Winter, Robert M., P.O. Box 484, 42975-287th St., Menno, SD 57045 / 605-387-5322

Wise Custom Guns, 1402 Blanco Rd, San Antonio, TX 78212-2716 / 210-828-3388

Wise Guns, Dale, 333 W Olmos Dr, San Antonio, TX 78212 / 210-828-3388

Wiseman and Co., Bill, PO Box 3427, Bryan, TX 77805 / 409-690-3456; FAX: 409-690-0156

Wisners Inc/Twin Pine Armory, P.O. Box 58, Hwy. 6, Adna, WA 98522 / 360-748-4590; FAX: 360-748-1802

Wolf (See J.R. Distributing)

Wolf's Western Traders, 40 E. Works, No. 3F, Sheridan, WY 82801 / 307-674-5352 patwolf@wavecom.net

Wolfe Publishing Co., 6471 Airpark Dr., Prescott, AZ 86301 / 520-445-7810 or 800-899-7810; FAX: 520-778-5124

Wolverine Footwear Group, 9341 Courtland Dr. NE, Rockford, MI 49351 / 616-866-5500; FAX: 616-866-5658

Wood, Mel, P.O. Box 1255, Sierra Vista, AZ 85636 / 602-455-5541

Wood, Frank (See Classic Guns, Inc.), 3230 Medlock Bridge Rd, Ste 110, Norcross, GA 30092 / 404-242-7944

Woodleigh (See Huntington Die Specialties)

Woods Wise Products, P.O. Box 681552, 2200 Bowman Rd., Franklin, TN 37068 / 800-735-8182; FAX: 615-726-2637

Woodstream, P.O. Box 327, Lititz, PA 17543 / 717-626-2125 FAX: 717-626-1912

Woodworker's Supply, 1108 North Glenn Rd., Casper, WY 82601 / 307-237-5354

Woolrich, Inc., Mill St., Woolrich, PA 17701 / 800-995-1299; FAX: 717-769-6234/6259

Working Guns, Jim Coffin, 1224 NW Fernwood Cir, Corvallis, OR 97330-2909 / 541-928-4391

World Class Airguns, 2736 Morningstar Dr., Indianapolis, IN 46229 / 317-897-5548

World of Targets (See Birchwood Casey)

World Trek, Inc., 7170 Turkey Creek Rd., Pueblo, CO 81007-1046 / 719-546-2121; FAX: 719-543-6886

Worthy Products, Inc., RR 1, P.O. Box 213, Martville, NY 13111 / 315-324-5298

Wosenitz VHP, Inc., Box 741, Dania, FL 33004 / 305-923-3748; FAX: 305-925-2217

Wostenholm (See Ibberson [Sheffield] Ltd., George)

Wright's Hardwood Gunstock Blanks, 8540 SE Kane Rd., Gresham, OR 97080 / 503-666-1705

WTA Manufacturing, P.O. Box 164, Kit Carson, CO 80825 / 800-700-3054; FAX: 719-962-3570

Wyant Bullets, Gen. Del., Swan Lake, MT 59911

Wyant's Outdoor Products, Inc., P.O. Box 9, Broadway, VA 22815

Wyoming Bonded Bullets, Box 91, Sheridan, WY 82801 / 307-674-8091

Wyoming Custom Bullets, 1626 21st St., Cody, WY 82414

Wyoming Knife Corp., 101 Commerce Dr., Ft. Collins, CO 80524 / 303-224-3454

X

X-Spand Target Systems, 26-10th St. SE, Medicine Hat, AB T1A 1P7 CANADA / 403-526-7997; FAX: 403-528-2362

Y

Yankee Gunsmith, 2901 Deer Flat Dr., Copperas Cove, TX 76522 / 817-547-8433

Yavapai College, 1100 E. Sheldon St., Prescott, AZ 86301 / 520-776-2353 FAX: 520-776-2355

Yavapai Firearms Academy Ltd., P.O. Box 27290, Prescott Valley, AZ 86312 / 520-772-8262

Yearout, Lewis E. (See Montana Outfitters), 308 Riverview Dr E, Great Falls, MT 59404 / 406-761-0859

Yee, Mike, 29927 56 Pl. S., Auburn, WA 98001 / 206-839-3991

Yellowstone Wilderness Supply, P.O. Box 129, W. Yellowstone, MT 59758 / 406-646-7613

Yesteryear Armory & Supply, P.O. Box 408, Carthage, TN 37030

York M-1 Conversions, 803 Mill Creek Run, Plantersville, TX 77363 / 800-527-2881 or 713-477-8442

Young Country Arms, William, 1409 Kuehner Dr #13, Simi Valley, CA 93063-4478

Yukon Arms Classic Ammunition, 1916 Brooks, P.O. Box 223, Missoula, MT 59801 / 406-543-9614

Z

Z's Metal Targets & Frames, P.O. Box 78, South Newbury, NH 03255 / 603-938-2826

Z-M Weapons, 203 South St., Bernardston, MA 01337 / 413-648-9501; FAX: 413-648-0219

Zabala Hermanos S.A., P.O. Box 97, Eibar, 20600 SPAIN / 43-768085 or 43-768076; FAX: 34-43-768201

Zander's Sporting Goods, 7525 Hwy 154 West, Baldwin, IL 62217-9706 / 800-851-4373 FAX: 618-785-2320

Zanoletti, Pietro, Via Monte Gugielpo, 4, I-25063 Gardone V.T., ITALY

Zanotti Armor, Inc., 123 W. Lone Tree Rd., Cedar Falls, IA 50613 / 319-232-9650

ZDF Import Export, Inc., 2975 South 300 West, Salt Lake City, UT 84115 / 801-485-1012; FAX: 801-484-4363

Zeeryp, Russ, 1601 Foard Dr., Lynn Ross Manor, Morristown, TN 37814 / 615-586-2357

Zero Ammunition Co., Inc., 1601 22nd St. SE, P.O. Box 1188, Cullman, AL 35056-1188 / 800-545-9376; FAX: 205-739-4683

Ziegel Engineering, 2108 Lomina Ave., Long Beach, CA 90815 / 562-596-9481; FAX: 562-598-4734 ziegel@aol.com www.ziegelerg.com

Zim's, Inc., 4370 S. 3rd West, Salt Lake City, UT 84107 / 801-268-2505

Zoli, Antonio, Via Zanardelli 39, Casier Postal 21, I-25063 Gardone V.T., ITALY

Zriny's Metal Targets (See Z's Metal Targets & Frames)

Zufall, Joseph F., P.O. Box 304, Golden, CO 80402-0304

Up-To-Date References From DBI Books

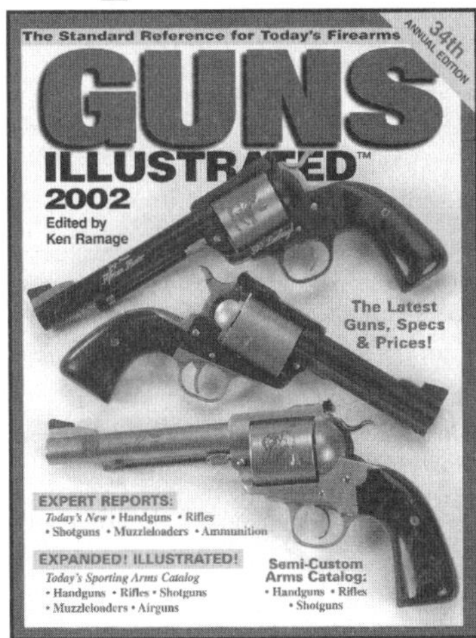

Guns Illustrated™ 2002
The Standard Reference for Today's Firearms, 34th Edition
edited by Ken Ramage

Consult the industry's standard reference for the most recent sporting firearms products. Feature articles cover developments in handguns, rifles, shotguns, muzzleloaders, and ammunition. Follow today's emerging firearm trends, and see the latest rifles, handguns, and shotguns in this extensively illustrated and updated catalog. The semi-custom and limited production arms catalog section has been expanded for this edition.

Softcover • 8-1/2 x 11 • 352 pages
1,500+ b&w photos
Item# GI2002 • $22.95

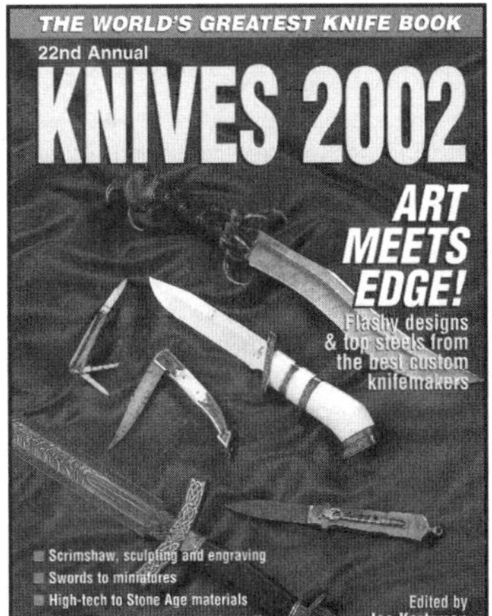

Knives 2002
22nd Edition
edited by Joe Kertzman

This 22nd annual edition is a showcase of stunning photos, completely updated directories and invaluable information regarding trends, state-of-the-art knives, services, supplies, knifemakers and dealers. Only the best knifemakers are found here. Join them as they explain their creative processes for scrimshaw, stonework, damascus blades, sheaths and much more.

Softcover • 8-1/2 x 11 • 304 pages
1,200 b&w photos
Item# KN2002 • $22.95

Gun Digest® 2002
The World's Greatest Gun Book, 56th Annual Edition
edited by Ken Ramage

Keep up-to-date on the latest collecting and accessory information the gun industry offers. This 56th edition showcases a new full-color section on engraved and custom guns, all-new feature articles, fresh new product reports and a completely updated catalog and reference section. Don't miss the expanded and updated Directory of the Arms Trade including directories of products, services and manufacturers.

Softcover • 8-1/2 x 11 • 560 pages
2,000 b&w photos
16-page color section
Item# GD2002 • $27.95

The Gun Digest® Book of Modern Gun Values
11th Edition
edited by Ken Ramage

Identify, evaluate and price any of the commonly encountered firearms made from 1900 to present. This specialized, heavily illustrated, expanded edition helps you easily identify and value older firearms found in gun shops, auctions, advertisements-or that old family gun you've just inherited. More than 7,500 post-1900 models are gathered by type then listed alphabetically. All prices are fully updated to mid-year. Includes more photos, and new sections covering mechanical inspection and (full-color) condition evaluation. New reference section lists books and associations for collectors.

Softcover • 8-1/2 x 11 • 640 pages • 3,000+ b&w photos
Item# MGV11 • $24.95

2002 Sporting Knives
edited by Joe Kertzman

This brand-new, heavily illustrated book provides complete coverage of today's sporting cutlery: folders & fixed designs, tactical, semi-custom, multi-tools, swords & fantasy designs and accessories. Read about the latest designs; view the current offerings of the sporting cutlery industry through the heavily illustrated pages of the comprehensive catalog section. Need more information? The reference section includes a complete directory of companies; the Library of Sporting Cutlery & Edged Weapons; periodical publications and a directory of collectors associations.

Softcover • 8-1/2 x 11 • 256 pages
700 b&w photos
Item# DGK01 • $21.95

Cartridges of the World
9th Edition, Revised and Expanded
by Frank C. Barnes,
Edited by M. L. McPherson

Whether you are searching for information on an obsolete cartridge or a new wildcat, a black powder round or a smokeless variety, you will find it here. Tables identify cartridges by measurement and offer ballistics and loading data. Learn the history of 1,500+ American and European cartridges in this single volume.

Softcover • 8-1/2 x 11 • 512 pages
627 b&w photos
Item# COW9 • $27.95

To place a credit card order or for a FREE all-product catalog call

800-258-0929 **Offer GNB1**

M-F 7am - 8pm • Sat 8am - 2pm, CST

Krause Publications, Offer GNB1
P.O. Box 5009, Iola WI 54945-5009
www.krausebooks.com

Shipping & Handling: $4.00 first book, $2.00 each additional. Non-US addresses $20.95 first book, $5.95 each additional.

Sales Tax: CA, IA, IL, PA, TN, VA, WI residents please add appropriate sales tax.

Satisfaction Guarantee: If for any reason you are not completely satisfied with your purchase, simply return it within 14 days of receipt and receive a full refund, less shipping charges.